Property and Conveyancing Library

EXECUTORS, ADMINISTRATORS
AND PROBATE

AUSTRALIA
The Law Book Company
Brisbane • Sydney • Melbourne • Perth

CANADA
Carswell
Ottawa • Toronto • Calgary • Montreal • Vancouver

Agents:
Steimatzky's Agency Ltd., Tel Aviv;
N.M. Tripathi (Private) Ltd., Bombay;
Eastern Law House (Private) Ltd., Calcutta;
M.P.P. House, Bangalore;
Universal Book Traders, Delhi;
Aditya Books, Delhi;
MacMillan Shuppan KK, Tokyo;
Pakistan Law House, Karachi, Lahore

PROPERTY AND CONVEYANCING LIBRARY

WILLIAMS, MORTIMER AND SUNNUCKS
ON
EXECUTORS, ADMINISTRATORS AND PROBATE

(Being the 17th edition of *Williams on Executors*
and the 5th edition of *Mortimer on Probate*)

by

J. H. G. SUNNUCKS, D.L., M.A.(Cantab.)
A Bencher of Lincoln's Inn

J. G. ROSS MARTYN, M.A., LL.M.(Cantab.)
of the Middle Temple and Lincoln's Inn, Barrister

K. M. GARNETT, Q.C., M.A.(Oxon.)
of the Middle Temple and Lincoln's Inn, Barrister

LONDON
STEVENS & SONS
1993

Published in 1993 by Sweet & Maxwell Ltd. of
South Quay Plaza, 183 Marsh Wall, London E14
Computerset by Promenade Graphics Ltd.,
Cheltenham, Gloucestershire
Printed and bound in Great Britain by Hartnolls Ltd., Bodmin

A CIP catalogue record
for this book is available
from the British Library

ISBN 0420–485–309

"I will the Law written in our vulgar language, for now it is an old, mix'd and corrupt Language, only understood by Lawyers, whereas every Subject ought to understand the law under which he lives."

—King James I

"For who almost is there who either is not, or may not be an Executor or Administrator; or at least hath not, or may not have to do with them, either to receive from them, or to pay to them Debts or Legacies? . . . How many know no more of these, than of the Way of a Ship upon the Sea?"

—Tho Wentworth, *Office and Duty of Executors*

WILLIAMS ON EXECUTORS AND ADMINISTRATORS

First edition	1832	By Rt. Hon. Sir E. V. Williams.
Second edition	1838	,, ,, ,, ,, ,, ,, ,,
Third edition	1841	,, ,, ,, ,, ,, ,, ,,
Fourth edition	1849	,, ,, ,, ,, ,, ,, ,,
Fifth edition	1856	,, ,, ,, ,, ,, ,, ,,
Sixth edition	1867	,, ,, ,, ,, ,, ,, ,,
Seventh edition	1873	By Rt. Hon. Sir E. V. Williams and W. V. Vaughan Williams.
Eighth edition	1879	By Hon. Sir Roland L. Vaughan Williams and W. V. Vaughan Williams.
Ninth edition	1893	By Hon. Sir Roland L. Vaughan Williams.
Tenth edition	1905	By Hon. Sir Roland L. Vaughan Williams and A. R. Ingpen, K.C.
Eleventh edition	1921	By Sydney E. Williams, assisted by H. Clifford Mortimer.
Twelfth edition	1930	By Professor David Hughes Parry and John Cherry.
Thirteenth edition	1953	By Sir David Hughes Parry, assisted by D. C. Potter.
Fourteenth edition	1960	By Professor G. W. Keeton, assisted by E. H. Scamell.
Fifteenth edition	1970	By J. H. G. Sunnucks.
Second impression	1974	
Sixteenth edition	1982	By J. H. G. Sunnucks, John Ross Martyn and Kevin Garnett.
Seventeenth edition	1993	By J. H. G. Sunnucks, John Ross Martyn and Kevin Garnett.

MORTIMER ON PROBATE

First edition	1911	By Clifford Mortimer.
Second edition	1927	By Clifford Mortimer and Hamish H. H. Coates.
Third edition	1970	By J. H. G. Sunnucks.
Fourth edition	1982	By J. H. G. Sunnucks, John Ross Martyn and Kevin Garnett.
Fifth edition	1993	By J. H. G. Sunnucks, John Ross Martyn and Kevin Garnett.

PREFACE

It might at first be thought that not much had changed in the law affecting personal representatives, or the administration and distribution of estates, in the 12 years since the last edition of this work. Such a thought would be wrong because quite apart from the introduction of the new Non-Contentious Probate Rules, there has been the substantial legislation in sections 17–28 of the Administration of Justice Act 1982, sections 47–51 of the Administration of Justice Act 1985 and the continuing development of case law.

The purpose of this edition has been to continue the task set by the former Vice-Chancellor Sir Robert Megarry in his review of the 14th edition: that it should be the leading practitioners' book on executors and administrators "full, accurate and within its proper sphere exhaustive" (see 78 L.Q.R. 114). This has involved some further small reorganisation combined with substantial cross-referencing to eliminate repetition as far as possible, and to try and follow a logical sequence of events as they are likely to occur, beginning with the appointment of the executor or administrator and ending with final distribution of the estate and the risks thereafter involved in the refunding and tracing of assets.

There has been some expansion of the chapter on the funeral and burial where there have now been a number of relevant Consistory Court decisions especially affecting monuments, memorials and cremation, all matters of potential importance to executors. Other increasingly common topics for the practitioner are matrimonial and joint property (sometimes involving ademption or election), international complications, family provision, tax (in all its variety), conveyancing chains, conditional gifts and of course conditional revocation. We much hope that *Williams* will be found to give guidance and practical help in the law in all these fields as they affect the executor or administrator.

The usual problems of terminology arise. "De-Latinisation" has been carried as far as we felt it feasible, and we have also, in the interests of brevity and accuracy, dropped, as far as statute law will really allow it, the adjective "personal" from the noun "representative" since personal representatives ceased to be solely "personal" as long ago as 1897.

A common complaint about a work such as this is the amount of quaint ancient law preserved. To the inexperienced observer much of this may seem superfluous, but it is surprising how often material of this nature can suddenly become important. We make no apology therefore for preserving some of these vivid illustrations of existing law such as the account of the widow's dealings in beer in *Wheeler* v. *Collier* (1595) Cro. Eliz. 406, or the judgment against the Sheriff for an escape in *Whiteacres* v. *Onsley* (1572) Dyer 322, or indeed the inclusion in the definition of assets of the proceeds of a menial office in the House of Lords for a term of years. See *Schellinger* v. *Blackerby* (1749) 1 Ves. Sen. 346. The human element intrudes in a spectacular manner where the testator attempts to state his wishes through a pack of cards (*Moore* v. *Moore* (1900)), or a barrister drafts a will and claims the residue as executor (*Seagrave* v. *Kirwan* (1828) 1 Beat. 157), or where the Probate Judge makes inappropriate remarks on the construction of the will (*Re Hawksley* [1934] Ch. 384).

We are grateful once again for the detailed help given us by Mr. A. K. Biggs, now of the Winchester Probate Registry, covering the bulk of the non-contentious probate material. For the contentious practice we are indebted to Master Gowers of the Chancery Division of the High Court whose knowledge and practical experience in this field have been of great value. Chapter 7 on death duties has been largely re-written by Mr. Ian Ferrier of Gray's Inn. Chapter 13 on substantial validity owes much to the medical knowledge and experience of Dr. Richard Fox, M.B., B.S.(Lond.), M.R.C.P., F.R.C.Psych., D.P.M., Consultant Psychiatrist and Diplomate of the American Board of Psychiatry and Neurology. Chapter 24 on Social Security has been largely re-written and owes everything to Professor David Williams, LL.M., Ph.D., Price Waterhouse Professor of International Business Taxation of the University of London. Chapter 50 on payment of debts involved substantial additional material as a result of the new insolvency legislation. For this we are indebted to Sir Patrick Sinclair and Mr. Nicholas Caddick of these Chambers.

Beyond this, help on special topics has come from many sources and we are particularly grateful to Mr. M. H. Boyd-Carpenter of Farrer & Co., Mr. M. J. Cotton of the Solicitor's Office of the Inland Revenue and Mr. H. N. de V. Mather of the Public Trustee Office. Prolonged support on an almost daily basis has also come from friends and colleagues in Chambers. In this connection we would like to mention particularly the late Mr. Edmund Skone James, Mr. Paul Dickens, Mr. Simon Barker, Miss Brenda Roller, Mr. Alexander Stewart, Mr. Gregory Banner, Mr. Gwilym Harbottle, Mr. Ian Duggan, Miss Gloria Stimson and Mr. Clive Nicholls, all of whom have given willing and patient help whenever troubled.

The Publishers have shown their usual forbearance especially in the later delays and complications in which the editorial team at Sweet and Maxwell have been particularly helpful. Last but not least, the typesetters' remarkable skill in the interpretation of some of the handwriting and in presentation of the material must be gratefuly acknowledged.

The law is stated as at November, 30 1992.

J. H. G. Sunnucks.
J. G. Ross Martyn.
K. M. Garnett.

Contents

xi

PART TWO B: THE GRANT (B) OF ADMINISTRATION

PART THREE: NON-CONTENTIOUS PRACTICE

PART FOUR: CONTENTIOUS PRACTICE

PART FIVE: DEVOLUTION AND LIABILITY

PART SIX: ADMINISTRATION OF ASSETS

PART SEVEN: FAMILY PROVISION

PART EIGHT: ADMINISTRATION AND OTHER ACTIONS

PART NINE: DISTRIBUTION OF ASSETS

APPENDIX ONE: STATUTES

APPENDIX TWO: RULES AND ORDERS

TABLES

TABLE OF CASES

TABLE OF STATUTES

TABLE OF S.R.s & O.s AND S.I.s

TABLE OF NON-CONTENTIOUS PROBATE RULES

TABLE OF RULES OF THE SUPREME COURT

Part One

FIRST STEPS

CHAPTER 1

HISTORY AND JURISDICTION

History

A person confronted for the first time with the often formidable duties of an executor or administrator may not at first appreciate the importance of an understanding of the historical development of these offices. As recently as 1975 a case decided by Archbishop Morton, sitting as Lord Chancellor, in 1489 was relevant and was cited to Brightman J.[1] The historical origins of the probate jurisdiction appear in two main authorities. These are *Dyke* v. *Walford*[2] and *Hewson* v. *Shelley*,[3] both concerned with administration rather than executorship. The principal text books before Sir Edward Vaughan Williams wrote the first edition of this work in 1832 were *Wentworth*[4] and *Toller*.[5] There has always been an overlap with the principal works on Wills of which *Swinburne*,[6] and *Jarman*,[7] *Hawkins* and *Theobald*[8] are the most prominent. The ecclesiastical jurisdiction seems to have stemmed from the church's encouragement of will-making[9] and the spiritual dangers of intestacy which the Ordinary would take it upon himself to guard against on behalf of the intestate. However this jurisdiction was limited to personal estate.[10] The jurisdiction over real estate belonged to the common law courts.[11] With the development of trust law the courts of equity began to impinge on both jurisdictions.[12] The effect of the Land Transfer Act 1897[13] was to extend to real estate the jurisdiction of the Probate Court which had, under the Court of Probate Act 1857, taken over the jurisdiction of the ecclesiastical courts in relation to personalty. The pres-

---

[1] *Fountain Forestry* v. *Edwards* [1975] Ch. 1, *post*, p. 690.
[2] (1848) 5 Moo.P.C. 434.
[3] [1914] 2 Ch. 13.
[4] First published in 1641. Wentworth is thought to be a pseudonym for Mr. Justice Dodderidge. The 1774 edition was said to be "not much indebted to its several editors."
[5] (1800) Samuel Toller was the first such writer to include reference to administrators.
[6] A judge of the prerogative court of York.
[7] (1841); 8th and last ed. 1951.
[8] (1876); 14th ed. 1982.
[9] See, *e.g.* the Prayer Book rubric in the Visitation of the Sick and *Hewson* v. *Shelley* [1914] 2 Ch. 13, 38.
[10] Constitutions of Clarendon (1164). See *Re St. Mary Faversham* [1986] Fam. 143 at p. 154.
[11] See *Hewson* v. *Shelley* [1914] 2 Ch. 13. The clergy never had a beneficial interest, *Dyke* v. *Walford* (1848) 5 Moo.P.C. 434. See also *post*, p. 4.
[12] See Holdsworth and Vickers, *Law of Succession*, pp. 1–21; Maitland, *Equity*, 2nd ed., pp. 248–249; 252, 254. Holdsworth, H.E.L., Vol. 1, p. 629.
[13] See *post*, p. 9.

3

ent Chancery and Family Divisions have thus inherited an ancient division of function.[14]

The ecclesiastical courts

As a rule the court in which the testament of a deceased person ought to have been proved was the Court of the Ordinary of the place wherein the testator dwelt, *i.e.* generally speaking, the bishop of the diocese. But if the deceased, at the time of his death, had effects to such an amount as to be considered notable goods, usually called *bona notabilia*, within some other diocese or peculiar[15] than that in which he died, then the will had to be proved before the Metropolitan of the province by way of special prerogative[16]; whence the courts where the validity of such wills was tried, and the offices where they were registered, were called the Prerogative Courts and the Prerogative Offices of Canterbury and York.[17]

Whatever may have been the case in earlier times,[18] it is certain that, at the time of the passing of the Court of Probate Act 1857, the ecclesiastical court was, apart from certain Courts Baron, the only court in which the validity of wills of personalty, or of any testamentary paper whatever relating to personalty, could be established or disputed.[19] Originally the ecclesiastical courts had no jurisdiction over wills of realty and no grant of probate was made.[20] Later, however, probate was granted of wills which disposed of both real and personal property.

Although the ecclesiastical courts have now no jurisdiction in probate, they do have power to decide all matters necessary to their existing jurisdiction including the existence or otherwise of a trust. If such a decision is not appealed it is binding on the parties.[21]

---

[14] As to present jurisdictions, see *post*, p. 7. As to the civil law concept of the universal heir and its origins, see *post*, p. 31.

[15] "Peculiars" are certain districts exempt from the jurisdiction of the Ordinary of the diocese, and are so called because they have a *peculiar* and special Ordinary of their own.

[16] 4 Inst. 335.

[17] The Prerogative Court of Canterbury extends in general over all the southern dioceses (and formerly those in Wales), and is generally known as the Court of Arches. In York the Prerogative Court is known as the Chancery Court of York. Both courts retain ecclesiastical but no probate jurisdiction. Decisions of those courts in probate matters before 1857 are of similar authority to decisions of the later Probate Court and Probate Division of the High Court.

[18] See Bac.Abr., Exors. E. 1; *Dyke* v. *Walford* (1848) 5 Moo.P.C. 434; see also Holdsworth, *Hist. of Eng. Law*, 34d ed., Vol. 1, p. 625; Pollock & Maitland, H.E.L., 2nd ed., Vol. 2, pp. 331 *et seq.*

[19] Fonblanq.Treat. on Eq., Pt. 2, c. 1, s.1, n. (*a*); Bac.Abr., Exors. E. 1; and see *ante*, p. 3; *Gascoyne* v. *Chandler* (1755) 2 Lee 241. See *post*, p. 119, as to the general question as to what instruments require probate.

[20] There have been contradictory attempts in the past to distinguish between the words "will" and "testament." Littleton suggested the former referred to personalty and the latter to realty, and Coke and others the reverse. See 12th ed. of this work, p. 4.

[21] *Re St. Mary Faversham* [1986] Fam. 143 at p. 154.

Practice of Prerogative Courts

The jurisdiction now vested in the High Court, so far as regards procedure and practice, is exercised in the manner provided by statute or by rules of court, and, where there is no special provision, as nearly as may be in the same manner as that in which it might have been exercised by the court to which it formerly appertained,[22] so that the practice of the Prerogative Courts may still be relevant.

Court of Probate

By the Court of Probate Act 1857,[23] all voluntary and contentious jurisdiction and authority of all ecclesiastical, peculiar, manorial, and other courts and persons in England then having jurisdiction or authority to grant or revoke probate of wills or letters of administration of the effects of deceased persons was abolished, and no jurisdiction or authority in relation to any matters or causes testamentary, or to any matter arising out of or connected with the grant or revocation of probate or administration, was thereafter to belong to or be exercised by any such court or person. By the same statute[24] all jurisdiction in relation to the grant and revocation of probate of wills and letters of administration in England and Wales was made exercisable in the Court of Probate thereby established.

High Court of Justice

By the Judicature Act 1873, the existing courts therein named (of which the Court of Probate was one) were united and consolidated together as one Supreme Court of Judicature in England and Wales.[25] Almost the whole of the Court of Probate Act 1857 and the Judicature Act 1873 were repealed and their provisions consolidated in the Supreme Court of Judicature (Consolidation) Act 1925,[26] which has now been replaced by the Supreme Court Act 1981.

Practice of the High Court

The Judicature Act 1925, s.99 (as amended) gave wide powers for making rules regulating the procedure and practice of the High Court generally, and section 100 for making rules and orders for the procedure and practice of the High Court in non-contentious probate business. These sections have been replaced by Supreme Court Act 1981, ss.84 and 127,

[22] See Supreme Court Act 1981, s.19, replacing Judicature Act 1925, s.32 which itself replaced Court of Probate Act 1857, s.29. Sir C. Cresswell appears to have been of the opinion that s.29 applied to the procedure only of the court, and not to the principles on which it was to act: *Re Oliphant* (1860) 1 Sw. & Tr. 525. See also *Belbin* v. *Skeats* (1858) 1 Sw. & Tr. 148; 27 L.J.P. & M. 56; *Braine* v. *Braine* (1860) 1 Sw. & Tr. 271; 29 L.J.P. & M. 151; *Druce* v. *Young* [1899] P. 84, 101.

[23] s.3.

[24] s.4.

[25] s.5.

[26] In this work referred to as the Judicature Act 1925.

respectively. By the Judicature Act 1925, s.103(1), it was provided that, save as otherwise provided by the Act or by rules of court, all forms and methods of procedure which were formerly in force in any of the courts the jurisdiction of which was then vested in the High Court, might, if not inconsistent, continue to be used. This section has been repealed and not replaced.

Under the powers conferred by the Court of Probate Act 1857, s.30 (now repealed), copious rules and orders were, in 1862 and 1863, made for the guidance of practitioners in the probate court. These rules have been superseded. Non-contentious business in now regulated by the Non-Contentious Probate Rules 1987[27] and is further governed by a considerable number of President's Directions and District Judge's Directions.[28] Contentious business is governed by Order 76[29] and, where this does not cover the procedure, by the other relevant Rules of the Supreme Court.

Jurisdiction of the High Court

The Supreme Court consists of the Court of Appeal, the High Court and the Crown Court.[30] The High Court is a Superior Court of Record,[31] and exercises:

(a) all such jurisdiction and authority in relation to probates and letters of administration as was at the commencement of the Court of Probate Act 1857 vested in or exercisable by any court or person in England, together with full authority to hear and determine all questions relating to testamentary causes and matters:

(b) all such powers throughout England in relation to the personal estate in England of deceased persons as the Prerogative Court of Canterbury had immediately before the commencement of the Court of Probate Act 1857 in the Province of Canterbury or in the parts thereof within its jurisdiction in relation to those testamen-

---

[27] See *post*, p. 1223.
[28] The Judicature Acts do not appear to have altered the procedure or practice of the probate court with respect to non-contentious business. Nor did they alter or enlarge the jurisdiction of the probate court in non-contentious matters: *Re Tomlinson* (1881) 6 P.D. 209; and see *Re Bristow* (1891) 66 L.T. 60; *Re Caspari* (1896) 75 L.T. 663. But before the passing of the Judicature Acts 1873–75, the probate court never recognised the doctrine of equitable conversion, and in the case of *Re Gunn* (1884) 9 P.D. 242, 244, Sir James Hannen said: "It appears to me that a very great change has been worked now by the fusion of all the courts into one. There is no difference between the law to be administered in this [Probate] Division and elsewhere, but each court is to ascertain what the law is, whether legal or equitable, and I think therefore it is open to me to establish a different basis to that which existed in the Probate Court. I am of opinion that where freehold property has had impressed upon it a changed character by reason of the doctrine of equitable conversion, it is to be treated as personalty, and probate duty is payable, and it therefore follows that probate must be granted." In *Att.-Gen. v. Marquis of Ailesbury* (1887) 12 App.Cas. 672, 696, Lord Macnaghten cited this case with approval.
[29] See *post*, p. 1254.
[30] Supreme Court Act 1981, s.1 (*post* p. 1193).
[31] *Ibid.* s.19.

tary causes and matters and those effects of deceased persons which were at that date within the jurisdiction of that court:

(c) such like jurisdiction and powers with respect to the real estate of deceased persons as were thereinbefore conferred with respect to the personal estate of deceased persons:

(d) all probate jurisdiction which, under or by virtue of any enactment which came into force after the commencement of the Act of 1873 and was not repealed by the 1981 Act, was immediately before the commencement of that Act vested in or capable of being exercised by the High Court constituted by the Act of 1873.

In the exercise of its probate jurisdiction the court "shall perform all such like duties with respect to the estate of deceased persons as were immediately before the commencement of the Court of Probate Act 1857 to be performed by ordinaries generally or by the Prerogative Court of Canterbury in respect of probates, administrations and testamentary causes and matters which were at that date within their respective jurisdictions."[32]

The jurisdiction vested in the High Court is exercised (so far as regards procedure and practice) in the manner provided by the Act or by such rules and orders of court as may be made from time to time pursuant to the Act, and where no special provision is contained in the Act or in any such rules or orders of court with reference thereto, the jurisdiction is exercised as nearly as may be in the same manner as that in which it might have been exercised by the court to which it formerly appertained.[33]

Rules of court are made by the Rules Committee,[34] and Practice Directions are given by the President or the Senior District Judge of the Division.

Although the earlier Acts have now been repealed[35] their effect is preserved by the Supreme Court Act 1981, s.25, under which the High Court has all the probate jurisdiction which it had immediately before the commencement of that Act.

Assignment of business in the High Court

Before the Administration of Justice Act 1970 the probate jurisdiction of the High Court was assigned to the "Probate Division." This included amongst other things:

"(a) All causes and matters which, if the Act of 1873 had not [been] passed, would have been within the exclusive cognizance of the Court of Probate . . . :

(c) All causes and matters which under, by virtue of or in pursuance of

---

[32] See Judicature Act 1925, s.20 (repealed) and Supreme Court Act 1981, ss.19(2)(b), 25.
[33] Judicature Act 1925, s.32, replacing s.23 of the Judicature Act 1873, and see Supreme Court Act 1981, s.25.
[34] See Supreme Court Act 1981, ss.84, 85, 87. See also the Statutory Instruments Act 1946.
[35] See Supreme Court Act 1981, Sched. 7.

any enactment for the time being in force are assigned to that Division."[36]

The Family Division

Under the Administration of Justice Act 1970 the Probate, Divorce and Admiralty Division was renamed the Family Division and the principal probate registry was renamed the Principal Registry of the Family Division.[37] It was then provided that non-contentious or common form probate business should continue to be assigned to the Family Division and all other probate business should be assigned to the Chancery Division.[38] Non-contentious or common form probate business is defined as

> "the business of obtaining probate and administration where there is no contention as to the right thereto, including the passing of probates and administrations through the High Court in contentious cases where the contest has been terminated, and all business of a non-contentious nature in matters of testacy and intestacy not being proceedings in any action, and also the business of lodging caveats against the grant of probate or administration."[39]

The Chancery Division

All other probate business (*i.e.* contentious business) is assigned to the Chancery Division.[40] The practical test is whether or not a writ has been issued. A useful consequence of this division of functions is that where, as sometimes happens, there is a dispute about probate and the interpretation of the will, if proved, both matters can be heard and decided in sequence at one hearing by the same judge. It will also sometimes be convenient to have claims for family provision[41] heard in sequence in this way. However, all jurisdiction vested in the High Court under the Supreme Court Act 1981 belongs to all Divisions alike,[42] so that any judge may in his discretion exercise jurisdiction in any matter not assigned to his Division. But though a judge in another Division would have jurisdiction to grant probate of a will, this would be so inconvenient that any judge would direct the parties to obtain probate in the Division to which such matters have been assigned.

Section 64 of the Supreme Court Act 1981, which gives a person commencing any cause or matter in the High Court liberty in the prescribed

[36] Judicature Act 1925, s.56(3).
[37] Administration of Justice Act 1970, s.1(1), now amended by the Supreme Court Act 1981, Sched. 7.
[38] *Ibid.* s.1(4). Application may be made for hearing of Chancery proceedings outside London in accordance with Practice Directions [1972] 1 W.L.R. 1; [1984] 1 W.L.R. 417 and [1988] 1 W.L.R. 630, 739.
[39] Judicature Act 1925, s.175(1); Supreme Court Act 1981, s.128.
[40] *Ibid.*, s.1(4).
[41] As to Family Provision see *post*, pp. 757 *et seq.*
[42] Judicature Act 1925, s.4(4), added by Administration of Justice Act 1928, and Supreme Court Act 1981, s.5(5).

manner to allocate it to whichever Division he thinks fit, is subject to and followed by section 65 which provides that any cause or matter may at any time and any stage be transferred as rules of court may direct from one Division to another.

The probate

As a general rule,[43] an executor cannot assert or rely on his right in any court without showing that he has previously established his executorship in the proper Division. The usual proof of his executorship is the production of the grant of probate which will contain a copy of the will by which he is appointed, bearing the seal of the court. This is usually called the probate. In other words, nothing but the probate (or letters of administration with the will annexed, when no executor is therein appointed, or the appointment of the executor fails) or other proof tantamount thereto of the admission of the will in the proper Division is legal evidence of the terms of the will.[44] Evidence of the existence of the will and of its terms, if these are not in issue, may however be accepted in the absence of a grant.[45] The will of a deceased Sovereign of the realm is no exception to this rule, notwithstanding no probate of such a will can be granted by the court. In the case of any claim under a Sovereign's will the proper course is to proceed by petition of right.[46]

Extent of probate

The Land Transfer Act 1897[47] empowered the court, in the case of a person dying after 1897, to grant probate or letters of administration in respect of real estate only, though there was no personal estate. And in the case of deaths after 1925 probate or administration in respect of the real estate of a deceased person, or any part thereof, was granted either separately or together with probate or administration of his personal estate, and was also granted in respect of a trust estate only where there was no personal estate, or in respect of a trust estate only, and a grant of letters of administration to real estate was limited in any way the court thought proper.[48] So the will of a person dying after the commencement of the Land Transfer Act 1897 disposing of real estate only is proved in the Family Division.[49] The court also has jurisdiction to issue a grant where the deceased left no estate.[50]

[43] As to what acts an executor may do before probate, see *post*, pp. 83 *et seq.*
[44] See *post*, pp. 83 *et seq.* As to the wills of persons domiciled abroad, see *post*, p. 11.
[45] See *Whitmore* v. *Lambert* [1955] 1 W.L.R. 495.
[46] *Ryves* v. *Duke of Wellington* (1846) 9 Beav. 579; Crown Proceedings Act 1947, s.40(1).
[47] S.1(3). See also *post*, p. 105.
[48] Judicature Act 1925, s.155(1), repealed and replaced by the Supreme Court Act 1981, s.113(1). See *post*, p. 1196. The phrase "Real Representative" was used only in the title to the Act. See *Re Chaplin, etc.* [1922] 2 Ch. 838. See as to the term "personal representative" p. 18, *post*.
[49] See *Re Gunn* (1884) 9 P.D. 242.
[50] Administration of Justice Act 1932, s.2(1). *Re Wayland* [1951] 2 All E.R. 1041, but see *Aldrich* v. *Att.-Gen.* [1968] P. 281. This Act has been repealed but its effect is preserved by s.25 of the Supreme Court Act 1981.

Construction

Where there is a will the primary consideration is the construction or interpretation of the will.[51] A court of equity considers a personal representative (*i.e.* an executor or administrator) as a fiduciary in relation to persons
interested in the distribution of the estate, including dependants entitled to
claim provision or maintenance,[52] and will compel the executor to perform
his testamentary duties with propriety. Hence, although in those courts, as
well as in courts of law, the probate seal is conclusive evidence of the *fac-
tum* of a will,[53] or of the right to administer, an equitable jurisdiction has
arisen of supervising the administration of the estate, whether testate or
intestate, in the Chancery Division, by construing the will or relevant legislation, in order to enforce a proper performance of the duties of the executor and the trusts of the will. The courts of equity when exercising this
jurisdiction are consequently sometimes called Courts of Construction.

So long as the ecclesiastical courts had exclusive testamentary jurisdiction, they were Courts of Construction as well as Courts of Probate,
because suits for legacies might have been brought there.[54] Indeed, the
cognizance of legacies in former times belonged exclusively to the ecclesiastical jurisdiction; for the Court of Chancery, until Lord Nottingham
extended the system of equity, administered no relief to legatees.[55] But the
Court of Probate was not a Court of Construction; for section 23 of the
Act, by which it was created,[56] expressly prohibited it from entertaining
any such suit. By section 56 of the Judicature Act 1925 all causes and
matters for "the administration of the estates of deceased persons," and
for "the execution of trusts charitable or private" were assigned to the
Chancery Division of the High Court. Thus, although the Probate Division, as a Division of the High Court of Justice, had jurisdiction to determine, as far as possible, all questions in controversy between the parties to
any cause or matter pending before it,[57] the court was still, in practice, not
a Court of Construction, and would generally speaking only construe testamentary documents so far as was necessary in order to determine whether

---

[51] For will precedents See Brighouse, *Precedents of Wills and Life Transfers*.

[52] As to how far a personal representative is a trustee, see *post*, p. 1049. As to persons
interested in distribution, see *post*, p. 931. As to claims for provision or maintenance.

[53] See *post*, p. 448.

[54] In practice, however, they retained jurisdiction only over grants of representations; see
Holds. H.E.L., Vol. 1, p. 629.

[55] *Deeks* v. *Strutt* (1794) 5 T.R. 690, 692. See also the judgment of the Court of Appeal in
Re Diplock [1948] Ch. 465, 484–487. This fact largely explains the "hybrid" nature of legacies
which are often treated as analogous rather to debts than to interests in residue and are still
often in practice excluded or ignored when claims under the family provision legislation are
considered, at least if they are small. See generally *post*, pp. 757 *et seq.*

[56] 20 & 21 Vict. c. 77; and see *Warren* v. *Kelson* (1859) 1 Sw. & Tr. 290.

[57] Judicature Act 1925, s.43, which took the place of Judicature Act 1873, s.24(7) and is
now itself replaced by the Supreme Court Act, s.49(2), and see Judicature Act 1925, s.4(4),
ante, and Supreme Court Act 1981, s.5(5). See also as to the conditions under which this jurisdiction will be exercised, *Re Tharp* (1878) 3 P.D. 76; *Betts* v. *Doughty* (1879) 5 P.D. 26; *Re
Marchant* [1893] P. 254; *Stone* v. *Hoskins* [1905] P. 194.

or not the document in question should be admitted to probate and to whom the grant should be made.[58] This necessity could however involve the Probate Division in deciding for instance upon the existence or otherwise of a residuary bequest, the proper recipient of such bequest and other questions such as whether or not an apparently external document is incorporated in the will. The same distinction still survives as between the Chancery Division exercising its probate jurisdiction and its jurisdiction as a court of construction[59] but the distinction is now clearly of less importance.

County courts: contentious business

The county court has jurisdiction in contentious business where an application has been made for a grant or revocation of a grant[60] and it is shown to the satisfaction of the county court that the value of the net estate does not exceed the county court limit[61] "Net estate" means the estate of the deceased person, exclusive of any property that the deceased was possessed of or entitled to as a trustee and not beneficially, but after making allowance for funeral expenses and for debts and liabilities.[62]

Where there is county court jurisdiction the High Court may order a transfer of proceedings to the county court.[63]

Jurisdiction and procedure in the county court

The jurisdiction of the county court in contentious probate matters is the same as it formerly was under the Court of Probate Acts 1857 and 1858; that is to say, the county court has jurisdiction in all probate matters limited only by the size of the deceased's estate.[64] It is not obligatory in such cases to apply through the county court for probate or administration, since the above jurisdiction is concurrent with that of the High Court and not exclusive.[65]

Probate jurisdiction—foreign domicile

Where the deceased dies domiciled abroad the English probate court applies different law to movable property from that which it applies to immovable property.

Immovables consist of real property, chattels real and leaseholds. Mov-

---

[58] *Re Heys* [1914] P. 192, 200; *Re Hawksley's Settlement* [1934] Ch. 384; and see *Re Lupton* [1905] P. 321; *Re Fawcett* [1941] P. 85; *Re Last* [1958] P. 137. See also *post*, p. 27.

[59] *Re Berger, decd.* [1990] Ch. 118. For will precedents see Brighouse, *Precedents of Wills and Life Transfers.*

[60] *i.e.* through the Principal Registry or a district probate registry under the Supreme Court Act 1981, s.105, *post*, p. 1194.

[61] County Courts Act 1984, s.32(1). The county court limit is currently £30,000.

[62] *Ibid.*, s.32(2).

[63] S.40 of the County Courts Act 1984 and *Practice Direction* [1988] 1 W.L.R. 741. See also as to jurisdiction in matrimonial guardianship, legitimacy and adoption matters, *Practice Direction* [1988] 1 W.L.R. 558.

[64] *Re Thomas* [1949] P. 336. *Zealley* v. *Veryard* (1866) L.R. 1 P. & D. 195.

[65] See *post*, p. 434 as to trial and procedure in the county court.

ables, besides chattels and money, include debts and other choses in action.

The principle, considered earlier, that, in ordinary cases, there must be property in England or Wales for a grant to issue here is to be borne in mind, and the proposed applicant or litigant must assure himself that movables forming part of the estate of the deceased are, in fact, situate here.

While, in most cases, there is no difficulty in determining whether or not movables are situate in England or Wales, debts and choses in action and claims may give rise to difficulty. The general rule is that goods are situate where they lie at any given moment, but debts, choses in action and claims are situate where the debtor or person against whom the claim exists resides. There are exceptions to this rule, but consideration of them is beyond the scope of this work.

1—JURISDICTION AS TO MOVABLE PROPERTY

Where a person who has died domiciled abroad leaves movable estate in England or Wales, the general rule followed by the courts of this country is to apply the law of the country or state in which the deceased died domiciled to determine whether he died testate or intestate or which documents constitute his will.[66] In this connection, however, it must be borne in mind that in respect of formalities the Wills Act 1963 may provide exceptions in the case of persons dying since 1963, and the Wills Act 1861 in the case of wills made before 1964.[67] A further exception to the general rule stated above is to be found where a person dies domiciled abroad leaving a will which exercises a power of appointment.[68]

In applying the law of the domicile of the deceased, the English courts look first to see whether the foreign court has made any decision about the estate of the deceased. If there has been such a decision, the English court will, in general, follow it, but if not, it will come to its own decision, applying the law of the domicile as given in evidence by experts in the foreign law in question. The following general principles apply:

(i) *The English courts follow the decision of the court of the domicile.* Where there is an express or implied decision by the court of the domicile of the deceased, the English court will hold itself bound by the decree, order, finding or grant made by that court and will refuse to entertain any proceedings impugning the substantial or formal[69] validity of any will

---

[66] *Price* v. *Dewhurst* (1838) 4 My. & Cr. 76, 82; *Enohin* v. *Wylie* (1862) 10 H.L.C. 1; *Crispin* v. *Doglioni* (1863) 3 Sw. & Tr. 96, 99; *Miller* v. *James* (1872) L.R. 3 P. & D. 4. On private international law in general, see Dicey and Morris, *The Conflict of Laws*, 11th ed., 1987. As to the administration of foreign estates see *Pugh* on this topic.

[67] For the Wills Act 1963, see *post*, pp. 151 *et seq.*; for the Wills Act 1861, see *post*, pp. 000 *et seq.*

[68] See *post*, pp. 120 *et seq.*

[69] *In the Estate of Yahuda* [1956] P. 388 (where the will admitted by the court of the domicile appeared to have been revoked).

established by it, or its express or implied finding that the deceased died intestate.[70]

The above rule applies even where the judgment proceeded upon a mistake as to English law[71] or where the whole facts were not before the foreign tribunal.[72] If the court of the domicile is alleged to have made a wrong decision, recourse must be had to the mode of appeal provided in that place.[73] But, although the courts here will follow the decision of the court of the domicile as to the validity or invalidity of any will (with the exceptions mentioned earlier), it will not necessarily make the grant here in the same form or to the same persons as it has been made or would be made by the court of the domicile.[74]

(ii) *Law of the domicile applies.* Where no recourse has been had to the court of the domicile, the English court applies the law of the place in which the deceased died domiciled (in the case of wills both as to formalities[75] and as to substance[76]) in determining whether he died testate or intestate and, in the former case, which documents constitute his testamentary papers. English law, save as to evidence and procedure, is excluded, whatever the nationality of the deceased and even where his residence was in England.[77]

Early cases holding that the English court could not decide such questions until resort had been had to the court of the domicile have not been followed.[78] But the English court is not bound to entertain the suit.[79] On the other hand it will not stay proceedings commenced in England merely because proceedings are pending in the court of the domicile.[80]

The English court will pronounce for a will which is valid in form and substance even if it lacks material validity, *i.e.* where it is wholly or partly ineffective.[81]

(iii) *Substantive law applicable.* In general, questions of substantive law are to be considered in accordance with the concepts thereof held in the

[70] *Doglioni* v. *Crispin* (1866) L.R. 1 H.L. 301; *Enohin* v. *Wylie* (1862) 10 H.L.C. 1; *Ewing* v. *Orr-Ewing* (1885) 10 App.Cas. 453.

[71] *Castrique* v. *Imrie* (1869) L.R. 4 H.L. 414; *Godard* v. *Gray* (1870) L.R. 6 Q.B. 139.

[72] *Brissac* v. *Rathbone* (1861) 6 H. & N. 301.

[73] *Bank of Australasia* v. *Nias* (1851) 16 Q.B. 717; *Re Trufort* (1887) 36 Ch.D. 600; *Pemberton* v. *Hughes* [1899] 1 Ch. 781, C.A.

[74] See *post*, p. 297.

[75] Except in the case of wills admissible under the Wills Act 1861 or 1963.

[76] The English court will admit to probate the will of a person not entitled by English law to make a will: *Re Maraver* (1828) 1 Hagg.Ecc. 498; see *Stanley* v. *Bernes* (1830) 3 Hagg.Ecc. 373.

[77] *Price* v. *Dewhurst* (1838) 4 My. & Cr. 76, 82.

[78] *Ewing* v. *Orr-Ewing* (1885) 10 App.Cas. 453.

[79] *Trimlestown* v. *Trimlestown* (1830) 3 Hagg.Ecc. 243.

[80] *Duprez* v. *Veret* (1868) 1 P. & D. 583; especially where there is no dispute over foreign law, *Surrey* v. *Perrin* [1912] P. 233.

[81] *Enohin* v. *Wylie* (1862) 10 H.L.C. 1.

country of the domicile. But it has been held that the English court is not compelled to follow the law of the domicile blindly.[82]

(iv) *Procedural law applicable.*   Evidence and procedure, by contrast, are governed by the law of England as being the *lex fori*. The question of the knowledge and approval by the deceased of his will has been held to be one of evidence and to be determinable by English law.[83]

(v) *Application of the law of the domicile in cases of renvoi.*   The law of the domicile to be applied is that which attaches to the particular deceased.[84] A number of countries, when determining a probate question where the deceased is of another nationality, apply not their own law but that of the nationality of the deceased. In such cases the English courts must apply that law.[85]

(vi) *Retrospective legislation ignored.*   The law of the domicile applied by the English courts is that which existed at the date of the death of the deceased; and if that law is changed retrospectively, the English courts will not recognise such change.[86]

(vii) *A foreign grant is no evidence of title in England.*   Although the English courts, in general, recognise foreign grants as impelling them to make a grant of the same or similar nature here, a foreign grant is no evidence in this country of title to the deceased's property. Consequently a person entrusted with a grant abroad must obtain one here before he may prove his title in proceedings brought in the English courts.[87]

   Important exceptions to this rule now apply in the case of certain grants made in Scotland and Northern Ireland which are to be treated for the purposes of the law of England as being grants made in this country.[88]

(viii) *An English grant has no effect abroad.*   Where the deceased dies domiciled abroad neither an English grant of movables[89] nor of immovables situate in England has any direct effect abroad. But certain foreign countries in certain circumstances require an English grant to be obtained (*e.g.* where the deceased was of British nationality) before they will make a grant. Where there is no property in England a grant may be made for the

---

[82] *Re Fuld, Hartley* v. *Fuld (No. 3)* [1968] P. 657.
[83] *Ibid.*
[84] *Re Annesley* [1926] Ch. 692; *Re Ross* [1930] 1 Ch. 377.
[85] *Collier* v. *Rivez* (1841) 2 Curt. 855. On *renvoi* generally, see Dicey and Morris, *The Conflict of Laws*, 10th ed., Chap. 6.
[86] *Lynch* v. *Provisional Government of Paraguay* (1871) L.R. 2 P. & D. 268; *Re Aganoor's Trust* (1895) 64 L.J.Ch. 521.
[87] *New York Breweries Co.* v. *Att.-Gen.* [1899] A.C. 62, considered in *Redwood Music Ltd.* v. *B. Feldman & Co. Ltd.* [1979] R.P.C. 1. In many countries there is, of course, no real equivalent to a "grant."
[88] Under The Administration of Estates Act 1971, s.1. See *post*, p. 368 *et seq.*, 1154.
[89] Under Wills Acts 1861 or 1963.

purpose of obtaining a foreign grant subsequently, by invoking the jurisdiction originally conferred by section 2 of the Administration of Justice Act 1932.[90]

2—JURISDICTION AS TO IMMOVABLE PROPERTY

Where the deceased dies domiciled abroad and leaves immovable property abroad, the grant in respect of that property must be obtained in the country or place where it is situated.

Where the whole or substantially the whole of the estate of the deceased in England and Wales consists of immovable property, a grant in respect of the whole estate may be made in accordance with the law which would have been applicable if the deceased had been domiciled in England.[91] Consequently, a will of immovables must be valid under the Wills Act 1837 or 1963 to be entitled to probate.[92] Where a will purports to dispose of both movable and immovable property but is duly executed by English law only and not by that of the domicile, difficult questions may arise as to how far the gifts of movables and immovables are interdependent. It seems that where gifts of movables are independent of gifts of immovables, a will purporting to dispose of both but invalid as to the former by the law of the domicile will, nevertheless, be valid as to the latter.[93]

Immovables situate in England and Wales devolve on intestacy according to English law, whatever may be the nationality or domicile of the deceased.[94]

A probate action as to a will of immovables is governed by English law and procedure and not the law of the domicile of the deceased.

3—JURISDICTION APPLICABLE TO THE REVOCATION OF WILLS

The revocation of wills by persons domiciled abroad requires special consideration. Revocation by such persons will often be governed by the Wills Act 1861 or the Wills Act 1963. Revocation under these Acts is considered later.[95] In other cases the validity of the purported revocation must depend on whether the will disposed of movables or immovables and on the method of revocation employed.

Where the deceased is domiciled abroad but purports to revoke a will which disposes entirely of immovables situate in England, that will is not revoked unless the revocation is effected by one of the modes recognised

---

[90] This has been repealed but its effect is preserved by the Supreme Court Act 1981, s.25. The proposition cited in the text was, however, doubted in *Aldrich* v. *Att.-Gen.* [1968] P. 281.

[91] N.-C.P.R. 1987, r. 30(3)(*b*).

[92] See *Freke* v. *Lord Carbery* (1873) L.R. 16 Eq. 461.

[93] See *Godham* v. *Godman* [1920] P. 261 and the cases there cited.

[94] *Doe* v. *Vardill* (1826) 5 B. & C. 438. *Re Collens* [1986] Ch. 505.

[95] See *post*, pp. 149, 151, respectively.

by English law; for, as already shown,[96] English law applies in all probate questions affecting immovables in this country.[97]

A later will of movables or other testamentary instrument is effective to revoke a will only if it is recognised as having that effect by the law of the domicile.[98] And revocation is also effective in spite of the fact that it is carried out by a mode not recognised by English law, *e.g.* a destruction not carried out by the testator in her presence.[99]

In considering whether a revocation has been validly effected the court must ascertain what the domicile of the testator was at the date of the revocation and not that at the date of his death.[1] Thus the will of a domiciled Frenchwoman was revoked on her marriage to a man domiciled in England and Wales.[2]

Where the court of the domicile has admitted a will in English form to probate and it can be shown that that will was revoked in a manner which would be effective by English law, the English court must uphold that will even though it can be shown that the principles of the English law of probate apply in the country of the domicile.[3]

The Hague Convention on Succession 1988. This convention, which is a compromise between the interests of "nationality" states and "domicile" states, will have a substantial effect on English law if and when adopted by statute.[4]

[96] See above.
[97] See *Re Cartwright* [1939] Ch. 90.
[98] *Cottrell* v. *Cottrell* (1872) 2 P. & D. 397.
[99] *Velasco* v. *Coney* [1934] P. 143.
[1] *cf. Re Reid* (1866) 1 P. & D. 74. (A case on Lord Kingsdown's Act.)
[2] *Re Martin* [1900] P. 211, C.A.; see *Re Groos* [1904] P. 269; *Re Von Faber* (1904) 20 T.L.R. 640.
[3] *Re Yahuda* [1956] P. 388.
[4] See (1987) 36 *International and Comparative Law Quarterly* 260, 266.

CHAPTER 2

DEFINITIONS AND CAPACITY TO ACT

This chapter is concerned first to explain the principal terms used in this work and secondly to consider what persons may be excluded from the functions of an executor or administrator. Technical Latin terms have been anglicised where possible alternatives exist but Latin cannot be entirely eliminated.

Executor

An executor[1] is the person appointed by the testator to execute the will.[2] "To appoint an executor," says Swinburne,[3] is to place one in the stead of the testator, who may enter to the testator's goods and chattels, and who hath action against the testator's debtors, and who may dispose of the same goods and chattels, towards the payment of the testator's debts, and performance of his will." Unless separate executors are appointed an executorship is indivisible.[4]

The bare nomination of an executor, without giving any legacy, or appointing anything to be done by him, is insufficient to make it a will, and as a will it is to be proved.[5]

A personal representative (not called an "executor") may however now be appointed by the court as an additional personal representative where there is only one personal representative, during the minority of a beneficiary or the subsistence of a life interest.[6] But the court's power to appoint new trustees does not of itself enable it to appoint an executor or administrator,[7] nor does the appointment of an additional personal representative have the effect of including him in any chain of representation.[8] However,

---

[1] As to executorship and trusteeship, see p. 1049 *post.* An executor is strictly executor of a person. Although appointed in the will he is not strictly executor of the will. See also p. 43 *post.*

[2] 2 Black.Comm. 503; *Farrington* v. *Knightly* (1719) 1 P.Wms. 544, 549; Toller 6th ed. 30. As to executor *de son tort,* see *post,* p. 93. As to executor by the tenor, see *post,* p. 29, and as to substituted executor, see *post.* As to transmission of the office, see *post,* p. 44. As to joint representation, see *post,* pp. 469, 690 *et seq.* As to universal heir. See p. 44 *post.* As to the Official Solicitor, see pp. 24, 890 *post.*

[3] Swinb., Pt. 4, s.2, pl. 2; *Brownrigg* v. *Pike* (1882) 7 P.D. 61–64.

[4] *Re Wells* [1968] 1 W.L.R. 44. See *Fountain Forestry* v. *Edwards* [1975] Ch. 1, 11, 12.

[5] Godolph., Pt. 2, c. 5, s.1; *Brownrigg* v. *Pike* (1882) 7 P.D. 61–64; *Re Lancaster* (1859) 1 Sw. & Tr. 464.

[6] Supreme Court Act 1981, s.114(4) replacing Judicature Act 1925, s.160(2). For the practice under this section, see *post,* pp. 236, 323, 343. See also under "Special Executor".

[7] See Trustee Act 1925, s.41. As to appointment of a judicial trustee in place of an executor, see *post,* p. 24.

[8] Supreme Court Act 1981, s.114(5). See *post,* pp. 44, 1196.

there is now power for the court to appoint a "substituted executor."[9] In Scotland an executor named in a will is called an executor nominate. An executor elective is a person appointed by the court.

Special executor

A testator may appoint, and in default of such express appointment is deemed to have appointed, as his special executors in regard to settled land the persons, if any, who are at his death the trustees of the settlement[10] thereof, and probate may be granted to such trustees specially limited to the settled land.[11] Special executors may also be appointed by a sole surviving trustee in respect of trust estate.[12] A special or additional representative in respect of settled land may also be appointed by the court.[13]

Administrator

An administrator is the person to whom a grant[14] is given by the court to administer the estate of the deceased. For the purposes of the Administration of Estates Act 1925 "Administration" means with reference to the real and personal estate of a deceased person, letters of administration whether general[15] or limited[16] or with the will annexed[17] or otherwise.[18]

The term "personal representative"

This derives from the distinction between the heir[19] (or "real" representative) in whom the real property of the deceased formerly vested and the executor or administrator in whom the personal property vested. It has become a collective term covering the offices of executor and administrator where the same principles of law apply to both.[20] For the purposes of the Administration of Estates Act 1925 the term personal representative

---

[9] See p. 27 post.

[10] For definition, see Administration of Estates Act 1925, s.55(1)(xxiv); Appendix, post, p. 1150; Settled Land Act 1925, ss.117(1)(xxiv), 30–34 as amended. Re Gibbings [1928] P. 28. Re Bridgett and Hayes [1928] Ch. 163. See post, pp. 37, 272, 544, 550.

[11] Administration of Estates Act 1925, s.22(1). See further post, pp. 327, 1122.

[12] See post, p. 38.

[13] Administration of Estates Act 1925, s.23(2). Re Clifton [1931] P. 222. See post, p. 1123 (Appendix).

[14] A grant may be a grant of probate (to an executor) or a grant of letters of administration (to an administrator). See post, pp. 104 et seq., 233 et seq.

[15] See post, pp. 233 et seq. For the text of the Administration of Estates Act 1925, see post, pp. 1112 et seq.

[16] See post, p. 316.

[17] See post, p. 245.

[18] Administration of Estates Act 1925, s.55(1)(i) "Administrator" means a person to whom administration is granted (ibid. s.55(1)(ii)). See Appendix, post, p. 1148. As to the statutory covenants for title where the conveyance is made "as personal representatives" see Law of Property Act 1925, s.76. As to the varieties of limited grant see pp. 316 et seq. post.

[19] See post, pp. 31, 460, 961.

[20] See Re Brooks [1928] Ch. 24.

includes as regards liability for death duties[21] any person who intermeddles with the property of a deceased person.[22] Since the personal representative is now the representative of the deceased for both realty and personalty the adjective "personal" has become pleonastic if not misleading. However the term "personal representative" remains a statutory definition. For the sake of brevity the adjective "personal" is frequently omitted in this work and the word "representative" is to be interpreted as having the same connotation as "personal representative." The question when a representative becomes a trustee is discussed in relation to assents.[23] The term "legal personal representatives" has been held for the purposes of section 5(2) of the Copyright Act 1911 to include the foreign executors of a foreign testator having personal property in England.[24] From the earliest time it has been a rule that every person may be an executor, saving such as are expressly forbidden.[25] Similarly there is no bar to the appointment of any person as an administrator, but the matter is at the court's discretion.[26]

The Sovereign

The Sovereign may be constituted executor: in which case the Sovereign appoints such persons as the Sovereign shall think proper to officiate the execution of the will, against whom such as have cause of action may bring their suits; also the Sovereign may appoint others to take the accounts of such executors.[27] Administration is granted to a nominee of the Crown where the Sovereign is interested on intestacy.[28] A similar, but not identical, practice applies where the duchies of Cornwall or Lancaster are so interested.[29]

Corporations

A corporation sole may be an executor,[30] but doubts were formerly entertained whether a corporation aggregate could be executor; principally because it could not take the oath for the due execution of the office.[31] But

---

[21] This expression includes capital transfer tax chargeable on the death of any person, Finance Act 1975, Sched. 12, para. 1.

[22] Administration of Estates Act 1925, s.ss (i)(xi). As to the executor *de son tort*, see *post*, pp. 93, 101.

[23] See *post*, p. 1049.

[24] See *Redwood Music Ltd.* v. *B. Feldman Ltd.* [1979] R.P.C. 1.

[25] Swinb., Pt. 5, s.1, pl. 1; and see 2 Black.Comm. 503. The right to take on distribution is similar. See *post*, p. 972.

[26] See *post*, pp. 233, 258, 343.

[27] Godolph., Pt. 2, c. 1, s.2; and see 4 Inst. 335.

[28] See *post*, pp. 265, 1068. As to the application to the Crown of Administration of Estates Act 1925 see *ibid.* s.57. As to *bona vacantia* arising on intestacy see generally *Ing* on *Bona Vacantia*, pp. 31 *et seq.*

[29] See fn. 26.

[30] Godolph., Pt. 2, c. 6; Wentw.Off.Ex., 14th ed., p. 39. See *Re Haynes* (1842) 3 Curt. 75. If there is a vacancy the successor can accept or renounce on his appointment (Law of Property Act 1925, s.180(3)). See also *post*, pp. 474, 540. As to the Public Trustee as executor, see Public Trustee Act 1906 and *post*, p. 24.

[31] 1 Black.Comm. 477; Com.Dig., Admon B. (2); Wentw.Off.Ex., 14th ed., p. 39.

there were authorities to the contrary.[32] Accordingly corporations on being named executors appointed persons styled "syndics," to receive administration with the will annexed, who were sworn like other administrators.[33] The syndic might be the manager of the corporation[34] but had to be appointed syndic before the grant could be made.[35] Notwithstanding the Bodies Corporate (Joint Tenancy) Act 1899[36] probate could not be granted to a syndic and individuals jointly.[37]

This practice was altered in 1920[38] when the court was empowered to grant to a corporation named as executor probate in its own name provided its principal place of business was in the United Kingdom.

The practice was again altered in 1926[39] when special provision was made as to trust corporations and subject to this the practice before 1920 was restored.[40] Thus the court may now grant representation to a trust corporation[41] whether acting alone or jointly with another person[42] and in the case of non-trust corporations, representation may be granted to a nominee or attorney of a corporation.[43] But representation will not be granted to a syndic or nominee on behalf of a trust corporation.[44]

Partners

The appointment of some or all the members of an unincorporated body such as a partnership is regarded as the appointment of the members or partners as at the date of the will, provided that such persons are identifiable. Thus where a testator in India nominated his brother, and "Messrs. Cockerell & Co., East India agents, London," and one A.B., to be his executors, and before his death the firm of Cockerell & Co., which consisted of four members, had been dissolved, it was held that the appointment was not of the firm collectively, but of the persons composing it individually, and that each of the members was entitled to be joined in the

---

[32] Swinb., Pt. 5, s.9; Godolph., Pt. 3, c. 1, s.1; 1 Roll.Abr., tit. Executors, T. 7, citing 12 E. 4, 9, b.

[33] 3 Bac.Abr. by Gwillim, p. 5, tit. Executors, A. 2; Toller 30, 31; *Re Darke* (1859) 1 Sw. & Tr. 516; *Re Rankine* [1918] P. 134.

[34] *Re Hunt* [1896] P. 288.

[35] *Re Rankine* [1918] P. 134.

[36] And see *Re Thompson* [1905] 1 Ch. 229.

[37] *Re Martin* (1904) 90 L.T. 264.

[38] Administration of Justice Act 1920, s.17.

[39] Administration of Estates Act 1925, Sched. 2, Pt. II, repealing s.17 of the Administration of Justice Act 1920. The repeal applies whether the death occurred before or after 1926: *ibid.*

[40] See Non-Contentious Probate Rules 1987, r. 36(4), *Practice Direction* [1956] 1 W.L.R. 127. See Appendix, *post*, p. 1237 and *post*, p. 240.

[41] As to the meaning of a "trust corporation," see Supreme Court Act 1981, s.128 and *Re Skinner* [1958] 1 W.L.R. 1043. See *post*, p. 240.

[42] Supreme Court Act 1981, s.115(1). The requisite formalities will be completed by an authorised officer of the trust corporation: Supreme Court Act 1981, s.115. See also Non-Contentious Probate Rules 1987, r. 36, *post*, pp. 1119, 1237.

[43] Non-Contentious Probate Rules 1987 r. 36(4)(*a*).

[44] Supreme Court Act 1981, s.115(2).

probate with the other executors.[45] However where a testator appointed "the firm of Rodgers Horsley & Burton . . . who may act through any partner or partners of that firm or their successors in business at the date of my death not exceeding two in number to be the Executors and Trustees of this my will," this was held to be an appointment of all the partners of the firm at the date of the testator's death, a grant to two and a power reserved to the others.[46]

Aliens

An alien has the same capacity of taking, acquiring, holding and disposing of property as if he were a British subject,[47] and is therefore capable of being a representative.[48] In wartime however it seems that administration will not be granted to an alien enemy.[49]

Infants

An infant appointed executor (or trustee[50]) cannot obtain probate until he attains the age of 18.[51] The appointment has no effect before probate is granted to him[52] but his right to probate may not be renounced on his behalf.[53]

Although an infant was originally[54] considered capable of the office at 17, he was until 1970 prevented from taking a grant before 21.[55] Administration may similarly be granted for the use and benefit of an infant who would otherwise be entitled to a grant of administration.[56]

---

[45] *Re Fernie* (1849) 6 Notes of Cas. 657; but after 1925 representation will not be granted to more than four persons in respect of the same property: Supreme Court Act 1981, s.114(1); *Re Holland* [1936] 3 All E.R. 13; and if an appointment does not specify which of a number of parties are appointed it may be void for uncertainty: see *Re Horgan* [1971] P. 50, and *post*, pp. 922, 1032 and 67 L.S.Gaz. 46, 340.

[46] *Re Horgan, supra.* As to the form of oath where partners in a firm of solicitors are appointed without naming them, see *Practice Direction*, June 12, 1990, and p. 288, *post*.

[47] Status of Aliens Act 1914, s.17, as amended by British Nationality Act 1948, s.34(3), and Sched. 4, Pt. II.

[48] For the practice as to enemy aliens during the war of 1939–45, see *Re Fischer* [1940] 2 All E.R. 252; and *Practice Notes*, October 18, 1939; June 12, 1940; May 10, 1951. See also p. 33 *post*.

[49] *Re Schiff* [1915] P. 86; *Re Grundt* [1915] P. 126.

[50] Law of Property Act 1925, s.20.

[51] See *post*, pp. 323, 1121.

[52] Supreme Court Act 1981, s.118, *post*, p. 1121.

[53] Non-Contentious Probate Rules 1987, r. 34(1). As to grants during the infancy, see *post*, p. 323.

[54] Godolph., Pt. 2, c. 9, s.2; Swimb., Pt. 5, s.1, pl. 6.

[55] Administration of Estates Act 1798, s.6; *Re Stewart* (1875) L.R. 3 P. & D. 244. Family Law Reform Act 1969. As to the use of the word "minor," see *Practice Direction* [1970] 1 W.L.R. 977; [1987] 1 W.L.R. 93.

[56] Non-Contentious Probate Rules 1987, r. 34(1). As to grants during the infancy, see *post*, p. 323.

Married women

Although a married woman could formerly not accept office without the consent of her husband she is now in no different position from any other person.[57]

Criminals

The distinction between felony and misdeameanour was abolished by the Criminal Law Act 1967, s.1, but even before this felony was never of itself in principle a bar to the appointment of a representative. A person who has by his own criminal act caused the death of a testator cannot of course claim an interest under the will,[58] but there was never a bar in principle to a felon or outlaw exercising the office of executor[59] because he does so *in auter droit.*[60] Similarly the conviction for felony of an existing personal representative did not affect property vested in him by right of his representative office.[61] The grant of administration to a convict is improbable in the exercise of the court's discretion.[62] and may be impracticable if a sentence is being served at the time in question.[63]

Bankrupts

Probate was never refused[64] or revoked[65] on the sole ground of insolvency or poverty. In consequence the Chancery Court assumed a jurisdiction[66] in appropriate cases to restrain an insolvent or bankrupt executor, to appoint a receiver and, if necessary, to compel the executor to allow the use of his name in proceedings at law.[67] In these circumstances it is thought that since the fusion of the courts by the Judicature Act 1873, the Family

---

[57] The relevant legislation in chronological order is: Married Women's Property Act 1882, s.18; Married Women's Property Act 1907, s.1; Law of Property Act 1925, s.170; Judicature Act 1925, ss.159–167 (where no distinction is drawn); Law Reform (Married Women and Tortfeasors) Act 1935, s.1. Supreme Court Act 1981, ss.112–120.

[58] See *post*, pp. 327 and 972.

[59] Wentw.Off.Ex., 14th ed., p. 36; Godolph., Pt. 2, c. 6, s.1; Vin.Abr. tit. Outlawry, n.a., pl. 2. Trustee Act 1925, s.65 (repealed by the Criminal Law Act 1967).

[60] *Smethurst* v. *Tomlin* (1861) 2 Sw. & Tr. 143. For the discretion of the court as to persons to whom administration is to be granted, see *post*, pp. 343 *et seq.*

[61] Trustee Act 1925, s.65 (repealed by the Criminal Law Act 1967). The Forfeiture Act 1870, ss.9, 10, were repealed by the Criminal Justice Act 1948, Sched. 10, Pt. I.

[62] As to the court's discretion, see *post*, pp. 343, 350.

[63] *Re S. decd.* [1968] P. 302.

[64] *R.* v. *Sir Richard Raines* (1698) 1 Lord Raym. 361; *ibid.* 1 Salk. 299; 3 Salk. 162; 1 Stra. 672; Carth. 457; Holt 310; *Hathornthwaite* v. *Russel* (1740) 2 Atk. 126; *ibid.* Barnard C.C. 334. See also 3 P.Wms. 337, note to *Slanning* v. *Style*. But as to the discetion of the court under s.116 of the Supreme Court Act 1981, see *post*, p. 343. *Re Ray* (1926) 96 L.J.P. 37.

[65] *Hill* v. *Mills* (1691) 1 Show. 293. The property comprised in the deceased's estate remains vested in the bankrupt and does not become vested in the trustee in bankruptcy. See, now, the Insolvency Act 1986, ss.306, 283.

[66] See *per* Lord Mansfield in *R.* v. *Simpson* (1764) 1 W.Black. 456. Maitland, *Equity*, 2nd ed., pp. 249–251.

[67] *Utterson* v. *Mair* (1793) 2 Ves.Jun. 95; *Scott* v. *Becher* (1817) 4 Price 346. In like manner it restrained the assignees of a bankrupt executor from paying over the fund to him, and this upon petition in the bankruptcy, from the peculiar authority it had over them: *ibid.*

Division, taking account of the position in equity would now refuse a grant in any case where the Chancery Division would intervene as above,[68] so long as there was an alternative applicant for a grant, under the discretionary powers of the court.

The general grounds for the appointment of receivers are considered later.[69] In particular the court will not intervene if the testator has appointed an executor whom he knew to be insolvent or bankrupt[70] or merely because the executor is poor.[71] Such knowledge will, however, not be readily inferred.[72]

The court may restrain the bankrupt executor, but will not appoint a receiver, where there is another executor willing to act.[73] The grant of administration to an insolvent or bankrupt person is improbable.[74]

Mental disorder

Persons incapable of managing their affairs are incapable of being executors or administrators; for the disability renders them incapable not only of executing the trust reposed in them, but also of determining whether they will take upon themselves the execution of the trust or not.[75] If there is another executor capable and willing to take probate, a grant may be made to him. Otherwise, administration may be granted to some person for the use and benefit of the incapable person until further representation be granted or otherwise as the court directs.[76] With certain exceptions, notice must first be given to the Court of Protection,[77] and a person authorised by that court to apply for a grant is given priority.[78] If an executor becomes incapable the court may, on account of this natural disability, commit administration to another[79] or more probably now appoint another in his place.[80] Where one of several executors who have taken probate becomes incapable, the former grant will either be revoked and a fresh grant issued to the other executors, power being reserved to the executor who has become incapable to

---

[68] See *Re Gunn* (1884) 9 P.D. 242, 244.

[69] See *post*, p. 846.

[70] *Gladdon* v. *Stoneman*, March 21, 1808, *coram* Lord Eldon C., reported in a note to 1 Madd. 143; *Langley* v. *Hawk* (1820) 5 Madd. 46; *Stainton* v. *The Carron Co.* (1854) 18 Beav. 146, 161.

[71] *Hathornthwaite* v. *Russel* (1740) 2 Atk. 126; *ibid.* Barnard.C.C. 334; *Anon.* (1806) 12 Ves. 4; *Howard* v. *Papera* (1815) 1 Madd. 142.

[72] *Langley* v. *Hawk* (1820) 5 Madd. 46 (mere failure to alter the will after the bankruptcy).

[73] *Bowen* v. *Phillips* [1897] 1 Ch. 174.

[74] As to the court's discretion, see *post*, p. 343, 350.

[75] Godolph., Pt. 2, c. 6, s.2; Bac.Abr.Exors. 135; 2 Robert. 133, 134.

[76] See Non-Contentious Probate Rules 1987, r. 35(2), *post*, pp. 325, 1236. See also, *Re Phillips* (1824) 2 Add. 335, 336n., *Re Cooke* [1895] P. 68; and *post*, p. 325. Alternatively a grant of administration with the will annexed may be made. See *post*, p. 245.

[77] See Non-Contentious Probate Rules 1987 r. 35(5) *post*, p. 1236.

[78] See *post*, p. 325 and Heywood and Massey, 12th ed., p. 237. As to grants at the discretion of the court, see *post*, p. 343, 350.

[79] *Hill* v. *Mills* (1691) 1 Salk. 36; *Evans* v. *Tyler* (1849) 2 Rob.Eccl. 128, 134; *Re Galbraith* [1951] 2 All E.R. 470n. See *post*, p. 362.

[80] *i.e.*, under the Administration of Justice Act 1985, s.50. See *post*, p. 34.

come in and prove when again capable[81] or, more probably now, the court will simply terminate his appointment or appoint another in his place.[82]

Judicial Trustee

Under section 1(2) of the Judicial Trustees Act 1896, the administration of the property of a deceased person is a "trust," and the executor is a "trustee," so that under subsection (1) the court can, in a proper case, remove the executor and appoint a judicial trustee in his place, to whom, under subsection (4), it can give directions as to the administration of the "trust."[83] It is not possible to appoint a judicial trustee of part of an estate unless separate executors have been appointed.[84] The appointment of a judicial trustee is one method of replacing a recalcitrant representative. It has the advantage that the order can normally be made by the master in chambers without reference to the judge.[85] The originating summons to appoint a judicial trustee may also be issued out of a district registry.

The procedure for appointment of a judicial trustee is governed by the Judicial Trustee Rules 1983. The Public Trustee or the Official Solicitor may be so appointed.[86]

The Public Trustee

The Public Trustee is a corporation sole created by statute with certain powers and duties[87] and subject to certain restrictions.[88]

(1) *Powers and duties*

The Public Trustee may under section 6(1) of the Public Trustee Act 1906 act as executor or administrator.[89] He is also empowered to act (a) in the administration of estates of small value,[90] (b) as custodian trustee,[91] (c) as an ordinary trustee,[92] and (d) to be appointed a judicial trustee.[93] He may act

[81] *Re Shaw* [1905] P. 92, see *post*, p. 362.
[82] *i.e.* under the Administration of Justice Act 1985, s.50. See *post*, p. 34.
[83] *Re Ratcliff* [1898] 2 Ch. 352; see also *Re Jones* [1934] W.N. 77 *post* and the Judicial Trustee Rules 1983. Normally an estate is said to be "administered" and a trust "executed."
[84] *Rowells* [1968] 1 W.L.R. 44.
[85] See *Supreme Court Practice*, Ord. 32, r. 14(1), and *Practice Direction* [1990] 1 W.L.R. 52. Probably the most convenient method now of replacing a representative is to apply under the Administration of Justice Act 1985, s.50 (see *post*, p. 34). On such an application, the court may proceed as if the application were one for the appointment of a judicial trustee. See ss.50(4) and 50(2) adding s.1(7) to the Judicial Trustees Act 1896.
[86] Public Trustee Act 1906, s.2(1)(*d*), and Judicial Trustees Act 1896; Judicial Trustee Rules 1983, r. 2, and *infra*.
[87] See Public Trustee Act 1906.
[88] A brief paraphrase only is possible of the Public Trustee's functions as a personal representative. For his functions as trustee, see *Lewin on Trusts*, 16th ed., p. 450.
[89] When administering an estate of small value he has the powers of a Supreme Court Master. Public Trustee Act, s.3(3); Public Trustee Rules 1912, r. 14.
[90] Public Trustee Act, ss.2(1)(*a*), 3. As to the grant, see *post*, p. 242.
[91] *Ibid.* ss.2(1)(*b*), 4.
[92] *Ibid.* ss.2(1)(*c*), 5, 6.
[93] *Ibid.* ss.2(1)(*d*) and see Judicial Trustees Act 1896 and *supra*.

alone or jointly with others and is in the same position as a "private trustee,"[94] which expression covers the duties of executorship and adminis- tration.[95] He may decline absolutely or impose conditions before accepting any "trust,"[96] but he must not decline on the ground only of the small value of the estate.[97]

He has a duty to act in the administration of solvent estates of a gross value of under £1,000 on the date in question (and of partially administered estates where there is less than £1000 left), where all the persons bene- ficially entitled are of small means, unless he sees good reason for refus- ing.[98] Similarly, where administration proceedings have been instituted in any court, that court may order administration by the Public Trustee on the ground that by reason of the smallness of the estate it can be more econ- omically administered by him or that this is expedient for any other reason.[99] The court may also, regardless of the size of the estate, after notice to the persons beneficially interested, sanction the transfer of an estate in course of administration to the Public Trustee for administration either solely or jointly with the continuing personal representatives, if any.[1] His appointment is not effective until he has sealed a consent to act.[2]

(2) *Restrictions*

The statutory restrictions fall under four heads, namely, management of businesses, insolvent estates, charities and those affecting a custodian trusteeship:

(a) *Business.* The Public Trustee may not accept any trust which involves the management or carrying on of any business[3] unless he obtains Treasury permission. In practice there is no difficulty in obtaining such permission where a successful business is carried on through a limited company. He may also, without Treasury consent, act as custodian trustee only of a trust which involves the management of a business, provided he does not act in the management himself and holds no property which might expose him to liability against which he cannot be fully indemnified or secured. In addition he will normally agree to act as personal representative in an estate which includes a business, even when the business is not carried on through the medium of a limited company, but he would not be able to retain the business on an indefinite basis without special Treasury consent.[4]

---

[94] *Ibid.* s.2(2).
[95] *Ibid.* s.15.
[96] *Ibid.* s.2(3).
[97] *Ibid.* s.2(3).
[98] *Ibid.* ss.2(4), 3(1); *Re Devereaux* [1911] 2 Ch. 545, 549. Under s.3 he must be satisfied as to (1) solvency, (2) the limit of £1,000, (3) that all beneficiaries are of small means. The Public Trustee acts under this section only where a grant has already been obtained. Estates under £1000 are now likely to be insolvent and the section is seldom operated.
[99] *Ibid.* s.3(5).
[1] See *ibid.* s.6(2). Application is by originating summons in the Chancery Division. The Public Trustee is not a party but his prior consent should be obtained in the form of an under- taking to seal his consent if the court appoints him. Application must be at the instance of the personal representative.
[2] *Re Shaw* [1914] W.N. 141.
[3] Public Trustee Act, s.2(4).
[4] See Public Trustee Rules 1912, r. 7(1), (2).

(b) *Insolvent estates.*   The Public Trustee may not accept any trust under a deed of arrangement for the benefit of creditors, nor the administration of any estate known or believed by him to be insolvent.[5]

(c) *Charities.*   The Public Trustee may not accept any trust exclusively for religious or charitable purposes.[6] This provision does not however preclude him from acting as executor or administrator with the will annexed of an estate wholly given to charitable purposes. He may also act as trustee where the trusts are substantially, but not exclusively, charitable.

(d) *Custodian trusteeship.*   Where the Public Trustee acts as custodian trustee[7] the trust property and documents of title must be transferred to him as if he were sole trustee, and the management must remain with the managing trustees, but he must concur in and perform all acts necessary to enable the managing trustees to exercise their proper powers.

(3) *Estates of persons domiciled abroad*

Since the Act is expressly confined to England and Wales[8] the Public Trustee has no power to accept trusts construed or governed by the laws of any other country.[9] From this it follows that he will never re-seal a grant and he can act in relation to the estates of persons domiciled abroad only in the following circumstances:

   (a) Where the grant is limited *ad colligenda bona.*[10]
   (b) Where the will is confined to land in England or Wales.
   (c) Where he is to act only as attorney administrator for personal representatives duly constituted in the country of domicile.
   (d) Where, although unable to act as representative, he is required to act also as trustee in the execution of English trusts properly constituted in accordance with the local law and expressed to be subject to the jurisdiction of the English courts. Thus if in any given circumstances the duties of representative and trustee can in practice be severed, he may accept the trusteeship while renouncing the executorship.[11]

---

[5] Public Trustee Act, s.2(4).

[6] *Ibid.* s.2(5). *Re Hampton* (1918) 88 L.J.Ch. 103; *Re Cherry's Trusts* [1914] 1 Ch. 83.

[7] See *ibid.* s.4. So long as he is acting as custodian he cannot be appointed a managing trustee or ordinary trustee but must first be discharged from the custodian trusteeship (*Re Squire's Settlement* (1946) 62 T.L.R. 133).

[8] *Ibid.* s.17(2).

[9] *Re Hewitt's Settlement* [1915] 1 Ch. 228.

[10] As to such grants, see *post*, p. 331. *Re Sanpietro* [1940] P. 16.

[11] See *Re Gordon* (1877) 6 Ch.D. 531, 534.

CHAPTER 3

APPOINTMENT OF EXECUTORS

This chapter is concerned with the appointment of executors. Where no executor has been appointed the court will have to appoint an administrator. The appointment of administrators is considered in Chapter 17.[1]

Express, constructive and qualified appointment of executors

An executor is normally appointed by express nomination in the body of the will.[2] He may also be appointed by implication[3] and in either case his appointment may be absolute or qualified.[4] These are questions of construction and the probate court will act as a court of construction for these purposes.[5]

Substituted executors

An executor may be appointed solely, or in conjunction with others; but in the latter case all are considered in law as an individual person and, in general, the acts of any one of them, done for the purposes of administration, are deemed to be the acts of all of them.[6] Likewise a testator may appoint several persons as executors in several degrees; as where he makes his wife executrix, but if she will not or cannot be executrix, then he makes his son executor, and if his son will not or cannot be executor, then he makes his brother, and so on.[7] In such a case the wife is said to be *instituted* executor in the first degree, B is said to be *substituted* in the second degree, C to be *substituted* in the third degree, and so on.[8] The substituted executor cannot propound the will till the claims of the person first named executor have been considered. Thus the first named executor must be cited to accept or refuse, or may be shown to have died in the testator's lifetime,[9] or power may be reserved to him to prove the will on his return from

---

[1] See p. 233, *post.*
[2] An appointment beneath the signature is not effective. See *Re Woods* (1868) L.R. 1 P. & D. 566. As to the position of the signature, see *post*, p. 136. See also n. 65, *post.* For forms see Brighouse, *Precedents of Wills and Life Transfers.*
[3] See *post*, p. 29.
[4] See *post*, p. 35.
[5] *Re Fawcett* [1941] P. 85; *Re Last* [1958] P. 137. See also *Re Tharp* (1878) 3 P.D. 76, C.A., and *ante*, p. 10.
[6] Toller, 6th ed. 37. See *post*, pp. 469, 690.
[7] Swinb., Pt. 4, s.19, pl. 1; Godolph., Pt. 2, c. 4, s.1.
[8] *Smith* v. *Crofts* (1758) 2 Cas.temp. Lee 557.
[9] See *Re Betts* (1861) 30 L.J.P.M. & A. 167. *Re Wilmot* (1852) 2 Rob.Eccl. 579.

abroad,[10] but only if this appears to be the intention of the will.[11] If an instituted executor once accepts the office, and afterwards dies intestate, the substitutes are, prima facie, all excluded, because the condition of law (if he will not or cannot be executor) was once accomplished by such acceptance of the instituted executor.[12] In one case, however, the court granted probate to a substituted executor, after one of the original executors had renounced, and the other, *having intermeddled with the estate*, had gone abroad after refusing to prove the will.[13] Where a testator appoints an executor, and provides that, *in case of his death*, another should be substituted, on the death of the original executor, although he has proved the will, the executor so substituted may be admitted to the office, if it appears to have been the testator's intention that the substitution should take place on the death of the original executor, whether happening in the testator's life-time or afterwards.[14] In *Re Foster*[15] the deceased appointed his wife sole executrix, and in her default he appointed two nephews executors. Lord Penzance held that on the death of the wife, who had taken probate, the two nephews were entitled to a grant of probate as substituted executors. It was a question of construction as to whether the substitution was to take place only in the event of the wife not acting at all, or, as had happened, in the case of her death after taking probate. The court would not construe the words in a technical spirit, but would endeavour rather to carry out the real object of the testator. Lord Penzance thought it reasonable to hold that the testator intended that his wife should administer so long as she could, and in the event of her death, either before or after taking probate, the testator intended to substitute other persons. A grant was made to the two nephews accordingly.

Delegated power for executors to appoint

A testatrix appointed A and B executors, and by her will directed generally that should one executor die the survivor was "to choose another to the best of his judgment, and so to continue to the true intent and meaning of two executors." Upon the death of A, B appointed C to be executor, to act with him. C did not take probate during the lifetime of B. Sir H. Jenner Fust held that probate might pass to C, and that he might appoint another executor to act with him.[16] So where a testator bequeathed his estate in trust to F and G, who were nominated executors, with directions conjointly with the testator's wife to appoint a third person as trustee and executor, it was held by Sir H. Jenner Fust that, though it appeared that there was no

---

[10] *Re Lane* (1864) 33 L.J.P.M. & A. 185. See also "Limitations in Point of Time," *post*, p. 35.

[11] *Re Langford* (1867) L.R. 1 P. & D. 458.

[12] Swinb., Pt. 4, s.19, pl. 10; Godolph., Pt. 2, c. 4, s.2.

[13] *Re Freeman* (1931) 146 L.T. 143.

[14] *Re Lighton* (1828) 1 Hagg.Ecc. 235; *Re Johnson* (1858) 1 Sw. & Tr. 17.

[15] (1871) L.R. 2 P. & D. 304.

[16] *Re Deichman* (1842) 3 Curt. 123.

probability of agreement between F and G and the testator's wife in the choice of such third person, the appointment of executors was not thereby void, but that F and G were entitled to probate, with a power reserved for the third person when appointed.[17]

Delegated power for legatees to appoint

In another case, where a person by his will directed that the legatees should appoint two persons to execute his testamentary bequests, probate was granted in the Prerogative Court to the nominees as executors; and on that occasion the deputy registrar informed the court that, in practice, instances had frequently occurred of granting probates to persons nominated by those authorised by the testator so to nominate.[18] A person authorised to nominate an executor may nominate himself if the terms of the will so allow.[19] The Wills Act does not preclude this practice.[20]

Executor according to the tenor

An executor appointed by implication is usually called executor *according to the tenor*; for although no executor is expressly nominated in the will by the word "executor," yet, if by any word or circumlocution the testator recommends or commits to one or more the charge and office, or the rights which appertain to an executor, it amounts to as much as the ordaining or constituting him or them to be executors.[21] Thus an executor may be appointed by necessary implication. Where the testator says "I will that A B be my executor if C D will not," C D may be admitted into the executorship.[22] Conversely, however, an appointment is not to be inferred from "conjecturals" so that A B would not be appointed by the words "If my son A B marry with C D let him not be my executor."[23] An executorship by the tenor will also be implied where the word "executor" is not used, but where the person in question is directed to pay debts,[24] provided such debts are payable out of the general estate and not out of a particular fund.[25]

---

[17] *Jackson & Gill* v. *Paulet* (1851) 2 Robert. 344.

[18] *Re Cringan* (1828) 1 Hagg.Ecc. 548. See *Re Ryder* (1861) 2 Sw. & Tr. 127, where the person authorised to nominate had nominated himself and probate was granted to him; but *cf. Re Sampson* [1906] 1 Ch. 435.

[19] *Re Ryder* (1861) 2 Sw. & Tr. 127. The terms of the statutory power to appoint a new trustee under the Trustee Act 1893 did not so allow (*Re Sampson* [1906] 1 Ch. 435).

[20] *Jackson & Gill* v. *Paulet* (1851) 2 Robert. 344.

[21] Swinb., Pt. 4, s.4, pl. 3; Godolph., Pt. 2, c. 5, s.2; Wentw.Off.Ex., 14th ed., p. 20; *Re Manly* (1862) 3 Sw. & Tr. 56.

[22] Godolph., Pt. 2, c. 5, s.3; Swinb., Pt. 4, s.4, pl. 6. For examples, see *Naylor* v. *Stainsby* (1754) 2 Cas.Temp. Lee 54 and *Brightman* v. *Keighley* (1585) Cro.Eliz. 43.

[23] Godolph., Pt. 3, c. 3, s.5.

[24] *Re Punchard* (1872) L.R. 2 P. & D. 369; *Re Lowry* (1874) L.R. 3 P. & D. 157; *Re Baylis* (1865) L.R. 1 P. & D. 21; *Re Stewart* (1875) L.R. 3 P. & D. 244; *Re Mackenzie* [1909] P. 305.

[25] *Re Davis* (1843) 3 Curt. 748; *Re Toomy* (1864) 3 Sw. & Tr. 562; *Re Fraser* (1870) L.R. 2 P. & D. 183.

Examples of appointment "by the tenor"

The following are examples of cases where an executor has been held to be appointed:

A B should have his goods to pay his debts[26]; his wife should pay all and take all[27]; "I commit all my goods to the administration of A B"[28]; to "the deposition of A B"[29]; "to pay debts, funeral charges, and the expenses of proving the will"[30]; "I appoint my nephew my residuary legatee, to discharge all lawful demands against my will"[31]; "I devise all my personal goods to my two daughters and my wife, whom I make executrix"[32]; "I appoint my sister A B my executrix only requesting that my nephews C D and E F will kindly act for and with this dear sister"[33]; "I appoint A B and C D" without stating in what capacity, but bequeathing legacies to "each of my executors," and giving to his "said executors" the residue of his property, with certain directions as to it.[34] Again, where a testator did not specifically appoint any executor, but nominated four persons to act as his trustees, and bequeathed to them his residuary estate, with power to receive any sums due to the residue, and to give a discharge for the same, and in the will gave directions to his "executors," using the terms "trustees" and "executors" indifferently, as referring to the same persons.[35] So where a military nurse's will consisted of a letter giving the addressee full liberty to deal with her affairs, and giving directions as to the disposal of her property, the addressee was held entitled to probate of the document as executor according to the tenor.[36]

Where the testator gave various legacies, and then appointed that, his debts and legacies being paid, his wife should have the residue of his goods, so that she put in security for the performance of his will, this was held to make her executrix.[37] Again, where the will said nothing of the testator's debts, but contained only gifts of real and personal legacies, to be paid within two months after his death, and concluded, without any bequest of the residue or express appointment of executors, in these words: "I appoint A B, C D, and E F, to receive and pay the contents above mentioned", Sir G. Lee held that the persons so named were executors accord-

---

[26] *Re Manly* (1862) 3 Sw. & Tr. 56; *Henfrey* v. *Henfrey* (1842) 4 Moo.P.C. 29.

[27] *Brightman* v. *Keighley* (1585) Cro.Eliz. 43.

[28] Godolph., Pt. 2, c. 5, s.3; *Browne on Probate* 3rd ed., 110.

[29] *Pemberton* v. *Cony* (1589) Cro.Eliz. 164; Godolph., Pt. 2, c. 5, s.3.

[30] *Re Fry* (1827) 1 Hagg.Ecc. 80. Also *Re Almosnino* (1859) 1 Sw. & Tr. 508; *Re Collett* (1857) Dea. & Sw. 274; *Re Baylis* (1865) L.R. 1 P. & D. 21; *Re Adamson* (1875) L.R. 3 P. & D. 253; *Re Bell* (1878) 4 P.D. 85; *Re Lush* (1887) 13 P.D. 20; *Re Fawcett* [1941] P. 85.

[31] *Grant* v. *Leslie* (1819) 3 Phill. 116.

[32] *Foxwist* v. *Tremain* (1670) 1 Ventr. 102. All three were held to be appointed. As to the combination of express and implied appointment, see *post*, p. 32.

[33] *Re Brown* (1877) 2 P.D. 110. All three were executors.

[34] *Re Bradley* (1883) 8 P.D. 215.

[35] *Re Leven and Melville* (*Earl*) (1889) 15 P.D. 22; *Re Wilkinson* [1892] P. 227; *Re Russell* [1892] P. 380; see also *Re Drumm* [1931] N.I. 12.

[36] *Re Stanley* [1916] P. 192.

[37] Wentw.Off.Ex., 14th ed., p. 24.

ing to the tenor, for they could not receive and pay the legacies without collecting in the effects, and a person cannot assent to a legacy unless he has the management of the estate, because legacies cannot be paid till after the debts, and he only who has the management of the estate knows whether the assets are sufficient.[38] So a direction to a person "to pay all my just debts,"[39] or "to hold and administer in trust my estate,"[40] will constitute such person executor according to the tenor.

Persons not executors according to the tenor

Where a testator, being entitled to many shares in the Sun Fire Office, and in mines in Scotland, and a lease of a coalmeter's place, gave the same, by a will containing no appointment of an executor, to trustees in trust for his daughter, and after several contingencies gave the remainder thereof to his son, and if he should die in his minority without issue, gave the remainder thereof to the trustees for their own use, and gave all the residue of his estate to the said trustees, to pay one moiety to his daughter, and the other moiety to his son, Sir G. Lee held that there were no words in this will that made the trustees executors, inasmuch as they had only power to pay what was vested in them as trustees to the particular persons for whose use they held it, but had not a general power to receive and pay what was due to and from the estate, which is the office of an executor.[41] So where the whole personal estate was left to a trustee on trust for a specific purpose, and no executor was named in the will, it was held by Sir C. Cresswell that such trustee was not entitled to probate as executor according to the tenor.[42]

"Universal heir"

It has been said[43] that a person named "universal heir"[44] would have a right to apply for probate. But the practice of the Prerogative Court was to grant administration with the will annexed to the universal legatee of a testamentary paper, and not to decree probate to him as executor according to the tenor. This practice was adhered to by Sir C. Cresswell,[45] and was held[46] not to have been altered by Part I of the Land Transfer Act 1897.[47]

[38] *Pickering and Towers* v. *Towers* (1757) 2 Cas.temp. Lee 401.
[39] *Re Cook* [1902] P. 114; *Re Kirby* [1902] P. 188.
[40] *Re Way* [1901] P. 345; but see *Re Mackenzie* [1909] P. 305.
[41] *Boddicott and Hamilton* v. *Dalzell* (1756) 2 Cas.temp. Lee 294. See also *Fawkener* v. *Jordan* (1756) 2 Cas.temp. Lee 327; and *Moss* v. *Bardswell* (1860) 3 Sw. & Tr. 187, and *post* as to the distinction between the offices of trustee and executor.
[42] *Re Jones* (1861) 2 Sw. & Tr. 155.
[43] By Lord Hardwicke, in *Androvin* v. *Poilblanc* (1745) 3 Atk. 299.
[44] For this and other terms in French and German law, see Amos and Walton, *Introduction to French Law*, 2nd ed., pp. 288–338, and E. J. Cohn, *Manual of German Law*, 2nd ed., Vol. 1, pp. 257–293. As to the origins of the concept of universal succession, see Maine, *Ancient Law*, pp. 179–193. For a different use of the term "universal successor" see *National Bank of Greece* v. *Westminster Bank* [1971] A.C. 945.
[45] *Re Oliphant* (1860) 1 Sw. & Tr. 525.
[46] *Re Pryse* [1904] P. 301.
[47] Repealed as to deaths after 1925 (Administration of Estates Act 1925, s.56), its provisions being replaced by Pt. I of the Administration of Estates Act 1925.

Appointment of coadjutor or overseer

Although it appears to have fallen into disuse, the office of coadjutor or overseer to an executor has ancient authority. He is not an executor and has no power to administer or intermeddle otherwise than to counsel, persuade and advise; and if that fails to remedy negligence or miscarrying in the executors, he may complain to the court, and his charges in so doing ought to be allowed out of the testator's estate.[48] If A is made an executor, and B a coadjutor, without more, he is not by this made a joint executor with A.[49] But if A be made executor, and subsequently the testator, in his will, directs that B shall administer also with him, and in aid of him, B is an executor as well as A, and may prove the will alone as executor, if A refuses.[50] Where an infant was made an executor, and A and B *overseers*, with this condition, that they should have the rule and disposition of his goods, and payment and receipt of debts till the full age of the infant, they were held to be executors in the meantime.[51]

There are, no doubt, still circumstances where a testator might usefully employ this device to ensure that some responsible person (perhaps unwilling to undertake the details of executorship) can nevertheless ensure satisfactory administration and reference to the court, if need be, while incurring no financial liability. The office is in some ways analogous to that of arbitrator, or a visitor in the case of a charitable trust.

Implied appointment

When there is an express appointment of an executor, it is less probable that there should be an indirect appointment to the same office. But an executor according to the tenor may be admitted to probate jointly with an executor expressly nominated. Thus in *Powell* v. *Stratford*[52] the testator's wife was expressly named as executrix: Lord H. was to assist her, but he was not called executor, and the court said he might be so according to the tenor. In *Grant* v. *Leslie*[53] the deceased left a will and four codicils. In the will he named certain persons executors, and his nephew residuary legatee. The last codicil, dated at a time when his nephew was on the point of attaining 21 years, contained the words: "I appoint my nephew my residuary legatee to discharge all lawful demands against my will and codicils signed of different dates." It was held that the nephew should be joined in the probate. In a subsequent case, where an executor was expressly nomi-

[48] Wentw.Off.Ex., 14th ed., p. 21.
[49] *Browne on Probate* 3rd ed. 115; Wentw.Off.Ex., 14th ed., p. 21; Godolph, Pt. 2, c. 2, s.4. The words in the Year Book, 21 Hen. VI, c. 6, are: "I will that A and B shall be my executors, and also that I and K be coadjutors of the same A and B to distribute my goods."
[50] *Browne on Probate* 3rd ed. 115; Wentw.Off.Ex., 14th ed., p. 21. Where a testator willed that A and B should be his executors, and that I and K should be the executors of A and B to dispose of his goods, they were all executors: Dyer 4, p. 10, in margin.
[51] Wentw.Off.Ex., 14th ed., p. 21.
[52] (1803) cited 3 Phill. 118; *Re Brown* (1877) 2 P.D. 110.
[53] (1809) 3 Phill. 116.

nated for general purposes, another person was held to be executor, according to the tenor, for limited purposes.[54]

Where a person had been expressly appointed executor for a limited purpose in a will, it was held that he was appointed general executor by a codicil, by implication merely, without express words.[55]

Appointment revoked by implication

Where the testator in his will appointed two persons his executors, and in a codicil named his wife "sole executrix of this my will," the court held that the appointment of executors in the will was revoked.[56] *Semble*, the reappointment in a subsequent will of one of the executors named in a former will with a new executor shows an intention to revoke the appointment of executors in the first will where the word "sole" is used in the subsequent will,[57] but not otherwise.[58]

Where the same persons are appointed trustees and executors of a will, a revocation of their appointment as executors is not necessarily a revocation of their appointment as trustees.[59]

Appointment revoked by divorce

Where, after a testator has made a will the marriage is dissolved, the will takes effect as if any appointment of the former spouse as executor or executor and trustee were omitted.[60] This is equivalent in its effect to the former spouse predeceasing the testator.[61]

Appointment bad for uncertainty

An appointment of "A as my executor with any two of my sons" was held bad, as to the sons, for uncertainty.[62] Where a testator, having three sisters living when he made his will, appointed "one of my sisters" sole executrix, and two of the sisters died in his lifetime, the appointment was

---

[54] *Lynch* v. *Bellew and Fallon* (1820) 3 Phill. 424.

[55] *Re Aird* (1828) 1 Hagg.Ecc. 337.

[56] *Re Lowe* (1864) 3 Sw. & Tr. 478.

[57] *Re Baily* (1869) L.R. 1 P. & D. 628.

[58] *Re Lesse* (1862) 31 L.J.P.M. & A. 169.

[59] *Graham* v. *Graham* (1853) 16 Beav. 550; *Cartwright* v. *Shepheard* (1853) 17 Beav. 301; *Worley* v. *Worley* (1854) 18 Beav. 58. As to the relationship between executorship and trusteeship.

[60] Administration of Justice Act 1982, s.18 inserting a new section 18A into the Wills Act 1837.

[61] *Re Cherrington* [1984] 1 W.L.R. 772. It is not clear whether this provision is intended to be subject to a contrary intention appearing in the will as is the case where a gift in such a will lapses under the section. See *post*, p. 941. *Re Cherrington* was not followed in *Re Sinclair* [1985] Ch. 446 in so far as it covered the dispositive effects of the section. See p. 194, *post*.

[62] *Re Baylis* (1862) 2 Sw. & Tr. 613. *Semble*, a grant "to A and/or B" would be valid; see *Re Lewis* [1942] Ch. 424.

held void for uncertainty.[63] In *Re Horgan*[64] Latey J. declined to construe the appointment by the testator of "the firm of Rodgers Horsley & Burton . . . who may act through any partner or partners of that firm or their successors in business at the date of my death not exceeding two in number to be the Executors and Trustees of this my will" as the appointment as executors of any two of however many partners might be surviving at the time of the testator's death without identifying them, and accordingly the appointment was not void for uncertainty.

Statutory appointment and appointment of representative by the court

Before 1926 an executor could derive his office from a testamentary appointment only.[65] This principle still applies except where statute has expressly provided otherwise. Thus, a scheme under the Companies Act cannot affect an executorship.[66] However the court now has power[67] to appoint a "substituted personal representative" in place of the existing representative or representatives or any of them. It may also terminate the appointment of one or more, but not all, where there are two or more existing representatives. A substituted representative may be authorised to charge for his services. This power is given in addition to the courts' previous powers. Thus, if there is only one executor (not being a trust corporation[68]), then during the minority of a beneficiary or the subsistence of a life interest the court may, on the application of any person interested, or of the guardian, committee or receiver of any such person, appoint one or more personal representatives in addition to the original personal representative, in accordance with probate rules and orders.[69] Again, a testator is deemed to have appointed the trustees of the settlement (unless they have been expressly appointed by the testator) to be his special representatives in regard to settled land.[70] Further, the court has power to appoint a special or additional personal representative in respect of the

---

[63] *Re Blackwell* (1877) 2 P.D. 72. As to the admission of parol evidence to correct an imperfect description of the executor contained in a will, see *Re De Rosaz* (1877) 2 P.D. 66; *Re Brake* (1881) 6 P.D. 217; *Re John Chappell* [1894] P. 98; parol evidence is admissible to resolve an ambiguity (*Re Ashton* [1892] P. 82) and, it seems, to explain a partial but not to fill in a total blank (*Re Dianah Hubbuck* [1905] P. 129); for a case of misdescription of an executor corrected by striking out the wrong surname, see *Re Cooper* [1899] P. 193.

[64] [1971] P. 50, and see *ante*.

[65] A will is the only bed where an executor can be begotten or conceived: Wentw.Off.Ex., 14th ed., p. 3.

[66] *Re Skinner* [1958] 1 W.L.R. 1043.

[67] Administration of Justice Act 1985, s.50.

[68] For definition of which, see Trustee Act 1925, s.68(18), as amended by Law of Property (Amendment) Act 1926, s.3.

[69] Supreme Court Act 1981, s.114(4); for procedure, see *post*, pp. 349 *et seq.*; Wolst. & Ch., 13th ed., Vol. 5, p. 29. Persons so appointed are still not strictly "executors," see *ante*, p. 17.

[70] Administration of Estates Act 1925, s.22(1), discussed *post*, pp. 37, 272. Appendix, *post*, p. 1122.

settled land.[71] The appointment of a judicial trustee has always had a similar effect[72] and where an application is made under the Administration of Justice Act 1985 the court may proceed as if on an application under the Judicial Trustees Act 1896.[73]

Absolute and qualified appointments

The appointment of an executor may be either absolute or qualified. It may be absolute, when he is constituted certainly, immediately, and without any restriction in regard to the testator's effects, or limitation in point of time.[74] It may be qualified, by limitations as to the time or place wherein, or the subject-matter whereon, the office is to be exercised; or the creation of the office may be conditional. In such cases more than one grant of probate may be necessary, but severance of the grant in this way is forbidden "except as regards a trust estate" where the estate of the deceased is known to be insolvent.[75]

Limitations in point of time

The time may be limited when the person appointed shall begin, or when he shall cease, to be executor. Thus if a testator appoints a man to be his executor at a certain time, as at the expiration of five years after his death,[76] or at an uncertain time, as upon the death or marriage of his son,[77] this is a good appointment. Where the deceased appointed two executors, and, in the case of the death of either of them, appointed two others to be executors in their stead, on the death of the original executor, who had alone proved the will, the substituted executors were admitted to the office upon the exhibition of a proxy of consent from the original executor who had not proved.[78] So, if a man appoints his son to be executor when he shall come to full age,[79] such qualified appointment is good; and in the meantime he has no executor.[80] Again, the testator may appoint the executor of A to be his executor, in which case, if he dies before A, he has no executor till A dies.[81] So a man may make A and B his executors, and appoint that A shall not intermeddle during the life of B. In such a case they will be executors successively, and not jointly.[82]

Likewise the testator may appoint a person to be his executor for a par-

---

[71] Administration of Estates Act 1925, s.23. *Re Clifton* [1931] P. 222; see also *Re Powell* [1935] P. 114.

[72] See *ante*.

[73] Administration of Justice Act 1985, s.50(4).

[74] Toller 6th ed. 36.

[75] Supreme Court Act 1981, s.113, *post*, p. 1119.

[76] Swinb., Pt. 4, s.17, pl. 1; Wentw.Off.Ex., 14th ed., p. 22.

[77] Swinb., Pt. 4, s.17, pl. 4.

[78] *Re Lighton* (1828) 1 Hagg.Ecc. 235. See also cases on substituted executors, *ante*, p. 27.

[79] Wentw.Off.Ex., 14th ed., pp. 22, 23.

[80] As to grants during infancy, see *post*, p. 323.

[81] Wentw.Off.Ex., 14th ed., pp. 22, 23; Godolph., Pt. 2, c. 2, s.4.

[82] Wentw.Off.Ex., 14th ed., p. 31. But see *post*, p. 38.

ticular period only, as during five years next after his decease,[83] or during the minority of his son, or the widowhood of his wife,[84] or until the death or marriage of his son.[85] Where[86] a widow was appointed executrix and residuary legatee for life, with remainder, as to the residue, to the nieces of the testator, and by a codicil it was provided that, in case she married again, she and the nieces should agree on proper persons to be trustees, to whom she was directed to assign all the real and personal estate, in trust for the uses of the will, but so as not to be liable for the debts, or subject to the power, of her second husband, it was held that her executorship expired on her second marriage.

In these cases, if the testator does not appoint a person to act before the period limited for the commencement of the office on the one hand, or after the period limited for its expiration on the other, the court may commit administration with the will annexed[87] to another person, until there is an executor, or after the executorship is ended.[88]

Limitations in point of place

In like manner, the appointment may be limited in point of place. Thus, the testator may make A his executor for his goods in Cornwall, B for those in Devon, and C for those in Somerset[89]; or he may make different executors for his goods in different dioceses, or different provinces[90]; or, which seems more rational and expedient, he may so divide the duty when his property is in various countries.[91] Thus an appointment of a Portuguese resident as executor "in Portugal"[92] or of an executor "in this country," referring to India,[93] has been held to refer to the estate in those countries, and separate grants were made confined to such estate. Power may however be reserved to such executors to prove in respect of the English estate,[94] and if an English will by ratification incorporates a Tasmanian will with different executors the grant may go to all the executors jointly.[95] If separate probates are granted the English executor can make title in England without the concurrence of other executors acting abroad under a different grant.[96]

---

[83] Swinb., Pt. 4, s.17, pl. 1.
[84] Wentw.Off.Ex., 14th ed., p. 29; Godolph., Pt. 2, c. 2, s.3.
[85] Swinb., Pt. 4, s.17, pl. 4.
[86] *Bond* v. *Faikney* (1757) 2 Cas.temp. Lee 371.
[87] As to the right to such a grant, see *post*, p. 245.
[88] Swinb., Pt. 4, s.17, pl. 2; Plowd. 279, 281.
[89] Swinb., Pt. 4, s.18, pl. 1; Godolph., Pt. 2, c. 2, s.3; Wentw.Off.Ex., 14th ed., p. 29; *Spratt* v. *Harris* (1833) 4 Hagg.Ecc. 405.
[90] Swinb., Pt. 4, s.18, pl. 4.
[91] *Spratt* v. *Harris* (1833) Toller 6th ed. 36; 4 Hagg.Ecc. 405.
[92] *Velho* v. *Leite* (1864) 3 Sw. & Tr. 456.
[93] *Re Wallich* (1864) 3 Sw. & Tr. 423.
[94] *Re Pulman* (1863) 3 Sw. & Tr. 269.
[95] *Re Harris* (1870) L.R. 2 P. & D. 83.
[96] *Re Cohen's Executors and L.C.C.* [1902] 1 Ch. 187. As to the appointment of trustees resident abroad see *Re Whitehead* [1971] 1 W.L.R. 833.

Limitations as to subject-matter

Again, the power of an executor may be limited as to the subject-matter upon which it is to be exercised. Thus the testator may make A his executor for his plate and household stuff, B for his sheep and cattle, and C for his real estate or any part thereof.[97] So a person may be made executor for one particular thing only and no more,[98] but if it appears that there will be no executor to administer the property excluded, the court may construe the appointment as general and direct an unlimited grant,[99] or may refuse probate altogether and direct administration with the will annexed.[1] The same will may contain the appointment of one executor for general, and another for limited, purposes.[2] Thus it is often convenient for an author to appoint a special "literary executor" in view of the special nature of property in his works, rather than involve his general executor in the employment and supervision of literary agents over long periods.[3] But probate will not be granted to more than four persons in respect of the same part of the estate.[4]

Where special executors have been appointed for settled land[5] a testator may appoint other persons, with our without such trustees, or any of them, to be his general executors for his other property and assets.[6] "Settled land" in the above context means land vested in the testator which was settled before his death and not by his will.[7]

Special representatives in respect of trust estate

Section 36 of the Trustee Act 1925 (which gives power to a sole surviving trustee to appoint new or additional trustees) does not enable a sole surviving trustee to appoint trustees *by his will* to carry on the trust in continuation to himself. But it is respectfully suggested, despite the remarks of Kekewich J. to the contrary in *Re Parker's Trusts*,[8] that there is nothing to prevent a sole surviving trustee from appointing by his will separate special

[97] Dyer 4*a*; Wentw.Off.Ex., 14th ed., p. 29; Godolph., Pt. 2, c. 3, pl. 2, 3.
[98] Wentw.Off.Ex., 14th ed., p. 29, *Davies* v. *Queen's Proctor* (1851) 2 Robert. 413.
[99] *Rose* v. *Bartlett* (1633) Cro.Car. 292.
[1] *Re Wakeham* (1872) L.R. 2 P. & D. 395.
[2] *Lynch* v. *Bellew and Fallon* (1820) 3 Phill. 424.
[3] As to copyright property, see *Copinger and Skone James on Copyright*, 13th ed., para. 5–2 *et seq.*
[4] Supreme Court Act 1981, s.114(1), *post*. The Judicature Act 1925, s.160(1), (repealed) limited the number in respect of the same "property," but Bucknill J. held the number was limited in respect of the same "estate" in an unreasoned judgment in *Re Holland* [1936] 3 All E.R. 13. Power may, of course, be reserved to excess executors if they are unwilling to renounce.
[5] See *ante*, p. 18.
[6] Administration of Estates Act 1925, s.22(2). Where a general grant of probate has been made, including settled land, the trustees of the settlement, if such exist, may still be appointed as special executors: a memorandum of the appointment will be indorsed on the general grant: *Re James* (1926) 162 L.T.J. 498.
[7] Administration of Estates Act 1925, s.22(1); and see *Re Egton S.E.* [1931] 2 Ch. 180; and Appendix, *post*, p. 1122.
[8] [1894] 1 Ch. 707.

executors for the purpose of the trust estate. If this is so, the court may, where such appointment has been made, grant probate to the special executors limited to the trust estate.[9]

Who may appoint new trustees

It is further submitted that it is only the representatives of such a sole surviving trustee who have obtained probate,[10] limited to or including the trust estate, who (as representatives of the last surviving or continuing trustee) have power to appoint new trustees under section 36. But if a general grant, including the trust estate, is made in the first instance to the general executors appointed by the will, such executors could appoint new trustees under section 36, in which case, should a subsequent grant be made to special representatives limited to the trust estate, such special representatives could be compelled to transfer the trust estate to the new trustees already appointed.[11]

Conditional appointment of executor

Lastly, the appointment may be conditional; and the condition may be either precedent or subsequent.[12] Thus it may be that, before he acts as such, the executor should give security to pay the legacies and in general to perform the will.[13]

Where an executor was appointed, provided he proved the will within three calendar months next after the death of the deceased, it was held that, in computing the time, the day of the death was to be excluded.[14] But if he fails to prove the will within three months, his appointment is void (at all events if there are substituted executors), though the failure is through the inadvertence of his solicitor, and though he has acted in the execution of the trust of the will.[15] If a person appoints A and B executors, with a proviso that B is not to administer, the proviso is void, and both A and B may apply for probate jointly.[16]

Conditional appointments of executors are fully discussed in Swinburne[17] and Godolphin.[18]

---

[9] Supreme Court Act 1981, s.113 (*post*, p. 1119); and see Non-Contentious Probate Rules 1987, r. 51, and compare *Re Mortifee* [1948] P. 274.

[10] Subject to the provisions of Trustee Act 1925, s.36(5) and s.18(2).

[11] See *Re Parker's Trusts, supra*. See also *Re Boucherett* [1908] 1 Ch. 180.

[12] Wentw.Off.Ex., 14th ed., p. 23; Godolph., Pt. 2, c. 2, s.1; and see *Stapleton and Truelock's Case* (1555) 3 Leon. 2, pl. 6; *Alice Frances' Case* (1527) 1 Dyer 4, pl. 8, in margin; Wentw.Off.Ex., 14th ed., p. 28. Should the executorship be determined by a breach of the condition, all acts done by the executor in pursuance of his office, before such condition is broken, are good: Godolph., Pt. 2, c. 2, s.1. See *post*, pp. 364 *et seq.*

[13] Godolph., Pt. 2, c. 2, s.1; Wentw.Off.Ex., 14th ed., p. 28.

[14] *Re Wilmot* (1834) 1 Curt. 1.

[15] *Re Day* (1850) 7 Notes of Cas. 553. See also *Re Lane* (1864) 33 L.J.P.M. & A. 185.

[16] 19 Hen. 8, pl. 8; Dyer, fol. 3. But see *ante*, p. 35, n. 82.

[17] Pt. 4, ss.5–16.

[18] Pt. 1, cc. 13, 14: Pt. 2, c. 2.

CHAPTER 4

ACCEPTANCE AND TRANSMISSION OF OFFICE

Executors cannot be compelled to accept office

The office of executor is a private one of trust. The executor is as a rule, named by the testator, not by the law, so the person nominated may refuse,[1] so long as he has not intermeddled,[2] though he cannot assign[3] the office; and even if in the lifetime of the testator he has agreed to accept the office, it is still in his power to refuse.[4] The persons deemed to have been appointed special representatives as regards settled land may likewise refuse to act as such.[5]

The Public Trustee

The Public Trustee may decline, either absolutely or except on the pre-scribed conditions, to accept any trust,[6] but he cannot decline to accept any trust on the ground only of the small value of the trust property.[7] He is also subject to a number of statutory restrictions previously considered.[8]

Citation to prove or renounce—conditional acceptance

Though the executor cannot be compelled unless he has intermeddled[9] to accept the executorship, he can be compelled to decide whether he will accept it or not, for the Family Division of the High Court[10] has power to summon any person named as executor in a will to prove or renounce pro-bate of the will, and to do such other things concerning the will as were cus-tomary before 1926.[11] The acceptance or refusal of office must be unconditional, but an executor is entitled before accepting to insist upon an indemnity from the beneficiaries.[12] Similarly, there is no objection to an agreement between a solicitor or other professional executor and the bene-

---

[1] Bac.Abr.Exors. E. 9. Dee *Douglas* v. *Forrest*, 4 Bing. 686, in the judgment of Best C.J. And see *Mohamidu Mohideen Hadjiar* v. *Pitchey* [1894] A.C. 437.

[2] As to the executor *de son tort*, see *post*, p. 93.

[3] See *post*, p. 43.

[4] *Doyle* v. *Blake* (1804) 2 Scho. & Lefr. 231.

[5] See the words "if willing to act" in Administration of Estates Act 1925, s.23(3). Appen-dix, *post*, p. 1123.

[6] This expression includes an executorship or administratorship: Public Trustee Act 1906, s.15. See *ante*, p. 24.

[7] Public Trustee Act 1906, s.2(3).

[8] See *ante*, pp. 24 *et seq*.

[9] See *post*, p. 93.

[10] As to the jurisdiction of the Family Division, see *ante*, p. 8.

[11] Supreme Court Act 1981, s.112, *post*, p. 1115, reproducing 21 Hen, 8, c. 5, s.8. For forms of citation, see Tristram & Coote 27th ed., pp. 1029 *et seq*. For practice as to citations, see *post*, p. 388.

[12] *Re Clay* [1919] 1 Ch. 66.

ficiaries for remuneration of such executor not otherwise chargeable,[13] if the beneficiaries are all *sui juris*.

Cessation of executor's rights

Section 5 of the Administration of Estates Act 1925[14] provides that where a person appointed executor by a will survives the testator but dies without having taken out probate of the will; or is cited to take out probate of the will and does not appear to the citation; or renounces probate of the will; his rights in respect of the executorship shall wholly cease, and the representation to the testator and the administration of his real and personal estate shall devolve and be committed in like manner as if that person had not been appointed executor.

This section applies where the executor is cited to take probate of a *copy* of a will and does not appear.[15] It appears to mean that the rights referred to cease as at the date of such executor's death, non-appearance or renunciation, but that the vesting and devolution of property operate as if he had not been appointed at all, otherwise doubt is thrown upon the acknowledged right of an executor to act before grant.[16] Where an executor to whom power has been reserved survives his acting co-executor, and does not appear to a citation, the case will stand as if his name had never appeared in the will, and the executor, if any, of the acting executor will be representative of the original testator.[17] Again, on the death of an executor, without having either renounced or taken probate, the executor of the survivor of two acting executors becomes the representative of the original testator.[18]

Executor who starts to act

Though an executor can elect whether he will accept or refuse the executorship, he may determine such election by acts which amount to an administration. For if he once administers, it is considered that he has already accepted the executorship.[19] The court must then compel him to prove the will,[20] and he becomes responsible for death duties and the attendant

---

[13] The need for such an agreement may arise from the absence of a charging clause in the will (see *post*, p. 51), or from the executor witnessing the execution of the will. See *post*, p. 977.

[14] This section reproduces Court of Probate Act 1857, s.79, and Court of Probate Act 1858, s.16. For text, see *post*, p. 1116.

[15] *Davis* v. *Davis* (1859) 31 L.J.P.M. & A. 216.

[16] See *post*, p. 83.

[17] *Re Noddings* (1860) 2 Sw. & Tr. 15, corrected, *ibid.* 473; *Re Reid* [1896] P. 129; and see *Re Boucherett* [1908] 1 Ch. 180.

[18] *Re Lorimer* (1862) 2 Sw. & Tr. 471. As to chain of representation, see *post*, p. 44, and as to the death of a sole non-proving executor, see *post*, p. 85.

[19] See *Cummins* v. *Cummins* (1845) 3 J. & L. 64; 8 Ir.Eq.R. 723; *Rogers* v. *Frank* (1827) 1 Y. & J. 409; *Kilbee* v. *Sneyd* (1828) 2 Moll. 186. See *post*, pp. 95 *et seq.* and 380.

[20] Godolph., Pt. 2, c. 19, s.2; Swinb., Pt. 6, s.22, pl. 1.; Bro.Exors., pl. 90; *Long and Feaver* v. *Symes and Hannam* (1832) 3 Hagg.Ecc. 771; *Mordaunt* v. *Clarke* (1868) L.R. 1 P. & D. 592; but see *post*, pp. 379, 381, 382; *Re Stevens* [1897] 1 Ch. 422; affirmed [1898] 1 Ch. 162. See *infra*, n. 25.

penalties.[21] If one of several executors, after intermeddling with the effects, renounces, the record of such renunciation on the probate granted to his co-executors ought to be cancelled.[22]

If the executor of an executor intermeddles in the administration of the effects of the first testator he cannot refuse the administration of the effects of the latter; and he cannot take upon himself the latter administration and refuse the former.[23] But with the sanction of the court an executor or an administrator may transfer the administration to the Public Trustee.[24]

Though there are old cases to the contrary, the law now is that if the executor has acted, and the court, not knowing it, commits administration to another, the administration may be revoked, and the executor compelled to prove the will; for an executor who has intermeddled cannot subsequently renounce nor has the court power to authorise him to do so[25]; but the grant of administration with the will annexed, until so revoked, is valid. Hence, a debtor to the testator cannot, in answer to a suit by such administrator, set up the act *in pais* of the executor against his renunciation, in order to delay or prevent a recovery by the administrator.[26]

The only sense in which the committing of the administration in such circumstances can now be said to be void is as respects the liability of the executor; for if he has once administered, he will remain liable to be sued as executor, both at law and in equity, in spite of his renunciation, and the consequent appointment of an administrator.[27] So if an executor administers part of the assets, he may be charged with the receipts, as executor, though he renounced the executorship, and paid the money to the other executor who proved the will.[28]

Acts which amount to administration or intermeddling

In general any act in relation to the testator's property which indicates an intention in him to take upon himself the executorship will constitute an acceptance of office by the nominated executor, provided such an act is not of so minimal a character as to amount only to[29] technical intermeddling.

---

[21] See *post*, p. 277.

[22] *Re Badenach* (1864) 3 Se. & Tr. 465, in which case one of several co-executors who had renounced after intermeddling was allowed, notwithstanding 20 and 21 Vict. c. 77, s.79 (reproduced by Administration of Estates Act 1925, s.5), to retract his renunciation on the ground that the renunciation was invalid after intermeddling; see also *Re Stevens* [1897] 1 Ch. 422; affirmed [1898] 1 Ch. 162; *Re Freeman* (1931) 146 L.T. 143.

[23] *Brooke* v. *Haymes* (1868) L.R. 6 Eq. 25; *Re Perry* (1840) 2 Curt. 655.

[24] Public Trustee Act 1906, s.6.

[25] *Jackson and Wallington* v. *Whitehead* (1821) 3 Phill. 577; and see *Re Stevens, supra*; 1 Roll.Abr.Exor.C. 2, p. 907; Wentw.Off.Ex., 14th ed., pp. 91, 92; Godolph., Pt. 2, c. 31, s.3; 2 Scho. & Lefr. 237. See *post*, p. 751. A person renouncing a grant limited to settled land need not state that he has not intermeddled.

[26] *Doyle* v. *Blake* (1804) 2 Scho. & Lefr. 231; *Hewson* v. *Shelley* [1914] 2 Ch. 13. See also Administration of Estates Act 1925, ss.27 and 37. Appendix, *post*, pp. 1125, 1131.

[27] Wentw.Off.Ex., 14th ed., p. 92.

[28] *Read* v. *Truelove* (1762) Ambl. 417. As to the liability to creditors and legatees of an executor renouncing after acts of administration, see *post*, pp. 751 *et seq.*

[29] *Holder* v. *Holder* [1968] Ch. 353, 392.

A further test is whether, if not nominated, he would be liable as an executor *de son tort*.[30] Common instances of such acts of administration as amount to acceptance of office are as follows:

(1) *Dealing with goods, or other assets—intention*

If the executor takes possession of the testator's goods and converts them to his own use, or disposes of them to others, this is an administration.[31] So, if he takes the goods of a stranger, under an apprehension that they belonged to the testator, and administers them, this amounts to an administration.[32] Thus, where the testator being tenant at will of certain goods, his executor seized the goods, supposing them to belong to the testator, with an intent to administer, it was held that this made him executor in law.[33] But if an executor seizes the testator's goods, claiming a property in them himself though afterwards it appears that he had no right, this will not make him executor; for the claim of property shows a different view and intention from that of administering as executor.[34]

(2) *Dealing with debts*

If an executor receives debts due to the testator, and especially if he gives acquittances for such debts, this amounts to an election of the executorship; so, if he releases a debt due to the testator[35]; or even if he writes to demand payment of a debt due.[36] However, if one of several executors merely joins in the payment of small debts, opens an account and indorses insurance policies, these acts of themselves are not sufficient to preclude his renunciation.[37]

(3) *Accepting legacy*

So if there are two executors and one of them is given a specific legacy, and he takes possession of it without the consent of his co-executor, this amounts to an administration; for a legatee cannot take a chattel bequeathed to him without the assent of the executor.[38]

(4) *Acknowledging executorship*

Where a man who was named as one of several executors, in answer to an inquiry as to who were the executors, wrote a letter saying that he and

[30] Godolph., Pt. 2, c. 8, s.1 and s.6; Bac.Abr., tit. Executors, E. 10; Toller 6th ed. 43; *Rayner* v. *Green* (1839) 2 Curt. 248. But see Wentw.Off.Ex., 14th ed., p. 94.
[31] Wentw.Off.Ex., 14th ed., p. 93; or even takes them into his hands, some say, without converting them; *ibid.*
[32] 1 Roll.Abr. 917, pl. 12; Bac.Abr., tit. Executors, E. 10; *I.R.C.* v. *Stype* [1982] Ch. 456.
[33] 1 Roll.Abr. 917, pl. 12; Vac.Abr., tit. Executors, E. 10.
[34] Bac.Abr., tit. Executors, E. 10.
[35] Wentw.Off.Ex., 14th ed., p. 94; Swinb., Pt. 6, s.22, pl. 2; 1 Roll.Abr. 917, pl. 7, 8; *Pytt* v. *Fendall* (1754) 1 Lee 553.
[36] *Re Stevens* [1897] 1 Ch. 422; affirmed [1898] 1 Ch. 162.
[37] *Holder* v. *Holder* [1968] Ch. 353, 392.
[38] 1 Roll.Abr. 917, tit. Exor., B. pl. 9; Bac.Abr., tit. Exor., E. 10. See *post*, p. 1051.

others were executors, this was held to afford sufficient evidence that he had acted as executor.[39] The insertion of an advertisement calling on persons to send in their accounts, and to pay money due to the testator's estate to A and B, "his executors in trust," was held to make them compellable to take probate, and to subject them personally to the costs occasioned by their resistance (the estate being small, and left for two years and a half without a representative).[40]

(5) Assisting co-executor

An executor who has not proved is not to be considered as acting by assisting a co-executor, who has proved, in writing letters to collect debts, nor by writing directly to a debtor of the testator, and requiring payment.[41]

(6) Taking the Oath

Taking the oath as executor is not such an intermeddling as to preclude renunciation.[42] Thus, if he has not administered, the court will, upon his own application, dismiss him and allow him to renounce probate even after the usual oath, and an appearance given as executor. Such a renunciation was permitted in *Jackson and Wallington* v. *Whitehead*,[43] so that the executor might be examined as a witness. But an executor cannot renounce after he has taken probate.[44] An executor cannot refuse by any act or declaration other than a formal renunciation in writing signed by him or his attorney and entered and recorded in the court.[45] But such renunciation need not be by deed.[46] A renunciation is not a conveyance within the Law of Property Act 1925, s.52, which requires conveyances to be by deed.[47]

An executor cannot assign

An executorship is an office of personal trust and cannot therefore be assigned.[48] The estate may, however, with the sanction of the court be transferred to the Public Trustee for administration,[49] and there is now

---

[39] *Vickers* v. *Bell* (1864) 10 Jur.(N.S.) 376; 4 De G.J. & S. 274.

[40] *Long and Feaver* v. *Symes and Hannam* (1832) 3 Hagg.Ecc. 771.

[41] *Orr* v. *Newton* (1791) 2 Cox 274. See also *Stacey* v. *Elph* (1833) 1 M. & K. 195; and *Holder* v. *Holder*, *supra*; but see *Harrison* v. *Graham* (1700) 3 Hill's MSS 239; 1 P.Wms. 241n. (y) to 6th ed.; *post*, p. 751.

[42] *M'Donnell* v. *Prendergast* (1830) 3 Hagg.Ecc. 212.

[43] (1821) 3 Phill. 577. See also *Long and Feaver* v. *Symes and Hannam* (1832) 3 Hagg.Ecc. 771.

[44] *Re Veiga* (1862) 32 L.J.P.M. & A. 9. As to renunciation generally, see *post*, p. 378.

[45] Wentw.Off.Ex., 14th ed., p. 88; *Long and Feaver* v. *Symes and Hannam*, *supra*, and see *Broker* v. *Charter* (1590) Cro.Eliz. 92; Wentw.Off.Ex., 14th ed., p. 88; Godolph., Pt. 2, c. 19, s.4. *Re Rosser* (1864) 3 Sw. & Tr., 490. In practice the renunciation is entered in the Probate Registry. See also *post*, pp. 378 *et seq.*

[46] *Re Boyle* (1864) 3 Sw. & Tr. 426.

[47] See 1 Wolst. & Ch., 12th ed., p. 319 and p. 1057 *post*.

[48] *Re Skinner* [1958] 1 W.L.R. 1043; *Bedell* v. *Constable* (1668) Vaugh 177. See also n. 1, p. 17 *ante*.

[49] Public Trustee Act 1906, s.6(2) and see *ante*, p. 24.

power for the court to appoint a substitute for, and to remove, a personal representative.[50] An executor may also, by power of attorney, appoint another to act for him for a period of up to 12 months.[51]

Chain of representation

But an executor of a sole or last surviving executor of a testator is the executor of that testator, so that the interest vested in the original executor by probate of the will of the testator is continued and kept alive, without a new probate of the original will,[52] by probate of the will of the executor.[53] The power of an executor is founded upon the special confidence and actual appointment of the deceased; and such executor is therefore allowed to transmit that power to another, in whom he has equal confidence. But the principle does not apply to an executor who does not prove the will of his testator, and, if an executor leaves surviving him some other executor of his testator who afterwards proves the will of that testator, it ceases to apply when such probate is granted.[54] So long as the chain of representation is unbroken, the last executor in the chain is the executor of every preceding testator.[55] Where it is broken an administrator *de bonis non* of the original testator must be appointed by the court.[56] The chain of such representation is broken by an intestacy,[57] or the failure of a testator to appoint an executor, or the failure to obtain probate of a will[58]; but it is not broken by a temporary grant of administration if probate is subsequently granted.[59] *Semble*, if probate is not subsequently granted, the chain of representation is broken as from the death of the original executor, but without prejudice to the intermediate acts of the temporary administrator.

Where a sole executor has died leaving a will and appointing an executor, who for some reason neither proves nor renounces probate, it has been held in Ireland that a grant can be made of the unadministered estate of the

[50] Administration of Justice Act 1985, s.50.

[51] See Trustee Act 1927, s.25, as amended by the Powers of Attorney Act 1971.

[52] *Wankford* v. *Wankford* (1704) 1 Salk. 299.

[53] Administration of Estates Act 1925, s.7(1), which reproduces in effect the law as it was before 1926; as to which, see Com.Dig., tit. Administration, G., tit. Administration, B. 6; Touchst. 464; stat. 25 Edw. 3, st. 5, c. 5; Wentw.Off.Ex., 14th ed., p. 461; 2 Black.Comm. 506. The rule is the same though the original probate was a limited one: *Re Beer* (1851) 2 Rob.Eccl. 349. See *post*, p. 695, as to whether a power given to an executor is transmissible to his executor, and Appendix, *post*, p. 1112, for the text of the Administration of Estates Act 1925.

[54] Administration of Estates Act 1925, s.7(1). As to joint representation see p. 469 *post*.

[55] *Ibid.* s.7(2). *Post*, p. 1116.

[56] See *Re Martin* (1862) 3 Sw. & Tr. 1; *Re Bridger* (1878) 4 P.D. 77 and *post*, p. 337.

[57] Administration of Estates Act 1925, s.7(3). The administrator of the executor is merely an officer of the court, and has no privity or relation to the original testator. See 2 Black.-Comm. 506.

[58] Administration of Estates Act 1925, s.7(3). Thus, if the person appointed executor dies before the testator, there must be administration with the will annexed: see *Brown* v. *Poyns* (1648) Sty. 147; *Pullen* v. *Sergeant* (1684) 2 Ch.Rep. 300. See also *Isted* v. *Stanley* (1580) 3 Dyer 372 a; *Hayton* v. *Wolfe* (1621) Cro.Jac. 614; *Day* v. *Chatfield* (1683) 1 Vern. 200; *Wankford* v. *Wankford* (1704) 1 Salk. 299; *Anon.* (1628) 3 Salk. 21. See *post*, pp. 245 *et seq.*

[59] Administration of Estates Act 1925, s.7(3). See *post*, pp. 476, 1116.

original testator to a residuary legatee under his will or to some other suitable person; such a grant is limited to continue until the executor shall obtain probate of his testator's will.[60] However, in England and Wales a discretionary grant would in such circumstances normally be made after citation of the executor.

The administrator during the minority of the executor of an executor is the representative of the first testator.[61] Hence, in an action by a creditor of the original testator, such an administrator is properly charged as the administrator during the minority of the second executor, and not as the administrator *de bonis non* of the original deceased.[62]

So also if administration with the will annexed has been granted to the attorney of an executor, the chain of representation is not thereby broken so long as the executor himself proves later.[63] Where a joint grant of administration with the will annexed is made to the nominee of a company (not being a trust corporation)[64] and an individual, who are appointed executors, under a will, no question as to the chain of representation arises unless the company ceases to exist during the life of the individual.[65] There is no chain of executorship through a special executor of settled land,[66] or through an additional personal representative appointed by the court.[67]

Where two or more executors are appointed, and prove the will, if one of them dies, leaving one or more of his co-executors living, no interest in the executorship is transmissible to his own executor, but the whole representation survives, and will be transmitted ultimately to the executor (if any) of the surviving executor. Thus, if A makes B and C executors, then B makes J his executor and dies, and afterwards C dies intestate, the executor of B is not the executor of A: the executorship is wholly and solely vested in C by the survivorship, so that there must be a grant of administration *de bonis non*.[68] *Secus* (otherwise) if C had not proved A's will.[69]

Effect of the chain

An executor of an executor, in however remote a series, has the same interest in the estate of the first testator as the first and immediate execu-

[60] *Re Gilkinson* [1948] N.I. 42.
[61] *Anon.* (1675) 1 Freem.K.B. 288; confirmed by Administration of Estates Act 1925, s.7(3). Also *Norton* v. *Molyneux and Ford* (1608) Hob. 246; and see note by Mr. Smirke in the 2nd ed. of Freeman's Reports (K.B.) at p. 288.
[62] See *Norton* v. *Molyneux and Ford, supra.*
[63] *Re Bayard* (1849) 1 Robert. 768; 7 Notes of Cas. 117; *Re Murguia* (1884) 9 P.D. 236; and see as to the effect of a grant for the use and benefit of the executrix during her incapacity, *Re Frengley* [1915] 2 Ir.R. 1. It is now necessary for such an executor to prove in view of s.7(1) of the Administration of Estates Act 1925. This was not formerly so.
[64] See *ante*, p. 20.
[65] See Senior Registrar's Directions, May 18, 1927.
[66] See Senior Registrar's Direction, July 21, 1936.
[67] See *ante*, p. 17.
[68] Wentw.Off.Ex., 14th ed., p. 215; *Re Smith* (1842) 3 Curt. 31. *Cf.* Trustee Act 1925, s.18(2), as to the devolution of powers and trusts given to or imposed on trustees: *post*, pp. 695 *et seq.*
[69] See Administration of Estates Act 1925, s.5, *post*, p. 1116. See also *post*, p. 388, n. 3.

tor.[70] Every person in the chain of representation to a testator has the same rights in respect of the real and personal estate of that testator as the original executor would have had if living and is, to the extent to which the estate whether real or personal has come to his hands, answerable as if he were an original executor.[71]

Effect of power to prove being reserved

If power to prove is reserved to an executor, and his co-executor dies having proved the will and acted, the chain continues in the executor of the acting executor who becomes the executor of the original testator until probate is granted to the executor to whom power was reserved[72]; similarly, if a grant of administration is applied for in respect of the original testator's estate, the non-proving executor must be cited.[73]

Surviving executor incapable

A grant for the use and benefit of an executor during his incapacity is equivalent to a grant of probate to him and, should such executor survive his co-executor, the executor of the latter will not represent the original testator.[74]

Uncertainty as to the chain

Where it is uncertain who is the personal representative of a deceased trustee[75] who was entitled to or possessed of any interest in land the court may make a vesting order.[76]

Grants other than those obtained in England and Wales

The chain of representation is broken where the executor does not prove the will of the testator[77] and a grant of probate other than one obtained in

[70] Wentw.Off.Ex., 14th ed., c. 20, pp. 462, 463; Com.Dig. Administration, G.; Administration of Estates Act 1925, s.7. At common law, an executor of an executor could not bring actions in respect of the *choses in action* of the original testator. But by statute 25 Edw. 3, stat. 5, c. 5, it was enacted that executors of executors should have actions of debts, accompts and of goods carried away by the first testators. An executor was within the equity of the statute 32 Hen. 8, c. 37, with respect to remedies for rent in arrear in certain cases, and conversely, by statute 4 Will. & M. c. 24, the executor of an executor who wasted his testator's estate was rendered chargeable in the same manner as the testator might have been.

[71] Administration of Estates Act 1925, s.7(4). The earlier enactments were repealed by Administration of Estates Act 1925, s.56, Sched. 2, Pt. 1, for all cases where death occurs after 1925.

[72] *Re Reid* [1896] P. 129 notice must normally be given to the executor to whom power is reserved. N.-C.P.R. 1987 r. 27. *Practice Direction* [1988] 1 W.L.R. 195.

[73] See Administration of Estates Act 1925, ss.5, 6, 7. In a proper case renunciation may be retracted. (*Re Stiles* [1898] P. 12.)

[74] *Re Frengley* [1915] 2 Ir.R. 1.

[75] See *ante*, p. 24 as to meaning of "trustee"

[76] Trustee Act 1925, s.44.

[77] Administration of Estates Act 1925, s.7(1), (3). A grant will in many cases be obtained under N.-C.P.R. 1987, r. 30.

England or Wales is therefore normally not sufficient to create or continue the chain.[78]

However, where a person dies domiciled in Northern Ireland a grant of probate obtained there will be treated for the purposes of the law of England and Wales as if it had been originally made by the High Court in England and Wales[79] and therefore such a grant will apparently be sufficient to establish or maintain the chain. This rule applies whenever the deceased died,[80] and apparently therefore the chain of representation may have been created and be continued indefinitely by grants obtained in Northern Ireland.

Although in certain circumstances where a person dies domiciled in Scotland a confirmation or a certificate of confirmation may be recognised for the purposes of the law of England and Wales as a grant of representation to the executors named therein,[81] section 7 of the Administration of Estates Act 1925 does not apply on the death of such an executor,[82] and it therefore appears that a chain of representation cannot be created or continued by such a confirmation or certificate.

Where a Court of Probate in a British Possession to which the Colonial Probates Act 1892 applies[83] has granted probate to an executor or executors and that grant has been resealed in England, a chain of executorship arises where subsequently the same court has granted probate of the executor (or last surviving executor) to his executor as executor and this grant has also been resealed in England.[84]

Administrator de bonis non (unadministered assets)

An administrator appointed to administer the unadministered assets of an estate is not within the chain of representation. He is however entitled, subject to the terms of his grant, to such real and personal estate as remains *in specie* and has not been administered by the first executor or administrator.[85] Also it has been held that if an executor receives money in right of his testator, and lays it up by itself, and dies intestate, this money goes to

---

[78] *Re Gaynor* (1869) L.R. 1 P. & D. 723.
[79] Administration of Estates Act 1971, s.1(4). See *post*, pp. 368, 1155.
[80] *Ibid.* s.1(6).
[81] *Ibid.* s.1(1). See *post*, p. 1154.
[82] *Ibid.* s.1(3).
[83] See *post*, p. 370.
[84] See *Senior Registrar's Direction*, February 24, 1949.
[85] *Wankford* v. *Wankford* (1704) 1 Salk. 299, by Lord Holt; Bac.Abr. Executors, B, 2, 2. L was possessed of furniture and other property, and on his death, intestate, in 1827, the furniture was removed by his widow to another house, in which she resided, until her death in 1832, with her daughter E, and continued during that period to use the furniture. In October 1829, the widow caused the furniture to be valued, with a view to her taking out administration to L, which she afterwards did. In 1838, the furniture was sold by the defendant (who had married another daughter of L), with E's concurrence. In 1840 (disputes having arisen about the distribution of the proceeds), E took out administration to her mother. It was held, that E could not maintain trover for the furniture without having taken out administration *de bonis non* to L: *Elliot* v. *Kemp* (1840) 7 M. & W. 306; *Tingrey* v. *Brown* (1798) 1 Bros. & P. 310. As to grants *de bonis non*, see also *post*, p. 337.

the administrator *de bonis non*, being as easily distinguished to be part of the testator's effects as goods *in specie*.[86] And wherever assets are in the hands of a third person, at the death of an administrator, or executor intestate, the administrator *de bonis non* may sue for their recovery.[87] Similarly, he may sue, or be sued, on contracts made with the former executor or administrator.[88] He is thus in practice for many purposes in the same position as an executor within the chain of representation.

Assets disposed of fraudulently

If the original executor or administrator has fraudulently disposed of the assets for his own use in collusion with a purchaser,[89] such assets will be considered, in equity, as unadministered, and will consequently pass as such to the administrator *de bonis non*, who, in that character, may apply to the court to have the sale set aside, and to have the legal estate conveyed to him. Thus, in *Cubbidge* v. *Boatwright*,[90] a testatrix had directed that a leasehold property should be sold, and the money divided among five persons, but the administrator with the will annexed, alleging that he had become entitled to it by agreement with the legatees, assigned it over for valuable consideration, the purchase-money being paid for his own personal use, and not in order to be administered as assets of the testatrix. It was held that, at his death, it remained assets unadministered; and that the purchaser must be directed to convey it to the administratix *de bonis non*, though the persons beneficially interested were not all parties to the suit. But if the administrator, in his character of administrator, had sold the property, and the purchaser had been ignorant of the real nature of the transaction, the sale could not have been set aside.[91]

Assets disposed of lawfully

If, however, the original executor has fully administered the estate in accordance with the law, a subsequent administrator *de bonis non* cannot recover from a beneficiary assets which have been paid to him in a due course of administration.[92]

Assets not passing on grant de bonis non

If by some of the means specified in a later part of this work,[93] the property in any of the effects of the deceased has been changed by the original

---

[86] *Wankford* v. *Wankford, supra*; Bac.Abr. Executors, B, 2, 2.
[87] *Lady Langford* v. *Mahony* (1843) 4 Dr. & Warr. 81, 107. See *post*, p. 50.
[88] *Hirst* v. *Smith* (1797) 7 T.R. 182; *Moseley* v. *Rendell* (1817) L.R. 6 Q.B. 338. See *post*, p. 876. See also Administration of Estates Act 1925, s.39(1)(iii).
[89] See *post*, pp. 680 *et seq.*
[90] (1826) 1 Russ. 549.
[91] See *infra*.
[92] *Re Aldhous* [1955] 1 W.L.R. 459. Where notices for claims in the usual (though not entirely correct) form had been issued under Trustee Act 1925, s.27, no claims from possible next-of-kin were received. See further, *post*, p. 605.
[93] *Post*, pp. 1051 *et seq.*

executor or administrator, and has vested in him in his individual capacity, such effects will go to his own administrator or executor, and not to the administrator *de bonis non*.

Thus, under the old law, if a personal representative granted an under-lease of a term of years of the deceased, reserving the rent to himself, his executors, etc., though he had the head term wholly in right of the deceased, yet if he died, the rent was at law payable to his personal representative,[94] and not to the administrator *de bonis non* of the original deceased[95]; but the rents reserved in such leases were assets of the original deceased, and applicable in due course of administration.[96] It is conceived that at the present time, in the absence of notice of the grant *de bonis non*, the under-lessee might still be protected if he paid the rent to the representatives of the original executor or administrator, though his proper course on receiving such notice would seem to be to pay the rent to the administrator *de bonis non*.[97]

Mortgage by prior representative

After 1925, a mortgage of a freehold can only take effect at law as a term of years,[98] and a mortgage of a leasehold as a sub-term,[99] or in either case, by means of a charge by deed expressed to be by way of legal mortgage.[1] Thus, if the original representative creates a mortgage, the freehold reversion or the head term, as the case may be, remains in him, and in the case of a charge by deed by way of legal mortgage no term at all is vested in the mortgagee. It follows that the land subject to the mortgage will devolve upon the administrator *de bonis non*, and a right to redeem will pass with it.[2]

Promissory note taken by original representative

Again, the administrator *de bonis non* is entitled to all debts due and owing to the original testator or intestate[3]; but in this instance also, the original executor or administrator may, in some cases, have so altered the property in a *chose in action* as to transmit it to his own representative, and

---

[94] It seems, however, that they could not have distrained: *Drue* (or *Drew*) v. *Bailie* (or *Bayly*) (1675) 1 Freem.K.B. 402, 403.

[95] *Drue* (or *Drew*) v. *Bailie* (or *Bayly*) (1675) 1 Freem.K.B. 402; 2 Lev. 100; *Norton* v. *Harvey* (1674) 1 Ventr. 259; *Cowell* v. *Watts* (1805) 6 East 405. See, however, *Catherwood* v. *Chabaud* (1823) 1 B. & C. 150; *post*, p. 50.

[96] Bac.Abr. Leases, 1, 7.

[97] See Administration of Estates Act 1925, s.39(1). And see Law of Property Act 1925, ss.78, 80(2), 141.

[98] Law of Property Act 1925, s.85.

[99] *Ibid.* s.86.

[1] *Ibid.* s.87.

[2] As to the liability of the administrator *de bonis non* on the covenants in the mortgage, see Law of Property Act 1925, s.80(2). For the position before 1925, see *Skeffington* v. *Whitehurst* (1837) 3 Y. & C.Exch. 1; doubted but affirmed *sub nom. Skeffington* v. *Budd* (s.c.) (1842) 9 Cl. & F. 219; and *cf. Butler* v. *Bernard* (1674) 1 Chan.Cas. 224; Freem.Ch. 139.

[3] See Administration of Estates Act 1925, s.21.

not to the administrator *de bonis non.* Thus, where A died intestate, and his son took out administration to him, and received part of a debt, being rent in arrear to the intestate, and accepted a promissory note for the residue, and then died intestate, it was held that this acceptance of the note was such an alteration in the property as vested it in the son, and, therefore, on his death, it went to *his* administrator, and not to the administrator *de bonis non.*[4] But even in this case, it is conceived, the administrator *de bonis non* would now be entitled to recover on the promissory note.[5]

Where administrator de bonis non may sue

It would seem from the case of *Catherwood* v. *Chabaud*[6] that where the substituted cause of action is such that the first executor or administrator may sue in his representative character, the right of action devolves upon the administrator *de bonis non* of the original deceased; for he succeeds to all the legal rights which belonged to the first executor or administrator in his representative capacity.[7] Therefore, where a bill of exchange was indorsed generally, but delivered to S. C., as administratix of I. C., for a debt due to the intestate, and S. C. died before the bill became due and before it was paid, it was held that the administrator *de bonis non* of I. C. might sue upon the bill.[8] In such cases it does not follow, because the administrator *de bonis non* may sue, that the representative of the original executor or administrator may not sue; there may be instances where the latter might and ought to sue: *e.g.* if the first administrator or executor has made himself a debtor to the estate of the original deceased for the amount of a bill received in payment of a debt due to that estate.[9]

Judgment obtained by the original representative

The rights of the administrator *de bonis non* to enforce judgments obtained by the original representative are governed by Ord. 46, r. 2[10] under which the leave of the court is required.

If the original executor or administrator, in his own name, brings trespass for goods taken out of his possession, which were the testator's or intestate's, and dies, his own executor or administrator must take execution of the judgment; but the executor of an executor holds the proceeds of the execution as assets of the first testator, and the executor or administrator of an original administrator, or of an administrator of an original intestate executor, can be compelled in equity to pay them to the administrator *de bonis non.*[11]

---

[4] *Barker* v. *Talcot and Shaw* (1687) 1 Vern. 473; Bac.Abr. Executors, B, 2, 2.
[5] See Administration of Estates Act 1925, s.39(1)(iii).
[6] (1823) 1 B. & C. 150.
[7] See *post*, p. 876.
[8] *Catherwood* v. *Chabaud* (1823) 1 B. & C. 150.
[9] *Ibid.* 156.
[10] See *post*, p. 871.
[11] *Yaites* v. *Gough* (1603) Yelv. 33.

CHAPTER 5

REMUNERATION AND PAYMENTS

1—REMUNERATION

An executor is not obliged to accept his appointment as such but if he does accept he is bound by the rule "that no one who has a duty to perform shall place himself in a situation to have his interests conflicting with that duty."[1] Thus he is entitled to no allowance at law or in equity, for personal trouble and loss of time in the execution of his duties.[2] This is not altered by the executor's renunciation of the executorship, and his afterwards assisting in it; nor by the fact that he deserves more, and has benefited the estate to the prejudice of his own affairs.[3] A surviving partner, being executor, is not entitled, without express stipulation, to any allowance for carrying on the trade after the testator's death[4]; and even where there is an express power the executor is not entitled to an allowance as against creditors.[5] The only exceptions to this general principle arise from (1) an express agreement to allow remuneration, (2) an express authority contained in the will, (3) the express authority of the court or (4) statutory authority. In practice problems generally arise in relation to solicitors' charges. Here there is no distinction between contentious and non-contentious costs.[6]

Where there are several executors the rule is modified to the extent that if a solicitor acts for himself and his co-executors or co-trustees and the work which he has done for himself and the others has been of benefit to the estate but no additional expense has been incurred by his acting for himself then he is entitled to claim and to charge for his professional services.[7]

(1) Authorisation by express agreement

The rule preventing a solicitor-trustee from claiming more than out-of-pocket costs does not prevent him from claiming strictly professional

---

[1] *Per* Lord Cranworth L.C. in *Broughton* v. *Broughton* (1855) 5 De G.M. & G. 160, 164. In general the same rules apply here as to both representatives and trustees and as to remuneration and profit. As to trustees, see *Lewin on Trusts* (16th ed.) pp. 191–212. "The strictness of the rule depends on the circumstance that the trustee is both master and servant at the same time" (*per* Evershed M.R. in *Dale* v. *I.R.C.* [1952] Ch. 704, 715.)

[2] *Robinson* v. *Pett* (1734) 3 P.Wms. 249; *Scattergood* v. *Harrison* (1729) Mosely 128; *Brocksopp* v. *Barnes* (1820) 5 Madd. 90; *Forster* v. *Williams Deacon's Bank Ltd.* [1935] Ch. 359.

[3] *Robinson* v. *Pett* (1734) 3 P.Wms. 249.

[4] *Burden* v. *Burden* (1813) 1 Ves. & B. 170; *Stocken* v. *Dawson* (1843) 6 Beav. 371. Nor is an executor and legatee of such surviving partner: *ibid.* As to partnership, see further *post*, p. 472.

[5] *Re Salmen* (1912) 107 L.T. 108, and see *Broughton* v. *Broughton* (1855) 5 De G.M. & G. at p. 165.

[6] See *Broughton* v. *Broughton* (1855) 5 De G.M. & G. at p. 164. .

[7] *Cradock* v. *Piper* (1850) Mac. & G. 664; *Re Worthington* [1954] 1 W.L.R. 526, 529. This "anomaly" appears to depend on principles of contribution or subrogation in equity. *Cf. Re Downer Enterprises* [1974] 1 W.L.R. 1460. See also p. 605 *post*.

51

charges under a special contract. Where however the execution of the office was likely to be attended with trouble, and the executor, who had no legacy and who at first declined to act in the executorship, but afterwards agreed with a residuary legatee to act in consideration of a hundred guineas, died before the execution of the trust was completed, the court refused the claim of his executors to be allowed that sum out of the trust money in their hands. The court observed that, apart from the fact that the executor had died before the trust was executed, such bargains oughts to be discouraged, as tending to dissipate the property.[8]

A solicitor who takes a grant as administrator at the request of the next of kin should agree his right to charge before taking the grant.

(2) Authorisation by will

Similarly, a solicitor-executor or trustee may be authorised by the will to charge for his professional services only or for his time and trouble in addition.[9] Such a clause is strictly construed.[10] To enable a solicitor-trustee to charge for services not strictly professional,[11] there must be express words in the will showing that such was the testator's intention.[12] The words of the will may be sufficient to authorise him to charge even for the time and trouble involved, though this is not solicitor's work at all.[13] If a trustee was given remuneration by the will for so long as he held office as trustee, his beneficial interest was "as holder of an office"[14] so that estate duty was not payable on his death.[15] Similar provisions now apply so that where a person is entitled to reasonable remuneration as a trustee his "interest" is left out of account in determining the value of his estate and tax is not charged when the interest comes to an end.[16]

A direction in a will enabling a solicitor-trustee to charge for work done as solicitor amounts to a legacy of profit costs. Thus, if the solicitor attests the will,[17] or the estate proves to be insolvent,[18] he can claim for no more

[8] *Gould* v. *Fleetwood* (1732) 3 P.Wms. 251, n. (A). See also *Ayliffe* v. *Murray* (1740) 2 Atk. 58.
[9] *Re Sherwood* (1840) 3 Beav. 338; *Christophers* v. *White* (1847) 10 Beav. 523. See also *Broughton* v. *Broughton* (1855) 5 De G.M. & G. 160; *Harbin* v. *Darby* (1860) 28 Beav. 325; *post* p. 51. The charge constitutes a "bounty." It is not earned. *Dale* v. *I.R.C.* [1952] Ch. 704.
[10] *Re Orwell* [1982] 1 W.L.R. 1337.
[11] As to which, see *Harbin* v. *Darby*, *supra*.
[12] *Re Chapple* (1884) 27 Ch.D. 584; *Clarkson* v. *Robinson* [1900] 2 Ch. 722; *Re Chalinder and Herington* [1907] 1 Ch. 58. *Re Orwell* [1982] 1 W.L.R. 1332. A solicitor should not insert such a clause in a will appointing him executor or trustee unless the testator has expressly instructed him to do so: *Re Chapple*, *supra*. Nor should he employ a secret trust: *Re Pugh* [1967] 1 W.L.R. 1262, 1267.
[13] *Re Ames* (1883) 25 Ch.D. 72; *Re Fish* [1893] 2 Ch. 413; *Clarkson* v. *Robinson* [1900] 2 Ch. 722, 726.
[14] Finance Act 1894, s.2(1)(*b*). As to death duty generally, see *post*, p. 71.
[15] *Public Trustee* v. *I.R.C.* [1960] A.C. 398.
[16] Inheritance Tax Act 1984, ss. 89, 90. Reference should be made to the exact wording of the paragraph.
[17] See *post*, p. 976.
[18] *Re Thorley* [1891] 2 Ch. 613; *Re White* [1898] 1 Ch. 297; [1898] 2 Ch. 217; *Re Brown* [1918] W.N. 118. As to death duties, see *Public Trusteee* v. *I.R.C.* [1958] Ch. 866.

than out-of-pocket costs. This rule applies to all professional trustees.[19] The effect of a legacy or gift to an executor or trustee is considered later.[20] If difficulties arise in the interpretation of a will prepared by the solicitor in question he will not normally be allowed to benefit.[21]

When executor entitled to commission

An agent, who is appointed executor of his principal, is not entitled to charge commission on business done after the testator's death,[22] even, it seems on goods transmitted by the testator in his lifetime, if not received by the agent-executor until after the death.[23] An executor, who is a member of a banking firm, cannot charge the ordinary banker's commission against his testator's estate.[24] An executor, who acts as auctioneer in the sale of assets, is not entitled to charge commission.[25] But where a testator, a victualler, directed his trade to be carried on by his executors, brewers and spirit merchants, who had been in the habit of serving him in his lifetime, and supplies were furnished for that purpose by them, the court would not declare that the executors were entitled to receive the cost price only for these supplies, but directed an inquiry whether the supplies were proper, and furnished at the ordinary market price.[26] Again, the terms of the will may authorise an executor to charge for professional assistance, etc., and for loss of time occasioned by the administration.[27]

Fees of trust corporations

When a trust corporation is appointed by will to be executor, or executor and trustee, it is usual to provide in the will that the appointments is made on the terms and conditions upon which the particular trust corporation undertakes such duties.[28] Such terms vary as between one corporation and another but in character and incidence the chief fees are similar. They are capital fees (including an acceptance fee and a withdrawal fee), which are chargeable to the capital of the estate, and income fees which are assessed on the income received or collected.[29] These fees are exclusive of all other fees and costs which may be payable, such as legal fees or fees on sales of stock. It is normal for the will to provide for the scales of fees in force at the

---

[19] *Ibid.*

[20] See *post*, p. 56.

[21] *Re Rees* [1950] Ch. 204; 211; *Re Pugh* [1967] 1 W.L.R. 1262.

[22] *Sheriff* v. *Axe* (1827) 4 Russ. 33.

[23] See *Hovey* v. *Blakeman* (1799) 4 Ves. 596. But contrast *Scattergood* v. *Harrison* (1729) Mosely 128.

[24] *Heighington* v. *Grant* (1840) 5 M. & Cr. 258, 262.

[25] *Kirkman* v. *Booth* (1848) 11 Beav. 273. Nor, if he is a partner with others, can the partnership make a charge; *Matthison* v. *Clarke* (1854) 3 Drew. 3.

[26] *Smith* v. *Langford* (1840) 2 Beav. 362, disapproved in *Sykes* v. *Sykes* [1909] 2 Ch. 241.

[27] See *Willis* v. *Kibble* (1839) 1 Beav. 559 (land surveyor held entitled to charge); and *ante*, p. 52.

[28] *Re Campbell* [1954] 1 W.L.R. 516.

[29] As to the incidence of income fees in special cases: see *Re Hulton's Will* [1936] Ch. 536; *Re Riddell* [1936] Ch. 747; *Re Roberts' Will Trusts* [1937] Ch. 274; *Re Goodwin* [1938] Ch. 341; *Re Evans' Will Trusts* [1948] Ch. 185.

date of the testator's death to apply and such a provision is valid. However any attempt to enable the corporation to vary the scale unilaterally without the consent of beneficiaries after the death is probably an uncertain or an unauthorised delegation or an infringement of the Wills Act 1837, s.9 in that such variation will not have complied with the requirements of signature and witnesses.[30]

(3) Remuneration under the express authority of the court

On a proper application[31] the court can in special circumstances[32] allow an executor or trustee remuneration or an increase in remuneration[33] including director's fees,[34] past and future, for acts done in connection with the estate.[35] Thus a liberal scale of payment may be allowed to trustees held accountable to a trust for a substantial profit made.[36] When the court, in its discretion, has appointed a trustee to be consignee with usual profits, and the appointment has been acted upon, the court will not afterwards withdraw its sanction from it.[37] Where a trust corporation is granted administration,[38] or is appointed executor under the Administration of Estates Act 1925, s.23(2), whether solely or jointly with another person, the court can, under section 42 of the Trustee Act 1925, authorise such personal representative to charge.[39] An administrator *pendente lite* appointed under the Supreme Court Act 1981, s.117 may be assigned reasonable remuneration.[40] A person appointed as substitute representative under the Administration of Justice Act 1985, s.50,[41] may also be authorised to charge remuneration for his services.[42]

Remuneration for assets overseas

Although no commission is allowed to a trustee in this country for what he does, however laborious his duty may be, the court will allow a commission to trustees acting in certain foreign countries so as to induce persons to act there as trustees. Thus, the court allowed a commission to

[30] As to uncertainty, see p. 58 *post*, n. 75. As to incorporation of documents, see p. 153, *post*.
[31] See *Re Barbour* [1974] 1 W.L.R. 1198, 1202.
[32] *Re Codd's Will Trusts* [1975] 1 W.L.R. 1139 where Graham J. authorised an increase in the remuneration of the bank trustee but only, apparently, with the consent of all the beneficiaries.
[33] *The Duke of Norfolk* [1982] Ch. 61.
[34] *Re Keeler* [1981] Ch. 156.
[35] *Marshall* v. *Holloway* (1820) 2 Swanst, 432; *Forster* v. *Ridley* (1864) 4 De G.J. & Sm. 452; *Re Freeman's Settlement Trusts* (1887) 37 Ch.D. 148. *Re Duke of Norfolk's Settlement Trusts* [1982] Ch. 61. See also article by F. Glover, 129 New L.J. 501.
[36] *Phipps* v. *Boardman* [1967] 2 A.C. 46, 104, 112. See also *Re Wright, ex p. Wood* [1959] C.L.Y. 1231 (solicitor-executors allowed substantial remuneration for management of business whereby benefits had accrued to an insolvent estate).
[37] *Morison* v. *Morison* (1838) 4 My. & Cr. 215.
[38] See the Supreme Court Act 1981, s. 115.
[39] *Re Young* [1934] W.N. 106; 151 L.T. 221; *Re Masters* [1953] 1 W.L.R. 81.
[40] See *post*, p. 333.
[41] See p. 27, *ante*.
[42] s.50(3).

trustees who actually discharged their duties in the East and West Indies, as by remitting assets to this country.[43] But no commission is payable where the remittant himself is actually, at the time of the remittance, in this country.[44] He must be actually in the country where the remittance was made: for if, by any means, money which has not been received by him upon the spot and remitted by him from the spot to this country is remitted to this country, no commission will be allowed.[45]

In Australia a commission or percentage may be and generally is allowed to executors and administrators, and in many parts of the Commonwealth there are incorporated companies which act as executors and charge commission.

The English executors of a testator domiciled in England and Wales, who obtained an ancillary grant in New York State, were allowed not to account to beneficiaries for executorial remuneration received in New York.[46]

(4) Statutory authority for remuneration

The Judicial Trustees Act 1896, s.1(5), provides that, where a judicial trustee is appointed, there may be paid to him out of the trust property such remuneration, not exceeding the limits prescribed by the rules for the time being in force under the Act, as the court may assign in each case, subject to any rules under the Act respecting the application of such remuneration where the judicial trustee is an official of the court, and that the remuneration so assigned to any judicial trustee shall, save as the court may for special reasons otherwise order, cover all his work and personal outlay.

The Public Trustee Act 1906, s.9, enables the Public Trustee to charge fees for his services.

The Trustee Act 1925, ss.23 and 30 are referred to later.[47]

2—OTHER PAYMENT TO AN EXECUTOR

Money advanced by executor

If an executor borrows money, or advances it out of his own pocket, to pay the debts of his testator which carry interest, or to satisfy of his testator's creditors who are very importunate and threaten to bring actions, he is entitled not only to be paid in full in priority to the creditors,[48] but also to an allowance of interest for the money so advanced or borrowed.[49]

---

[43] *Denton* v. *Davy* (1836) 1 Moo.P.C. 15.
[44] *Ibid.* And see *Chetham* v. *Lord Audley* (1798) 4 Ves. 72; *Hovey* v. *Blakeman* (1799) 4 Ves. 596.
[45] *Chambers* v. *Goldwin* (1801) 5 Ves. 834; *Denton* v. *Davy* (1836) 1 Moo.P.C. 15, 32; *Campbell* v. *Campbell* (1842) 13 Sim. 168.
[46] *Re Northcote's W.T.* [1949] 1 All E.R. 442.
[47] See p. 746 *et seq. post.*
[48] *Spackman* v. *Holbrook* (1860) 2 Giff. 198; *Re Jones* [1914] 1 Ch. 742, *post*, p. 000.
[49] *Small* v. *Wing* (1730) 5 Bro.P.C. 66, Toml.ed. And see *Finch* v. *Pescott* (1874) L.R. 17 Eq. 554.

Interest is calculated only on the balance found due to him on the master's certificate.[50] Interest is not allowed to an executor on costs paid by him pending a suit about the estate.[51]

Legacies to executors

Where legacies are given to persons, in the character of executors, and not as marks of personal regard only, such bequests are treated as given upon the implied condition that the parties clothe themselves with the character in respect of which the benefits were intended for them.[52] "Nothing is so clear," said Lord Alvanley, in *Harrison* v. *Rowley*,[53] "as that if a legacy is given to a man as executor, whether expressed to be for care and pains, or not, he must, in order to entitle himself to the legacy, clothe himself with the character of executor." This rule, however, does not extend to a gift of residue to an executor.[54]

Two questions then arise: First, when is a legacy to be regarded as given to a person in the character of executor. Secondly, what is a sufficient assumption of the character of executor to entitle the legatee, when a legacy is so given.

Gift to executor as such

A legacy to a person appointed executor is presumed to be given to him in that character, and it is on him to show something in the nature of the legacy, or other circumstances arising on the will, to repel that presumption.[55] Thus, in *Stackpoole* v. *Howell*,[56] the testator devised his real and personal estates to the plaintiff, and the defendants H and M, upon various trusts, and appointed them executors. He afterwards made two codicils by which he gave to those three persons legacies, not expressly as trustees or executors, but by their names and descriptions: and the legacies by the first codicil were classed together, and of equal amounts, as were those in the second. The plaintiff renounced probate, and his claim to the legacies was disallowed.[57]

But this presumption will be rebutted if it appears, as a matter of interpretation[58] that the bequest to a person who is named executor is given to him independently of that character; and then the legatee will be entitled to receive the legacy, whether he accepts the office or not. Thus, in *Hum-*

---

[50] *Gordon* v. *Trail, infra.*

[51] *Gordon* v. *Trail* (1820) 8 Price 416; *Lewis* v. *Lewis* (1850) 13 Beav. 82.

[52] *Abbot* v. *Massie* (1796) 3 Ves. 148; *Freeman* v. *Fairlie* (1812) 3 Meriv. 29.

[53] (1798) 4 Ves. 212.

[54] *Griffiths* v. *Pruen* (1840) 11 Sim. 202; *Christian* v. *Devereux* (1841) 12 Sim. 264. See also *Compton* v. *Bloxham* (1845) 2 Coll. 201; *Hillerdon* v. *Grove* (1856) 21 Beav. 518; *Re Maxwell* [1906] 1 Ir.R. 386.

[55] *Stackpoole* v. *Howell* (1807) 13 Ves. 417; *Re Appleton* (1885) 29 Ch.D. 893.

[56] (1807) 13 Ves. 417. See, too, *Piggott* v. *Green* (1833) 6 Sim. 72.

[57] See also *Walne* v. *Hill* [1883] W.N. 171, where the same result followed on revocation of the appointment of the executor.

[58] Query, whether parol evidence is admissible to rebut the presumption. See *Re Appleton* (1885) 29 Ch.D. 893, *per* Cotton L.J.; *cf. ibid., per* Fry L.J.

berston v. *Humberston*,[59] the testator, as an encouragement to his executors (who were four) to accept the trust and executorship, gave to each of them £100 and £12 for mourning, and to each a ring, and £10 a year for their trouble. Lord Cowper C. held that, notwithstanding the condition of the acceptance might seem to run to all the legacies, yet the executors, though they did not act, should have their rings and mourning, these being intended for them immediately, and not to wait their time of acceptance; but that they should not have their £100 and the annuity of £10 each. So in *Bubb* v. *Yelverton*,[60] where a testator appointed his "friend" P his executor, and gave him a legacy "as a remembrance," and P did not act as executor, it was held by Lord Romilly M.R. that he was entitled to the legacy without proving the will.

So in *Burgess* v. *Burgess*,[61] a legacy given to the testator's trustees and executors, as a mark of his respect for them, was held by Knight Bruce V.-C. not to be revoked by a codicil appointing other trustees and executors in their place, and giving a legacy of equal amount to the newly appointed trustees and executors, in similar language.[62]

If a legacy given to a person who is appointed executor is made payable after the death of a tenant for life the presumption that the legacy was given to him in his character of executor is rebutted.[63] The mere fact, however, that the gift of the legacy precedes the appointment of the legatee as executor, or that the legacies to several persons appointed executors differ either in their amount or subject-matter is not enough by itself to rebut the presumption.[64]

How executor qualifies

Secondly, before a legatee to whom a gift has been made in the character of executor can claim his legacy, he must have either proved the will with the intention of acting under it (though he may do this at any time, even after the hearing of his claim[65]), or taken some step which shows unequivocally his intention to act in the executorship,[66] as by giving directions about the funeral of the testator.[67] If he proves the will,[68] or does such an unequi-

---

[59] (1716) 1 P.Wms. 332. See, too, *Dix* v. *Reed* (1823) 1 Sim. & Stu. 237.

[60] (1871) L.R. 13 Eq. 131. *Cf. Reed* v. *Devaynes* (1791) 2 Cox 285, which does not seem to be in accordance with the more recent authorities.

[61] (1844) 1 Coll. 367.

[62] See also *Compton* v. *Bloxham* (1845) 2 Coll. 201, 202, where the same judge said that the courts had struggled against the effect of a general rule, the propriety of which had been doubted. See also *Re Denby* (1861) 3 De G.F. & J. 350; *Cockerell* v. *Barber* (1826) 2 Russ. 585; *Wildes* v. *Davies* (1853) 1 Sm. & G. 475; 22 L.J. Ch. 495, as explained in *Re Apppleton* (1885) 29 Ch.D. 893.

[63] *Re Reeve's Trusts* (1877) 4 Ch.D. 841.

[64] *Re Appleton, supra.*

[65] *Reed* v. *Devaynes* (1791) 2 Cox 285.

[66] *Lewis* v. *Mathews* L.R. 8 Eq. 277, where an executor was held entitled to his legacy although he died in Australia without having proved the will, for he had sent over a power of attorney under which another person was adminstering the estate.

[67] *Harrison* v. *Rowley* (1798) 4 Ves. 212.

[68] *Angermann* v. *Ford* (1861) 29 Beav. 349.

vocal act,[69] his representatives can claim the legacy though he died before
the administration of the estate had been concluded. If, however, he is
incapacitated from proving or acting by old age,[70] or illness,[71] he has no
claim to the legacy.

In *Hollingworth* v. *Grasett*,[72] a testator bequeathed his residuary estate
to A, his executor and trustee of his will, with a gift over in case of the
death of A, so that he might not be enabled to perform the duties thereby
required of him. A proved the will, but died before he had fully performed
the trusts of it. It was held by Shadwell V.-C. that A, by merely proving the
will, entitled himself to the residue absolutely.

But the conduct of an executor, after proving the will, may be such as to
demonstrate that, instead of a bona fide intention to execute the trusts, he
procured probate as a means of enabling him to violate, in the grossest
manner, the confidence reposed in him by the testator. In such a case, the
mere act of proving the will cannot entitle him to the legacy meant for him.
Thus, in *Harford* v. *Browning*,[73] M (one of four executors) had a legacy of
£1,500 and an annuity of £100 given to him by the testator, upon proving
the will, and taking upon himself the execution of it. M concurred in
the probate, and shortly afterwards eloped with, and married abroad, the
infant daughter of the testator, who was beneficially interested under the
will. With the exception of probate, M never acted as executor, and in consequence of his misconduct he was restrained by the Court of Chancery
from interfering in the trusts of the will. It was held that M's concurrence in
the probate, under these circumstances, did not entitle him either to the
legacy or the annuity.

Gift "for his trouble"

In *Baker* v. *Martin*,[74] a testator directed that £100 should be paid annually to one of his executors, for his trouble in superintending his concerns,
until a final settlement of his affairs should take place. The executor proved
and acted. Some time after the testator's death, a suit was instituted for the
administration of his estate, but no receiver was appointed, and some of
the assets were still outstanding. Shadwell V.-C. held that the annuity did
not cease on account of the institution of the suit.

A request by a testator that a handsome gratuity should be given to each
of his executors is void for uncertainty.[75] But a gift of reasonable remuner-

---

[69] *Harrison* v. *Rowley, supra; Lewis* v. *Mathews, supra.*
[70] *Hanbury* v. *Spooner* (1843) 5 Beav. 630.
[71] *Re Hawkin's Trusts* (1864) 33 Beav. 570. Query, whether the representatives of an
executor who died without knowing that he had been appointed can claim a legacy given to
him in his official capacity; *Harrison* v. *Rowley* (1798) 4 Ves. 212. *Semble*, the representative
of a trustee can if the trustee had no active duties to perform: *Brydges* v. *Wotton* (1812) 1 V. &
B. 134; *Browne* v. *Browne* [1912] 1 Ir.R. 272.
[72] (1845) 15 Sim. 52.
[73] (1787) 1 Cox 302.
[74] (1836) 8 Sim. 25.
[75] *Jubber* v. *Jubber* (1839) 9 Sim. 503.

ation to an executor for his trouble is effectual, and the court will act on the measure of the bequest supplied by the testator, and ascertain how much ought to be expended.[76]

Acceptance of Trusts

Where personal property is bequeathed to executors as trustees, and they prove the will, this imports an acceptance of the trusts[77]; and after 1897, the same is true of devises of real estate made to executors as trustees. But probate or letters of administration granted to the representative of a sole or last surviving trustee will not constitute him trustee of the settlement or will creating the trust unless he elects to act as trustee[78]; having elected to act, he becomes trustee for all purposes.[79] He cannot, however, insist upon acting if new trustees are appointed.[80] On the other hand, he can refuse to act.[81]

---

[76] *Jackson* v. *Hamilton* (1846) 3 J. & Lat. 702; *Buckley* v. *Buckley* (1888) 19 L.R.Ir. 544.
[77] *Mucklow* v. *Fuller* (1821) Jacob 198. And see *post*, p. 731.
[78] *Re Benett* [1906] 1 Ch. 216.
[79] *Re Waidanis* [1908] 1 Ch. 123; *Re Howarth* [1909] W.N. 30.
[80] *Re Routledge* [1909] 1 Ch. 280; and see Trustee Act 1925, s.18, *post*.
[81] *Re Benett, supra.*

CHAPTER 6

FUNERAL, INVENTORY AND COLLECTION OF ASSETS

1—THE FUNERAL

The Corpse

The primary responsibility for the funeral falls upon the executors[1] of the deceased, if and when these are known.[2] Subject to this the next of kin are responsible. In some of the relevant legislation the term "relative" is used. This has been defined as "a husband or wife, parent or grand-parent or child or grandchild, including a legitimate child and any person who is, or is the child of, a brother, sister, uncle or aunt."[3] There can be no property in a dead body but the executors are entitled to possession for the purpose of disposal.[4] Directions given by the deceased in the will are not legally enforceable as such.[5] Directions given in the form of a conditional gift may be enforceable if possible and if not contrary to public policy.[6] However, effect should be given so far as possible to the wishes of the deceased and if he has left no directions his body is entitled to Christian burial.[7] There is no legal objection to the burial of cremated remains.[8]

Death overseas

Where death occurs abroad local advice will be needed, but the general considerations are set out in Pugh, *The Administration of Foreign Estates*.[9]

---

[1] *Williams* v. *Williams* (1882) 20 Ch.D. 659, 664. As to heirlooms and the shroud and coffin, see *post* p. 508, fn. 94. On this topic generally see 10 Halsbury's Laws, paras. 1001–1243.

[2] It has been decided in Australia that a Solicitor who retains a deceased's will owes a duty to take reasonable steps to find the executor and inform him of the content of the will: *Hawkins* v. *Clayton* (1988) 164 C.L.R. 539. *Sed quaere*.

[3] See the Disused Burial Grounds (Amendment) Act 1981, s.9. When a child is in care or fostered the right to bury falls to the natural parent. Subject to this right the local authority has power to bury where the deceased child was in its care immediately before death (Child Care Act 1980, s.25), *Re B*, *Daily Telegraph* April 12, 1991.

[4] See n. 1.

[5] *Williams* v. *Williams* (1882) 20 Ch.D. 659, 665. But see the Anatomy Act 1984 and the Cremation Regulations 1920, 1952 and 1965. *Re Grandison*, *The Times*, July 10, 1989.

[6] A condition precedent may be enforceable if there is an effective gift over. See generally *Re Berens* [1926] Ch. 596; *Re Thomas* [1930] 2 Ch. 67; *Re Elliott* [1952] Ch. 217; *Roper on Legacies* 651–675; Sheperd's Touchstone 132.

[7] *Gilbert Buzzard* (1821) 1 Hagg. Con. 333, 343; *Rustewart* (1840) 12 A. & E. 773.

[8] *Re Dixon* [1892] P. 393. The interment of ashes in the church will normally be refused (*Re St. Peters* [1982] 1 W.L.R. 1283).

[9] See pp. 245, 255.

The Burial

Burial may be in consecrated or unconsecrated ground,[10] and in a churchyard or a public burial place or cemetery.[11] After burial in consecrated ground the corpse comes under the protection of the ecclesiastical court of the Diocese and cannot lawfully be removed except under a faculty.[12] A non-parishioner may not be buried in the churchyard of the parish without the consent of the incumbent,[13] unless at the date of his death his name is entered on the church electoral roll of the parish.[14] An incumbent, however, is obliged to bury the corpse or ashes of any person within his cure.[15] A petitioner for a faculty who is not an executor or administrator has no right to be heard as against the representative.[16]

After burial in unconsecrated ground a body may not be removed without the licence of a Secretary of State under the Burial Act 1857.[17] Such a licence is also necessary for removal from consecrated to unconsecrated ground and vice versa but is not necessary if a faculty is obtained for removal from one consecrated place to another or this is done under a coroner's order. The removal of remains from one part of a closed burial ground to another part is not prohibited by section 3 of the Burial Act 1853.[18] Where a churchyard has been closed by order in council, burials may nevertheless sometimes take place there if the exact terms of the order allow this.[19]

The provision and maintenance of cemeteries and crematoria is governed by the Local Government Act 1972.

The representatives of a person whose remains are buried in a church or churchyard declared redundant have a right to be notified and to arrange for the removal of the remains under section 65 of and Schedule 6 to the Pastoral Measure 1968. There is, however, no right to notification if the burial was more than 25 years before the date stipulated.

---

[10] The Cemeteries Clauses Act 1847, provided a special code but is now applicable only to cemetery companies which are not local authorities. See Local Government Act 1972.

[11] Ibid.

[12] Williams v. Williams (1882) 20 Ch.D. 659.

[13] Re St. Nicholas [1983] Fam. 1, 5. Having given consent the incumbent may be estopped from later refusal. In deciding whether to give such consent the incumbent must have regard to any general guidance given by the Church Council (Church of England (Miscellaneous Provisions) Measure 1976, s.6(2)).

[14] Church of England (Miscellaneous Provisions) Measure 1976, s.6(1).

[15] Canon B. 38.2.3. There is no distinction in canon law between a corpse and ashes. See Re Church Norton [1989] Fam. 37.

[16] Re St. Nicholas [1983] Fam. 1, 8 and see Rees v. Hughes [1946] 1 K.B. 517, 524; Re Grandison, The Times, July 10, 1989.

[17] Re Talbot [1901] P. 1. See as to Licence and Fee s.1, 1982 No. 364.

[18] Re St. Mary's, Barnes [1982] 1 W.L.R. 531. As to prescriptive rights of burial, see article 1991 E.L.J. p. 133 (P. Sparkes). An exclusive right of burial can exist in perpetuity and confer a cause of action enforceable by injunction and damages, subject to the jurisdiction of the Home Office to grant or refuse a licence (Reed v. Maldon [1989] Ch. 408).

[19] See Opinions of the Legal Board III/26.

Cremation

It is not illegal at common law to burn a dead body instead of burying it, unless it is so done as to amount to a public nuisance,[20] or it is done against the known written directions of the deceased to the contrary.[21] The burial service in the Book of Common Prayer does not contemplate cremation though cremation has now a statutory sanction.[22] Where a body has been consumed in a fire, it has been customary to collect the ashes and to bury them in a churchyard, accompanied with the use of the Order for the Burial of the Dead, and the same course is usually followed where there has been a previous service.[23]

The form of application for cremation must be signed by the executor or nearest relative unless the cremation authority is given a satisfactory reason to the contrary.[24]

Medical directions

There are detailed provisions in the Anatomy Act 1984 allowing for anatomical examinations of the body if directed by the deceased in writing or in the presence of two witnesses, subject to the wishes of the next-of-kin, and for cases where the deceased wishes his body or specified parts to be used for therapeutic purposes or for purposes of medical education or research.

Military Remains

It is an offence under the Military Remains Act 1986 to tamper with, damage, move, remove or unearth military or associated human remains without a licence under that Act. However it is further provided that the grant of such a licence is "without prejudice to the rights of any person including the Crown . . . as the owner of or the person entitled . . . to claim an interest in any such remains." This must presumably include an executor or administrator.[25]

Monuments and Memorials in Churchyards

The extent of the executor's functions and authority in the erection of monuments is uncertain. In practice it is necessary to consult those beneficially interested in the estate on whose interests the cost is likely to fall. The incumbent may give permission, but if he refuses this the matter comes

[20] *R.* v. *Price* (1884) 12 Q.B.D. 247, and see Cremation Acts 1902 and 1952.
[21] Cremation Regulations 1930, r. 4; but see *ibid.* r. 14, making r. 4 inapplicable in cases of plague, etc. See also Reservation Regulation 1952 (S.I. 1952 No. 1568) and S.I. 1965 No. 1146.
[22] Cremation Acts 1902 and 1952.
[23] *Re Dixon* [1892] P. 386, 394; Cremation Regulations 1920, r. 16. For a more detailed consideration of this topic, see 10 Halsbury's Laws, paras. 1001–1243.
[24] Cremation Regulations 1952 (S.I. 1952 No. 1568).
[25] See the Protection of Military Remains Act 1986, s.4(6).

under the faculty jurisdiction of the consistory court.[26] This jurisdiction is normally exercised on the basis of diocesan guidelines and covers design,[27] materials, and the wording of inscriptions.[28] The leading object is the convenience of the parishioners so that the unanimous decision of the vestry, and now presumably of the Parochial Church Council, carries great weight.[29] The court will in exercising its jurisdiction decide questions of ownership and trust law[30]; but it must be doubted how far the consistory court can properly better its own jurisdiction or the legislative functions of the synods by means of procedural regulations.[31] The erection of "buildings" on disused churchyards is forbidden by section 3 of the Disused Burial Grounds Act 1884, but a scheme under the Pastoral Measure 1968 may allow this if no person has been buried there for 50 years or no relative or personal representative has objected.[32] See also the Disused Burial Grounds (Amendment) Act 1981.

Funeral expenses

The deceased should be buried in a manner suitable to the estate he leaves behind.[33] Funeral expenses, according to the degree and quality of the deceased, are allowed out of the estate of the deceased, before any debt or duty whatsoever.[34] Where the assets prove to be insufficient for the payment of all debts, then, as against creditors, the representative is only entitled to incur such expenses as are, in the particular circumstances of the case, absolutely necessary.[35]

The executor is entitled to be allowed reasonable expenses, according to the testator's condition in life, and if he exceeds those, he is to take the chance of the estate turning out insolvent. No precise sum can be fixed to

[26] See Re Woldingham Churchyard [1957] 1 W.L.R. 811; Keet v. Smith (1876) 1 P.D. 73; Hopper v. Davis (1754) 1 Lee 648.

[27] See Re St. Nicholas [1983] Fam. 1, 9. Photographs are not encouraged (Re St. Marks Haydock [1981] 1 W.L.R. 1164).

[28] Keet v. Smith (1876) 1 P.D. 73 (addition of word "Rev" to the name of a non-conformist minister allowed on appeal); St. Mark's Haydock [1981] 1 W.L.R. 1167 (inscription must not be controversial).

[29] Sharpe and Sangster v. Hansard (1830) 3 Hagg. 337.

[30] Re St. Mary's Faversham [1986] Fam. 143, 154.

[31] Regulations purporting to control memorials after interment of ashes have caused concern in this respect.

[32] Pastoral Measure 1968, s.30.

[33] 2 Black. Comm. 508. As to liability to pay for the funeral expenses, see post p. 721. As to death grant, post p. 497.

[34] 3 Inst, 202 R. v. Wade (1818) 5 Price 621. A husband executor appointed by his wife's will made under a testamentary power of appointment is entitled to retain out of her estate the expenses of her funeral though such estate is insufficient for creditors and her will does not contain any charge for debts and funeral expenses. Re M'Myn (1886) 33 Ch.D. 575.

[35] In strictness, said Lord Holt, no funeral expenses are allowed in the case of an insolvent estate, except for the coffin, ringing the bell, and the fees of the parson, clerk and bearers: but not for the pall or ornaments: Shellys Case (1693) 1 Salk. 296. Perhaps, observes Dr Burn, the expenses of the shroud and digging the grave ought to have been added: 4 Burn E.L., 8rh ed., p. 348. See also note to East India Co. v. Skinner (1695) Comberb. 342; Stag v. Punter (1744) 3 Atk. 119; Hancock v. Podmore (1830) 1 B. & Ad. 260; Yardley v. Arnold (1842) Carr. & M. 434, 438. See post, p. 633.

govern executors in all cases. It must obviously vary in every instance, not only with the station in life of each particular testator, but also with the price of the requisite articles at the particular time and place.[36]

When the estate is solvent then as against beneficiaries the representative is not justified, in the absence of a direction in the will, in incurring extravagant funeral expenses.[37]

The question is one of fact.[38] Thus the cost of a tombstone was allowed (within the terms of the Assurance Companies Act 1909) in one case[39] but not in another.[40] The cost of mourning was allowed in one case[41] but not in another.[42] The cost of reinterment in order to fulfil the last wishes of the deceased has been allowed in Canada.[43] A payment of £93 odd for mourning rings distributed among relations and friends of the deceased was allowed by Lord Eldon where the will gave no directions, but committed "anything not specified" to the discretion of the executors.[44] In another case £600 was allowed on the funeral in his own country of a wealthy local celebrity.[45]

Similar principles apply for purposes of death duty under which allowance is made for "reasonable funeral expenses"[46] if those are in fact paid out of the estate.[47] A married woman's funeral expenses were payable primarily out of her estate, not by her husband as such.[48]

The question of the liability of an executor or administrator for the expenses of the funeral of the deceased is considered later.[49]

2—INVENTORY AND ACCOUNT

Inventory and account

A representative is under a duty, when required to do so by the court, to exhibit on oath in the court a full inventory of the estate and when so

---

[36] *Edwards* v. *Edwards* (1834) 2 Cr. & M. 612; *Reeves* v. *Ward* (1835) 2 Scott 390; *Bissett* v. *Antrobus* (1831) 4 Sim. 512; *Re Walter* [1929] 1 Ch. 647, 655.

[37] See *Stacpoole* v. *Stacpoole* (1816) 4 Dow. 209.

[38] *Goldstein* v. *Salvation Army Assurance* [1917] 2 K.B. 291, 297; *Mullick* v. *Mullick* (1829) 1 Knapp. 245 (P.C.).

[39] *Goldstein* v. *Salvation Army Assurance*, *ante*.

[40] *Bridge* v. *Brown* 2 Y. & C.C.C. 181.

[41] *Pritt* v. *Pritt* (1758) 2 Lee 508.

[42] *Johnson* v. *Baker* (1825) 2 C. & P. 207.

[43] *Re Oldfield* [1949] 2 D.L.R. 175.

[44] *Paice* v. *The Archbishop of Canterbury* (1807) 14 Ves. 364.

[45] *Offley* v. *Offley* (1691) Prec. Chance. 26.

[46] I.H.T Act 1984 s.172 and see *Encyclopaedia of Capital Taxation* p. 1.12. *Cf.* Finance Act 1894, s.7(1), Dymond's *Capital Taxes*, para. 25.200.

[47] *Re Barnes* [1939] 1 K.B. 316. The costs of a tombstone is now allowed. S.P. 7/87.

[48] *Rees* v. *Hughes* [1946] 1 K.B. 517.

[49] *Post*, p. 721.

required render an account of the administration of the estate to the court.[50] Formerly the exhibition of a true and perfect inventory and account of the estate was automatically required by statute, but the change introduced by the Administration of Estates Act 1971[51] apparently recognised the modern practice not to require an inventory or account unless an application had been made to the court for the purpose by some party interested.[52]

An executor, upon taking probate, and an administrator, on taking out letters of administration, takes an oath that he will (amongst other things) when required to do so by the court exhibit to the court a full inventory of the said estate and render an account thereof to the court. A similar promise was included in the surety's guarantee which the registrar could require as a condition of granting administration under the former non-contentious probate rules.[53] Guarantees are no longer required under any of the new rules.

Who may demand inventory and account

A representative, whether or not he is still in office,[54] may be compelled to exhibit an inventory on the application of any person having an interest, or even the appearance of an interest.[55] Thus the representative of the residuary legatee of a person who was the residuary legatee of the original testator may have a sufficient interest for the purpose of calling on the representative of the original testator to exhibit an account.[56] Even a probable or contingent interest will justify a party in calling for an inventory and account.[57]

Thus, there is an obligation to produce an inventory to a creditor who swears to certain sums due from the deceased to him, though the debt is contested[58]; to the assignee of a bankrupt who had made an affidavit of a debt from the deceased to the bankrupt, notwithstanding that the Limitation Acts had run out since the administration was granted[59]; to a credi-

---

[50] Administration of Estates Act 1925, s.25 as substituted by the Administration of Estates Act 1971, s.9 (*post* p. 1124). The provision reproduces in limited form 21 Hen. 8, c.5. as extended to personal representatives generally and to real estate. As to the invalidity of directions in a will which conflict with this duty, see *post* p. 1033. An administrator *pendente lite* is always required to exhibit accounts. See *post*, p. 335.

[51] s.9.

[52] As to the state of the law before the passing of this Act, see the 15th edition of this work. In practice the Inland Revenue Account performs the function of the inventory in many cases.

[53] N.-C.P.R. 1954, r. 38(3). See also p. 73, *post*, and N.-C.P.R. 1987, r. 40.

[54] *Re Thomas* [1956] 1 W.L.R. 1516; *Taylor* v. *Newton* (1752) 1 Lee 15.

[55] *Phillips* v. *Bignell* (1811) 1 Phil. 239; *Gale* v. *Luttrell* (1824) 2 Add. 234.

[56] *Winchlow* v. *Smith* (1753) 1 Lee 417.

[57] *Salter* v. *Sladen* (1792) Prerog. M.T. 1792; *Snow* v. *Strutt* (1793) Prerog. H.T. 1793, cited 1 Phil. 241; *Myddleton* v. *Rushout* (1797) 1 Phil. 244; *Reeves* v. *Freeling* (1812) 2 Phil. 57; *Burgess* v. *Marriott* (1843) 3 Curt. 424. The procedure is by summons under the N.-C.P.R. 1987, r. 16(2).

[58] *Smith* v. *Pryce* (1754) 1 Lee 569; *Hackman* v. *Black* (1755) 2 Lee 251.

[59] *Philipson and D'Escherney* v. *Harvey* (1757) 3 Lee 344. See also *Wainford* v. *Barker* (1697) 1 Ld. Raym. 232.

tor by a bond of the testator, though it was alleged to be invalid, and though an action on the bond was then pending,[60] for such an applicant is entitled to ascertain whether there are any assets before he incurs any further expense, and, in such circumstances, though the representatives may insist that the estate of the deceased is not liable it is their duty either to exhibit an inventory and account or to admit assets sufficient to answer the claim.[61] Again an inventory and account may be demanded by a residuary legatee who has given a release, for, on such an application, the court will not consider the question whether or not the release is valid.[62] An executor who is also residuary legatee may call on his co-executor for an inventory[63]; and so he may, perhaps, without any special interest.[64]

On the other hand, where a creditor has proceeded in the Chancery Division for the discovery of assets, he probably cannot proceed also in the Family Division for an inventory or an account.[65] And where a legacy was to be paid in three instalments, and the executor having made two and tendered the third was cited[66] by the legatee to bring in an inventory, it was held that there was no need for an inventory in this instance.[67] Similarly, where the executor has admitted sufficient assets the court has refused to compel the exhibition of an inventory.[68] And a declaration of the estate containing sufficient particulars has in several cases been accepted by the court instead of an inventory.[69]

Delay in applying for an Inventory

There is no statute or rule of positive law limiting the period within which an application for an inventory and account must be made, and time alone does not preclude such an application.[70] But where there has been a great lapse of time since the death, the court has frequently refused to enforce the exhibition of an inventory, for reason and justice prescribe some limitation.[71] Thus, an application to compel an administratrix to

---

[60] *Gale* v. *Luttrell* (1824) 2 Add. 234. See also 1 Oughton, tit. 240 ss.9, 10.

[61] *Jickling* v. *Bircham* (1843) 2 Notes of Cas. 463 (account and inventory ordered 24 years after death).

[62] *Kenny* v. *Jackson* (1827) 1 Hagg. Ecc. 105. See also *Acaster* v. *Anderson* (1848) 1 Rob.Ecc. 672.

[63] *Paul* v. *Nettlefod* (1824) 2 Add. 237.

[64] *Huggins* v. *Alexander* (1736) Prerog. 1736; 2 Add. 238, n.(a).

[65] *Myddleton* v. *Rushout* (1797) 1 Phil. 244. *Secus*, if the proceedings in the Chancery Division are instituted by a third party: *Brotherton* v. *Hellier* (1755) 2 Lee 131.

[66] An application to the registrar on summons is now the practice.

[67] *Boon's Case* (1672) Raym. 470.

[68] *Fleet* v. *Holmes* (1755) 2 Lee 101; *Burgess* v. *Marriott* (1843) 3 Curt. 424.

[69] *Leighton* v. *Leighton* (1757) 2 Lee 356; *Akerman* v. *Gybbon* (1758) 2 Lee 511; *Higgins* v. *Higgins* (1832) 4 Hagg.Ecc. 242.

[70] See *Jickling* v. *Bircham* (1843) 2 Notes of Cas. 463 (account and inventory ordered 24 years after death).

[71] *Burgess* v. *Marriott* (1843) 3 Curt. 424.

exhibit an inventory after the lapse of 18 years was rejected, and the applicant, in the circumstances, condemned in costs.[72]

Who must exhibit an inventory

The persons who may be compelled to exhibit an inventory and account are not confined to the representative himself, or even to those who, upon the death of the representative, succeed to the representation of the original testator or intestate.

Thus, the representatives of a deceased administrator with the will annexed, though not at the same time those of the first testator, were compelled to exhibit an inventory and account, upon a reasonable presumption being raised that any part of the estate of the first testator had got into their hands,[73] and a person, having an interest in the estate, may call upon such representatives for the inventory without first taking a *de bonis non* grant to the first testator. So the executors of a deceased executor, though not the representatives of the original testator (there being an executor of the original testator still surviving) are compellable to bring in an inventory of the effects of the original testator.[74] Although an administrator pending suit may be compelled to exhibit an inventory,[75] the executors of such an administrator cannot be so compelled in proceedings concerning the administrator's own will at the instance of persons claiming under the original will where neither will has been pronounced for.[76]

An attorney who takes administration in the name of another may be compelled by the latter to exhibit an inventory and account.[77]

Delay in exhibiting an inventory

The ecclesiastical court discouraged delay in production of an inventory when called for, and generally condemned the parties who were guilty of it in costs.[78] The order to exhibit an inventory or render an account may be enforced by committal.[79]

---

[72] *Scurrah* v. *Scurrah* (1841) 2 Curt. 919. See also *Ritchie* v. *Rees & Rees* (1822) 1 Add. 144 (lapse of 45 years); *Pitt* v. *Woodham* (1828) 1 Hagg.Ecc. 247 (lapse of 24 years from death; acquiescence for seven years by assignee in bankruptcy of beneficiary; other facts tending to show insolvent had received more than his share); *Bowles* v. *Harvey* (1832) 4 Hagg.Ecc. 241 (lapse of 35 years); *Higgins* v. *Higgins* (1832) 4 Hagg.Ecc. 242 (lapse of 17 years: declaration instead of inventory held sufficient).
[73] *Ritchie* v. *Rees & Rees* (1822) 1 Add. 144, 158. See *Holland* v. *Prior* (1834) 1 M. & K. 237, 245, 246, 247.
[74] *Gale* v. *Luttrell* (1824) 2 Add. 234.
[75] *Brotherton* v. *Helier* (1755) 2 Lee 131.
[76] *Lascelles* v. *Jobber* (1753) 1 Lee 443.
[77] *Bailey* v. *Bristowe* (1850) 2 Rob. 245.
[78] *Phillips* v. *Bignell* (1811) 1 Phil. 239, 241, 243 and *Griffiths & Trinder* v. *Bennett & Taylor* (1816) 2 Phil. 364.
[79] *Marshman* v. *Brookes* (1863) 32 L.J.P.M. & A. 95.

Form and contents of inventory

The inventory exhibited by an executor or administrator ought to contain a full, true and perfect description and valuation of all the estate, real and personal, in possession and in action, to which the executor or administrator is entitled in that character. It is sufficient if the estate of the deceased is valued by any honest persons in the neighbourhood, and reduced into an inventory,[80] which when exhibited at the instance of a party interested, must be verified by special oath, either personally or by virtue of a commission; for the formal general oath of the executor or administrator will not be sufficient.[81]

The court can only require that all property possessed by the deceased upon death should be included in the inventory. It cannot under this jurisdiction call for an account of the subsequent profits in his business.[82]

After the passing of the Finance Act 1894 it would seem that an inventory should also include all estate situated in a foreign country in respect of which estate duty is payable, since such foreign assets then came within the cognisance of the court.[83] These provisions, however, were repealed and replaced by section 28(2) of the Finance Act 1949, and since the introduction of Capital Transfer Tax and Inheritance Tax[84] the inventory will include property outside the United Kingdom if the deceased died domiciled within the United Kingdom.

In some instances, particularly in complicated cases, the court will exercise a discretion as to the sort of inventory it will accept.[85]

Objections to inventories

The court will entertain objections to inventories,[86] but it has been held that witnesses should not be examined in order to falsify the inventories.[87] The foundation for this distinction was that, if the answers to the objections admit more assets than were inserted in the inventory, the court may order the inventory to be amended by the insertion of these; but if further assets might be established by witnesses in opposition to the answers, the court could not order them to be inserted in the inventory, which is required by the statute to be upon oath; nor could it compel the executor

---

[80] 1 Oughton, *tit.* 233, ss.1, 2; 4 Burn E.L. 8th ed. p. 310.

[81] 1 Oughton, *ubi ante*, n. (*d*), 2; Toller (6th ed.) 250.

[82] *Pitt* v. *Woodham* (1828) 1 Hagg.Ecc. 247.

[83] *Raymond* v. *Von Watteville* (1758) 2 Lee 551; *Wilson* v. *Ogle* (1737) Orerog. 1737, cited 2 Lee 555. See the Finance Act 1894, s.2(2), as amended by the Finance Act 1923, s.37; the Finance Act 1936, s.24 (repealed by the Finance Act 1948, Sched. XI, P. IV, as respects persons dying after July 30, 1949. See the Finance Act 1949, s.28(2) and the Finance Act 1962, s.28).

[84] See p. 72, *post.*

[85] *Reeves* v. *Freeling* (1812) 2 Phil. 56.

[86] *Telford* v. *Morison* (1824) 2 Add. 319; *Shackleton* v. *Lord Barrymore* (1798) cited 2 Add. 329.

[87] *Telford* v. *Morison, supra.*

or administrator to swear to assets, the possession of which he has twice already upon oath denied.[88]

However, it is not thought that this reasoning would prevail at the present day for the representatives may be the only persons who can explain what has become of an item alleged to be missing.

Practice

Application for an inventory and account is made by applying to the Principal Registry of the Family Division by summons, supported by affidavit.[89]

After investigating the account, if the court finds it true and perfect, it will vouch it (*i.e.* pronounce for its validity), and if all parties interested have been served with the summons the order of the court is final, so that the personal representatives cannot be subjected to further suits in that behalf.[90]

Costs and expenses

If compelled to account in the Family Division the representative will be allowed all reasonable expenses, calculated so that he receives no profit, but incurs no loss.[91] Thus he is allowed his expenses of litigation in another court over and above such costs as were there allowed[92]; and it would seem that the decisions pointed out elsewhere,[93] respecting the accounts and allowances of representatives in equity, would be regarded as authorities in the Family Division.

3—COLLECTION AND PRESERVATION OF ASSETS

Due diligence required

It is the duty of a representative, after a grant has been made to him, to collect, with due diligence,[94] all the estate of the deceased.[95] If by unduly delaying to bring an action the executor or administrator has enabled a debtor of the deceased to plead the Limitation Acts, he will be personally

---

[88] *Ibid.* It is suggested in a note to *Brogden* v. *Brown* (1825) 2 Add. 441, by the reporter, that where the executor is also the party before the court propounding the will, the court might perhaps permit depositions to be taken on the allegations, if the answers shoud prove unsatisfactory.

[89] N.-C.P.R. 1987, r. 61(2).

[90] 4 Burn E.L. 9th ed. p. 609.

[91] *Ibid.* p. 608.

[92] *Ibid.*

[93] *Post*, p. 919 *et seq.*

[94] See *Re Tankard* [1942] Ch. 69 As to time for distribution and the executor's year, see *post*, p. 112.

[95] Administration of Estates Act 1925, s.25(*a*), as substituted by the Administration of Estates Act 1971, s.9 (*post* p. 1124).

liable.[96] He has a general duty to preserve and protect the assets of the estate.[97]

Formerly, the executor or administrator was obliged, within a convenient time,[98] to remove all the personal property of the deceased left on any land which went to the heir, or to a reversioner or remainder-man; otherwise such property might be distrained as *damage feasant*.[99] This rule would seem still to apply to the general representatives of a deceased person whose goods were on settled land vested in the deceased's special representatives.

The vesting of the Executor's or Administrator's estate and the devolution of property are considered at p. 449 and the following chapters.

[96] *Hayward* v. *Kinsey* (1701) 12 Mod.Rep. 568, 573; *post*, p. 735 *et seq.*
[97] As to preservation grants, see p. 331 *post.*
[98] See *Stodden* v. *Harvey* (1608) Cro.Jac. 204 (removal of cattle by executors of lessee for life within six days considered reasonable).
[99] See *post*, p. 666.

CHAPTER 7

DEATH DUTIES

The assessment and payment of death duty whether in the form of estate duty, capital transfer tax, or now, inheritance tax is often one of the main concerns of a representative. The subject is too complex for anything beyond an initial summary of the main considerations. The case law on all these taxes remains inter-changeably relevant especially where the testator has made gifts "free of tax."[1] Reference should be made to the specialist works on these taxes.[2] This Chapter is confined to death duties as they directly affect the administration of the estate or as their ultimate burden may affect the distribution of the estate among those beneficially interested. Reference in any document to estate duty or to death duties are by statute construed as referring to inheritance tax.[3]

HISTORY

There have been a number of changes in recent years. Estate duty, introduced in 1894 as a stamp duty payable on death, came to be extended to apply to gifts made by the deceased within various periods preceding the death. Capital transfer tax, which replaced estate duty when death occurred on or after March 13, 1975, imposed a cumulative tax on gifts whether or not made more than seven years before death.[4] In 1986 there was a return to the principle of exemption for gifts made during lifetime, known as "potentially exempt transfers," provided the donor survived seven years, with a tapering relief for periods between three and seven years before the death.[5] In recognition of these significant changes, the tax was renamed "inheritance tax" as from July 25, 1986,[6] although the basic structure of capital transfer tax was retained. Estate duty will now only be directly relevant in a limited number of cases, for example where the surviving spouse exemption is applicable or where heritage property exemption had been accorded.[7]

---

[1] See *post* p. 78. As to income tax, see p. 583 *post* (before death) and p. 932 (after death).

[2] See *British Tax Encyclopedia* Part 3c; *Dymond's Capital Taxes*; *McCutcheon on Inheritance Tax* (3rd ed.).

[3] See Inheritance Tax Act 1984, Sched. 6, para. 1; Finance Act 1986, s.100.

[4] Finance Act 1975, s.19.

[5] Finance Act 1986, s.101; Inheritance Tax Act 1984, ss.3A and 7(4). The concept of "gifts with reservation" was re-introduced from the estate duty legislation by Finance Act 1986, s.102 and Sched. 20.

[6] Finance Act 1986, s.100.

[7] Inheritance Tax Act 1984, Sched. 6. However, to prevent avoidance of inheritance tax, provisions under estate duty regarding gifts with reservation of benefit were re-introduced, by Finance Act 1986, s.102 and Sched. 20, and decisions which had become irrelevant under capital transfer tax may once more be in point.

Inheritance tax

Tax is imposed on the value transferred by a "chargeable transfer"[8] which is defined as any transfer of value other than an exempt transfer.[9] A transfer of value is any disposition made by a person as a result of which the value of his estate immediately after the disposition is less than it would be but for the disposition. The amount by which it is less is the value transferred by the transfer.[10] In determining whether the value of a person's estate has been reduced no account is taken of the value of excluded property ceasing to form part of the estate as a result of a disposition.[11]

Exempt transfers include transfers between spouses,[12] small transfers,[13] small gifts (up to £250) to the same person,[14] normal expenditure out of income,[15] wedding gifts,[16] transfers allowable for income tax,[17] charitable gifts,[18] political gifts,[19] and national or public gifts.[20-21] On death, tax is charged as if immediately before his death the deceased had made a transfer of value and the value transferred by it had been equal to the value of his estate immediately before his death.[22] A person's estate is defined as the aggregate of all the property to which he is beneficially entitled except that the estate of a person immediately before his death does not include "excluded property".[23] Excluded property is a term which in general covers property outside the United Kingdom if the person beneficially entitled is domiciled outside the United Kingdom, reversionary interests (with exceptions),[24] and certain other exemptions such as the estates of persons dying on active service, cash options under annuity schemes, certain government securities in foreign ownership, overseas pensions, Manx and Channel Island savings, the estates of visiting forces and staffs, and property covered by arrangements made for double taxation relief.[25]

---

[8] Inheritance Tax Act 1984, s.1.

[9] *Ibid.* s.2(1).

[10] *Ibid.* s.3(1). There are of course further complex provisions covering connected persons and dealings in reversions. See *ibid.* ss.10 and 55, and *McCutcheon on Inheritance Tax*, (3rd ed.), 2–41, 15–35.

[11] Inheritance Tax Act 1984, s.3(2).

[12] *Ibid.* s.18.

[13] Up to £3,000 in any one year. *Ibid.*, s.19.

[14] *Ibid.*, s.20.

[15] *Ibid.* s.21.

[16] *Ibid.* s.22.

[17] *Ibid.* s.12.

[18] *Ibid.* s.23. It has been held in the context of income tax that the exemption for charities applied only to those established in the United Kingdom: *Camille and Henry Dreyfus Foundation Inc.* v. *I.R.C.* [1956] A.C. 39, *I.R.C.* v. *Gull* (1937) 21 T.C. 374. A charity is so established if the trustees are resident.

[19] *Ibid.* s.24.

[20-21] *Ibid.* ss.25–26.

[22] *Ibid.*, s.4(1).

[23] *Ibid.* s.5(1). As to powers exercisable by the deceased, see p. 73 *post*.

[24] *Ibid.* ss.6(1), 48(1).

[25] As to excluded property generally see *McCutcheon, on Inheritance Tax*, (3rd ed.), pp. 15–16–15–36.

Liability and accountability

The personal representative (including an intermeddler)[26] is liable or accountable for inheritance tax on all property which devolves upon or vests in him[27] or in which he has intermeddled but not beyond this[28] and where there is more than one personal representative they are all jointly and severally liable.[29] This liability is an original liability which is in terms imposed on the representative and accordingly an order in the *de bonis propriis* form rather than the *de bonis testatoris* form is appropriate where the liability arises on the death of the testator.[30] The personal representative must deliver an account specifying to the best of his knowledge and belief all property which formed part of the deceased's estate immediately before his death.[31] This includes property subject to a general power of appointment or to a power to charge money on the property.[32] However, it seems that the omission of the former criterion of "competency to dispose,"[33] will give rise to difficulties where property passes as a result of the perfection of an imperfect gift,[34] or in some cases of estoppel.[35] The liability of the personal representative does not affect the liability of the persons beneficially interested or their respective interests for inheritance tax and the latter have accordingly to account for or repay the same as the case may require.[36]

Inland revenue account

An account must be produced before any grant is issued or resealed by the High Court and it must show by means of such receipt or certification as may be prescribed by the Commissioners of Inland Revenue that the tax has been paid or that no tax is payable.[37] The personal representatives

[26] Inheritance Tax Act 1984, ss.199(4), 200(4). See generally *McCutcheon on Inheritance Tax*, (3rd ed.), pp. 22–23. As to intermeddling see *post*, p. 93.

[27] *Ibid.* s.200(1). Special executors for settled land are liable on this basis and there is no longer any special statutory provision for settled land. Settlements in general are subject to special provisions in Inheritance Tax Act 1984, ss.43–85.

[28] *Ibid.* s.204(1) which limits the liability of a personal representative to the tax liability arising in respect of assets which have been received or might have been received but for the neglect or default of the personal representative.

[29] *Ibid.* s.205.

[30] *I.R.C.* v. *Stannard* [1984] 1 W.L.R. 1039, applying *Berry* v. *Gaukroger* [1903] 2 Ch. 116.

[31] Inheritance Tax Act 1984, s.216. As to excluded property see *ante*, p. 72.

[32] *Ibid.* s.5(2); and see *Re Penrose* [1933] Ch. 793; *Re Parsons* [1943] Ch. 12, *Re Jones* [1945] Ch. 105; *Re Stratton's Disclaimer* [1958] Ch. 42.

[33] See Finance Act 1894, s.22(2)(*a*).

[34] See *Strong* v. *Bird* (1874) L.R. 18 Eq. 315 and *post*, p. 650. In such cases the donor remained competent to dispose up to the date of his death, but the gift is perfected on death and does not devolve on the personal representative as such but beneficially. See also, Dymond, *Capital Taxes*, 5.332, 5.350.

[35] If an imperfect "gift" is perfected by estoppel the exact date of perfection may be unascertainable. See *e.g. Crabb* v. *Arun D.C.* [1976] Ch. 179 following *Ramsden* v. *Dyson* (1866) L.R. 1 H.L. 129.

[36] See Inheritance Tax Act 1984, s.211(3).

[37] Supreme Court Act 1981, s.109; Inheritance Tax Act 1984, s.216. See also *post*, p. 294; see further *Practice Direction* [1981] 1 W.L.R. 1185.

must deliver their account before the expiration of the period of 12 months from the end of the month in which the death occurs, or, if it expires later, the period of three months beginning with the date on which the personal representatives first act as such.[38] Material errors must be corrected by further account within six months of discovery.[38] The tax is payable on delivery of the account[39] and the personal representatives may also then pay tax chargeable on the death for which they are not liable, if so requested by the persons liable.[40] However, the tax may be paid by instalments where it is attributable to the value of land,[41] to shares or securities of a company which gave the deceased control of the company immediately before his death or to certain other shares and securities and business interests if the statutory conditions are satisfied.[42] Except in certain cases where the tax is payable by instalments, interest runs after six months from the end of the month in which the death occurred and is adjusted by further payment or repayment on final account.[43] The Board has extensive power to require information.[44]

Where representative not liable for inheritance tax

Although the general[45] representatives have in their account to show to the best of their knowledge and belief all property which formed part of the deceased's estate immediately before his death,[46] they are liable only to pay inheritance tax on the property which devolves on them.[47] The knowledge is confined to the personal knowledge of the person who has to deliver the accounts, including the information contained in all the documents which he possesses or of which he has custody, or to which he is entitled but no further; he is not required to act as an information gatherer.[48] Liability for the tax on other property falls on the trustees of settlements,[49] persons in whom property is vested at any time after the death, and the persons beneficially entitled to interests in possession after the

[38] *Ibid.* ss.216(6), 217.
[39] *Ibid.* s.226(2).
[40] *Ibid.* s.226(2).
[41] "Land" includes land held jointly in fee simple for tenants in common. *Att.-Gen.* v. *Public Trustee & Tuck* [1929] 2 K.B. 77 decided under the Finance Act 1894, s.6(8). As to registered land see the Land Registration Act 1925, s.73, *post*, p. 552 as amended by the Finance Act 1975, Sched. 12, para. 5. For special rules as to interest where tax is payable by instalments see Inheritance Tax Act 1984, s.234.
[42] *Ibid.* ss.227–228. If the property is sold the tax becomes immediately payable.
[43] *Ibid.* s.233; *I.R.C.* v. *Raphael* [1935] A.C. 96. The rate is specified by the Board of Inland Revenue from time to time in accordance with a formula contained in The Taxes (Interest Rate) Regulation 1989 (S.I. 1989 No. 1297), made pursuant to the Finance Act 1989, s.178.
[44] *Ibid.* s.219.
[45] Special executors have only to account for property on which they are liable.
[46] *Ibid.*, s.216.
[47] See *ante*, p. 73.
[48] *Re Clore* (*No.* 3), *I.R.C.* v. *Stype Trustees* (*Jersey*) *Ltd.* [1985] 1 W.L.R. 1290.
[49] See *post*, p. 81, n. 17.

death.[50] Similarly, unless there is agreement to the contrary a donee is responsible for any original or additional tax liability arising from a gift made before the death to that donee.[51] This personal liability is reinforced by an Inland Revenue charge on the property in question[52] registrable as a land charge[53] in the case of land. The charge does not apply to personal or movable property in the United Kingdom which was beneficially owned by the deceased immediately before his death and which vests in his personal representatives.[54] A purchaser in good faith for consideration in money or money's worth other than a nominal consideration is not liable unless the property is subject to an Inland Revenue charge.[55] Even then the purchaser is not liable if the property was situated outside the United Kingdom or was personal property situated in the United Kingdom and the purchaser had no notice of the facts giving rise to the charge or in the case of land it is not protected by registration.[56] Where two or more persons are liable for inheritance tax, each is liable for the whole.[57] Where personal representatives pay tax for which a charge has been imposed the tax is repayable by the person in whom the property is vested.[58]

Ultimate burden

The fact that a person is liable for inheritance tax to the Crown does not mean that the duty must ultimately be borne by him. The incidence of the ultimate burden of inheritance tax is in the first place a matter of interpretation of the will.[59] There may be express directions affecting inheritance tax or there may be directions as to "testamentary expenses."[60] Subject to this the inheritance tax payable on freehold land,[61] property appointed by will under a general power of appointment,[62] property comprised in a *donatio mortis causa*,[63] property situated outside the United Kingdom, or property subject to a joint tenancy immediately before the death must ulti-

[50] See *Ibid.* ss.200(1), 201(1); *Re Avery* [1913] Ch. 208; Dymond, *Capital Taxes*, para. 26.300; *McCutcheon on Inheritance Tax*, 3rd ed., 22.28, 22.29.
[51] See, *e.g. ibid.* s.199(2).
[52] *Ibid.* ss.257, 258; *cf. O'Grady* v. *Wilmot* [1916] 2 A.C. 231.
[53] See the Land Charges Act 1972, ss.2, 3, 4, 17 and the Land Registration Act 1925, ss.20, 23, 59, 64, 73 as amended by the Finance Act 1975, Sched. 12; *cf.* the Law of Property Act 1925, s.16; *Re Palmer* [1900] W.N. 9; *Re Sharman* [1901] 2 Ch. 280; *Re Previté* [1931] 1 Ch. 447; *Re Morris* [1927] W.N. 146; *Re Owens* [1941] Ch. 17.
[54] *Ibid.* s.237(3).
[55] *Ibid.* ss.200(2), 272.
[56] *Ibid.* s.238(1).
[57] *Ibid.* s.205.
[58] *Ibid.* s.211(3); *Christies' Trustees* v. *Christies' Trustees*, 1943 S.C. 97; *McCutcheon on Inheritance Tax*, 3rd ed., 22–44.
[59] *Re Lomer* [1929] 1 Ch. 731; *Re Previté* [1931] 1 Ch. 447; *Re Ridley* [1950] Ch. 415; *Re Matthews' Will Trusts* [1961] 1 W.L.R. 1415; *Re Paulet's Will Trusts* [1969] 1 Ch. 552.
[60] As to the inclusion of inheritance tax in this term, see *post*, p. 77.
[61] *Re Palmer* [1900] W.N. 9; *Re Sharman* [1901] 2 Ch. 280; *Re Morris* [1927] W.N. 146; *Re Previté* [1931] 1 Ch. 447; *Re Owers* [1941] Ch. 17. *Re Rosenthal decd.* [1972] 1 W.L.R. 1273.
[62] *O'Grady* v. *Wilmot* [1916] 2 A.C. 231. Property subject to a general power is treated as property to which the deceased was beneficially entitled. (*Ibid.* s.5(2) and see *ante*.)
[63] *Re Hudson* [1911] 1 Ch. 206.

mately be borne by the persons beneficially entitled in proportion to their interests.[64] In effect the person beneficially entitled will bear the tax unless the property is free personal estate[65] situated in the United Kingdom. And if legacies are charged on real estate, the legatees must contribute rateably to the inheritance tax payable on the real estate.[66] Difficulties as to where the burden ultimately falls will if necessary be resolved in administration proceedings[67] and where any duty or tax is unpaid the court makes provision for payment out of any property in the possession or control of the court.[68]

Options

Whether a person who purchases real estate in the exercise of an option given him by will is entitled to take it free from liability to inheritance tax is not yet clear. A purchaser is generally entitled to take free from incumbrances,[69] and in *Re Fison's Will Trusts*[70] Romer J. held that this principle enabled the purchaser to take free even of a mortgage raised to pay estate duty. In *Re Lander*,[71] however, Roxburgh J. held that the purchaser under an option to buy at less than the market value must bear a proportionate amount of the estate duty.

The latter decision appears to be correct in principle and if *Re Fison's Will Trusts* be regarded as incorrect the other cases cited in both reports can be reconciled by reference to the extent of the testator's bounty involved. This criterion, however, was rejected by Romer J.

Personalty

In the absence of a contrary intention in the will, English[72] death duty on leaseholds[73] and all moveable personal property situated in the United Kingdom,[74] which devolves upon or vests in the representatives must ultimately be borne as a testamentary expense by the general estate (including

[64] *Re Orford* [1896] 1 Ch. 257; *Berry* v. *Gaukroger* [1903] 2 Ch. 116, 113; *Re Charlesworth's Trusts* [1912] 1 Ch. 319; *Re Hicklin* [1917] 2 Ch. 278; *Re Tollemache* [1930] W.N. 138. There is no longer any legislation to correspond with s.14 of the Finance Act 1894 which expressly covered the imposition of a testamentary charge on gifts made by the will. Under s.14 the beneficiary of the charge was made liable for the death duty. It seems that the principle in *Berry* v. *Gaukroger* [1903] 2 Ch. 116 would not apply in such a case so that ultimate liability would fall on the donee and not on the beneficiary of the charge.
[65] For these purposes personal estate includes leaseholds and undivided shares in land held on trust for sale, see the Inheritance Tax Act 1984, s.237(3).
[66] *Re Spencer Cooper* [1908] 1 Ch. 130; *Re Owers* [1941] Ch. 17.
[67] As to which see *post*, pp. 821.
[68] *Ibid.* s.232.
[69] *Re Wilson* [1908] 1 Ch. 839.
[70] [1950] Ch. 394.
[71] [1951] Ch. 546. Neither *Re Wilson* nor *Re Fison's Will Trusts* was cited in this case.
[72] Foreign duties are not generally administration expenses.
[73] *Bain* v. *Brand* (1876) 1 App.Cas. 762; *Re Culverhouse* [1896] 2 Ch. 251.
[74] *Re Scott* [1916] 2 Ch. 268.

realty as well as personalty) of the deceased in the order mentioned in the Administration of Estates Act 1925, Sched. 1, Pt. II.[75]

Realty

The principle became established under estate duty that real property, wherever situated, and personal property situated outside the United Kingdom bore its own tax, while the tax on personal property situated in the United Kingdom was a testamentary expense.[76] Following doubts raised by the decision in a Scottish case,[77] the legislation was amended to make it clear that where representatives are liable for tax, it is to be treated as part of the general testamentary and administration expenses of the estate, subject to any contrary intention shown by the deceased in his will.[78] Where such tax does not fall to be so borne, the tax is repayable, where occasion requires, by the person in whom the property to the value of which the tax is attributable is vested.[79]

Contribution

It is clear that, in the absence of a contrary intention, no contribution is required from legatees either of leaseholds or other personal property specifically bequeathed or of pecuniary legacies, whether settled or unsettled,[80] or from annuitants whose annuities are payable out of the deceased's personalty.[81]

Once the death has occurred, the persons liable for tax cannot transfer their liability by disposing of their interests, and it would seem that trustees, beneficiaries and others who have parted with their interests lawfully before the death upon which a claim to tax arises cannot be charged with tax, since the persons liable are those in possession, or who are entitled to possession, or who have acquired an interest in the property.[82]

These propositions are reinforced now by the Inheritance Tax Act 1984 which provides for repayments to the personal representatives by the persons in whom the property is vested where the tax does not fall to be borne as part of the testamentary expenses[83] or where there is a right to pay by instalment.[84] There is power to raise the necessary amount by sale or mort-

[75] *Re Anstead* [1943] Ch. 161; *Re Ridley* [1950] Ch. 451; *Re Buesst's Will Trusts* [1963] Ch. 419; *Re Wilson* [1967] Ch. 53; *Re Thompson* [1936] Ch. 676; *Re Owers* [1941] Ch. 17. It has been held that legacies are primarily payable out of personalty: *Re Beaumont's Will Trusts* [1950] Ch. 462; *Re Wilson* [1967] Ch. 53.

[76] *Re Clemow* [1900] 2 Ch. 182; *Re Spencer Cooper* [1908] 1 Ch. 130.

[77] *Re Dougal* [1981] S.T.C. 514.

[78] Finance (No. 2) Act 1983, s.13(1). See now Inheritance Tax Act 1984, s.211(1), (2).

[79] *Ibid.* s.211(3). For the application of this rule, see Dymond, *Capital Taxes*, 27.802 and *McCutcheon on Inheritance Tax*, (3rd ed.), 22.44. For the equitable right to reimbursement see *Re Latham* [1962] Ch. 616, 641.

[80] *Re Webber* [1896] 1 Ch. 914; *Re Culverhouse* [1896] 2 Ch. 251.

[81] *Re Trenchard* [1905] 1 Ch. 82.

[82] See *Re Hall-Dare* [1916] 1 Ch. 272; *Taylor* v. *Poncia* [1901] W.N. 87; *Re Snape* [1915] 2 Ch. 179.

[83] *Ibid.* s.211(3).

[84] *Ibid.* s.213.

gage[85] by a limited owner taking a charge on the property[86] and by expending other money subject to the same trusts as the property to which the tax is attributable.[87] The Board issues to persons not ultimately liable conclusive certificates showing the tax paid or borne.[88]

Variation or Disclaimer

The fixing of the inheritance tax liability on a person at the date of the death is subject, however, to variation if there is a disclaimer or variation[89] of the disposition of the deceased's estate within two years of the death[90] or a transfer of property within that period in accordance with the wishes of the deceased.[91] The Capital Taxes Office may challenge a purported variation if this is not genuine and amounts merely to a tax-saving operation involving collusion between the beneficiaries.

Gifts free of tax

The rules which formerly assisted in the construction of the words "free of tax," or similar words, are obsolescent, in so far as they referred to English succession duty or legacy duty[92]; but since inheritance tax is sometimes a testamentary expense and sometimes a charge on particular property, questions may yet arise, particularly in devises of land, where a "free of tax" provision may operate, so as to exonerate a devise or other gift from the charge of tax it would otherwise have borne.[93]

A direction in a will to pay testamentary expenses and duties out of residue may exonerate from the charge to tax realty which is specifically devised,[94] but this will only be where there is some clear disposition which in effect gives the specific devisee of realty an additional legacy of the amount of the tax payable on his devised property.[95] Again, where there was a direction to pay all legacies free of death duties, and the testator specifically devised his freehold house, both the estate duty and the succession duty on the freehold house were payable out of the residue, "legacies" being construed in the context to include all the preceding gifts of person-

---

[85] *Ibid.* s.212(1).

[86] *Ibid.* s.212(2).

[87] *Ibid.* s.212(3). The amount in question includes interest and costs properly incurred. *Ibid.* s.212(4).

[88] *Ibid.* s.214.

[89] There can be only one such variation. *Russell* v. *I.R.C.* [1988] 1 W.L.R. 834. A variation takes effect as soon as it is communicated to the representatives. See *Crowden* v. *Aldridge* [1992], *The Times*, November 30, 1992.

[90] *Ibid.* s.142.

[91] *Ibid.* s.143.

[92] See the 12th ed. of this work, Pt. 4, Bk. 4, Chap. 4, s.7. And see *Re NcNeill* [1958] Ch. 259; *Re Paterson's Will Trusts* [1963] 1 W.L.R. 623. But see *Re Sebba* [1959] Ch. 166.

[93] See *e.g. Re Walley* [1972] 1 W.L.R. 257.

[94] *Re Pimm* [1904] 2 Ch. 345; *cf. Re Ridley* [1950] Ch. 415 (general devise); *Re Wilson* [1967] Ch. 53.

[95] See *per* Wilberforce J. in *Re Phuler's Will Trusts* [1965] 1 W.L.R. 68, 69; *Re Neeld (No. 2)* [1965] 1 W.L.R. 73n; both distinguished in *Re Williams* [1974] 1 W.L.R. 754.

alty and realty in the will.[96] The general rule is established that a devise of realty "free of tax" means free of inheritance tax.[97]

Where a tenant for life under a settlement exercised a power of appointment by conferring on the appointee an annuity "free of all deductions," it was held that the annuity was free of liability to contribute to the tax payable on the death of the tenant for life.[98]

The operation of the "grossing up" rule means that it may be undesirable to make gifts "free of tax."[99]

Inheritance tax on settled legacies

Where a testator directs that legacies are to be paid free of tax, the question may arise as to whether this includes tax payable on settled legacies on the death of the first legatee.[1] This is a matter of interpretation[2] but there is a presumption that a testator only intends to provide for such tax as is payable by reason of his own death and to rebut this presumption a clear intention to provide for further tax must be found.[3] In some cases it has been held that the testator intended to provide only for the payment of the tax which became payable in consequence of his death[4]; in others, that he intended to include all tax payable in consequence of the dispositions made by his will.[5] This may put the executors in an embarrassing situation if the residue is given absolutely, because they cannot tell at the date of the death of the testator what the amount of duty on the death of the life tenant in a settled legacy would be.[6] Subject to what is said in the following paragraph, the latter construction includes tax payable on the death of a legatee in respect of that legacy.

Tax imposed by subsequent legislation

Intimately connected with this is the question whether the testator intended to provide for tax which should, or might, be imposed by legislation after his decease. Again there is no general rule, and each will must

---

[96] *Re Previté* [1931] 1 Ch. 447.
[97] *Re King* [1942] Ch. 413; *Re Ridley supra*; *Re Dawson's Will Trusts* [1957] 1 W.L.R. 391.
[98] *Re Smith-Bosanquet* [1940] Ch. 954; *Re Sebright* [1944] Ch. 287.
[99] Inheritance Tax Act 1984, s.38(3)–(5). See Dymond, *Capital Taxes*, 12.630 *et seq.* and *Lake* v. *Lake* [1989] S.T.C. 865.
[1] See Dymond, *Capital Taxes*, 27.432.
[2] See *Re Palmer* [1916] 2 Ch. 391; *Re Wedgwood* [1921] 1 Ch. 601; *Re Paterson's Will Trusts* [1963] 1 W.L.R. 623; *Re Embleton's Will Trusts* [1965] 1 W.L.R. 840.
[3] *Re Laidlaw* [1930] 2 Ch. 392; *Re Shepherd* [1949] Ch. 116; *Re Howell* [1952] Ch. 264.
[4] See *Re D'Oyly* [1917] 1 Ch. 556; *Re Wedgwood, supra*; *Re Beecham* [1924] W.N. 21; *Re Sarson* [1925] Ch. 31.
[5] See *Re Pimm* [1904] 2 Ch. 345; *Re Stoddart* [1916] 2 Ch. 444; *Re Parker* [1917] W.N. 233; *Re Eve* [1917] 1 Ch. 562; *Re Jones* [1928] W.N. 227; *Re Trimble* [1931] 1 Ch. 369; *Re Hicks* [1933] Ch. 335.
[6] See *per* Cross J. in *Re Embleton's Will Trusts* [1965] 1 W.L.R. 840, 846. This consideration has operated to induce the courts to come down on the side of saying, in cases of doubt, that future tax is not covered by the words in the will (*ibid.*).

be construed according to the actual words used therein.[7] In the majority of cases the testator is supposed to have referred only to those taxes in existence at the date of his death,[8] or at the time the legacy is severed from the rest of the estate.[9] In some cases, however, his words have been construed widely so as to include any tax subsequently imposed.[10] But "it is for the legatees who seek the benefit of this extended exoneration to establish affirmatively that the words used give them this benefit."[11]

Foreign taxes

"Free of tax" provisions in an English will refer only to taxes imposed by English law, unless there are words in the will extending the provisions so as to include foreign taxes.[12] Nevertheless, it would seem that many foreign taxes will be borne by residue as a testamentary expense, if it is necessary for the executors to pay the tax before they can get in and make the foreign assets available for application under the will. The distinction seems to lie, in the words of Jenkins L.J., between[13] "a specific gift of property situated in a foreign country and attracting duty by the laws of that country, or a gift to a legatee domiciled or resident abroad which attracts duty in the hands of the legatee under the law of his or her domicile or place of residence" and "a case in which property in Canada has passed under a general residuary devise and bequest in the English will of a testatrix domiciled and resident here, and in which this country is the appropriate forum of administration." In the former two instances the donee pays the tax. In the latter instance it may be paid out of the estate (*i.e.* residue).[14]

Where an English testator by an English will gave a pecuniary legacy "free of duty," in the absence of any contrary intention expressed in the will, the only taxes payable out of his estate in respect of the legacy were those imposed by English law.[15] But where a British subject, ordinarily resident in Turkey, by his will devised "free of all duties" certain freehold land in France, French duty, *mutation*, in respect of such property was held to be payable out of the estate, and not by the devisee, for there was no

---

[7] See *Re Palmer* [1916] 2 Ch. 391; *Re Wedgwood* [1921] 1 Ch. 601. As to the fund from which duty on settled legacies is payable, see *Re Weigall's Will Trusts* [1956] Ch. 424, 432 *et seq.*, where Harman J. applied the reasoning in *Re Palmer*, and did not follow the decision of Romer J. in *Re Cassel's Will Trusts* [1947] Ch. 1.

[8] See *Re Beecham, supra*; *Re D'Oyly, supra*; *Re Snape* [1915] 2 Ch. 179.

[9] *Re Palmer, supra*; *Re Wedgwood, supra*; *Re Sutherland* [1922] 2 Ch. 782; *Re Shepherd, supra.*

[10] *Re Stoddart, supra*; *Re Tinkler* [1917] 1 Ch. 242; *Re Parker, supra*; *Re Eve, supra*; *Re Lomer* [1929] 1 Ch. 731.

[11] *Per* Sargant J., in *Re Sutherland, supra*, at p. 789; *Re Fenwick* [1922] 2 Ch. 775.

[12] *Re Norbury* [1939] Ch. 528; *Re Frazer* [1941] Ch. 326; *Re Cunliffe-Owen* [1951] Ch. 964; *Re Goetze* [1953] Ch. 96.

[13] [1953] Ch. 111; [1959] Ch. 175.

[14] *Re Goetze* [1953] Ch. 96; *Re Sebba* [1959] Ch. 166.

[15] *Re Norbury, supra.*

other tax, in England or elsewhere, payable in respect of the property out of the estate.[16]

Tax on settlements

A direction in a will to pay all inheritance tax out of residue does not extend to tax which is ultimately payable by the trustees of a settlement. Such tax must be borne, in the ordinary way, by the settled property. A person entitled to an interest in possession in the residuary estate of a deceased person upon the completion of the administration of that estate is treated as being entitled on the basis that the administration was completed immediately upon death.[17]

Certificate of discharge

Where land has been charged with payment of duty the vendor will have to prove the discharge by means of a certificate of discharge unless the abstract of title recites payment, in which case the burden of verification falls upon the purchaser.

Where application is made to the Commissioners of Inland Revenue by a person liable for any tax on the value transferred by a chargeable transfer which is attributable to the value of property specified in the application the Board must give a certificate to the effect that the tax has been or will be so paid if satisfied that this is so.[18] There is also provision for a certificate to be obtained where tax is or may be chargeable after two years from the death on delivery of a full statement.[19] Such a certificate gives no discharge in case of fraud or failure to disclose material facts, nor does it affect further tax if further property comes to light.[20]

Inheritance tax litigation

The procedure is now governed by the Inheritance Tax Act 1984, sections 221 to 225. After the accounts[21] and any corrective accounts[22] have been delivered (and if applicable) the Board has exercised its power to require information[23] it may then give a written notice of determination.[24] From this there is a right of appeal by written notice giving grounds of appeal within 30 days.[25] Unless the appeal is substantially confined to ques-

---

[16] *Re Quirk* [1941] Ch. 46; distinguishing *Re Norbury.*

[17] *Re Briggs* [1914] 2 Ch. 413. The provisions governing inheritance tax on settled property are contained in the Inheritance Tax Act 1984, Part III, ss.43–93 and are beyond the scope of this work. For the position of residuary beneficiaries, see *ibid.* s.91. See generally Dymond, *Capital Taxes*, chapters 16–21.

[18] Inheritance tax Act 1984, s.239(1).

[19] *Ibid.* s.239(2).

[20] *Ibid.* s.239(4).

[21] *Ibid.* s.216.

[22] *Ibid.* s.217; see *post*, p. 296.

[23] *Ibid.* s.219.

[24] *Ibid.* s.221.

[25] *Ibid.*, s.222. As to appeals out of time, see *ibid.*, s.223.

tions of law it is heard in the first instance by the Special Commissioners.[26] Neither the High Court nor the Special Commissioners can decide matters of land valuation.[27] This is reserved to the Lands Tribunal. The jurisdiction of the Lands Tribunal extends not only to the intrinsic value of the land, but to such collateral matters as the deduction to be made in relation to the potential liability to repay discount on property acquired pursuant to the "right to buy" provisions in the Housing Acts.[28] Proceedings in the High Court are begun by originating summons in the Chancery Division.[29] Proceedings before the Special Commissioners are governed by section 224 of the Inheritance Tax Act 1984, are heard in private and are less formal than in the High Court. Within 30 days of the determination of the case by the Special Commissioners they may be required to state a case for the High Court[30] on any question of law.[31] It follows that the evidence adduced before the Special Commissioners and their findings of fact are of major importance. The Board is precluded from taking any legal proceedings for recovery of tax unless the amount has been agreed in writing or determined and specified under the procedure indicated above.[32] Such a certificate can be obtained even if the estate is so small that no duty is payable.[33]

Commissioners' powers to commute or accept payment in kind

It is outside the scope of this work to discuss the practice and the powers of the Board.[34] It should, however, be mentioned that the Board has powers to accept property in satisfaction of duty,[35] and to mitigate penalties.[36]

Tax avoidance

The "new approach" by the courts to tax avoidance schemes may be relevant to dispositions made with a view to saving inheritance tax.[37] The attitude of the courts may be influenced by whether the dispositions were carried out over a reasonable time-scale (*i.e.* months rather than days) and whether the parties involved had independent legal advice.[38]

---

[26] *Ibid.*, s.222(2), (3).

[27] *Ibid.*, s.222(4). As to inspection to ascertain value, see *ibid.*, s.220.

[28] *Alexander* v. *I.R.C.* [1991] S.T.C. 112.

[29] See R.S.C., Ord. 91, r. 2.

[30] Inheritance Tax Act 1984, s.225(1).

[31] *Ibid.*, s.225(4). Subsequent alterations in the law after payment has been made will not disturb the position. See *Ibid.*, s.255.

[32] *Ibid.*, s.242. As to previous Crown practice, see *Re Park* [1970] 1 W.L.R. 626, 631.

[33] See 56 L.S. Gaz. 479.

[34] See generally, the Inland Revenue Regulation Act 1890, ss.1–4 and the Inheritance Tax Act 1984, s.215; *McCutcheon on Inheritance Tax*, 3rd ed., Chapter 22. The address for correspondence is Capital Taxes Office, Commerce Square, The Lace Market, Nottingham NG1 1HS.

[35] Inheritance Tax Act 1984, s.230.

[36] *Ibid.* s.253. There is no longer power to remit tax (*cf.* the Finance Act 1894, s.8(11)), but there are time limits for the recovery of tax—Inheritance Tax Act 1984, s.240(2), (3).

[37] See *W.T. Ramsay Ltd.* v. *I.R.C.* [1982] A.C. 300; *Furniss* v. *Dawson* [1984] A.C. 474; *Craven* v. *White* [1989] A.C. 398; *Countess Fitzwilliam* v. *I.R.C.* [1992] S.T.C. 185 and also Inheritance Tax Act 1984, s.268, applied in *I.R.C.* v. *Macpherson* [1989] A.C. 159.

[38] See *Hatton* v. *I.R.C.* [1992] S.T.C. 140, and *Countess Fitzwilliam* v. *I.R.C.* [1992] S.T.C. 185.

CHAPTER 8

ACTION BEFORE GRANT—ACTION WITHOUT GRANT

1—ACTION BEFORE GRANT

Distinction between probate and administration

Although different considerations apply, it is convenient to consider in one chapter the validity of acts done by executors and administrators before grant of probate or administration has been obtained and the position of persons who intermeddle without title to a grant at all. The differences between executors and administrators stem from the fact that an executor derives his title from the will whereas the grant provides the only title of the administrator. But a grant of administration with the will annexed is of course proof of the will in question,[1] and probate is the necessary evidence of an executor's title.

Executor derives title from will

Where an executor is appointed by a will, he derives title from the will,[2] and the property of the deceased vests in him from the moment of the testator's death,[3] so that probate is said to have relation to the time of the testator's death.[4] Thus, though he cannot rely on his title in any court without production of probate or a grant of administration with the will annexed, the grant is merely operative as the authenticated evidence of the executor's title.[3] For this reason a court would be likely to grant interim relief in an urgent case upon a proper undertaking by an executor to take out a grant of probate.

This principle applies where the testator died domiciled abroad, provided, in the case of immovables, that the law of the domicile is the same as English Law on this point.[5] In the case of movables, it is submitted that the

---

[1] See *Redwood Music Ltd.* v. *B. Feldman & Co. Ltd.* [1979] R.P.C. 1.

[2] As to the statutory power for the court to appoint a personal representative, see *ante*, pp. 17, 34.

[3] *Smith* v. *Milles* (1786) 1 T.R. 475, 480; *Comber's Case* (1721) 1 P.Wms. 766; *Woolley* v. *Clark* (1822) 5 B. & A. 744. *Semble*, the same may be said of a special representative, who is deemed to have been appointed in respect of "settled land" under the Administration of Estates Act 1925, s.22 (see *post*, pp. 272, 1122).

[4] Wentw.Off.Ex., 14th ed., p. 115; *Whitehead* v. *Taylor* (1839) 10 A. & E. 210; *Ingle* v. *Richards* (*No.* 2) (1860) 28 Beav. 366.

[5] *Redwood Music Ltd.* v. *B. Feldman & Co. Ltd.* [1979] R.P.C. 1.

principle applies irrespective of the law of the domicile.[6] In either case the production of an English grant would of course still be necessary to prove title in an English court.

What executor may do before grant

From this it follows that an executor who is of full age at the date of the testator's death,[7] before he proves the will, may do almost all the acts which are incident to his office, except only some of those which relate to actions.[8] Thus he may seize and take into his hands any of the testator's effects.[9] He may pay, or take releases of debts owing from the estate[10]; he may receive or release debts which are owing to it[11] and distrain for rent due to the testator.[12] If, before probate, the day occurs for payment upon bond made by, or to, the testator, payment must be made to, or by, the executor, though the will is not then proved, upon like penalty as if it were.[13] So he may at his discretion sell or otherwise deal with the testator's undisposed goods.[14] Formerly he could even give away such goods[15] but this is no longer within his powers because he is no longer beneficially entitled to the undisposed residue.[16] He may assent to, or pay, legacies[17] and he may enter on the testator's land.[18]

It follows that if a cause of action arises in favour of the estate of a deceased person at or after his death, time will at once begin to run, if there is an executor, even though probate has not been obtained.[19]

---

[6] As to the distinction between movable and immovable property in this context, see *ante*, p. 11.

[7] For the position of an infant who is appointed executor, see the Supreme Court Act 1981, s.118; *ante*, p. 21, *post*, p. 1121.

[8] Godolph., Pt. 2, c. 20, s.1; Wentw.Off.Ex., 14th ed., p. 81; Treat. on Eq. B. 4, Pt. 2, c. 1, s.2; *Wankford* v. *Wankford* (1704) 1 Salk. 299, 301; *Humphreys* v. *Ingledon* (1721) 1 P.Wms. 752. Much of the material in this and the following paragraph received judicial approval in *Re Stevens* [1897] 1 Ch. 422, 429.

[9] Godolph., Pt. 2, c. 20, s.1; Wentw.Off.Ex., 14th ed., p. 81; *Anon.*, Lofft. 81.

[10] Godolph., Pt. 2, c. 30, s.3; Wentw.Off.Ex., 14th ed., p. 81.

[11] Co.Litt. 292b; *Graysbrook* v. *Fox* (1564) 1 Plowd. 275; *Middleton's Case* (1603) 5 Co. 28a; Godolph., Pt. 2, c. 20, s.1; Wentw.Off.Ex., 14th ed., p. 81; *Wankford* v. *Wankford* (1704) 1 Salk. 299, 306, 307; *Wills* v. *Rich* (1742) 2 Atk. 285; *Re Stevens* [1897] 1 Ch. 422, 430.

[12] *Whitehead* v. *Taylor* (1839) 10 A. & E. 210.

[13] Godolph., Pt. 2, c. 2, s.3; Wentw.Off.Ex., 14th ed., p. 18.

[14] Godolph., Pt. 2, c. 20, s.3; Wentw.Off.Ex., 14th ed., p. 82. He may release or assign any part of the personal estate before probate: by Lord Macclesfield, 1 P.Wms. 768, *Comber's Case* (1721). It is consequently no objection to the title of an assignee of a patent that the assignors, the executors of the grantee, had omitted to register the probate until after the date of the assignment: *Elwood* v. *Christy* (1864) 17 C.B.(N.S.) 754. But as to a purchaser's right to withhold payment, see *post*, p. 85.

[15] Wentw.Off.Ex., p. 18.

[16] See *post*, p. 935.

[17] Godolph., Pt. 2, c. 29, s.1; Wentw.Off.Ex., 14th ed., p. 82; *Anon.* (1677) Freem.Ch. 23. As to assents in respect of a legal estate in land, see *post*, pp. 1055 *et seq*.

[18] *R.* v. *Stone* (*Inhabitants of*) (1795) 6 T.R. 295; 3 Dyer 367a.

[19] *Knox* v. *Gye* (1872) L.R. 5 H.L. 656; but if there is no executor, time will only run from the actual grant of letters of administration: *Murray* v. *East India Co.* (1821) 5 B. & Ad. 204. See *post*, p. 897.

If executor dies before grant

If the executor should die, after any of these acts, without proving the will, such acts will stand firm and good.[20] Where a termor devised his term to another whom he made his executor and died, and the devisee entered and died before 1926, without any probate, it was held that the term was legally vested in the executor by his entry, and an execution of the devise, without any probate.[21] So if an executor assents to a legacy, and dies before probate, the assent is good.[22] Thus the executor of a person who has died after 1925 can (though as regards a legal estate in land he should not in practice) validly convey, assign or assent to the vesting of the real estate or chattels real of such person,[23] and such conveyance, or assignment, or assent will be valid even if the executor should die before obtaining probate. So all payments made to an executor before probate are good, and will not be defeated, though he dies and never proves the will.[24] In a word, the executor's not proving the will, upon his death, determines the executorship, but does not avoid it.[25]

But probate is a document of title

Though an executor may, before probate, by conveyance, assignment or assent give valid title to the grantee, assignee or person in whose favour the assent is made, yet, if it be necessary to support that title by deducing it from the conveyance, assignment or assent, it also becomes requisite to show the right to make the conveyance or assignment, or give the assent. This can only be effected by producing the probate, or other evidence of the admission of the will in the court.[26] If a sole executor dies after the conveyance, assignment or assent, without having obtained probate, letters of administration with the will annexed must be produced instead.[27]

Again, though an executor can, before probate, give a binding receipt for purchase-money, yet a purchaser is not bound to pay the purchase-

[20] Wentw.Off.Ex., 14th ed., p. 82; Anon. (1677) 2 Freem.Ch. 23; *Brazier* v. *Hudson* (1836) 8 Sim. 67. The substance of the above passages was treated as authoritative and followed by North J. in *Re Stevens* [1897] 1 Ch. 422, 429, and by Eve. J. in *Kelsey* v. *Kelsey* (1922) 91 L.J.Ch. 382, 384 (where a notice, required to be given to the "personal representatives" of a deceased partner, given to executors before they had obtained probate, was held to have been properly given).

[21] 3 Dyer 367*a*; *R.* v. *Stone* (*Inhabitants*) (1795) 6 T.R. 298; *Fenton* v. *Clegg* (1854) 9 Exch. 680. As to the need for a written assent since 1925, see *post*, p. 1055. As to penalties for not obtaining a grant, see *post*, p. 277.

[22] *Johnson* v. *Warwick* (1856) 17 C.B. 516. *Redwood Music Ltd.* v. *B. Feldman & Co.* [1979] R.P.C. 1, 5.

[23] Administration of Estates Act 1925, s.2(1); *Brazier* v. *Hudson, supra.* After probate is obtained, however, a memorandum of the conveyance, assignment or assent should be indorsed thereon: see *post*, p. 679.

[24] *Wankford* v. *Wankford* (1704) 1 Salk. 299, 306, 507.

[25] By Lord Holt in *Wankford* v. *Wankford* (1704) 1 Salk. 299, 309. As to statutory cesser of the executorship, see *ante*, p. 39, and as to chain of representation, *ante*, p. 44.

[26] See *ante*, p. 9.

[27] *Johnson* v. *Warwick* (1856) 17 C.B. 516. As to the position if such executor is not sole executor, see *ante*, p. 46.

money till probate, because until the evidence of title exists, the executor cannot give a complete indemnity[28]; nor can notice of the conveyance be indorsed.[29]

The production of a grant of representation or confirmation made by a court in the United Kingdom is necessary to establish the right to recover or receive any part of the deceased's estate situated in the United Kingdom.[30] Thus it has been said that the court has not the legal optics to look at the will before probate.[31] But where a life policy is effected by a person who dies domiciled abroad, the production of a grant is not necessary to prove the existence of the right to receive the policy money.[32]

Actions before probate

An executor[33] cannot maintain actions before probate except those founded on his *actual* possession; for in actions where he sues in his representative character, he may be compelled, by the course of pleading, to produce the probate at the trial or, in some cases, by an application to the court, at an earlier stage of the action[34]; and in those actions where he sues in his individual capacity, relying on his *constructive* possession as executor, though he does not plead as executor, it will generally be necessary for him to prove himself executor at the trial,[35] which he can only do by showing the probate. For example, where an executor brings trespass *de bonis asportatis*, or trover,[36] upon his testator's possession, and a conversion in his lifetime, he necessarily describes himself as executor in his pleadings, and his character as such may be traversed. Where the goods were taken or converted after the testator's death, although, since the property in the goods draws to it a possession in law, he might formerly have relied on this *constructive* possession of his own, notwithstanding he had never had actual possession, still, if his title to the property were put in issue by the pleadings, he had to show his title as executor at the trial by producing the probate, properly stamped in order to prove his constructive possession.[37] By Order 6, r. 3, if the plaintiff sues in a representative capacity, the indorsement of claim on the writ of summons must show in what capacity he sues.

---

[28] *Newton* v. *Metropolitan Ry.* (1861) 1 Dr. & Sm. 583; *Re Stevens* [1897] 1 Ch. 422, 430.

[29] See *post*, p. 679.

[30] Revenue Act 1884, s.11; extended to real estate by the Administration of Estates Act 1925, s.2(1). See also the effect of Administration of Estates Act 1971, *post*, p. 368.

[31] *Per* Jervis C.J. in *Johnson* v. *Warwick* (1856) 17 C.B. 516, 522.

[32] Revenue Act 1884, s.11 proviso, Revenue Act 1889, s.19. *Haas* v. *Atlas Assurance Co.* [1913] 2 K.B. 209; *Redwood Music Ltd.* v. *Feldman & Co. Ltd.* [1979] R.P.C. 1. See *post*, p. 106.

[33] The position of an executor *de son tort* is analogous in this respect. See *post*, pp. 93.

[34] *Webb* v. *Adkins* (1854) 14 C.B. 401; *Tarn* v. *Commercial Bank of Sydney* (1884) 12 Q.B.D. 294; *Re West* [1947] W.N. 2. As to the effect of a grant, see *post*, p. 449.

[35] *Blainfield* v. *March* (1702) 7 Mod. 141, by Holt C.J.; 2 Saund. 47z, note to *Wilbraham* v. *Snow* (1670).

[36] See now the Torts (Interference with Goods) Act 1977.

[37] *Hunt* v. *Stevens* (1810) 3 Taunt. 113.

Where, however, the executor has had actual possession of the property which is the subject of the action, before it came to the hands of the defendant, such possession, according to the general principle, establishes a prima facie title in him so as to enable him to sue for his remedy in tort,[38] or contract,[39] as the case may be. In such cases the actual possession of the plaintiff is a prima facie title, without reference to the circumstances in which that possession has been obtained, whether as executor or by any other means.[40] It has elsewhere[41] been suggested that an executor may, before grant, maintain actions of trespass or trover[36] for effects of the testator which have never come into his actual possession although taken or converted after the death. This, it is submitted, is incorrect.

The law is the same for the grantee of the executor. Thus, in an action of trover for a horse and gig, which the plaintiff claimed as the purchaser from an executor, it was held, that as at the time of the trial probate had not been granted, and the executor had never had actual exclusive possession of the gig and horse, the plaintiff could not make out his title, though he produced the will appointing his vendor executor.[42] In this case, the plaintiff and defendant both claimed title to the property; and Lord Tenterden, in his address to the jury, observed, that if the plaintiff had proved a clear and undisputed possession, it might have been sufficient; but it appeared that the defendant, before and after the sale to the plaintiff, used the gig and horse.

Executor may commence action before probate

Though an executor cannot *maintain* actions before probate, except upon his actual possession, yet he may *commence* the action before probate,[43] and may continue the same as far as that step where the production of the probate becomes necessary, and it will be sufficient if he obtains the probate in time for that exigency.[44] Thus where a reversion of a term comes to him, he may sue before probate for such rent as has accrued after the death of the testator,[45] and if such an issue is joined that it becomes necessary for him to prove his title by executorship (as, for instance, if *non*

---

[38] Wentw.Off.Ex., 14th ed., p. 84; 1 Plowd. 281, in *Graysbrook* v. *Fox.* See *Elliott* v. *Kemp* (1840) 7 M. & W. 306, 312, 314.

[39] Wentw.Off.Ex., 14th ed., pp. 84, 85.

[40] *Oughton* v. *Seppings* (1830) 1 B. & Ad. 241. See also *White* v. *Mullett* (1851) 6 Exch. 713, 715; *Waller* v. *Drakeford* (1853) 1 E. & B. 749.

[41] See Toller (6th ed.) 47; 2 *Roberts on Wills*, 172, 173.

[42] *Pinney* v. *Pinney* (1828) 8 B. & C. 335.

[43] 1 Roll.Abr. 917, A. 2; *Martin* v. *Fuller* (1696) Comb. 371; *Wankford* v. *Wankford* (1704) 1 Salk. 302, 303; *Webb* v. *Adkins* (1854) 14 C.B. 401. But in cases where the defendant does not dispute his liability or the title of the executors to probate, but merely requires production of the probate before paying the executor, the executor ought not to sue, and the court will stay the action if he does. See *Tarn* v. *Commercial Bank of Sydney* (1884) 12 Q.B.D. 294.

[44] *Wills* v. *Rich* (1742) 2 Atk. 285; *Easton* v. *Carter* (1850) 5 Exch. 8, 14; *Meyappa Chetty* v. *Supramanian Chetty* [1916] 1 A.C. 603, 608; *Biles* v. *Caesar* [1957] 1 W.L.R. 156. The probate is a court order and proves itself.

[45] *Wankford* v. *Wankford* (1704) 1 Salk. 307, *per* Holt C.J.; *Whitehead* v. *Taylor* (1839) 10 A. & E. 210.

tenuit—no title—should be pleaded), it will be sufficient if he obtains probate in time to produce it in evidence at the trial.

In order to protect the defendant in such cases, the court, on being shown that the plaintiff who claims as executor has not obtained probate, will stay proceedings until probate has been taken out and a reasonable time has elapsed after it has been submitted to the inspection of the defendant.[46]

The same principles apply to all proceedings whether in the Chancery Division,[47] or elsewhere including bankruptcy petitions[48] and winding-up petitions.[49]

Notices affecting land

Such notices may be invalid if the estate owner proves to be dead. There may then be no person on whom the notice can be served before grant. Even after grant it may be difficult to obtain the names of the representatives on whom such notices must be served.[50]

Executor may be sued before probate

On the other hand, if an executor has elected to administer, he may, before probate, be sued at law or in equity by the deceased's creditors, whose rights are not impeded by his delay, and to whom, as executor *de jure* or *de facto*, he has made himself responsible.[51] So an action may be commenced against an executor before probate by a residuary legatee or devisee for an account of the estate and effects of the testator, and to have the assets secured,[52] and to discover the estate of the testator, though an action is pending respecting the validity of the will.[53] But a creditor of a deceased debtor cannot sue a person named as executor in the will unless he has elected to administer by intermeddling or proving the will, conse-

---

[46] *Webb* v. *Adkins, supra*; *Tarn* v. *Commercial Bank of Sydney, supra.*

[47] *Humphreys* v. *Humphreys* (1734) 3 P.Wms. 349. And see *Ingall* v. *Moran* [1944] 1 K.B. 160, 168, 170; *Patten (Executrix)* v. *Panton* (1793) 3 Bac.Abr. 53, by Gwillim, Executors, E. 14. *Simons* v. *Milman* (1828) 2 Sim. 241. *Jones* v. *Howells* (1843) 2 Hare 342. In *Newton* v. *Metropolitan Ry.* (1861) 1 Dr. & Sm. 583, notice of motion for an injunction was given, and at that time when the motion, but for the press of business, would have been heard, there was no probate; but when the motion was actually heard, the probate was in court; and it was held by Kindersley V.-C. that the defendants could not resist the motion upon the ground of demurrer. See also *Beardmore* v. *Gregory* (1865) 34 L.J.Ch. 392.

[48] See *Ex p. Paddy* (1818) 3 Madd. 241; *Rogers* v. *James* (1816) 7 Taunt. 147, cases decided under the old Bankruptcy Acts.

[49] *Re Masonic and General Life Assurance Co.* (1885) 32 Ch.D. 373.

[50] See Law Com. 184 and 140 N.L.J. 95.

[51] Wentw.Off.Ex., 14th ed., pp. 86, 87; Plowd. 280; Toller (6th ed.) 49. It is clear upon the grounds which have been stated, that if he has administered, he will be liable, not only before probate, but though he should refuse to take probate and administration should be committed to another. See the observations of Best C.J. in *Douglas* v. *Forrest* (1828) 4 Bing. 704. As to what amounts to an election to administer.

[52] *Blewitt* v. *Blewitt* (1832) 1 Younge 541; *Re Stevens* [1897] 1 Ch. 422.

[53] *Dulwich College* v. *Johnson* (1688) 2 Vern. 49. See also *Phipps* v. *Steward* (1737) 1 Atk. 285; Fonbl.Treat. on Eq., Bk. 4, Pt. 2, c. 1, s.2, n.(*b*). Since the passing of the Judicature Acts, actions for the sole purpose of obtaining discovery have become rare. See, however, *Norwich Pharmacal Co.* v. *Customs and Excise Comrs.* [1974] A.C. 133.

quently the seizure and sale of part of a testator's assets, under an execution founded upon a judgment in an action so constituted, was ineffectual to bind the testator's estate.[54]

In *Loudon* v. *Ryder (No. 2)*[55] it was held that a defendant, who asserts a right as next-of-kin of a deceased person, and who could be entitled to a grant of administration, may be sued if he sets up a wrongful claim, since otherwise the defendant would be able to profit by his failure to obtain a grant.

Administrator derives title from grant

It has been shown that an executor may perform most of the acts appertaining to his office, before probate.[56] But for an administrator, the general rule is that a party entitled to administration can do nothing as administrator before letters of administration are granted to him, inasmuch as he derives his authority entirely from the appointment of the court.[57] Before his appointment the property vests in the President.[58] He then has the same rights and liabilities and is accountable as if he were the executor.[59] However, if a foreign domiciled testator makes a will appointing an executor the will can be proved by a grant with the will annexed to an English attorney administrator and this is sufficient to prove the will in England.[60] This can prove the document from which the foreign executor derives his title.

At law, letters of administration must issue before the commencement of legal proceedings by a person entitled to administration for he has no right of action until he has obtained them, and even if he obtains a grant afterwards, it does not for this purpose relate back.[61] An administrator with the will annexed has no more right in this respect than any other administrator.[62] The proceedings are a nullity and cannot be validated by a later grant of administration.[63]

If a person purports to release a debt or claim and afterwards takes out letters of administration, it will not bar him; for the right was not in him at

---

[54] *Mohamidu Mohideen Hadjiar* v. *Pitchey* [1894] A.C. 437.
[55] [1953] Ch. 423.
[56] *Ante*, p. 88.
[57] *Wankford* v. *Wankford* (1704) 1 Salk. 301, by Powys J.; and see *Creed* v. *Creed* [1913] 1 Ir.R. 48; *Woolley* v. *Clark* (1822) 5 B. & A. 744–746; *Chetty* v. *Chetty* [1916] 1 A.C. 603.
[58] See p. 461, *post.*
[59] Administration of Estates Act 1925, s.21. See *post*, p. 1122.
[60] See *Redwood Music Ltd.* v. *B. Feldman & Co. Ltd.* [1979] R.P.C. 1.
[61] *Martin* v. *Fuller* (1696) Comb. 371 Comb.Dig., Admon.B. 9; 1 Salk. 303, by Powell J.; *Wooldridge* v. *Bishop (1827) 7 B. & C. 406; Ingall* v. *Moran* [1944] K.B. 160; and see *Hilton* v. *Sutton Steam Laundry* [1946] K.B. 65. But a mere misdescription, not appearing in the indorsement of the writ will not be fatal: *Bowler* v. *John Mowlem & Co.* [1954] 1 W.L.R. 1445. See also *Stebbings* v. *Holst & Co.* [1953] 1 W.L.R. 603; *Finnegan* v. *Cementation Co.* [1953] 1 Q.B. 688.
[62] *Phillips* v. *Hartley* (1827) 3 C. & P. 121.
[63] *Hilton* v. *Sutton Steam Laundry, supra; Burns* v. *Campbell* [1952] 1 K.B. 15.

the time of the release.[64] So an assignment of a term of years,[65] or an agreement to suffer the term to be surrendered and to give possession to the landlord,[66] by an administrator before letters is, it seems, of no validity.[65] Again, if the deceased was a tenant from year to year, a surrender of this leasehold interest cannot be made by a next-of-kin before taking out letters of administration.[67]

An administrator is not estopped by a mortgage he had made of the premises in dispute at a time before he became administrator.[68] And it may be doubted whether admissions made by a representative before he was clothed with that character are receivable in evidence against him in an action brought by or against him in his representative capacity.[69]

Where it had been agreed by articles of partnership that the executor or administrator of a deceased partner should have the option of succeeding to the share of the deceased in the partnership business on giving notice within three calendar months of the death to the surviving partners, it was held that a notice given by the administrator of the deceased partner within the three months of his death, but before taking out letters of administration, was not an effectual notice within the meaning of the agreement, because the letters of administration had no relation back to the act of giving notice, so as to clothe him with the character of administrator at that time.[70]

What an administrator may do before grant

The general proposition that letters of administration do not relate back to the date of death is subject to a number of exceptions or apparent exceptions which apply by statute or at common law where this is for the benefit of the estate.[71] The test is objective, that is to say, the grant will "relate back" only if this actually benefits the estate and not because the expected administrator thinks it will benefit the estate.[72] Although there is no authority on the question it is thought that the test of "benefit" must be as at the date of the act in question regardless of supervening events.[73]

Statute

Under section 26 of the Limitation Act 1980 an administrator claiming recovery of land (including leases) is deemed to claim as if there had been

---

[64] *Middleton's Case* (1603) 5 Co. 28b.
[65] 3 Preston on Abst. 146. See *Bacon* v. *Simpson* (1837) 3 M. & W. 78.
[66] See *Doe* v. *Glenn* (1834) 1 A. & E. 49.
[67] *R.* v. *Great Glen (Inhabitants of)* (1833) 5 B. & Ad. 188.
[68] *Metters* v. *Brown* (1863) 1 H. & C. 686.
[69] See *Stewart* v. *Edmonds*, Sittings after Hil.Term 1828, *coram* Abbott C.J.; *Fenwick* v. *Thornton* (1827) M. & M. 51. But see *Smith* v. *Morgan* (1839) 2 M. & Rob. 257.
[70] *Holland* v. *King* (1848) 6 C.B. 727; and see *Dibbins* v. *Dibbins* [1896] 2 Ch. 348; *Re Kinahan's Trusts* [1907] 1 Ir.R. 321. *Cf. Kelsey* v. *Kelsey* (1922) 91 L.J.Ch. 382; *ante*, p. 85, n. 20.
[71] *Mills* v. *Anderson* [1984] Q.B. 704.
[72] See *Mills* v. *Anderson* [1984] Q.B. 704 at p. 710.
[73] *Cf.* [1984] Q.B. 704 at p. 712.

no interval of time between the death and the grant of letters of administration.

Under section 2 of the Administration of Estates Act 1925 an intending applicant for administration can bring an action for trespass against real estate[74] in the interval between the death of a testator and the grant of administration with the will annexed[75] and may obtain the appointment of a receiver to prevent a wrong to the estate.[76]

Common law

Cases may, however, be found, where the letters of administration have been held to relate back to the death of the intestate, so as to give a validity to acts done before the letters were obtained.[77] Thus if a man takes the goods of the intestate as executor *de son tort*, and sells them, and afterwards obtains letters of administration, it seems the sale is good by relation and the wrong is purged.[78] So in *Whitehall* v. *Squire*,[79] where an intestate had delivered to the defendant a horse to depasture, and the plaintiff, before administration granted, desired the defendant to bury the intestate decently, who thereupon buried him, and the plaintiff agreed that the defendant should keep the horse in part satisfaction of the charges; and afterwards the plaintiff took administration, and brought trover for the horse; it was held by Dolben and Eyre JJ. (Holt C.J. dissenting), that the plaintiff was bound by the agreement and could not maintain the action.[80] The principle, however, of this decision appears to have been that the plaintiff, being a *particeps criminis* in the very act of which he complained, should not be permitted to recover upon it against the person with whom he colluded.[81] An administrator can recover in trespass or trover against a wrongdoer who has seized or converted goods before the grant.[82] The reason for this is that otherwise there would be no remedy for this wrong-

---

[74] Including chattels real: Administration of Estates Act 1925, s.3(1).

[75] *Re Pryse* [1904] P. 301 (decided under the Land Transfer Act 1897); *Ingall* v. *Moran* [1944] K.B. 160, 171 (*per* Goddard L.J.). In the interval, the estate vests in the President; see p. 460, *post*.

[76] *Ibid.*

[77] See *Mills* v. *Anderson* [1984] Q.B. 704 at p. 709.

[78] *Kenrick* v. *Burges* (1583) Moor. 126; Godolph., Pt. 2, c. 8, s.5, p. 99, 4th ed.; *Foster* v. *Bates* (1843) 12 M. & W. 226; *Hill* v. *Curtis* (1865) L.R. 1 Eq. 90, 100; as to executor *de son tort*, see *post*; Godolph. Pt. 2. C. 205, 6; 2 Roll. Abr. 399 tit. Relation, A pls. Rolls le 544, Trespass T. pl. 1; *Middleton's Case* (1603) 5 Co. 28b; Com.Dic.Administrator B. 10. Weston 6 ff. Ex. 14th ed., 115, 116; *Fred Long* v. *Burgess* [1949] 2 All E.R. 484, 488.

[79] (1703) 1 Salk. 295.

[80] Contrast *Stewart* v. *Edmonds, supra*. And see *Parsons* v. *Mayesden* (1676) 1 Freem. 152, where it was laid down that if a man takes the goods of the deceased by the consent of him to whom administration is afterwards granted, this is no defence if he is sued as executor *de son tort*. But see *Hill* v. *Curtis, supra*.

[81] *Mountford* v. *Gibson* (1804) 4 East 446, by Lord Ellenborough. See also *Morgan* v. *Thomas* (1853) 8 Exch. 305, by Parke B., and cases mentioned in last note. As to the right founded on mere possession, to bring actions against wrongdoers without producing letters of administration, see *ante*, pp. 86 *et seq.*

[82] *Foster* v. *Bates* (1843) 12 M. & W. 226, 233.

doing.[83] Further, it has been held that where the administrator might sue in trover for a conversion between the death of the intestate and the grant of administration, he may waive the tort and recover as on contract. Thus, where money belonging to an estate at the time of the intestate's death, or due to him and paid in after his death, or proceeding from the sale of his effects after his death, has, before the grant of administration, been applied by a stranger to the payment of the intestate's debts and funeral expenses, the administrator may recover it from such stranger as money had and received to his use as administrator.[84]

Again, where goods had been sold after the death of an intestate and before the grant of letters of administration, avowedly on account of the estate of the intestate, by one who had been the intestate's agent, it was held that the administrator might ratify the sale and recover the price from the purchaser as for goods sold and delivered.[85] It would also seem that whenever anyone acting on behalf of the intestate's estate, and not on his own account, makes a contract with another before any grant of administration, the administration will have relation back, so that the benefit of the contract is not lost and the administrator may sue upon it, as made with himself.[86] Similarly, if during the time when there is no personal representative, services have been rendered which not only were for the benefit of the estate, but also were rendered under a contract with someone who subsequently by becoming administrator became authorised to bind the estate, and who ratified the contract, the estate of the deceased is liable for such services.[87] It seems also that the grant of administration vests leasehold property in the administrator by relation, so as to enable him to bring actions for all matters affecting that property after the death of the intestate, and so to render him liable to account for the rents and profits of it from the death of the intestate.[88]

Such relation back exists only in those cases where the act done is for the benefit of the estate.[89] Accordingly, where the widow of an intestate had remained in possession of her husband's property for some time after his decease, and the intestate's son had not interfered in any way with the property, which was seized under a writ of *fi. fa.* issued against the widow,

---

[83] *Foster* v. *Bates, supra*; *Searson* v. *Robinson* (1860) 2 Fost. & F. 351; and see *Re Pryse, supra*.

[84] *Welchman* v. *Sturgis* (1849) 13 Q.B. 552.

[85] *Foster* v. *Bates, supra*; and see *Re Pryse, supra*.

[86] *Bodger* v. *Arch* (1854) 10 Exch. 333. The same principle is applied to an executor *de son tort*. See *post*, p. 102. *Mills* v. *Anderson* [1984] Q.B. 704 at 710.

[87] *Re Watson, ex p. Phillips* (1886) 18 Q.B.D. 116; affirmed (1887) 19 Q.B.D. 234. See, however, the remarks of Lord Esher M.R., who doubted whether an administrator, after becoming administrator and while acting in the interests of other persons, could have ratified a prior contract made with himself.

[88] *R.* v. *Horsley* (1807) 8 East 405, 410. *Youngmin* v. *Heath* [1974] 1 W.L.R. 135. See also *post*, p. 575.

[89] *Mills* v. *Anderson* [1984] Q.B. 704 at 710. The relation back does not necessarily apply for all purposes and cannot make wrong an act which was lawful at the time. See *Tharpe* v. *Stallwood* (1843) 5 M. & G. 760. Detinue did not lie if the defendant had ceased to hold assets before the grant: *Crossfield* v. *Such* (1852) 8 Ex. 333.

and the son afterwards took out administration, it was held that there was no evidence from which the administrator's consent to the widow's taking the property could be implied, and by Parke B. that even if there had been, the estate was not bound by it, as the act to which the consent was given did not benefit the estate.[90]

Security before administration granted

Where a question was pending in the ecclesiastical court, as to a party's right to a grant of letters of administration, and such party possessed himself of a portion of the goods of the deceased before he had established his title, Sir G. Lee decreed that he should give such security for the safety of the goods as the court should approve.[91]

Tort executor not compellable

Though a next-of-kin may have intermeddled with the effects, and made himself liable as executor *de son tort*, he cannot be compelled by the court to take upon himself the office of administrator.[92]

2—ACTION WITHOUT TITLE TO A GRANT

Executor de son tort—Intermeddling

A person not lawfully appointed executor or administrator and without title to a grant may by reason of his own intrusion upon the affairs of the deceased be treated for some purposes as having assumed the executorship: such an intermeddler is called a tort executor or an executor *de son tort* (*i.e.* of his own wrong).[93] The same term is used whether the deceased died testate or intestate, for the law knows no such appellation as "administrator *de son tort*."[94]

The expression is used to include an executor named in the will who intermeddles before probate[95]; but this usage has been criticised[96] on the ground that such intermeddling, though it precludes renunciation, is not in itself unlawful. The concept is derived from the principle that a person who has assumed authority where he has none is accountable as if he had that authority.[97]

---

[90] *Morgan* v. *Thomas* (1853) 8 Exch. 302.

[91] *Jones* v. *Yarnold* (1728) 2 Lee 570. As to injunctions restraining intermeddling with assets before administration, see *Cassidy* v. *Foley* [1904] 2 Ir.R. 427.

[92] *Ackerley* v. *Oldham* (1811) 1 Phill. 248; *Ackerley* v. *Parkinson* (1815) 3 M. & S. 411; *Re Fell* (1861) 2 Sw. & Tr. 126. *Secus*, an executor who has administered.

[93] Similar definitions are found in Swinb., Pt. 4, s.23, Pl. 1; Godolph., Pt. 2, c. 8, s.1; Wentw.Off.Ex., 14th ed., c. 14, p. 320. See also *Degazon* v. *Barclays Bank* [1988] 1 F.T.L.R. 17.

[94] Godolph., Pt. 2, c. 8, s.2.

[95] As in *Webster* v. *Webster* (1804) 10 Ves. 93. Lord Dyer in *Stokes* v. *Porter* (1558) 2 Dyer 166b applies the term to a lawful executor who maladministers; but the usage is rare and misleading.

[96] *Sykes* v. *Sykes* (1870) L.R. 5 C.P. 113.

[97] See *per* Denning M.R. in *Phipps* v. *Boardman* [1965] Ch. 992, 1018.

Rationale

Two principles are involved. The first (and most frequently emphasised) is that no one should be permitted, by refraining from taking out probate or administration, to obtain possession of the deceased's property free from his liabilities.[98] The second is that where a person does acts characteristic of an executor the natural inference to be drawn is that he is named as executor in a will which he has not yet proved[99]; and third parties should be able to rely on this assumption.[1]

Basis of liability

The liability of an executor *de son tort* is now defined by section 28 of the Administration of Estates Act 1925, which provides that if any person to the defrauding of creditors *or* without full and valuable consideration obtains, receives or holds any real or personal estate of a deceased person, or effects the release of any debt or liability due to the estate of the deceased, he shall be charged as executor *de son tort* to the extent of the real and personal estate received or coming into his hands, or the debt or liability released, after deducting (i) any debt for valuable consideration and without fraud due to him from the deceased at the time of death and (ii) any payment by him which might properly be made by a personal representative.

The Elizabethan statute[2] which this section replaces covered only the case where the next-of-kin procured a grant of administration to "some stranger of mean estate" as his agent or attorney, in order to take the property free from the deceased's liabilities; the executor *de son tort* was never in other contexts regarded as a creature of the statute.[3] The present section, however, is wide enough to cover all cases in which liability could in practice arise[4]: it might be difficult to contend that there survives a concurrent and independent liability at common law.[5]

The main practical importance of this[6] is that at law an executor *de son tort* had no right to retain for his own debt,[7] whereas under section 28 he is entitled to deduct debts owed to him by the deceased. He will have this right, however, only in proceedings brought by a legatee or fellow creditor; if he is sued by the lawful representative his liability depends not on his having made himself chargeable *as executor*, and therefore not on section

---

[98] *cf.* the Administration of Estates Act 1925, s.28. See Appendix *post*, p. 1125.

[99] 2 Black.Comm. 507, 508; Wentw.Off.Ex., 14th ed., p. 322.

[1] *Parker* v. *Kett* (1701) 1 Ld.Raym. 658; 12 Mod. 466; *Thomson* v. *Harding* (1853) 2 El. & Bl. 630.

[2] (1601) 43 Eliz. 1, c. 8.

[3] Except, apparently *per incuriam*, by Sir. R. Malins V.-C. in *Coote* v. *Whittington* (1873) L.R. 16 Eq. 534.

[4] Since liability is limited to assets received: see *post*, p. 597.

[5] But see *I.R.C.* v. *Stype Investments* [1981] Ch. at p. 381 (reversed on appeal [1982] Ch. 456).

[6] But see also *post*, pp. 98, 99.

[7] *Coulter's Case* (1598) 5 Co. 30a; Cro.Eliz. 630; *Curtis* v. *Vernon* (1790) 3 T.R. 587; 2 H.Bl. 18; *Alexander* v. *Lane* (1608) Yelv. 137. As to retainer, see *post*, pp. 640, 641.

28, but on his having committed a trespass to or other actionable interference with the deceased's property.

Acts giving rise to liability

Any act which, if done by an executor named in the will, would preclude him from renouncing probate will make one not so named an executor *de son tort*[8]; though the liability of the latter, if in fact he has had no assets in his hands, is purely theoretical.[9]

Taking, using, or disposing of goods

The slightest intermeddling with goods is, in principle, sufficient to create liability—the old authorities instance the taking of a Bible, or a bedstead of small value[10]; a common case is that of carrying on the deceased's trade.[11]

"Incorporeal" property

There may be an intermeddling with a chose in action, as by demanding, receiving or releasing debts due to the deceased[12]; or where a company registers a transfer of the deceased's shares to someone other than the lawfully constituted personal representative.[13]

Land

It is clear that there may now be an executor *de son tort* of either a freehold or a leasehold interest in land.[14] It has been held, however, that an executor *de son tort* of a lease does not automatically incur personal liability on the covenants. His liability thereunder depends on attornment or estoppel.[15]

Express claim

A person who makes an express claim to act as executor, as by bringing or defending an action in that character, is also liable as executor *de son tort*.[16] The receipt or payment of debts, or the payment of legacies, should,

[8] Godolph., Pt. 2, c. 8, s.6; *I.R.C. v. Stype* [1982] Ch. 456. As to such acts of administration, see *ante*, p. 41; *post*, p. 380.

[9] See *infra*, p. 96. But his defence is *plene administravit*, not *ne unques executor*.

[10] *Robbin's Case* (1601) Noy. 69.

[11] As in *Padget v. Priest* (1787) 2 T.R. 97; *Hooper v. Summersett* (1810) Wightw. 16. Contrast *Serle v. Waterworth* (1838) 4 M. & W. 9 (continuing to live in house without carrying on trade), affirmed on this point *sub nom. Nelson v. Serle*, 4. M. & W. 795.

[12] Godolph., Pt. 2, c. 8, s.1; Swinb., Pt. 6, s.22. See also *Stokes v. Porter* (1558) 2 Dyer 166b.

[13] *Att.-Gen. v. New York Breweries Co.* [1899] A.C. 62, affirming [1898] 1 Q.B. 205.

[14] Administration of Estates Act 1925, s.28; *I.R.C. v. Stype* [1982] Ch. 456.

[15] *Stratford-upon-Avon v. Parker* [1914] 2 K.B. 562, where, however, it was found as a fact that the defendant had never taken possession of the lease. The contrary view was assumed to be correct in *Paull v. Simpson* (1846) 9 Q.B. 365 and *Williams v. Heales* (1874) L.R. 9 C.P. 177.

[16] Godolph., Pt. 2, c. 8, s.1; Wentw.Off.Ex., 14th ed., p. 326; Swinb., Pt. 6, s.22.

it seems, be regarded as prima facie constituting an express claim, rather than as mere intermeddling.[17]

Fraud of creditors

Where a conveyance or assignment is voidable as being in fraud of creditors,[18] a person who after the death of the grantor takes or remains in possession thereunder may be sued by such creditors as executor *de son tort*.[19] The transaction is valid, however, as against the personal representatives of the deceased.[20]

Cases where liability is excluded

(a) Mere intermeddling by a stranger after probate or administration has been granted will not make him an executor *de son tort*: creditors and legatees can then look for payment to the lawful representative and have no need of a remedy against the person intermeddling.[21] A person, however, who makes an express claim to act as executor, or does some act equivalent to such a claim, will even at this stage become liable as executor *de son tort*.[22] Lord Kenyon[23] and Sir Thomas Plumer[24] are both reported as saying that there can *never* be a lawful executor and an executor *de son tort* at the same time; but neither appears to have been considering the question of an express claim, and the other authorities are quite unequivocal.

(b) Acts of humanity and necessity: such acts as locking up the goods of the deceased for safekeeping, retaining these in one's custody at the time of death until one may lawfully be discharged of them, doing urgent repairs to his property, feeding his livestock, providing sustenance for his children, arranging and paying for a suitable funeral[25] (and getting in debts for that purpose[26]) will not of themselves make the doer an executor *de son tort*.

Similar acts may be done by an executor named in the will without precluding renunciation; as may merely preparatory acts such as taking an account or making an inventory[27]; and, probably, such minimal acts as joining with the other named executors to open a bank account, sign small cheques for necessary expenses or indorse insurance policies.[28]

---

[17] *Ibid.*

[18] See now Insolvency Act 1986, s.423.

[19] Godolph., Pt. 2, c. 8, s.1; 1 Sid. 31, pl. 9; 1 Roll.Abr. 549 (C. 1), pl. 3; *Stamford's Case* (1574) 2 Leon. 223; *Hawes* v. *Leader* (1611) Cro.Jac. 271; *Edwards* v. *Harben* (1788) 2 T.R. 587.

[20] *Hawes* v. *Leader, supra.*

[21] *Anon.* (1702) 1 Salk. 313; Godolph., Pt. 2, c. 8, s.1.

[22] *Ibid.*; *Read's Case* (1604) 5 Co. 33b; Wentw.Off.Ex., 14th ed., p. 325; Swinb., Pt. 4, s.23; Com.Dig. Administrator (C. 1). See also p. 98, n. 43, *infra.*

[23] *Hall* v. *Elliot* (1791) Peake N.P.C. 119.

[24] *Tomlin* v. *Beck* (1823) 1 Turn. & R. 438.

[25] Dyer 166b, in margin; Fitz. Executors, pl. 24; 1 Roll.Abr. 918, Executors (C. 2), pl. 4; Wentw.Off.Ex., 14th ed., c. 14, p. 323; Godolph., Pt. 2, c. 8, s.6; *Harrison* v. *Rowley* (1798) 4 Ves. 212.

[26] *Camden* v. *Fletcher* (1838) 4 M. & W. 378.

[27] Godolph., Pt. 2, c. 8, s.6.

[28] *Holder* v. *Holder* [1968] Ch. 353.

(c) Claiming under some other colourable title: a person is not liable as executor *de son tort* who claims possession in his own right in some way distinct from and paramount to the deceased's title[29]; as where goods have been pledged to him,[30] or where he claims a lien on them, notwithstanding that he cannot completely make out his title,[31] or even where he takes them in mistake for his own.[32]

Special cases

Agents

Where one person intermeddles as agent for another, both are liable as executors *de son tort*[33]; it is no defence for the agent to show that he has accounted to his principal.[34]

Sharland v. *Mildon*[35] suggests that the agent is liable even if he believes that his principal had authority to act; the defendant there pleaded unsuccessfully that he believed his principal to have taken out letters of administration. Where, however, such a belief is honest and reasonable in the light of the principal's conduct, it is submitted that the agent should be protected by the general rule concerning dealings by third parties with an executor *de son tort* as laid down in *Thomson* v. *Harding*.[36] *Padget* v. *Priest*[37] is sometimes cited as authority for the view that even a mere servant intermeddling on his master's instructions is liable as executor *de son tort*; but the case does not really support that proposition, since the servant had in effect admitted to holding assets on his own behalf.

As to the position of one who before probate acts as agent for an executor named in the will, the authorities are conflicting. Probate once granted will legalise previous acts done by the agent[38]; but difficulty arises if at the date of the hearing probate has still not been obtained. The view taken in *Sykes* v. *Sykes*[39] was that an agent for a named executor can never be liable as executor *de son tort*, since the acts of his principal, even before probate, cannot properly be characterised as unlawful; but *Att.-Gen.* v. *New York Breweries Co. Ltd.*[40] seems clear authority to the contrary. The testator in the latter case died domiciled in New York and his executors only obtained probate there; at their request, the defendant English company registered

---

[29] Godolph., Pt. 2, c. 8, s.6.
[30] *Ibid.*
[31] *Femings* v. *Jarrat* (1795) 1 Esp.N.P.C. 336.
[32] Godolph., Pt. 2, c. 8, s.6; Swinb., Pt. 6, s.22; Com.Dig. Administrator (C. 2).
[33] *Sharland* v. *Mildon* (1846) 5 Hare 468.
[34] *Hill* v. *Curtis* (1865) L.R. 1 Eq. 90.
[35] *Supra.*
[36] (1853) 2 E. & B. 630. See *post*, p. 102.
[37] (1787) 2 T.R. 97.
[38] *Sykes* v. *Sykes* (1870) L.R. 5 C.P. 113.
[39] *Supra.*
[40] [1899] A.C. 62.

a transfer to their names of the testator's shares: the House of Lords held that the company was liable as executor *de son tort* for payment of English probate duty. The fact that the will was governed by a foreign law cannot, it is submitted, affect the issue: the executors would nevertheless have been entitled to a grant of probate in England.[41] In this case, however, the company was aware that the executors had in fact no intention of obtaining an English grant; and it may be that the decision can be distinguished on that ground.[42]

Again, where a person employed as agent by a lawful executor continues to act after the agency has been revoked by his principal's death, it is uncertain whether he is chargeable as executor *de son tort*. It was held in *Cottle* v. *Aldrich*[43] that he was; in *Tomlin* v. *Beck*[44] that he was not. In the former case there had been an express claim by the agent to be acting as executor: this seems to be the only ground on which the two cases can be distinguished.

Recipients

A person who received property from an executor *de son tort* without being party to the original intermeddling was not under the old law himself liable as executor *de son tort*,[45] even if a mere volunteer.[46] (Though he might be liable to an action for conversion of goods by the lawful representative.[47]) Now, however, it seems that a person who in fraud of creditors or without full and valuable consideration receives property from an executor *de son tort* may be liable under section 28 of the Administration of Estates Act 1925.

Transmission

It was held in *Meyrick* v. *Anderson*[48] that an executor *de son tort* to a lawful executor is chargeable as executor *de son tort* to the original testator; though if he has not in fact intermeddled with any assets of the original testator, and the lawful executor had committed no devastavit, his liability will be purely technical.[49] The reasoning by which the decision is supported is applicable only where the lawful executor was the sole, or sole surviving, executor of the original testator.

In *Wilson* v. *Hodson*,[50] on the other hand, it was held that the lawful

---

[41] See *infra* (foreign grants).

[42] *Redwood Music Ltd.* v. *B. Feldman & Co. Ltd.* [1979] R.P.C. 1, 9.

[43] (1815) 4 Maule & Selw. 175.

[44] (1823) 1 Turn. & R. 438.

[45] Godolph., Pt. 2, c. 8, s.1; Com.Dig. Administrator (C. 2); *Hursell* v. *Bird* (1891) 65 L.T. 709.

[46] *Paull* v. *Simpson* (1846) 9 Q.B. 365. It may be that he would be liable in equity: see *Hill* v. *Curtis* (1865) L.R. 1 Eq. 90, 101.

[47] cf. *Fyson* v. *Chambers* (1842) 9 M. & W. 468.

[48] (1850) 14 Q.B. 719.

[49] See *infra*.

[50] (1872) L.R. 7 Ex. 84.

executors of an executrix *de son tort* of a lease could not be sued for breaches of covenant committed by the original deceased. Since, however, the liability of the representatives could clearly not exceed that of their testatrix, and it is doubtful whether the executrix *de son tort*, merely as such, would herself have been liable on the covenants,[51] the decision cannot be relied on as establishing any general principle. It seems clear, in any case, that any right of action available against a person as executor *de son tort* would now be available against his personal representatives by virtue of the Law Reform (Miscellaneous Provisions) Act 1934.[52]

Foreign grants

A foreign[53] grant of probate or administration or other foreign authority cannot be used to establish title to English property[54]; thus a foreign representative who intermeddles with English assets without any intention of obtaining an English grant will be liable as executor *de son tort*.[55] Conversely, a person who takes possession of foreign assets under a foreign grant cannot be sued in England as executor *de son tort* if he has not intermeddled with any English property.[56]

Letters ad colligendum[57]

An administrator *ad colligendum* who exceeds his powers is liable as executor *de son tort*; but the court has power under section 116 of the Supreme Court Act 1981 to attach additional powers to such a grant.[58]

Infants

There can be no liability as executor *de son tort* for acts done during infancy.[59]

Liability to creditors and legatees

It is commonly said that a tort executor has all the liabilities, but none of the privileges, that belong to the character of executor[60]; but this statement cannot be accepted without qualification. His liability to pay debts and

---

[51] *Stratford-upon-Avon* v. *Parker* [1914] 2 K.B. 562.

[52] As to which, see *post*.

[53] As to the effect of Scottish confirmations and Northern Ireland grants, see *post*.

[54] See *ante*.

[55] *Att.-Gen.* v. *New York Breweries Co.* [1899] A.C. 62 affirming [1898] 1 Q.B. 205, and as explained in *Redwood Music Ltd.* v. *B. Feldman & Co. Ltd.* [1979] R.P.C. 1.

[56] *Beavan* v. *Lord Hastings* (1856) 2 K. & J. 724.

[57] As to grants *ad colligenda*, see *post*.

[58] *Whitehead* v. *Palmer* [1908] 1 K.B. 151; *Re Sanpietro* [1941] P. 16. The old rule was that the court had no jurisdiction to attach a power to sell to such a grant, so that an administrator acting under such a power was liable as executor *de son tort*; *Anon.* (1566) 3 Dyer 256a; Wentw.Off.Ex., 14th ed., c. 14, p. 324; Godolph., Pt. 2, c. 8, s.1; Swinb., Pt. 4, s.23.

[59] *Stott* v. *Meanock* (1862) 31 L.J.Ch. 746.

[60] *Carmichael* v. *Carmichael* (1846) 2 Ph.C.C. 103, *per* Lord Cottenham.

legacies depends, it is true, on his being treated as if he were indeed the lawful executor; and in any action by a creditor or legatee he should be sued as such.[61] He is under no duty, however, to get in the assets of the deceased; and in equity, no general order for administration can be made against him: such an order can be made only where there is a lawfully constituted representative before the court.[62]

A person sued as a tort executor may at the same time plead that he never was an executor (*ne unques executor*) and that he has completed the administration (*plene administravit*).[63] The old rule was that one who pleaded *ne unques executor* alone and failed to establish the plea was liable for the whole of the amount sued for[64]; provided he pleaded *plene administravit*, however, he was liable only to the extent of assets actually received by him, even if he in fact still had unadministered assets in his hands.[65] Under section 28 of the Administration of Estates Act 1925 an executor *de son tort* is liable only "to the extent of the real and personal estate received or coming to his hands, or the debt or liability released"; but even apart from this, an English court would not today allow substantive liability (as opposed to any question of costs) to depend on a technicality of pleading.[66]

To establish a plea of *plene administravit* an executor *de son tort* may show either that he has accounted for all assets received by him to the lawful personal representative[67] (though a lawful executor cannot discharge himself by accounting to a co-executor) or that he has applied them in a due course of administration.[68]

Where the defendant claims that he has accounted to the lawful representative he must show that he did so before action brought[69]; he cannot rely on a payment made after the issue of the writ, even if at that date no administration had yet been granted to anyone.[70] (If it were otherwise, the plaintiff would be unfairly prejudiced by having to bring a fresh action

---

[61] *Coulter's Case* (1598) 5 Co. 30a; Godolph., Pt. 2, c. 8, s.2; 1 Saund. 265, n. 2 to *Osborne* v. *Rogers*.

[62] *Cary* v. *Hills* (1872) L.R. 15 Eq. 79. But an executor *de son tort* is liable to account in equity for assets actually received: *Coote* v. *Whittington* (1873) L.R. 16 Eq. 534.

[63] *Hooper* v. *Summersett* (1810) Wightw. 20, *per* Wood B.

[64] Wentw.Off.Ex., 14th ed., pp. 331–332; 1 Saund. 336, n. 10 to *Hancocke* v. *Prowde*.

[65] Dyer 166b, in margin; 1 Saund. 265, n. 2 to *Osborne* v. *Rogers*; *Hooper* v. *Summersett* (1810) Wightw. 16 *per curiam*; *Yardley* v. *Arnold* (1842) Car. & M. 434; *Degazon* v. *Barclays Bank* [1988] 1 F.T.L.R. 17.

[66] The rule still seems to be applied with some strictness in Canada: see *Charron* v. *Montreal Trust Co.* [1959] C.L.Y. 1241; 15 D.L.R. (2d) 240. The defence, however, must be raised before judgment on the issue of liability: *Midland Bank Trust Co.* v. *Green (No. 2)* [1979] 1 W.L.R. 460.

[67] *Anon.* (1702) 1 Salk. 313; *Padget* v. *Priest* (1787) 2 T.R. 97, *per* Ashurst J. and Buller J.; *Curtis* v. *Vernon* (1790) 3 T.R. 590, *per* Lord Kenyon.

[68] Wentw.Off.Ex., 14th ed., c. 14, pp. 331, 332; *Mountford* v. *Gibson* (1804) 4 East 454, *per* Le Blanc J.; *Oxenham* v. *Clapp* (1831) 2 B. & Ad. 309; 2 Black.Comm. 508; Bac.Abr. Exors. B. 3, 2.

[69] *Padget* v. *Priest* (1787) 2 T.R. 97; *Curtis* v. *Vernon* (1790) 3 T.R. 587, affirmed 2 H.Bl. 18.

[70] *Curtis* v. *Vernon, supra.*

against the lawful representative.) The same principles apply where an executor *de son tort* is sued in equity for an account.[71]

Where the executor *de son tort* claims to have applied the assets in a due course of administration, he may rely on payment before action of debts of equal or superior degree to the plaintiff's, and on payment even *pendente lite* of debts of superior degree[72]; but whether he may also after action brought pay a creditor of equal degree remains doubtful.[73]

It has already been pointed out[74] that under section 28 of the Administration of Estates Act 1925 an executor *de son tort* appears in effect to have a right to deduct for his own debt. A grant of administration *pendente lite* formerly legalised a retainer in the strict sense.[75]

Liability for death duties

For the purposes of liability to death duties,[76] section 55(1)(xi) of the Administration of Estates Act 1925 includes in the definition of personal representative "any person who takes possession of or intermeddles with the property of a deceased person without the authority of the personal representatives or the court." The liability of an executor *de son tort* is thus similar in this respect to that of a lawful representative.[77] The same effect is produced by sections 199(4) and 200(4) of the Inheritance Tax Act 1984.

Liability to lawful representative

A person who intermeddles without authority with the property of the deceased will generally be liable to an action by the lawful representative. His liability in this case, however, depends not on his having so acted as to make himself chargeable as executor, but on the general law about interference with the property of another.[78]

To an action in trespass by the lawful representative it is not a defence to show that the assets concerned have been applied in a due course of administration[79]; payments which the lawful representative would in any case have been bound to make may be pleaded in mitigation of damages,[80] since it is

---

[71] *Hill* v. *Curtis* (1865) L.R. 1 Eq. 90 (payment before action); *Layfield* v. *Layfield* (1834) 7 Sim. 172 (payment *pendente lite*).

[72] *Oxenham* v. *Clapp* (1831) 2 B. & Ad. 309.

[73] *Oxenham* v. *Clapp, supra.*

[74] See *ante.*

[75] *Pyne* v. *Woolland* (1690) 2 Ventr. 180; *Williamson* v. *Norwitch* (1652) Sty. 337; *Vaughan* v. *Brown* (1739) 2 Stra. 1106; Andr. 328; 1 Saund. 265, n. 2 to *Osborne* v. *Rogers*; but see *Whitehead* v. *Sampson* (1679) 1 Freem.K.B. 265.

[76] As to which, see *ante*, pp. 73.

[77] *I.R.C.* v. *Stype* [1982] Ch. 456, 473.

[78] As to which, see Torts (Interference with Goods) Act 1977.

[79] *Whitehall* v. *Squire* (1703) Carth. 104, *per* Holt C.J.; 2 Black.Comm. 508; *Elworthy* v. *Sandford* (1864) 3 Hurl. & C. 330.

[80] *Padget* v. *Priest* (1787) 2 T.R. 100, *per* Buller J.; *Mountford* v. *Gibson* (1804) 4 East 454, *per* Le Blanc J.; 2 Black.Comm. 508; Bac.Abr.Exors. B. 3.1; *Fyson* v. *Chambers* (1842) 9 M. & W. 468. In *Woolley* v. *Clark* (1822) 5 B. & A. 744, the executor was allowed to recover full damages with no allowance for assets duly administered; but the case is generally regarded as having been decided *per incuriam* and not to be authoritative.

no detriment to him that they have been made by another[81]; but even if all the assets in the defendant's hands are shown to have been so applied the plaintiff is still entitled to nominal damages.[82]

Where the plaintiff sues only in conversion it may be that he will lose the action if all assets possessed by the defendant are shown to have been applied in a due course of administration,[83] but the correctness of the authorities for this proposition has long been doubted.[84]

In either case, it was formerly the rule that such payments could only be pleaded by the defendant where the estate was solvent, for otherwise the lawful representative would have been prejudiced in the exercise of his rights of preference and retainer.[85] With the abolition of such rights[86] it is doubtful whether such a rule still applies to the estates of persons dying on or after January 1, 1972.[87]

Where the defendant has received debts due to the deceased the action of the lawful representative must be for moneys had and received to his use. This remedy is not discussed in the authorities, but presumably the same principles would be applicable as to an action for wrongful interference with goods.

Position of alienee from executor de son tort

It is laid down in *Coulter's Case*[88] that "all lawful acts which an executor *de son tort* doth are good." Again, the statement cannot be accepted without qualification; a solitary act of wrongdoing by one taking upon himself to hand over the goods of the deceased to a creditor will not give the creditor a good title to them as against the lawful representative.[89] The true principle is stated in *Thomson* v. *Harding*,[90] where, delivering the judgment of the Court of King's Bench, Lord Campbell C.J. said:

> "We are by no means of opinion that, as against a person who becomes the rightful representative of a person deceased, every payment from the assets of the deceased shall be valid, if made by a person who has so intermeddled with the property as to render himself liable to be sued as executor *de son tort*. . . . But, where the executor *de son tort* is really acting as executor, and the party with whom he deals has fair reason for supposing that he has authority to act as such, his acts shall bind the rightful executor, and shall alter the property."

[81] *Mountford* v. *Gibson* (1804) 4 East 451, *per* Lawrence J.

[82] *Anon.* (1701) 12 Mod. 441; 2 *Phillips on Evidence*, 7th ed., p. 234, n. 6.

[83] Buller's *Nisi Prius*, 7th ed., p. 48. See also *Parker* v. *Kett* (1701) 12 Mod. 466, *per* Holt C.J. at p. 471 (but not as reported in 1 Ld.Raym. 658).

[84] See all previous editions of this work.

[85] Wentw.Off.Ex., 14th ed., c. 14, p. 335; *Mountford* v. *Gibson* (1804) 4 East 453, *per* Lawrence J.; 2 Black.Comm. 507, 508; *Elworthy* v. *Sandford* (1864) 3 Hurl. & C. 330.

[86] By the Administration of Estates Act 1971, s.10(1), but only in respect of the estates of persons dying on or after January 1, 1972. *Ibid.* ss.12(6), 14(2).

[87] *Ibid.* ss.12(6), 14(2).

[88] (1598) 5 Co. 30a.

[89] *Mountford* v. *Gibson* (1804) 4 East 441; *Mills* v. *Anderson* [1984] Q.B. 704.

[90] (1853) 2 E. & B. 630. See, too, *Parker* v. *Kett* (1701) 12 Mod. 466; 1 Ld.Raym. 658.

In that case a person employed by an intestate during his life to collect the rents of certain properties continued to do so after the death and therewith discharged the deceased's overdraft with his bank, together with certain other of his liabilities; in an action for moneys had and received by a person who had later taken out letters of administration the bank was held entitled to retain the sums so paid. In *Mountford* v. *Gibson*,[91] on the other hand, the defendant had sold and delivered to an intestate in his lifetime a quantity of iron; after the death he applied to the widow for payment, she redelivered the iron to him in satisfaction of his debt, but there was no evidence of her having done any other act characteristic of an executrix; the administrator succeeded in an action in trover for recovery of the iron.

The rule applies only to lawful acts. The true executor is not entitled to charge the property of the deceased as security for his own debt and if an executor *de son tort* attempts to do the same his unlawful act will be equally ineffective.[92]

An executor *de son tort* cannot give a good title to land, for the grant must be produced for this purpose.

---

[91] (1804) 4 East 451.
[92] *Buckley* v. *Barber* (1851) 6 Exch. 164.

CHAPTER 9

PROPERTY FOR WHICH A GRANT IS REQUIRED

In general a grant is necessary to establish title to all property of the deceased within the jurisdiction of the English court. The grant is conclusive, so long as it stands, of the appointment of the executor or administrator, and of the validity and contents of the proved will. Without a grant the executor cannot prove his title and a relative or next of kin however much entitled to a grant of administration has no title at all, for an administrator's authority derives from the court alone.[1] The only two exceptions to this proposition at common law are: (a) the estates of the Sovereign and members of the Royal Family[2] and (b) the survivorship principle in joint tenancy.[3] By statute there are a number of exemptions mainly directed to saving of cost where the estate within the jurisdiction is relatively small and the safeguards are sufficient.[4]

Property in England the basis of jurisdiction

Broadly speaking, the basis of the jurisdiction of the High Court over the estate of a deceased person is that property of some kind is situate in England or Wales at the time of his death or at the time when proceedings are commenced[5] or a grant applied for. If, therefore, it disposes only of property in a foreign country a will is not, in ordinary circumstances, admissible in England and Wales.[6]

But, as previously stated,[7] the court has power to make a grant of probate or administration to an estate the deceased notwithstanding that left no property in England or Wales. This power is only likely to be exercised in special circumstances.[8] It seems that the court may reseal a grant though there is no property in England or Wales.[9]

---

[1] See p. 449 *post* as to the effect of a grant.
[2] See p. 106 *post.*
[3] See p. 545 *post.*
[4] See *post.* Liability to death duties is not affected by these exemptions and recipients may be liable as representatives or executors or otherwise if the estate is large enough to attract such duties. Creditors may of course be affected where there is no grant or where assets do not come into the hands of the representative. See p. 597 *post.*
[5] Where some of the deceased's property abroad had been brought to England before the proceedings, the court admitted to probate a will disposing only of property abroad: *Stubbings* v. *Clunies-Ross* (1911) 27 T.L.R. 127.
[6] *Re Coode* (1867) 1 P. & D. 449.
[7] See *ante*, p. 9.
[8] See *Re Wayland* [1951] 2 All E.R. 1041; and *Aldrich* v. *Att.-Gen.* [1968] P. 281.
[9] *Saunders* v. *Bibby Hesketh* (1900) 45 S.J. 11.

Where there are two wills, one disposing of property in England or Wales

If two or more independent wills are made, one disposing of property in England and Wales and the other of property abroad, only the former will can be admitted to probate in this country.[10] Where the deceased's only will was expressly limited to property abroad, but there was property in England, administration was granted for his property here.[11]

But where wills affecting the property of the deceased in England and Wales and abroad are not independent, the English will, if last, may incorporate the foreign will by reference, and both, or the relevant portion of the foreign will,[12] be admitted to probate.[13] So also the foreign will may incorporate the English will and so extend its operation to England and Wales.[14]

Real and personal property

As already shown,[15] the ecclesiastical and probate courts formerly had no jurisdiction to make grants for real property alone.

In 1881 chattels real and trust and mortgage estates were vested in the personal representative and grants could be made in respect thereof.[16]

In 1897 by section 1 of the Land Transfer Act of that year it was provided that real restate vested in any person without a right in any other person to take by survivorship should vest in his personal representatives, even if a grant was not sought to real estate only. The Act, which governs cases where the death occurred after 1897 and before 1926, did not extend to copyholds or customary freeholds (both now abolished), nor did it bind the Crown.

The main provisions of this statute were re-enacted by section 1 of the Administration of Estates Act 1925, but the Crown is now bound.[17]

Probate or administration (with or without the will) may be granted for real or personal property either separately or together; but where the estate is known to be insolvent a grant is not to be severed, except for trust estate.[18]

At present there is little distinction in probate law and practice between real and personal property, save that in many cases a separate grant is still necessary for settled land.[19] An important distinction is to be made

[10] *Re Coode, supra*; *Re Astor* (1876) 1 P.D. 150; *Re Smart* (1884) 9 P.D. 64; *Re De la Rue* (1890) 15 P.D. 185; *Re Murray* [1896] P. 65.
[11] *Re Mann* [1891] P. 293.
[12] *Re Tamplin* [1894] P. 39.
[13] *Re Todd* [1926] P. 173.
[14] *Re Howden* (1874) 43 L.J.P. & M. 26; *Re Harris* (1870) 2 P & D. 83; *Re Murray, supra*. *Re Western* (1898) 78 L.T. 49; *Re Green* (1899) 79 L.T. 738.
[15] See *ante*, p. 9.
[16] By the Conveyancing Act 1881, s.30.
[17] Administration of Estates Act 1925, s.57(1). See *post*, p. 471 and Appendix, *post*, pp. 1112, 1151.
[18] Supreme Court Act 1981, s.113, and see *post*, 327, 1119.
[19] See *post*, pp. 272 *et seq. cf. Sen* v. *Headley* [1991] Ch. 425.

between movable and immovable property where the deceased died domiciled abroad.[20]

The Sovereign and members of the Royal Family

The court has no jurisdiction to make a grant for the estate of a deceased Sovereign of England.[21] A will of the private estate of the Sovereign does not require publication.[22]

A special practice applies to the estates of members of the Royal Family. Although the wills of royal consorts and other members of the Royal Family are admitted to probate, special application may be made to the President of the Family Division for an order that they be sealed up without making a copy for record purposes. The application is made by summons, issued out of the Principal Registry, which is served on the Treasury Solicitor. The will and Inland Revenue account are examined at the Capital Taxes Office before the papers to lead the grant are lodged. No copy of the will is annexed to the grant.

Where an order for sealing up is made, the will and oath are sealed in an envelope enclosed with a note as to its contents and handed to the Record Keeper of the Principal Registry for safekeeping. No copy will issue thereafter nor may the envelope be opened save by leave of the President.

Life policies of persons who die domiciled abroad

Where a person dies domiciled abroad and his sole assets in England consist of moneys payable on policies of assurance, no grant is required,[23] but such moneys were liable to estate duty,[24] and now, apparently, to Inheritance Tax.

Miscellaneous small assets

A large number of provisions, made by statute or statutory instrument, enable sums generally not exceeding £5,000 to be paid to the persons entitled without any grant of representation to the estate of the deceased being taken out.

Nearly all these enactments are set out in the Schedules to the Administration of Estates (Small Payments) Act 1965. The various maximum payments payable without a grant were raised to £1,500 in cases where the death or nomination occurred on or after August 10, 1975 and to £5,000 for deaths on or after May 11, 1984.[25] The limit in the cases where the death

---

[20] See *ante*, pp. 11 *et seq*.

[21] *Re King George III* (1822) 1 Add. 255; *Re King George III* (1862) 3 Sw. & Tr. 199.

[22] Crown Private Estates Act 1862, s.5.

[23] Revenue Act 1884, s.11 proviso, Revenue Act 1889, s.19. As to the Hague Convention on Succession, see generally p. 16, *ante*.

[24] *Haas* v. *Atlas Assurance Co.* [1913] 2 K.B. 209.

[25] Administration of Estates (Small Payments) (Increase of Limit) Orders 1975 and 1984 (S.I. 1984 No. 539).

occurred on or after September 5, 1965 but before August 10, 1975 was £500.[26]

These assets fall into two categories; assets in particular funds and accounts due to the deceased or his estate because of his employment, former employment or his special situation, and assets of the deceased in particular funds unrelated to his employment.

Assets in particular funds payable because of the deceased's service, employment, etc., include:

(i) Sums on account of pay, pensions or grants due to members or retired members of the Armed Forces and the auxiliary and nursing services and to certain of their dependants.[27]

(ii) Amounts due for pensions or refunds of pension contributions of members of the House of Commons which may be paid to a personal representative on production of a grant or confirmation issued by any court in the United Kingdom. If the amount does not exceed £5,000 it may be paid by the trustees of the Members' Pension Fund, without the production of a grant, to such persons as would be entitled on intestacy, subject to certain restrictions where there are claims on the estate.[28]

(iii) Sums on account of pay, superannuation, allowances or gratuities due to those entitled to the estates of civil servants,[29] members of the police force,[30] firemen,[31] teachers and other specified members of the education services[32] members of various other specified public services[33] and employees of local authorities.[34]

(iv) Where the Minister of Social Security by agreement with the Administrator of Veterans' Affairs holds money or investments on trust for a United States veteran resident in England, such sums may be paid to the person entitled to the latter's estate, except in cases of escheat or *bona vacantia*.[35]

(v) The Court of Protection may provide for the funeral expenses of a

---

[26] Administration of Estates (Small Payments) Act 1965, s.1.
[27] See the Army Pensions Act 1830, s.5, applied by the Army (Artillery, etc.) Pensions Act 1833, s.2; Pensions and Yeomanry Pay Act 1884, s.4, applied to the Air Force by the Air Force (Application of Enactments) (No. 2) Order 1918, and to the women's forces by the Army and Air Force Women's services (Adaptation of Enactments) Order 1949, and to pensions due to Commonwealth servicemen by the Military Pensions (Commonwealth Relations Office) Regulations 1959. See also the Regimental Debts Act 1893, ss.7 and 9, applied to the Air Force as above. See also the Navy and Marines (Property of Deceased) Act 1865, s.6; Naval Pensions Act 1884, s.2, and see art. 64 of the Royal Warrants of May 24, 1949, H.C. Pap. No. 259 of 1949 (Air Force) and Order in Council of September 29, 1959 (Naval Forces).
[28] Parliamentary and other Pensions Act 1972, s.24.
[29] Superannuation Act, 1972, s.4.
[30] Police Pensions Regulations 1973.
[31] Firemen's Pension Scheme Order 1973; Fire Services Act 1951, ss.1 and 2; Reserve and Auxiliary Forces (Protection of Civil Interests) Act 1951, ss.42 and 44.
[32] Superannuation Act 1972, s.9(1), and Teacher's Superannuation Regulations 1976.
[33] Superannuation (Various Services) Act 1938, s.2, and regulations made thereunder.
[34] Local Government Act 1972, s.19.
[35] U.S.A. Veterans' Pensions (Administration) Act 1949, s.1(3).

deceased patient out of any funds in court where it appears that the net value of the estate does not exceed £5,000, and order that any such funds or the balance thereof or any other property under its control be paid or transferred to the personal representative of the patient, when constituted, or to the person who appears to be entitled to representation to the estate.[36]

(vi) Property of a deceased seaman not exceeding £5,000 in the hands of the Minister of Social Security may be paid or delivered by him to certain specified persons, including any person appearing to be the next of kin, or his widow or child, or anyone beneficially entitled to a grant.[37]

(vii) Sums due to deceased seamen under schemes to compensate them for war damage and other loss or damage to their effects[38] or payable under certain war pensions granted to members of the merchant marine.[39]

(viii) The Ionian Bank may register a Greek subject as the owner of shares on the death of a Greek shareholder, but estate duty or Inheritance Tax must be paid. There is no limit in value.[40]

4. *Assets in particular funds where the deceased was not in a particular category*

(i) *Government stock.* Government, British Transport, British Electricity and British Gas stock up to any amount may be transferred as if there were an English grant where a grant has been made in the Isle of Man or the Channel Islands and the grant or a copy thereof is produced, together with a certificate from the Commissioners of Inland Revenue as to payment of any death duties.[41]

Government stock in the name of a deceased person not exceeding £1,500 in nominal or actual value (whichever is the less), may be transferred by the Bank of England or the Bank of Ireland to the National Savings Stock Register.[42]

Government stock inscribed on the National Savings Stock Register may be paid to the grantees of a grant made in the Isle of Man or the Channel Islands without limit of amount on the production of the grant, or a certi-

---

[36] Court of Protection Rules 1984, r.73(2).

[37] Merchant Shipping Act 1970, s.66(2).

[38] Pensions (Navy, Army, Air Force and Mercentile Marine) Act 1939, s.6(3), (as extended by Pensions (Mercantile Marine) Act 1942, s.1, and see the Compensation to Seamen (War Damage to Effects) Scheme 1949.

[39] War Pensions (Mercantile Marine) Scheme 1949.

[40] Ionian Bank (Limited) Act 1899, s.2.

[41] Finance Act 1949, s.48, and see the British Transport Stock Regulations 1947, para. 14(3), Electricity Stock Regulations 1948, para. 13(3), and Gas Stock Regulations 1949, para. 12(3).

[42] National Debt Act 1972, s.6.

fied copy, together with a certificate from the commissioners of Inland Revenue as to payment of death duties.[43]

Provided the nomination was made before May 1, 1981 the holder of stock inscribed on the National Savings Stock Register might nominate the whole or any part of his holding to some other person on his death, in which event the nominee's name will be inscribed in place of that of the nominor without a grant being taken out, but if the value of the stock added to post office assets exceeds £5,000, a certificate as to the payment of estate duty or capital transfer tax must be produced.[44]

(ii) *Government and bank annuities.* Sums not exceeding £5,000 due in respect of National Debt annuities[45] or savings bank annuities may be paid without a grant.[46]

Sums up to any amount in respect of these annuities may be paid on production of a grant issued in the Isle of Man or the Channel Islands.[47]

(iii) *Savings bank deposits and savings certificates.* Provided the nomination was made before May 1, 1981 a depositor in a savings bank or a holder of savings certificates who had attained the age of 16 years might nominate a person to whom such sums as may be due in them at the death of the depositor or holder shall be paid. Such nominee may be paid these sums without a grant whatever the amount in the case of national savings bank deposits or savings certificates.[48] In the case of trustee savings banks the power for a depositor to make a nomination pursuant to the Trustee Savings Banks Regulations 1972, was withdrawn as from May 1, 1979.[49] Any deposits held may be repaid without a certificate from the commissioners of Inland Revenue as to capital transfer tax liability in respect of those deposits.[50] In all other cases the production of a certificate as to Tax is required if the total of such assets exceed £5,000 when aggregated with any government securities on the post office register.

Sums in savings certificates or in a savings bank not dealt with by nomination may be paid to the persons beneficially entitled thereto on the death of the deceased without a grant, but the maximum amount is £1,500.

(iv) *Premium bonds.* A grant of representation issued in the United Kingdom, the Isle of Man or the Channel Islands is sufficient authority to the Director of Savings to pay over premium savings bonds up to any amount.[51] Premium bonds up to £5,000 in value may be paid without a

[43] National Debt Act 1972, s.7(1).
[44] National Savings Stock Register Regulations 1976 reg. 42: Trustee Savings Bank Act 1981, ss.27(4), 55.
[45] Government Annuities Act 1929, s.21.
[46] *Ibid.* s.57.
[47] Government Annuities Act 1929, ss.20 and 56.
[48] Trustee Savings Banks Act 1969. (Repealed by Trustee Savings Bank Act 1981 s.55).
[49] Trustee Savings Bank (Amendment) Regulations 1979.
[50] *Ibid.*
[51] Premium Savings Bonds Regulations 1972.

grant.[52] Premium bonds owned by persons domiciled in Northern Ireland, the Channel Islands or the Isle of Man are treated as not being situate in England. Should a prize be won on a bond held by the deceased after his death, the amount of the prize is added to the holding to determine the total holding.

(v) *Registered societies.*   Where the deceased dies testate or intestate on or after September 5, 1965, sums not exceeding £5,000 may be paid without a grant by the trustees of a loan society or the committee of management or directors of a building society.[53]

At the age of 16 years a member of a trade union, an industrial, provident or friendly society may nominate a person to receive moneys up to £5,000 payable by these institutions at his death. Where such sums do not exceed £5,000 no grant is necessary.[54]

(vi) *National insurance.*   National insurance benefit which has been claimed by a deceased or to which he was entitled may be paid and distributed to or among those who claim as personal representatives or to be entitled under a will or on intestacy, or, where the deceased was illegitimate, among other persons, and strict proof of title may be dispensed with.[55]

(vii) *Funds in court.*   Where an intestate is entitled to a fund in court or a share in such fund and the whole estate does not exceed £5,000 payment out of court may be made without a grant.[56]

Limitation of amount

Although the limit for deaths on or after September 5, 1965 is £500 (increased to £1,500 by the Administration of Estates (Small Payments) (Increase of Limit) Order 1975 in respect of deaths occurring on or after August 10, 1975) and £5,000 for deaths after May 11, 1984 except where otherwise indicated, in cases of death before that date the maximum amount varied in different cases between £50 and £500.

The Treasury may, in future, specify higher maxima.[57]

It is to be noted that the dispensation from the necessity of obtaining a grant in the cases mentioned above does not exempt the various assets mentioned from inheritance tax where there are other assets which bring

---

[52] *Ibid.*

[53] Building Societies Act 1962, s.46, as amended by Administration of Estates (Small Payments) Act 1965.

[54] Trade Union Amendment Act 1876, s.10, as subsequently amended; and Industrial and Provident Societies Act 1965, s.25.

[55] National Insurance (Claims and Payments) Regulations 1948, reg. 18, as amended, and National Insurance (Industrial Injuries) (Claims and Payments) Regulations 1964, reg. 25 and Sched. 2.

[56] R.S.C., Ord. 22 r. 11.

[57] Administration of Estates (Small Payments) Act 1965, s.6.

the total value of the estate above the appropriate limit. Many of the provisions mentioned above expressly require a certificate from the Capital
Taxes office as to the payment of Tax.

Pension funds

Nominations made by the deceased under pension and insurance
schemes do not on general require a grant since the nominator while alive
has no control over the funds in question.[58] Whether or not a given nomination constitutes a testamentary paper so as to be governed by wills legislation is a matter of construction of the scheme in question.[59]

[58] See *Re Danish Bacon Co.* [1971] 1 W.L.R. 248. As to death duty on such schemes see
Encyclopaedia of Capital Taxation, 4B–088. As to the effect of nominations on claims for
family provision see pp. 801, 804, *post.*
[59] *Baird* v. *Baird* [1990] A.C. 548.

CHAPTER 10

THE EXECUTOR'S YEAR

A representative is not bound to distribute the estate before the expiration of one year from the death,[1] but an assent should not be postponed merely because of duties, debts or liabilities if reasonable arrangements for discharge have been made.[2] Quite apart from statute, however, an executor cannot be compelled to pay a legacy before the end of a year from the testator's death, during which period it is presumed that he may fully inform himself of the state of the property.[3] Within that period he cannot be compelled to pay a legacy, even where the testator directs it to be discharged within six months after his death.[4]

This allowance, however, to executors is merely for convenience, so that the debts of the testator may be ascertained, and the executors made acquainted with the amount of assets, so as to be able to make a proper distribution of them,[5] Therefore, if the executors can discharge legacies at an earlier period, they have authority to do so.[6] They should, however, exercise special caution where a claim under the Inheritance (Provision for Family and Dependants) Act 1975 is likely to be brought.[7]

If executors fail to realise any property within the executor's year, the onus is on the executors to show some valid reason for the delay.[8]

Where a legacy is given to A to be paid at 21, and if he should die before attaining that age, then to B—should A die before attaining 21, but more

---

[1] Administration of Estates Act 1925, s.44 (*post*, p. 1137.) As to the practice of due diligence in collecting the estate, see *ante*, p. 69. Executors should do the best they can for the estate as a whole (see *Re Hayes* [1971] 1 W.L.R. 758) and where there is power to postpone sale a considerable delay may be justified.

[2] Administration of Estates Act 1925, s.36(10), and see *post*, p. 1060.

[3] *Wood* v. *Penoyre*, 13 Ves. 325, 333, 334; *Pearson* v. *Pearson* (1833) 1 Scho. & Lefr. 11; Toller 312. As to time for payment of debts, see *post*, p. 886. As to interest, see *post*, pp. 1035 *et seq*.

[4] See *Benson* v. *Maude* (1821) 6 Madd. 15; *Re Lord Llangattock* (1918) 34 T.L.R. 341. In *Brooke* v. *Lewis* (1822) 6 Madd. 358, the testator gave certain legacies, which he directed to be paid within six months after his decease; and he directed the residue to be divided among certain persons named, or such of them as should be living at the time the same should be distributed. It was held that the residue was to be divided among the legatees named who were living at the end of one year after the death of the testator.

[5] *Garthshore* v. *Chalie* (1804) 10 Ves. 1, 13; *Grayburn* v. *Clarkson* (1868) 3 Ch.App. 605; *Sculthorpe* v. *Tipper* (1872) L.R. 13 Eq. 232; *Brown* v. *Gellatly* (1867) L.R. 2 Ch.App. 751, 759; *Re Tankard* [1942] Ch. 69.

[6] *Pearson* v. *Pearson* (1833) 1 Scho. & Lefr. 12; *Angerstein* v. *Martin* (1823) 1 Turn. & R. 232, 241; *Garthshore* v. *Chalie*, *ante*.

[7] *Re Simson* [1950] Ch. 38; *Re Ralphs* [1968] 1 W.L.R. 1522. See *post*, pp. 757 *et seq*.

[8] *Per* Wood L.J. in *Grayburn* v. *Clarkson* (1868) L.R. 3 Ch.App. 605. As to the discretion to postpone conversion, see *post*, p. 739.

than a year from the testator's death, B will be entitled to receive his legacy immediately. There is only allowed one period of a year, and that period starts from the testator's death.[9]

Date of valuation

Difficult questions of valuation can sometimes arise where there is a substantial alteration in values between the date of death and the end of the executor's year. Where there is a will this question will normally be a matter of construction, but subject to this it seems that the proper date is the end of the executor's year when distribution ought to occur.[10] If estate duty had to be taken into account, different properties or funds had to be regarded as divided up before payment of such duty. Presumably the same will apply under inheritance tax.

Practice in administration action

According to the ordinary practice in an action to administer the assets of a deceased testator, the court in the first place waits until all the claims on the estate are settled, and until the clear fund is ascertained; and then the particular legatees are paid.[11] They are paid their principal, and if entitled to interest, they are paid interest at the rate of 6 per cent. per annum up to that time.[12]

But if it clearly appears that a surplus will remain, after discharging all the testator's debts and liabilities, though the exact amount of the surplus cannot be ascertained for a considerable time, the court will, by anticipation, direct proportional payments to be made to pecuniary legatees, as far as that can be done with safety to the creditors.[13] In the absence of any direction to the contrary in the testator's will, the rule of administration is that each such payment must be appropriated first to interest at 6 per cent. per annum, and after satisfying all interest due, to principal.[14] This rule also applies where payments on account are made to legatees owing to difficulties in realising a testator's estate.[15]

In a case[16] where it appeared, upon affidavits, that the estate was large, with but few debts or charges thereon, the court ordered the jointure of the widow of the testator and annuities given by his will to be paid out of the income of the estate, before decree, but refused to direct the payment of the pecuniary legacies.

[9] *Laundy* v. *Williams* (1728) 2 P.Wms. 478.
[10] See *Re Slee* [1962] 1 W.L.R. 496 and cases there discussed.
[11] *Thomas* v. *Montgomery* (1830) 1 Russ. & M. 729, 737.
[12] See Ord. 44, r. 10; *Re Gardner* (1892) 67 L.T. 552; *Re Campbell* [1892] 3 Ch. 468; *Re Inman, Ibid.* 518; *Re Snaith* (1894) 71 L.T. 318; and see *post*, p. 1035.
[13] *Thomas* v. *Montgomery, supra*, at p. 729, Ord. 29, r. 8.
[14] *Thomas* v. *Montgomery, supra*; *Re Prince* (1935) 51 T.L.R. 526.
[15] *Ibid.*; *Re Morley's Estate* [1937] Ch. 491.
[16] *Digby* v. *Boycott* (1845) 4 Hare 444.

Legacy liable to be divested

Where a legacy is given generally, subject to a limitation over upon a subsequent event, the divesting contingency will not prevent the legatee from receiving his legacy at the end of the year from the testator's death; and he is not bound to give security for repayment of the money, in case the event should happen. Thus, where a legacy was given on condition to be void in case the legatees should succeed to an estate in the event of the death of A without issue of her body, payment was decreed in the lifetime of A, and without security for refunding.[17] But where a legacy was given to a father, on condition that he did not interfere with the education of his daughter, on an application by the father for his legacy, the court required from him security to that effect, to be approved by the master, and directed the costs of the proceedings to be paid out of the legacy.[18]

Annuity: first payment

If an annuity is given by will, it begins immediately from the testator's death, so the first payment should be made at the expiration of a year next after that event.[19] Where an annuity is expressly directed to commence within the year, as at the first quarter-day after the testator's death,[20] or where an annuity is given with a direction that it shall be paid monthly,[21] the money will be due at the first quarter-day in the former case, and at the end of the first month after testator's death in the latter, though not payable by the executor till the end of the year. Where a testator gives an annuity to A for life, and directs the first payment to be made within one month from his, the testator's death, the annuity commences from the death of the testator; and though the first year's payment is due at the appointed time, the payment for the second year does not become due till the end of that year.[22] Where a testator gives an annuity to A for life, payable quarterly, the first payment to be made within 18 months after his death, the annuity does not commence till 15 months from the death of the testator.[22]

Where a testatrix had directed that two annuities be paid subject to a life interest in the residuary income, the first payment to be made three months after the death of the tenant for life, and the tenant for life disclaimed, it was held that the annuities were accelerated so as to take effect from the death of the testatrix.[23]

---

[17] *Fawkes* v. *Gray* (1811) 18 Ves. 131. See also *Griffiths* v. *Smith* (1790) 1 Ves. 97; 1 Rop.-Leg., 3rd ed., 752.

[18] *Colston* v. *Morris* (1819) 6 Madd. 89.

[19] By Lord Eldon in *Gibson* v. *Bott* (1802) 7 Ves. 96, 97, and in *Fearns* v. *Young* (1804) 9 Ves. 553; *Stamper* v. *Pickering* (1838) 9 Sim. 176; *Re Robbins* [1907] 2 Ch. 8, 13. See also *Houghton* v. *Franklin* (1823) 1 Sim. & Stu. 390, 392. As to annuities generally see p. 1008 *et seq. post.*

[20] *Storer* v. *Prestage* (1818) 3 Madd. 167.

[21] *Houghton* v. *Franklin* (1823) 1 Sim. & Stu. 390.

[22] *Irvin* v. *Ironmonger* (1831) 2 Russ. & M. 531.

[23] *Re Hodge* [1943] Ch. 300.

Legacy for life

A distinction was taken by Lord Eldon, in *Gibson* v. *Bott*,[24] between an annuity and a legacy for life. "If an annuity," said his lordship, "is given, the first payment is paid at the end of the year from the death: but if a legacy is given for life, with remainder over, no interest is due till the end of two years. It is only interest of the legacy; and till the legacy is payable, there is no fund to produce interest."[25]

Residue—Rule in Allhusen v. Whittell

However, a different doctrine prevails where there is a bequest of the residue of personal estate for life, with remainder over. Since the value or amount of the residue is *ex hypothesi* unascertainable before administration is complete its income is also unascertainable. The person taking the residue for life is entitled to income,[26] in some shape or other, from the date of the death of the testator.[27] But if there are debts to be paid he is not entitled to the whole actual income accruing during the first year. The rule is that the executors, when they have dealt with the estate, will be taken by the court as having applied in payment of debts, legacies, and other charges such portion of the fund as, together with the income of that portion for one year, was necessary for the payment thereof.[28] And when eventually the whole estate is realised, it becomes necessary to ascertain retrospectively what was the residue at the end of the year, attributing a due proportion of the sum realised after the end of the year to capital and a due proportion to interest.[29] But the rule laid down in *Allhusen* v. *Whittell* is not to be slavishly followed in every case where residue is settled. Being an equitable rule adopted for giving effect to a presumed intention of the testator, it can be displaced by any language of the will which shows an intention to displace it.[30] It does not apply to contingent legacies,[31] and

[24] (1802) 7 Ves. 89, 96.

[25] A sum of money directed to be placed out to produce an annuity is to be considered as a legacy payable at the end of a year, not as an annuity payable from the death; *ibid.* 97; *Re Friend* (1898) 78 L.T. 222.

[26] Sums due to a deceased person under a service agreement are capital not income of the estate: *Re Payne* [1943] W.N. 250. Dividends in a public company earned before the testator's death, but declared afterwards, form income and not *corpus*: *Bates* v. *Mackinley* (1862) 31 Beav. 280; *Maclaren* v. *Stainton* (1861) 3 De G.F. & J. 202 *Gilly* v. *Burley* (1856) 22 Beav. 618; *Lock* v. *Venables* (1859) 27 Beav. 598. As to whether a bonus is to be regarded as capital or income, see *post*, p. 535.

[27] *Angerstein* v. *Martin* (1823) 1 Turn. & R. 232; *Hewitt* v. *Morris* (1824) 1 Turn. & R. 241; *La Terriere* v. *Bulmer* (1827) 2 Sim. 18; *Dimes* v. *Scott* (1828) 4 Russ. 195; *Douglas* v. *Congreve* (1836) 1 Keen 410; *Taylor* v. *Clark* (1841) 1 Hare 161; *Macpherson* v. *Macpherson* (1852) 1 Macq. H. of L. 243. But see *contra, Taylor* v. *Hibbert* (1820) 1 Jac. & Walk. 308; *Stott* v. *Hollingworth* (1818) 3 Madd. 161; and *Amphlett* v. *Parke* (1827) 1 Sim. 275.

[28] *Allhusen* v. *Whittell* (1867) L.R. 4 Eq. 295; *Lambert* v. *Lambert* (1873) L.R. 16 Eq. 320; *Re Shee* [1934] Ch. 345. "Income" includes profits of the testator's business: *Re Elford* [1910] 1 Ch. 814.

[29] *Wightwick* v. *Lord* (1857) 6 H.L.C. 217, 226. This rule was applied to real estate in *Marshall* v. *Crowther* (1874) 2 Ch.D. 199.

[30] *Re Darby* [1939] Ch. 905, 915; but see *Re Ullswater* [1952] Ch. 105.

[31] *Re Fenwick* [1936] Ch. 720.

should not be applied where large sums have been expended in clearing the estate at periods long before the end of the first year.[32] And if the nature of the property concerned, or the circumstances affecting it, are such that the rule cannot be applied according to its terms then the rule is not applicable to the case at all.[30]

Where a testator has covenanted to pay an annuity, the rule in *Allhusen* v. *Whittell* applies so that each instalment of the annuity as it becomes payable is to be paid by means of a piece of capital together with the income on that piece of capital as from the date of the testator's death down to the date of payment.[33] If, however, the liability to pay an annuity originates not in a personal covenant or obligation on the part of the testator but in a charge created by his predecessor in title, the rule in *Allhusen* v. *Whittell* does not apply.[34]

These principles, however, are subject to modification where the executors are under an express or implied obligation to convert the residue into money and invest it in specified securities.

Delay by executor—notional payment

Where a legatee, by express direction or otherwise is not to take a gift unless he lives to receive it, his interest vests the moment he might have received it, for the court will not, by adopting too literal a construction,[35] suffer the rights of legatees to be prejudiced by the fraudulent or unnecessary delays of executors or trustees, and may order an inquiry as to the period at which the legacy might have been paid.[36] This does not apply, however, where the testator shows clearly that the legacy is not to vest until actual receipt thereof, as where he adds the words "whether the same shall become due and payable or not."[37]

Where a testatrix directed that the legacies given by her will were not to vest until they became payable, and that they should be paid within six months from her death, the representatives of a legatee who died within the six months were entitled to the legacy; for there was nothing to prevent the legacies from being payable immediately after the death of the testatrix.[38]

---

[32] *Re McEuen* [1913] 2 Ch. 704.

[33] *Re Perkins* [1907] 2 Ch. 596; *Re Poyser* [1910] 2 Ch. 44; and see *Re Darby* [1939] Ch. 905, 915; *Re Berkeley* [1968] Ch. 744.

[34] *Re Darby, ante.* See also *Re Leicester's Settled Estates* [1939] Ch. 77 (tithe redemption annuity).

[35] *Johnson* v. *Crook* (1879) 12 Ch.D. 639 (where the authorities are discussed); *Re Collison* (1879) 12 Ch.D. 834; *Re Chaston* (1881) 18 Ch.D. 218, 227; *Re Goulder* [1905] 2 Ch. 100; *Re Petrie* [1962] Ch. 355.

[36] *Re Dodgson's Trusts* (1853) 1 Drewr, 440; *Law* v. *Thompson* (1827) 4 Russ. 92; *Re Arrowsmith's Trusts* (1860) 2 De G.F. & J. 474. See also *Re Chaston* (1881) 18 Ch.D. 218; *RetttWilkins* (1881) 18 Ch.D. 634.

[37] *Johnson* v. *Crook, ante.*

[38] *Lucas* v. *Carline* (1840) 2 Beav. 367. See also *Packham* v. *Gregory* (1845) 4 Hare 396; *Re Arrowsmith's Trusts, ante.*

Part Two A

THE GRANT

(A) of Probate

CHAPTER 11

THE NEED FOR PROBATE

Having carried out or prepared to carry out his duties to arrange the funeral and burial or cremation,[1] the preparation of the inventory and account,[2] the collection of assets,[3] and the preparation of the Inland Revenue account,[4] the executor or prospective administrator is concerned, where there is property for which a grant is required, to obtain a grant of probate or administration, as the case may be.

Will

A will is the aggregate of a man's testamentary intentions so far as they are manifested in writing duly executed according to the Wills Act 1837.[5] It is an instrument by which a person makes a disposition of his property to take effect after his death and which is in its own nature ambulatory and revocable during his life.[6] The will is the aggregate or net result of a man's testamentary wishes. In this sense it is inaccurate to speak of a man leaving two wills; he does leave and can leave but one will.[7] That will also comprises documents to which it refers provided these exist at the date of the last properly executed document.[8] Under the probate jurisdiction incorporated documents ought to be included in the probate but in practice the Chancery Division has, under its jurisdiction to construe documents, always given effect to documents which as a matter of construction it has held to be incorporated even if these have not been included in the probate.[9]

Probate

Probate is necessary of every testamentary instrument and act[10] which disposes of real or personal property in England.[11] Without probate such instruments and acts cannot be recognised by any court in this country.[12]

---

[1] See *ante*, pp. 60–64.
[2] See *ante*, pp. 64–69.
[3] See *ante*, pp. 69–70.
[4] See *ante*, p. 73.
[5] *Lemage* v. *Goodban* (1865) L.R. 1 P. & D. 57; *Re Berger* [1990] Ch. 118, 131. For forms see Brighouse, *Precedents of Wills and Life Transfers*.
[6] *Jarman on Wills* (8th ed.) p. 26.
[7] *Douglas-Menzies* v. *Umphelby* [1908] A.C. 224, 233; *Re Berger* [1990] Ch. 118, 133.
[8] *Re Berger* [1990] Ch. 118, 135. As to incorporation of documents, see p. 153 *post*.
[9] See p. 155 *post*.
[10] *i.e.* a nuncupative will.
[11] It seems that the Chancery Court may order an inquiry for the purpose of sending testamentary papers to be proved, see *Brenchley* v. *Lynn* (1852) 2 Rob. 441, 458 *et seq*.
[12] *Ibid.*

Even a will which merely confirms another will which has already been proved must be admitted to probate.[13] A will which contains no dispositive provisions but merely appoints executors is admissible to probate.[14] But a will which does not appoint executors and has no dispositive effect is not admissible to probate.[15]

A conditional will which is ineffective because the condition has not been fulfilled is not admissible to probate.[16] Early cases held that an instrument which merely revoked all former wills was admissible to probate; but it is now well settled that such an instrument is not entitled to probate.[17] However, such instrument must be brought into the registry when a grant is applied for which depends on the execution thereof. Where a revocatory instrument does not effect a total intestacy, it is entitled to probate.[18] Also, where a will having no apparent dispositive effect is construed as implying a variation of the rights to distribution on intestacy, probate is necessary.[19]

An instrument which merely appointed a guardian was held not entitled to probate.[20]

As has already been shown it is the right and duty of the probate court to construe testamentary documents with a view to determining which documents and what part of them should be admitted to probate.[21]

There are several kinds of wills admissible to probate which require detailed consideration. These are wills exercising a power of appointment,[22] duplicate wills,[23] conditional or contingent wills[24] and joint and mutual wills.[25]

A. WILLS EXERCISING A POWER OF APPOINTMENT

By section 10 of the Wills Act 1837 it is enacted that no exercise of a power of appointment by will shall be valid unless it is executed in the same manner as other wills under the Act. Every will so executed constitutes a valid exercise of a power of appointment notwithstanding an express requirement by the instrument creating the power that the will should be executed with some additional or other form of execution or solemnity.

It is incumbent on the probate court, if it has all persons interested before it, not merely to consider the probate aspects of a will exercising a

[13] *Weddall* v. *Nixon* (1853) 17 Beav. 160.
[14] *Re Jordan* (1868) L.R. 1 P. & D. 555; *Re Leese* (1862) 2 Sw. & Tr. 442; see *Brownrigg* v. *Pike* (1882) 7 P.D. 61.
[15] See *Re Thomas* [1939] 2 All E.R. 567.
[16] *Re O'Connor* [1942] 1 All E.R. 546.
[17] *Re Fraser* (1870) L.R. 2 P. & D. 40; see *Toomer* v. *Sobinska* [1970] P. 106.
[18] *Re Spracklan's Estate* [1938] 2 All E.R. 345.
[19] *Jarman on Wills*, 8th ed., p. 684; *Lett* v. *Randall* (1855); *Bund* v. *Green* (1879) 12 Ch.D. 819; 3 Sim & G. 83, 89; *Re Wynn* [1984] 1 W.L.R. 237, 241.
[20] *Re Morton* (1864) 3 Sw. & Tr. 345, 422.
[21] See *ante*, pp. 10, 27.
[22] See *infra*.
[23] See *post*, p. 124.
[24] See *post*, p. 124.
[25] See *post*, p. 127.

power but to decide whether there was a power and whether it was well executed.[26] It seems that, as where trustees exercise a power, a testator is under a fiduciary duty to consider all the issues pertinent to an appointment before executing the power, and if he is unaware of a discretion or did not understand the powers may not have been validly exercised.[27]

English wills executing English powers where the testator dies domiciled abroad

A will disposing of movable property situate in England or Wales under a power of appointment in an English settlement is admissible to probate if duly executed according to English law, even if not duly executed by the law of the place in which the deceased died domiciled.[28] "The document," said Lord Loreburn in *Murphy* v. *Deichler*,[29] "may be admitted to probate as a will for the purpose of the appointment, though it may not be admissible for other purposes." The reason for this is that a will may be a good execution of the power, which is a question to be decided by the court of construction,[30] but being a testamentary instrument it must be proved as a valid will.[31]

The exercise of a special power of appointment is not a disposition of property belonging to the testator and is not therefore affected by any disability under which the testator may be by the law of his domicile to dispose of his own property.[32]

In general no restriction placed on the exercise of a general power of appointment by the law of a testator's domicile can have any effect, whether the testator so executed the power as to make the property his own or not,[33] but if by blending the settled funds with other assets he shows an intention that the former should be treated as part of the latter and the latter are affected by the law of his domicile, that law may apply.[34]

Foreign wills executing English powers

A power to appoint by will which does not require any special form of execution is well executed if the will is valid by the law of the testator's

---

[26] *Re Tharp* (1878) 3 P.D. 76, C.A.

[27] See *Turner* v. *Turner* [1984] Ch. 100. This principle may not apply to a general power.

[28] *Murphy* v. *Deichler* [1909] A.C. 446. Wills Act 1963, s.2(1)(*d*), *post*, p. 151.

[29] *Murphy* v. *Deichler*, *supra*, p. 448.

[30] *D'Huart* v. *Harkness* (1865) 34 Beav. 324; *Pouey* v. *Hordern* [1900] 1 Ch. 492; *Re Mégret* [1901] 1 Ch. 547; *Re Baker's Settlement Trusts* [1908] W.N. 161.

[31] *D'Huart* v. *Harkness*, *supra*; *Bradford* v. *Young* (1884) 26 Ch.D. 656.

[32] *Pouey* v. *Hordern* [1900] 1 Ch. 492. As to special, general and hybrid powers, see *post*, p. 596.

[33] *Re Mégret* [1901] 1 Ch. 547; *Re Waite's Settlement Trusts* [1958] Ch. 100, but see *Re Hadley* [1909] 1 Ch. 20, 35. See also *Re Pryce* [1911] 2 Ch. 286; *Re Lewal* [1918] 2 Ch. 391 and nn. 32, *supra*, and 34, *infra*.

[34] *Re Pryce*, *supra*; *Re Khan* [1966] Ch. 567, not following *Re Waite*, *supra*.

domicile, even if not validly executed by the law of England, and this applies whether the power to appoint is general or special.[35]

As section 10 of the Wills Act 1837 does not apply where the testator dies domiciled abroad the will must, in general, be executed not merely to comply with the law of the domicile but also to comply with the terms of the power.[36] But defective execution in this respect may be remedied for the benefit of persons for whom, and in circumstances in which, it is the practice of courts of equity to aid the defective execution of a power.[37]

A general bequest exercises a power of appointment in a foreign will

By section 27 of the Wills Act 1837 a general bequest or devise in a will includes property over which the testator has a general power of appointment, unless a contrary intention appears in the will. This rule has been held to apply where the will was not executed in accordance with the Wills Act 1837 but was validly executed by the law of the domicile.[38] Here the proper approach is to construe the will in accordance with its proper law in order to find the testator's intention. It is then a matter of English law whether such intention amounts to a "bequest" under section 27 of the Wills Act 1837.[39]

Application of Lord Kingsdown's Act to powers of appointment

Where a power of appointment is exercised by a will valid neither by the law of the domicile nor under the Wills Act 1837 but only under Lord Kingsdown's Act,[40] there is doubt whether such exercise is a valid one.[41] It is tentatively suggested that it is. Cases raising the point are likely to be extremely rare following the repeal of Lord Kingsdown's Act.

Effect of the Wills Act 1963 on powers of appointment

Where a will is duly executed in accordance with section 1 of the Wills Act 1963,[42] any power of appointment exercised in it will be held to be well executed. Additionally section 2(1)(d) of the Act provides that "a will so far as it exercises a power of appointment, if the execution of the will conformed to the law governing the essential validity of the power" is to be

[35] *D'Huart* v. *Harkness* (1865) 34 Beav. 324; *Re Price* [1900] 1 Ch. 442, 447; *Re Wilkinson's Settlement* [1917] 1 Ch. 620, 626.

[36] *Barretto* v. *Young* [1900] 2 Ch. 339.

[37] *Re Walker* [1908] 1 Ch. 560.

[38] *Re Simpson* [1916] 1 Ch. 502; *Re Lewal, supra*; *Re Strong* (1925) 95 L.J.Ch. 22. *Re D'Este* [1903] 1 Ch. 898 must be considered to have been incorrectly decided. As to the administration of foreign estates see Pugh on this topic.

[39] *Re Fenston's Settlement* [1971] 1 W.L.R. 1640.

[40] As to which see *post*, p. 149.

[41] *Re Simpson, supra*, and *Re Wilkinson's Settlement, supra*, are to be preferred to *Re Kirwan* (1883) 25 Ch.D. 373.

[42] As to which see *post*, p. 151.

treated as properly executed. Furthermore section 2(2) of the Act provides that "a will so far as it exercises a power of appointment shall not be treated as improperly executed by reason only that its execution was not in accordance with any formal requirements contained in the instrument creating the power."

The effect of these provisions in relation to wills exercising a power of appointment which are not valid under the Wills Act 1837 is that they and the powers of appointment exercised by them will, except in rare cases, be valid under the Wills Act 1963.

Revocation of a will exercising a power of appointment

Whereas the ordinary rules of English law apply to the revocation, by a testator domiciled in England and Wales, of a will exercising a power of appointment,[43] a person domiciled abroad may revoke such will by the methods recognised by the law of his domicile even if such methods would not be recognised by the Wills Act 1837.[44]

Practice

In ordinary circumstances a will which exercises a power of appointment is admitted to proof in the same way as any other will. But a will may be revoked save in so far as it exercises a power of appointment,[45] or the court may be satisfied that a revocation clause did not extend to the power of appointment.[46]

In such cases, if there is no valid will, a grant of administration with so much only of the revoked will annexed as relates to the appointed fund is made to the person entitled on intestacy.[47] But if there is another, valid, will which is proved, the relevant part of the revoked will may be proved by the appointees or by one of them with the consent of the others. The grant is limited to property over which the power of appointment extends.

A will may be valid only in so far as it exercises an appointment.[48] In such case the grant is not generally made to the executor, for he takes nothing, *jure representationis*.[49] Administration (with the will) may be granted to the appointee limited to the property covered by the power of appointment, unless those interested on intestacy consent to a general grant.[50]

The invalidity of a will by the law of the domicile and, where applicable, under the Wills Act 1963 must be established by an affidavit of law. The oath refers to the instrument creating the power.

---

[43] Including the special rule as to marriage only revoking the exercise of a power of appointment in particular circumstances, see Wills Act 1837, s.18, and see *post*, p. 191.
[44] *Velasco* v. *Coney* [1934] P. 143.
[45] See *post*, p. 191.
[46] *Ibid.*
[47] *Re Poole* [1919] P. 10; *Re Gibbes* (1887) 37 Ch.D. 143.
[48] See *ante*, p. 120.
[49] *Re Tréfond* [1899] P. 247; *Re Vannini* [1901] P. 330.
[50] *Ibid.*

B. Duplicate Wills

A will may be executed in duplicate. In some respects the two documents are thereupon regarded as one will. Thus when one part is destroyed by the testator, *animo revocandi*, the whole will is revoked[51] and where one part is traced into the deceased's possession and is not forthcoming at his death, there is a presumption that it has been destroyed *animo revocandi*.[52] A duplicate will is a duly executed document and not to be confused with a copy which is not.

Practice

The executors need only prove one part of a duplicate will. But the other part must be produced on the application for a grant so that its identity with the part to be proved may be checked. If the other part cannot be produced its absence will have to be accounted for by affidavit, so as to overcome the presumption of revocation.[53]

C. Conditional or Contingent Wills

A will may be so expressed as to take effect only if some contingency occurs or some condition is fulfilled and if a will is so expressed and the contingency does not happen or the condition fails, the will is not entitled to probate.

But for wills of this kind to be refused probate on the ground that the contingency to which the testator referred has not occurred, it must plainly appear from the terms of the will that the testator intended so to limit its operation.[54] It is not enough for the testator to refer to a future event merely by way of ascribing his reason for making a will.[55] Extrinsic evidence may be received to show that a will not expressed to be conditional was in fact so intended.[56] The will may need to be read as a whole to ascertain the nature of the condition, as to which a clause may be misleading.[57]

Phrases importing a condition into the will

The following expressions were held to make the wills conditional and, as the event had not happened, probate was refused:

"If I die before my return from my journey to Ireland I wish. . . . "[58]
"Being on the eve of embarking for San Francisco . . . in the case of my

---

[51] See *post*, p. 203. As to revival by codicil of duplicate wills, see *post*, p. 220.

[52] See *post*, p. 203.

[53] See N.-C.P.R. 1987, r. 15 (*post*, p. 1229).

[54] *Re Porter* (1869) L.R. 2 P. & D. 22, 23. The court must construe the testamentary papers: *Re Thomas* [1939] 2 All E.R. 567.

[55] *Ibid.* and see *Edmondson* v. *Edmondson* (1901) 17 T.L.R. 397.

[56] *Re Govier* [1950] P. 237.

[57] *Re Whitrick* [1957] 1 W.L.R. 884.

[58] *Parsons* v. *Lanoe* (1748) 1 Ves.Sen. 189.

decease during my absence being fully ascertained and proved. . . . ."[59]
"Being obliged to leave England to join my regiment in China . . . should anything unfortunate happen to me while abroad . . . everything I may be in possession of at that time . . . to be equally divided."[60] "In case anything should happen to me during the remainder of the voyage. . . . ."[61] "Instructions to be followed if I die at sea or abroad. . . . ."[62] A joint will by spouses "in case they should be called out of the world at one and the same time and by one and the same accident"[63] "In case of a sudden or accidental death befalling me in India."[64] "In the event of our two deaths" in a joint will was held, in the circumstances, to mean in the event of their simultaneous deaths.[65] A will conditional on simultaneous deaths operates if, in the ordinary understanding of that phrase, death occurred at virtually the same time.[66]

Phrases not importing a condition into the will

Wills containing the following phrases were held to be unconditional: (where a testator was about to make a voyage) "Therefore as I may easily die, I think it my duty to inform you what you have to do with my property in case I should die."[67] "All men are mortal and no one knows how soon his life may be required of him. Lest I die before the next sun I make this my last will."[68] "In the prospect of a long journey, should God not permit me to return home, I make this my last will."[69] "In the event of my death while serving in this horrid climate, or any accident happening to me, I leave . . . I consider that every person should be prepared for the worst and particularly in such a treacherous climate as this . . . which has compelled me to write this."[70] "In case of any fatal accident happening to me, being about to travel by railway. . . . ."[71] In a soldier's will: "The chances are in favour of more of us being killed, and, as I may not have another opportunity of saying what I wish to be done . . . in case of an accident I wish to make over everything I possess to you."[72] In a soldier's will: "If I do buy it, you must see that the few quids I have at Holts go to J.S."[73] "As

---

[59] *Re Winn* (1861) 2 Sw. & Tr. 147; see *Roberts* v. *Roberts* (1862) 2 Sw. & Tr. 337.
[60] *Re Porter, supra.*
[61] *Re Robinson* (1870) L.R. 2 P. & D. 171. Contrast *Re Martin* (1867) L.R. 1 P. & D. 380; *Re Mayd* (1880) 6 P.D. 17.
[62] *Lindsay* v. *Lindsay* (1872) L.R. 2 P. & D. 459.
[63] *Re Hugo* (1877) 2 P.D. 73.
[64] *Jobson* v. *Ross* (1873) 42 L.J.P. & M. 58. Contrast *Re Vines* [1910] P. 147.
[65] *Re Govier* [1950] P. 237.
[66] *Re Pringle* [1946] Ch. 124, but see *Re Rowland* [1963] 1 Ch. 1.
[67] *Strauss* v. *Schmidt* (1820) 3 Phill. 209.
[68] *Burton* v. *Collingwood* (1832) 4 Hagg.Ecc. 176.
[69] *Re Cawthron* (1863) 3 Sw. & Tr. 417.
[70] *Re Thorne* (1865) 4 Sw. & Tr. 36; see *Re Spratt* [1897] P. 28, 32.
[71] *Re Dobson* (1866) L.R. 1 P. & D. 88.
[72] *Re Spratt, supra.*
[73] *Winter* v. *Pawle* (1918) 34 T.L.R. 437.

I am about to leave home for Bangor, should any accident, etc., take me
out of this world. . . . "[74]

Criteria in deciding whether a will is conditional

Sir F. H. Jeune in the case of *Re Spratt*[75] said[76]: "But if it be not clear
whether the words used import a reason for making a will or impress a conditional character on it, the whole language of the document and also the
surrounding circumstances[77] must be considered.[78] In such cases there are
two criteria which are especially useful for determining the problem: first,
whether the nature of the disposition made appears to have relation to the
time or circumstances of the contingency; and, secondly, where the contingency is connected with a period of danger to the testator, whether it is
coincident with that period, because, if it is, there is ground to suppose that
the danger was regarded by the testator only as a reason for making a will,
but, if it is not, it is difficult to see the object of referring to a particular
period, unless it be to limit the operation of the will."

A will is not contingent unless it is clear that the testator intended that it
should only operate in a certain event or during a certain period.[79] Nor will
the court allow an impossible condition to limit the will.[80]

Where a contingency has failed, the will must be re-executed to give it
effect. Even the revocation clause is inoperative.[81] But a codicil, in other
respects contingent on an event which has not happened, may, it seems,
revive a will to which it refers, or render that will operative if it has not
been duly executed.[82]

In deciding whether the will is contingent the court cannot take into
account declarations made by the testator after the failure of the contingency which express adherence to the will, unless the language of the
will is ambiguous.[83]

A will may be conditional on the assent of some person to its provisions,
and, if that assent is withheld, the instrument is not entitled to probate.[84]

A will intended to take effect as the exercise of a power of appointment
is not necessarily contingent on the existence of the power. So, if it turns
out that the power was either not well created or was defeated by the hap-

[74] *Re Stuart* (1888) 21 L.R.Ir. 105.
[75] [1897] P. 28.
[76] At p. 29.
[77] *Re Govier* [1950] P. 237; see *Re Thomas* [1939] 2 All E.R. 567.
[78] In the following cases dealing with death on a voyage or journey the language was held to
be unclear and the wills to be unconditional: *Re Martin* (1867) L.R. 1 P. & D. 380; *Re Mayd*
(1880) 6 P.D. 17, compare *Re Vines* [1910] P. 147; *Halford* v. *Halford* [1897] P. 36.
[79] *Re Dobson* (1866) L.R. 1 P. & D. 88; see *Re Winn* (1861) 2 Sw. & Tr. 147; *Roberts* v.
Roberts (1862) 2 Sw. & Tr. 337, 339.
[80] *Bunbury* v. *Doran* (1873) Ir.R. 8 C.L. 516; (1875) Ir.R. 9 C.L. 284, Ex.Ch.
[81] *Roberts* v. *Roberts, supra*; *Parsons* v. *Lanoe* (1748) 1 Ves.Sen. 189; *Re Winn, supra*; *Burton* v. *Collingwood* (1832) 4 Hagg.Ecc. 176; see *Re Cawthron* (1863) 3 Sw. & Tr. 417. As to
the revocation clause, see *Re Hugo* (1877) 2 P.D. 73.
[82] *Re Mendes Da Silva* (1861) 2 Sw. & Tr. 315.
[83] *Re Vines, supra*.
[84] *Re Smith* (1869) L.R. 1 P. & D. 717.

pening of some contingent event after the will, the disposition will not fail if the testator had a bequeathable interest in the property independent of the power.[85]

Practice

Probate will be granted at once (it seems) when, on the death of the testator, the event on the happening of which the will is contingent is still in suspense, but such probate operates subject to the happening of the event and only enables the estate to be administered in the meantime.[86]

Affidavit evidence is required as to the fulfilment or otherwise of the condition, unless it is obviously inoperative. All wills which may be conditional must be shown to the registrar for his directions.

A conditional document, though not submitted for probate, must be filed with the oath and other documents. Consideration must be given to possible revival or incorporation by a conditional will.[87]

D. JOINT AND MUTUAL WILLS

Joint wills

A joint will is a single instrument whereby two or more persons give effect to their testamentary dispositions. If the will is duly executed by the testators it is as much the will of each of them as if they had made separate wills each dealing with that person's own property.[88] Such a will is revocable at any time by any of the testators during their joint lives, and by the survivor after the death of one of them[89]; but if it is not altered or revoked, it will take effect as the will of the survivor.[90] A joint will may operate a power of appointment.[91]

Mutual wills

A mutual will is one of two testamentary papers made respectively by two persons, each giving the other rights in his property as identical as they can be, for the purpose of carrying out the intention of the two testators.[92]

But although mutual wills are revocable,[93] they may amount to a compact in equity. There may thus be a breach of contract and of trust[94] where two persons have made an arrangement or agreement as to the disposal of

---

[85] *Southall* v. *Jones* (1858) 1 Sw. & Tr. 298; *Sing* v. *Leslie* (1864) 2 H. & M. 68.

[86] *Re Cooper* (1855) Dea. & Sw. 9; *Re Bangham* (1876) 1 P.D. 429.

[87] *Registrar's Direction*, March 10, 1941.

[88] See *Re Stracey* (1855) Dea. & Sw. 6; *Re Piazzi-Smyth* [1898] P. 7.

[89] *Hobson* v. *Blackburn and Blackburn* (1822) 1 Add. 274.

[90] *Re Lovegrove* (1862) 2 Sw. & Tr. 453; *Re Fletcher* (1883) 11 L.R.Ir. 359.

[91] *Re Duddell* [1932] 1 Ch. 585.

[92] See, generally, article by R. Burgess (1970) 34 Conv.(N.S.) 230. Also "Relative of the Secret Trust" 1988 (May 20) N.L.:J. 351.

[93] See *Re Heys* [1914] P. 192; *Hobson* v. *Blackburn* (1822) 1 Add. 274.

[94] See 1988 N.L.J. 351 (May 20).

their property and have executed mutual wills in pursuance of that agreement and then, after the death of the first to die, the survivor has revoked
that will.[95]

But the mere fact that, *e.g.* spouses happen each to have left the other all
their property does not form the basis of a compact, for though the wills
are mutual they must be shown to have been made as the result of an
agreement or arrangement.[96]

Even if the wills are made as the result of an agreement there is no compact in equity if one testator revokes his will in the lifetime of the other and
so informs him; for that other testator can then revoke his will if he
wishes.[97] Similarly there is no breach of contract where the will of the survivor is revoked by operation of law, for example by re-marriage.[98]

Where there is a compact in equity the personal representatives of the
surviving testator will be directed under the Chancery jurisdiction to hold
the estate on the trusts of the revoked will.[99]

But no directions will be given under the probate jurisdiction to the personal representative of the surviving testator so to hold the estate; for such
a matter is one for determination by the court of construction.[1]

Where two testatrices made mutual wills in favour of their two sisters
and directed that the will should not be proved until after the death of the
two sisters, the will of the first testatrix to die was then, on her death,
admitted to proof omitting the direction.[2]

Joint and mutual wills

Joint and mutual wills are mutual wills in the form of a single instrument.
They are governed by the same principles as apply to joint wills and to
mutual wills.

Practice

A joint will disposing of property jointly owned by the testators is normally proved on the death of the survivor, unless there is some special
reason for obtaining a grant on the death of the first to die. But in ordinary
cases the will is proved as his will on the death of the first to die. It has been
held that a will providing that it should take effect on the death of both tes-

---

[95] *Dufour v. Pereira* (1769) 1 Dick. 419; *Walpole v. Lord Orford* (1797) 3 Ves. 402; *Gray v. Perpetual Trustee* [1928] A.C. 391. See also article by J. D. B. Mitchell (1951) 14 M.L.R. 136; *Re Cleaver* [1981] 1 W.L.R. 939; (1980) Cmnd. 1902; 1980 *Conveyancer* 64, 101.

[96] The wills themselves may give clear indication of a contract, *Re Green* [1951] Ch. 148. But see *Re Oldham* [1925] Ch. 75 and *Vine v. Joyce* [1963] C.L.Y. 3627.

[97] *Stone v. Hoskins* [1905] P. 194.

[98] *Re Marsland* [1939] Ch. 820.

[99] Under such trusts a legatee may take a vested interest which does not lapse if he predeceases the surviving testator: *Re Hagger* [1930] 2 Ch. 190. And see *Jarman on Wills*, 8th
ed., pp. 41–42.

[1] *Re Heys, supra.* See 34 *Conveyancer* 230.

[2] *Re O'Connor* [1942] 1 All E.R. 546.

tators could not be proved until both were dead,[3] but later cases indicate that this is not correct.[4]

Unless the joint will affects property jointly owned, it is proved a second time on the death of the last testator to die.

Where a joint will is proved on the death of the first testator to die, the date of birth of the other testator must be supplied to the registry. On the death of the survivor the grant must be obtained at the registry where the grant to the other testator's estate was obtained.[5] If an affidavit of due execution is required on the first death, it should establish due execution by both testators.[6]

It is not clear whether the surviving testator's re-marriage will revoke a mutual will. The obligation not to revoke may apply only to the testator's own actions and not to the operation of statute law.[7]

---

[3] *Re Raine* (1858) 1 Sw. & Tr. 144.
[4] *Re Piazzi-Smyth* [1898] P. 7; *Re Heys* [1914] P. 192; *Re Hack* (1930) 169 L.T.J. 285.
[5] Secretary's Circular, August 10, 1962.
[6] *Ibid.*
[7] See *Re Marsland* [1939] Ch. 820 and 1980 Cmnd. 7902.

CHAPTER 12

THE FORMAL VALIDITY OF WILLS

The formal validity of a will depends upon compliance with certain statutory requirements whereas substantial validity depends upon matters such as capacity,[1] knowledge and approval,[2] undue influence, fraud and forgery.[3]

A will need not be in legal language or in any particular form. Any duly executed document is entitled to operate as a will and to be admitted to probate, provided that the person executing it intended that it should not take effect until after his death, and that it is dependent on death for its vigour and effect.[4]

Extrinsic evidence

If the document itself is equivocal or silent, it may be proved by extrinsic circumstances to have been intended to operate as a testamentary disposition[5]; for evidence to show the intention (*quo intuitu*) with which a paper was executed has always been received in the court of probate.[6] The court may admit parol evidence[7] if the language of the paper is insufficient.[8] The onus of proving that a document is a will lies on those who set it up where on the face of it there is no testamentary import.[9] But if a document is executed in accordance with the Wills Act 1837, the presumption is that it is intended to be testamentary.[10]

In numerous cases documents not testamentary in form have been admitted to probate, on proof of due execution, where the evidence showed that they were intended to operate as wills. Among the documents admitted have been instructions for a will,[11] orders on bankers (including

---

[1] See p. 158, *post.*
[2] See p. 170, *post.*
[3] See p. 183, *post.*
[4] *Cock* v. *Cooke* (1866) L.R. 1 P. & D. 241; *Robertson* v. *Smith* (1870) L.R. 2 P. & D. 43, 45; *Re Coles* (1871) L.R. 2 P. & D. 362. As to nominations under pension and insurance schemes see *ante*, p. 111.
[5] *King's Proctor* v. *Daines* (1830) 3 Hagg.Ecc. 218, 221.
[6] *Jones* v. *Nicolay* (1850) 2 Rob. 288, 292.
[7] *Re English* (1864) 3 Sw. & Tr. 586; *Cock* v. *Cooke, supra.*
[8] *Robertson* v. *Smith, supra*; *Re Slinn* (1890) 15 P.D. 156, 158.
[9] *King's Proctor* v. *Daines, supra*; see *Whyte* v. *Pollock* (1882) 7 App.Cas. 400, 406.
[10] *Re Meynell* [1949] W.N. 273; *Re Berger* [1990] Ch. 118, C.A.
[11] *Torre* v. *Castle* (1836) 1 Curt. 303; *Bone and Newsam* v. *Spear* (1811) 1 Phill. 345; *Hattatt* v. *Hattatt* (1832) 4 Hagg.Ecc. 211; *Barwick* v. *Mullings* (1829) 2 Hagg.Ecc. 225; *Re Fisher* (1869) 20 L.T. 684; *White* v. *Pollock, supra*; see *Burton* v. *Collingwood* (1832) 4 Hagg.Ecc. 176; *Re Slinn* (1890) 15 P.D. 156; *Re Meynell, supra.* Probate was refused in *Matthews* v. *Warner* (1798) 4 Ves. 186; *Rymes* v. *Clarkson* (1809) 1 Phill. 22; *Blewitt* v. *Blewitt* (1833) 4

savings banks),[12] cheques,[13] letters,[14] promissory notes,[15] receipts for stock and bills endorsed,[16] endorsed bonds,[17] documents making gifts,[18] deeds[19] and nominations.[20] Packets directed to be given unopened to named persons were, in one case,[21] ordered to be opened in the presence of a registrar and, on being found to contain bank notes, a schedule was made which was ordered to be added as a codicil to the will.

DOCUMENTS NOT INTENDED AS WILLS MAY BE SUCH

In addition to the cases where papers were intended by their makers to operate as wills there may be documents disposing of a deceased's estate only after his death which are not intended to be testamentary. Such documents may, however, be operative as wills if they have been duly executed.[22] As Sir John Nicholl said in *King's Proctor* v. *Daines*[23]:

> "If there is any proof either in the paper itself or from clear evidence dehors, first, that it was the intention of the writer of the paper to convey the benefits by the instrument which would be conveyed by it, if considered as a will; and, secondly, that death was the event that was to give effect to it, then, whatever be its form, it may be admitted to probate as testamentary."

But no case has gone the length of deciding that because an instrument cannot operate in the form given to it, it must operate as a will.

An instrument coming into operation immediately, especially if it involves anything in the nature of consideration, cannot operate as a will.[24]

Hagg.Ecc. 4101; *Elsden* v. *Elsden* (1832) 4 Hagg.Ecc. 183; *Gillow* v. *Bourne* (1831) 4 Hagg. Ecc. 192; *Bragge* v. *Dyer* (1830) 3 Hagg.Ecc. 207; *Coventry* v. *Williams* (1844) 3 Curt. 787; see *Re Pascall* (1868) L.R. 1 P. & D. 606; *Boughton-Knight* v. *Wilson* (1915) 32 T.L.R. 146; see the review of these cases in *Godman* v. *Godman* [1920] P. 261, C.A. at 281 *et seq.*

[12] *Jones* v. *Nicolay*, *supra*; *Re Marsden* (1860) 1 Sw. & Tr. 542; *Cock* v. *Cooke*, *supra*.

[13] *Bartholomew and Brown* v. *Henley* (1820) 3 Phill. 317; *Sotheran* v. *Dening* (1881) 20 Ch.D. 99, C.A.

[14] *Re Mundy* (1860) 2 Sw. & Tr. 119; *Towers* v. *Hogan* (1889) 23 L.R.Ir. 53; see *Drybutter* v. *Hodges* (1793) cited in 2 Hagg.Ecc. 247; *Passmore* v. *Passmore* (1811) 1 Phill. 216; *Denny* v. *Barton and Rashleigh* (1818) 2 Phill. 575.

[15] *Gough* v. *Findon* (1851) 7 Ex. 48; see *Maxee* v. *Shute* (1799) cited 2 Hagg.Ecc. 247.

[16] *Sabine* v. *Goate* (1782) citd 2 Hagg.Ecc. 247.

[17] *Musgrave* v. *Down* (1784) cited 2 Hagg.Ecc. 247.

[18] *Robertson* v. *Smith* (1870) L.R. 2 P. & D. 43; *Re Slinn* (1890) 15 P.D. 156; *Re Coles* (1871) L.R. 2 P. & D. 362; *Cock* v. *Cooke* (1866) L.R. 1 P. & D. 241.

[19] *Hixon* v. *Whytham* (1675) 1 Ch.Cas. 248; *Green* v. *Proude* (1674) 1 Mod. 117; *Re Slinn*, *supra*; *Habergham* v. *Vincent* (1793) 2 Ves.Jun. 204; *Peacock* v. *Monk* (1748) 1 Ves.Sen. 127; *Masterman* v. *Maberley* (1829) 2 Hagg.Ecc. 235; *Emley* v. *Davidson* (1881) 45 L.T. 418; *Re Morgan* (1866) L.R. 1 P. & D. 214; *Fielding* v. *Walshaw* (1879) 27 W.R. 492; *Re Colyer* (1889) 14 P.D. 48; *Re Cosnahan* (1866) L.R. 1 P. & D. 183; *Doe* d. *Cross* v. *Cross* (1846) 8 Q.B. 714; *Re Anziani* [1930] 1 Ch. 407.

[20] *Re Baxter* [1903] P. 12; *Re Barnes* [1940] Ch. 267.

[21] *Pelham* v. *Newton* (1754) 2 Lec. 46.

[22] *Masterman* v. *Maberley* (1829) 2 Hagg.Ecc. 235; see also the cases at n. 19, *supra*, from *Habergham* v. *Vincent* onwards.

[23] (1830) 3 Hagg.Ecc. 218, 221.

[24] *Re Robinson* (1867) L.R. 1 P. & D. 384; see *Jeffries* v. *Alexander* (1860) 8 H.L.C. 594.

On the other hand if a deed or document is in part clearly testamentary it seems that such part may take effect as a will, though other parts are not testamentary.[25]

If an instrument is not testamentary either in form or substance and if the operation thereof is not postponed until the death of the maker, and if no extrinsic evidence is adduced to prove that it was intended to operate as a will, probate will not be granted.[26]

DOCUMENTS APPARENTLY INTENDED AS WILLS MAY NOT BE SUCH

However clearly a paper may appear to be testamentary on the face of it, it will not be admitted to probate if extrinsic evidence proves that it was not made *animo testandi*, *e.g.* a will made in jest[27] or a sham will,[28] or a will executed by mistake.[29] But the evidence to prove that an apparently valid will is not so must be cogent and conclusive.[30]

If the testator intended the paper to be testamentary the court cannot look to its effect or the testator's intention as to the effect he wished it to have.[31] But if the testator expressly says on a paper that it is not to operate as a will it is not valid as such.[32]

Burden of proof

Where the paper is not clearly testamentary on the face of it, the burden of proving that it was intended as a will is on those who propound it.[33] But unimportant ambiguities cannot overthrow a paper the legal character and effect of which is clear, even if they justify inquiry.[34] Even serious defects in a will, *e.g.* that it makes a gift to named persons but does not state what is being given do not necessarily preclude the document from having testamentary effect.[35]

[25] *Re Robinson, supra*; *Doe* d. *Cross* (1846) 8 Q.B. 714; *Re Anziani* [1930] 1 Ch. 407, 424.
[26] *King's Proctor* v. *Daines, supra*; see *Glynn* v. *Oglander* (1829) 2 Hagg.Ecc. 428; *Shingler* v. *Pemberton* (1832) 4 Hagg.Ecc. 356; *Griffin and Amos* v. *Ferard* (1835) 1 Curt. 97; *Marjoribanks* v. *Hovenden* (1843) Dru.*t*.Sug. 11, 27; *Langley* v. *Thomas* (1857) 26 L.J.Ch. 609; *Hodson* v. *Barnes* (1926) 43 T.L.R. 71 ("will" on an egg-shell).
[27] *Nichols* v. *Nichols* (1814) 2 Phill. 180.
[28] *Lister* v. *Smith* (1863) 3 Sw. & Tr. 282.
[29] *Re Hunt* (1875) L.R. 3 P. & D. 250; *Re Meyer* [1908] P. 353.
[30] *King's Proctor* v. *Daines, supra*; see *Re Meynell* [1949] W.N. 273. A nomination is not normally intended to operate as a will. See *Re Danish Bacon Co.* [1971] 1 W.L.R. 248. *Baird* v. *Baird* [1990] 2 A.C. 548.
[31] *King's Proctor* v. *Daines* (1830) 3 Hagg.Ecc. 218; see *Beech* v. *Public Trustee* [1923] P. 46.
[32] *Ferguson-Davie* v. *Ferguson-Davie* (1890) 15 P.D. 109.
[33] *Thorncroft and Clarke* v. *Lashmar* (1862) 2 Sw. & Tr. 479, 484; *King's Proctor* v. *Daines, supra*.
[34] *Whyte* v. *Pollock* (1882) 7 App.Cas. 400.
[35] *Re Stevens* [1952] Ch. 323; see *Re Messenger's Estate* [1937] 1 All E.R. 355.

Practice

Where any unorthodox document is lodged for probate, affidavit evidence that it was intended as a will is, in many cases, essential, *e.g.* where an executed draft is being set up as the actual will.[36]

The Wills Act 1837

Formal validity depends upon compliance with section 9 of the Wills Act 1837. This section was amended by the Wills Act Amendment Act 1852 and more recently by the Administration of Justice Act 1982.[37]

For deaths on or after January 1, 1983 the provisions are as follows:

"**9. Signing and attestation of wills.** No will shall be valid unless—

(a) it is in writing and signed by the testator, or by some other person in his presence and by his direction; and

(b) it appears that the testator intended by his signature to give effect to the will; and

(c) the signature is made or acknowledged by the testator in the presence of two or more witnesses present at the same time; and

(d) each witness either—

(i) attests and signs the will; or

(ii) acknowledges his signature in the presence of the testator (but not necessarily in the presence of any other witness),

but no form of attestation shall be necessary."

For deaths before January 1, 1983 the provisions under the Wills Act 1837 as amended by the Wills Act Amendment Act 1852 are as follows:

"**9.** No will[38] shall be valid unless it shall be in writing and executed in manner hereinafter mentioned; (that is to say;) it shall be signed at the foot or end thereof by the testator, or by some other person in his presence and by his direction, and such signature shall be made or acknowledged by the testator in the presence of two or more witnesses present at the same time, and such witnesses shall attest and shall subscribe the will in the presence of the testator, but no form of attestation shall be necessary."[39]

Thus for deaths on or after January 1, 1983 it is not necessary that the

---

[36] See *Re Meynell* [1949] W.N. 273; *Re Berger* [1990] Ch. 118.

[37] Administration of Justice Act 1982, s.17.

[38] "Will" includes testament, codicil, an appointment by will in exercise of a power and any other testamentary disposition: Wills Act 1837, s.1.

[39] A survey conducted by the Principal Registry of all wills submitted to probate in England and Wales between September 4, 1978, and December 1, 1978, revealed that 0.123 per cent. were rejected for failure to comply with s.9. The Law Reform Committee rejected the suggestion that the court be given a dispensing power to admit a will to probate despite a formal defect under s.9. See Cmnd. 7902, 1980.

testator's signature should be "at the foot or end" of the will, but rather that the testator "intended by his signature to give effect to the will."[40]

By section 13 of the Wills Act 1837 "Every will executed in manner here-inbefore required shall be valid without any other publication thereof."

The question whether or not the Wills Act has been complied with is not subject to any presumptions,[41] but there is a presumption that a signature appearing after that of a testator is the signature of a witness to the will.[42]

A will must be in writing

The first provision of section 9 is "No will shall be valid unless it shall be in writing."

This is construed, unless the contrary intention appears, as including references to typing, printing, lithography, photography, and other modes of representing or reproducing words in a visible form.[43]

A will may be written wholly or partly in pencil[44] or in shorthand.[45] It may be written in any language.[46]

The testator's signature

Section 9 of the Act further provides that the will must be signed by the testator, or by some other person in his presence and by his direction.

The words "Your loving Mother" have been held to be a valid signature.[47] A testator's initials have been held to be his signature.[48] A signature uncompleted because of the testator's weakness has been held sufficient where the completed part was intended to be his signature.[49] To constitute a signature, the name should be put on the paper with the purpose of authenticating the document. Thus where a testator wrote his own name as part of the heading to a holograph will, this constituted a signature.[50]

A mark.   It is a sufficient signing if a testator put his mark on his will, even though he could write[51] and even where his hand is guided.[52] It is

---

[40] This change to s.9 of the Wills Act 1837, as itself altered by the Wills Act Amendment Act 1852 (*infra*), followed the recommendations of the Law Reform Committee. See Cmnd. 7902, 1980.

[41] See *per* Russell L.J. in *Re Bravda* [1968] 1 W.L.R. 479, 490H. See further pp. 146 *et seq.*, *post*.

[42] See *per* Salmon L.J. in *Re Bravda* [1968] 1 W.L.R. 479, 492H.

[43] Interpretation Act 1978, s.5 and Sched. 1.

[44] *Rymes* v. *Clarkson* (1809) 1 Phill. 22, 35.

[45] *Orin* v. *Orin, The Times*, December 20, 1921.

[46] *Whiting* v. *Turner* (1903) 89 L.T. 71; see *Reynolds* v. *Kortright* (1854) 18 Beav. 417.

[47] *Re Cook* [1960] 1 W.L.R. 353.

[48] *Re Savory* (1851) 15 Jur. 1042; see *Re Christian* (1849) 2 Rob. 110; *Re Blewitt* (1880) 5 P.D. 116.

[49] *Re Chalcraft* 1948] P. 222; compare *Re Colling* [1972] 1 W.L.R. 1440.

[50] *Wood* v. *Smith* [1991] 2 All E.R. 939 and on appeal, [1992] 3 W.L.R. 583, (C.A.). *cf. Re Young* [1969] N.Z.L.R. 454.

[51] *Baker* v. *Dening* (1838) 8 A. & E. 94; *Re Field* (1843) 3 Curt. 752.

[52] *Wilson* v. *Beddard* (1841) 12 Sim. 28 (although this was a case in which the will was treated as signed at the testator's direction).

immaterial that the testator's name is not put against the mark, even though the name does not appear anywhere on the face of the will[53]; or even though a wrong name is written against the mark by another person.[54] But probate will not be granted where there is no evidence, or only highly suspicious evidence, to identify the person affixing the mark with the testator.[55]

Wrong name.   If a testator, intentionally or unintentionally, signs under a wrong or assumed name, provided he signs *animo testandi*, that is a sufficient signature, for the name so written may stand as the mark of the testator.[56]

Sealing.   Signature by a seal with the testator's initials[57] or a stamp with his name[58] have been held sufficient and probably sealing with a plain seal would suffice.[59] In these cases it would be necessary to show that the testator intended to make his signature. A thumb print has been accepted as a signature,[60] as has an undecipherable scrawl.[61]

Signature for the testator by another.   The section provides that the will may be signed by some other person in the presence of the testator and by his direction. Such person may be (*inter alios*) an attesting witness[62] or the person who drew the will.[63] There is good signature if the person signing for the testator signs in his own name.[64] A mark, whether a cross or facsimile name, is enough,[65] but not a name pencilled in beforehand.[66]

When the will is signed by a third party in the presence of the testator and of the attesting witnesses, the testator must, by act or word, in some way indicate to the two attesting witnesses that the signature was placed there at his request. If a previous positive direction had been given to the agent to sign the will the testator need not repeat it, but he must do something to show that he understood at the time that the other party was signing for him.[67] Affirmative evidence that a signature made by another was

---

[53] *Re Bryce* (1839) 2 Curt. 325.
[54] *Re Clark* (1859) 1 Sw. & Tr. 460; *Re Douce* (1862) 2 Sw. & Tr. 593.
[55] *Edmonds* v. *Lewer* (1865) 11 Jur.(N.S.) 911.
[56] *Re Redding* (1850) 2 Rob. 339; *Re Glover* (1847) 11 Jur. 1022.
[57] *Re Emerson* (1882) 9 L.R.Ir. 443.
[58] *Jenkins* v. *Gaisford* (1863) 3 Sw. & Tr. 93.
[59] *Ibid.*
[60] *Re Finn* (1935) 154 L.T. 242.
[61] *Re Kieran* [1933] Ir.R. 222.
[62] *Re Bailey* (1838) 1 Curt. 914; *Smith* v. *Harris* (1845) 1 Rob. 262.
[63] *Re Elcock* (1869) 20 L.T. 757.
[64] *Re Clark* (1839) 2 Curt. 329; *Re Blair* (1848) 6 N.C. 528.
[65] *Jenkins* v. *Gaisford* (1863) 3 Sw. & Tr. 93.
[66] *Reeves* v. *Grainger* (1908) 52 S.J. 355.
[67] *Re Marshall* (1866) 13 L.T. 643; see *Re Summers* (1850) 2 Rob. 295; *Morritt* v. *Douglas* (1872) L.R. 3 P. & D. 1.

made in the testator's presence and by his direction is not essential.[68] The cases relating to the presence of witnesses[69] apply to the presence of the testator where a will is signed for him.

Time when signature made

Although the strict requirements as to the place of the testator's signature have now been relaxed, it is still essential that the signature be placed on the paper after the testamentary dispositions have been put there, unless the appending of the signature and writing of the will were all part of one operation.[70]

Position of the testator's signature

Although it is no longer necessary that the testator's signature should be "at the foot or end" of the will where the death has occurred on or after January 1, 1983, there will still be cases where wills of testators dying before that date fall to be proved also. Some of the case law could be relevant to the requirement that "the testator intended by his signature to give effect to the will." The material covering the position of the testator's signature is not therefore deleted in this edition.

The will had to be signed "at the foot or end thereof." This provision was narrowly construed in early cases and caused extensive injustice. To remedy this the Wills Act Amendment Act 1852 provided by section 1:

" . . . every will shall, so far only as regards the position of the signature of the testator, or of the person signing for him as aforesaid, be deemed to be valid . . . if the signature shall be so placed at or after, or following, or under,[71] or beside,[72] or opposite[73] to the end of the will, that it shall be apparent on the face of the will that the testator intended to give effect by such his signature to the writing signed as his will,[74] and no such will shall be affected by the circumstance that the signature shall not follow or be immediately after the foot or end of the will,[75] or by the circumstance that a blank space shall intervene between the concluding word of the will and the signature,[76] or by the

---

[68] *Gaze* v. *Gaze* (1843) 3 Curt. 451.

[69] See *post*, p. 141.

[70] *Wood* v. *Smith*, *The Times*, March 4, 1992, approving dicta in *Re, White* [1991] Ch. 1. See also [1983] *Conveyancer* 21.

[71] *Re Woodley* (1864) 3 Sw. & Tr. 429; *Re Powell* (1865) 4 Sw. & Tr. 34.

[72] *Re Jones* (1865) 4 Sw. & Tr. 1; *Re Wright* (1865) 4 Sw. & Tr. 35; *Re Coombs* (1866) L.R. 1 P. & D. 302; *Re Ainsworth* (1870) L.R. 2 P. & D. 151; *Re Usborne* (1909) 25 T.L.R. 519; *Re Roberts* [1934] P. 102; *Re Hornby* [1946] P. 171.

[73] *Re Williams* (1865) L.R. 1 P. & D. 4; *Re Hughes* (1887) 12 P.D. 107; *Royle* v. *Harris* [1895] P. 163.

[74] *Re Beadle* [1974] 1 W.L.R. 417.

[75] *Page* v. *Donovan and Hankey* (1857) Dea. & Sw. 278 (a notarial minute interposed).

[76] See n. 80.

circumstance that the signature shall be placed among the words of the testimonium clause,[77] or of the clause of attestation,[78] or shall follow, or be after or under the clause of attestation, either with or without a blank space intervening, or shall follow or be after or under, or beside the names or one of the names of the subscribing witnesses,[79] or by the circumstance that the signature shall be on a side or page or other portion of the paper or papers containing the will whereon no clause or paragraph or disposing part of the will shall be written above the signature, or by the circumstance that there shall appear to be sufficient space on or at the bottom of the preceding side or page or other portion of the same paper on which the will is written to contain the signature[80]; and the enumeration of the above circumstances shall not restrict the generality of the above enactment[81]; but no signature . . . shall be operative to give effect to any disposition or direction which is underneath or which follows it,[82] nor shall it give effect to any disposition or direction inserted after the signature shall be made."[83]

Section 2 covered wills made before the amending Act and section 3 gave the word "will" the same meaning as in section 1 of the Wills Act 1837.[84]

Where words followed the testator's signature[85] but were not brought into the will in one of the ways set out above, they could not be included in the probate though written with testamentary intention before the execution of the will.[86]

The court might admit to proof all that was written above the signature of the testator and reject what was written below, but only if satisfied that such signature was intended to give effect to the words preceding the signa-

---

[77] *Re Mann* (1858) 28 L.J.P. 19; *Trott* v. *Skidmore* (1860) 2 Sw. & Tr. 12; see *Winsor* v. *Pratt* (1821) 5 J.B.Moore 484.
[78] *Re Walker* (1862) 2 Sw. & Tr. 354; *Re Huckvale* (1867) L.R. 1 P. & D. 375; *Re Casmore* (1869) L.R. 1 P. & D. 653; *Re Pearn* (1875) 1 P.D. 70; *Re Harris* (1875) 23 W.R. 734.
[79] *Re Puddephat* (1870) L.R. 2 P. & D. 97; *Re Jones* (1877) 46 L.J.P. 80; *Re Horsford* (1874) L.R. 3 P. & D. 211.
[80] *Re Wright* (1865) 4 Sw. & Tr. 35; *Re Williams* (1865) L.R. 1 P. & D. 4; *Hunt* v. *Hunt* (1866) L.R. 1 P. & D. 209; *Re Coombs* (1866) L.R. 1 P. & D. 302; *Re Fuller* [1892] P. 377; *Millward* v. *Buswell* (1904) 20 T.L.R. 714; *Re Moore* [1901] P. 44.
[81] Signature at the back: *Re Hammond* (1863) 3 Sw. & Tr. 90; *Re Archer* (1871) L.R. 2 P. & D. 252. Signature on a separate sheet: *Re Gausden* (1862) 2 Sw. & Tr. 362; *Cook* v. *Lambert* (1863) 3 Sw. & Tr. 46; *Re Horsford, supra; Lewis* v. *Lewis* [1908] P. 1; *Foster* v. *Cooper* [1960] 1 W.L.R. 495. Will in envelope: *Re Lambert* (1862) 31 L.J.P. 118; *Re West* (1863) 32 L.J.P. 273; *Re Nicholls* [1921] 2 Ch. 11; *Re Mann* [1942] P. 146; *Re Bean* [1944] P. 83; *Re Beadle* [1974] 1 W.L.R. 417: see *Re Davis* [1952] P. 279. Signature at the top: *Re Stalman* (1931) 145 L.T. 339, C.A.; *Re Harris: Murray* v. *Everard* [1952] P. 319; *Re Bercovitz* [1962] 1 W.L.R. 321; *Re Beadle, supra* (in which cases the wills were held invalid).
[82] See *post,* p. 138.
[83] *Re Arthur* (1871) L.R. 2 P. & D. 273.
[84] See *ante,* p. 133, n. 38.
[85] The signature must have been intended to give testamentary effect to the document. See *ante,* n. 75 and text thereto.
[86] *In the Goods of Evans* (1923) 128 L.T. 669 and see *post.*

ture as the testator's will[87] and not merely to authenticate them.[88] It would not take this course where to do so would defeat the testator's intention and make nonsense of his testamentary dispositions.[89]

Where a will was written on several sheets only the last needed to be executed. So where the attesting witnesses to a will of this type only observed the last sheet, there was a presumption of due execution.[90] This rule did not extend to a series of separate and independent documents.[91] In cases where a will consisted of separate sheets these had to be attached at the time of execution, but the attachment might consist of as little as the holding of the sheets between finger and thumb[92] or a pressing on them by the thumb.[93]

Sheets found after the death of the testator bound together were presumed to have been so bound at the time of execution, even though the numbering of the sheets was not consecutive.[94] In an Irish case[95] it was held that if a will was written on several disconnected sheets and only the last was executed, the presumption was that the whole will was in the room and under the control of the testator at the time of execution and ought to be admitted to probate.

Where a will was in several sheets, any signatures by the testator and the witnesses on earlier sheets were, prima facie, to be regarded as in authentication (to guard against interpolation) and not in execution.[96] But where a will had been duly executed and there followed additions, duly executed at the end of them, the presumption was that all the dispositions are valid.[97]

Where, from the obvious sequence and sense of the context, it appeared to the satisfaction of the court that the signature of the deceased really followed the dispositive part of the will, though it occupied a place on the paper literally above or before the dispositive part or parts thereof, such part or parts might be admitted to proof.[98]

---

[87] *Re Anstee* [1893] P. 283; *Royle* v. *Harris* [1895] P. 163; *Millward* v. *Buswell* (1904) 20 T.L.R. 714; see *Re Gee* (1898) 78 L.T. 843.

[88] *Sweetland* v. *Sweetland* (1865) 4 Sw. & Tr. 6; *Phipps* v. *Hale* (1874) L.R. 3 P. & D. 166; *Re Dilkes* (1874) L.R. 3 P. & D. 164; *Margary* v. *Robinson* (1886) 12 P.D. 8.

[89] *Sweetland* v. *Sweetland, supra*; *Margary* v. *Robinson, supra*.

[90] *Gregory* v. *The Queen's Proctor* (1846) N.C. 620, 639; *Marsh* v. *Marsh* (1860) 1 Sw. & Tr. 528; *Re Little, deceased* [1960] 1 W.L.R. 495.

[91] *Re Pearse* (1867) L.R. 1 P. & D. 382; *Re Hatton* (1881) 6 P.D. 204.

[92] *Lewis* v. *Lewis* [1908] P. 1.

[93] *Re Little, deceased, supra.*

[94] *Rees* v. *Rees* (1873) L.R. 3 P. & D. 84, 86.

[95] *Re Tiernan* [1942] I.R. 572.

[96] *Ewen* v. *Franklin* (1855) Dea. & Sw. 7; *Sweetland* v. *Sweetland* (1865) 4 Sw. & Tr. 6; *Re Dilkes* (1874) L.R. 3 P. & D. 164; *Phipps* v. *Hale* (1874) L.R. 3 P. & D. 166; see *Leonard* v. *Leonard* [1902] P. 243.

[97] *Re Cattrall* (1863) 3 Sw. & Tr. 419.

[98] *Re Kimpton* (1864) 3 Sw. & Tr. 427; *Re Wotton* (1874) L.R. 3 P. & D. 159, distinguished in *Royle* v. *Harris* [1895] P. 163. See also *Re Gilbert* (1898) 78 L.T. 762; *Re Malen* (1885) 54 L.J.P. 91; *Re Stalman* (1931) 145 L.T. 339, C.A.; *Re Roberts* [1934] P. 102 (signature in the margin); *Re Long* [1936] P. 167; *Re Hornby* [1946] P. 171; *Murray* v. *Everard* [1952] P. 319; *Re Bercovitz* [1961] 1 W.L.R. 892; [1962] 1 W.L.R. 321, C.A.; *Gilbert* v. *Heining* (1965) 109 S.J. 112. *Re Smith* [1931] P. 225 has not been followed.

Words which followed the signature of the testator were admitted to proof if they could fairly be regarded as interlineations in the body of the will,[99] or as incorporated by reference therein.[1] It had to be established that what was written after the signature was written before execution and that there were words of reference to bring the clause into the will.[2] The mere fact that the executed part of the will ended with an incomplete sentence was not sufficient to allow the admission of words following the signature of the testator.[3]

Acknowledgment of his signature by the testator

Section 9 of the Wills Act 1837 further provides that his signature must be made "or acknowledged by the testator in the presence of two or more witnesses present at the same time."

Where the will is not signed by the testator or by another on his behalf in the presence of the attesting witnesses, he may acknowledge the previously written signature to such witnesses. For a valid acknowledgment the signature of the testator must have been on the will, the witnesses must have seen the signature or have had the opportunity of seeing it, and some words must have been spoken by the testator or some act done by him (or suffered by him to be spoken or done by another in his presence and on his behalf) as may properly be regarded as an acknowledgment of his signature.

As to the signature, in *Re Gunstan*[4] Jessel M.R. said, quoting *Jarman on Wills*:

" 'There is no sufficient acknowledgment unless the witnesses either saw or might have seen the signature,[5] not even though the testator should expressly declare that the paper to be attested by them is his will'; and I may add in my opinion, it is not sufficient even if the testator were to say 'My signature is inside the paper' unless the witnesses were able to see the signature."[6]

It is immaterial whether the witnesses actually saw the signature or not.[7]

While it is not essential that there should be positive evidence that the testator's signature was on the document before acknowledgment, the court must be satisfied that it was, in fact, there.[8] Where positive evidence

---

[99] *Re Birt* (1871) L.R. 2 P. & D. 214; see *Re White* (1860) 30 L.J.P. 55; *Re Malen, supra; Re Greenwood* [1892] P. 7; *Re Hornby, supra.*

[1] *Re Watkins* (1865) L.R. 1 P. & D. 19; *Re Dallow* (1866) L.R. 1 P. & D. 189; *Palin v. Ponting* [1930] P. 185.

[2] See cases in previous note.

[3] *Re Anstee* [1893] P. 283; *Re Gee* (1898) 78 L.T. 843; *Palin v. Ponting, supra.*

[4] (1882) 7 P.D. 102, 107.

[5] It is sufficient if part of the signature is visible: *Hocking v. Glass* (1961) 105 S.J. 612.

[6] See also *Hudson v. Parker* (1844) 1 Robb.Eccl. 14. See also *Re Groffman* [1969] 1 W.L.R. 733.

[7] *Daintree v. Butcher and Fasulo* (1888) 13 P.D. 102, 103; *Re White* [1991] Ch. 1. See also p. 208, *post.*

[8] *Fischer v. Popham* (1875) L.R. 3 P. & D. 246; *Wright v. Sanderson* (1884) 9 P. D. 149.

is lacking the court must have regard to all the circumstances.[9] If the witnesses at the time of the alleged acknowledgment neither saw nor had the opportunity of seeing the signature there is no valid acknowledgment.[10]

As to acknowledgment, in *Hudson* v. *Parker*[11] Dr. Lushington said:

> "Acknowledgment may be expressed in words that will adequately convey that idea, if the signature be proved to have been then existent; no particular form of expression is required either by the word 'acknowledge' or by the exigency of the act to be done. It would be quite sufficient to say 'that is my will,' the signature being there and seen at the time, for such words do import an owning thereof; indeed, it may be done by any other words which naturally include within their true meaning acknowledgment and approbation."

Sir H. J. Fust went further in *Re Thomson*[12] where he said, "When a paper is produced by a testator to the witnesses, with his name signed thereto, and they have an opportunity of seeing his name, and they attest the same by subscribing the paper, they being present at the same time, this is a sufficient acknowledgment of his signature by the testator." The witnesses need not be told that the document is a will.[13] They may even be deceived by the testator into believing that the document is a deed.[14]

If the witnesses are asked to sign the document by some person in the presence and hearing of the testator, and see or have an opportunity of seeing the signature, that is a valid acknowledgment by the testator though he himself speaks no word; for the request of another in the presence of the testator may be regarded as the equivalent of a request by the testator himself.[15] Similarly it has been said in an Irish case that if a silent testator whose signature is physically visible to himself and the witnesses has the will brought in and can see and acquiesce in their action of signing the will as his witnesses from his point of view that is an acknowledgment that it is his signature.[16]

If, however, the signature has not been written by the testator, but by some person in his presence or by his direction, the former must by word or act indicate that the signature was put there at his request and that the other person was signing for him.[17] The testator must not remain entirely passive.[18]

---

[9] *Blake* v. *Knight* (1843) 3 Curt. 547; *Re Huckvale* (1867) L.R. 1 P. & D. 375.

[10] *Ilott* v. *Genge* (1842) 3 Curt. 160, (1844) 4 Moo.P.C. 265; see *Re Gunstan* (1882) 7 P.D. 102.

[11] (1844) 1 Rob. 14, 25; see *Re Gunstan, supra*; *Henderson* v. *Priestman* [1918] 2 Ir.R. 90.

[12] (1846) 4 N.C. 643, 644; approved in *Daintree* v. *Butcher and Fasulo* (1888) 13 P.D. 102.

[13] *Daintree* v. *Butcher and Fasulo, supra*.

[14] *Re Benjamin* [1934] All E.R. 359.

[15] *Faulds* v. *Jackson* (1845) 6 N.C.Suppl.i; *Inglesand* v. *Inglesand* (1874) L.R. 3 P. & D. 172; *Re Marshall* (1866) 13 L.T. 643.

[16] *Cooke* v. *Henry* [1932] I.R. 574, 579 and see *Kavanagh* v. *Fegan* [1932] I.R. 566.

[17] *Re Marshall, supra*; see *Re Summers* (1850) 2 Rob. 295.

[18] *Re Marshall, supra*; *Morritt* v. *Douglas* (1872) L.R. 3 P. & D. 1.

The testator may acknowledge his signature by means of gestures.[19] As little as a nod of the head has been held sufficient.[20]

The witnesses must be conscious of the act done. Bodily presence is not enough, nor the possibility of being able to see the testator's signature if the attention of the witnesses was taken up by some other matter.[21]

If the witnesses see the testator writing what the court is satisfied is his signature to his will, that is sufficient, although they do not see the signature and the testator does not acknowledge it.[22]

The attestation of wills

Section 9 of the Act now provides that each witness must either attest and sign the will or acknowledge his signature in the presence of the testator (but not necessarily in the presence of any other witness) but no form of attestation is necessary.[23] The provision allowing for acknowledgment of his signature by a witness is new and would have saved the will in question in *Re Colling*,[24] but such acknowledgment is not effective where the testator died before 1983.[25]

The new provisions also omit the requirement that the witness shall "subscribe."[26] This requirement made a distinction between attestation and subscription,[27] described as somewhat barren. It did not mean that attestation could be independent of subscription.[28] The person signing must intend his signature in attestation and must not append it for other reasons.[29]

The presence of the testator

The witnesses must be in the visual presence of the testator,[30] within reach of the organs of sight.[31] It is not necessary that the testator should actually see the witnesses sign, provided that he is in such a situation that he might see them if he chose to look.[32]

.

[19] *Re Davies* (1850) 2 Rob. 337.
[20] *Goodall* v. *Hadler, The Times*, October 20, 1960.
[21] *Hudson* v. *Parker* (1844) 1 Rob. 14, 24; *Brown* v. *Skirrow* [1902] P. 3.
[22] *Smith* v. *Smith* (1866) L.R. 1 P. & D. 143.
[23] See p. 133, *ante.*
[24] [1972] 1 W.L.R. 1440.
[25] See p. 133, *ante.*
[26] See p. 133, *ante.*
[27] *Hudson* v. *Parker, supra.*
[28] *Hindmarsh* v. *Charlton* (1859) 1 Sw. & Tr. 433, 439.
[29] See *post*, p. 143.
[30] The Law Reform Committee recommended this requirement be retained. See Cmnd. 7902, 1980.
[31] *Brown* v. *Skirrow, supra*; see *Doe* d. *Wright* v. *Manifold* (1813) 1 M. & S. 294, 295.
[32] *Hudson* v. *Parker, supra*, p. 35; *Shires* v. *Glasscock* (1685) 2 Salk. 688; *Casson* v. *Dade* (1781) 1 Bro.C.C. 99 (perhaps the most extreme case); *Newton* v. *Clarke* (1839) 2 Curt. 320; *Tribe* v. *Tribe* (1849) 1 Rob. 775; *Re Trimnell* (1865) 11 Jur.(N.S.) 248; wills were pronounced against in *Doe* d. *Wright* v. *Manifold, supra*; *Re Newman* (1838) 1 Curt. 914; *Re Ellis* (1840) 2 Curt. 395; *Re Colman* (1842) 3 Curt. 118; *Jenner* v. *Ffinch* (1879) 5 P.D. 106; *Carter* v. *Seaton* (1901) 85 L.T. 76; *Betts* v. *Gannell* (1903) 19 T.L.R. 304.

If a testator is in a state of insensibility when his will is attested, the will is not duly executed, although he is corporally present when the witnesses subscribe their names.[33] He must be aware of the presence of the witnesses.[34] Where the testator is blind it must be shown that he could, had he had his eyesight, have seen the witnesses sign.[35] But the witnesses must not themselves be blind even if the testator has his sight.[36]

Both attesting witnesses must be present at the signature or acknowledgment

Whether the testator signs his will or acknowledges his signature on it, he must do so when both witnesses are present. Where the death occurred before January 1, 1983, the will was invalid, unless both witnesses attested and subscribed after the testator's signature had been made or acknowledged. This was not expressly provided for by section 9 of the Wills Act, but it was implicit from the requirement that the testator's signature "shall be made or acknowledged . . . in the presence of two or more witnesses. . . . and such witnesses *shall* attest and *shall* subscribe the will . . ." The words "shall" were prospective[37] and were to be construed as "shall then."[38] Many wills were refused probate for failure to comply with these requirements. The most common circumstance was where the testator signed in the presence of only one witness, W1, who then duly attested and subscribed, and the testator later acknowledged his signature in the presence of W1 and a second witness, W2, who then also attested and subscribed. The will failed because it was witnessed by W1 before the testator acknowledged his signature to W2.[39] The position was the same where W1 traced over his signature with a dry pen on the occasion when W2 was present.[40] Where either[41] or both[42] witnesses signed the will before the testator signed, the will was again invalid. If a witness was present when a testator started to sign but then left, it was not sufficient unless the part which he had seen written constituted the testator's name or mark.[43]

In the case of deaths on or after January 1, 1983, it seems that a will made in any of these circumstances will now be valid, provided each of the

---

[33] *Right* v. *Price* (1779) 1 Doug. 241.

[34] *Re Killick* (1864) 3 Sw. & Tr. 578; *Jenner* v. *Ffinch, supra.*

[35] *Re Piercy* (1845) 1 Rob. 278.

[36] *Re Gibson* [1949] P. 434.

[37] *Cooper* v. *Bockett* (1843) 3 Curt. 648.

[38] *Re Allen* (1839) 2 Curt. 331.

[39] *Moore* v. *King* (1842) 3 Curt. 243; *Cooper* v. *Bockett, supra*; *Hindmarsh* v. *Charlton* (1861) 8 H.L. 160; *Wyatt* v. *Berry* [1893] P. 5; *Brown* v. *Skirrow* [1902] P. 3; *Re Davies' Estate* [1951] 1 All E.R. 920; *Re Colling* [1972] 1 W.L.R. 1440; *Re Schewchuk* (1968) 1 D.L.R. (3rd) 288.

[40] *Re Cunningham* (1860) 4 Sw. & Tr. 194; *Re Maddock* (1874) L.R. 3 P. & D. 169.

[41] *Chesline* v. *Hermiston* [1928] 4 D.L.R. 786; *Re Young* [1969] N.Z.L.R. 454.

[42] *Re Olding* (1841) 2 Curt. 865; *Re Byrd* (1842) 3 Curt. 117; *Pennant* v. *Kingscote* (1843) 3 Curt. 642; *Brenchley* v. *Still* (1850) 2 Rob. 162; *Re Hoskins* (1863) 1 New Rep. 569; *Re Winter* [1926] V.L.R. 300.

[43] *Re Colling, supra*, distinguishing *Re Chalcraft* [1948] P. 222. See *ante*, p. 134.

witnesses acknowledges his signature to the testator after the testator has made or acknowledged his signature.

The attesting witnesses need not sign or acknowledge in the presence of each other

Although it is essential that both witnesses should be present with the testator when he signs or acknowledges his will, it is not essential that both witnesses should be present when they sign or acknowledge their signatures,[44] provided that each does so in the presence of the testator. The cases supporting this proposition were few and old[45] and there was a decision to the contrary.[46] Nevertheless the proposition was again and again held in unreported cases to have been a correct one. It is now expressly confirmed by statute.[47]

The signatures of the witnesses

The witnesses may sign their names or make their mark or sign in such other way (including signature with initials) as is descriptive of the witness.[48] A mark is a good signature even though another person writes the witness's name[49] or even writes a wrong name.[50] A witness may sign with a mark although he can write. He may sign with initials. A description is a good signature, e.g. "servant to X."[51]

It has been held that witnesses do not validly attest by placing their seals alone upon the paper,[52] but the decision would seem to be incorrect in view of the cases in which it as been held that a testator may sign with a seal.[53]

The hand of the witness may be guided[54] but he must sign himself. Another cannot do so for him.

Whatever form the attestation may take the court must be satisfied that what was written upon the will by the witness was intended to represent his name. Thus the mere correction of an initial is not enough[55]; nor the addition of an address.[56] The word "witness" written by the second attesting witness against the name of the first was held not to be a valid subscrip-

---

[44] Although witnesses usually do sign in each other's presence, the Law Reform Committee recommended that this practice should not be a statutory requirement. See Cmnd. 7902, (1980).

[45] *Faulds* v. *Jackson* (1845) 6 N.C.Suppl.i; *Cooper* v. *Bockett, supra*, p. 659; *Re Webb* (1855) Dea. & Sw. 1.

[46] *Casement* v. *Fulton* (1845) 5 Moo.P.C. 130.

[47] See p. 133, *ante.*

[48] *Re Christian* (1849) 2 Rob. 110; *Hindmarsh* v. *Charlton, supra*, p. 171.

[49] *Harrison* v. *Harrison* (1803) 8 Ves. 185.

[50] *Re Ashmore* (1843) 3 Curt. 756; see *Re Duggins* (1870) 39 L.J.P. & M. 24.

[51] *Re Sperling* (1863) 3 Sw. & Tr. 272.

[52] *Re Byrd* (1842) 3 Curt. 117.

[53] See *ante.*

[54] *Harrison* v. *Elvin* (1842) 3 Q.B. 117; *Re Frith* (1858) 1 Sw. & Tr. 8; *Lewis* v. *Lewis* (1861) 2 Sw. & Tr. 153.

[55] *Hindmarsh* v. *Charlton* (1861) 8 H.L.C. 160.

[56] *Re Trevanion* (1850) 2 Rob. 311.

tion.[57] But where a witness had written the word "executors" against his signature it was held, on the evidence, that he had signed in the character of witness as well as in that of executor.[58] Where a witness, through feebleness, wrote only part of his signature this was held to be an insufficient attestation.[59] But the decision seems to be incorrect since, as already pointed out,[60] the incomplete signature of a testator is sufficient.

The signature must have been written for the purpose of attesting the due execution of the will and not for other reasons. Thus where a will contains two signatures of the testator, one sufficient, the other insufficient for the purposes of section 9 of the Wills Act 1837, there will be no proper attestation if the witnesses intend to witness the insufficient signature only.[61]

Position of the signatures of the attesting witnesses

In the case of *Re Braddock*[62] Sir James Hannen said[63]: "The law does not require that the attestation should be in any particular place, provided that the evidence satisfies the court that the witnesses in writing their names had the intention of attesting."[64] The signatures may even be on a different page from that of the testator.[65]

But in considering whether persons have attested as witnesses the position of the signatures may be most material. If they are placed against a particular clause in the will the inference is, prima facie, that they were put there to give effect or testify to the words of that clause,[66] or to give effect to alterations.[67]

If the witnesses have not signed on the same sheet as the testator, the sheet on which they sign must be physically connected with that signed by him. No mode of affixing one piece of paper to another is laid down.[68] They may be pinned together[69] or even held in the testator's fingers or under the pressure of his hand.[70] The will may be in an envelope which alone is signed by the witnesses.[71] It does not matter if the sheets sub-

[57] *Re Eynon* (1873) L.R. 3 P. & D. 92.
[58] *Griffiths* v. *Griffiths* (1871) L.R. 2 P. & D. 300.
[59] *Re Maddock* (1874) L.R. 3 P. & D. 169.
[60] See *ante*, p. 134.
[61] *Re Bercovitz* [1962] 1 W.L.R. 321; *Re Beadle* [1974] 1 W.L.R. 161.
[62] (1876) 1 P.D. 433.
[63] *Ibid.* 434.
[64] See *Phipps* v. *Hale* (1874) L.R. 3 P. & D. 166, 168; *Re Bercovitz* [1961] 1 W.L.R. 894 (affirmed on appeal [1962] 1 W.L.R. 321).
[65] *Re Chamney* (1849) 1 Rob. 757; *Re Davis* (1843) 3 Curt. 748; *Roberts* v. *Phillips* (1855) 4 El. & Bl. 450; *Re Streatley* [1891] P. 172; *Re Danning, Harnett* v. *Elliot* [1958] 2 All E.R. 1 (signatures on back of page).
[66] *Re Wilson* (1866) L.R. 1 P. & D. 269, 271; see *Ewen* v. *Franklin* (1855) Dea. & Sw. 7; *Phipps* v. *Hale* (1874) L.R. 3 P. & D. 166; see also *Re Dilkes* (1874) L.R. 3 P. & D. 164; *Sweetland* v. *Sweetland* (1865) 4 Sw. & Tr. 6.
[67] *Re Martin* (1849) 1 Rob. 712; *Re White* [1991] Ch. 1.
[68] *Re Braddock* (1876) 1 P. & D. 433.
[69] *Re Braddock, supra.*
[70] *Lewis* v. *Lewis* [1908] P. 1; *Foster* v. *Cooper* [1960] 1 All E.R. 387.
[71] *Re Nicholls* [1921] Ch. 11; compare *Re Beadle* [1974] 1 W.L.R. 161.

sequently become detached.[72] But, it seems, that where there is nothing from which some such connection can be inferred, probate must be refused.[73] A duplicate will, one part of which was signed by the testator and another by the witnesses was held to be invalid[74]; as was the second of two wills written on one piece of paper of which only the first was attested.[75]

Attestation by persons "incompetent" to give evidence

Section 14 of the Wills Act 1837, which appears to allow persons not competent (in the modern sense) to give evidence to act as attesting witnesses, refers to those persons who in 1837 were incompetent to give evidence, *e.g.* the parties, their spouses, persons of no religious belief, etc.

Attesting witnesses and their spouses take no benefit under a will

Section 15 of the Wills Act 1837 deprives attesting witnesses and their spouses of any benefit under the will, but expressly permits them to give evidence of the validity or invalidity of the will.[76]

An attesting witness formerly lost his benefit even if his signature was superfluous because two witnesses had previously attested the will before he came to sign.[77] But by the Wills Act 1968, s.1[78]:

"For the purposes of section 15 of the Wills Act 1837 (avoidance of gifts to attesting witnesses and their spouses) the attestation of a will by a person to whom or to whose spouse there is given or made any such disposition as is described in that section shall be disregarded if the will is duly executed without his attestation and without that of any such person."

The section applies to the will of any person dying after May 29, 1968, whether it was executed before or after the passing of the Act.[79]

If it could be established that the third or subsequent signature was not placed on the will in attestation, the signatory did not lose his benefit.[80] In a clear case the probate court will order the omission of the signature from probate.[81] In older cases the question in what capacity a person signed the

---

[72] *Lewis* v. *Lewis, supra.*

[73] *Re Pearse* (1867) L.R. 1 P. & D. 382, but see *Re Tiernan* [1942] I.R. 572.

[74] *Re Hatton* (1881) 6 P.D. 204.

[75] *Re Taylor* (1851) 2 Rob. 411.

[76] For detailed consideration of this section and the destination of the interest forfeited see *post*, pp. 975 *et seq.* The Law Reform Committee recommended that this rule be retained. See Cmnd. 7902, 1980. See also 100 L.Q.R. 453; 133 S.J. 613.

[77] *Randfield* v. *Randfield* (1863) 32 L.J.Ch. 668; see *Wigan* v. *Rowland* (1853) 11 Hare 157; *Re Bravda* [1968] 1 W.L.R. 479, C.A.

[78] Passed in consequence of the decision in *Re Bravda, supra.*

[79] subs. (2).

[80] *Re Sharman* (1869) L.R. 1 P. & D. 661; *Re Smith* (1889) 15 P.D. 2; *Kitcat* v. *King* [1930] P. 266.

[81] *Re Smith, supra*; *Kitcat* v. *King, supra.*

will was left to the chancery jurisdiction,[82] but this is not now the practice. In any case in which the applicant for a grant desires that a signature should be omitted as not written in attestation or as one which should, under the Wills Act 1968, be disregarded, the registrar's direction must be taken.

Presumption of the due execution of a will

There is no absolute necessity for positive evidence of due execution in order to enable the court to pronounce for a will. The court will take into account the circumstances and judge from them collectively whether or not there was due execution.[83] What those circumstances are may be gathered from the words of Dr. Lushington in *Thomson* v. *Hall*[84]:

> "The character of the witnesses, the length of time which has elapsed since the transactions took place, the nature of the facts deposed to— whether they are likely or not to have made an impression on the minds of the witnesses—are circumstances to be taken into account, to which is to be added this consideration also, whether the case admits of the principle—the presumption—*omnia rite esse acta.*"

In addition the court will consider the testator's desire to execute a valid will; his knowledge of what was necessary for that purpose; and the inherent improbability of his neglecting or omitting the formalities which he knew to be essential.[85] If the converse of these circumstances be proved that will weaken the case in favour of the will.[86]

The presumption that everything was properly done (*Omnia rite et solemniter esse acta*), arises whenever a will, regular on the face of it and apparently duly executed, is before the court, and amounts to an inference, in the absence of evidence to the contrary, that the requirements of the statute have been duly complied with.[87] The presumption applies with more or less force according to the circumstances of each case.[88] When there is a regular attestation clause,[89] with the names of two witnesses appended thereto, leading to the conclusion that the will was duly executed by a person who knew the requirements of the Wills Act, the principle applies directly[90]; for the court will assume that no one would have signed his name to the statement contained in such clause unless it were true.[91] Where there is an informal attestation clause, which leads to the conclusion

---

[82] See *Re Mitchell* (1841) 2 Curt. 916; *Re Forest* (1861) 2 Sw. & Tr. 334.

[83] *Blake* v. *Knight* (1843) 3 Curt. 547. As to compliance with the Statute see p. 134, *ante*.

[84] (1852) 2 Rob. 426, 432.

[85] *Cooper* v. *Bockett* (1843) 3 Curt. 648, (1846) 4 Moo.P.C. 419; *Wright* v. *Sanderson* (1884) 9 P.D. 149; *Lloyd* v. *Roberts* (1858) 12 Moo.P.C. 158.

[86] See *Harris* v. *Knight* (1890) 15 P.D. 170, 178.

[87] *Lloyd* v. *Roberts, supra; Burgoyne* v. *Showler* (1844) 1 Rob. 5, 10; *Smith* v. *Smith* (1866) L.R. 1 P. & D. 143, 145.

[88] *Vinnicombe* v. *Butler* (1864) 3 Sw. & Tr. 580, 582; *Harris* v. *Knight, supra.*

[89] See *Re Moore* [1901] P. 44.

[90] *Vinnicombe* v. *Butler, supra,* p. 582.

[91] *Per* Cotton L.J. in *Harris* v. *Knight* (1890) 15 P.D. 170, 178. See *Wright* v. *Rogers* (1869) 38 L.P.J. 67.

that the testator did not know the requirements of the Act the presumption still applies, but with less force[92] and even though the document be informal, and contains no attestation clause whatever, yet in the absence of evidence to the contrary, the presumption will apply.[93] But irregularity may be so marked that the presumption has little application.[94]

In considering the presumption in the case *Re Peverett*[95] Sir Francis Jeune P. said: "Two things may be laid down as general principles. The first is that the court is always extremely anxious to give effect to the wishes of persons, if satisfied that they really are their testamentary wishes; and, secondly, the court will not allow a matter of form to stand in the way if the essential elements of execution have been fulfilled."

> " 'The maxim *omnia praesumuntur rite esse acta*,' said Lindley L.J. in *Harris* v. *Knight*,[96] is an expression in a short form, of a reasonable probability, and of the propriety in point of law of acting on such probability. The maxim expresses an inference which may be reasonably drawn when an intention to do some formal act is established; when the evidence is consistent with that intention having been carried into effect in a proper way; but when the actual observance of all due formalities can only be inferred as a matter of probability . . . . The maxim only comes into operation where there is no proof one way or the other, but where it is more probable that what was intended to be done was done as it ought to have been done to render it valid; rather than that it was done in some other manner which would defeat the intention proved to exist, and would render what is proved to have been done of no effect."

Probate judges have been long accustomed to give great weight to the presumption of due execution arising from the regularity, *ex facie*, of the testamentary paper produced where no suspicion of fraud has occurred. And Fry L.J. in *Wright* v. *Sanderson*[97] stated that in doing so they have, in his opinion, acted rightly and wisely. It seems, therefore, that it is not strictly necessary to prove a testator's intention to make a will before the presumption applies. Indeed, in many cases nothing whatever is known about the testator's testamentary intentions at the date when he placed his signature on the paper in question.

Presumption of due execution when the witnesses are dead

Where a will bears on it the signature of the testator and of two wit-

---

[92] *Vinnicombe* v. *Butler* (1864) 3 Sw. & Tr. 580; *Re Rees* (1865) 34 L.J.P.M. & A. 56; see *Clery* v. *Barry* (1887) 21 L.R.Ir. 152 (signature for the testator).
[93] *Re Peverett* [1902] P. 205, approved in *Re Denning* [1958] 2 All E.R. 1, distinguished in *Strong* v. *Hadden* [1915] P. 211.
[94] *Re Bercovitz* [1962] 1 W.L.R. 321.
[95] See fn. 93, *supra*.
[96] (1890) 15 P.D. 179.
[97] (1884) 9 P.D. 149, 163.

nesses, even if there is no attestation clause[98] and it is proved that both witnesses are dead or they cannot be traced[99] the court will presume due execution,[1] if the handwritings can be proved and provided there is nothing irregular on the face of the will of such a kind as to raise a contrary presumption.[2] The presumption has been applied to a case of a will lost after the death of the testator which had to be proved by parol evidence and of which the witnesses were dead,[3] and even to a case where the signature of the deceased appeared under the signatures of the attesting witnesses, both of whom were dead.[4] The presumption has also been applied where there was a delay of some 20 years in proving the will.[5]

Presumption of due execution where the witnesses have forgotten the circumstances, or negative due execution

The court will not allow defective memory alone to overturn a will which is upon the face of it duly executed. If the witnesses are forgetful of the facts, the presumption of due execution will prevail.[6]

Even if one or more witnesses profess to remember the transaction and state that the will was not, for some reason, duly executed, this negative evidence may be rebutted by that of other attesting witnesses[7] or of other persons present,[8] and, if their evidence is accepted, the will may be admitted to probate.

Furthermore, the court may pronounce for the will though all the attesting witnesses who give evidence negative due execution and there is no other available evidence, provided that the court is satisfied that they are not to be credited or that their memories fail them.[9]

But where the evidence of the attesting witnesses directly negatives due execution and is not rebutted by direct or circumstantial evidence, the court must pronounce against the will.[10]

---

[98] *Re Peverett* [1902] P. 205, extended in *Re Denning* [1958] 2 All E.R. 1, but see *Strong* v. *Hadden* [1915] P. 211.

[99] *Re Phibbs* [1917] P. 93.

[1] *Trott* v. *Skidmore* (1860) 2 Sw. & Tr. 12; *Burgoyne* v. *Showler* (1844) 1 Rob. 5, 10; *Re Thomas* (1859) 1 Sw. & Tr. 255; *Re Spain* (1915) 31 T.L.R. 435.

[2] *Trott* v. *Skidmore, supra*; *Re Swinford* (1869) L.R. 1 P. & D. 630; *Re Bercovitz, supra*.

[3] *Harris* v. *Knight* (1890) 15 P.D. 170.

[4] *Re Puddephat* (1870) L.R. 2 P. & D. 97.

[5] *Davis* v. *Mayhew* [1927] P. 264, C.A. (where the previous cases are reviewed).

[6] *Burgoyne* v. *Showler, supra*; *Re Gunstan* (1882) 7 P.D. 102, 115; see *Wright* v. *Sanderson* (1884) 9 P.D. 149, 160; *Re Hare* (1842) 3 Curt. 54; *Thomson* v. *Hall* (1852) 2 Rob. 426; *Woodhouse* v. *Balfour* (1887) 13 P.D. 2; *Whiting* v. *Turner* (1903) 98 L.T. 71; see also *Vinnicombe* v. *Butler* (1864) 3 Sw. & Tr. 580 (where there was also an incomplete attestation clause); *Re Webb* [1964] 1 W.L.R. 509; *Re Coghlan* [1948] 2 All E.R. 68.

[7] *Chambers* v. *Queen's Proctor* (1840) 2 Curt. 415.

[8] *Young* v. *Richards* (1840) 2 Curt. 371; *Vere-Wardale* v. *Johnson* [1949] P. 395.

[9] *Cooper* v. *Bockett* (1843) 3 Curt. 648; (1846) 4 Moo.P.C. 419; *Lloyd* v. *Roberts* (1858) 12 Moo.P.C. 158; *Re Moore* [1901] P. 44; *Pilkington* v. *Gray* [1899] A.C. 401; *Neal* v. *Denston* (1932) 147 L.T. 460.

[10] *Burgoyne* v. *Showler* (1844) 1 Rob. 5, 10; *Owen* v. *Williams* (1863) 4 Sw. & Tr. 202; *Croft* v. *Croft* (1865) 4 Sw. & Tr. 10; *Wyatt* v. *Berry* [1893] P. 5; *Dayman* v. *Dayman* (1894) 71 L.T. 699; *Strong* v. *Hadden* [1915] P. 211; see *Pennant* v. *Kingscote* (1843) 3 Curt. 642.

Lord Kingsdown's Act

The Wills Act 1861, commonly known as Lord Kingsdown's Act, though now repealed,[11] still governs the formal validity of certain wills made before January 1, 1964. Wills valid under the Act are not invalidated by the fact that the testator died after the date of the repeal of the Act, *i.e.* December 31, 1963.[12] The Act will, however, have a diminishing importance. By section 1 of the Act a will of personal[13] estate made out of the United Kingdom[14] by a British subject,[15] whatever his domicile at the date of the will or at his death, is well executed and admissible to proof if it was validly executed (i) by the law of the place where it was made,[16] (ii) by the law of the place where the testator was domiciled at the time he made the will, or (iii) by the law of that part of Her Majesty's Dominions where the testator had his domicile of origin. By section 2 of the Act a will of personal estate made in the United Kingdom by a British subject, whatever his domicile at the date of the will or at his death, is well executed and admissible to proof if it was executed according to the forms required in that part of the United Kingdom where it was made.[17] Under section 3 of the Act subsequent change of domicile does not revoke a will or render it invalid or alter its construction. By section 4 no will is revoked or rendered invalid as regards personal estate which would have been valid if the Act had not been passed, except in so far as it is revoked or altered by a subsequent will valid under the Act.

British nationality

The law relating to British nationality is governed by the British Nationality Act 1981. The subject can only be properly treated at a length beyond the scope of this work. It may, however, be mentioned that many former British colonies and protectorates which have attained independence have expressly retained for their nationals the status of commonwealth citizens. The expression is used as an alternative to "British subject." Lord Kingsdown's Act applies to such persons.

The position of married women with regard to British nationality is somewhat complicated and requires careful consideration.

---

[11] By the Wills Act 1963, s.7(3).

[12] *Ibid.* s.7(4).

[13] Including leaseholds, *Re Grassi* [1905] 1 Ch. 584, and land on trust for sale, *Re Lyne* [1919] 1 Ch. 80, but not the proceeds of sale of settled land, *Re Cartwright* [1939] Ch. 90.

[14] The United Kingdom now consists of England, Wales, Scotland and Northern Ireland, but not the Isle of Man, the Channel Islands or the Republic of Ireland.

[15] Including a naturalised British subject, *Re Gally* (1876) 1 P.D. 438; but not British born persons who have married aliens, *Re Von Buseck* (1881) 6 P.D. 211; *Bloxham* v. *Favre* (1884) 9 P.D. 130.

[16] Where no special form of will is required, the will is valid if it would be upheld by the law of the place where it was made, *Stokes* v. *Stokes* (1898) 78 L.T. 50.

[17] *Re S.* (1962) 106 S.J. 313.

Application of Lord Kingsdown's Act

For the Act to apply the testator must have been a British subject at the time the will was made.[18] If a British subject is, by the law of his domicile, incapable of making a will, that will is not valid under the Act.[19] The provision that a change of domicile does not revoke or render a will invalid has been held to apply to wills generally and not merely to the wills of British subjects.[20]

The international effect of the Act has raised some difficult problems. Where the court of the domicile has granted administration to executors of a will valid by that law and there is also a will valid under the Act but invalid by the law of the domicile, the grant will be made in England to the grantees appointed by the court of the domicile and not to the executors appointed by the will valid under the Act.[21] But in such a case, probate of a will in English or Welsh will be granted to the executors of that will.[22]

Where proceedings are in progress abroad as to the validity of a will which is invalid by English law, the English court will grant probate of a will valid under the Act to the executors named therein.[23] Where a will valid by English law and by the law of the domicile and admitted to probate by the court of the domicile was revoked by a will valid under the Act but invalid in the country of the domicile, both wills having been admitted to probate in England, it was held in the Chancery Division that the later will revoked the former and that the executors of the later will must hold the estate on the principles of English law and not of the law of the domicile.[24] Where a testator made a will disposing of capital moneys from the sale of settled lands, and also some wills valid by French law, it was held that as the former dealt with realty, it did not come within the Act.[25] Although a will may be admissible to probate under the Act, it may be invalid or inoperative.[26]

Practice

An affidavit must be filed showing that the testator was a British subject. Except where it is shown that the testator had a domicile of origin in England (which must be proved by affidavit) there must be an affidavit of foreign law showing the validity of the will by the law applicable. Unless the will is in English form the grant will be limited to personalty.[27]

---

[18] *Bloxham* v. *Favre* (1884) 9 P.D. 130.

[19] *Registrar's Direction*, May 5, 1953.

[20] *Re Groos* [1904] P. 269. *Loustalan* v. *Loustalan* [1900] P. 211 (marriage held not to revoke a will where it would not revoke it by the law of the domicile though the deceased married and later acquired an English domicile).

[21] *Re Meatyard* [1903] P. 125. *Re Manifold* [1962] Ch. 1.

[22] See N.-C.P.R. 1987, r. 30, 3(*a*) (*post*, p. 1234).

[23] *Re Cocquerel* [1918] P. 4.

[24] *Re Manifold* [1962] Ch. 1.

[25] *Re Cartwright* [1939] Ch. 90.

[26] *Re Grassi* [1905] 1 Ch. 584; *Lyne* v. *De la Ferté* (1910) 102 L.T. 143.

[27] *Registrar's Direction*, May 5, 1953.

The Wills Act 1963

This Act was passed in pursuance of an international convention, and it, therefore, follows that the foreign signatories have passed corresponding legislation. The conflict of laws inherent in Lord Kingsdown's Act has thus, to a large extent, been avoided.

The Act, where it applies, governs only the wills of testators who die after December 31, 1963.[28]

Wills treated as properly executed

By section 1 of the Act "A will[29] shall be treated as properly executed if its execution conformed to the internal law[30] in force in the territory where it was executed,[31] or in the territory where, at the time of its execution or of the testator's death, he was domiciled or had his habitual residence,[32] or in a state[33] of which, at either of those times, he was a national."

By section 2:

"(1) Without prejudice to the preceding section, the following shall be treated as properly executed:

(a) a will executed on board a vessel or aircraft of any description, if the execution of the will conformed to the internal law in force in the territory with which, having regard to its registration (if any) and other relevant circumstances, the vessel or aircraft may be taken to have been most closely connected;

(b) a will so far as it disposes of immovable property, if its execution conformed to the internal law in force in the territory where the property was situated[34];

(c) a will so far as it revokes a will which under this Act would be treated as properly executed or revokes a provision which under this Act would be treated as comprised in a properly executed will, if the execution of the later will conformed to any law by reference to which the revoked will or provision would be so treated[35];

(d) a will so far as it exercises a power of appointment, if the

---

[28] Wills Act 1963, s.7.

[29] "Will" includes any testamentary instrument or act, s.6(1).

[30] For the meaning of "internal law," see *post*, p. 152.

[31] For a case where this requirement was not satisfied, see *Re Kanani* (1978) 122 S.J. 611.

[32] "Habitual residence" may be equivalent to the concept of domicile held in many foreign countries and to the English concept of ordinary residence, see *Stransky* v. *Stransky* [1954] P. 428. See also Dicey and Morris, *Conflict of Laws*, 11th ed., p. 1012.

[33] "State" means territory or group of territories having its own law of nationality, s.6(1).

[34] As s.2 is without prejudice to s.1, a will of immovable property may also be valid under s.1.

[35] Thus even if a dispositive provision in a will is invalid, a revocatory clause may be valid. It seems that marriage, not being a testamentary act, would not revoke a will made under the Act.

execution of the will conformed to the law governing the essential validity[36] of the power.

(2) A will so far as it exercises a power of appointment shall not be treated as improperly executed by reason only that its execution was not in accordance with any formal requirements contained in the instrument creating the power."

Special requirements for the execution of a will

Section 3 of the Act provides that where any law in force outside the United Kingdom requires special formalities to be observed by testators of a particular description or attesting witnesses to possess particular qualifications, such requirements are to be treated as formal and not substantial.

Internal law

This phrase is defined in section 6(1) as meaning the law which would apply where no question of the law in any other territory or state arose, *i.e.* renvoi is not to be applied.

Where more than one system of internal law dealing with the formal validity of wills exists in any state or territory

"(*a*) if there is in force throughout the territory or state a rule indicating which of those systems can properly be applied in the case in question, that rule shall be followed; or (*b*) if there is no such rule, the system shall be that with which the testator was most closely connected at the relevant time, and for this purpose the relevant time is the time of the testator's death where the matter is to be determined by reference to circumstances prevailing at his death, and the time of the execution of the will in any other case."[37]

Subsection (3) of section 6 enacts:

"In determining for the purposes of this Act whether or not the execution of a will conformed to a particular law, regard shall be had to the formal requirements of that law at the time of execution, but this shall not prevent account being taken of an alteration of law affecting wills executed at that time if the alteration enables a will to be treated as properly executed."[38]

---

[36] The essential validity of a special power, though not necessarily of a general power, is the validity of the provision in the settlement or will conferring the power. For the law governing this validity, see Dicey and Morris, *Conflict of Laws*, 11th ed., p. 1072.

[37] s.6(2). The subsection covers the case of a citizen of the United Kingdom and Commonwealth to whom a number of different systems might be applicable. It also covers states where different systems apply according to religion, caste or tribe.

[38] Thus retrospective legislation which purports to invalidate a will which was valid when it was made is to be disregarded, but may validate a will which was invalid for formal reasons when it was made.

Construction

The construction of a will is not altered by a change of domicile after execution.[39]

Practice

Where the will has been executed in accordance with the Wills Act 1837, no affidavit of foreign law[40] is required if (i) the execution took place in England, (ii) the testator's habitual residence at the time of the execution was in England, (iii) the testator's domicile at the time of the execution was English, (iv) the testator was of British nationality whose closest connection at the date of the execution or the date of his death was with England and the English system of internal law as to the formal validity of wills.

No affidavit of law is normally required (i) if the will was made in Northern Ireland, the Republic of Ireland, the Australian states (including Tasmania), Canada or New Zealand, (ii) the testator's habitual residence at the date of the execution of his will or of his death was in any of these countries and states, (iii) the testator was a national of one of the many countries mentioned or, (iv) the testator was at the date of the execution of his will or of his death domiciled in any part of these countries and territories.[41]

In all cases there should be an affidavit of facts and in cases other than those set out above an affidavit of law is also required except where the will has been admitted to probate or its equivalent in the country or territory in which the deceased died domiciled. If the will has been proved in some other country or territory it must be shown that no *renvoi* has been applied.

Where section 6(2) applies, the affidavit must show whether subsection (*a*) or (*b*) is applicable, and where the closest connection with a particular system of law is relied on, the grounds for doing so should be set out.

Incorporation of documents

A document not formally executed as a will may in some circumstances be treated as part of the will. It is then said to be incorporated therein by reference.[42]

The following three conditions must be satisfied: (i) The unexecuted document must be in existence at the time of the execution of the testamentary instrument in which it is to be incorporated; (ii) there must be a reference in the will or codicil to the informal document as an existing, not as a future document; (iii) the unexecuted document must be so described as to leave no doubt, in the circumstances, as they are proved to have existed, that the document referred to is that propounded. The burden of

---

[39] s.4.
[40] See N-C.P.R. 1987, r. 19 (*post*, p. 1230).
[41] *Registrar's Direction*, November 20, 1972.
[42] *Croker* v. *Marquis of Hertford* (1844) 4 Moo.P.C. 339, 365; *Allen* v. *Maddock* (1858) 11 Moo.P.C. 427, 444 *et seq. Re Berger* [1990] Ch. 118. See also p. 119 *ante*.

proving these three conditions is upon those who contend for incorporation.[43] It should here be remembered that documents not incorporated
and not referred to in the will may affect distribution under the doctrine of
secret trusts.[44]

Admissibility of extrinsic evidence

A reference in a will may be in such terms as to exclude parol evidence,
as where it is to papers not yet written,[45] or where the description is so
vague as to be incapable of being applied to any instrument in particular.
But where there is a reference to any written document described as then
existing, in such terms that it is capable of being ascertained, parol evidence is admissible to ascertain it, and the only question then is whether
the evidence is sufficient for the purpose.[46]

There is a distinction between evidence of surrounding circumstances
and direct evidence of intention, e.g. the declarations of the testator. Evidence must necessarily be received to show whether the document referred
to in the will is in existence and whether that produced was in existence at
the date of the execution of the will.

In general, however, evidence of intention cannot be received.[47] "There
is but one case" said Lord Abinger in Doe v. Hiscocks[48] "in which this sort
of evidence of intention can be properly admitted, and that is . . . where
the devise is on the face of it perfect and intelligible, but, from some of the
circumstances admitted to proof, an ambiguity arises as to which of two or
more things, or which of two or more persons (each answering the words in
the will), the testator intended to express."

On this principle direct evidence has been admitted to show which of two
unexecuted papers, equally fulfilling the description in the will, the testator
meant to incorporate.[49]

Consideration of the three conditions

1. The existence of the unexecuted document at the time of the execution

A testator cannot reserve to himself a power of disposing of his property
by any paper not executed in accordance with section 9 of the Wills Act
1837. Accordingly an unexecuted paper made after the will can never form
part of it.[50] The onus is on those who allege the incorporation of an unexe-

---

[43] Singleton v. Tomlinson (1878) 3 App.Cas. 404.
[44] See Re Snowden [1979] Ch. 528 and Theobald on Wills, 14th ed., Chap. 11.
[45] See University College v. Taylor [1908] P. 140, 144–145.
[46] Allen v. Maddock, supra.
[47] Ibid. 440.
[48] (1839) 5 M. & W. 363, 368.
[49] Paton v. Ormerod [1892] P. 247, 252; see Re Greves (1858) 1 Sw. & Tr. 250; Re Almosnino (1859) 1 Sw. & Tr. 508, 510.
[50] See Re Bateman's Will Trusts [1970] 1 W.L.R. 1463.

cuted paper in a will to prove that that paper was in existence before the execution of the will.[51]

2. *Reference to an existing document in the will*

The will must refer to the unexecuted paper as an existing document. So that if the will refers to a future document evidence is not admissible to show that the testator meant an existing one.[52] To effect incorporation the words in the will need not expressly state that it exists, but they must be unambiguous and the words "such rules and regulations as are contained and specified in any memorandum amongst my papers . . . " were held possibly to refer to future documents, and parol evidence was excluded.[53] Where a deed which provided for part of the estate to be distributed in accordance with possible subsequent memoranda was referred to in a will, the deed was held to be incorporated but the clause as to subsequent memoranda was declared inoperative.[54]

3. *Identification of the unexecuted document*

The unexecuted document must be so described as to leave no doubt that the document referred to in the will is that propounded.[55] "Certainty and identification" said Dr. Lushington in *Croker* v. *Marquis of Hertford*[56] "is the very essence of incorporation. If any doubt can exist as to the instrument to be incorporated, then the principle of incorporation by relation would fail."

The words of reference may be so vague as to be incapable of being applied to any document in particular, and, in such case, it seems, parol evidence is inadmissible to show that the testator intended to refer to a particular document.[57] Where, however, there is a reference to any written document described as then existing, so that it is capable of being ascertained, parol evidence is admissible to ascertain it, and the only question then is the sufficiency of the evidence.[58]

---

[51] *Singleton* v. *Tomlinson* (1878) 3 App.Cas. 404, 414; *Ferraris* v. *Hertford* (1843) 3 Curt. 468, 492 *et seq.* and *sub nom. Croker* v. *Hertford* (1844) 4 Moo.P.C. 339, 365.

[52] *Re Sunderland* (1866) L.R. 1 P. & D. 198; *Re Bateman's Will Trusts* [1970] 1 W.L.R. 1463.

[53] *University College* v. *Taylor* [1907] P. 228; see *Blackwell* v. *Blackwell* [1929] A.C. 318, 329; *Re Keen's Estate* [1937] Ch. 236.

[54] *Re Edwards' W.T.* [1948] Ch. 440; see 67 L.Q.R. and *Re Schinz's W.T.* [1951] Ch. 870; *cf. Re Jones* [1942] Ch. 328; and see *Barclays Bank* v. *Treasury Solicitor* [1939] 2 All E.R. 416.

[55] *Allen* v. *Maddock* (1858) 11 Moo.P.C. 427, 444.

[56] (1844) 4 Moo.P.C. 366.

[57] *Allen* v. *Maddock* (1858) 11 Moo.P.C. 427, 454, and the cases there cited.

[58] *Ibid.* Proof of identity was held sufficient in *Re Smith* (1841) 2 Curt. 796j; *Re Claringbull* (1844) 3 N.C. 1; *Ingoldby* v. *Ingoldby* (1846) 4 N.C. 493; *Allen* v. *Maddock, supra*; *Re Almosnino* (1859) 3 Sw. & Tr. 6; *Re Daniell* (1882) 8 P.D. 14; *Re Heathcote* (1881) 6 P.D. 30. Proof of identity was held insufficient in *Re Sotheran* (1841) 2 Curt. 831; *Ferraris* v. *Hertford* (1843) 3 Curt. 468, 4 Moo.P.C. 339; *Re Phelps* (1849) 6 N.C. 695; *Haynes* v. *Hill* (1849) 7 N.C. 256; *Re Greves* (1858) 1 Sw. & Tr. 250; *Re Drummond* (1860) 2 Sw. & Tr. 8; *Van Straubenzee* v. *Monck* (1862) 3 Sw. & Tr. 6; *Re Allnutt* (1863) 3 Sw. & Tr. 167; *Re Brewis* (1864) 3 Sw. & Tr. 473; *Singleton* v. *Tomlinson* (1878) 3 App.Cas. 404; *Paton* v. *Ormerod* [1892] P. 247; *Re Garnett* [1894] P. 90; *Eyre* v. *Eyre* [1903] P. 131; *University College* v. *Taylor* [1908] P. 140, C.A.

Effect of a codicil on an unexecuted testamentary paper

Where a testamentary paper intended to operate as a will or codicil has not been validly executed and a further document referring to it and describing itself as a codicil has been duly executed the question of its effect has to be considered. In such case, where the codicil states that it is a codicil to the testator's last will, the unexecuted document will be incorporated,[59] provided that there is clear evidence that it is indeed the paper referred to in the executed codicil[60] and that the testator believed it to be his will.[61] There must be express reference in the executed codicil; it is not enough that the codicil is on the same piece of paper as the unexecuted will.[62] A codicil does not incorporate unattested additions made to the will to which it refers even if these documents call themselves codicils,[63] and even if they are all written on the same piece of paper, unless it refers to them.[64]

A duly executed codicil calling itself a second codicil may validate an earlier unexecuted codicil,[65] but there must be a reference to the first codicil in the second.[66] A bare enumeration, e.g. "This is the second codicil" without evidence connecting the codicil to some unexecuted document has been held sufficient to incorporate the earlier document.[67]

Words written on the same sheet of paper as the will

Where words, written on the same sheet of paper as the will, follow the operative signature of the testator, the court will first examine whether they can be held to form part of the will. If satisfied that they cannot, it will then consider whether they are incorporated in it.[68]

Dispositive instructions in an unincorporated document

Where a will shows that a testator has given instructions as to the disposal of some of his property in an unexecuted document which cannot be treated as incorporated, the court may grant probate of the will with a direction to the executor to administer the estate in accordance with the trusts set out in that document.[69] In an old case sealed parcels which a tes-

---

[59] See *Allen* v. *Maddock*, supra; *Re Heathcote*, *supra*. Contrast *Re Phelps*, *supra*; *Haynes* v. *Hill*, *supra*.

[60] *Ibid.*

[61] The testator must refer to the unexecuted document as his will or codicil.

[62] *Re Drummond* (1860) 2 Sw. & Tr. 8; *Re Tovey* (1878) 39 L.T. 235.

[63] *Haynes* v. *Hill*, *supra*.

[64] *Re Willmott* (1858) 1 Sw. & Tr. 36.

[65] *Re Smith*, *supra*.

[66] *Re Drummond*, supra; *Re Tovey*, *supra*.

[67] *Ingoldby* v. *Ingoldby*, *supra*; *Re Heathcote*, *supra*. *Stockil* v. *Punshon* (1880) 6 P.D. 9 appears to be incorrectly decided.

[68] *Re Watkins* (1865) L.R. 1 P. & D. 19; *Re Dallow* (1866) L.R. 1 P. & D. 189.

[69] *Re Marchant* [1893] P. 254; see *Inchiquin* v. *French* (1744) 1 Cox 1; *Smith* v. *Attersoll* (1826) 1 Russ. 266.

tatrix in her will directed to be delivered to certain persons were ordered to be opened in court and treated as legacies.[70]

Revival as affecting incorporation

The doctrine of revival (discussed later in this book[71]) in so far as it holds that the execution of a codicil revives a will, has important consequences when applied to incorporation by reference. The court must treat the codicil as if the testator had at the same time sat down and re-executed his will.[72]

The rule was thus stated by Sir Gorell Barnes in the case of *Re Smart*[73]:

"If the document is not existing at the time of the will, but comes into existence afterwards, and then, after that again there is a codicil confirming the will . . . the will may be treated, by the confirmation given by the codicil, as executed again, and speaking from the date of the codicil; and if the informal document is existing then, and is referred to in the will as existing, so as to identify it, there will be incorporation; but if the will, treated as being re-executed at the date of the codicil, still speaks in terms which show it to be referring to a future document, then it appears to me there is no incorporation."

Where a document is referred to in terms consistent with its being a future document it will not be incorporated, even if it might refer to an existing document.[74]

Statement for the purposes of the Inheritance (Provision for Family and Dependants) Act 1975[75]

A statement referred to in a will as being made for the purposes of the Inheritance (Provision for Family and Dependants) Act 1975 as to the testator's reasons for not benefiting, *e.g.* his wife is not to be treated as incorporated unless dispositive.[76]

Statutory will forms

Under section 179 of the Law of Property Act 1925 certain will forms have been prescribed which may be incorporated by reference only.

Practice

Practice in cases of incorporation or possible incorporation is considered elsewhere.[77]

[70] *Pelham* v. *Newton* (1754) 2 Lee 46.
[71] See *post*, pp. 218 *et seq.*
[72] *Re Lady Truro* (1866) L.R. 1 P. & D. 201, 205; *Re Berger* [1990] Ch. 118.
[73] [1902] P. 238 and contrast *Re Lady Truro, supra*, on the facts.
[74] *Re Smart* [1902] P. 238; See *Re Reid* (1868) 38 L.J.P. 1; *Durham* v. *Northen* [1895] P. 66; contrast *Re Stewart* (1863) 3 Sw. & Tr. 192 which appears to be wrongly decided.
[75] See s.21.
[76] As to family provision, see *post*, pp. 757 *et seq.*
[77] See *post*, p. 309.

CHAPTER 13

THE SUBSTANTIAL VALIDITY OF WILLS

The substantial as distinct from the formal[1] validity of a will raises the questions of (1) testamentary capacity, (2) knowledge and approval,[2] (3) undue influence,[3] (4) fraud[4] and (5) forgery.[5] These are considered in that order. The underlying principle is that the testator's mind[6] must go with his testamentary act, whether in making or revoking a will.

Where a will is admitted to probate in common form it is assumed, in the absence of indications to the contrary,[7] that the testator was free to make it, was mentally capable of doing so and knew and approved its contents, but in probate actions the court must examine these matters broadly or closely according to the circumstances.

There are a number of ways in which a testator's mind may not go with his testamentary act. He may lack, or be deemed to lack, testamentary capacity; he may not know and approve of the contents of the will; he may be deceived into making it by fraud or constrained to make it by force, threats or other forms of undue influence. Another person may forge a will and propound it as that of the deceased. Wherever any of the above matters are proved in relation to a testamentary instrument, the document purporting to be executed by the deceased has no validity and cannot be admitted to probate, save that in cases where part of the will was not affected by the matters mentioned above, such part is admissible.

Where there is any doubt about the testator's capacity, the will should be witnessed if possible by a doctor and a lawyer who should be reasonably satisfied of the testator's capacity.[8]

1. TESTAMENTARY CAPACITY

Infants

In general, infants lack testamentary capacity. It was enacted by section 7 of the Wills Act 1837 that "no will made by any person under the age of 21 years shall be valid." The age of 18 years is now substituted for that of

---

[1] As to formal validity see pp. 130 *et seq. ante.*
[2] p. 170 *post.*
[3] p. 183 *post.*
[4] p. 187 *post.*
[5] p. 189 *post.*
[6] As to medical evidence and witnesses, see pp. 159 *et seq. post.*
[7] See N.-C.P.R. 1987, rr. 12–16, as to the circumstances in which registrars make inquiries where probate in common form is applied for (*post,* pp. 1228, 1229).
[8] See 1970 B.M.J. p. 801 (Raymond Jennings Q.C. and n. 35 below).

21.[9] But, members of the armed forces and sailors, when entitled to make privileged wills,[10] may do so although under the age of 18[11] and in Scots law a boy of 14 and a girl of 12 have testamentary capacity.

Mental capacity needed to make a will

No person is capable of making a will who is not of sound mind, memory and understanding. The testator's mind must be sound to be capable of forming the testamentary intentions embodied in the will; his memory must be sound to recall the several persons who ought to be considered as his possible beneficiaries; his understanding must be sound so that he may comprehend their various ties with him by blood or friendship, and their claims on these or other grounds upon his testamentary bounty.[12]

In *Banks* v. *Goodfellow*[13] Cockburn C.J. said[14]

"It is essential . . . that a testator shall understand the nature of his act and its effects; shall understand the extent[15] of the property of which he is disposing; shall be able to comprehend and appreciate the claims to which he ought to give effect, and, with a view to the latter object, that no disorder of the mind shall poison his affections, pervert his sense of right, or prevent the exercise of his natural faculties, that no insane delusion shall influence his will in disposing of his property and bring about a disposal of it which, if his mind had been sound, would not have been made.[16]"

The law does not call for a perfectly balanced mind, nor is a will to be pronounced against merely because the testator was moved by capricious, frivolous, mean or even bad motives.[17] A testator may disinherit his children to gratify his spite or benefit charity to gratify his pride but the court must nevertheless uphold his will.

Testamentary capacity thus calls for particular mental characteristics.[18]

[9] Family Law Reform Act 1969, s.3(1)(*a*).

[10] See pp. 224 *et seq.*

[11] Wills (Soldiers and Sailors) Act 1918, ss.1, 3, as amended by the Family Law Reform Act 1969, s.3(1)(*b*). The minimum age is 14 years for males and 12 years for females, see *post*, p. 225.

[12] Based on the charge of Sir J. Hannen in *Boughton* v. *Knight* (1873) L.R. 3 P. & D. 64, 65. There is now statutory power for the court to make a will for a patient under the Mental Health Act 1983, ss.96, 97. See Heywood and Massey, *Court of Protection Practice*, 12th ed., p. 314 *et seq. Practice Note* (1970) 1 W.L.R. 228 and Article 34, *Conveyancer* (N.S.) 150. 13, Fam. Law 135. *Re Davey* (1981) 1 W.L.R. 164. In making such a will the Court of Protection proceeds on the assumption that the patient would have been a normal decent person acting in accordance with contemporary standards of morality. See *per* Hoffmann J. in *Re C.* [1991] 3 All E.R. 866, See also *Re L* (*W.J.G.*) [1966] Ch. 135; *Re D* [1982] Ch. 237.

[13] (1870) L.R. 5 Q.B. 549.

[14] At p. 565.

[15] There is no case decided on the question of knowledge of the extent of the property. See 35 *Conveyancer* 303.

[16] *Boughton* v. *Knight, supra*, at p. 66. *Re K* [1988] Ch. 310.

[17] *Ibid.*

[18] *Ibid.* at p. 72, as explained in *Burdett* v. *Thompson* (1873) 3 P.D. 72, n. 1. *Re Beaney* [1978] 1 W.L.R. 770.

A man may have the mental capacity to marry and yet, on his wedding day, be incapable of making a will.[19]

Conversely a patient[20] whose affairs are the subject of an order of the Court of Protection may be capable, subject to safeguards, of making a valid will.[21]

It has been held[22] that the tests for registration of an enduring power of attorney under section 6(5)(*a*) of the Enduring Powers of Attorney Act 1985 are that the donor must understand:

(a) that the attorney would be able to assume complete authority over the donor's affairs;

(b) that he could do anything with the property that the donor himself could have done;

(c) that the authority would continue if the donor became mentally incapable; and

(d) that the authority would in that event become irrevocable without confirmation by the court.

This decision was based on the general proposition that capacity to perform any juristic act exists when the person who has purported to do the act had at the time the mental capacity, with the assistance of such explanation as he may have been given to understand the nature and effect of that particular transaction.[23] This is in general similar to the specific tests applied in probate and affords a useful analogy.

Causes of Mental Incapacity

In relation to probate cases it is not helpful to base opinions upon the varieties of mental disorder defined in the Mental Health Act 1983[24] or the diagnoses current in psychiatry, because the particular mental capacities required may be present or absent in all these categories according to the degree of their severity and from time to time in the course of an illness. This is not to say that a psychiatrist called to account for testamentary capacity or lack thereof should not be expected to do so in precise nosological terms. However, decided cases which based themselves on the medical knowledge of their time are apt to be misleading, while those which have dealt with aspects of the topic in a more general way may still give

[19] *Park v. Park* [1954] P. 89, 112 (C.A.), unless that will is a simple one, see *per* Singleton L.J. at 122. Conversely however it has been held that although a lunatic so found could dispose by will in a lucid interval he could not dispose *inter vivos*: *Re Walker* [1905] 1 Ch. 160, 169, 173; *Re Marshall* [1920] 1 Ch. 284. See *Mental Health Law*: Hoggett, B. (2nd ed.), 314, 323. See also *Re T.* [1992] *The Times*, August 21, 1992.
[20] See Mental Health Act 1983, s.94.
[21] See Heywood and Massey, *Court of Protection Practice*, 12th ed., p. 187 *et seq.*
[22] In *re K* (*Enduring Powers of Attorney*) [1988] Ch. 310.
[23] *Re Beaney* [1978] 1 W.L.R. 770.
[24] These definitions are primarily directed at questions of medical treatment and compulsion. In cases of doubt doctors "approved by the Secretary of State as having special experience in the diagnosis or treatment of mental disorder" under s.12(2) of the Mental Health Act 1983, can be of particular help.

useful guidance today. Further study of mental illness may well make the theories and terminology of today as out of date as those of many of the doctors of the last century.

In broad terms it may be said that there are two grounds on which a person may be held to lack testamentary capacity; (i) that his mind has never developed sufficiently; and (ii) that his mind has become impaired, temporarily or permanently.

1. Failure of the mind to develop

Many persons are born with or acquire very limited mental capacity and their minds do not develop sufficiently to entertain the notion of making a will. There are, however, many persons of limited mental powers who attain the borderline of mental·capacity and these latter may be capable of making a will if it is in simple terms. Even if the will is not in simple terms, e.g. one prepared by a solicitor in legal phraseology, a person of limited intelligence may understand its provisions if they are carefully explained to him in simple language. The question in these cases is whether the deceased had attained sufficient capacity to fulfil the requirements previously considered.[25]

2. Impairment of the mind

There are two groups of causes of mental impairment. (1) Organic (physical) causes which impair the operation of the brain. (2) Functional disorders, i.e. mental illnesses without established physical cause. Each is revealed by thorough mental and physical examination: objective laboratory or other tests (e.g. C.T. scans) are almost always helpful with the former but not the latter.

(1) There are a great many causes of physical impairment of the mind—physical injury to the brain; alcohol and other drugs; the products of disease especially of the liver, kidneys, or endocrine glands; shrinkage of the brain in senile or prematurely senile disorders (e.g. Alzheimer's disease); brain deterioration due to poor blood supply in arteriosclerosis, or after a burst or blocked blood vessel (stroke). The faculties principally affected are consciousness, memory, attention, concentration, calculation and the ability to appreciate the significance of events and recall them. These are systematically tested in a full mental examination.

(2) The functional disorders without (so far) proven physical cause refer to morbid changes in mood (excessive cheerfulness or sadness) or of thinking (delusions, i.e. false beliefs, which are absurd and cannot be shaken by proof or argument a train of thought so

[25] The mental states considered in this paragraph approximate to those defined in the Mental Health Act 1983 as "severe mental impairment" and "mental impairment." Terms in everyday use include mental "handicap", "retardation", "subnormality", "defect" and the euphemistic "learning disability" (now increasingly used).

disordered that the listener has difficulty in following it, leading ultimately to incoherence) or of sensations of sight, hearing or bodily state (hallucinations, or false sensations).

These categories are not mutually exclusive and may occur together, as, for example, a demented individual may fail to recognise his wife and also have delusions of poverty. The most common causes of testamentary incapacity are as follows:

(a) Physical injury. Injury directly affecting the brain, *e.g.* through motor accident, is capable of causing a person to lose testamentary capacity. In probate cases it is rare for such injury to be alleged as the sole cause but physical injuries, particularly in the elderly, often indirectly affect the mind and can be at least a contributory cause of lack of testamentary capacity. Furthermore, physical injury received long ago may cause the mental deterioration associated with old age to set in earlier. Projection through a windscreen or from a motorcycle is particularly prone to injure the frontal lobes of the brain, producing impairment of emotional control and changes in personality.

(b) Physical illness. It is rare for physical illness alone to be pleaded as having reduced the deceased to a state of mental incapacity except when the disputed will was made during the deceased's last illness.[26] It should be noted, however, that advanced disease of the liver, kidneys, heart or lungs may either poison the brain or deprive it of oxygen, so rendering the patient incapable. Cancer and a number of rarer causes may damage the brain and disease of the temporal lobes may produce a paranoid psychosis very similar to schizophrenia (*infra*).

But even when a testator is on his death-bed and so enfeebled that he cannot speak or write he may use signs[27] or even through the medium of a pack of cards[28] express his testamentary wishes and make a valid will, when, for instance, unable to speak after a stroke.

If, while in health, the testator has given instructions for a will and it is prepared in accordance with those instructions, only a very slight degree of mental capacity is required at the time of execution. Though a testator is moribund and unable to remember or understand the instructions he has given, yet if he is capable of understanding and does understand that he is executing a will for which he has given instructions, that is sufficient.[29] However, terminal illness has in many cases been held so far to have impaired the mental capacity of the deceased as to cause the court to pronounce against the last will.

---

[26] But as an example, see *Battan Singh* v. *Amirchand* [1948] A.C. 161, P.C.

[27] *Gillett* v. *Rogers* (1913) 108 L.T. 732.

[28] *Moore* v. *Moore*, *The Times*, February 13, 1900.

[29] *Parker* v. *Felgate* (1883) 8 P.D. 171; see *Goodacre* v. *Smith* (1867) L.R. 1 P. & D. 351, 361; *Perera* v. *Perera* [1901] A.C. 354, 361; *Solicitor for the Duchy of Cornwall* v. *Batten* [1952] 2 T.L.R. 925. These cases are sometimes considered under the head of knowledge and approval but, it is submitted, are really pertinent to the question of testamentary capacity.

(c) Abuse of alcohol or drugs. An habitual heavy drinker may well be capable of making a will. Although, during a drinking bout, he may lack that capacity,[30] this may return to him when sober. Even if the deceased is shown to have been to some degree under the influence of alcohol, it may be proved that he was still able to appreciate the testamentary act in all its bearings.

Nevertheless medical evidence has often shown that alcohol abuse has caused such deterioration of the mental faculties (alcoholic dementia) so as to have removed testamentary capacity,[31] particularly if intemperate habits have been coupled with advancing age. It has also to be borne in mind that alcohol abuse may result in delusions (particularly of paranoid type) and hallucinations and merge into mental illness. In an interesting but rare condition, pseudo-memories, often of great complexity, are invented by the patient to fill gaps in the memory (Korsakoff syndrome).

Abuse of drugs is less commonly alleged in probate cases, but such abuse may cause a person to lose testamentary capacity, particularly when he is under their proximate influence. As with alcohol, delusions may occur. Delusions of persecution or of the unfaithfulness of a spouse are particularly characteristic of both.

(d) Dementia. Progressive intellectual loss due to death of brain cells occurring in pre-senile, or senile, phases, formerly known as senile dementia, is now usually referred to as Alzheimer's disease since most cases show the cellular changes typical of that condition. Of unknown origins, it is by far the most common cause of probate actions. Dementia impairs all intellectual function and, in particular, memory of recent events. Memory of remote events, on the contrary, is for a time often preserved or even enhanced. Consequently, old people frequently make fresh wills, mindful of the fact that a will made years ago no longer embodies their testamentary intentions, but forgetful that they have recently made a will to correct this.

The other common form of dementia, known as multi-infarct dementia, is due to blockage of the arteries to the brain, producing small areas of brain death. It is this type that is particularly prone to spells of confusion and lucid intervals.[32] Both types of dementia frequently co-exist and the assessment of testamentary capacity at the time the will is made, let alone retrospectively, may be extremely difficult.

The personality of old people is often well preserved and, at a casual interview, they may give every appearance of being capable of making a will although, in fact, they lack capacity.

---

[30] See *Re Heinke, The Times*, January 22, 1959.
[31] In criminal law the test is whether the craving for alcohol has or has not become involuntary. See *R. v. Tandy* [1989] 1 W.L.R. 350.
[32] See n. 33 below and text thereto.

The degree of capacity which must be retained by the old is discussed in *Den* v. *Vancleve*[33]:

> "By the terms 'a sound and disposing mind and memory' it has not been understood that the testator must possess these qualities of mind in the highest degree; otherwise, very few would make testaments at all; neither has it been understood that he must possess them in as great a degree as he may have formerly done, for even this would disable most men in the decline of life; the mind may be in some degree debilitated, the memory may have become in some degree enfeebled, and yet there may be enough left clearly to discern and discreetly to judge, of all those things and all those circumstances which enter into the nature of a rational, fair, and just testament. But if they have so far failed as that these cannot be discerned and judged of, then he cannot be said to be of sound and disposing mind and memory."

One of the most difficult features where wills made by old people are in question is their varying state of mental capacity. At some times they may be confused while, at others, they are completely lucid. Fluctuant confusion of this nature is particularly characteristic of dementia caused by arterial blockage. Alzheimer cases usually hold a steady, if deteriorating, state and both conditions may co-exist. Evidence which conclusively shows that within a few days of his testamentary act a person was quite incapable of making a will does not necessarily prove that he was incapable at the time he actually made it. For this reason the evidence of those present when the deceased gave instructions for his will or at its execution (if they were not merely witnesses called into his presence for a few moments) is of considerable weight. This is particularly so where such persons were unprejudiced and where the court is satisfied that they took pains to assess the mental state of the deceased and where they give evidence of facts and matters which support their assessment.[34]

In many cases the evidence of such lay witnesses has been preferred to medical evidence as to capacity based on attendances on the deceased on other occasions. Such evidence has in particular been preferred to conclusions as to testamentary capacity drawn by medical men from the evidence given and not from personal medical knowledge of the deceased. It has been said that when a solicitor is drawing up a will for an aged testator or one who has been seriously ill, it should be witnessed or approved by a medical practitioner who ought, then, to record his examination. This is the "golden if tactless rule." Other precautions are that if there was an

---

[33] 2 Southard at p. 660, cited with approval by Cockburn C.J. in *Banks* v. *Goodfellow* (1870) L.R. 5 Q.B. 549, 567.

[34] See *infra*, for the practice which should be adopted in cases where a person's testamentary capacity is in doubt.

earlier will it should be examined and any proposed alterations should be discussed with the testator.[35]

(e) "Functional" mental illness. Illnesses of this type serious enough to affect testamentary capacity are usually psychoses, characterised by distortion of the sense of reality and lack of insight into this change. The commonest psychoses are schizophrenia or affective, *i.e.* mood (manic or depressive) disorders. Schizophrenia involves distortion of thought and emotion with delusions, often of persecution, hallucinations, usually auditory, and indifference to important matters, with over-concern for trivialities. Bizarre and unpredictable behaviour may occur, including suicide. Persons suffering from schizophrenia not infrequently exclude from their wills those who have a legitimate claim in their testamentary bounty. The disease tends to progress with phases of at first complete and later partial recovery.[36] There is withdrawal from the world without—social isolation—and disruption of the world within.

Mood disorders take two forms: in the manic form abnormal happiness, loquacity and perhaps irritability are displayed and conduct in social, financial and sexual spheres may become irresponsible. A person afflicted may spend or dispose of immense wealth, which generally exists only in his imagination. The depressive form of the illness is much more common and may be manifested in delusions of guilt, sinfulness and hopelessness. In the elderly, delusions of poverty, even in the very rich, are characteristic. Single attacks of the disorder or repeated attacks with complete recovery are a particular feature and its incidence rises with age whereas schizophrenia starts usually during adolescence or early adult life.

While the distinctions made above are of great importance from the medical point of view, the question to be determined in probate cases is seldom what form of mental illness afflicts the testator, but whether its degree is such as to remove testamentary capacity. In both schizophrenia and affective disorders an acute onset generally carries the most hopeful outlook under modern treatment. In *Mudway* v. *Croft*[37] Sir H. J. Fust said:

> " . . . it has frequently been attempted to furnish some general rules which might serve as guides to courts of law in the investigation and decision of cases of (alleged unsoundness of mind) but all endeavours to do so have failed. . . . It is absolutely and essentially necessary to look to the peculiar circumstances of each individual case; and to judge from the whole character of the person whose mental capacity is the subject of enquiry, what was the state and condition of mind of

---

[35] *Kenward* v. *Adams*, *The Times*, November 29, 1975; *Re Simpson* (1977) 121 S.J. 224: See also *Re Cummins* [1972] Ch. 62, 67: "It was witnessed by a consultant psychiatrist and a solicitor. We must assume that he was of sufficient testamentary capacity."

[36] For detailed, internationally accepted, descriptions of mental disorders, see International Classification of Diseases, 10th Revision, Chapter V(F): World Health Organization, 1990 (I.C.D.–10) and/or Diagnostic and Statistical Manual of Mental Disorders (3rd Ed.)—Revised, American Psychiatric Association, Washington, DC, 1987 (DSM-III-R).

[37] (1843) 3 Curt. 671, 676.

that individual; not only with respect to the immediate times at which a will is executed, but at the intermediate stages of his life."

This approach to cases of disputed mental capacity is particularly useful where the deceased has suffered from mental illness. Mental illness may be so mild as not to affect testamentary capacity or so severe as to remove it altogether. As Lord Cranworth said in *Boyse* v. *Rossborough*[38]:

"Between . . . an extreme case (of mental illness) and that of a man of perfectly sound and vigorous understanding, there is every shade of intellect, every degree of mental capacity. There is no possibility of mistaking midnight for noon; but at what precise moment twilight becomes darkness is hard to determine."

In the majority of cases involving probate, the mental illness advances slowly and, where it recedes, its cure is likely to be equally slow. Consequently it is particularly difficult to determine when mental illness has removed testamentary capacity. Epilepsy was treated as a "disease of the mind" in *R.* v. *Sullivan*.[39]

Lucid intervals

This time-honoured term refers to fluctuations in most mental illnesses, originally spontaneous, but nowadays much more likely to be induced by treatment. It is increasingly likely, therefore, that testamentary capacity can be induced, if only for a short period, by the available physical treatments. These add to the difficulty of determining whether a person who is mentally ill has testamentary capacity at the time of making his will. It is recognised that a person who, in general, has lost testamentary capacity by reason of mental illness may have what have been termed "lucid intervals." These are periods when, even though all symptoms of mental illness have not been eradicated, the mind has returned temporarily to a sufficiently balanced state to weigh up the considerations which should guide a testator in making his will. Lucid intervals are a particular feature where disease of the brain causes mental illness, when it may be well known to the family doctor or attendant nurse that the testator is quite lucid early in the morning or in the evening, but is confused at other times. They should be consulted or asked to be present when the will is to be prepared or executed.

Once it has been proved or admitted that a testator has, in general, lost testamentary capacity through mental illness at a date before the purported will, the burden of proving that it was executed during a lucid interval lies on those who so allege.[40] The proposition laid down in *Smith* v. *Tebbitt*[41] to

---

[38] (1857) 6 H.L.C. 2, 45.

[39] [1984] A.C. 156.

[40] *Per* Lord Thurlow in *Att.-Gen.* v. *Parnther* (1792) 3 Bro.C.C. 441, 444; *Hall* v. *Warren* (1804) 9 Ves. 605, 611; *Groom* v. *Thomas* (1829) 2 Hagg.Ecc. 443, 434; a principle repeatedly acted upon in later unreported cases.

[41] (1867) L.R. 1 P. & D. 354, 398.

the effect that once long-standing unsoundness of mind has been proved, it is not necessary to carry proof of it up to the moment of execution is no doubt correct, but it must not be assumed from this that once long-standing mental illness has been proved at any time in a testator's life, any special burden lies on those propounding a will made years after recovery to establish soundness of mind. But where mental illness has been proved to have existed at times both before and after the purported making of the disputed will, the allegation that it was made in a lucid interval must be established by evidence as strong as that which is required to prove that testamentary capacity has been lost through mental illness.[42] The reason for insisting on convincing proof of a lucid interval is that in many forms of mental illness the sufferer in many situations, on many occasions and to many people may give every appearance of normality. This is particularly the case where a person suffers from circumscribed delusions; for it not infrequently happens that only certain circumstances will cause him to evince the delusion in question.

Where it is proved that a person suffers from delusions the test of a lucid interval is that no symptom of that delusion can be called forth at the time when the will is made, even when the testator's mind is directed to the subject-matter of the delusion.[43] The testator should be able to describe his feelings and talk of the subject of his delusion without betraying any sign of unnecessary vehemence or excitement. In many circumstances, however, such a test would not be practicable.

Contents of the will may show a lucid interval

If a testator makes a will after the onset of mental illness, it is strong proof of a lucid interval that he does so in a rational way and without assistance and that he makes rational provisions in it as to the disposal of his property.[44] This is particularly so if his will contains provisions similar to those in wills made before the illness began. But such proof is far from conclusive, for it may be proved that the underlying mental illness prevents the sufferer from considering the nature and extent of his property and the claims of his relations on his testamentary bounty.

Delusions

In early cases it was held that the presence of delusions, *i.e.* false beliefs, precluded the possibility of testamentary capacity.[45] This doctrine must however be regarded as over-ruled. Medical practice recognises that iso-

---

[42] *Per* Lord Thurlow in *Att.-Gen.* v. *Parnther* (1792) 3 Bro.C.C. 441; see *Ayrey* v. *Hill* (1824) 2 Add. 206, 209.

[43] *Nichols and Freeman* v. *Binns* (1858) 1 Sw. & Tr. 239.

[44] See *Cartwright* v. *Cartwright* (1793) 1 Phill. 90, 100; *Bannatyne* v. *Bannatyne* (1852) 2 Rob. 472; *Nichols and Freeman* v. *Binns, supra.*

[45] See e.g. *Dew* v. *Clark* (1826) 3 Add. 79 (irrational antipathy to only daughter).

lated delusions or delusional systems may not deprive a person of such capacity. In *Banks* v. *Goodfellow*[46] Cockburn C.J. said:

> "No doubt, where the fact that the testator has been subject to any insane delusion is established, a will should be regarded with great distrust and every presumption should in the first instance be made against it. Where insane delusion has once been shown to have existed, it may be difficult to say whether the mental disorder may not possibly have extended beyond the particular form or instance in which it has manifested itself. It may be equally difficult to say how far the delusion may not have influenced the testator in the particular disposition of his property. And the presumption against a will made under such circumstances becomes additionally strong where the will is . . . one in which natural affection and the claims of near relationship have been disregarded. But where in the result a jury are satisfied that the delusion has not affected the general faculties of the mind, and can have had no effect upon the will, we see no sufficient reason why the testator should be held to have lost his right to make a will, or why a will made under such circumstances should not be upheld."

This view of the law on this topic has been followed ever since.[47]

Test of the presence of delusion

Delusion has been variously defined, but to almost every definition some objection can be raised.[48] Perhaps the best test for determining whether delusion is present in a person's mind is that laid down by Sir J. Hannen in *Boughton* v. *Knight*[49]:

> "You must not arbitrarily take your own mind as the measure (saying) 'I do not believe such and such a thing, and, therefore, a man who believes it is insane.' Nay more; you must not say 'I should not have believed such and such a thing; therefore the man who did believe it is insane.' But you must of necessity put to yourself this question and answer it, 'Can I understand how any man in possession of his senses could have believed such and such a thing?' And if the answer you give is, 'I cannot understand it,' then it is of the necessity of the case that you should say that the man is not sane."

In practice it is often difficult to draw a line between unreasonable belief, overvalued idea, suspicion or fear, and delusion. What starts as an

---

[46] (1870) L.R. 5 Q.B. 549, 570.

[47] See *Boughton* v. *Knight* (1873) L.R. 3 P. & D. 64; *Smee* v. *Smee* (1879) 5 P.D. 84, 89. An example of a delusion which has no effect on testamentary capacity would be the belief that cogwheels were interfering with the patient's intestinal functions. Juries are now unknown in probate actions, but the right to a jury remains and it is thought that the appropriate procedure would be to transfer the case to the Queen's Bench Division.

[48] See the consideration of these definitions in *Smith* v. *Tebbitt* (1867) L.R. 1 P. & D. 354, 398, 401 *et seq.*

[49] (1873) L.R. 3 P. & D. 64, 68.

unreasonable belief may develop into an irrational belief. But merely because a person has extraordinary ideas he is not to be presumed to be suffering from a delusion.[50]

In some cases where the delusion is of a limited nature and only exists in relation to a particular person or persons,[51] the testator being quite rational in general, the court may hold that only part of the will must be rejected, but that the rest can be pronounced for.[52]

Burden of proving unsoundness of mind

Although those propounding the will must satisfy the court that the testator was of sound disposing mind,[53] yet if the will is rational on the face of it and is shown to be duly executed and no other evidence is offered, the court will pronounce for it, presuming that the testator was mentally competent.[54] Slight evidence of mental incapacity will not disturb this presumption.[55]

It has, therefore, been said that the burden of proving unsoundness of mind lies on those who allege it.[56] But when the whole evidence is before the court, the decision must be against the validity of the will, unless it is affirmatively established that the deceased was of sound mind when he executed it.[57]

The burden of proof may shift from one party to another in the course of a case.[58] Where grave suspicion of incapacity arises in the case of those propounding the will, they must dispel that suspicion by proving testamentary capacity.[59] Thus where it is admitted by those propounding the will that the deceased suffered from serious mental illness at a period before the will,[60] or where its terms are incoherent, irrational or strange,[61] a presumption is raised against it, though not a conclusive one.

The fact that the deceased became mentally ill after the will was executed does not necessarily raise a presumption against it, but this fact may throw an adverse light on antecedent behaviour of an ambivalent character.[62]

It is doubtful whether the mental illness or even complete insanity of

---

[50] *Austen* v. *Graham* (1854) 8 Moo.P.C. 493.

[51] Irrational hostility to close friends or relatives is not uncommon in old age.

[52] *Re Bohrmann* [1938] 1 All E.R. 271.

[53] *Per* Lord Brougham in *Waring* v. *Waring* (1848) 6 Moo.P.C. 341.

[54] *Symes* v. *Green* (1859) 1 Sw. & Tr. 401; *Sutton* v. *Sadler* (1857) 3 C.B.(N.S.) 87, 98. A testator is entitled to be capricious or improvident, see *Bird* v. *Luckie* (1850) 8 Hare at p. 306.

[55] See *Sutton* v. *Sadler*, *supra*.

[56] *Dew* v. *Clark and Clark* (1826) 3 Add. 79; *Wheeler and Batsford* v. *Alderson* (1831) 3 Hagg.Ecc. 574.

[57] *Symes* v. *Green*, *supra*; *Sutton* v. *Sadler*, *supra*; *Smith* v. *Tebbitt* (1867) L.R. 1 P. & D. 354, 398; see *Harmes* v. *Hinkson* (1946) 90 S.J. 515, P.C.

[58] *Waring* v. *Waring* (1848) 6 Moo.P.C. 341.

[59] *Ibid.* p. 356.

[60] *Bannatyne* v. *Bannatyne* (1852) 2 Rob. 472.

[61] *Austen* v. *Graham* (1854) 8 Moo.P.C. 493.

[62] *Burrows* v. *Burrows* (1827) 1 Hagg.Ecc. 109; *Hoby* v. *Hoby* (1828) 1 Hagg.Ecc. 146, 150; *Wheeler and Batsford* v. *Alderson* (1831) 3 Hagg.Ecc. 574.

relatives of the deceased is admissible to show that he suffered from mental illness.[63]

Where delusions exist the burden is on those propounding the will to show that they did not affect the making of it.[64] Unless the court is satisfied that there is no reasonable connection between the delusion and the bequests in the will, it must pronounce against the will.[65]

Where a lucid interval is alleged to have existed when the will was made, the burden of so proving lies on those propounding the will.[66]

Testamentary capacity where the deceased died domiciled abroad

Where the deceased died domiciled abroad his testamentary capacity must be determined according to the law of his domicile,[67] but the court will apply the *lex fori, i.e.* English law, as to evidential matters.[68]

2. KNOWLEDGE AND APPROVAL[69]

A party who puts forward a document as being the true last will of the deceased must establish that the testator knew and approved of its contents at the time when he executed it.[70] The testator's knowledge and approval of the contents of the will are part of the burden of proof assumed by everyone who propounds a testamentary document.[71]

In ordinary circumstances the burden of proof is discharged by proof of testamentary capacity and of due execution, from which knowledge and approval by the testator of the contents of his will are assumed.[72] But, in one of the kinds of circumstances considered below,[73] knowledge and approval must be proved affirmatively by those propounding the will.

Proof of knowledge and approval

Affirmative proof of knowledge and approval may take any form, pro-

---

[63] See *Marsh v. Tyrrell and Harding* (1828) 2 Hagg.Ecc. 84; (1832) 3 Hagg.Ecc. 471; *Frere v. Peacocke* (1843) 3 Curt. 664, 670.

[64] *Smee* v. *Smee* (1879) 5 P.D. 84; see *Banks v. Goodfellow* (1870) L.R. 5 Q.B. 549, 570. The observations of Lord Haldane in *Sivewright v. Sivewright*, 1920 S.C.(H.L.) 63, 64 are generally considered to be *obiter*.

[65] *Smee* v. *Smee, supra*, at p. 92.

[66] See *ante*, pp. 166 *et seq.*

[67] *Re Maraver* (1828) 1 Hagg.Ecc. 498; *Re Fuld, Hartley v. Fuld (Fuld Intervening)* (No. 3) [1968] p. 675.

[68] *Re Hartley, Hartley v. Fuld (Fuld intervening) (No. 3) supra.*

[69] Knowledge and approval is here treated as part of the substantive validity of a will, but is, perhaps, strictly merely an evidential matter: *Re Fuld, Hartley v. Fuld (Fuld intervening) (No. 3)* [1968] P. 675.

[70] *Barry v. Butlin* (1838) 2 Moo.P.C. 480; *Guardhouse v. Blackburn* (1866) L.R. 1 P. & D. 109, 116; *Atter v. Atkinson* (1869) L.R. 1 P. & D. 665, 670; *Cleare v. Cleare* (1869) L.R. 1 P. & D. 655, 657. As to pleading see *post*, p. 000 and *Re Stott deceased* [1980] 1 W.L.R. 246.

[71] *Cleare* v. *Cleare, supra.*

[72] *Barry v. Butlin, supra*, at p. 484; *Guardhouse v. Blackburn, supra*, at p. 116; *Cleare v. Cleare, supra. Re Morris* [1971] P. 62.

[73] See *post*, pp. 172 *et seq.*

vided it is strong enough to satisfy the court. The fact that the deceased gave instructions for his will, or that it was read over to him or by him is, no doubt, the most satisfactory, but not the only satisfactory form of proof.[74] The court will naturally look for such evidence. It may be impossible to establish a will without it, but the court does not require it in every case[75] and has, in numerous cases, been satisfied as to the knowledge and approval of the testator without such evidence, provided that other evidence and the circumstances of the case warrant such a conclusion.

There must be a proper and sufficient reading over of the will. It might not be a proper reading of the will by the testator if he were merely to cast an eye over it[76] or if a draft has been sent him for his perusal, accompanied by a letter to the effect that there had been no material departure from his instructions.[77] Clearly reading over the will at such a speed as to make it virtually impossible for the testator to follow it would not be enough; nor, in the case of a somewhat deaf man, would it suffice to read it over in such a low voice that the testator could not properly hear it.

It is not essential to prove that a will originated with the testator and, therefore, proof of instructions may be dispensed with, provided that it is proved that the testator completely understood, adopted and sanctioned the disposition proposed to him, and that the instrument itself embodied that disposition.[78] Where circumstances excite the vigilance and suspicion of the court a very high degree of proof may be required.[79]

Where a mistake either on the part of the testator or his draftsman is alleged, the burden of proof is on those setting up the mistake and varies according to the circumstances.[80] There is no rule that in the absence of fraud a testator who reads over a will must be taken to have known and approved its contents.[81]

Instructions while the testator is in health; execution when he is in extremis

Where a testator, in a state approaching insensibility, executes a will drawn up in accordance with previous instructions, though he may not remember them and could not understand the will even if read to him clause by clause, yet, if he is capable of understanding and does understand that he is engaged in executing the will for which he has given instructions, he has been held to know and approve of its contents.[82]

---

[74] *Guardhouse* v. *Blackburn, supra.*
[75] *Barry* v. *Butlin, supra,* at p. 485.
[76] *Garnett-Botfield* v. *Garnett-Botfield* [1901] P. 335, 343.
[77] *Brisco* v. *Baillie and Hamilton* [1902] P. 234.
[78] *Constable and Bailey* v. *Tufnell and Mason* (1833) 4 Hagg.Ecc. 465, 477.
[79] See *post,* p. 173.
[80] See *post,* pp. 177 *et seq.*
[81] *Re Morris* [1971] P. 62.
[82] *Parker* v. *Felgate* (1883) 8 P.D. 171; see *Goodacre* v. *Smith* (1867) L.R. 1 P. & D. 351, 359, 361; *Perera* v. *Perera* [1901] A.C. 354, 361; *Solicitor for Duchy of Cornwall* v. *Batten* [1952] 2 T.L.R. 925. *Re Flynn* [1982] 1 W.L.R. 310, 320.

Want of knowledge and approval of part of a will

The principles set out above apply equally to a portion of a will as to the whole.[83] If, therefore, it can be proved that any word or clause in the will has been introduced without the testator's knowledge and approval, such word or clause may be rejected and the remainder of the will only admitted to probate.[84] The broad proposition just laid down has, however, been the subject of much judicial consideration and is considered in detail later.[85]

When affirmative proof of knowledge and approval must be given

Knowledge and approval must be affirmatively proved by those propounding the will if those who oppose it, by cross-examination or otherwise, succeed in meeting the prima facie case raised by proof of execution.[86] But certain circumstances, in themselves, once admitted, raise doubts as to knowledge and approval and oblige those setting up the will to call evidence to dispel them.

If instructions are given by a deaf and dumb person by signs and not in writing[87] the court will require to be satisfied that the testator made his meaning clear and that his intentions are embodied in his will. Where a testator cannot speak or write[88] or is paralysed[89] the court must be satisfied that the deceased knew and approved of his will. Where the will of a blind or illiterate person contains no statement to the effect that the will was read over to him the court must also be satisfied as to knowledge and approval. Although it is preferable that the will should have been read over to such testators or, at least, the substance of it explained to them, this is not essential in all cases. If the court is satisfied that the testator gave instructions for his will and that these instructions were embodied in it, the will may be upheld although it was not read over.[90]

Affirmative evidence of knowledge and approval may be required where a will is alleged to have been signed by another person for the deceased and at his direction. The form of the will itself may raise doubt, e.g. where a legacy to a named person is incomplete: "I leave X £. . . . "

Where the burden falls on those propounding the will its weight varies with the circumstances. In some cases very little is required to satisfy the court that the deceased knew and approved of his will. But in cases where

---

[83] *Guardhouse* v. *Blackburn* (1866) L.R. 1 P. & D. 109, 116.
[84] See *Rhodes* v. *Rhodes* (1882) 7 App.Cas. 192, 198. See *Re Austin* (1929) 73 S.J. 545 where the court was not satisfied as to the righteousness of the transaction in relation to one clause. See also *Re Morris* [1971] P. 62; *Re Phelan* [1972] Fam. 33.
[85] See *post.*
[86] *Cleare* v. *Cleare* (1869) L.R. 1 P. & D. 655, 658.
[87] See *Re Geale* (1864) 3 Sw. & Tr. 431.
[88] *Re Owston* (1862) 2 Sw. & Tr. 461; *Gillett* v. *Rogers* (1913) 108 L.T. 732.
[89] *Gillett* v. *Rogers, supra.*
[90] *Fincham* v. *Edwards* (1842) 3 Curt. 63; 4 Moo.P.C. 198 (on appeal, *sub nom. Edwards* v. *Fincham*); see *Re Axford* (1860) 1 Sw. & Tr. 540.

the vigilance and suspicion of the court are aroused the burden of proof may be so heavy that it can hardly be removed.[91]

Circumstances which excite the vigilance and suspicion of the court

"If a party writes or prepares a will under which he takes a benefit," said Parke B. in *Barry* v. *Butlin*,[92] "That is a circumstance that ought generally to excite the suspicion of the court, and call upon it to be vigilant and jealous in examining the evidence in support of the instrument, in favour of which it ought not to pronounce unless the suspicion is removed, and it is judicially satisfied that the paper propounded does express the true will of the deceased."

In *Fulton* v. *Andrew*[93] Lord Hatherley said[94]: "There is one rule which has always been laid down by the courts having to do with wills, and that is that a person who has been instrumental in the framing of a will, and who obtains a bounty by that will, is placed in a different position from ordinary legatees who are not called upon to substantiate the truth and honesty of the transaction as regards their legacies. It is enough in their case that the will was read over to the testator and that he was of sound mind and memory and capable of comprehending it. But there is a further onus on those who take for their own benefit, after being instrumental in preparing or obtaining a will. They have thrown on them the onus of showing the righteousness of the transaction."

In the earlier case of *Barry* v. *Butlin*[95] it was laid down by Parke B.[96] that "it cannot be that the simple fact of a party who prepared the will being himself a legatee is in every case and under all circumstances to create a contrary presumption" (*i.e.* against the will) "and to call upon the court to pronounce against the will unless additional evidence" (*i.e.* evidence beyond the proof of testamentary capacity and due execution) "is produced to prove knowledge of its contents by the deceased." The learned judge pointed out that in some cases such a circumstance would have no weight at all, *e.g.* where the legacy was small in relation to the size of the estate. The word "bounty" used by Lord Hatherley in the extract from his speech in *Fulton* v. *Andrew*[97] quoted earlier must, it is submitted, mean a benefit that is substantial in relation to the size of the estate.

It is clear from *Fulton* v. *Andrew*[98] that it is not merely where a person writes or prepares a will under which he so benefits that the suspicion of the court is aroused. For example a person may be instrumental in obtaining a

---

[91] *Wintle* v. *Nye* [1959] 1 W.L.R. 284.
[92] (1838) 2 Moo.P.C. 480, 481. For a comparable principle in matters of construction, see *Re Pugh's Will Trusts* [1967] 1 W.L.R. 1262 and cases there cited.
[93] (1875) L.R. 7 H.L. 448; see *Brown* v. *Fisher* (1890) 63 L.T. 465.
[94] (1875) L.R. 7 H.L. 448, 471.
[95] (1838) 2 Moo.P.C. 480.
[96] At p. 484.
[97] *Supra.*
[98] (1875) L.R. 7 H.L. 448.

will when he suggests terms benefiting himself and accompanies the testator to a solicitor of his own choosing, especially if he remains present while the instructions for the will are given. A variety of other circumstances may combine to show that a person has procured a will for his own benefit.

Evidence where the righteousness of the transaction is in question

Some early cases[99] might appear to lay down that wherever any person has procured a substantial benefit for himself he must dispel suspicion by proving that the deceased gave instructions for the will or that it was read over to him. But in *Barry* v. *Butlin*[1] Parke B. said[2]: "Nor can it be necessary that in all cases, even if the testator's capacity is doubtful, the precise species of evidence of the deceased's knowledge of the will is to be in the shape of instructions for or reading over the instrument. They form, no doubt, the most satisfactory, but they are not the only satisfactory description of proof by which the cognisance of the contents of the will may be brought home to the deceased. The court would naturally look for such evidence, in some cases it might be impossible to establish a will without it, but it has no right in every case to require it."

Conversely, as is shown later,[3] the mere fact that instructions were given for the will and that the will was read over to the testator may not be enough to remove suspicion.

Conduct of the beneficiaries may amount to fraud

In *Fulton* v. *Andrew*[4] Lord Cairns said[5]: "How does the qualification that there must be no fraud bear on the present case? It is very difficult to define the various grades and shades of fraud; but it is an important qualification to engraft upon the general state of things that the reading over of a will to a competent testator must be taken to have apprised him of the contents. If your Lordships find a case in which persons who are strangers to the testator, who have no claim upon his bounty, have themselves prepared, for their own benefit, a will disposing in their favour of a large portion of the property of the testator, and if you submit that case to a jury, it may well be that the jury may consider that there was a want, on the part of those who propounded the will, of the execution of the duty which lay upon them, to bring home to the mind of the testator the effect of his testamentary act and that that failure in performing the duty which lay on them amounted to a greater or lesser degree of fraud on their part."

[99] *e.g. Billinghurst* v. *Vickers* (1810) 1 Phill. 187.
[1] (1838) 2 Moo.P.C. 480.
[2] At p. 485.
[3] See next paragraph.
[4] (1875) L.R. 7 H.L. 448.
[5] At p. 463.

Failure to Plead Fraud

This view was approved by the House of Lords in *Wintle* v. *Nye*,[6] in which case lack of testamentary capacity and want of knowledge and approval were pleaded, but fraud and undue influence were not. It was further held that despite the absence of any express plea of fraud or undue influence a solicitor who, having little or no claim on the testatrix, had procured a large benefit in her will, might be cross-examined to the effect that if the testatrix did not know and approve of her will it was because of fraud. It was laid down that, in some cases, suspicion may be so grave that it can hardly be removed.

Fraud not the sole or vital issue

The court must not address itself solely to the question of fraud and decide the case on whether or not those opposing the will have made out a case of fraud.[7] The vital and essential issue in cases of this kind is whether those propounding the will have discharged the burden of showing the righteousness of the transaction and that the paper propounded expresses the true will of the deceased.[8]

It may not be strictly correct to say that those propounding the will must show that it was not obtained by fraud or undue influence[9]; but in some cases the circumstances may raise such suspicion that if it is not dispelled the court will refuse to be satisfied as to the righteousness of the transaction.

It has been said[10] that it is the duty of anyone who expects a will to be made in his favour to see that the testator receives independent advice and that such a person should take care that the evidence in support of the will should not be that of himself alone, but be independent and impartial. No doubt it is a counsel of prudence to take the steps advocated, but it may not always be possible to do so and failure to take them is not necessarily a reason for refusing to be satisfied as to the righteousness of the transaction, though it may be so in particular circumstances.

Particular matters which arouse suspicion

Where a person is active in the preparation or at the execution of a will under which he benefits, a variety of circumstances increase suspicion. Where a testator gives instructions in answer to questions, particularly leading questions, the court will require more stringent proof than in other cases that the will embodies the unprompted testamentary intentions of the deceased.[11] The fact that the deceased has given no instructions for the will

---

[6] [1959] 1 W.L.R. 284. See also *Re Fuld (No. 3)* [1968] P. 675, 722, *post*, p. 432, R.S.C. Ord. 18, r. 8(1). Compare text to n. 59, *post*.

[7] *Tyrrell* v. *Painton* [1894] P. 151; see *Re Scott, Huggett* v. *Reichman* (1966) 110 S.J. 852.

[8] *Finny* v. *Govett* (1908) 25 T.L.R. 186, C.A.

[9] See *Spiers* v. *English* [1907] P. 122, 124.

[10] In *Parker* v. *Duncan* (1890) 62 L.T. 642.

[11] *Green* v. *Skipworth* (1809) 1 Phill. 54, 58.

requires explanation, especially where the beneficiary himself prepared it[12]; and so does the fact that the deceased was without independent advice, legal or otherwise, and that his relations and friends were kept from him.

A radical departure from testamentary dispositions, long adhered to, requires explanation, especially if the person in whose favour the change is made possesses great influence and authority with the deceased and originates and conducts the whole transaction[13]; and such facts may raise strong suspicion that the change was not the result of the free volition of the deceased.[14] But that suspicion may be dissipated by proof of a change of circumstances since the earlier wills.[15]

The testator's feebleness of body or mind may not be relied on to question the righteousness of the transaction.[16]

Although, as is shown later,[17] persons standing in certain special relationships to others, e.g. doctor and patient, solicitor and client, do not have to disprove undue influence where they obtain a substantial benefit under the will, they will be called upon to show the righteousness of the transaction where they have been active in procuring the will.[18]

Putting to proof the righteousness of the transaction

In many of the older cases the righteousness of the transaction was raised under the plea of undue influence and there can be no doubt that it can still be raised in this way. In modern practice, however, it is usual to put a party to proof of the righteousness of the transaction under the plea of want of knowledge and approval. By this means the burden of proof is placed on those who propound the will, without the party attacking the will assuming the formidable task of proving undue influence. Moreover, even if those propounding the will succeed in satisfying the court as to the righteousness they will not necessarily be given costs against their opponents, whereas if undue influence is unsuccessfully pleaded, those who do so only rarely escape having to pay the costs.[19]

What circumstances do not raise the righteousness of the transaction

At one time a belief was prevalent that general circumstances surrounding the preparation and execution of a will might be adduced in pleading

[12] *Middleton* v. *Forbes* (1787) cited in *Ingram* v. *Wyatt* (1828) 1 Hagg.Ecc. 384, 395.
[13] *Marsh* v. *Tyrrell and Harding* (1828) 2 Hagg.Ecc. 84, 87.
[14] *Marsh* v. *Tyrrell, supra,* at p. 110; see *Wintle* v. *Nye* [1959] 1 W.L.R. 284.
[15] *Constable and Bailey* v. *Tufnell and Mason* (1833) 4 Hagg.Ecc. 465.
[16] See *Re R. deceased* [1951] P. 10, 16. This is the clear inference of the reference to *Barry* v. *Butlin* (1838) 2 Moo.P.C. 480, though the question did not arise in *Re R. deceased.* But see *per* Slade J. in *Re Stott* [1980] 1 W.L.R. 246, 251.
[17] See *post*, p. 183.
[18] See *Atter* v. *Atkinson* (1869) L.R. 1 P. & D. 665, 688; *Wintle* v. *Nye* [1959] 1 W.L.R. 284 (as to solicitors); *Greville* v. *Tylee* (1851) 7 Moo.P.C. 320 (as to medical men).
[19] See also *post*, p. 432. *Re Flynn* [1982] 1 W.L.R. 310, 321.

and evidence to excite the suspicion and vigilance of the court and to throw upon those propounding the will the onus of showing the righteousness of the transaction. This view was based largely on a misinterpretation of part of the judgment of Lindley L.J. in *Tyrrell* v. *Painton*.[20]

A practice arose of pleading a wide range of circumstances, including the intemperance, illness or great age of the deceased and the immorality of his relations with the beneficiary as showing want of knowledge and approval on the part of the deceased.

In *Re R. deceased*[21] Willmer J. carefully considered what circumstances could raise the question of the righteousness of the transaction. He exposed the error of the notions that had been entertained of the effect of *Tyrrell* v. *Painton*[22] and, after reviewing the authorities, said[23]: "The conclusion I draw from these authorities to which I have referred is that, when it is a question of knowledge and approval of the contents of a will the circumstances which are held to excite the suspicions of the court must be circumstances attending, or at least relevant to, the preparation and execution of the will itself." The learned judge based his judgment on the decision of the Court of Appeal in *Davis* v. *Mayhew*[24] to this effect and on the principle laid down in *Low* v. *Guthrie*[25] that the rule in *Barry* v. *Butlin*[26] and *Fulton* v. *Andrew*[27] is not to be used as a screen behind which a man is at liberty to charge another with fraud and dishonesty without assuming the responsibility of making that charge in plain terms.

It was pointed out in *Re R. decd.*[28] that surrounding circumstances not attending or relevant to the preparation and execution of the will may well be relevant to other issues such as testamentary capacity and undue influence.

Mistake[29]

A person may not know and approve of a will or of part thereof because of a mistake. Mistakes fall into three main categories: 1. Mistake as to the document signed; 2. mistake in relation to the revocation or revival of a will; 3. mistake as to particular words or dispositions contained in a will. In the latter case the mistake may give rise to the doctrine of election[30]

1. Mistake as to the document signed or destroyed

A person does not know and approve of a will which he does not intend

---

[20] [1894] P. 151, 157.
[21] [1951] P. 10.
[22] *Supra.*
[23] [1951] P. 10, 17.
[24] [1927] P. 264.
[25] [1909] A.C. 278.
[26] (1838) 2 Moo.P.C. 480.
[27] (1875) L.R. 7 H.L. 448.
[28] [1951] P. 10. See also *Re Stott deceased* [1980] 1 W.L.R. 249.
[29] As to rectification see p. 182 *post.*
[30] As to election see p. 979 *post* and 1990 L.Q.R. 487, 571.

to execute. Accordingly when a testator executes a will prepared for another, the document is not his will,[31] even if some of the provisions therein were intended by the signatory.[32]

Where a testator destroys a will intending to revoke his will but actually destroys the will of another living person, that will is not revoked.[33]

2. Mistakes in relation to the revocation and revival of wills

This topic is considered in those parts of this work on the revocation and the revival of wills.[34]

3. Mistake as to particular words or dispositions in a will

The fact that words or dispositions have been inserted in a will by mistake does not necessarily mean that the testator must be taken not to have known and approved of them or that, consequently, they may be omitted from probate.

In *Taylor* v. *Kershaw*[35] Greene M.R. said[36]:

"The jurisdiction of the Court of Probate to grant probate of a will textually different to the actual document signed by the testator is a strictly limited one. If the testator himself approved the words to which he put his signature (and the presumption is that he approved them), those words must stand. If the words were selected by the draftsman to whom the testator confided the task of drafting his will, similarly the words so selected must stand, even if the testator was ignorant of the actual words used. The mistake of the testator or of the draftsman employed by him as to the legal effect of the words used is immaterial. The jurisdiction, where it exists, is admittedly confined to the exclusion of words, since the insertion of words would run counter to the provisions of the Wills Act."

A testator may also be taken not to have known and approved the contents of a will where words have been omitted. In such circumstances the court may as a matter of construction supply the missing words or omit further words to give better effect to the testator's intention.

This outlines the law but the topic requires more detailed consideration.

Where the mistake is that of the testator

If a testator approves the words used in his will those words must stand, even if they do not have the legal effect that the testator intends. A testator cannot be understood to be saying that he approves the words he uses if,

[31] *Re Hunt* (1875) L.R. 3 P. & D. 250; *Re Meyer* [1908] P. 353.
[32] *Re Meyer, supra.*
[33] *Re Penson* [1960] C.L.Y. 1232.
[34] See *post*, pp. 190 and 218, respectively.
[35] [1939] P. 198.
[36] [1939] P. 198, 216. See also *Morrell* v. *Morrell* (1882) 7 P.D. 68.

and only if, they have the meaning he desires.[37] But the testator must know and approve of the words used and if, by a slip of the pen or other mistake, he writes one word or phrase intending to have written another it seems that the same principles apply as where a draftsman introduces mistakes into a will.[38] But it would be more difficult to satisfy the court of a mistake than where a draftsman had prepared the will.

The court has allowed printed words to be omitted from probate where the testator has used a printed will form, even where he has himself written the will. Thus an unintended gift printed in a somewhat misleading will form was ordered to be omitted.[39] Again, where a testator executed three printed will forms on the same day under the impression that three separate units of his property had to be dealt with by separate wills, each will form containing a revocation clause, the wills were admitted to probate without the revocation clauses, for these had been left in by inadvertence or a misunderstanding as to their effect.[40]

Where the words are selected by the draftsman

Words selected by a draftsman cannot be omitted from probate merely because he or the testator[41] mistakes or forgets their legal effect.[42]

If the draftsman inserts a provision in the will not fully carrying out the testator's instructions,[43] or even if he inserts it without any instructions at all and without reason,[44] that alone will not be a ground for omitting words. Even if the testator objects to the words being inserted but is persuaded to agree to this by entirely wrong advice as to their effect, the mistake must stand.[45]

But the testator must know of the words used. The court ordered the omission of a gift printed in a will form procured for the testator by a friend who did not read that clause over to him when reading the rest of the will.[46] The reading by the testator of his will must be a proper one and where it is read to him the will must be properly read,[47] but subject to this and to the circumstances being such as to raise the question of the righteousness of the transaction or where there is fraud,[48] a testator who has read his will or to whom it has been read must be presumed to have known and approved

---

[37] *Beech* v. *Public Trustee* [1923] P. 46, 53.
[38] See below.
[39] *Re Garroway* (1866) 116 N.L.J. 1061.
[40] *Re Phelan* [1972] Fam. 33 and *post*, p. 195.
[41] See above.
[42] *Morrell* v. *Morrell, supra*; *Gregson* v. *Taylor* [1917] P. 256; *Beech* v. *Public Trustee, supra*; see *Rhodes* v. *Rhodes* (1882) 7 App.Cas. 192. *Re Morris* [1971] P. 80 (approving a passage in Mortimer on which this and the succeeding paragraph are based).
[43] *Harter* v. *Harter* (1873) L.R. 3 P. & D. 11.
[44] *Rhodes* v. *Rhodes* (1882) 7 App.Cas. 192.
[45] *Collins* v. *Elstone* [1893] P. 1.
[46] *Re Duane* (1862) 2 Sw. & Tr. 590.
[47] See *ante*, p. 171.
[48] *Allen* v. *M'Pherson* (1847) 1 H.L.C. 191.

of it, even though the court finds it impossible to suppose that he had any intelligent appreciation of the effect of the words at all.[49]

Words introduced by a draftsman into a will through inadvertence

Where a draftsman writes words in a will which he does not intend or where they are typed in wrongly and the mistake is not noticed, the court will order them to be omitted. Thus where a testator gave instructions for a bequest of all his shares in a company to be made to a nephew, but the draftsman by inadvertence wrote "forty shares," the word "forty" was ordered to be omitted.[50] Where a testator gave instructions for a bequest of £10,000 to each of his daughters Georgina and Florence, but the draftsman omitted the name Florence and wrote that of Georgina in each bequest, the latter name was ordered to be omitted from the second bequest.[51] Where the number "103" was inserted in mistake for "105" it was ordered to be omitted[52]; as was the word "British" (where "Bristol" was substituted)[53]; and the word "including" in mistake for "excluding"[54]; the word "revenue" in mistake for "residue"[55] and the word "real" in mistake for "said."[56]

Where the relationship between persons mentioned in the will has been wrongly given, such description, e.g. "my uncle," may be omitted,[57] and so may the wrong name of an executor.[58]

But the rule is a narrow one. The court will not strike out a word introduced by inadvertence where to do so would effect a disposition not intended by the testator.[59] It has, however, been held that words may be omitted even if such omission will not give full effect to the testator's wishes and will render part of the will ambiguous or lacking any meaning.[60]

Omission of words in an attestation clause

Words in an attestation clause were held not to form part of the will and where a mistaken statement as to revocation was made in such clause it was ordered to be omitted.[61]

[49] See *Rhodes* v. *Rhodes, supra.*
[50] *Morrell* v. *Morrell* (1882) 7 P.D. 68. See also *Re Morris* [1971] P. 62 (and *ante*, n. 42).
[51] *Re Boehm* [1981] P. 247.
[52] *Re Walkeley* (1893) 69 L.T. 419. In this case the will was read over to the testator.
[53] *Re Bushell* (1887) 13 P.D. 7. But see *infra.*
[54] *Re Huddleston* (1890) 63 L.T. 255. In this and in the previous case words were substituted, but incorrectly; see *infra*, p. 181.
[55] *Re Schott* [1901] P. 190.
[56] *Vaughan* v. *Clerk* (1902) 87 L.T. 144.
[57] *Re Bowker* [1932] P. 93; *Re Clark* (1932) 147 L.T. 240.
[58] *Re Cooper* [1899] P. 193.
[59] *Taylor* v. *Kershaw* [1939] P. 198; see *Rhodes* v. *Rhodes* (1882) 7 App.Cas. 192. As to the application of the principle *ut res magis valeat* in contract and trust law see *per* Sachs L.J. in *Re Leek* [1969] 1 Ch. 563, 586.
[60] *Re Boehm* [1891] P. 247. *Re Morris* [1971] P. 62.
[61] *Re Atkinson* (1883) 8 P.D. 165.

Omission and substitution generally

Although the court may, in the circumstances already considered, order words introduced by mistake to be omitted it cannot substitute the words intended by the testator, for to do so would run counter to the Wills Act 1837.[62] Earlier decisions to the contrary[63] have been disapproved expressly[64] or by implication,[65] but it is sometimes possible for the equity jurisdiction to be used so that a wrongly named legatee is held to be a trustee for the person shown to have been intended.[66]

Apart from the limited provisions of the Administration of Justice Act 1982,[67] a court may not rectify a will by inserting words; to do so would be contrary to the Wills Act 1837.[68] Where, however, it is clear that words have been omitted from a will and it is clear as a matter of construction what those words are then the court of construction may read the necessary words into the will[69] or rearrange the existing words to give effect to the testator's intention.[70] However it cannot do so if, on the construction of the will, there is any real doubt as to the testator's true intention,[71] but in such circumstances the court may omit further words from the will if by doing so better effect can be given to the testator's known intention, even though the result is still different from that intended by the testator.[72] It has been said that the court is not to be detered by any accidental omission from putting the true signification on the will or to substitute what "some blundering attorney's clerk or law stationer" has written and treat that blunder as the intention of the testator.[73]

Mistake as to the date of the will

An incorrect date in a will cannot be corrected.[74] The procedure in an application for the probate of an incorrectly dated will is considered later.[75]

The burden of proof of mistake

As indicated in the passage from *Taylor* v. *Kershaw* cited earlier, if the

---

[62] *Re Schott, supra; Taylor* v. *Kershaw, supra.*
[63] *Re Bushell, supra; Re Huddleston, supra.*
[64] *Re Schott, supra.*
[65] *Taylor* v. *Kershaw, supra; Re Morris* [1971] P. 62.
[66] See *post,* p. 182. This may depend on not deleting the wrong name in the grant.
[67] See s.20.
[68] *Taylor* v. *Kershaw* [1939] P. 198; *Re Reynette-James* [1976] 1 W.L.R. 161.
[69] *Re Whitrick* [1957] 1 W.L.R. 844. But in *Re Cory* [1955] 1 W.L.R. 725, the court added words even though it could not be said precisely what the testator had intended. See also *Whitrick on Wills,* 7th ed. 556 and *Re Smith* [1948] Ch. 49, 53.
[70] *Re Bacharach's Will Trusts* [1959] Ch. 245.
[71] *Re Fallett* [1953] 1 W.L.R. 429. See also *Re Weald* [1962] Ch. 643 and *Re Murray* [1955] Ch. 69.
[72] *Re Boehm* [1891] P. 247; *Re Morris* [1971] P. 62; *Re Reynette-James* [1976] 1 W.L.R. 161.
[73] *Mello R.* v. *Daintree* (1886) 33 Ch.D. 198, 207; *Re Smith* [1948] Ch. 49.
[74] *Re Thomson* (1865) L.R. 1 P. & D. 8; *Reffell* v. *Reffell* (1866) L.R. 1 P. & D. 139.
[75] *Post,* p. 311.

testator has duly executed his will the presumption is that he knew and approved of all its contents, and that presumption becomes a very grave and strong one and only to be rebutted by the clearest evidence in cases where the will was read over to the testator.[76] It is, however, going too far to say[77] that it must be established beyond all doubt that the words which a party seeks to have omitted did not form part of the testator's will. Furthermore, the reading over must be a proper one.[78]

But where the will was not read over to the testator and the mistake is made in circumstances in which the court may omit words or dispositions, the mistake may be established on a balance of probabilities.[79]

Rectification

The will of a testator who dies after December 31, 1982 may be rectified by the court under section 20 of the Administration of Justice Act 1982[80] if it fails to carry out the testator's intentions in consequence of a clerical error or a failure to understand his instructions. In this context "clerical error" is not restricted to an error made by a clerk. It includes an error made by the testator in writing out or typing his own will.[81] The words should be construed as applying to an error made in the process of recording the intended words of the testator in the drafting or transcription of his will, as contrasted with an error made in carrying his intention into effect through a mistaken choice of words.[82] The application to rectify must be made within six months of the date of grant although the court may give "permission" for a later application. The personal representative of the testator is not liable for distributing any part of the estate after the end of the six month period but the power for a beneficiary to recover any part of the estate so distributed is not prejudiced by this provision.[83] Limited grants to settled land or trust property are not taken as affecting the date of grant, nor are grants limited to real estate or to personal estate unless a grant limited to the remainder of the estate has previously been made or is made at the same time.

Where the mistake is as to the ownership of property by the testator or somebody else the doctrine of election may provide a remedy in equity.[84]

[76] *Gregson* v. *Taylor* [1917] P. 256. But see *Crerar* v. *Crerar*, 106 L.J. 694, approved in *Re Morris* [1971] P. 62.
[77] As was said in *Gregson* v. *Taylor* [1917] P. 256, 261.
[78] See *ante*, p. 171.
[79] *Taylor* v. *Kershaw* [1939] P. 198.
[80] For full text see Appendix p. 1203 *post*.
[81] *Re Williams* [1985] 1 W.L.R. 905.
[82] *Wordingham* v. *Royal Exchange Trust Co. Ltd.*, *The Times*, December 11, 1991. See also *R.* v. *Comptroller General of Patents, ex p. Martin* (1953) 89 C.L.R. 381.
[83] See also 1983 Conveyancer 21.
[84] As to election see *post* p. 979 and 1990 L.Q.R. 487, 571.

3. UNDUE INFLUENCE

Definition

Undue influence has been defined in a number of cases,[85] but perhaps the best short definition is that of Sir J. P. Wilde in *Hall* v. *Hall*[86] "Pressure of whatever character . . . if so exercised as to overpower the volition without convincing the judgment." Pleas of undue influence, fraud and forgery are discouraged. It is open to a defendant to cross-examine to this effect on a plea of want of knowledge and approval.[87]

Chancery definition of undue influence does not apply in probate

Before enlarging on the definition given above it may be well to distinguish between undue influence as understood in probate and as understood in equity.[88]

In equity persons standing in certain relationships to others are liable to have undue influence presumed against them in relation to certain transactions, *e.g.* a father benefiting from a child, a doctor from his patient or a solicitor from his client. In consequence the erroneous view has sometimes been formed, strengthened by a misapprehension as to the effect of the Judicature Acts, that where the Chancery court would presume undue influence the probate court would do likewise.

The error of this view is clear from *Parfitt* v. *Lawless*[89] where Lord Cranworth's dictum in *Boyse* v. *Rossborough*[90] "Undue influence cannot be presumed" was quoted with approval.

The Chancery Division will not, on the grounds of fraud or undue influence, set aside or refuse to enforce provisions of a will pronounced valid by the probate court,[91] but in authorising dispositions under section 96 of the Mental Health Act 1983 the court will pay attention to relationships from which undue influence will be presumed.[92]

Undue influence as understood in probate

Speaking of undue influence in his charge to the jury in *Wingrove* v. *Wingrove*[93] Sir James Hannen said: "There is no subject upon which there

---

[85] *Williams* v. *Goude* (1828) 1 Hagg.Ecc. 577, 596; *Barry* v. *Butlin* (1838) 2 Moo.P.C. 480, 491; *Boyse* v. *Rossborough* (1857) 6 H.L.C. 2, 48.

[86] (1868) L.R. 1 P. & D. 481, 482.

[87] See *Re Fuld* [1968] P. 722 and *ante*, p. 175; *post*, p. 432; R.S.C. Ord. 76, r. 9(3) (*post* p. 1257); *Re Stott* [1980] 1 W.L.R. 246.

[88] For an example of the equitable jurisdiction see *Re Craig* [1971] Ch. 95. See also note 11, p. 185 *post.*

[89] (1872) L.R. 2 P. & D. 462, 468.

[90] *Supra*, at p. 49.

[91] *Allen* v. *M'Pherson* (1847) 1 H.L.C. 191, 210. As to the position in equity, see *Snell's Equity*, 29th ed., pp. 550–558. See also as to legacies to solicitors, *ante* p. 52.

[92] *Re C.M.G.* [1970] Ch. 574. See generally Heywood & Massey: *Court of Protection Practice*, 12th ed., pp. 191–196.

[93] (1885) 11 P.D. 81, 82.

is a greater misapprehension. . . . We are all familiar with the use of the word 'influence'; we say that one person has an unbounded influence over another, and we speak of evil influences and good influences, but it is not because one person has an unbounded influence over another that there-fore, when exercised, even though it may be very bad indeed, it is undue influence in the legal sense of the word. A young man may be caught in the toils of a harlot, who makes use of her influence to induce him to make a will in her favour, to the exclusion of his relatives. . . . A man may be the companion of another, and may encourage him in evil courses, and so obtain what is called an undue influence over him, and the consequence may be a will in his favour. But that again, shocking as it is, will not amount to undue influence. To be undue influence in the eye of the law there must be—to sum it up in one word—coercion. It must not be a case in which a person has been induced, by means such as I have suggested to you, to come to a conclusion that he will make a will in a particular person's favour, because if the testator has only been persuaded or induced by con-siderations which you may condemn, really and truly to intend to give his property to another, though you may disapprove of the act, yet it is strictly legitimate in the sense of its being legal. It is only when the will of the per-son who becomes a testator is coerced into doing that which he does not desire to do, that it is undue influence."

"The coercion may of course be of different kinds, it may be in the grossest form, such as actual confinement or violence, or a person in the last days or hours of life may have become so weak and feeble, that a very little pressure will be sufficient to bring about the desired result, and it may even be that the mere talking to him at that stage of illness and pressing something upon him, may so fatigue the brain, that the sick person may be induced, for quietness' sake, to do anything.[94] This would equally be coer-cion, though not actual violence."

Thus undue influence is not bad influence but coercion.[95] Persuasion and advice do not amount to undue influence so long as the free volition of the testator to accept or reject them is not invaded.[96] Appeals to the affections or ties of kindred, to a sentiment of gratitude for past services, or pity for future destitution or the like may fairly be pressed on the testator.[97] The testator may be led but not driven and his will must be the offspring of his own volition, not the record of someone else's.[98] There is no undue influence unless the testator if he could speak his wishes would say "this is not my wish but I must do it."[99]

[94] *Hacker* v. *Newborn* (1654) Style 427; *Lamkin* v. *Babb* (1752) 1 Lee 1; *Kinleside* v. *Harri-son* (1818) 2 Phill. 449, 551; *Constable* v. *Tufnell* (1833) 4 Hagg.Ecc. 465, 485. See also *Re Flynn* [1982] 1 W.L.R. 310, 320.
[95] See *Williams* v. *Goude* (1828) 1 Hagg.Ecc. 577, 581, 596.
[96] *Parfitt* v. *Lawless* (1872) L.R. 2 P. & D. 462, 474.
[97] *Hall* v. *Hall* (1868) L.R. 1 P. & D. 481, 482.
[98] *Hall* v. *Hall, supra,* at p. 482.
[99] *Wingrove* v. *Wingrove* (1885) 11 P.D. 81, 83; *Baudains* v. *Richardson* [1906] A.C. 169, 184. *Re Flynn* [1982] 1 W.L.R. 310, 320.

Although force and coercion are sometimes pleaded as such, they are really only alternative pleas for that of undue influence. It also seems clear that as in contract there can be such a thing as economic coercion or duress in probate law.[1]

In some cases[2] it has been held that undue influence may be exercised by fraud, but this view has not received acceptance.[3] Furthermore, the present Rules of Court require that fraud should be expressly pleaded.[4]

Undue influence as to part of a will

If it is proved that part of a will only has been obtained by undue influence, that part may be rejected and the remainder pronounced for,[5] at least in cases where the part which is rejected is distinct and severable.[6] It seems, however, that even where the rejection of part of a will would render ambiguous or insensible some other part not obtained by undue influence, the court should not reject that other part.[7]

How far undue influence must be exercised only in relation to the will

Strictly, to upset a will the undue influence must be shown to have been exercised in relation to the will itself.[8] Where, however, there is evidence that the testator was so far under the influence of persons benefiting from his will that he was not a free agent, the conclusion may be warranted that undue influence was exercised in relation to the will, even if there is no direct evidence.[9]

Alteration of Will prevented—Equity

In these circumstances it seems that the court will uphold the will but hold those exercising undue influence to be trustees for the persons who would have benefited had the alteration to the will been made.[10] This will arise under the equity jurisdiction, so that undue influence in the Chancery sense might here apply.[11]

[1] See *Atlas Express* v. *Kaflo* [1989] Q.B. 833.
[2] *Barry* v. *Butlin* (1838) 2 Moo.P.C. 480, 491; *Boyse* v. *Rossborough* (1857) 6 H.L.C. 2, 48.
[3] See *Parfitt* v. *Lawless* (1872) L.R. 2 P. & D. 462, 471.
[4] Ord. 18, r. 8(1). But as to cross-examination without such a plea see *ante*, p. 175. The distinction lies in the fact that probate is an order *in rem*.
[5] *Billinghurst* v. *Vickers* (1810) 1 Phill. 187; *Allen* v. *M'Pherson* (1847) 1 H.L.C. 191, 209; *Fulton* v. *Andrew* (1875) L.R. 7 H.L. 448; *Farrelly* v. *Corrigan* [1899] A.C. 563.
[6] *Rhodes* v. *Rhodes* (1882) 7 App.Cas. 192, 198.
[7] See *Re Boehm* [1891] P. 247, 251.
[8] *Per* Lord Cranworth L.C. in *Boyse* v. *Rossborough* (1857) 6 H.L.C. 2, 48; see *Wingrove* v. *Wingrove* (1885) 11 P.D. 81, 83; *Baudains* v. *Richardson* [1906] A.C. 169; *Craig* v. *Lamoureux* [1920] A.C. 349.
[9] *Per* Lord Cranworth L.C. in *Boyse* v. *Rossborough, supra*, p. 51; *Craig* v. *Lamoureux, supra*, at p. 356.
[10] *Betts* v. *Doughty* (1879) 5 P.D. 27 (where a compromise was reached).
[11] That is to say a presumption might arise, or undue influence be much easier to prove. See *ante*, p. 183.

Burden of proof in cases where undue influence is alleged

While the overall burden of proving a will lies on those who propound it,[12] such burden is, in general, discharged by showing that the will was duly executed and that the testator had testamentary capacity.[13] On these matters being shown, those alleging undue influence must prove it; for, as already stated, undue influence cannot be presumed.[14] It is not sufficient to show that the circumstances attending the execution are consistent with its having been procured by undue influence. It must be shown that they are inconsistent with any other hypothesis.[15]

Nevertheless in many cases in which the court has not been satisfied that there was undue influence, and even in cases where undue influence has been positively disproved, the court has pronounced against the will propounded.[16] The court in those cases has refused to pronounce for the will because circumstances have excited its suspicion and vigilance, and it has not been satisfied as to the righteousness of the transaction.[17]

These circumstances are frequently raised under the plea of want of knowledge and approval of his will on the part of the testator,[18] and they have, therefore, been discussed under this subject.[19] But there has been no change in the law laid down by authorities of great weight that the question of the righteousness can be raised and considered when undue influence is pleaded. It must be borne in mind that putting a party to the proof of the righteousness of the transaction is not to be used as a screen behind which a man may make veiled charges of fraud and dishonesty without assuming the responsibility of making those charges in plain terms.[20]

Statements by a person deceased charged with undue influence

Where a person who was alleged to have used undue influence to procure a will had died a few days before the execution thereof, it was held that statements made by him but not in the presence of the deceased were admissible as to undue influence.[21]

Undue influence where the deceased was domiciled abroad

Where the deceased died domiciled abroad the court in England applies the *lex domicilii* in deciding what constitutes undue influence or its nearest

[12] *Baker* v. *Batt* (1838) 2 Moo.P.C. 317, 319; *Barry* v. *Butlin* (1838) 2 Moo.P.C. 480, 484.
[13] *Barry* v. *Butlin, supra.*
[14] *Boyse* v. *Rossborough, supra* at p. 49.
[15] *Ibid.* at p. 51; *Craig* v. *Lamoureux, supra.*
[16] See *Barry* v. *Butlin, supra*; *Fulton* v. *Andrew, supra*; *Re Fuld, Hartley* v. *Fuld (Fuld intervening)* (*No. 3*) [1968] P. 675.
[17] See *Barry* v. *Butlin* (1838) 2 Moo.P.C. 480; *Fulton* v. *Andrew* (1875) L.R. 7 H.L. 448; *Re Hartley, Hartley* v. *Fuld (Fuld intervening)* (*No. 3*) [1965] 3 All E.R. 776 (*Re Fuld* [1968] p. 675).
[18] For example, in *Wintle* v. *Nye* [1959] 1 W.L.R. 284, H.L. As to cross-examination to establish fraud on a plea of want of knowledge and approval see *ante* p. 175.
[19] See *ante*, p. 175.
[20] *Low* v. *Guthrie* [1909] A.C. 278, 281. *Cf.* p. 175, *ante.*
[21] *Radford* v. *Risdon* (1912) 28 T.L.R. 342. See also the Civil Evidence Act 1968.

equivalent by that law; but the *lex fori*, *i.e.* English law is applied as to evidential matters.[22]

Costs where undue influence is pleaded

Although there are reported cases in which those who have unsuccessfully pleaded undue influence have been given their costs out of the estate, such cases are a rarity unless the righteousness of the transaction has also been raised and the court has not been satisfied about it. Where the court has not been so satisfied, those pleading undue influence have not infrequently been granted their costs against the other side. But it cannot be made too clear that where a charge of undue influence is unsuccessfully made the great probability is that those who make it will be condemned in costs.[23]

4. FRAUD

From early times fraud has been a ground for setting aside a will.[24] Fraud has sometimes been regarded as a species of undue influence, which, no doubt, it is in a general sense. But as already shown,[25] undue influence as understood in the probate court involves a degree of coercion, while fraud does not. Furthermore from a pleading point of view fraud and undue influence are regarded as separate and distinct.[26] Fraud must be specifically pleaded[27] and cannot be raised indirectly under the head of undue influence.[28]

Leave to amend to allege fraud may be given during the trial,[29] even after the case of the party on whom lay the burden of proof has been closed.[30] In an action alleging want of knowledge and approval but not fraud a party may be cross-examined to show that if the deceased did not know and approve of the will it was because that party was fraudulent.[31]

Fraud does not necessarily vitiate the entire will. If a bequest is obtained by fraud but no fraud is used in relation to the rest of the will, the will may be pronounced for, omitting that bequest.[32]

---

[22] *Re Hartley, Hartley* v. *Fuld (Fuld intervening) (No. 3), supra.*
[23] See *post*, p. 440, as to costs in cases of undue influence.
[24] *Lord Donegal's Case* (1751) 2 Ves.Sen. 408.
[25] See *ante*, p. 183.
[26] See Ord. 18, r. 12(1) and Ord. 76, r. 9(3)(*c*).
[27] Ord. 18, r. 8(1).
[28] *White* v. *White* (1862) 2 Sw. & Tr. 504. But suspicion of fraud may cause the court to pronounce against a will, see *Fulton* v. *Andrew* (1875) L.R. 7 H.L. 448; *Wintle* v. *Nye* [1959] 1 W.L.R. 284, H.L.
[29] *White* v. *White, supra.*
[30] *Riding* v. *Hawkins* (1889) 14 P.D. 56.
[31] *Wintle* v. *Nye, supra* and *ante*, p. 175.
[32] *Allen* v. *M'Pherson* (1847) 1 H.L.C. 191; *Plume* v. *Beale* (1717) 1 P.W. 388 and see *post*, p. 452.

Fraudulent calumny

There cannot be a stronger instance of fraud than a false representation about the character of an individual, made to the testator for the purpose of inducing him to revoke a bequest made in favour of that individual, or to exclude the person so calumniated from any benefit in his will.[33] So if some person raises prejudices in the mind of the testator against those who would be the natural objects of his bounty, and by contrivance keeps him from intercourse with his relatives, to the end that these impressions thus formed to their disadvantage may never be removed, such contrivance may be equivalent to positive fraud, and may render invalid any will executed under false impressions so kept alive.[34] The deceit must be compared with the capacity or understanding of the person deceived in order to decide whether the fraud is such as to nullify the will.[35] The court has pronounced against an alleged last will fraudulently propounded.[36]

Righteousness of the transaction and fraud

Where a person is active in the procuring of a will under which he benefits it is his duty to bring home to the mind of the deceased the effect of his testamentary act; and failure to do so may amount to fraud.[37]

Will pronounced for by reason of fraud

A decree pronouncing for a will may be set aside if it is proved that the decree was obtained by fraud.[38] But evidence of fraud discovered since the decree must be adduced and must be sufficient to raise a reasonable probability of success, or the action will be stayed.[39] Although in most cases a judgment obtained by fraud can be set aside only as against the fraudulent person, this limitation does not apply to probate, since a will must be either good or bad as against all the world.[40]

Burden of proof in fraud

Although it is not entirely correct to say that fraud must be proved with the strictness of a criminal charge, there is no doubt that a very high degree of proof is needed to establish it.[41]

---

[33] *Per* Lord Lyndhurst in *Allen* v. *M'Pherson* (1847) 1 H.L.C. 191, 207; *White* v. *White* (1862) 2 Sw. & Tr. 504.
[34] *Boyse* v. *Rossborough* (1857) 6 H.L.C. 2.
[35] See *Marsh* v. *Tyrrell and Harding* (1828) 2 Hagg.Ecc. 84, 123.
[36] *Re Peppar, The Times*, December 16, 1960.
[37] *Fulton* v. *Andrew* (1875) L.R. 7 H.L. 448, 463; endorsed in *Wintle* v. *Nye* [1959] 1 W.L.R. 284, 295.
[38] *Birch* v. *Birch* [1902] P. 130, C.A.; see *Priestman* v. *T,iomas* (1884) 9 P.D. 70.
[39] See *Birch* v. *Birch, supra.*
[40] *Ibid.* at p. 138. See p. 270 *post* and as to the effect of a grant, p. 449, *post.*
[41] *Bater* v. *Bater* [1951] P. 35, 36; see *Hornal* v. *Neuberger Products* [1957] 1 Q.B. 247.

5. FORGERY

Cases in which wills are alleged to have been forged in whole or in part are uncommon and there seems to be no reported case on the principles which govern such actions.[42] Forgery is, no doubt, a form of fraud, but it should be specifically pleaded and, in pleading, particulars can be demanded and a mere substance of the case is not enough.

Forgery of a whole will in imitation of the testator's handwriting is rarely attempted unless the will is very short. More usually the forgery is of the signature of the deceased and the attesting witnesses to a typed document.

Forgery is a criminal offence, but as a probate action is a civil and not a criminal proceeding, the standard of proof is not the same as in a criminal prosecution.[43] Nevertheless a very high standard of proof is required to establish so serious a charge.[44]

---

[42] If forgery is established those who have propounded a forged will are estopped and the will must be revoked. See *Priestman* v. *Thomas* (1884) 9 P.D. 210.

[43] See cases in n. 41, *supra. cf. R.* v. *Ewing* [1983] Q.B. 1039 (C.A.) (computer print-out admissible).

[44] *Ibid.*

Chapter 14

THE REVOCATION OF WILLS

As testamentary intention is ambulatory until death, a will is in its nature a revocable instrument; so that even if the testator makes his will irrevocable by express words therein, yet he may revoke it. The question whether a will has been revoked or not is primarily a matter for the probate jurisdiction as such but the court of construction may also when interpreting documents admitted to probate in effect also decide whether or not a revocation has occurred. Since the merger of the probate jurisdiction with that of the Chancery Division the distinction is less important than formerly.[1]

Although a will is always revocable a contract not to revoke it is a binding one although the contract may not be specifically enforceable[2] damages are recoverable for the breach thereof, on principles similar to those which govern contracts to make a will in a particular form.

Mutual wills may, in certain circumstances, be regarded as irrevocable in equity to the extent that on the death of the survivor of the two testators who has revoked his part of a mutual will after the death of the first to die, his personal representatives may be directed to hold the property in trust for the beneficiaries under the revoked will.[3]

Where a testator is prevented by force or threats from altering or revoking his will, or from executing a later will leaving his property to others, the court may, it seems, declare that the executors of the earlier will are trustees for the persons who would have benefited had the later will been executed.[4]

A testator cannot delegate his power of revoking his will to another by inserting a clause in his will authorising him to destroy it after his death.[5] He may, however, make the validity of the will contingent on the assent of a third person after his death, and, if that assent is withheld, probate of the instrument will be refused.[6]

Under the Wills Act as amended there are six modes in which a will may

---

[1] See p. 8 *ante* and *Re Finnemore* [1991] 1 W.L.R. 793, 814.

[2] See *Robinson* v. *Ommaney* (1883) 23 Ch.D. 285 (affirming 21 Ch.D. 780) *Jarman on Wills*, 8th ed., p. 27. *Theobald on Wills*, 14th ed., p. 92 *et seq*. Questions of part performance and estoppel may often arise in this connection. See in addition to the cases cited in Jarman, *Loffus* v. *Maw* (1862) 3 Giff, 592; *Central London Property Trust Ltd.* v. *High Trees House Ltd.* [1947] K.B. 130; *Wakeham* v. *Mackenzie* [1968] 1 W.L.R. 1175; *Jones* (*A.E.*) v. *Jones* (*F.W.*) [1977] 1 W.L.R. 438; article "Estoppel as a Sword" by David Jackson (1965) 8 L.Q.R. 84, 223. *Crabb* v. *Arun D.C.* [1976] Ch. 179. *Re Basham* [1986] 1 W.L.R. 1498; *Snells Equity*, 29th ed., p. 568 *et seq*.

[3] See *ante*, p. 128 and Article in 1988 N.L.J. 351 (May 20).

[4] *Betts* v. *Doughty* (1879) 5 P.D. 26.

[5] *Stockwell* v. *Ritherdon* (1848) 1 Rob. 661; *Re Smith* (1869) L.R. 1 P. & D. 717, 719.

[6] *Re Smith* (1869) L.R. 1 P. & D. 717.

be revoked, whether in whole or in part: (A) by marriage, (B) by divorce, (C) by another will or codicil, (D) by a writing, duly executed, declaring an intention to revoke, (E) by the testator or some other person in his presence and by his direction, burning, tearing or otherwise destroying his will with the intention of revoking it, (F) by the revival of a previous will.

In addition (G) there are two modes by which a will or codicil may be partially revoked, namely by a duly executed obliteration, interlineation or other alteration, or by such an unexecuted obliteration as renders what is obliterated no longer "apparent."[7] Conditional revocation is considered under head (H).

A. REVOCATION BY MARRIAGE

Following recommendations of the Law Reform Committee,[8] section 18 of the Administration of Justice Act 1982 has substituted a new section 18 of the Wills Act 1837, governing revocation by marriage. The substituted section applies to wills made on or after January 1, 1983. The position relating to wills made before this date is considered first.

1. Wills made before January 1, 1983

Section 18 of the Wills Act 1837 as originally enacted provided that "every will made by a man or a woman shall be revoked by his or her marriage (except a will made in exercise of a power of appointment, when the real and personal estate thereby appointed would not in default of such appointment pass to his or her heir, customary heir, executor or administrator, or the person entitled as his or her next-of-kin, under the Statute of Distributions)."[9] Another exception appears to be a privileged will.[10]

Wills exercising a power of appointment

So far as a will coming into operation after 1925 is concerned, the reference to the Statute of Distributions is to be taken as a reference to the persons entitled to benefit on intestacy under the present law.[11] Thus if the trust instrument provides that the property vests in the persons entitled on intestacy (including the widow[12] in the case of deaths before 1926) or in the executor or administrator of the deceased, the will is revoked by marriage. If the property would under the trust instrument pass to other persons the will is not revoked.

The tendency of cases decided under the section is strongly in favour of

---

[7] See *post*, p. 209.
[8] Cmnd. 7902, 1980. As to revocation of mutual wills by re-marriage of the survivor, see p. 129 *ante*.
[9] See *Re Paul* [1921] 2 Ch. 1, 4.
[10] See *post*, p. 225.
[11] Administration of Estates Act 1925, s.50(1).
[12] *Re Gilligan* [1950] P. 32.

the validity of an exercise of a power of appointment.[13] If a will, in addition to exercising a power of appointment of the excepted class, disposes of other property, the portion of the will which disposes of the property is revoked by marriage, and administration with the will annexed, limited to the property over which the testator had a power of appointment, will be granted to the appointee or the person entitled on intestacy, according to the circumstances.[14]

Wills made in contemplation of marriage

By section 177 of the Law of Property Act 1925 wills made after 1925 expressed to be made in contemplation of marriage are not revoked by the solemnisation of the marriage contemplated. Before the coming into force of this provision marriage revoked even wills made in contemplation thereof.[15]

The will must show with whom the marriage is contemplated,[16] though it need not expressly state that it is made in contemplation of marriage if the intention is clear.[17] Expressions such as "my fiancée"[18] and "my wife"[19] have been held sufficient. Contemplation of marriage in a general way is not enough.[20] The will must show that a particular marriage was in the testator's mental view.[21] The will as a whole must be made in contemplation of marriage, and the fact that certain gifts in the will are made in contemplation of marriage may not be sufficient to bring the will within the section.[22] The testator's intention must be gathered from the will itself, and no extrinsic evidence is admissible on this issue.[23]

A man whose wife has not been heard of for seven years may make a will in contemplation of marriage with another woman.[24]

2. Wills made on or after January 1, 1983

The substituted section 18 of the Wills Act 1837 provides that, subject to exceptions, "a will shall be revoked by the testator's marriage."[25]

The first exception updates the operation of the section on powers of appointment, by providing that "a disposition in a will in exercise of a

---

[13] *Re Fitzroy (1858) 1 Sw. & Tr. 133; Re Renwick (1867) L.R. 1 P. & D. 319; Re McVicar* (1869) L.R. 1 P. & D. 671; *Re Russell* (1890) 15 P.D. 111; *Smith* v. *Thompson* (1931) 146 L.T. 14.
[14] *Re Russell, supra*; see *Poole* v. *Poole* [1919] P. 10. See *ante*, p. 120, as to the practice in admitting to probate wills of this type.
[15] *Re Cadywold* (1858) 1 Sw. & Tr. 34.
[16] *Sallis* v. *Jones* [1936] P. 43.
[17] *Re Gray* (1963) 107 S.J. 156.
[18] *Re Langston* [1953] P. 100; *Re Coleman* [1976] Ch. 1. Compare *Public Trustee* v. *Crawley* [1973] 1 N.Z.L.R. 695; *Re Whale* [1971] 2 N.Z.L.R. 1.
[19] *Pilot* v. *Gainfort* [1931] P. 103.
[20] *Sallis* v. *Jones, supra.*
[21] *Re Gray, supra.*
[22] *Re Coleman, supra*, which contains a useful review of the Commonwealth authorities.
[23] *Ibid.* Cmnd. 7902, 1980.
[24] *Pilot* v. *Gainfort, supra.*
[25] S.18(1).

power of appointment shall take effect notwithstanding the testator's subsequent marriage unless the property so appointed would in default of appointment pass to his personal representatives."[26]

The second exception provides that "where it appears from a will that at the time it was made the testator was expecting to be married to a particular person and that he intended that the will should not be revoked by the marriage, the will shall not be revoked by his marriage to that person."[27] It appears that, as previously, the intention must be gathered from the will itself.[28]

The third exception provides that:

"Where it appears from a will that at the time it was made the testator was expecting to be married to a particular person and that he intended that a disposition in the will should not be revoked by his marriage to that person,—

(a) that disposition shall take effect notwithstanding the marriage; and

(b) any other disposition in the will shall take effect also, unless it appears from the will that the testator intended the disposition to be revoked by the marriage."[29]

This provision follows the recommendation of the Law Reform Committee following the decision in *Re Coleman*.[30] Its effect is to reverse the burden of proof in such cases.

3. What marriages revoke wills

To revoke a will the marriage must be valid by the laws of this country,[31] and the testator must, at the time of his marriage, be domiciled in a country where marriage has the effect of revoking a previous will.[32] A marriage ceremony may be presumed to have taken place though no certificate can be found, and such marriage will revoke a will.[33] A voidable marriage, being a valid subsisting marriage until it is annulled[34] is effective to revoke a will.[35] On the other hand, a void marriage, being a marriage which the court will treat as never having taken place,[36] will not, it is submitted, revoke a will.

---

[26] S.19(2). See the recommendations of the Law Reform Committee, Cmnd. 7902, 1980.

[27] S.18(3).

[28] *Cf.* the Law Reform Committee's recommendation (Cmnd. 7902, 1980) that extrinsic evidence should be admissable on this issue. If, however, the language used in the will is ambiguous, extrinsic evidence, including evidence of the testator's intention, is now admissable. See the Administration of Justice Act, 1982, s.21.

[29] S.18(4), Wills Act 1837.

[30] [1976] Ch. 1. See p. 191, *supra.*

[31] *Mette* v. *Mette* (1859) 1 Sw. & Tr. 416; *Warter* v. *Warter* (1890) 15 P.D. 152.

[32] *Re Reid* (1866) L.R. 1 P. & D. 74; *Re Martin* [1900] P. 211.

[33] *Rumsey* v. *Stern* (1967) 111 S.J. 113.

[34] Matrimonial Causes Act 1973, s.16. *De Reneville* v. *De Reneville* [1948] P. 100.

[35] *Re Roberts* [1978] 1 W.L.R. 653.

[36] *De Reneville* v. *De Reveville*, *supra.*

It would seem that marriage does not effect a revocation under the Wills Act 1963.[37]

B. EFFECT OF DIVORCE

Before 1983 there was irony in the fact that a will was revoked by marriage but not by divorce. Now, under the Administration of Justice Act 1982, the provisions in any will of a testator dying on or after January 1, 1983, in so far as they relate to the former spouse, will not survive a decree of divorce or similar decree.[38] Thus where after a testator has made a will a decree of a court of civil jurisdiction in England and Wales[39] dissolves or annuls his marriage or his marriage is dissolved or annulled and the divorce or annulment is entitled to recognition in England and Wales by virtue of Part II of the Family Law Act 1986, the will takes effect as if any appointment of the former spouse as an executor or as the executor and trustee in the will were omitted and any devise or bequest to the former spouse lapses except in so far as a contrary intention appears by the will. The right of the former spouse to claim family provision is expressly preserved.[40] Where by the terms of the will there is a life interest which lapses under these provisions the remainder is accelerated whether it be vested or contingent on the termination of the life interest.[41] When a gift lapses it falls into residue and a lapsed gift of residue passes as on intestacy. The word "lapse" in section 18A is not to be equated with a provision in the will as to the effect of the spouse in question predeceasing the testator.[42]

C. REVOCATION BY A SUBSEQUENT WILL OR CODICIL

Section 20 of the Wills Act 1837 provides that a will or codicil[43] or any part thereof may be revoked "by another will or codicil executed in manner hereinbefore required."

The words "in manner hereinbefore required" have been held to apply not only to section 9 of the Wills Act but to privileged wills under section 11.[44]

The mere fact of making a subsequent testamentary paper does not work a total revocation of a prior one unless the latter expressly or in effect revokes the former, or the two are incapable of standing together. Any

---

[37] See ante, p. 151.

[38] See s.18A of the Wills Act 1837 inserted by s.18 of the Administration of Justice Act 1982; 1983 Conveyancer 21.

[39] Family Law Act 1986, s.53.

[40] S.18A(2) of the Wills Act 1837.

[41] S.18A(3) of the Wills Act 1837.

[42] Re Sinclair [1984] 1 W.L.R. 1240 affirmed on appeal [1985] Ch. 446, overruling Re Cherrington [1984] 1 W.L.R. 772. Theobald on Wills, 14th ed., p. 655.

[43] As to the equation of a codicil with a dinghy see Re Sebag-Montefiore [1944] Ch. 331, 342.

[44] Wood v. Gossage [1921] P. 194, C.A.

number of instruments, whatever their relative dates or in whatever form they may be (so long as they are clearly testamentary), may be admitted to probate as together containing the last will of the deceased. A later will or codicil partially inconsistent with one of earlier date will revoke it in so far as they are inconsistent.[45] Where the deceased has left several testamentary papers, the question is what dispositions did he intend, not what papers did he desire or expect to be admitted to probate.[46]

Revocation where there is a revocation clause

In general a clause of revocation, where it is in clear words, revokes all former wills just as if they never existed and leaves no operation to any former will.[47] But this is not an inflexible rule. In *Gladstone* v. *Tempest*[48] Sir Herbert Jenner said[49]: "Generally speaking there is no doubt that by a general clause of revocation there is a revocation of all prior testamentary acts. But it has been over and over again laid down that probate of a paper may be granted of a date prior to a will with a revocatory clause, provided the court is satisfied that it was not the deceased's intention to revoke that particular legacy or benefit."

Where a codicil revoked bequests and dispositions in a will the appointment of executors in the will was held not to be revoked.[50]

Where there is a revocation clause and the will proceeds to exercise a power of appointment or expressly refers to it, the exercise of the power in a previous will is revoked.[51] And even general words of revocation revoke a will exercising a power of appointment,[52] unless there is cogent evidence to the contrary.[53] But a revocation clause in an English will did not revoke a will expressly dealing with the testator's Belgian estate.[54]

Revocation clause inserted by mistake

Where the will has been read over to a testator or its contents have been brought to his notice in any other way, he will usually be held to have known and approved its contents[55] including any revocation clause. Even if

---

[45] Based on the quotation from an earlier edition of *Williams on Executors*, approved in *Lemage* v. *Goodban* (1865) L.R. 1 P. & D. 57, 62. See *Re Petchell* (1874) L.R. 3 P. & D. 53, 156; *Townsend* v. *Moore* [1905] P. 66, 67.

[46] *Lemage* v. *Goodban*, *supra*.

[47] See *Southern* v. *Dening* (1881) 20 Ch.D. 99, 105, C.A.

[48] (1840) 2 Curt. 650.

[49] At p. 653.

[50] *Re Howard* (1869) L.R. 1 P. & D. 636; contrast *Cottrell* v. *Cottrell* (1872) L.R. 2 P. & D. 397; and see *Henfrey* v. *Henfrey* (1840) 2 Curt. 468; 4 Moo.P.C. 29, 36.

[51] *Richardson* v. *Barry* (1830) 3 Hagg.Ecc. 249; *Re Eustace* (1874) L.R. 3 P. & D. 183.

[52] *Southern* v. *Dening* (1881) 20 Ch.D. 99, C.A.; *Re Kingdon* (1886) 32 Ch.D. 604; *Cadell* v. *Willcocks* [1898] P. 21, 26.

[53] *Lowthorpe-Lutwidge* v. *Lowthorpe-Lutwidge* [1935] P. 151, distinguishing *Smith* v. *Thompson* (1931) 47 T.L.R. 603.

[54] *Re Wayland* [1951] 2 All E.R. 1041.

[55] *Guardhouse* v. *Blackburn* (1866) L.R. 1 P. & D. 109; *Atter* v. *Atkinson* (1869) L.R. 1 P. & D. 665. However there is no irrebuttable presumption to that effect: *Re Morris* [1971] P. 62.

the revocation clause was introduced through the error of the draftsman it must stand,[56] unless it was introduced without the instructions of the deceased and without his knowledge.[57]

But a revocatory clause introduced through the inadvertence of the testator or the partial revocation of an earlier will from this cause may be omitted.[58] Thus where a testatrix omitted a charging clause from her second will and inadvertently copied in a revocation clause it was held that the revocation clause might be omitted.[59] Where a testatrix, following an incorrect draft of her will, revoked clauses in it referring to them by number but intending to revoke clauses numbered differently, it was held that the words of revocation might be omitted.[60]

Where a codicil revoked provisions in a revoked will, intending to alter provisions in the will revoking that will, all three documents were admitted to probate together.[61] In a number of cases the revocation is of a conditional nature and the doctrine of dependent relative (conditional) revocation, considered later, will apply.[62]

Inference as to the revocation of an earlier will by a lost will

If the contents of a later will which has been lost cannot be proved, the earlier will stands, even if it can be shown that the provisions of the lost will were, in unknown respects, different from those of the earlier one.[63] To revoke the first will there must be clear, stringent and conclusive evidence that there was either a revocation clause in the lost will or that its provisions were inconsistent with those of the prior will.[64]

In one case where a solicitor had drawn a will which was lost, it was held that the correct inference was that he must have included a revocation clause in it.[65] In a later case, however, the court refused to draw that inference in the same circumstances.[66]

Revocation where there is no revocation clause

Prima facie every document purporting to be a will which is duly

---

[56] *Morrell* v. *Morrell* (1881) 7 P.D. 68. Although see now, as to rectification, the Administration of Justice Act 1982, s.20.

[57] *Re Oswald* (1874) L.R. 3 P. & D. 162; *Re Moore* [1892] P. 378; *Marklew* v. *Turner* (1900) 17 T.L.R. 10.

[58] See *Re Phelan* [1972] Fam. 33.

[59] *Re Cocke* [1960] 1 W.L.R. 491.

[60] *Re Swords* [1952] P. 368. See *Re Morris* [1971] P. 62.

[61] *Re Stedham* (1881) 6 P.D. 205; *Re Dyke* (1881) 6 P.D. 205; *De Chilcott* [1897] P. 223; see *Re Robinson* (1934) 143 L.T. 593.

[62] See p. 211, *post.*

[63] *Cutto* v. *Gilbert* (1854) 9 Moo.P.C. 131, 143; *Hellier* v. *Hellier* (1884) 9 P.D. 237.

[64] *Cutto* v. *Gilbert, supra,* at p. 140; *Barkwell* v. *Barkwell* [1928] P. 91; *Re Wyatt* [1952] 1 All E.R. 1030.

[65] *Re Hampshire* [1951] W.N. 174.

[66] *Re Wyatt, supra.*

executed ought to be admitted to probate, and, where there is more than one such document, the court will endeavour so to read their contents as to support the admissibility of them all to probate.[67] The court will not readily conclude that a later will was intended to revoke an earlier one when it contains no revocation clause.[68]

Thus where the residuary clause in the last will was unintelligible and that in the earlier will was clear, the court admitted both wills to probate.[69] And where the earlier will contained a residuary bequest and the later will did not, both were held admissible to probate.[70]

Where two testamentary documents are proved to have been executed on the same occasion or where there are two undated documents and in neither case can it be established which was executed first, then if the documents are so inconsistent that they cannot stand together, neither will be admitted to probate.[71] Nevertheless if two wills, made in such circumstances, are too inconsistent for them to be admitted to probate, a revocation clause contained in both of them revokes any previous will.[72] But if it is possible to construe the two documents (there being no revocation clause in either) so that they can stand together in spite of some inconsistencies, both will be admitted to probate.[73]

The position where the testator makes one will disposing of property in England and another governing property abroad has already been considered.[74]

Extrinsic evidence as to revocation where there is no revocation clause

In considering whether a later will revokes an earlier one or whether the two should be admitted to probate together the court will first examine provisions and construe them.[75]

Where there is something which on the face of the later instrument raises doubt or ambiguity whether it was intended to be in substitution for or in addition to a previous will, the court has always had recourse to external evidence to ascertain the testator's intention. But this evidence, it seems, was confined to that which put the court in the same position as the testator

---

[67] *Townsend* v. *Moore* [1905] P. 66, 80. For the practice as to admitting two or more wills to probate, see *post*, p. 311.

[68] See *Stoddart* v. *Grant* (1852) 1 Macq.H.L. 163, 175.

[69] *Lemage* v. *Goodban* (1865) L.R. 1 P. & D. 57.

[70] *Re Petchell* (1874) L.R. 3 P. & D. 153.

[71] *Townsend* v. *Moore* [1905] P. 66, 84.

[72] *Re Howard* [1944] P. 39.

[73] *Townsend* v. *Moore* [1905] P. 66, C.A.; see *Re Brown* [1946] W.N. 115 (where slightly differing duplicate wills had been admitted to probate).

[74] See *ante*, p. 105.

[75] *Re Petchell* (1874) L.R. 3 P. & D. 153, 156; *Townsend* v. *Moore, supra*; *Re Fawcett* [1941] P. 85. However even where both documents are in the event admitted to probate, a court may later construe the later will as virtually revoking the earlier: *Re Plant* [1952] Ch. 298.

when he made his will.[76] Certainly the court was not permitted to receive evidence of what those present at the execution of the will thought the testator intended.[77] In the case of deaths occurring on or after January 1, 1983, however, extrinsic evidence, including that of the testator's intention, may be now admitted to assist interpretation in so far as the language used in the will is ambiguous.[78]

Intrinsic evidence of revocation where there is no revocation clause

In *Birks* v. *Birks*[79] Sir J. P. Wilde said "I repudiate the notion that there are any particular words or any particular forms of expression on which one's finger can be put as an universal test of revocation." This statement has found general acceptance. The court has to deduce what the testator's intention was, from the words used by him, looked at as a whole. If that intention was to dispose of his property in a different manner in the last will from that in the prior will, that will is revoked, even if the later will does not in all particulars cover the whole subject-matter of the prior will,[80] *e.g.* where it does not dispose of the residue.[81] The words "All for mother" have been held to revoke all previous wills[82]; as has the word "ungültig," for which "cancelled" was substituted.[83]

The fact that a paper is described as a "last will and testament"[84] or even as a "last and only will"[85] is not conclusive or even presumptive evidence of an intention to revoke all previous wills.

The fact that a devisee in a later will is incapable of benefiting has been held not to prevent it revoking an earlier inconsistent will.[86] And the mere fact that the later document disposes of residue,[87] or appoints executors does not effect a revocation.[88] Conversely the fact that the earlier will appoints executors while the last will does not will not prevent the revocation *in toto* of the earlier will, including the appointment of executors.[89]

---

[76] *Re Bryan* [1907] P. 125, 130; see *Chichester* v. *Quatrefages* [1895] P. 186 (where evidence of the death of the testator's wife was admitted). Earlier authorities to the effect that the court might investigate in a general way *quo animo* to the testator executed his last will were not followed *eg. Thorne* v. *Rooke* (1841) 2 Cart 799; *Jenner* v. *Ffinch* (1879) 5 P. & D. 106.

[77] *Townsend* v. *Moore, supra.*

[78] Administration of Justice Act 1982, s.21.

[79] (1865) 4 Sw. & Tr. 23, 30.

[80] *Dempsey* v. *Lawson and Lawson* (1877) 2 P.D. 98, 115.

[81] *Dempsey* v. *Lawson and Lawson, supra*; *Re Bryan* [1907] P. 125.

[82] *Thorn* v. *Dickins* [1906] W.N. 54.

[83] *Jones* v. *Treasury Solicitor* (1932) 49 T.L.R. 75.

[84] *Cutto* v. *Gilbert* (1854) 9 Moo.P.C. 131, 142; *Lemage* v. *Goodban* (1865) L.R. 1 P. & D. 57, 61; *Re Summers* (1901) 84 L.T. 271; *Kitcat* v. *King* [1930] P. 266; *Re Hawksley* [1934] Ch. 384.

[85] *Simpson* v. *Foxon* [1907] P. 54.

[86] *Ex. p. Earl Ilchester* (1803) 7 Ves. 348, 379.

[87] *Lemage* v. *Goodban, supra*; *Re Petchell* (1874) L.R. 3 P. & D. 153; *Townsend* v. *Moore* [1905] P. 66, C.A.

[88] *Stoddart* v. *Grant* (1852) 1 Macq.H.L. 163, 173.

[89] *Henfrey* v. *Henfrey* (1842) 4 Moo.P.C. 29.

Revoked will not revived by revoking the instrument of revocation

Section 22 of the Wills Act provides that no will or codicil or any part thereof, which shall be in any manner revoked, shall be revived otherwise than by there re-execution thereof, or by a codicil executed as required by the Act, and showing an intention to revive the same. Consequently there can be no revival of a will unconditionally revoked by the execution of another will, except by the modes indicated in section 22. So the destruction of a second will, which revoked an earlier will, cannot revive or reinstate the earlier document, or any part thereof which has been duly revoked.[90]

D. Revocation by a Revocatory Instrument

The relevant positions of section 20 of the Wills Act 1837 read: "No will or codicil, or any part thereof, shall be revoked otherwise than . . . by some writing declaring an intention to revoke the same and executed in the manner in which a will is hereinbefore required to be executed."

The words "executed in the manner in which a will is hereinbefore required to be executed" refer, not only to section 9 of the Wills Act (which prescribes the formalities for the due execution of wills) but also to the proviso in section 11 relating to privileged wills. Thus an unexecuted letter written by a person while privileged operates to revoke his will.[91]

The intention to revoke must be declared, though no set form of words is required.[92] An attested deed which is void is insufficient,[93] but an obliteration, duly executed and with words of attestation was held sufficient,[94] as was an attested letter directing destruction of the will.[95]

A writing declaring an intention to revoke, by which the deceased in no way disposes of any property, is neither a will nor a codicil and cannot be admitted to probate[96] unless it contains some provisions of a testamentary character, e.g. the appointment of executors.[97]

E. Revocation by Burning, Tearing, etc.

The relevant part of section 20 of the Wills Act 1837 reads: "No will or codicil, or any part thereof, shall be revoked otherwise than . . . by the

---

[90] Cutto v. Gilbert, supra; Re Hodgkinson [1893] P. 339; Sanger v. Hart (1897) 77 L.T. 374.
[91] Wood v. Gossage [1921] P. 194, C.A.
[92] Ford v. De Pontès (1861) 30 Beav. 572, 594; see Benchley v. Still (1850) 2 Rob. 162; Re Hicks (1869) L.R. 1 P. & D. 683; Re Fraser (1869) L.R. 2 P. & D. 40.
[93] Ford v. De Pontès, supra.
[94] Re Gosling (1886) 11 P.D. 79.
[95] Re Durance (1872) L.R. 2 P. & D. 406; Re Spracklin's Estate [1938] 2 All E.R. 345.
[96] Re Fraser (1869) L.R. 2 P. & D. 40, not following earlier cases which must be considered incorrectly decided.
[97] Re Durance, supra.

burning, tearing or otherwise destroying the same by the testator, or by some person in his presence and by his direction, with the intention of revoking the same."

The act of destruction

It is not necessary that the will be totally destroyed, burnt, or torn in pieces. If the will be burnt or torn in the slightest manner, this, joined with the declared intent, will be a good revocation.[98]

Although no sheet of paper is completely divided, the tearing may be sufficient to revoke, if done with that intention.[99] But there must be an actual, not a symbolical burning or tearing of the paper upon which the will is written.[1] An unsuccessful attempt to destroy does not revoke.[2] The will itself must be damaged, not merely an envelope in which it is contained.[3]

Furthermore the act of destruction, in order to be effectual must not be inchoate and incomplete. The testator must have done all that he intended in order to effect destruction. If he is interrupted from completing the act or acts of destruction which he was performing there is no revocation.[4]

Section 20, after referring to burning and tearing a will, continues, "or otherwise destroying the same." These words must be understood as intending some mode of destruction *ejusdem generis*, not an act which is not a destroying in the primary sense of the words.[5] Thus cancelling a will by striking it through with a pen is not a destruction of the will.[6] Cutting a will with the intention of revocation is effective,[7] and it has been suggested that if a will was written in pencil and the words were removed with a rubber, that would be sufficient revocation.[8]

Destruction of the signature to the will effects revocation

Destruction of the essence of the instrument, not of the material on which it is written, effects revocation.[9] Thus if the signature of the testator is removed from the will by burning, tearing or cutting it away, the entirety of the will is destroyed and the act, if performed with intent to revoke

---

[98] *Bibb* v. *Thomas* (1775) 2 W.Black. 1043 (a decision under the Statute of Frauds 1677, s.6). *Re Jones* [1976] Ch. 200. As to the apparently odd effect of the Theft Act 1968, see *post*, p. 728.

[99] *Elms* v. *Elms* (1858) 1 Sw. & Tr. 155, 157.

[1] *Cheese* v. *Lovejoy* (1877) 2 P.D. 251, 253. (Held not sufficient to write "This is revoked" over the back of the will and then screw it up and throw it in the waste paper basket.)

[2] *Doe* v. *Harris* 6 A. & E. 209, 216.

[3] *Ibid.*; *Hobbs* v. *Knight* (1838) 1 Curt. 769, 778.

[4] *Elms* v. *Elms, supra*; *Doe* v. *Perkes* (1820) 3 B. & A. 489, 491; see *Re Colberg* (1841) 2 Curt. 832.

[5] *Stephens* v. *Taprell* (1840) 2 Curt. 459, 465; *Re Rose* (1845) 4 N.C. 101; *Re Brewster* (1859) 29 L.J.P. 69; *Cheese* v. *Lovejoy, supra.*

[6] *Ibid.*

[7] *Hobbs* v. *Knight* (1838) 1 Curt. 769, 779; *Clarke* v. *Scripps* (1852) 2 Rob. 563, 570.

[8] *Hobbs* v. *Knight, supra*; *Re Morton* (1887) 12 P.D. 141, 142.

[9] *Hobbs* v. *Knight, supra.*

(*animo revocandi*), revokes the will.[10] Furthermore, if the signature of the testator, which is essential to the will, is so obliterated that it can no longer be made out, it has been held that the will is revoked,[11] provided that the act was done with that intention.[12]

If the signatures of the attesting witnesses are completely erased by the testator with intent to revoke, the will would, it seems, be revoked.[13] In such a case, however, there would be greater difficulty in proving that the erasure was done with intent to revoke.[14]

Although a seal is not a necessary part of a will, yet where the testator has made it so by the words "In witness whereof I have set my hand and seal," and later tore off the seal, *animo revocandi*, the will was held to be revoked.[15]

Where the will is written on several sheets of paper, and each of the sheets was signed by the testator and the attesting witnesses, and the last sheet, bearing the operative signatures, is not forthcoming at his death, it will be presumed that the testator destroyed it with intent to revoke and the whole will be treated as revoked.[16] Where a will was on several sheets of paper, each signed by the testator, as mentioned in the testimonium clause, the fact that the testator had torn his signature off every sheet except the last was held to revoke the will.[17]

Destruction by some person in the testator's presence

The presence of the testator is essential and if destruction at his request does not take place in his presence[18] the act is ineffectual in revoking the will.[19] The revocation must be done with the testator's authority, and he cannot acquiesce in a destruction done without his authority, even if done in his presence.[20]

A testator cannot delegate his power of revoking his will by inserting a clause in it conferring on another authority to destroy it after his death.[21]

---

[10] *Hobbs* v. *Knight, supra*; *Clarke* v. *Scripps, supra*; *Re Lewis* (1858) 1 Sw. & Tr. 31; see *North* v. *North* (1909) 25 T.L.R. 322; compare *Christmas and Christmas* v. *Whinyates* (1863) 3 Sw. & Tr. 81.

[11] *Hobbs* v. *Knight* (1838) 1 Curt. 769, 779; *Clarke* v. *Scripps* (1852) 2 Rob.Eccl. 563; *Re Morton* (1887) 12 P.D. 141; *Re Godfrey* (1893) 69 L.T. 22 (scratching out with a knife); *Re Adams* [1990] Ch. 601 (overscoring with ball point pen).

[12] *Re King* (1851) 2 Rob. 403.

[13] *Hobbs* v. *Knight, supra*; see *Margary* v. *Robinson* (1886) 12 P.D. 8; *Re Coleman* (1861) 2 Sw. & Tr. 314; *Re Adams, supra*.

[14] *Playne* v. *Scriven* (1849) 7 N.C. 122; *Re Coleman, supra*; *Re Greenwood* [1892] P. 7.

[15] *Price* v. *Price* (1858) 27 L.J.Ex. 409; *Williams* v. *Tyley* (1858) Johns. 530, 533.

[16] *Re Gullan* (1858) 1 Sw. & Tr. 23.

[17] *Williams* v. *Tyley, supra*; *Re Harris* (1864) 3 Sw. & Tr. 485; but see *Clarke* v. *Scripps, supra*. As to interpolated sheets see *post*, p. 211.

[18] As to presence, see *ante*, p. 200.

[19] *Re Dadds* (1857) Dea. & Sw. 290; *Lunbeck* v. *De Kremer* (1965) 110 S.J. 18.

[20] *Mills* v. *Millward* (1889) 15 P.D. 20; see *Gill* v. *Gill* [1909] P. 157; *Booth* v. *Booth* [1926] P. 118, 132.

[21] *Stockwell* v. *Ritherdon* (1848) 1 Rob. 661; see *Re Durance* (1872) L.R. 2 P. & D. 407.

Partial revocation by destruction

Although, as has been seen, the destruction of part of the will may operate to revoke the entire instrument, yet it is clear from the wording of the section that a part only of the will may be revoked in the manner described.[22] The intention of the testator must govern the extent and measure of the operation to be attributed to the act of destruction, and determine whether the act revokes the whole or only part, and what part, of an instrument.[23]

Where part of a will is destroyed but the part bearing the signatures is not destroyed, those alleging revocation must prove their case, unless the part preserved is so unintelligible as to be impracticable as a testamentary instrument.[24]

Proof of the intention of the testator to revoke a will

"The intention of the testator to revoke wholly or in part," said Sir John Dodson in *Clarke* v. *Scripps*,[25] "may be proved:

1. By evidence of the expressed intention of the testator, especially if such declaration was contemporaneous with the act. . . .

2. The intention may, in the absence of any express declaration, be inferred from the nature and extent of the act done by the testator; *i.e.* it may be inferred from the state and condition to which the instrument has been reduced by the act. From the face of the paper itself it may be inferred either that he did intend to destroy it altogether, or that he did not.

3. The intention may, in some degree at least, be inferred from intrinsic circumstances. There may have been declarations, not directly as to the revocation, but such as would lead to the inference whether he did intend to revoke the will or did not."

Where the middle of a sheet was cut away and a wafer joined the top and bottom of it, it was held that only the piece cut out was revoked.[26] Where there was severe mutilation coupled with unattested alterations, the court held that the paper was a draft of a new will and as, partially revoked, intended to stand until such new will was executed.[27] Probate was granted omitting the alterations.[28] Where the first few lines of a will were cut off it was held that it was partially revoked.[29] But mutilation may be so extensive as to show revocation, especially if the surviving part is practically unintelligible.[30]

[22] *Clarke* v. *Scripps* (1852) 2 Rob.Eccl. 563, 567; *Re Lambert* (1841) 1 N.C. 131.
[23] *Clarke* v. *Scripp, supra*; see *Scruby* v. *Fordham* (1822) 1 Add. 78.
[24] *Ward* v. *Bond* (1962) 106 S.J. 1034.
[25] (1852) 2 Rob. Eccl. 563, 567.
[26] *Re Lambert* (1841) 1 N.C. 131; see *Christmas* v. *Whinyates* (1863) 3 Sw. & Tr. 81.
[27] As to conditional revocation, see p. 211 *post.*
[28] *Clarke* v. *Scripps* (1852) 2 Rob.Eccl. 563; see *Williams* v. *Tyley* (1858) Johns. 530.
[29] *Re Woodward* (1871) L.R. 2 P. & D. 206; see *Re Nunn* [1936] 1 All E.R. 555; see also *Re Maley* (1887) 12 P.D. 134 and *Re Everest* [1975] Fam. 44.
[30] *Ward* v. *Bond* (1962) 106 S.J. 1034.

Destruction of a duplicate will

Where one part of a duplicate will is destroyed by a testator with the intention of revoking the whole, his intention takes effect. There is a presumption of revocation of the whole by the destruction of one part.[31] But it may be shown that the destruction was done, *diverso intuitu*, or by accident, or while of unsound mind, or for the sake of peace and to deceive importunate persons.

The presumption of an intention is strongest where only one part of the duplicate will is in the testator's possession.[32] It applies, but less strongly where he destroys one of two duplicates in his possession,[33] and weakly where he alters one duplicate and later destroys it, preserving the other.[34] The presumption is at its weakest where a testator destroys a duplicate in the hands of his solicitor but preserves his own part.[35] Where the testator so mutilates one part of his will as would ordinarily amount to partial revocation but preserves the other part it has been held that there is no revocation at all.[36]

Declarations of the testator have been held inadmissible to prove that a will was executed in duplicate.[37]

Revocation of interlineation

Similar reasoning to that governing duplicate wills has been applied where a testator has interlineated a fresh provision in his will and executed a codicil to the same effect.[38] On revocation of the codicil the interlineation was held to be revoked.[39]

Revocation of a will does not revoke a codicil

Section 20 of the Wills Act 1837 expressly provides that no will or codicil or any part thereof shall be revoked otherwise than as there provided. Accordingly revocation of a will cannot revoke a codicil.[40] Earlier cases to the contrary have been disapproved and in spite of non-judicial criticism the later decisions appear the better reasoned.[41]

Where both will and codicil were executed on the same sheet of paper

---

[31] *Colvin v. Fraser* (1829) 2 Hagg.Ecc. at pp. 266, 329; see *Burtenshaw v. Gilbert* (1774) 1 Cowp. 49, 54; *Pemberton v. Pemberton* (1807) 13 Ves. 290, 308; *Jones v. Harding* (1887) 58 L.T. 60.

[32] *Pemberton v. Pemberton, supra.*

[33] *Ibid.*

[34] *Ibid.*

[35] *Payne v. Trappes* (1847) 1 Rob. 583, 591.

[36] *Roberts v. Round* (1830) 3 Hagg.Ecc. 548, 553.

[37] *Atkinson v. Morris* [1897] P. 40; *Eyre v. Eyre* [1903] P. 131, 157.

[38] See *post*, pp. 221 *et seq.*

[39] *Utterson v. Utterson* (1814) 3 V. & B. 122.

[40] *Re Turner* (1872) L.R. 2 P. & D. 403.

[41] *Black v. Jobling* (1869) L.R. 1 P. & D. 685; *Re Savage* (1870) L.R. 2 P. & D. 78; *Re Turner, supra; Gardiner v. Courthorpe* (1886) 12 P.D. 14.

and the testator tore his signature off the will, upon proof that he thereby intended to revoke both will and codicil, both were held to be revoked.[42]

A codicil which has not been revoked will be admitted to probate even though, because of the destruction of the will, it is largely unintelligible.[43]

Burden of proof of the revocation of a will or codicil

In general once a will is proved to have been duly executed, the party alleging revocation must prove his allegation, and, in the absence of proof his case falls to the ground.[44] To this rule there are three important exceptions:

1. *Will found destroyed after the testator's death*

If a will which has been in the custody of the testator during his lifetime is found in his house or repository after his death torn or so mutilated as to destroy the evidence of due execution, the prima facie presumption is that the document was so torn or mutilated by the testator, with an intention to revoke. The onus is then upon the person propounding the will to show either that the act was not done by the testator, or that he did not intend by such tearing or mutilation to revoke the will.[45] But partial tearing which leaves all the words distinct and legible does not necessarily show an intention to revoke the will, and the burden of proving that such tearing was done *animo revocandi* is on those who allege revocation.[46]

2. *Will in testator's possession missing at his death*

Where a will, or codicil,[47] is last traced into the testator's possession and is not forthcoming at his death after all reasonable search and inquiry, the presumption arises that he has destroyed it *animo revocandi*.[48] The burden of proving, in these circumstances, that the will was not destroyed *animo revocandi* is upon the party propounding its contents.[49]

"The presumption," said Parke B, in *Welch* v. *Phillips*,[50] "is founded on good sense; for it is highly reasonable to suppose that an instrument of so much importance would be carefully preserved by a person of ordinary caution in some place of safety, and would not be lost or stolen; and if, on the death of the maker, it is not found in his usual repositories, or else where he resides, it is in a high degree probable that the deceased himself

[42] *Re Beckley* (1883) 8 P.D. 169.

[43] *Re Turner, supra*; *Gardiner* v. *Courthorpe, supra*.

[44] *Benson* v. *Benson* (1870) L.R. 2 P. & D. 172, 176.

[45] *Lambell* v. *Lambell* (1831) 3 Hagg.Ecc. 568, 569; *Bell* v. *Fothergill* (1870) L.R. 2 P. & D. 148, 150; see *Re Thornton* (1889) 14 P.D. 82.

[46] *Jinkin* v. *Cowling* [1924] P. 113; see *Re Mackenzie* [1909] P. 305.

[47] See *Re Donisthorpe* [1947] W.N. 226.

[48] *Welch* v. *Phillips* (1836) 1 Moo.P.C. 299; *Re Mitcheson* (1863) 32 L.J.P. 202; *Sugden* v. *Lord St. Leonards* (1876) 1 P.D. 154, 217; *Drake* v. *Sykes* (1907) 23 T.L.R. 747.

[49] *Colvin* v. *Fraser* (1829) 2 Hagg.Ecc. 266, 325; *Lillie* v. *Lillie* (1829) 3 Hagg.Ecc. 184, 185n.

[50] (1836) 1 Moo.P.C. 299, 302.

has purposely destroyed it.'' It cannot be presumed that the destruction has taken place without his knowledge or authority, for that would be to presume a crime.[51]

Before any presumption arises the court must be satisfied that the will was not in the testator's repositories, or elsewhere. In most cases the repositories of the deceased are duly searched by those whose good faith is not impugned.[52] But where the repositories of the deceased were clearly accessible to and were proved to have been investigated first by the only person interested in destroying the will the court has refused to presume that the missing will was destroyed by the testator unless satisfied that it was not in existence at his death.[53] These decisions, however, are in substance based on an inference or suspicion of fraudulent abstraction. As stated above, destruction of another's will is a criminal offence and ought not to be found without the strongest evidence.[54] It is doubtful, therefore, whether they are correct. Direct evidence of the destruction of the will is not essential; the court may act on a properly drawn inference.[55]

3. *Will destroyed by testator of unsound mind*

Where a will is known to have been destroyed by a testator thought to have been of unsound mind at the time of destruction the burden lies on the person propounding the will to establish that she was of unsound mind at the time of destruction.[56]

Rebuttal of the presumption of the revocation of a missing will

The strength of the presumption as to the revocation of a missing will traced into the testator's possession varies according to the character of the custody which the deceased had over the will.[57] It is a presumption which may always be rebutted by adducing evidence which raises a higher probability to the contrary.[58] It may be shown that the testator had no opportunity or was incapable of destroying the will, or may establish a combination of circumstances leading to the conclusion that the testator did not himself destroy the will. It may be shown that the will was in existence after the testator's death, that he destroyed it while of unsound mind or in error or under duress; or that it was destroyed in his lifetime by some person without his approbation or consent.[59]

[51] *Rickards* v. *Mumford* (1812) 2 Phill. 23, 24.
[52] *Prodmore* v. *Whatton* (1864) 3 Sw. & Tr. 449, 451.
[53] *Ibid.*; *Finch* v. *Finch* (1867) L.R. 1 P. & D. 371, but see *per* Buckley L.J. in *Drake* v. *Sykes* (1907) 23 T.L.R. 747, 749.
[54] *Wargent* v. *Hollings* (1832) 4 Hagg.Ecc. 245, 249; *Colvin* v. *Fraser, supra*; *Allan* v. *Morrison* [1900] A.C. 604.
[55] *Botting* v. *Botting* [1951] 2 All E.R. 997.
[56] *Re Sabatini* (1969) 114 S.J. 35.
[57] *Sugden* v. *Lord St. Leonards* (1876) 1 P.D. 154. As to conditional revocation in such circumstances see p. 217, n. 83 and text, *post.*
[58] *Welch* v. *Phillips* (1836) 1 Moo.P.C. 299, 302.
[59] *Wargent* v. *Hollings* (1832) 4 Hagg.Ecc. 245, 249.

The older cases lay down that the evidence in rebuttal must reasonably produce moral conviction.[60] But in modern cases the court has again and again held the presumption to be rebutted on a balance of probabilities and has leaned towards testacy.

The acts, declarations and conduct of the deceased may show the improbability of his having destroyed the will *animo revocandi*.[61] Declarations of unchanged affection and intention may rebut the presumption; and as Sir H. Jenner Fust said in *Saunders* v. *Saunders*.[62] "The strongest proof of adherence to the will, and of the improbability of its destruction arises from the contents of the will itself."

It is not incumbent on those propounding a missing will to show how it was destroyed or lost,[63] though evidence showing how it might have been lost or destroyed naturally assists the case of those propounding the will.

Evidence of declarations by the testator showing an intention to adhere to the will is admissible to rebut the presumption, as is contrary evidence to strengthen it.[64] Before the Evidence Act 1938 a statement by the testator that he had revoked a will was held to be evidence of his intention to revoke but not of revocation itself.[65] But a letter in such terms written by the testator was admitted under the Evidence Act 1938[66] to prove revocation and not merely an intention to revoke.[67]

But declarations alone unsupported by circumstances showing their sincerity may be misleading. "Few Declarations," said the sceptical Lord Eldon in *Pemberton* v. *Pemberton*,[68] "deserve less credit than those of men as to what they have done by their wills. The wish to silence importunity, to elude questions from persons who take upon themselves to judge of their own claims, must be taken into consideration." In *Sugden* v. *Lord St. Leonards*,[69] however, Cockburn C.J. expressed the contrary view. Certainly declarations coupled and consistent with conduct are of weight in proof of intention. So too is the tenor of an extended conversation, especially if it is not liable to the suspicion of insincerity; still more so are declarations made in confidential communications.[70]

The presumption discussed above does not apply where the testator became insane after the execution of the will. In such case the burden of proving revocation lies on those who seek to prove it.[71] If a will has been in

---

[60] See *Davis* v. *Davis* (1824) 2 Add. 223, 226; *Colvin* v. *Fraser* (1829) 2 Hagg.Ecc. 266.

[61] *James* v. *James* (1829) 3 Hagg.Ecc. 185n.; *Patten* v. *Poulton* (1858) 1 Sw. & Tr. 55.

[62] (1848) 6 N.C. 522; see *Sugden* v. *Lord St. Leonards*, *supra*.

[63] *Patten* v. *Poulton*, *supra*.

[64] *Keen* v. *Keen* (1873) L.R. 3 P. & D. 105; *Bell* v. *Fothergill* (1870) L.R. 2 P. & D. 148; *North* v. *North* (1909) 25 T.L.R. 322; *Re Wilson* (1961) 105 S.J. 531.

[65] *Drake* v. *Sykes* (1907) 23 T.L.R. 747, C.A.

[66] The provisions of this Act referred to were repealed by the Civil Evidence Act 1968, but the 1968 Act contains provisions of a somewhat similar nature.

[67] *Re Bridgewater* [1965] 1 W.L.R. 416.

[68] (1807) 13 Ves. 290, 301.

[69] (1876) 1 P.D. 154, 225.

[70] *Colvin* v. *Fraser* (1829) 2 Hagg.Ecc. 266, 345.

[71] *Sprigge* v. *Sprigge* (1868) L.R. 1 P. & D. 608; *Re Crandon* (1901) 84 L.T. 330; *National Provincial Bank* v. *Taylor* (1920) 64 S.J. 148; see *Re Yule* (1965) 109 S.J. 317.

the custody of a testator at times when he was sometimes of sound and at other times of unsound mind the burden of proving revocation again lies on those alleging it.[72]

Where a will, to which a codicil has been executed, is found at the death of the testator in a mutilated state, and there is no evidence as to the date of mutilation, the presumption is that the will was mutilated after the execution of the codicil.[73]

It seldom happens that cases, which set out upon legal presumptions, require to be decided on the mere presumptions. The general circumstances of the case usually lead to a tolerably satisfactory conclusion of the real fact, either confirming or repelling the presumption. The presumptions are to be treated as indications of inferences to be drawn and not as rigid rules.[74]

The testator's intention to revoke

The burning, tearing or otherwise destroying the will must be done with the intention of revoking the same.[75] "All the destroying in the world without intention," said James L.J. in *Cheese* v. *Lovejoy*[76] "will not revoke a will, nor all the intention in the world without destroying; there must be the two." So a destruction *sine animo revocandi* cannot, it seems, be rendered effective by subsequent ratification.[77]

If a testator is of unsound mind when he destroys his will, the will is not revoked[78]; nor if he is so drunk as not to be responsible for his actions.[79] The mental capacity required to revoke a will in such circumstances is the same as that required to make a will.[80]

The intention of the testator is particularly crucial in cases of revocation by destruction, since the destruction may be by accident or mistake.[81] In case of mistake it matters not whether the mistake is of fact or law.

F. REVOCATION BY REVIVAL

The revival of a will or codicil may operate to revoke another will, executed after the original execution, but before the revival of the will so republished.[82]

---

[72] *Harris* v. *Berrall* (1858) 1 Sw. & Tr. 153; *Benson* v. *Benson* (1870) L.R. 2 P. & D. 172, 176.

[73] *Christmas* v. *Whinyates* (1863) 3 Sw. & Tr. 81.

[74] See *Re Yule, supra.*

[75] See *Clarke* v. *Scripps* (1852) Rob.Eccl. 563, 567. *Re Jones* [1976] Ch. 200.

[76] (1877) 2 P.D. 251, 263.

[77] *Mills* v. *Millward* (1889) 15 P.D. 21; *Gill* v. *Gill* [1909] P. 157.

[78] *Brunt* v. *Brunt* (1873) L.R. 3 P. & D. 37, 38.

[79] *Re Brassington* [1902] P. 1.

[80] *Re Sabatini* (1969) 114 S.J. 35.

[81] *Burtenshaw* v. *Gilbert* (1774) 1 Cowp. 49, 52; *Smith* v. *Cunningham* (1823) 1 Add. 448, 455; *Thynne* v. *Stanhope* (1822) 1 Add. 52, 53; *Giles* v. *Warren* (1872) L.R. 2 P. & D. 401, 402; see *Perrott* v. *Perrott* (1811) 14 East 423, 439.

[82] See, *post*, pp. 221 *et seq.*

G. REVOCATION BY OBLITERATION, INTERLINEATION AND ALTERATION

A will may be revoked, almost always partially, by obliteration, interlineation or alteration.

Requirements

Section 21 of the Wills Act 1837 provides that "No obliteration, interlineation, or other alteration made in any will after the execution thereof shall be valid or have any effect, except so far as the words or effect of the will before such alteration shall not be apparent, unless such alteration shall be executed in like manner as hereinbefore is required for the execution of the will; but the will, with such alteration as part thereof, shall be deemed to be duly executed if the signature of the testator and the subscription of the witnesses be made in the margin or on some other part of the will opposite or near to such alteration, or at the foot or end of or opposite or near to such alteration, or at the foot or end of or opposite to a memorandum referring to such alteration, and written at the end or some other part of the will."

There is a marked distinction between interlineations and alterations. The former are generally used merely to complete an imperfect sentence, while the latter make a change in the original disposition.

Where unattested alterations occur in a will the presumption is that such alterations were made after the execution of the will and, in the absence of evidence rebutting the presumption, probate will be granted of the will, as executed, omitting the alterations.[83]

The court is more ready to hold that interlineations were written before execution,[84] especially if other testamentary papers, e.g. a previous will or draft of the will in question embodies the words interlineated.[85]

Where alterations appear in a will made by a person under privilege, the presumption is that alterations therein were made during the continuance of privilege.[86]

The presumption against the validity of alterations and interlineations stated above may be rebutted by proof or internal evidence to the contrary.[87]

Evidence

The court may come to the conclusion that alterations were in the will before its execution upon any reasonable evidence and need not insist

---

[83] *Cooper* v. *Bockett* (1844) 4 Moo.P.C. 419; *Greville* v. *Tylee* (1851) Moo.P.C. 320, 328; *Re Adamson* (1875) L.R. 3 P. & D. 253.
[84] See *Re Cadge* (1868) L.R. 1 P. & D. 543; *Birch* v. *Birch* (1848) 1 Rob. 675.
[85] *Callow* v. *Sutton* [1946] 2 All E.R. 735.
[86] *Re Tweedale* (1874) L.R. 3 P. & D. 204.
[87] *Re Adamson* (1875) L.R. 3 P. & D. 253, 255.

upon evidence from the attesting witnesses, or on any other particular species of evidence.[88]

The evidence of an expert in handwriting is entitled to consideration[89] as is the fact that the testator knew the formalities required for making a will, and that the alterations appear to have been written (or not to have been written) with the same pen and ink as the will.[90] But no presumption arises where names and amounts in the body of the will are written in a different ink from the main part of the will.[91] Nor does the fact that words interrupt the grammatical structure of a passage in the will raise a presumption against them.[92]

Inspection of the will and the character of the alterations may satisfy the court that they were made before execution.[93] But the mere fact that dates before that of the will have been placed against the alterations by the testator will not, in itself, justify their inclusion in the probate.[94]

The presumption may be rebutted by evidence of declarations made by the testator before the execution of the will, showing an intention on his part which appears to have been carried into effect by the will as altered, and not as it originally stood.[95] But evidence of declarations made by the testator after the execution of the will have been held inadmissible to show that alterations were made before the will was executed.[96]

A mere general statement by the testator that he had made unspecified alterations is insufficient to give validity to the alterations found upon his will.[97]

Where alterations cause words in a will to be no longer apparent

Although, in general, unattested alterations in a will made after execution cannot be admitted to probate, section 21 of the Wills Act 1837 contains an exception in cases where the words or effect of the will before alteration shall not be "apparent." If, therefore, words are completely obliterated, the obliteration is effectual, and probate must be granted as if there were blanks in the will, even if the original words can be scientifically deciphered.[98]

Words beneath obliterations, erasures or alterations on a will are appar-

---

[88] *Re Hindmarch* (1866) L.R. 1 P. & D. 307, 308; *Greville* v. *Tylee, supra.*
[89] *Re Hindmarch, supra.*
[90] *Ibid.*
[91] *Greville* v. *Tylee, supra.*
[92] *Re Swindin* (1850) 2 Rob. 192.
[93] *Birch* v. *Birch, supra; Re Swindin, supra; Re Cadge, supra; Re Tonge* (1891) 66 L.T. 60.
[94] *Re Adamson* (1875) L.R. 3 P. & D. 253.
[95] *Williams* v. *Ashton* (1860) 1 J. & H. 115; *Re Sykes* (1873) L.R. 3 P. & D. 27; *Re Adamson* (1875) L.R. 3 P. & D. 253, 256; *Re Jessop* [1924] P. 221.
[96] *Doe* v. *Palmer* (1851) 16 Q.B. 747, 756; see *Sugden* v. *Lord St. Leonards* (1876) 1 P.D. 154, 228.
[97] *Williams* v. *Ashton, supra.*
[98] *Re Itter* [1950] P. 130.

ent within the meaning of the section, if experts, using magnifying glasses[99] when necessary, can decipher them; but it is not allowable to resort to any physical interference with the document, by chemicals or otherise,[1] so as to render clearer what has been written on it. Words revealed by infra-red photography are not apparent within the section.[2] But the court has allowed paper pasted over the back of a codicil to be removed in order to ascertain whether it had been revoked by the words covered up.[3]

When words in a will are so completely obliterated as not to be apparent no extrinsic evidence may be admitted to show what they originally were.[4]

Executed alterations

All alterations when made after the execution of the will are to be executed in the same manner as a will,[5] save that the signatures (which includes initials)[6] may be made in the margin or on some other part of the will opposite or near to the alterations, or at the foot or end of or opposite to a memorandum referring to the alteration[7] and written at the end or some other part of the will.[8]

A duly executed codicil will give effect to unattested alterations in a will, and that, it seems, whether or not the codicil be expressly confirmatory of the will to which it refers.[9] For a codicil is a revival of a will and validates the dispositions of the will as they stand at the time of the execution of the codicil.[10]

It will generally be presumed, in the absence of evidence to the contrary, that alterations on a will were made not only after its execution but also after the execution of any codicil.[11]

Declarations by a testator made before the execution of a codicil which revives the will may be admitted to show that the alterations made in the will were made before the execution of the codicil.[12] Statements in a codicil are admissible to determine whether an interlineation in the will was made before of after its execution.[13]

---

[99] Re Ibbetson (1839) 2 Curt. 337; Re Horsford (1874) L.R. 3 P. & D. 211, 215; Ffinch v. Combe [1894] P. 191, 201; Re Brasier [1899] P. 36.

[1] Re Itter [1950] P. 130.

[2] Ibid., but see p. 217, n. 78 and text, post.

[3] Re Gilbert [1893] P. 183. Contrast Re Horsford, supra, and Ffinch v. Combe, supra (in which cases it was held that paper pasted over writing might not be removed).

[4] Townley v. Watson (1844) 3 Curt, 761, 768; see Re McCabe (1873) L.R. 3 P. & D. 94, 96; Re Horsford, supra; Ffinch v. Combe, supra; Re Adams [1990] Ch. 601.

[5] Re Hay [1904] 1 Ch. 317, 321; Re White [1991] Ch. 1. As to execution of wills see ante, pp. 133 et seq.

[6] Re Blewitt (1880) 5 P.D. 116.

[7] See Re Treeby (1975) L.R. 3 P. & D. 242.

[8] Wills Act 1837, s.21.

[9] Neate v. Pickard (1843) 2 N.C. 406; Skinner v. Ogle (1845) 4 N.C. 74, 79; Re Wyatt (1862) 2 Sw. & Tr. 494.

[10] See post, p. 218.

[11] Re Sykes (1873) L.R. 3 P. & D. 26.

[12] Ibid. at p. 28.

[13] Re Heath [1892] P. 253.

Deliberative alterations

Alterations in a will, especially where pencil writing is used, may be deliberative and not final, and, in such case, are not confirmed by a codicil.[14] It has been held that the presumption is that pencil alterations are deliberative but that alterations in ink are final.[15]

Interpolated sheets

Where a testator substitutes unattested sheets for those in his will as executed, even if the substituted sheets are signed and witnessed, those sheets cannot be admitted to probate and the will is revoked.[16] Where, however, several sheets of paper constituting a connected disposal of the estate are found together after the death of the testator, the last sheet being duly executed, the presumption is that they all formed part of the will at the time of its execution.[17] This presumption, it seems, is not rebutted by the mere fact that the sheets do not constitute a consistent disposal of the estate.[18] In this, as in other circumstances, the court leans towards the validity of the testamentary instrument.

The statements of the testator are admissible to show whether any, and what, sheets were constituent parts of the will at the time of execution.[19]

In certain cases words written below the signature of the testator before execution of his will, and referred to in the body thereof, have been regarded as interlineations and admitted to probate.[20]

Where the construction of the will may be affected by the appearance of the original paper, the court will order the probate to pass in facsimile.[21]

H. CONDITIONAL REVOCATION

Although a testator may intend to revoke his will or codicil,[22] the intention may be conditional upon some matter being true or some event occurring. For example, he may revoke a will conditionally upon setting up some other testamentary instrument in the place of that revoked, or in an erroneous belief as to the validity of the will revoked or the effect of the revocatory act. In such circumstances the will or codicil remains unrevoked while the condition is unsatisfied. This proposition of law is known as the doctrine of conditional revocation.[23]

---

[14] *Re Hall* (1871) L.R. 2 P. & D. 256, 258; *Re Adams* (1872) L.R. 2 P. & D. 367.

[15] *Hawkes* v. *Hawkes* (1828) 1 Hagg.Ecc. 321; see *Re Mardon* [1944] P. 109.

[16] *Treloar* v. *Lean* (1889) 14 P.D. 49; *Leonard* v. *Leonard* [1902] P. 243.

[17] *Gregory* v. *Queen's Proctor* (1846) 4 N.C. 620; *Marsh* v. *Marsh* (1860) 1 Sw. & Tr. 528; *Rees* v. *Rees* (1873) L.R. 3 P. & D. 84.

[18] *Marsh* v. *Marsh, supra*, at p. 531.

[19] *Gould* v. *Lakes* (1880) 6 P.D. 1; *Re Hutchison* (1902) 18 T.L.R. 706.

[20] *Re Birt* (1871) L.R. 2 P. & D. 214; *Re Greenwood* [1892] P. 7.

[21] *Re Raine* (1865) 34 L.J.P. 125; see *Re Smith* (1864) 3 Sw. & Tr. 589; *i.e.* by way of a fiat copy.

[22] As to the necessary revocatory intention, see *ante*, p. 139.

[23] More cumbersomely known as the doctrine of dependant relative revocation.

Origins

The doctrine has been criticised as having developed on misapprehension, unjustifiable inference, and faulty analogy.[24] The concept is probably derived from the civil law.[25] Three early cases turn on the identity of the gifts in an earlier will with those contained in a later (invalid) will.[26] The later "will" is in such cases construed as a confirmation of the gifts in the earlier will and the revocation (whether verbally expressed, implied, or derived from an act of destruction[27]), is construed as conditional on the effectiveness of the later (invalid) will.

The doctrine developed on the criterion of "paramount intention"[28] but this could not be applied where the intention was clear but a will was partially defeated by, for instance, attestation by a beneficiary. Here the principle of "mistake" was invoked,[29] applying both to mistake of law and of fact. The concepts of intention and mistake are complementary because a mistake vitiates the intention and the court then has to proceed on supposition or inference however much disguised.

Statute Law

The doctrine of conditional revocation undoubtedly qualifies the express provisions of statute law.[30] As established by the cases, it has been referred to as a gloss for purposes of interpreting the Wills Act 1837.[31] Section 5 of the Statute of Frauds required devises and bequests of land to be in writing signed by the testator and attested and subscribed in the testator's presence by three or four credible witnesses. The difference between this and section 6 was, "most singular."[32] Section 6 provided that no devise of land in writing should be revocable otherwise than by another will or codicil in writing or by burning, cancelling, tearing or obliterating the same. Before the Statute of Frauds, a will of land had to be in writing but could be revoked by parol.[33] Section 5 of the Statute of Frauds was re-placed by section 9 of the Wills Act 1837[34] but section 6 was substantially re-enacted in section 20 of the Wills Act 1837. To this were added section 19 (no revocation by pre-

---

[24] See 71 L.Q.R. 374.

[25] "Tunc prius testamentum rumpitur, cum posterius perfectum est." See *ex p. Ilchester* (1803) 7 Ves.Jun. 348, 375, 379.

[26] *Eccleston* v. *Speake* (1689) 3 Mod. 258; *Onions* v. *Tyrer* (1716) 1 P. Wms. 343; *Hyde* v. *Hyde* (1708) 3 Ch.Rep. 155. See also *Re Finnemore* [1991] 1 W.L.R. 793, 804 (alternative ground for decision).

[27] The form of revocation is immaterial. See *Re Bernard* [1916] 1 Ch. 552; *Ward* v. *Van Der Loeff* [1924] A.C. 653, 677, 684; *Re Hawksley* [1934] Ch. 384, 401.

[28] *Ex p. Ilchester* (1803) 7 Ves.Jun. 348, 372, 378; *Tupper* v. *Tupper* (1855) 1 K. & J. 665, 670; *Re Robinson* [1930] 2 Ch. 332, 336; *Re Hawksley* [1934] Ch. 384, 401.

[29] *Perrott* v. *Perrott* (1811) 422, 438; *Re Finnemore* [1991] 1 W.L.R. 793, 806, 827.

[30] *i.e.* The Statute of Frauds 1677, s.6; Wills Act 1837, ss.20, 21, 22.

[31] See *per* Atkin L.J. in *Re Southerden* [1925] P. at 185: "The case depends on the Wills Act 1837 and therefore it would not be proper to determine it upon cases decided before that Act was passed." See also *Re Finnemore* [1991] 1 W.L.R. 793, 809.

[32] See *per* Lord Alvanley in *ex p. Ilchester* (1803) 7 Ves.Jun. 348, 371.

[33] See the argument in *ex p. Ilchester* (1803) 7 Ves.Jun. 356 (Romilly).

[34] See *ante.*

sumption), section 21 (alterations to be executed as for a will) and section 22 (revival of wills only by re-execution). Nowhere is there express provision for the doctrine of conditional revocation. The doctrine appears at its most forceful where the statute forbids a person to take (*e.g.* a witness) but the doctrine allows him to do so.[35]

Jurisdiction

Numerous cases have arisen in the probate jurisdiction under which the issue is whether or not a given will or wills are to be admitted to probate and in what form.[36] However the question can equally well arise under the Chancery jurisdiction where the court acts on the probate but imposes trusts in the terms of the will held to be wholly or partially unrevoked.[37] In the former case the question will be largely one of intention or mistake. In the latter it will be largely a matter of construction.[38]

Application

The questions to be asked when it is sought to apply this doctrine, once it has been established that the testator had the necessary revocatory intention, were set out by Buckley L.J. in *Re Jones*[39] as follows:

"If he had an intention of revoking the will, was his intention absolute or qualified, so as to be contingent or conditional? If it was absolute, that is the end of the investigation, for the act takes effect as a revocation.

If, however, it was qualified, the further question which arises is, what was the nature of the qualification? The testator's intention may have been dependent upon an intent to revive an earlier testamentary document, founded on an erroneous belief that the cancellation of the later will would have that effect, as in *Powell* v. *Powell* (1866) L.R. 1 P. & D. 209, or it may have been wholly and solely dependent upon an intention to displace it by some new testamentary disposition. An example of this may be taken to be *Dixon* v. *Treasury Solicitor* [1905] P. 42 where there was evidence that the testator thought that the cancellation of an earlier will was a necessary precondition of making a new one.

If the testator's intention is found to have been a qualified one, subject to some condition or contingency, the final question arises: has that condition or contingency been satisfied or occurred? If the condition or contingency to which the intention to revoke was subject has not been satisfied or occurred, the revocation is ineffective; if it has been satisfied or occurred, the revocation is effective."

[35] *Re Robinson* [1930] 2 Ch. 382. *Re Finnemore* [1991] 1 W.L.R. 793.
[36] See *e.g. Re Jones* [1976] Ch. 200.
[37] See *e.g. Re Hawksley* [1934] Ch. 384, 395; *Re Finnemore* [1991] 1 W.L.R. 793, 814.
[38] *Re Finnemore* [1991] 1 W.L.R. 793, 804.
[39] [1976] Ch. 200; see also *Re Finnemore* [1991] 1 W.L.R. 793, 810.

Types of conditional revocation

1. *Mistake whether of law or fact or both may annul cancellation or revocation*[40]

A testator often seeks to revoke his will because he is labouring under a mistake of fact; *e.g.* that a will has been lost,[41] that the legatees were dead,[42] that he had not previously disposed of a particular asset,[43] that he would have no property to leave.[44] The revocation will take effect unless as a matter of construction the revocation was contingent upon the fact being true.[45]

In many cases a testator seeks to revoke a will because he misunderstands the law applicable in the circumstances, as where he revokes his will believing that his wife will be the sole person to benefit on intestacy,[46] that the destruction of a will revives an earlier will,[47] that the will which is destroyed is invalid,[48] that the destruction of a codicil will leave his revived will operative,[49] that a settlement would operate in spite of the revocation of a will although it would not in fact do so in the circumstances,[50] that other arrangements for disposal of a testator's property were effective,[51] that a provision in the later instrument was valid, whereas it was void for remoteness.[52] There is no distinction between invalidity of the will itself and incapacity to take.[53]

2. *Purported revocation conditional on making a fresh, valid will*

Sometimes a testator revokes his will as a preliminary to making a fresh will. In doing so he may intend that the revocation be conditional on a new valid will being made, in which case the doctrine of conditional revocation applies, or he may intend that the will be revoked whether or not a later will is made, in which case it does not. The mere fact that at the time of the revocation the testator intended to make a new will is not by itself sufficient to establish that the revocation was conditional. The position was summarised by Buckley L.J. in *Re Jones*[54] as follows:

---

[40] *Perrott* v. *Perrott* (1811) 14 East 422, 438.
[41] *Re Moresby* (1828) 1 Hagg.Ecc. 378.
[42] *Campbell* v. *French* (1797) 3 Ves. 321.
[43] *Goddard* v. *Overend* [1911] 1 R. 469; *Re Churchill* [1917] 1 Ch. 206 is probably wrongly decided, see *Re Feis* [1964] Ch. 106.
[44] *Re Carey* (1977) 121 S.J. 173; *Re Casey* (1971) 111 S.J. 123.
[45] *Re Feis* [1964] Ch. 106.
[46] *Adams* v. *Southerden* [1925] P. 177, C.A.; *Re Greenstreet* (1930) 74 S.J. 188.
[47] *Powell* v. *Powell* (1866) L.R. 1 P. & D. 209; *Cossey* v. *Cossey* (1900) 82 L.T. 203; *Re Bridgewater* [1965] 1 W.L.R. 416.
[48] *Giles* v. *Warren* (1872) L.R. 2 P. & D. 401.
[49] *James* v. *Shrimpton* (1876) 1 P.D. 431.
[50] *Stamford* v. *White* [1901] P. 46.
[51] *Re Feis* [1964] Ch. 106.
[52] *Ward* v. *Van der Loeff* [1924] A.C. 653.
[53] *Re Robinson* [1930] 2 Ch. at p. 337, but *cf. Tupper* v. *Tupper* (1855) 1 K. & J. 665, 669.
[54] [1976] Ch. 200.

"A testator who has made a will in favour of A may become disenchanted with A and decide not to benefit him. He may well at the same time decide that in these circumstances he will benefit B instead of A. It does not by any means follow that his intention to disinherit A will be dependent on his benefiting B, or making a will under which B could take.

If he were told that for some reason B could not or would not benefit under his new will, would the testator say, 'In that case, I want my gift to A to stand,' or would he say, 'Well, even so, I do not wish A to benefit?' In the former case, his *animus revocandi* at the time of the destruction or mutilation of his will could properly be regarded as dependent on the execution of a new will, but not in the latter."

If the revocatory act is conditional in this sense, then if the testator dies before making a fresh will, the original will remains unrevoked.[55]

Occasionally a testator purports to make a fresh will, but for some reason it is invalid or ineffective. For example, it may not be duly executed,[56] it may be ineffective in part by being witnessed by a beneficiary[57] or it may be left in an obviously incomplete state.[58] In all such cases, provided that the revocatory act was conditional, the earlier will remains unrevoked. The revocation may even be conditional on a contingency occurring as expressed in a fresh, valid will.[59]

3. *Purported revocation effected as a preliminary to making alterations*

The doctrine may also apply where a testator has sought to alter his will, for example by erasure or obliteration of part followed by substitution of a new provision,[60] but has ineffectively done so, as where the new provision is unattested[61] or he has omitted to make it at all.[62] Provided the court is satisfied that the testator would have intended to restore the original words in such a case, they will remain unrevoked.

4. *Cancellation or destruction*

Different considerations apply where a will is destroyed or physically cancelled by for example obliteration or writing across it. The matter is

---

[55] *e.g. Dixon* v. *Treasury Solicitor* [1905] P. 42.

[56] *Onions* v. *Tyrer* (1716) 1 P. Wms. 343; *Scott* v. *Scott* (1859) 1 Sw. & Tr. 258; *Clarkson* v. *Clarkson* (1862) 2 Sw. & Tr. 491; *Dancer* v. *Crabb* (1873) L.R. 3 P. & D. 98; *Durber* v. *Bunn* (1926) 134 L.T. 669; *Re Davies* [1951] 1 All E.R. 920; *Re Botting* [1951] 2 All E.R. 997.

[57] *Mansell* v. *Crannis* (1978) 122 S.J. 489; *Ward* v. *Van der Loeff* [1924] A.C. 653.

[58] *Re Hope-Brown* [1942] P. 136; *Re Allen* (1962) 106 S.J. 115; *Re Irvine* [1919] I.R. 485 *Re Cocke* [1960] 1 W.L.R. 491.

[59] *Re Allen* (1962) 106 S.J. 115.

[60] See *ante*, p. 189.

[61] *Re Zimmer* (1924) 40 T.L.R. 502.

[62] *Re Horsford* (1874) L.R. 3 P. & D. 211.

then not so much one of construction as of satisfying the court of (a) the act in question and (b) the intention behind this act.[63]

5. *Express unconditional revocation*

Although it has been said that an express revocation "will stand" so that the doctrine does not apply in such cases[64] this does not seem to be correct and the courts have applied the doctrine even in the face of an express categorical revocation.[65] The question is not determined by the presence or absence of express words of revocation.

Evidence—Presumption against intestacy

All the circumstances surrounding the apparent revocation must be examined to see whether the testator's intention when revoking his will was absolute or qualified.[66] It is a matter of drawing the proper inference from those circumstances, and no particular burden lies on the party alleging that the revocation was conditional.[67] However, the usual presumption against intestacy[68] applies in cases where an intestacy would result if the doctrine were not applied. There is a golden rule of construction that when a testator has executed a will in solemn form you must assume that he did not intend to make it a solemn farce.[69] In this context it has to be remembered that at the time of the earlier cases there was no such presumption. The heir was the "darling of the law" and the courts were not so reluctant to upset a will which displaced the heir.[70] Thus the earlier cases in which the doctrine was applied should perhaps be given even greater force than later cases where the presumption against intestacy reinforced the doctrine. Even where there is no evidence about the act of revocation at all, as where revocation is presumed from the fact that the will was last seen in the testator's possession but was not found on his death,[71] the court may nevertheless draw the necessary inference from the known facts.[72] Where, however, the only evidence is that of a person interested in setting up the earlier will, whose conduct throws doubts upon his credibility, such evidence may be disregarded.[73] Evidence of statements made by the testator as to his intention when committing the act of revocation is admissible.[74] Any lapse of time between the forming of the necessary intention by the

---

[63] See *per* Lord Mansfield in *Burtenshaw* v. *Gilbert* (1774) Cowp. 49, 53.

[64] See *per* Lord Dunedin in *Ward* v. *Van der Loeff* [1924] A.C. at p. 671, but the other speeches do not seem to take this view. *Re Finnemore* [1991] 1 W.L.R. 793, 807.

[65] *Re Hawksley* [1934] Ch. 384; *Re Bernard* [1916] 1 Ch. 552.

[66] *Re Jones* [1976] Ch. 200; *Re Finnemore* [1991] 1 W.L.R. 793, 805, 823.

[67] *Re Jones*, *supra*, 218. *Cf. Re Murray* [1956] 1 W.L.R. 605.

[68] See *e.g. Re Harrison* (1885) 30 Ch.D. 390.

[69] *per* Esher M.R. *Ibid*. at p. 393.

[70] See 71 L.Qp.R. 387.

[71] See *ante*, p. 204.

[72] *Re Botting* [1951] 2 All E.R. 997 considering *Homerton* v. *Hewett* (1872) 25 L.T. 854. *Cf.* *Ward* v. *Bond* (1962) 106 S.J. 1034.

[73] *Eckersley* v. *Platt* (1866) L.R. 1 P. & D. 281.

[74] *Powell* v. *Powell* (1866) L.R. 1 P. & D. 209.

testator and his subsequent act of revocation would be an important factor to take into account but would not necessarily be conclusive one way or the other.[75] It would not of course be sufficient if the testator formed the necessary intention after the act of revocation.[76] It may be easier to reach the conclusion that revocation was conditional where a testator has revoked a previous will merely to make small changes, for example a condition attached to a gift, but not the gift itself, or matters of machinery, such as the appointment of different trustees.[77]

In the case of conditional revocation by obliteration, infra-red rays may be used to restore the original words of the will[78] and extrinsic evidence is admissible to show what the words originally were.[79]

Application of the Doctrine

The doctrine has been applied where the intention was clear from earlier dispositions,[80] where revocation was based on mistake of law or fact,[81] where there was no express revocation,[82] in order to rebut the presumption of revocation where a known will was not forthcoming on the death of the testator[83] and where the residue in the second will was undisposed of.[84]

Conversely the doctrine has been held not to apply where the intention to revoke and reason for doing so are clear,[85] where the application of the doctrine would be making a will for a testator so as to perfect an imperfect gift[86] and where the mere intention to make a new will was insufficient to indicate that the mutilation of the will was intended to be conditional.[87]

The doctrine may also be applied so as to have a distributive effect and confirm some gifts and vary others.[88]

---

[75] *Re Bromham* [1951] W.N. 603.

[76] *Re Weston* (1869) L.R. 1 P. & D. 633.

[77] *Re Murray* [1956] 1 W.L.R. 605.

[78] *Re Itter* [1950] P. 130.

[79] *Brooke* v. *Kent* (1841) 3 Moo.P.C. 334; *Re McCabe* (1873) L.R. 3 P. & D. 94.

[80] *Onions* v. *Tyrer* (1716) 1 P. Wms. 343; *ex p. Ilchester* (1803) 7 Ves. 348, 372; *Re Finnemore* [1991] 1 W.L.R. 793.

[81] *Perrott* v. *Perrott* (1811) 18 East 422, 438; *Re Southerden* [1925] P. 177; *Re Finnemore* [1991] 1 W.L.R. 793, 826 (alternative ground for decision).

[82] *Ward* v. *Van der Loeff* [1924] A.C. 653, 666; *Alexander* v. *Kirk Patrick* L.R. 2 H.L.Sc. 397; *Duguid* v. *Fraser* (1885) 31 Ch.D. 449; *Morley* v. *Rennoldson* [1895] 1 Ch. 449; *Re Robinson* [1930] 2 Ch. 332; *Re Hawksley* [1934] Ch. 384.

[83] *Re Botting* [1951] 2 A.E.R. 997. See p. 205 *ante.*

[84] *Re Cocke* [1960] 1 W.L.R. 491.

[85] *Burtenshaw* v. *Gilbert* (1774) Cowper 49; *Tupper* v. *Tupper* (1854) 1 K. & J. 665; *Re Feis* [1964] Ch. 106.

[86] *Re Churchill* [1917] 1 Ch. 206, 211.

[87] *Re Jones* [1976] Ch. 200.

[88] *Re Finnemore* [1991] 1 W.L.R. 793, 821, 824, 827.

CHAPTER 15

THE REVIVAL OF WILLS

Definition

This chapter is concerned with the revival of a revoked will. The word "republication" has been wrongly used in the past in this context, but "republication" is now meaningless as explained in *Berkeley* v. *Berkeley*.[1] Before the Wills Act 1837[2] a will generally operated only on real property of the testator at the date of his will, so that "republication" by a later codicil was important where a testator had acquired further land after the date of his original will. A codicil still has the effect of confirming the will and making it operate as from the date of the codicil in so far as it does not speak "with reference to property."[3]

Revival

Section 22 of the Wills Act 1837 provides, "No will or codicil, or any part thereof, which shall be in any manner revoked, shall be revived otherwise than by the re-execution thereof, or by a codicil executed in manner hereinbefore required, and showing an intention to revive the same . . . "[4]

Although before the Wills Act 1837 a will of personalty might be republished by declaration, since the Act there must be re-execution to revive a will or the execution of a codicil which shows an intention to revive it. Destruction of an instrument revoking a will does not revive that will.[5]

Re-execution as reviving a will

The same considerations apply to the re-execution of a will as apply to its execution. In determining whether there has been re-execution, the purpose for which the signatures were placed on the document may require to be ascertained. They must be placed there *animo testandi* and not for some other reason.[6]

Revival of a will by a codicil

For a codicil to effect the revival of a will, the intention to revive must

---

[1] [1946] A.C. 555, 575. But *cf.* Wills Act 1837, s.34, *post*, p. 221.
[2] See s.24.
[3] See Wills Act 1837, s.24 and *post*, p. 948.
[4] As to the remainder of the section see *post*, p. 223.
[5] *Major* v. *Williams* (1843) 3 Curt. 432; *Re Brown* (1858) 1 Sw. & Tr. 32; *Re Hodgkinson* [1893] P. 339.
[6] *Dunn* v. *Dunn* (1866) L.R. 1 P. & D. 277.

appear on the face of the codicil.[7] A clause confirming a codicil may not be enough to revive a revoked will.[8]

Previously, unless there was a latent ambiguity in the codicil, extrinsic evidence of the intention to revive the instrument was inadmissible[9]; but the court would receive such evidence of the surrounding circumstances as, by placing it in the position of the testator, would better enable it to read the true sense of the words used.[10] In the case of deaths occurring on or after January 1, 1983, it appears that by virtue of section 21 of the Administration of Justice Act 1982 it will now be permissable to introduce extrinsic evidence, including that of the testator's intention, to assist in the interpretation of a codicil, where either:

(a) the language of the codicil is ambiguous on its face (a patent ambiguity); or

(b) in so far as evidence, other than that of the testator's intention, shows that the language used is ambiguous in the light of the surrounding circumstances (a latent ambiguity).

Although the wording of the section refers only to a "will,"[11] it is thought the section will be construed as extending to a codicil.

The intention to revive must be in express words referring to the will as revoked and importing an intention to revive it, by a disposition which is inconsistent with any other intention, or by some other expressions conveying with reasonable certainty the existence of the intention in question.[12]

A reference in a codicil may revive a will[13] though it does not state the date of that will,[14] or description.[15] A codicil which merely refers to the testator's "will" may revive a revoked will if it is shown that there was not more than one will in existence[16]; but where a testator refers in a codicil to his "last will," and there is nothing in the codicil to point to any particular will, the reference is construed as being to the last will in legal existence, and not to a revoked will.[17]

The mere physical annexation, e.g. by a piece of tape, of a duly executed codicil of a later date to revoked testamentary papers is not in itself a ground for inferring an intention to revive.[18]

Even ungrammatical language, if its meaning is clear, may revive a

---

[7] *Re Steele* (1868) L.R. 1 P. & D. 575, 578.

[8] *Re Sebag-Montefiore* [1944] Ch. 331.

[9] *Re Goodenough* (1861) 2 Sw. & Tr. 141; *Re Steele, supra*, at p. 576.

[10] *Re Steele* (1868) L.R. 1 P. & D. 575; *Re Davis* [1952] P. 279.

[11] *Cf.* Wills Act 1837, s.1.

[12] *Re Steele, Supra*; see *Re Smith* (1890) 45 Ch.D. 632; *Re Sebag-Montefiore* [1944] Ch. 331.

[13] *Re McCabe* (1862) 2 Sw. & Tr. 474.

[14] *Re Houblon* (1865) 11 Jur. (N.S.) 549; *Re Green* (1899) 79 L.T. 738.

[15] *Thomson* v. *Hempenstall* (1849) 1 Rob. 783.

[16] *Neate* v. *Pickard* (1843) 2 N.C. 406; *Marsh* v. *Marsh* (1860) 1 Sw & Tr. 528, 533.

[17] *Hale* v. *Tokelove* (1850) 2 Rob. 318, 326; *Marsh* v. *Marsh, supra*; *Re Steele, supra*.

[18] *Marsh* v. *Marsh, supra*.

revoked will.[19] Where the testator's will was revoked by marriage it was revived by an indorsement duly executed on the envelope containing it to the effect that the principal beneficiary was now the testator's wife.[20]

Whether reference in a codicil revives a revoked will

Whether a mistaken reference in a codicil to a later will revives an earlier will of which it merely gives the date was considered by Sir J. P. Wilde in the case of *Re Steele*,[21] in which he said "The court ought to be slow to conclude that a testator has manifested in this indirect way a desire to revoke his last will, and it should scrutinise narrowly the language of a codicil which is said to show such an intention, lest in the desire to follow the testators' wishes too blindly it should set them at naught altogether." This decision has been followed in a number of later cases[22] in which mistaken references to revoked wills by their dates have been made in codicils. In such cases the mistaken reference to the revoked will should be omitted from the probate.[23] Earlier authorities holding that a reference to a revoked will by date in a codicil is in itself sufficient to revive it must be considered to be wrongly decided.

Where, however, a revoked will is mistakenly referred to in a codicil not merely by date but by its provisions, such will is revived.[24] For even if the mistake is that of the draftsman it must be treated as the mistake of the testator.[25] But where a draftsman applied his mind to a part only of the revoked will when drafting a codicil, that part only was revived,[26] and the revived part of the will, a later will and the codicil were admitted to probate.[27]

It may now also be possible to rectify a codicil if the court is satisfied that it fails to carry out the testator's intentions in consequence of either a clerical error or a failure to understand his instructions.[28]

Where a codicil refers to a revoked will, intending to revive it, but such will has been destroyed, *animo revocandi*, the codicil cannot revive it[29]; nor can a draft of the will be admitted to probate.[30] But it seems that where one part of a will in duplicate has been destroyed on being revoked, but the

---

[19] *Re Terrible* (1858) 1 Sw. & Tr. 140.

[20] *Re Davis, supra.*

[21] (1868) L.R. 1 P. & D. 575, 579; see *Re May* (1868) L.R. 1 P. & D. 575, 581.

[22] *Re Wilson* (1868) L.R. 1 P. & D. 575, 582; *Re Ince* (1877) 2 P.D. 111; *Re Lady Isabella Gordon* [1892] P. 228; *Jane* v. *Jane* (1917) 33 T.L.R. 389; *Goldie* v. *Adam* [1938] P.85; *Re White* (1961) 105 S.J. 259.

[23] *Lady Isabella Gordon, supra; Goldie* v. *Adam, supra.*

[24] *Re Stedham* (1881) 6 P.D. 205; *Re Dyke* (1881) 6 P.D. 207; *Re Chilcott* [1897] P. 223; see *Re Baker* [1929] Ch. 668; *Re Pearson* [1963] 1 W.L.R. 1358.

[25] *Goldie* v. *Adam, supra.*

[26] *Re Mardon* [1944] P. 109.

[27] *Ibid.*; see *Re Carleton* [1915] 2 I.R. 9.

[28] Administration of Justice Act 1982, s.20.

[29] *Hale* v. *Tokelove* (1850) 2 Rob. 318, 328; *Rogers* v. *Goodenough* (1862) 2 Sw. & Tr. 342; *Re Steele* (1868) L.R. 1 P. & D. 575, 576; *Re Reade* [1902] P. 75.

[30] *Hale* v. *Tokelove, supra.*

other part is in existence, the will may be revived by a codicil.[31] It was at one time held that although the destroyed will was not revived, any intermediate will was revoked; but this view has since been discredited.[32]

Whether the rule applies to a will which has been accidentally destroyed is still an open question, but the circumstances which would call for it to be answered are unlikely to arise.

Where a revoked will was revived by a codicil and the latter was destroyed by the testator it was held that the destruction was not done *animo revocandi* as he could not have intended to have left his will inoperative, and probate was granted of the will and of the codicil as contained in a draft.[33] But it seems that if a testator destroys a codicil, intending to revoke both will and codicil, such destruction will be inoperative to revoke the will.

A codicil expressed to take effect only upon an event which does not happen revives a will to which it refers by date, and is on that account entitled to probate.[34] And when a codicil revives a revoked will, subject to the happening of a contingency which is in suspense at the date of the testators's death, the revoked will is entitled to probate immediately upon his death.[35]

Consequences of revival

Section 34 of the Wills Act 1837 provides: "Every will re-executed or republished, or revived by any codicil shall, for the purposes of this Act, be deemed to have been made at the time at which the same shall be so re-executed, republished or revived."

In general the revival of the will is tantamount to making it *de novo*; it brings down the will to the date of the revival and makes it speak as at that time.[36] The will and codicil are, in these circumstances, one document in effect.[37] It is to be noted, however, that the date on which any disposition is made within the meaning of any particular enactment may not be governed by this rule but by the special provisions of the enactment.[38]

But there are exceptions to the general rule stated above. The court has declined to enforce it strictly where exact compliance would defeat the testator's intention.[39] Nor will revival so apply as to make void a valid restriction merely because of the passing of a statute after the date of the will.[40]

Revival of a will may extend its operation to persons and property to

[31] *Payne* v. *Trappers* (1847) 1 Rob. 583. As to duplicate wills, see *ante*, p. 124.
[32] *Rogers* v. *Goodenough, supra.*
[33] *James* v. *Shrimpton* (1876) 1 P.D. 431.
[34] *Re Da Silva* (1861) 2 Sw. & Tr. 315; see *Re Hugo* (1877) 2 P.D. 73.
[35] *Re Bangham* (1876) 1 P.D. 429.
[36] *Re Champion* [1893] 1 Ch. 101; *Re Fraser* [1904] 1 Ch. 726.
[37] *Re Reeves* [1928] 1 Ch. 351, 355.
[38] See *Berkeley* v. *Berkeley* [1946] A.C. 555; *Re Heath's W.T.* [1949] Ch. 170.
[39] *Re Fraser, supra.*
[40] *Re Heath's W.T., supra.*

whom or to which the description therein was not applicable when the will was made, provided the will spoke of them as existing.[41]

The revival of a will which itself contains a clause revoking former testamentary instruments revokes any wills executed between the dates of the original execution and of the revival.[42] Where the revived will contains no revocation clause the intermediate wills are not necessarily revoked and all the documents may be admitted to probate. If there is contention as to the testator's intention as to revocation, the court of construction will consider all the testamentary instruments and may determine their effect when interpreted together.[43]

Effect of revival of wills on codicils

Difficult questions arise in determining the effect of the revival of a will upon codicils thereto. Where the instrument which effects the revival expressly refers to the codicils, no difficulty arises; but assuming a testator to have made a will, then a first codicil modifying the will and later a second codicil confirming the will but not mentioning the codicil, the question arises whether the second codicil revives the will as it originally stood, or confirms the will as modified by the first codicil.

Where the first codicil has been duly executed and neither it nor the will has been revoked, prima facie the will as modified by the first codicil is confirmed and the first codicil is not revoked.[44] But in every case it is a question of the intention of the testator, and although a reference simply to the date of the will is not sufficient in itself to restrict the confirmation to that particular document, yet if other words and surrounding circumstances convey that intention with reasonable certainty, the first codicil will be treated as revoked, and the will together with the second codicil only admitted to probate.[45]

Where the first codicil was duly executed but the will and the first codicil have been revoked, a reference in the reviving codicil to the will alone will not, it seems, be a sufficient expression of an intention to revive the first codicil.[46]

Where the first codicil was never duly executed, it can only have force and effect (if at all) if incorporated in and set up by the later codicil.[47]

Section 22 of the Wills Act 1837 further[48] provides, "When any will or codicil which shall be partly revoked, and afterwards wholly revoked, shall be revived, such revival shall not extend to so much thereof as shall have

[41] *Re Hardyman* [1925] Ch. 287.
[42] *Rowling* v. *Crowther* [1963] 1 W.L.R. 1358; see *Re Baker* [1929] Ch. 668.
[43] *Re Sted* (1881) 6 P.D. 205; *Re Dyke* (1881) 6 P.D. 207; *Deakin* v. *Garvie* (1919) 36 T.L.R. 122, C.A.; *Goldie* v. *Adam* [1938] P. 85; *Re Baker, supra*; *Re Mardon* [1944] P. 109.
[44] *Re De La Saussaye* (1873) L.R. 3 P. & D. 42; *Green* v. *Tribe* (1878) 9 Ch. D. 231; *Follett* v. *Pettman* (1833) 23 Ch.D. 337.
[45] *Upfill* v. *Marshall* (1843) 3 Curt. 636; *McLeod* v. *McNab* [1891] A.C. 471.
[46] *Re Reynolds* (1873) L.R. 3 P. & D. 35; see *Re Sebag-Montefiore* [1944] Ch. 331.
[47] See *ante*, pp. 219 *et seq.*
[48] As to the beginning of the section see *ante*, p. 218.

been revoked before the revocation of the whole thereof, unless an intention to the contrary shall be shown."[49]

The execution of a codicil which revives a will may give effect to unattested alterations in a will, or render the will effective to incorporate documents which have come into existence subsequent to its execution, or render valid an unexecuted will or other paper.[50] It may also extend the operation of the will to persons and property to whom or to which the description is applicable at the date of revival.[51]

Finally, if a testator makes a will while of unsound mind, and afterwards recovers mental capacity and revives it, he doubtless makes it a valid will, though the mere fact of his recovery, without more, cannot give it any force or strength. In the same way an adult testator can ratify a will made during infancy.

---

[49] See *Neate* v. *Pickard* (1843) 2 N.C. 406; *Re Hodgkinson* [1893] P. 339.
[50] See *ante*, p. 156.
[51] See *Re Hardyman* [1925] Ch. 287.

CHAPTER 16

PRIVILEGED WILLS

Exemption from formalities

Men or women serving in the Royal Navy, the Army, the Royal Marines or the Royal Air Force, may, in circumstances hereafter described, make valid wills without complying with the formalities laid down in ordinary circumstances. The same privilege is accorded to sailors "at sea."[1]

History

The Statute of Frauds 1677 (which first made it necessary that wills of personalty should be made in writing) by section 22 enacted that "any soldier, being in actual military service, or any mariner or seaman" might dispose of his personal estate as he might have done before the passing of the Statute. Section 11 of the Wills Act 1837 in effect re-enacted section 22 of the Statute of Frauds 1677. Personal estate includes personalty over which the testator has a power of appointment whether special or general.[2]

The categories of those entitled to make privileged wills were widened by the Wills (Soldiers and Sailors) Act 1918, section 2 of which extended them to include members of the Royal Naval and Marine forces, not only when at sea but in cases where, if they had been soldiers, they would have been on actual military service. By section 5(2) of the Act the expression "soldier" in section 11 of the Wills Act 1837 was extended to include members of the Royal Air Force.

By section 3 of the Wills (Soldiers and Sailors) Act 1918 privileged wills may be made of realty as well as of personalty in cases of persons embraced by that Act and by section 11 of the Wills Act 1837 who die after February 6, 1922. If the death was after this date it is immaterial that the privileged will was made before that date.[3]

Since no formalities were required for making a will of personalty before the passing of the Statute of Frauds 1677, none are required for privileged wills. Such wills may be in writing or even oral.

Oral or nuncupative wills

In the case of an oral, sometimes called a nuncupative, will the court must be satisfied as to the exact words used, or at least as to their sub-

---

[1] See generally 83 L.S. Gazette 2078.
[2] *Re Chichester* [1946] Ch. 289.
[3] *Re Yates* [1919] P. 93. Where the death occurred before the passing of the Act, a will of personalty and realty where the gift of the former was dependent on the latter was held not to be admissible: *Godman* v. *Godman* [1920] P. 261.

stance, and that it was the deceased's intention to make a disposition on his death.[4] The deceased must be shown to be conveying a request that his wishes should be acted on at his death, not merely imparting information as to his wishes.[5] He must make clear what his wishes are.[6] It is immaterial whether the deceased knew that his declaration would have testamentary effect.[7]

Written wills

A written will need not be signed by the testator, nor need it be attested in any way. As attesting witnesses are not required, it seems that a gift to an attesting witness is valid.[8] But the matter is not beyond doubt.[9]

A will and two letters have been admitted as together constituting the testamentary disposition of the deceased.[10] A letter to solicitors stating how the testator wished his will to be altered and asking them to destroy his will and make a fresh one as indicated by his letter was admitted to probate in an unreported case. In another unreported case a draft will as altered by a soldier and sent to his solicitor with a covering letter and a memorandum was admitted to probate. The court must be satisfied that the document in question is intended as a will and is not merely a draft.[11]

Where a will already exists a codicil may be made on the same principles.

Revocation of a privileged will

Privileged wills can be revoked as informally as they were made.[12] But an inaccurate summary of his will by a testator will not be interpreted as a revocation of it.[13]

It seems that marriage or divorce will not revoke a privileged will.[14]

Appointment of a guardian

By section 4 of the Wills (Soldiers and Sailors) Act 1918, the appointment of a guardian in a privileged will is valid where the testator dies after the date of the Act.[15]

Infant testators

By section 1 of the Wills (Soldiers and Sailors) Act 1918 a person entitled

---

[4] *Re Donner* (1917) 34 T.L.R. 138; *Dalrymple* v. *Campbell* [1919] P. 7.
[5] *Re Knibbs, Flay* v. *Trueman* [1962] 1 W.L.R. 852.
[6] *Re MacGillivray* [1946] 2 All E.R. 301.
[7] *Spicer* v. *Richardson* [1949] P. 441; *Dalrymple* v. *Campbell, supra.*
[8] *Re Limond* [1915] 2 Ch. 240.
[9] See *Re Priest* [1944] Ch. 58, a case under Lord Kingsdown's Act (Wills Act 1861).
[10] *Re Vernon* (1916) 33 T.L.R. 11.
[11] *Boughton-Knight* v. *Wilson* (1915) 32 T.L.R. 146.
[12] *Wood* v. *Gossage* [1921] P. 194, which by implication overrules *Re Wardrop* [1917] P. 54.
[13] *Re Beech* [1923] P. 46, C.A.; see *Re MacGillivray, supra.*
[14] *Wood* v. *Gossage, supra.*
[15] See *Re Chichester* [1946] Ch. 289.

to make a privileged will may dispose of personalty as he might have done
before the Wills Act 1837, even though he is under the age of majority. By
section 3 of the Act such person may dispose of realty in his will in the same
way as personalty, even though under the age of majority. The effect of
these sections combined with section 22 of the Statute of Frauds 1677[16] is
to make common law applicable to the age at which a privileged will can be
made.

At common law a male could make a will on attaining the age of 14 years
and a female on attaining the age of 12 years. Accordingly infants entitled
to make privileged wills may make them from these ages according to their
sex.

An infant serving with the British Army of the Rhine in 1954 was held to
be entitled to make a privileged will, because he was a soldier in actual
military service, although the will was made in England during a period of
leave[17]; as was an infant who was a sailor and made his will while ashore
between voyages.[18]

An infant may exercise a power of appointment by a privileged will.[19]

Wills of members of the armed forces

Two matters need particular consideration in the case of members of the
armed forces: (i) who may be considered a member of such forces and (ii)
what is meant by the phrase "in actual military service" used in section 11
of the Wills Act 1837.

(i) *Who is a member of the armed forces*

As already stated, those serving in the Royal Navy, the Royal Marines
and the Royal Air Force, if in actual military service, are entitled to make
privileged wills. In *Andrews* v. *Wingham*[20] Denning L.J. stated[21] that many
other categories of persons engaged on war service were entitled to make
privileged wills. These categories "include all our men serving, or called up
for service, in the wars: and women too for that matter. It includes not only
those actively engaged with the enemy but all who are trained to fight him.
It also includes those members of the forces who, under stress of war, both
work at their jobs and man the defences, such as the Home Guard.[22] It
includes not only the fighting men but also those who serve in the forces,
doctors, nurses, chaplains, WRNS, ATS, and so forth."

Before this decision the following were held to be soldiers; a surgeon in

[16] See *ante*, p. 224. As to the age of majority after 1969, see the Family Law Reform Act
1969, s.3.
[17] *Re Colman* [1958] 1 W.L.R. 457.
[18] *Re Newland* [1952] P. 71.
[19] See *Wernher* v. *Beit* [1918] 2 Ch. 82.
[20] [1949] P. 187, C.A.
[21] At p. 196.
[22] See *Blyth* v. *Lord Advocate* [1944] 2 All E.R. 375.

the service of the East India Company,[23] a cook in that service,[24] a volunteer,[25] a member of a force of irregular troops,[26] a Territorial officer called up before the outbreak of war,[27] a member of the Women's Auxiliary Air Force,[28] a Queen Alexandra nurse.[29] But a member of the St. John's Ambulance Corps was held not to be entitled to make a privileged will.[30]

(ii) *Meaning of the words "in actual military service"*

Earlier decisions as to the meaning of these words identified them with the phrase *in expeditione* which was used in the Roman law of privileged wills. But this limited interpretation was overruled in the case of *Andrews v. Wingham*,[31] in which the testator, serving in the Royal Air Force, made his will in Canada while in course of training there. Bucknill L.J., having pointed out that the word "actual" has the same meaning as "active," explained the tests whether a person was in actual military service as follows[32]: "In my opinion the tests are: (a) was the testator 'on military service'? (b) was such service, 'active'?"

The Court of Appeal upheld a decision that a soldier in camp in England who was killed by a bomb was entitled to make a privileged will.[33] It disapproved cases in which a member of the Home Guard,[34] and an officer of the Army Dental Corps killed by a bomb on his home[35] were held not to be on actual military service.

In a later case[36] it was held that a soldier who was obliged by his conditions of service to go out on patrol against a "clandestine force of assassins" while serving in Northern Ireland was in "actual military service." His oral declaration to his officer "If I don't make it make sure Anne gets all my stuff" was held to be a universal bequest of personalty and his declaration was admitted to probate.

The *ratio decidendi* in *Andrews v. Wingham*[37] was followed in a case in which a soldier serving with the British Army of the Rhine in 1954 was held entitled to make a privileged will while on leave in England.[38]

[23] *Re Donaldson* (1840) 2 Curt. 386.
[24] *Shearman* v. *Pyke* (1724) unrep. Described in *Re Jones* [1981] Fam. 7.
[25] *Re Hiscock* [1901] P. 78.
[26] *Re Cory* (1901) 84 L.T. 270.
[27] *Re Rippon* [1943] P. 61.
[28] *Re Rowson* [1944] 2 All E.R. 36.
[29] *Re Stanley* [1916] P. 192. The deceased in this case might well be thought to have qualified as a sailor, see *Re Hale* [1915] 2 I.R. 362.
[30] *Anderson* v. *Downes* [1916] P. 49.
[31] [1949] P. 187, C.A., overruling *Drummond* v. *Parish* (1843) 3 Curt. 522.
[32] At p. 192.
[33] *Re King Spark* [1941] P. 115.
[34] *Re Anderson* [1943] P. 1.
[35] *Re Gibson* [1941] P. 118n.
[36] *Re Jones* [1981] Fam. 7. See also [1982] *Conveyancer* 185.
[37] *Supra*, p. 203.
[38] *Re Colman* [1958] 1 W.L.R. 457; see *Re Limond* [1915] 2 Ch. 240. It is doubtful whether the case of *Re Grey* [1922] P. 140 (in which probate was refused of a will made in a military hospital a year and a half after returning from service) would be so decided since *Andrews* v. *Wingham, supra.*

Cases of difficulty are likely to arise when the armed forces are engaged in paramilitary operations. Each case must be judged on its own facts. When there is a doubt the benefit should be given in favour of the will.[39] The right view is the expansive view.[40]

It is clear from the case of *Andrews* v. *Wingham*[41] and other cases[42] that it is not necessary that the testator should be *inops consilii* at the time he made the will. It is also clear that return to civilian life does not *per se* revoke a privileged will.[43] Provided there is service, provided that it is military, and provided that it is active it is not of consequence whether its purpose is to fight off a foreign enemy or to suppress a rebellious group of subjects.[44]

Wills of sailors

The words "mariner or seaman" in section 11 of the Wills Act 1837 extend to officers of whatever rank.[45] The phrase applies to men and women of the merchant marine as well as of the Royal Navy.[46] An admiral,[47] a naval surgeon,[48] a naval purser[49] and even a female typist aboard a merchant ship[50] have been held to be within the phrase.

Meaning of "at sea"

A wide interpretation has always been given to the words "at sea." The earlier cases were reviewed in *Re Newland*[51] where an infant who made a will at home between voyages while a seaman under direction to serve at sea, whenever and wherever called on, was held to be "at sea." Where, however, an apprentice seaman made his will after discharge from one ship and before instructions to join another, he was not "at sea."[52] In earlier cases a will made ashore during a voyage was held to be made "at sea,"[53] as was a will made aboard ship in the Thames before a voyage[54] and a will made aboard ship in a river by an admiral engaged on naval operations.[55]

---

[39] *Andrews* v. *Wingham* [1949] P. 187, 196.
[40] *Re Jones* [1981] Fam. 7.
[41] *Supra.*
[42] *Re Colman* [1958] 1 W.L.R. 457.
[43] *Re Coleman* [1920] 2 Ir.R. 332; see *Re Booth* [1926] P. 118.
[44] *Re Jones* [1981] Fam. 7. *Re Tweedale* (1874) L.R. 3 P. & D. 204; *Re Booth* [1926] P. 118; *Re Anderson* (1958) 75 W.N.(N.S.W.) 334. See also 126 S.J. 424.
[45] *Euston* v. *Seymour* (1802) cit. 2 Curt. 339 and 340; *Re Saunders* (1865) L.R. 1 P. & D. 16, 18.
[46] *Re Parker* (1859) 2 Sw. & Tr. 375; *Re Newland* [1952] P. 71.
[47] *Euston* v. *Seymour, supra.*
[48] *Re Saunders, supra.*
[49] *Hayes* (1839) 2 Curt. 338, 340.
[50] *Re Hale* [1915] 2 Ir.R. 362.
[51] *Supra*; see also *Wilson* v. *Colclough* [1952] P. 92.
[52] *Re Rapley* [1983] 1 W.L.R. 1069, distinguishing *Re Newland* [1952] P. 71.
[53] *Re Lay* (1840) 2 Curt. 375.
[54] *Re Patterson* (1898) 79 L.T. 123.
[55] *Re Austen* (1853) 2 Rob.Eccl. 611.

But where a sailor made a will in port on joining his ship 15 days before she sailed he was held not to be "at sea."[56]

A will made aboard a gunnery ship permanently stationed in Portsmouth harbour was held to have been made "at sea,"[57] as was a will made by a naval surgeon aboard the ship in which he was being invalided home.[58] But an admiral who lived ashore in the West Indies was held not to be "at sea"[59]; nor was a canal pilot[60] or the captain of a crosschannel ship[61] whose wills were made ashore. But the latter decision is of doubtful correctness.[62]

Naval assets

Wills made by seamen and marines[63] who died before August 14, 1953, were not valid to pass naval assets[64] unless executed in accordance with section 9 of the Wills Act 1837, or under section 11 where this covers the execution.[65] Special formalities were required to be laid down to cover the wills of seamen and marines made while prisoners of war.[66]

But such persons may now make wills in the ordinary way[67] and even wills made before August 14, 1953, but not complying with the formalities mentioned are valid to pass naval assets if the Admiralty so directs.[68]

By the Navy and Marines (Property of Deceased) Order 1956, made under the Navy and Marines (Property of Deceased) Act 1865, the wills of seamen and marines may be deposited with the Inspector of Seamen's Wills.

Merchant seamen

The Board of Trade may refuse to hand over the property of a merchant seaman to those claiming under his will if that will was made aboard ship and did not comply with the formalities prescribed for such wills by section 66 of the Merchant Shipping Act 1970.[69]

Practice

To prove a privileged will an affidavit is required showing that at the date of the will the deceased was a member of the armed forces in actual military service or a sailor at sea, and the full facts supporting these conten-

[56] *Re Corby* (1854) 1 Spinks Ecc. & Adm. 292.
[57] *Re McMurdo* (1868) L.R. 1 P. & D. 540.
[58] *Re Saunders, supra.*
[59] *Euston* v. *Seymour, supra.*
[60] *Re Barnes* (1926) 43 T.L.R. 71.
[61] *Barnard* v. *Birch* [1919] 2 I.R. 404.
[62] In view of *Re Newland* [1952] P. 71. The decision in *Re Thomas* (1918) 34 T.L.R. 626 is likewise to be doubted.
[63] Navy and Marines (Wills) Act 1865, s.2, p. 2.
[64] *Ibid.*, s.5.
[65] *Ibid.*
[66] *Ibid.*, s.6.
[67] See Navy and Marines (Wills) Act 1953, s.1.
[68] Navy and Marines (Wills) Act 1939, s.1.
[69] Merchant Shipping Act 1970, s.65.

tions must be set out. The domicile of the deceased at the time the will was made must be sworn to.[70] Domicile at this date in England or some other country recognising privileged wills is essential to the validity of the will.[71]

Written wills

Affidavit evidence of the deceased's signature or, where the will is not signed, of his handwriting will generally be required[72] but not if the will is signed and witnessed by two witnesses, *i.e.* where the testator is an infant. Where the testator has placed a mark on the will instead of signing it, affidavit evidence is required that he had knowledge of the contents.[73]

Where there are alterations or interlineations on a will, these must be proved to be in the deceased's handwriting or to have been made with his approval. In the absence of evidence to the contrary the presumption is that the alterations were made during the continuance of the privileged period, provided the will was made during such period.[74]

Letters

As much of a letter which contains the provisions of a privileged will is often not of a testamentary nature, district judges or registrars have a discretion as to what part of such letters shall be admitted to probate. The parts to be admitted are set out in a fiat copy in such cases and are signed by the district judge or registrar. The original letter is filed but is not open to public inspection without the leave of a district judge or registrar.[75]

Nuncupative Wills

Application for the admission to probate of a nuncupative will is made *ex parte* to a district judge of the Principal Registry or registrar of a district probate registry.[76] The district judge or registrar may direct that the application be made by summons to a district judge or registrar in chambers or a judge, in chambers or in open court.[77] The application must be supported by an affidavit setting out the grounds of the application together with the available evidence as to the contents of the will.[78] The district judge or registrar may require that notice be given to persons who would be prejudiced by the application.[79]

---

[70] President's Direction, May 7, 1945. As to the Hague Convention on Succession see generally p. 15 *ante*.
[71] Registrar's Direction, November 7, 1955.
[72] See the N.-C.P.R. 1987 r. 18, *post*, p. 1230.
[73] *Re Hackett* (1859) 4 Sw. & Tr. 220 and see the N.-C.P.R., r. 13, *post*. See also *ante*, p. 158, *post*, p. 205.
[74] *Re Tweedale* (1874) L.R. 3 P. & D. 204.
[75] President's Direction, October 20, 1939; see *Re Heywood* [1916] 1 P. 47.
[76] N.-C.P.R. 1987, r. 54(1).
[77] N.-C.P.R. 1987, r. 61.
[78] N.-C.P.R. 1987, r. 54(3).
[79] *Ibid.*, r. 54(4).

Part Two B

THE GRANT

(B) of Administration

CHAPTER 17

CHOICE AND APPOINTMENT OF ADMINISTRATOR

An administrator[1] is a person to whom representation of the deceased is committed by the court in default of an executor.[2] His office resembles that of an executor but, since he has not been selected by the deceased, different provisions as to the vesting of the estate apply.[3]

Administrators are appointed in certain cases where the deceased left a will and in all cases where he died intestate and a grant is applied for. If the deceased left a will, administrators are appointed where the deceased did not appoint executors, where the appointment of executors in a will is void because of uncertainty as to the appointment, where a sole executor has died or renounced, where the application is made by the attorney of an executor, where executors are incapable of performing the office or where executors have failed to take a grant after having been cited to accept or refuse a grant of probate or cited to propound a will.[4] In special circumstances an executor may be passed over by the court[5] and an administrator appointed.

Different rules apply as to the entitlement to administration where the deceased left a will (which is known as administration with the will annexed) and where he died wholly intestate.[6]

Administrators are not entitled to take a grant immediately on the death of the deceased.[7] There is a presumption against intestacy for it has been said that where the testator has executed a will in solemn form you must assume that he did not intend to make it a solemn farce.[8]

Vesting of the estate before a grant of administration

Where the deceased dies wholly intestate, his estate vests in the Probate Judge, *i.e.* the President of the Family Division of the High Court, until a grant of administration is taken out.[9] Where the deceased dies leaving a will but the whole estate is not disposed of, the undisposed estate vests in

---

[1] See *ante*, p. 18.
[2] As to the appointment of executors, see *ante*, p. 27.
[3] See below.
[4] See *post*, p. 388 for these citations.
[5] See *post*, pp. 258, 388 *et seq.*
[6] N.-C.P.R. 1987, rr. 20 and 22, respectively (*post*, p. 1230).
[7] As to the earliest time at which a grant may be taken out, see *post*, p. 277.
[8] *Re Harrison* (1985) 30 Ch.D. 390, 393; and see *Theobald on Wills* (14th ed.) 785.
[9] See the Administration of Estates Act 1925, ss.9 and 55(1)(xv) as amended by the Administration of Justice Act 1970, s.1(6) and Sched. 2, para. 5 (*post*, pp. 1117, 1149). See also p. 461 *post*.

the Probate Judge[10] until a grant of letters of administration with the will annexed has been taken out. There is no provision for the case where the deceased, having disposed of his whole estate appoints no executor or appoints one who has pre-deceased him or is incapable of acting or is unwilling to do so.[11]

Where the estate of the deceased vests in the Probate Judge a notice to quit, served upon him, is effective to determine a tenancy.[12] The method of service is by sending the notice to him, care of the Treasury Solicitor.[13]

It is considered that the Chancery Division in its bankruptcy jurisdiction now has power to make an order for administration of a deceased bankrupt's estate where there is no personal representative.[14]

Who may be appointed administrators

Generally speaking the same persons are capable of being administrators as are capable of being executors,[15] provided that they are entitled to a grant under the Rules. Not only may individuals be appointed administrators, but also a number of public officials such as the Treasury Solicitor and the Solicitors to the Duchies of Lancaster and Cornwall.[16] The Public Trustee is entitled to be an administrator.[17] In this connection it should be noted that an executor or administrator who has taken a grant may, with the sanction of the court, transfer the deceased's estate to the Public Trustee for administration either solely or jointly with the continuing executors or administrators.[18]

A grant of administration may be made to a trust corporation[19] either solely or with an individual, whenever the death occurred.[20] But administration is not granted to the nominee of a trust corporation.[21]

An attorney may act as administrator[22] of any person entitled to apply for a grant under the Rules, including an executor, wherever the person entitled resides.[23]

Persons who may not act as administrators

An infant or person who is mentally incapable of managing his affairs

---

[10] *Ibid.* ss.9 and 55(1)(iv). "Partially intestate" would, it seems, cover intestacy as to real property only or personal property only, see *Whitmore* v. *Lambert* [1955] 1 W.L.R. 495, C.A.

[11] It may be that the estate vests in the Probate judge, see *Harper* v. *Taylor* (1949) 100 L.J. 108.

[12] *Earl of Harrowby* v. *Snelson* [1951] 1 All E.R. 140.

[13] Practice Direction [1985] 1 W.L.R. 310.

[14] See p. 625, n. 6, *post.*

[15] As to who may be an executor, see *ante,* p. 17.

[16] These solicitors take grants on behalf of the Crown or the Duchies in cases where the deceased leaves no kin within the Administration of Estates Act 1925; see *post,* p. 265.

[17] Public Trustee Act 1906, s.6(1). See *ante,* p. 24.

[18] *Ibid.* s.6(2).

[19] As to trust corporations, see *post,* pp. 240 *et seq.*

[20] Supreme Court Act 1981 s.115 (*post* p. 1197).

[21] *Ibid.* subs. (2).

[22] As to grants to attorneys, see *post,* pp. 319 *et seq.*

[23] N.-C.P.R. 1987 r. 31.

may not act as an administrator, but grants of administration may be made for the use and benefit of such persons.[24]

No person guilty of criminally killing the deceased is in practice likely to be given a grant to his estate.[25]

Acceptance or refusal of office

A person entitled to a grant of administration accepts office by applying for and obtaining a grant. Unlike an executor such a person cannot be compelled to take a grant, even if he has intermeddled.[26]

A person entitled to administration may renounce his right.[27] If he neither takes a grant nor renounces, he may be cited to accept or refuse a grant and if he fails to appear to the citation the grant may be made to the citor, if entitled, in his stead.[28]

The court has power in its discretion to pass over the persons primarily entitled to administration and to give the grant to persons having a lower title, and even to persons having no title at all.[29]

Where a dispute arises as to which person among those entitled in the same degree should be granted administration, the court will decide the dispute by summons to a district judge or registrar.[30] The title of any person to be granted administration is decided in an interest action.[31]

Number of administrators

Administration is not granted to more than four persons in respect of the same property.[32] It is unusual for so large a number to obtain a grant.

Where more than one administrator has taken a grant and it is sought to obtain a representative grant to an estate which the deceased was entitled to represent, all co-administrators must apply for such grant unless any of them renounce or consent to the others taking the grant.[33]

Number of administrators where there is a minority or life interest

It is enacted[34] that administration shall, if there is a minority or if a life interest arises under the will or intestacy, be granted either to a trust corporation, with or without an individual, or to not less than two individuals, unless it appears that it is expedient in all the circumstances to appoint an individual. On any application for a grant of administration, with or with-

---

[24] See *post*, p. 323.
[25] See *ante*, p. 22 and *post*, pp. 327, 348.
[26] *Re Davis* (1860) 4 Sw. & Tr. 213; *Re Fell* (1861) 2 Sw. & Tr. 126.
[27] See *post*, p. 378.
[28] See *post*, pp. 388 *et seq.*
[29] See *post*, pp. 343 *et seq.*
[30] N.-C.P.R. 1987, r. 27(5) and see *post*, pp. 1233 *et seq.*
[31] See *post*, p. 406.
[32] Supreme Court Act 1981 s.114(1) (*post*, p. 1196).
[33] *Re Nayler* (1851) 2 Rob. 409; *Hancock* v. *Lightfoot* (1864) 3 Sw. & Tr. 557.
[34] Supreme Court Act 1981 s.114(2), (*post*, p. 1196).

out the will, the oath must state whether any minority or life interest arises.[35] The rule applies whether the grants are limited or unlimited, but there are three clear exceptions[36]: first, in the case of an administrator *pending suit*[37]; second, where the grant is to a consular official under the Consular Conventions Act 1949[38]; third, where the grant is limited to settled land.[39]

Where the deceased dies wholly intestate leaving a spouse and infant children, a life and minority interest only arise if at the date of grant the total estate is more than enough to satisfy the statutory entitlements of that spouse.[40] If in the course of administration this limit is exceeded the proper course is to apply for appointment of a second administrator.[41]

Single administrator where there is a minority or life interest

The court has power to make a grant of administration to an individual (not being a trust corporation) as sole administrator in the case of a minority or life interest if "it appears to the court to be expedient in all the circumstances."[42] No provision is made by the rules for such an application, but it should be made to the district judge or registrar supported by an affidavit setting out the reason for the application, or, alternatively, the reason may be included in the oath to lead the grant.[43] It has been suggested[44] that the types of cases in which the application will be allowed will include cases where the proposed administrator is a solicitor or accountant; where the proposed administrator is a surviving spouse and the spouse's entitlement narrowly fails to exceed the value of the estate; where the minor in question will shortly attain his majority; and where the proposed administrator is a representative of a local authority.

Selection of administrators where there is a minority or life interest

The two administrators should, where practicable, be equally entitled to a grant. But it often happens that there is only one of the class entitled in priority. In such case the person entitled in priority may obtain a grant with a person next in priority, *e.g.* a residuary legatee with a specific legatee or a spouse with a child.

Where the second administrator is in the next class to the first, the latter

---

[35] N.-C.P.R. 1987 r. 8(4) (*post*, p. 1227).
[36] For a further possible exception in the case of discretionary grants, see article in 212 L.T. at p. 224.
[37] *Re Haslip* [1958] 1 W.L.R. 583; and see *post*, p. 333.
[38] See *po st*, p. 322.
[39] See *post*, p. 272.
[40] See *post*, pp. 258 *et seq.* for these entitlements.
[41] This seems the necessary intendment of the section but there is no authority. See *post*, p. 260.
[42] Supreme Court Act 1981, s.114(2).
[43] *Registrar's Direction*, March 16, 1982.
[44] *Tristram and Coote's Probate Practice*, (27th ed.), p. 262.

being the sole member of his class, the grant to the two of them is made without an order. Similarly, no order is required where the person next entitled after the first administrator has renounced and it is desired to join the person next entitled after the renunciant[45]; or where the proposed second administrator is a trust corporation.[46] With this last exception an application to join a person who has no right or no immediate right to a grant with the person entitled must be made to a district judge or registrar *ex parte*, supported by an affidavit by the person entitled, the consent of the person proposed to be joined and such other evidence as the registrar may direct.[47]

Where the grant must be made to two persons it is immaterial that the applicants represent the interest of a single individual, *e.g.* as guardians, attornies, etc.[48]

Nomination of a co-administrator

If there is only one person competent and willing to take a grant on behalf of an infant, administration may, unless a district judge or registrar otherwise directs, be granted to such person jointly with any fit and proper person nominated by him.[49] A common case under this rule is the nomination of a co-administrator by a surviving spouse. It should be noted, however, that in this case, although a child *en ventre sa mère* may be entitled to share in the estate, the mother does not have parental responsibility[50] until after the child's birth and may not nominate a co-administrator.

Where there is no spouse, but several children of whom only one is not under age, an application should be made to the district judge or registrar to appoint a person to join with the child of full age in taking the grant. Application to be appointed is made *ex parte* on application to a district judge or registrar.[51]

Attorney as second administrator

A limited grant of administration, with or without the will may be made to the person first entitled and the attorney of the person equally entitled or next entitled. Although no order is required for such grant, the consent of the person first entitled must be given in writing and must be lodged. But if the first person entitled does not consent to taking a grant with the attorney of the person equally entitled or next entitled, application must be made on summons for the joinder of the attorney in the grant.[52] If such an

---

[45] N.-C.P.R. 1987, r. 25(1) (*post*, p. 1232).
[46] *Ibid.* r. 25(3)(b).
[47] N.-C.P.R. 1987, r. 25(2) (*post*, p. 1232).
[48] *President's Direction*, November 1925.
[49] N.-C.P.R. 1987, r. 32(3) (*post*, p. 1236).
[50] Children Act 1989, s. 2.
[51] N.-C.P.R. 1987, r. 32(2).
[52] *President's Direction*, February 22, 1949.

order is made the donor has no right to displace the attorney and apply for a grant himself. Consequently the consent of the donor of the power is required, unless the attorney was appointed expressly to be joined with the person first entitled.

Where a surviving spouse is the donor of the power and the attorney applies with a person having a vested interest in the estate, the grant is limited for the use and benefit of that spouse until further representation be granted, thereby preserving the priority of the spouse.

Representation of several branches of a family

Where several branches of a family are under age and equally entitled to a grant, the applicants for a grant should, when practicable, represent the various branches of the family. If a member of one branch is of age and entitled to a grant, it is desirable that the other grantee should represent one of the other branches.[53]

Preference for living interest and for persons sui juris

Unless a registrar otherwise directs, administration is granted to a living person entitled thereto in preference to the personal representative of a deceased person and to a person of full age entitled thereto in preference to a guardian of a minor.[54]

Second administrator where the whole estate vests in one person

A person solely entitled to a grant sometimes wishes to have a co-administrator. In such case any kin of the deceased in order of priority applicable on intestacy[55] may be joined without any order as a person entitled to share in the event of an accretion in the value of the estate. But if it is desired to join some other person application is made *ex parte* on affidavit with the consent of the proposed co-administrator.[56]

Foreign domicile

In cases of foreign domicile, whether there is a minority or life interest depends on the law of that country, and the statement in the oath as to such interests is, therefore, based on that law.[57] But as already stated[58] English procedural law applies so that even if the law of the domicile allows a grant, where there is a minority or life interest, to be made to one individual, the grant in England must be made on the principles obtaining here.

---

[53] Registrar's Circular, May 14, 1926.
[54] N.-C.P.R. 1987, r. 27(5) (*post*, p. 1233).
[55] See N.-C.P.R. 1987, r. 22 (*post*, p. 1231).
[56] See N.-C.P.R. 1987, r. 25 (*post*, p. 1232).
[57] Registrar's Direction, May 5, 1953. As to the Hague Convention on Succession see generally p. 16 *ante*.
[58] See *post*, p. 297.

Addition of a personal representative after a grant has issued

It is enacted[59] that if there is only one personal representative (not being a trust corporation[60]) then, during the minority of a beneficiary or the subsistence of a life interest, and until the estate is fully administered, the court may, on the application of any person interested or of the guardian, committee or receiver of any such person, appoint one or more personal representatives in addition to the original representative.

The additional personal representative (who is known by this title) may be added not merely where there is an administrator but where there is a sole or sole surviving executor.[61]

Practice

Applications to add a personal representative are made *ex parte* to a district judge or registrar[62] and are supported by an affidavit.[63] The consent in writing of the person to be added is required.[64] The affidavit gives details of the grant, the reason for the addition of another grantee and shows that a minority or life interest still exists or has lately arisen, where such is the case.

On such application the district judge or registrar may direct that the original grant be noted with the addition of a further representative, or he may impound or revoke the grant or make such further order as the case may require.[65]

Administrators' powers to appoint new trustees

Administrators who have cleared the estate and completed administration are trustees for the beneficiaries under any will, for those interested on intestacy, and for those others in whose favour an order has been made under the Inheritance (Provision for Family and Dependants) Act 1975.[66]

Where there is a minority or life interest their duties as administrators and trustees may continue for a long period. In a number of cases administrators do not wish to act as trustees and, they appoint new trustees,[67] but in default of doing so they are trustees in the full sense.[68]

---

[59] Supreme Court Act 1981 s.114(4) (*post*, p. 1196).
[60] See *post*, p. 240.
[61] *Registrar's Direction*, December 31, 1971. As to the meaning of the expression "personal representative," see *ante*, p. 18 and *post*, p. 1049.
[62] N.-C.P.R. 1987 r. 26.
[63] N.-C.P.R. 1987 r. 26(1) (*post*, p. 1233).
[64] *Ibid.*
[65] *Ibid.* sub-r. (2).
[66] See *post*, p. 757.
[67] Trustee Act 1925, s.36.
[68] *Re Cockburn* [1957] Ch. 438. See further on this topic, *post*, p. 1049.

Trust corporations

As has been seen,[69] the need for a second administrator does not arise where administration is in the hands of a trust corporation.

Various statutes and statutory instruments lay down the persons and bodies which are trust corporations:

1. The Public Trustee.[70]
2. The Treasury Solicitor, the Solicitor for the affairs of the Duchy of Lancaster and the Official Solicitor.[71]
3. Any person holding any official position prescribed by the Lord Chancellor.[72]
4. In relation to bankruptcy and to property subject to a deed of arrangement, the trustee in bankruptcy and the trustee under the deed respectively.[73]
5. In relation to charitable, ecclesiastical and public trusts, any local or public authority prescribed by the Lord Chancellor and any corporation constituted under the laws of the United Kingdom or any part thereof which satisfies him that it undertakes the administration of such trusts without remuneration or is obliged to apply all its net income for charitable, ecclesiastical or public purposes and is authorised by him to act as a trust corporation.[74]
6. The Church of England Pensions Board.[75]
7. A corporation appointed by the court in a particular case to be trustee.[76]
8. A custodian trustee.[77]
9. The Administrators of German and Japanese Enemy Property in relation to such property.[78]

Custodian trustees

Besides the custodian trustees who are included in the list given above, companies in the United Kingdom[79] incorporated by Special Act or by Royal Charter, certain companies in the United Kingdom or in another Member State of the European Economic Community[80] with an issued capital of not less than £250,000 (of which not less than £100,000 must have

---

[69] See *ante*, pp. 235 and 239.
[70] Supreme Court Act 1981, s.128.
[71] Law of Property (Amendment) Act 1926, s.3.
[72] *Ibid.* Although no such persons have ever been prescribed or rules made under this head the provision is not regarded as obsolete.
[73] *Ibid.*
[74] *Ibid.*
[75] Church of England Pensions Board (Powers) Measure 1952, s.6.
[76] Supreme Court Act 1981, s.128.
[77] *Ibid.*
[78] *Registrar's Directions*, April 18, 1951, January 31, 1952, and April 14, 1953.
[79] See Public Trustee Rules 1926, r. 30, as amended. Public Trustee Act 1906, s.4.
[80] The decision in *Re Barlow* [1933] P. 184 that the Bank of Ireland is not entitled to a grant of probate in England is no longer good law. *Re Bigger* [1977] Fam. 203.

been paid up) or, its equivalent in the relevant currency, are the most important class of custodian trustees. The Public Trustee Rules 1912, rule 30 contains the complete list of such custodian trustees.

Grants to trust corporations

A trust corporation may obtain probate when named as executor, and it may act as administrator.[81] In both cases it may act alone or jointly with another person.[82] No grant may be made to a syndic or nominee on behalf of a trust corporation.[83]

A trust corporation may be empowered by the court to charge for its services as a personal representative.[84] The public trustee has statutory power to charge.

Any officer authorised for the purpose by a trust corporation or the directors or governing body thereof may, on behalf of the corporation, swear affidavits, give security and do any other act or thing which the court may require with a view to the corporation obtaining a grant, and the acts of such officer bind the corporation.[85] Where the trust corporation in the holder of an official position, any officer whose name is included on a list filed with the Senior District Judge of persons authorised to make affidavits and sign documents on behalf of the office holder may act as the officer through whom the trust corporation applies for the grant.[86] Otherwise, a certified copy of the resolution authorising the officer to make the application must be lodged, or alternatively the oath must state that such certified copy has been lodged, the office in question is identified then by the position he holds and that such resolution is still in force.[87]

The officer must depose in the oath that the corporation is a trust corporation as defined by Rule 2(1) of the Non-Contentious Probate Rules 1987 and has power to accept the grant[88] and must show how it is entitled to the grant sought. If the corporation applies as attorney, it may do so even where it represents one individual only and there is a minority or life interest.

Where a trust corporation applies for a grant of administration (with or without the will) other than as a beneficiary or the attorney of some person

[81] Supreme Court Act 1981, s.115(1) (*post*, p. 1197). As to the dispensation from explaining a change of name necessitated by the Companies Acts or evidence about this, see *Practice Direction* [1982] 1 W.L.R. 214. Where the will contains conditions which might limit the corporation's power to take a full grant the oath should state whether or not these still apply. *Practice Direction* [1981] 2 All E.R. 1104.
[82] *Ibid.*
[83] *Ibid.* subs. (2).
[84] By virtue of Trustee Act 1925, s.42. The power may be invoked where the beneficiaries are infants, see *Re Masters* [1953] 1 W.L.R. 81. The trust corporation must be empowered by its constitution to charge. See also *Re Campbell* [1954] 1 W.L.R. 516 (Bank executor under a codicil).
[85] Supreme Court Act 1981 s.115(3).
[86] N.-C.P.R. 1987, r. 36(2)(a).
[87] *Ibid.*, r. 36(2)(b).
[88] N.-C.P.R. 1987, r. 36(1).

the consents of all persons entitled to a grant and of all persons interested in the residuary estate must be lodged unless the district judge or registrar dispenses with them on such terms as he thinks fit.[89]

The consents of persons who, in the case of intestacy, would be entitled to share in the estate in the event of an accretion need not be lodged, but only that of the surviving spouse. Where consents which are required have not been obtained, the persons concerned must be shown to have renounced or to have been cited.

Grants where minors are beneficially entitled

Where persons of full age and minors are beneficially entitled under a will or an intestacy, the former, in addition to consenting to a grant to the trust corporation, renounce their right to a grant. This enables a grant to be made to the trust corporation limited until the minors apply for a grant or until further representation be granted, thus preserving their rights.[90] A district judge or registrar may dispense with renunciation in such a case. The person(s) with parental responsibility[91] for a minor may consent to a trust corporation applying for a grant for the use and benefit of that minor.

Where there is no person with parental responsibility for a minor a trust corporation may apply to be appointed to take administration as if an individual. The grant will be limited until one of the minors applies for a grant on attaining full age or until further representation.

Where all the executors named in the will are under age, a grant may be made to a trust corporation on the consent of the persons entitled to the residuary estate; but if the latter are minors consents on their behalf may be accepted (as above). Where all the persons entitled are under age the grant is made to the corporation in its own right and not for the use and benefit of the minors.[92]

Grants to the Public Trustee

The Public Trustee is authorised to accept in his official name grants of probate and administration.[93] In the case of administration, with or without the will, the Public Trustee is, in general, considered as equally entitled to a grant with any class; but the consent or citation of the Public Trustee is not required for a grant to some other person and the spouse or next-of-kin of the deceased are preferred unless good cause is shown to the contrary.[94] As executor the Public Trustee continues the chain of executorship.[95]

On application for administration with the will, the Public Trustee must

---

[89] *Ibid.* sub-r. (3).
[90] *President's Direction*, June 19, 1947.
[91] Children Act 1989, s.2.
[92] *Registrar's Direction*, February 25, 1952.
[93] Public Trustee Act 1906, s.6(1). See generally *ante*, pp. 24 *et seq.*
[94] *Ibid.* see *Re Woolley* (1911) 55 S.J. 220. N.-C.P.R. 1987 r. 36.
[95] President's Instructions, March 27, 1908.

clear off the executors in the usual way. He notifies the persons entitled to administration with the will, that unless they apply for a grant or enter a caveat within eight days, he will apply for a grant. The time mentioned above is increased where the addressee is abroad to allow time for an answer by post.[96]

In applications for administration, without the will, similar notice is given to those entitled to a grant.

Administration of estates of under £1,000

Any person who in the opinion of the Public Trustee would be entitled to apply to the court for administration by the court of a solvent estate of which the Public Trustee is satisfied that the gross capital is under £1,000, may apply to him to administer the estate. The Public Trustee will then administer it, if satisfied that all the beneficiaries are of small means, unless he sees good reason for refusing to do so.[97] The undertaking of the Public Trustee to administer is filed at the Principal Registry and any existing grant is noted with the fact. No duplicate of a grant thus noted may be issued without the direction of a district judge or registrar.[98] As a result of inflation this section has fallen into disuse.

Various grants to the Public Trustee

The Public Trustee may take a limited grant, *e.g.* as attorney.[99] He may take a grant in the case of persons dying domiciled abroad.[1] Where the Public Trustee has been appointed an executor, a grant will not be made to a co-executor until it has been ascertained whether the former wishes to act.[2]

Grants to the Treasury Solicitor

The Treasury Solicitor and the Solicitor for the Duchy of Lancaster do not swear an oath to lead the grant,[3] but they file a signed statement. They deliver an Inland Revenue Account in the normal way except (i) where the gross value of the estate is below the level at which tax is payable when a statement giving the name, address and date of death of the deceased is completed and inserted inside the account and (ii) where the domicile of the deceased is outside Great Britain when the normal requirement to send accounts to the Capital Taxes Office does not apply.[4]

---

[96] *Ibid.*
[97] Public Trustee Act 1906, s.3(1), see *ante*, p. 24.
[98] *Registrar's Direction*, March 3, 1920.
[99] See *Registrar's Direction*, March 24, 1936.
[1] See *ante*.
[2] *Registrar's Direction*, November 18, 1920.
[3] Administration of Estates Act 1925, s.30(3) (*post*, p. 1126).
[4] Secretary's Circular, November 15, 1972.

Grants to administrators of enemy property

As already mentioned[5] the Administrators of German and of Japanese Enemy Property are trust corporations. They are respectively to be treated as equally entitled to a grant with any person or class.[6]

---

[5] See *ante*, p. 240.

[6] See *Registrar's Directions*, April 18, 1951, and January 31, 1952. The administrator's oath shows that all or part of the estate is German or Japanese enemy property. Where there is a will the executor must be cleared off before a grant is made to the administrator. The oath contains a brief account of the facts on which the administrator relies. Translations of wills and other documents certified by the Board of Trade will be accepted. (Secretary's Circular, February 13, 1952.) No sureties were required. The administrators only act in respect of the estates of persons who died before October 6, 1952, but this situation could still arise.

CHAPTER 18

ADMINISTRATION WITH THE WILL ANNEXED

Administration with the will annexed (*cum testamento annexo*) is the grant made where a will is proved by any person other than an executor.[1] The present chapter covers only grants where the deceased died domiciled in England[2] after 1925.[3] The circumstances in which such a grant is made are:

(1) Where no executor has been appointed.
(2) Where the executor appointed has died in the lifetime of the testator, or after his death without taking probate.
(3) Where the executor has renounced probate, or, having been cited to accept or refuse a grant of probate, has not appeared to the citation.
(4) Where the appointment of an executor is void for uncertainty.
(5) Where the court under its discretionary powers passes over the executor and makes a grant to some other person.
(6) Where the executor is incompetent to take probate by reason of his minority or mental or physical incapacity.[4]
(7) Where an executor applies for a grant to be made to his attorney.
(8) Where a corporation, association or charitable body which is not a trust corporation (and so is incapable of taking a grant of probate) is appointed sole executor, when a grant is made to its nominee or attorney.

Order of priority of right to a grant where the deceased has left a will

This order of priority is laid down by rule 20 of the Non-Contentious Probate Rules 1987 (as amended) and is as follows:

(a) The executor (unless a non-trust corporation[5]);
(b) Any residuary legatee or devisee holding in trust for any other person;
(c) Any residuary legatee or devisee (including one for life), or where the residue is not wholly disposed of by the will, any person entitled to share in the undisposed of residue (including the

---

[1] Supreme Court Act 1981, s.119 (*post*, p. 1198).
[2] For administration where the deceased died domiciled abroad, see *post*, p. 299. The effect of such a grant may be to prove the title from which a foreign executor derives his authority. See *ante*, p. 83.
[3] As to grants where the death occurred before 1926, see *Mortimer on Probate*, 2nd ed., p. 347.
[4] See *Re D. and B.* (1979) 10 Fam.Law 55.
[5] See *post*, p. 250.

Treasury Solicitor when claiming *bona vacantia* on behalf of the Crown), provided that—

   (i) unless a district judge or registrar otherwise directs, a residuary legatee or devisee whose legacy or devise is vested in interest shall be preferred to one entitled on the happening of a contingency, and

  (ii) where the residue is not in terms wholly disposed of, the registrar may, if he is satisfied that the testator has nevertheless disposed of the whole or substantially the whole of the known estate, allow a grant to be made to any legatee or devisee entitled to, or to share in, the estate so disposed of, without regard to the persons entitled to share in any residue not disposed of by the will;

  (d) the personal representative of any residuary legatee or devisee (but not one for life, or one holding in trust for any other person), or of any person entitled to share in any residue not disposed of by the will;

  (e) any other legatee or devisee (including one for life or one holding in trust for any other person) or any creditor of the deceased, provided that, unless a registrar otherwise directs, a legatee or devisee whose legacy or devise is vested in interest shall be preferred to one entitled on the happening of a contingency;

  (f) the personal representative of any other legatee or devisee (but not one for life or one holding in trust for any other person) or of any creditor of the deceased.

Each of these classes is further considered below.

Interest in the residue

In many cases a right to a grant under this rule depends on the applicant having an interest in the residue of the estate. A great variety of words and phrases have been held to constitute a gift of residue and many others have been held insufficient. It is not within the scope of this book to discuss such questions of construction, and works on wills should be consulted.[6]

Section 33 of the Wills Act 1837[7] often requires consideration in deciding who is entitled to the residue. In the case of deaths occurring on or after January 1, 1983, the section provides that where:

  (a) a will contains a devise or bequest to a child or remoter descendant of the testator; and

---

[6] See *Theobald on Wills*, 14th ed., p. 770.

[7] As now amended, in the case of deaths occurring on or after January 1, 1983 by the Administration of Justice Act 1982. For the position relating to deaths before this date, see the previous edition of this work, p. 222. One of the effects of the amendment is to reverse the effect of such decisions as *Re Hurd* [1941] Ch. 196 and *Re Basioli* [1953] Ch. 367 so as to create a truly substitutional gift in favour of the issue in question.

(b) the intended beneficiary dies before the testator, leaving issue; and

(c) issue of the intended beneficiary are living at the testator's death,

then, unless a contrary intention appears by the will, the devise or bequest shall take effect as a devise or bequest to the issue living at the testator's death.

The section applies to class gifts and to children *en ventre*.[8] The illegitimacy of any person is to be disregarded.[9]

Forfeiture of benefit

Beneficiaries under wills may lose their benefit thereunder and so not be entitled to a grant. Under section 15 of the Wills Act 1837 if beneficiaries or their spouses witness a will the former cannot in general benefit from the will.[10] Any person who has criminally killed a testator loses all benefit from his estate and cannot take a grant to it.[11] In such circumstances the grant is made to another under the discretionary powers of the court.[12]

Class (a) The Executor[13]

Grants for the use and benefit of executors who are infants,[14] or incapable of managing their affairs.[15]

Clearing off executors and others entitled in priority to the applicant

Every application for administration with the will annexed must show why an executor is not applying. This procedure is termed "clearing off" and applies not only to executors but to all cases where an applicant for a grant is not *prima facie* entitled.[16] The court will not grant administration, with the will, to a residuary legatee on the mere consent of the executor[17] and the same principle applies in other cases. There must either be a renunciation by the surviving persons with a prior right or they must have been cited to accept or refuse a grant and have not entered an appearance.[18]

The court has power to pass over the persons primarily entitled to a

[8] See s.33(3) and (4)(*b*) and *Theobald on Wills* (14th ed.), Supplement pp. 770–774.
[9] See s.(4)(*a*).
[10] See *ante*, p. 145. Even if the attesting witness cannot take a grant as beneficiary, he may do so as, *e.g.* a person interested in the undisposed-of estate. N.-C.P.R. 1987, r. 21. A superfluous witness is no longer disentitled (Wills Act 1968, s.1). See *ante*, p. 145.
[11] Subject to the provisions of the Forfeiture Act 1982.
[12] See *post*, pp. 348, 1074.
[13] As to priorities see N.-C.P.R. 1987, r. 20.
[14] See *post*, p. 323.
[15] See *post*, p. 325.
[16] The oath must show in what way persons entitled in priority have been cleared off, N.-C.P.R. 1987, r. 8(4) (*post*, p. 1227).
[17] See *Garrard* v. *Garrard* (1871) L.R. 2 P. & D. 100.
[18] For citations, see *post*, pp. 388 *et seq.*

grant and to grant administration to persons entitled in a lower degree or even to persons having no right.[19]

Class (b) Any residuary legatee or devisee holding in trust

On clearing off executors, administration with the will may be granted to any legatee or devisee in trust. If any of these persons have power under the will to nominate a trustee in their stead, a grant will be to the substituted trustee on the renunciation of the trustee named in the will being produced, together with the nomination of the substitute. Where the Chancery Division has appointed a trustee in substitution for the surviving trustees named in the will, the grant may be made to the appointees.[20] The order of the Chancery Division should be lodged with the application for a grant.

Class (c) Any other residuary legatee or devisee or a person entitled to share in undisposed of estate, etc.

On the clearing off of executors and the residuary legatees or devisees in trust, a grant is made to the residuary legatees or devisees (including those for life) or those entitled to share in the undisposed of estate. All have an equal right to the grant. A residuary legatee or devisee whose interest is vested is to be preferred to one whose interest is contingent.[21]

Where there is a life interest, two administrators or a trust corporation alone or with an individual must be appointed.[22] If there is only one residuary legatee or devisee for life a grant must be made to him and an ultimate legatee or devisee. If there are two legatees or devisees for life, a joint grant is made to them in preference to a residuary legatee or devisee substituted.[23]

Where a person is given and exercises a power to appoint the ultimate residuary legatees and devisees, the latter have the same right to a grant as if they had been directly named.[24] If the residue of the personalty is given to two persons in common and the share of one has lapsed, the grant may be made to the surviving residuary legatee or the person entitled on intestacy. Conversely, if joint tenants have survived the testator and died, there is no lapse and the grant is made to the personal representative of the last to die.

Where a dispute arose as to who was the residuary legatee, the court granted administration to a specific legatee, leaving it to the court of construction to decide who was the residuary legatee.[25]

---

[19] See *post*, pp. 343 *et seq.*
[20] *Cresswell* v. *Cresswell* (1824) 2 Add. 342; *Woodfall* v. *Arbuthnot* (1873) L.R. 3 P. & D. 108.
[21] N.-C.P.R., 1987, r. 20(c)(i).
[22] See *ante*, p. 235.
[23] *Brown* v. *Nicholls* (1851) 2 Rob. 399, 402.
[24] *In the Goods of Martindale* (1858) 1 Sw. & Tr. 9.
[25] *Brown* v. *Nicholls* (1851) 2 Rob. 399.

Persons entitled to the undisposed estate

The expression "residue not wholly disposed of by the will"[26] includes cases where there is no disposition of residue, an incomplete disposition thereof or the lapse of a share of residue.

The principles which govern entitlement to an estate on intestacy are considered later.[27] Where a spouse entitled to the whole estate has died after the testator, a grant may be made to his personal representative. Grants may also be made to the personal representatives of persons in other classes entitled, subject, however, to the preference for other persons in the class who are living.

It may happen that the ultimate disposition of the estate is not ascertainable. If this is because there are persons who are only entitled on the happening of a contingency, e.g. where the residue is left to such persons of a class as shall attain the age of 21, then such persons are entitled to apply for a grant in the same class of priority as those persons having a vested interest.[28] In all other cases the matter should be put before the district judge or registrar for his directions.

Where there has been disposition of the whole or substantially the whole estate

Where the whole estate is not in terms disposed of but the whole or substantially the whole of it as ascertained at the time of the application has been disposed of, a grant may be made to any legatee or devisee without regard to the persons entitled to share in the undisposed of residue.[29]

This provision does not affect the right of a person entitled to the undisposed of residue to apply for a grant. It is useful to enable those with a substantial interest in the estate to administer it where those entitled to only a small interest are not known or are not easily traceable. In clear cases such applications are granted as of course. Where it appears doubtful whether the dispositions amount to virtually the whole of the estate or there are other difficulties the direction of a district judge or registrar is taken.

Unless it is clear that there are kin entitled to share in the undisposed of residue, notice must be given to the Treasury Solicitor of the application and the district judge or registrar may then direct that no grant shall issue for 28 days.[30]

Class (d) The personal representative of any residuary legatee or devisee, etc

On clearing off of all prior classes, a grant may be made to the personal

---

[26] N.-C.P.R. 1987, r. 20(c) (post, p. 1230).

[27] See post, pp. 253 et seq.

[28] N.-C.P.R. 1987, r. 20, although a residuary beneficiary whose interest has vested is normally to be preferred to one whose interest is contingent: N.-C.P.R. 1987, r. 20.

[29] N.-C.P.R. 1987, r. 20.

[30] Ibid. r. 38 (post, p. 1238).

representative of any residuary legatee or devisee (but not one for life, or one holding in trust for any other person) or of any person entitled to share in any residue not disposed of by the will.[31] All have an equal right to the grant.

Class (e) Specific legatee, devisee or creditor

On clearing off all prior classes, a grant may be made to any other legatee or devisee (including one for life or one holding in trust for any other person) or any creditor of the deceased.[32] Again, a legatee or devisee whose interest is vested is to be preferred to one whose interest is merely contingent.[33]

Class (f) Personal representative of specific legatee, devisee or creditor

Finally, when all other classes have been cleared off, a grant may be made to the personal representative of any other legatee or devisee, or any creditor of the deceased.[34] A grant may not be made to the personal representative of such a legatee or devisee who is one for life or holding in trust for any other person.[35] Where the estate is not wholly disposed of, the persons in this class must not only clear off the persons entitled in priority but also those entitled to be constituted the personal representatives of any persons who, having acquired an interest in the disposed of residue or any undisposed of part thereof, have died but no grant to their estate has been taken out. Where the whole of the undisposed estate has vested in a spouse who has since died, a person who may have a child of the deceased who is also a child of the spouse should constitute himself the personal representative of the surviving spouse, take a leading grant in that estate and then apply for a grant in the estate of the first spouse to die.

In all applications by persons in this class where the deceased died without kin or without known kin, the Crown must be specifically cleared off by renunciation or citation.[36]

Grants to persons not in the specified classes

1. *Grant to a trust corporation*

On the renunciation of the executors and with the consent of all those entitled to a grant and interested in the residuary estate, administration (with the will) may be granted to a trust corporation, including the Public

---

[31] *Ibid.* r. 20(*d*).
[32] *Ibid.* r. 20(*e*).
[33] *Ibid.*
[34] *Ibid.* r. 20(*f*).
[35] *Ibid.*
[36] *Ibid.* r. 38 and Ing on *Bona Vacantia*, pp. 72 *et seq.*

Trustee.[37] The district judge or registrar has power, in his discretion, to dispense with the consents of any persons entitled.

2. *Grant to the nominee or attorney of a non-trust corporation*

Although administration, with or without the will, may not be granted to a nominee on behalf of a trust corporation[38] the rule does not apply to a non-trust corporation. Where such a corporation, if it were an individual, would be entitled to a grant, administration for its use and benefit is granted to its nominee or attorney, limited until further representation be granted.[39] If there is a minority or life interest the grant is made to two nominees or attorneys.

Practice. The nominee or attorney must swear in the oath that the corporation is not a trust corporation.[40] A sealed or otherwise authenticated copy of the resolution or instrument by which the corporation appoints such persons must be lodged.[41] Where the corporation is entitled as executor it must be established that it has power to take a grant through its nominee, by producing a copy of its constitution.[42] Where the corporation is appointed jointly with an individual, the right of that individual must first be cleared off. Alternatively, administration may be granted to their attorney for their use and benefit until further representation.[43]

3. *Grant to an assignee*

Where all the persons entitled to the estate have assigned their whole interest therein to one or more persons, the assignees replace in the order of priority for a grant the assignor or the assignor with the highest priority.[44] Where there are two or more assignees, administration, with the will, may be granted with the consent of the others to any one or more of them not exceeding four.[45] The assignee must produce the original instrument of assignment and lodge a copy.[46] Where a consent is necessary, it must be lodged.

4. *Grant to a trustee in bankruptcy or under a deed of arrangement*

A trustee in bankruptcy has no title to a grant under the rules but he may apply for a grant under the discretionary powers of the court.

---

[37] See *ante*, p. 242.
[38] See Supreme Court Act 1981, s.115(2) (*post*, p. 1197).
[39] N.-C.P.R. 1987, r.36(4)(*a*) (*post*, p. 1237). See also *ante*, p. 19.
[40] *Ibid*. r. 36(4).
[41] *Ibid*. r. 36(4)(*b*).
[42] Registrar's Direction [1956] 1 W.L.R. 127.
[43] N.-C.P.R., 1987, r. 36(4)(*d*).
[44] *Ibid*. r. 24(1) (*post*, p. 1232).
[45] *Ibid*. sub-r. (2).
[46] *Ibid*. sub-r. (3).

A trustee under a deed of arrangement has no title to a grant. In some cases, provided the terms of the deed of arrangement permit it, he may be able to establish a title as the assignee of the only person entitled to the estate. Failing this he may apply for a grant under the discretionary powers of the court. The grant describes him as trustee under the deed and is limited to the period during which he remains trustee.[47]

5. *Limited grant (with the will)*

Besides the cases of limited administrations (with the will) mentioned above, limited grants are made in a number of circumstances. These grants are considered later.[48] Grants *de bonis non* and cessate grants may also be made with the will annexed.[49]

Practice in obtaining grants of administration (with the will)

In general the practice in obtaining a grant of administration (with the will) is the same as in obtaining a grant of probate,[50] but certain special points must be noted. The oath must clear off all persons with a prior right to a grant[51] and show the capacity in which the applicant is entitled. It must show what the position is as to executors, *e.g.* that none were appointed or that they predeceased the testator or have renounced. It must state whether there is a minority or life interest.

An administrator (with the will) will not now be required to provide a guarantee.[52] Fees are payable as on a grant of probate.

---

[47] Registrar's Direction, July 24, 1956.
[48] See *post*, pp. 316 *et seq.*
[49] See *post*, pp. 337 and 340 respectively, for these grants.
[50] See *post*, pp. 306 *et seq.*
[51] N.-C.P.R 1987, r. 8(4) (*post*, p. 1227).
[52] But see p. 291, *post*, as to the residual power.

CHAPTER 19

ADMINISTRATION ON TOTAL INTESTACY

The right to a grant of administration on intestacy depends in general on the beneficial interests on distribution on intestacy so that much of the material following is relevant also to Chapter 79.[1] The present chapter concerns the obtaining of letters of administration where the deceased died, domiciled in England and Wales,[2] after 1925[3] and wholly intestate.[4] Grants of letters of administration are made in the following circumstances:

(1) Where the deceased died without executing a will.
(2) Where the only testamentary instrument revokes all previous testamentary dispositions and makes no disposition.[5]
(3) Where the will of the deceased appointed no executor and disposed only of property abroad, though he left property in England.
(4) Where, although a possibly valid will exists, the executors and persons entitled thereunder have been cited to propound it but have not appeared to the citation, or, have not proceeded to propound the will with reasonable diligence. In this case administration is granted as on intestacy, for the will is treated for this purpose as if it were invalid.[6]

It is necessary after noting the general considerations affecting such grants to consider the rights of the surviving spouse,[7] of children and issue,[8] of other relatives,[9] of the Crown[10] and of creditors.[11]

---

[1] *Post*, p. 1065.
[2] As to grants of administration where the deceased died domiciled abroad, see *post*, p. 299.
[3] As to grants in the case of deaths before 1926, see *Williams on Executors*, 12th ed. In the rare case where a person was of unsound mind and of age before 1926 a grant to his estate is made on the same principles as if he had died before 1925; see the Administration of Estates Act 1925, s.56, Sched. 1, Pt. 2. As to distribution on intestacy before and after 1925, see *post*, pp. 1065 *et seq.*
[4] For grants on partial intestacy, see *ante*, p. 250.
[5] For the presumption against intestacy see p. 216, *ante*.
[6] See N.-C.P.R. 1987, r. 48(2), (*post*, p. 1244).
[7] *Post*, p. 258.
[8] *Post*, p. 261.
[9] *Post*, p. 263.
[10] *Post*, p. 265.
[11] *Post*, p. 266.

A. General Considerations Affecting Grants and Distribution on Intestacy

Divorce

A person who has been divorced has no title to a grant to his former spouse's estate.[12-13]

Where the intestate died in the early hours of the day on which a decree was made absolute it was held that no doctrine of relation back applied and the "wife" was entitled on intestacy.[14]

Spouses who are commorientes

Where spouses die in circumstances which make it uncertain which survived the other and the deaths occurred before 1953, the elder is presumed to have predeceased the younger.[15] In the case of deaths both intestate occurring since 1952 each estate devolves as if the husband or wife had not survived the other.[16]

Effect of a decree of judicial separation or a separation order

Where a decree of judicial separation or a separation order in the magistrates' court was in force at the death of a wife intestate before August 1, 1970, then whether the husband or the wife obtained the order or decree, any property acquired by the wife or which devolved on her since the date of the decree or order devolved as if her husband had predeceased her.[17] Where the decree or order was obtained by the wife the rule applied also to property to which she was entitled in remainder or reversion at the date of the decree or order.[18] Such decree or order did not affect the devolution of the estate of an intestate husband.[19] Where the death occurs on or after August 1, 1970, the property of either spouse, as to which he or she dies intestate devolves as if the other spouse were then dead. A separation order obtained in magistrates' court does not deprive the husband of his right on intestacy to the wife's estate acquired since the making of the order.[20]

Adoption

Where the death occurs after December 31, 1975 an adopted child is treated as the lawful child of the adopter or adopters[21] and is therefore

---

[12-13] As to the recognition of foreign decrees of divorce, annulment and separation, see now the Family Law Act 1986, s.45.

[14] *Seaford* v. *Seifert* [1968] P. 53.

[15] Law of Property Act 1925, s.184 and see *post*, pp. 352 *et seq.*

[16] Administration of Estates Act 1925, s.46(3), as amended by the Intestates' Estates Act 1952, s.1(4).

[17] Matrimonial Causes Act 1965, s.20(3)(*a*) now replaced by the Matrimonial Causes Act 1973, s.18(2) in respect of death on or after August 1, 1970.

[18] *Ibid.*

[19] *Ibid.*

[20] Matrimonial Causes Act 1973, s.18(3).

[21] Adoption Act 1976, s.39.

entitled to a grant in accordance with the terms of rule 22 of the Non-Contentious Probate Rules 1987. Adoption means adoption by an adoption order, by an order made under the Children Act 1975, the Adoption Act 1958, the Adoption Act 1950 or any enactment repealed by the Adoption Act 1950, by an order made in Scotland, Northern Ireland, the Isle of Man or in any of the Channel Islands, an overseas adoption[22] or an adoption recognised by English law under the law of any other country.

The position is the same where the death occurred after December 31, 1949 but before 1976.[23]

If the death occurred before January 1, 1950 the adopted person has no statutory rights of succession so neither the adopter nor the adopted person has a right to a grant to the other's estate.

Practice

The oath refers to the adoption order, its effect, and that it is still subsisting.[24] The applicant is described as the lawful adopted son or daughter of the deceased or the lawful brother or sister by adoption.[25]

Legitimacy

The policy of the Family Law Reform Act 1987 is that references to any relationship between two persons shall, unless the contrary intention appears, be construed without regard to whether or not the father and mother of either of them, or the father and mother of any person through whom the relationship is deduced have or had been married to each other at any time.[26] Thus where death occurs on or after April 4, 1988 the intestacy provisions of the Administration of Estates Act 1925 are construed without reference to illegitimacy and illegitimate children take as if legitimate.[27] Similarly dispositions inter vivos made on or after April 4, 1988 are construed as above, as are dispositions by will or codicil where the will or codicil is made on or after that date.[28] Trustees and personal representatives are no longer relieved of the responsibility of ascertaining whether illegitimate relationships might affect the distribution of assets.[29] Protection should be sought under section 27 of the Trustee Act 1925. There is also a statutory rebuttable presumption for the purpose of obtaining grants of probate or administration that the deceased left no illegitimate relations.[30] Reference should be made to the detailed wording of this complex legislation.

[22] See Adoption Act 1976 s.72, as amended by the Children Act 1989, s.88 and Schedule 10.
[23] The relevant statute is then the Adoption Act 1958.
[24] See *Tristram and Coote on Probate Practice*, 27th ed., Form 99, p. 1056.
[25] *Ibid*. p. 232.
[26] Family Law Reform Act 1987 s.1(1). See Appendix p. 1216 *post*.
[27] *Ibid*. s.18. See Appendix p. 1217 *post*.
[28] *Ibid*. s.19. See Appendix p. 1217 *post*.
[29] *Ibid*. s.20. See Appendix p. 1218 *post*.
[30] *Ibid*. s.21. See Appendix p. 1218 *post*.

Legitimation

Before the Family Law Reform Act 1987 took effect as described above the law depended on questions of legitimation. Where the 1987 Act does not apply the position is as follows.

Where parents married after their children were born, the latter were legitimated provided that the father was domiciled in England at the date of the marriage.[31] Where either parent was married to a third person at the date of the birth[32] the child was only legitimated from October 29, 1959 or the date of the marriage of its parents, whichever was later. In other cases the legitimation dates from January 1, 1927, or the marriage, whichever was later.[33]

A legitimated person, his spouse, children or remoter issue were entitled to take any interest in the estate of the deceased dying after the date of legitimation as if such person had been born legitimate,[34] save that real or personal property devolving with a dignity or title of honour did not pass to a legitimated person.[35] Subject to the same provision as to property devolving with a dignity or title of honour, where a legitimated person or his child or remoter issue died intestate in respect of all or any of his real or personal property, the same persons were entitled to take the same interests therein as if the legitimated person had been born legitimate.[36]

If an illegitimate person died after 1926, but before the subsequent marriage of his parents, leaving a spouse, children or remoter issue living at the date of such marriage, then if that person would, if living at the date of the marriage of his parents, have become a legitimated person, he was treated as if legitimated as from the date of the marriage; if he was born when either of his parents were married to a third person, he was only so treated if he died on or after October 29, 1959. Consequently his spouse, children and remoter issue were entitled to take interests in property on that basis.[37]

Children of void and voidable marriages

A child of a void marriage, born after the marriage,[38] was treated as a legitimate child of its parents if, at the time of the act of intercourse resulting in the birth, or at the time of the celebration of the marriage, if later, both or either of its parents reasonably believed that the marriage was valid.[39] But the father must have been domiciled in England and Wales at

[31] Legitimacy Act 1976, s.2.
[32] The date of conception is not material: *Re Heath* [1945] Ch. 417.
[33] Legitimacy Act 1926 as amended by the Legitimacy Act 1959 and preserved by the Legitimacy Act 1976, Sched. 1, para. 1.
[34] Legitimacy Act 1976, s.5(3). *Re Hepworth* [1936] Ch. 750; *Re Brodie* [1967] Ch. 818; *Re Billson* [1984] Ch. 409, C.A.
[35] *Ibid.*, Sched. 1.
[36] *Ibid.* s.5(3).
[37] *Ibid.* s.6.
[38] *Re Spence* [1990] 1 Ch. 197.
[39] Legitimacy Act 1976, s.1(1).

the date of the birth or, if he died before the birth, at the date of his death.[40] So far as affects the succession to a dignity or title or honour or the devolution of any property settled therewith, only such children as were thus legitimated after October 29, 1959, were entitled to succeed.[41] Rights under the intestacy of a person who died before October 29, 1959, were not affected.[42]

Any child of a voidable marriage which was annulled who would have been the legitimate child of the parties had the marriage been dissolved were deemed to be legitimate.[43]

Effect of foreign legitimation

Where the parents of an illegitimate person married at any time and the father was domiciled outside England and Wales, and where by the law of the domicile the child became legitimated by such marriage, such child was recognised by English law as legitimated from January 1, 1927, or the date of the marriage, whichever was later, notwithstanding that at the date of birth his father was not domiciled in a place where legitimation by subsequent marriage was permitted by law.[44] Apart from statute an illegitimate person was legitimated by the subsequent marriage, even if polygamous,[45] of his parents or by an act of recognition by the father, if at the time of birth or conception and at the date of the subsequent marriage or act of recognition the law of the domicile of the father recognised the legitimation.[46] Such a person was entitled to share in the estate of an intestate and to take a grant.

Practice

A copy of any declaration of legitimacy or of the amended birth certificate should be produced. If there is no such declaration and the birth has not been re-registered and it appears that the applicant can obtain such declaration or re-registration, he will be required to do so. If re-registration is impossible and to obtain a declaration of legitimacy is impossible or would impose undue hardship, evidence in support of legitimacy should be put before the district judge or registrar who may direct that an application be made to the court on motion or to a judge by summons with notice to the Attorney General,[47] and, where the Crown is or could be beneficially

---

[40] *Ibid.* s.1(2).
[41] *Ibid.* s.3(a).
[42] *Ibid.* s.4(1).
[43] Matrimonial Causes Act 1973, s.16.
[44] Legitimacy Act 1976, s.3.
[45] *Bamgbose* v. *Daniel* [1955] A.C. 107.
[46] *Re Luck* [1940] Ch. 864; *Re Marshall* [1957] Ch. 263, affd. *ibid.* 507. See *Udny* v. *Udny* (1869) L.R. 1 Sc. & Div. 441; *Re Goodman* (1881) 17 Ch.D. 266; *Re Grove* (1889) 40 Ch.D. 216; *Re Askew* [1930] 2 Ch. 259; *Re Bischoffsheim* [1948] Ch. 79. Dicey and Morris, *Conflict of Laws*, 11th ed. pp. 846–859.
[47] *Practice Direction*, May 24, 1965; [1965] 1 W.L.R. 955. As to hardship involved in a public hearing see *Barritt* v. *Att.-Gen.* [1971] 1 W.L.R. 1713.

interested, the Treasury Solicitor must be notified.[48] The oath must show that any person in any declaration of legitimacy or certificate of re-registration is the person claimed to be legitimate.[49]

Illegitimate persons[50]

Before 1970, with one exception, illegitimate persons could only take a grant on the intestacy of their lawful next of kin, *e.g.* a spouse or a child. After 1969, however, an illegitimate child is entitled on intestacy to share in his parent's estate as if he were legitimate, and his parents have a corresponding right to share in the estate of their illegitimate children.[51]

Order of priority of right to a grant

The rules lay down an order of priority of right to a grant of letters of administration.[52] It is to be noted that the right to a grant is dependent on the various classes of persons having a beneficial interest in the estate.[53]

Any person not primarily entitled to a grant may obtain one if all persons entitled in priority to him have been cleared off by renunciation[54] or on their failure to take a grant after citation to accept or refuse one.[55]

The court has power, in its discretion, to pass over the persons primarily entitled to administration and to make a grant to persons having a lower title or even to persons having no title at all.[56] Where a person otherwise entitled to a grant to the estate of the deceased has been guilty of criminally killing him, his right is abrogated.[57]

B. THE RIGHT OF THE SURVIVING SPOUSE TO A GRANT[58]

Sole and joint grants

The surviving spouse will be entitled to a grant alone where no life interest arises under the intestacy (and assuming there is no minority interest).[59] He or she takes a joint grant with some other person in all other cases. The other person is generally someone also beneficially interested in the estate.

In order to ascertain whether a surviving spouse is entitled to take a grant alone or whether he must take it with another person, it is thus necessary to consider the beneficial rights of the persons entitled on intes-

---

[48] See the N.-C.P.R. 1987, r. 38 and *ante*, p. 249.
[49] Practice Direction, May 24, 1965, *supra*.
[50] See *post*, pp. 263 and 265.
[51] Family Law Reform Act 1969, s.14; the N.-C.P.R. 1987, r. 22.
[52] N.-C.P.R. 1987, r. 22 (p. 1231 *post*).
[53] See *ante*, p. 235, *post*, p. 406. N.-C.P.R. 1987, r. 22.
[54] For renunciation, see *post*, p. 378.
[55] For citations to accept or refuse a grant, see *post*, p. 358.
[56] See *post*, p. 343.
[57] Subject to relief under the Forfeiture Act 1982. See *post*, p. 348. The beneficial interest is lost, see *post*, p. 1074.
[58] For tables, see *post*, p. 1287. See also as to distribution on intestacy. *post*. pp. 1065 *et seq*.
[59] *i.e.* where the fixed net sum absorbs the whole estate.

tacy although this is really a matter of distribution.[60] These rights vary according to the period in which the death of the deceased took place as follows, but in all cases the surviving spouse takes the personal chattels of the deceased.[61]

The fixed net sum

The amount of the lump sum ("the statutory legacy") to which the surviving spouse is entitled on intestacy is now varied by statutory instrument under the Family Provision Act 1966 from time to time. The figure is larger where the intestate leaves no issue. These figures are as follows:

Date of Death	Leaving Issue	Leaving no issue
After May 1987[62]	£75,000	£125,000
After February 1981[63]	£40,000	£ 85,000
After March 14; 1977[64]	£25,000	£ 55,000
After June 1972[65]	£15,000	£ 40,000
After December 1966[66]	£ 8,750	£ 30,000
After December 1952[67]	£ 5,000	£ 20,000
After December 1925[68]	£ 1,000	£ 1,000

The fixed net sum is charged upon the residuary estate free of tax and costs. Interest is payable as from the date of death at the rate specified by the Lord Chancellor,[69] payable out of income but charged upon corpus.[70]

The life interest

In addition to the personal chattels and the fixed net sum the surviving spouse takes a life interest in half the residue left after deduction of the fixed net sum where there are children or issue; the issue receive the other half absolutely. Where there are no issue the surviving spouse takes half the residue absolutely, the remainder (the other half) passing to the next of kin, in equal shares if to more than one person.

Meaning of "Residuary Estate"

The residuary estate of the intestate as referred to in section 46 of the Administration of Estates Act 1925 covers only assets the succession to which is regulated by English law. It follows that a surviving spouse may be

[60] See post, pp. 1065–1075.
[61] For the definition of "pesonal chattels," see post, pp. 498, 1149.
[62] 1987 S.I. 799. For tables of distribution see p. 1287 post. See also pp. 1065 et seq. post.
[63] 1981 S.I. 255.
[64] 1977 S.I. 415.
[65] 1972 S.I. 916.
[66] Family Provision Act 1966, s.1. See also p. 1066 post.
[67] Intestates Estates Act 1952.
[68] Administration of Estates Act 1925, s.46.
[69] See Administration of Justice Act 1977, s.28. Currently six per cent.
[70] Re Saunders [1929] 1 Ch. 674; and see 81 S.J. 643.

entitled to the whole of the fixed net sum charged on the English residue while at the same time benefiting under the law of his or her domicile, for there is no "hotchpot" provision on a total intestacy.[71]

Priority of surviving spouse's right to a grant

A surviving spouse is entitled to grant in priority to all other persons.[72] Unless he is an infant, a grant may be made to him alone where he is entitled to the whole estate or, after 1952, where the intestate leaves no children or issue.[73]

Where the estate does not exceed the fixed net sum, the oath may so state, but where it exceeds the sums referred to but is reduced to or below them after taking into account the permitted deductions, i.e. personal chattels, debts and incumbrances, inheritance tax costs (see below) and fees for the grant, the oath must show the value of the gross estate and state the net value after the deductions which should be mentioned seriatim with the amount of the costs and interest stated. Costs of administering a trust or holding an estate during a minority or life interest are not to be included nor any costs which cannot be forecast with reasonable accuracy.[74] Interest on the fixed net sum is payable from income, and is not a permitted deduction save where the income is insufficient to pay the interest.[75]

Changes in the value of the estate

Although the date at which the value of the estate is to be taken is that of payment or appropriation and not of the death, it is in general assumed that the value is the same on both dates. Any substantial change between the two dates which clearly gives some person as well as the surviving spouse an interest in the estate will necessitate an application by two grantees where a minority or life interest arises.

A surviving spouse may in any case join in a grant with a person in the class next in order of priority[76] and, where it can be foreseen that an increase in the value of the estate will give rise to a minority or life interest, it is advisable to apply for a joint grant. Alternatively a trust corporation may be joined as second administrator[77] or a grant may be made to a trust corporation alone on the lodging of the consent of those beneficially entitled to the estate[78]. No renunciation is necessary. In the case of a minority, the spouse may also nominate a fit and proper person to join with him.[79]

[71] *Re Collens* [1986] Ch. 505.
[72] N.-C.P.R. 1987. r. 22(1) (*post*, p. 1231).
[73] Unless any person entitled to share in the estate is an infant.
[74] Registrar's Direction, June 28, 1960.
[75] Administration of Estates Act 1925, s.46(4) (as amended) and Registrar's Direction, November 17, 1960.
[76] N.-C.P.R. 1987, r. 25 (*post*, p. 1232). See also *ante*, p. 258.
[77] N.-C.P.R. 1987, r. 25(3)(*b*).
[78] N.-C.P.R. 1987, r.36/3.
[79] N.-C.P.R. 1987, r. 25(3)(*a*), 32(3).

Renunciation by or citation of a surviving spouse

If a surviving spouse is entitled to the whole estate no matter what its value and is cleared off by renunciation or citation,[80] a grant may be made to a creditor or to a person in the class of kin with the highest priority entitled to share in the event of an accretion having an equal right.[81]

On renunciation by a spouse who has a life interest, a grant may be made to not less than two individuals or to a trust corporation either alone or with a beneficiary. If there is only one person entitled in priority to a grant he may take a grant with the person next in priority even though the latter has no beneficial interest.[82]

Death of surviving spouse

The representatives of a spouse entitled to the whole estate have the same right to a grant as had the spouse while alive.[83] They must, therefore, be cleared off before a person who may have a beneficial interest (by an accretion), or a creditor, may take a grant. Where no personal representative has been constituted, renunciation by those entitled to be so constituted is necessary before any other person may take a grant. Where both spouses have died and no grant has been taken out their child or other applicant cannot obtain a grant in the estate of the first to die without taking a leading grant in the estate of the survivor. A "leading" grant is a grant which "leads" to entitlement to a further grant to another estate. Without the leave of a district judge or registrar, a potential personal representative of the survivor may not renounce in that capacity and then obtain a grant as one beneficially interested in the estate.[84]

Where a spouse survives and dies but was not entitled to the whole estate a grant may be made to one or more of the other persons beneficially entitled to a share. A grant may in this case be made to the personal representatives of the surviving spouse only if all other persons entitled to share in the estate are cleared off.[85]

Where the surviving spouse and all kin entitled to share in the estate have died, the representatives of the former are entitled in priority to the personal representatives of the latter.[86]

C. The Right of Children or Issue to a Grant

Where there is a surviving spouse, half the residue of the estate after payment to the spouse of his statutory entitlements[87] is held on statutory trusts

---

[80] There is now no provision for a *spes successionis* grant in the rules.
[81] See the N.-C.P.R. 1987, r. 22(1) (*post*, p. 1231).
[82] *Ibid*. r. 25(1).
[83] N.-C.P.R. 1987, r. 22(4) (*post*, p. 1232).
[84] See the N.-C.P.R. 1987, r. 37(2) (*post*, p. 1238).
[85] N.-C.P.R. 1987, r.22(4), proviso.
[86] N.-C.P.R. 1987, r. 22(4), *Registrar's Direction*, November 7, 1955.
[87] See *ante*, pp. 258 *et seq.*, and further as to distribution on intestacy, *post*, p. 1065.

for the children of the deceased or for their issue where a child has died in the lifetime of the deceased. After the death of the spouse the other half is held for the children or issue on the same trusts. A child *en ventre sa mère* (unborn child) is included among children or issue.[88]

Where the deceased leaves no surviving spouse, the whole of the estate is held on statutory trusts for the children or remoter issue.

The statutory trusts

(i) Where there are children or remoter issue the estate (or the residue thereof) is held in trust in equal shares for the children of the intestate living at his death, who attain the age of 18 years or marry under that age; and for such issue of any child of the intestate who predeceases him as are living or *en ventre sa mère* at the death of the intestate and attain the age of 18 years or marry under that age, such issue taking *per stirpes* through all degrees in equal shares. However, no issue may take whose parent is living at the date of the death of the intestate.[89]

The representative must bring into account any money or property which by way of advancement or on marriage has been paid by the intestate to such child, or settled by him for the benefit of such child (including any life or lesser interest and including property covenanted to be paid or settled). Subject to any contrary intention expressed or appearing from the circumstances, such benefits to a child are to be taken in satisfaction of the child's share if living at the date of the death of the intestate and the value is to be reckoned as at that date.[90]

The statutory powers of advancement, maintenance and accumulation apply, but an infant, on marriage, is entitled to give valid receipts for the income of his share.[91]

The representatives may permit any infant contingently interested to have the use of the personal chattels on such terms as they consider reasonable and without being liable to account for any consequential loss.[92]

(ii) These trusts apply where the whole of the residuary estate is held on the statutory trusts for relatives, save for the provision for bringing money or property into account.[93]

Failure of the statutory trusts

On failure of the statutory trusts in favour of issue the estate devolves as if the deceased had died without leaving issue.[94] On failure of the statutory trusts in favour of any class of relatives, the estate devolves as though the deceased had left no relative of that class.

[88] Administration of Estates Act 1925, s.55(2) (*post*, p. 1150).
[89] Administration of Estates Act 1925, s.47(1) (*post*, p. 1141).
[90] *Ibid.*
[91] *Ibid.*
[92] Administration of Estates Act 1925, s.47(1).
[93] *Ibid.* s.47(3).
[94] *Ibid.* s.47(2).

Illegitimate children and their issue

These now take as if legitimate.[95]

Before 1926 illegitimate children had no interest in their parent's intestate estate. Where after 1926 and before 1970 the mother of an illegitimate child dies wholly or partially intestate and does not leave any legitimate issue, the illegitimate child or, if dead, his issue is entitled to take the same interest in the estate as he would if he had been born legitimate.[96] Where either parent of an illegitimate person dies intestate after December 31, 1969, that person has the same right to inherit his parent's estate as if he were legitimate.[97] Consequently an illegitimate child may take a grant to the estate of either of his parents and his issue will have the same rights to take a grant as legitimate issue have. The position of adopted and legitimated children has already been considered.[98]

Grants to children or remoter issue

A child or other issue if of age and entitled to share in the intestate's estate is entitled to a grant thereto. Where there is a surviving spouse the grant will be made to the spouse and the child or issue; otherwise it will be made to such children or issue as join in applying.[99] Although a child who marries under the age of 18 has an absolutely vested interest in the estate he cannot take a grant until of full age.

Unless otherwise directed by a district judge or registrar any person beneficially interested in the estate has a right to a grant in priority to the personal representatives of a child who has died after surviving the intestate.[1]

Where an intestates' illegitimate child or remoter issue are entitled to the estate they are also entitled to take a grant.[2]

D. THE RIGHT OF OTHER RELATIVES TO A GRANT

1. Death before 1953 where there is a surviving spouse but no children or issue[3]

In such case the estate of the deceased is held (subject to the statutory entitlements of the spouse[4]) for the spouse for life and then for those of his next-of-kin who come within the following degrees, each class after that of the parents only benefiting if there is no member of the class above.[5]

---

[95] See p. 255 *ante*.
[96] Legitimacy Act 1926, s.9(1).
[97] Family Law Reform Act 1969, s.14. Legitimacy Act 1976, s.5.
[98] See *ante*, pp. 255–258.
[99] Subject to a maximum of four, see *ante*, p. 235.
[1] N.-C.P.R. 1987, r. 27(5) (*post*, p. 1233).
[2] Family Law Reform Act 1987, s.18. Legitimacy Act 1976, s.5.
[3] Administration of Estates Act 1925, s.46(1), as originally enacted.
[4] See *ante*, pp. 258 *et seq*.
[5] Administration of Estates Act 1925, ss.46(1), 47(5), as amended by the Intestates' Estates Act 1952.

    (i) The parents in equal shares or the surviving parent.

    (ii) On the statutory trusts for the brothers and sisters of the whole blood in equal shares, or where such brother or sister has died in the lifetime of the deceased, for their surviving issue, taking *per stirpes*.

    (iii) On the statutory trusts for the brothers and sisters of the half blood and their issue as in (ii).

    (iv) The grandparents in equal shares or for the surviving grand-parent.

    (v) On the statutory trusts for the uncles and aunts of the whole blood and their issue as in (ii).

    (vi) On the statutory trusts for the uncles and aunts of the half blood and their issue as in (ii).[6]

2. Death after 1952 where there is a surviving spouse but no children or issue

In such case the spouse is entitled[7] (in addition to his statutory entitlements previously discussed[8]) to half the estate, and the next-of-kin who come within the following degrees to the other half absolutely in the following order of priority:

    (i) The parents in equal shares or the surviving parent.

    (ii) The brothers and sisters of the whole blood in equal shares, or where such brother or sister has died in the lifetime of the deceased, their surviving issue taking *per stirpes*. The other classes set out under (1) do not benefit.

3. Death at any time after 1925 where there is no surviving spouse, child or issue[9]

In such case the estate of the deceased devolves to the next-of-kin set out in (1), but each class after that of parents only benefits if there is no member of the class above.

Grants to next-of-kin

Where there is a surviving spouse and kin are interested in the estate, those in the class entitled may join with the surviving spouse in a grant in cases where the deceased died before 1953, as a life interest arises. Where, in the same circumstances, the deceased died after 1952, kin are only entitled to join in a grant with the spouse where a minority interest arises.

---

[6] In spite of the wording of the Administration of Estates Act 1925, s.47(5) (repealed), issue of uncles and aunts were entitled where all uncles and aunts are dead, *Re Lockwood* [1958] 1 Ch. 231. See also *20 Conveyancer* 399.

[7] Administration of Estates Act 1925, s.46(1), as amended by the Intestates' Estates Act 1952. For tables of distribution, see *post*, p. 1287.

[8] See *ante*, p. 259.

[9] Administration of Estates Act 1925, s.46(1) (*post*, p. 1137).

Where there is no surviving spouse, any members (not exceeding four[10]) of the class entitled to share in the estate may take a grant and the issue of deceased members of the class are equally entitled. In all cases next-of-kin applying must show that there is no person in a class having priority to theirs or that such persons have renounced or been cited to take a grant.

The mother of an illegitimate child who died before 1970 was entitled to take the same share in his estate as she would have, had he been legitimate and his only surviving parent,[11] and she was entitled to a grant where she would be entitled as his surviving parent.[12] After 1969 both parents are entitled to share in the estate of their illegitimate child.[13]

E. THE RIGHT OF THE CROWN TO A GRANT[14]

If an intestate dies without leaving a spouse, issue or the relatives set out above the Crown, the Duchy of Lancaster[15] or the Duke of Cornwall,[16] as the case may be, are entitled to his estate,[17] by statute and not by the prerogative right.[18]

The Treasury Solicitor takes a grant as nominee on behalf of the Crown, and the Solicitors for the Duchies on their behalf. Unless it is positively known that there are no next-of-kin the procedure is by way of application under section 116 of the Supreme Court Act 1981.[19] Grants to the Treasury Solicitor and the Solicitor for the Duchy of Lancaster devolve on their successors in office, but not grants to the Solicitor for the Duchy of Cornwall. New grants[20] are made to successors of the latter.

Subject to the Family Law Reform Act 1987[21] the Crown and the Duchies take the estates of illegitimate persons who die intestate without leaving the limited classes who are entitled to share in their estates, *i.e.* spouse, issue or natural parents. Grants to the estates of foundlings are made under the discretionary powers of the court[22] and in the case of those brought up at the Foundling Hospital evidence is required from the secretary and the solicitor to the Governors.

[10] See *ante*, p. 235. For rights on distribution, see further, *post* p. 1068.

[11] See *ante*, p. 258.

[12] See the N.-C.P.R. 1954, r. 21(1)(iii) before the 1969 amendment.

[13] Family Law Reform Act 1969, s.14. I is to be noted, however, that the Act made no provision for a brother or other relative of an illegitimate person to inherit his estate. The present position is governed by the 1987 Act. See p. 263 *ante*.

[14] Administration of Etates Act 1925, s.46(1)(vi). See further on this topic, *post* p. 1068 and *Ing on Bona Vacantia*, pp. 19 *et seq.*

[15] *Dyke* v. *Walford* (1848) 5 Moo.P.C. 434.

[16] *Solicitor of the Duchy of Cornwall* v. *Canning* (1880) 5 P.D. 114.

[17] But though entitled to the estate, the Crown or the Duchees may make *ex gratia* payments to the dependants of the deceased and other persons for whom the intestate might reasonably have been expected to make provision. Administration of Estates Act 1925, s.46(1)(vi) and see *post*, p. 1069.

[18] *Re Mitchell*, [1954] Ch. 525.

[19] See p. 1117, *post*.

[20] In practice these are very rare.

[21] See p. 255 *ante*.

[22] Registrar's Direction, December 23, 1948.

The claims of the Crown and the Duchies may, however, be defeated where residue is left to a company which has been dissolved and the deceased left no kin, by an order of the Chancery Division[23] setting aside the dissolution.[24]

F. THE RIGHT OF A CREDITOR TO A GRANT

If all persons entitled to share in the estate have been cleared off by renunciation or citation a grant may be made to a creditor of the deceased,[25] even if his debt is statute-barred.[26] Where a surviving spouse is entitled to the whole estate as ascertained at the time of the application, the renunciation of the spouse (or, if dead, of his personal representatives) is sufficient to allow a grant to be made to a creditor. He need not clear off the persons who would be beneficially entitled if there were an accretion.

Where the Crown is interested in the estate, the renunciation of the Treasury Solicitor or of the Solicitors to the Duchies is required. If the estate is insolvent, such renunciation is appropriate and a grant may be made to a creditor. In the case of the Duchies, however, if the estate proves to be solvent and a creditor is granted administration, then the effect of renunciation regarding the residue after all debts have been paid is unclear. The residue would constitute *bona vacantia*, but *quaere* whether or not it would pass to the Crown. Where the creditor cannot be positive that there are no kin he may proceed by citation and give notice to the Treasury Solicitor.[27]

Though a creditor in equity may be granted administration,[28] a person who has bought up a debt of the deceased after his death will not.[29]

Grants will be made to nominees of public departments, local authorities and the Commissioners of Inland Revenue when they are creditors. The Official Receiver or a liquidator of a company may be granted administration as a creditor, as may be the trustee in bankruptcy or personal representative of a creditor.[30]

An undertaker is not as such a creditor of the deceased but of his estate and authority which appears to imply the contrary[31] is not, it is submitted, to be followed on this point. In modern practice a grant to an undertaker is made under the discretionary powers of the court.

---

[23] Under Companies Act 1948, s.352; Companies Act 1985 ss.651, 655.

[24] *Re Servers of the Blind* [1960] 1 W.L.R. 564. See *Ing on Bona Vacantia*, pp. 125, 148 *et seq.*

[25] N.-C.P.R. 1987, r. 22(3). If alternative remedies are available a creditor may be wise to avoid this course.

[26] *Coombs* v. *Coombs* (1866) L.R. 1 P. & D. 288.

[27] Application under the Supreme Court Act 1981, s.116, is usually cheaper (*post*, p. 1117).

[28] *Fairland* v. *Percy* (1875) 3 P.D. 217.

[29] *Baynes* v. *Harrison* (1856) 1 Dea. & Sw. 15; *Re Coles* (1863) 3 Sw. & Tr. 181.

[30] *Downward* v. *Dickinson* (1864) 3 Sw. & Tr. 564; the N.-C.P.R. 1954, rr. 19(v), 21(5).

[31] *Newcombe* v. *Beloe* (1867) L.R. 1 P. & D. 314.

Part Three

NON-CONTENTIOUS PRACTICE

CHAPTER 20

FORMS OF PROBATE

Probate in common and in solemn form

Wills may be proved in two ways, in common form or in form of law. The latter is usually termed proof in solemn form and sometimes proof *per testes*.

A will is proved in solemn form when it is propounded in an action to which persons interested under another will or on intestacy are made parties and for the validity of which the court pronounces after hearing the evidence.

A will is proved in common form (i) where its validity is not questioned, (ii) where the court allows it to be admitted to probate after a hearing on motion or summons. In general the distinction is reflected in the assignment of business in the High Court already discussed.[1]

Difference in effect between the two forms of probate

Where a will is proved in common form, those whose interests are adversely affected may later challenge its validity in an action.[2] If such challenge succeeds, the probate originally granted will be revoked. But if a will is proved in solemn form, no person who has been a party or privy to the proceedings (or indeed is aware of them and does nothing) can afterwards put the executor to proof of the will, unless there is evidence of fraud or a later will has been discovered.[3]

Acquiescence as a bar to challenging a will proved in common form

Mere acquiescence on the part of the next-of-kin or those interested under another will in allowing an executor to take a grant of probate in common form is not, in general, a bar to their afterwards calling in such probate and putting the executor to proof in solemn form.[4] An executor may even prove a will in common form and then attack it in his capacity as next-of-kin.[5] Even a person who has taken his legacy under a will may afterwards contest it.[6] But before being permitted to do so he must bring

---

[1] See *ante*.

[2] There is no statutory limitation period for a probate action so that it seems that the equitable principles of laches and estoppel would apply to a late claim. *Re Flynn* [1982] 1 W.L.R. 310. See p. 271 *post*.

[3] *Ritchie* v. *Malcolm* [1902] 2 I.R. 403.

[4] *Bell* v. *Armstrong* (1822) 2 Add. 365, 373; *Goddard* v. *Smith* (1873) L.R. 3 P. & D. 7.

[5] *Williams* v. *Evans* [1911] P. 175.

[6] *Bell* v. *Armstrong, supra*, at p. 374; *Merryweather* v. *Turner* (1844) 3 Curt. 802, 811.

his legacy into court,[7] unless he is a minor.[8] Extreme cases of laches and acquiescence may bar an action in solemn form,[9] but it seems only where the action is frivolous and vexatious.[10] Words contained in a common form grant, as for instance a statement of domicil or that certain persons are the only persons entitled to share in an estate are not binding in law or conclusive,[11] although the probate is in principle an order of the court.

Who are bound by a decree in solemn form

Where an executor or person benefiting under a will proves it in solemn form and all persons adversely affected by it have been made parties or are privy to the proceedings, such persons and those claiming under them are, in general, for ever barred from contesting it. Nor will it avail that the second action is brought by these persons in a representative capacity.[12]

Not only are the principal parties bound by the judgment of the court, but so also are privies, *i.e.* those who being of full age and *sui juris*, elect to stand aside though notified of their interest in the suit.[13] But if a person, though cognisant of the suit, did not know of his interest therein, he cannot be held bound by its result if at a later date he discovers facts which would have given him a right to intervene had he known of them at the time.[14] Although it has been said that the judgment in a probate action is a judgment *in rem*,[15] it is clear that it does not bind all the world.[16]

A person to whom notice of the action has been given under R.S.C. Ord. 15, r. 13A is a privy and may also be bound by the judgment.

If a person not bound by the decree succeeds in securing a pronouncement against the will proved earlier in solemn form, the parties and privies in the first action can benefit from it.[17]

Although the decree of the court after hearing evidence is generally binding, where judgment is given in the absence of a person at the trial it may be set aside in proper circumstances.[18]

---

[7] *Ibid.*

[8] *Goddard* v. *Norton* (1846) 5 N.C. 76.

[9] *Braham* v. *Burchell* (1826) 3 Add. 243, 256; *Merryweather* v. *Turner, supra*; *Mohan* v. *Broughton* [1899] P. 211; [1900] P. 56, C.A.; but see *Re Coghlan* [1948] 2 All E.R. 68 (where an action to prove a will after 20 years' delay was not struck out).

[10] *Re Coghlan, supra.*

[11] *Re Ward* [1917] 1 W.L.R. 1376.

[12] *Re Langton* [1964] P. 163, C.A.

[13] *Newell* v. *Weeks* (1814) 2 Phill. 224; *Ratcliffe* v. *Barnes* (1862) 2 Sw. & Tr. 486; *Wytcherley* v. *Andrews* (1871) L.R. 2 P. & D. 327, 328.

[14] *Young* v. *Holloway* [1895] P. 87; see *Peters* v. *Tilly* (1886) 11 P.D. 145

[15] *Re Langton, supra, per* Danckwerts L.J., but this observation is contrary to previous cases and must be regarded as *obiter*. See also n. 20 below and text thereto. As to the effect of a grant see also p. 419 *post.*

[16] See *Concha* v. *Concha* (1886) 11 App.Cas. 541; *Beardsley* v. *Beardsley* [1899] 1 Q.B. 746. See also p. 188 *ante.*

[17] *Young* v. *Holloway, supra.*

[18] See Ord. 35, r. 2; *Barraclough* v. *Young* [1967] P. 1.

Who is bound by a decree pronounced after a compromise

On a compromise, those who are parties to the compromise are bound.[19] Cognisance of the suit or even of the compromise is not enough to bind persons who have stood by not knowing that the suit was not proceeding.[20] But those who are interested in the suit and are in court when the compromise is announced and approved are bound.[21]

The practice as to compromise is considered later.[22]

Effect of order obtained by fraud and of the discovery of a later will

If an order, whether pronouncing for or against a will, is obtained by fraud, it may be set aside not only as against the persons who so obtained it but as against the persons interested thereunder, for the will is either good or bad against all the world.[23] There is no limitation period in probate.

If, after an order, a will or a will later than that pronounced for, is discovered, the parties having an interest which has been adversely affected by the order may obtain its revocation.

Special forms of probate

In some circumstances special forms of probate (generally in common form) are issued. These are as follows:

1. Double probate

Where there are several executors named in a will, upon the grant of probate to one (or some) of them only it is the practice to reserve the power to make a like grant to the others. Since a grant may not be made to more than four persons,[24] where more than that number are appointed executors, power is reserved to such executors over that number as are competent to act and have not renounced. In the first case, if an executor to whom power is reserved applies for a grant, a grant of double probate is made to him. Double probate is also given in the second case, but only as vacancies occur. Where an executor who has renounced is allowed to retract his renunciation,[25] but a grant has already been made, double probate may issue to him.

The grant of double probate confers the same rights as the original grant. An executor to whom power has been reserved may take a grant of probate of a codicil found after the original executor has died. Where both proving executors have died, a grant may be made to the executor of the survivor of

---

[19] See *Re King* [1917] 2 Ch. 420.

[20] *Wytcherley* v. *Andrews, supra.* But see *Re King* [1917] 2 Ch. 420, where charities were held bound by a compromise entered into by the Attorney-General on their behalf, of which they were ignorant.

[21] See *Tiger* v. *Handley* [1948] W.N. 432.

[22] See *post.*

[23] *Birch* v. *Birch* [1902] P. 130, C.A. See also n. 13 above.

[24] Supreme Court Act 1981 s.114(1).

[25] For retraction, see *post.*

the executors if such grant is necessary (there being a possible chain of representation).

Where there is a grant of administration with the will annexed with power reserved to an executor to prove there can be no "double" grant.[26]

Procedure.   Double probate may be extracted from the principal registry or from any district registry.[27] The application may be made by post.[28]

The oath, in addition to covering the usual matters, gives particulars of the former grant, shows that power was reserved and, in a case where more than four executors were appointed, sets out this fact and shows that an executor (naming him) has died on a particular date. The amount of the estate shown in the grant and Inland Revenue Account or affidavit is that remaining unadministered. It seems that there would be no power to grant and little purpose in granting double probate after administration is complete.

2. Cessate or second probate

Where the original grant of probate was limited for any specified period or until the happening of some event, a new grant, called a cessate probate, is made on the effluxion of that time or the happening of that event.[29]

3. Limited probate

Limited grants of probate are made where the will is lost[30] or unobtainable and when the testator has limited the executor's appointment.[31]

4. Probate caeterorum

Where an executor appointed for a special purpose has taken his grant and the general executor then applies for a grant, the grant made is of probate *caeterorum*.[32]

Settled land grants

Grants are still sometimes necessary where a person died before 1926. In such cases no special grant is required for settled land forming part of his estate. But where a person dies after 1925 in whom land was vested before

---

[26] *Re Mathew* [1984] 1 W.L.R. 1011, 1014. It should be noted that the decision that executors may have power reserved to take probate on granting administration (with will annexed) has not been followed. The original decision, of which the case referred to was the appeal, followed a discretionary order made under section 116 of the Supreme Court Act 1981. The grant which issued was of letters of administration (with will annexed) limited until the executors obtained probate: it being accepted that "power reserved" means power reserved to take a like grant. Supreme Court Act 1981, s.116, *post.*
[27] Administration of Justice Act 1969, s.28.
[28] See *post*, p. 288.
[29] See *ante*, p. 275.
[30] See *ante*, p. 248.
[31] See *ante*, p. 263.
[32] See *post*, p. 264.

his death and not by his will which remained settled land notwithstanding his death, a special grant is required.[33] This grant, which is known as a settled land grant, is made not to his general executors or administrators but to special personal representatives. Where there are several settlements with different or varying trustees, a grant is made in respect of each settlement, limited to the settled land comprised in that settlement.

It is beyond the scope of this work to discuss the somewhat complicated topic of settled land and where any question arises whether the land in question is or is not settled land or as to the settlement, trustees or other matters, reference should be made to the textbooks on the subject.[34]

Priority in applications for grants to settled land

1. Executors

"A testator may appoint, and in default of such express appointment shall be deemed to have appointed, as his special executors in regard to settled land, the persons, if any, who are at his death the trustees of the settlement thereof, and administration may be granted to such trustees specially limited to settled land."[35] A testator may appoint other persons with or without such trustees to be his general executors.[36]

The special executors have a prior right to a grant in respect of settled land.[37] Where there would otherwise be no trustee of the settlement, the personal representatives of the settlor are the trustees until other trustees are appointed.[38]

Subject to the limitation of their office to dealing with settled land, special executors have the same rights and duties as other executors, but there is no chain of executorship through such an executor.[39]

2. Administrators

Priority for a grant of administration to settled land is, first to the special executors (see above), then the trustees of the settlement at the time of the application for the grant, and thirdly the personal representative of the deceased.[40]

Whereas administration in respect of settled land may only be granted to the special executors named in the will, administration may be granted to the trustees of the settlement at the time of the application. Thus trustees appointed since the date of the death are entitled to administration. The

---

[33] Administration of Estates Act 1925, s.22(1), the N.-C.P.R. 1987, r. 29(2). See *post*, pp. 523, 1000, 1059.

[34] See, *e.g. Lewin on Trusts*, 16th ed., pp. 468–509; *Megarry and Wade on Real Property*, 5th ed., p. 311 *et seq.*

[35] Administration of Estates Act 1925, s.22(1).

[36] *Ibid.* subs. (2).

[37] N.-C.P.R. 1987 r. 29(2)(i).

[38] Settled Land Act 1925, s.30(3).

[39] Registrar's Direction, July 21, 1936.

[40] N.-C.P.R. 1987, r. 29(2).

order of priority of entitlement to apply prescribed by rule 29 of the Non-Contentious Probate Rules must be followed.

Where the deceased died intestate, the trustees at the date of the death and those appointed later are equally entitled to a grant. Where there are no trustees or they have been cleared off, the representatives of the deceased are entitled to a grant in respect of settled land on the same principles as govern ordinary applications on intestacy.[41]

Grants including settled land

Where the persons entitled to the free estate of the deceased are also entitled to a grant to settled land, a separate grant limited to the settled land may be made to them.[42] Since the amendment of rule 29, from October 14, 1991, there can no longer be any grant "including" settled land.[43] A grant of administration only (limited to settled land) may be made to those entitled in priority under the rule as now amended.

Grants limited to settled land

Grants of this nature were formerly made because those entitled to them were not also entitled to the free estate. But now the persons entitled to a general grant must apply separately for a grant limited to settled land to which they are also entitled.

1. Probate limited to settled land

Since the amendment to rule 29 referred to above, there can no longer be *probate* limited to settled land.

The special executors may apply for a grant of administration limited to the settled land. They may apply before or after a grant of probate to the general estate. When the application is made before that by the general executors, the will must be lodged, but is not marked in the usual way. Where the general grant has already been made an office copy of the will should be lodged where application is made to a Registry other than that which issued the general grant.

Where the surviving trustee of the settlement has appointed another trustee after the death of the deceased, probate limited to settled land cannot be granted to both trustees but only to the surviving trustee. This is because it is only the trustees of the settlement at the death of the deceased who are his special executors.[44]

2. Administration with the will annexed limited to settled land

Since the amendment to rule 29 referred to above there can no longer be administration with the will annexed limited to settled land.

[41] See *ante.*
[42] N.-C.P.R. 1987, r. 29 as amended with effect from October 14 1991 by S.I. 1991 No. 1876 (*post*, p. 1234).
[43] *Ibid.*
[44] Administration of Estates Act 1925, s.22(1).

3. Letters of administration limited to settled land

The circumstances in which administration may be granted limited to settled land and the classes entitled have already been considered.[45]

4. Ad colligenda grants limited to settled land

Orders for a grant *ad colligenda* limited to settled land have been made where it was requisite to sell the land in pursuance of a contract.

5. Administration pending suit limited to settled land

In a proper case administration pending suit may be granted limited to settled land.

Grants save and except settled land

Where there is settled land for which a separate grant must be taken, the person entitled to the free estate will take a grant expressly excluding the settled land.[46]

If there has been no previous grant, the practice is the same as in ordinary applications for probate or administration; but if a grant limited to settled land has been taken, the oath must give details of it and an office copy of the settled land grant must be lodged. Where there is a will an office copy should be lodged. The will does not require marking as the grant is of administration only.[47]

Amendment to exclude settled land grants

A general grant may be amended to except settled land where the value of that land was not included in the amount for which the grant was made. A district judge or registrar may, in his discretion, allow an amendment where the value was mistakenly included. In both cases an affidavit must support the application.[48]

Application for amendment should be made to the registry from which the grant was issued.

Appointment of special or additional personal representatives in respect of settled land

In certain circumstances, *e.g.* when a grantee has died or retired from the trust, it is requisite to make application for the appointment of a special or additional personal representative in respect of settled land.[49]

In such case notice of intention to make such application must be given to the Record Keeper at the principal registry. Next a direction must be

[45] N.-C.P.R. r. 29.
[46] N.-C.P.R. 1987 r. 29(3).
[47] N.-C.P.R. 1987, r. 10(2).
[48] Registrar's Circular, November 24, 1926.
[49] See the Administration of Estates Act 1925, s.23(2).

obtained in the Chancery Division that such an application be made. This direction and the grant are then lodged in the principal registry[50] and a summons is taken out returnable before a district judge supported by an affidavit setting out the grounds on which the appointment of the personal representative is sought. If the order is made the district judge decides any question as to further security.

---

[50] See *Re Clifton* [1931] P. 222.

CHAPTER 21

GRANTS IN COMMON FORM—GENERAL PRACTICE

This chapter covers the method of obtaining grants where the deceased died domiciled in England.[1] The general practice applies to all grants whether of probate or of administration (with or without the will). The special considerations which apply in applications for probate are considered later.[2] The practice in applications for administration (with or without the will) is considered in the chapters on those topics.[3] Practice in special types of grant, *e.g.* limited grants, has been mentioned when these topics have been considered. By virtue of s.74 of the Courts and Legal Services Act 1990 "registrars" of the principal registry were renamed "district judges." As the majority of probate matters are dealt with in district probate registries, and for ease of reference, the term registrar (unless the context otherwise requires) is retained throughout this Part. The term registrar denotes a district judge if application is made to the Principal Registry.

How soon a grant may issue

Except with the leave of a registrar no grant of probate or letters of administration with the will annexed may issue within seven days of the death of the deceased and no grant of letters of administration within 14 days of the death.[4] An application for leave for a grant to issue within those times is made *ex parte* and special reasons must be shown in the supporting affidavit.

Although the earliest times for the issue of grants are laid down, no latest time is specified and no limitation period applies. In respect of deaths after March 12, 1975, a penalty of £100 is laid down for administering an estate without a grant.[5]

---

[1] For the practice where the deceased died domiciled abroad, see *post*, pp. 297, 305.

[2] See *post*, p. 306.

[3] See *ante*.

[4] N.-C.P.R. 1988, r. 6(2). For the origins of this rule, see *Hewson* v. *Shelley* [1914] 2 Ch. 13, 45. See also *post*, p. 1226.

[5] By the Stamp Act 1815, s.37, as amended by the Finance Act 1975, s.52(2) and Sched. 13. For deaths before this date, see the Stamp Act 1815, s.37 (before amendment) and the Customs and Inland Revenue Act 1881, s.40. As to the object of s.37 of the Stamp Act 1815, see *Bodger* v. *Arch* (1854) 10 Exch. 333, 337.

Preparation of Papers

The categories of persons entitled to prepare papers for probate has been enlarged by the Courts and Legal Services Act 1990.[6]

A. WHERE GRANTS MAY BE OBTAINED

1. The Principal Registry

In every case a grant may, if desired, be obtained at the principal registry of the Family Division, Somerset House, Strand, London, WC2R 1LP.[7]

The application may be made by a solicitor,[8] provided he gives an address within the jurisdiction of the High Court.[9] Application may also be made in person.

2. The District Registries and sub-registries

The district registries are empowered to make grants in common form[10] and, in general, district probate registrars have the same powers as regards grants as the district judges of the principal registry.[11] Second or subsequent grants may be made in the registry in which the first grant was made or in any other registry.[12] This rule applies to settled land grants after a "save and except" grant and vice versa.[13] It also applies to a further grant following one which has been revoked or become cessate.

No grant, however, can be made by a district registrar in any contentious case or in any case in which it appears to the district registrar that a grant ought not to be made without the direction of the court.[14] Thus a grant of administration pending suit must be obtained from the principal registry.[15]

District registries have been established at a number of places in England and Wales[16] and these places may be varied by order. Some of the district registries have sub-registries. The latter are open full time. Sub-registries have no power to issue grants and the necessary papers are

---

[6] See s.23 of the Solicitors Act 1974, as amended by ss.54 and 55 of the Courts and Legal Services Act 1990.

[7] Supreme Court Act 1981, s.105.

[8] N.-C.P.R. 1987, r. 4 (*post*, p. 1225). See also n. 6, *supra*.

[9] *Ibid.* sub-r. (2).

[10] Supreme Court Act 1981, s.106; Administration of Justice Act 1985, s.51.

[11] N.-C.P.R. 1987, r. 2.

[12] Administration of Justice Act 1969, s.28.

[13] *Registrar's Direction*, June 27, 1932.

[14] N.-C.P.R. 1987, r. 7(1).

[15] *Registrar's Direction* 1935.

[16] The location of district registries is currently as follows: Birmingham, sub-registry, Stoke-on-Trent; Brighton, sub-registry Maidstone; Bristol, sub-registries Bodmin and Exeter; Ipswich, sub-registries Norwich and Peterborough; Leeds, sub-registries Lincoln and Sheffield; Liverpool, sub-registries Chester and Lancaster; Llandaff, sub-registries Bangor, Carmarthen and Gloucester; Manchester, sub-registry Nottingham; Newcastle, sub-registries Carlisle, Middlesborough and York; Oxford, sub-registry Leicester; Winchester (no-sub registry). The registry at Llandaff is known as the Probate Registry of Wales.

forwarded after preliminary examination to the parent district registry for the grant to be issued. Probate offices, run from the main registries and sub-registries, are open, usually for one day each week, for personal applications. Solicitor applications cannot be processed through these offices. There is no limit to the value of the estate in these applications.

As in the case of the principal registry, application for a grant may be made by a solicitor or in person.

In general personal applications are made in the same way as other applications[17] but forms of application should first be obtained through the post on application by letter or telephone from the nearest probate registry or by calling at such registry. On completion, the forms, the death certificate and any will should be forwarded to the registry at which the form was issued with an intimation which probate office the applicant wishes to attend.

Records of district registries which have been closed are preserved, and are available for inspection in other registries.

District registries notify the registry which maintains the index of pending applications of all applications for grants.[18] This registry is currently the District Probate Registry at Leeds.

The county court

When a probate action is heard in a county court the testamentary papers are, on its conclusion, sent to the probate registry from which they came and the grant is made there.

B. MODES OF APPLICATION FOR GRANTS

1. Applications at the principal registry

(i) *Applications made through a person entitled to prepare papers for probate*[19]

Applications for a first grant are made by leaving at the Receiver's Department the necessary papers to lead the grant, *viz.* any will or codicils, the Oath, the Inland Revenue account or affidavit and such other papers as the nature of the case may require. The *ad valorem* fee is paid and a fee sheet is impressed. The applicant must give the address of his place of business within the jurisdiction.[20]

Drafts of papers may be submitted to the probate department for settling. Affidavits of fact, where these are requisite, will not be settled by the department.

Applications for grants may also be made by post at the principal

---

[17] See *post*, p. 950.
[18] See N-C.P.R. 1987, rr. 44(4) and 57 (*post*, pp. 1241, 1247).
[19] Applications for grants by solicitors at the principal registry and at district registries are governed by the N.-C.P.R. 1987, r. 4 (*post*, p. 1225).
[20] N.-C.P.R. 1987, r. 4(2).

registry, by sending the necessary papers addressed to: The Receiver of Papers, Principal Registry of the Family Division, Somerset House, Strand, London WC2R 1LP (Dx 396 London/Chancery).[21] The staff at the registry will answer simple queries by telephone or by post, as far as this is practicable.

(ii) Personal applications

Applications at the principal registry are made to the Personal Application Department, at Somerset House.[22] The forms of application are obtainable on request from any registry or sub-registry. After completion by the applicant they may be lodged personally or by post in the registry at which the applicant wishes to attend. If an appointment at a probate office is required the applicant should request this on lodging the papers. Where a request for forms is made a booklet, giving details of the procedure and the addresses of the registries and probate offices, is supplied.

A district judge has a discretion to direct that a personal application be not received or be not proceeded with.[23] Applications will not be accepted where a probate action or motion is necessary or where an outstanding application has already been made by a solicitor on behalf of the applicant which has not been withdrawn.[24]

Personal applications for resealing are made through the Principal Registry or any district registry or sub-registry.[25]

The applicant must lodge a death certificate or other evidence of death and any testamentary documents, and must supply full particulars of the property passing on the death of the deceased and of any other property liable to inheritance tax valued as at the date of death, as well as a list of debts and funeral expenses.

The papers to lead the grant are prepared in the registry.[26]

There is no longer any requirement for personal applicants to obtain an administration guarantee or bond or give a surety.

Unless otherwise directed by a district judge, the papers to lead the grant must be sworn before one of the officers authorised to administer oaths in the Personal Application Department.[27]

(iii) Procedure after an application has been lodged

When an application, whether by a solicitor or in person, has been lodged, any will (or codicil) is photographed and the copy filed for record purposes, and the records are searched to see whether any other grant has

---

[21] *Practice Note* [1975] 1 W.L.R. 662.
[22] Personal applications are governed by the N.-C.P.R. 1987, r. 5. Local probate offices have been set up in Greater London and elsewhere (*post*, pp. 281, 1225).
[23] N.-C.P.R. 1987, r. 5(3).
[24] *Ibid.*
[25] N.-C.P.R. 1987, r. 39.
[26] N.-C.P.R. 1987, r. 5(6).
[27] N.-C.P.R. 1987, r. 5(7).

been made in respect of the same estate or any *caveat* has been entered. The papers are examined and a grant prepared to which a photographic copy of any will or codicil is attached. No grant may be made until a certificate has been received from the registry which maintains the grant index (Leeds) that no other application has been made and there is no other impediment to the grant's issue. The grant is signed by a District Judge, or a Probate Officer, authorised in that respect by the President of the Family Division, and sealed with the seal of the Family Division. A photographic copy of the grant is filed for record purposes.

Grants are sent by post unless the application has been made by a law agent on behalf of a solicitor. A grant is regarded as issuing at 10 a.m. on the day for which it has been dated.

2. Applications at a district registry or sub-registry

Where the application is made by a solicitor he may attend at the district registry or send the appropriate papers by post. Personal application may also be made in much the same way as at the principal registry.[28]

The procedure after papers have been lodged is similar to that at the principal registry. No grant can be made at a district registry until a certificate has been received from the registry which maintains the grant index (Leeds) that no other application has been made and that there is no *caveat* or other impediment to the grant's issue.[29] On this certificate being received the grant is issued and a photographic copy thereof and of any will is sent to the principal registry. A calendar of every grant issued in England and Wales each year can be inspected at a district registry.[30] The practice as regards the papers to be lodged is similar to that at the principal registry.

Appeal from a district registrar is by summons to a judge in any non-contentious matter, including refusal to make a grant.[31]

C. GENERAL PRACTICE AS TO GRANTS

Having considered the particular practice in obtaining grants at the principal registry and at district registries it is now proposed to consider the general practice as to grants.

Expediting grants

The issue of grants may be expedited where circumstances justify it; but it must be shown that hardship would result if expedition were not granted.[32] An affidavit is not required but the registrar must be apprised of the grounds for expedition.

---

[28] N.-C.P.R. 1987, r. 5(1).
[29] See the N.-C.P.R. 1987, r. 57, (*post*, p. 1247).
[30] Supreme Court Act 1981, s.111.
[31] N.-C.P.R. 1987, r. 65, (*post*, p. 1248).
[32] Secretary's Circular, November 13, 1951.

Stamp Duty

Where an original instrument has to be produced and adjudication for stamp duty is likely to delay the issue of a grant the procedure can be expedited by giving an undertaking to the controller to re-submit the instrument for adjudication after the grant has issued.[33]

Issue of grants

As already stated, grants are sent by post or through the document exchange unless arrangements are made for their collection.

Where two applications are lodged in the same estate, and one applicant opposes the application of the other, each being equally entitled, a summons to a registrar is necessary.[34]

Where, after papers have been lodged by a solicitor, the conduct of the matter is transferred to another solicitor, there must be lodged a letter of consent by the solicitor who lodged the papers and an authority for the new solicitor to act.

Errors in grants

Where a grant, after passing the seal, is found to be defective through an official error, it should be returned to the registry for correction by rewriting, within 14 days, provided it has not been registered. In all other cases the correction is made by order of a registrar.[35]

Death of the grantee before the official issue of the grant

A grant sealed after the death of the grantee is a nullity. Where the death occurs on the date of the grant, the registrar may require an affidavit in order that he may decide whether to exercise his discretion to revoke the grant.[36] If the registry is notified of the death on the day the grant issues, the document is unofficially destroyed and the records of it are expunged. Otherwise revocation of the grant is necessary.[37]

Notice to the Crown of application for a grant

In any case in which it appears that the Crown is or might be beneficially interested in the estate, notice of the intended application for a grant must be given to the Treasury Solicitor, and the registrar may direct that no grant shall issue within 28 days after such notice has been given.[38]

---

[33] *Practice Direction* [1978] 1 W.L.R. 430.

[34] N.-C.P.R. 1987, r. 27(6).

[35] *Registrar's Direction*, November 14, 1940.

[36] *i.e.* under the N.-C.P.R. 1987, r. 41, *Registrar's Direction*, June 19, 1975. And see *Re Seaford* [1968] P. 53.

[37] *Registrar's Direction*, June 18, 1951.

[38] N.-C.P.R. 1987, r. 38. See *ante*, p. 1238.

Copy grants

An executor or administrator may obtain copies of the grant sealed with the seal of the registry on payment of the appropriate fee. Such copies are useful in expediting the registration of the grant. Application for copy grants may be made with the application for the grant or at any time thereafter. Sealed copies are accepted as evidence of the grant in all parts of the United Kingdom without further proof.[39]

Fees payable on issue of grant

With the exceptions hereafter dealt with, no fee is payable where the asset value of the estate does not exceed £10,000; a fee of £40 is payable where the net estate exceeds £10,000 but does not exceed £25,000; £80 where the net estate exceeds £25,000 but does not exceed £40,000; £150 where the net estate exceeds £40,000 but does not exceed £70,000; £215 where the net estate exceeds £70,000 but does not exceed £100,000; £300 where the net estate exceeds £100,000 but does not exceed £200,000; and where the net estate exceeds £200,000, £300 plus £50 for each additional £100,000 or part thereof.[40]

Fees on grants are paid by cash or cheque. At the principal registry payment is shown by a machine imprint on a fee sheet.

Where an application is abandoned and later renewed, the registrar has a discretion to reduce or remit the fee.[41] Normally half the fee may be remitted.

Probate fees are payable on the net estate, including reversionary interests.

Gratuities to the personal representatives of civil servants are exempt from fees.[42]

In addition a fee, the departmental fee, is payable on personal applications. This fee is: net estate not more than £500—£1; net estate not more than £1,000—£2; net estate not more than £5,000—£5 and if the net estate exceeds £5,000, £1 for every £1,000 or part thereof.[43]

Fees where a member of the armed forces died on service

In relation to a member of any of the armed services or certain associated persons dying after March 12, 1975, no capital transfer tax or inheritance tax is payable by reason of his death if it is certified by the Defence Council or the Secretary of State that he died from a wound inflicted, accident occurring or disease contracted while he was on active service or other service of a warlike nature.[44] In such circumstances a fixed fee of £2 is charged.[45]

---

[39] Supreme Court Act 1981, s.132.
[40] See the Non-Contentious Probate Fees Order 1981 (*post*, p. 1271); Practice Direction [1981] 1 W.L.R. 1185.
[41] Non-Contentious Probate Fees Order 1981, para. 5(3).
[42] Non-Contentious Probate Fees Order 1981, para. 4.
[43] *Ibid.*, fee 2.
[44] Finance Act 1975, Sched. 7, para. 1(1).
[45] Non-Contentious Probate Fees Order 1981, fee 3.

Papers to be lodged on application for a grant

With every application for a grant there must be lodged an Oath and, unless the estate qualifies as an "excepted estate,"[46] an Inland Revenue account. In the case of administration (with or without the will) a guarantee is not now required.[47]

A registrar will not allow a grant to issue until all inquiries he may see fit to make have been answered.[48] In particular cases affidavits are always required, in others the circumstances of the case may make affidavits necessary. Other documents are necessary in cases of a particular type or may be required in special circumstances to support the averments in the Oath. These requirements are dealt with *passim* in this work.

D. THE OATH

Every executor or administrator is required to swear or affirm a document known as the Oath. Although certain matters in the Oath are laid down by rule,[49] there are a number of other matters which under the practice must be covered in the Oath. Because of this the Oath may be submitted in draft for settling by the registry.

The Oath must cover the following matters:

1. The name, address and description of the deponent

The true full name of the deponent must be given. Where the name of an executor applicant has been wrongly given or misspelt in the will, the Oath corrects this by reciting *e.g.* "William Bailey (in the Will and usually known as Bill Bailey)." Where the misspelling is minor, *e.g.* "Brown" for "Browne," or where a second forename has been omitted no further evidence of identity is usually required, but where a wrong surname or first forename is given or where the description might apply to some other person, *e.g.* "Mr. Green" a statement in the Oath or a separate affidavit may be required.[50] The grant will issue in the correct name.

Where the will merely appoints "my husband" or "my wife" as executor, the Oath must state that the deponent is the lawful husband or wife or the testator/testatrix at the date of the will. If the executor has changed his name from that given in the will, he should show that that name was formerly his. Any deed poll which changed the name should be referred to and produced; otherwise he should set out when the change of use took place, that he has abandoned the name given in the will and now uses his current name. An executrix who has married or married again gives her

---

[46] Capital Transfer Tax (Delivery of Accounts) Regulations 1981 (as amended).
[47] See *post*, p. 291.
[48] N.-C.P.R. 1987, r. 6(1) (*post*, p. 1226).
[49] N.-C.P.R. 1987, r. 8. See also *Practice Direction, (Fam D) (Probate: Oath)* [1988] 1 W.L.R. 610.
[50] See the N.-C.P.R. 1987, r. 6(1). See *post*, p. 1226.

present description and her former name and description, *e.g.* "Jane White, wife of John White, formerly Jane Grey, spinster."

The address given must be the true place of residence and, except in special circumstances, a business or accommodation address or a club is not accepted unless the Oath or a certificate from a solicitor establishes that the deponent has no permanent or better address.[51] A professional person *e.g.* a solicitor or accountant who is an executor may, however, give his professional address.[52] The address of an executor given in the will is not mentioned in the Oath except to establish identity, *e.g.* "Mr. Black of The Orchard, Littley."

The deponent, if male, must give his occupation; if female, her status, or, where she has one, her profession or occupation.[53] A retired man gives his former occupation and adds "retired." The expression "of no occupation" is permitted[54] and so is "Knight," "Peer of the Realm,"[55] etc., but not such expressions as "of independent means," "gentleman or esquire." The wife of a baronet is strictly described as "Dame," but "Lady," the correct title of the wife of a knight, is accepted except where she has a higher title in her own right[56] or by courtesy.

2. The name, address, age and description of the deceased

The Oath gives the true name of the deceased and, where he used an alias, he should be described as "AB otherwise YZ." The grant is made in the true name of the deceased, but an alias may be added for special reason, *e.g.* some part of the estate was held in another name or that the will was executed in the alias name.[57] The Oath explains the position as to an alias.[58] Change of name is explained *mutatis mutandis*, as in the case of a change of name by an applicant.[59]

Where the heading in the will gives the true name of the testator but the signature gives merely one forename or one of his initials, no alias is necessary in ordinary circumstances. But if the names or initials differ, except in minor respects, from the name in the heading, an alias is necessary.[60] The Oath must state specifically which is the true name,[61] but alternatively, an affidavit of alias may be sworn.

Where the deceased is described in the will as "the elder" but has not so signed the will, such description is not inserted in the grant, but the reverse is the case where he is described as "the younger."

---

[51] *Registrar's Direction*, July 22, 1941.
[52] Rules of the Supreme Court, Ord. 41, r. 1(4).
[53] Secretary's Circular, May 12, 1967.
[54] *Registrar's Direction*, May 26, 1936.
[55] *Registrar's Direction*, December 8, 1936.
[56] Secretary's Circular, March 2, 1955.
[57] N.-C.P.R. 1987, r. 9. See *post*, p. 1227.
[58] *Ibid.*
[59] See previous paragraph.
[60] *Registrar's Direction*, March 27, 1931.
[61] *Ibid.*

The same rules as to the address of the deceased apply as in the case of a deponent. Where the deceased's last address was other than that given in his last testamentary instrument, the Oath shows that he was formerly of that address or that the address was a temporary one. Where the address of the deceased is uncertain, the best address that is known should be given and, unless a registrar otherwise directs, it should be sworn that no better address can be given; and the domicile of the deceased must be sworn to.[62] Unless it is specifically requested only the last address of the deceased will appear in the grant. If good reason can be shown a former address may be included, or a second address, if this is relevant.

If it is sought to have set out in the grant more than the last address of the deceased and that set out in his last testamentary instrument, a written request for the addition of any other address must be lodged; but not more than four addresses will be allowed in the grant.[63] The age of the deceased must be given. Where it is not known the best estimate must be given.[64]

The rules applying to the description of the deponent[65] apply to the description of a testator.

3. The date of death of the deceased

Where known, the precise date of death must be given in the Oath. If the fact of death is known but the exact date is not, the Oath states when the deceased was last seen alive or last known to be alive and when his body was found.[66] Where leave has been obtained to swear the death, the Oath states that the deceased died on or since the date when he was last known to be alive and gives particulars of the order made.

The date of death given in a grant is not prima facie evidence of death.[67]

Evidence of death

In the case of the armed forces of the Crown, the certificate of the Ministry of Defence, giving a specific date of death is sufficient proof and it should be filed with the Oath but may be redelivered on a note of it being made on the Oath.[68] Where a definite date cannot be given or the deceased is "missing believed killed," the certificate must still be lodged for consideration whether a grant can issue or whether application must be made to swear death.

Death certificates issued by the Registrar General of Shipping and Seamen[69] are accepted as proof of death in the case of known death, and also

[62] *Registrar's Direction*, August 1, 1925.
[63] *Registrar's Direction*, January 23, 1939.
[64] *Practice Direction* [1981] 1 W.L.R. 1185.
[65] See previous paragraph.
[66] *Re Long-Sutton* [1912] P. 97.
[67] *Moons* v. *De Bernales* (1826) 1 Rus. 301.
[68] *Registrar's Direction*, July 15, 1943.
[69] Under the Merchant Shipping Act 1970.

in the case of presumed deaths, provided they are properly endorsed.[70] A certified copy of entry in the Marine Register under the Offshore Installations (Logbooks and Registration of Death) Regulations 1972 is also accepted. Certificates of death issued by the Secretary of State for Trade are accepted as proof of death.[71] Certificates of death or presumed death are issued by the Ministry of Defence and the former India Office, Colonial Office and the Commonwealth Relations Office and are accepted. The Senior District Judge has a discretion to accept other certificates of death or presumption of death as sufficient proof.[72]

4. The place of death

Since the place of death is no longer included in the grant, it is not necessary to state it in the Oath.

5. The domicile of the deceased

The Oath must state the domicile of the deceased, unless the registrar otherwise directs.[73] This requirement results from the passing of the Administration of Estates Act 1971 under which a grant in respect of the estate of a person who died domiciled in England and Wales will be recognised in Scotland and Northern Ireland provided the grant contains a note of the domicile.[74]

6. Settled land: Life or minority interest

The Oath must state to the best of the knowledge, information and belief of the deponent whether there was land vested in the deceased which was settled before his death (and not by his will) and which remained settled land notwithstanding his death. On application for a grant of administration with or without will the Oath shall state whether any life or minority interest arises.[75]

7.(1) Orders made in probate actions

If, following a probate action, a will has been pronounced for, an office copy of the order should be lodged with the papers. The wording of any order admitting the will to probate must be followed in referring to it in the Oath.

Where the omission of part of the will from probate has been ordered,[76] a copy of the will omitting that part is lodged together with the order.[77] The fiat is then written officially in the margin of the copy.

---

[70] *Registrar's Direction*, February 1, 1973.
[71] Under Civil Aviation Act 1949, s.55, as amended.
[72] President's Direction, March 19, 1943.
[73] N.-C.P.R. 1987, r.8(2).
[74] Administration of Estates Act 1971, ss.2, 3 and see *post*, p. 1114, 1115.
[75] N.-C.P.R. 1987, r. 8(3) (*post*, p. 1227).
[76] For the circumstances in which part of a will may be omitted, see *post*, p. 314.
[77] *Practice Direction* [1968] 1 W.L.R. 987.

(2) Orders made to rectify a will

If, following an application to rectify a will,[78] the Registrar directs rectification, an engrossment of the will in its rectified form should be lodged
for the registrar's fiat. Applications may be made to rectify where the will
as executed failed to carry out the testator's intentions through clerical
error or failure to understand his instructions.[79]

8. Relationship

In the case of probate it is not necessary to set out the relationship
between the executor and the deceased, except where there would otherwise be ambiguity or doubt. Thus where an executor is referred to merely
as "my husband" or "my son" the Oath should state that the desponent
was the lawful husband or son at the date of the will.

In application for administration on intestacy the will the relationship of
the applicant to the deceased is set out, as it is in those cases in which it is
relevant to give title to apply for grant.

9. Description of executors

The deponent shows that he is the sole executor or one of the executors,
the surviving executor or one of the surviving executors. A woman describes herself as executrix. Where power is reserved to an executor or he
renounces, the executor applying describes himself as one of the executors
of the deceased. Any limitation in the appointment must be mentioned, *e.g.*
that the appointment is for life. An executor for the English estate of the
deceased describes himself as "executor for England." Where an executor
has been appointed on his coming of age the Oath states that he has
"attained the age of 18 years." An executor substituted is so described, but
where an executor for whom another is substituted in the event of his death
applies, he is described as the executor named in the will.[80] This expression
is also used where the codicil cancels the appointment of an executor named
in the will. Where the substitution is to take place in certain eventualities,
the description is "the executor named in the will as therein mentioned."[81]

Where an individual and a non-trust corporation are named executors in
a will, the former recites in the Oath that the latter is a non-trust corporation.

Where partners in a firm of solicitors are appointed executors without
naming them individually, and not all wish to apply, it is sufficient for the
oath to recite that the applicant is or was a partner at the relevant date.[82]
The oath need not now recite that notice of the application has been given
to all the other non-applying partners to whom power is to be reserved.[83]

[78] Administration of Estates Act 1982, s.20 (*post*, p. 1203).
[79] N.-C.P.R. 1987, r. 55 (*post*, p. 1246).
[80] *Registrar's Direction* June 20, 1910.
[81] *Practice Direction*, June 12, 1990.
[82] *Ibid.*, so as to comply with N.-C.P.R. 1987, r. 27(1).
[83] N.-C.P.R. 1987, r. 27(1A), April 25, 1912.

10. Clearing off persons with a prior right to a grant

Executors and administrators who are not primarily entitled to a grant must show in the Oath in what way those with prior rights have been cleared off.[84] On an application for probate, an executor substituted shows that the event in case of which he was substituted has occurred. Where two persons are named as executors but another is substituted if one of them is unwilling to act, power cannot be reserved to the executor with a substitute; he must either take a grant or renounce and so allow the substitute to take a grant.[85]

11. The amount of the estate

The Oath states the gross value of the estate as shown in the Inland Revenue Account, unless the amount is under that for which an Inland Revenue Account is required, in which case this is stated.[86] Where the Capital Taxes Office alters the amount of the estate shown in that account, it is not normally necessary to amend the figure given in the Oath. The statement of provisional figures is considered below.

Where the sole asset of the estate is a claim under the Law Reform (Miscellaneous Provisions) Act 1934 a figure of "nil" as the value of the estate is only permitted if the solicitor applying shows that he cannot give a better estimate. It is usual, however, for an estimate of the ultimate value of the estate to be given.

Where a person died domiciled in England or Wales, the property covered is the estate in the United Kingdom.[87] Where a person died domiciled outside England and Wales, the property covered is the estate in England and Wales. All property which is covered by the grant must be included in the total of the estate, even where it is exempt from inheritance tax as must reversionary interests.

Property not included

The mere fact that property was aggregated with the estate for the purposes of taxation did not make it part of the estate. Thus gifts *inter vivos*, property held on joint tenancy and property passing under a settlement were not included in the amount given in the Oath. Where the deceased had a general power of appointment, the property comprised in it was only included if the power was exercised by will or if it belonged to the deceased's estate in default of appointment.[88] Aggregation does not arise under the legislation affecting inheritance tax.[89]

Payments under the Fatal Accidents Act 1976, or the Fatal Accidents

[84] N.-C.P.R. 1987, r. 8(4).
[85] Senior Registrar's Instruction, November 1962.
[86] See *Practice Direction* [1981] 1 W.L.R. 1185.
[87] *i.e.* England, Wales, Scotland and Northern Ireland. This follows from the Administration of Estates Act 1971, ss.2, 3.
[88] *O'Grady* v. *Wilmot* [1916] 2 A.C. 231.
[89] See generally *ante*, pp. 71 *et seq.*

Acts 1846–1959 are not included, nor are payments under the Social Security Act 1980.

12. Proper Description of Persons Interested on Intestacy

The proper description of the surviving spouse, the issue and other relatives has been laid down[90] and must be followed in the oath.[91] The applicant must show in what way he is entitled to a grant.

13. Minority or life interest on intestacy

The deponent must state whether there is a minority or life interest and whether there was land vested in the deceased which was settled previously to his death and remains settled land notwithstanding his death.[92]

14. True Name

Where the deceased used an alias, the oath must depose to the facts, setting out the true name and showing that some specified part of the estate was held in the other name.[93]

15. Court Orders

Where any decree or order of a judge or registrar has been obtained enabling the application for a grant, *e.g.* under the discretionary powers of the court or giving leave to swear death, particulars of the decree or order must be included in the oath and must be lodged with the papers, as must the supporting papers in *ex parte* applications.

16. Notice to the Treasury Solicitor

Where it appears that the Crown is or may be beneficially interested in the estate, notice must be given by the applicant to the Treasury Solicitor. The registrar may direct that no grant shall issue within 28 days after such notice has been given.[94]

---

[90] President's Direction (Non-Contentious Probate) 1925 and *Registrar's Direction*, July 16, 1951, as amended by *Practice Direction (Probate D.) (Succession Rights: Illegitimate Children)* [1969] 1 W.L.R. 1863 and *Practice Direction (Fam D.) (Probate: Oath)* [1988] 1 W.L.R. 610. In brief the descriptions are:
A husband is described as "the lawful husband," a wife as "the lawful widow" or, if she has remarried, as "the lawful relict." In cases where an accretion is possible the surviving spouse is described as "the only person now entitled to the estate" where such is the case, but where there are no other kin, he is described as "the only person entitled to the estate." Other persons are described as "the son" (etc.) and one of the persons, or "the only person," entitled to share in the estate." Where a person's claim depends on the death of a parent in the lifetime of the deceased, this should be shown. Brothers, etc., should be described as "a brother of the whole, or 'half,' blood of the deceased." Cousins entitled are referred to as "cousins german." Adopted children are described as "the lawful adopted son/daughter etc."
[91] The form of oath used by the Solicitor in the affairs of the Duchy of Cornwall is slightly different.
[92] N.-C.P.R. 1987, r. 8(3).
[93] N.-C.P.R. 1987, r. 9 (*post*, p. 1227).
[94] N.-C.P.R. 1987, r. 38. (See *ante*, p. 1238.)

17. Wills of persons on military service and seamen

Where the deceased died domiciled in England and Wales and it appears the will of the deceased is one for which privilege can be claimed it is admitted to proof on the registrar being satisfied that the will is in the testator's handwriting.[95]

E. THE GUARANTEE

The former general requirement[96] that an administrator give a bond for the due administration of the estate was abolished with effect from January 1, 1972.[97] However, as a condition of granting administration to any person the High Court may require one or more sureties to guarantee that they will make good, within any limit imposed by the court on the total liability of the surety or sureties, any loss which any person interested in the administration of the estate of the deceased may suffer in consequence of a breach by the administrator of his duties as such.[98]

Discretion to Require a Guarantee

This discretion was formerly exercised in the light of rule 38(1) of the Non-Contentious Probate Rules 1954 which provided that a registrar should not require a guarantee except where it was proposed to grant administration to a creditor,[99] a person who might have an interest if there were an accretion,[1] a person who would be entitled if the person beneficially entitled died intestate,[2] an attorney of a person entitled[3] a person taking for the use and benefit of an infant,[4] or an incapable person[5] or to a person resident outside the United Kingdom.[6] Even in these cases a guarantee was not normally required for a trust corporation, a practising solicitor, a Crown Servant acting in his official capacity or the nominee of a public department or local authority.[7] Although rule 38 has been abolished and not repeated in the 1987 rules the discretion continues under the Statute and its exercise must be subject to the right to be heard.[8]

---

[95] N.-C.P.R. 1987, r. 18 and Wills Act 1837, s.11 (p. 1089, *post*).
[96] See the 15th edition of this work.
[97] Administration of Estates Act 1971, ss.8, 14(2), passed following the recommendation of the Law Commission in its Report on *Administration Bonds, Personal Representatives' Rights of Retainer and Preference, and Related Matters*, Cmnd. 4497 (1970).
[98] Supreme Court Act 1981, s.120.
[99] See N.-C.P.R. 1987, r. 22(3).
[1] See N.-C.P.R. 1854, r. 19(v). The provision for accretions is now contained in N.-C.P.R. 1987, r. 22(3).
[2] See N.-C.P.R. 1954, r. 27.
[3] See N.-C.P.R. 1987, r. 31.
[4] See N.-C.P.R. 1987, r. 32.
[5] See N.-C.P.R. 1987, r. 35.
[6] See N.-C.P.R. 1954, r. 38(1).
[7] See N.-C.P.R. 1954, r. 38(2).
[8] *cf.* N.-C.P.R. 1954, r. 5(4) (Abolished and not repeated).

Exemptions

Section 120(5) of the Supreme Court Act 1981 expressly excludes the Treasury Solicitor, the Official Solicitor, the Public Trustee, the Solicitors for the two Duchies, the Crown Solicitor for Northern Ireland and Consular Officers of the foreign states.

Who might be sureties

Unless the registrar otherwise directed, a surety had to be resident in the United Kingdom.[9] An application for the acceptance of sureties not so resident was made *ex parte* to a registrar. No officer of a registry or sub-registry could become a surety.[10]

A corporation or company might be a surety, but had to file an affidavit by its proper officer to the effect that it had power to act as surety and had executed the guarantee in the manner prescribed by its constitution. The affidavit might contain sufficient information as to its financial position to satisfy the registrar that its assets were sufficient to satisfy all claims which might be made against it under any guarantee which it had given or was likely to give for the purposes of section 167 of the Administration of Estates Act 1971.[11] Instead of making such an affidavit on every occasion, the Senior Registrar might allow a corporation to make it once a year on giving an undertaking to notify any change in its constitution affecting its power to become a surety.[12]

Number of sureties

Unless the registrar otherwise directed, two sureties were required, except that where the proposed surety was a corporation, or where the gross value of the estate did not exceed £500, one would suffice.[13]

Liability of sureties

The guarantee enures for the benefit of every person interested in the administration of the estate and is enforceable by such persons against the surety or sureties as if the guarantee were contained in a contract under seal between them. The liability of two or more sureties is joint and several.[14]

Unless the registrar otherwise directed, the limit of liability of a surety or sureties under a guarantee was the gross amount of the estate as sworn on the application for the grant.[15]

Justification by sureties

Except where the proposed surety was a corporation, or where the regis-

[9] N.-C.P.R. 1954, r. 38(5)(*b*).
[10] N.-C.P.R. 1954, r. 38(5)(*c*).
[11] N.-C.P.R. 1954, r. 38(6).
[12] *Ibid.* proviso.
[13] N.-C.P.R. 1954, r. 38(5)(*a*).
[14] Supreme Court Act 1981, s.120(2).
[15] N.-C.P.R. 1954, r. 38(5)*d*).

trar otherwise directed, every surety must justify,[16] that is, swear an affidavit showing that he was worth in real or personal property the amount of the limit of his liability.

Form and execution of the guarantee

A special form was laid down for the guarantee,[17] and except where the surety was a corporation the signature of the surety must be attested by an authorised officer of a probate registry or sub-registry, commissioner for oaths or other person authorised by law to administer an oath.[18] A corporation must execute the guarantee in the normal manner, by affixing its seal to the guarantee.

Stamp duty is not chargeable on the guarantee.[19]

Enforcement of the guarantee

As already stated, an action may be brought against the surety or sureties by any person interested in the administration of the estate as if the guarantee were contained in a contract under seal between them.[20] However, no action may be brought without the leave of the High Court,[21] which should, unless a registrar otherwise directs under Rule 61, be sought by a summons to a registrar.

Enforcement of administration bonds

Since the passing of the Administration of Estates Act 1971 the former procedure for taking an administration bond from an administrator has been replaced by taking a guarantee from sureties, in the manner described. The Act, however, preserved the right to enforce such a bond given before the commencement of the Act.[22]

For a detailed consideration of administration bonds, reference should be made to the fifteenth edition of this work. Generally, however, an administrator was required to give a bond, in double the amount of the gross estate for the due administration thereof. As a rule, two sureties to the bond were required.

Where the condition of an administration bond has, prima facie, been broken, the court has power to assign the bond (even after administration is complete), and the assignee may then sue upon it in his own name as if it had been originally given to him, and may recover thereon, as trustee, for all persons interested, the full amount recoverable in respect of the breach

---

[16] N.-C.P.R. 1854, r. 38(5)(e).
[17] N.-C.P.R. 1954, r. 38(3).
[18] N.-C.P.R. 1954, r. 38(4), r. 2(2).
[19] Supreme Court Act 1981, s.120(4).
[20] Supreme Court Act 1981, s.120(2).
[21] Supreme Court Act 1981, s.120(3) N.-C.P.R. 1987, r. 40, *post*, p. 1239).
[22] Administration of Estates Act 1971, s.12(5). The Act commenced on January 1, 1972.

of the condition.[23] The assignee brings the action to recover in the Queen's Bench Division.

Where a person interested in the estate believes that a condition of the bond has been broken by the administrator, *e.g.* that the administrator has converted any part of the estate to which he was not entitled to his own use, he may apply by summons to a registrar of the Principal Registry for the bond to be assigned to himself or some other person whom he must name.[24] The summons must be supported by an affidavit setting up the breach complained of and the facts of the case. It must be served on the administrator and on every surety.[25]

The order, if made, is itself the assignment of the bond. Where an order is made, the usual order is that the costs shall follow those in the subsequent action in the Queen's Bench Division, for that is where the substantive issue is decided.

When assignment will not be ordered

An application for the assignment of a bond may be resisted by showing that there has been no breach of any condition. It may be shown that the breach has been consented to by those interested in the estate. A notice under section 27 of the Trustee Act 1925 by the administrator will protect the sureties from liability for the acts of an administrator which are protected by such notice.[26]

It has been held that a registrar has a discretion to refuse to assign a bond.[27] But where there has been a breach of the bond which has not been consented to, it is doubtful whether such a discretion exists. The substantive issue is not a matter for a registrar but for a judge of the Queen's Bench Division.[28]

THE INLAND REVENUE ACCOUNT[29]

Unless the estate is an excepted estate there must be lodged a document, known as the Inland Revenue Account, setting out particulars of the estate of the deceased.[30] In the case of applications for letters of administration,

---

[23] Supreme Court Act 1981, s.120 and 1925 s.167, as originally enacted and amended by the Administration of Justice Act 1928, s.19 and Sched. 1.

[24] Former N.-C.P.R. 1954, r. 38(8).

[25] *Ibid.*

[26] See *Newton* v. *Sherry* (1876) 1 C.P.D. 246 and *post*, p. 605.

[27] *In the Estate of Weiss* [1962] P. 136. See also *post*, p. 319.

[28] See *Harvell* v. *Foster* [1954] 2 Q.B. 368 (C.A.). This decision was not cited in *In the Estate of Weiss*, *supra*. As to attorney administrators, see *post*, pp. 319, 937.

[29] To be "excepted" the estate must not exceed £125,000, it must comprise only property which passes by will or intestacy, there must be not more than £15,000 value outside the United Kingdom and the deceased must have died domiciled in the U.K. having made no lifetime chargeable transfer. See S.I. 1981 No. 880; S.I. 1983 No. 1039; S.I. 1987 No. 1128 and S.I. 1990 No. 1110.

[30] In the case of a death occurring before March 13, 1975, a sworn Inland Revenue affidavit is required. In such cases, see the 15th edition of this work. See Supreme Court Act 1981, s.109 and Inheritance Act 1984, s.216.

with or without the will, by the Treasury Solicitor or the solicitors for the Duchies of Lancaster and Cornwall a statement is lodged in lieu of an oath to lead the grant. As in other cases an Inland Revenue Account must be delivered.[31]

This topic has already been mentioned,[32] but an adequate exposition of the considerations to be borne in mind when an Inland Revenue Account is to be settled is beyond the scope of this work and reference should be made to the specialised books[33] on inheritance tax.

Necessity for the account

Payment of inheritance tax is a condition precedent to the issue of a grant of representation.[34] The representative of the deceased must specify, in appropriate accounts annexed to the account, all the property in respect of which tax is payable on the death of the deceased, and he is accountable for such tax.[35]

Statement of provisional figures

A testator cannot prevent the swearing of a full Inland Revenue account by a direction in his will.[36]

Only in exceptional cases and with the concurrence of the Capital Taxes Office will an amount "so far as can at present be ascertained" be allowed to be sworn to, and this must not be merely a nominal figure.

To this rule there are two exceptions, (i) where the personal representative does not know the amount or value of certain assets of the deceased he may swear that such assets exist, that he does not know the value and that he undertakes as soon as this has been ascertained to deliver a further account and to pay any further tax to which he may be liable[37]; (ii) tax on an interest in expectancy may, at the option of the person accountable, be paid either with the tax then payable or when it falls into possession.[38]

Where the raising of the full tax at once would cause excessive sacrifice, the Commissioners of Inland Revenue may allow a postponement of all or part of the payment. Application for such postponement is made to the Capital Taxes Office.

Forms of account

There are now four main forms of Inland Revenue account which are

[31] See the Administration of Estates Act 1925, s.30(3), (*post*, p. 1126). N.-C.P.R. 1987 r. 42. (*post* p. 1239) *Practice Direction (Fam D) (Probate: Representation Grant)* [1981] 1 W.L.R. 1185.
[32] See *ante*, p. 73.
[33] See *Encyclopaedia of Capital Taxation*, para. 2A–079.
[34] Supreme Court Act 1981, s.109, p. 1195, *post.*
[35] See the Finance Act 1975, s.12, *I.R.C.* v. *Stype* [1985] 1 W.L.R. 1290. As to accountability for capital transfer tax/inheritance tax, see *ante*, pp. 73, 289 *et seq.*
[36] *Re Beech, The Times*, August 9, 1904.
[37] Finance Act 1975, Sched. 4, para. (2)(2)(*a*).
[38] *Ibid.* Sched. 4, para. 13.

current: IHT Forms 200, 201, 202 and A–5C. The first is used on application for an original grant where the deceased died domiciled in some part of the United Kingdom on or after March 27, 1981; the second for an original grant where the deceased died domiciled outside the United Kingdom on or after March 27, 1981; the third for an original grant where the deceased died on or after March 27, 1981, domiciled in the United Kingdom and left gross estate in the United Kingdom not exceeding the contempory threshold at which tax becomes payable; the fourth for a grant *de bonis non*, of double probate or a *cessate* grant. These forms are obtainable from the Capital Taxes Office and most head post offices. An explanatory booklet for completion of IHT Forms 200 and 201 is also obtainable.

Examination of the account

The Inland Revenue Account is not generally examined until after the grant has issued. However, the account should be sent to the Capital Taxes Office for examination and assessment where either the deceased died domiciled outside the United Kingdom or exemption from tax is claimed in respect of property of special historic, scientific or national interest; or payment of tax is to be made from a National Savings Bank account, National Savings Certificates or Premium Savings Bonds; or the grant is to be one of *de bonis non*, double probate, or *cessate* or in respect of settled land, or in respect of assets transferred to this country from abroad since the death of the deceased and the deceased was domiciled outside Great Britain and left no estate in Great Britain.

Certificate of delivery of the affidavit

Where the deceased died before March 13, 1975, the grant will bear an endorsement as to the delivery of the Inland Revenue Affidavit and payment of duty.[39] No such endorsement is made in respect of Inland Revenue Accounts and tax where death occurred on or after March 13, 1975.

Corrective accounts

Where further estate is discovered or a correction is required for other reasons in the figures already included, a corrective account, form D–3, is completed. This form should be forwarded to the Capital Taxes Office for assessment.

---

[39] See the Customs and Inland Revenue Act 1881, s.30, and the N.-C.P.R. 1987, r. 42; 1239 *post*.

CHAPTER 22

GRANTS WHERE THE DECEASED DIED DOMICILED ABROAD

Property in England

Where the deceased dies domiciled abroad leaving property in England, special rules govern the making of grants in respect of that property.[1] To some extent grants are made to the persons to whom they have been made or would be made by the law of the domicile of the deceased, but there are important exceptions.

Reciprocal Recognition of United Kingdom Grants

Under the provisions of the Administration of Estates Act 1971, Scottish confirmations and Northern Ireland grants for the estates of persons dying domiciled in Scotland and Northern Ireland respectively may be recognised under English law without the necessity for a separate grant in this country or for resealing, provided that they contain a notation of the domicile. Reference should be made to the chapter in this work dealing with resealing and reciprocal recognition of grants.[2]

Limits to the application of foreign law

As already shown, where the whole or substantially the whole estate of the deceased in England and Wales consists of immovables, the grant is made according to the law applicable as if the deceased had died domiciled in England.[3] In the case of movable property the court has power to override the person entrusted with administration by the court of the domicile or the person beneficially entitled to share in the estate by that law and to make the grant to others.[4]

Although a foreign court has made a grant to an infant, the English court will not do so,[5] since by English law an infant is incapable of administering an estate. Where there is a minority or life interest, the grant here will not necessarily be made to a single individual though entrusted to such by the court of the domicile.[6] In no case will a grant be made to more than four persons.[7] Where a grant was made abroad to nominees of a person entitled

---

[1] N.-C.P.R. 1987, r. 30 (*post*, p. 1234). See also Pugh, *Administration of Foreign Estates*.
[2] *Post*, p. 368.
[3] N.-C.P.R. 1987, r. 30(3)(*b*); See *Re Collens* [1986] Ch. 505; [1988] *Conveyancer* 30.
[4] N.-C.P.R. 1987, r. 30(1)(*c*).
[5] *Re Duchess D'Orleans* (1859) 1 Sw. & Tr. 253; *Re Meatyard* [1903] P. 125, 129.
[6] Because of the provisions of the Supreme Court Act 1981, s.114(2) (*post*, p. 1196).
[7] Because of the Supreme Court Act 1981, s.114(1).

by her consent, the court in England refused to make a grant without her further consent.[8]

Where a limited grant has been made by the court of the domicile, the English court has made a general grant.[9] But where the limitation is as to time, a similar limitation will be made here, provided the registrar is satisfied that the grant is required for the collection of the English assets, that this can be done in the time limited, and that there are no debts.[10]

Where the will of a person who dies domiciled abroad consists wholly or partly of movables in England and Wales, it will be admissible to probate (i) if its validity can be established in accordance with the Wills Act 1963,[11] (ii) where, in cases where it is still applicable, the Wills Act 1861 (Lord Kingsdown's Act) operates to make the will valid.[12]

The English court will admit testamentary documents to proof in spite of the fact that they are not strictly wills in the English sense, provided that they have been admitted by the court of the domicile[13] or would be recognised by such court.[14]

Grants to executors

Where the will of a testator who died domiciled abroad is admissible to proof under section 1 of the Wills Act 1963 and is in English or Welsh, probate may be granted to the executor named therein.[15] The grant may be made to the executor or his attorney and no order therefor is required.

Where the will is in English and executed in the manner of a will under section 9 of the Wills Act 1837, it will normally be accepted as duly executed if the deceased was domiciled in Northern Ireland, the Republic of Ireland, any state of Australia (including Tasmania), Canada or New Zealand.[16] Similar principles apply where questions of foreign law are relevant in considering whether the will is valid by virtue of the provisions of the Wills Act 1863. In other cases an affidavit of law is required unless the registrar is satisfied by other evidence.[17]

The oath must contain a statement as to the place of domicile of the deceased. The grant will only cover the estate of the deceased in England and Wales.

Grants to executors according to the tenor

If a will in English or Welsh is in such terms as would, by English law,[18]

---

[8] *Re Weaver* (1866) 36 L.J.P. & M. 41.
[9] *Re Levy* [1908] P. 108.
[10] *Registrar's Direction*, November 20, 1972.
[11] For the Wills Act 1963, see *ante*, pp. 151 *et seq.*
[12] For the Wills Act 1861, see *ante*, pp. 149 *et seq.*
[13] *Re Oldenburg* (1884) 9 P.D. 234 (an *acte definitif*).
[14] *Re Queen Marie of Roumania* [1950] W.N. 457 (an *acte de partage*).
[15] N.-C.P.R. 1987, r. 30(3)(*a*)(i). See also *Redwood Music Ltd.* v. *B. Feldman & Co. Ltd.* [1979] R.P.C. 1.
[16] *Registrar's Direction*, November 20, 1972.
[17] See *post*, p. 301.
[18] *Re Cosnahan* (1866) L.R. 1 P. & D. 183; *Re Earl* (1867) L.R. 1 P. & D. 450.

constitute a person named therein executor according to the tenor, such person may obtain probate thereof in that capacity either personally or by his attorney.[19]

Where the will is in a language other than English or Welsh, even the most express words will not constitute him executor. But if the will names an executor or refers to him in such terms as would constitute him an executor according to the tenor by English law, a grant may be made to him in the latter capacity.[20] No order for a grant is necessary and the procedure is as set out in the preceding paragraph.

Where a foreign corporation has been appointed executor, it may appoint an attorney to take a grant for its use and benefit, unless some person has been entrusted with administration by the court of the domicile and has already applied for an English grant.[21]

The renunciation of probate by an executor elsewhere does not deprive him of his right to probate in England. Unless he specifically renounces probate in England, he may take a grant in England, and, where an executor who has not renounced does not apply for a grant in England, power to do so must be reserved to him.

Grants of administration

Except as set out above, probate is not granted where the deceased died domiciled abroad. In all other cases the grant is of administration with or without the will, as the case may be, and the normal rules of priority do not apply.[22] Such grants are made, (a) to the person entrusted with the administration of the estate by the court of the deceased's domicile, or (b) where there is no person so entrusted, to the person beneficially entitled to the estate by the law of the place where the deceased died domiciled or if there is more than one person so entitled to such of them as the registrar may direct; or (c) if in the opinion of the registrar the circumstances so require, to such a person as he shall direct.[23]

(a) *Grant to the person entrusted by the court of the domicile*

A person entrusted by the court of the domicile who applies for a grant, whether directly or through an attorney, takes precedence over all others and it is not necessary for him to clear off an executor.[24] But an executor may obtain probate in spite of the fact that the court of the domicile has entrusted some other person with the administration of the estate, provided that he is not disentitled by the law of the domicile. Where the same person is both an executor and the person entrusted he may obtain a grant in either capacity.

[19] N.-C.P.R. 1987, r. 30(3)(*a*)(ii).
[20] *Ibid.* As to executors by the tenor, see *ante*, p. 29.
[21] *Registrar's Direction*, November 20, 1972.
[22] N.-C.P.R. 1987, r. 28(2).
[23] N.-C.P.R. 1987, r. 30(1).
[24] *Registrar's Direction*, November 20, 1972.

To qualify as a person entrusted by the court of the domicile, the applicant must have obtained a grant, decree or order of that court conferring upon him virtually the same authority as is possessed by an English personal representative.[25] Thus the mere declaration by such court as to who are the heirs of the deceased is not sufficient. Cases of doubt should be put before the registrar for his decision on the point.

A registrar's order must be obtained in all cases. A district registrar may make the order.[26]

Where a will has been proved abroad, probate of any codicils must be granted by the court of the domicile before they can be admitted to probate here.[27]

The grant is made to the applicant as the person entrusted by the court of the domicile no matter who he is or on what ground he has been clothed with that power, and not on the basis of any right to a grant he would have had if the deceased had been domiciled in England and Wales.[28]

(b) *Grant to a person beneficially entitled to the estate by the law of the place of domicile*

Any person(s) beneficially entitled to share the estate of the deceased by the law of the place where he died domiciled may apply for an order for a grant[29] either directly or through an attorney where there is no person entrusted with the administration by the court of the place of domicile.

The affidavit of law or notarial certificate or act[30] which must accompany the application recites the facts of the case and shows that the applicant is a person or one of the persons beneficially entitled to the estate by the law of the domicile. The affidavit should show the validity of any will and the admissibility of any copy will produced. The applicant for the grant or other suitable person must set out the facts in the oath or in an affidavit.[31]

(c) *Grants made in the discretion of a registrar*

Where there is no person entrusted with administration by the court of the country domicile of the deceased and no person is beneficially entitled to the estate by that law (which is unlikely) the registrar may make an order for a grant to such person as he thinks fit.[32] Such order may also be

---

[25] A Scottish judicial factor does not have this authority. Since January 1, 1974, grants of probate and letters of administration under the Law of Sri Lanka are issued by the Public Trustee and not by a court, and it is therefore thought that such grants would not entitle a person to a grant by virtue of the N.-C.P.R. 1987, r. 30. Orders to Administer in favour of the Public Trustee of New Zealand, Western Australia, Victoria, Tasmania and the Public Curator of New Zealand may be treated as entrusting these officials: Registrar's Direction, November 20, 1972; Secretary's Circular, January 29, 1975.

[26] N.-C.P.R. 1987, r. 30.

[27] *Re Miller* (1883) 8 P.D. 167.

[28] *Re Humphries* [1934] P. 78.

[29] N.-C.P.R. 1987, r. 30(1)(*b*).

[30] N.-C.P.R. 1987, r. 19.

[31] *Registrar's Direction*, November 20, 1972.

[32] N.-C.P.R. 1987 r. 30(1)(*c*).

made, if special circumstances require it, to a person other than the person
entrusted with administration by the court of the country of the domicile.

The most usual reason for applying for this order is that the deceased has
died in a country where a grant of administration is required but, because
there is no estate there, it is not desired to take out a grant in that place.
Where there are difficulties of administration a person with prior entitlement may be passed over, but otherwise this provision is rarely needed
because there is inevitably a person beneficially interested.

In effect rule 30(1)(c) in foreign domicile applications equates with section 116 of the Supreme Court Act 1981 for English and Welsh domiciles.[33]

Death before 1926

Where the death took place before 1926, the applicant may still take a
grant as if the deceased had died domiciled in England and Wales.[34] But he
may also take a grant under the present rule.[35]

Practice where the deceased died domiciled abroad

1. *Affidavits of foreign law*

In non-contentious applications, evidence of foreign law is given either
on affidavit or by certificate by or act before a notary practising in the
country or territory concerned.[36] The affidavit of any person may be
accepted whom, having regard to the particulars of knowledge or experience given in the affidavit, the registrar regards as suitably qualified to give
such evidence.[37]

There is no automatic bar on the acceptance of an affidavit of law made
by the person claiming to be entitled to the grant or his attorney or the
spouse of either. The acceptability of an affidavit of law made by any such
person is a matter for the decision of the registrar in the light of the circumstances of each particular case.[38]

2. *Translations of wills*

Translations of wills in the Welsh language can be made by an official of
the Probate Registry of Wales. If the applicant lodges a notarial translation
or one verified by the affidavit of a qualified private individual, such will be
accepted.[39]

In other cases the translation should be notarial or one certified by a
British consul. Other translations may be accepted at the discretion of the
registrar, but the translator must file an affidavit showing his qualifications.

---

[33] For applications under s.116 see p. 343 *post.*
[34] By virtue of the N.-C.P.R. 1987, r. 68 (*post*, p. 1249).
[35] *Registrar's Direction*, June 25, 1956.
[36] N.-C.P.R. 1987, r. 19 (*post*, p. 1230).
[37] *Ibid.*, giving effect to the Civil Evidence Act 1972, s.4(1).
[38] Secretary's Circular, April 26, 1974.
[39] Secretary's Circular, June 16, 1960 (amended October 14, 1974).

Where a will is in English it is often translated into the language of the place of the testator's domicile. Strictly, where the original will is not obtainable, this translation with a re-translation into English is the document to be admitted to probate here in cases where the court abroad has admitted a translation to probate or its equivalent,[40] but, in practice, a photographic or verified copy of the original will is called for. Where this is not produced the registrar may order the re-translation to the checked with the original[41] and may, it seems, correct the re-translation, as may the Chancery Division when construing the will.[42]

Although the probate copy of a foreign will is usually photographic, an engrossment may be ordered if the will contains extraneous matter or is unsuitable for photography.

3. *Papers to be lodged on application for a grant*

When a person entrusted by the court of the deceased's domicile applies, the original decree, order or grant or an officially certified copy is lodged, together with an official copy of the will, if any, with a notarial or other sufficient translation. Guarantees are not now required.

Where the application is by a person beneficially entitled by the law of the deceased's domicile, there must be an affidavit of law setting out briefly the facts of the case and the law applicable to them. The affidavit must show who is beneficially entitled to the estate by the law of the domicile. Subject to the deponent's qualifications an affidavit will be accepted without further inquiry. There must be an affidavit of facts by the applicant or a statement of them in the oath including a statement that there is no person entrusted with administration by the court of the place of domicile,[43] and unless otherwise directed by the registrar the oath must state the place where the deceased died domiciled.[44]

A decree of divorce or nullity pronounced by a court in an overseas country will be recognised if the oath states that the deceased was domiciled in that country at the commencement of the proceedings giving rise to the decree; or either spouse was habitually resident in that country; or either spouse was a national of that country. In all other cases, including a case where it is alleged the decree was obtained by extra-judicial proceedings a full statement of the facts should be submitted to a registrar for decision.[45] Where more than one person is beneficially entitled any or all persons entitled may apply. No grant can be made to more than four persons,[46] but any number may join in appointing an attorney. Where there is

---

[40] *Re Rule* (1878) 4 P.D. 76.
[41] *Registrar's Direction*, November 20, 1972.
[42] See *Re Cliff's Trusts* [1892] 2 Ch. 229; *Re Manners* [1923] 1 Ch. 220.
[43] See *Registrar's Direction*, February 19, 1957.
[44] N.-C.P.R. 1987 r. 8(2) (*post*, p. 1227).
[45] *Registrar's Direction*, December 10, 1971. See also the Family Law Act 1986, s.46.
[46] Supreme Court Act 1981, s.114(1).

a minority or life interest a grant will not be made to a single individual unless it is expedient to do so.[47] Guarantees are not now required.

In applications for a grant in the registrar's discretion, an affidavit of facts must be filed and, if it is sought to obtain a grant here without having taken a grant available in the place of the domicile, the reason must be given. An affidavit of law is required to show who is beneficially entitled to the estate by the law of the domicile and why such person cannot apply. It should establish the validity of the will, if any. The oath is not sworn until after the order is made.

4. *Modes of application for a grant on an order being made*

There are two modes of application. The first is to lodge the papers before the grant application at the registry. If the application is granted the order will be served by post and the oath is then completed reciting details of the order. This mode of application must be adopted where a discretionary grant is sought.

The second mode of application is suitable for cases where application is made under the provisions of rule 30(1)(*a*) or (*b*). The oath and other necessary documents are prepared in advance of the order, the oath itself requesting the order. If the registrar makes an order the grant will be sent out in the normal way.

In all cases of foreign domicile the Inland Revenue Account in Form IHT 201 must be sent for control before the application for the grant and lodged, controlled, with the grant application.

5. *Wills and copies of wills*

Where available, the original will is lodged. Often, however, the original will is in the custody of a foreign court or official and in such case a copy under seal (where a seal is used) and duly authenticated by the official having custody of the original is accepted and no order for the admission to proof of such copy is necessary.[48] If the will has been proved in a foreign court or is held by a foreign official, the fact should be stated in the affidavit of law which should establish the admissibility of the copy lodged.

In the case of Scottish wills the original of a registered will cannot be obtained, but the original of a recorded will is obtainable. Unless it can be established that confirmation has been issued, there must be an affidavit of law.[49]

In the case of Irish wills which were destroyed together with the grants when the Four Courts were burnt, the sealed copy made by the Irish Principal Probate Registry is accepted as proof in England.

In the case of wills recorded in the former India Office, copies under the seal of the Foreign and Commonwealth Office are accepted.[50]

---

[47] Supreme Court Act 1981, s.114(2) (*post*, p. 1196). See also *ante*, p. 235.
[48] N.-C.P.R. 1987, r. 54(2) (*post*, p. 1246).
[49] Secretary's Circular, November 7, 1955, amended November 19, 1956.
[50] *Registrar's Direction*, March 18, 1950, as amended, 1954.

Where wills were proved in the former Supreme Court in China (the British court with extraterritorial powers in China), copies may be obtained from the Treaty and Nationality Department of the Foreign Office and these are accepted in proof.

The surviving spouse of a domiciled Dane may take a grant of administration in that country, notwithstanding any will left by the deceased. In such cases a grant of administration with the will annexed will be made in this country upon a registrar's order to such spouse as the person entrusted by the Danish court or by Danish law, as the case may be.[51]

Where the original will is lost or unobtainable and no official copy is available, the procedure is the same as where the deceased died domiciled in England.[52]

6. *The oath*

Unless otherwise directed by the registrar, the oath must specifically state the place of the domicile,[53] including the state or province where there is a federal system with different laws in different parts of the country; but where the legal system is uniform, it is enough to state the country.[54] The oath covers the English assets only. The oath should describe the applicant as the person entrusted with the administration of the estate by the court having jurisdiction at the place of the domicile of the deceased or as beneficially entitled to it by that law, as the case may be.

Where a discretionary order has been made, the applicant is described in the oath as the person authorised by the order under Non-Contentious Probate Rule 30(1)(c) of which the date is given.[55] Where the oath has been executed before the order, re-execution may be dispensed with if it is so drawn as to give a sufficient title to the grant and not to be inconsistent with the order.[56]

Grants where there is a minority or life interest; grants to a second administrator

Where a single individual has been entrusted with administration by the court of the domicile, but a minority or life interest arises, it is advisable for a trust corporation or two individuals to be appointed attorneys. But if the individual entrusted wishes to apply direct he must do so with a second person, and both should swear the oath, so that the registrar's order may join such second person.[57] This also applies where there is only one person of full age beneficially entitled or the only person beneficially entitled has a life interest in part or all of the estate.

[51] *Registrar's Direction*, November 20, 1972.
[52] See *post*, pp. 316 *et seq.*
[53] N.-C.P.R. 1987, r. 8(2).
[54] *Registrar's Direction*, November 20, 1972.
[55] *Ibid.*
[56] *Registrar's Direction*, November 20, 1972.
[57] See N.-C.P.R. 1987, r. 30(2).

The joinder of a second administrator is not limited to the case above referred to. In any discretionary grant the registrar may appoint two or more persons as administrators.

Replacement of attorney by his principal

Where the grant has been made to an attorney and the person entrusted or beneficially entitled by the law of the domicile later wishes to take a grant himself, he must lodge an affidavit showing that the order entrusting administration is still in force or that he is still beneficially entitled by the law of the domicile; upon which a further registrar's order may be made.[58]

Notice to the Treasury Solicitor

Where the Crown is or may be beneficially interested in the estate, notice of the application must be given to the Treasury Solicitor, whether the deceased died abroad or in England and Wales.[59] Unless there is affirmative evidence that there are successors who, by the law of the domicile, inherit the estate, the consent of the Treasury Solicitor to the making of a grant to the applicant must be produced.[60] The reason for this procedure is that although *bona vacantia* in the place of the domicile may vest in that country, it does not follow that they vest in that country as successors. If the country of the domicile is merely entitled to *bona vacantia* by the equivalent of a *jus regale*, the Crown is entitled to such property in England and Wales.[61]

Miscellaneous

Affidavits of law and oaths to lead grants may be submitted in draft form for prior approval of the Registrar before being sworn. Indeed, it is often advisable to have such documents approved before being sent abroad for swearing as re-submission for re-swearing can be costly.

The Inland Revenue Account must be submitted to and assessed by the Capital Taxes Office, before the application for the grant.[62]

Applications for grants where the deceased died domiciled abroad may be accepted in the Personal Application Department of any registry. However, where there is or may be doubt as to the domicile of the deceased a registrar may decide than an application for a grant is not suitable to be dealt with as a personal application. The Personal Application Department will refer any doubtful case to a registrar for decision.

---

[58] *Registrar's Direction*, November 20, 1972.
[59] N.-C.P.R. 1987, r. 38.
[60] *Registrar's Direction*, November 20, 1972.
[61] See *Re Maldonado* [1954] P. 223; Dicey and Morris, *Conflict of Laws*, 11th ed., p. 1005.
[62] *Registrar's Direction*, November 20, 1972.

CHAPTER 23

APPLICATIONS TO ADMIT WILLS TO PROOF

In this chapter the special matters of practice which apply to an application for probate in common form, and, so far as the will itself is concerned, to letters of administration (with will annexed) are considered. The general practice on obtaining grants has already been considered.[1]

Document to be lodged

In every application for probate or letters of administration (with the will annexed) there must be lodged the Oath, the Inland Revenue Account, where an Account is necessary and, unless they are unobtainable, the original will and any codicils thereto. In certain cases, as shown later, it will be necessary to lodge affidavits and other documents, *e.g.* a translation of a will in a foreign language.

Marking of wills

Every will in respect of which an application for a grant is made must be marked by the signatures of the applicant and the person before whom the Oath is sworn, and is to be exhibited to any affidavit which may be required as to the validity, terms, condition or date of execution of the will; save that if the registrar is satisfied that such marking might result in the loss of the will, he will allow a photographic copy to be marked or exhibited in lieu of the will itself.[2]

Engrossment for the purpose of record

Where the registrar considers that a facsimile copy of the will would not be satisfactory for the purposes of record, he may require an engrossment suitable for facsimile reproduction to be lodged.[3] Where a will contains alterations not admissible to probate or has been ordered to be rectified by virtue of section 20(1) of the Administration of Justice Act 1982, an engrossment of the will in the form in which it is to be proved (a fiat copy) must be lodged.[4] Such engrossments must reproduce the punctuation, spacing and division into paragraphs of the will and, where there are alterations, restore the original wording as far as this is possible. Where it is

---

[1] See *ante*, p. 277 *et seq.* As to caveats see p. 383 *post.*
[2] N.-C.P.R. 1987, r. 10.
[3] N.-C.P.R. 1987, r. 11(1).
[4] *Ibid.* para. (2).

not, a blank space should be left. The engrossment must be made bookwise on durable paper following continuously from page to page on both sides of the paper.[5] As an alternative to a typewritten engrossment, a facsimile copy of the will produced by photography may be lodged where a complete page or pages of the will are to be excluded, where words on the same page below the testator's signature can be masked out, or where the original has been altered but not re-executed or republished and there exists a photo-copy of the original executed document.[6]

Affidavit of due execution

Where a will contains no attestation clause or where that clause is insufficient or where it appears to the registrar that there is some doubt as to due execution, he will require an affidavit of due execution from one or more of the attesting witnesses or, if no attesting witness is conveniently available, from any other person who was present at the execution of the will.[7] If no such affidavit can be obtained the registrar may direct an affidavit from some person who can identify the handwriting of the deceased or which will establish any other matter raising a presumption in favour of due execution.[8] However, where the distribution of the estate is unaffected by proof of the will *i.e.* the distribution is the same under an intestacy or an earlier will, the will may be accepted to proof without any evidence in support of due execution.[9]

Affidavits of due execution are required, *inter alia*, where the testator has signed in the attestation or testimonium clause, where he has signed twice, where he has signed below the witnesses' signatures, or where the signature is in an unusual place on the will.

Such affidavits are not required for minor irregularities, *e.g.* "his or her" in a will form, but major irregularities call for an affidavit of due execution as do wills which raise suspicion that they were not duly executed.[10] An affidavit is not required where witnesses are stated in the will to have "attested" it.[11]

Where an affidavit of due execution is required from a witness abroad, a copy and not the original will may be exhibited, if the registrar so directs[12]

Where evidence of due execution is unobtainable, a will is normally admitted to proof on the filing of an affidavit to show who would be prejudiced by the admission of the will, exhibiting the consents of those persons.

An attesting witness who refuses to make an affidavit of due execution

---

[5] *Ibid.* para. (3).
[6] *Practice Direction* [1979] 3 All E.R. 859.
[7] N.-C.P.R. 1987, r. 12(1).
[8] *Ibid.* para. (2).
[9] *Ibid.* para. (3).
[10] See *Registrar's Direction*, May 31, 1951.
[11] *Re Selby-Bigge* [1950] 1 All E.R. 1009.
[12] N.-C.P.R., r. 10(2).

may be ordered to attend before the court for examination[13] and to pay the costs of such examination.[14]

Affidavits of due execution must not merely state that the will was or was not duly executed; they must give an account of the salient facts in connection with the execution.[15]

Knowledge and approval by the deceased

Before admitting to proof a will which appears to have been signed by a blind or illiterate testator or by another person by direction of the testator, or which for any other reason raises doubt as to the knowledge and approval of the testator, the registrar will satisfy himself as to his matter.[16] He may require affidavit evidence on the point.[17]

Further evidence is not usually required where the attestation clause states that the will was read over to a blind or illiterate testator or where it states that the will was signed by the direction of the testator who appeared to understand the contents.

Possible revocation by the testator

Any appearance of attempted revocation of a will by burning, tearing or otherwise destroying, and every other circumstance leading to a presumption of revocation by the testator, must be accounted for to the registrar's satisfaction.[18] Affidavit evidence is usually required in such a case.

Revocatory instruments

Although an instrument which only revokes a will is not entitled to probate,[19] it must be brought into the registry on an application for a grant. Such an instrument is only relevant to an application for probate when it only partially revokes a will or revokes a later codicil.[20]

A codicil revoked by a later codicil must be proved if it alters the will or an earlier codicil.[21] If it is known that a codicil has been thus revoked but it is not brought in, its production will be called for.[22] Where a revocation of a codicil was by destruction, a copy or reconstruction may be admitted on the order of a registrar. The codicil will be marked "The codicil of which this is a copy/reconstruction was revoked by destruction." The grant is not limited until a more authentic copy is proved.[23]

---

[13] Supreme Court Act 1981, s.122.
[14] Re Sweet [1891] P. 400; Re Bays (1910) 54 S.J. 200; cf. Shepheard v. Beetam (1872) L.R. 2 P.& D. 384.
[15] See the N.-C.P.R. 1987, r.16. See ante, p. 158.
[16] N.-C.P.R. 1987, r. 13. See ante, pp. 158, 230.
[17] N.-C.P.R. 1987, r. 16.
[18] N.-C.P.R 1987, r. 15. See ante p. 124.
[19] Toomer v. Sobinska [1907] P. 106.
[20] Re Sprocklan [1938] 2 All E.R. 345.
[21] President's Direction, March 11, 1943.
[22] Ibid.
[23] Registrar's Direction, July 30, 1940.

Obliterations, interlineations and other alterations

Where any obliteration, interlineation or other alteration is not authenticated in the manner prescribed by section 21 of the Wills Act 1837, or by the re-execution of the will or by a codicil, the registrar will require evidence to show whether the alteration was made before execution and will give directions as to the form in which the will is to be proved, unless the alteration is of no practical importance.[24]

Generally an affidavit is obtained from the attesting witnesses, but occasionally the person who wrote, typed or drafted the will can deal with the matter.

When obliterations, interlineations or other alterations are not admissible to proof, the copy of the will (which omits them) is called the fiat copy and is made in accordance with the registrar's direction. In the old phrase the will is said to "pass in facsimile."

Incorporation of documents

Three main issues arise over the incorporation of documents in a will. The first is a question of construction as to whether the document is or is not to be treated as part of the will. The second is the procedural issue as to whether such a document ought to be included in the probate. The third issue is whether a document physically attached to or associated with the will ought to be included in the grant.

The requirements for a document not itself executed to be treated as part of the will are (1) that it can be strictly identified[25] by extrinsic evidence if necessary,[26] (2) that it was in existence at the date of the will[27] and (3) that it is referred to in the will as an existing document.[28] Thus reference to the scale fees of a trust corporation is inneffective to incorporate such a scale if it is variable in the future.[29]

The inclusion of the document, if properly incorporated, in the probate itself seems to be a matter of discretion and convenience. Thus lengthy documents[30] or trust deeds affecting other people[31] need not be included, but in general it has been said to be desirable that the document should be set out in the probate for the benefit of those interested and so that the registry should know the ultimate destination of the residue in case the chain of representation is broken and it becomes necessary to issue a grant

[24] N.-C.P.R. 1987, r. 14.
[25] *Allen* v. *Maddock* (1858) 11 Moo. P.C. 427; *University College of N. Wales* v. *Taylor* [1908] P. 140, 145.
[26] *Allen* v. *Maddock* (1858) 11 Moo. P.C. 427; *Eyre* v. *Eyre* [1903] P. 131.
[27] *Re Mardon* [1944] P. 109.
[28] *Re Walkins* (1865) 1 P. & D. 19. Extrinsic evidence is not admissible to prove the existence of the document at the date of the will, see *Re Sunderland* (1886) 1 P. & D. 198. As to revival affecting incorporation of documents see *ante*, p. 157.
[29] It seems reliance would have to be placed on the reasonableness of such fees on the same lines as a professional trustee charging clause.
[30] *Sheldon* v. *Sheldon* [1844] 1 Rob. Ecc. 81; *Bizzey* v. *Flight* (1876) 3 Ch.D. 269.
[31] *Re Sibthorp* (1866) L.R. 1 P. & D. 108; *Re Jones* (1920) 36 T.L.R. 294.

for further distribution.[32] In practice it is sometimes convenient for the sake of privacy to leave property in a will to the trustees of a family trust upon the trusts of an existing settlement which is not included in the probate. If incorporation is directed the oath refers to the last will and testament " e.g. contained in the paper writings marked "A" and "B" or "A, 'B' and C" as appropriate.

If from any mark on a will it appears that some other document has been attached to the will, or if a will contains any reference to another document in terms suggesting that it ought to be incorporated, the registrar requires the document to be produced and may call for such evidence about the attaching or incorporation of the document as he may think fit.[33] Marks include those of a pin, paper-clip, fastener, seal or wafer. Where a solicitor is aware that some non-testamentary document was attached to the will his certificate to that effect is normally accepted. In other cases an affidavit of plight and condition may be required, although this is now rarely called for.

Practice

Evidence may be called for, on affidavit if necessary, to establish that the document produced is that referred to in the will. If a document incorporated by the will cannot be found, evidence, which may be directed to be by affidavit, is required to show what searches and inquiries have been made and that they have proved fruitless. The registrar will decide whether an incorporated document is dispositive.[34] A statement in a will indicating an intention to make a disposition by list or memorandum will not require evidence to lead to incorporation, the list/memorandum not existing at the time of the will. However, if a codicil is made which republishes the will at its own date after a list/memorandum was made, the document must be considered for incorporation.

A deed or other document, if short, may be incorporated (though this is not often done), but it is undesirable that part of a deed should be incorporated; in other cases an examined copy of the deed verified on affidavit is filed.[35] Where documents have been lost probate has been granted on the filing of an affidavit which describes the document.[36] Where only part of a document is material, that part only need be lodged.[37]

If a person who has power over the deed will not produce it, the court will grant probate without its production but a copy must be lodged if available.

---

[32] *Ibid.*
[33] N.-C.P.R. 1987, r. 14(3).
[34] *Re Jones* (1920) 123 L.T. 202.
[35] *Registrar's Direction*, July 21, 1936. The Chancery Court has ordered a settlement as varied by the court to be included in the grant: *Re Sibthorp* (1866) L.R. 1 P. & D. 106.
[36] *Re Lansdowne* (1863) 3 Sw. & Tr. 194; *Re Dundas* (1863) 32 L.J.P.M. & A. 165.
[37] *Re Limerick* (1850) 2 Rob.Ecc. 313.

Where a will incorporates a will which has already been proved, probate of that earlier will should be produced for notation.

Incorporation where there is a foreign will

Where an English will incorporates a foreign will, both, or the relevant portion of the foreign will, may be admitted to proof.[38] But a foreign will may be released for proof abroad.[39] If the foreign will is abroad and is not available, a copy will be admitted to proof.[40]

Date of will

Where there is doubt as to the date on which a will was executed, the registrar may require such evidence as he thinks necessary to establish the date.[41] Usually affidavits from the attesting witnesses or other persons present at the execution are required either to establish a definite date or, failing that, as to execution between definite dates.

If no date can be established an affidavit is usually required stating that, in spite of searches, no will has been found which is or might be of a later date.

If the date on the will is wrong or different dates are given, similar affidavits are required, unless in the latter case the discrepancy is slight and unimportant.

Where a codicil misrecites the date of the will or of an earlier codicil, an explanatory affidavit must be filed and an account must be given of the searches and inquiries made for a document of the date misrecited. Where it is clear that there has been a misrecital, the will and the probate copy thereof will be noted with the filing of the affidavit and as to misrecital.

Revival of wills

The question whether a will has been revived is often a difficult one. Except in clear cases the direction of a registrar should be taken.[42]

Application to have probate refused

Where the latest or only testamentary document is invalid and the applicant desires to prove an earlier will or (in applications for administration) that there was no valid will, the document in question may be lodged at the registry. This is often done in connection with the application for a grant to another will but may be done before such application.

If the document is patently invalid, *e.g.* attested by only one witness, no affidavit is required, but if the document is apparently duly executed, affidavit evidence must be filed showing in what respect the will was not so

---

[38] *Re Tamplin* [1894] P. 39.
[39] *Re Todd* [1926] P. 173.
[40] *Re Mercer* (1870) L.R. 2 P. & D. 91; see the N.-C.P.R. 1987, r. 54(2).
[41] N.-C.P.R. 1987 r. 14(4).
[42] As to revival of wills see *ante*, pp. 218 *et seq.*

executed. If the Registrar is satisfied the will was not duly executed he will mark it "Probate Refused."[43]

Generally, a testamentary document will only be marked "Probate Refused" if there has been an attempt to prove it. If it is obviously invalid the solicitor need not lodge it.

Procedure for proving codicils

Any codicils must, in general. be proved with the will, and if a will has been proved in a district registry, the codicil must also be proved in that registry. But where a codicil which does not alter the appointment of executors is in dispute, the will may be proved before the codicil is adjudicated upon if administration of the estate is urgently needed. But this does not empower the executors to distribute the estate, except perhaps to the extent agreed upon by all persons who might be affected. Similarly, a will and codicil may be admitted to probate where the sole contest is as to the validity of another codicil.[44]

Probate has been granted of a will and certain codicils where there were known to be other codicils abroad. It was left to the executors to prove the latter when they should be transmitted to England.[45]

Where a will was not forthcoming at the testator's death, probate of a codicil was granted.[46] And where a will and codicil were not forthcoming, probate was granted of a second codicil.[47] Where a will was revoked by destruction, the court granted probate of the codicil alone.[48]

Separate probate of a codicil

If a codicil has been discovered after a will has been admitted to probate, a separate probate thereof is granted, provided that it does not affect the appointment of executors.[49] If the executor who proved the will is dead, the executor of that person may prove the codicil. But if different executors are appointed by the codicil, the probate of the will must be brought in and revoked.[50] When letters of administration (with the will) have been granted and a codicil is later discovered, the grant must be revoked and a new grant taken out of administration with both will and codicil annexed.

Where a will was proved abroad, a codicil subsequently found was not allowed to be proved in England until proved in the court where probate had been obtained.[51] However in view of the provisions of the Wills Act

---

[43] N.-C.P.R. 1987, r. 12(1).
[44] *Re Day* [1940] 2 All E.R. 544.
[45] *Re Robarts* (1873) L.R. 3 P. & D. 78; *Re Clements* [1892] p. 254.
[46] *Re Savage* (1870) L.R. 2 P. & D. 110.
[47] *Black* v. *Jobling* (1869) L.R. 1 P. & D. 685, see *Gardiner* v. *Courthope* (1886) 12 P.D. 14.
[48] *Re Turner* (1872) L.R. 2 P. & D. 403. As to revocation see *ante*, pp. 360 *et seq.*
[49] *Langdon* v. *Rooke* (1841) 1 N.C. 254.
[50] *See post.*
[51] *Re Miller* (1883) 8 P.D. 167; *Re Crawford* (1890) 15 P.D. 212.

1963 there is reasonable doubt whether this decision would now be followed.

A codicil which has been revoked by a later codicil must be proved if it alters the terms of an earlier will or codicil.[52] If it is known that a codicil has been revoked and it is not brought in, its production will be called for.[53]

Particular kinds of will

The special practice applicable to lost wills[54] joint and mutual wills,[55] conditional wills[56] and duplicate wills[57] is considered under these heads.

Where a will is expressed to be made in contemplation of marriage and that the will is not to be revoked by the marriage the Oath must state that the marriage was duly solemnised and give the date of the ceremony.[58] If the deceased did not contract any marriage, this should be stated.

Where two or more documents together form the sum of the testator's testamentary intentions, all are admitted to probate and are marked "A," "B," etc., and are described as the "true and original last will and testament as contained in the paper writings marked 'A,' 'B,' etc."

Where a testator makes one will relating to his estate in England and another to his estate abroad and these are independent, the English will alone is admitted to probate,[59] but a copy of the other will, which if proved should be a court certified copy, should be lodged.[60]

Where a testator makes one will dealing with his universal estate and another limited to estate in England and Wales it is usual to prove both wills provided they are mutually compatible. It is the practice of the probate registrar to accept to proof all testamentary documents leaving it to the Chancery Division to decide, if necessary, the proper construction.

Wills in a foreign language

The procedure is the same for translations as where a person dies domiciled abroad.[61]

Description of wills in the Oath

All wills and codicils submitted for probate must be described in the Oath and the dates thereof given. Where a lost will is admitted to proof the

---

[52] President's Direction, March 11, 1943.
[53] *Registrar's Direction*, July 30, 1949.
[54] See *post*, p. 316.
[55] See *ante*, p. 128.
[56] See *ante*, p. 124.
[57] See *ante*, p. 124.
[58] Wills Act 1837, s.18 (as substituted by the Administration of Justice Act 1982 with effect from January 1, 1983), pp. 192, 1090.
[59] *Re Astor* (1876) 1 P.D. 150; *Re Callaway* (1890) 15 P.D. 147; *Re De la Rue* (1890) 63 L.T. 253.
[60] *Re Murray* [1896] P. 65, *Re Todd* [1926] P. 173.
[61] See *ante* p. 301.

fact that it is "as contained in a draft thereof" or "as proved by parol evidence," if such is the case, must be deposed to. Where documents are incorporated the will is described "as contained in the paper writings marked 'A' and 'B.' "

Omission of words from probate

Offensive, libellous and blasphemous words

A testator has the right to explain the reasons for his testamentary dispositions, especially where he has made little or no provision for his widow or his dependent children, for the court may have a duty to consider such reasons.[62] But he must not use his will as a vehicle for slander.[63]

The court will exclude from probate words which are of an atrocious, offensive or libellous character,[64] or which are blasphemous. Probate may be refused until an application has been made for such words to be excluded.

But the court will not lightly interfere with a person's testamentary intention and must be fully satisfied that the words complained of come within one of the categories above mentioned.[65] Dispositive words may not be omitted,[66] unless, perhaps, those merely intended to be offensive.[67] Nor will words be omitted which assist in construing the will.[68] Although the words excluded are generally directed against some person or body, the court has ordered the omission of words relating to the testator's funeral and the disposal of his remains which were offensive to his family and might have been reported in the press.[69]

Offensive words may not be expunged from the will itself, but are omitted from the probate copy thereof.[70]

Words not of an offensive nature

The circumstances in which words alleged to have been inserted in a will by mistake may be omitted have already been considered.[71]

Practice

Contested applications for the omission of words must be made by summons to a district judge of the Principal Registry. Such application

---

[62] Both in general and under specific enactments, *e.g.* the Inheritance (Provison for Family and Dependants) Act 1975, s.21.

[63] *Re Hall* [1943] 2 All E.R. 159; *Re T. deceased* (1961) 105 S.J. 325. See 35 *Conveyancer* 303.

[64] *Re Wartnaby* (1846) 4 N.C. 476; *Marsh* v. *Marsh* (1860) 1 Sw. & Tr. 528; *Re White* [1914] P. 153; *Re Bohrmann* [1938] 1 All E.R. 271; but see *Re Rawlings* (1934 78 S.J. 338.

[65] *Curtis* v. *Curtis* (1825) 3 Add. 33; see *Re Caie* (1927) 43 T.L.R. 697.

[66] See also *Re Honywood* (1871) L.R. 2 P. & D. 251; *Beech* v. *Public Trustee* [1923] P. 46.

[67] As (in unreported case) "I bequeath to my butler my cellar key of which he has made such frequent and unauthorised use."

[68] *Re Rawlings* (1934) 78 S.J. 338.

[69] *Re Bowker* [1932] P. 93.

[70] *Re Maxwell* (1929) 140 L.T. 471.

[71] See *ante*, pp. 177 *et seq.*

may be the subject of a probate action in the Chancery Division or may be referred to a judge on summons or to the court on motion.[72] Uncontested applications are made to the registrar of the registry at which it is proposed to apply for the grant. The application is made *ex parte* supported by an affidavit of facts and exhibiting the will and the consent of persons not under a disability who could be prejudiced by the order.[73] With any application for probate is lodged a copy of the order to omit the words complained of, together with a copy of the will omitting those words. The fiat is written in the margin of this copy.[74]

Order of executors in a grant of probate

In the ordinary course executors are named in a grant of probate in the same order as they are mentioned in the will. But where the names appear in a different order in the Oath, that order is followed.

Wills not governed by section 9 of the Wills Act

Although certain of the rules governing the admission of wills to proof in common form[75] do not apply to privileged wills,[76] the terms and validity of other wills, *e.g.* wills valid by the law of the domicile of the deceased, must be established to the registrar's satisfaction.[77]

[72] *Practice Direction* [1968] 1 W.L.R. 987. In this case the application may be self-defeating unless a hearing in private can be ordered under R.S.C., Ord. 33, r. 4.
[73] *Practice Direction* [1968] 1 W.L.R. 987.
[74] *Ibid.*
[75] N.-C.P.R. 1987, rr. 12 to 15 inclusive.
[76] See *ante*, p. 224.
[77] N.-C.P.R. 1987, r. 17.

CHAPTER 24

LIMITED GRANTS

It is often expedient for grants to be limited either in duration, in property or for special purposes. In some cases the order of a registrar or judge is required, but not in others, *e.g.* grants to attorneys or for the use of minors or persons with mental disability. Only by special leave is a person entitled to a general grant permitted to take a limited grant.[1]

The limitations discussed relate to: lost, damaged or unobtainable wills, attorneys,[2] minors,[3] mental disability,[4] incarceration,[5] testamentary limitation,[6] time or place,[7] powers of appointment,[8] married women in certain circumstances,[9] litigation,[10] absence abroad,[11] and preservation of the estate.[12]

A. Lost, Damaged or Unobtainable Wills

Where an original will or codicil is lost, destroyed or damaged, application may be made for an order admitting it to proof as contained in a copy, draft, photostat or in accordance with parol evidence.[13] If the will is lost, the grant made is limited until the original or a more authentic copy is proved.[14]

Where part of a will is missing a copy which reproduces the missing portion will be admitted to probate on lodgment of the surviving portion. Where the writing has become indecipherable the will is admitted to probate in the form of an engrossment containing the words of the original will as they can be best ascertained. This engrossment is endorsed with the registrar's fiat.

---

[1] *Re Von Brentano* [1911] P. 172. As to the liability as *executor de son tort* of a limited administrator who exceeds his powers, see *ante*, p. 319.
[2] *Post*, p. 323.
[3] *Post*, p. 325.
[4] *Post*, p. 327.
[5] *Post*, p. 327.
[6] *Post*, p. 329.
[7] *Post*, p. 330.
[8] *Ante*, p. 114.
[9] *Post*, p. 330.
[10] *Post*, p. 331.
[11] *Post*, p. 331.
[12] *Post*, p. 331.
[13] See N.-C.P.R. 1987, r. 54 (*post*, p. 1246).
[14] The limitation used to be "until the original or a more authentic copy be brought in." The change in practice allows the original grant to stand until a new grant issues and thus avoids a gap in the administration and the difficulties which could arise if the supposedly more authentic copy "brought in" were not ultimately proved.

Procedure where the will is lost, destroyed or damaged

Unless the matter is obviously of such difficulty that it must be heard by a judge on summons or motion, application should be made to the Probate Department of the Principal Registry or district registrar in the first instance.[15] There must be evidence to rebut the presumption that the will, now missing, was revoked by destruction by the deceased in his lifetime.

Where all those who might be prejudiced by the admission to probate of the will are *sui juris* and consent, a registrar, if satisfied as to the facts, may make an order whether the will was destroyed in the lifetime of the testator or after. Where such consent is not available a registrar will make an order in a plain case where the destruction or loss took place after the testator's death. Only in a clear case will a registrar without consent make an order where the will was lost or destroyed in the testator's lifetime.

Where there is opposition to the admission of the will to probate, it should be propounded in an action. Where, although there is no opposition, it is unclear what has happened or where the will may have been destroyed with intent to revoke (*animo revocandi*) the court will hear the matter on motion.

Cases in which a will is to be proved by parol evidence may be referred to a judge.

Applications to the registrar

Applications for the admission to probate of a lost will as contained in a copy, etc., may be made *ex parte* to a registrar.[16]

The affidavit in support must set out the grounds of the application with such evidence as is available as to the due execution of the will, its existence or otherwise after the death, as shown by the efforts made to trace it, and the accuracy of any copy or draft (which must be annexed[17]). The affidavit must show who would be prejudiced by the admission of the will to probate, and the registrar may direct that notice be given to such persons.[18]

Evidence

Declarations, whether oral or in writing, made by the testator before or after the execution of the will are admissible to show the contents of a lost will but declarations made after execution are not admissible as to the fact of execution itself. This must be shown in some other way because of the statutory requirements as to execution.[19] The cogency of such evidence

[15] *Re Nuttall* [1955] 1 W.L.R. 847. Cases of damaged wills may be referred to the Senior District Judge: *Registrar's Direction*, January 22, 1941 as amended by Secretary's Circular, June 27, 1975.
[16] N.-C.P.R. 1987, r. 54(1).
[17] *Re Riley* [1896] P. 9.
[18] N.-C.P.R. 1987, r. 54(4).
[19] *Walker* v. *Solicitor for affairs of H.M. Treasury* (1961) 105 S.J. 531. *Barkwell* v. *Barkwell* [1928] P. 91, 96.

depends upon the nearness in time of the execution and the declaration.[20] A lost will may be proved by a single witness, even if interested and though the attesting witnesses cannot be traced.[21] The standard of proof is that applicable in other civil cases.[22]

When the complete contents of a missing will cannot be proved, probate may be granted of such part as can be proved, *e.g.* where a copy of only part of the will exists or where parol evidence covers only some of the dispositions.[23] A will may be proved partly by an incomplete draft and partly by parol evidence.[24]

Although the court formerly admitted to probate a will as contained in the declaration[25] of a party, it is necessary to supply a reconstruction of its contents[26] where no draft or copy can be found, and this reconstruction should be exhibited to the affidavit in support of the application to admit the will to probate. A privileged will has been admitted to probate as contained in a letter to the principal beneficiary.[27]

Codicils

The same principles apply to lost or damaged codicils as to lost or damaged wills. Where the contents of a codicil are unknown the will is admitted to probate, limited until the codicil or a more authentic copy is proved. Probate of a codicil alone may be granted where the will has been lost and its contents are unknown, with the equivalent limitation.[28]

Representative unable to make oath

A person entitled on intestacy who wishes to take a grant occasionally has reason to believe that the deceased made a will which has been lost and of which the contents are unknown. Consequently he may feel unable to swear that the deceased died intestate. To overcome this difficulty a grant of administration limited until the will or a copy thereof is proved may be made in such a case. Alternatively a grant may be made as on intestacy. Cases under this alternative are heard on motion. A similar procedure may be followed where an executor believes there is a later will.

Unobtainable wills

Where a will is in the custody of a foreign court or official, *e.g.* a notary,

---

[20] *Sugden* v. *Lord St. Leonards* (1876) 1 P.D. 154, 242, 252. Earlier cases to the contrary must be taken as wrongly decided in spite of the reservations expressed in *Woodward* v. *Goulstone* (1886) 11 App.Cas. 469; see *Re MacGillivray* (1946) 62 T.L.R. 538, C.A.
[21] *Sugden* v. *Lord St. Leonards, supra.*
[22] *Re Wippermann* [1955] P. 59.
[23] *Re Phibbs* [1917] P. 93.
[24] *Burls* v. *Burls* (1868) L.R. 1 P. & D. 472.
[25] The old equivalent of the statement of claim.
[26] *Wildmore* v. *Wildmore* (1938) 185 L.T.J. 297.
[27] *Brigstocke* v. *Brooking* (1963) 107 S.J. 216.
[28] *Re Greig* (1866) L.R. 1 P. & D. 72.

and such court or official will not part with it, duly authenticated copies may be admitted to probate without order,[29] with or without limitation.

Where persons abroad have custody of a will but will not transmit it to England, a copy may be admitted to probate until the original or a more authentic copy is proved.[30]

If it is impossible to obtain any copy of the will, a grant may be made limited to a known gift in the will.[31]

Where it is known that there was a will and that it may be in existence, a grant of administration (with the will) has been made.[32]

Copies of foreign documents which are the equivalent of wills in the country where the deceased died domiciled have been admitted to probate until the originals or more authentic copies are proved.[33]

B. Grants to Attorneys and Consular Officers

Any person entitled to a grant of probate or administration may appoint an attorney[34] to take the grant for his use and benefit, limited until further representation be granted, or in such other way as a registrar directs.[35] Where, however, such person entitled is an executor, a grant is not made to his attorney without notice being given to the other executors, unless such notice is dispensed with by a registrar.[36]

Where the donor of the power is mentally incapable and the attorney is acting under an enduring power of attorney, application is made under rule 35.[37]

Procedure

A person residing abroad is not obliged to apply for a grant by his attorney; he may take the grant himself.

The power of attorney is generally for the express purpose of obtaining a grant to the deceased's estate, but the authority of a general power of attorney may extend to obtaining a grant,[38] although given before the death of the deceased.[39] This procedure differs from that in force under the 1954 rules in that any person entitled may appoint an attorney irrespective of residence.

[29] N.-C.P.R. 1987, r. 54(2) proviso (*post*, p. 1246).
[30] *Re Lemme* [1892] P. 89; *Re Von Linden* [1896] P. 148; *Re Robinson* (1941) 191 L.T.J. 267. See also *post*, p. 331.
[31] *Re Dost Aly Khan* (1880) 6 P.D. 6.
[32] *Re Von Wrochem* (1964) 108 S.J. 240.
[33] *Re Prince Oldenburg* (1884) 9 P.D. 235; *Re Queen Marie of Roumania* [1950] W.N. 457.
[34] Including an Attorney registered under s.6 of the Enduring Powers of Attorney Act 1985. See N.-C.P.R. 1987, rr. 31(3), 35.
[35] N.-C.P.R. 1987, r. 31(1) (*post*, p. 1235). See also as to attorney administrators, *post*, p. 937.
[36] *Ibid.*, r. 31(2).
[37] *Ibid.* r. 31(3), and see p. 325 for grants where the person entitled is mentally incapable of managing his affairs.
[38] See the Powers of Attorney Act 1971, Sched. 1 for a suitable general power of attorney.
[39] *Re Barker* [1891] P. 251.

Residence of the attorney

The attorney need not reside in England. Executors in different countries may, by separate powers, appoint the same attorney. No form of guarantee is now required.

Form and execution of the power of attorney

Although a power of attorney should be a formal document, a registrar has a discretion to allow such informal documents as a memorandum[40] or letter.[41]

If a power is in a foreign language a duly certified translation is required. If the power is in English, but is given in a non-English-speaking country, it must be shown that the deceased understood English, unless it has been witnessed by a notary or the British consul. The Republics of Ireland and of South Africa are treated as English-speaking. Where there is a doubt as to language in any part of the Commonwealth the matter should be referred to a registrar.[42]

A notarial copy of a power deposited with a notary or in a court of law and shown to be valid by an affidavit of law will be accepted as having the force and validity that the original has in the court of the domicile. Office copies of powers of attorney deposited in the Central Office of the Supreme Court (before October 1, 1971)[43] or in the Supreme Court of Northern Ireland or registered in the books of Council and Session in Scotland are accepted without proof.[44]

If a power of attorney contains a power of substitution and the attorney has exercised it, the substitute may take a grant.[45] Substitution, if allowed by the law of the deceased's domicile, is also accepted.[46] An individual or a trust corporation must be appointed directly. Where a firm is appointed, the member of it applying must show that he was a member of the firm at the date of the power.

Where A is appointed attorney and failing him B, the former must be cleared off before a grant is made to the latter. An executor who renounces probate may take a grant as attorney of another executor, provided he has not renounced this right as well.[47]

Where a minority or life interest arises a grant cannot be made to a single individual as attorney,[48] but two attorneys may obtain a grant, though representing the interests of a single principal. A power of attorney limited

---

[40] *Re Elderton* (1832) 4 Hagg.Ecc. 210.
[41] *Re Ormond* (1828) 1 Hagg.Ecc. 145.
[42] *Registrar's Direction*, November 17, 1949.
[43] The procedure for deposit in the Central Office of the Supreme Court was abolished by Powers of Attorney Act 1971, s.2.
[44] See the Evidence and Powers of Attorney Act 1940, s.4.
[45] *Palliser* v. *Ord* (1724) Bunb.Exch.Rep. 166.
[46] *Re Abdul Hamid Bey* (1898) 78 L.T. 202.
[47] See the N.-C.P.R. 1987, r. 37(1).
[48] *Registrar's Direction*, May 23, 1952.

to a specific portion of the estate is only accepted if good reason is shown to a registrar.

Representative grants

A power of attorney expressed to be for the purpose of obtaining a grant of administration (with or without the will) to the estate of one person will enable the attorney to obtain a grant to which the representative, as such, is entitled in another estate. Where it is thought likely that a grant in another estate will be necessary, the power should be worded so as to authorise a grant to the attorney in both estates.[49]

Filing the power of attorney in the registry

A power limited to obtaining a grant is filed permanently in the registry and is not returnable.[50] A general power is stamped and returned upon production of a copy for filing. This copy must be certified as a true and complete copy.

Grants to attorneys of executors

A grant made to the attorney of an executor is of administration (with will) for the use and benefit of the executor and is limited until further representation be granted. The grant makes the attorney agent for the donor but it is virtually for the use and benefit of all those interested in the estate.[51]

If all the executors appoint the same attorney, the grant is limited for their use or benefit and until further representation be granted. If some of the executors later wish to take probate and the others have not intermeddled through the attorney, the grant may be revoked and a new grant made to the executor applying, with power reserved to the others. If over four executors are appointed the power given by them must be limited so that no more than four attorneys apply.[52] If a surviving executor revokes the power granted by him and his deceased co-executor, the court will revoke the grant to the attorney and make a fresh grant to any new attorney the surviving executor appoints.[53]

Where more than one executor is appointed but an attorney is not appointed by all of them, notice of the application for a grant to an attorney must be given to any executor who has not appointed him, unless notice is dispensed with by a registrar.[54] Such notice must be left at the last known address of the executor or sent to that address by registered post.[55]

---

[49] *Registrar's Direction*, October 11, 1974.
[50] *Registrar's Direction*, March 14, 1952.
[51] *Re Cassidy* (1832) 4 Hagg.Ecc. 360; *Chambers* v. *Bicknell* (1843) 2 Hare 536; *Re Manifold* [1962] Ch. 1; *Re Weiss* [1962] P. 136 and 26 *Conveyancer* 154. See also *post*, p. 937.
[52] *Registrar's Direction*, October 14, 1952.
[53] *In the Estate of Dinshaw* (1930) P. 180.
[54] N.-C.P.R. 1987, r. 31(2) (*post*, p. 1235).
[55] N.-C.P.R. 1987, r. 67 (*post*, p. 1249).

The oath or other evidence shows that this has been done and it is advisable for the copy notice and any document received in answer to be lodged. The attorney of a residuary legatee may take a grant without notice to the other residuary legatees.

Where two or more executors each appoint an attorney a joint grant is made limited until the death of either executor or of the attorneys or until either executor applies for probate. While a proving executor is alive a grant is not made to the attorney of an executor to whom power has been reserved.

Grants to attorneys of trust corporations are made in their official capacity, *e.g.* "the Public Trustee of Queensland" and not to "John Smith," who holds that position.

Death of the donor or the attorney

If, on the death of a donor, part of the estate remains unadministered a grant *de bonis non* will be necessary. On the death of the attorney before completion of administration a *cessate* grant is necessary. The donor, unless he applies for a grant himself, appoints a fresh attorney.[56]

Oath

In the oath the applicant is described as the lawful attorney of the person entitled and includes the limitation "for the use and benefit of . . . and until further representation be granted." Where application is made by a person entitled and the attorney of another person equally entitled the grant will be "limited until further representation be granted." The oath must contain the consent of the applicant entitled himself to apply to the grant being so limited.

Grants to consular officers

Grants may be made to the consular officers of a number of countries for the estates of nationals of those countries who are resident out of England.[57] This is an alternative to a grant to that person or his attorney. The grant is made to the consular officer by his official title and is limited for the use and benefit of the national until further representation be granted.[58] Even in the case of a minority or life interest a grant may be made to the officer alone.[59] The court has power to postpone a grant to a consular officer for such period as it considers appropriate in the circumstances.[60]

---

[56] See *post.*

[57] Consular Conventions Act 1949, s.1. The countries which are covered by Orders in Council made under this Act are: Austria, Belgium, Bulgaria, Czechoslovakia, Denmark, the Federal German Republic, France, Greece, Italy, Japan, Mexico, Mongolia, Norway, Poland, Spain, Sweden, U.S.S.R. and Yugoslavia. A similar procedure applies under the now repealed Domicile Act 1861. See also *ante*, p. 21, and Pugh, *Administration of Foreign Estates.*

[58] *Registrar's Direction*, January 31, 1952.

[59] Consular Conventions Act 1949, s.1(4).

[60] *Ibid.* proviso.

Practice

The oath shows that the applicant is the consular officer of a country covered by Order in Council, that the person[61] for whom he applies is a national of the same country and resides out of England, that he is entitled to a grant and has not appointed an attorney. No consent or authority from the person concerned is required. No guarantee will be required in the case of a grant to a consular officer.[62]

C. GRANTS FOR THE USE OF MINORS

Grants cannot be made to persons under age, but must be made to the person(s) with parental responsibility for them or to the person(s) deemed to have such responsibility,[63] for their use and benefit until they attain the age of 18.[64] Where there is more than one minor the grant (formerly described as *durante minore aetate*) is limited until one of them attains the age of 18.

Unless a registrar otherwise directs a grant will be made to a person of full age in preference to the guardian of a minor entitled in the same degree as that person.[65]

While two guardians (persons with parental responsibility) may represent the interests of a single individual,[66] where there are several branches of a family all being under age and equally entitled to a grant, it is desirable that the applicants should represent the several branches of the family.[67] The procedure since the Children Act 1989 is governed by rule 32 of the Non-Contentious Probate Rules 1987, as amended by the 1991 amendment.[68]

Oath

The oath deposes to the fact that those entitled to the grant are minors and gives their ages.[69] The oath must state the applicant's title to apply and contain a statement that the grant is for the use and benefit of the minor(s) and until he/she/one of them attains the age of 18 years.[70]

Where a minor is executor

Where a minor is sole executor, administration with the will annexed is granted in the order of priority prescribed by rule 32(1) until he comes of age, when a grant may be made to him.[71] This applies only where the

---

[61] "Person" includes a charity: *Registrar's Direction*, October 13, 1954.
[62] Supreme Court Act 1981, s.120(5).
[63] N.-C.P.R. 1987, r. 32(1) of the Childrens Act 1989, s. 2(1), (2) or 4, Sched. 14, para. 4 or 6.
[64] Family Law Reform Act 1969, s.1 and Sched. 1, Pt. II, reduced full age from 21 to 18 years.
[65] N.-C.P.R. 1987, r. 27(5). See also *ante*, p. 21, *post*, p. 475.
[66] President's Direction, November 1925.
[67] *Registrar's Direction*, May 14, 1926.
[68] S.I. 1991 No. 1876 and see *Practice Direction* [1991] 1 W.L.R. 1069.
[69] *Registrar's Direction*, August 18, 1863.
[70] See the Children Act 1989, s.5 as to the appointment of guardians.
[71] Supreme Court Act 1981, s.119(1), Appendix, *post*, p. 1198, and see p. 35 *ante*.

minor has an interest in the residuary estate; where he has no such interest the grant, unless a registrar otherwise directs, is made for his use and benefit to the person interested in the residue.[72]

Where one of several executors is a minor probate may be granted to any others not under disability, with power reserved to the minor on attaining the age of 18.[73] Administration (with will) for the use and benefit of a minor executor may only be granted to those having parental responsibility or his guardians[74] if the other executors renounce or do not apply for a grant after being cited to accept or refuse one.[75]

The right of a minor executor to probate on attaining full age may not be renounced by any person on his behalf.[76] His right to administration (with or without will) may only be renounced by a person appointed by a registrar and authorised by him to renounce.[77]

Where a minor would be entitled to administration

Where a person who would otherwise be entitled to a grant of administration (with or without will) is a minor, two classes of persons are primarily, *i.e.* without order, entitled to a grant on his behalf: (i) a parent who has, or is deemed to have parental responsibility;[78] (ii) the guardian of the minor who is appointed or deemed to be appointed guardian in accordance with section 5 of the Children Act 1989.[79]

Any person in these classes may be passed over and the grant made by order of a registrar to any person he appoints to obtain administration, to act either alone or jointly with any person or persons in the classes mentioned.[80]

(i) The parents

The person entitled to apply for the grant on behalf of his minor child is the parent with parental responsibility.[81] Where both parents have such responsibility they should apply together, but where one only has parental responsibility that parent may nominate his co-administrator.[82] Parent includes adoptive parents and the mother of an illegitimate child,[83] or his father if he has acquired parental responsibility under the Act.

---

[72] N.-C.P.R. 1987, r. 32(1) proviso. (*post*, p. 1235).

[73] N.-C.P.R. 1987, r. 33(1).

[74] See Children Act 1989, ss.2–6 and r .33(1).

[75] N.-C.P.R. 1987, r. 33(2).

[76] N.-C.P.R. 1987, r. 34(1). If the infant dies a grant *de bonis non* is necessary, see *post*, p. 475.

[77] N.-C.P.R. 1987, r. 32(1) applying s.2(1), 2(2) or 4, para. 4 or 6 of Sched. 14 to the Children Act 1989 or s.12(1) of the Adoption Act 1976.

[78] N.-C.P.R. 1987, r. 34(2).

[79] The Children Act 1989 repealed and replaced a number of earlier Acts. Section 5 covers the appointment of guardians by the court and by the parent "in the event of his death". Guardians of the estate can only be appointed in accordance with rules of court. (s. 5(11) & (12)).

[80] N.-C.P.R. 1987, r. 32(2).

[81] Children Act 1989, s.2.

[82] N.-C.P.R. 1987, r. 32(3).

[83] Children Act 1989, s.2(2).

Elected guardians

The procedures for an infant over the age of 16 years (known as a "minor") to elect a guardian has been abolished.

D. Grants where a Person otherwise Entitled is under a Disability (Disability Grants)

Where a person who would otherwise be entitled to a grant is, by reason of mental incapacity, unable to manage his affairs, administration may be granted for his use and benefit during such incapacity.[84]

A grant of administration is not made in such cases, unless a registrar otherwise directs, until all persons entitled in the same degree as the incapable person are cleared off.[85]

If one of several executors is incapable, probate is granted to the others, power being reserved to the executor who is incapable on recovery of his capacity.[86] Where one executor is incapable and the other appoints an attorney, a grant is made to the latter's attorney limited until the former shall recover and apply for a grant or until further representation be granted.

Where a person otherwise entitled to a grant is mentally incapable

Subject to what has been said in the preceding paragraph any person authorised by the Court of Protection to apply has the prior right to a grant on behalf of a person who is mentally incapable.[87] Where no person has been so authorised the grant is made to the lawful attorney of the incapable person acting under a registered enduring power of attorney.[88] Where there is no such attorney. entitled to act, the grant is made to the person entitled to the residuary estate.[89]

Notice of intended application for a grant must be given to the Court of Protection.[90]

The mere appointment by the Court of Protection of a receiver for a patient does not authorise the person appointed to apply for a grant. An express authority is required, contained either in the original order or in a subsequent order or direction. If the patient has a beneficial interest in the estate, it is the normal practice of the court to give this authority, and provision is made for the appointment of another (unnamed) person as co-administrator in case there should be a minority or life interest. The person

---

[84] N.-C.P.R. 1987, r. 35. Such grants were formerly described as *durante dementia*. On recovery the incapable person may obtain a cessate grant. See *post*, pp. 339, *et seq.*

[85] *Ibid.* sub-r. (1).

[86] *Evans* v. *Tyler* (1849) 2 Rob.Ecc. 128, 131.

[87] N.-C.P.R. 1987, r. 35(2)(*a*). See *ante*, p. 23.

[88] *Ibid.* sub-r. (2)(*b*).

[89] *Ibid.* sub-r. 2(*c*).

[90] N.-C.P.R. 1987, r. 35(5).

named in the order of the Court of Protection, the attorney, or the person
entitled to the residuary estate may nominate a co-administrator where the
grant is required to be made to not less than two administrators unless a
registrar otherwise directs.[91]

Where a patient resides in an institution, a certificate of the responsible
medical officer is sufficient to prove incapacity.[92] But where the patient is
not so residing, a certificate from his doctor certifying the period he has
attended him and stating that in his opinion the patient is incapable of
managing and administering his property and affairs and is unlikely to be
so capable within three months, will normally be accepted. In cases where
such a certificate cannot be given the directions of a registrar should be
obtained.[93]

Grant to a person appointed by a registrar

In cases of mental incapacity where no person has been authorised by
the Court of Protection to take a grant, and there is no person acting under
a registered enduring power of attorney[94] or if such attorney renounces,
and the person entitled to the residue cannot apply (usually because this
person is the incapable person), the court has power to appoint administrators even though they have no interest in the estate.[95] In such cases the
application is *ex parte* by an affidavit of the facts. The affidavit should be
made by all proposed grantees.

Where the deceased died domiciled abroad an applicant for a grant for
the use and benefit of an incapable person must obtain an order from a
registrar. If he is neither the person entrusted with administration nor himself beneficially entitled to share, he may still obtain a grant under the
registrar's discretionary powers.[96] Administration has been granted to a
Scottish curator.

Incapacity arising after a grant has issued

Where one of two or more grantees becomes incapable after obtaining a
grant, the grant is revoked. A new grant is made[97] to the person(s) equally
entitled with the incapable grantee whether they were the other original
grantees or not. Where two executors prove a will and one becomes incapable the grant is revoked and a new grant made to the capable executor
with power reserved to the incapable executor on regaining his capacity.
The application for revocation and the new grant may be contained in the
same affidavit referring to the will as already proved. The will need not be

[91] N.-C.P.R. 1987, r. 35(3).
[92] *Practice Note* [1962] 2 All E.R. 613.
[93] *Registrar's Direction*, [1969] 1 All E.R. 494.
[94] See the Enduring Powers of Attorney Act 1985 and *Practice Direction* [1986] 1 W.L.R. 419.
[95] N.-C.P.R. 1987, r. 35(4) and see *Re Penny* (1846) 1 Rob. 426; *Re Hastings* (1877) 4 P.D. 73.
[96] See N.-C.P.R. 1987, r. 30(1)(c). See *post*, pp. 343, *et seq*.
[97] See *post*, pp. 362, 366.

remarked and no new form of Inland Revenue Account need be delivered. Where a sole grantee becomes incapable the grant is no longer impounded. A new grant, *de bonis non*, to the unadministered estate will be made to the person of equal or next entitlement.

Capacity Regained

If the grant is limited during incapacity, it ceases to operate as soon as recovery can be proved either by production of an order of the Court of Protection or (if that Court is not seised of the matter) by doctor's affidavit. A cessate grant will then be made to the former patient.

A grant limited until further representation will continue until the former patient applies upon proof of recovery as above and will then cease upon issue of the new grant.

E. GRANTS FOR A PERSON SERVING A PRISON SENTENCE

A sentence of imprisonment does not deprive the prisoner of his right to a grant. But a grant may be made, preferably to his attorney, for the use and benefit of a prisoner under the discretionary powers of the court.[98] In proper circumstances the court may pass over a prisoner who is primarily entitled to a grant and appoint another person to administer, also under its discretionary powers.[99] Since a murderer forfeits his beneficial interest he is not entitled to a grant.[1]

F. GRANTS LIMITED AS TO PROPERTY

A grant to the real estate of a deceased person or a part thereof may be made separately from, or together with, a grant to his personal estate; and a grant may be made in respect of real estate where there is no personal estate or in respect of trust estate only, and a grant of administration maybe limited in any way the court thinks proper.[2] It is further provided that where the estate is insolvent the grant shall not be severed except as regards trust estate.[3]

Procedure

Application may be made to a registrar whatever the amount of the estate.[4] The application is made *ex parte* and is supported by an affidavit

---

[98] Registrar's Direction, March 3, 1963. As to the appointment of criminals as personal representatives, see *ante*, p. 22.

[99] *Re Drawmer* (1913) 108 L.T. 732; *Re S. deceased* [1968] P. 302 and see Supreme Court Act 1981, s.116.

[1] *Re Crippen* [1911] P. 108.

[2] Supreme Court Act 1981, s.113. As to special executors, see *ante*, p. 18.

[3] *Ibid.* See also *ante*, p. 105, *post*, p. 1119.

[4] N.-C.P.R. 1987, r. 51. See pp. 321.

showing whether it is made in respect of real estate or any part thereof only, or of real estate together with personal estate, or in respect of trust estate only; whether the estate is known to be insolvent; and that all persons entitled to a grant in respect of the whole estate in priority to the applicant have been cleared off.[5] The grantee must be entitled by the ordinary rules of priority, otherwise the discretionary powers of the court must be invoked.[6]

A grantee entitled to the whole estate may apply for a grant to a part only, but a person entitled to a limited grant only in respect of part of the estate has a right to take such grant. Where a grant has been made limited to part of the estate, a further grant in respect of the remainder will be issued without an order.[7]

The court has granted administration to a beneficiary limited to that fund in which he was interested where the trustee was dead and there was no personal representative or his personal representative consented.[8] Grants have been made to legatees limited to their legacies[9]; to the trustee in bankruptcy of the owner of certain shares put in the name of the deceased, limited to those shares[10]; to a stranger limited to administration with the will annexed, where the will disposed only of part of the estate.[11] Grants have been made limited to land which ceased to be settled land at the death of an intestate, the remainder of the estate being granted to the Treasury Solicitor.[12] Where on a contested application one applicant for a grant to the whole estate was only interested in a part thereof it was held that the grant must be limited to that part.[13] Grants have also been made limited to carrying on a suit in Chancery and to receiving the fund that was the subject of the suit.[14] But a grant limited to part of the estate will not be made to the nominee of a debtor.[15]

Grant limited to trust property, there being no other

An application may be made for a "nil" grant in such a case.[16] The oath must show that the grant is required to administer trust property. Where the trust is created by will, a grant is made to the personal representative of the original testator, not to the beneficiary. Where the trust was created by

---

[5] *Ibid.*

[6] In *Re Powell* [1935] P. 114 the grant was made under s.155 of the Judicature Act 1925, but should have been made under the Judicature Act, s.162. The corresponding provisions of the Supreme Court Act 1981 are ss.113 and 116.

[7] *Registrar's Direction*, March 24, 1958.

[8] *Pegg* v. *Chamberlain* (1860) 1 Sw. & Tr. 527; *Re Ratcliffe* [1899] P. 110.

[9] *Re Steadman* (1828) 2 Hagg. 59; *Re Watson* (1858) 1 Sw. & Tr. 110. A grant was refused in *Re Watts* (1860) 1 Sw. & Tr. 538.

[10] *Re Agnese* [1900] P. 60.

[11] *Re Jackson* [1892] P. 257.

[12] *Re Mortifee* [1948] P. 274.

[13] *Re Dodgson* (1859) 1 Sw. & Tr. 259; see *Poole* v. *Poole* [1919] P. 10.

[14] *Re Elector of Hesse* (1827) 1 Hagg.Ecc. 93; *Re Dodgson, supra.*

[15] *Re Rivers* (1832) 4 Hagg.Ecc. 355.

[16] See the Administration of Justice Act 1932, s.2. This Act has been repealed but the jurisdiction is preserved by the Supreme Court Act 1981, s.25. See p. 9, n. 50 *ante*, and p. 15, n. 90 *ante*.

deed the trustees are preferred as grantees. Where all the trustees are dead, application may be made by the personal representative of the last surviving trustee or, failing any such personal representative by the person beneficially entitled to the trust fund.

G. Grant Limited in Accordance with the Terms of the Will

Where a testator appoints a general executor and another for a special purpose, as for instance a "literary executor," and both apply for probate at the same time, one grant is made but the powers of the executors are distinguished. Where the general executor applies first a general grant is usually made[17] to him. He is described in the grant as the general executor. It is not necessary to reserve power to a special executor as he is entitled to apply in respect of his part of the estate as of right.

Grants "save and except"

Where one executor has been appointed for a special purpose or fund[18] as well as a general executor, the latter may take a grant save and except the special purpose or fund. If the general executor fails or renounces, administration (with the will) save and except may be granted to the residuary legatee or devisee. Where a testator has made a will limited to a particular purpose only or limited his will to dispose of his estate in one country only and has died intestate as to the rest of his estate, the persons entitled to the rest of the estate, without waiting for the executor to take his grant, may obtain administration save and except the property disposed of by will.[19]

H. Grants "Caeterorum" (Remainder Grants)

Where a grant limited to part of the estate or a particular purpose has been made, the grant to the rest of the estate is known as a grant *caeterorum*, *i.e.* of the remainder. Such a grant may be of probate or of administration with or without the will.

Probate *caeterorum* is granted where the executor for the special purpose has taken his grant and the general executor later applies. Where two executors thus differentiated have been appointed but the general executor is cleared off by death or renunciation, the residuary legatee or devisee or other person entitled under the normal rules may obtain administration (with the will) *caeterorum*. Similarly where the executor for special purposes has taken his grant and the testator died otherwise intestate those entitled on intestacy may obtain administration *caeterorum*. Where a grant

---

[17] But see *Re Wallich* (1864) 3 Sw. & Tr. 423.
[18] *Ibid.*
[19] For grants save and except settled land, see p. 275, *ante*.

has been made under section 113 of the Supreme Court Act 1981 or a limited grant has been made under the discretionary powers of the court, the person entitled to the rest of the estate may take a grant *caeterorum*.

Procedure

A grant *caeterorum* may be applied for at a district registry or from the principal registry.[20] The oath includes particulars of the previous grant and where application is made at a registry other than that from which the previous grant issued, an office copy of the grant must be lodged with the papers.

I. GRANTS LIMITED AS TO TIME OR PLACE

Occasionally an appointment of an executor is limited in the will to take effect after a lapse of time, *e.g.* after five years. In such cases a grant of administration (with the will) is made limited until the appointment of the executor begins. A grant of administration may be necessary until a will can be brought to England,[21] though this circumstance must be rare in modern times. Where a will is shown to have existed at the time of the testator's death but cannot be found and its contents are unknown, administration may be granted until the will or a copy is found and brought into the registry.[22]

Administration may be limited to a country or a place.[23]

Where a will is not in dispute but there is litigation as to the validity of a codicil, the former may be admitted to probate and the grant limited to the termination of the litigation.[24] Where there is no litigation in progress but only the will is available, the court may admit the will to probate on the executor undertaking to prove the codicils when they come to hand.[25]

J. WILLS EXERCISING A POWER OF APPOINTMENT

In certain circumstances limited grants are made in respect of wills exercising a power of appointment. The topic has already been considered.[26]

K. GRANT TO THE ESTATE OF A MARRIED WOMAN ACQUIRED AFTER SEPARATION

As already set out,[27] property acquired by a married woman after judicial

---

[20] Administration of Justice Act 1969, s.28.
[21] See *Re Brown* (1899) 80 L.T. 360. See also *ante* pp. 318, 319.
[22] *Re Wright* [1893] P. 21; *Re Ponsonby* [1895] P. 287; and see *ante*, p. 316.
[23] *Re Mann* [1891] P. 293; see *Re Tamplin* [1894] P. 39; *Re Von Brentano* [1911] P. 172.
[24] *Re Day* [1940] 2 All E.R. 544.
[25] *Re Robarts* (1873) L.R. 3 P. & D. 110.
[26] See *ante*, p. 120.
[27] See *ante*, p. 254.

separation, or an order having the same effect, passed not to her husband on her death intestate before 1970, but as if he had predeceased her. A grant limited to this property may be taken out by those entitled, the husband being entitled to a grant *caeterorum*. But now the property of a spouse thus separated devolves as if the other spouse were dead.[28]

L. Grants Limited to an Action

Limited grants, known as grants of administration *ad litem*, are made constituting a person a party to a suit and limited to this purpose. The topic is discussed later.[29]

M. Absentee Grants ("Durante Absentia")

The jurisdiction to make absentee grants under section 164 of the Judicature Act 1925 has been succeeded by a wider discretion under section 116 of the Supreme Court Act 1981[30] so that such grants are no longer made as such. Under this practice the court could order the transfer into court of any money or securities belonging to the estate.[31] If the representative capable of acting as such, returned while legal proceedings to which the administrator was party were in progress, he was to be made a party to the proceedings, and the costs of the administration and the proceedings were paid by such person or out of such fund as the court should direct.[32] A returning executor could not bring an action until he had obtained the revocation of the grant[33] and was only made a party to proceedings in progress.

The section applied to a case where the executor of an executor was abroad.[34] Where the executor, the residuary legatee, was a prisoner of war, a grant has been made under the section to a legatee limited to his legacy.

N. Grants Ad Colligenda Bona (Preservation Grants)

The court has a general power to make a grant for the preservation of the estate without waiting until those entitled to a grant have applied. Grants made for the preservation of the estate are grants *ad colligenda bona defuncti*, usually known as *ad colligenda* grants. Such a grant is often useful where the person entitled to a full grant is abroad or temporarily incapacitated and some urgent step needs to be taken (*e.g.* the removal of valuables

---

[28] Matrimonial Causes Act 1973, s.18(2).
[29] See *post*, p. 346.
[30] See p. 1197, *post*.
[31] Judicature Act 1925, s.164 subs. (2).
[32] *Ibid.* subs. (3).
[33] Administration of Estates Act 1925, s.15 (*post*, p. 1120).
[34] *Re Grant* (1876) 1 P.D. 435.

from an empty house or more commonly nowadays the sale of a house or stocks and shares).

Procedure

Application for the grant is made *ex parte* to a registrar.[35] The usual limitation imposed in an order for such a grant to issue is for the purpose only of collecting and receiving the estate and doing acts necessary for its preservation. Any particular act in relation to the estate which it is desired to do but which is not covered by this general formula must be specifically requested and will be set out in the order. In any case where a series of acts have to be done in relation to the estate, or where it is not known precisely what steps will have to be taken, it is advisable to obtain a grant under the discretionary powers of the court rather than a grant *ad colligenda bona*.

The grant may be made to entire strangers in a proper case,[36] and the Treasury Solicitor or the solicitors for the Duchies may obtain grants where it is necessary for the preservation of the estate that some act should be done at once and without waiting for fuller inquiries as to the existence of next-of-kin.

Grants have been made to a creditor limited to collecting the estate in order to pay his debts and to renewing his lease,[37] to a creditor where no next-of-kin could be found[38] and to the Official Solicitor where the executors were attempting to move the proceeds of sale of estate assets outside the jurisdiction.[39] Grants have been made for the benefit of absent or unknown next-of-kin with extended powers to pay debts, deal with real estate and to sell the property of the deceased.[40] It is not essential for kin of the deceased to apply, for the grants may be made to friends.[41]

All preservation grants are limited until further representation be granted. The oath to lead the grant need not contain any statement as to the existence of a will or whether the deceased died intestate neither will it be necessary to recite the normal "clearings off"[42] but will recite the details and date of the order. The usual rule as to the number of administrators where there is a life or minority interest applies. These grants are always of administration (without the will) only, and if there is a will it is not proved or annexed to the grant. The grant will not state whether the deceased was testate or intestate.[43]

When the purpose of the preservation grant has been attained a general grant may issue to the person entitled. No order is necessary to obtain this

---

[35] N.-C.P.R. 1987, r. 52(*b*).

[36] *Re Wyckoff* (1862) 3 Sw. & Tr. 20.

[37] *Re Clarkington* (1861) 2 Sw. & Tr. 380; *Re Stewart* (1869) L.R. 1 P. & D. 727.

[38] *Re Ashley* (1890) 15 P.D. 120.

[39] *I.R.C.* v. *Stype* [1982] Ch. 456, 476.

[40] *Re Schwerdtfeger* (1876) 1 P.D. 424; *Re Bolton* [1899] P. 186; see *Re Roberts* [1898] P. 149. See also *Re Sanpietro* [1940] P. 16 (grant in respect of English estate of an alien enemy).

[41] *Re Radnall* (1824) 2 Add. 232; *Re Gudolle* (1835) *cit.* 3 Sw. & Tr. 22; *Re Bolton, supra.*

[42] *Registrar's Direction*, October 12, 1979.

[43] *Ibid.*

grant which then supersedes the grant *ad colligenda*. The general grant may be applied for at any registry.[44]

Where an Inland Revenue Account is required to be delivered this must be done. Any tax payable must be paid before the grant can issue.

O. ADMINISTRATION PENDING SUIT (*pendente lite*)

Where a probate action has begun, but not before,[45] application may be made to the court to grant administration limited to the continuance of the litigation[46] or pending suit. The object of such a grant is to ensure that the estate of the deceased is managed and preserved for the benefit of those found to be entitled thereto. Applications for the appointment of an administrator pending suit are most commonly made in connection with the sale, lease or repair of a house, but there are many other matters, *e.g.* dealings with stocks and shares or the running and management of a business, which necessitate such an application. The practice where an administrator pending suit has been appointed is now subject[47] to many of the rules of court governing the appointment of a receiver.[48]

Who may apply for the grant

Usually the application is made by one of the parties, but the court may appoint an administrator pending suit on the application of any person interested in the estate, *e.g.* a creditor.[49] A single individual may be appointed although there is a minority or life interest.[50]

Who will be appointed as administrator pending suit

If the parties are agreed on the necessity of the appointment they usually agree on an administrator. But if they propose rival candidates, the master will choose. It is often the case that a solicitor for each of the disputing parties is appointed.

A person unconnected with the suit is the most proper person to be appointed to the office.[51] Often an accountant is proposed. A party may be appointed where all parties consent. Even where all parties do not consent the court may still appoint a party where circumstances make it advisable.[52]

---

[44] See the Administration of Justice Act 1969, s.28. As to such grants to the Public Trustee in the case of foreign estates, see *ante*, p. 24. As to the liability of a limited administrator who exceeds his powers, see under *executor de son tort, ante*.

[45] *Salter* v. *Salter* [1896] P. 291.

[46] Supreme Court Act 1981, s.117.

[47] Ord. 76, r. 14(2).

[48] *i.e.* Ord. 30, rr. 2, 4, 6 and (subject to the Supreme Court Act 1981, s.117. See Ord. 76, r. 15(2).

[49] *Tichborne* v. *Tichborne* (1869) L.R. 1 P. & D. 730; *Re Cleaver* [1905] P. 319.

[50] *Lindley* v. *Lindley* [1953] P. 203; *Re Haslip* [1958] P. 275. See *ante*, pp. 235, 236.

[51] *De Chatelain* v. *Pontigny* (1858) 1 Sw. & Tr. 34.

[52] *Re Griffin* [1925] P. 38; and see *Wright* v. *Rogers* (1870) L.R. 2 P. & D. 179, where executors were appointed administrators *pendente lite* during an appeal.

When an administrator pending suit will not be appointed

The court will not appoint an administrator pending suit unless it is satisfied that such appointment is expedient in the circumstances. Thus where the appointment of an executor in a will was not affected by a disputed codicil, the application was refused.[53] Similarly, an application was refused where there was no evidence that the assets were being wasted.[54]

Although in an exceptional case the Probate Division appointed an administrator pending suit when the Chancery Division had already appointed a receiver,[55] this was contrary to the usual practice. Once a person has been appointed to manage the estate, an application to make a parallel appointment will be refused.[56]

Special cases of appointments of an administrator pending suit

Where a will was not in dispute in a probate action administration with the will annexed was granted during the pendency of the suit.[57]

Where an action was in progress over the estate of a widow the court appointed an administrator pending suit not only of her estate, but of the estate of her deceased husband of whom she was the universal legatee.[58] In modern practice, however, the court would make a grant to the estate of the husband, in such circumstances, under its discretionary powers and not appoint an administrator pending suit.

Procedure

The application is made by summons in the Chancery Division[59] in the proceedings, returnable before the master. The summons should name the proposed administrator and should be supported by an affidavit showing that there is some step which it is expedient should be taken to preserve or protect some asset of the estate, and the value of the property likely to be administered. Scripts are not required except in so far as they may be necessary exhibits to any affidavit.[60] There must be affidavit evidence of the fitness of the proposed administrator and his consent to act must be filed. The order may limit the grant to dealing with specified property.[61]

When the order has been made, the papers to lead the grant must be lodged in the principal registry.[62] The fee for the grant is payable in full, as

---

[53] *Mortimer* v. *Paull* (1870) L.R. 2 P. & D. 85.
[54] *Horrell* v. *Witts* (1866) L.R. 1 P. & D. 103.
[55] *Tichborne* v. *Tichborne* (1869) L.R. 1 P. & D. 730; *Re Cleaver* [1905] P. 319. As to appointment of receivers by the Chancery Division, see *post*, p. 846.
[56] *Veret* v. *Duprez* (1868) L.R. 6 Eq. 329; *Re Oakes* [1917] 1 Ch. 230.
[57] *Misigaes* v. *Misigaes* [1950] W.N. 232.
[58] *Re Dawes* (1870) L.R. 2 P. & D. 147; *Re Fawcett* (1889) 14 P.D. 152; *Re Shorter* [1911] P. 184.
[59] Ord. 76, r. 14(1).
[60] Establishment Circular, January 24, 1942.
[61] See *Stanley* v. *Bernes* (1828) 1 Hagg.Ecc. 221.
[62] Ord. 76, r. 14(2); Ord. 30, r. 2(1).

is inheritance tax. The administrator may be required to give security which will be by guarantee unless the court otherwise directs.[63]

On the determination of the proceedings a full (not a *cessate*) grant is made on lodging at the registry[64] an office copy of the final order of the court and the usual papers required in order to obtain a grant.

Powers and duties of an administrator pending suit

The administrator has all the rights and powers of a general administrator, other than the right to distribute. He is subject to the control of the court and must act under its direction.[65] He is an officer of the court, under the direction of which he represents the deceased.[66]

The powers and duties of an administrator pending suit begin on the date on which the grant is obtained and end with the final order in the proceedings.[67] The grant is not revoked by such final order but ceases, reviving if there is an appeal, until that appeal is disposed of.[68]

An administrator pending suit may only pay a legacy or an annuity with the consent of all persons who might be adversely affected by his doing so.[69] Where there was a dispute as to alleged debts the administrator was not allowed to pay them until they had been passed by the court.[70]

Where a dispute arises between the parties as to what course the administrator should take over any matter, the directions of a master should be sought on summons. In cases of difficulty or importance the master will adjourn the summons to the judge.

The administrator's account

Unless the parties otherwise agree, the administrator will normally be ordered to bring in an account at the end of his first year of administration, whereafter no further account may be needed, at any rate until he is discharged.[71] The account, which should be verified by affidavit,[72] should consist of a cash account and an inventory of assets in his hands.[73]

Remuneration of an administrator pending suit

The court may direct that an administrator pending suit shall receive out of the estate of the deceased, or the income thereof, such reasonable

---

[63] Ord. 30, r. 2(3).
[64] Principal or district.
[65] Supreme Court Act 1981, s.117 *post*, p. 1197.
[66] *Re Graves* (1828) 1 Hagg.Ecc. 313.
[67] *Wieland* v. *Bird* [1894] P. 262.
[68] See *Taylor* v. *Taylor* (1881) 6 P. & D. 29.
[69] See *Whittle* v. *Keats* (1866) 35 L.J. 54.
[70] *Charlton* v. *Hindmarsh* (1859) 1 Sw. & Tr. 433.
[71] *Practice Direction* (*Probate Actions*) [1973] 1 W.L.R. 627.
[72] *Ibid.*
[73] *Practice Direction* (*Probate Actions*) [1973] 1 W.L.R. 627. See also pp. 64 *et seq.*, *ante*.

remuneration as it shall think fit.[74] The remuneration will be fixed on the taking of the accounts.

In estimating what is a reasonable remuneration, the court may direct that the remuneration be fixed by reference to such scales or rates of professional charges as it thinks fit.[75] The master takes into account the total work done in receiving and paying out moneys and the duration and complexity of the administration. Allowance is to be made for professional skill, business knowledge and similar special qualifications. The degree of responsibility borne is to be taken into account and, to a lesser extent, the amount of the estate.

Summary of account

Before the costs are taxed, the accounts passed and the remuneration fixed, vouchers and receipts for all payments made must be produced to the master's clerk. A summary should then be made showing in the first column the total receipts and, parallel with it, the total payments, the filing fee for the affidavit, the remuneration asked, the taxed costs, the fee on passing the account and the balance in hand.

Thereupon the master certifies the balance in the hands of the receiver. This balance must be paid to the persons entitled.

Costs

Where a party is condemned in the costs of an action or the costs are ordered to be paid out of the estate, the order covers the charges of an administrator pending suit, including the costs of applying for his appointment.[76] But where part of the work done was necessary in an ordinary administration of the estate, costs ordered against a party should, in respect of the administrator, be apportioned.[77]

---

[74] Supreme Court Act 1981, s.117(3); and Ord. 76, r. 14(2); Ord. 30, r. 3.
[75] Ord. 30, r. 3.
[76] *Fisher* v. *Fisher* (1878) 4 P.D. 231.
[77] *Howlett* v. *Howlett* [1950] P. 177.

CHAPTER 25

SPECIAL GRANTS

A. Unadministered Assets

Where all the persons to whom a grant of probate or administration has been made have died without completing administration and where, in the case of probate, no chain of executorship continues, a grant is made to a new representative to enable the administration of the estate to be completed. This type of grant is generally known by the first three words of the full Latin title *"De bonis non administratis"* although of course it now applies to land as well as to personal property.

The new grant is made on the principles which apply respectively to administration with the will annexed and to administration without a will. Whereas, however, the probate registry makes the original grant on its own interpretation of the will, *e.g.* to the next-of-kin of a testator on the basis of a partial intestacy, the grant for unadministered assets will be made on the basis of any other interpretation of the will made meantime by the Chancery Division which affects the right to a grant.[1]

Administration (with will) for unadministered assets

Where the first grant was made to an executor and the chain of executorship has been broken, the grant of administration (with will) *de bonis non* is made to the residuary legatee or devisee in trust. Failing a residuary legatee or devisee in trust the order of priority continues in the same way as in a first grant of administration (with will).[2]

Where an executor has performed some acts of administration but has died before taking a grant, the grant made to the person thereafter applying is an ordinary grant and not a grant *de bonis non*. The acts done are good,[3] but the administering cannot be noticed by the court of Probate.[4]

If the original grant was made to a creditor or legatee, any other creditor or legatee may take administration (with will) *de bonis non* without obtaining the renunciation of the residuary legatees. Where, however, the latter were cited and did not appear when the original grant was made, they must be cited again.

A grant *de bonis non* may be made to the representative of a deceased residuary legatee who renounced when the original grant was made or did

---

[1] See *Warren* v. *Kelson* (1859) 1 Sw. & Tr. 290. See also as to this grant and the chain of representation, *ante*, p. 47.

[2] N.-C.P.R. 1987, r. 20, *ante*, pp. 233, *et seq.*, 245 *et seq.*

[3] See *ante*, pp. 83 *et seq.*

[4] *Wankford* v. *Wankford* (1704) 1 Salk. 299, 303; S.C. 3 Salk, 162, 164.

not appear after citation to accept or refuse a grant. As in the case of an original grant, it is the general rule that a grant *de bonis non* will be made to a living person rather than to the representative(s) of a deceased person entitled in the same degree, and to a person of full age rather than to the guardian of a minor.[5]

In the ordinary way of grant of administration (with will) *de bonis non* includes the testamentary papers originally admitted to probate. But if a codicil has been found since the original grant, it will be included in the new grant.

As set out hereafter, where an order is made under the Inheritance (Provision for Family and Dependants) Act 1975 it must be recorded in the grant of probate.[6] The same procedure, *mutatis mutandis*, in relation to these orders is followed in grants *de bonis non*.

Administration for unadministered assets

Where an administrator dies without having wholly administered the deceased's estate, priority of right to a grant is given to those beneficially entitled to share in the estate.[7] Accordingly where the administrator was the sole person beneficially interested in the estate the grant is made to his executors or, failing them, to his administrators.

But where there are persons alive who are beneficially interested in the unadministered estate, they are entitled to a grant *de bonis non* in preference to the representative of the administrator, unless a registrar otherwise orders[8] and, of course, unless the personal representative also has a beneficial interest in the original estate.

In considering whether a surviving spouse took a beneficial interest in the whole estate it is to be borne in mind that that interest is in the estate as ascertained at the time of the application for the grant *de bonis non* and not at the date of the death of the original intestate. Thus an accretion to the estate may affect the entitlement to a grant *de bonis non*.

Where the surviving spouse and all the next-of-kin entitled to share in the estate have died, the representative of the spouse is entitled to a grant in preference to that of the next-of-kin.[9]

Limited grants de bonis non

Grants *de bonis non* may be limited in the same way as other grants,[10] *e.g.* for the use and benefit of a minor or to taking legal proceedings.

Where an estate has been completely administered save for a legacy, administration *de bonis non* (with the will) has been granted to the legatee

---

[5] N.-C.P.R. 1987, r.27(5).
[6] See *post*.
[7] See the N.-C.P.R. 1987, r. 22(4).
[8] N.-C.P.R. 1957, r.27(5).
[9] *Registrar's Direction*, November 7, 1955.
[10] See *ante*.

on the consent or after the citation of the residuary legatee,[11] but in modern practice such legatee would have to seek a grant under the discretionary powers of the court or after the renunciation or citation of those entitled to a general grant. Where the deceased died bankrupt, a grant was made to the Official Receiver on the renunciation of the widow and children. Later the debts having been paid and the Official Receiver not wishing to continue as administrator, the widow and children were allowed to retract their renunciation, the grant was revoked and a grant *de bonis non* was made to them.[12]

Where an administrator *caeterorum* (with or without the will) or an administrator save and except settled land dies without fully administering the estate, a grant *de bonis non* will be made to the persons who would have been competent to take the original grant.

A *de bonis non* grant where the deceased died domiciled abroad may be obtained on the death of the person to whom the grant was issued and is made in accordance with the principles applicable in the country in which the deceased died domiciled.[13]

A *de bonis non* grant may be made in respect of a resealed grant.

Grants de bonis non and cessate grants distinguished

Where a grant is taken by one person for the use and benefit of another, *e.g.* by an attorney for the use and benefit of the donor of the power, a grant *de bonis non* is made on the death of the latter in the lifetime of the former. A *cessate* grant is made where the grantee dies in the lifetime of the person for whose use and benefit he has taken a grant.

Procedure

Grants *de bonis non* may be applied for at the principal registry or at a district registry.[14] In general the practice as to the Oath and Inland Revenue account is the same as in an application for an original grant, but the following differences are to be noted.

The Oath gives particulars of the original grant, the date of the death of the grantee, and shows that part of the estate which remains unadministered. Where probate was originally granted it must be shown how the chain of executorship has been broken. Where a grant is required only to make title, the Oath states that the administration has not been completed.

In cases of administration (with the will) the applicant is sworn to and marks the original will, the probate copy annexed to the previous grant or an office copy issued by the registry in which the original is deposited. If the probate copy is marked by the applicant, it is retained in the registry and in many cases it is preferable that it should not be marked. In the case

[11] *Re Steadman* (1828) 2 Hagg.Ecc. 59; *Re Biou* (1843) 3 Curt. 739, 741.
[12] *Re Thacker* [1900] P. 15.
[13] See *Re Gaynor* (1869) L.R. 1 P. & D. 723.
[14] Administration of Justice Act 1969, s.28.

of a foreign will the applicant may be sworn to and mark the copy already filed, a fresh notarial copy, or the copy annexed to the former grant. In the case of a lost will the Oath states that it has not been found.

If the original grant was obtained at a district registry and the new application is made at the Principal Registry, notice of the issue of the *de bonis non* grant is transmitted to the district registrar.

Where the original grant issued on the basis of the estate's being an "excepted estate," *i.e.* where no form of Inland Revenue Account was required, the same figures may be used as the values for the unadministered estate.

Where an Account was delivered for the original grant, an Account in Form A5C need no longer be sent to the Capital Taxes office for control before the application for the grant *de bonis non*. The Account will be submitted with the other papers to lead the grant.

A *de bonis non* grant being a second or subsequent grant to the same estate carries a fee of £2.[15]

B. Cessate or Second Grants

Cessate grants are made in two sets of circumstances: (a) where the original grant was limited in time or until the happening of some event, and that time has flowed or that event has happened, (b) where the original grant was made for the use and benefit of another and the grantee has died.[16]

A *cessate* grant is a re-grant of the whole grant, though the estate to be administered is sworn in the Oath as the unadministered estate.

Cessate grants after the effluxion of time or the happening of an event

Where a grant has been limited until the original will or a more authentic copy is proved and such will or copy is discovered and, if the document originally admitted does not correspond in all respects with the will or copy subsequently found, it may be more convenient to apply for a *cessate* grant.[17] The Oath recites the making of the original grant and shows that it has expired on the discovery of the will or more authentic copy. If in the meantime the original grantee has died the will must be proved by the person who is next entitled to a grant. Where a grant has been limited to acting as a party to an action, a *cessate* grant may be made to those entitled on it being shown that the action has terminated.

A *cessate* grant is required where an executorship limited for life, until remarriage or in some other way ceases on the happening of the limiting event.

---

[15] Non-Contentious Probate Fees Order 1981, Fee No. 3(*e*).

[16] Where, however, the person for whose use and benefit the grant was made has died, the grant is *de bonis non* and not *cessate*: see *ante*, p. 339.

[17] *Registrar's Direction*, April 21, 1971.

Where a grant has been made to an attorney, it ceases when the donor of the power makes application for a direct grant to himself for the original grant is always limited until further representation be granted. Where the attorney acts for a person entrusted to administer by the law of the domicile or beneficially entitled by that law, an affidavit must be filed showing in the former case that the order entrusting is still in force. A further order will be necessary.[18]

Minors

Grants for the use and benefit of minors cease on their attaining full age when they may obtain a grant for themselves with another administrator if there is a continuing life interest. Where a grant has been made for the use and benefit of minors and the administrators, in their representative character, afterwards take administration in another estate, both grants cease on one of the infants attaining majority.

Mental Incapacity

A grant of administration for the use and benefit of an incapable person ceases on that person's recovery, and the latter may take a *cessate* grant. Where the administration has been granted to a person authorised by the Court of Protection, recovery is proved by the production of the order of that court determining the proceedings. Where the grant has been made to some other person recovery is proved by the affidavit of the doctor. Notice of the application must be given to the administrator, but his consent is not required.

Death of the grantee

On the death of an attorney the grant ceases and a *cessate* grant may be made to another attorney or directly to the person entitled.[19]

A *cessate* grant has been made, on notice to the donor of the power to the deceased attorney, to the attorney of another person interested in the estate.[20] Where one of two attorneys appointed severally dies, a *cessate* grant may be made to the other on an affidavit of facts.

Minors

Where the person with parental responsibility for or the guardian of an executor dies during the minority, *cessate* administration (with the will) may be granted. If one administrator for the use and benefit of an infant dies during the minority, application may be made for the appointment of another administrator.[21]

---

[18] *Registrar's Direction*, November 20, 1972 (*i.e.* a further order under N.-C.P.R. 1987, r. 30(1).
[19] See *ante*, p. 322.
[20] *Re Barton* [1898] P. 11.
[21] See the N.-C.P.R. 1987, r. 26, and *ante*, p. 324.

Mental Incapacity

On the death of the administrator for the use and benefit of an incapable person, a *cessate* grant is made to some other person. The continuing incapacity of the former must be proved in the same way as for an original grant.[22]

In the cases above the oath sets out the original grant, the death of the attorney or administrator and, in the case of incapacity, the continuance of the incapacity.

Where the person who dies is the person for whose use and benefit the grant was made, the new grant is not a *cessate* grant but a grant *de bonis non*.

---

[22] See pp. 325, 341, *ante*.

CHAPTER 26

DISCRETIONARY GRANTS

Previous chapters have covered the ordinary rules of priority in obtaining grants of administration (with the will)[1] and administration on intestacy,[2] and the ordinary right of an executor to obtain a grant of probate.[3] Circumstances, however, arise in which it is inexpedient to follow the ordinary rules and, where this is the case, the court has statutory power in its discretion to grant administration to persons who are not primarily entitled to a grant, or even to persons who have no title at all. Thus the court may refuse to allow an executor to take a grant of probate and may commit administration of the estate to another.

Even where there are a number of persons equally entitled to a grant of administration (with or without the will) the court has an inherent or judicial power to refuse a grant to some of them and commit it to others. This power is exercised where disputes have arisen between such persons.

Cases also arise where, because deaths have occurred at or about the same time, or because of other circumstances, it is doubtful who is entitled to a grant. In such cases the court determines the question under its inherent jurisdiction.

Somewhat akin to these powers is that of allowing a grant of probate or administration to issue on the basis that a missing person is dead. The court does not presume the death, but allows the person who would be entitled to a grant if the missing person were dead to swear that he died on or since the date of his disappearance.

These are all matters involving the exercise of the court's discretion and they are considered in this sequence in this chapter.

A. THE STATUTORY DISCRETION

Where the deceased died before 1926

The discretionary powers of the court where the deceased died before 1926 were exercised under section 73 of the Court of Probate Act 1857 by virtue of section 162(2) of the Judicature Act 1925 but since the Supreme Court Act 1981[4] the general statutory discretion is exercised in all cases under the 1981 Act.[5]

---

[1] See *ante*, pp. 245 *et seq.*
[2] See *ante*, pp. 253 *et seq.*
[3] See *ante*, p. 306.
[4] See s.116 (*post*, p. 1197).
[5] In the case of death before 1926 the court had power under the statute 21 Hen. 8, c. 5, to pass over the widow in cases of intestacy and grant administration to the next-of-kin. For the last reported case see *Re Frost* [1905] P. 140.

Where the deceased died after 1925

Originally such discretionary powers were conferred by section 162 of the Supreme Court of Judicature (Consolidation) Act 1925. But these were soon found to be too limited and were enlarged by section 9 of the Administration of Justice Act 1928. Section 116 of the Supreme Court Act 1981 now provides as follows:—

"**116.** *Power of court to pass over prior claims to a grant.*

(1) If by reason of any special circumstances it appears to the High Court to be necessary or expedient to appoint as administrator some person other than the person who, but for this section, would in accordance with probate rules have been entitled to the grant, the court may in its discretion appoint as administrator such person as it thinks expedient.

(2) Any grant of administration under this section may be limited in any way the court thinks fit."

The wording of this section, though differing from the earlier legislation, has the same effect, and cases decided under the earlier sections are authorities under the later. For example the court has the same power to pass over an executor as it had before 1926, in spite of the absence of any reference in the present enactment to the case where the deceased left a will and there is no willing and competent executor.[6]

The word "administrator" above quoted includes an administrator with the will annexed.[7] In spite of the use of the word "administrator" in the singular, where there is a minority or life interest there must be two administrators.[8]

Limits to the statutory discretion

The discretionary powers of the court both before and after 1925 are wide and extend beyond circumstances connected with the estate or its administration.[9] The grant may be limited in any way in which the Court thinks fit.[10] Executors may be passed over with power reserved to them to apply for a grant of probate.[11] The powers are not, however, unlimited. It seems that a general grant cannot be made where a limited grant would be made in ordinary circumstances.[12] The discretion of the court must be properly exercised and where a girl of 21 was passed over on the ground of immaturity and a temporary grant made to a trust corporation, this was

---

[6] *Re Biggs* [1966] P. 118.
[7] See *Re Massey* [1899] P. 270 made under the similar wording of the Court of Probate Act 1857, s.73. As to the Hague Convention on Succession, see generally p. 16 *ante*.
[8] Supreme Court Act 1981, s.114.
[9] *Re Clore dec'd* [1982] Fam. 113; [1982] Ch. 456, 476.
[10] Supreme Court Act 1981, s.116(2).
[11] *Re Mathew* [1984] 1 W.L.R. 1011.
[12] See *Re White, supra.* at p. 83.

held not to be a proper exercise of the discretion.[13] The discretionary powers of the court have been exercised in a number of classes of case:

Passing over an executor

An executor may be passed over on account of his bad character,[14] attempts to avoid tax,[15] his neglect of his duties,[16] where he has intermeddled and refuses to take a grant,[17] because of his absence abroad,[18] imprisonment,[19] ill-health,[20] unsoundness of mind,[21] incompetence to take probate,[22] disappearance[23]; or where the estate is insolvent.[24] All these constitute "special circumstances" within the section.

Passing over those primarily entitled to administration

(i) *Grants made by consent.* To a nominee,[25] including a nominee of the Law Society to the estate of a deceased solicitor to enable the practice to be carried on,[26] to a person agreed on by the parties or the persons interested in the estate,[27] to a stranger without citing the next-of-kin on the consent of some of the beneficiaries,[28] to a claimant whose legitimacy was doubtful.[29] Cases holding that a grant cannot be made merely because there is a consent[30] must be taken to have been overruled.

(ii) *Persons abroad.* The court has frequently passed over persons primarily entitled to a grant who were abroad,[31] particularly in cases of

[13] *Re Taylor* [1950] 2 All E.R. 446, C.A.
[14] *Re Wright* (1898) 79 L.T. 473; *Re Drawmer* (1913) 108 L.T. 732; *Re S.* [1968] P. 302. *Re Samson* (1873) L.R. 3 P. & D. 48 must be considered incorrectly decided. See also *post*, p. 351.
[15] *I.R.C.* v. *Stype* [1982] Ch. 456.
[16] *Re Ray* (1926) 96 L.J.P. 37; *Re Potticary* [1927] P. 202.
[17] *Re Biggs* [1966] P. 118. Such an executor is not entitled to renounce. See *post*, p. 380. This case was decided before the Rules were altered to provide for a grant to a citor. The practice in such cases would now normally be for the complainant to cite the intermeddler under r. 47(3) of the N.-C.P.R. 1987, and subsequently apply for a grant under r. 47(5)(c).
[18] *Re Cooper* (1869) L.R. 2 P. & D. 21; *Re Batterbee* (1889) 14 P.D. 39; *Re Taylor* [1892] P. 90; *Re Crawshay* [1893] P. 108; *Re Massey* [1899] P. 270; *Re Williams* [1918] P. 122; *I.R.C.* v. *Stype* [1982] Ch. 456.
[19] *Re S.* [1968] P. 302, and see *ante*, p. 22.
[20] *Re Galbraith* [1951] P. 422.
[21] *Re Atherton* [1892] P. 104.
[22] *Re Stewart* (1875) L.R. 3 P. & D. 244.
[23] *Re Sawtell* (1862) 2 Sw. & Tr. 448.
[24] *Re Leguia* [1934] P. 80 (in this case the deceased died domiciled abroad). (Now the provision of N.-C.P.R., r.3 would be applied.)
[25] *Re Roberts* (1858) 1 Sw. & Tr. 64; *Re Davis* [1906] P. 330; *Re Morgans* (1931) 145 L.T. 392.
[26] See President's Direction, March 15, 1965.
[27] *Re Hopkins* (1875) L.R. 3 P. & D. 235; *Re Potter* [1899] P. 265.
[28] *Re Moffatt* [1900] P. 152.
[29] *Re Minshull* (1889) 14 P.D. 151.
[30] *e.g. Teague* v. *Wharton* (1871) L.R. 2 P. & D. 360.
[31] *Re Hagger* (1863) 3 Sw. & Tr. 65; *Re Hughes* (1873) L.R. 3 P. & D. 140; *Re Webb* (1888) 13 P.D. 71; *Re Nares* (1888) 13 P.D. 35; *Re Wallas* [1905] P. 326. In *Re Cooke* (1859) 1 Sw. & Tr. 267 the application was refused.

urgency.[32] Application for a discretionary grant in such cases is often preferable to an application for a preservation grant.

(iii) *Small or insolvent estate.*   Where the estate is small or is insolvent the court is often prepared to pass over the persons primarily entitled and, in such cases, has not insisted on their being cited,[33] especially where they have had notice of the application[34] or where advertisements have not been answered.[35] In such cases grants are often made to creditors or to undertakers[36] who are not creditors.[37]

(iv) *Persons missing or believed to be dead.*   Where the person primarily entitled to a grant has been missing for a number of years he has often been passed over in favour of the person next entitled or with an inferior title.[38] In some cases the applicant has been given leave to depose in the Oath that he believes that he is the sole next-of-kin.[39]

(v) *Settled land.*   Where a life-tenant died leaving no kin and a very small personal estate, a general grant to the estate of the life-tenant has been made to the remainderman on citation of the next-of-kin,[40] or even without their being cited.[41]

(vi) *Constituting a party to an action.*   It is often necessary, mainly in the Queen's Bench Division, but also in the Chancery Division, to constitute a party, particularly a defendant, to the action. Thus where a person injures another by negligently driving a motorcar and then dies leaving little or no property, no grant is taken out to his estate and the proposed plaintiff, having no one to sue, cannot recover damages from the deceased's insurers. In such a case the injured person can apply for a nominee to be appointed administrator *ad litem*, *i.e.* to represent the deceased only in respect of the proposed action.[42]

Preferably one grant only should be made in respect of the estate and so where an action lies by the surviving spouse against the estate of the other spouse it is best for the surviving spouse not to apply but for some disinterested person to apply for a discretionary order, but in exceptional cases two grants may be made, the grant of administration *ad litem* being made

[32] *Re Jones* (1858) 1 Sw. & Tr. 13; *Re Escot* (1858) 4 Sw. & Tr. 186; *Re Drinkwater* (1862) 2 Sw. & Tr. 611; *Re Cholwill* (1866) L.R. 1 P. & D. 192.
[33] *Re Wilde* (1887) 13 P.D. 1; *Re Everley* [1892] P. 50.
[34] *Re Teece* [1896] P. 6; *Re Bishop* (1913) 108 L.T. 928.
[35] *Re Heerman* [1910] P. 357.
[36] See *Newcombe v. Beloe* (1867) L.R. 1 P. & D. 314.
[37] *Newcombe v.Beloe, supra,* which held that the undertaker in that case was a creditor must be taken to be incorrectly decided on that point.
[38] *Re Peck* (1860) 2 Sw. & Tr. 506; *Re Harling* [1900] P. 59. See also *Re Moore* [1891] P. 299; *Re Shoosmith* [1894] P. 23; *Re Harper* [1899] P. 59; *Re Chapman* [1903] P. 192.
[39] *Re Reed* (1874) 29 L.T. 932; *Re Callicott otherwise Smith* [1899] P. 189.
[40] *Re Bordass* [1929] P. 107; see *Re Dalley* (1926) 70 S.J. 839.
[41] *Re Birch* [1929] P. 164; see *Re Mortifee* [1948] P. 274.
[42] See *Re Simpson*; *Re Ganning* [1936] P. 40.

first. Where the surviving spouse has already taken a grant this must be revoked in cases where two grants are to be made, and where a spouse has intermeddled, probate can be granted to any co-executor with power reserved to the spouse.[43]

A grant has frequently been made to the Official Solicitor limited to defending proposed proceedings.[44] The Official Solicitor may be prepared to take a grant for the purpose of a claim being made against an estate under the Inheritance (Provision for Family and Dependants) Act 1975.[45] This is frequently the case where the surviving spouse is the only person entitled to the grant and the person seeking relief under the Act.

Where no grant has been made, an alternative procedure is now to bring the action against the estate under the Proceedings Against Estates Act 1970. This Act is considered later.[46] Consideration should also be given to applying for an order that the case proceed in the absence of a representative or for the appointment of some person to represent the estate in the proceedings.[47] But the procedure is not applicable where the estate to which it is desired to appoint a representative is the estate which is the subject of the dispute.[48]

(vii) *Creditors.* Grants have been made to creditors of the estate, passing over those primarily entitled,[49] in some cases without citation after notice had been given[50] or after advertisement.[51] Furthermore, grants have been made to the creditors of persons entitled to a grant who have died without taking one.[52] Grants have also been made to the trustee in bankruptcy of a person entitled to the deceased's estate.[53] Undertakers are not creditors, but grants may be made to them in a proper case.[54] They must first apply for a discretionary order under section 116 of the Supreme Court Act 1981. A creditor should be so described in the affidavit and in the grant.[55]

(viii) *Grants (with the will) made where there is doubt as to the person entitled.* The wording of the will sometimes raises a difficult question of construction in determining who is, *e.g.* the residuary legatee (where no executor is appointed). In such cases the court may make a grant under its discretionary powers, leaving it to the court of construction to construe the

[43] Registrar's Circular, February 2, 1967, and see *Re Newsham* [1967] P. 230 (where a grant was made to a stranger under s.162 of the Judicature Act 1925 as the widow's claim against her husband's insurance company might have been prejudiced by a grant to her).
[44] See *Re Knight* [1939] 3 All E.R. 928.
[45] Secretary's Circular, November 11, 1976. For Family Provision see pp. 757 *et seq., post.*
[46] See *post*, p. 904.
[47] See Ord. 15, r. 15.
[48] *Silver* v. *Stein* (1852) 21 L.J.Ch. 312.
[49] *Re Atherton* [1892] P. 104.
[50] *Re Bishop* (1913) 108 L.T. 928.
[51] *Re Heerman* [1910] P. 357.
[52] *Re Fraser* (1867) L.R. 1 P. & D. 327; *Re Wensley* (1882) 7 P.D. 13.
[53] *Re Turner* (1886) 12 P.D. 18.
[54] In *Newcombe* v. *Beloe.*
[55] *Registrar's Direction*, June 7, 1935.

will[56] unless to do so would be unduly onerous on the estate.[57] But if all the parties interested in the question involved are before the court and the question is absolutely involved in the granting of administration, the probate court must act as the court of construction.[58]

(ix) *Persons of bad or criminal character.*   The court has frequently passed over persons of bad or criminal character. In one case the court passed over the husband of the deceased because of his intemperance[59]; in another a widow who had propounded a will found to be a forgery was passed over in favour of her daughter.[60] Where a sole executor was in prison and refused to renounce, the court passed him over in favour of a residuary legatee.[61]

Criminal killing

A murderer is debarred on grounds of public policy from benefiting from or taking a grant to the estate of his victim.[62] On the same grounds a person who has committed manslaughter is debarred from a grant to the estate of the person whom he has killed[63] subject to the limited relief given by the Forfeiture Act 1982. It has been held in several unreported cases that diminished responsibility does not so far excuse the killer as to allow him to take a grant.

Where, however, a killer is found guilty but insane, he retains his right to a grant.[64] The presumption is that the killer is of sound mind, and it must be shown that he had no felonious intent to enable him to take a grant.[65] Thus where a man killed his wife and then committed suicide, and there was no evidence as to his state of mind, his personal representative was not allowed to make any claim on her estate.[66]

Although the findings of a coroner's inquest are not proof of criminal killing,[67] the crime may now be proved by putting in evidence the certificate of any conviction therefore, unless the convicted person disputes his guilt.[68] If he disputes guilt the certificate is not evidence.[69] Unless, therefore, it can be proved by the evidence of a person who heard the plea that the alleged killer pleaded guilty, it may well prove impossible to establish

[56] See *Re Last* [1958] P. 137.
[57] *Re Cherrington* [1984] 1 W.L.R. 772, where the estate was small and the division of estate agreed, the only question being who should take the grant.
[58] See *Re Tharp* (1878) 3 P.D. 76, C.A.
[59] *Re Arden* [1898] P. 147.
[60] *Re Paine* (1916) 115 L.T. 935.
[61] *Re Drawmer* (1913) 108 L.T. 732; *Re S. decd.* [1968] P. 302.
[62] *Re Crippen* [1911] P. 108. See 1973 L.Q.R. 235.
[63] *Hall* v. *Knight & Baxter* [1914] P. 1.
[64] *Re Houghton* [1915] 2 Ch. 173; *Re Pitts* [1931] 1 Ch. 546; *Re Batten's Will Trusts* (1961) 105 S.J. 529.
[65] See *R.* v. *Huntbach* [1944] K.B. 606.
[66] *Re Pollock* [1941] Ch. 219.
[67] *Re Sigsworth* [1935] Ch. 89; see *Bird* v. *Keep* [1918] 2 K.B. 692.
[68] Civil Evidence Act 1968, s.11.
[69] *Hollington* v. *Hewthorn* [1943] K.B. 587.

the crime in an application to pass over the alleged killer. There is a heavy burden of proof on those who seek to establish an unlawful killing.[70] But the fact that a killer is in prison on a long sentence has been held sufficient ground for passing him over.[71]

Since a criminal killer is also debarred from benefiting from his victim's estate, he is not permitted to contest a probate action concerning that estate[72] and the fact that he is debarred from benefiting may be pleaded against him.[73]

Where a person is debarred from sharing in the estate of a person whom he has killed, it does not necessarily pass to the Crown as *bona vacantia*; a specific or pecuniary legacy lapses, and a residuary gift which fails may give rise to an intestacy or acceleration of interests, but there is no lapse in a class gift.[74] The court will not deem the killer to have predeceased his victim so as to enable a substituted gift to take effect.[75]

Procedure

Applications for grants under the discretionary powers of the court may be made to a registrar.[76] The application is made *ex parte* supported by an affidavit of facts and any other relevant documents. In cases of difficulty registrars may refer the matter to be heard by a judge on summons.[77] If the matter is clearly contentious, the more appropriate procedure is in open court, and the registrar should be asked to give directions for pleadings in order to identify the issues and for placing some limit on the affidavit evidence.[78] Details of the order must be included in the Oath.

Where a person has a direct interest in the estate, *e.g.* a legatee or creditor, his best method of obtaining a grant is to cite, by advertisement if necessary, the person having a superior right to accept or refuse a grant.[79] But where a person's only right to share in the estate depends on the death of a person with a prior right who cannot be traced, citation is not the correct procedure.[80] In such case application should be made for a discretionary grant. Advertisements may be ordered and the applicant may be ordered to take out an indemnity policy to cover any claim on the estate by the person to be passed over. This enables the grantee to receive the assets of the estate, if entitled.

---

[70] *Re Dellow's Will Trusts* [1964] 1 W.L.R. 451.

[71] *Re S. decd., supra.*

[72] *Hall* v. *Knight & Baxter, supra.*

[73] *M.* v. *L.* [1946] P. 183.

[74] See *Re Callaway* [1956] Ch. 559; *Re Peacock* [1957] Ch. 310; *Re Scott* [1975] 1 W.L.R. 1260. 1270.

[75] *Marsden* v. *Marsden* (1963) 107 S.J. 318.

[76] N.-C.P.R. 1987, r. 52(*a*).

[77] Under the N.-C.P.R. 1987, r. 61.

[78] *Van Horn* v. *Van Horn, The Times,* November 30, 1978. Contentious matters still come within the jurisdiction of the Family Division where they arise before or without the need for the issue of a writ. See *ante,* p. 8.

[79] *Registrar's Direction,* February 19, 1957.

[80] *Ibid.*

Where the estate is small, grants have been made under the discretionary powers of the court without citing the persons entitled in priority if the
court is satisfied that those persons had consented to the application, that
they had been apprised of it but had not objected, or where citation
(especially by advertisement) would be an unreasonable expense because
the estate is so small.

In a few cases a person who has no right at all to a grant wishes to obtain one
for the benefit of those interested in the estate. In such a case renunciation by
those interested in the estate or their citation will not give the applicant any
right to a grant. But although the application should be made without any
citation, the applicant must show that those entitled to a grant consent, or at
least that they know of the application and have not objected.

B. Exercise of Discretion as between Applicants in the same Degree

This jurisdiction of the court is exercised solely in grants of administration.
One executor cannot claim that another is unfit for his office even if he is
convicted of a serious crime, for the testator has chosen them both. An
executor may be passed over by the court,[81] not at the instance of a co-
executor as such, but only in the interests of those entitled to the estate. If
in such a case there are a number of executors a grant of administration will
go to those who are acceptable.

Disputes between persons entitled to administration in the same degree

A grant of administration may be made to any person entitled thereto without notice to other persons entitled in the same degree.[82] Accordingly, in the
ordinary course, the grant is made to the first applicant who is entitled without
notice to others entitled in the same degree.[83] But a dispute between persons
entitled in the same degree as to which of them shall take the grant must be
brought before a registrar for determination. The application is made by
summons.[84] If the issue of such a summons is known to a registrar he will not
allow a grant to be sealed until the summons is determined.[85]

In such disputes, as in other cases, regard must be had to the rule that
unless a registrar otherwise directs administration is to be granted to a living person entitled in preference to the representatives of a deceased person who would have been entitled, and to a person not under disability in
preference to a minor entitled in the same degree.[86]

---

[81] See *ante*, p. 345.
[82] N.-C.P.R. 1987, r. 27(4).
[83] See *Cordeux* v. *Trasler* (1865) 4 Sw. & Tr. 48, 51. The applicant should disclose all
material facts, but need do no more than this (*Lemos* v. *Lemos* [1992] unreported).
[84] N.-C.P.R. 1987, r. 27(6).
[85] N.-C.P.R. 1987, r. 27(8).
[86] N.-C.P.R. 1987, r. 27(5).

Objections to an applicant

Objections are made on the following grounds: (i) the bad character, financial position or ineptitude for business of an applicant, (ii) the fact that he has an interest incompatible with the proper administration of the estate, (iii) his minor interest in the estate, (iv) that he is personally objectionable to other persons entitled to share in the estate.

If objections exist against an administrator the court will not compel an unobjectionable person to join in a grant with him.[87]

1. *The bad character, etc., of an applicant*

Not only the bad character of the applicant,[88] but bankruptcy or insolvency[89] are sufficient grounds for refusing him a grant. Even ill-health in a severe degree has been held to disqualify an applicant on the objection of another. Complete disregard of business matters or ineptitude in such matters are also grounds for refusing a grant.

2. *Incompatible interest of the applicant*

The court will exclude an applicant who has an interest which conflicts with the proper administration of the estate. Thus where the son of the applicant had a claim on the estate, his father was refused a grant lest he should not support the case of the estate against his son with sufficient strength.[90] A grant *de bonis non* was refused to an applicant entitled and granted to the representative of a next-of-kin because the only assets left in the estate were those to which the deceased's next-of-kin might be entitled in an action.[91]

3. *Majority of interest*

Where there is animosity between members of the class entitled but no specific ground of objection to the applicants can be alleged, it is the practice to prefer the applicant with the largest interest or who is supported by the majority of interest.[92] But the rule is one of practice and not of law.[93]

Similarly the court will generally prefer the creditor with the largest debt, except where creditors with a larger aggregate debt support some other applicant.[94]

A next-of-kin who was a legatee has been preferred to a next-of-kin who was not.[95]

[87] *Bell* v. *Timiswood* (1812) 2 Phill. 22.
[88] *Re Frost* [1905] P. 140.
[89] *Bell* v. *Timiswood, supra.*
[90] *Budd* v. *Silver* (1813) 2 Phill. 115.
[91] *Re Carr* (1867) L.R. 1 P. & D. 291.
[92] *Dampier* v. *Colson* (1812) 2 Phill. 54; *Iredale* v. *Ford* (1859) 1 Sw. & Tr. 305.
[93] *Re Stainton* (1871) L.R. 2 P. & D. 212.
[94] See *Re Smithson* (1866) 36 L.J.P. & M. 77.
[95] *Dobson* v. *Cracherode* (1756) 2 Lee 326.

4. *Personal objection where applicants have equal interests*

Where two applicants are equally entitled to share in the whole of the estate but each objects to the other, the dispute can sometimes be settled by their agreeing on the appointment of the solicitors representing each of them or a neutral third party, *e.g.* a trust corporation. Failing agreement the court may appoint such neutral person under its discretionary powers.[96]

C. SURVIVORSHIP

Where two or more persons in immediate succession to one another, either under a will or on intestacy, die in circumstances which make it uncertain which survived the other, the court is called upon to decide the order of death as governing the entitlement to a grant. Persons dying in such circumstances are called *commorientes*. This decision may have important consequences far beyond the question of who is to administer the estates. The distribution and taxation of both estates may be directly affected by the decision.

Presumption of survival

Before 1926 there was no presumption as to the order of death between two or more persons who died in circumstances making it uncertain who was the survivor or whether they died simultaneously.[97] After 1925 there is a presumption of death in order of seniority,[98] but this is qualified where the *commorientes* are husband and wife.[99]

Practice

Where, bearing in mind the presumptions above mentioned, there is still uncertainty as to the order of the deaths, the decision of the registrar is required and the available evidence should be submitted at the first opportunity so that he may decide whether the grant shall issue or whether further evidence is required. An affidavit by the person who found the bodies and of a doctor may be sufficient. Although the depositions at an inquest are not evidence[1] they may assist the registrar in some cases, but the application should not be delayed in order to obtain them.[2]

If, after consideration of the evidence, the order of deaths remains doubtful, the registrar will either direct the matter to be put before the court by summons or, where a conflict of evidence arises, that an action be commenced.[3]

---

[96] See *Re Morgans* (1931) 145 L.T. 392 (where there was agreement as to the grant to nominees).

[97] See *post*, p. 353.

[98] See *post*, p. 353.

[99] See *post*, p. 353.

[1] *Bird* v. *Keep* [1918] 2 K.B. 692; *Re Sigsworth* [1935] Ch. 89.

[2] *Registrar's Direction*, June 11, 1964.

[3] See *Taylor* v. *Kershaw* [1939] P. 198 at p. 208 (which was not a case of *commorientes*).

Even where the will of a *commoriens* is entirely inoperative, it must be proved.[4]

In the case of spouses *commorientes* before 1953 the grant in the estate of the younger should be obtained first and then one in respect of the elder spouse. Thus where the estate of the elder spouse dying intestate does not exceed £1,000 (after the permitted deductions) the representative may apply for a grant to his estate. But if it exceeded this amount, his next-of-kin should apply.[5]

Where spouses are *commorientes* after 1952 and die intestate, the grant is made to the persons entitled on the basis that neither spouse survived the other.

Where several members of a family are *commorientes* and die intestate, a grant is made to the persons entitled to the estate of the youngest.

Where a *commoriens* is an unmarried minor, the estates of any elder *commorientes* cannot pass to him on intestacy.[6] But where a minor *commoriens* is given a benefit under the will of a person whom he is deemed to have survived which vests in him in spite of his minority, the person entitled to his estate may obtain a grant. If he clears prior rights, that grantee may also, in his representative capacity, obtain a grant to the estate of the testator.

Foreign domicile of commorientes

The presumptions in the case of *commorientes* which have been discussed above only apply where the deceased died domiciled in England. Where *commorientes* are of foreign domicile, the law of their domicile concerning *commorientes* must be applied.[7]

Other circumstances in which the court decides who is entitled to a grant

The court may be called upon to decide who is the representative of the deceased in cases other than those of *commorientes*, *e.g.* where it was doubtful whether an intestate had died before the decree of dissolution of marriage made against him had been made absolute.[8]

The court may have to construe a will in order to decide whether a person named therein is an executor according to the tenor or whether (where no executor has been appointed) a person named in the will or referred to therein is a residuary legatee, or is in some other way given a title to a grant by a will.[9]

---

[4] *Re Ford* [1902] 2 Ch. 605.
[5] See the N.-C.P.R. 1987, r. 22(4).
[6] See the Administration of Estates Act 1925, s.47.
[7] *Re Cohn* [1945] Ch. 5.
[8] *Re Seaford* [1968] P. 53.
[9] *Re White* (1882) 7 P.D. 65 (and the cases there cited); *Re Last* [1958] P. 137. See also *Re Posner* [1953] P. 277. *cf. Re Cherrington* [1984] 1 W.L.R. 772, not followed in *Re Sinclair* [1984] 1 W.L.R. 1240.

The court might have to decide whether a person claiming to be an executor or administrator was an imposter.

D. LEAVE TO SWEAR DEATH

As the court decides the order of death of two or more persons in cases of doubt, so it decides whether a person's death is so far to be assumed as to allow the person who would be entitled to a grant to his estate if he died to swear as to belief that he died on or since a particular date.

This decision is made in cases where the applicant for a grant, whether of probate or administration, is unable to swear to the death of the presumed deceased because of lack of direct evidence. The court does not presume the missing person to be dead[10] and should he prove to be alive, he may apply to a registrar or judge (according to who made the order) for its rescission and for revocation of the grant.[11]

The principal circumstances in which the application is made are: (i) that the presumed deceased has not been heard of for a considerable period by those with whom he might be expected to communicate; or (ii) that he has disappeared in circumstances pointing to suicide or accidental death.

(i) Persons who have not been heard of for a long period

Where a person has not been heard of for a period of seven years and upwards there may be a presumption that he is dead, but the question is generally one of the inference to be drawn from the facts.[12] Thus, while in ordinary cases a person might be expected to communicate with his friends and relatives, there may sometimes be good reasons for his not doing so.

Although the court is more ready to give leave to swear death when the presumed deceased has not been heard of for seven years, leave has been given after shorter periods where full inquiries have been made.[13]

Where the person entitled to a grant to the estate of the presumed deceased has died since the disappearance, it has been held that for the purpose of deciding who is entitled to a grant the date to be taken as the date of the death of the presumed deceased depends on the circumstances of the case.[14] In some cases, e.g. where a surviving spouse's statutory entitlements to the fixed net sum on intestacy have to be considered, a change of law, e.g. the raising of the entitlement from £40,000 to £75,000 from June 1, 1987 will affect the right to a grant.

There may be sufficient evidence to show whether the presumed

[10] Re Jackson (1902) 87 L.T. 747.
[11] Re Napier (1809) 1 Phill. 83.
[12] Chard v. Chard [1956] P. 259; Re Watkins [1953] 1 W.L.R. 1323.
[13] Re Matthews [1898] P. 17; Re Winstone [1898] P. 143.
[14] Re How (1858) 1 Sw. & Tr. 53, 54; Re Jackson [1907] 2 Ch. 354. Those who assert that the deceased was alive or dead on a particular date must prove it: Doe v. Nepean (1833) 5 B. & Ad. 86; Re Phene's Trust (1870) 5 Ch.App. 139. Cross on Evidence, 7th ed., p. 128, 730 et seq. Phipson on Evidence, 12th ed. 2124–2126.

deceased or the person with the prior right to a grant to his estate died first, but it is often impossible to establish the order of deaths. Grants to the estates of a presumed deceased in the latter type of case are made under the discretionary powers of the court.[15] The application for leave to swear death is combined with an application for the discretionary grant.[16]

The court cannot give leave to swear the death of any person except the presumed deceased.[17] Thus where the person entitled to a grant on the death of the presumed deceased has also disappeared in circumstances which make it appear probable that he too is dead, the proper course is to apply for leave to swear the death of both in one application.

(ii) Circumstances pointing to suicide or accidental death

Sometimes people disappear after threats of suicide, but their bodies are never found. If the evidence strongly points to suicide, leave to swear death may be granted before a long period has elapsed since the presumed deceased was last heard of. The same principles apply where there is a clear indication that an accident has befallen the missing person.

Most cases where accidental death is probable are of drowning either in a swimming or sailing accident, where a ship sinks or is overdue and presumed to have sunk, or where aircraft disappear during a flight.

Practice

Application for leave to swear death is made to a registrar. The application is made *ex parte* and must be supported by an affidavit setting out the grounds of the application and containing particulars of any policies of assurance effected on the life of the presumed deceased.[18]

The affidavit should also set out the circumstances in which the presumed deceased was last heard of and give his age; it should depose to the applicant's belief that the presumed deceased is dead.[19] Any relevant letters from the presumed deceased should be exhibited.[20] Details of searches and inquiries should be given, and, if there has been advertisement for him the relevant newspapers should be annexed. Where the deceased died testate his will should be annexed; where he died intestate the affidavit should state who are his next-of-kin. Particulars of any bank accounts or credit cards should be given including the dates when they were last operated.

Where a county court has made an order similar to that sought, it is sufficient if the application is supported by an affidavit of facts.[21] Although a

---

[15] *Re Peck* (1860) 2 Sw. & Tr. 506; *Re Harling* [1900] P. 59; *Re Lever* (1935) 154 L.T. 270.

[16] *Re Lever* (1935) 154 L.T. 270.

[17] See *Re Clark* (1889) 15 P.D. 10.

[18] N.-C.P.R. 1987, r. 53. Suicide may affect the claims on the policy. As to the meaning of suicide since the Suicide Act 1961 see *R. v. Inner West London Coroner* [1989] Q.B. 249.

[19] *Re Hurlston* [1898] P. 27.

[20] *Re Clarke* [1896] P. 287.

[21] *Re Rishton* (1921) 125 L.T. 863.

decree of presumption of death and dissolution of marriage has no direct application, the fact that such a decree has been made should be mentioned in the affidavit.

Where ships or aircraft are missing particulars of the circumstances in which this occurred should be given. Any certificate given pursuant to regulations 3 or 4 and 5 of the Merchant Shipping (Returns of Births and Deaths) Regulations 1972 and 1979 will be accepted as proof of death.[22] An affidavit by the owners of the ship or aircraft should be filed, except where orders have already been made in respect of persons missing aboard that ship or aircraft.

The principal registry keeps a record of disasters in which a number of persons have been killed, with lists of the victims in each case. Where the presumed deceased is thought to have died in such a disaster, proof of his presumed death may not require elaborate evidence. In some instances of multiple deaths as the result of a disaster the Senior District Judge of the Principal Registry of the Family Division will issue a circular listing the deceased and stating that no proof of death is required and application for leave to swear death will not be necessary on application for grants to the estates of the deceased named therein. Information as to such a circular may be obtained from the Secretary of the Principal Registry. Practitioners should inquire as to the evidence acceptable in such cases.

Where leave to swear death is given, no precise date of death is stated in the Oath, but it is merely sworn that it is believed the presumed deceased died on, before or since a particular date or, where a particular date cannot be given, on or since an approximate date.

Foreign domicile of the presumed deceased

A registrar may decide applications where the presumed deceased died domiciled abroad. Where, however, the evidence appears untrustworthy such applications are referred to a judge.[23] Where the court of the domicile makes an order presuming death and vests the estate in the persons entitled thereto, the English court will not require any independent evidence showing the death.[24] But where there is an order of the court of domicile presuming death but not vesting the estate, the court will require evidence to show the death of the presumed deceased.[25]

In all these cases leave to swear death must be obtained. Where, however, the court of the domicile had actually made a declaration that a presumed deceased had died on a certain day and in consequence thereof a death certificate had been issued, it was held that no leave to swear death was required.[26]

---

[22] *Registrar's Direction*, April 14, 1980.
[23] *Re Dowds* [1948] P. 256.
[24] *Re Schulhoff, Re Wolf* [1948] P. 66; see *Re Spenceley* [1892] P. 255.
[25] *Re Schulhoff, Re Wolf, supra.*
[26] *Re Schlesinger* [1950] C.L.C. 3853.

CHAPTER 27

AMENDMENT, NOTATION, REVOCATION AND IMPOUNDING OF GRANTS

A. AMENDMENT OF GRANTS

After the issue of a grant, amendment may become necessary because (i) an error may have been discovered therein; (ii) an error may have been discovered in the probate copy of the will or a further document found which must be incorporated; (iii) settled land may have been wrongly excluded. In such circumstances a registrar, if satisfied that the grant should be amended, will make an order accordingly, provided that (save in special circumstances) the application is made by the grantee or with his consent.[1]

Errors in the grant

An error may be so serious that the grant must be revoked[2] but in many cases amendment of the grant is sufficient.

Amendment is allowed in some cases where the forename, address,[3] status or the date or place of death of the deceased is incorrect. But an incorrect surname, unless the error is in the spelling, entails revocation. An error in the first or only forename (other than one of spelling) requires revocation of the grant, but the omission of any other forename or an error in such name can be cured by amendment.

An alias may be added by amendment, but where it is sought to add the true name to the grant made under an alias, the grant is generally revoked. Where a grantee's name or address is incorrectly stated, amendment is usually allowed.

Where limitations have been omitted, *e.g.* for the use and benefit of a minor, amendment is allowed. Misdescriptions of property or of a deed in limited grants may be corrected by amendment in most cases.

No grant which has passed the seal may be altered without an order of a registrar, and where unauthorised alterations have been made, the grant will be impounded and a corrected duplicate made. Where the alteration is of a serious nature, the grant will be revoked.

Where the date of the will is given incorrectly the court has ordered the grant to be corrected by a memorandum endorsed with the correct date.[4] If

---

[1] N.-C.P.R. 1987, r. 41.
[2] For revocation of grants, see *post*, p. 360. As to the effect of an error see *Re Ward* [1971] 1 W.L.R. 1376 and *post*, p. 363.
[3] An additional address may be inserted by amendment, *Re Towgood* (1872) L.R. 2. P. & D. 408.
[4] *Allchin* (1869) L.R. 1 P. & D. 664.

a grant is found to be inaccurate because of an official error it will be corrected (provided it has not been registered) on return to the registry within 14 days of sealing. In other cases correction must be made by registrar's order.[5]

Error on the probate copy of the will

Where an error has been made in the engrossment of a will, the necessary amendment is made by registrar's order on lodgement of the grant.

Error as to settled land grants

Amendment in such cases has already been discussed.[6]

Practice

Application for amendment is made to the registry which issued the grant. The grantee lodges or sends by post an affidavit by him showing the nature of the error and the need for its correction, together with the grant and any additional copies which were issued. If satisfied, the registrar then makes an order for the correction of the grant.

B. Notation of Grants

A variety of circumstances make it necessary for a notation of a grant to be made. These are as follows:

Orders under the Inheritance (Provision for Family and Dependants) Act 1975

Where any order is made under this Act a copy is sent by the court which made it to the Principal Registry of the Family Division for entering and filing and a memorandum of the order is endorsed on or annexed to the grant,[7] which is also sent. The same procedure applies to variation orders. Although a consent order made in proceedings under the Act where all parties are *sui juris* may to a pedant not be an order under the Act, nevertheless a note of the order should be endorsed on the grant.[8] After notation the grant is returned to the person who lodged it.

Alteration in the value of the estate

Where the value of the estate or the amount of the deductions therefrom is altered, the grant may, if desired, be lodged at the Capital Taxes Office so that the amendment may be noted. Where death occurred before March

---

[5] *Registrar's Direction*, November 14, 1940.

[6] See *ante*, p. 275.

[7] Inheritance (Provision for Family and Dependants) Act 1975, s.19(3); R.S.C., Ord. 99, r. 7; C.C.R. Ord. 48, r. 8. See generally pp. 357 *et seq.*, *post*.

[8] *Practice Direction (Family Provision: Endorsement of Order)* [1979] 1 W.L.R. 1.

13, 1975, the grant will contain a statement of the amount of estate duty paid,[9] and any amendment to this may similarly be noted.

Election by a spouse to have a life interest redeemed

Where on a death after 1952 a surviving spouse elects to have the life interest redeemed[10] and is the sole representative of the deceased, the election is not effective unless written notice thereof is given to the senior district judge of the Family Division within 12 months of the grant being taken out. The notice[11] must be filed in the principal registry or in the registry which issued the grant. If the notice is lodged in a district registry it must be lodged in duplicate. The notice is then noted on the grant and record and is open to inspection.[12]

Administration by the Public Trustee

Where the Public Trustee is prepared to administer an estate of under £1,000 in value,[13] his undertaking to do so is filed and the grant noted accordingly.

Where an executor is permitted to retract a renunciation

In such case a notation of the grant to him is made on the original grant, if available, and on the record thereof.[14]

Notation of domicile

If no statement as to domicile in England and Wales was included in the grant, it may be added later on application supported by an affidavit. The grant is then noted at the registry. Such an application may be necessary particularly because the provisions of the Administration of Estates Act 1971, under which grants which note the domicile as being in England and Wales are to be recognised in Scotland and Northern Ireland and *vice versa*,[15] apply to grants issued before as well as after the passing of the Act.[16] Grants issued before the coming into effect of the Act may well not contain a statement as to domicile.[17]

---

[9] In the case of deaths after March 12, 1975, the grant will not contain a statement of any tax paid, following the repeal of the Stamp Act 1815, s.42 by the Finance Act 1975, s.59 and Sched. 13. As to Inheritance Tax see *ante*, pp. 71 *et seq.*

[10] As to such election, see *post*, p. 1067.

[11] For the form, see the N.-C.P.R. 1987, Sched. 1, Form 6.

[12] See the N.-C.P.R. 1987, r. 56(3), (*post*, p. 365).

[13] See *ante*, pp. 241/242.

[14] See *post*, p. 308.

[15] See *post*, p. 308 *et seq.*

[16] Administration of Estates Act 1971, ss.2(5), 3(2). See Pugh on *Administration of Foreign Estates*.

[17] See *ante*, pp. 301, 368.

Addition of a further representative

Where an order on summons has been made by a registrar for a further representative to be added, the order and the grant are lodged. The appointment of the additional representative is then noted on the grant and the record.

Notation of transfer of representative powers

Where an order is made under the Insolvency legislation[18] or section 1 of the Judicial Trustees Act 1896, which transfers the power of the personal representative to the person named in the order, the court which makes the order will notify the principal registry of the terms of the order. The record copy of the grant is noted as to the effect of the order and, if the grant issued from a district registry, that registry is notified of the order and its record copy grant noted.[19]

C. REVOCATION OF GRANTS

The court has power to revoke grants of probate and letters of administration.[20] Such revocation is effected (i) by decree or order in an action; (ii) by order of a judge on motion; (iii) by order of a registrar. In addition the court has power, of its own motion, to call in a grant where it appears that it should not have been made or that it contains an error, and if satisfied that it would be revoked at the instance of a party interested, to revoke it.[21] A grant may be revoked even if it is not possible to call it in.[22] A personal representative has a statutory duty when required to do so by the High Court to deliver up the grant of probate or administration to that court.[23]

Revocation by order in an action

Where the plaintiff succeeds in an action for revocation of a grant,[24] the judge orders the grant to be revoked. In the rare case where a grant has been obtained after a probate action but before an appeal, the Court of Appeal, if it reverses the decision, may revoke the grant.

Revocation by the court on motion

Revocation by this procedure is uncommon. Where, however, a grant has been obtained on the basis of an incorrect or false statement and the

---

[18] Insolvency Act 1986 and the Administration of Insolvent Estates of Deceased Persons Order 1986 (S.I. 1986 No. 1999).

[19] Secretary's Circular, May 18, 1953 (as amended) and Secretary's Circular, July 6, 1953.

[20] Supreme Court Act 1981, s.25. No statutory limitation period applies. See *Re Flynn* [1982] 1 W.L.R. 310, 314.

[21] Administration of Justice Act 1956, s.17(1).

[22] *Ibid.* subs. (2).

[23] Administration of Estates Act 1925, s.25 as substituted by s.9 of the Administration of Estates Act 1971.

[24] For actions for revocation of grants, see *post*, p. 407.

grantee, though not asserting that the grant was correctly made, will not consent to its revocation, the person seeking its revocation may apply to a judge on motion.

Revocation by a registrar

This procedure applies where the grantee applies for or consents to revocation.[25] A registrar may revoke a grant without consent only in exceptional circumstances.[26] He may also revoke a grant on an application for the addition of a personal representative.[27] He may revoke a grant without any application where it was wrongly made because of an official error.[28]

Grounds for revoking a grant

The principal grounds for revoking a grant are: (i) That it was obtained by a false or incorrect statement. (ii) That there is a supervening defect in the grant. (iii) That the grant was in effect a nullity. (iv) That the name of the deceased was wrongly stated in the grant. This latter ground is rarely used. An amendment is more appropriate.

1. Grant obtained by a false or incorrect statement

Examples of revocation ordered under this head are:

(a) Where a will has been discovered after a grant of administration or a later valid will discovered after a grant of probate of an earlier will.

(b) Where, after a grant of probate, a codicil is discovered altering or revoking the appointment of executors. In this case a new grant is made of probate of the will and codicil, but if the appointment of executors is not affected, separate probate of the codicil is granted.

Where a codicil is discovered after a grant of administration (with the will) the grant is revoked and a fresh grant of administration with the will and codicil annexed is made.

(c) Where administration has been granted to a guardian of a minor without those with prior rights being cleared off.[29]

(d) Where the executor of an invalid, revoked or forged will obtains probate.

(e) Where the executor obtained probate in England[30] of a will the validity of which was being contested in the court of the domicile.

(f) Where a minor obtains a grant on the basis that he is of full age.

(g) Where a grant to the estate of a living person is obtained, *e.g.* a supposed death on active service,[31] or the presumed deceased is found alive after leave has been given to swear his death.

---

[25] N.-C.P.R. 1987, r. 41(1).
[26] N.-C.P.R. 1987, r. 41(2).
[27] N.-C.P.R. 1987, r. 26(2).
[28] Administration of Justice Act 1956, s.17.
[29] *Re Morris* (1862) 2 Sw. Tr. 360.
[30] *Trimlestown (Lord)* v. *Trimlestown (Lady)* (1830) 3 Ecc. 243, 248.
[31] *Re Napier* (1809) 1 Phill. 83.

(h) Where a grant is made to a person falsely claiming to be the widow of the deceased or his next-of-kin.[32]

(i) Where a grant is made to the Crown, but next-of-kin are discovered.[33]

2. Supervening defect in the grant

(a) *Where a grantee becomes incapable.*   Where one of two or more grantees becomes incapable, the grant must be revoked and a new grant made. Where one of two or more executors becomes incapable the new grant is made to the capable executor, power being reserved to the incapable executor to take a grant on his recovery.[34] Where there is only one executor or both executors become incapable, the court revokes the grant and makes a new grant to person(s) next entitled in priority.[35]

Where one of two or more administrators becomes incapable, the new grant is made to any co-grantee.[36] Where the incapable grantee had a superior title to take of his co-grantee, the new grant by limitation reserves the right of the former to a grant on his recovery. If the new administrator has an inferior title to the incapable grantee, the new grant will be for the use and benefit of the latter.[37] Where the sole grantee becomes incapable the grant may be impounded[38] and not revoked.

(b) *Where the grantee disappears.*   The grant is revoked and a new grant *de bonis non* is issued to a person interested in the estate.[39]

(c) *Grantees wishing to be relieved of their duties.*   Grants are occasionally revoked because grantees wish to be relieved of their duties,[41] but special circumstances must be shown. The normal procedure is to apply to the Chancery Division for the removal of the grantees and substitution of new grantees.[42]

(d) *Where a grantee is no longer interested in the estate.*   Grants have been revoked when the grantee has ceased to be interested in the estate, *e.g.* a grant to a trustee in bankruptcy or a creditor on the debts being paid in full.[43]

---

[32] *Re Moore* (1845) 3 N.C. 601; *Re Bergman* (1842) 2 N.C. 22. Fraud need not be proved, see *Evan* v. *Stevenson* (1963) 107 S.J. 893. See also *Warren* v. *Kelson* (1859) 1 Sw. & Tr. 290.

[33] As to claims arising after administration by the Crown see *Ing on Bona Vacantia*, pp. 81 *et seq.*

[34] *Re Sowerby* (1891) 65 L.T. 764; *Re Shaw* [1905] P. 92.

[35] *Re Galbraith* [1951] P. 422.

[36] *Re Newton* (1843) 3 Curt. 428.

[37] *Registrar's Direction*, July 16, 1956.

[38] The practice of impounding grants has been abandoned: *Registrar's Direction* July 9, 1985. It is usual for the grant to be held in abeyance pending the original grantee's recovery.

[39] *Re Loveday* [1900] P. 154; see *Re Covell* (1889) 15 P.D. 8.

[40] *Re Jenkins* (1819) 3 Phill. 33.

[41] *Re Hoare* (1833) 2 Sw. & Tr. 361n; *Re Galbraith, supra*; constrast *Re Heslop* (1846) Rob. Eccl. 457, which would probably not be followed.

[42] Administration of Justice Act 1985, s.50.

[43] *Re Thacker* [1900] P. 15; *Re Hoare, supra*; see *Re Ferrier* (1828) 1 Hag.Ecc. 241.

3. Where the grant is, in effect, a nullity

(a) *Where a grantee has died*   before the grant has passed the seal it will be revoked.

(b) *Will not duly executed.*   Where, since the making of the grant, it is discovered that the will was not duly executed and proof thereof is provided, the grant will be revoked.

(c) *Grant made too soon.*   Where, through inadvertence, a grant of probate or of administration (with the will) is made without special leave within seven days of the death of the deceased or a grant of administration within 14 days of death,[44] it will be revoked but a new grant will be made to the same grantees.

4. Name of the deceased wrongly stated in the grant

Where the surname or the first forename of the deceased in the grant is seriously incorrect, the grant will be revoked. Minor spelling mistakes are corrected by amendment.[45]

Revocation by the court of its own motion

The statutory power[46] of the court to revoke grants of its own motion is usually applied to correct official errors. It is also used where a grantee is no longer entitled to act as the result of his criminal conduct, but no one is willing to take any action to revoke the grant.

Courts refusal to revoke

The court will not revoke a grant limited to taking proceedings in another Division merely to enable a general grant to issue,[47] or merely to preserve the right to sue of a person who has been guilty of laches.[48] A grant was not revoked merely because it misstated the persons entitled to share in the estate.[49] The failure of an administrator to disclose all the assets of the estate to the Inland Revenue and to give satisfactory particulars of the estate when requested is not enough to entail the revocation of the grant.[50] Where probate in common form was granted by consent, it was held that it could not be revoked on the allegation that conditions on which that consent had been given had not been complied with, no fraud being alleged.[51] The revocation of a grant may be rescinded in a proper case.[52]

---

[44] See the N.-C.P.R., 1987 r. 6.
[45] See *ante*, p. 357.
[46] Under the Supreme Court Act 1981, s.25(1)(*b*); s.121.
[47] *Re Brown* (1872) L.R. 2 P. & D. 455.
[48] *Willis* v. *Beauchamp (Earl)* (1886) 11 P.D. 59.
[49] *Re Ward* [1971] 1 W.L.R. 1376.
[50] *Re Cope* [1954] 1 All E.R. 698.
[51] *Nicol* v. *Askew* (1837) 2 Moo.P.C. 88.
[52] *Re Stables* (1831) 3 Hag.Ecc. 560.

Practice

Where the grantee is the applicant or consents to revocation, the application is made to the registry where the grant was issued.

Where a grantee refuses to allow revocation then the person desiring it must make application by summons to a registrar supported by an affidavit of facts. A probate action may be necessary.

Although a grant may be revoked on the application of a grantee who has no right to a fresh grant, the usual practice is for the person seeking the revocation to take a fresh grant. A creditor may obtain the revocation of a grant.[53] A grant may be revoked even after the death of the grantee or the ceasing of the grant.[54]

Applications to a registrar are supported by an affidavit giving details of the first grant and the ground for revocation, and showing the right to a fresh grant. The consent of the grantee (if he is not the applicant) must be lodged. The grant must be produced unless the person in whose custody it is has failed to obey the order (which must be served on him) to bring in the grant, and it is impossible or impracticable to secure its production. Where solicitors had a lien on a grant of administration they were allowed to retain it after its revocation.[55] A lost grant may be revoked, but the grantee may be put on terms to bring it in if it should be found.[56]

Any will or codicil of later date than that already proved must be produced and, where the grantee has died before the grant was issued, a certificate of death is required. The incapacity of a grantee is proved by the certificate of the responsible medical officer where the patient is in a mental hospital; or by an affidavit from the patient's doctor.[57]

Where one executor has become incapable, one application may be made to cover the revocation of the grant and the issue of a new grant to the remaining executors who took probate.[58] Otherwise the grant must be revoked before the new one is issued.

Effect of revocation

Conveyances

All conveyances of any interest in real or personal estate made to a purchaser by a grantee are valid notwithstanding the revocation or variation of the grant of probate or administration.[59] A "purchaser" is defined[60] as a lessee, mortgagee or other person who in good faith acquires an interest in property for valuable consideration. The provision applies without preju-

---

[53] See *Re French* [1910] P. 169.
[54] *Registrar's Direction*, July 15, 1924.
[55] *Barnes* v. *Durham* (1869) L.R. 1 P. & D. 728.
[56] *Re Carr* (1858) 1 Sw. & Tr. 11.
[57] *Practice Direction (Representation: Mental Incapacity)* [1962] 1 W.L.R. 738.
[58] See *Re Phillips* (1824) 2 Add. 335; *Re Marshall* (1836) 1 Curt. 297.
[59] Administration of Estates Act, s.37(1) and see *ante*, p. 40.
[60] Administration of Estates Act 1925, s.55(1)(xviii). A purchaser of settled land is covered, see *Re Bridgett and Hayes* [1928] Ch. 163; *Re Taylor* [1929] P. 260, 263.

dice to any order of the court made before 1926 and whenever the testator or intestate died.[61]

Persons acting on the grant

Persons who in good faith act under a grant of representation are protected despite its revocation by section 27 of the Administration of Estates Act 1925, and despite the fact that the supposed deceased proves to be alive.[62]

But a grantee who makes payments after having notice of the existence of a later will or of other facts casting doubt on the correctness of the grant made to him will be liable.[63] Where an executor pays a charitable bequest to the trustee thereof named in the will who bona fide applies it in accordance with the will and the grant is afterwards revoked, the new grantee cannot compel the trustee to repay the money to him.[64]

Orders of the court

By section 204(1) of the Law of Property Act 1925: "An order of the court under any statutory or other jurisdiction shall not, as against a purchaser, be invalidated on the ground of want of jurisdiction, or want of any concurrence, consent, notice, or service, whether the purchaser has notice of any such want or not."

A grant of probate[65] or letters of administration[66] is an order of the court within this section, but the wording is not conclusive.[67]

Payment after revocation

A purchaser or other person who makes payment to a personal representative after the grant has been revoked will not be protected under the provisions above mentioned unless at the time he made the payment he had no knowledge of the revocation, in which case it may be that protection would extend to him.

Payments to agents of personal representative

Where a personal representative employs an agent, e.g. an auctioneer, and the grant is revoked and a fresh grant made to another person, it seems that the latter is bound by any contract made by the agent and by the contract of agency itself "as if it had been entered into by himself."[68] It seems, therefore, that a person who had previously dealt with the agent and was

---

[61] Administration of Estates Act 1925, s.37(2) 1125.
[62] Re Bloch, The Times, July 2, 1959. For the terms of s.27, see ante, p. 40.
[63] Woolley v. Clark (1822) 5 B. & Ald. 744.
[64] Fitzpatrick v. M'Glone [1897] 2 Ir.R. 542.
[65] Re Bridgett and Hayes, supra. See also post, p. 449 et seq., 883.
[66] Hewson v. Shelley [1914] 2 Ch. 13. See, post, p. 449 et seq., 455.
[67] Re Ward [1971] 1 W.L.R. 1376.
[68] See the Administration of Estates Act 1925, s.39(1)(iii).

ignorant that the new personal representative had rescinded the contract of agency would be protected as to any payment made to the agent.

Effect of appeal on intermediate acts

It seems that all acts protected by the provisions mentioned above would still be protected if done between the issue of a grant after a probate action and its revocation as the result of a successful appeal, unless a pending action had been registered in respect of proceedings affecting land.[69]

Legal proceedings to continue

If an action is brought by an administrator and, while it is pending, the grant is revoked and administration is committed to another, the court may order that the proceeding be continued by or against the new personal representative in like manner as if the same had been originally commenced by or against him. The court may impose conditions in making such an order.[70] Such an order may be obtained *ex parte* upon an allegation of transmission of interest to the new administrator by the fresh grant.[71]

If an administrator, before his grant is revoked, obtains judgment for a debt due to the estate, the new administrator may apply for leave to issue execution.[72]

Defence after grant has been revoked

Where a person is sued as personal representative after the grant to him has been revoked, he should allege in his defence not only the facts but that he has fully administered all the assets in his hands, or delivered them to the new representative.[73]

D. IMPOUNDING OF GRANTS

Where the sole grantee or sole surviving grantee becomes incapable of managing his affairs and the new grant is made to the person authorised by the Court of Protection to apply for it, the old grant is not revoked and remains at large. The grant is no longer impounded.[74] As already shown,[75] where one of several grantee becomes incapable, the grant is revoked.

Where the deceased dies domiciled abroad and his executor becomes incapable, a new grant may be issued to the persons appointed by the court of the domicile to manage his affairs.

---

[69] Land Charges Act 1972, s.5; the Law of Property Act 1925, s.198.

[70] Administration of Estates Act 1925, s.17.

[71] R.S.C., Ord. 15, r. 7.

[72] R.S.C., Ord. 46, r. 2.

[73] This seems to be the principle deducible from the old system of pleading. See *Garter* v. *Dee* (1671) 1 Freem. K.B. 13; *Palmer* v. *Litherham* (1627) Latch. 267; *Lawson* v. *Crofts* (1658) 1 Keb. 114. See *post*, 894.

[74] The former practice of impounding grants has been discontinued: *Registrar's Direction*, July 9, 1985.

[75] See *ante*, p. 362.

Practice

An order to impound a grant is obtained on production of the grant together with an affidavit of facts by the proposed grantee. This is rarely used but can still be ordered on an application to add another personal representative under rule 26(2). Incapacity is proved as already set out.[76] If the grant cannot be produced in spite of all reasonable efforts to do so the registrar will usually accept an undertaking to bring it in if it later comes to hand.[77]

In applications for the revocation of a grant and for a fresh one to issue, one affidavit should be so drafted as to cover both applications.

The new grant is a grant *de bonis non* or, in the case of double probate, a grant to the whole estate. The value of the estate shown in the Oath and grant is of the part still unadministered.

On the recovery of the incapable person, both the temporary grant and the original grant (if at large) are brought in and the recovery of the grantee proved by production of the order of the Court of Protection or by a medical affidavit. The consent of the temporary grantee must be shown and the temporary grant will be noted with the fact that it had ceased by reason of the recovery of the original grantee.

Where the sole or sole surviving grantee dies without having recovered capacity, the grant having been impounded, and his will is proved by his executors, the original grant may, on a registrar's order, be delivered to them so that they can show a chain of executorship.

---

[76] See ante, pp. 325 *et seq*.
[77] *Registrar's Direction*, October 6, 1961.

CHAPTER 28

RECOGNITION AND RESEALING

A grant issued in one part of the United Kingdom is recognised in another part of the United Kingdom under the provisions for reciprocal recognition of grants contained in the Administration of Estates Act 1971.[1] Resealing of such grants is therefore no longer required.

Grants issued in the United Kingdom, together with those issued in the majority of the countries of the Commonwealth are made effective in most other parts of the Commonwealth by resealing, *i.e.* sealing the grant again with the seal of the court of the confirming country or territory.

A. RECIPROCAL RECOGNITION WITHIN THE UNITED KINGDOM

Scotland

Where a person dies domiciled in Scotland, a confirmation[2] granted in respect of all or part of his estate and noting his Scottish domicile, and a certificate of confirmation[3] noting his Scottish domicile and relating to one or more items of his estate, shall be treated for the purposes of the law of England and Wales as a grant of representation to the executors[4] named in the confirmation or certificate.[5] In such circumstances the grant will be treated as a grant of probate, where it appears that the executors are named in the certificate as executors nominate, and in all other cases, as a grant of letters of administration.[6]

A confirmation, which will contain an inventory of the estate of the deceased[7] or a certificate of confirmation,[8] is to be treated under the law of

---

[1] See also *Practice Direction (Probate Grants: Sureties)* [1971] 1 W.L.R. 1790. The Act is set out at p. 1154, *post.*

[2] A confirmation is the equivalent under Scottish law of a grant of probate or letters of administration.

[3] A certificate of confirmation is a certificate issued by the Scottish Court on request showing that a specific item or items are included in the estate.

[4] The term "executors" here is to be construed according to the law of Scotland; Administration of Estates Act 1971, s.1(7).

[5] *Ibid.* s.1(1).

[6] *Ibid.* s.1(2).

[7] Which may include real estate of the deceased situated in England and Wales or Northern Ireland. *Ibid.* s.6(1) amending the Confirmation of Executors (Scotland) Act 1858. The confirmation may also contain a note or statement, signed by the Sheriff Clerk, of property in England and Wales and Northern Ireland held by the deceased in trust. The Administration of Estates Act 1971, s.1 will apply to such property as it applies to the property specified in the confirmation. Administration of Estates Act 1971, s.5(2).

[8] See n. 35, *supra.*

England and Wales as a grant in respect of the property specified in the confirmation or certificate, as the case may be.[9]

A confirmation includes an additional confirmation,[10] which itself includes an eik, a confirmation *ad non executa* and a confirmation *ad omissa vel male appretiata*.

The Act applies to confirmations granted before as well as after the commencement[11] of the Act.[12] In relation to a confirmation granted before the commencement of the Act, the relevant part of the Act takes effect as if it had come into force immediately before the grant was made.[13]

A document purporting to be a confirmation, additional confirmation or certificate, or a duplicate, given under seal will be accepted as such unless the contrary is proved.[14]

Section 7 of the Administration of Estates Act 1925 is not, by virtue of the 1971 Act, to apply on the death of an executor named in a confirmation or a certificate.[15] Thus the chain of representation will not continue by virtue of such an instrument on the death of an executor.[16]

The 1971 Act provides for the reciprocal recognition of English grants in Scotland.[17]

A person who is a personal representative by virtue of the Act may not be required to deliver up his grant.[18] The effect of this is to exclude section 25(*c*) of the Administration of Estates Act 1925 in such cases.[19]

Northern Ireland

Similarly the Act provides for the recognition of Northern Irish grants in England and Wales. Thus where a person dies domiciled in Northern Ireland a grant of probate of his will or letters of administration in respect of his estate, or any part of it, is to be treated for the purposes of the law of England and Wales as if it had originally been made by the High Court in England and Wales, provided it bears a note of the domicile.[20]

The Act applies to probates and letters of administration granted before as well as after the commencement[21] of the Act,[22] and, unless the contrary is proved such instruments, or copies, will be accepted without further proof if they purport to be issued under seal.[23]

---

[9] Administration of Estates Act 1971, s.1(1).
[10] *Ibid.* s.1(7).
[11] January 1, 1972. *Ibid.* s.14(2).
[12] *Ibid.* s.1(6).
[13] *Ibid.*
[14] *Ibid.* s.4(1)(*a*).
[15] *Ibid.* s.1(3).
[16] See *ante*, p. 44.
[17] Administration of Estates Act, 1971, s.3(1).
[18] *Ibid.* s.1(6).
[19] See p. 360 *ante*.
[20] *Ibid.* s.1(4).
[21] January 1, 1972. *Ibid.* s.14(2).
[22] *Ibid.* s.1(6).
[23] *Ibid.* s.4(2).

Again, a personal representative by virtue of the Act may not be required to give up his grant[24] but the chain of representation may be continued by virtue of a Northern Irish grant.

The Act provides for the reciprocal recognition of English grants in Northern Ireland.[25]

B. RESEALING OF GRANTS

Commonwealth grants in the United Kingdom

The resealing of grants made in member countries of the Commonwealth and in some former Member Countries is governed by the Colonial Probates Acts 1892 and 1927.[26] Section 1 of the 1892 Act provides that where any British possession recognises grants made in the United Kingdom, it may be directed by Order in Council that (subject to any exceptions or modifications) the Act shall apply to that possession. Section 2(1) provides for the resealing in England of grants made by the courts of the possessions to which the Act applies.

The countries and territories to which the Act at present applies are those laid down by the Colonial Probate Act Application Order 1965.[27] In addition grants made in the Republic of South Africa may be resealed.[28]

Following the repeal of the Probates and Letters of Administration (Ireland) Act 1857 by the Administration of Estates Act 1971, it is no longer possible to reseal any grant issued in The Republic of Ireland,[29] or in practice in Aden.[30]

Although the court may require evidence of domicile,[31] the statement in the Inland Revenue account is usually accepted.

---

[24] *Ibid.* s.1(5).

[25] *Ibid.* s.2.

[26] See also N.-C.P.R. 1987, r. 39.

[27] As amended by other orders to cover the change of name in certain territories. The countries and territories covered are: Alberta, Antigua, Australian Capital Territory, Bahamas, Barbados, Belize, Bermuda, Botswana, British Antarctic Territory, British Columbia, British Sovereign Base Areas in Cyprus, Brunei, Cayman Islands, Christmas Island (Australian), Cocos (Keeling) Islands, Cyprus (Republic), Dominica, Falkland Islands, Falkland Islands Dependencies, Fiji, Gambia, Ghana, Gibraltar, Grenada, Guyana, Hong Kong, Jamaica, Kenya, Kiribati, Lesotho, Malawi, Malaysia, Manitoba, Montserrat, New Brunswick, New Guinea (Trust Territory), New South Wales, New Zealand, Newfoundland, Nigeria, Norfolk Island, Northern Territory of Australia, North-West Territories of Canada, Nova Scotia, Ontario, Papua, Prince Edward Island, Queensland, St. Christopher, Nevis and Anguilla, St. Helena, St. Lucia, St. Vincent, Saskatchewan, Seychelles, Sierra Leone, Singapore, Solomon Islands, South Africa, South Australia, Sri Lanka, Swaziland, Tanzania, Tasmania, Tortola (formerly Virgin Islands), Trinidad and Tobago (Republic), Turks and Caicos Islands, Tuvalu (formerly Ellice Islands), Uganda, Victoria, Western Australia, Zambia, Zimbabwe as to which see *Practice Direction* (*Probate Grants: Zimbabwe*) [1980] 1 W.L.R. 553).

Although some of the above countries are no longer members of the Commonwealth, those listed have not repealed the legislation which governs resealing.

[28] South Africa Act 1962, s.2 and Sched. 2.

[29] As to the former position, see the 15th edition of this work.

[30] See *Tristram and Cootes Probate Practice* (27th ed.), p. 471–473.

[31] Colonial Probates Act 1892, s.2(2).

Except by the leave of a registrar, no grant may be resealed unless made under the Non-Contentious Probate Rules 1987 r. 30[32] (1)(a) or (b). If grant has been made to a person entrusted by the court of the domicile it may be resealed although it is not such a grant as would be made in England.[33] When resealing is applied for by a person beneficially entitled by the law of the domicile, no affidavit of law is now required.

Practice

The application is made at any registry or sub-registry by the grantee or a person on his behalf authorised in writing.[34] It may be made personally or by post.[35]

The original grant, a sealed duplicate grant or a copy grant certified by the proper officer of the court must be lodged and the grant must either include any copy will or be accompanied by a certified copy.[36] An exemplification of an original grant is treated as a copy.[37] Any power of attorney or authorisation of an agent must be lodged.

An Inland Revenue Account in Form IHT201 must be lodged.[38] No guarantee or surety is now required.

No limited or temporary grant may be resealed without the leave of a registrar,[39] except a grant to personal estate.[40] A grant limited to estate within the jurisdiction of the issuing court may not be resealed,[41] nor a grant to an attorney limited to estate out of England.[42] The nature of other limitations must be shown as must the character of the estate.[43]

Any power of attorney must expressly authorise the application for resealing. Any authorisation to apply to reseal must be in writing.[44] Where a trust corporation applies to reseal, no copy of the resolution appointing a nominee to apply need be lodged.[45]

The Public Trustee of New Zealand may in certain circumstances obtain a grant or order to administer an estate in that country. In the case of small estates he may file an election to administer. In the former case resealing is done in the ordinary way; but in the latter, before the election is resealed, the Public Trustee must certify that the election is still in force and undertake not to act further if the value of the estate exceeds the limits of a small

[32] N.-C.P.R. 1987, r. 39(3). As to the N.-C.P.R. 1987, r. 3, see *ante*, p. 299 *et seq.*
[33] *Re McLaughlin* [1922] P. 235.
[34] N.-C.P.R. 1987, r. 30(1).
[35] See *ante*, p. 280.
[36] N.-C.P.R. 1987, r. 39(5).
[37] President's Direction, March 13, 1902.
[38] N.-C.P.R. 1987, r. 39(2). See *ante*, p. 370 and see p. 1249 *post.*
[39] N.-C.P.R. 1987, r. 39(4).
[40] *Registrar's Direction*, May 26, 1936.
[41] *Registrar's Direction*, July 16, 1951.
[42] *Registrar's Direction*, September 23, 1930.
[43] *Registrar's Direction*, January 31, 1951.
[44] N.-C.P.R. 1987, r. 30(1).
[45] Senior Registrar's Decision, January 1956.

estate.[46] The Public Trustee of Queensland (formerly the Public Curator of Queensland)[47] may similarly obtain an order to administer or file an election, and these may be resealed in the same way.[48] There are also provisions for the filing of elections to administer small estates in Tasmania, Victoria and Western Australia, but in these cases the practice is for the elections to lead a grant to the Public Trustees of these states as the person entrusted.[49] These elections are not resealed without evidence in the particular case that they qualify as grants.

Where a grant has been made to more than one person, it cannot be resealed without authority from the others. Where a grant has been made to two or more executors and one has died, the death of that executor must be proved on resealing. The fiat and the record of resealing will show that the resealing was done at the instance of the others. Where a grant of probate has been made to an executor and resealed and a subsequent grant made to his executor on his death and resealed, a chain of executorship exists and no further grant to the original estate can be made in England.[50]

Resealing will be allowed in "nil" estates if the reason is given in writing.[51] In the case of settled land an English grant should be obtained.

Where, after resealing, another grantee has been added or the grant has been amended whereby an executor to whom power was reserved is deemed to be an executor, the amended grant may be resealed. Amendments to grants which have not been resealed cannot be resealed. Duplicate grants are resealed without any reason being given.[52] They bear the date when they are signed and no reference to the original resealing is made.[53]

English grants in Commonwealth countries

Enactments reciprocal to the Colonial Probates Acts 1892 and 1927 allow English grants to be resealed in those countries and territories to which the Colonial Probates Act Application Order 1965 applies.

---

[46] *Registrar's Direction*, March 24, 1958.
[47] Name and title changed by the Queensland Australia Statute entitled The Public Trustee Act 1978.
[48] *Registrar's Direction*, January 31, 1974.
[49] *Registrar's Direction*, November 20, 1972.
[50] *Registrar's Direction*, February 24, 1949.
[51] President's Direction, March 4, 1942.
[52] *Registrar's Direction*, July 18, 1941.
[53] *Registrar's Direction*, January 27, 1942.

CHAPTER 29

SEARCHES, COPIES, EXEMPLIFICATIONS, DUPLICATES AND DEPOSIT OF WILLS OF LIVING PERSONS

Searches and copies

All wills and other documents under the control of the High Court in any probate registry are to be deposited and preserved in such places as the Lord Chancellor may direct and, subject to the control of the High Court and the probate rules, are to be open for inspection,[1] but an original will or other document referred to in section 124 of the Supreme Court Act 1981 is not open to inspection if in the opinion of a registrar such inspection would be undesirable or otherwise inappropriate.[2] A record of grants is kept in the registries and is open to inspection.[3]

Any will proved in England and Wales since 1857 can be searched for, and a copy read, in the Principal Registry. Searches can also be made in the district registries. A copy of the whole or any part of a will may be obtained, (i) from the registry at which it is preserved, (ii) where not preserved at a registry, from the Principal Registry, (iii) subject to the approval of the Senior District Judge of the Family Division, from that registry in cases in which the will was proved in a district registry.[4]

A procedure exists for the making of a "standing search." On payment of the prescribed fee, an office copy will be sent of any grant which corresponds with the particulars contained in the application, and is issued either not more than 12 months before the application is received or within six months thereafter. The application is made to the Record Keeper at the Principal Registry, or to any district registry or sub-registry, and may be renewed on payment of the prescribed fee for further periods of six months.[4]

Copies may be facsimile copies sealed with the seal of the court and issued either as office copies or certified under the hand of a registrar to be true copies.[5] Copies must include all documents admitted to probate, whether proved together or separately.[6] Certain countries require special forms of certificate in respect of copy wills and these are obtainable on application. A sealed and certified copy of an original document in a

---

[1] Supreme Court Act 1981, s.124. As to deposits of wills of living persons, see *post*, p. 375.
[2] N.-C.P.R. 1987, r. 58.
[3] Supreme Court Act 1981, s.111.
[4] N.-C.P.R. 1987, r. 43 (as amended with effect from October 14, 1991).
[5] N.-C.P.R. 1987, r. 59.
[6] *Registrar's Direction*, July 19, 1935.

foreign language may also be obtained, unless the document is a notarial or other certified copy of the original.

All probates, letters of administration, orders and other instruments and copies thereof, as well as exemplifications are receivable in evidence in all parts of the United Kingdom without further proof.[7]

Copies of documents in proceedings

Any person may, on payment of the prescribed fee, take copies of any writ or other originating process, any judgment or order given or made in court, or the copy thereof, and (with the leave of a registrar on *ex parte* application) of any other document.[8]

Wills proved before 1858

Wills of this period are preserved in a number of places. The only records preserved in the High Court are those of the Prerogative Court of Canterbury and certain others of minor importance. Some of these records are kept at the Principal Registry and some at the Public Record Office and may be searched on special conditions. Inquiries as to these records should be directed to the Record Keeper of the Principal Registry. Copies may be taken.

Exemplifications

An exemplification is a document (usually obtained because of the requirements of a foreign court) which contains an exact copy of any will and what is virtually a copy of the grant. A testimonium clause is signed by a registrar and the document is then sealed. Exemplifications of grants which have been resealed in England are not issued.

Exemplifications of grants issued in a district registry must be applied for in the registry which issued them. In the Principal Registry application may be made on personal attendance or by post.

In this connection it may be mentioned that there is no jurisdiction to allow an original will which has been admitted to proof to be sent out of the jurisdiction.[9]

Duplicate grants

Duplicate grants are only issued to grantees. Application for a duplicate grant is made *ex parte* to a registrar. The usual reason for applying for duplicate grants is that the original has been lost or destroyed. In this case the application may be made by letter from the applicant's solicitor. In other cases the grantee must himself write and state the reason why a duplicate is sought.

---

[7] Supreme Court Act 1981, s.132.
[8] See R.S.C., Ord. 63, r. 4(1) as applied to probate causes of matters by R.S.C., Ord. 76, r. 1.
[9] *Re Greer* (1929) 73 S.J. 349.

The application must be made at the registry from which the original grant was issued. The letter of request must be lodged and, at the Principal Registry—but not at a district registry—the original grant or an office copy thereof. Special conditions apply in respect of grants issued before 1935. Save that these grants are headed "Duplicate Grant" they are the same as the original.[10] They bear any official amendment or notation which has been made.[11]

Deposit of the wills of living persons

A depository for the wills of living persons is provided at the Principal Registry of the Family Division.[12] Wills may be deposited by sending them there by post, or by depositing them there or at a district registry on payment of the prescribed fee.[13] Although a will which has been thus deposited may be revoked by another testamentary instrument, except with leave it cannot be handed out again nor can the testator attend to destroy it.

A testator who attends a registry to deposit his will signs an endorsement on a sealed envelope containing it.[14] This endorsement gives the name and address of the executors and contains an undertaking by the testator to notify the executors of their appointment and of the deposit.[15] The date of the testator's birth is given to assist identification, and the endorsement is signed in the presence of an officer of the registry, who also signs the endorsement.[16] A will may be sent by post to the Principal Registry for deposit. It will be accepted if it is in a sealed envelope bearing an endorsement in the above form which purports to be signed by the testator.[17] A will may be presented for deposit at any registry by an agent. It will be accepted if the registrar is satisfied that the agent has authority to deposit the will.[18]

When a will is deposited, an officer of the registry gives or sends to the testator (and, if applicable, his agent) a certificate which states the names of the testator and executors, and the date of the will and that, except by leave, the will may not be taken out.[19] A copy of the certificate is filed with the will.[20]

When a will is lodged at a district registry for deposit, it is forwarded to

---

[10] *Registrar's Direction*, January 27, 1942.

[11] *Registrar's Direction*, July 30, 1941.

[12] See the Supreme Court Act 1981, s.126, prospectively repealed and to be replaced by the Administration of Justice Act 1982, ss.23–26.

[13] See generally, the Wills (Deposit for Safe Custody) Regulations 1978 (S.I. 1978 No. 1724).

[14] *Ibid.* reg. 4.

[15] *Ibid.* reg. 3(1).

[16] *Ibid.* reg. 4.

[17] *Ibid.* reg. 5(1).

[18] *Ibid.*

[19] *Ibid.* regs. 4 and 5(2).

[20] *Ibid.*

the Principal Registry together with a copy of the certificate.[21] Whenever a will is deposited at the Principal Registry, a sufficient record of the deposit will be made to enable the fact to become known when any application is made for a grant to the testator's estate.[22]

Wills of incapable persons

The Court of Protection may authorise the deposit of the will of a patient, in which case the person authorised to make the deposit signs the endorsement on the envelope containing the will and gives the particulars which a testator depositor is required to give. A certificate of deposit is drawn up and signed by the registrar and delivered to the depositor.

At a district registry a certificate is given to the depositor but the copy is sent to the Principal Registry.

Withdrawal of deposited will

A deposited will may not be withdrawn before the death of the testator without leave.[23] The request for the return of the will is made to the Principal Registry and should be accompanied by the certificate of deposit.[24] If the district judge is satisfied of the identity of the testator and that it would be proper to return the will, he will do so, and the record of the original deposit will be noted accordingly.[25]

Procedure on death of testator

A deposited will is not to be released until the death of the testator is established to the satisfaction of the district judge.[26] There should be produced to him the death certificate of the testator, or such other evidence of death as may satisfy him, and, unless the district judge otherwise directs, the certificate of deposit.[27] The district judge may then open the envelope containing the will and subject to any precautions which he thinks necessary, deliver the will to the executor of any other person who the district judge is satisfied intends to prove the will or, where the will has been revoked or no grant is required, to the person entitled to possession of the will.[28] The person receiving the will is required to give a written undertaking to lodge the will on any application for a grant.[29]

Deposit of the wills of persons subject to military law

Where the will of a person who dies while subject to military law comes

[21] Wills (Deposit for Safe Custody) Regulations 1978 (S.I. 1978 No. 1724), reg. 6.
[22] *Ibid*. reg. 7.
[23] *Ibid*. reg. 8(4).
[24] *Ibid*. reg. 8(1).
[25] *Ibid*. reg. 8(2).
[26] *Ibid*. reg. 8(4).
[27] *Ibid*. reg. 9(1).
[28] *Ibid*.
[29] *Ibid*. reg. 9(2).

into the hands of a Secretary of State and representation to the estate is not taken out, he may, where the domicile of the deceased appears not to have been Scottish or Irish, cause it to be deposited in the Principal Registry.[30]

Where such person dies intestate, the Secretary of State may, where any property of the deceased comes into his hands and representation is not taken out, deposit at the Principal Registry a declaration of the deceased's intestacy.[31]

In either case the Secretary of State may also deposit an inventory of the personal property of the deceased, showing how it has been applied.[32] Such wills, declarations and inventories are preserved and may be inspected in the same way as other documents preserved in the Registry.

The term "living will" has no legal significance but is generally used to describe a document expressing a wish that if the "testator" becomes so seriously ill that there is no prospect of recovery, procedures to sustain life should be withheld. The draftsman of such a document is torn between the duty to the client and the risk of prosecution under the Suicide Act 1961.[33]

International Wills

Under the 1973 Convention on International Wills[34] a will made in the form required has international validity as prescribed.[35] When these sections come into force the United Kingdom will be able to ratify the Convention.

---

[30] Regimental Debts Act 1983, s.21.
[31] *Ibid.*
[32] *Ibid.*
[33] See p. 972 *post* and article by D. A. Lush, 86 *Law Society's Gazette*, 21.
[34] See Sched. 2 to the Administration of Justice Act 1982.
[35] Administration of Justice Act 1982, s.27. The procedure is set out in s.28.

CHAPTER 30

RENUNCIATION AND RETRACTATION

Renunciation

Renunciation must be absolute and not conditional and is a formal act in writing[1] whereby a person having a right to probate or administration waives and abandons that right. Although renunciation takes effect from signature,[2] it may be withdrawn at any time up to filing.[3] The court may allow a renunciation to be retracted.[4]

Renunciation by an executor binds his personal representative, but renunciation by any other person does not. Consequently the personal representatives of a person who has renounced administration may take a grant *de bonis non*.

Persons having a superior right must renounce (or be otherwise cleared off) before those having an inferior right to a grant may take it; the mere consent of the renunciant is not enough.[5]

Form of renunciation

The renunciation may be signed by any number of renunciants. It need not be under seal. A renunciation in English by a person of a non-English speaking race will not be accepted unless it is executed before a notary public, or the registrar is satisfied in some other way that the renunciant understood the nature and effect of his act.

Renunciation by a person entrusted with administration by the law of the domicile of the deceased does not affect his right to a grant in England unless he specifically renounces that right.

A trust corporation renounces under seal or by an official appointed to execute renunciations,[6] and in the latter case the resolution of the corporation appointing the official or a certified copy thereof must be produced. A non-trust corporation should, by resolution, appoint a nominee to renounce on its behalf. The resolution or a certified copy should be lodged. In many cases a resolution by the board of management may be accepted as an alternative.

Renunciation on terms

Executors are not entitled to a formal release from liability as a term of

---

[1] The seal of a corporation is equivalent to writing.
[2] *Munday* v. *Slaughter* (1839) 2 Curt. 72.
[3] *Re Morant* (1874) L.R. 3 P. & D. 151.
[4] See *post*, p. 381.
[5] *Garrard* v. *Garrard* (1871) L.R. 2 P. & D. 238.
[6] Secretary's Circular, July 19, 1955.

their renunciation or of their handing over the documents relating to the estate.

Renunciation before the application for a grant

Although it is not a common practice, an executor may renounce before the application for a grant and, indeed, as soon as the testator is dead. His renunciation must be accompanied by the original will, both of which documents are then filed in the registry to which they are sent. Where an executor who renounces is entitled also to a grant of administration with will annexed, his renunciation will not be accepted unless he also renounces administration (with will annexed).[7] Where the will cannot be found, the renunciation must be accompanied by a verified copy, if available, and an affidavit accounting for the non-production of the original.

Where no executor is named in the will, the persons entitled to the residue may renounce but must file the will.

Renunciations before the application for a grant are filed in the registry, a district registry notifying the Principal Registry of renunciations filed in it.

Upon any subsequent application for a grant the applicant must swear the Oath and mark the will before the authorised officer of the registry in which the will is filed, unless arrangements are made for this to take place at another registry. In cases of difficulty application may be made for an official copy of the will to be marked instead of the original.[8]

Renunciation on application for a grant

Most renunciations are made in connection with an application for a grant. In this case the renunciation is lodged with the papers to lead the grant.

Effect of renunciation

An executor's renunciation of probate does not affect any right he has to take administration unless he renounces that right as well.[9] Consequently where he wishes to renounce his rights in both capacities, the renunciation should cover both. But where a bare executor had renounced probate he was allowed to take administration (with the will) as the attorney of his co-executors.[10]

Renunciation of probate is a renunciation in respect of all wills of the testator and of those of which he was executor in consequence of a chain of executorship.[11] Any executor or administrator may renounce any administration to which he would be entitled in his representative capacity. The

---

[7] *Registrar's Direction*, October 5, 1954.
[8] N.-C.P.R. 1987, r. 10(2).
[9] N.-C.P.R., 1987 r. 37(1).
[10] *Re Russell* (1869) L.R. 1 P. & D. 634.
[11] *Re Perry* (1840) 2 Curt. 655. See also *post*, p. 577 (as to leases).

renunciation of an acting executor without that of a co-executor to whom power has been reserved is enough, it would seem, to allow a person entitled in a lower degree to take a grant.

An attorney may renounce on behalf of a person living abroad if the power of attorney specifically authorises him to do so.[12]

Although an executor who has renounced probate abroad only may take a grant as administrator, an administrator who has renounced in any capacity may not take a grant in some other capacity (*i.e.* a lower one) unless a registrar otherwise directs.[13]

The appointment of a minor as executor does not constitute him a personal representative for any purpose until probate has been granted to him.[14] Consequently he may renounce on attaining full age even if a grant has been taken out for his use and benefit during his minority.

Renunciation by an executor to whom power has been reserved

Where an executor to whom power has been reserved wishes to renounce after the grant has issued, the renunciation (which need not refer to the grant) may be brought into the Principal Registry or a district registry. An office copy of the grant may be produced if the original is not available for production. At the Principal Registry the renunciation is filed on a district judge's order; at a district registry the registrar signs a minute and notifies the Principal Registry of the renunciation. A notation of the renunciation is made on the record but not on the grant.

Renunciation on behalf of minors and incapable persons

A minor's right to administration may be renounced, but only by a person appointed under rule 32(2) and authorised to renounce by a district judge or district registrar. The mother of an unborn minor has been appointed his guardian for the purpose of renouncing. The right of a minor to probate on attaining full age may not be renounced by any person on his behalf.[15]

Where a person is incapable of managing his affairs, a person so authorised by the Court of Protection may renounce probate or administration on his behalf, unless the incapable person is an infant executor.

The next-of-kin of a person incapable of managing his affairs may not renounce a grant on his behalf.

An intermeddler may not renounce

If an executor has intermeddled in his deceased's estate, his renunciation

---

[12] *Re Rosser* (1864) 3 Sw. & Tr. 490, 492.

[13] N.-C.P.R. 1987, r.37(2). For the exercise of the registrar's discretion, see *Re Toscani* [1912] P. 1 and the cases there cited.

[14] Supreme Court Act 1981, s.118 (*post*, p. 1198).

[15] N.-C.P.R. 1987 r. 34(1).

will not be accepted and will be declared invalid.[16] But it is now possible for a person, after citing such executor to take probate, to ask for a grant to himself or to some other person,[17] and this course will probably be adopted in most cases of intermeddling by an executor. Alternatively application may be made to pass over the intermeddling executor's prior right.[18]

Renunciation is not rendered ineffective if the intermeddling is only of a technical nature.[19] An executor who is competent cannot be precluded from renouncing on any ground save that of intermeddling.[20] Persons, other than executors' who have intermeddled may renounce, since only executors are compellable to take a grant.[21]

The acts of an executor which amount to intermeddling have been discussed earlier.[22]

Grant to a further estate

Where a leading grant has been made to two administrators, one of whom does not wish to take a grant to a further estate which they have become entitled to administer in a representative capacity, such administrator may either renounce or give consent to the other one applying for a second grant. In the case of two executors, no renunciation or consent is required of the other if only one of them applies for a grant.

Non-appearance to a citation

Non-appearance by a person with a superior right to a grant, after service on him of a citation to accept or refuse a grant extracted by a person with an inferior right, has the same effect as renunciation by the citee and his rights wholly cease.[23]

Retractation

A renunciation cannot be countermanded by the person renouncing. It may, however, be retracted at any time by the order of a registrar.[24] Only in exceptional cases will leave be given to an executor to retract a renunciation of probate after a grant has been made to some person entitled in a lower degree.[25]

---

[16] *Re Biggs' Estate* [1966] P. 118; [1966] 1 All ER 358. *Re Badenach* (1864) 3 Sw. & Tr. 465; *Mordaunt* v. *Clarke* (1868) L.R. 1 P. & D. 592. Even if the intermeddling were confined to property abroad, *Re Lord and Fullerton's Contract* [1896] 1 Ch. 228. See also *ante*, pp. 40, 95 *post*, p. 389. As to the exercise of the jurisdiction to make a discretionary grant in such cases see *ante*, p. 345.
[17] See the N.-C.P.R. 1987 r. 47(5)(c).
[18] Supreme Court Act 1981, s.116.
[19] *Holder* v. *Holder* [1968] Ch. 353.
[20] *Jackson* v. *Whitehead* (1821) 3 Phill. 577.
[21] *Re Fell* (1861) 2 Sw. & Tr. 126; *Re Davis* (1860) 4 Sw. & Tr. 213.
[22] See *ante*, p. 40.
[23] Administration of Estates Act 1925, s.5.
[24] N.-C.P.R. 1987, r. 37(3).
[25] *Ibid.* proviso.

An executor wishing to retract must show that his retractation would be for the benefit of the estate or of those interested under the will of the deceased.[26] An executor, who is also a residuary legatee and has renounced in both capacities, may, in special circumstances, be permitted to retract his renunciation in the latter capacity.[27] An executor who has renounced probate has been refused an order to retract his renunciation, but has been permitted to take a grant *de bonis non* as a creditor.[28]

An administrator has been allowed to retract in special circumstances.[29]

Effect of retractation

Where an executor is permitted to retract his renunciation and proves the will, probate is deemed to take effect and always to have taken effect without prejudice to the previous acts and dealings of and notices to any other personal representative who has previously proved the will or taken out letters of administration.[30] A notation of the subsequent probate is made on the original grant, if available, and on the record. The grant when noted, is retained unless otherwise directed.

Persons, other than executors, must show that the retractation is necessary or expedient, *e.g.* because of difficulty in constituting any other person as administrator.[31]

Renunciation of administration by a person does not bind his personal representatives and they need not, therefore, apply to retract if they wish to obtain a grant.

Practice

Application for leave to retract a renunciation is made *ex parte* to a registrar.[32] An affidavit of facts must be filed in support, showing that the retractation is necessary or expedient. The former grant, if available, or an office copy, if it is not, together with the registrar's order and the affidavit are lodged at the Principal Registry or a district registry when the application for a fresh grant is made after retractation has been permitted.

---

[26] *Re Gill* (1873) L.R. 3 P. & D. 113. *sed quaere.*
[27] *Re Richardson* (1859) 1 Sw. & Tr. 515; *Re Wheelwright* (1878) 3 P.D. 71.
[28] *Re Toscani* [1912] P. 1.
[29] *Re Thacker* [1900] P. 15; see *Melville* v. *Ancketill* (1909) 100 L.T. 863.
[30] See the Administration of Estates Act 1925, s.6 (*post*, p. 1116).
[31] *Re Blake* (1866) 35 L.J.P. & M. 91.
[32] See the N.-C.P.R. 1987, r. 37(3) (*post*, p. 1238).

CHAPTER 31

CAVEATS AND DISCONTINUANCE

A. CAVEATS

A caveat[1] is a notice in writing that no grant is to be sealed in the estate of the deceased named, without notice to the caveator. No grant can be sealed if the registry is aware of the caveat, but it will not prevent the sealing of a grant on the day the caveat is entered.[2]

The main object of a caveat is to enable a person who is considering opposition to a grant to obtain evidence or legal advice in the matter. It is sometimes a preliminary to the issue of a writ or citation.

Where the real object of the person entering a caveat is not to prevent a grant being issued but merely to have notice of it,[3] it is more appropriate to apply for a standing search to be made.[4]

The effect of a caveat is that no grant can issue after its entry until it is removed or ceases to have effect. The entry of a caveat does not make the caveator liable to give security for costs in a subsequent action in which he is a defendant.[5]

Any person may apply for a search to be made for any effective caveat in the estate of any deceased person.

Entry of a caveat

Any person wishing to enter a caveat or a solicitor on his behalf may effect entry of a caveat by completing Form 3 in the appropriate book at the registry or sub-registry or by sending by post at his own risk a notice in Form 3 to any registry or sub-registry.[6] The proper officer provides an acknowledgment of the entry.[7] Notice of the entry of a caveat in the Principal Registry or in a district registry is immediately given to the registry which maintains the current index of grant applications. This is currently the Leeds District Probate Registry.[8]

---

[1] Caveats are regulated by s.108 of the Supreme Court Act 1981 and the N.-C.P.R., 1987, r. 44 (*post*, p. 1240). For form of caveat, see *post*, p. 250.

[2] N.-C.P.R. 1987, r. 44(1).

[3] For example, before making an application under the Inheritance (Provision for Family and Dependants) Act 1975.

[4] See *ante*, p. 373. A caveat should not be used when the only reason is a potential claim for family provision.

[5] *Re Emery* [1923] P. 184; *Rose* v. *Epstein* [1974] 1 W.L.R. 1565.

[6] N.-C.P.R. 1987, r. 44(2).

[7] *Ibid.*

[8] Supreme Court Act 1981, s.108; *Practice Direction* [1988] 3 All E.R. 544.

Duration and effect

A caveat normally remains in force for six months unless a registrar otherwise directs.[9] Any caveat in force when a summons for directions[10] is issued, remains in force until the summons is disposed of unless the registrar directs that it should cease to have effect.[11] Unless a District Judge of where application to discontinue is made by consent a registrar otherwise directs a caveat in respect of which an appearance to a warning has been entered remains in force until the commencement of a probate action.[12] The commencement of a probate action, though not extending the duration of a caveat, prevents the sealing of any grant (except a grant to an administrator pending suit), whether or not a caveat has been entered, until application for a grant made by the person shown to be entitled by the decision of the court[13]; whereupon any caveat entered by the plaintiff in the action, and any caveat in respect of which notice of the action was given, ceases to have effect.[14] A caveat may also cease to have effect by its withdrawal.[15] The death of a caveator does not automatically withdraw the caveat and a summons to do so is necessary. The court may order a grant to be issued despite the presence of a caveat or the issue of a writ where the procedure adopted by the caveator is vexatious and an abuse of the process of the court.[16]

Extension and renewal of a caveat

An application may be made within the last month of the six month period during which a caveat remains in force for its renewal for a *further* six months.[17] The application must be made to the registry in which the caveat was entered and must be in writing, but no special form is prescribed. The further six month period runs from the date of the expiry of the previous period. Successive applications may be made.

Except with leave of a district judge of the Principal Registry, no further caveat may be entered by a caveator whose caveat is either in force, or has ceased to have effect following the caveator's failure to enter an appearance, a district judge or a registrar's direction that the caveat should cease to have effect, or the court's decision in a probate action or in proceedings by way of citation or motion.[18] A further caveat, accepted in ignorance of such circumstances, is of no effect.[19] A further caveat, entered with leave,

---

[9] N.-C.P.R. 1987, r. 44(3).
[10] See *post*, p. 19.
[11] N.-C.P.R. 1987, r. 44(8).
[12] N.-C.P.R. 1987, r. 44(13) (as amended).
[13] See N.-C.P.R. 1987, r. 45(3).
[14] N.-C.P.R. 1987, r. 45(4).
[15] *Ibid.* sub-r. 11. The old term "subduct" has become obsolete.
[16] *Re Hancock decd.* (1978) C.L.Y. 1443.
[17] N.-C.P.R. 1987, r. 44(3).
[18] N.-C.P.R. 1987, r. 44(14).
[19] Registrar's Direction, January 28, 1958.

expires six months from entry and not six months from the expiry of the original caveat.[20]

Papers to lead grant retained on a caveat being entered

Although no grant is issued when a caveat is found to have been entered and to be still in force, the papers to lead the grant are retained in the registry until the caveat has been removed.

Warning of caveats

When an applicant for a grant finds that it has been stopped by the entry of a caveat, he may issue a warning in prescribed form.[21] This is a notice issued out of the Leeds District Probate Registry warning the caveator to enter an appearance at that Registry within eight days inclusive of the day of service, setting out his interest[22] or, if he has no contrary interest but wishes to show cause against the sealing of a grant, to issue and serve in the same period a summons returnable before a registrar.[23] He must give an address for service within the jurisdiction. The warning is served in the manner prescribed by Order 65, r. 5 of the Rules of the Supreme Court 1965.[24]

Withdrawal of caveats

A caveator may withdraw his caveat at any time before entering an appearance to the warning,[25] notwithstanding that proceedings are in progress by way of writ, citation or motion.[26] If the caveat has been warned, he must give notice of withdrawal forthwith to the person who has warned it.[27]

Notice that a caveat has been withdrawn is given by the registry to the applicant for the grant or his solicitors. The caveat must be withdrawn at the registry at which it was entered.

Non-appearance to warning

If a caveator takes no steps within eight days of service of the warning, the application for a grant may proceed on the applicant filing an affidavit showing that the warning has been duly served and that he has not received a summons for directions. The caveat thereupon ceases to have effect provided there is in fact no pending summons.[28]

---

[20] *Registrar's Direction*, January 28, 1958.
[21] See *post*, p. 1251.
[22] N.-C.P.R. 1987, r. 44(5); *Practice Direction* [1988] 3 All E.R. 544.
[23] See N.-C.P.R. 1987, r. 44(6).
[24] See N.-C.P.R. 1987, r. 67.
[25] N.-C.P.R. 1987, r. 44(11).
[26] *Registrar's Direction*, January 28, 1958.
[27] N.-C.P.R. 1987, r. 44(11).
[28] N.-C.P.R. 1987, r. 44(12); *Practice Direction* [1988] 3 All E.R. 544.

Appearance to warning

A caveator having an interest contrary to the person warning, and who wishes to enter an appearance to a warning, must do so within eight days of the warning, or later provided that the affidavit mentioned in the preceding paragraph has not been filed.[29] If such an affidavit has been filed, a further caveat may only be entered with leave.[30]

The caveator or his solicitor files the prescribed form Form 5 and enters an appearance in the Leeds District Probate Registry[31] in which the name and address of the caveator, and the interest of the caveator contrary to that of the person warning the caveat, are stated. Appearance may be entered by post. A sealed copy of the appearance must be served on the person warning the caveat.[32] Where a person who enters an appearance is interested under a will or codicil he must give the date thereof and show his interest, *e.g.* as residuary legatee. Where he claims to be interested under an intestacy, he must show how his interest arises.[33] A claim to provision under the Inheritance (Provision for Family and Dependants) Act 1975 is a claim against the estate and not an "interest" for this purpose, although a successful claimant will of course have the status of a beneficiary under the trusts of the will or intestacy. If a person entering an appearance does not show an interest, the entry of the appearance may be refused or struck out on application by summons of the person warning the caveat.

Appearance on behalf of minors or other persons under a disability is entered on the same principles as is an acknowledgment of service on their behalf to a writ.[34]

Summons for directions by a caveator

Where a caveator has no interest contrary to that of the person warning the caveat but wishes to show cause against the issue of a grant, he does not enter an appearance but may, within eight days of the service of the warning or before the applicant for a grant has filed his affidavit of service as to no summons for directions having been taken out, issue and serve such summons returnable before a registrar. On the hearing of this summons, the caveator asks for the relief which he requires.

Effect of appearance

Once an appearance has been entered no grant can be issued except to the caveator himself without an order of the court for the withdrawal of the caveat, unless a registrar otherwise orders.[35]

---

[29] *Ibid.*, sub-r. (10).
[30] See *ante*, p. 384.
[31] *Practice Direction* [1988] 3 All E.R. 544.
[32] *Ibid.* For form of appearance, see *post*, p. 1252.
[33] See *Ibid.*
[34] See *post*, pp. 411, 414.
[35] N.-C.P.R. 1987, r. 44(13).

Notification of probate actions to caveators

Upon the commencement of a probate action a copy of the writ is sent by a Chancery Master to the Senior District Judge of the Family Division, who then gives every caveator, other than the plaintiff, notice of the commencement of the action,[36] and upon the entry of a caveat during the pendency of the suit the caveator is similarly notified of the existence of the action.[37] A similar procedure applies where, in a non-probate action, a counter-claim is brought for a grant, or the revocation of a grant of representation.[38]

B. DISCONTINUANCE

The next step after appearance to a warning is normally the issue of a writ in the Chancery Division. However, it may be decided to discontinue the proceedings at this stage. This may happen in three sets of circumstances, first where it is alleged that the appearance dicloses no interest contrary to that of the person warning the caveat, secondly, where agreement has been reached as to the division of the estate between those claiming an interest, and thirdly, where a person has been cited to bring in a grant and, having obeyed, finds that no further step is taken.

No contrary interest shown

Occasionally it is alleged that the appearance shows no interest contrary to that of the person warning the caveat or is frivolous or vexatious. In such case a summons to discontinue proceedings may be taken out before a district judge of the Principal Registry. The summons must be taken out before the writ is issued.

Consent

Discontinuance of proceedings by consent before a writ has been issued is effected by a summons. Discontinuance of contentious proceedings is considered elsewhere.[39]

After citation

A person cited to bring in a grant who obeys the citation but finds that the citor takes no further step may apply to a registrar on summons for the discontinuance of the proceedings and for the delivery out to him of the grant.

---

[36] N.-C.P.R. 1987 r. 45(1).

[37] *Ibid.*, r. 45(2).

[38] Secretary's Circular, April 14, 1976. As to a probate counterclaim in a non-probate action, see *post*, p. 420.

[39] See *post*, p. 427. As to enforcement of consent orders see *Green* v. *Rozen* [1955] 1 W.L.R. 741; *McCallum* v. *Country Residences* [1965] 1 W.L.R. 657; *Wilson* v. *Express* [1969] 1 W.L.R. 197.

CHAPTER 32

CITATION

A citation is an instrument, signed by a registrar and issued under seal of the court, reciting that a cause or matter is before the court and the interest of the person extracting the citation and calling upon the party cited to enter an appearance and, in certain cases, to take some other step therein specified. Where the party cited is not called to take any step, an intimation is given that if he does not appear or, having appeared, does not show cause to the contrary, the court will proceed to make the order or declaration asked for in the citation. Citations are only issued on the application of a person interested in the estate. They are not issued by the court of its own motion.[1]

Types of citation

1. To accept or refuse a grant of probate or administration[2]

Where a person who has a prior right to a grant of probate or administration delays or declines to take it, but will not renounce his right, he may be cited by a person having an inferior right to accept or refuse a grant. If the citee does not then take a grant the citor may take one. If an executor does not appear to the citation, his rights as executor wholly cease, but if he has rights to a grant in a lower capacity, *e.g.* as residuary legatee, these do not cease unless he is cited in that capacity also.[3] Where power has been reserved to an executor, the executors who have proved or the survivor of them, or the executors of the last survivor of them may cite the executor to whom power was reserved to accept or refuse a grant.[4] Such procedure is adopted in order to preserve a particular chain of executorship.[5]

In cases of intestacy, persons beneficially interested in the estate, including creditors, may cite all persons having a superior right to a grant of administration and may apply for a grant if the citees do not appear. But registrars are not in favour of the issue of citations by persons whose only real interest in the estate depends upon the death of an untraced proposed citee who, if alive, would be entitled to the whole estate.[6] In such cases application should be made for a grant under the discretionary powers of

---

[1] *Burroughs* v. *Griffiths* (1754) 1 Cas.temp.Lee 544.

[2] See N.-C.P.R. 1987, r. 47.

[3] Administration of Estates Act 1925, s.5. The section speaks of a person being "cited to take out a grant of probate," but this has been understood to mean cited to accept or refuse a grant of probate. For text, see *post*, p. 1116.

[4] N.-C.P.R. 1987, r. 47(2).

[5] For chain of executorship, see *ante*, p. 44.

[6] *Registrar's Direction*, February 19, 1957. The practice for citations is governed by the N.-C.P.R. 1987, rr. 46–48.

the court.[7] But citations may issue at the instance of those who have an immediate interest, *e.g.* legatees or creditors.[8]

2. *To take probate*

Where an executor has intermeddled[9] in the estate of the deceased and has not taken a grant within six months of the death, he may be cited to show cause why he should not be ordered to take a grant by any person interested in the estate, unless proceedings as to the validity of the will are pending.[10] If the executor fails to enter an appearance or fails to apply for a grant, the citor may apply for an order requiring the executor to take a grant. If such executor still refuses to take a grant he will be liable, even if the estate is outside the jurisdiction,[11] to committal.[12] But an executor cannot be cited to take probate where he has merely neglected to take a grant without intermeddling.

Citation to take probate is the appropriate course where there is reason to think that an intermeddling executor will regularise his position by taking probate, or will not appear to the citation. In the latter case the citor should apply on summons for a grant to be made to himself or some other person.[13] But where there is reason to fear that the executor will take a grant and maladminister the estate, application should be made for him to be passed over under the discretionary powers of the court.[14]

3. *To propound a will*[15]

Where a person genuinely believes[16] that a will which has not been proved[17] is invalid, and he himself is interested under an earlier will or on intestacy, he may cite the executors and beneficiaries to propound it. Where an executor is doubtful of the validity of a codicil, it is not the practice for him to cite those interested under it to propound it. He should prove the will and ask the court to pronounce against the codicil, in solemn form, making those interested under the codicil parties.[18]

Initial procedure

One citation may be issued against several parties who have different interests and a number of sealed copies may be obtained with the original to facilitate service.

---

[7] Under the Supreme Court Act 1981, s.116. See *ante*, p. 343.
[8] *Registrar's Direction*, February 19, 1957.
[9] As to intermeddling, see *ante*, pp. 93, 380.
[10] N.-C.P.R. 1987, r. 47(3).
[11] *Re Lord and Fullerton's Contract* [1896] 1 Ch. 228.
[12] See, *e.g. Re Biggs* [1966] P. 118.
[13] N.-C.P.R. 1987, r. 47(5)(c).
[14] See *Re Biggs* [1966] P. 118; *Re Potticary* [1927] P. 202, *ante.*
[15] See N.-C.P.R. 1987, r. 48.
[16] *Morton* v. *Thorpe* (1863) 3 Sw. & Tr. 179; *Re Bootle* (1901) 84 L.T. 570.
[17] *Jolley* v. *Jarvis & Sands* [1964] P. 262.
[18] *Re Benbow* (1862) 2 Sw. & Tr. 488; *Re Muirhead* [1971] P. 263.

Any citation may issue from the Principal or a District Registry and must be settled by a registrar.[19] The original will[20] and other essential papers, *e.g.* renunciations, must be lodged.

An affidavit of facts is sworn in support by the citor but, in special circumstances, a registrar may give leave for the citor's solicitor to swear it.[21] The affidavit should not be sworn before the citation is settled, so that it may be corrected if it does not cover the facts set out in the citation. In cases where service by advertisement is sought, the affidavit sets out the searches and inquiries made and shows that personal service is impracticable. Where the citee is out of the jurisdiction the affidavit sets out the circumstances including the place or country in which the citee is and states the deponent's belief that he has a good cause of action. In the case of a citation to take probate, the main instances of intermeddling should be set out and it should be stated that the deceased has been dead for more than six months. A creditor who applies must give the value of the estate, the nature and amount of the debt and state (where appropriate) that he holds no security for it, or the nature of the security held.

Where it is alleged that there are no known next-of-kin, the affidavit must set out the steps which have been taken to trace them. The citor must enter a caveat[22] before the issue of the citation.[23]

Service   must be effected personally unless a registrar otherwise directs.[24] A certificate of service should be endorsed.[25]

Citations may be served abroad, though where the citee does not reside in the United Kingdom, the Isle of Man or the Channel Islands, it is preferable to obtain leave to serve a copy citation. If a citee has an agent in England he should be served with a copy citation.

Where the deceased had no known kin a creditor must serve a copy of the citation on the Treasury Solicitor or (if appropriate) on the Solicitor for the Duchy of Lancaster or of Cornwall.

Where personal service cannot reasonably be effected the registrar may order substituted service, usually by advertisement.[26] He will direct in which papers the advertisements are to be inserted, the number of insertions and the time for appearance. A short form of newspaper advertisement is used for citations to accept or refuse a grant and a draft abstract is lodged to be settled by the registrar.

---

[19] N.-C.P.R. 1987, r. 46(1).

[20] A will referred to in a citation must be lodged before the citation is issued unless this is impracticable in which case a photographic copy should be lodged. (See N.-C.P.R. 1987, r. 46(5)).

[21] N.-C.P.R. 1987, r. 46(2).

[22] For caveats, see *ante*, p. 383.

[23] N.-C.P.R. 1987, r. 46(3).

[24] N.-C.P.R. 1987, r. 46(4).

[25] *Goodburn* v. *Bainbridge* (1860) 2 Sw. & Tr. 4.

[26] N.-C.P.R. 1987, r. 46(4).

Appearance is entered at the Registry from which the citation issued. In non-contentious business the ordinary rule applies as to an address for service.[27] In addition, when an interest is claimed under a will or codicil, their dates must be given and where an interest in the estate of an intestate is claimed the grounds on which such claim is founded must be set out. The person appearing files his appearance by lodging it in Form 5. He must serve a sealed copy of the appearance on the citor[28] by leaving it at the latter's address for service or by sending it there by post or otherwise.[29] The time for appearance is eight days inclusive of the day of service[30] unless the citee is abroad or the service is by advertisement, in which cases the registrar fixes the time for appearance.

Procedure after appearance or non-appearance

The procedure after appearance varies according to the type of citation.

(i) *Citation to accept or refuse a grant.* Where there has been personal service but no appearance has been entered, the server makes an affidavit of service, exhibiting the citation endorsed with a certificate of service signed by the deponent[31] and stating the means by which he knew the identity of the citee.[32] Where the citation was served abroad the affidavit shows that it has also been served on the citee's agent in England and Wales or that he has no attorney, agent or correspondent in England and Wales.[33] Where the service was by advertisement, the newspapers, the citation and the abstract settled by the registrar are filed. Application for a grant is then made *ex parte*.[34]

If the party cited renounces after being cited, the citor may obtain a grant in the ordinary way without taking any steps in respect to the citation, since the caveat does not prevent the caveator from obtaining a grant.

If the party cited wishes to obtain a grant, he must appear and apply for a grant *ex parte*, filing an affidavit to show that he has appeared to the citation, and that the citor has had notice of the appearance but has not served the citee with notice of application for a grant to himself.[35]

If before service, whether personal or by advertisement, the citor and party cited agree that the latter shall have a grant, the former withdraws his caveat.

Where the Crown has obtained an order for a grant on the footing that there are no kin, but before the grant is issued kin are discovered, the

---

[27] N.-C.P.R. 1987, r. 49 (*post*, p. 1245).
[28] N.-C.P.R. 1987, r. 46(6).
[29] N.-C.P.R. 1987, r. 67 (applying R.S.C. Ord. 65, r. 5).
[30] N.-C.P.R. 1987, r. 46(6).
[31] *Harenc* v. *Dawson* (1863) 3 Sw. & Tr. 50.
[32] *Registrar's Direction*, April 21, 1964.
[33] *Evans* v. *Burrell* (1859) 4 Sw. & Tr. 185; *Kenworthy* v. *Kenworthy* (1863) 3 Sw. & Tr. 64.
[34] N.-C.P.R. 1987, r. 47(5)(*a*).
[35] N.-C.P.R. 1987, r. 47(4).

order may be rescinded on the application of the Treasury or Duchy Solicitor or of the next-of-kin on *ex parte* application supported by an affidavit of
facts. If the grant has been made, it may be revoked,[36] but the order itself
is not revoked if the revocation of the grant is made at the instance of the
Crown.[37]

Where it is found that a citee is dead but his personal representative is
entitled and prepared to take a grant, an order may be made on summons
to a registrar for a grant to issue notwithstanding the citation. The consent
of the citor is filed.

If a party cited appears but takes no step to obtain a grant or has not
prosecuted his application with reasonable diligence, the citor may apply
for a grant to himself notwithstanding the steps already taken.[38]

Where an executor to whom power has been reserved is cited to take a
grant of double probate and does not appear, the citor applies to a registrar
on summons that it be noted on the grant that the executor has not
appeared and that his rights as executor have wholly ceased.[39] The summons is supported by an affidavit of service of the citation.[40] If such executor appears but does not apply for a grant or does not prosecute his
application with reasonable diligence, the citor applies to a registrar on
summons for the appearance to be struck out and the grant noted as in the
case where no appearance has been entered.[41]

(ii) *Citation to take probate.*   If an intermeddling executor who has been
cited wishes to take probate, he must enter an appearance and apply for a
grant *ex parte* in the same way as a person cited to accept or refuse a
grant.[42]

If the citee does not appear the citor files affidavits of service as in the
case of a person cited to accept or refuse a grant and applies to a registrar
on summons either for an order directing the citee to take a grant within a
specified time, or for a grant to himself or some other named person.[43] The
procedure is similar where the citee enters appearance but takes no further
step or is not reasonably diligent in his application. If an order is made for
the citee to take a grant it must be endorsed with a penal notice.

(iii) *Citation to propound a will.*   A party cited in this case should issue a
writ if he wishes the will under which he is interested to be admitted to probate. If the citee appears but does not proceed to propound the will with
reasonable diligence the citor should apply to the registrar for an order for
a grant as if the will were invalid.[44] The application is made by summons,

---

[36] See *ante*, p. 360.
[37] President's Direction, October 21, 1952.
[38] N.-C.P.R. 1987, r. 47(7)(*a*) (*post*, p. 1244).
[39] N.-C.P.R. 1987, r. 47(5)(*b*).
[40] N.-C.P.R. 1987, r. 47(6).
[41] N.-C.P.R. 1987, r. 47(7)(*b*).
[42] N.-C.P.R. 1987, r. 47(4).
[43] N.-C.P.R. 1987, r. 47(7)(*c*).
[44] N.-C.P.R. 1987, r. 48(2)(*b*).

which must be served on the citee who has entered an appearance. If the citee does not appear, the citor files affidavits of service, and applies to the registrar *ex parte* for an order for a grant on the basis that the will is invalid.[45]

Parties under a disability

No special provisions are made by the Non-Contentious Probate Rules for serving a citation on a person under a disability or for the appointment of a next friend or guardian *ad litem*.[46] The general provisions of Order 80 of the Rules of Supreme Court are applicable.[47]

In a probate action if there is default of appearance to the writ by a defendant under a disability, the plaintiff must apply for a guardian *ad litem* to be appointed of such defendant.[48] This rule is not specifically applicable in the case of citations, but such application should be made in the case of citations where a person under a disability is in default of appearance.

[45] N.-C.P.R. 1987, r. 48(2)(*a*).

[46] Before the transfer of contentious probate business to the Chancery Division (see *ante*, p. 8) the procedure was the same as in a probate action, (see Registrar's Direction, October 6, 1960) for which there were special provisions under R.S.C. Ord. 80. These provisions have now been revoked.

[47] See *post*, p. 411.

[48] Ord. 80, r. 6.

CHAPTER 33

APPLICATIONS, SUMMONSES AND MOTIONS

In non-contentious matters circumstances often arise which make it necessary to obtain the decision, direction or order of a registrar or a judge.

Decision or direction of a registrar

There are many matters on which it necessary to take the decision or direction of a registrar. It is impossible to give an exhaustive list of these matters. Examples are: as to the due execution of a will; whether by the terms of the will the applicant for a grant of administration (with the will) is the residuary legatee; whether alterations or interlineations are entitled to probate; whether a document is to be treated as incorporated in a will; whether an affidavit of foreign law is sufficient; whether a grant may be expedited.

Such matters of doubt are usually referred informally to a district judge by the Principal of the Probate Department of the Principal Registry or, in the case of a district registry, to the district registrar by the Chief Clerk. In cases of exceptional doubt or difficulty a district registrar may obtain the directions of a district judge of the Principal Registry.[1] Any registrar may require any application to be made by summons to a registrar in chambers or to a judge in chambers or in open court.[2]

When a matter is referred to a registrar informally, he either gives a decision or a direction as to the further steps which are to be taken.

Ex parte applications

A large number of matters are heard by a registrar *ex parte*. These are mentioned *passim* in this work and the special practice applicable is set out in each case. In every case such applications should be supported by an affidavit and in many cases other documents must be lodged. There is a special responsibility to the court to be frank and fair in all *ex parte* applications. In the Principal Registry *ex parte* applications should be referred, at first instance, to the appropriate probate section. Some applications may be dealt with by the principal of the probate department who may refer them to a district judge. In a district registry all *ex parte* applications are referred to the registrar. A registrar may refer any such application to a judge[3] in which case it is almost always heard on summons.

---

[1] Supreme Court Act 1981, s.106(4).
[2] N.-C.P.R 1987, r. 61(1).
[3] *Ibid.*

A district registrar has, for most purposes, the same jurisdiction as a district judge of the Principal Registry.[4]

Summonses to a registrar

A number of applications in non-contentious business are heard by way of summons to a registrar, either because the rules so provide or following a direction by a registrar to that effect.[5] These are considered *passim* throughout this work. A summons for hearing by a registrar must be issued out of the registry in which it is to be heard. A summons to be heard by a judge must be issued out of the Principal Registry.[6]

Summonses to a judge

A number of matters, formerly heard on motion, are now heard on summons to a judge. Summonses to a judge are of two kinds: (i) matters referred to him by a registrar,[7] (ii) appeals from a registrar.[8] A motion is appropriate if the matter is highly contentious.[9]

During the long vacation all the powers exercisable under the Non-Contentious Probate Rules by a judge in chambers may be exercised by a district judge of the Principal Registry.[10]

Procedure on summons

In non-contentious probate matters, all summonses, must be drawn up in duplicate and a copy left at the Registry. The sealed copy with the return day and time placed on it is returned to the applicant.

A registrar or judge may direct that a summons in a non-contentious probate matter for the service of which no other provision is made under the Non-Contentious Probate Rules shall be served on such persons as he may direct.[11]

In non-contentious proceedings a summons is served in the manner prescribed by Order 65, rule 5.[12]

Hearing before a registrar

Summonses are heard from 10.30 a.m. from Mondays to Fridays by district judges and registrars. Their clerks should be notified as to the prob-

---

[4] N.-C.P.R. 1987, r. 2(2).
[5] *i.e.* under the N.-C.P.R. 1987, r. 6(1).
[6] N.-C.P.R. 1987, r. 61(4).
[7] Under the N.-C.P.R. 1987, r. 61.
[8] Under the N.-C.P.R. 1987, r. 65. Appeals from a district registrar are to a judge and not, as formerly, to a (now) district judge of the Principal Registry, see *ante*, p. 279.
[9] See *post*, p. 396. For the definition of non-contentious business see p. 8 *ante*.
[10] N.-C.P.R 1987, r. 64. It follows that during the long vacation a district judge may now hear a matter brought before the Court on motion.
[11] N.-C.P.R. 1987, r. 66(1).
[12] N.-C.P.R. 1987, r. 67.

able length of the hearing so that a special appointment may be made
where necessary; failure to do so may result in an adjournment.[13]

Summonses to be attended by counsel should be so marked. Where a
summons is not so marked but the party served intends to be represented
by counsel, he must notify the applicant of his intention and fix a fresh time
for hearing, of which he must notify the applicant.[14] Unless the registrar
grants a certificate for counsel's attendance, no costs of such attendance
are allowed.[15]

Orders on all summonses in contentious matters are drawn up at the
Registry.

Hearing before a judge

In general, summonses to a judge are heard in chambers. Occasionally a
summons is adjourned into open court.

Motions[16]

Few probate matters are now heard on motion. Most of those formerly
heard in this way are now decided on summons. The 1987 rules make no
provision for motions.

A registrar may require any application to be made to the court on
motion, rather than by summons, but it is uncommon for him to do so. The
procedure may be suitable in the case of a highly contentious matter, in
which case consideration should be given to obtaining the registrar's directions for service of pleadings in order to identify the issues, and for some
restriction to be placed on the affidavit evidence.[17]

The motion procedure is still appropriate to obtain an injunction and for
committals for contempt and release from prison.[18]

Procedure on motion

During the term motions are heard on a day fixed by the Clerk of the
Rules. Papers for all motions, whether original or adjourned, must be
deposited in the Probate Department of the Principal Registry not less
than seven clear days before the motion is to be heard. These papers
include the case on motion, the notice of motion, affidavits and exhibits
and original wills. The Department must be informed if any relevant documents are on the file of any other proceedings, so that such documents may
be procured.

If it is desired to bring on a motion during the long vacation the Probate

---

[13] *Registrar's Direction*, October 30, 1942.
[14] *Registrar's Direction*, July 18, 1961.
[15] Ord. 62, Appendix 2. Part I, para. 2(2)(*a*).
[16] For the motion procedure generally. See R.S.C. Ord. 8, for the practice in the Chancery
Division see *post* pp. 425, 849, 853.
[17] *Van Horn* v. *Van Horn, The Times*, November 30, 1978. As to the Chancery jurisdiction
see p. 8 *ante*.
[18] R.S.C. Ord. 52, r. 4(1).

Department should be consulted as to the practice. Where necessary a district judge will direct the matter to come before the Vacation Judge. This will depend on the circumstances and especially on the need for urgency.

All requisite papers must be filed, for a district judge may strike out any motion where the papers are defective. The heading in motions after setting out the Division is "In the estate of A.B. deceased." The names of the parties are not set out.

The case on motion sets out the relevant facts, the relief or remedy sought and details of any proceedings which have taken place. The case on motion must be verified by affidavit evidence.[19]

Notice of motion

In motions in non-contentious business a judge or registrar may direct that notice of motion for the service of which no other provision is made by the Rules, be served on such person as he may direct. The usual rules for service in non-contentious matters apply.[20] Motions are heard in open court as in the Chancery Division. Appeal from an order on motion is made to the Court of Appeal. The practice is the same as in other Divisions.

---

[19] As to practice see *Tristram and Coote's Probate Practice* 27th ed., p. 680.
[20] *i.e* N.-C.P.R. 1987, r. 67. See *ante*, p. 395.

CHAPTER 34

COSTS

No fixed scale

In non-contentious business there are no fixed items or scales of costs. A solicitor is entitled to such sum as is fair and reasonable having regard to all the circumstances of the case and in particular (i) the complexity of the matter or the difficulty or novelty of the questions raised; (ii) the skill, labour, specialised knowledge and responsibility involved on the part of the solicitor; (iii) the number and importance of the documents prepared or perused, without regard to length; (iv) the place where, and the circumstances in which, the business or any part of it is transacted; (v) the time expended by the solicitor; (vi) the nature and value of the property involved; and (vii) the importance of the matter to the client.[1]

These matters are cumulative, but there must be no overlap in the charge, so that if one matter is brought in under one head, it should not also be brought in under another.[2]

Usually the logical starting point will be head (v) since this will be easily computed and will indicate the weight of the matter. However, it will often result in an undercharge since a solicitor will frequently continue to consider a matter outside his strict working hours,[3] thus the final figure will always be a matter of judgment and not arithmetical calculation, so that the time expended should be used only as a cross check. In particular, it should not be used as a foundation to calculate the charge where the factors under the other heads are of much greater significance.[4]

Where the estate is large, the most important head will be (vi).[5] Where a large estate consists of many small parcels of property rather than a few large blocks it will as a matter of practice be more convenient to reflect the extra work involved under head (i), although this is a matter which affects the "nature" of the estate under head (vi).[6]

It is appropriate to calculate a charge by means of sliding scale of percentages on the value of the property.[7] A scale which has been applied is 1

---

[1] Supreme Court (Non-Contentious Probate Costs) Rules 1956, r. 1. Compare the similar Solicitor's Remuneration Order 1972. See *post*, p. 1271. For the Law Society's recommended charges see 1971 L.S. Gazette 133.
[2] *Maltby* v. *Freeman* [1978] 1 W.L.R. 431.
[3] *Ibid.*
[4] *Treasury Solicitor* v. *Regester* [1978] 1 W.L.R. 446.
[5] *Maltby* v. *Freeman, supra.*
[6] *Ibid.*
[7] *Ibid.* See also *Property and Reversionary Investment Corporation Ltd.* v. *Secretary of State for the Environment* [1975] 1 W.L.R. 1504.

1/2 per cent. on the band up to £0.25m, 6 1/2 per cent. on the band between £0.25m and £1m and 1/6 per cent. on the band between £1m and £2.5m.[8]

Taxation

Without prejudice to the right of the solicitor or the client to have the bill of costs taxed under the Solicitors Act 1974,[9] the client may require the solicitor to obtain a certificate from the Law Society as to the amount charged being a fair and reasonable sum. The sum so certified if less than that charged in the bill is, in the absence of taxation, to be the sum payable.[10]

Before a solicitor brings proceedings to recover costs he must, unless costs have been taxed under the Solicitors Act 1974, draw the client's attention, in writing, to his right to the above-mentioned certificate and to the provisions of the Solicitors Act 1974 as to the taxation of costs between solicitor and client.[11] A client is not entitled to require a solicitor to obtain a certificate from the Law Society after the bill of costs has been taxed under the Solicitors Act, nor after it has been paid.[12]

On a taxation of costs the solicitor must satisfy the Taxing Master of the fairness and reasonableness of his charges.[13] If less than one-half the amount charged is allowed by the Taxing Master he must bring the matter to the notice of the Law Society.[14]

Taxations under the Solicitors Act 1974 should be heard by the Supreme Court Taxing Master.[15] However the Taxing Master may, if he considers it appropriate refer a taxation to a district judge of the Principal Registry with that judge's concurrence. The bill and supporting documents should be lodged with the taxing Master's clerk at first instance. If a referral is appropriate the document will be forwarded by the clerk.

Bills of Costs which do not fall to be taxed under the Solicitors Act but follow an order made in proceedings on summons are taxed; where the order for taxation was made by a district judge or a taxing officer[16] authorised to tax costs[17]; or where the order is made by a registrar by that register.[18] The compromise of a claim for costs may include provision for the payment of interest.[19]

---

[8] See n. 2, above.

[9] ss. 70–72.

[10] Supreme Court (Non-Contentious Probate Costs) Rules 1956, r. 1, proviso (*a*), (*post*, p. 1271).

[11] Supreme Court (Non-Contentious Probate Costs) Rules 1956, r. 1, proviso (*b*), (*post*, p. 1271). See *Walton* v. *Egan* [1982] Q.B. 1232.

[12] *Ibid.* proviso (*c*).

[13] *Ibid.* proviso (*d*).

[14] *Ibid.* proviso (*e*).

[15] Under the Solicitors Act 1974, s. 72(2).

[16] N.-C.P.R. 1987, r. 60(*a*).

[17] See R.S.C., Ord. 62, r. 19.

[18] N.-C.P.R. 1987, r. 60(*b*).

[19] *Walton* v. *Egan* [1982] Q.B. 1232.

Legal aid

Legal aid may be given in non-contentious probate matters. Taxation takes place in accordance with the procedure set out above. Where the taxation does not arise through an order but from the discharge or revocation of a legal aid certificate, the costs will be taxed by a district judge (taxing officer) or registrar of the Registry where the summons proceedings were issued.

Part Four

CONTENTIOUS PRACTICE

CHAPTER 35

PRELIMINARY STEPS AND PARTIES

A. GENERAL

As has been seen[1] under the Administration of Justice Act 1970 non-contentious or common form probate business continued to be assigned to the Family Division of the High Court and all other probate business was assigned to the Chancery Division. Thus contentious probate or probate in solemn form[2] falls now within the Chancery jurisdiction. The procedure is in general the same as in other Chancery actions but the provisions of Order 76 of the Rules of the Supreme Court have particular application. Since the Chancery Division also has jurisdiction in Family Provision[3] and in the interpretation of Wills economies can sometimes be achieved by arranging when the matter is before the Chancery Master for consecutive hearings before the same judge of one or all of these issues affecting the same estate.[4]

Definition of a probate action

A probate action is defined[5] as an action for the grant of probate of the will, or letters of administration to the estate, of a deceased person, or for the revocation of such a grant, of for a decree pronouncing for or against the validity of an alleged will, not being an action which is non-contentious or common form business.[6]

Limitation

Since there is no statutory limitation period for probate actions the court has a wide discretion under Order 18, rule 19 of the Rules of the Supreme Court in allowing or disallowing delayed probate claims but in general it seems that once administration is in progress and certainly when distribution is complete the court will need very strong reasons indeed to upset an existing grant. In *Re Hassan*[7] an action was struck out where the death was

---

[1] See *ante*, p. 7.

[2] For the distinction between solemn and common form see *ante*, p. 269. For instances where common form issues come before a judge of the Family Division see *ante*, pp. 395.

[3] See *post*, pp. 757 *et seq*.

[4] As to the arrangements for hearings outside London, see *Practice Direction* [1988] 1 W.L.R. 630.

[5] Ord. 76, r. 1(2) (*post*, p. 1254).

[6] For the definition of non-contentious or common form business, see the Supreme Court Act 1981, s.128 and p. 8, *ante*, 20 *post*.

[7] [1981] Guardian Gazette 842. It has been argued that the absence of a statutory limitation period should lead to a shortening and not a lengthening of the allowable delays, bearing in mind the executor's year and the time limits for family provision claims, but see *Re Flynn* [1982] 1 W.L.R. 310, 315, 318.

in March 1972, the grant in November 1972 and the action had begun in February 1974. In *Re Flynn*[8] proceedings were first taken just within six years of the grant of probate in the mistaken belief that the statutory limitation period applied. The court refused to strike out the action on the ground of mere delay where the claim was not clearly frivolous or vexatious.

Forms of probate action

There are three forms of probate action: (a) actions asking the court to pronounce for or against a will in solemn form of law; (b) interest actions, sometimes known as interest suits; (c) actions for the revocation of probate or letters of administration.

(a) Actions for pronouncing for or against a will

(i) *Action begun on the plaintiff's initiative.*　An executor or a beneficiary under a will may, for his own protection (particularly in cases where doubts have been raised by those interested under another will or on intestacy), desire to prove the will in solemn form. By doing so he obtains a decision which ensures that no future contest arises over the validity of will and that a decision is obtained while the witnesses are still available.

In such case the executor or a beneficiary should issue a writ and make defendants the executor and principal beneficiaries of any immediately prior will who would be adversely affected by the proving of the will propounded. Where there are doubts as to the validity of the will immediately prior to that propounded, it may be advisable to join persons interested in a yet earlier will, or on intestacy. Any beneficiaries entitled to lesser interests in the will immediately before that propounded, if adversely affected, should be notified and given an opportunity to appear. Where there is no other will those interested on intestacy should be made defendants.

If none of the defendants serves an acknowledgment of service showing intention to defend[9] or having done so, does not serve a defence, the case is brought on as a short cause.[10] If any of them serves a defence, the action proceeds as a defended cause.

Where executors or beneficiaries are aware of a later document of testamentary purport which they do not believe to be valid, two courses are open to them. The first, which is adopted where it is not expected that anyone will contend for the purported will, is to cite the executor and the persons interested thereunder to propound it.[11] The second is for the person interested under the earlier will to issue a writ, making defendants the persons interested under the later will. In this case he must show the invalidity of the later will if he wishes to have the earlier will pronounced

---

[8] [1982] 1 W.L.R, 310. See also p. 269 (acquiescence), *ante*.
[9] See Ord. 2, r. 3(*e*).
[10] See *post*, p. 427 for short causes.
[11] For procedure, see *ante*, pp. 389, 391.

for. If he finds that he cannot do this the plaintiff may ask the court to admit the will he propounds to probate in common form. This will be done on the basis that the writ is equivalent to a citation to propound the later will.

Where a person (including the Crown) interested on intestacy knows of a will which he believes to be invalid, the same procedure is open to him as is open to a person interested under an earlier will.

(ii) *Actions brought about by persons entering a caveat.* Actions for the pronouncing for or against a will generally arise because an applicant for a grant of probate in common form finds that a caveat has been entered by some person opposed to the will. Usually the applicant warns the caveat and after appearance has been entered to the warning, issues a writ.

The interest of a caveator. Those who are interested on intestacy have an interest in the estate of the deceased. Where the deceased died without known kin the Treasury Solicitor has an interest in his estate unless he died domiciled or possessed of property in the Duchy of Lancaster or of Cornwall, in which case the solicitors for those Duchies have an interest.

The executor or beneficiary under another will has an interest in the estate of the deceased,[12] and so has any beneficiary under a will from which those propounding it seek to have the clause under which he benefits omitted. A creditor has an interest in an estate to which he has obtained a grant.[13]

An executor who has obtained a grant of probate in common form cannot take proceedings in his capacity of executor to have the grant revoked; nor can his executor.[14] But an executor who was also the next-of-kin of the deceased but had obtained probate in common form was held not to be disentitled to take proceedings to revoke his grant where he gave a satisfactory explanation of his reasons for having taken probate.[15]

Whether an Executor can be compelled to prove a will in solemn form. It is often said that persons interested in one of the ways discussed above may compel an executor to prove the will in solemn form. This is not, however, a correct statement of the law. There is no procedure by which an executor can be compelled to commence a probate action. In practice many executors who are prepared to undertake their duties if the will is not contested are unwilling to be involved in a probate action. In many instances it would be most unjust if an executor could be compelled to prove a will in solemn form, *e.g.* in a case where he has been shown evidence that the will was procured by undue influence.

---

[12] But a legatee who disputes a will under which he has obtained a benefit may be called on to pay his legacy into court; *Bell* v. *Armstrong* (1822) 2 Add, 365, 374; *Braham* v. *Burchell* (1826) 3 Add. 243, 256; unless he is an infant: *Goddard* v. *Norton* (1846) 5 N.C. 76.

[13] *Menzies* v. *Pulbrook* (1841) 2 Curt. 845; see *Dabbs* v. *Chisman* (1810) 1 Phill. 155, 159.

[14] *Re Chamberlain* (1867) L.R. 1 P. & D. 316.

[15] *Williams* v. *Evans* [1911] P. 175.

Even if an executor has obtained probate, he is not bound to uphold the validity of the will in a probate action. Indeed it would, in some instances, be most improper for him to do so, *e.g.* where a later will has been discovered which revokes the will proved. Similarly administrators, including creditors and appointees of the court, are not obliged to uphold grants made to them.

But, as already shown, any person interested under a will may commence an action to prove it in solemn form should he wish to do so.[16]

Grant to an Executor who has refused to propound a will. An executor who has refused to propound a will on his own initiative or after having been made defendant to an action may yet take a grant of probate if that will is etablished. His acknowledgment of service showing intention not to defend or his failure to serve an acknowledgment of service at all does not preclude his taking the office as non-appearance to a citation to accept or refuse probate does. Consequently an executor may let beneficiaries under the will contend for it without losing his right to a grant.

Decree for or against a will. At the end of a probate action or short cause the court pronounces for or against the validity of such will or wills as are set up by each party. This pronouncement is called the decree. Where a will is upheld, probate thereof is decreed in whole or in part in solemn form of law. When the will is pronounced for, the executor may obtain a grant of probate; where there is no executor, the persons entitled to a grant of administration with the will annexed may apply for it in the probate registry.

Where the court pronounces against one or more wills and does not pronounce for the validity of any will or of any will of which there are executors, it does not (except in special circumstances) order that the grant shall issue to any particular person, but leaves the persons entitled to apply for a grant at the registry.[17]

(b) Interest actions

Interest actions mainly arise as the result of a dispute as to who is entitled to a grant on intestacy. They often arise from disputes as to whether the marriage of the deceased was valid[18] but they may also result from personation. In many cases the legitimacy of one or more of the parties is involved. In this case a declaration of parentage, legitimacy or legitimation will be necessary.[19] This may be decided on inquiry under Order 85 of the Rules of the Supreme Court.

Occasionally, the party who propounds a will denies the interest of the party opposing it, who sets up another will or claims on intestacy. The pro-

---

[16] See generally *Jolley* v. *Jarvis* [1964] P. 262, and *ante*, p. 39, 389.
[17] See *Practice Note* [1938] W.N. 222.
[18] See *Vardy* v. *Smith* (1932) 49 T.L.R. 36.
[19] See Family Law Act 1986, s.56.

ponent may contend that even if the other will is valid or there is an intestacy the opposing party has no interest.[20] In this case the question of the defendant's interest may be tried as a separate issue.

The parties to an interest action and those claiming through them cannot reopen the same question after it has been determined by the court. But other persons who have an interest almost identical with those of one of the parties are not bound if they do not claim through such party.[21]

(c) Action for the revocation of grants

Where a will has been proved in common form an action may be commenced for the revocation of the grant (whether of probate or of administration with the will annexed), (i) where it is alleged that the will was not a valid one, (ii) where a later will revoking it or a duly executed revocatory instrument has been discovered since the grant was made, (iii) where it has been discovered that the deceased married since the date of the will so that it was revoked, (iv) where it is alleged that the grant was obtained by a person not entitled.

A bare executor or his executor who has taken probate in common form cannot afterwards take proceedings to contest that will. However, it is well established that an executor who has an interest in the estate under another will or on intestacy and who has taken probate may institute an action for the revocation of the grant, if he has a reasonable explanation for his action in taking the grant.[22]

Where any of the four grounds for the revocation of a grant mentioned above exist, an action for revocation is only begun if there is a contest as to the grounds alleged. The procedure where there is no such contest has already been set out.[23]

An action for revocation of letters of administration may be instituted (i) on the discovery of a will the validity of which is disputed by the grantee, or (ii) where it is alleged that the grantee had no title because persons nearer in title were alive. Even a grant to the Crown may be revoked if kin entitled to a grant come forward.

Lodgement of grants

In any action for the revocation of a grant the plaintiff must, if he is the person to whom the grant was made, lodge the grant in Chancery Chambers within seven days of the issue of the writ if it is not already lodged in the principal or a district registry.[24] Similarly, a defendant must, if the grant is in his possession or under his control, lodge it in Chancery

---

[20] *Posner* v. *Miller* [1953] P. 277.
[21] *Spencer* v. *Williams* (1871) L.R. 2 P. & D. 230.
[22] *Williams* v. *Evans* [1911] P. 175.
[23] See *ante*, pp. 360 *et seq.*
[24] Ord. 76, r. 4(1), (*post*, p. 1254).

Chambers within 14 days after service of the writ on him, if it has not already been lodged in a registry.[25] In default of compliance with these requirements a person may be ordered, on the application of any party to the action, to lodge the grant within a specified time, and until the grant is lodged he may not take any step in the action without the leave of the court.[26]

B. PRELIMINARY STEPS IN AN ACTION

Bringing in scripts[27]

In some cases it is known that a script is in the possession of a person who will not allow another to inspect it or have a copy. In order that the latter may have an opportunity to ascertain his rights under the document, the Court can, whether or not proceedings are pending, issue a subpoena to bring in the document.[28]

Where no action has been commenced, the application is made *ex parte* in the Principal Registry or a district probate registry supported by an affidavit setting out the grounds of the application.[29] The subpoena may command the script to be brought into the Principal Registry or into a district registry as the Court may direct.[30] If satisfied, the district judge or registrar will order the subpoena to issue. It must be served personally and endorsed with a penal notice. It is doubtful whether such a subpoena can issue for service out of the jurisdiction.

Where an action has been commenced the procedure is similar, but is made *ex parte* to the appropriate Chancery Master, again supported by an affidavit.[31] The subpoena requires that the script be brought into Chancery Chambers.[32]

If the person served with the subpoena does not have the script in his possession or control he should file an affidavit in the registry from which the subpoena is issued or in chambers to that effect.[33] If a subpoena is disobeyed it may be enforced by committal; but only after ordering the person served to attend court to be examined with regard to the script.[34] A solicitor cannot refuse to produce a will on the ground that he has a lien on it.[35]

---

[25] *Ibid.*
[26] Ord. 76, r. 4(2), (*post*, p. 1254).
[27] For the definition of the word script, see *post*, p. 414.
[28] Supreme Court Act 1981, s.123.
[29] N.-C.P.R. 1987 r. 50(2).
[30] Supreme Court Act 1981, s.123.
[31] Ord. 76, r. 13(4).
[32] Ord. 76, r. 13(3).
[33] *i.e.* in the registry, where no action has been commenced (N.-C.P.R. 1987, r. 50(2)), and in chambers if it has been (Ord. 76, r.13(6)).
[34] *i.e.* under the Supreme Court Act 1981, s.122, *infra. Parkinson* v. *Thornton* (1867) 37 L.J.P. & M. 3; *Re Floyd* (1909) 53 S.J. 790.
[35] *Georges* v. *Georges* (1811) 18 Ves. 294.

Examination of persons believed to have knowledge of a script

Where it appears that there are reasonable grounds for believing that any person has knowledge of any document which is or purports to be a testamentary document, the High Court may, whether or not any legal proceedings are pending order him to attend for the purpose of being examined in open court.[36] The court may require him to answer any question about the document and order him to bring in the document.[37] Disobedience constitutes a contempt[38]

The application is made where it is believed that a person has knowledge of a script but either will not make any statement on the matter or makes one which appears misleading or deliberately incomplete.

The application is made by summons to a district judge of the Principal Registry of the Family Division or a district probate registrar where no action has been commenced,[39] and where an action has been commenced, by summons in the action.[40] The summons must be served on the person against whom the order is sought.[41] If an order is made for the attendance of a person, a date is fixed for his attendance and he is then examined by counsel for the applicant. He is not the witness of the applicant and leading questions may be asked. This hearing is in open court.[42]

It is rare for interrogatories to be ordered. In special circumstances evidence may be ordered to be taken before an examiner.[43]

The examination is for the purpose of tracing a script and must not be used to obtain from attesting witnesses an account of the circumstances attending the execution of the will.[44] Where attesting witnesses refused to make an affidavit of due execution the court[45] ordered them to attend for examination under the powers conferred on it by section 24 of the Court of Probate Act 1857.[46] The section is hardly ever invoked in modern probate practice and the procedures laid down by it are virtually obsolete.

C. PARTIES TO AN ACTION

Where a person can show that the court has jurisdiction to make an order in a probate action which may affect his interest or possible interest in the

---

[36] Supreme Court Act 1981, s.122.
[37] *Ibid.*
[38] *Ibid.*
[39] N.-C.P.R. 1987 r. 50(1).
[40] Ord. 76, r. 13(2).
[41] N.-C.P.R. 1987 R. 50(1); Ord. 76, r. 13(2).
[42] *Re Laws* (1872) L.R. 2 P. & D. 458; *Re Shepherd* [1891] P. 323. The witness, it seems, is entitled to conduct money: *Re Harvey* [1907] P. 239, not following *Re Wyatt* [1898] P. 15; and can claim representation by counsel, *Re Cope* (1867) 36 L.J.P. & M. 83.
[43] *Banfield* v. *Pickard* (1881) 6 P.D. 33.
[44] *Evans* v. *Jones* (1867) 36 L.J.P. & M. 70.
[45] See n. 44.
[46] *Re Sweet* [1891] p. 400; *Re Bays* (1910) 54 S.J. 200.

estate of the deceased, however slightly, such person has a right to be a party to that action.[47]

But a person who has criminally killed the deceased has no right to his estate and is not, therefore, entitled to be a party.[48] Where the killer dies before the criminal trial, the court will order an inquiry as to his entitlement under the will.

A creditor has no interest in whether the court pronounces for one will or another, or for an intestacy, and cannot be a party,[49] unless he has obtained administration.[50]

In an action for revocation of a grant of probate or letters of administration the plaintiff must join all those who are entitled to administer the estate under such grant.[51]

Plaintiffs and defendants

In probate actions the rule[52] requiring a plaintiff to make all persons parties to the suit where such persons are jointly entitled with him does not apply. In other respects the general position of and practice regarding plaintiffs and defendants are the same as in other actions.

The parties should join all other persons whom they wish to be bound by the decision of the court. If it is inconvenient to join all such persons, the Master may order that notice of the proceedings be served on them, leaving them to intervene[53] or a representation order may be sought.[54] The former practice of citing a party to the proceedings, thereby binding him, is no longer provided for.

A person who has not been made a party to a probate action and whose interest may be affected by the result of the suit may apply to be added as a defendant. If he is cognisant of the proceedings and of an interest in them and does not so apply he will be bound by the proceedings although he is not a party to them.[55] Such person, however, will not be bound by a compromise even if an order is made.[56] The interest of a person who wishes to intervene is not confined to one arising under a will or on intestacy.[57] The purchase of part of the estate from the administrator after the death of the deceased has been held to give an interest to intervene in an action to revoke the grant of administration.[58]

---

[47] *Hingeston* v. *Tucker* (1862) 2 Sw. & Tr. 596; *Crispin* v. *Doglioni* (1863) 3 Sw. & Tr. 96.
[48] *Re Hall* [1914] P.1. See also *ante*, pp. 22 and *post*, p. 1074.
[49] *Menzies* v. *Pulbrook* (1841) 2 Curt. 845.
[50] *Dabbs* v. *Chisman* (1810) 1 Phill. 155, 159, 160.
[51] Ord. 76, r. 3.
[52] Ord. 15, r. 4(2).
[53] See section 47 of the Administration of Justice Act 1985 and R.S.C. Ord. 15, r. 13A. If they do not intervene they will be bound by the Order.
[54] Ord. 15, r. 13.
[55] See *ante*, p. 4, *post*, p. 448.
[56] *Wytcherley* v. *Andrews* (1871) L.R. 2 P. & D. 327; *Young* v. *Holloway* [1895] P. 87. See *post*, p. 427.
[57] *Lindsay* v. *Lindsay* (1872) L.R. 2 P. & D. 459.
[58] *Ibid.*

Application for leave to be joined is made by summons in the action to the Master, supported by an affidavit showing the interest of the applicant in the estate.[59] The summons must be served on the plaintiff and such other parties as are not in default of appearance.[60]

Where a party is joined the court may and, in practice, does give directions as to the service of pleadings, the filing of an affidavit of scripts and other relevant matters. Where such a party wishes to serve separate pleadings he should include in his summons an application to do so. In the ordinary way he adopts the pleadings of the party who has the same interest as himself.

As in other actions a person under a disability sues by his next friend and defends by his guardian *ad litem*. The normal rules apply to the appointment of next friends and guardians *ad litem* in a probate action.[61]

The addition or change of parties is governed by the ordinary rules of court.[62]

---

[59] Ord. 65, r. 9.
[60] See Ord. 80, r. 2(1).
[61] *i.e.* those of Ord. 80.
[62] See Ord. 15. As to whether after a scheme of amalgamation a bank executor may continue to act, see *Re Skinner* [1958] 1 W.L.R. 1043.

CHAPTER 36

THE WRIT, ACKNOWLEDGMENT AND AFFIDAVIT OF SCRIPTS

A. THE WRIT

A probate action is begun by a writ of summons, which must be issued out of the Chancery Chambers or a Chancery District Registry.[1a] If by accident a writ is issued out of any other district registry, application should be made forthwith to transfer the action to London, where the appropriate steps can be taken under Order 2 of the Rules of the Supreme Court to regularise matters.

Any caveat in force at the date of the writ remains in force, unless a registrar otherwise orders or unless it is withdrawn, until the application for a grant is made by the person shown to be entitled thereto by the decision of the court in the action.[2]

The commencement of the action operates to prevent the sealing of a grant in the estate of the deceased until application for a grant is made by the person shown to be entitled by the decision of the court[3]; consequently it is not necessary for the plaintiff to enter a caveat before he commences a probate action. A copy of the writ is sent by the Chancery Master to the Senior District Judge of the Principal Registrar of the Family Division.[4]

Although after a caveat has been warned and an appearance entered to the warning either side is entitled to issue a writ, this is usually done by the person who warned the caveat.

The leave of the court in no longer required to issue the writ.[5] Nevertheless the court has a residual discretion to refuse to allow the writ to be issued if there are grounds for concluding that it is an abuse.[6]

Heading of the writ

The writ must be headed with the name of the deceased as well as the names of the parties.[7]

The endorsement on the writ

Before a writ in a probate action is issued it must be endorsed with a statement showing the nature of the interest of the plaintiff and of the

---

[1] Ord. 76, r. 2(1) (*post*, p. 1254).
[1a] See Rules of the Supreme Court (Amendment No. 2) Regulations (S.I. 1992 No. 1907).
[2] N.-C.P.R. 1982, r. 45(3) (*post*, p. 1242).
[3] *Ibid.*
[4] See *ante*, p. 387.
[5] See the previous edition of this work, p. 385.
[6] *Re Langton* [1964] P. 163.
[7] *Practice Direction (Chancery: Procedure)* [1983] 1 W.L.R. 4. See *post*, p. 417, for the form of heading.

defendant in the estate of the deceased.[8] In the usual way, the writ may also be endorsed with a statement of claim.[9]

The endorsement shows either that the plaintiff sues as executor or sets out the nature of his interest in the estate, *e.g.* as residuary legatee or as entitled to share in the estate on intestacy. The character or interest of the defendant must be similarly described. Where a defendant has entered a caveat it is customary, after setting out his character or interest, to add "and because you have entered a caveat."

The usual rules apply as to the endorsement of the writ with the name and address of the plaintiff (if in person) or of his solicitors.[10]

Service

Service of the writ is effected in the same way as in other actions.[11] In probate actions a writ (or notice of writ) may be served out of the jurisdiction, but only with the leave of the court.[12] Probate actions are not affected by the Civil Jurisdiction and Judgments Act 1982.[13]

B. ACKNOWLEDGMENT OF SERVICE

The acknowledgment of service is subject to the normal rules of court.[14]

Failure to acknowledge service

In probate actions failure to serve an acknowledgment of service showing an intention to defend does not allow the plaintiff to enter judgment against a defendant in default.[15]

Where one of several defendants so fails the plaintiff should file an affidavit of service of the writ or notice of writ on that defendant, and then proceed with the action as if that defendant had acknowledged service.[16]

Where no defendant serves an acknowledgment of service showing an intention to defend, the plaintiff may apply for an order to discontinue the contentious proceedings.[17] As, however, the plaintiff usually wishes to have a binding decision of the court in his favour, the more common procedure is to apply for an order for trial of the action.[18] Before doing so, the plaintiff must file an affidavit of service of the writ or notice of writ on the defendant or defendants, and, if no statement of claim is indorsed on the writ, he must lodge a statement of claim in the Judges' Chambers.[19] If the

---

[8] Ord. 76, r. 2(2).
[9] Ord. 6, r. 2(1)(*a*). As to pleadings see *post*, p. 417.
[10] Ord. 6. r. 5.
[11] See Ord. 10.
[12] Ord. 11, r. 1(1)(*b*).
[13] See Article 1 of the 1968 Convention, set out in Schedule 1 of the Act.
[14] See Ord. 12.
[15] Ord. 76, r. 6(1).
[16] Ord. 76, r. 6(2).
[17] See p. 387 *ante*, p. 429 *post*.
[18] Ord. 76, r. 6(3).
[19] Ord. 76, r. 6(4).

Master is then satisfied that the formalities have been complied with, he will adjourn the case into court in the Short Probate List.[20] The Master may, and usually will, direct that the action be tried on affidavit evidence.[21] Unless the court otherwise directs, a plaintiff must file his affidavit of scripts before the order is made.[22]

Where no acknowledgment of service is served on behalf of a person under a disability, the plaintiff applies for the appointment of a guardian *ad litem* on summons to the Master, supported by an affidavit setting out the facts.[23] The Master has power to dispense with service of the summons on a person under a disability.[24] The affidavit in support shows that the defendant is a person under disability who has been served with the writ or defence and counterclaim, that the proposed guardian *ad litem* is a proper person to act, that he is willing to act and that he has no interest adverse to the person under disability and that, the time for acknowledgment having expired, the summons has been duly served on the person under disability at least seven days before the return day.[25] The Official Solicitor is usually prepared to act as guardian *ad litem* if no other person is able and willing to act.

C. THE AFFIDAVIT OF SCRIPTS

Unless the court otherwise directs, the plaintiff and every defendant who has acknowledged service must file an affidavit of testamentary scripts.[26]

A testamentary script is a will or codicil or draft thereof, written instructions for a will or codicil made by or at the request, or under the instructions, of the testator,[27] and any document purporting to be evidence of the contents, or to be a copy, of a will or codicil which is alleged to have been lost or destroyed.[28]

The affidavit must describe any script of the deceased in the action of which the deponent has knowledge. If the deponent knows of no script he must say so. In the case of a script in the possession or control of another person the deponent must state the name and address of that person or, if such be the case, that he does not know the name or address of such person.[29] The script is merely described in the affidavit; it is not annexed to it. The script should not be marked, stapled, pinned or bent.

The present rule lays down that the affidavits of scripts must be sworn by the plaintiff and defendant personally. It seems, therefore, that they may not, in any circumstances, be sworn by the solicitor of these parties.

---

[20] See *post*, p. 427.
[21] Ord. 76, r. 6(5).
[22] Ord. 76, r. 5(2). See *post*, p. 415.
[23] See Ord. 80, r. 6.
[24] *Ibid.* r. 6(6).
[25] *Ibid.*, r. 6(5).
[26] Ord. 76, r. 5(1).
[27] A solicitor's attendance notes recording the testator's instructions are scripts.
[28] Ord. 76, rr. 1(3) and 5(5).
[29] Ord. 76, r. 5(1).

The parties must file their affidavits of scripts within 14 days of the acknowledgment of service by a defendant.[30] If no defendant acknowledges service and the court does not otherwise direct, a plaintiff must file his affidavit before an order is made for the trial of the action.[31] A party may, if necessary, file a supplemental affidavit of scripts voluntarily; or he may be ordered to do so.[32]

Within the same time limits, a party must also lodge in Chambers any testamentary script referred to in his affidavit which is in his possession or under his control,[33] and a copy.[34] Where a script is not lodged by a party, because, for example, it has been forwarded by the Family Division to the Chancery Division, a copy should nevertheless be lodged before the first hearing at which the script has to be considered.[35]

Where a script or any part of it is in pencil, a facsimile copy thereof or of any page bearing pencil writing must, unless otherwise directed, be lodged with the script, the words which are in pencil in the original being underlined in red in the copy.[36]

Inspection of scripts and obtaining copies of scripts

Except by leave of the court, no party to a probate action is allowed to inspect the affidavit of scripts of another party or the scripts themselves unless and until he has filed his own affidavit of scripts.[37] Inspection takes place in Chambers.

Photographic copies of scripts may be ordered, but such copies will not be made where the document is unsuitable for photography.[38] Pencil writing is sometimes impossible to photograph satisfactorily, and, in such case, the facsimile copy will be photographed.

Attesting witnesses

If the court orders the trial of a probate action on affidavit evidence, it may be necessary for an attesting witness to swear an affidavit of due execution of a will or codicil which it is desired be admitted to probate. The original will or codicil cannot be handed out of court to enable this to be done. The attesting witness should attend the Royal Courts of Justice to swear the affidavit in the presence of an officer of the court. Alternatively, it may be more convenient to bespeak a photographic copy from the Chief Master's Secretariat. The clerk who has custody of the original document will certify the copy as authentic, and it may then be exhibited to the affidavit of due execution instead of the original. The affidavit should state

[30] Ord. 76, r. 5(2).
[31] *Ibid.*
[32] See *Peacock* v. *Lowe* (1867) L.R. 1 P. & D. 311n, 478n.
[33] Ord. 76, r. 5(2).
[34] *Practice Direction* (*Probate Actions*) [1973] 1 W.L.R. 627.
[35] *ibid.*
[36] Ord. 76, r. 5(3).
[37] Ord. 76, r. 5(4).
[38] Registrar's Circular, February 28, 1939.

that the exhibited document is an authenticated copy of the document sought to be admitted.[39]

Transmission of scripts in cases tried outside London

Where a probate action is set down in a district registry without the assistance of the Cause Clerk, the solicitor concerned must forthwith notify the Chief Master's Secretary in writing and request him to forward the scripts to the registrar concerned.[40]

---

[39] *i.e.* under Ord. 76, r. 10 or r. 12.
[40] *Practice Direction* (*Probate*: *Contentious Actions*) [1974] 1 W.L.R. 1349.

CHAPTER 37

PLEADINGS

Peculiarities

The procedure as to pleadings in a probate action is in outline the same as in other actions but there are a number of important respects in which they differ. Pleadings in a probate action are headed:

In the High Court of Justice   CH 199.. D No. ....
Chancery Division (Probate)
In the estate of *AB* deceased[1]
Between

CD   Plaintiff
and
EF   Defendant

Any other parties are added to the title as they come into the action. Pleadings in a probate action are now subject to the normal rules of pleading, with the following exceptions:

(i) Where a plaintiff in a probate action disputes the interest of a defendant,[2] such a denial must be specifically pleaded in the statement of claim.[3]

(ii) Where a party claims to be entitled to a grant of letters of administration, another party is not entitled to dispute that interest unless he can show in his pleading that if the allegations made there are true, he would be entitled to an interest in the estate.[4]

(iii) A party pleading want of knowledge and approval must specify the nature of the case on which he intends to rely.[5] In doing so he is not entitled to rely on any allegation which would be relevant in support of any of the pleas that:

(a) The will was not duly executed, or
(b) at the time of the execution of the will the testator was not of sound mind, memory and understanding, or
(c) the execution of the will was obtained by undue influence or fraud,

unless that other plea is also pleaded.[6]

This does not mean that when alleging want of knowledge and approval

---

[1] Proceedings should be entitled in this way in all probate actions: *Practice Direction (Chancery: Procedure)* [1983] 1 W.L.R. 4. If there are numerous defendants these should be numbered, but for short titles "and others" will suffice.

[2] As to interest actions, see *ante*, p. 406.

[3] Ord. 76, r. 9(1), (*post*, p. 1257).

[4] Ord. 76, r. 9(2).

[5] Ord. 76, r. 9(3).

[6] *Ibid.*

matters may not be pleaded which might also be relevant on one of the above pleas unless that other plea is also made. Often, of course, such matters as a testator's senility or the involvement of a beneficiary in the preparation of the will may be directly relevant in a case of want of knowledge and approval. The above words of Order 76, rule 9 of the Rules of the Supreme Court are to be read in a restricted sense as preventing one of the pleas mentioned there from being raised under the cover of a plea of want of knowledge and approval. The test appears to be that matters should not be pleaded which, if true, would affirmatively prove one of the other pleas, as opposed to merely providing evidence in support of that plea, unless that plea is also made.[7]

Particulars

The normal rules as to the service of particulars apply.[8] Thus a party must in his pleading give full particulars of any fraud or undue influence relied on[9] and must give particulars of the facts relied on when pleading any disorder or disability of mind of a testator.[10]

Amendment

The same rules as to amendment[11] apply in probate actions as in other actions.

Default

The normal rules as to default of pleadings do not apply to a probate action.[12] Where any party in a probate action fails to serve on any other a pleading which he is required by the rules to serve on him, application may be made for an order for the discontinuance or dismissal of the action. The alternative is to apply for an order for trial of the action.[13] The procedure is similar to that where all the defendants fail to acknowledge service.[14] The application should be made to the Master, supported by an affidavit showing that the relevant pleading has not been served. If satisfied, the Master will order the action to be tried in the Short Probate List, and will usually direct it to be heard on affidavit evidence.[15]

Statement of claim

Unless the court gives leave to the contrary or the statement of claim is endorsed on the writ the plaintiff must serve a statement of claim on every

[7] *Re Stott* [1980] 1 W.L.R. 246.
[8] Ord. 18, r. 12.
[9] Ord. 18, r. 12(1)(*a*).
[10] Ord. 18, r. 12(1)(*b*).
[11] See Ord. 20.
[12] Ord. 76, r. 10(1).
[13] Ord. 76, r. 10(2).
[14] See *ante*, p. 413.
[15] Ord. 76, r. 10(2).

defendant who has acknowledged service. The statement of claim must be served before the expiration of six weeks from the acknowledgment of service by the defendant, or of eight days after he has filed his affidavit of scripts, whichever is the later.[16] As mentioned earlier, where a short statement of claim is endorsed on a writ, *e.g.* "the plaintiff is the executor of the last will of the deceased," it is common to add the statement "The above is the plaintiff's statement of claim," but under current practice a claim should be fully pleaded, so that the issues become clear as soon as possible.

It is not necessary to serve a statement of claim on a defendant who has not acknowledged service.[17]

Where the plaintiff disputes the interest of a defendant he must allege this in his statement of claim, and where he disputes the interest by which another party claims to be entitled to a grant of letters of administration, he must show in his pleading that if the allegations which he makes are proved, he would be entitled to an interest in the estate.[18]

In other respects the rules governing statements of claim[19] are the same in probate as in other actions.

Defence

As in other actions the defendant in a probate action must, unless the court gives leave to the contrary, serve his defence on the plaintiff before the expiration of 14 days after the time limited for acknowledgment of service or after the statement of claim is served on him, whichever is later.[20] In other respects, too, the practice as to defences and counterclaims is similar to that in other actions.

In his defence the defendant should not merely set out a paper case which answers the allegations in the statement of claim; he should set out how his interest really arises. Thus where the statement of claim sets up only the last of two or more wills and the defendant wishes to set up an intestacy, believing that the deceased left no valid will, he should not merely plead against the will set up but mention the other wills and set out his case against them.

Qualified defence

A defendant may, with his defence, serve the plaintiff with notice that he merely insists upon the will being proved in solemn form and only intends to cross-examine the witnesses produced in support of the will.[21] This procedure has a very important effect on the question of costs and is discussed under that topic.[22]

---

[16] Ord. 76, r. 7.
[17] *Ibid.*
[18] Ord. 76, r. 9(1) and (2).
[19] See Ord. 18.
[20] Ord. 18, r. 2.
[21] Ord. 62, r. 4(3).
[22] See *post*, p. 438.

Counterclaim

In a probate action, a defendant who alleges that he has any claim or is entitled to any relief or remedy in respect of any matter relating to the grant of probate of the will, or letters of administration to the estate, of the deceased, must add to his defence a counterclaim in respect of that matter.[23] In practice the majority of defences have a counterclaim added to them, *e.g.* setting up an earlier will, or claiming a grant of letters of administration.

If the plaintiff fails to serve a statement of claim, a defendant who has such a claim may, with the leave of the court, serve a counterclaim and the action then proceeds as if the counterclaim were the statement of claim.[24] This prevents delay on the part of the plaintiff by giving carriage of the action to the defendant.

Probate counterclaim in a non-probate action

A defendant may claim relief appropriate to a probate action[25] in an action where no such relief is claimed by the plaintiff.[26] Where a defendant does so, it is the intention of the rules to bring such an action into line with a normal probate action.[27] Thus the counterclaim should contain a statement of the defendant's and the plaintiff's interests in the estate in question.[28] In whatever Division or place the action is proceeding, the counterclaim must be produced, before it is served, to a Chancery Master and three copies of it lodged with him. An undertaking will be extracted from the defendant's solicitor to serve the counterclaim on a specified date, which will fix the commencement of the probate action. The Principal Registry will then be notified of the commencement of the probate action in the normal way so that no grant will be issued. A copy of the counterclaim will be sent to the Division in which the action is proceeding.[29]

The party against whom the counterclaim is made may then, if he considers it appropriate, make an application to strike out the counterclaim on the grounds that the counterclaim ought to be disposed of by a separate action.[30] Unless he does so within seven days after service of the counterclaim, and the application is granted, the court will, if necessary of its own motion, order that the action be transferred to the Chancery Division in London, or a Chancery District Registry if not already there.[31] If the action is not already proceeding in the Chancery Division in London, the Master with whom the probate counterclaim has been lodged will already have sent a copy to the Senior

---

[23] Ord. 76, r. 8(1).
[24] Ord. 76, r. 8(2).
[25] For the definition of a probate action, see *ante*, p. 403.
[26] Ord. 76, r. 15.
[27] *Ibid.* r. 15(2).
[28] *Ibid.* r. 15(3). This is similar to Ord. 76, r. 2(2)(*a*).
[29] See the notes to the Supreme Court Practice, para. 76/15/1.
[30] *i.e.* under Ord. 15, r. 5(2).
[31] Ord. 76, r. 15(5).

Master of the Queen's Bench Division, Senior District Judge of the Family
Division or registrar, as the case may be, to enable this to be done.

Reply and subsequent pleadings

The rules as to reply and defence to counterclaim[32] which apply in other
actions apply also in probate actions. It is rare for a plaintiff to seek to file a
reply except in conjunction with a defence to counterclaim. Occasionally a
rejoinder is necessary in a probate action, but later pleadings are most
uncommon.

---

[32] See Ord. 18, r. 3.

CHAPTER 38

INTERLOCUTORY MATTERS

Summons for directions

A summons for directions in a probate action follows the normal rules.[1] It is heard by the Master or Chancery District Judge. Usually all matters raised under the summons can be disposed of at one hearing. If not, the court will dispose of all those matters which it can, and adjourn the remainder of the summons.[2]

Discovery[3]

While the practice as to discovery follows the general pattern of discovery in other actions, the relevant period, especially in cases where testamentary capacity is in issue, is often a considerable one and there are a great number of matters, *e.g.* the business transactions of the deceased, which may be of importance. Those advising the party giving discovery must try to place themselves in the position of their opponents when considering what documents may be relevant. This is particularly the case where they act for the party who has the papers of the deceased in his possession; for this position ought not to give that party an advantage over his opponent.[4] It should be borne in mind that it is the practice of the probate court to order discovery of all documents which might have any bearing on the issues raised.

The court has wide powers for ascertaining the nature and whereabouts of the testamentary papers of the deceased and of compelling their production.[5]

As already stated the plaintiff and defendant must file affidavits of scripts. In addition there are often documents affecting testamentary matters which, though not covered by the definition of testamentary scripts, are of the utmost importance in the case. Such documents must be disclosed.

A rare and macabre form of discovery which has been allowed in probate cases is the opening of the coffin of the deceased to settle the question of his identity.[6]

Interrogatories

The facts relating to the making and execution of a will are often solely in the knowledge of one party, *e.g.* where the deceased makes a home-

[1] See Ord. 25.
[2] Ord. 25, r. 2(3).
[3] See Ord. 24.
[4] See *Hunt* v. *Anderson* (1868) L.R. 1 P. & D. 476.
[5] Under ss.122 and 123 of the Supreme Court Act 1981, see *ante*, pp. 408 *et seq.*
[6] See *R.* v. *Dr. Tristram* [1898] 2 Q.B. 371; *Druce* v. *Young* [1899] P. 84.

made will benefiting a person who lives with him. In such cases interrogatories may be most valuable. Where there is a suspicion of undue influence or of an unrighteous transaction, answers to interrogatories may either strengthen such suspicions or so dispel them as to cause the interrogating party to come to terms or abandon his action. Interrogatories may be of increasing use now that they can be served without leave.

The practice as to interrogatories is the same as in other actions.[7] Where undue influence was alleged against the executor and the universal legatee, interrogatories were allowed as to whether the executors (who received no benefit under the will) had received loans or gifts from the deceased and whether, by arrangement in the lifetime of the deceased, they had received any property from the universal legatee after the death.[8]

Privilege

The death of the client does not terminate the relationship of privilege between solicitor and client. It survives for the benefit of the client's successors in title[9] but cannot be claimed as between such successors. If the privilege was shared jointly with the client and some other person, that other person's consent must be obtained before any disclosure even to the dead client's successors in title.[10] It follows that if privilege is claimed the solicitor should not make disclosure until compelled and of course if he is not a party he cannot be forced to answer interrogatories. Where there is a genuine dispute and no claims to privilege are raised the proper course is for such a solicitor to make a statement available to all parties, whether or not he is acting for some of them.[11]

Evidence

Evidence in a probate action may be given on affidavit. Application for this mode of giving evidence should, where possible, be made in the summons for directions; otherwise it must be made on summons to the Master. In actions in the "Short Probate List"[12] it is common for the evidence to be given on affidavit. Where the estate is small the whole of the evidence in an uncontested action may be so given.[13]

Statements made by persons who have died before the hearing of the case are not infrequently put in in probate cases. To a lesser extent statements admissible under the Evidence Acts[14] in other circumstances than the death of the maker of the statement have been adduced in evidence.

[7] See Ord. 26.
[8] *Young* v. *Holloway* (1887) 12 P.D. 167, C.A.
[9] *Bullivant* v. *A. G. Victoria* [1901] A.C. 196.
[10] *Rochefoucald* v. *Boustead* [1897] 1 Ch. 196; (1896) 65 L.J. Ch. 794.
[11] See *Re Sanders* (1961) 105 S.J. 324; 56 L.S.Gaz. 619; *A Guide to the Professional Conduct of Solicitors*, issued by the Council of the Law Society, p. 49. The guidance remains valid although omitted from the current loose-leaf guide.
[12] See *post*, pp. 427, 430.
[13] *Re Baldwin, Fletcher* v. *Roulston* (1964) 108 S.J. 921.
[14] *i.e.* the Evidence Act 1938 and the Civil Evidence Act 1968.

Before the Civil Evidence Act 1968 came into force the rules of evidence in probate cases allowed witnesses to give evidence of statements made by the deceased bearing on his testamentary acts, instruments and intentions, with certain exceptions as to the latter.[15] The effect of the Civil Evidence Act 1968[16] and the rules made thereunder[17] is to preserve this rule. Although a statement by a testator that he has destroyed his will is inadmissible to prove that fact, it has been held that a letter written by him to that effect was admissible under the Evidence Act 1938.[18]

Although, in general, documents requiring attestation may, instead of being proved by an attesting witness, be proved as if no attesting witness were alive, this does not apply to wills or other testamentary documents.[19]

Witness statements

The new rules providing for the service of witness statements[20] apply to probate actions as to other actions. They should help to identify the real issues of fact or evidence in the case and, by forcing parties to disclose their hands at an earlier stage, lead to an earlier settlement of the action.

Examination of witnesses

As many witnesses are of advanced age and unable to come to court applications for the examination of such persons before the hearing are frequent. The application is made to the Master and the practice is the same as in other actions.[21] The depositions must be returned by the examiner to the Senior Master. Applications for the issue of letters of request are also made to the Master, as are applications for the examination of witnesses abroad before a special examiner, *e.g.* the British consul. All such evidence is given *de bene esse* and there is no order that the depositions shall be read at the trial. This is a matter for the trial judge.[22] It is not proper for the examiner to give his opinion as to the credibility of witnesses, but he may make a special report to record facts, for example that the witness fainted or rose to his feet and tried to assault counsel.[23]

Orders

Orders made in probate actions are drawn up in accordance with the normal practice in the Chancery Division.[24] They are enforced in the usual way.[25]

---

[15] This has already been considered *passim*.
[16] s.2.
[17] Ord. 38, r. 21(3).
[18] *Re Bridgewater* [1965] 1 W.L.R. 416. See now the Civil Evidence Act 1968, s.2.
[19] Evidence Act 1938, s.3.
[20] Ord. 38, r. 2A.
[21] See Ord. 39.
[22] President's Direction, December 1931.
[23] *Wissler* v. *Wippermann* [1955] P. 59; Ord. 39, r. 13.
[24] For this, see Ord. 42, r. 6.
[25] See Ord. 45.

Injunctions

Applications for injunctions are made on motion in open court to a judge.[26] If there is urgency, an injunction may be made *ex parte* before the writ in the action is issued.[27] Where an executor, before taking probate, prepared to dispose of assets of the estate, the court granted an injunction against him and appointed a receiver on the application of his co-executor.[28]

Similarly an application may be made for an injunction if maladministration is alleged against an executor after he has taken a grant of probate.[29]

Committal

Where a person has omitted to do some act that he has been ordered to do or has done some act which he has been ordered not to do he may be committed for contempt of court. Applications to commit are made in the same way as in other actions.[30]

An executor who has intermeddled in the estate of the testator and has not taken a grant within six months of his death may be cited to take probate[31] and, if he refuses to do so, may be committed.[32] Any person who, having been required by the court to do so under section 122 of the Supreme Court Act 1981, fails to attend for examination, answer any question or bring in any document, is guilty of contempt of court[33] and may be punished by committal.

---

[26] See Ord. 29. *Practice Direction* [1988] 1 W.L.R. 632. See p. 396 *ante*.
[27] *Ex p. Earl of Sandwich* [1962] C.L.Y. 2432 and see Ord. 29, r. 1.
[28] *Re Moore* (1888) 13 P.D. 36.
[29] *Re Moxley* [1916] 2 I.R. 145; *Colebourne v. Colebourne* (1876) 1 Ch.D. 690.
[30] See Ord. 52.
[31] See *ante*, p. 389.
[32] *Mordaunt v. Clarke* (1868) L.R. 1 P. & D. 592; *Re Lister* (1894) 70 L.T. 812; *Re Coates* (1898) 78 L.T. 820.
[33] Supreme Court Act 1981, s.122(3).

CHAPTER 39

TRIAL AND APPEAL

A. TRIAL IN THE HIGH COURT

Place of trial

An action brought in the High Court may be tried either in or outside London. The matter is decided on the summons for directions, but if circumstances change, an application may be made to the Master on a summons to change the venue.[1] The court has a discretion as to the place of trial, save that in actions by or against the Crown the hearing must be in London unless the Crown consents to the hearing elsewhere or requests a local venue.[2]

In fixing the venue the court has regard to all the circumstances, including the convenience of the parties and their witnesses and the date at which the trial can take place. Probate actions are not set down for London as of course.[3]

Trials of actions in the Chancery Division outside London are authorised to be held in Leeds, Liverpool, Manchester, Newcastle-upon-Tyne and Preston.[4] Where the circumstances justify it hearings can be arranged elsewhere. The parties' solicitors should ascertain through the circuit administrator whether a local venue will be available before the Master is approached on the matter.[5]

Where the trial is to be in London an order will be made on the summons for directions for trial before a judge, and a period will be fixed within which the plaintiff must set the action down for trial.[6]

Mode of trial

In the High Court a probate action may be tried by a judge alone or by a judge and jury like any other action in the High Court.[7] Since the transfer of contentious business to the Chancery Division, however, applications for trial by a judge and jury are unknown.

---

[1] Ord. 33, rr. 1 and 4(1).
[2] Ord. 77, r. 13.
[3] *Re Walters* (1964) 108 S.J. 220.
[4] *Practice Directions* (*Chancery: Proceedings Outside London*) [1972] 1 W.L.R. 1; [1984] 1 W.L.R. 417; [1988] 1 W.L.R. 630.
[5] *Ibid.*
[6] As to setting down, see Ord. 34. See also Ord. 33, rr. 4, 5 and notes thereto in the *Supreme Court Practice*.
[7] Ord. 33, r. 2. It has been suggested that if a jury were to be required the hearing would have to be transferred to the Queen's Bench Division.

The Witness List

If the estimate of length of the trial given to the Master on the summons for directions is three days or less, the action will be set down in Part II of the Witness List. Otherwise it will be set down in Part I. If required, an application may be made to fix the date of the hearing.

The Short Probate List

Where a party is in default of acknowledgment of service or pleadings, or where the action is to be compromised, discontinued or dismissed, it is often necessary for a will to be pronounced either for or against in solemn form. In such circumstances the Master will adjourn the matter into court for trial in the Short Probate List, at a date and time to be fixed. The Master will usually order the case to be heard on affidavit evidence.

Default of acknowledgment of service or pleading

The procedure here has already been considered.[8]

Compromise

Where, whether before or after service of the defence, the parties agree to compromise, they may apply for the action to be tried in the Short Probate List.[9] The application should be made by summons to the Master who will, if satisfied that the matter is in order, set the case down to be tried in the Short Probate List, usually on affidavit evidence.[10] The court has no inherent power to bind absent parties,[11] but if the action comes within Rules of the Supreme Court, Order 15, r. 13 the court can make a representation order and then approve the compromise so as to bind absent parties.[12] A sum may be set aside to answer the maximum claims of those who dissent.[13]

Although solicitors for the parties or counsel may sign the terms on behalf of the parties they represent, this has proved unsatisfactory and has given rise to allegations by the lay clients that they did not understand the agreement come to or that it was never submitted for their approval. Except in special circumstances therefore, the parties should always sign the terms. Nevertheless a compromise entered into by solicitors for a party

---

[8] *Ante*, pp. 413 and 418.

[9] Ord. 76, r. 12, (*post*, p. 1258). See also 137 N.L.J. 721. The Court has an interest in upholding a genuine compromise. See *Colchester Borough Council* v. *Smith* [1992] 2 W.L.R. 728.

[10] *Ibid*. Where litigation has been occasioned by some other party the terms of compromise will, if reasonable, be taken as the measure of damages against that party. See *Biggin* v. *Permanite* [1951] 2 K.B. 314.

[11] *Re Knowles* [1966] Ch. 386: a case on family provision. *Collingham* v. *Sloper* [1894] 3 Ch. 716. Absent parties can now be bound in such proceedings where Ord. 15, r. 13 applies: Ord. 99, r. 4(2).

[12] *Re Archibald* [1974] C.L.Y. 1592. Administration of Justice Act 1985, s.49. The requirements of this section are so wide as usually to defeat its reputed intention.

[13] *Collingham* v. *Sloper* [1894] 3 Ch. 716.

is binding unless the solicitors, to the knowledge of the other side, had no authority to take such a step.[14] A court cannot without evidence pronounce against the last will by consent.[15]

Minutes of order

Where it is desired to include the terms of a compromise in an order of the court, they should be set out in a schedule to the proposed order in normal Tomlin form.[16]

Minutes of order, in duplicate, should be lodged with the Master at least two days before the application comes before him.[17] By the terms of the minutes of order, the court should be invited to pronounce for a particular will or against the will or wills propounded. If required, the terms of the compromise may provide that whether or not the court pronounces for the will put forward the estate should be divided in the manner thereafter set out in the terms, but full regard should always be paid to the interests of absent parties.[18]

Where it is agreed that a particular person should be the grantee, the terms should so specify. Where it can be proved that the proposed grantee is solely entitled to the grant without requiring the exercise of the court's discretion under the Non-Contentious Probate Rules, or all persons who should be entitled to a grant are before the court, then to the term specifying that person as grantee, there should be added the words "if entitled thereto." Otherwise, this term will be disregarded on the application for a grant.[19]

Costs should be provided for in the terms, but those of the proving executor which are to come out of the estate should not be mentioned.[20]

Parties under a disability

Where any party to a proposed compromise is under a disability[21] it is necessary to apply to the court by summons to approve the terms of the settlement on behalf of that party. Where, therefore, it is also desired to have a will pronounced for or against in solemn form, the two applications should be combined. The application to have the compromise approved on behalf of the person under a disability will be heard by the judge in Chambers and the action in the Short Probate List can be heard immediately thereafter.

The practice on seeking the court's approval is that the application is

---

[14] *Welsh* v. *Roe* (1918) 118 L.T. 529, contrast *Tower* v. *Cox* (1822) 2 Add. 219 (where the solicitors did not proceed). As to discontinuance by consent, see *ante*, p. 387.
[15] See p. 430 *post*.
[16] *Practice Directions* (*Probate: Compromise Action*) [1972] 1 W.L.R. 1215.
[17] *Ibid*.
[18] *Re King* [1917] 2 Ch. 420, 432.
[19] *Practice Note* [1938] W.N. 222.
[20] See *Barclays Bank* v. *Cole* (1962) 106 S.J. 837. See *post*, p. 441.
[21] As to the practice where a patient is under the Court of Protection, see Heywood and Massey, *Court of Protection Practice* 12th ed., pp. 255 *et seq*.

supported by an affidavit by the next friend or guardian *ad litem* exhibiting the opinion of counsel that the settlement is for the benefit of the infant.[22]

The Master now has a limited jurisdiction to approve a compromise on behalf of a person under a disability.[23] Since, however, a will can only be pronounced for or against in solemn form before a judge in open court, it is thought that the most convenient course will be in any event to deal with both matters before the judge. If pronouncement in solemn form is not required then the matter may of course, be within the Master's jurisdiction.

Charities

Where a specified individual charity is a party to a compromise it should agree the terms through its duly authorised officer. Where there is a bequest for a charitable purpose generally, *e.g.* the establishment of a school, the Attorney-General should have been made a party to the action and will be able to approve the compromise on behalf of charity generally.[24] If a particular charity has been made a party and yet does not appear, the Attorney-General may bind that charity to the compromise.[25]

Discontinuance or dismissal

The normal rules as to withdrawal or discontinuance[26] do not apply to a probate action.[27]

Discontinuance of proceedings after the entry of a caveat but before the issue of a writ has already been considered.[28] At any stage after the issue of a writ the court may, on the application of a plaintiff or of any party who has acknowledged service, order the action to be discontinued or dismissed on such terms as to costs or otherwise as it thinks just.[29] When doing so, the court may order that a grant be made to the person entitled thereto.[30]

Discontinuance of contentious proceedings after a writ has been issued will be uncommon, and will usually be part of a compromise.[31] It might be appropriate, for example, where the parties have come to terms and wish, with the Court's approval, to avoid a formal pronouncement by the court as to the validity or otherwise of the will or wills in question.

Dismissal of a probate action might be appropriate, for example, where

[22] *Re Birchall* (1880) 16 Ch.D. 41.
[23] A master may approve a compromise on behalf of a person under a disability where his interest in the estate (as certified by counsel) does not significantly exceed £30,000. *Practice Direction (Chancery: Masters' Powers)* [1990] 1 W.L.R. 52.
[24] *Boughey* v. *Minor* [1893] P. 181. Where the Attorney-General agrees to the compromise of a claim by or against a charity, he will "consent" to the compromise. Otherwise it is the practice for him "not to object" to it.
[25] *Re King* [1917] 2 Ch. 240.
[26] Ord. 21.
[27] Ord. 76, r. 11(1).
[28] *Ante*, p. 387.
[29] Ord. 76, r. 11(2).
[30] *Ibid.*
[31] See *ante*, p. 427; *Re Barraclough* [1967] P. 1.

a party failed to disclose any necessary interest in his pleadings or they were otherwise frivolous or vexatious, or a party had failed to comply with an order of the court or was guilty of undue delay. In such circumstances the party seeking dismissal of the action or the court might well require formal pronouncement for or against a will.

The application may be made by motion or summons (including the summons for directions), but where formal pronouncement is required, it will usually be by the latter course. The summons is in the first instance to the Master, supported by any necessary affidavit evidence, who may then adjourn the matter into court, normally to be heard in the Short Probate List on affidavit evidence.

Evidence on trial in the Short Probate List[32]

Where a will is being set up, evidence of one of the attesting witnesses should be adduced.[33] Affidavit evidence will usually be sufficient. Where the circumstances raise strong doubt as to the testamentary capacity of the deceased it is advisable to call medical evidence, if available, to show capacity.

Where the court is asked to pronounce against what purports to be the last will of the deceased, evidence must be called to show lack of due execution, incapacity or whatever ground is alleged for the invalidity of the will. It is the duty of the probate court to give effect if it can to the wishes of the testator as expressed in testamentary documents and it should not, therefore, pronounce against what it knows to be the last will in date without making an inquiry as to its validity.[34] A court cannot pronounce against a will by consent[35] and therefore *a fortiori* cannot pronounce against a will in a case of default without sufficient evidence. Although it has been suggested that where there is a genuine belief in the invalidity of a later will and the action has become undefended the court may pronounce against a will in solemn form without further evidence, this suggestion, based on an extension of the principle in *Morton* v. *Thorpe*[36] is, it is submitted, wrong.[37]

Trial in a contested action

The course of the hearing of a probate action follows that of other actions[38] but with some important differences.

The right to begin

The rules of court lay down that, subject to any direction of the judge, the plaintiff should begin by opening his case, unless the burden of proof of

[32] See also *post*, p. 431.
[33] *Winwood* v. *Lemon* (1961) 105 S.J. 1107.
[34] *Re Muirhead* [1971] P. 263.
[35] *Re Watts* (1837) 1 Curt. 594.
[36] (1863) 3 Sw. & Tr. 179. See also *ante*, p. 389.
[37] See also *Re Muirhead, supra*.
[38] Ord. 35.

all issues in the action lies on the defendant in which case the latter has the right to begin.[39] Thus the trial judge has an unfettered discretion[40] to depart from the rule. It was suggested in a previous edition of this work that in probate cases the judges would follow the practice which had hitherto obtained. This practice was that that party had the right to begin who was setting up the last or the only will.[41] To this rule there were two exceptions: (i) where the validity of the will was not in issue and the sole issue was revocation, in which case the party alleging revocation had the right to begin[42]; (ii) where, apart from the question of formal proof of due execution, the sole issues were fraud, undue influence or forgery, where the party making these allegations had the right to begin.[43] These rules applied in revocation actions as in other probate actions.[44] This suggestion has, however, been disapproved so that the discretion is unfettered although no guidance as to its exercise has been given.[45] Nevertheless, the reasons for the former practice will no doubt sometimes give good guidance as to the exercise of the discretion. These reasons stem from the fact that where there is a contest as between two wills the party propounding each will has to establish it to the court's satisfaction. In such cases there never can be a situation where *all* the issues have to be proved by the defendant, so the defendant could *never* have the right to begin. This would be an unfortunate and costly consequence in some cases for as Sir J. Hannen says in *Hutley* v. *Grimstone*[46] "A testator often executes numerous wills, and the court might be engaged in investigating the validity of a series, all of which would be of no importance whatever if the last will were established to be the true will; if the inquiry begins at any other point in the series, much time and labour might be thrown away, and it might be still necessary to investigate the last will."

Discovery

It is important that the court should have all available information so the court leans in favour of the fullest discovery.[47]

Evidence

The general rules of evidence apply in probate actions as they do in other actions. There are, however, a number of special rules as to the evidence which is admissible and the evidence which is required to prove special matters, *e.g.* due execution, revocation, testamentary capacity, knowledge

---

[39] R.S.C. Ord. 35, r. 7.
[40] See *Re Parry* [1977] 1 W.L.R. 93.
[41] *Hutley* v. *Grimstone* (1879) 5 P.D. 24.
[42] *North* v. *North* (1909) 25 T.L.R. 322.
[43] *Hutley* v. *Grimstone* (1879) 5 P.D. 24.
[44] *Cross* v. *Cross* (1864) 3 Sw. & Tr. 292; *Tate* v. *Tate* (1890) 63 L.T. 112.
[45] *Re Parry* [1977] 1 W.L.R. 93, 95.
[46] (1879) 5 P.D. 24. In that case the parties had not by their pleadings required proof of the wills, so that it was only needed by the court.
[47] *Re Maitland* (1981) 125 S.J. 865.

and approval, undue influence and fraud. This evidence is considered where the various topics are discussed. In addition there are a number of special points as to evidence which apply in all probate cases or in the greater part of them.

At least one attesting witness must be called, if available,[48] in a defended case. Where an action has been set down in the Short Probate List[49] evidence of due execution will usually be ordered to be given on affidavit, particularly where the estate is small.[50] A will has been pronounced for without any evidence as to due execution where none was available.[51] Affidavits originally sworn in support of grants in common form have been accepted in proof.[52]

No notice under Order 38, rule 21 need be given of an intention to adduce hearsay evidence of a statement alleged to have been made by the deceased in a probate action.[53]

Attesting witnesses are not the witnesses of any party, but of the court.[54] In that capacity it is their duty to give to any party who asks for it an account of the circumstances in which the will was executed. The evidence of attesting witnesses is of course often of great importance on issues of testamentary capacity, knowledge and approval, and undue influence. In a probate action the court is entitled to see statements as to the execution of the will even though obtained by the solicitor for a party and otherwise privileged.[55]

Where one attesting witness fails to prove due execution, the party propounding the will is bound to call the other attesting witness, even if he is hostile.[56] But an attesting witness may be asked leading questions by the counsel who calls him and even cross-examined.[57] However, unless counsel is satisfied that the witness is being recalcitrant and that his evidence can only be obtained by cross-examining, the examination should be conducted in the normal way.

Although in general an instrument of which attestation is requisite may, instead of being proved by the attesting witnesses, be proved as if they were dead, this principle does not apply to the proof of wills or other testamentary documents.[58]

The burden of proof

The burden of proof in probate cases lies, in general, upon those who

---

[48] *Belbin* v. *Skeats* (1858) 1 Sw. & Tr. 148; *Oakes* v. *Uzzell* [1932] P. 19.
[49] See *ante*, p. 427.
[50] *Re Baldwin, Fletcher* v. *Roulston* (1964) 108 S.J. 921.
[51] *Winwood* v. *Lemon* (1961) 105 S.J. 1107.
[52] *Palin* v. *Ponting* [1930] P. 185; *Trotman* v. *Trotman* (1964) 108 S.J. 159.
[53] Ord. 38, r. 21(3).
[54] *Jones* v. *Jones* (1908) 24 T.L.R. 839; *Oakes* v. *Uzzell, supra*; *Re Fuld, Hartley* v. *Fuld (No. 2)* [1965] P. 405.
[55] *Re Fuld, Hartley* v. *Fuld, supra*.
[56] *Vere-Wardale* v. *Johnson* [1949] P. 395 and the cases there cited.
[57] *Jones* v. *Jones, supra*; *Oakes* v. *Uzzell, supra*; *Re Fuld, Hartley* v. *Fuld, supra*.
[58] Evidence Act 1938, s.3.

propound a will. But the burden of proving fraud, undue influence and forgery lies on those who allege it. Where fraud is not alleged in the pleadings it is nevertheless open to a defendant who challenges a will on the ground of want of knowledge and approval to cross-examine as if fraud had been pleaded.[59] The burden of proof in many cases shifts during the course of the case. The question of the burden of proof has been considered under the headings of testamentary capacity, knowledge and approval, fraud, undue influence, etc.[60]

The hearing

At the close of the plaintiff's case or at the close of the case of the party who began, the defendant, or the plaintiff if the defendant began, may open his case and will call his witnesses. If any other defendant has served any pleading which puts forward a case different from those of the plaintiff and the defendant, that party opens his case and calls his witnesses after the defendant has closed his case, unless the judge otherwise directs. The final speeches are made in reverse order from that in which the parties opened the case.

The former rule that witnesses in a probate action should remain out of court until they give their evidence,[61] is no longer applicable.[62]

Executors are specifically made competent witnesses.[63] Attesting witnesses who forfeit their benefit are nevertheless competent witnesses.[64]

Judgment

At the end of the judgment the judge pronounces for or against the will, or, in interest suits, for or against the interest of the parties involved.[65]

Where judgment is reserved the judge may accede to a motion to call evidence which was not available at the hearing.[66]

The person seeking to obtain a grant must obtain an office copy of the judgment, and when this is lodged in the Principal Registry the original will (in the case of a grant or probate) will be handed out and the usual procedure in common form grants followed.[67]

Where a grant of representation was made before the action and the title to it is confirmed by the action the judge should be asked at the hearing for the grant to be handed out to the grantee or his solicitor.[68] A grant of pro-

---

[59] *Wintle* v. *Nye* [1959] 1 W.L.R. 284; *Re Fuld* [1968] p. 727, and *ante*, pp. 125. As to costs see *post*, p. 440.

[60] See *ante*, pp. 158 *et seq.*

[61] *Practice Note* (1908) 24 T.L.R. 263.

[62] *Green* v. *Nightingale* [1975] 1 W.L.R. 80.

[63] Wills Act 1837, s.17.

[64] Wills Act 1837, s.15. See *ante*, p. 145.

[65] As to the effect of the judgment see p. 270 *ante* and p. 450 *post*.

[66] *Sugden* v. *Lord St. Leonards* (1876) 1 P.D. 154, applied in *Acosta* v. *Longsworth* [1965] 1 W.L.R. 107, P.C.

[67] See *ante*, p. 277.

[68] *Registrar's Direction*, October 18, 1950.

bate is marked by the registrar to show that the validity of the will has been pronounced for. After notation and re-photographing the grant is returned to the probate registry and then handed out to the applicant or his solicitor.

The power of the court to set aside a judgment where a party does not appear at the trial[69] applies in a probate action.[70]

The judgment can be made specifically binding on non-parties under Order 15, rule 13A of the Rules of the Supreme Court.

Adjournment from the Master

A party dissatisfied with an order of the Master should appeal to the judge. The normal rules as to appeals from the Master apply.[71]

B. Trial in the County Court

Jurisdiction

Although it is uncommon for probate actions to be tried in the county court there is jurisdiction where the net value of the estate after making allowance for funeral expenses, debts and liabilities does not exceed £30,000.[72] The jurisdiction is founded where on an application for grant or revocation of probate in the principal or a district registry it is shown to the satisfaction of a county court that the value of the net estate does not exceed this county court limit.[73] Transfer from the High Court to the county court is governed by section 40 of the County Courts Act 1984.[74]

Place of Trial

The county court having jurisdiction in the place of abode of the deceased was originally the only court having jurisdiction[75] but this limitation has been abolished and the rules make no specific provision.[76]

Costs

After transfer the High Court has no power to order costs incurred before transfer.[77] The county court has complete jurisdiction within the statutory limits.[78]

---

[69] Under Ord. 35, r. 2.

[70] *Barraclough* v. *Young* [1967] P. 1.

[71] See *Practice Direction (Chancery: Procedure)* [1983] 1 W.L.R. 4; *Practice Direction (Chancery Applications: Change of Name)* [1984] 1 W.L.R. 447; and R.S.C. Ord. 58, r. 1.

[72] County Courts Act 1984, s.32; Administration of Justice Act 1985; County Courts Jurisdiction Order 1981.

[73] *Ibid.*

[74] The High Court has a discretion regardless of the wishes of the parties: *Dunn* v. *Dunn* (1860) 1 Sw. & Tr. 521.

[75] See County Courts Act 1959, s.62.

[76] See County Court Rules 1981, Ord. 41.

[77] *Macleur* v. *Macleur* (1868) 1 P. & D. 604.

[78] *Re Thomas* [1949] P. 336.

Procedure

Except where the county court rules otherwise provide, the provisions of the Rules of the Supreme Court relating to contentious probate proceedings apply so far as appropriate to probate actions in the county court.[79] On the issue of a summons the proper officer of the county court sends a notice to the principal registry requesting all documents relating to the matter to be sent to him.[80] A copy of any judgment must be sent to every party to the proceedings.[81] The registrar of the county court transmits to the principal registry or a district probate registry as he thinks convenient a certificate under the seal of the court certifying that the order for grant or revocation has been made and the probate registry then gives effect to the order on the application of the party in whose favour the order has been made.[82]

C. APPEALS

Appeals from a judge in chambers

The same rules as to appeals from a judge in chambers apply in probate actions as in other actions.[83]

Appeals from a judge in court

The same rules as to appeals from a judge in court apply in probate actions as in other actions.[84]

The Court of Appeal has an inherent jurisdiction to strike out a probate appeal which is an abuse of the process of the court.[85]

The size of the estate, the number of parties and the great cost of the proceedings at first instance may together amount to special circumstances which justify the Court of Appeal in ordering a substantial security for costs from the appellant.[86]

Appeals from county courts

The general rules governing appeals from a county court[87] apply where that court has exercised its probate jurisdiction. No appeal lies from the

---

[79] C.C.R. Ord. 41, r. 4. See in particular R.S.C. Ord. 76.
[80] C.C.R. Ord. 41, r. 2.
[81] C.C.R. Ord. 41, r. 3.
[82] County Courts Act 1984, s.33.
[83] See Ord. 58, r. 6.
[84] See Ord. 59.
[85] *Re Fuld, Hartley* v. *Fuld (No. 4)* (1966) 110 S.J. 150. (On appeal).
[86] *Ibid.* As to parties on appeal, see *post*, p. 928.
[87] See Ord. 59, r. 19.

Court of Appeal to the House of Lords in probate proceedings decided in a
county court.[88]

Appeals to the House of Lords

The procedure in such appeals is the same in probate matters as in other
appeals from the Court of Appeal.

[88] County Courts Act 1984, s.82.

CHAPTER 40

COSTS

Court's discretion

Costs in probate actions are at the discretion of the court.[1] It is the general rule in probate actions, as in other actions, that costs follow the event.[2] The notion, sometimes entertained, that the costs of unsuccessful parties will generally be ordered out of the estate in a probate action, is erroneous.[3] A large part of this chapter is taken up by a consideration of the exceptions to the rule that costs follow the event. The impression may, therefore, be formed that the rule is more honoured in the breach than in the observance. It should be made clear that this is not so. Cases which form an exception to the rule are usually reported as to costs, while those in which the general rule is followed are not. Practitioners advising those about to embark on a probate action should not, in ordinary circumstances, advise them that their costs are likely to be ordered out of the estate of the deceased if they fail.

Subject to specific rules, a party may only recover costs from another under an order of the court.[4] Costs should be asked for at the hearing after judgment is given.[5] In a case where no order for costs was made at the trial, the court subsequently allowed costs to be paid out of the estate.[6] Several different orders for costs may be made where there are a number of parties to whom different considerations apply.[7] Although costs may be ordered to be paid on an indemnity basis, this is unusual in the absence of consent.

It is the practice to allow the costs of the caveat, warning and appearance to the warning when they lead to a probate action as costs in the contentious proceedings.[8]

Exceptions to the general rule

There are several important exceptions to the rule that costs follow the event in probate actions:

---

[1] Supreme Court Act 1981, s.51, as substituted by s.4 of the Courts and Legal Services Act, 1990.

[2] Ord. 62, r. 3(3). See *Twist* v. *Tye* [1902] P. 92; *Spiers* v. *English* [1907] P. 122.

[3] *Page* v. *Williamson* (1902) 87 L.T. 146, 147. Gorell Barnes J. expressed the view in this case that departures from the rule that costs follow the event only occurred under rare and exceptional circumstances, but this view is to be accepted with considerable reserve since cases to the contrary are far from being rare or exceptional. It is in special rather than in rare and exceptional circumstances that the general rule is departed from.

[4] Ord. 62, r. 3(2).

[5] *Dyke* v. *Williams* (1871) L.R. 2 P. & D. 239 (costs asked for nine years after the trial refused).

[6] *Wilkinson* v. *Corfield* (1881) 6 P.D. 27.

[7] *Re Fuld, Hartley* v. *Fuld* (*No.* 3) [1965] 3 All E.R. 776, 783.

[8] *Moran* v. *Place* [1896] P. 214; *Salter* v. *Salter* [1896] P. 291.

1. Where notice to cross-examine has been given

Where a party opposing a will has given notice (which must be served with the defence[9]) that he merely insists on the will being proved in solemn form and intends only to cross-examine the witnesses called in support of the will, such party is not liable to pay the costs of the other party unless the court is of opinion that there was no reasonable ground[10] for opposing the will.[11] Although a party who thus limits his opposition will not in most cases be condemned in the costs if he fails,[12] it does not follow that he will be granted his costs out of the estate.

The notice may be conditional upon particular witnesses being called.[13] It may also be confined to the witnesses called to prove a particular matter, *e.g.* testamentary capacity. But though the notice gives protection as to costs where the party who gives it pleads against due execution, testamentary capacity and knowledge and approval,[14] protection does not extend to cases where the party giving the notice pleads undue influence or fraud,[15] nor does the protection apply to a party who seeks to call in and obtain revocation of probate[16] or to a mere legatee (as distinct from the executor) under a previous will.[17]

2. Where the litigation has been caused by the conduct of the testator

This is the rule which also applies to the construction of an ambiguous will. Where the state of his testamentary papers, the habits and mode of life or (doubtfully) where the testator's own statements have brought about the litigation, costs of unsuccessful parties may be ordered out of the estate.

Thus where owing to the confusion in which his papers were left it was doubtful whether the deceased intended entirely to revoke an earlier will[18]; or where it was doubtful whether an apparently duly executed document was intended to be testamentary[19] the court ordered the costs of both parties to be paid out of the estate.

Where the conduct and habits and mode of life of a testator have given

[9] *Bone* v. *Whittle* (1866) L.R. 1 P. & D. 249.

[10] *Perry* v. *Dixon* (1899) 80 L.T. 297 (even a trustee may be condemned in costs); see *Spicer* v. *Spicer* [1899] P. 38.

[11] Ord. 62, r. 4(3).

[12] Failure in a suit does not necessarily mean that the opposition was unreasonable, *Davies* v. *Jones* [1899] P. 161, 164.

[13] *Leeman* v. *George* (1868) L.R. 1 P. & D. 542.

[14] *Cleare* v. *Cleare* (1869) L.R. 1 P. & D. 655; *Re Sanders* (1961) 105 S.J. 324.

[15] *Ireland* v. *Rendall* (1866) L.R. 1 P. & D. 194.

[16] *Tomalin* v. *Smart* [1904] P. 141.

[17] *Hockley* v. *Wyatt* (1882) 7 P.D. 239. It seems that the executor under a former will had the same right as the next of kin who were the 'favourites of the Court.' See Williams: *Executors* (8th ed.), 344.

[18] *Jenner* v. *Ffinch* (1879) 5 P.D. 106; *Lemage* v. *Goodban* (1865) L.R. 1 P. & D. 57, 63; see *Orton* v. *Smith* (1873) L.R. 3 P. & D. 23. The principle here is similar to that in the Chancery Division where a will requires the interpretation of the court.

[19] *Thorncroft & Clarke* v. *Lashmar* (1862) 2 Sw. & Tr. 479.

ground for questioning his testamentary capacity, the costs of the unsuccessful opponents of the will must be paid out of the estate.[20]

Conversely, if an executor is led into litigation by the fact that the testator gave every appearance of being able to manage his affairs he is entitled to his costs out of the estate even if he fails.[21] But where executors are in a fiduciary relationship to the deceased they must exercise the utmost vigilance in the interest of his estate and, if they do not do so, will be condemned in costs.[22]

In earlier cases it was held that where the testator's own statements had induced litigants unsuccessfully to plead undue influence, costs must be paid out of the estate.[23] These cases were not cited in *Re Cutcliffe*[24] in which Hodson L.J. said[25]: "While it would not be possible to limit the circumstances in which a testator is said to have promoted litigation by leaving his own affairs in confusion, I cannot think that it should extend to cases where a testator by his words, either written or spoken, has misled other people, and perhaps inspired false hopes in their bosoms that they may benefit after his death."

3. Where litigation has been caused by the conduct of principal beneficiaries

If a party supporting the will is a principal beneficiary and has by unreasonable or improper conduct induced litigation which the court considers reasonable, the costs of the litigation should come out of the estate,[26] *e.g.* where a residuary legatee would not produce a will until after administration had been obtained, though called on to do so.[27]

Under this rule the court will allow the costs of a party who contests testamentary capacity, knowledge and approval[28] by the deceased and even undue influence[29] and fraud. Whether such pleas are justified is to be judged on the merits of each case.[30] The court must consider whether sufficient doubt and suspicion have been caused by the conduct of beneficiaries to justify any of these pleas. Where beneficiaries have been active in the preparation of the will suspicion will easily be aroused.[31] But even this circumstance does not necessarily warrant a charge of undue influence.[32]

---

[20] *Mitchell* v. *Gard* (1863) 3 Sw. & Tr. 75, 77; *Davies* v. *Gregory* (1873) 3 P.D. 28, 31; *Roe* v. *Nix* [1893] P. 55; *Spiers* v. *English* [1907] P. 122, 123.

[21] See *Spiers* v. *English, supra. Boughton* v. *Knight* (1873) L.R. 3 P. & D. 64, 79.

[22] *O'Donnell* v. *Bruce* (1962) 106 S.J. 432.

[23] *Cousins* v. *Tubb* (1891) 65 L.T. 716; *Shortman* v. *Shortman* (1892) 67 L.T. 71.

[24] [1959] P. 6.

[25] At p. 19.

[26] *Michell* v. *Gard* (1863) 3 Sw. & Tr. 75, 77; *Spiers* v. *English, supra.*

[27] *Smith* v. *Smith* (1865) 4 Sw. & Tr. 3.

[28] *Child* v. *Osment* [1914] P. 129; *Goodacre* v. *Smith* (1867) L.R. 1 P. & D. 351; *Orton* v. *Smith* (1873) L.R. 3 P. & D. 23.

[29] *Williams* v. *Henery* (1864) 3 Sw. & Tr. 471.

[30] *Orton* v. *Smith, supra.*

[31] See *Goodacre* v. *Smith* (1867) L.R. 1 P. & D. 351; *Orton* v. *Smith* (1873) L.R. 3 P. & D. 23; *Aylwin* v. *Aylwin* [1902] P. 203 (where no order for costs was asked for or made).

[32] *Wilson* v. *Bassil* [1903] P. 239, 242; *Spiers* v. *English* [1907] P. 122; *Re Cutcliffe* [1959] P. 6, C.A.

The existence of some suspicious circumstances which were not, in fact, the cause of the litigation will not entitle an unsuccessful party to his costs, *e.g.* a failure to mention instructions for a will in an affidavit of scripts.[33]

4. *Where circumstances afford reasonable grounds for opposing a will*

Where there are reasonable grounds for opposing a will, other than those mentioned above, the unsuccessful party, though not usually granted his costs out of the estate, will not be condemned in costs.

"It is the function of this court," said Sir J. P. Wilde in *Mitchell* v. *Gard*,[34] "to investigate the execution of a will and the capacity of the maker, and having done so to ascertain and declare what is the will of the testator. If fair circumstances of doubt and suspicion arise to obscure this question, a judicial enquiry is, in a manner, forced upon it. Those who are instrumental in bringing about and subserving this enquiry are not wholly in the wrong, even if they do not succeed; and so it comes that this court has been in the practice on such occasions of deviating from the common rule in other courts, and of relieving the losing party from costs, if chargeable with no other blame than that of having failed in a suit which was justified by good and sufficient grounds for doubt."

Thus where a will was unsuccessfully opposed because a doctor, who attested it, expressed doubts as to the testator's testamentary capacity, the court refused to condemn the next-of-kin in costs.[35] There are cases where a party is entitled to demand proof in solemn form, but not justified in fully contesting the action.[36]

But parties should not be tempted into fruitless opposition to a will by a belief that their costs will be defrayed by others, or that they will escape condemnation in costs.[37]

Pleas of fraud or undue influence

A plea of undue influence or fraud ought never to be put forward unless the party who pleads it has reasonable grounds on which to support it.[38] Failure to establish such pleas will, as a general rule, be followed by condemnation in costs.[39]

But the losing party may be relieved of paying costs if there is reasonable

---

[33] *Foxwell* v. *Poole* (1862) 3 Sw. & Tr. 5.

[34] (1863) 3 Sw. & Tr. at p. 78, a passage approved in *Re Cutcliffe, supra.*

[35] *Tippett* v. *Tippett* (1865) 1 P. & D. 54; see *Bramley* v. *Bramley* (1864) 3 Sw. & Tr. 430 (where the balance of probabilities was only just against the will); *Ferrey* v. *King* (1861) 3 Sw. & Tr. 51 (where conflicting evidence was given by attesting witnesses).

[36] *Gillett* v. *Rogers* (1913) 108 L.T. 732.

[37] *Mitchell* v. *Gard, supra*; see *Re Cutcliffe* [1959] P. 6, C.A.

[38] *Mitchell* v. *Gard, supra*; *Spiers* v. *English, supra.* As to cross-examination without a plea of fraud see *ante*, p. 175.

[39] *Summerell* v. *Clements* (1862) 3 Sw. & Tr. 35; *Leo* v. *Levy* (1909) 25 T.L.R. 717; *Re Cutcliffe, supra.* See also *per* Scarman J. in *Re Fuld (No. 3)* [1968] P. 675, at p. 722.

ground for contesting the case on these issues.[40] The question whether such pleas are justified must be judged upon the merits of each case.[41] Costs have even been allowed out of the estate where the circumstances were such as to arouse the vigilance and suspicion of the court by the residuary legatee seeking to obtain from the deceased, who was insane, a deed vesting all his property in her,[42] where the principal beneficiary had taken instructions for the will himself and it was never read over to the deceased,[43] where the principal beneficiary had obtained a will in his favour and had procured a person to write the testator's signature on two cheques,[44] and where there were other circumstances requiring investigation.[45] Costs have been ordered to be paid out of the legacies of those who were the real cause of the litigation.[46]

Where costs had been allowed to a party who had unsuccessfully pleaded undue influence it was held on appeal that the order must stand where there are any grounds on which it can be based.[47]

Interest suits

Unless there are special circumstances, the party who fails to prove his case in an interest suit is condemned in costs.[48]

A. COSTS OF PARTICULAR PARTIES

Executors

An executor in a probate action is in a different position from an established executor applying to the court in administration proceedings. In the latter case he is almost invariably entitled to his costs on an indemnity basis.[49] In probate his title as executor is itself generally in doubt. He is not obliged to propound the will and if he does so he will be wise to obtain an indemnity from the persons beneficially interested if he is not so interested himself.[50]

An executor who successfully proves a will in solemn form is, as a rule, entitled to his costs out of the estate.[51] Apart from the order of the court he has a right to take them out of the estate as costs of obtaining probate. He should not ask for costs out of the estate, if successful, as an order of the

---

[40] *Mitchell* v. *Gard* (1863) 3 Sw. & Tr. 75; *Summerell* v. *Clements* (1862) 3 Sw. & Tr. 35; *Bramley* v. *Bramley* (1864) 3 Sw. & Tr. 430; *Smith* v. *Smith* (1866) L.R. 1 P. & D. 239.

[41] *Orton* v. *Smith* (1873) L.R. 3 P. & D. 23, 25.

[42] *Williams* v. *Henery* (1864) 3 Sw. & Tr. 471.

[43] *Goodacre* v. *Smith* (1867) L.R. 1 P. & D. 351.

[44] *Orton* v. *Smith, supra.*

[45] *Wilson* v. *Bassil* [1903] P. 239; but see *Spiers* v. *English* [1907] P. 122.

[46] *Child* v. *Osment* [1914] P. 129.

[47] *Cummins* v. *Murray* [1906] 2 I.R. 509.

[48] See *Northey* v. *Cock* (1824) 2 Add. 326; *Tucker* v. *Westgarth* (1824) 2 Add 352; *Wiseman* v. *Wiseman* (1866) L.R. 1 P. & D. 351.

[49] See *post*, 915, 921.

[50] See *post*, n. 59 and text.

[51] *Headington* v. *Holloway* (1830) 3 Hag.Ecc. 280, 282; *Wild* v. *Plant* [1926] P. 139; and see Ord. 62, r. 6(2).

court involves a taxation,[52] but he must, of course, ask for any order he seeks against any other party.

Where through the negligence of the executrix the original will was lost, the court condemned her in the costs of the defendants and only allowed her such costs as she would have incurred in proving the original will in solemn form.[53]

Where an executor is partially successful he may be given his costs if he has not acted unreasonably.[54] But where the residuary gift to an executrix was held to have been procured by her undue influence, but the rest of the will was upheld, she was condemned in the costs, save those of proving in solemn form.[55] Where a verdict establishing a will was set aside and a new trial granted, the executors were allowed their costs out of the estate up to the time when the rule for a new trial was made absolute.[56]

An executor is prima facie justified in propounding a will,[57] but he is not bound to do so.[58] The fact that he is a bare executor is no ground for his not being condemned in costs.[59] If an executor must or ought to have known that he was propounding a document that could not be supported he will be condemned in costs.[60] An executor's right to costs will be lost or curtailed by inequitable conduct amounting to a violation or culpable neglect of his duty.[61] And an executor has been condemned in costs where he was exonerated of undue influence and his co-executor found guilty.[62]

Where executors have ample opportunity to observe the behaviour of a testator and propound a will they will be condemned in costs if they are unsuccessful,[63] especially where they are in a fiduciary relationship with him.[64] But an executor who has no opportunity of observing the strange behaviour of a testator may be given his costs although he fails to establish the will.[65]

Executors who unreasonably opposed a third codicil, which they insisted should be propounded in solemn form, were condemned in the costs.[66]

---

[52] *Barclays Bank* v. *Cole* (1962) 106 S.J. 837.

[53] *Burls* v. *Burls* (1868) L.R. 1 P. & D. 472; see *Smith* v. *Atkins* (1870) L.R. 2 P. & D. 169.

[54] *Wild* v. *Plant* [1926] P. 139, C.A. *cf. Holding* v. *Property Trust* [1989] 1 W.L.R. 1313, 1324.

[55] *Smith* v. *Atkins* (1870) L.R. 2 P. & D. 169; see *Thomas* v. *Jones* [1928] P. 162.

[56] *Boulton* v. *Boulton* (1867) L.R. 1 P. & D. 456.

[57] *Boughton* v. *Knight* (1873) L.R. 3 P. & D. 64, 77; see *Wild* v. *Plant, supra.*

[58] *Rennie* v. *Massie* (1866) L.R. 1 P. & D. 118, 119.

[59] *Ibid.*

[60] *Boughton* v. *Knight, supra*; see *Dodge* v. *Meech* (1828) 1 Hag.Ecc. 612; *Clarkson* v. *Waterhouse* (1860) 2 Sw. & Tr. 378; *Richards* v. *Humphreys* (1860) 29 L.J.P. & M. 137; *Rennie* v. *Massie, supra*; *Cottrell* v. *Cottrell* (1872) L.R. 2 P. & D. 397; *Rogers* v. *LeCocq* (1896) L.J.P. 68; *Twist* v. *Tye* [1902] P. 92; *Bliss Hill* v. *Jeffries* [1916] W.N. 394, C.A.; *Saint* v. *Tuckfield* (1961) 105 S.J. 511; *Huggett* v. *Reichman* (1966) 110 S.J. 852.

[61] *Turner* v. *Hancock* (1882) 20 Ch.D. 303, 305, as applied to probate cases in *Thomas* v. *Jones* [1928] P. 162.

[62] *Haydon* v. *Pring* [1919] P. 131, C.A., and see *Thomas* v. *Jones, supra.*

[63] See *Boughton* v. *Knight, supra.*

[64] *O'Donnell* v. *Bruce* (1962) 109 S.J. 432.

[65] *Boughton* v. *Knight, supra.*

[66] *Speke* v. *Deakin* (1913) 109 L.T. 719.

An executor who has failed to prove a will has no contractual or quasi-contractual right to costs out of the estate.[67]

Where a legatee propounds a will

Where a legatee propounds a will and establishes it, thereby fulfilling the duty of an executor, he is entitled to have his expenses paid out of the residuary estate.[68] If he obtains a grant of administration (with the will) he is entitled to recoup himself out of the estate for these expenses without an order of the court. Where a legatee is not entitled to such a grant he should apply for costs out of the estate.[69]

Where an executor proved the will only, a legatee who successfully proved a codicil was held entitled not only to his party and party costs against the executor but also to such further sum as would cover his additional expenses out of the estate.[70] But costs out of the estate were refused to a legatee who had successfully propounded a codicil but had unwisely delayed in producing it.[71]

Parties who successfully oppose probate

A litigant having successfully opposed a will, on becoming legal representative of the deceased, either on intestacy or under an earlier will, is entitled to recoup himself out of the estate for his expenses, and also to proceed against his opponent, provided the latter has been condemned in costs.

But where a will is set aside at the instance of a person who has no title to be constituted legal personal representative, a distinction appears to exist between cases in which the unsuccessful litigant has or has not been condemned in costs. In the latter case the successful litigant may be allowed his costs out of the estate,[72] in the former he must rely on the party who has been condemned in the costs for payment.[73]

Additional parties

It is the general practice of the court to allow only one set of costs.[74] Consequently a party who is added at his own request will not usually be allowed costs where he pleads in an action,[75] unless there is such diver-

---

[67] *Re Barlow* [1919] P. 131.
[68] *Sutton* v. *Drax* (1815) 2 Phill. 323; *Williams* v. *Goude* (1828) 1 Hag.Ecc. 577, 610; *Thorne* v. *Rooke* (1841) 2 Curt. 799, 830.
[69] *Bewsher* v. *Williams & Ball* (1861) 3 Sw. & Tr. 62. Costs should be asked for on an indemnity basis.
[70] *Bremer* v. *Freeman* (1856) Dea. & Sw. 192, 258; *Wilkinson* v. *Corfield* (1881) 6 P.D. 27; *Speke* v. *Deakin* (1913) 109 L.T. 719.
[71] *Headington* v. *Holloway* (1830) 3 Hag.Ecc. 280.
[72] *Crichell* v. *Crichell* (1863) 3 Sw. & Tr. 41; *Bewsher* v. *Williams & Ball, supra*; see *Dyke* v. *Williams* (1871) L.R. 2 P. & D. 239.
[73] *Nash* v. *Yelloly* (1862) 3 Sw. & Tr. 59; but see *Cross* v. *Cross* (1864) 3 Sw. & Tr. 292.
[74] *Bagshaw* v. *Pimm* [1900] P. 148; *Tennant* v. *Cross* (1886) 12 P.D. 4.
[75] *Twist* v. *Tye* [1902] P. 92; *Shawe* v. *Marshall* (1858) 1 Sw. & Tr. 129.

gence between his interests and those of the other parties as to justify a separate pleading.[76] If his interests are already represented in the action, his reasonable course is to support the side that represents them.[77]

Where an intervener was cited by the unsuccessful defendants and charged with undue influence he was given his costs against them.[78]

The court has power to condemn in costs a caveator who has not been cited or made a party.[79]

The Treasury Solicitor may, in the discretion of the court, be condemned in costs.[80] The Official Solicitor may be ordered to pay costs. He was not infrequently granted costs on a common fund basis but unless he asked for costs on this scale he only got party and party costs if successful.[81] Under current practice it seems he would seldom be allowed costs on the indemnity basis.

Successful creditors will be allowed their costs, including those of the appointment of an administrator *pendente lite*.[82]

A party to any probate proceedings in the capacity of trustee, representative or mortgagee is, unless otherwise ordered, entitled to the costs of the proceedings in so far as they are not recovered from or paid by any other person, out of the fund held by the trustee, representative or mortgagee, as the case may be. The court may otherwise order only on the ground that he has acted unreasonably or in the case of a trustee or representative, has in substance acted for his own benefit rather than for the benefit of the fund,[83] in which case there is a right of appeal on costs.

The costs of an administrator *pendente lite* are included in the costs ordered against a party.[84] The costs of ordinary work in winding up the estate are not of course included.[85]

Legal aid is available in probate actions but where a settlement is being negotiated, it must be borne in mind that the legal aid fund has a first charge for costs on all moneys and property recovered or preserved for a legally aided person.[86]

Apportionment of costs

The court has power to apportion costs. Costs have been ordered to be paid out of certain real estate,[87] out of the legacies given to the successful

---

[76] *Bagshaw* v. *Pimm, supra*; *Burgoyne* v. *Showler* (1844) 1 Rob.Eccl. 5, 13; *Jenner* v. *Ffinch* (1879) 5 P.D. 106.

[77] *Twist* v. *Tye, supra*.

[78] *Tennant* v. *Cross* (1886) 12 P.D. 4.

[79] *Ratcliffe* v. *Barnes* (1862) 2 Sw. & Tr. 486. See also now, as to the jurisdiction to make a costs order against a non-party, *Aiden Shipping Co. Ltd.* v. *Interbulk Ltd.* [1986] A.C. 965.

[80] Administration of Justice (Miscellaneous Provisions) Act 1933, s.7.

[81] *Eady* v. *Elsdon* [1901] 2 K.B. 460.

[82] *Tichborne* v. *Tichborne* (1869) L.R. 1 P. & D. 730.

[83] Ord. 62, r. 6(2).

[84] *Fisher* v. *Fisher* (1878) 4 P.D. 231.

[85] *Howlett* v. *Howlett* [1950] P. 177.

[86] Legal Aid Act 1988, s.16(6).

[87] *Dean* v. *Bulmer* [1905] P. 1.

parties whose conduct had caused the litigation,[88] and out of the shares of residue given to unsuccessful parties.[89]

Where a large number of parties was involved, the court made orders for costs varying in accordance with their success or otherwise and their conduct.[90]

Where issues are found distributively, the court may condemn the unsuccessful party in the costs of those issues alone upon which he failed, but only, it seems, where the exact amount of such costs, as distinguished from the costs of the issues upon which he was successful, can be ascertained on taxation.[91]

The court may make an order charging the costs of a solicitor incurred in a probate action upon the interest of his client under a will or on intestacy as upon property recovered or preserved through the solicitor's instrumentality.[92]

Conditional order for costs

While it seems that orders for costs may be made upon proper conditions, the court will not make a grant of administration conditional on the payment of costs.[93]

Security for costs

Security for costs is given on the same principles as in other actions.[94] A caveator, who has been made a defendant following the entry by him of an appearance, is not thereby placed in the position of plaintiff so as to become liable to give security for costs.[95]

Security may be ordered for the costs of an appeal from the decision of the judge.[96]

Taxation of costs

Costs in probate actions are taxed as in other actions in the Chancery Division.

Difficult questions as to taxation may arise on a dispute between a litigant in a probate action who has been awarded costs out of the estate, and his solicitors.[97]

[88] *Child* v. *Osment* [1914] P. 129.
[89] *Harrington* v. *Butt* [1905] P. 3n.
[90] *Re Fuld, Harltey* v. *Fuld* (*No. 3*) [1968] P. 675, 719 *et seq.*
[91] *Rayson* v. *Parton* (1869) L.R. 2 P. & D. 38, and see *Fyson* v. *Westrope & Cutting* (1859) 1 Sw. & Tr. 279, 283; *Smith* v. *Atkins* (1870) L.R. 2 P. & D. 169.
[92] Solicitors Act 1974, s.73; *Hyde* v. *White* [1933] P. 105.
[93] *Sawbridge* v. *Hill* (1871) L.R. 2 P. & D. 219.
[94] See Ord. 23.
[95] *Re Emery* [1923] P. 184; *Rose* v. *Epstein* [1974] 1 W.L.R. 1565.
[96] See *Re Fuld, Hartley* v. *Fuld* (*No. 4*) [1968] P. 727.
[97] *Re Fuld, Hartley* v. *Fuld* (*No. 4*) [1968] P. 727.

A successful litigant must include in his bill for taxation all the costs to which the judgment entitles him; he is not entitled to tax one bill and then present another which contains items which should have been contained in the first bill.[98]

[98] *Re Segalov* [1952] P. 241.

Part Five

DEVOLUTION AND LIABILITY

CHAPTER 41

THE EFFECT OF A GRANT

Once the exercise of the probate jurisdiction is complete the effect of its exercise has to be considered. Although the grant is conclusive,[1] rectification of a will is now possible under section 20 of the Administration of Justice Act 1982 so that complete reliance on the terms of a will admitted to probate is no longer possible at least for the period of six months after grant within which the application for rectification should be made.[2]

Rectification of wills

Rectification may be ordered where a court is satisfied that the will fails to carry out the testator's intentions in consequence of a clerical error or failure to understand instructions. Thus the traditional rule that a testator's intentions are to be inferred from the wording of the will itself is now qualified to the extent that extrinsic evidence is admissible to show clerical errors or misunderstanding of instructions. Such evidence would seem to be admissible even where it would not otherwise qualify under the terms of section 21 of the Administration of Justice Act 1982.[3] A clerical error is an error made in the process of recording the intended words of the testator in the drafting or transcription of the will.[3a]

Conditions for rectification

There is a time limit of six months after the date of first grant of representation within which an application for rectification of a will must be made unless the court permits a later application.[4] If after this period of six months the personal representatives distribute any part of the estate, they are not thereby rendered liable on the ground that they ought to have taken account of the possibility that the court might permit an application after the end of the six month period. This does not however, prejudice any power to recover any part of the estate so distributed.[5] The date of the first grant of representation for the purposes of section 20 is decided by leaving out of account any grants limited to settled land or trust property and a grant limited to real or personal estate is also left out of account unless a grant limited to the remainder of the estate has previously been made or is made at the same time.[6]

---

[1] See p. 450 *post.*
[2] Administration of Justice Act 1982, s.20(2). As to the effect of mistake in the will, see also p. 177 *ante.*
[3] See p. 824 *post*, and *Re Williams* [1985] 1 W.L.R. 905.
[3a] *Wordingham* v. *Royal Exchange Trust* [1992] 2 W.L.R. 496.
[4] Administration of Justice Act 1982, s.20(2).
[5] Administration of Justice Act 1982, s.20(3). As to refunding and tracing see p. 1026 *post.*
[6] Administration of Justice Act 1982, s.20(4). For the text see Appendix p. 1204 *post.*

Grant conclusive

Subject to this a probate, even in common form, unrevoked, is conclusive both in the courts of law and of equity,[7] as to the appointment of an executor, and the validity and contents of a will, so far, as to cases before the Land Transfer Act 1897, as it extends to personal property, and as to wills coming into operation after that Act, as to both real and personal property (except the legal estate in copyholds); and the will cannot be impeached by evidence even of fraud.[8]

It also seems that the grant of probate is sufficient to confirm the executor as trustee,[9] as well as executor, where he is appointed "executor and trustee," and conversely it has been held that renunciation of probate is conclusive evidence of disclaimer of the trusteeship.[10]

It cannot be proved that another person was appointed executor, or that the testator was insane, or that the will of which the probate has been granted was forged; for that would be directly contrary to the seal of the court.[11]

In short, no court can take notice of the rights of representation to personal property, or to real estate in cases of death after the passing of the Land Transfer Act 1897 unless the jurisdiction in probate has been exercised either by the Family Division in non-contentious matters or by the Chancery Division in contentious matters[12]; and when that jurisdiction has been exercised by the grant of probate or letters of administration, no other court can permit it to be gainsaid.[13] The court is bound to assume that all documents admitted to probate are testamentary documents.[14]

Executor not to act while administration in force

Similarly a grant of administration precludes anyone other than the grantee from acting as personal representative until the grant has been recalled or revoked.[15]

---

[7] *Allen* v. *Dundas* (1789) 3 T.R. 125: *Griffiths* v. *Hamilton* (1806) 12 Ves. 298; *Jones* v. *Jones* (1817) 3 Meriv. 171. All the then cases on this subject will be found collected and commented on with great ability in Hargrave's *Law Tracts*, pp. 459 *et seq.* A probate obtained, as a matter of course, on a Scottish confirmation, under stat. 21 & 22 Vict. c. 56, or the Judicature Act 1925, s.168 (which replaced the earlier enactment), stood on the same footing; and it made no difference that proceedings were pending in Scotland for a reduction of the confirmation: *Cumming* v. *Fraser* (1860) 28 Beav. 614. See also *ante*, pp. 9, 368 (as to resealing).

[8] *Griffiths* v. *Hamilton* (1806) 12 Ves. 298, 307. It is at least in this sense a judgment in rem, binding on all concerned (*Re Langton* [1964] P. 163) as well as being binding 'in personam' on all parties (and possibly all who had the opportunity to intervene) as in *The Gemma* [1899] P. 285; *The August.8.* [1983] 2 A.C. 450. See also the Administration of Justice Act 1985, s.47.

[9] *Re Sharman* [1942] Ch. 311, 317, and see *post*, p. 731.

[10] *Re Gordon* (1877) 6 Ch.D. 531, 534; *Re Clout & Frewer's Contract* [1924] 2 Ch. 230; *Re Birchall* (1889) 40 Ch.D. 436.

[11] *Noel* v. *Wells* (1668) 1 Sid. 359.

[12] See *ante*, p. 8.

[13] *Att.-Gen.* v. *Partington* (1864) 3 Hurl. & C. 193, 204; *Re Ivory* (1878) 10 Ch.D. 372.

[14] *Re Barrance* [1910] 2 Ch. 419, 421; *Re Wernher* [1918] 1 Ch. 339; [1918] 2 Ch. 82, C.A.

[15] See the Administration of Estates Act 1925, s.15, *post*, p. 1120; *Re West* [1947] W.N. 2.

English grant not evidence of English domicile

A probate or administration with the will annexed is conclusive evidence that the instrument proved was testamentary according to the law of this country, but it proves nothing else.[16] Therefore the fact that a grant has been obtained in an English court is not conclusive that the testator was domiciled in England,[17] even though the will is in such form that, though admissible as a testamentary instrument according to English law, it would not have been entitled to probate according to the law of the country of the true domicile of the deceased.[18] Further, it would seem from the decision of the House of Lords in *Concha* v. *Concha*[19] that the decree of the probate court based on its decision as to domicile is not conclusive in rem or inter partes as to domicile for any other purpose.

Grant determining next-of-kin conclusive

In *Bouchier* v. *Taylor*,[20] the House of Lords decided that after a sentence in the ecclesiastical court determining who were the next-of-kin of the intestate, and granting letters of administration to the person found to be such next-of-kin, the Court of Chancery was precluded from directing any issue to try that question. Further, where the sentence of the ecclesiastical court, in a suit for a grant of administration, turned upon the question which of the parties was next-of-kin to the intestate, such sentence was conclusive upon that question in a subsequent suit in the Court of Chancery, between the same parties, for distribution.[21] Thus, so long as letters of administration remain in force they are conclusive evidence that the administrator to whom as next-of-kin, or one of them, they were granted is in fact such next-of-kin.[22] However, they are not conclusive evidence that the next-of-kin to whom they expressly or impliedly refer are the only next-of-kin.[23]

Grant gives no beneficial interest

A grant gives no beneficial interest to those entitled under the will or intestacy before the completion of administration. This topic is considered later.[24]

---

[16] *Whicker* v. *Hume* (1858) 7 H.L.C. 124; and see *ante*, n. 8 and text thereto and *post*, p. 456.

[17] For this reason if the matter is in dispute the applicant in Family Provision proceedings will have to prove the domicile of the deceased even though it is stated in the grant. See *post*, p. 763.

[18] *Bradford* v. *Young* (1884) 26 Ch.D. 656; 29 Ch.D. 617.

[19] (1886) 11 App.Cas. 541.

[20] (1776) 4 Bro.P.C. 708, Toml. ed.; discussed and distinguished in *Concha* v. *Concha*, *supra*. See Hargrave's *Law Tracts*, pp. 472–476.

[21] *Barrs* v. *Jackson* (1845) 1 Phil. C.C. 582; reversing *ibid.* 1 Y. & C.C.C. 585; and see *Spencer* v. *Williams* (1871) L.R. 2 P. & D. 230. As to distribution, see *post*, p. 1065.

[22] *Re Ivory* (1878) 10 Ch.D. 372, 374.

[23] *Ibid.*

[24] See *post*, p. 1050.

Payment to executor of forged will good discharge

Upon this principle it was decided that payment of money to an executor, who had obtained probate of a forged will, was a discharge to the
debtor of the deceased, notwithstanding the probate was afterwards
declared null in the ecclesiastical court, and administration granted to the
intestate's next-of-kin,[25] for if the executor had brought an action against
the debtor, the latter could not have controverted the title of the executor
as long as the probate was unrepealed; and the debtor was not obliged to
wait for a suit, when he knew that no defence could be made to it.[26] But
where S. procured probate in the name of H., the executor named in a
forged will, and obtained a transfer of stock and payment of dividends, it
was held that the probate could authorise a transfer or payment to H.
alone, and that a party giving faith to the probate was bound to see that the
person claiming under it was the real H.[27]

Probate conclusive as to will

The question whether particular legacies given by a will are cumulative
or substituted, may be influenced by the question whether they have been
given by distinct instruments. In such a case probate *as of a will and codicil*
is conclusive even though the will and codicil are written on the same
papers.[28]

The probate is also conclusive as to every part of the will of which it has
been granted; for example, in *Plume* v. *Beale*,[29] where an executor proved
a will of personal property, and then brought a bill in equity to be relieved
against a particular legacy, on the ground that it had been interlined in the
will by forgery, Lord Cowper dismissed the bill with costs, observing that
the executor might have proved the will in the ecclesiastical court, with a
particular reservation as to that legacy.[30]

Trusts affecting will

Though courts of equity were bound to receive, as testamentary, a will,
in all its parts, which had been proved in the proper Probate Court, in certain cases they affected with a trust a particular legacy or a residuary
bequest obtained by fraud.[31] Such a trust may even be for the benefit of the

---

[25] *Allen* v. *Dundas* (1789) 3 T.R. 125. See also *Prosser* v. *Wagner* (1856) 1 C.B.(N.S.) 289,
and the Administration of Estates Act 1925, s.27(2) replacing the Court of Probate Act 1857
(20 & 21 Vict. c. 77), s.77, *post*, p. 1125.

[26] *Allen* v. *Dundas* (1789) 3 T.R. 125, 129.

[27] *Ex p. Jolliffe* (1845) 8 Beav. 168.

[28] *Baillie* v. *Butterfield* (1787) 1 Cox 392.

[29] (1717) 1 P.Wms. 388.

[30] See *ante*, p. 189.

[31] Mitf.Pl. 257, 4th ed. As to the executor's beneficial interest, see *post*, p. 935.

next-of-kin if it is clear that the residuary legatees were not to benefit and the intended trusts are unascertainable.[32] Similarly, documents which have not been proved may be incorporated in equity.[33]

There are clear limits to the jurisdiction of courts of equity in this matter. "I think it will be found upon examining the cases in which this court has declared a legatee or executor to be a trustee for other persons, that they have been either questions of construction,[34] or cases in which the party had been named as trustee, or had engaged to take as such,[35] or in which the Court of Probate could afford no adequate or proper remedy. If there be any decision that goes beyond this, I must with all deference be permitted to doubt its correctness."[36]

A case in which the probate jurisdiction cannot afford an adequate or proper remedy is where the draftsman of a will fraudulently inserts his own name instead of that of a legatee. In such a case a court of equity treats him as a trustee for the real legatee[37]; for if probate were refused because of the fraud the real legatee would lose his legacy.[38]

Again, though it is now settled that a will cannot, either before or after probate, be set aside in equity on the ground that the will was obtained by fraud on the testator,[39] yet where probate has been obtained by fraud on the next-of-kin, equity interferes and either converts the wrongdoer into a

[32] *Re Hawksley* [1934] 1 Ch. 384, 400.

[33] See pp. 153 and 309 *ante*.

[34] *Kennell* v. *Abbott* (1799) 4 Ves. 802; *cf. Meluish* v. *Milton* (1876) 3 Ch.D. 27.

[35] *Thynn* v. *Thynn* (1684) 1 Vern. 296; and see *Re Pugh* [1967] 1 W.L.R. 1262 and cases there cited. The gift may amount to a fiduciary power of appointment. *Re Beatty* [1990] 1 W.L.R. 1508.

[36] *Per* Lord Lyndhurst in *Allen* v. *McPherson* (1847) 1 H.L.C. 191, 214.

[37] *Marriot* v. *Marriot* (1725) 1 Stra. 666; Mitf.Pt., 4th ed., 258. In *Seagrave* v. *Kirwan* (1828) 1 Beat. 157, the executor, who was a barrister, had himself prepared the will, the rule of law at the time being that the executor was entitled to the residue unless otherwise disposed of, or unless a legacy was bequeathed to him. Sir A. Hart held that it was the duty of the executor to have informed the testator that such was the rule, and that he could not be allowed to profit from this omission, but must be decreed to be a trustee for the next-of-kin. See also *Bulkeley* v. *Wilford* (1834) 2 Cl. & F. 102; *ibid.* 8 Bligh 111. It was held by Stuart V.-C. (notwithstanding the case of *Allen* v. *McPherson, post*), that the court, under its equitable jurisdiction, has authority to declare an attorney a trustee for the heir-at-law and next-of-kin of real and personal estate given him by a will prepared by himself, where he has improperly taken advantage of the testator's ignorance, or allowed him to remain under a mistaken impression which influenced the gift; *Hindson* v. *Weatherill* (1854) 1 Sm. & G. 609. But this decision was reversed on appeal, on the facts, the Lords Justices declining to give any opinion on the law of the case. Turner L.J., however, distinguished it from *Seagrave* v. *Kirwan*, observing that in that case the testator had no intention to benefit Kirwan the counsel: (1854) 5 De G.M. & G. 301. See also *Walker* v. *Smith* (1861) 29 Beav. 394.

[38] *Allen* v. *McPherson* (1847) 1 H.L.C. 191, 212. As to omission of words from grant see *ante*, p. 314 and as to partial revocation *ante*, pp. 202 *et seq*. It seems that on proof of fraud the name might be deleted but the true name could not be inserted. See *ante*, pp. 172 and 177 *et seq*.

[39] *Kerrich* v. *Bransby* (1727) 7 Bro.P.C. 437, as interpreted by Lord Hardwicke in *Barnesly* v. *Powel* (1749) 1 Ves.Sen. 284, 287, and by Lord Eldon in *Ex p. Fearon* (1800) 5 Ves. 647. *Semble*, the view of Abinger C.B. in *Middleton* v. *Sherburne* (1841) 4 Y. & C.Ex. 358, as to the grounds of decision in *Kerrich* v. *Bransby* is not acceptable: see *Allen* v. *McPherson* (1847) 1 H.L.C. 191, 211, 212.

trustee of such probate, or obliges him to consent to a repeal or revocation of it in the court in which it was granted.[40]

The transfer of the contentious probate jurisdiction to the Chancery Division will probably reduce the significance of the points discussed above.

Will construed as inoperative

Further, a court construing an instrument of which probate has been obtained may hold that it is in the particular circumstances and on its true construction ineffectual.[41] And where several instruments are admitted to probate as constituting the last will of a testator, one of such instruments may nevertheless on its true construction virtually revoke a former one.[42] Where the machinery provided by the will is defective in a non-essential respect the Court can and should make good the deficiency.[43]

Material validity of foreign will

Even where a will has been admitted to probate, it may, being a will of movables, still be ineffectual, by the law of the domicile of the deceased, to dispose of the estate. This may be expressed by saying that although the will is formally valid, it lacks material validity.[44] In *Thornton* v. *Curling*[45] Lord Eldon C. expressed his opinion that if a British subject domiciled in a foreign country by his will appoints an executor, but makes a disposition of his personal property, which, though valid by the law of England, is invalid by the law of that foreign country, the Court of Chancery is at liberty, notwithstanding probate may have been granted in this country, to hold that the will has no operation beyond appointing the executor. His Lordship observed that although, as the ecclesiastical court had granted probate of the will, he must take it to be a will, yet what part of the contents of that will was effectual, and in what way the court should determine on the property, was quite a different thing.[46]

---

[40] *Barnesly* v. *Powel* (1749) 1 Ves.Sen. 119, 284, 287. The distinction between a fraud on the testator in obtaining the will and a fraud on the next-of-kin in obtaining probate, taken by Lord Hardwicke in *Barnesly* v. *Powel* was recognised by Lord Apsley in *Meadows* v. *Duchess of Kingston* (1775) Ambl. 756, 764, by Lord Cottenham in *Price* v. *Dewhurst* (1838) 4 M. & Cr. 76, 85, and by Lord Lyndhurst in *Allen* v. *McPherson* (1847) 1 H.L.C. 191, 213. See also *Gingell* v. *Horne* (1839) 9 Sim. 539; Mitf.Pl., 4th ed., p. 357; 2 Roper Leg., 3rd ed., p. 688. In *Priestman* v. *Thomas* (1884) 9 P.D. 210, in an action in the Probate Division, T. and G. propounded an earlier and P. a later will. The action was compromised, and by consent verdict and judgment were taken for establishing the earlier will. Subsequently P. discovered that the earlier will was forgery, and in an action in the Chancery Division, to which T. and G. were parties, obtained the verdict of a jury to that effect and judgment that the compromise should be set aside. In another action in the Probate Division for revocation of the probate of the earlier will it was held, affirming the decision of the President of the Probate Division (9 P.D. 70), that T. and G. were estopped from denying the forgery.
[41] See *Gawler* v. *Standerwick* (1788) 2 Cox Eq.Cas., 15.
[42] See *Campbell* v. *Earl Radnor* (1783) 1 Bro.C.C. 271; *Walsh* v. *Gladstone* (1843) 13 Sim. 261; affirmed 1 Phil.C.C. 294; *Re Hawksley's Settlement* [1934] Ch. 384.
[43] *Re Malpass* [1985] Ch. 42, 50.
[44] See *ante*, p. 13.
[45] (1824) 8 Sim. 310; 59 E.R. 123, L.C.
[46] See *Concha* v. *Concha* (1886) 11 App.Cas. 541; *Bradford* v. *Young* (1885) 29 Ch.D. 617.

So, in *Campbell* v. *Beaufoy*,[47] a plea by an executor who had proved a will, that "the testator was at the date of his will, and also at the time of his death, domiciled in France, and that all the bequests of the personal estate affected to be made by it are by the law of France null and void," was held by Wood V.-C. to be a good plea in bar to a suit by a legatee under the will for payment of his legacy and for administration of the personal estate of the testator. Similarly, in *Loffus* v. *Maw*,[48] a revoking codicil, though it had been admitted to probate, was not allowed under the circumstances to have any revoking effect.

Criminal proceedings

On an indictment for forging a will, probate of that will unrevoked is not conclusive evidence of its validity so as to be a bar to the prosecution.[49]

Collateral matters

Though the order of the probate court is conclusive of the right directly determined, it is not so of any collateral matter, which may possibly be collected or inferred from the order by argument.[50] Therefore letters of administration which have been granted to a person as administrator of A. B., deceased, are not prima facie evidence of A. B.'s death.[51] But, in default of circumstances giving rise to suspicion, probates and letters of administration are accepted as sufficient conveyancing evidence of death.[52]

In construing the will a court is not bound by remarks made under the probate jurisdiction which are not necessary to the exercise of that jurisdiction.[53]

Where Probate Court lacked jurisdiction

Likewise, though no evidence is receivable to impeach the probate or the letters of administration, being the judicial acts of a court having competent authority, yet it might be proved that the court which granted them

[47] (1859) Johns. 320. See also *Re Ross* [1930] 1 Ch. 377; and *cf. Re Priest* [1944] Ch. 58.
[48] (1862) 3 Giff. 592. There was no foreign element in this case.
[49] *R.* v. *Buttery* (1818) Russ. & Ry.C.C.R. 342. It is said in *R.* v. *Vincent* (1721) 1 Stra. 481, that the probate was admitted as conclusive evidence on a similar prosecution; but that case must now be considered as overruled. See *R.* v. *Gibson* (1802) Russ. & Ry.C.C.R. at p. 343, n. (*a*). As to the Theft Act 1968, see *post*, p. 189. See also p. 42 *ante*, and p. 728.
[50] *Blackham's Case* (1709) 1 Salk. 290.
[51] *Thompson* v. *Donaldson* (1799) 3 Esp.N.P.C. 63; *Moons* v. *De Bernales* (1826) 1 Russ. 301 (but see *French* v. *French* (1755) 1 Dick. 268, where Lord Hardwicke, in particular circumstances, admitted the probate as proof of the testator's death). However, if the plaintiff sues an executor or administrator, and there is no plea of *ne unques executor* or *administrator*, the plaintiff's right to sue is admitted, and therefore no evidence can be required of the death of the testator or intestate: *Lloyd* v. *Finlayson* (1797) 2 Esp. 564. Where money was ordered to be paid to A. or his representatives, the mere production of the probate was not formerly sufficient to enable the reprsentative to obtain payment; proof of the death was required, and that the testator was the party in the cause: *Clayton* v. *Gresham* (1804) 10 Ves. 289. See S.C.F.R. 1987, r. 43.
[52] See the Law of Property Act 1925, Sched. 6, Spec. 1, note.
[53] *Re Hawksley* [1934] Ch. 384.

had no jurisdiction, and that therefore its proceedings were a nullity.[54] So it may be proved that the supposed testator or intestate is alive; for in such case the probate court can have no jurisdiction, nor its sentence any effect.[55] And it may be shown that the seal attached to the supposed probate has been forged; for that does not impeach the judgment of the probate court[56] or that the grant has been revoked; for this is in affirmance of its proceedings.[57]

Original English will as evidence

The question has arisen how far a court can in construing an English will look at the original document.[58]

In *Havergal* v. *Harrison*,[59] where the words in the probate were "brother and sister," and it was suggested that in the original will the words were "brothers and sister," Lord Langdale M.R. said he was bound by the probate, but if, on the production of the original will, a doubt existed as to the accuracy of the probate copy, the court would give an opportunity to the parties to apply to the probate court to set it right. Accordingly, in *Oppenheim* v. *Henry*,[60] where the probate copy of a will was in these words: "I release my sons from all claims due to me by bonds *on* moneys advanced to them by me," and the court was desired to look at the original will, in order to ascertain whether the word written "*on*" in the probate was not "*or*" in the will, Wood V.-C. declined to do so, and said that looking at the will to ascertain the alleged inaccuracy of the probate was quite different from the case of a question arising on the punctuation of the will, or on the introduction of a capital letter, or other mark indicating where a sentence was intended to begin, and which might affect its sense. So, also, in *Gann* v. *Gregory*,[61] where the probate court had granted a facsimile probate of a will, made after the Wills Act came into operation, with cross lines drawn in ink over the bequest of certain legacies (the decree in the Prerogative Court having been pronounced for the will as contained in the document, "with several alterations, interlineations, and erasures, appearing therein"), it was suggested, that if the original will were looked at, it would be seen that the pencil alterations made in the legacies contained under the cross lines must have been made after those lines were drawn, and it might thence be inferred that the testator meant the legacies to remain part of the will. Lord Cranworth C. said that he was not of those who thought it was competent for the Court of Chancery on every occasion to look at the original will, though he was aware Lord Eldon did it in some instances, but in

---

[54] *Ibid.*

[55] *Allen* v. *Dundas* (1789) 3 T.R. 125, 130. But see as to purchasers, the Law of Property Act 1925, s.204(1); *ante*, p. 365.

[56] *Mariot* v. *Mariot* (1725) 1 Stra. 666, 671.

[57] Bull.N.P. 247.

[58] As to rectification see s.20 of the A.J.A. 1982 p. 182/449 *ante*, and 1983 *Conveyancer* 21.

[59] (1843) 7 Beav. 49.

[60] (1853) 9 Hare 802, n. (*b*) to *Walker* v. *Tipping* (1853) 1 W.R. 126.

[61] (1854) 3 De G.M. & G. 777.

each there were special circumstances. As probate had been granted of the will, with the alterations in it, it must be taken as conclusively settled by the probate court that the will was at its execution in its present state; that is, that the testator executed the instrument with the lines drawn over it, mèaning thereby, that the legacies were not to stand part of the will. Again, in *Taylor* v. *Richardson*,[62] where the probate had been delivered out with blanks in course of the will, and it was suggested that it might be construed as if the words ran continuously, Kindersley V.-C. observed that the probate court had said that the will was an instrument in such and such words, and in certain places, and such and such blanks, and that the Court of Chancery was bound to look at the blanks as part of the will.

The court will, however, look at the will itself in order to derive aid in its construction from the punctuation, or manner of writing, or from other appearances on the face of it. In *Compton* v. *Bloxham*,[63] Knight Bruce V.-C. relied, in construing a will, on the fact that certain words in the original will began an entirely new sentence.[64] Again, in *Shea* v. *Boschetti*,[65] where a facsimile probate of a will, with certain passages of it struck through, had been granted, Romilly M.R. expressed his opinion that, whether the Court of Probate grants a facsimile probate or not, the Court of Chancery is bound to look at anything in the original will itself which may aid and assist it in coming to a correct conclusion as to the construction to be put upon the contents of the will. So, in *Manning* v. *Purcell*,[66] it appears that the Lords Justices, in construing a will of personalty, ordered the original will to be produced, and had regard to certain erasures appearing therein, which had been omitted in the probate. In *Re Harrison*,[67] a testatrix in making her will used a law stationer's form which was partly in print, blanks being left in it which were to be filled up by the person who made use of it, and after directing that her debts and funeral and testamentary expenses should be paid by her executrix thereinafter named gave all her property both real and personal "unto . . . to and for her own use and benefit absolutely, and I nominate, constitute, and appoint my niece Catherine Hellard to be executrix of this my last will and testament." The Court of Appeal held that there was an effectual gift of the residue to Catherine Hellard, and that for the purpose of construing a will the court is entitled to look at the original will, as well as at the probate copy. Lord Esher M.R. said: "The main argument in this case is founded on there being a blank in the will, and how can you tell that there is a blank without looking at the will? I know of no rule that for the purpose of construing a will you may not look at the original will itself." Baggallay L.J. concurred, saying: "I fully agree that for many purposes the first thing to be looked at is the probate

---

[62] (1853) 2 Drewr. 16.
[63] (1845) 2 Coll. 201.
[64] See also *Re Steel* [1978] 2 W.L.R. 950.
[65] (1854) 18 Beav. 321.
[66] (1855) 7 De G.M. & G. 55.
[67] (1885) 30 Ch.D. 390. See also *Reeves* v. *Reeves* [1909] 2 Ir.R. 521, 533; *Re Messenger's Estate* (1937) 81 S.J. 138; *Re Stevens* [1952] Ch. 323.

copy of the will. But when I look at the probate copy in this case I find that there is a blank space in it. This is consistent either with an accidental omission to fill up the blank, or with an intention not to fill it up. It then becomes very material to look at the original will."

In *Re Battie-Wrightson*,[68] a testatrix, who had an account at seven banks, bequeathed her balance "at the said bank" to a legatee. A clause immediately preceding this bequest and containing the name of the bank had been formally erased, and no bank was named in the specific legacy as evidenced by the probate copy. It was held that the court, in order to ascertain what bank was intended, was entitled to look at the original will to see the erased portion.[69]

In *Re Steel*[70] Megarry V.-C. said that "it seems clear that in construing a will the court is entitled to examine the original will and give the proper weight to any punctuation in it (or lack of punctuation) and also, I think, the arrangement of it." Arrangement includes any indentation or lack of indentation.

The principle to be derived from the cases would appear to be that the original will may be looked at to assist the construction, but not to alter or vary or displace anything determined in the granting of the probate; and that if it is sought to do this, application must be made under the probate jurisdiction to rectify the probate. Since the contentious probate jurisdiction and qestions of construction are both now comprised in the Chancery jurisdiction it seems that the problem will seldom now arise and that if it does the court will be in a position to amend the grant if necessary on application in the proceedings for construction.

---

[68] [1920] 2 Ch. 330.

[69] The court suggested that the original will was admissible as evidence on another ground, namely, as extrinsic evidence to explain a latent ambiguity.

[70] [1979] Ch. 218.

CHAPTER 42

VESTING IN THE PERSONAL REPRESENTATIVE

After considering the appointment of personal representatives and the operation and effect of the probate jurisdiction it is necessary to consider the vesting of the estate in the representative and in some cases in others[1] the effect of Social Security Legislation[2] the devolution of various types of property and the incidence of liabilities of the deceased.[3]

Estate of executor vests on testator's death

As the interest of an executor in the estate of the deceased is usually derived from the will,[4] so it vests in the executor from the moment of the testator's death.[5] Thus where a testator had given a bailiff authority to distrain, but died almost immediately before the distress was taken, and, after it had been taken in his name, his executor ratified the distress, it was held that the plaintiff might plead as the bailiff of the executor, because the rent was due to the estate, and the law knows no interval between the testator's death and the vesting of the right in his executor. As soon as the executor obtains probate, his right is considered as accruing from the date of death.[6] Similarly the death of a lunatic determined the jurisdiction in lunacy,[7] and the death of a child in care determines the prior rights of the Local Authority.[7a]

All moveable goods, no matter where situated, have always been regarded as vesting in possession in the executor immediately on the testator's death,[8] the rule of law being that the property of personal chattels draws to it possession.[9] It was considered otherwise of things immovable, as leases for years of land or houses; for of these the executor or administrator was not deemed to be in possession before entry.[10] So of leases for

---

[1] See pp. 478 et seq. post.

[2] See pp. 489 et seq. post.

[3] See pp. 553 et seq. post.

[4] *Biles* v. *Caesar* [1957] 1 W.L.R. 156. But note certain new exceptional cases: the Administration of Estates Act 1925, ss.22, 23(2); the Judicature Act 1925, s.160(2), Supreme Court Act 1981, ss.114(4), discussed *ante*, p. 34.

[5] Com.Dig. Administration, B. 10; *Woolley* v. *Clark* (1822) 5 B. & A. 744–746. As to what a personal representative may do before grant, see *ante*, p. 83.

[6] *Whitehead* v. *Taylor* (1839) 10 A. & E. 210.

[7] *Re Bennett* [1913] 2Bh 318.

[7a] See p. 60 *ante* (Right to bury).

[8] Wentw.Off.Ex., 14th ed., p. 228; 11 Vin.Abr. 240.

[9] 2 Saund. 47 b, n. (1) to *Wilbraham* v. *Snow*. In other words the property gives a sufficient right to possession to enable the owner to exercise possessory remedies. He can choose between trespass and trover.

[10] Wentw.Off.Ex., 14th ed., p. 228. See the observations of Parke B. in *Barnett* v. *Earl of Guildford* (1855) 11 Exch. 32. But a *reversion* of a term, which the testator granted for a part of the term, is in the executor immediately by the death of the testator: *Prattle* v. *King* (1681) T. Jones 169.

years of a rectory, consisting of glebe lands and tithes for years, it was doubtful if there could be actual possession without entry into the glebe land.[11] It would seem that as leases can now take effect in possession without actual entry,[12] chattels real of a testator, immediately on his death, vest in possession in his executor (without the necessity for actual entry); and the same principle would seem to apply to his real estate.[13]

Rights of beneficiaries

The rights of persons entitled under a will or intestacy are subsidiary to the rights of the representative for purposes of administration, so that a beneficiary cannot in the absence of maladministration force an executor to exercise a power (as for instance, to assent subject to mortgage[14]). On the other hand a beneficiary in possession is not a trespasser but a person who, subject to the claims of administration, is entitled in equity to a share of the proceeds of sale and rents and profits until sale. If, therefore, such a beneficiary is given notice to quit, mesne profits are allowed to the executor only from the date of expiry of the notice to quit.[15]

Estate of administrator vests from time of grant

Conversely no right of action accrues to an administrator until he has taken out letters of administration. Thus where an administrator sues on a cause of action arising after the death of the intestate, it is no defence that the defendant committed the act complained of or relied upon more than six years previously (or whatever the appropriate period of limitation may be), if the grant of administration was made within this period.[16]

Vesting in the heir

Where real estate came within the operation of the Land Transfer Act 1897, s.1,[17] in the absence of and until the constitution of a personal representative of the deceased, the legal estate devolved on the heir-at-law.[18] Upon administration the grant vested the land in the administrator by relation so as to enable him to bring actions for matters affecting that property after the death of the intestate.[19]

---

[11] Wentw.Off.Ex., 14th ed., p. 229; 11 Vin.Abr. 240.

[12] Law of Property Act 1925, s.149(2); *cf. ibid.* s.51(1), which applies to "conveyances."

[13] Administration of Estates Act 1925, s.2(1); *Biles* v. *Caesar* [1957] 1 W.L.R. 156. See *post* p. 1114.

[14] *Williams* v. *Holland* [1965] 1 W.L.R. 739. See *per* Lord Upjohn at p. 744, and see *post*, pp. 684, 1050.

[15] *Ibid.*

[16] See *Murray* v. *E.I. Company* (1821) 5 B. & A. 104; *Pratt* v. *Swaine* (1828) 8 B. & C. 285; and *post*, p. 83. As to the relation back of a grant see p. 91 *ante*.

[17] See *ante* p. 105.

[18] See dicta in *John* v. *John* (1898) 2 Ch. 573; *Re Griggs* [1914] 2 Ch. 547 (which no longer apply to deaths after 1925).

[19] See *per* Stirling L.J., *Re Pryse* [1904] P. 301, 305.

Vesting in the probate judge

Where a person dies intestate after 1925, his real and personal estate, until administration granted, vest in the President of the Family Division "in the same manner and to the same extent as formerly in the case of personal estate it vested in the Ordinary."[20] This is a matter of necessary convenience and protection and no duties attach to the judge[21] nor is he a trustee for any of the purposes of the Trustee Act 1925.[22] A notice to quit served upon the President before administration granted is effective[23] and is not affected by the doctrine of relation back.[24] Such a notice is necessary to terminate a tenancy after the tenant's death intestate.[25]

Other effects of "relation back"

The relation of the grant of administration back to the death of the intestate will not divest any right legally vested in another between the death of the intestate and the grant of administration.[26]

The doctrine of "relation back" must be applied only to protect the estate from wrongful injury occurring in the interval before grant. A title cannot relate back if it is a title to something which has perished or been extinguished without fault or wrong on the part of anyone in the interval.[27] Similarly a man cannot be made a trespasser by relation back if the act complained of was lawful at the time.[28]

There is in some instances, the same relation back of the title of the representative where the deceased had only a special property in the goods as where he had the absolute property. Thus, if an undischarged bankrupt acquired goods after his bankruptcy, and died possessed of them, having been allowed to retain possession by the assignees, his administrator might maintain trover against a third party who had sold the goods between the period of the death of the intestate and the grant of the administration; for there was a good title in the bankrupt as against all the world but the assignees, and this title passes to his administrator.[29] But there is no such relation back as to chattels in which the deceased had no personal interest, but held merely as the administrator of another. The bare circumstance of

---

[20] Administration of Estates Act 1925, s.9, (*post*, p. 1117). As to the former manner and extent of such vesting in the Ordinary, see 13 Edw.1. c. 19, as amended by the Court of Probate Act 1857, s.19. See also *ante* and 140 N.L.J. 95.

[21] *Re Deans* [1954] 1 W.L.R. 332. The Ordinary had an obligation to discharge debts but the President has no such obligation. (*Ibid. per* Wynn-Parry J. p. 335).

[22] *Ibid.*

[23] *Smith* v. *Mather* [1948] 2 K.B. 212; and see *post*, p. 545.

[24] *Fred Long & Sons Ltd.* v. *Burgess* [1950] 1 K.B. 115. Notice is served on the Treasury Solicitor. See *Practice Direction* [1985] 1 W.L.R. 310.

[25] *Wirral* v. *Smith* (1982) 43 P. & C.R. 312 (C.A.). A land charge may also have to be registered against the President as estate owner under section 34 of the L.C. Act 1972.

[26] *Waring* v. *Dewsbury* (1710) Gilb.Eq.Rep. 223, cited by Strange, *arguendo*, in *R.* v. *Mann, ibid.* 1 Stra. 97; 2 Stra. 749. See also *R.* v. *Horsley* (1807) 8 East 405. As to relation back see also p. 91 *ante*.

[27] *Ibid.*

[28] *Tharpe* v. *Stallwood* (1843) 5 M. & Gr. 760.

[29] *Fyson* v. *Chambers* (1842) 9 M. & W. 468. See also *post*, p. 473.

his dying in possession will not enable his personal representative to maintain trover (conversion) even against a mere wrongdoer; for it will be a good defence that the right to the goods in question has devolved on the administrator *de bonis non* of the original intestate.[30]

Commorientes

It is not relevant here to consider all the issues affecting *commorientes* for which reference should be made to works on wills.[31]

If the testator and legatee died before 1926 from the same cause and in the same circumstances, as where both perished in a shipwreck, the representatives of the legatee could make no claim to the legacy unless they could prove, by the production of positive evidence, that the legatee survived the testator.[32] The question in each case was one of fact, and the burden of proof was on the party attempting to prove an affirmative, for the law raised no presumption whatsoever.[33] So if the evidence, in any particular case, did not establish the survivorship the law treated it as a matter incapable of being determined.[34] After 1925, however, there is a presumption,[35] for all purposes affecting the title of property,[36] that where two or more persons have died in circumstances rendering it uncertain which of them survived the other or others, the younger person survived the elder one,[37] subject to an order of the court to the contrary.[38] This presumption may, of course, be rebutted by evidence leading to a defined and warranted conclusion that the elder person was in fact the survivor[39]; but the court has no discretion to displace the presumption on the ground that its operation may be unfair,[40] and the presumption applies even if the deaths are found to be simultaneous[41] and even if the deaths occurred in different places and not in the same disaster.[42] The presumption may be excluded by the terms of the will.[43]

---

[30] *Elliott* v. *Kemp* (1840) 7 M. & W. 306. As to relation back under the Limitation Acts, see *post*, p. 897, n. 3.

[31] See Theobald, *Wills*, 14th ed. 775 and the discussion of *Re Rowland* [1963] 1 Ch. 1 in 79 L.Q.R. 1–5 and 26 M.L.R. 353–366 by M.J. Albery, Q.C. See also as to appointment of administrators in this connection *ante*, pp. 352 *et seq.*

[32] *Underwood* v. *Wing* (1855) 4 De G.M. & G. 633; *ibid. sub nom. Wing* v. *Angrave* (1860) 8 H.L.C. 183; 19 Beav. 459; *Taylor* v. *Diplock* (1815) 2 Phill.Ecc. 261; *Satterthwaite* v. *Powell* (1838); 1 Curt. 705; *Barnett* v. *Tugwell* (1862) 31 Beav. 232.

[33] *Re Shilling* (1856) Dea. & Sw. 183. See also cases mentioned in 12th ed. of this work at p. 779, n. (g).

[34] *Re Nightingale* (1927) 71 S.J. 542.

[35] This is a rule of substantive law; *Re Cohn* [1945] Ch. 5.

[36] But not the incidence of inheritance tax: Inheritance Tax Act 1984, s.4(2).

[37] Law of Property Act 1925, s.184; *Hickman* v. *Peacey* [1945] A.C. 304; *Re Callaway* [1956] Ch. 559. *Re Rowland* [1963] 1 Ch. 1, and see *supra*. n. 31 and *ante*. p. 352.

[38] *Hickman* v. *Peacey* [1945] A.C. 304, 316.

[39] *Re Bate* [1947] 2 All E.R. 418.

[40] *Re Lindop* [1942] Ch. 377.

[41] *Ibid.* n. 38.

[42] *Ibid.* n. 38.

[43] *Re Guggenheim, The Times,* June 20, 1941 (cited Tristram & Coote, 25th ed., p. 451). See also *Re Pringle* [1946] Ch. 124; *Re Rowland* [1963] Ch. 1.

Where after January 1, 1953, a husband and wife have died wholly or partially intestate in circumstances which make it uncertain which of them survived the other, and the intestate's husband or wife is by virtue of section 184 of the Law of Property Act 1925 deemed to have survived the intestate, the section nevertheless has effect as respects the intestate as if the husband or wife had not survived the intestate.[44] Thus where a husband leaves part of his estate to his wife but dies intestate as to part, if he is the elder, the part left by the will passes to the wife's estate, but the other part passes as if she had predeceased him.

Lapse of legacies

Other problems as to lapse, which are frequently ones of interpretation, are more appropriately considered in the leading works on wills and are accordingly omitted from this work.[45]

The effect of the vesting—auter droit

The interests vesting in the personal representative do not vest in him beneficially. Although he is not necessarily a trustee[46] he is said to hold "in auter droit" so that his interest is different from the absolute and ordinary interest which everyone has in his own property.[47] Thus a claim against an executor as such is different from a claim against him personally and the issues are different, in particular with reference to pleadings and limitation.[48] It has even been held that an executor can contract with himself in his personal or private capacity.[49] It has been said that he has his estate merely as the minister or dispenser of the property of the dead. Conversely, however, an executor is not to be treated for all purposes as if there were a 'cleavage of personality' and he may be liable to discover documents in both capacities whatever the form of the pleadings.[50]

Executorship and Trusteeship (creditors)[51]

An executor is a trustee for creditors only in a loose sense.[52] However he may be an express trustee for creditors either if the will says so or if the testator was himself trustee for persons claiming as creditors.[53]

This principle is well illustrated by the position as to the debts or bank-

---

[44] Administration of Estates Act 1925, s.46(3), as amended by the Intestates' Act 1952, s.49(1). For text see *post*, p. 1140.

[45] See *Theobald, Wills*, 14th ed., p. 766 and article "Lapse of Devises and Bequests" by H.A.J. Ford in 78 L.Q.R. 88–106.

[46] See p. 1049 *post*.

[47] Wentw.Off.Ex., 14th ed., p. 192; *Beswick* v. *Beswick* [1968] A.C. 58.

[48] See *Fannon* v. *Backhouse* [1987] *The Times*, August 22, 1990; R.S.C. Ord. 15, r. 1 and p. 892 *post*.

[49] *Holmes* v. *Barber* [1977] 1 W.L.R. 371. See also R.S.C. Ord. 6, r. 3.

[50] *Buchanan & Michaelson* v. *Rubinstein* [1965] Ch. 258, 263.

[51] *Ibid.* n. 46.

[52] *Re Davis* [1891] 3 Ch. 124; see also *Re Thomas* [1912] 2 Ch. 350 (fiduciary).

[53] *Re Lacy* [1899] 2 Ch. 149.

ruptcy of the representative, his rights and duties as to the assets of the estate[54] and his relations with his co-executors or co-administrators.[55]

Bankruptcy of representative

If the executor or administrator becomes bankrupt, with any property in his possession belonging to the testator or intestate, distinguishable from the general mass of his own property, it is not distributable under the bankruptcy.[56] The trustee cannot seize even *money* which can be specifically distinguished and ascertained to belong to the deceased, and not to the bankrupt himself.[57]

Reputed ownership

Under the "reputed ownership" provisions of the Bankruptcy Act 1914[58] the property of the bankrupt divisible among his creditors included all goods being at the commencement of the bankruptcy, in the possession, order or disposition of the bankrupt, in his trade or business, by the consent and permission of the true owner. In the case of a given representative mere possession gave no indication of the beneficiary's consent, so that the trustee in bankruptcy required the strongest evidence of consent by the beneficiary to assets remaining in the hands of the personal representative after completion of the administration, if he were to claim such assets for the creditors.[59] The principle of reputed ownership was applied in favour of creditors where a person entitled to a grant remained in possession of goods for 12 years without obtaining a grant.[60] The reputed ownership principle was abandoned in the Insolvency Act 1986.[61]

Executor continuing the business

Executors who continue to carry on the testator's business in the firm name, under a power in the will, are not partners, and cannot be made

[54] *Post*, p. 466.
[55] *Post*, p. 469.
[56] See the Bankruptcy Act 1914, s. 38. Williams and Muir Hunter, *Bankruptcy* 19th ed., pp. 242 *et seq*; Insolvency Act 1986, s. 208.
[57] By Lord Mansfield in *Howard* v. *Jemmett* (1768) 3 Burr. 1369, cited by Lord Kenyon in *Farr* v. *Newman* (1792) 4 T.R. 621, 648. Under the bankruptcy of an executor and trustee, directed by the will to carry on a trade, a limited sum to be paid to him by the trustees for that purpose, the general assets beyond that fund are not liable: *Ex p. Garland* (1801) 10 Ves. 110. As to tracing assets in equity, see *post*, p. 1081.
[58] See the Bankruptcy Act 1914, s.38(2)(c). Things in action other than debts due are not goods: see *ibid.*
[59] *Kitchen* v. *Ibbetson* (1873) L.R. 17 Eq. 46.
[60] *Fox* v. *Fisher* (1819) 3 B. & A. 135; *Re Thomas* (1842) 1 Phil. C.C. 159. As to the right of a trustee in bankruptcy to claim the executor's right of indemnity against the testator's estate, see *post*, p. 1076.
[61] See *Muir Hunter on Personal Insolvency* 3–145. The 1986 Act took effect on December 29, 1986.

bankrupt as such, but they may be individually proceeded against as joint debtors.[62]

Lease vested in executor

Although a testator's lease vested in the executor does not pass to the executor's trustee in bankruptcy, a proviso avoiding the lease on the bankruptcy of the lessee takes effect on the bankruptcy of the executor.[63]

Powers of the court

The court has jurisdiction even where property has gone to the trustee in bankruptcy under mistake of law, to order its return to the bankrupt or to appoint a receiver because the trustee is an officer of the court.[64] This jurisdiction does not extend to the executor of a deceased solicitor because such executor is not an officer of the court.[65]

Where a bankrupt is an executor and residuary legatee, and has paid the debts and particular legacies out of part of the assets, if he refuses to collect the rest, notwithstanding the trustee in bankruptcy has not the legal interest vested in him, the court will assist the trustee to get in the remainder in the name of the executor.[66]

Execution for debts of representative

Again, the goods of a deceased person in the hands of his representative cannot be seized in execution of a judgment against the personal representative in his own right.[67] So if an executor, in pursuance of the directions in the testator's will, carries on the testator's business and in so doing contracts debts, the fact that he has carried on the business in his own name, and that the testator's assets employed in it are ostensibly the executor's own property, will not entitle a judgment creditor of the executor to take in execution the testator's assets.[68] However a testator's goods may be taken in execution of a judgment against the executor if the executor acquiesces,[69] if he has by *devastavit* or otherwise converted the goods to his own use[70] or if by lapse of time he has precluded himself from pleading the

---

[62] *Re Fisher & Sons* [1912] 2 K.B. 491; *post*, p. 724. See also Lindley, *Partnership* (16th ed.) pp. 62, 684.

[63] *Doe d. Bridgman* v. *David* (1834) 1 Cr.M. & R. 405.

[64] See *Ex p. James* (1874) L.R. 9 Ch. 609, and *Ex p. Simmons* (1885) 16 Q.B.D. 308; but see *Re Sandiford (No. 2)* [1935] Ch. 681.

[65] *Re Sandiford (No. 2)* [1935] Ch. 681.

[66] *Ex p. Butler* (1749) 1 Atk. 213. See also the Bankruptcy Act 1914, s.38.

[67] *Farr* v. *Newman* (1792) 4 T.R. 621, where all the former authorities are collected and discussed. *M'Leod* v. *Drummond* (1810) 17 Ves. 152, 169; *Kinderley* v. *Jervis* (1856) 22 Beav. 1, 23.

[68] *Re Morgan* (1881) 18 Ch.D. 93; see also *post*, pp. 679, 726.

[69] *Whale* v. *Booth* (1784) 4 Term Rep. 625n.

[70] *Quick* v. *Staines* (1798) 1 Bos. & Pul. 293.

executorship,[71] or from proceeding in equity by injunction to restrain the creditor.[72] So after a lapse of six or seven years, equity will not restrain by injunction a creditor of an executor from taking in execution property of the testator which is assets in equity.[73] However, where goods of an intestate had been taken possession of and used by an administrator in the house of the intestate for three months after the death of the intestate, Lord Tenterden held that they could not be taken in execution for the administrator's own debt, the time, in this case, not being sufficient to make the goods the administrator's property.[74] Where an insolvent executor has a right of indemnity against the testator's estate this right may pass to the creditor or trustee in bankruptcy.[75]

Disposing of assets of deceased

A personal representative cannot by his will dispose of any of the property vested in him as such[76]; though if a sole or last surviving executor appoints an executor the property passes to him as the representative of the first testator[77]; but an administrator cannot as such transmit any interest in the property of the intestate to his own personal representative.[78]

On the other hand, an executor or administrator can, during his own lifetime, dispose of the assets of the testator; he has absolute power over them for this purpose, and they cannot be followed by the creditor of the deceased.[79] This rule, however, is subject to some qualifications, which will be pointed out in the general discussion of the powers of executors and administrators.[80]

It has been held that if an executor or administrator grants all his own goods (*omnia bona sua*), the goods of the deceased will not pass, unless the grantor has no goods except as executor or administrator.[81] So if an executor releases all actions, suits and demands whatsoever, which he had for any cause whatever, this extends only to such as he has in his own right, and not to such as he has as executor.[82]

---

[71] *Aylesbury* v. *Harvey* (1684) 3 Lev. 204.

[72] *Ray* v. *Ray* (1815) Coop.C.C. 264 (lapse of six or seven years). Upon this case, in *Re Morgan* (1879) 18 Ch.D. 93, 101, Fry J. remarks that "the court thought the circumstances were such as to raise an inference of a gift by the testator's creditor to the executor."

[73] *Ibid.* n. 72.

[74] *Gaskell* v. *Marshall* (1831) 1 Mood. & Rob. 132; *ibid.* 5 C. & P. 31. The learned judge, upon *Quick* v. *Staines* being cited, observed that the marriage in that case made all the difference.

[75] See *Jennings* v. *Mather* [1902] 1 K.B. 1 and Williams and Muir Hunter, *Bankruptcy* (18th ed.) p. 290.

[76] *Bransby* v. *Grantham* (1577) 2 Plowd. 525; Godolph., Pt. 2, c. 17, s.3.

[77] *Ante*, p. 44.

[78] See *ante*, pp. 44 *et seq*. As to the transmission of beneficial interests, see *post*, p. 1051.

[79] By Lord Mansfield, in *Whale* v. *Booth* (1784) 4 T.R. 625, note to *Far* v. *Newman*.

[80] See *post*, pp. 664 *et seq*.

[81] *Hutchinson* v. *Savage* (1709) 2 Ld.Raym. 1307; Wentw.Off.Ex. (14th ed.), p. 193. But an executor may have trespass for taking goods in his time, *quare bona et catalla sua*, because of the possession: by Holt C.J. in *Knight* v. *Cole* (1690) 1 Show. 150, 155.

[82] *Knight* v. *Cole* (1690) 1 Show. 150, 153.

Merger

At law when two estates vested in the same person in the same right they merged automatically,[83] but since a personal representative held the estate of the deceased in a different right there could be no merger between that estate and estates held in his own right.[84] Since 1873 however the rule at equity has prevailed[85] that the intention of the parties must be regarded.[86] In deciding this intent the interest and duty of the parties is considered[87] but there can still be no merger between estates held by the same person in different rights.[88] Thus, if after administration is complete the personal representative is beneficially entitled, equity may infer a merger, but not before.[89]

At law the ready money of the deceased became the property of the personal representative when it ceased to be kept apart or was passed into currency.[90] Hence where the specific coin was intermixed with the executor's own money a creditor of the testator could not, by *fieri facias* on a judgment recovered against the executor, take such money as *de bonis testatoris* in execution.[91] In equity, however, the money can be followed so long as it, or that which represents it, is identifiable and not wholly spent or dissipated so that nothing remains that could be subject to the trust or fiduciary duty.[92] Since the Judicature Acts, it would seem that the creditor would be entitled to have the judgment debt satisfied out of such intermixed moneys to the amount of the testator's money.[93]

Compensation for payment of deceased's debt

If the testator died indebted to the executor, or the executor not having ready money of the testator, or for any other good reason, paid a debt of the testator's with his own money, he could elect to take any specific chattel as compensation; and if it was not more than adequate, the chattel by such election became his own.[94] If by such election he acquired the absolute ownership of the chattel, and died, his executor could defend himself in

---

[83] See *post*, n. 86.

[84] 2 Black.Comm. 177; *Jones* v. *Davies* (1860) 5 H. & N. 767.

[85] See the Law of Property Act 1925, s. 185, s.185, and the Judicature Act 1925, s.44, re-enacting the Judicature Act 1873, s.25(4)(11). See also *post*, p. 548.

[86] See Snell, *Equity*, 29th ed., p. 423, *Whiteley* v. *Delaney* [1914] A.C. 132.

[87] *Capital and Counties* v. *Rhodes* [1903] 1 Ch. 631, 652.

[88] *Chambers* v. *Kingham* (1878) 10 Ch.D. 743; *Re Radcliffe* [1892] 1 Ch. 227, 231.

[89] 3 Preston on Conv. 310, 311; *Re French-Brewster* [1904] 1 Ch. 713; and see *post*, pp. 1051, as to when an assent by an executor in his own favour may be implied.

[90] *Taylor* v. *Plumer* (1815) 3 M. & S. 562.

[91] Wentw.Off.Ex. (14th ed.), c. 7, p. 196; Toller 6th ed., p. 185.

[92] *Re Hallett's Estate* (1880) 13 Ch.D. 696, 719. And see *Mutton* v. *Peat* [1900] 2 Ch. 79; *Re Hallett & Co.* [1894] 2 Q.B. 237; *Ministry of Health* v. *Simpson* [1951] A.C. 251. *Space Investments* v. *Canadian Imperial Bank* [1986] 1 W.L.R. 1072.

[93] *Re Hallett's Estate* (1880) 13 Ch.D. 696, 711, 712. See also *post*, pp. 1082 *et seq.*

[94] Toller 6th ed., p. 185; Wentw.Off.Ex. 14th ed., c. 7, pp. 196, 199; *Elliott* v. *Kemp* (1840) 7 M. & W. 306, 313 *per* Parke B. It would seem, however, that this proposition should be strictly confined to chattels of an inexpensive nature in the light of the rules affecting purchase of trust assets by a personal representative or trustee. See *post*, p. 707.

an action of detinue brought for the same by the surviving executor of the first testator. There are dicta in the older cases that if an executor paid with his own money the debts of the testator in such order as the law appoints, to the value of the whole of the personal assets, he acquired an absolute right to them; and he could dispose of them as he pleased without being guilty of any *devastavit*.[95] This was, however, true only if the assets spoken of could be identified and appropriated to the debt which they had satisfied.[96] Thus it was held[97] that, in equity at least, the mere intention so to appropriate the assets was not enough. After the Judicature Acts this rule presumably prevailed. If the debt due to the executor exceeded the value of the assets the executor was not bound to sell. He could keep the assets *in specie*. But if the debt was less than the assets there had to be a clear appropriation of specific assets and a sale of the remainder.[98]

Because these rights of the executor were derived from, if not indeed part of his right of retainer, it seems that they are affected by the abolition of that right, and can now only be exercised under the provisions of section 10(2) of the Administration of Estates Act 1971.[99]

Assent

The nature of an executor's interest changes where an executor who is also a legatee assents to his own legacy.[1] So an administrator who is also entitled to share in the residue as one of the next-of-kin may acquire a legal title in his own right to goods of the deceased, by taking them in exercise of his power of appropriation,[2] or by an agreement with the parties entitled to share with himself under the statute.[3]

All assents made after 1925, whether by an executor or by an administrator, must be in writing in order to be effectual to transfer legal estates in land.[4]

Purchase

Similarly if the testator's goods are sold under a *fieri facias*, the executor, as well as any other person, may buy such goods of the sheriff; and if he does so, the property, which was vested in him as executor is turned into a property in his own right (*in jure proprio*.)[5]

---

[95] *Merchant* v. *Driver* (1669) 1 Saund. 307; *Chalmer* v. *Bradley* (1819) 1 Jac. & Walk. 51, 64; *Vanquelin* v. *Bouard* (1863) 15 C.B. (N.S.) 341, 372.

[96] *Re Rhoades* [1899] 2 Q.B. 347, 352.

[97] *Hearn* v. *Wells* (1844) 1 Coll. 333.

[98] See p. 1158 *post*; *Re Gilbert* [1898] 1 Q.B. 282, approved by C.A. in *Re Rhoades*, *ante*; *Re Broad* (1911) 105 L.T. 719.

[99] For the abolition of retainer, see *post*, pp. 640 *et seq.*

[1] See *post*, p. 1051.

[2] See the Administration of Estates Act 1925, s.41 *post*, p. 1133. As to appropriation in satisfaction of a legacy or share in residue, see *post*, pp. 685, 1020, 1026.

[3] See *Elliott* v. *Kemp* (1840) 7 M. & W. 306.

[4] See *post*, pp. 1049 *et seq.*

[5] Wentw.Off.Ex. 14th ed., c. 7, p. 200; Toller 6th ed., p. 239.

If the executor among the testator's goods finds and takes some which were not the testator's, and the owner recovers damages for them in an action of trespass or trover, and the judgment is followed by satisfaction, in this, as in all similar cases, the goods become the trespasser's property, because he has paid for them.[6]

Doctrine of notice

The interest of a personal representative in the property of the deceased is not however so different from the interest of a beneficial owner that the normal doctrines of notice cease to apply. Thus where A, one of the executors of B, had notice of a transaction because of his partnership with one G, it was held that the executors of B were not bona fide holders for valuable consideration without notice[7] because A could not sever his character of executor from his character as partner. The executors were therefore affected with notice. The converse is the position where an executor has notice derived from another executorship or trust.[8]

Joint representation

Where more than one executor or administrator is appointed the joint office is treated as that of an individual person.[9] Each executor represents the estate for all purposes[10] subject only to the statutory exceptions.[11] They have a joint and entire interest in the estate (real[12] and personal) of the testator or intestate, which is incapable of being divided; and in case of death such interest vests in the survivor[13] without any new grant by the court.[14] Consequently, if one of two executors or administrators purports to grant or release his interest in the testator's or intestate's estate to the other, nothing passes: because each was possessed of the whole before.[15] Similarly, the act of one in possessing himself of the effects is the act of the others, so as to entitle them to a joint interest in possession and a joint right of action if needed.[16] The relationship appears to be similar to that of joint trustees.[17] Statutory exceptions to this principle now apply on the

---

[6] Wentw. *supra*; Toller 6th ed., p. 239; *Brinsmead* v. *Harrison* (1871) L.R. 6 C.P. 584; L.R. 7 C.P. 547; *Ex p. Drake, re Ware* (1877) 5 Ch.D. 866.

[7] *Anon* v. *Adams* (1830) 1 Younge 117.

[8] See Trustee Act 1925, s.28, (*post*, p. 1107).

[9] 3 Bac.Abr. 30, tit. Exors., D. 1; and see *post*, p. 690 as to powers.

[10] *Re Houghton* [1904] 1 Ch. 622, 626.

[11] See below.

[12] *Anon.* (1536) 1 Dryer 23 *b*; Com.Dig.Admon., B, 12; the Administration of Estates Act 1925, Pt. I.

[13] See the judgment of Parke B. in *Nation* v. *Tozer* (1834) 1 Cr.M. & R. 172, 174.

[14] *Ante*, pp. 44 *et seq.*

[15] Godolph., Pt. 2, c. 16, s.1.

[16] *Nation* v. *Tozer* (1834) 1 Cr.M. & R. 172, 174; 4 Tyrwh. 563, *per* Parke B. See also *post*, p. 693.

[17] See *Dawson* v. *I.R.C.* [1990] A.C. 1.

sale of real estate[18] and of stocks and shares.[19] Actions between joint representatives are considered later.[20]

General and special representation

There is of course no joint interest or obligation as between the general and special representatives of the deceased, whether the separate grants arise from the terms of appointment in the will[21] or from statute law.[22] Anomalous situations can arise from the existence of two or more grants,[23] but in general the division is clearly defined and the obligations and duties are quite separate. Thus, the general executors can make title to the testator's real estate situated in England without the concurrence of the special executors.[24] And special personal representatives who have obtained a grant limited to settled land[25] may dispose of such settled land without the concurrence of the general representatives, "who may likewise dispose of the other property and assets of the deceased without the concurrence of the special personal representatives."[26]

Estate of administrator same as executor's

After the administration is granted, the interest of the administrator in the property of the deceased is equal to and with the interest of an executor.[27] Executors and administrators differ in little else than in the manner of their constitution.[28]

Devolution before 1926

Both at law and in equity the whole personal estate of a deceased person devolves on his personal representative.[29] In the case of deaths which occurred after 1897 and before 1926, the whole of the deceased's real estate (including real estate over which he had exercised by will a general power of appointment), other than and except copyholds and customary freeholds, where admission or any act of the lord of the manor was

---

[18] See *post*, p. 691.

[19] See *post*, p. 692.

[20] See *post*, p. 693. As to powers see p. 690 *post*.

[21] See *ante*, p. 37.

[22] See *ante*, p. 18.

[23] As to estates *pur autre vie*, see *post*, p. 547. See also *post*, p. 533.

[24] *Re Cohen* [1902] 1 Ch. 187.

[25] See the Administration of Estates Act 1925, ss.22, 23; the Supreme Court Act 1981, ss.114, 116.

[26] Administration of Estates Act 1925, s.24.

[27] Touchs. 474; *Blackborough* v. *Davis* (1701) 1 P.Wms. 41, 43, Holt C.J.; the Administration of Estates Act 1925, s.21 and see, as respects real estate, the Administration of Estates Act 1925, ss.1(2), 55(1)(xi).

[28] Fonbl.Treat.Eq.Bk. 4 Pt. 2, c. 1, s.1. As to limited grants, see *ante*, p. 316.

[29] Com.Dig.Biens, C.; Co.Litt. 388 *a*.

required to perfect the title of a purchaser from the customary tenant,[30] but including equitable estates or interests in copyholds,[31] devolved on the personal representative.[32]

Devolution after 1925

Since 1925 the personal estate devolves as before. The real estate to which a person dying after 1925 was entitled for an interest not ceasing on his death devolves from time to time on his personal representative in the same way as chattels real previously devolved.[33]

"Real estate" for this purpose includes land in possession, remainder or reversion, and every interest in or over land to which a deceased person was entitled at the time of his death[34]; and also real estate held on trust[35] (including settled land) or by way of mortgage or security, but not money to arise under a trust for sale of land, nor money secured or charged on land.[36]

The words "from time to time" contained in the Administration of Estates Act 1925, s.1(1), provide for the devolution of the deceased's estate from an executor or administrator who ceases to be such (for example, by death or efflux of time or the happening of some condition) to the new personal representative when constituted, so that on any change occurring in the representation of the deceased there will automatically occur at the same time a devolution of the real estate on the new personal representative.

Interests not ceasing on death

A testator is deemed to have been entitled at his death to any interest in real estate passing under any gift contained in his will which operates as an appointment under a general power to appoint by will, or operates under the testamentary power conferred by statute[37] to dispose of an entailed interest.[38] An entailed interest not so disposed of is deemed an interest

---

[30] Copyhold land and land by customary tenure have been enfranchised: the Law of Property Act 1922, s.128. As to the executor's liability to pay a fine on death of former copyholder after enfranchisement but before extinguishment of manorial incidents, see *Att.-Gen. to Prince of Wales* v. *Bradshaw* [1930] 2 Ch. 279.

[31] *Re Somerville and Turner's Contract* [1903] 2 Ch. 583.

[32] Land Transfer Act 1897, Pt. I, repealed as respects death after 1925 by the Law of Property (Amend.) Act 1924, s.1, and Sched. 1. Before 1897 questions arose as to when the real estate of a deceased person vested in his executors as trustees. Such questions cannot arise as to death since the Land Transfer Act 1897. On this subject generally, see 11th edition of this work, pp. 498 *et seq.*

[33] Administration of Estates Act 1925, s.1(1). For the full text of this Act, see *post*, p. 1112. As to the meaning of "chattels real" see *post*, p. 543. Since the personal representative has then become also the 'real' representative the word 'personal' ceases to be significant. See p. 18 *ante*.

[34] *Ibid.* s.3(1)(i).

[35] This provision replaces Conveyancing Act 1881, s.30.

[36] Administration of Estate Act 1925, s.3(1)(ii).

[37] Law of Property Act 1925, s.176; *Acheson* v. *Russell* [1951] Ch. 67.

[38] Administration of Estates Act 1925, s.3(2).

ceasing on the deceased's death[39]; so also is a deceased person's interest under a joint tenancy where another joint tenant survives the deceased.[40]

Even before 1926 personal property in which the deceased had but a joint estate or possession survived to his companions, and his executor or administrator was not entitled to a moiety of it[41]; for a survivorship was recognised as well between joint tenants of goods and chattels in possession or in right, as between joint tenants of inheritance or freehold.[42]

In some circumstances, although at common law there would be survivorship between joint tenants, equity will imply a trust as to a proportionate share of the beneficial interest in favour of the representatives of the deceased joint tenant. Such an implied trust, however, may be rebutted by evidence of an intention to benefit the survivor. Thus, where a woman paid money into a joint account with her nephew, and then during her lifetime alone made payments in and withdrawals, evidence was admitted to show that she intended the beneficial interest to pass on death to the nephew.[43] Conversely where there is a purchase of land in unequal shares[44] or there is other evidence of an intent to hold in severalty[45] the representative will be entitled in equity to the beneficial interest of the deceased as against the survivor.[46]

Partnership property

Subject to contrary agreement a partnership is dissolved by the death of a partner.[47] There is a continuing authority in the survivor to bind the firm[48] and the deceased partner's share is a debt accruing at the date of death.[49]

The wares, merchandise, debts or duties which joint merchants have as joint merchants or partners, do not pass by survivorship but go to the executors of the deceased; for the rule is that for the benefit of commerce there is no place among merchants for the arrival of benefits by survivorship.[50] This part of the *lex mercatoria* has been extended to all traders

---

[39] *Ibid.* subs. (3).

[40] *Ibid.* subs. (4).

[41] Swinb. Pt. 3, s.6, pl. 1.

[42] Co.Litt. 182a (*Harris* v. *Fergusson* (1848) 16 Sim. 308; *Crossfield* v. *Such* (1852) 8 Exch. 825.

[43] *Young* v. *Sealey* [1949] Ch. 278.

[44] *Lake* v. *Gibson* (1729) 1 Eq.Cas.Abr. 291, on appeal *Lake* v. *Craddock* (1732) 3 P.Wms. 158.

[45] *Harrison* v. *Burton* (1859) 1 J. & H. 287 (parol evidence admitted despite Statute of Frauds); *Aveling* v. *Knipe* (1815) 19 Ves. 441.

[46] On this subject generally, see Snell, *Equity*, 29th ed., pp. 36–39, 177–190.

[47] Partnership Act 1890, s.33. See generally Lindley, *Partnership*, 16th ed., p. 598.

[48] *Ibid.* s.38.

[49] *Ibid.* s.43. See also *post*, pp. 566, 705.

[50] "*Jus accrescendi inter mercatores pro beneficio commercii locum non habet.*" Co.Litt. 182a. *R.* v. *Collectors of Customs* (1813) 2 M. & S. 225. Lindley, *Partnership* 15th ed., p. 519. But with respect to *choses in action*, though the *right* of the deceased joint tenant devolves on his personal representative, the *remedy* survives to his companion, who alone must enforce the right by action; see *post* p. 515.

(including manufacturers),[51] and, as it would seem, to all persons engaged in joint undertakings in the nature of trade.[52]

The result is that on the death of a partner, subject to the terms of the partnership, the personal representatives of the deceased partner are in equity equally entitled to the partnership assets with the surviving partners. This interest devolves as personalty.[53]

The legal estate in partnership land will devolve according to the normal principles of real property law. Other partnership assets will, at law, pass to the surviving partners. In the absence of agreement or special provision in the terms of partnership the rights of the personal representatives of the deceased partner can only be enforced by sale of the assets.[54]

Joint mortgage

Where two persons advance a sum of money by way of mortgage and take the mortgage to them jointly and one of them dies, when the money is paid the survivor will not have the whole, but the representative of the deceased mortgagee will have his share.[55] For though a joint debt belongs at law to the survivor, yet in equity the presumption is that money advanced by two or more persons is owned by them in separate shares and not jointly. Thus on a joint mortgage, whether the sum is advanced in equal or unequal shares, there is in equity a tenancy in common between the mortgagees. At law, however, as between the mortgagees and the mortgagor the sum is deemed to have been advanced on a joint account and the last survivor can give a complete discharge.[56] Such survivor then holds in trust for the personal representatives of the deceased mortgagee.

Joint gift

Where, however, two become joint tenants, or jointly interested, in personal property, by way of gift, there the same is subject to all the consequences of the law of survivorship.[57]

In *Morris* v. *Barrett*,[58] the residue of real and personal estate was devised by a testator to his two sons as joint tenants. The two sons, for 20 years after the father's decease, carried on the business of farmers with such estates, and kept the moneys arising therefrom in one common stock, and with part of such moneys purchased other estates in the name of one of

---

[51] *Buckley* v. *Barber* (1851) 6 Exch. 164.

[52] *Hamond* v. *Jethro* (1611) 2 Brownl. & Gold. 999.

[53] *Re Bourne* [1906] 2 Ch. 427, 433. This authority confers a lien on the surplus assets after realisation: the Partnership Act 1890, s.22.

[54] See generally Lindley, *Partnership*, 16th ed., p. 648 onwards. For an instance of partners holding land on joint tenancy not subject to partnership, see below.

[55] Fonbl.Treat B.2, c. 4, s.2, n. (*g*); *Vickers* v. *Cowell* (1839) 1 Beav. 529;. *Re Jackson* (1887) 34 Ch.D. 732 (tenancy in common in equity upheld despite express joint account in deed affecting the position in equity and in law).

[56] Law of Property Act 1925, s.111, which replaces s.61 of the Conveyancing Act 1881.

[57] *Jeffereys* v. *Small* (1683) 1 Vern. 217.

[58] (1829) 3 Y. & J. 384.

them, but never in any manner entered into any agreement respecting such farming business, or ever accounted with each other. It was held, in the circumstances, that they continued, till the death of one of them, joint tenants of all the property that passed by the will of their father, but were tenants in common of the after-purchased estates.[59]

Devolution of estate of undischarged bankrupt

The property of a bankrupt divisible among his creditors includes (with certain exceptions) all property vested in him at the commencement of the bankruptcy[60] and all property acquired after this date and before discharge.[61] He has, however, certain powers to deal with after-acquired property without reference to the trustee in bankruptcy[62] and a right to protect such property against third parties.[63] Despite substantial earlier authority[64] it has been held that such rights do not constitute a property in the bankrupt.[65] Whatever the usefulness or otherwise of this distinction it seems plain that whatever rights or property may exist in the bankrupt will vest in his representative.[66] But it would seem that the bare circumstance of the deceased having died in possession of goods will not give his representatives a title to them even against a mere wrongdoer, if it can be shown that, in truth, the title is elsewhere.[67]

Options and rights of selection

The devolution of options and powers of selection is considered later.[68]

Corporator sole

On the death of a corporator sole[69] his interest in the corporation's real and personal estate is deemed to be an interest ceasing on his death and devolves to his successor.[70] Though a lease granted to a bishop or other corporation sole, and his successors, devolved before 1926 upon the per-

---

[59] For the distinction between partnership and part ownership, see *Steward* v. *Blakeway* (1868) 4 Ch.App. 603 and Lindley, *Partnership*, 16th ed., p. 63.

[60] This is the date when the bankruptcy order is made (Insolvency Act 1986, s.278).

[61] See the Bankruptcy Act 1914, s.38; Williams and Muir Hunter, *Bankruptcy*, 19th ed., pp. 242 *et seq.* Insolvency Act 1986, s.203.

[62] See the Bankruptcy Act 1914, s.47.

[63] *Re Pascoe* [1944] Ch. 219, 226. It will be noted that the cases cited in the next footnote were not referred to in *Re Pascoe* and Lord Greene M.R. appears to misquote s.38 (at p. 226). *cf.* Williams and Muir Hunter, *Bankruptcy*, 19th ed., p. 370.

[64] *Fyson* v. *Chambers* (1842) 9 M. & W. 468; *ante*, p. 461; *Morgan* v. *Knight* (1864) 15 C.B. (N.S.) 669.

[65] *Ibid.* n. 63.

[66] *Ibid.* n. 64.

[67] *Elliott* v. *Kemp* (1840) 7 M. & W. 306; *ante*, p. 461.

[68] See *post*, p. 699.

[69] As to corporations sole, see *ante*, p. 19 and *post*, p. 540; and Maitland, *Selected Essays*, pp. 73–103 and *Collected Papers*, Vol. III, pp. 210–243.

[70] Administration of Estates Act 1925, s.3(5). This subsection applies on the demise of the Crown as respects all property, real and personal, vested in the Crown as a corporation sole; *ibid.* the Law of Property Act 1925, s.180(1).

sonal representatives of the lessee, not his successor,[71] it is now "deemed always to have passed and devolved to or vested in the successors from time to time of such corporation."[72]

Property of married women

A representative may often be faced with problems arising from the purchase of property by the deceased in his wife's name, or in joint names, joint bank accounts and housekeeping moneys. These are not problems peculiar to a personal representative and the reader is accordingly referred to other works.[73]

Limited grants

Limited grants have already been discussed.[74] The limitations contained in the grant will of course limit the interest of the personal representative in the estate, but subject to these every person to whom administration is granted has the same rights and liabilities, and is accountable in like manner as if he were the executor of the deceased.[75]

Grants during minority

A grant of administration *durante minore aetate* usually contains the limitation "until he shall attain the age of eighteen," or, if the grant is made during the minority of two or more persons who if of full age would be entitled to probate or letters of administration, "until one of them shall attain the age of eighteen." Thus when the infant or one of two or more such infants[76] attains full age the grant determines, and until a new grant is made there is no person who can act as the personal representative of the deceased.[77]

If the grant is made during the minority of two or more minors, one of whom dies before coming of age, this will not determine the administration.[78] But if all the minors, for whose use and benefit the administration was granted, die under age the grant to their guardians ceases, and administration *de bonis non* to the estate of the deceased is taken out.[79]

---

[71] Co.Litt. 46b; *Fulwood's Case* (1591) 4 Co. 65a.

[72] Law of Property Act 1925, s.180(1). Before 1926 a lease could not vest in a corporation sole.

[73] See, *e.g.* Lewin, *Trusts* 16th ed., pp. 139–141; Snell, *Equity* 29th ed., pp. 177–190. Money or property derived from a housekeeping allowance made by the husband belongs to both parties in equal shares in the absence of contrary agreement: The Married Women's Property Act 1964, s.1.

[74] See *ante*.

[75] Administration of Estates Act 1925, s.21.

[76] See 4 Burn.E.I. 385, Phillimore's edition.

[77] The minor who has attained full age cannot act until probate has been granted to him: see the Supreme Court Act 1981, s.118.

[78] *Anon.* (1613), Brownl.47; *Jones* v. *Strafford* (1730) 3 P.Wms. 79, overruling the opinion in *Brudnel's Case* (1592) 5 Co. 9a.

[79] See also *ante*, pp. 323 *et seq*.

Rights and liabilities of administrator during minority

"The limit to his administration is no doubt the minority of the person, but there is no other limit. He is an ordinary administrator: he is appointed for the very purpose of getting in the estate, paying the debts, and selling the estate in the usual way; and the property vests in him."[80] Thus he may sell the deceased's property for the purposes of administration, and may make an assent if there are sufficient assets to pay debts.[81]

A power of sale given by a testator to his executors or administrators may be exercised by an administrator *durante minore aetate*.[82] If an action is brought against him, and the administration determines pending the action, he ought to retain assets to satisfy the debt which attached to him by the action.[83]

Chain of representation is not broken

A grant of administration during the minority of an executor of an executor does not break the chain of representation to the original testator if the executor, after attaining full age, proves the testator's will.[84] Hence an administrator during minority can act as executor for the original testator.

Practice: pleading

In an action brought by an administrator during minority, he must plead that the minor is still under the age of 18 years; because it is a matter within his cognisance, and which entitles him to the action.[85] But if an action is brought *against* such an administrator, the plaintiff is not obliged to plead that the minor is still under age; for this is a matter more properly within the cognisance of the defendant, and, if his power is determined, he ought to show it.[86]

Duty to account

An administrator during minority, after such administration is determined, may be compelled to account to the minor[87] after he has attained

---

[80] *Per* Jessel M.R. in *Re Cope* (1880) 16 Ch.D. 49, 52. And see *Hewson* v. *Shelley* [1914] 2 Ch. 13.

[81] See Bac.Abr.Exors. V. 1, 2; *Prince's Case* (1599) 5 Co. 29b; *Anon*, 1 Freem.K.B. 288. *Ante*, p. 432.

[82] *Monsell* v. *Armstrong*, L.R. 14 Eq. 423. As to retainer see *post*, p. 640 and as to the former right of such an administrator to retain see *Roskelley* v. *Godolphin*, T.Raym. 483; Com.-Dig.Admon.F.

[83] *Sparks* v. *Crofts* (1698) Comberb. 465, by Lord Holt. *cf.* Administration of Estates Act 1925, s.15.

[84] Administration of Estates Act 1925, s.7(3); and see *ante*, p. 44.

[85] *Piggot's Case*, 5 Co.Rep. 29a.

[86] *Beal* v. *Simpson*, 1 Ld.Raym. 409, by Powell J.

[87] See *Fotherby* v. *Pate*, 3 Atk. 603.

full age and has obtained a grant,[88] or, it seems, to any other person, including a creditor,[89] who has obtained a subsequent grant.

Where the administrator during minority has duly administered the assets, and has paid over the surplus to the person who has obtained a subsequent grant, the remedy of a creditor is against the executor or subsequent administrator.[90] In such circumstances, the administrator *durante minore aetate*, if sued by a creditor,[91] may plead *plene administravit*,[92] except, possibly, where he has committed a *devastavit*.[93] But as the court would allow a party to follow assets into any hands, if it were shown that he had not accounted to the person who subsequently obtained a grant, but fraudulently and by collusion had detained any part, in such a case an action might be maintained against the administrator during minority without joining the executor or subsequent administrator.[94]

---

[88] See the Supreme Court Act 1981, s.118.

[89] *Taylor* v. *Newton*, 1 Lee 15.

[90] See Bac.Abr.Exors. B. 1, 2. See also *Fotherby* v. *Pate, supra*, and *Brooking* v. *Jennings*, 1 Mod 175.

[91] A creditor cannot sue such an administrator as an executor *de son tort*: *Palmer* v. *Litherland* (1627) Latch. 267; *Lawson* v. *Crofts* (1658) 1 Sid. 57.

[92] *Anon.*, 1 Freem. 150. See also *Brooking* v. *Jennings, supra*.

[93] Bull N.P. 145, citing *Palmer* v. *Litherland, ante*; *Packman's Case*, 6 Co. 19b; and it has been said even though he should have obtained a release from the minor on attaining full age; *Anon.*, 1 Freem. 150; Com.Dig.Admon.F. But *quaere*. See the Trustee Act 1925, ss.14, 15 (*post*, p. 1098).

[94] See *Fotherby* v. *Pate*, 3 Atk. 603.

CHAPTER 43

VESTING OF ASSETS IN OTHERS

As has been seen[1] all assets of the deceased do not vest in the personal representative. The principal exceptions are gifts conditional on death (*"donationes mortis causa"*),[2] survivorship under joint tenancy,[3] and nominations.[4] Vesting of the estate in the heir[5] and in the President of the Family Division[6] have already been considered.

Gifts Conditional on Death

Some of the most difficult problems of devolution arise from gifts or purported dispositions made by the deceased at the time of or shortly before death. If such a gift amounts to a perfected[7] gift or a gift *mortis causa* the property does not of course devolve on the personal representative.

Definitions

A *donatio mortis causa* is thus defined in the civil law, from which both the doctrine and the denomination are borrowed: *Mortis causa donatio est, quae propter mortis fit suspicionem; cum quis ita donat, ut si quid humanitus ei contigisset, haberet is qui accepit: sin autem supervixisset qui donavit, reciperet, vel si eum donationis poenituisset aut prior decesserit is cui donatum sit.*[8] The description of a *donatio mortis causa* given by Lord Cowper is: "Where a man lies in extremity, or being surprised with sickness, and not having an opportunity of making his will; but lest he should die before he could make it, he gives with his own hands his goods to his friends about him: this, if he dies, shall operate as a legacy; but if he recovers, then does the property thereof revert to him."[9] This description has, however, been criticised on the grounds that (1) although the lack of opportunity to make a will is the reason for the doctrine it has never been adopted as a test, (2) the gift does not operate in the same way as a legacy, and (3) the decision was reversed in the House of Lords.[10]

---

[1] See p. 459 *ante.*
[2] See below.
[3] See p. 545 *post.*
[4] See p. 115 *ante.*
[5] See p. 460 *ante.*
[6] See p. 461 *ante.*
[7] As to the distinction between a gift *mortis causa* and a perfected gift *inter vivos*, see p. 479 below.
[8] Inst.lib. 2, tit. 7. The correctness of this definition, and the inaccuracy of that given by Swinburne, Pt. 1, s. 7, pl. 2, is noticed by Lord Loughborough in *Tate* v. *Hilbert* (1793) 2 Ves. 111, 119.
[9] *Hedges* v. *Hedges* (1852) Prec.Chanc. 269; (on appeal 2 Bro.P.C. 457, 462).
[10] See article by Mr. R. E. Megarry Q.C. (as he then was) in (1965) 81 L.Q.R. 21.

In *Re Beaumont*[11] Buckley J. says: "A *donatio mortis causa* is a singular form of gift. It may be said to be of an amphibious nature being a gift which is neither entirely *inter vivos* nor testamentary. It is an act *inter vivos* by which the donee is to have the absolute title to the subject of the gift not at once but if the donor dies. If the donor dies the title becomes absolute not under but as against his executor. In order to make the gift valid it must be made so as to take complete effect on the donor's death. The court must find that the donor intended it to be absolute if he died, but he need not actually say so."

It is useful to consider how it is to be distinguished from a legacy on the one hand and gift *inter vivos* on the other.

Donatio mortis causa and legacy

A *donatio mortis causa* differs from a legacy in these respects:

1. Probate of it is unnecessary. The gift takes effect from delivery and the donee claims the subject of it as a gift from the donor in his lifetime, and not under a testamentary act.[12]

2. It follows that no assent or (except, possibly, in the case of inchoate or incomplete delivery[13]) other act on the part of the executor or administrator is necessary to perfect the title of the donee.[14] In fact the distinction between a *donatio mortis causa* and a legacy is that the former is claimed against the executor, and the other from the executor.

A *donatio mortis causa* is liable for the debts of the deceased on a deficiency.[15] It is also subject to the rules of satisfaction and ademption.[16]

Donatio mortis causa and gift inter vivos

A *donatio mortis causa* differs from a gift *inter vivos* in these respects,[17] in which it resembles a legacy.

1. It is incomplete and revocable during the donor's life. The revocation may either be effected by the recovery of the donor,[18] or by resumption of the possession (other than for mere safe custody[19]) of the subject.[20] But the donor cannot revoke the donation by a subsequent will; for, on the death of the donor, the title of the donee becomes, by relation, complete

---

[11] [1902] 1 Ch. 889, 892.
[12] 1 Rop.Leg., 3rd ed., p. 12; *Rigden* v. *Vallier* (1751) 2 Ves.Sen. 252, 258; *Kelly* v. *O'Connor* [1917] 1 Ir.R. 312.
[13] *Re Wasserberg* [1915] 1 Ch. 195, 202.
[14] *Tate* v. *Hilbert* (1793) 2 Ves.Jr. 111, 120.
[15] See below.
[16] See *post*, pp. 941 *et seq.*
[17] There was formerly another distinction in that a *donatio mortis causa*, unlike a gift *inter vivos*, might be made to the wife of the donor. This difference no longer exists since the Married Women's Property Act 1882.
[18] *Ante*, p. 478. As to imperfect gifts and declarations of trust, see (1968) 118 N.L.J. 769.
[19] *Re Hawkins* [1924] 2 Ch. 47.
[20] *Ward* v. *Turner* (1752) 2 Ves.Sen. 431; *Bunn* v. *Markham* (1816) 7 Taunt. 232, by Gibbs C.J.

and absolute from the time of delivery.[21] It may, however, be satisfied by a legacy given to the donee[22] if the testator intended it so to be, but the mere fact that the legacy is of equal amount to the *donatio* does not in itself raise the presumption that it was intended to be in satisfaction of the *donatio*.[23]

2. It forms part of the estate of the donor for the purposes of inheritance tax. This follows from its incomplete nature. Therefore it ought on principle to enjoy the exemptions on death, but not those for lifetime gifts.[24] Similarly the persons liable to pay the tax on it and to be the persons liable ought to be the persons liable in respect of a transfer on death.[25] Estate duty on a *donatio* was not a testamentary expense, and was therefore not payable by the executor under a direction to pay testamentary expenses out of residue.[26] Presumably, however, inheritance tax would be so payable if the *donatio* (as suggested above) forms part of the estate of the donor.[27]

3. It is liable for the debts of the testator upon deficiency of other assets.[28]

Distinction in conflict of laws

Where on the administration of the estate of a person who dies abroad but domiciled in England the validity of a gift made by him *mortis causa* is in issue, there is a difference of opinion on the question whether there is involved a transfer *inter vivos* or a matter of succession,[29] that is to say, whether the matter should be determined according to the law of the *lex situs* or according to the domicile. In any case, if the acts relied on as constituting a parting with the dominion over the property take place outside England, the efficacy of such acts for the purpose of parting with the dominion must be determined in accordance with the law of the place where they occur.[30]

Origins

Although, as has been seen,[31] the doctrine is derived from the civil law[32] the requirements of English law have diverged, especially in the requirement that the donor must have acted "in contemplation of death."[33] In the

---

[21] *Jones* v. *Selby* (1710) Prec.Chanc. 300.

[22] *Ibid.* and see *Johnson* v. *Smith* (1749) 1 Ves.Sen. 314.

[23] *Hudson* v. *Spencer* [1910] 2 Ch. 285.

[24] Dymond, *Capital Taxes* 13–110.

[25] *i.e.*, under the Inheritance Tax Act 1984, s.4(1).

[26] *Re Hudson* [1911] 1 Ch. 206.

[27] For the liability for and incidence of inheritance tax generally, see *ante*, pp. 75–76.

[28] *Smith* v. *Casen* (1718) mentioned in *Drury* v. *Smith*, 1 P.Wms. 406; *Ward* v. *Turner* (1752) 2 Ves.Sen. 431, 434. But see [1978] *Conveyancer* 130. (Shân Warnock-Smith).

[29] See *Re Craven's Estate* (*No.* 1) [1937] Ch. 423; and *cf. Re Korvine's Trusts* [1921] 1 Ch. 343. Dicey and Morris, *Conflict of Laws*, (11th ed.) 1987, p. 946.

[30] *Ibid.* n. 29.

[31] See *ante*, p. 478.

[32] See *per* Lord Hardwicke in *Ward* v. *Turner* (1751) 2 Ves.Sen. 431, 438.

[33] See *per* Plumer M.R. in *Walter* v. *Hodge* (1818) 2 Sw. 92, 100 and *post*, p. 481.

civil law there is no such requirement. The gift has to be simply conditional on death.[34] Although this additional emphasis is well established it leads to complications[35] and since its utility is doubtful it is submitted that greater emphasis in English law might usefully be placed on the conditional nature of the gift rather that upon "contemplation." Some degree of "contemplation" is, of course, intrinsic to any gift conditional on death, but in Scottish law it has been held that there need be no immediate apprehension of death.[36]

Requirements

There are three requirements[37] of a valid *donatio mortis causa*, namely:

1. The gift must be made in contemplation of the donor's death.
2. The gift must be conditional only on the death of the donor.
3. The donor must part with dominion over the subject-matter of the gift.[38]

In addition the donor must have the necessary mental capacity to make a gift. This is not necessarily of such a high degree as that required for a will, but it varies with the circumstances of the transaction. Thus for a trivial gift a low degree of understanding may be sufficient, but if the donor is disposing of his only or main asset the same high degree will be required as for a will.[39]

1. Contemplation of death

The gift must be made in contemplation of the donor's death,[40] "by which is meant not the possibility of death at some time or other, but death within the near future, what may be called death from some reason believed to be impending."[41] Although it has never been expressly decided in England[42] the test would seem to be subjective and not objective as to whether there was contemplation of death. It is the donor's state of mind

---

[34] D. 39, 6, 2; 39, 31, 2 (at end); 39, 35, 4 (*extra suspicionem ullius periculi a sano et in bona valetudine posito et cui ex humana sorte mortis cogitatio est*). See also French Code Civil, art. 944, German BGB, § 23d, Swiss Code of Obligations, art. 245(2), Austrian AGBGB, art. 956; see also Windscheid, *Pandekten*, 9th ed., § 369 and Lee-Honoré, *South-African Law of Obligations* (1950), § 281.

[35] See below.

[36] *Blyth* v. *Curle* (1885) 12 Retty 674.

[37] The statement of claim must state facts amounting to a *donatio mortis causa* (*Re Parton* (1882) 45 L.T. 755).

[38] See *per* Mummery J. in *Sen* v. *Headley* [1990] Ch. 728, 735 (reversed on other issues [1991] Ch. 425).

[39] See *Re Beaney* [1978] 1 W.L.R. 770 following *Gibbons* v. *Wright* (1954) 91 C.L.R. 423, 438. It seems that the principles applicable to any gift *inter vivos*, as indicated in those cases must also apply to a *donatio mortis causa*. As to testamentary capacity see *ante*, p. 158.

[40] *Duffield* v. *Elwes* (1827) 1 Bligh (N.S.) 497, 530, but see above.

[41] *Re Craven's Estate (No. 1)* [1937] Ch. 423, 426; see also *Wilkes* v. *Allington* [1931] 2 Ch. 104, 110.

[42] It appears that an objective test has been adopted at least *obiter* in Canada: see (1965) 81 L.Q.R. 21.

and not the actual circumstances which must logically be treated as material. In the decided cases death has always been apprehended from illness or from a surgical operation necessitated by illness, but there is no reason why it should not be apprehended from other sources[43] nor apparently need the donor be in extremis.[44]

A gift made in expectation of death from a probable cause (e.g. cancer) will not be invalidated by reason of death occurring from another and possibly unsuspected cause (e.g. pneumonia), unless the gift is expressly made conditional upon death from the apprehended cause (i.e. cancer).[45] There must be clear evidence that the gift was made in contemplation of death. The burden of proof is necessarily on the donee, and no gift ought to be recognised unless it is supported by evidence of the clearest and most unequivocal character.[46] But it may be established solely on the evidence of the donee if such evidence is considered trustworthy[47]; and where it appears that the donation was made whilst the donor was in his last illness and only a few days or weeks before his death, it will be presumed that the gift was made in contemplation of death.[48] It has been held that a gift made in contemplation of suicide is not a valid donatio mortis causa, because if the donor was insane at death there was no capacity to complete the gift and if sane there was an intention to complete the gift by crime so that in either event the gift could not stand.[49] This reasoning no longer applies since suicide is no longer a crime[50] but since a suicide has control of the timing of death and thus an opportunity to make a will it remains unlikely that such a gift will normally be valid at least in favour of a donee with knowledge of the donor's intentions.

2. Conditional on death

The gift must be conditioned to take effect only on the death of the donor; when the peril is ended the gift is revoked.[51] But it is not essential that the donor should expressly attach this condition to the gift; for if a gift

---

[43] Agnew v. Belfast Banking Co. [1896] 2 Ir.R. 204, 221. cf. Thompson v. Mechan (1958) 13 D.L.R. (2d) 103 (risks of air travel not sufficient).

[44] The contrary suggestion is made in Thompson v. Mechan (1958) 13 D.L.R. (2d) 103, but this seems incorrect. For a similar suggestion, see Canada Trust Co. v. Labadie [1962] O.R. 151. The test of "in extremis" fails to cover situations of extreme external danger as distinct from serious illness or injury. It has been suggested that the test should be "real and substantial apprehension of premature death." See (1965) 81 L.Q.R. 21 and Plumer M.R. in Walter v. Hodge (1818) 2 Sw. 92, 100.

[45] See Wilkes v. Allington [1931] 2 Ch. 104; Mills v. Shields [1948] I.R. 367.

[46] Cosnahan v. Grice (1862) 15 Moo.P.C. 215.

[47] Re Dillon (1890) 44 Ch.D. 76, 80; Re Farman (1887) 57 L.J.Ch. 637; M'Gonnell v. Murray (1869) 3 Ir.R. Eq. 460; Re Weston [1902] 1 Ch. 680, 684; as between spouses the evidence must be beyond suspicion; Walter v. Hodge (1818) 2 Sw. 92; Re Whittaker (1882) 21 Ch.D. 657.

[48] Gardner v. Parker (1818) 3 Madd. 184; Re Lillingston [1952] 2 All E.R. 184.

[49] Re Dudman [1925] Ch. 553, following Agnew v. Belfast Banking Co. [1896] 2 Ir.R. 204.

[50] Suicide Act 1961. See pp. 518, 972 post.

[51] Irons v. Smallpiece (1819) 2 B. & Ald. 551; Tate v. Leithead (1854) Kay 658; Staniland v. Willott (1852) 3 Mac. & G. 664, 675.

is made during the donor's last illness and in contemplation of death, the law infers the condition that the donee is to hold the donation only in case the donor dies.[52] Thus, in *Gardner* v. *Parker*,[53] A, being confined to his bed, gave to B a bond for £1,800 two days before his death, in the presence of a servant, saying: "There, take that, and keep it." Leach V.-C. decided in favour of the gift, observing that the doubt originated in that the donor had not expressed that the bond was to be returned if he recovered; but that the bond having been given in the extremity of sickness, and in contemplation of death, the intention of the donor was to be inferred that the bond should be treated as a gift only in case of his death; and that if a gift is made in the expectation of death, there is an implied condition that it is to be held only on the happening of that event.

Still, if from all the circumstances of the gift there is sufficient evidence to rebut the ordinary presumption, and to make it appear that the gift was unconditional, it cannot be supported as a *donatio mortis causa*.[54] Thus, in *Edwards* v. *Jones*,[55] Lord Cottenham C. held that in order to be good as a *donatio mortis causa*, the gift must have been made in contemplation of death, and intended to take effect only on the donor's decease; and that if it appeared from the circumstances of the transaction that the donor intended to make an immediate and irrevocable gift, that would destroy the title of the party who claimed as a donee *mortis causa*. His Lordship further observed that a party making a *donatio mortis causa* does not part with the whole interest, save only in a certain event, and it is of the essence of such a gift that it shall not otherwise take place. Such a gift leaves the whole title in the donor, unless the event occurs which is to divest him. In this case, however, there was an actual assignment, by which the donor transferred all her right, title and interest to the donee. This was in itself sufficient to exclude the possibility of treating the transfer as a *donatio mortis causa*.

3. Dominion and delivery

The donor must part with dominion over the subject-matter of the gift.[56] The general rule is that, to substantiate the gift, there must be an *actual* or *constructive* tradition or delivery of the thing to the donee himself,[57] or to someone else for the donee's use.[58]

Actual delivery occurs where the purse, the ring, the jewel or the watch is given into the hands of the donee, either by the donor himself or by his

---

[52] 1 Rop.Leg., 3rd ed., p. 4; *Wilkes* v. *Allington* [1931] 2 Ch. 104.
[53] (1818) 3 Madd. 184.
[54] See *Walter* v. *Hodge* (1818) 2 Swanst. 92; *Re Lillingston* [1952] 2 All E.R. 184.
[55] (1835) 1 My. & Cr. 226.
[56] *Re Johnson* (1905) 92 L.T. 357; *Re Craven's Estate* (*No.* 1) [1937] Ch. 423.
[57] *Ward* v. *Turner* (1752) 2 Ves.Sen. 431; *Irons* v. *Smallpiece* (1819) 2 B. & Ald. 551; *Powell* v. *Hellicar* (1858) 26 Beav. 261; *Re Cole* [1964] Ch. 175.
[58] *Drury* v. *Smith* (1717) 1 P.Wms. 404; *Re Korvine* [1921] 1 Ch. 343.

order. Thus, in *Bunn* v. *Markham*,[59] Sir G. Clifford had written upon the parcels containing the property in question the names of the parties for whom they were intended, and had requested his natural son to see the property delivered to the donees. It was, therefore, manifestly his intention that it should pass to them; but as there was no actual delivery, the Court of Common Pleas held that it was not a valid gift.

Constructive delivery occurs where the donor hands over the means of coming at the possession of the property, the most usual example being the delivery of the key to the receptable or place in which the property is kept. It was at one time thought that constructive delivery was limited to bulky goods which were not easily capable of manual delivery, but this view was rejected in *Mustapha* v. *Wedlake*,[60] and its revival in *Re Wasserberg*[61] must be considered as erroneous. Thus the delivery of the key of a trunk has been held to amount to the delivery of the trunk and its contents.[62] The delivery of title deeds may amount to a parting with dominion over land. The question is one of fact.[63] The delivery of the key of a warehouse or other place, in which goods of bulk were deposited, has been determined to be a valid delivery of the goods for the purpose of a *donatio mortis causa*.[64] In these cases the key is not to be considered in the light of a symbol representing the thing itself; but the delivery of it has been allowed as the delivery of the possession, because it is the *way* of coming at the possession or to make use of the thing.[65] An antecedent delivery made *alio intuitu* to the donee is sufficient,[66] as is a subsequent obtaining of possession by the donee before the donor's death.[67]

Though a delivery to a third party for the donee's use may be good,[68] a mere delivery to an agent, in the character of agent *for the giver*, is not sufficient.[69]

Passing of dominion necessary. It is essential that the deceased should have parted with dominion, and not merely with possession.[70] Thus, in *Reddel* v. *Dobree*,[71] A, being in a declining state of health, delivered to C. R. a locked cash-box, and at the same time told her to go at his death to his son for the key, and that the box contained money for herself, and

---

[59] 7 Taunt. 231; *cf. Re Harrison* [1934] W.N. 25.

[60] (1891) 8 T.L.R. 160.

[61] [1915] 1 Ch. 195. See 59 S.J. 282.

[62] *Jones* v. *Selby* (1710) Prec.Chanc. 300; *Ward* v. *Turner, ante; Re Wasserberg* [1915] 1 Ch. 195; *Re Lillingston* [1952] 2 All E.R. 184.

[63] *Sen* v. *Headley* [1991] Ch. 425, 438; *Birch* v. *Treasury Solicitor* [1951] Ch. 298.

[64] *Ward* v. *Turner* (1752) 2 Ves.Sen. 431, 443; *Smith* v. *Smith* (1740) 2 Stra. 955.

[65] *Ward* v. *Turner, ante; Bunn* v. *Markham* (1816) 7 Taunt. 224.

[66] *Cain* v. *Moon* [1896] 2 Q.B. 283; *Birch* v. *Treasury Solicitor* [1951] Ch. 298. See *Re Stoneham* [1919] 1 Ch. 149.

[67] *Re Weston* [1902] 1 Ch. 680.

[68] See *ante*, n. 58 and text thereto.

[69] *Farquharson* v. *Cave* (1846) 2 Coll. 356.

[70] *Hawkins* v. *Blewitt* (1798) 2 Esp.N.P.C. 663; and see *Re Harrison* [1934] W.N. 25.

[71] 10 Sim. 244; *Treasury Solicitor* v. *Lewis* [1900] 2 Ch. 812; *Re Johnson* (1905) 92 L.T. 357; *Re Craven's Estate* [1937] Ch. 423.

entirely at her disposal after he was gone, but that he should want it every three months whilst he lived. The box was twice delivered to the deceased by his desire, and he delivered it again to C. R., and it was in her possession at his death. The key, though it had attached to it a piece of bone on which was engraved C. R.'s name, remained throughout in A's possession. On A's death his son refused to deliver the key to C. R. The box was then broken open under the directions of C. R. It was found to contain, inside a cover on which was written C. R.'s name, a cheque for £500 drawn by a third party in favour of A. Shadwell V.-C. held that there was no *donatio mortis causa*, for A had done no more than, to a certain extent, to put C. R. in possession of the box, retaining to himself the absolute power over its contents.[72]

But if there has been delivery of the subject-matter of the gift, the fact that the donor has, with the consent of the donee, taken back the property for safe custody does not invalidate the gift.[73]

Thing in action: indicia of title. Where the subject of the gift was a thing in action, there was a doubt as to the conditions required to make a sufficient passing of dominion. It now appears, however, that it is not necessary that a document be handed over containing a record of all the essential documents or information through which the claim arises. The real test, it appears, is whether the instrument handed over amounts to the essential indicia of title and is such as would have to be produced in court in an action on the chose.[74] The delivery of the instrument does not of itself pass the legal title to the subject-matter, but the donor's personal representative will be required by the court to perfect the gift.[75]

In *Ward* v. *Turner*,[76] Lord Hardwicke held that the delivery of *receipts* for South Sea annuities was not such a delivery of the annuities themselves as to support the gift of them as a *donatio mortis causa*; but that an actual transfer of the stock would have been sufficient to effectuate the intended donation.[77] Again, the giving of a power of attorney is not, of itself, a sufficient delivery of the subject-matter; but if the donee of the power, acting on the donor's instructions, obtains a transfer of debts or securities into his own name, then there is sufficient parting with the dominion.[78]

In *Moore* v. *Darton*,[79] a receipt had been given by a borrower to a lender as follows: "Received of D. £500 to bear interest at 4 per cent. per annum." Knight Bruce V.-C. held that the delivery of this receipt to an agent of the borrower by the lender on his deathbed, stating that he wished

---

[72] See also *Trimmer* v. *Danby* (1856) 25 L.J.Ch. 424.
[73] *Re Hawkins* [1924] 2 Ch. 47.
[74] *Birch* v. *Treasury Solicitor* [1951] Ch. 298, 308–311, *per* Evershed M.R. (disapproving dicta in *Re Weston* [1902] 1 Ch. 680 and *Delgoffe* v. *Fader* [1939] Ch. 922).
[75] *Re Dillon* (1890) 44 Ch.D. 76, 82–83.
[76] (1851) 2 Ves.Sen. 431.
[77] As in *Staniland* v. *Willmott, post*, n. 1.
[78] *Re Craven's Estate (No. 1)* [1937] Ch. 423.
[79] 4 De G. & Sm. 517.

the debt to be cancelled, was a sufficient *donatio mortis causa*, on the ground, *semble*, that the document was essential to the proof of the contract of loan.

4. Property capable of being the subject-matter of a donatio mortis causa

In general any form of property is now capable of being the subject-matter of such a gift but special considerations attach to:

(a) Land. Until 1991 it was generally and it seems universally accepted that land or real estate could not be the subject matter of such a gift.[80] However, since the reversal of Mummery J.'s decision in *Sen* v. *Headley*[81] the law is unsettled on this point. The Court of Appeal, discounting the need for judicial caution and referring to the infrequent invocation of the doctrine, held that since the doctrine was anomalous anomalous exceptions were not justified.[82] A trust arises on the death of the donor[83] by operation of law.[84] This amounts to the creation or operation of a resulting, implied or constructive trust within s.53(2) of the Law of Property Act 1925, so that a written document is not necessary.[85]

(b) Negotiable instruments. Bank notes may be the subject of *donatio mortis causa*, because the property is transferred by the delivery.[86] On the same principle it would seem that all negotiable instruments which require nothing more than delivery to pass to the donee the money secured by them (for example, exchequer notes or promissory notes payable to bearer,[87] or bills of exchange or exchequer bills indorsed in blank) may be the subjects of donations *mortis causa*.[88]

Unindorsed negotiable instruments payable to order may be the subject of a *donatio mortis causa*.[89] In *Re Mead*,[90] a person shortly before his death gave to his wife two bills of exchange payable to himself or order. The bills

---

[80] It seems clear from *Duffield* v. *Elwes* (1827) 1 Bligh (N.S.) 497, 542 *Sen* v. *Headley* [1990] 2 W.L.R. 620, that real estate cannot be the subject of a *donatio mortis causa* because there can be no "delivery." In the case of a mortgage there is sufficient delivery because "whatever would pass the money will carry the estate along with it for every purpose," *per* Lord Mansfield as quoted by Lord Eldon. *Ibid.* p. 541.

[81] See *Sen.* v. *Headley* [1990] Ch. 737–741.

[82] *Sen.* v. *Headley* [1991] Ch. 425, 440.

[83] *Snellgrove* v. *Baily* (1744) 3 Atk. 213.

[84] *Duffield* v. *Elwes* (1827) 1 Bli. (N.S.) 497.

[85] *Sen.* v. *Headley* [1991] Ch. 425, 439. Leave to appeal was given by the House of Lords, but the case was compromised before hearing in that House.

[86] *Miller* v. *Miller* (1735) 3 P.Wms. 356; and see *Re Hawkins* [1924] 2 Ch. 47.

[87] It was suggested in *Re Leaper* [1916] 1 Ch. 579 that a donor's own promissory note cannot be the subject-matter of a *donatio mortis causa*, but it would seem that the same principles apply as to the donor's own cheque.

[88] 1 Rop.Leg., 3rd ed., p. 16.

[89] *Veal* v. *Veal* (1867) 27 Beav. 303 (promissory note payable to order); *Rankin* v. *Weguelin* (1832) 29 L.J.Ch. 323n.; *Re Mead, infra*; *Clement* v. *Cheeseman* (1884) 27 Ch.D. 631 (cheque payable to donor or order); and see *Duffield* v. *Hicks* (1827) 1 Bligh (N.S.) 498.

[90] 15 Ch.D. 651.

did not fall due until after the donor's death; nor had they been indorsed by him. There was held to have been a valid *donatio mortis causa*. It seems that the ground on which unindorsed negotiable instruments may be the subject of a gift *mortis causa* is not that property is transferred at law by delivery, but that the property is so transferred by the delivery of the instrument as to give a title to the donee to the assistance of a court of equity to make the gift complete.[91]

(c) Cheques. Mere delivery[92] to the donee of a cheque drawn by the donor himself is not enough to constitute a good *donatio mortis causa*.[93] There must be in addition to such delivery either actual payment of the cheque by the drawee,[94] or due presentation to him for payment,[95] or a negotiation made for value to a third party,[96] before the donor's death; in the case of negotiation, it is sufficient if the value is received immediately after the donor's death and before the person giving value was apprised of the death.[97] Furthermore, the giving of a cheque does not operate as an appropriation *inter vivos* in favour of the donee.[98]

(d) Bonds. A bond may be the subject of a *donatio mortis causa*, because the property in the debt is considered to pass in equity by the delivery of the document.[99]

(e) Mortgage deeds. The property in the deeds and the right to recover the money secured by them passes by the delivery followed by the death of the donor. The personal representatives of the donor are trustees for the donee to make the gift effectual.[1]

(f) Policies of insurance. Like a mortgage or bond, a policy of insurance[2] can be made the subject of a *donatio mortis causa*.

---

[91] See *Duffield* v. *Hicks, ante*; *Re Dillon*, 44 Ch.D. 83.

[92] Contrast case of promissory note, bond, or cheque of a third person, *ante*, p. 484.

[93] *Hewitt* v. *Kaye* (1868) L.R. 6 Eq. 198; *Re Beak*, L.R. 13 Eq. 734 (where the cheque was accompanied by the bank pass-book); also *Tate* v. *Hilbert*, 2 Ves.Jr. 111, 120; *Tate* v. *Leithead* (1854) Kay 658; *Re Beaumont* [1902] 1 Ch. 889.

[94] *Bouts* v. *Ellis* (1853) 17 Beav. 121, affirmed 4 De G.M. & G. 249; and see *Lawson* v. *Lawson* (1718) 1 P.Wms. 441 (but see remarks of Lord Loughborough in 2 Ves. 121).

[95] *Re While* [1928] W.N. 182 (where a cheque was handed by the donee in her own house to the sub-manager of the bank shortly before the donor died: gift held completed on the acceptance by the sub-manager of the cheque in exercise of his authority as a bank official).

[96] *Rolls* v. *Pearce* (1877) 5 Ch.D. 730.

[97] *Tate* v. *Hilbert, supra*.

[98] *Hopkinson* v. *Forster* (1874) L.R. 19 Eq. 74.

[99] *Snellgrove* v. *Baily* (1744) 3 Atk. 214; *Ward* v. *Turner* (1752) 2 Ves.Sen. 431, 442; *Gardner* v. *Parker* (1818) 3 Madd. 184; *Re Richards* [1921] 1 Ch. 513 (registered Victory Bonds passing by deed registered at the Bank of England).

[1] *Duffield* v. *Elwes* 1 Bligh (N.S.) 497. See also *Staniland* v. *Wilmott* (1852) 3 Mac. & G. 664, 676; *Re Dillon* (1890) 44 Ch.D. 76, 82; *Re Beaumont* [1902] 1 Ch. 889; *Wilkes* v. *Allington* [1931] 2 Ch. 104, and *ante*, n. 77.

[2] *Witt* v. *Amis* (1861) 1 Best & Sm. 109, adopted by Romilly M.R. in *Amis* v. *Witt* (1863) 33 Bess. 619.

(g) Savings books. The delivery of a Post Office Savings Bank (now National Savings Bank) deposit book,[3] or National or War Savings Certificates,[4] may constitute good gifts *mortis causa* of the balance standing to the credit of the depositor or of the value of the certificates delivered, as the case may be. But where a deposit is invested by the Post Office Savings Bank in Government Stock under the regulations contained in the deposit book, by having the stock placed on the Savings Bank Investment Account of the National Debt Commissioners and credited to the depositor, the delivery of the investment certificate and the deposit book cannot constitute a good *donatio mortis causa* of the Government Stock.[5] Nor does the delivery of certificates of building society shares constitute a good *donatio mortis causa* of the shares.[6]

(h) Deposit accounts. It has been held that the delivery of a deposit account book showing a sum standing to the credit of the deceased on deposit account at the bank constituted a valid gift.[7] But where the account, though technically a deposit account, was in fact operated by the deceased as a current account, so that the deposit account book did not constitute the essential *indicia* of title, it was held that no valid gift had been made.[8]

(i) Gifts subject to trusts or incumbrances. It is no objection that the gift was not made to the donee free from incumbrance, but was charged with the performance of a particular purpose.[9] Thus, a gift may be good as a *donatio mortis causa*, though it is coupled with a trust that the donee shall provide for the funeral of the donor[10]; but, of course, there must be present the element of gift.[11]

[3] *Re Weston* [1902] 1 Ch. 680; *Re Andrews* [1902] 2 Ch. 394; *Birch* v. *Treasury Solicitor* [1951] Ch. 298.
[4] *Darlow* v. *Sparks* [1938] W.N. 146; 2 All E.R. 235; *Re Ward* [1946] 2 All E.R. 206.
[5] *Re Andrews, supra*; but see *Re Lee* [1918] 2 Ch. 320, where the delivery of an "Exchequer Bond Deposit Book," issued by the Post Office, and containing a certificate of the holder's title to registered Exchequer Bonds acquired through the Post Office, was held to constitute a good *donatio mortis causa*, *Re Andrews* being distinguished.
[6] *Re Weston, supra*. Railway stock cannot be the subject of *donatio mortis causa*: *Moore* v. *Moore*, L.R. 18 Eq. 474.
[7] *Moore* v. *Moore* (1874) L.R. 18 Eq. 474; *Re Dillon*, 44 Ch.D. 76; *Birch* v. *Treasury Solicitor* [1951] Ch. 298; see also *Amis* v. *Witt*, 1 Best & Sm. 109; 33 Beav. 619.
[8] *Delgoffe* v. *Fader* [1939] Ch. 992. (But see as to this case *ante*, p. 485, n. 74.)
[9] *Blount* v. *Burrow*, 4 Bro.C.C. 75. See *Hambrooke* v. *Simmons*, 4 Russ. 25.
[10] *Hills* v. *Hills*, 8 M. & W. 401; *Treasury Solicitor* v. *Lewis, ante*; see also *Re Korvine* [1921] 1 Ch. 343; *Re Ward* [1946] 2 All E.R. 206.
[11] *Re Harrison* [1934] W.N. 25.

CHAPTER 44

SOCIAL SECURITY

Although the sums involved are normally not great an executor is concerned with increasingly complex legislation in this field.[1] It is therefore necessary to consider the aspects of social security law affected by a death, and those benefits to which a person may become entitled or which a person may claim as a result of a death. The schemes and benefits covered are: (1) social security contributions and benefits, (2) widows' benefits, (3) children's benefits, (4) war pensions, (5) income support. All means-tested benefits such as income support and housing benefits will be affected by the death of a recipient or another earner in the recipient's family. Any resulting reduction in resources of a surviving spouse or dependants may make them eligible for such benefits, but no special points arise, and reference should be made to the general law.[2]

Two general points apply to all the benefits described below. First, regulations operate to remove any overlapping of benefit, that is, to prevent a person claiming two or more benefits at the same time for the same cause, or to prevent two or more persons claiming benefit in some circumstances as a result of the same event or contributor's contributions.[3] Secondly, every assignment of, or charge on, a benefit, and every agreement to assign or charge a benefit, is void. Similarly, the benefit cannot pass to any other person on bankruptcy.[4]

(1) National Insurance contributions and benefits

Contributions

National insurance contributions due from and payable by a person at death[5] remain payable by his personal representative and are preferred

---

[1] For general discussions of social security law see Ogus and Barendt, *The Law of Social Security* (referred to in this chapter as Ogus and Barendt). See also Nelligan, *Social Security Case Law: Digest of Commissioners' Decisions*, 1980. Reference may also be made to the series of explanatory leaflets produced by the Department of Social Security. These are listed in leaflet NI 146, obtainable from Social Security offices, or from: D.S.S. (Leaflets), P.O. Box 21, Stanmore, Middlesex HA7 1AY. For the updated legislation and valuable commentary, see Mesher, *Income Support, The Social Fund and Family Credit: The Legislation*, published annually by Sweet & Maxwell (Mesher) and Bonner, Hooker, Smith and White, *Non-Means Tested Benefits: The Legislation*, a companion volume also published annually (Bonner *et al.*).

[2] See note 1 above.

[3] Social Security Administration Act 1992, ss.73, 74, and Social Security (Overlapping Benefits) Regulations 1975 (S.I. 1975 No. 554) as amended. See Ogus and Barendt, pp. 437–443.

[4] Social Security Administration Act 1992, s.187.

[5] Under the general rules in Social Security Contributions and Benefits Act 1992, Part I (referred to below).

debts on the estate where a person dies insolvent.[6] This applies equally to collection by the Inland Revenue or by the Department of Social Security. Contributions are not due after a death for any payments made to the estate of the deceased for sums earned, but not paid, before the death.

Regulation 43 of the Social Security (Contributions) Regulations 1979[7] preserves the right for voluntary Class 2[8] and Class 3[9] contributions to be made in respect of the contribution record of a deceased contributor notwithstanding the death. Such contributions must be made within the time limits which would have applied to the contributor.[10] Class 3 contributions may be paid in all cases for the two contribution years before the death and in certain cases for six or more years before the death.[11] Generally, however, benefit cannot be claimed for any period before the time when contributions are paid. While contribution conditions for benefits vary, a timely payment to make good deficiencies in the contribution record of a deceased contributor may result in additional benefit for the surviving spouse or dependants.

Women who were married on April 6, 1977, and who thereafter became widows (or women who were widows on that date, subsequently remarried, but have again become widows) may, by reason of their marriage, have elected to pay Class 1 contributions at the reduced rate and to be under no liability to pay Class 2 contributions.[12] Subject to the Contributions Regulations,[13] entitlement to pay at the reduced rate ends because of the death of the husband. Unless brought to an end for other reasons, the election to reduced rate contributions ceases, where the husband died during the period April 6 to September 30, in any year, on the following April 5 and where the husband died on any other day, it ceases on the last day of the tax year following the one in which he died.[14] However, if at the end of that period the woman is again married, or is a "qualifying widow"[15] within the meaning of the Regulations, the election will continue to have effect.[16] If the widow decides to pay contributions at the standard rate on her husband's death, liability and entitlement to pay will start at the beginning of the following tax year.[17] Revocation of election to reduced rate, once made, cannot be reversed.[18]

---

[6] Insolvency Act 1986, s.382 & Sched. 6, paras. 6, 7.
[7] S.I. 1979 No. 591.
[8] Under Social Security Contributions and Benefits Act 1992, s.11.
[9] Under Social Security Contributions and Benefits Act 1992, s.13.
[10] Time for payment is provided by Social Security (Contributions) Regulations 1979 (S.I. 1979 No. 591), reg. 54 (hereafter referred to as Contributions Regulations).
[11] *Ibid.* reg. 38.
[12] Social Security Pensions Act 1975, s.3, and Contributions Regulations, reg. 100.
[13] See reg. 101(1).
[14] *Ibid.* reg. 103(2)(b).
[15] As defined by *ibid.* reg. 100(8).
[16] *Ibid.* reg. 103(4).
[17] *Ibid.* reg. 101(1)(d).
[18] *Ibid.* reg. 100(1), (4).

Benefits to which the deceased was entitled

Where the deceased was receiving periodic social security benefits immediately before the death, entitlement will in most cases cease after the week in which the death occurred. In the case of invalidity benefit, sickness benefit, income support and unemployment benefit, entitlement ceases on the day of death.[19] The Department of Social Security should be notified promptly of the death, and any pension and allowance books or uncashed giro cheques returned.

A claim to, or entitlement to make a claim for, a national insurance benefit for a period before the death of a deceased does not fail because of the death. Instead the Secretary of State may appoint such person as he may think fit to proceed with or make a claim for benefit in place of the deceased, subject to the usual time limits. Any payments authorised after a death will be made, at the discretion of the Secretary of State, to or for the benefit of the executor, administrator, legatee or next of kin or creditor.[20] Similar rules apply to child benefit[21] and income support.[22] An undetermined claim for family credit will lapse on the death of both the man and woman in a claimant family, or the adult in a single parent family. A claim which has been determined but which remains unpaid at the death is still payable, the payment being made to a suitable person for the benefit of the recipient family.

Repayment of benefits

Where the deceased has received benefit in circumstances where, had the deceased survived, benefit would have been recoverable by the Department, any liability on the part of personal representatives or others to repay the overpaid benefit depends on the benefit involved. All social security benefits can be recovered from the beneficiary, or from any other person, if that person has misrepresented or failed to disclose a material fact as a result of which there has been an overpayment of benefit. In the case of a deceased claimant, recovery can be made from the estate of the deceased, or personally from the deceased's personal representatives under this rule.[23] This liability was challenged in the Court of Appeal in *Secretary of State for Social Services* v. *Solly*.[24] The deceased had applied for national assistance claiming that her resources were only £400. On her death five years later her estate proved to be worth £2,000. By her will she appointed her son S as executor. The Department sought explanations from S as to the source of the money, but S refused to co-operate with inquiries. Finally the Department referred the matter to an Appeals Tri-

---

[19] This derives from the definition of entitlement to each of the benefits.
[20] Social Security (Claims and Payments) Regulations 1987; (S.I. 1987 No. 1968), reg. 30.
[21] *Ibid.*, n. 20.
[22] *Ibid.*, n. 20.
[23] Social Security Administration Act 1992, ss.71–79.
[24] [1974] 3 All E.R. 922.

bunal. The Tribunal confirmed the Department's claim, based on the size of the estate, that the deceased had been overpaid £832 in benefit. After further non-co-operation by S the Department took action in the High Court against S as executor to recover the money. Summary judgment was given against S by the judge on appeal. That decision was confirmed unanimously and shortly by the Court of Appeal, which confirmed that the Department had power to refer a question as to overpayment to a Tribunal after the death of a beneficiary.

In a subsequent unreported decision[25] resulting from a similar situation[26] the Department sought to recover from an executor the money overpaid to a deceased after the executor had distributed the estate. A county court judge decided that the executor, who had acted without consulting solicitors or advertising for creditors, had committed *devastavit* but had acted honestly and reasonably and could be excused under section 61 of the Trustee Act 1925. Judgment was given to the Department in the sum of £50, the amount appropriated by the executor from the estate as his costs, and costs.

Family credit, which is paid to a family rather than to an individual, can be reclaimed on the death of a member of a family, from any surviving adult member of the family,[27] if there has for any reason been an overpayment.

Pneumoconiosis and similar diseases

Under the Pneumoconiosis etc. (Workers' Compensation) Act 1979 compensation[28] is payable, where a person immediately before he died was disabled by pneumoconiosis, byssinosis or diffuse mesothelioma, to a dependant, if the Secretary of State is satisfied that the conditions of entitlement under the Act are present. These conditions are:

  (a) that no payment under the Act has been made to the deceased in respect of the disease;
  (b) that industrial disablement benefit was payable to the deceased in respect of the disease immediately before he died, or that death benefit is payable to the dependant by reason of the death;
  (c) that every employer by whom the deceased was employed during the period in which he was developing the disease and against whom he might have had a claim for damages has ceased to carry on business; and

---

[25] *Secretary of State* v. *Blackie*, Liverpool County Court, January 27, 1975, noted at [1975] C.L.Y. 3126.

[26] In the *Solly* case (n. 24 above), Lord Denning noted that "it is business on a big scale" in that the amount of benefit recovered this way had been £6 million up to that year (1974).

[27] See n. 23 above.

[28] The amounts payable are defined in the Pneumoconiosis etc. (Workers' Compensation) (Payment of Claims) Regulations 1979, (S.I. 1979 No. 1726).

(d) that no action has been brought nor claim compromised in respect of the death or disablement.[29]

The dependants who may claim are:

(a) a spouse residing with him or maintained by him, and if none
(b) the non-self-supporting children of the deceased, and if none
(c) a reputed spouse residing with the deceased, and if none
(d) any relative wholly or mainly dependent on the deceased at the date of death.[30]

(2) Widows' benefits[31]

Widow's payment

A widow[32] is entitled[33] to a lump sum of £1,000 in respect of the death of her husband if at the time of his death he satisfied the contributions condition[34] for the benefit and either the widow was under 60 at the time of the death or the late husband was not entitled at death to a Category A retirement pension.

Widowed mother's allowance

A weekly allowance, commencing immediately after the death of a husband, is payable[35] to the widow[36] of the deceased if at some time after the death:

(a) she was entitled to child benefit[37] for a child of herself and her late husband, or
(b) she was entitled to child benefit[38] for a child for whom her late husband was claiming child benefit at his death, or

[29] s.2(2) of the Act.
[30] Ibid., s.3, which defines the terms used.
[31] See generally Ogus and Barendt, Chap. 6. See also D.S.S. leaflets NP. 35 and NP. 36. Claims must be made within three months of the death, on form BW. 1 available at social security offices. A widow criminally responsible for the death of her husband is not entitled to the benefit. R. v. Chief National Insurance Commissioner [1981] 2 W.L.R. 412.
[32] But not a widower or dependent female living with the deceased as an unmarried couple. Entitlement as a widow ceases on remarriage, and is suspended while the widow is cohabiting with a man as his wife: Social Security Contributions and Benefits Act 1992, s.36(2).
[33] By s.30 of the Social Security Contributions and Benefits Act 1992. The widow's payment replaced the previous widow's allowance (a weekly benefit) in respect of husbands who died on or after April 4, 1988: Social Security Act 1986, s.36.
[34] The condition is provided by the Social Security Contributions and Benefits Act 1992, Sched. 3, para. 4. It is a minimal requirement that in any one year 25 Class 2 or Class 3 contributions, or the equivalent of Class 1 contributions, have been paid.
[35] Social Security Contributions and Benefit Act 1992, s.37.
[36] See n. 32 above.
[37] Entitlement is defined by Child Benefit Act 1975, s.2.
[38] Ibid.

(c) she was entitled to child benefit[39] for a child for whom she was claiming that benefit whilst residing with her late husband, or

(d) she was pregnant by her late husband or by A.I.D., but was living with her husband at his death.

In each case the late husband must have satisfied the contribution conditions.[40] The allowance continues, once awarded, until the widow ceases to be entitled to child benefit for any child covered in the above provisions, or she earlier remarries or cohabits with a man as his wife. If she cohabits the award is suspended and will recommence when cohabitation ends.

Widow's pension

A widow[41] who is over 45 but under 65 at her husband's death is entitled[42] to a weekly pension when widowed mother's allowance ceases to be payable or, if none is payable, when widow's allowance ceases to be payable. The rate payable depends on the age of the widow at the time of the husband's death. In any event it is only payable if the husband's contribution record meets the requisite conditions[43] for the benefit. Categories of pensions are set out in sections 43–55 and 78–79 of the Social Security Contributions and Benefits Act 1992.

Category A.   A widow[44] who does not herself satisfy, or fully satisfy, the contribution conditions for a Category A retirement pension is entitled[45] subject to limitations to require that her late husband's contribution record be treated as if it were her contribution record so as to satisfy the conditions.[46]

Category B.   A widow[47] is entitled to a Category B retirement pension if her late husband died after she became 60 and at his death they were still married, if he satisfied the contribution conditions.[48] A widow is also entitled to a Category B pension where she has retired from regular employment, but where her husband died before she reached 60 and she was, in consequence of his death, entitled to widow's pension.[49]

---

[39] *Ibid.*

[40] The conditions are defined by Social Security Contributions and Benefits Act 1992, Sched. 3, para. 5.

[41] See n. 32 above.

[42] By Social Security Contributions and Benefits Act 1992, s.38.

[43] These are the same as for widowed mother's allowance, see n. 35 above.

[44] This applies equally to widowers.

[45] Social Security Contributions and Benefits Act 1992, s.48.

[46] On retirement pensions generally see Ogus and Barendt, Chap. 5.

[47] A widower may claim if he is retired and the wife died after both were over retirement age, and she had been entitled to a Category A retirement pension: Social Security Pensions Act 1975, s.8(2).

[48] Social Security Contributions and Benefits Act 1992, s.49(1).

[49] *Ibid.*, s.49(5).

Category C.   Where a widow's late husband was over 65 on July 5, 1948, and was entitled to a Category C retirement pension at death, and the widow was then over 40, or at the time of claim is over 60 and has retired from regular employment, she is entitled to a Category C retirement pension.[50]

(3) Children's benefits

Child's special allowance[51]

A divorced former wife[52] of a deceased man is entitled to a weekly benefit where, after his death, she is entitled to child benefit[53] for a child for whom either she or her deceased former husband was entitled to claim at the time of his death, if he has satisfied the contribution condition[54] and provided that he was contributing at not less than a stated level[55] to the costs of providing for the child, or the claimant was entitled to receive payment from him under a court order, trust or agreement at not less than that level.[56] However, no new claims can be made in respect of this benefit since April 6, 1987.[57]

Guardian's allowance[58]

Any person entitled to claim child benefit[59] for an orphan is also entitled[60] to guardian's allowance, payable weekly. Claims may also be made for children one of whose parents has died if the other parent has disappeared or is in custody. Regulations[61] provide for further claims for adopted or illegitimate children or for children whose parents are divorced so that effectively they only have one parent.

---

[50] *Ibid.*, s.78(1).

[51] Ogus and Barendt, p. 239.

[52] A woman whose voidable marriage to the deceased has been annulled (but not a party to a void marriage) is also entitled: Social Security (Child's Special Allowance) Regulations 1975 (S.I. 1975 No. 497), reg. 3. Entitlement ceases if the claimant marries, and is suspended if she cohabits with a man as his wife.

[53] For entitlement see Child Benefit Act 1975, s.2.

[54] As contained in Social Security Contributions and Benefits Act 1992, Sched. 3, para. 6.

[55] 25p a week: Social Security (Child's Special Allowance) Regulations 1975 (S.I. 1975 No. 497), reg. 2.

[56] Social Security Contributions and Benefit Act 1992, s.56.

[57] *Ibid.*

[58] See Ogus and Barendt, p. 256, leaflet N.I. 14. Claims are made on form B.G. 1 at the local social security office, and must be made within three months of entitlement arising.

[59] See Child Benefit Act 1975, s.2.

[60] Social Security Contributions Benefits Act 1992, s.77. There are no contribution conditions, but a parent of the child must have satisfied certain residence and similar conditions before the allowance can be claimed: see Social Security (Guardian's Allowance) Regulations 1975 (S.I. 1975 No. 515), reg. 6, as amended.

[61] Guardian's Allowance Regulations, n. 60 above.

(4) War pensions[62]

Where the death of a member or former member of the armed forces is due or related to service with the forces, a widow or dependants of the deceased may claim a war pension.[63] A claim may be made where:

(a) the death occurred during service or not later than seven years after the end of service, and the death is due to or hastened by an injury which was attributable to service, or the aggravation by service of an injury which existed before or arose during service; or

(b) the death occurred more than seven years after the end of service, and the death was due to or substantially hastened by such injury or aggravation of injury.[64]

A widow whose late husband's death is within the above provision may claim a war pension.[65] A claim may also be made by an unmarried female dependant living with the deceased as his wife, if she is looking after a child of his.[66] A child of the deceased may be awarded a pension up to the age of 16 and, in certain circumstances, over that age.[67] This may be supplemented by an education allowance.[68]

A discretionary pension may be payable to a widower of a female member of the forces where her death occurred through service as stated above, if he was dependent on her and is unable to support himself and in financial need.[69] A discretionary pension may also be paid to a parent of the deceased where that parent is over pensionable age and is in pecuniary need by reason of infirmity or other permanent condition, and by any dependent child aged under 16, or any one other dependent adult, if the claimant is in pecuniary need and incapable of self-support.[70]

---

[62] See generally Ogus and Barendt, Chap. 9 and leaflets MPL 151 and 152 (available from war pensions offices). Pensions are administered through the D.S.S. North Fylde Central Office, Norcross, Blackpool FY5 3TA.

[63] Strictly, there is no entitlement to these pensions, as they are paid under the Royal Prerogative and conditions were set out in Royal Warrants (for the Army), Orders in Council (for the Royal Navy) and Orders by Her Majesty (for the Royal Air Force). Under Social Security (Miscellaneous Provisions) Act 1977, s.12, it is provided that powers in this respect may, in addition to their exercise in the traditional manner, also be exercised by Order in Council under that section. This power has now been used both to amend and consolidate the provisions extant at the time of enactment of that section. See now Naval Military and Air Forces etc. (Disablement and Death) Service Pension Order 1978 (S.I. 1978 No. 1525), as amended by S.I. 1978 No. 1902; S.I. 1979 No. 113; S.I. 1979 No. 1312; S.I. 1980 No. 1080 and 1081; S.I. 1981 Nos. 1070 and 1672; S.I. 1982 Nos. 845 and 1077.

[64] Note that the burden of proof shifts to the claimant after the seven year period has expired. See *Dickinson* v. *Minister of Pensions* [1953] 1 Q.B. 228.

[65] S.I. 1978 No. 1525, regs. 27, 29, 32, 33.

[66] *Ibid.* regs. 30, 31, 32, 33.

[67] *Ibid.* regs. 35, 36, 37.

[68] *Ibid.* reg. 38.

[69] *Ibid.* reg. 34.

[70] *Ibid.* regs. 40, 41.

(5) Means-tested benefits—funeral

A recipient of a means-tested benefit may claim a funeral payment from the Social Fund if he or she (or a member of his or her family) takes responsibility for a funeral.[71] This applies to recipients of income support, family credit, housing benefit and community charge benefit. However, if the claimant has realisable capital of over £500 (or £1,000 if the claimant [or his partner if there is one] is over 60), then a claim can only be made insofar as the amount of the claim exceeds the amount by which the claimant's free capital exceeds the £500 or £1,000 limit. For example, if the claimant has "free" capital of £2,000 and is aged over 60, a social fund payment will only be made if the total cost of the funeral exceeds £1,000.

The maximum amount of payment is the cost of an ordinary coffin and the usual accompanying costs and fees for a modest burial or cremation.[72] From that must be deducted any assets of the deceased available to the claimant, and any sums received such as insurance policies, burial club payments or contributions from charities.[73]

---

[71] Social Fund Maternity and Funeral Expenses (General) Regulations 1987 (S.I. 1987 No. 481).

[72] *Ibid.*, note 79, reg. 7.

[73] *Ibid.*, note 79, reg. 8. As to funeral and burial in general, see p. 60 *et seq.*, *ante*.

CHAPTER 45

THE DEVOLUTION OF CHATTELS

Chattels personal defined

Chattels personal[1] have been described as things *movable*, which may be annexed to, or attendant on, the person of the owner, and carried about with him. Such are animals, household stuff, money, jewels, corn, garments, motor-vehicles, and everything else that can be put in motion and transferred from place to place.[2] All these, and other things of the same nature, generally speaking, devolve at common law on the executor or administrator. For the purposes of the Administration of Estates Act 1925 "personal chattels" mean carriages, horses,[3] stable furniture and effects (not used for business purposes), motorcars and accessories (not used for business purposes), garden effects, domestic animals, plate,[4] plated articles,[5] linen,[6] china, glass, books,[7] pictures, prints, furniture,[8] jewellery,[9] articles of household or personal use[10] or ornament, musical and scientific instruments and apparatus, wines, liquors and consumable stores, but do not include any chattels used at the death of the intestate for business purposes[11] nor money or securities for money. This definition[12] does not directly affect the devolution of property. Its purpose is to prevent unnecessary sale of such chattels[13] and to ensure that they pass to the sur-

---

[1] For definition of *"personal chattels"* for the purposes of the Administration of Estates Act 1925 (unless the context otherwise requires), see *ibid*. s.55(1)(x), *post*, p. 1149 and below.

[2] See 2 Black. Comm. 387, 388.

[3] Including racehorses (*Re Hutchinson* [1955] Ch. 255).

[4] See *Holden* v. *Ramsbottom* (1863) 4 Giff. 205; *Re Grimwood* [1946] Ch. 54; *Re Lewis* [1910] W.N. 6.

[5] *Ibid*. n. 4.

[6] See *Hunt* v. *Hort* (1791) 3 Bro. C.C. 311.

[7] This has been held to include literary and musical manuscripts (*Willis* v. *Curtois* (1838) 1 Beav. 189; *Re Plowden* (1808) 24 T.L.R. 883; *Re Barratt* (1915) 31 T.L.R. 502; *Re Tomline* [1931] Ch. 521), but not a stamp album (*Re Masson* (1917) 86 L.J. Ch. 753).

[8] Including a collection of clocks: *Re Crispin* [1975] Ch. 245.

[9] Including unmounted but cut diamonds (*Re Whitby*) [1944] Ch. 210) but not coins (*Sudbury* v. *Brown* (1856) 4 W.R. 736; *Att.-Gen.* v. *Harley* (1828) 5 Russ, 173).

[10] Including stamps (*Re Reynolds* [1966] 1 W.L.R. 19; *Re Collins* [1971] 1 W.L.R. 37; *Re Crispin*, and see 82 L.Q.R. 18, above, at p. 251) and a yacht (*Re Chaplin* [1950] Ch. 507); a coin collection (*Re Collins*, above, in which the two cases on coins referred to in n. 8 above do not seem to have been cited); and a collection of watches (*Re Ogilby*, [1942] Ch. 288).

[11] A herd of cattle even if not run for profit is "used for business purposes" (*Re Ogilby* [1942] Ch. 288).

[12] See the Administration of Estates Act 1925, s.55(1)(x), *post*, p. 1149 and Statutory Will forms, Form 2.

[13] See *post*, p. 688. As to the power of executors to dispose of chattels specifically bequeathed see n. 44, *post*, p. 667.

viving spouse,[14] but it is frequently adopted in wills[15] and necessarily influences the meaning of "chattels personal" at common law. It is still of importance in considering the devolution of property, to distinguish chattels from realty, since part or the whole of the realty of which the deceased was seised may pass to special executors, as being settled land.

Since in general realty and personalty now devolve on the personal representatives the ancient distinctions between the categories of property have become less important, but the distinctions are still relevant in many cases and for many purposes.

Animals

Chattels animate may be subdivided into the tame and the wild. A person may have an absolute property, in such as are of a nature tame and domestic (as horses, dogs, cattle, sheep, poultry, and the like) and they are therefore capable of being transmitted, like any other personal chattel, to his executor or administrator. In those of a wild nature, i.e. such as are usually found at liberty and wandering at large, generally speaking, a person can have no property transmissible to his representatives.

But there may be a qualified property in animals of the latter class through the work of man (per industriam hominis) by a man's reclaiming them and making them tame by art, industry or education, or by so confining them within his own immediate power, that they cannot escape and use their natural liberty,[16] and the animals so reclaimed or confined go to the executor or administrator. Thus, tame pigeons, deer, rabbits, pheasants or partridges, will go to the executors or administrators; and though they were not tame, yet if they were kept alive, in any room, cage or such like place, they devolve upon the personal representative.[17] But if at any time such animals regain their natural liberty, the property instantly ceases, unless they have the intent to return (animum revertendi) which is only ascertainable by their usual custom of returning.[18] A qualified property may also subsist in wild animals (ferae naturae) (because of incapacity) (propter impotentiam;) as in young pigeons, which though not tame, being in the dove-house, are not able to fly out; and they will go to the executors or administrators.[19]

Animals incidental to realty

Similarly under the old laws of inheritance animals which a person owned by way of privilege (ratione privilegii) were considered as incident to the freehold and inheritance, and did not formerly pass to the executor

---

[14] See ante, p. 258; post, p. 1065 et seq. Note that the value of the chattels appears to be irrelevant, Re Crispin, above, at p. 250.

[15] For forms of Will see Brighouse, Precedents of Wills and Life transfers.

[16] 2 Black.Comm. 390, 391.

[17] Wentw.Off.Ex,. 14th ed., p. 143.

[18] 2 Black.Comm. 392.

[19] Ibid. n. 16.

or administrator. Thus deer in a park[20] (*i.e.* in a park properly so called, which must be either by grant or prescription),[21] rabbits in a warren, doves in a dove-house, did not formerly go to the executor or administrator.[22] The reason assigned for this by Lord Coke was that, without them, the inheritance would be incomplete. Another obvious reason mentioned by Lord Coke in the same case was that the deceased had not any property in them.[23] If the former was the true reason they would now go with the real estate; while if the latter was the true reason there was no interest of the deceased in them to devolve upon his personal representatives, as personalty.

Similarly, if a person buys fish, as carp, bream, tench, etc., and puts them into his pond, on his death they devolve with the real estate.[24]

But if a person has only a term of years in the land in which the park, warren, dove-house, or pond is situated, the deer, rabbits, doves and fish go to the executor or administrator as accessory chattels following the estate of their principal, *viz.* the park, warren, dove-house, or pond.[25] But the executor or administrator can have no further interest than the deceased had in them, *i.e.* a right to take as many as he pleases, during his term, provided he leaves enough for the stores; otherwise, it is waste.[26]

Timber and Crops

Here the main criterion is severance in the case of timber but more sophisticated distinctions apply to crops.

Timber

Personal effects of a vegetable nature are the fruit or the parts of a plant or tree, when severed from the body of it, or the whole plant or tree itself, when severed from the ground.[27] Unless they have been severed, trees,

---

[20] Co.Litt. 8a; Wentw.Off.Ex., 14th ed., p. 127. See *Inglewood* v. *Forestry Commission* [1988] 1 W.L.R. 959, 1278. (Deer not "game")

[21] *Davis* v. *Powell* (1738) Willes 46, where it was held that deer in an enclosed ground, in which deer had been usually kept, and which was therefore called a park, might be distrained for rent. And it has been held that deer on an ancient and *legal* park *may* be so tame as to pass to executors as personal property: *Morgan* v. *Earl of Abergavenny* (1849) 8 C.B. 768; *Ford* v. *Tynte* (1861) 2 J. & H. 150. A tenant for life of deer is bound to keep up the herd: *Paine* v. *Warwick* [1914] 2 K.B. 486.

[22] Com.Dig.Biens, B.; Wentw.Off.Ex., 14th ed., p. 127.

[23] The case of swans, 7 Co. 17b. But though animals *ferae naturae* are not, while living, the personal chattels of the owner of the soil, yet if they are found and killed on the land by a trespasser the qualified property in them *ratione soli* becomes absolute in the owner of the soil: *Blades* v. *Higgs* (1861) 12 C.B.(N.S.) 501; 13 C.B.(N.S.) 844; affirmed in Dom.Proc. 11 Jur.(N.S. 701. As to bees, see 2 Black.Comm. 393; *Hannam* v. *Mockett* (1824) 2 B. & C. 944; *Kearry* v. *Pattinson* [1939] 1 All E.R. 65. See also *Treatise on the Law of Fixtures, etc.*, by Messrs. Amos and Ferard.

[24] Co.Litt. 8a. *Secus*, as to fish in a tank; Bac.Abr.tit.Exors.H. 3, vol. 3, p. 64.

[25] Wentw.Off.Ex., 14th ed., p. 127; Godolph. Pt. 2, c. 13, s.4.

[26] Co.Litt. 53a.

[27] 2 Black.Comm. 389.

and the fruit produce of them,[28] as well as hedges, bushes, etc., from their intimate connection with the soil, follow the nature of their principal, and therefore, when the owner of the land dies, they devolve as real estate.[29]

However, even growing timber trees are, in some cases, considered as chattels. Thus, if a tenant in fee simple grants away the trees, they become vested in the grantee; and if the latter should die before they are felled, they will go to his executor or administrator as chattels; for in consideration of law, they are divided from the freehold.[30] So where a tenant in fee simple sells the land and reserves the trees from the sale, the trees are in property divided from the land, although in fact, they remain annexed to it, and will pass as chattels to the executors or administrators of the vendor.[31] But if the person so entitled to the trees distinct from the land afterwards purchases the inheritance, the trees will be re-united to the freehold in property, as they are de facto.[32] If the tenant in fee simple leases the land, excepting the trees, and afterwards grants the trees to the lessee, they are not by this means re-annexed to the inheritance, but the lessee has an absolute property in them, which will go to his executors or administrators as personalty.[33]

So if a tenant in tail sells the trees to another, they vest in the purchaser as chattels, and on his death pass to his executors or administrators; and in such a case also, by legal fiction they are severed from the land; but if the tenant in tail dies before actual severance, as to the issue in tail, they are part of his inheritance, and will go with it, and the purchaser or his executor cannot take them.[34] The law, it may be presumed, is the same for the purchaser from a tenant in tail after possibility of issue extinct, or a tenant for life without impeachment of waste.[35] And it seems that equity would not afford relief.[36] But if the sale is made in exercise of the powers conferred upon limited owners of the Settled Land Act 1925, the persons entitled in remainder would be bound by the sale, so that on the death of the purchaser the trees, whether or not severed from the land, would devolve upon his representative as personal estate.[37]

Trees and bushes when severed, are in some cases timber and in some not timber according to the general law of the land, or the custom of the country where they grow. Timber belongs to the owner of the first estate

---

[28] Before 1898 such produce always went direct to the heir; see Swinb. Pt. 7, s.10. Pl. 8; Wentw.Off.Ex., 14th ed., pp. 146, 147; *Rodwell* v. *Phillips* (1842) 9 M. & W. 501.

[29] Thus formerly they always went to the heir and not to the deceased's executor or administrator; Swinb. Pt. 7, s.10, pl. 8; *Re Ainslie* (1855) 30 Ch.D. 485.

[30] *Stukeley* v. *Butler* (1614) Hob. 173; Wentw.Off.Ex., 14th ed., p. 148; Com.Biens, H.

[31] *Herlakenden's Case* (1589) 4 Co. 63b; Wentw., *ante.*

[32] 4 Co. 63b; *Anon.* (1593) Owen 49.

[33] 4 Co. 63b.

[34] *Liford's Case* (1614) 11 co. 46b, 50a, for, it was said, timber trees cannot be felled with a goose quill.

[35] *Pyne* v. *Dor* (1785) 1 T.R. 55; *Bishop of London* v. *Webb* (1718) 1 P. Wms. 527.

[36] See Fonbl. Treat. on Equity, B. 1, c. 4, s.19, that no act of tenant in tail shall be carried into execution in a court of equity any further than at law, for this would be to repeal the statute *De Donis.*

[37] See the Settled Land Act 1925, ss.66, 90.

of inheritance in the land.[38] Thus if a tenant for life or years, unless he is so without impeachment of waste, cuts down timber trees, or a stranger does so, or the wind blows them down, the trees so severed do not belong to the tenant, although the tenant is entitled to interest.[39] On the other hand, if such a tenant cuts down hedges or trees, not timber, or they are severed by the act of God, the tenant will have them[40]; and, consequently, they will devolve upon his executor or administrator as chattels. So if trees are blown down, which are in their nature timber, but are dotards without any timber in them,[41] or if such they are wrongfully severed by the lessor, they belong to the tenant, and will pass to his representatives.[42]

Crops—emblements

There are certain vegetable products called emblements[43] which, though annexed to and growing upon the land at the time of the occupier's death, are considered by the law as chattels, and will pass as such. Emblements may be seised and sold under a *fieri facias*. Their sale is not a contract for sale of land but is a sale of goods and if they are separately assigned they are personal chattels within the Bills of Sale Acts.[44]

Emblements include not only corn and grain of all kinds, but everything of an artificial and annual profit that is produced by labour and manurance,[45] such as hemp, flax, saffron, and the like,[46] melons of all kinds,[47] also hops, though they spring from old roots, because they are annually manured, and require cultivation,[48] and potatoes.[49] Hence they are called industrial crops (*fructus industriales.*) When the occupier of the land, whether he is the owner of the fee simple or of an estate determining with his own life, has sown or planted the soil with the intention of raising a crop

---

[38] *Herlakenden's Case* (1589) 4 Co. 63a; *Berwick* v. *Whitfield* (1734) 3 P. Wms. 268; *Lushington* v. *Boldero* (1851) 15 Beav. 1; *Ormonde* v. *Kynnersley* (1820) *ibid.* 10.

[39] *Tooker* v. *Annesley* (1832) 5 Sim. 235; *Consett* v. *Bell* (1842) 1 Y. & C.C.C. 569. As to the rights of a tenant for life and remainderman, see *Lewin on Trusts*, 16th ed., p. 536 and generally.

[40] Com.Dig.Biens, H.; *Berriman* v. *Peacock* (1832) 9 Bing. 384; *Re Ainslie* (1855) 30 Ch.D. 485; *Re Harker* [1938] 1 Ch. 323.

[41] *Herlakenden's Case* (1589) 4 Co. 63a, b; *Countess of Cumberland's Case* (1610) Moore 812.

[42] *Channon* v. *Patch* (1826) 5 B. & C. 897.

[43] See Megarry and Wade. *Real Property*, 5th ed., 1984, pp. 101, 703.

[44] *Evans* v. *Roberts* (1826) 5 B. & C. 829; *Scorrell* v. *Boxall* (1827) 1 Y. & J. 398; *Jones* v. *Flint* (1839) 10 A. & E. 753.

[45] Co.Litt. 55b.

[46] *Ibid.*; Wentw.Off.Ex., 14th ed., p. 147.

[47] Wentw.Off.Ex., 14th ed., p. 153. Query as to artichokes; see *ibid.*

[48] The authorities, however, do not prove that the person who *planted* the young hops, or his personal representatives, will be entitled to the first crop, whenever produced: *Graves* v. *Weld* (1833) 5 B. & Ad. 105, 120. As to teazles, see *Kingsbury* v. *Collins* (1827) 4 Bing. 202.

[49] *Evans* v. *Roberts* (1826) 5 B. & C. 829, 832, Bayley J. It has been said (see *Godolph. Pt. 2, c. 14, s.1* and *Wentw.Off.Ex., 14th ed., p. 152*) *that things underground such as carrots, turnips, etc., go with the inheritance; but according to Coke if a tenant plants roots*, they form part of his personal estate; Co.Litt.55b. Coke's view seems the more acceptable: see 2 Black. Comm. 123.

of such a nature and dies before harvest time, the law gives to his representatives the profits of the crop, *emblavence de bled*, or emblements, to compensate for the labour and expense of tilling, manuring and sowing the land.[50]

But the rule does not apply to fruit growing on trees[51]; nor to planted trees; for the general rule is that whatever is fixed or planted in the soil belongs to the soil (*quicquid plantatur solo, solo cedit.*) The case of trees, shrubs, and other produce of their grounds planted by gardeners and nurserymen, with an express view to sale, may be mentioned as an exception; for they are removable by them or their representatives, as emblements are.[52]

The growing crop of grass, even if sown from seed, and though ready to be cut for hay, cannot be taken as emblements.[53] If seems, however, that artificial grasses, such as clover, sainfoin and the like, by reason of the greater care and labour necessary for their production, are within the rule as to emblements.[54] It is suggested that under modern farming methods this latter rule would normally apply.

The doctrine of emblements extends to a crop of that species only which ordinarily repays the labour by which it is produced within the year in which that labour is bestowed.[55] Nor can a second crop be taken as an emblement in a succeeding year even though the first crop taken during the first year did not fully suffice to repay the cost of sowing and acts of cultivation performed in that year.[56]

The right to emblements includes, of course, an ancillary right of entry and exit limited to this purpose.[57]

Fee simple owners

Generally, on the death of the owner of the fee simple, the emblements devolve on his personal representatives.[58] But where a person is seised of the soil as joint tenant, and dies, the corn, etc., sown goes to the survivor, because joint tenants are supposed to cultivate by a joint stock.[59] The survivor will be beneficially entitled if there is mere joint ownership, but will

---

[50] Swinb.Pt. 7, s.10, pl. 8

[51] *Ante*, p. 500.

[52] *Penton* v. *Robart* (1801) 2 East 88, 90; *Lee* v. *Risdon* (1816) 7 Taunt. 191, in judgment of Gibbs C.J.; and see the remark of Lawrence J. in 3 East 44, n. (*c*); *Wyndham* v. *Way* (1812) 4 Taunt. 316.

[53] Gilb.Ev. 215, 216, *Evans* v. *Roberts* (1826) 5 B. & C. 829, 832.

[54] 4 Burn, E.L. 299. No case seems to have occurred where these matters have come in question. The general right seems to have been admitted in *Graves* v. *Weld, post.*

[55] *Graves* v. *Weld* (1833) 5 B. & Ad. 105, 118; and see Woodfall *Landlord and Tenant*, 28th ed., 1978, para. 2–0064.

[56] *Ibid.* n. 54.

[57] Co.Litt. 56*a. cf. Hayling* v. *Okey* (1853) 8 Exch. 545; *Evans* v. *Roberts* (1826) 5 B. & C. 829, 840.

[58] See *Lawton* v. *Lawton* (1743) 3 Atk. 13, 16; Wentw.Off.Ex., 14th ed., p. 145.

[59] Gilb.Ev. 212, 213.

hold in trust as to a moiety for the deceased if there is a partnership or other indication of severance.[60]

If a person seised in fee sows the land and then conveys it away, and dies before severance, the crops will not go to the representative of the grantor, but will pass with the soil as appertaining to it.[61]

In like manner, if the land itself is devised, the growing crops pass as part of it to the testator's representative in the first instance, and then to the devisee,[62] because in the absence of a contrary direction[63] the testator is presumed so to intend; every man's donation will be taken most strongly against himself,[64] to the disadvantage of the residuary estate.

If there is an express legatee of the growing crops, or any specific bequest in the will which can apply to emblements, they will vest in the executor, and, after his assent, the specific legatee.[65]

Limited owners

The privilege of taking the emblements is, however, by no means confined to the case of the representatives of a person seised of the inheritance, but the rule is general, that, in the absence of express agreement to the contrary,[66] everyone who has an uncertain estate or interest, if his estate determines by the act of God and not by his own act[67] before severance of the crop, will take the emblements, or they will go to his executor or administrator.[68]

Settled land

On the death of a tenant for life,[69] emblements devolve as part of his general estate to the exclusion of the remainderman or reversioner, because in this case the estate of the tenant is determined by the act of God.[70] Thus, if the legal estate in the land was vested in the tenant for life as trustee estate owner, and on his death after 1925 the trustees of the settlement take out special representation as respects the settled land, the

---

[60] See *ante*.

[61] Gilb.Ev. 214; the Law of Property Act 1925, s.63.

[62] Before 1898 the executor was excluded, the devisee took directly: *Cooper* v. *Woolfitt* (1857) 2 H. & N. 122.

[63] *West* v. *Moore* (1807) 8 East 339; *Cox* v. *Godsalve* (1699) 6 East 604n.; *Blake* v. *Gibbs* (1825) 5 Russ. 13, *in notis*; *Rudge* v. *Winnall* (1849) 12 Beav. 357; *Re Roose* (1880) 17 Ch.D. 696.

[64] Gilb EV. 214.

[65] *Cox* v. *Godsalve* (1699) 6 East 604, note to *Crosby* v. *Wadsworth*. See Jarman, *Wills*, 8th ed., p. 1297.

[66] *Leschallas* v. *Woolf* [1908] 1 Ch. 641.

[67] *e.g.* by surrender, marriage, forfeiture, condition broken, etc: Com.Dig.Biens, G. 2; *Davis* v. *Eyton* (1830) 7 Bing. 154.

[68] Com.Dig.Biens, G. 2; See also 1 Roll.Abr.Emblements, A. pl. 12, p. 727.

[69] As to the right to emblements of a tenant by the curtesy, a tenant in dower, and a jointress, see 11th ed. of this work, pp. 549, 550.

[70] See Co.Litt. 55*b*.

emblements do not vest in them, but in the deceased's general representatives. But there may be a case where emblements do not devolve as part of the general estate of the tenant for life, because the deceased was not the actual party who sowed the land and the consequent failure of the reason upon which the right is founded.[71] In such a case, so far as the beneficial interest is concerned, the right to the emblements goes with the land from which they arise. Thus, if A sows land and then settles it upon, or devises it to, B for life, remainder to C for life, and B dies before the corn is reaped, the beneficial interest in the corn will pass with the beneficial interest in the land to C.[72]

Tenancy at will

A tenancy at will (in the strict sense of the expression) is determined by the death of the lessee, and his representatives will be entitled to the emblements.[73]

Agricultural Holdings Act 1986

Where the tenancy of an agricultural holding[74] held by a tenant at a rack-rent[75] determines by the death or cesser of the estate of any landlord entitled for his life, or for any uncertain interest, instead of claims to emblements the tenant is to hold and occupy the holding until the occupation is determined by a 12 months' notice to quit, expiring at the end of a year of the tenancy.[76] A tenant is defined to include, for the purposes of the Act, the executors and administrators of a tenant.[77]

Further, a tenant, on quitting his holding at the determination of his tenancy, is entitled under the same Act to obtain from his landlord compensation for disturbance of his tenancy by his landlord and also for improvements which he has effected; and these rights enure for the benefit of his personal representatives.[78]

Under section 86 the general personal representatives of a landlord who was not an absolute owner of a holding, but who was compelled under the Act to pay compensation for improvements or for disturbance to an outgo-

---

[71] But if a disseisor sows the land of the tenant for life and the latter dies, the corn forms part of the general estate of the tenant for life: see *Knevit* v. *Pool* (1601), Gould, 143, 146.

[72] Formerly the legal as well as the beneficial interest would have gone direct to the remainderman: see *Grantham* v. *Hawley* (1615) Hob. 132. See also *Knevit* v. *Pool* (1601) Cro.Eliz. 463; *Spencer's Case* (1622) Winch 51; Co.Litt. 55*b*, n. (2), from Hal.MSS.; Gibb.Ev. 250.

[73] Co.Litt. 55*b*.

[74] As to the meaning of a "holding" for the purposes of the Agricultural Holdings Act 1986 see *ibid*. s.1(1).

[75] See *Re Sawyer and Withall* [1919] 2 Ch. 338.

[76] Agricultural Holdings Act 1986, s.21. As to provision for fixtures under this Act, see *post*, pp. 513, 514. As to further extention of the tenancy by succession see Part IV of the Agricultural Holdings Act 1986.

[77] *Ibid*. s.96(1).

[78] *Ibid*. ss.1, 60–78, 96(1).

ing tenant whose tenancy determined before the death of the landlord, are entitled to obtain from the Minister an order charging the holding with the repayment of the amount so paid.[79]

Glebe land

The executors or administrators of an incumbent would probably at common law be entitled to the emblements of the glebe, for the deceased had an uncertain interest in the land, which was determined by the act of God.[80] The right, however, was fully established by 28 Hen. 8, c. 11, which provided that any incumbent who happened to die, and before his death had caused any of his glebe lands to be manured and sown at his own proper costs and charges with any corn or grain, might make his testament of all the profits of the corn growing upon the said glebe so manured and sown. This statute has been repealed, but the repeal probably does not affect the rights of the representative of an incumbent.[81]

Inanimate Chattels

These pass as a rule to the general representatives. Except for some documents relating to real estate[82] all papers and documents devolve as chattels. Relevant papers must be included in an affidavit sworn in answer to an order for discovery notwithstanding that they may be held by an executor in his private capacity.[83] If any chattel is specifically bequeathed to a legatee, it will not vest in him till the representatives have assented. There are, however, some chattels personal inanimate, including heirlooms and fixtures, which may not pass to the general representatives.

Heirlooms

Heirlooms, in the strict sense, are such goods and personal chattels as went *by special custom* to the heir along with the inheritance, and not to the executor or administrator of the last proprietor.[84]

Brooke says[85] that heirlooms are those things which have continually gone with the capital messuage, by *custom*, which is the best thing of every sort, as of beds, tables, pots, pans, and such like of dead chattels move-

---

[79] See *Gough* v. *Gough* [1891] 2 Q.B. 665, decided on the Agricultural Holdings Act 1883 (now repealed).

[80] See general principle for limited owners as stated *ante*. Glebe is now vested in the Diocesan Board of Finance. See the Endowments and Glebe Measure 1976.

[81] A parson who resigns his living is not entitled to emblements: *Bulwer* v. *Bulwer* (1819) 2 B. & A. 470. See *ante*, p. 504, n. 67.

[82] As to which, see *post*, p. 508.

[83] *Buchanan-Michaelson* v. *Rubinstein* [1965] Ch. 258. See also *post*, p. 766.

[84] On the Saxon origin of the term, see 2 Black.Comm. 427, and *Byng* v. *Byng* (1826) 10 H.L.C. at p. 183.

[85] Discent. pl. 53.

able. Coke says,[86] that heirlooms are due by *custom*, and not by the common law, and that the heir had an action for them at common law, and could not sue for them in the Ecclesiastical Court.[87] An heirloom, in the strict sense, could only go to the heir by force of a custom, and in its nature it was a chattel distinct from the freehold. Blackstone,[88] however, said that heirlooms were "generally such things as cannot be taken away without damaging or dismembering the freehold"; and Lord Holt is reported to have said at Nisi Prius, that goods in gross could not be an heirloom, but had to be things fixed to the freehold, such as old tables, benches, etc.[89] This proposition is not only adverse to the authorities above cited, that an heirloom is a detached chattel, but is also liable to the objection that the heir would not then have taken it by custom, but as a thing annexed to the freehold at common law.[90]

The custom which entitled the heir had to be strictly proved.[91]

Whether heirlooms devisable

It seems that though the owner of heirlooms may sell or dispose of them during his lifetime, as he may of the timber of the estate,[92] yet he could not before 1926 bequeath them by will away from the heir upon whom the estate, with which the heirlooms had gone by custom from heir to heir, had descended.[93]

After 1925, it would seem that heirlooms absolutely vested in the owner of an estate of inheritance devolve with that estate upon his representatives. But whether it is now within the power of a testator by his will to bequeath heirlooms away from the land with which they have by custom descended remains to be decided.

Chattels in the nature of heirlooms

Besides heirlooms, properly so called, there were other instances of inanimate personal chattels, which the law gave to the heir, as part of his inheritance, and which might be considered as chattels in the *nature* of

---

[86] Co.Litt. 18*b*. See also Spelman's *Glossary*, *Heirloom* and *Les Termes de la Ley*, Treat.on *Fixtures*, 162.

[87] As to the divisions of jurisdiction between the courts, see *ante*, p. 1.

[88] 2 Black.Comm. 427.

[89] *Lord Petre* v. *Heneage* (1701) 12 Mod. 520.

[90] According to the report of *Lord Petre* v. *Heneage*, by Lord Raymond (1 Ld.Raym. 728), Lord Holt merely said: "a jewel cannot be an heirloom, but only things ponderous, as carts, tables, etc.," which agrees with the definition by Spelman, "*omne utensile robustius*." Blackstone, Vol. 2, p. 17, says: "an heirloom or implement of furniture, which by custom descends to the heir together with a house, is neither land nor tenements, but a mere moveable."

[91] 2 Black.Comm. 428.

[92] *Ibid.* 429.

[93] See Co.Litt. 18*b*; *Pusey* v. *Pusey* (1684) 1 Vern. 273. See also *Tipping* v. *Tipping* (1721) 1 P.Wms. 730; 2 Black.Comm. 420; Com.Dig.Biens, B. See, however, Woodd.Vin.Lect. vol. 2, p. 380.

heirlooms. Thus monuments, coat-armour, the sword, pennons, and other ensigns of honour set up in memory of the deceased, went to the heir of the deceased, as heirlooms in the manner of inheritance.[94] There is no faculty jurisdiction under ecclesiastical law to authorise the sale of such chattels unless the heir has abandoned all claims.[95]

Charters and deeds affecting real estate

Charters or deeds relating to the inheritance are considered so much to savour of the realty, that the law for some purposes does not account them to be chattels,[96] but provides that they shall follow the land to which they relate.[97] So far has the doctrine of charters and other written assurances concerning the realty not being chattels been carried, that larceny could not have been committed of them at common law, the taking of them being considered (as of other things which were part of the freehold) merely as a trespass and not a felony.[98] An action for conversion would, however, lie even at common law. The very box or chest which has usually been employed for keeping them partakes of their nature, and devolves with them[99]; and of that also, at common law, no larceny could have been committed.

Deeds and writings which relate to terms of years, goods, chattels or debts are not within the above rule, and go to the executor or administrator as personalty whenever the death took place.[1]

---

[94] *Corven's Case* (1612) 12 Co. 105; even though they were annexed to the freehold of a church vested in the parson: Co.Litt. 18n.; 1 Gibs.Cod. 544; 2 Black.Comm. 420. See *Stubs* v. *Stubs* (1862) 1 H. & C. 257, as to the heir's right to an exemplification of a grant of arms from the Herald's College. And as to his right to Journals of the House of Lords delivered to peers, see *Upton* v. *Ferrers* (1801) 5 Ves. 801. If the executor laid a gravestone on the testator in the church, and set up coat-armour, and the vicar or parson removed them or carried them away, an action on the case lay for either the executor or the heir; Godb. 200, by Coke, *i.e.* (*semble*), if they were originally set up with a faculty: *Seager* v. *Bowle* (1823) 1 Add 541; and see *Spooner* v. *Brewster* (1825) 3 Bingh. 136. The property of the shroud and coffin remains in the executors or other person having charge of the funeral. As to property in the corpse or its ashes, and exclusive rights of burial *ante*, p. 60.

[95] *Re St. Andrews Thornhaugh* [1976] Fam. 230.

[96] By a grant of *omnia bona et catalla*, charters concerning the land do not pass: Perks, s.115; Touchst. 97, 98.

[97] See as to devolution before 1897, Godolph Pt. 2, c. 14, s.1; Wentw.Off.Ex., 14th ed., p. 153; Co.Litt. 6a, where Lord Coke calls them the sinews of the land. And see n. 00, *post*, and *Clayton* v. *Clayton* [1930] 2 Ch. 12, 17. They do not, however, *necessarily* follow the estate. See (1970) 33 M.L.R. 131–143.

[98] Russell, *Crime*, 12th ed., p. 892. But this defect of the common law was remedied by 7 & 8 Geo. 4, c. 29, s.23, the place of which is now taken by ss.1–6 and 20 of the Theft Act 1968.

[99] See as to devolution direct to the heir before 1897, Godolph, *supra*; Wentw.Off.Ex., 14th ed., p. 156; Com.Dig.Biens, B. Contrast Swinb. Pt. 6, s.7, pl. 5 (where it is said that the heir is only entitled to the chest if it be shut or sealed). The deeds and chest would now devolve in the first instance under the Administration of Estates Act 1925, Pt. I.

[1] Wentw.Off.Ex., 14th ed., p. 153; Bac.Abr.tit.Exors., H. 3. If the writings of an estate are pawned or pledged for money, they are considered as chattels in the hands of the creditor, and in case of his decease, they went, even before 1898 to his personal representatives as the party entitled to the benefit accruing from the load: Touchst. 469.

Chattels settled as heirlooms

Personal property may also be bequeathed or limited in strict settlement to devolve with land to one for life, with remainder to the sons and daughters entitled to the land in tail, so as to be transmissible like heirlooms.[2] Thus a testator may devise or limit in strict settlement a capital mansion and estate, together with personal property, such as the plate, pictures, library, furniture, etc., therein, such plate, etc., to be enjoyed, together with the house and estate, inalienable by the devisees in succession, as far as the law will allow. But, in the case of dispositions taking effect before 1926, the chattels, whether trustees were interposed or not, were the absolute property of the first adult person seised in tail, and on his death devolved on his executors or administrators.[3]

Chattels entailed, etc.

After 1925 chattels can be entailed.[4] A mere direction that chattels shall be enjoyed or held with, or upon, trusts, corresponding with trusts affecting entailed land, is sufficient for this purpose.[5] In fact, the usual[6] method of settling personal chattels, after 1925, is to assign them to trustees to hold upon trust to allow them to devolve and be enjoyed as heirlooms along with the settled land.[7] In this case such chattels are governed by the rules affecting estates tail in reality before 1926, so that income is not accumulated and a presumptive remainder is accelerated.[8]

Where chattels are now settled, the interest therein of a tenant for life, or of a tenant in tail who has not barred the entail during his lifetime or by his will,[9] ceases on his death.[10] But on the death of a tenant in tail who has disposed of the entailed chattels by his will, the beneficial interest in them devolves on his general representatives.[11]

Preservation of heirlooms

Lord Eldon, in *Clarke* v. *Earl Ormonde*,[12] said that heirlooms are a kind of property that is rather a favourite of the court, and that, although no tes-

---

[2] Co.Litt. 18*b*, n. (109), by Hargrave.

[3] Co.Litt. 18*b*, n. (190), by Hargrave; *Carr* v. *Lord Erroll* (1808) 14 Ves. 478; *Scarsdale* v. *Curzonv* (1860) 1 John. & Hem. 40; *Hill* v. *Hill* (1902) 71 L.J.Ch. 417. *Jarman on Wills*, 8th ed., p. 698.

[4] Law of Property Act 1925, s.130; see 1 Wolst. & Ch., 13th ed. pp. 237 *et seq.*

[5] Law of Property Act 1925, s.130(3); *Re Jones* [1934] Ch. 315. (The words of the section must be exactly complied with.)

[6] See 3 Prid., 25th ed., pp. 308 *et seq.*

[7] *Ibid.* n. 5.

[8] *Re Crossley* [1955] Ch. 627.

[9] See Law of Property Act 1925, s.176.

[10] Administration of Estates Act 1925, s.3(3) (*post*, p. 1115).

[11] See *ibid.*, s.3(2).

[12] (1921) 1 Jacob 108, 114, 115; as to personal chattels, see *ante*, p. 498 and *post*, p. 667, n. 44.

tator can in any way exempt any part of his personal estate from applicability to the payment of his debts, nor can he put into the hands of his executors the means of defending themselves at law; yet where a testator makes a will, providing that certain portions of his effects shall be treated as heirlooms, it is the duty of the executors, as far as possible, to preserve those parts of his property, and unless compelled, they ought not to apply them to the payment of debts.

Chattels of a corporation sole

Since 1925 these devolve upon the successor. The relevant provisions are considered later.[13]

Fixtures

When an inanimate chattel comes to be used with land it may lose its chattel nature and become part of the land. It is then known as a "fixture" but in some cases may still be removed by a person who is not owner of the land. The question whether it is a fixture does not depend entirely upon either physical affixing[14] or intent[15] but upon a combination of both. It is ultimately a question of fact.[16] The question whether, being a fixture, it is yet removeable depends upon whether it falls into certain exceptive categories.[17]

In any given case a personal representative may thus have to decide (*a*) is this a fixture? If not it remains a chattel. If it is then (*b*) is it removeable? If so, it becomes a chattel again on removal. If not, it passes with the land. The question can arise, *inter alia*, in the context of mortgage.[18] lease.[19] life tenancy,[20] will,[21] sale,[22] or bankruptcy[23] and in most such cases the problem before the representative is not peculiar. The reader is therefore referred generally to the principal works within the relevant field. The following attempts only to state the general principles and cover the problems peculiar to a personal representative.

---

[13] See *post*, p. 540.

[14] See, *e.g. D'Eyncourt* v. *Gregory* (1866) 3 Eq. 382 where "unfixed" statues, etc., were held to be fixtures as part of an architectural design.

[15] *Leigh* v. *Taylor* [1902] A.C. 157; *Hulme* v. *Brigham* [1945] 1 K.B. 152. *Berkley* v. *Poulett* (1976) 241 E.G. 911; 120 S.J. 836.

[16] See n. 15.

[17] See *post*, pp. 512, *et seq.*

[18] See Coote, *Mortgages*, 9th ed., p. 144; *Fisher and Lightwood on Law of Mortgage*, 10th ed., 1988, pp. 89 *et seq.*

[19] See Woodfall, *Landlord and Tenant*.

[20] Here the principles may be the same as for a lease. See Adkin, *Fixtures*, 3rd ed., p. 41. Megarry and Wade, *Real Property*, 5th ed. p. 737 but see *post*, p. 512.

[21] This will normally be a matter of construing the will. Adkin, *Fixtures*, 3rd ed., p. 37.

[22] See Megarry and Wade, *Real Property*, 5th ed. p. 737. Adkin, *Fixtures*, 3rd ed., p. 127.

[23] Adkin, *Fixtures*, 3rd ed., p. 167; Williams and Muir Hunter, *Bankruptcy*, 19th ed.; Muir Hunter, *Personal Insolvency*.

Annexation

Since physical "fixing" is not the sole test the word "annexation" has come to describe the process whereby a chattel becomes in law a part of the land. The existence or otherwise of physical fixing would seem from the authorities to raise a presumption in favour of,[24] or against,[25] annexation, as the case may be, but such presumption will give way to proof of intent. Was the chattel intended to form part of the realty[26] or was it although "fixed" intended simply to be enjoyed better as a chattel by means of such fixing?"[27] In the former case it is regarded as annexed,[28] but not in the latter. Similarly, although not fixed at all, it will be regarded as annexed if it forms part of an ornamental or architectural scheme.[29]

The devisee

Generally a devisee takes the land in the same condition as it would have descended to the heir.[30] He is, therefore, entitled to all articles so annexed to the land as to become part of the freehold, whether the annexation takes place before or subsequently to the date of the devise. Thus, where a picture and tapestry had been fixed as part of a general scheme of decoration of a house and not for their better enjoyment as chattels, they passed under a devise of the house.[31]

Conversely the devisee is not entitled to those fixtures which would not have devolved with the inheritance to the heir.[32]

Testator's intention paramount

In all these cases, however, the rights of the persons claiming the fixtures as chattels or as part of the land respectively, will be subject to the intention of the testator as expressed in the will.[33] If, from the nature or condition of the property devised, it is apparent that the intention is that the fixtures should go along with the freehold to the devisee, they will pass to

[24] *Smith* v. *City Petroleum* [1940] 1 All E.R. 260; *Penry* v. *Brown* (1818) 2 Stark N.P.C. 403, *Sheffield & S. Yorkshire B.S.* v. *Harrison* (1884) 15 Q.B.D. 358; *Ellis* v. *Glover* [1908] 1 K.B. 388.
[25] *Naylor* v. *Collinge* (1807) 1 Taunt, 19; *Culling* v. *Tufnal* (1694) Bull N.P. 34; *R.* v. *Londonthorpe* (1795) 6 T.R. 377; *R.* v. *Otley* (1830) 1 B. & Ad. 161; *Wansborough* v. *Maton* (1835) 4 A. & E. 884; *Webb* v. *Bevis* [1940] 1 All E.R. 247; *Jordan* v. *May* [1947] K.B. 427; *Hulme* v. *Brigham* [1943] 1 K.B. 152.
[26] *e.g.* a millstone, keys, doors, windows, rings, etc.: *Walmsley* v. *Milne* (1859) 7 C.B.(N.S.) 115, 138; *R.* v. *Crosse* (1664) 1 Sid. 204, 207.
[27] *Spyer* v. *Phillipson* [1931] 2 Ch. 183.
[28] *Leigh* v. *Taylor* [1902] A.C. 157.
[29] *D'Eyncourt* v. *Gregory* (1866) L.R. 3 Eq. 382.
[30] See *Norton* v. *Dashwood* [1896] 2 Ch. 497, 500.
[31] *Re Whaley* [1908] 1 Ch. 615; *Norton* v. *Dashwood* [1896] 2 Ch. 497; *Re Chesterfield* [1911] 1 Ch. 237.
[32] Amos & Ferard, *Fixtures*, 3rd ed., p. 323; *cf.* as to emblements, *ante*, p. 502.
[33] As to what passed under a bequest of "fixtures and fixed furniture," see *Birch* v. *Dawson* (1834) 2 A. & E. 37.

him, though they are of such a sort that the heir would not have been entitled to them.[34]

Settled land

The old law on the claims of the heir as against the personal representative to fixtures can still be relevant on the death of a tenant for life of settled land as between his general and his special personal representatives, for the latter as trustees for the remaindermen may have to claim as fixtures chattels which the life tenant and his general personal representatives claim not to have been annexed. The old law strongly favoured the heir whose inheritance must not be damaged.[35] The relaxations in the strict rule were made to encourage limited owners to benefit the estate during the continuance of their interest.[36] It was said by Chitty J. that:[37] "As between landlord and tenant, the claim of the tenant to remove fixtures set up by himself is the most favoured; as between tenant for life and remainderman, the claim of the tenant for life to remove fixtures set up by himself is less favoured; and as between executor and heir, where both claim under the same owner, the claim of the executor to remove fixtures set up by the owner is still less favoured." Thus it is strictly incorrect to equate the position of tenant for life and remainderman either with that of tenant and landlord or that of executor and heir[38] although in practice the results will normally be similar.

Ornamental and domestic fixtures

It does not seem to be clear, but equally it does not matter,[39] whether chattels used for ornamental and domestic purposes are regarded as not annexed (upon the principles stated above) or as being annexed but removable. Upon either view it is clear that chattels put up for ornamentation, and for the enjoyment of the tenant for life so fixing them while occupying the house, can be removed by his executor.[40]

---

[34] *Wood* v. *Gaynon* (1761) Ambl. 395. As to what passes under a "conveyance" (which includes an assent, but not a will: the Law of Property Act 1925, s.205(1)(ii), see s.62 of that Act; 1 Wolst & Ch., 13th ed., p. 136 *et seq.*

[35] Godolph. Pt. 2, c. 14, s.1; Touchstone, p. 470; Wentw.Off.Ex., 14th ed., 149–151; *Herlakenden's Case* (1589) 4 Co. 64a; *Cave* v. *Cave* (1705) 2 Vern. 508; *Bishop* v. *Elliott* (1856) 11 M. & W. 113.

[36] *Lawton* v. *Lawton* (1743) 3 Atk. 13, 14; *Re de Falbe* [1901] 1 Ch. 523, 538 *et seq.*

[37] *Norton* v. *Dashwood* [1896] 2 Ch. 497, 500: see also *Lawton* v. *Lawton* (1743) 3 Atk. 13; *Dudley* v. *Warde* (1751) Ambl. 113.

[38] See *ante*, p. 511 and Megarry and Wade, *The Law of Real Property*, 5th ed. p. 737. *Re de Falbe* [1901] 1 Ch. 523, 539; *Re Whaley* [1908] 1 Ch. 615, 619.

[39] The only respect in which the distinction might be material is in the time allowed for removal (see below). This rule appears to apply only to chattels annexed but removable. It presumably cannot apply to chattels not annexed in which case "abandonment" would be the issue. See *Smith* v. *City Petroleum* [1904] 1 All E.R. 260.

[40] *Leigh* v. *Taylor* [1902] A.C. 157. *cf. D'Eyncourt* v. *Gregory* (1866) L.R. 3 Eq. 382 (tapestry, etc., which had become essentially part of the house, not removable by tenant for life); but see as to this case, *Re de Falbe*, *ante*.

Trade fixtures

In *Re Hulse*,[41] which was the last of a series of cases[42] in which the rights of the personal representatives of a tenant for life or in tail to remove trade fixtures were considered, it was decided that the principle which as between landlord and tenant enables the latter to remove trade fixtures applies also to the case of a tenant for life and remainderman, and allows the former or his (general) personal representatives to remove machinery affixed by the tenant for life. There is no material difference in this respect between the position of a tenant for life and that of a tenant in tail,[43] but there was never any right for an executor to remove trade fixtures as against the heir.[44]

Agricultural trade fixtures

In *Elwes* v. *Maw*[45] it was decided that the privilege established in favour of tenants in trade did not extend to agricultural tenants, so as to entitle them to remove things which they had erected for the purpose of husbandry. This decision was, however, to some extent in conflict with a decision of Lord Kenyon[46] and it has been held that glasshouses erected by a nurseryman are removable as trade fixtures.[47] However, in practice the position will now be governed by statute[48] in most cases.

Time allowed for removal

In the absence of special contract, and in cases not within section 10 of the Agricultural Holdings Act 1986 tenants' fixtures cannot be removed after the termination of the lease, and this rule applies whether the lease determines by effluxion of time or by re-entry on forfeiture.[49] It has been suggested[50] that the tenant may remove fixtures "within a reasonable time" after termination of the lease but this is quite contrary to the well-

---

[41] [1905] 1 Ch. 406.

[42] See *Lawton* v. *Lawton, ante*; *Dudley* v. *Warde, supra*, in both of which cases a fire engine set up in a colliery by a limited owner was held to form part of his personal estate as against the remainderman. These cases were recognised in *Lawton* v. *Salmon* (1782) 1 H.Black. 260, *in notis*; *Penton* v. *Robart* (1801) 2 East 88, 91; *Elwes* v. *Maw* (1802) 3 *ibid.* 38, 54.

[43] See *Dudley* v. *Warde, ante*.

[44] *Fisher* v. *Dixon* (1845) 12 Cl. & F. 312; *Lawton* v. *Salmon* (1782) 1 H.Black 260n.; *Mather* v. *Fraser* (1856) 2 K. & J. 536; *Bain* v. *Brand* (1876) 1 App.Cas. 762.

[45] (1802) 3 East 28. As to emblements, see *ante*, p. 502.

[46] *Penton* v. *Robart* (1801) 2 East 88, and see *Wake* v. *Hall* (1883) 8 App.Cas. 195, 210.

[47] *Mears* v. *Callender* [1901] 2 Ch. 388.

[48] Agricultural Holdings Act 1986, s.10. See Woodfall *Landlord and Tenant*, 1990. See also the Allotments Act 1922, s.3, and the Allotments Act 1950, s.3. See Woodfall *Landlord and Tenant* (1990).

[49] *Pugh* v. *Arton* (1869) L.R. 8 Eq. 626. The tenant's right has been defined to continue during his original term and such further period of possession by him as he holds the premises under a right still to consider himself a tenant: *Mackintosh* v. *Trotter* (1838) 3 M. & W. 184.

[50] See *Smith* v. *City Petroleum* [1940] 1 All E.R. 260. It seems that the concept of "reasonable time" is derived from the definition of the right as given in n. 43, above or the necessary rule upon the determination of a life tenancy stated below. See *Ex p. Brook* (1878) 10 Ch.D. 100, 109, C.A.

established principle stated above which appears to have been overlooked. If the tenant forbears to exercise this privilege within this period, the law may presume that he voluntarily relinquishes his claim in favour of his landlord.[51] Hence it follows that if a tenant from year to year of a house dies, and his personal representative gives a notice to quit, he should take care to remove the fixtures, or dispose of the right of the deceased to them, before such notice expires. In the case of a tenant for life, or in tail, his general representative must, it would seem, remove the fixtures to which he is entitled within a reasonable time after the death of the deceased.

---

[51] *Lyde* v. *Russell* (1830) 1 B. & A. 394; *Smith* v. *City Petroleum Co. Ltd.* [1940] 1 All E.R. 260. See n. 39, *ante.*

CHAPTER 46

DEVOLUTION OF CLAIMS

A *thing* or *chose in action* is a right to be asserted, or property reducible into possession by an action, either at law or in equity. The expression includes the inchoate right of a person interested under a will or intestacy to enforce the proper administration of the estate. Thus the personal representative of a person interested in another estate in course of administration will have such a claim or *thing in action* vested in him.[1]

The subject of the present chapter will be considered firstly as to the general question as to what claims (including actions which arise by reason of the death) survive to the executor or administrator. Secondly, particular instances where the executor or administrator is entitled to claims, which the deceased might have put in suit, and where he is not so entitled. Since the rights which devolve are complemented by the liabilities which survive this chapter should be read in conjunction with Chapter 48.[2]

1.—WHAT CLAIMS DEVOLVE ON OR ACCRUE TO THE EXECUTOR OR ADMINISTRATOR

Causes of action, survive

The general rule has been established from the earliest times, that the right of action on which the testator or intestate might have sued in his lifetime survives his death, and is transmitted to his executor or administrator.[3] The rule was recognised by statutes,[4] and later by the Law Reform (Miscellaneous Provisions) Act 1934, s.1, as formerly amended by the Law Reform (Limitation of Actions) Act 1954, s.4,[5] so that on the death of any

---

[1] *Commr. of Stamp Duties* v. *Livingston* [1965] A.C. 694, 717; *Re Leigh* [1970] Ch. 277; *Re K.* [1986] Ch. 188; *Ayerst, V.C. & K. (Construction) Ltd.* [1976] A.C. 167, 177. As to such inchoate right, see *post*, p. 1050. As to the continuation of actions begun by the deceased in his lifetime see *post*, p. 868 *et seq.*, and as to choses in action which arise *after* death see *post*, pp. 874 *et seq.*

[2] See *post*, p. 553.

[3] (1699) 1 Saund. 216a; n. (1) to *Wheatly* v. *Lane*. The right of executors to sue was extended to administrators, by stat. 31 Edw. 3, stat. 1, c. 11. It was held in *Cobbett* v. *Clutton* (1826) 2 C. & P. 471 that an executor was entitled to possession and contents of a deed box of the deceased without giving a schedule of contents to solicitors to whom it had been passed by a third party. As to survival of actions against the personal representative, see *post*, pp. 553 *et seq.* For a recent example of an administratrix suing on the contract of the deceased, see *Beswick* v. *Beswick* [1968] A.C. 58, 77, 81, 87, 100–102. See also *post*, p. 518.

[4] Edw. 1, stat. 1, c. 23; 4 Edw. 3, c. 7; and 31 Edw. 3, stat. 1, c. 11. These statutes were replaced by the Administration of Estates Act 1925, s.26(1), which was repealed by the Law Reform (Miscellaneous Provisions) Act 1934, s.1(7).

[5] Now repealed. See the Proceedings Against Estates Act 1970, *post*, p. 904.

person after July 25, 1934, all causes of action vested in him survive for the benefit of his estate. This includes, but is not confined to, rights that can be enforced by action so long as they are rights and not mere hopes or contingencies.[6] The criterion is the loss to the deceased and not the loss to the estate.[7]

Thus an executor or administrator may recover debts of every description due to the deceased, either debts of record as judgments, or recognisances, or debts due on special contracts, as for rent, or arrears of a rentcharge; or on bonds and covenants under seal; or debts on simple contracts and promises not in writing, either express or implied.[8] He may proceed to taxation and enforcement of an order, including an order for costs,[9] even if the proceedings in question were not an "action" and were purely "personal" (e.g. matrimonial) so long as the order has actually been made before the death.[10] Again, where the goods of the testator taken away continued in specie in the hands of the wrongdoer, it was decided under the old procedure that replevin and detinue would lie for the executor to recover back the specific goods, etc.,[11] and, in case they were sold, an action for money had and received to recover their value.[12] Similarly, a personal representative may obtain an order for specific performance,[13] but can only stand in the shoes of the deceased and cannot escape a plea of laches by pleading want of knowledge.[14]

Contract broken in deceased's lifetime

Where a breach of a contract, to which the deceased was a party, took place during his lifetime, the cause of action thereby arising in favour of the deceased will, by virtue of the Law Reform (Miscellaneous Provisions) Act 1934, s.1(1) (as amended), survive for the benefit of his estate. The wide terms of the enactment clearly make obsolete a number of former rules of law on the survival of the right to sue on a broken contract; but the general rule before 1934 was that a cause of action arising from a breach of contract survived for the benefit of the estate of the deceased, unless the action was in substance an action for injuries to the person.[15]

Even where the contract which was broken during the lifetime of the deceased was a mere personal contract, it is clear that the cause of action

[6] See R.S.C. Ord. 15, r. 7, and *Sugden* v. *Sugden* [1957] P. 99. As to rights of a purely personal nature which do not survive, see *post*, p. 517. As to claims against the estate, see *post*, p. 808 *et seq*.

[7] *Adsett* v. *West* [1983] 1 Q.B. 826, 841.

[8] Wentw.Off.Ex., 14th ed., p. 159; Com.Dig. Administration, B.; Toller 6th ed. p. 157.

[9] *Kelly* v. *Kelly and Brown* [1961] P. 94.

[10] *Maconochie* v. *Maconochie* [1916] P. 326; *Dipple* v. *Dipple* [1942] P. 65.

[11] *Le Mason* v. *Dixon* (1628) Sir W. Jones 173, 174; 1 Saund. 217, n. (1).

[12] 1 Saund. 217, n. (1).

[13] *Beswick* v. *Beswick* [1968] A.C. 58, 102. A third party may enforce such an order under R.S.C. Ord. 45, r. 9.

[14] *M.E.P.C. Ltd.* v. *Christian-Edwards* [1979] 3 W.L.R. 713, H.L.

[15] See 12th ed. of this work, pp. 501, 502.

thereby vested in the deceased will survive for the benefit of his estate.[16]
This reverses the common law rule as stated in earlier editions of this work,
that, as a result of the decision in *Raymond* v. *Fitch*,[17] a personal representative could probably sue for any breach of contract in the lifetime of the
deceased unless it was a mere personal contract, when the rule *actio personalis moritur cum persona* applied.

Actions survive to the executor or administrator only

The executor or administrator is the only representative of the deceased
that the law will regard in respect of his personalties, and no word introduced into a contract or obligation can transfer to another his exclusive
rights derived from such representation.

The representation of the deceased, in matters of contract, by his executor or administrator is so complete that it is not necessary, in order to transmit to the executor or administrator a right of enforcing a contract, that he
should be named in the terms of it. Thus if money be payable to B., without naming his executor, his executor or administrator will have an action
for it.[18] So if money be payable to A., *or his assigns*, his executor will take
it; for he is assignee in law.[19]

"Personal" contracts

However, contractual rights based upon personal considerations do not
devolve[20] and it must be appreciated that the executor's right to enforce a
contract does not extend the contractual rights of the deceased.

A good illustration of this is the old case of *Neal* v. *Hanbury*,[21] where a
testator gave an annuity of £5 to his nephew Thomas Neal, without adding
the words "and his executors and administrators," the legacy to be paid
half-yearly during the life of the testator's wife, on condition that the
nephew behaved civilly to her, "for he was a very lewd, dissolute man."
Thomas Neal died during the lifetime of the testator's widow, and it was
held that the annuity died with him, the condition added making it plain
that the annuity was personal to Thomas Neal. The cessation of the annuity
would not, however, affect the right of Thomas Neal's executor to claim
any arrears of the annuity.

There is no general rule that divorce proceedings must abate on the
death of one of the parties.[22]

---

[16] Law Reform (Miscellaneous Provisions) Act 1934, s.1(1), as amended.
[17] (1835) 2 C.M. & R. 588; followed in *Ricketts* v. *Weaver* (1844) 12 M. & W. 718.
[18] Com.Dig. Administration, B. 13.
[19] *Pease* v. *Mead* (1613) Hob. 9; Wentw.Off.Ex., 14th ed., p. 215; the Administration of
Estates Act 1925, s.1(2).
[20] As to contracts of this nature, see *post*, pp. 527, 528, *et seq.* and *ante*, p. 556 *et seq.*
[21] (1701) Pr.Ch. 173. See also *Barford* v. *Stuckey* (1823) 1 Bing. 225.
[22] *Barder* v. *Caluori* [1988] A.C. 20.

Contract for benefit of third party

A personal representative may sue for specific performance and damages for the breach of an enforceable contract entered into by the deceased, though made exclusively for the benefit of a third party.[23]

Life assurance

It is contrary to public policy for the personal representative of an assured person to recover on a policy of assurance on the assured's life if the death of the assured was caused by suicide.[24]

Tort

Originally actions in tort died with the person.[25] Since 1934[26] such causes of action survive with the exception of causes of action for defamation. Where the cause of action survives for the benefit of a deceased person's estate, the damages recoverable must not include any exemplary damages, and "where the death of that person has been caused by the act or omission which gives rise to the cause of action," the damages recoverable are "calculated without reference to any loss or gain to his estate consequent on his death, except that a sum in respect of funeral expenses may be included."[27]

Under this provision damages can be recovered by the representatives[28] of a deceased person for the deceased's diminished expectation of happiness,[29] (but not for loss of expectation of life[29a]) as well as for the pain and suffering of the deceased between the time of the wrong and the death,[30] so long as there is clear evidence of reasonably prolonged suffering.[31] The provision, however, does not abrogate the common law rule in *Baker* v. *Bolton*,[32] that no one can maintain an action in tort against a person who by his wrongful act, neglect or default has caused the death of another.[33] Damages for lost years do not

---

[23] See *Anon.* (*Bafeild* v. *Collard*) (1646) Sty. 6; *Beswick* v. *Beswick* [1968] A.C. 58, 100–102.

[24] *Beresford* v. *Royal Insurance Co. Ltd.* [1938] A.C. 586. This rule does not exclude a widow personal representative from recovering in her own right under the Fatal Accidents Act. *Pigney* v. *Pointer* [1957] 1 W.L.R. 1121. Suicide is no longer a crime. See the Suicide Act 1961 and p. 972 *post*. *Quaere*, the effect of this on the rule: (1962) 25 M.L.R. 60.

[25] See *ante* p. 559. An action for damage to property, as for defamation of title, does not die: *Hatchard* v. *Mege* (1887) L.R. 18 Q.B.D. 771.

[26] Law Reform (Miscellaneous Provisions) Act 1934, s.1(1). As to Crown liability, see *Bell* v. *Secretary of State* [1986] 1 Q.B. 322.

[27] *Ibid.* subs. (2).

[28] A compromise reached before grant is not binding if not for the benefit of the estate: *Mills* v. *Anderson* [1984] Q.B. 304. See p. 92 *ante*.

[29] *Rose* v. *Ford* [1937] A.C. 826; *Benham* v. *Gambling* [1941] A.C. 157. For further cases, see *Annual Survey of English Law*, 1937, pp. 172–174, and (1941) 4 M.L.R. 81 *et seq*. Expectation of happiness has been held to be less in the case of a criminal: *Burns* v. *Edman* [1970] 2 Q.B. 541. See also *Gammell* v. *Wilson* [1981] 2 W.L.R. 248. (The claim comprises future earnings but not earnings lost before death for which a separate claim vests in the executors.)

[29a] See further s. 1 of the Administration of Justice Act 1982.

[30] *Rose* v. *Ford* [1936] 1 K.B. 90; [1937] A.C. 826; *Kandalla* v. *B.E.A.* [1981] 1 Q.B. 158.

[31] *Bishop* v. *Cunard White Star* [1950] P. 240.

[32] (1808) 1 Camp. 493.

[33] *Ibid.* n. 29.

include sums that the deceased would have spent on himself.[34] A personal representative may also enforce the deceased's rights of contribution against a joint tortfeasor.[35]

Continuing injury to freehold

Since the Land Transfer Act 1897 a personal representative may, apart from the above provisions, bring an action for an injury to the freehold of the deceased if that injury continues after the death. He is also, it seems, entitled to all equitable remedies in this respect subsisting in the deceased.[36]

Fatal Accidents Act 1976

Under the Fatal Accidents Act 1976[37] the executor or administrator of a deceased person,[38] including an alien,[39] may bring or continue[40] an action for the benefit of the wife, husband, or former wife or husband parent and child of the deceased and (since July 29, 1959) for the benefit also of or the issue of a brother, sister, uncle or aunt,[41] including adopted and illegitimate children and treating affinity as consanguinity and half-blood as whole. 1, If there is no executor or administrator or if he brings no such action within six months of the death, action may be brought by and in the name of any person for whose benefit it might have been brought.[42] The action is for damages for negligence[43] or breach of contract[44] where death has been caused by such neglect or default as would have entitled the injured party if alive to claim such damages.[45] Only one action lies[46] and this must be brought[47] within three

---

[34] *Kandalla* v. *B.E.A.* [1981] 1 Q.B. 158; *Adsett* v. *West* [1983] 1 Q.B. 826.

[35] *Ronex* v. *John Laing* [1983] Q.B. 398.

[36] See, *Jones* v. *Simes* (1890) 43 Ch.D. 607.

[37] Consolidating the Fatal Accidents Acts, 1846 to 1959 (except certain provisions of the 1959 Act, as amended by section 3 of the Administration of Justice Act 1982). As to these Acts see further *Clerk & Lindsell on Torts*, 16th ed., pp., 6–10.

[38] Fatal Accidents Act 1976, s.2(1). A plaintiff's suing as administrator must have an English grant (*Finnegan* v. *Cementation Co.* [1953] 1 Q.B. 688).

[39] *The Explorer* [1870] L.R. 3 Adm. & Ecc. 289; *Davidson* v. *Hill* [1901] 2 K.B. 606 (dissenting from the decision of Darling J. in *Adam* v. *British & Foreign Steamship Co.* [1898] 2 Q.B. 430).

[40] See *Pickett* v. *B.R.E. Ltd.* [1980] A.C. 136.

[41] Fatal Accidents Act 1976, s.1.

[42] Fatal Accidents Act 1976, s.2(2). Such person is responsible for informing and naming all other defendants: *Cooper* v. *Williams* [1963] 2 Q.B. 567.

[43] Fatal Accidents Act 1976, s.1(1) (wrongful act, neglect or default). See, *e.g. Kirkham* v. *Manchester Police* [1990] 2 W.L.R. 1987 (avoidable suicide).

[44] *Grein* v. *Imperial Airways* [1937] 1 K.B. 50.

[45] Fatal Accidents Act 1976, s.1(1) (see s. 3 of the Administration of Justice Act 1982). The claim may be barred by discharge in the lifetime of the deceased (*Read* v. *G.E.R.* (1868) L.R. 3 Q.B. 555).

[46] Fatal Accidents Act 1976, s.2(3). Full particulars of the claim and persons on whose behalf it is made must be given (s.2(4)): *Chapman* v. *Rothwell* (1858) 1 E.B. & E. 168; *Cooper* v. *Williams* [1963] 2 Q.B. 567; *Stebbings* v. *Holst* [1953] 1 W.L.R. 603. A claim may now be included for bereavement limited at present to a sum of £3500). See Administration of Justice Act 1982, s.3.

[47] A second defendant cannot be added by the plaintiff out of time, but such a person may still be liable to contribution under third-party notice from the original defendant, notwithstanding expiration of time (*Morgan* v. *Ashmore* [1953] 1 W.L.R. 418).

years of the death, subject to the power of the court to extend that period if material facts of a decisive nature were outside the knowledge of a person entitled to benefit by the action.[48] However, the claim should always be made as soon as possible, and in cases where the Merchant Shipping Acts apply, a failure at least to claim may result in total or partial loss of the remedy.[49] Care should be taken to distinguish between a claim by a personal representative in such capacity and a claim by a dependant for the time limit may preclude a widow, wrongly described as administrator, from claiming later under the Act.[50]

The remedy given by the Act is to individuals and not to a class, so that if a death results in no loss of property to the family of the deceased but changes the mode of distribution among the members, those adversely affected can claim.[51]

Effect

The effect is to give the representative a cause of action beyond that which the deceased would himself have had,[52] for the damages are to be "proportioned to the injury resulting from the death to the dependants respectively."[53] These Acts, therefore, give an additional right to that which devolves upon the death, but are conveniently discussed in this context.

Damages[54]

Damages are recoverable only on evidence[55] of actual pecuniary loss[56] arising as a direct consequence of the death.[57] No account is taken of benefits which have accrued or will or may accrue as a result of the death.[58]

---

[48] Limitation Act 1963, s.3, as amended by the Law Reform (Miscellaneous Provisions) Act 1971, s.20).

[49] *The Alma* [1903] P. 55.

[50] *Finnegan* v. *Cementation Co.* [1953] 1 Q.B. 688; *Bowler* v. *John Mowlem* [1954] 1 W.L.R. 1445; *Stebbings* v. *Holst* [1953] 1 W.L.R. 603.

[51] *Pym* v. *G.N. Ry.* (1863) 4 B. & Sm. 396.

[52] *Pym* v. *G.N. Ry.* (1862) 2 B. & Sm. 767; 4 *ibid.* 406; *Nunan* v. *Southern Ry.* [1924] 1 K.B. 223; *Grein* v. *Imperial Airways* [1937] 1 K.B. 50. Summary procedure may be appropriate (*Dummer* v. *Brown* [1953] 1 Q.B. 710).

[53] See s.3(1) of the Fatal Accidents Act 1976 (as substituted by s.3 of the Administration of Justice Act 1982).

[54] For a fuller treatment, reference should be made to Clerk and Lindsell, *Torts*, 16th ed., Chap. 6.

[55] *Duckworth* v. *Johnson* (1859) 4 H. & N. 653; *Barnett* v. *Cohen* [1921] 2 K.B. 461; *Burns* v. *Edman* [1970] 2 W.L.R. 1005.

[56] *Blake* v. *Midland Ry.* (1852) 18 Q.B. 93.

[57] *Burgess* v. *Florence Nightingale Hospital* [1955] 1 Q.B. 349; *Smith* v. *Leech Brain & Co.* [1962] 2 Q.B. 405.

[58] s.4 of the Act. *Pidduck* v. *Eastern Scottish* [1989] 1 W.L.R. 817; [1990] 1 W.L.R. 993 C.A.

"Benefit" includes benefit under the enactments relating to social security including enactments in force in Northern Ireland, and any payment by a friendly society or trade union for the relief or maintenance of a member's dependants.[59] Thus no account is taken of widow's benefit, guardian's allowance, retirement pension payable to a widow by virtue of her husband's insurance death grant, or death benefit under the Social Security Act 1975; nor can a jury take into consideration mental suffering, loss of society or voluntary payments made out of generosity, charity or a sense of moral obligation.[60] Account must, however, be taken of all other circumstances as at date of trial,[61] including the prospect of a Crown pension payable to the dependants,[62] the effect of an adoption order,[63] funeral expenses incurred by the dependants claiming,[64] all pecuniary advantages which would have flowed from the survival of the deceased,[65] so long as there was a reasonable expectation of these and not a mere speculative possibility,[66] any benefit to be derived from the estate of the deceased[67] or as a direct consequence of the death,[68] the tax that would have had to be paid on the earnings of the deceased, the tax that will have to be paid upon any annuity purchased out of the sum awarded,[69] and estate duty (and now, presumably, inheritance transfer tax) not saved on a gift.[70] When "account" is so taken, this must be on a broad basis and not necessarily "pound for pound."[71]

---

[59] See s.3 of the Administration of Justice Act 1982, substituting new sections.

[59] *Ibid.* n. 58.

[60] *Peacock* v. *Amusement Equipment Co.* [1954] 2 Q.B. 347; *Rawlinson* v. *Babcock & Wilcox* [1967] 1 W.L.R. 481; *Mead* v. *Clarke Chapman* [1956] 1 W.L.R. 76.

[61] *Mead* v. *Clarke Chapman* [1956] 1 W.L.R. 76; *Voller* v. *Dairy Produce Ltd.* [1962] 1 W.L.R. 960.

[62] *Baker* v. *Dalgleish, etc., Co.* [1922] 1 K.B. 361; *Johnson* v. *Hill* [1945] 2 All E.R. 272. The position is otherwise in a claim for negligence at common law; see *Payne* v. *Railway Executive* [1952] 1 K.B. 26.

[63] *Watson* v. *Willmott* [1991] 1 Q.B. 140.

[64] s.3(3) of the Act. *Burns* v. *Edman* [1970] 2 W.L.R. 1005. Reasonable expenses only are allowed (*Stanton* v. *Ewart F. Youldon Ltd.* [1960] 1 W.L.R. 543).

[65] *Franklin* v. *S.E. Ry.* (1858) 3 H. & N. 211; *Dalton* v. *S.E. Ry.* (1851) 4 C.B.(N.S.) 296; *Duckworth* v. *Johnson, supra; Pym* v. *G.N. Ry.* (1863) 4 B. & Sm. 396; *Sykes* v. *N.E. Ry.* (1875) 44 L.J.C.P. 191; *Hetherington* v. *N.E. Ry.* (1882) 9 Q.B.D. 160; *Berry* v. *Humm & Co.* [1915] 1 K.B. 627. *White* v. *L.T.E.* [1982] 1 Q.B. 489. Advantages flowing from crime are discounted; *Burns* v. *Edman* [1970] 2 W.L.R. 1005.

[66] *Barnett* v. *Cohen* [1921] 2 K.B. 461; *Davies* v. *Taylor* [1974] A.C 207 (divorce in prospect).

[67] *Grand Trunk Ry.* v. *Jennings*, 13 App.Cas. 800; *Roughead* v. *Ry. Executive* [1949] W.N. 280; *Whittome* v. *Coates* [1965] 1 W.L.R. 1285; *Voller* v. *Dairy Produce Ltd.* [1962] 1 W.L.R. 960.

[68] *Jenner* v. *Allen West* [1959] 1 W.L.R. 554. A voluntary gift is not within this category (*Peacock* v. *Amusement Equipment* [1954] 2 Q.B. 347). See further, *post*, p. 523.

[69] *British Transport Commission* v. *Gourley* [1956] A.C. 185; *Taylor* v. *O'Connor* [1971] A.C. 115.

[70] *Davies* v. *Whiteways Cyder Co. Ltd.* [1975] 2 Q.B. 262.

[71] See *Daniels* v. *Jones* [1961] 1 W.L.R. 1103. The elements of estimate should be weighed sympathetically and fairly and with a sense of proportion: *Mallett* v. *McMonagle* [1970] A.C. 166.

Account is not now to be taken of a widow's remarriage or prospects of remarriage.[72] The practice under the Fatal Accidents Act is generally to follow the principles set out by Lord Wright in *Davies* v. *Powell Duffryn Associated Collieries Ltd.*[73] Lord Wright said: "It is a hard matter of pounds, shillings and pence, subject to the element of reasonable future probabilities. The starting point is the amount of wages which the deceased was earning, the ascertainment of which to some extent may depend on the regularity of his employment. Then there is an estimate of how much was required or expended for his own personal and living expenses. The balance will give a datum or basic figure which will generally be turned into a lump sum by taking a certain number of years' purchase. That sum, however, has to be taxed down by having due regard to uncertainties."

Living expenses are assessed as a percentage of the available surplus after deducting from the net earnings the cost of maintaining the deceased in his station of life.[74]

Interest on damages

There is a distinction between damages under the Fatal Accidents Acts[75] and damages for non-economic loss in personal injury cases.[76] In both categories of case the courts offer guidelines[77] and in neither is account taken of inflation[78] or a high rate of interest allowed.[79]

In the normal fatal accident case, the damages are split into two parts: (a) the pecuniary loss which the dependants have sustained from date of death to date of trial and (b) the pecuniary loss which they will sustain after date of trial. Interest on the "pre-trial" loss is estimated at half the short-term interest rates during the period in question, no interest is allowed on the "future" loss nor is any allowance made for inflation. These factors will have been considered in fixing the multiplicand used to assess the annual dependency at date of trial.[80] Interest was formerly at the discretion of the court.[81] Income tax is not payable on such interest.[82] Interest may be reduced to reflect the plaintiffs delay.[83]

---

[72] s.3(2) of the Act.
[73] [1942] A.C. 601, 617.
[74] *Harris* v. *Empress Motors Ltd.* [1984] 1 W.L.R. 212.
[75] *Cookson* v. *Knowles* [1979] A.C. 556, 573, 579.
[76] *Wright* v. *British Railways Board* [1983] 2 A.C. 773.
[77] *Spittle* v. *Bunney* [1988] 1 W.L.R. 847.
[78] *Auty* v. *National Coal Board* [1985] 1 W.L.R. 784.
[79] *Birkett* v. *Hayes* [1982] 1 W.L.R. 816; *Roberts* v. *Johnstone* [1989] 1 Q.B. 878, 892. Known facts are however taken into account *Corbett* v. *Barking Health Authority* [1991] 2 Q.B. 408.
[80] *Cookson* v. *Knowles* [1979] A.C. 556, 573; *Jefford* v. *Gee* [1970] 2 Q.B. 130; *Graham* v. *Dodds* [1983] 1 W.L.R. 808; the Administration of Justice Act 1969, s.22.
[81] Law Reform (Miscellaneous Provisions) Act 1934, s.3. As to the former practice on summary judgment see *Gardner* v. *Sheffield Bros.* [1978] 1 W.L.R. 916, 918.
[82] Income & Corporation Taxes Act 1988, s.329.
[83] *Spittle* v. *Bunney* [1988] 1 W.L.R. 847.

Distribution of damages and compromise

When the damages have been assessed the defendant is not concerned with the distribution among the dependants.[84] If proceedings under the Acts are compromised and a lump sum paid to the executors the Chancery Division has jurisdiction to apportion this sum among the dependants and will apply the same principles as a jury would be directed to apply under the Acts.[85] A compromise involving a dependent who is not *sui juris* must be sanctioned by the court.[86]

Duplication of remedies

The rights conferred by the Law Reform (Miscellaneous Provisions) Act 1934 for the benefit of the estates of deceased persons are expressly declared[87] to be in addition to and not in derogation of any rights conferred on the dependants of deceased persons by what are now the Fatal Accidents Act 1976 or the Carriage by Air Act 1961. Damages recovered under the 1934 Act form part of the estate and are answerable for debts and death duties. Damages under the Fatal Accidents Act do not form part of the estate and are not so answerable. They are for the benefit of the dependants only. Since, however, the object of the Fatal Accidents Act is "to compensate the recipient on a balance of gains and losses for the injury sustained by the death"[88] it follows that if a dependant benefits from the estate (in consequence of the 1934 Act, or indeed otherwise[89]) the net[90] benefit so obtained from the estate must be deducted from the measure of damages under the Fatal Accidents Act. However, it has been held that where an award under the Law Reform Act includes a sum for earnings lost by the deceased between injury and death this should not normally be deducted.[91]

Carriage by Air 1961: Carriage by Railway Act 1972: Carriage of Passengers by Road Act 1974

These Acts give the force of law to a number of international conventions. The provisions of the conventions are in effect limited to international carriage, but the Carriage by Air Act, unlike the other two Acts, applies to

[84] *Eifert* v. *Holt's Transport* [1951] 2 All E.R. 655n. This decision is open to criticism on the ground that a distribution to a dependant who benefits from the estate is *pro tanto* reduced (see below), so that damages cannot properly be assessed in a "total" sum without first assessing the distributions and deducting all relevant "net benefits." See further Clerk and Lindsell, *Torts*, 16th ed., para. 6–20.
[85] *Bulmer* v. *Bulmer* (1883) 25 Ch.D. 409.
[86] For procedure, see R.S.C. Ord. 80, and the notes thereto in the *Supreme Court Practice*.
[87] s.1(5); *The Oropesa* [1943] P. 32. It had already been established before 1954 that proceedings under the Fatal Accidents Acts were different in character from the claim of an administrator at common law. *Leggott* v. *G.N.R.* (1876) 1 Q.B.D. 599.
[88] *Davies* v. *Powell Duffryn Collieries Ltd.* [1942] A.C. 601, 623.
[89] See *ante*, p. 521.
[90] See *per* Lord Wright [1942] A.C. 601, 613; *Feay* v. *Barnwell* [1938] 1 All E.R. 31.
[91] See *Murray* v. *Shuter* [1976] 1 Q.B. 972, 984.

non-international carriage as well. However, a passenger travelling in England and Wales by either air, rail or road may of course be engaged in an international journey. For details of the provisions of the Acts reference should be made to Clerk and Lindsell, *Torts*.[92]

Parliamentary Commissioner Act 1967

There is a statutory right for the personal representative to make a complaint where the deceased was entitled to do so.[93]

2.—PARTICULAR INSTANCES AND EXCEPTIONS

Covenants relating to land

A covenant relating to any land of the covenantee, made after 1925,[94] is deemed to be made with the covenantee and his successors in title and the persons deriving title under him or them,[95] but this is not of itself sufficient to effect annexation of the benefit to the land in question.[96] It follows that such covenants made after 1925 can be enforced by the personal representatives of the covenantee (before any assent is made) whether or not they are expressly named in the covenant, so long as such covenants touch and concern the land.

Again, covenants for title which, by section 76[97] of the Law of Property Act 1925, are implied into certain conveyances of land, enure for the benefit of the covenantee and all persons deriving title under him.[98] Accordingly, such covenants are enforceable by the personal representatives of the covenantee before assent made, although they are not of themselves sufficient to effect annexation.[99]

The benefit of restrictive covenants annexed to land passes to the assigns of the covenantee, but the benefit of covenants not so annexed cannot be separately assigned after the land benefited has been conveyed.[1] An executor, being an assign in law, can enforce covenants though the benefit

---

[92] 16th ed., 6–25—6–27.
[93] s.6(2).
[94] If the covenant was entered into before 1926, *semble*, since the Land Transfer Act 1897, the personal representative could, before making an assent or conveyance, enforce the covenant. *cf. Sainsbury* v. *Enfield* [1989] 1 W.L.R. 590.
[95] Law of Property Act 1925, s.78, replacing, in case of covenants made after 1925, Conveyancing Act 1881, s.58; *Smith and Snipes Hall Farm* v. *River Douglas Catchment Board* [1949] 2 K.B. 500; *Roake* v. *Chadha* [1984] 1 W.L.R. 40.
[96] *Sainsbury* v. *Enfield* [1989] 1 W.L.R. 590. See also Megarry & Wade, 5th ed., *The Law of Real Property* 785–787.
[97] Replacing Conveyancing Act 1881, s.7.
[98] See the Law of Property Act 1925, Sched. 2. And see also s.77.
[99] See n. 96.
[1] See *Re Rutherford's Conveyance* [1938] Ch. 396; *Chambers* v. *Randall* [1923] 1 Ch. 149. A restrictive covenant made after 1925 is void as against a purchaser of the land restricted unless registered under the Land Charges Act 1925, s.10(1), Class D (ii).

of them may not be so definitely attached to the land as to pass by a mere conveyance.[2]

As the benefit of a covenant to pay a rentcharge does not run with the rentcharge, the representatives of a deceased rentchargee cannot sue on such a covenant.[3]

If a covenant relating to freehold land of the covenantee is broken during the lifetime of the covenantee and the damage arising from such breach accrues before his death, any damages recovered by his personal representatives will be held by them as part of his personal estate.[4] But where the substantial damage takes place after the death of the covenantee, the damages recovered by his personal representatives will (subject to the purposes of administration) be held by them for the person entitled to the freehold land to which the covenant was annexed, even though the formal breach of the covenant occurred in the lifetime of the covenantee.[5]

It would seem that similar principles would apply on the breach of a covenant for title or indemnity relating to leasehold land of the covenantee.[6]

The benefit of covenants and powers given by way of indemnity against rent or breaches of covenants or conditions in relation to land are enforceable by the estate owner, including a representative, of the land affected.[7]

Annuities

An annuity in its original sense is a yearly payment of a certain sum of money granted to another in fee, for life, or for years, charging the person of the grantor only.[8] As it concerns no land, it is so far considered personal property that, although granted to a person and his heirs or the heirs of his body, it is not an hereditament within the Statute of Mortmain, 7 Edw. 1 stat. 2,[9] nor entailable within the statute *de donis*[10]; though it can now be entailed by virtue of section 130 of the Law of Property Act 1925. Thus, in *Lord Stafford* v. *Buckley*,[11] Lord Hardwicke decided that an annuity in fee of £1,000, granted by King Charles the Second out of the Barbados duties, was not realty within the statute *de donis*, or the Statute of Frauds, but a

---

[2] *Ives* v. *Brown* [1919] 2 Ch. 314. *Newton Abbot Co-operative Society* v. *Williamson and Treadgold* [1952] Ch. 286. And see the Law of Property Act 1925, ss.78 and 80(2); 1 Wolst. & Ch., 13th ed., pp. 162–165. For restrictive covenants generally, see Preston and Newsom *Restrictive Covenants Affecting Freehold Land.*

[3] *Grant* v. *Edmondson* [1931] 1 Ch. 1.

[4] Even at common law the executor (not the heir) could enforce such covenants: *Lucy* v. *Levington*, 2 Lev. 26; even though there was no allegtion of damage to the personal estate: *Ricketts* v. *Weaver*, 12 M. & W. 718. See also 2 Dart., 8th ed., p. 674.

[5] At common law the heir (not the executor) could recover such damages: *Kingdom* v. *Nottle*, 1 M. & S. 355; *King* v. *Jones*, 5 Taunt. 418; affirmed, 4 M. & S. 188.

[6] As to the recovery of rent by personal representatives, see *post*, pp. 531 *et seq.*

[7] Law of Property Act 1925, s.189(2).

[8] Co.Litt. 144b.

[9] *Ibid.* 2a, n. (1), by Hargrave.

[10] *Ibid.* 20a, and n. (4), by Hargrave.

[11] (1759) 2 Ves.Sen. 170.

personal inheritance.[12] In *Aubin* v. *Daly*,[13] it was held that the annuity which was the subject of Lord Hardwicke's decision in *Lord Stafford* v. *Buckley* was personal property and duly passed under a residuary clause to the executors.

But an annuity when granted with words of inheritance partakes of the nature of real property in that formerly it went to the heir to the exclusion of the executor.[14] Unless, however, words of inheritance were employed in the grant, it was held that the annuity passed to the executors as personal estate.[15]

Lord Coke calls an annuity granted to a man and his heirs[16] a fee simple personal.[17] Being of the nature of personal estate it did not devolve on personal representatives under Part I of the Land Transfer Act 1897; nor, *semble*, does it fall within Part I of the Administration of Estates Act 1925. On the other hand, the rules of succession applicable before 1926 to a personal inheritance have been abolished[18] and the succession to a personal inheritance (including an annuity formerly limited to a person and his heirs),[19] on an intestacy after 1925, is governed by Part IV of the Administration of Estates Act 1925.[20] But query whether such a personal inheritance forms part of the personal estate of a deceased person within Part III of that Act so as to be held by his personal representatives as part of his assets. It is conceived that that is the case.[21]

The above-mentioned annuities were held to be personal property on the ground that they were in no way connected with land. But where an annuity charged upon land is vested in a person for an interest not ceasing on his death, being of the nature of real property, it devolves, on his death, upon his personal representatives.[22]

Shares

Similarly, where an inheritance is granted, which arises out of land, it is considered real property. Thus, in *Buckeridge* v. *Ingram*,[23] shares in the navigation of the River Avon, under the statute 10 Anne, c. 2, were held

---

[12] 2 Ves.Sen. 178; and see *Lady Holdernesse* v. *Lord Carmarthen* (1784) 1 Bro.C.C. 377. *cf. Turner* v. *Turner* (1783) 1 Bro.C.C. 316, 325; *Re Rivett-Carnac* (1885) 30 Ch.D. 136, 141.

[13] (1820) 4 B. & A. 59.

[14] *Turner* v. *Turner* (1885) Ambl. 782, 783; *Stafford* v. *Buckley* (1750) 2 Ves.Sen. 170, 179, as to devolution of real estate, see *post*, pp. 543 *et seq.*

[15] *Taylor* v. *Martindale* (1841) 12 Sim. 158; *Parsons* v. *Parsons* (1869) L.R. 8 Eq. 260.

[16] In a limitation of such a character made after 1925 the heirs could only take as purchasers: the Law of Property Act 1925, s.131.

[17] Co.Litt. 2a.

[18] Administration of Estates Act 1925, s.45.

[19] *Ibid.* n. 16.

[20] See definition of real and personal estate for the purposes of this Part of the Act, s.52.

[21] *cf.* however, the definition of real estate for the purpose of Pt. III of the Act, s.55(1)(xix).

[22] Administration of Estates Act 1925, ss.1, 3, (1)(i).

[23] (1795) 2 Ves. 653.

real estate.[24] But in *Bligh* v. *Brent*[25] the Court of Exchequer held that shares in the Chelsea Water Works were to be considered as personal property. It was formerly usual when Acts of Parliament were obtained for the making of navigable canals, and similar works, to procure a clause to be inserted, directing that the shares, should be deemed to be personal estate.[26]

By section 182 of the Companies Act 1985 it is expressly provided that the shares or other interest of any member in a company are personal and not real estate.[27]

Stock in the public funds

Such stock, having been made personal property by the statutes, is like all other personal property, assets in the hands of the executor; and devolves upon him.[28] It is transferable by instrument in writing in accordance with the Stock Transfer Act 1963 delivered to the Bank of England.[29] The National Debt Act 1870[30] expressly provided that the interest of a stockholder is transferable by his executors and administrators, the grant must be produced for registration and all proving executors may be required to join in any transfer.

Servants and apprentices

By the death of a master his servant is discharged; hence the executors and administrators of the former could bring no action to enforce the contract of service after his death.[31] Nor had the executor or administrator, generally speaking, any interest in an apprentice bound to the deceased.[32] The master's interest was a right to his service only. So in *Rex* v. *Peck*,[33] Eyre J. said: "an apprenticeship is a personal trust between the master and servant, and determines by the death of either of them. And by the death of either of them, the end and design of the apprenticeship cannot be obtained; and it may be the executor is of another trade." This was the position at common law, and it appears still to be the position since the Law Reform (Miscellaneous Provisions) Act 1934 because although "personal"

---

[24] *Portmore* v. *Bunn* (1823) 1 B. & C. 699, 702; *Howse* v. *Chapman* (1799) 4 Ves. 543; and see *Drybutter* v. *Bartholomew* (1723) 2 P.Wms. 127; *Davall* v. *New River Co.* (1849) 3 De G. & Sm. 394. A lease of a lighthouse, and the tolls thereof, by the Corporation of Trinity House has been held to be a chattel real: *Ex p. Ellison* (1837) 2 Y. & C.Ex. 528.

[25] (1837) 2 Y. & C.Ex. 268. See *Hayter* v. *Tucker* (1858) 4 K. & J. 248.

[26] See *Thompson* v. *Thompson* (1844) 1 Coll. 381; *Robinson* v. *Addison* (1840) 2 Reav. 515.

[27] See *post* as to transfer of shares by personal representatives.

[28] *Bank of England* v. *Moffatt* (1791) 3 Bro.C.C. 260; *Bank of England* v. *Parsons* (1800) 5 Ves. 665; *Bank of England* v. *Lunn* (1809) 15 Ves. 569; *Franklin* v. *Bank of England* (1826) 1 Russ. 575; 9 B. & C. 156. See also *Churchill* v. *Bank of England* (1843) 11 M. & W. 323.

[29] See Stock Transfer Act 1982.

[30] s.23.

[31] Wentw.Off.Ex., 14th ed., p. 141. As to principal and agent, see *post*, p. 542. As to "personal" contracts, see *ante*, pp. 517.

[32] *Baxter* v. *Burfield* (1747) 1 Bott.P.L., 6th ed., pl. 696; 5th ed., pl. 819.

[33] (1698) 1 Salk. 66.

contracts are not excepted from the statutory "survival" thereby enacted there would seem in such cases to be, *ex hypothesi*, no right to action to survive.

However, in *Cooper* v. *Simmons*,[34] an infant, with the consent of his father, bound himself apprentice by indenture to a tradesman, "his executors and administrators such executors or administrators carrying on the same trade or business, and in the town of W., and with him, *and them*" to serve for the term of seven years; and the master, in consideration of the service of the apprentice, covenanted to teach and instruct him or cause him to be taught and instructed during the term. It was held that the apprentice was bound to serve the widow, who was executrix, whilst she carried on the same business in the town of W., and that she was bound to teach the apprentice. In such a case it would seem that the widow could sue independently of the conditions in the 1934 Act.

Difficulties have in the past arisen, when contracts for articles of apprenticeship have terminated by death of one party, as to return of premiums.[35] Such cases would now normally fall within the terms of the Law Reform (Frustrated Contracts) Act 1943 under which the court can award recovery of the whole or part of any sums paid or payable. For a solicitor the court's inherent jurisdiction might be used.[36]

Copyright

Copyright is personal property and vests in the representative of the deceased owner. It is therefore subject to the normal rules relating to personal property, with important an exception relating to copyright in original documents or other material things embodying unpublished works.

Section 93 of the Copyright, Designs & Patents Act 1988 provides that where under a bequest (whether specific or general) a person is entitled, beneficially or otherwise, to (a) an original document or other material thing recording or embodying a literary, dramatic, musical or artistic work which was not published before the death of the testator, or (b) an original material thing containing a sound recording or film which was not published before the death of the testator, the bequest is to be construed as including the copyright in the work in so far as the testator was the owner of the copyright immediately before his death unless a contrary intention is indicated in the testator's will or a codicil thereto.

This provision does not apply where the testator died before June 1,

---

[34] (1862) 7 H. & N. 707.

[35] See *Whincup* v. *Hughes* (1871) L.R. 6 C.P. 78; *Ferns* v. *Carr* (1885) 28 Ch.D. 409; *Re Thompson* (1848) 1 Ex. 864; *Hirst* v. *Tolson* (1850) 2 M. & G. 134; *Newton* v. *Rowse* (1687) 1 Vern. 460. See also *post*, p. 579.

[36] See Cordery's *Law of Solicitors*, 8th ed.

1957. Where the testator died on or after that date and before August 1, 1989, it applies only in relation to an original document embodying a work.[37]

Where an author died before June 1, 1957, the ownership after his death of a manuscript of his of a work which has not been published or performed in public is prima facie proof that the copyright is with the owner of the manuscript, provided that the manuscript was acquired under the author's testamentary disposition.[38]

Moral rights

The Copyright, Designs & Patents Act 1988 confers extensive new moral rights upon authors of copyright literary, dramatic, musical and artistic works and copyright films[39]: the right to be identified as author; the right to object to derogatory treatment; and rights in respect of false attribution of authorship (rights in relation to false attribution having existed under the Copyright Act 1956[40]). A right to privacy of certain photographs and films was also introduced by the 1988 Act.[41]

These rights are not assignable, [41a] but on the death of a person entitled to the right to be identified as author or director,[42] the right to object to derogatory treatment of a work,[43] and the right to privacy in certain photographs and films,[44] the right passes to such person as the deceased owner of the right may by testamentary disposition specifically direct. If there is no such direction, but the copyright in the work in question forms part of his estate, the right passes to the person to whom the copyright passes. If or to the extent that the right does not pass under either of these provisions, it is exercisable by his representatives.[45]

Where copyright forming part of a person's estate passes in part to one person and in part to another (as for example where a bequest is limited so as to apply to one or more but not all of the things the copyright owner has the exclusive right to do or authorise, or to part but not the whole of the period for which the copyright is to subsist), any right which passes with the copyright by virtue of the provisions mentioned in the preceding paragraph is correspondingly divided.[46] There are provisions dealing with the situation where a right which thus passes becomes exercisable by more than one person.[47]

---

[37] Copyright, Designs & Patents Act 1988, Sched. 1, para. 30(1).
[38] *Ibid.* para. 30(2). It is not clear that this would include intestacy. See also Copinger and Skone James on *Copyright*, 13 ed., para. 5–4.
[39] *Ibid.* ss.77–89 and Schedule 1, paras. 22–24.
[40] Copyright Act 1956, s.43.
[41] Copyright, Designs & Patents Act 1988, s.85.
[41a] *Ibid.* s.94.
[42] *Ibid.* s.77.
[43] *Ibid.* s.80.
[44] *Ibid.* s.85.
[45] *Ibid.* s.95(1). See Copinger and Skone James on *Copyright*, 13th ed., para. 22–64.
[46] *Ibid.* s.95(2).
[47] *Ibid.* s.95(3).

Any infringement after a person's death of the right to protection from false attribution of authorship under section 84 of the 1988 Act is actionable by his representatives.[48] The Copyright Act 1956, s.43 continues to apply for acts of false attribution done before August 1, 1989.[49]

The right to be identified as author or director and the right to object to derogatory treatment of a work do not apply, in relation to literary, dramatic, musical and artistic works the author of which died before August 1, 1989, or in relation to a film made before that date.[50] The right to privacy of certain photographs and films does not apply to photographs taken or films made before that date.[51] No act done before August 1, 1989 is actionable as an infringement of moral rights.[52]

Any damages recovered by representatives by virtue of section 95 of the 1988 Act for an infringement after a person's death devolve as part of his estate as if the right of action had subsisted and been vested in him immediately before his death.[53]

It is often convenient to appoint a separate literary executor (who may be a professional literary agent) rather than involve the general executor in this often troublesome field, where the copyrights are numerous or valuable, especially if they are left on trust.

Patent

An interest may also vest in representatives by virtue of a patent granted to the testator for the invention of a new manufacture within the realm[54]; and the title of the representatives may be registered.[55] A patent may, it seems, be granted to the representatives of a deceased inventor, or his successors in title.[56]

Registered design

The copyright in a design registered under the Designs Act 1949 vests in the representatives of the registered proprietor; and they may apply to be registered as proprietors thereof.[57] The representatives may also apply for registration where the deceased had not registered the designs of which he was the owner.[58]

---

[48] *Ibid.* s.95(5).
[49] *Ibid.* Sched. 1, para. 22(2).
[50] *Ibid.* para. 23(1), (2).
[51] *Ibid.* para. 24.
[52] *Ibid.* para. 22(1).
[53] *Ibid.* s.95(6).
[54] Toller 6th ed., p. 152, Patents Act 1977, s.3(3).
[55] Patents Act 1977, ss.32, 33; Patents Rules 1978, rule 46(1).
[56] Patents Act 1977, s.7(2)(c).
[57] Registered Designs Act 1949 (as amended by the Copyright, Designs & Patents Act 1988) ss.2, 19.
[58] *Ibid.* s.2(2).

Rent

At common law if rent was reserved generally (without saying to whom)[59] it followed the reversion even where express words to the contrary were used in the reservation of the rent.[60] On the other hand, if a lessee for years made an underlease reserving rent, the rent accruing after his death went to his personal representative, and not to his heirs, even though the reservation was to him and his heirs without mentioning the executors.[61] Similarly where the reversion was in part freehold and in part leasehold, an apportionment was made between the heir and the personal representative.[62]

The position is now governed by statute[63] so that rent reserved by a lease and every covenant and condition referring to the subject-matter of the lease go with the immediate reversion. If by a sub-demise longer than his own term a lessee extinguishes his reversion, the sublessee remains liable during the head-term to pay rent to the lessee and his representatives, by virtue of the covenant.

Arrears of rent

A representative may sue for arrears of rent accrued in the lifetime of the deceased.[65] Further, even at common law, if the reversion (being leasehold) vested in the personal representatives of a deceased person, they could distrain for the arrears of rent which became due in the deceased's lifetime.[66] As by the Land Transfer Act 1897, the real estate was made to devolve on the representatives of a person who died after 1897, the personal representatives, having the reversion, whether freehold or leasehold, could distrain for arrears of rent annexed thereto.

A representative may now distrain for rent as the deceased might have done and after the termination of the lease he may distrain as if the lease

---

[59] *Whitlock's Case* (1608) 8 Co. 69b. See also Co.Litt. 47a; *Cother* v. *Merrick* (1657) Hardr. 95; 3 Bac.Abr. 62, Exors. H. 3; *Anon* (1578) 3 Dyer 363; Godolph., Pt. 2, c. 24, s.13, p. 191. And se *Drake* v. *Munday* (1631) Cro.Car. 207; but *cf. Hatherton* v. *Bradburne* (1843) 13 Sim. 599.

[60] Co.Litt. 47a. As to whether the heir could take it, see 2 Saund. 367b. See also *Dollen* v. *Batt* (1858) 4 C.B.(N.S.) 760; Foa, *Landlord and Tenant*, 7th ed., p. 99.

[61] (1671) 2 Saund. 371, n. to *Sacheverell* v. *Froggatt*. Where no reversion was left in the lessor and the rent was reserved to his executors, administrators and assigns, it went to them: 3 Cruise's Dig., 3rd ed., 321; *Jenison* v. *Lexington* (1719) 1 P.Wms. 555.

[62] Gilb.Rents 188; *Moodie* v. *Garnance* (1616) 3 Bulstr. 153; see also 4 Co. 120b; Co.Litt. 215a.

[63] See the Law of Property Act 1925, s.141 (replacing the Conveyancing Act 1881, s.10, and the Conveyancing Act 1911, s.2, with amendments). *Re King* [1963] Ch. 459. See Woodfall, *Landlord and Tenant*, 28th ed., para. 1–1727.

[64] *Baker* v. *Gostling* (1834) 1 Bing.N.C. 19.

[65] Law Reform (Miscellaneous Provisions) Act 1934, s.1 (as amended), and Administration of Estates Act 1925, s.26 as amended (*post*, p. 1125).

[66] *Wade* v. *Marsh* (1625) 1 Roll.Abr. 672, tit. Distress, O. 13; *ibid*. Latch. 211.

had not determined provided that distress is made within six months of the termination or while the lessee is still in possession.[67]

Two or more representatives may join in distraining, or one may distrain alone, for the whole rent due, for they are regarded in the light of an individual person.[68]

Though rent accruing after the death of the lessor goes with the reversion (so that if recovered by the lessor's personal representatives it will be held by them, subject to the purposes of administration, for the benefit of the person in whose favour an assent of the reversion is made), yet arrears of rent which accrued due in the lifetime of the lessor will, in all cases, form part of his personal estate.[69]

Overpayments under the Rent Acts

The right which the tenant had in a controlled tenancy under the Rent Acts to recover overpayments of rent, where he had paid rent in excess of the standard rent, was a right which passed on his death to his personal representatives.[70]

Bill of exchange payable to testator

A promissory note or bill of exchange made payable to the deceased or his order, may be indorsed by his representative.[71] And, generally speaking, there is no difference between an indorsement of a note by the deceased and one by his personal representative.[72]

"Blight" notices

The rights of a person who has served a notice under the Planning Legislation requiring the purchase of land affected by planning "blight" pass to his representatives under section 161 of the Town and Country Planning Act 1990. Although there is no statutory provision to enable a representative to serve such a notice himself there is no reason in principle why he should not do so since the general objective is the protection of property rights. It seems that a representative would normally be an "owner-

---

[67] Administration of Estates Act 1925, s.26(4) (reproducing the Civil Procedure Act 1833, ss.37, 38: and see 2 Wolst. & Ch., 11th ed., pp. 1447, 1448, where the enactments relating to distress are mentioned. There are special restrictions upon the right of distress in case of agricultural holdings: see the Agricultural Holdings Act 1986, ss.16–19.

[68] 3 Bac.Abr. 30, tit. Exors., D. 1; this is not affected by the restrictions contained in the Administration of Estates Act 1925, s.2(2), which only affect conveyances.

[69] See 3 Bac.Abr. 63, Exors., N. 3; Wentw.Off.Ex., 14th ed., p. 129; Godolph., Pt. 2, c. 13, s.3.

[70] *Dean* v. *Wiesengrund* [1955] 2 Q.B. 120.

[71] *Rawlinson* v. *Stone* (1746) 3 Wils. 1.

[72] *Watkins* v. *Maule* (1821) 2 Jac. & W. 243; *Bromage* v. *Lloyd* (1847) 1 Exch. 32; *Bishop* v. *Curtis* (1852) 18 Q.B. 879. If a person indebted to another gives him a blank acceptance for a certain sum, and the donee subsequently dies, his administrator may fill up the paper as a bill payable to drawer's order, insert his own name as drawer, and enforce payment thereof against the acceptor: *Scard* v. *Jackson* (1875) 34 L.T. 65.

occupier" but not a "resident owner-occupier" within the definitions in section 168.

Settled land: arrears of rent

If the deceased was a "trustee-estate-owner" of "settled land" and representation as respects such land is granted to his special representatives,[73] it will be for his general representatives to sue or distrain for the arrears of rent which accrued in his lifetime, whether or not the reversion is vested in them. Subsection (4) (dealing with the right to distrain) of section 26 of the Administration of Estates Act 1925 does not differentiate between general and special representatives. But it is clearly convenient that the representatives who alone are concerned with the collection of the deceased's assets should be the persons to enforce the payment of arrears of rent accruing in the lifetime of the deceased. If, however, such arrears should in fact be recovered by the special representatives they could be compelled to account to the general representatives.

Arrears of rentcharge

Again the representatives of a deceased rentchargee may sue for arrears of rent accrued in the deceased's lifetime. And though at common law the executors or administrators of a person seised of a rent-service, rentcharge, rent-seck, or fee-farm, in fee-simple, or fee-tail, or for his own life or *pur autre vie*, could not distrain for the arrears incurred in the lifetime of the testator or intestate,[74] this defect was remedied by statutes.[75]

A representative may thus distrain for arrears[76] in the same manner as the deceased might have done so long as the land remains in the possession of the person liable[77] or of those deriving title under him.

If the deceased has both general and special representatives it will be for the former to sue or distrain for the arrears of the rentcharge which accrued due in his lifetime.[78]

The Apportionment Act 1870

Since rent which accrues before the death of a person does not always devolve (either immediately or mediately) upon the same persons as the rent accruing after such death, it follows that an apportionment of rent or other payments is often necessary. This is provided for by the Apportionment Act 1870,[79] which enacts that unless apportionment is expressly

[73] Under the Administration of Estates Act 1925, s.22, or the Supreme Court Act 1981, s.116 (*post*, p. 1197).

[74] Co.Litt. 162*a*.

[75] Namely, 32 Hen. 8, c. 37; the Civil Procedure Act 1833, ss.37, 38. See on these statutes the 12th edition of this work, pp. 690 *et seq*.

[76] Administration of Estates Act 1925, s.26(3) (reproducing 32 Hen. 8, c. 37). See *post*, p. 1125.

[77] See the Law of Property Act 1925, s.121.

[78] *Ibid*. n. 77.

[79] 33 & 34 Vict. c. 35. As to equitable apportionment, see *post*, p. 1039.

excluded,[80] all rents,[81] annuities,[82] dividends[83] and other periodical payments[84] in the nature of income[85] are considered as accruing from day to
day and are apportionable accordingly.[86] Outgoings must equally be
apportioned.[87] Thus the representative of a life-tenant will be entitled to
an apportioned part of all apportionable payments made after the death in
so far as these relate to a period before death. A representative may also
be concerned with the Apportionment Act as a matter of distribution
between those entitled under the will or intestacy,[88] but the Act is conveniently considered here.

The Act applies only to payments recurring at fixed times, not at variable
periods, so it has been held not to apply to income of a share in a private
trading partnership regulated by a partnership deed under which the dividend was decided by the managing partner,[89] nor to newspaper profits
divisible at the discretion of trustees,[90] nor to interest "accruing" on compensation under Town and Country Planning legislation.[91]

Apportionment of dividends

If a payment falls within the definition of "dividends"[92] it is apportionable even if payment is occasional and variable. Thus payments to shareholders by way of bonus or surplus profits are apportionable as dividends[93]
if made or declared for a definite period.[94] When so declared they accrue
for that period only.[95] Thus dividends declared for a period ceasing before

[80] Apportionment Act 1870, s.7; *Re Oppenheimer* [1907] 1 Ch. 399; *Re Edwards* [1918] 1
Ch. 142; *Re Lysaght* [1898] 1 Ch. 115.
[81] "Rent" includes rent service, rentcharge and rent seck, and also tithes and all periodical
payments of renderings in lieu of or in the nature of rent or tithe, s.5.
[82] "Annuities" includes salaries and pensions, s.5.
[83] "Dividends" includes (besides dividends strictly so called) all payments made by the
name of dividend bonus or otherwise out of the revenue of trading or other public companies,
divisible between all or any of the members of such respective companies, whether such payments shall be usually made or declared at any fixed times or otherwise; and all such divisible
revenue is for the purposes of the Apportionment Act 1870 deemed to have accured by equal
daily increment during and within the period for or in respect of which the payment of the
same revenue is declared or espressed to be made, but the word "dividend" does not include
payments in the nature of a return or reimbursement of capital, s.5. "Public company" here
means any company registered under the Companies Acts: *Re White* [1913] 1 Ch. 231.
[84] As to what are "other periodical payments," see below.
[85] Annual sums payable in policies of assurance are not apportionable, s.6.
[86] Apportionment Act 1870, s.2.
[87] *Re Joel* [1967] Ch. 14.
[88] See *post*, p. 1074 as to equitable apportionment on intestacy and the exclusion of all rules
of apportionment under s.33 of the Administration of Estates Act 1925 (*post*, p. 1127).
[89] *Jones* v. *Ogle* (1872) L.R. 8 Ch. 192, but see as to dividends, *infra*, p. 534.
[90] *Re Cox's Trusts* (1878) 9 Ch.D. And see *Re Robbins* [1941] Ch. 434.
[91] *Re Sneyd* [1961] 1 W.L.R. 575; *cf. Re Chance* [1962] Ch. 593 and *post*, p. 1043.
[92] See *ante*, n. 83.
[93] *Re Griffiths* (1878) 12 Ch.D. 655.
[94] *Re Jowitt* [1922] 2 Ch. 442. The fact that dividends are cumulative and preferential gives
no later claim for a period for which no dividends were declared: *Re Sale* [1913] 2 Ch. 697.
[95] *Re Wakley* [1920] 2 Ch. 205; *Re Marjoribanks* [1923] 2 Ch. 307; *Re Joel* [1936] 2 All E.R.
962.

the death are capital of the estate but dividends covering a period before and after the death are apportionable.[96]

Apportionment of bonus issues—capital or income

Where a company makes a bonus issue of shares or debentures or declares a dividend of capital profits the recipient may yet be regarded as receiving "income" in this respect. Such income in the hands of a representative will be apportionable.

The question whether such receipts are income or capital for this purpose is in general answered according to the rules laid down in *Bouch* v. *Sproule*[97] and *Hill* v. *Permanent Trustee of N.S.W.*[98] which are as follows:

1. Where a company is in liquidation, and the assets, representing either paid-up capital or accumulated profits, are divided among the shareholders, such assets are capital in the hands of the shareholders; consequently no question of apportionment arises.[99]

2. A limited company not in liquidation can make no payment by way of return of capital to its shareholders except as a step in an authorised reduction of capital, or under the Companies Act 1985, s.130, which relates to payments out of the share premium account.[1] Any other payment of money to its shareholders, no matter by what name it is called, must still remain a payment on division of profits.[2]

3. Such moneys, if the shareholder is a representative, will prima facie be held by him to be income of the estate and, if necessary, apportioned. The will may itself give directions as to apportionment and these will be binding, so long as they are not repugnant to the benefits conferred and do not attempt to oust the jurisdiction of the court in matters of construction and administration.[3] But no statement by the company or its officers that moneys which are being paid away to shareholders as profits are capital, or are to be treated as capital, can have any effect on the ultimate destination of the moneys so paid.[4]

4. Where a limited company administers a fund of undivided profits so that no part of such profits leaves the possession of the company, but the whole is applied in paying calls on existing shares[5] or in paying up new shares or debentures, which are issued or allotted to the shareholders who

---

[96] *Re Winder* [1951] 2 All E.R. 362; *Re Muirhead* [1916] 2 Ch. 181. There is no apportionment on a mere change of investments by trustees: *Re Clarke* (1881) 18 Ch.D. 160.

[97] (1887) 29 Ch.D. 635, 653; 12 App.Cas. 385, 397; (1951) 67 L.Q.R. 195; (1952) 15 M.L.R. 180; (1975) 39 *Conveyancer* 355.

[98] [1930] A.C. 720.

[99] *Re Armitage* [1893] Ch. 337.

[1] See *Re Duff* [1951] Ch. 923.

[2] *Re Malam* [1894] 3 Ch. 578; *Re Sandbach* [1933] Ch. 505 (redeemable dividend certificates); *Re Sechiari* [1950] 1 All E.R. 417; *Re Kleinwort* [1951] Ch. 860; *Re Alsbury* (1890) 45 Ch.D. 237; *Re Thomas* [1916] 2 Ch. 331. For the basis of this statement, see [1930] A.C. 731.

[3] *Re Wynn's W.T.* [1952] Ch. 271.

[4] *Re Bates* [1928] Ch. 682; *Re Doughty* [1947] Ch. 263; *Re Harrison* [1949] Ch. 678; *Re Whitehead* [1959] Ch. 579.

[5] *Re Hatton* [1917] Ch. 357.

would have been entitled to receive the profits had they been distributed, such new shares or debentures whether or not redeemable[6] are held by a shareholder, who happens to be a trustee or representative, as capital for the purposes of the trust or estate.[7]

5. Where a company intends to capitalise undivided profits by the issue of shares, thus retaining the profits as part of its assets, the fact that the form of the transaction is one which gives to each shareholder an option to take cash in lieu of the shares is not necessarily a factor which determines that the issue of shares is income and not capital; on the contrary, that fact is immaterial if, from the other documents and facts, it reasonably and clearly appears that the company, notwithstanding the form, intended to capitalise.[8]

6. *Semble*, where a trustee or representative receives, as shareholder, shares representing capitalised profits, and such shares are to be treated as either income or capital, according to the foregoing rules, a court of equity has no inherent jurisdiction to order any apportionment to produce a fair distribution between income and capital.[9] Such jurisdiction is confined to cases of breaches of trust, and the fact that trustees ought to have foreseen the bonus does not mean that they ought to have sold cum dividend.[10]

Apportionment on a sale "cum dividend"

Where stock in a public company was settled upon trust for A for life, and after her death for other beneficiaries, and after the death of A the stock was sold "cum dividend" by order of the court, it was held that A's estate was not entitled, under the Apportionment Act, to any payment out of the purchase-money of the stock in respect of a dividend earned in part before sale, but declared and received by the purchaser after sale.[11] But in a later case[12] Clauson J. directed that on the death of a life tenant his representatives were entitled to an apportionment of the dividends on all securities comprised in the trust, whether or not they were sold for administration purposes. Farwell J., however, treated[13] Clauson J.'s decision as being one applicable only in special circumstances and refused to regard it as a departure from the general practice. The whole position was carefully reviewed by Morton J. in *Re Henderson*.[14] The conclusions of the learned judge were that: (1) if the investment in respect of which the interest or

---

[6] *Re Outen* [1963] Ch. 291; *I.R.C.* v. *Fisher* [1926] A.C. 395; *C.I.T. Bengal* v. *Mercantile Bank* [1936] A.C. 478.
[7] *I.R.C.* v. *Blott* [1921] 2 A.C. 171; *Re Wright* [1945] Ch. 211; *Re Speir* [1924] 1 Ch. 359. See in particular the speech of Lord Russell of Killowen in *Hill* v. *Permanent Trustee of N.S.W.* [1930] A.C. 720, 731 *et seq.*
[8] *Re Evans* [1913] 1 Ch. 23; *Re Taylor* [1926] Ch. 923, 930, *per* Tomlin J.
[9] *Re Maclaren's Settlement Trusts* [1951] 2 All E.R. 414; *Re Kleinwort's Settlement Trusts* [1951] 2 All E.R. 328.
[10] *Re Rudd's Will Trust* [1952] 1 All E.R. 254. *Re Hayes* [1971] 1 W.L.R. 758, 768.
[11] *Bulkeley* v. *Stephens* [1896] 2 Ch. 241.
[12] *Re Winterstoke's Will Trusts* [1938] Ch. 158.
[13] *Re Firth* [1938] Ch. 517; see also *Re Walker* [1934] W.N. 104.
[14] [1940] Ch. 368. And see *Re Maclaren* [1951] 2 All E.R. 414.

dividend is payable is still held by the trustees of the will when the dividend becomes due and payable, the trustees must pay over the proper apportioned part of the dividend to the representatives of the deceased; (2) if the investment in respect of which the interest or dividend is payable has been transferred (*e.g.* by appropriation) to a person absolutely entitled under the will, before the dividend became due and payable, the trustees ought not to have so transferred the investment without making some arrangement to ensure that the representatives of the tenant for life will be able to obtain payment of the proper apportioned part of the dividend, but if no such arrangement has in fact been made, the transferees are bound to pay a due proportion of the dividend to the tenant for life's estate; and (3) if the investment in respect of which the interest or dividend is payable has been sold by the trustees cum dividend, the dividend is received by the purchaser who cannot be called upon over any part of it to the tenant for life's representatives and there is no apportionment of the purchase price in favour of the life tenant's representatives.

Where upon a direction by a tenant for life trustees had invested capital money in their hands in the purchase of stocks on which at the date of purchase dividends had been earned and declared, but not paid, the tenant for life was not entitled to such dividends, which were treated as capital.[15]

Apportionment on savings certificates

In *Re Holder*[16] a testator directed that no part of the dividends, rents, interests or moneys of the nature of income actually paid after death should be apportioned or treated as capital. Some years before the testator had purchased 500 national savings certificates for £375. Roxburgh J. held that the monthly accretions of interest were capitalised at the end of each month, unless the holder called for repayment, so that so much of the gross sum received by the executors as represented the value of the certificates at the testator's death must be treated be as capital.

Apportionment of rent

The Apportionment Act has been held not to apply to rent accrued due before the tenant goes out of possession, so that if rent is payable in advance and the tenant fails to pay, the landlord after re-entry is entitled to the whole and not merely an apportioned part of the advance rent which accrued due before the tenant went out of possession.[17] Similarly, the Apportionment Act does not apply to rent which accrued due to a testator before his death,[18] but if a landlord dies on the day payment is due, no cause of action forms part of his estate at the moment of death because the

---

[15] *Re Peel's S.E.* [1910] 1 Ch. 389; for, since the vendor does not take the dividend, an additional sum, in effect equal to such dividend, is paid for the stocks out of capital.

[16] [1953] Ch. 468.

[17] *Ellis* v. *Rowbotham* [1900] 1 Q.B. 740; *Re Aspinall* [1961] Ch. 526.

[18] *Re Aspinall* [1961] Ch. 526; *Norris* v. *Harrison* (1817) 2 Madd. 268.

rent is not due until the last moment of that day.[19] These rents when received are thus income of the estate and are apportionable.[20]

Insurance money

Money received after 1925[21] under a policy of insurance against loss or damage (whether by fire or otherwise) of any property subject to a trust or to a settlement within the meaning of the Settled Land Act 1925 is capital money for the purposes of the trust or settlement, if the policy has been kept up under any trust or power or in performance of any obligation or by a tenant for life impeachable for waste.[22]

It seems that if a tenant for life unimpeachable for waste receives fire insurance money on a policy privately effected by himself this money does not go with the land,[23] but in practice this situation cannot arise[24] except possibly under a claim of lien by the life tenant or his executors after the insurance money has been applied,[25] or where the property insured consists of furniture or removable fixtures.[26]

Damages for breach of lessee's covenant

The spirit of the law is that, with respect to injuries to land for which damages are to be recovered by personal action, the person who brings the action is entitled to the damages.[27] Thus, where before 1926 a tenant for life recovered damages for breach of a covenant contained in a lease granted by a previous tenant for life, it was held that there was no equity to compel him to hand them over to the trustees.[28] But this principle is subject to the intention expressed in the settlement, and, *semble*, damages recovered by trustees were, even before 1926, treated as *corpus*, unless the tenant for life could make out a right to the money.[29]

---

[19] *Ibid.* n. 18.

[20] *Ibid.*

[21] Before 1925 insurance moneys in general went with the land if the tenant was impeachable for waste, but the income or interest on such moneys went to the tenant; *Rook* v. *Worth* (1750) 1 Ves.Sen. 460. Similar principles were applied to war damage payments in *Re Scholfield* [1949] Ch. 341.

[22] Trustee Act 1925, s.20 (*post*, pp. 1100).

[23] See *Norris* v. *Harrison* (1817) 2 Madd. 268, as discussed in *Noble* v. *Cass* (1828) 2 Sim. 343.

[24] See the Fires Prevention (Metropolis) Act 1774, s.83, which enables the insurer to require the money to be laid out in repairs to buildings, etc. This Act was not mentioned in the cases cited in n. 84 above, presumably because it was wrongly thought to apply only to the metropolis; see *Sinnott* v. *Bowden* [1912] 2 Ch. 414.

[25] See *Todd* v. *Moorhouse* (1874) L.R. 19 Eq. 69 and 28 Halsbury's *Laws*, 4th ed., p. 568. The relevant authorities do not seem to have been cited in *Re Quicke* [1908] 1 Ch. 887.

[26] To which the Act does not apply.

[27] *Noble* v. *Cass* (1828) 2 Sim 343 *ante*, p. 538.

[28] *Re Lacon's Settlement* [1911] 2 Ch. 17; *Re Dealtry* (1913) 108 L.T. 832.

[29] *Re Pyke* [1912] 1 Ch. 770. *Cf. Noble* v. *Cass*, *ante*, which is, however, distinguishable, as in that case the trustees who recovered the money were only trustees of the life estate and were not trustees for the remaindermen.

After 1925, money, not being rent, received by way of damages or compensation for breach of any covenant by a lessee or grantee contained in any lease or grant of settled land is, by virtue of section 80 of the Settled Land Act 1925 (and subject as therein mentioned), deemed capital money under that Act, unless the court otherwise directs. But in cases to which section 80(1) does not apply[30] the old rules would still seem to apply.

Contingent interests

Contingent and executory interests, whether in real or personal estate, devolve on the representative of a party dying before the contingency, upon which they depend, takes effect.[31] Although contingent and executory interests do not vest in possession, they may nevertheless vest in right so as to be transmissible to executors or administrators.[32] But it is obvious that where the contingency upon which the interest depends is the endurance of the life of the party entitled to it till a particular period, the interest itself will be extinguished by the death of the party before the period arrives, and will not be transmissible to his executors or administrators. The only case in which a contingent future interest is not transmissible would seem to be where the being in existence when the contingency happens is an essential part of the description of the person who is to take.[33]

Powers and discretionary trusts

The object of a special power of appointment or of a discretionary trust has no transmissible interest. Thus the executor or administrator of the object of a special power cannot without express provision be an appointee under it. Where a husband gives his wife a power of appointment of a fund in favour of his children, and a child dies without any appointment having been made to him, no part can be appointed to the child's executor or administrator.[34]

---

[30] See subss. (4), (5) and (6) for exceptions.

[31] Fearne, C.R. 554; 2 Saund. 388n.; note to *Purefoy* v. *Rogers*. The Wills Act 1837, s.3; and the Law of Property Act 1925, s.4(2).

[32] *Pinbury* v. *Elkin* (1719) 1 P.Wms. 564; *King* v. *Withers* (1735) Cas.temp.Talb. 117; *Chauncy* v. *Graydon* (1743) 2 Atk. 616; *Peck* v. *Parrot* (1749) 1 Ves.Sen. 236; *Barnes* v. *Allen* (1782) 1 Bro.C.C. 181; 3 Ves. 208; *Perry* v. *Woods* (1796) 3 Ves. 204; *Taylor* v. *Graham* (1878) 3 App.Cas. 1287; *Re Cresswell* (1883) 24 Ch.D. 102. *Secus*, in the case of a mere possibility or *spes successionis*, though it has been held that a possibility of reverter on failure of a fee simple conditional is devisable by virtue of s.3 of the Wills Act 1837: *Pemberton* v. *Barnes* [1899] 1 Ch. 544. Though a mere expectancy or possibility is not transmissible to executors or administrators, it is assignable in equity for value: *Tailby* v. *Official Receiver* (1888) 13 App. Cas. 523, 543; *Re Dallas* [1904] 2 Ch. 385. A person may dispose of a possibility coupled with an interest: in Law of Property Act 1925, s.4(2).

[33] *Per* Kay J. in *Re Cresswell* (1883) 24 Ch.D. 102, 107.

[34] *Maddison* v. *Andrew* (1747) 1 Ves.Sen. 57, 59. As to the distinction between powers and trusts see *Re Baden* (1971) A.C. 424 and *post*, p. 695 and *I.R.C.* v. *Berrill* [1981] 1 W.L.R. at p. 1454.

Corporator sole

Before the Law of Property Act 1925, it was held that a *thing in action* vested in a corporation sole[35] devolved, on the death of the corporator sole, upon his representatives, and did not, except by virtue of a custom,[36] charter[37] or statute,[38] pass to his successor.[39] But by virtue of section 180 of that Act any property (including a thing in action[40]), or any interest therein, which is or has been vested in a corporation sole (including the Crown), unless and until otherwise disposed of by the corporation, devolves, and is deemed always to have devolved to the successors, from time to time, of such corporation. This applies notwithstanding any temporary vacancy, but without prejudice to the right of the successor to disclaim.[41] Further, any transaction purported to be made with a corporation sole, or any purported appointment of such a corporation to be trustee, during a vacancy in the office, is deemed to have taken effect as if the vacancy had been filled before the transaction or appointment, but subject to the successor's right of disclaimer.[42]

On the death of a corporator sole (after 1925) his interest in the real and personal estate of the corporation devolves to his successor.[43] This provision applies on the demise of the Crown as respects all property, real and personal, vested in the Crown as corporation sole[44] including the Crown Jewels.[45]

Bankrupt

The executor of a bankrupt is not entitled to his claims, for they are deemed to have been duly assigned to the trustee in bankruptcy.[46]

Arrears of maintenance pending suit

Again, it does not appear to have been satisfactorily settled that the court would allow the representatives of a wife to enforce payment of the

---

[35] See also *ante*, pp. 19, 474.

[36] See, *e.g. Byrd* v. *Wilford* (1596) Cro.Eliz. 464, 682; *Fulwood's Case* (1591) 4 Co. 65a.

[37] See, *e.g. Atkins* v. *Gardener* (1607) Cro.Jac. 159.

[38] *e.g.* in the case of the Treasury Solicitor or the Public Trustee.

[39] *Fulwood's Case, ante.* See also *Howley* v. *Knight* (1849) 14 Q.B. 240 (administration bond to ordinary).

[40] Law of Property Act 1925, s.205(1)(xx).

[41] *Ibid.* s.180(2).

[42] *Ibid.* s.180(3).

[43] Administration of Estates Act 1925, s.3(5); *Corven's Case* (1612) 12 Co. 105, 106; 4 Burn E.L., 8th ed., p. 304. See *ante*, p. 474.

[44] *Ibid.* n. 70.

[45] See Co.Litt. 18b. They are not devisable but may be disposed of by letters patent; *Hastings* v. *Douglas* (1634) Cro.Car. 344, by Berkerley and Jones.

[46] Bankruptcy Act 1914 (4 & 5 Geo. 5, c. 59), s.48(5). See Williams and Muir Hunter, *Bankruptcy*, 19th ed. p. 375 and Insolvency Act 1986, ss.283, 306, 436. *Muir Hunter on Personal Insolvency*, para. 3–146.

arrears of alimony against the husband; and it was held that they could not sustain a bill in equity for that purpose.[47]

There is no general rule that where one of the parties to a divorce suit has died, the suit abates, so that no further proceedings can be taken in it. The real question is whether further proceedings in the suit can or cannot be taken.[48] This depends in all cases on two matters and in some cases also on a third. The first is the nature of the further proceedings to be taken. The second is the true construction of any relevant statutory provisions. The third is the applicability of the Law Reform (Miscellaneous Provisions) Act 1934, s.1.[49] It therefore seems that where property is at stake the representative of the deceased spouse would be entitled to claim.[50]

Contribution in equity

Just as he may be liable in equity[51] the representative of a joint contractor or person with whom the deceased was jointly liable may be entitled to rights of contribution or reimbursement for tax paid on liabilities met by the deceased.[52]

Joint interests

As a general rule, the interest which the deceased had in a claim jointly with another does not pass to his representative.[53]

Partnership

Where one of two partners dies, an action on a contract made with the firm must be brought in the name of the survivor, and the executor or administrator of the deceased cannot be joined,[54] nor can he sue separately. The general rule is that though the right of a deceased partner devolves on his executor,[55] the remedy survives to his companion, who alone must enforce the right by action, and will be liable, on recovery, to account to the executor or administrator for the share of the deceased.[56]

---

[47] *Stones* v. *Cooke* (1835) 8 Sim. 321 n. (*q*), reversing *ibid.* 7 Sim. 22; *De Blaquiere* v. *De Blaquiere* (1830) 3 Hagg.Ecc. 322; *Vandergucht* v. *De Blaquiere* (1838) 5 M. & Cr. 229, 241. As to the rights of the wife to enforce payment of arrears of alimony after the husband's death, see *post*, p. 561.

[48] *Barder* v. *Calvori* [1988] A.C. 20, 37.

[49] See p. 515 *ante*.

[50] *Barder* v. *Calvori* [1988] A.C. 39; *Purse* v. *Purse* [1981] Fam. 143, 155.

[51] See p. 541 *post*.

[52] See *Re Latham* [1962] Ch. 616, 641; *Leedale* v. *Lewis* [1982] 1 W.L.R. 1335. See also as to subrogation *Re Downer Enterprises* [1974] 1 W.L.R. 1460.

[53] See *Southcote* v. *Hoare* (1810) 3 Taunt. 87. And see Administration of Estates Act 1925, s.3(4), which is not limited to joint tenancies in land. See p. 472 *ante* and p. 1115 *post*.

[54] See generally as to joinder of parties, R.S.C., Ord. 15.

[55] *Ante*, p. 472.

[56] *Martin* v. *Crompe* (1698) 1 Lord Raym. 340; *Kemp* v. *Andrews* (1691) Carth. 171; *Golding* v. *Vaughan* (1782) 2 Chit.Rep. 437; *R.* v. *Collectors of Customs* (1813) 2 M. & S. 225; (1670) 2 Saund. 117, note to *Coryton* v. *Lithebye*. See Lindley, *Partnership*, 15th ed., p. 520.

Principal and agent

A contract of agency if of a purely personal nature terminates with the death of either party.[57]

Joint covenants

Where two persons have the legal interest in the performance of a contract, though the performance thereof accrues only for the benefit of one of them, as where there is a covenant with two persons to pay an annuity to one of them and his assigns, on the death of the latter the remedy survives, and the executor or administrator of the deceased person cannot be made a party or sue separately.[58] And wherever the interest of the covenantees is joint, this rule of survivorship applies, though the covenant is in terms joint and several.[59] It follows, that where a contract is made jointly with several persons, or where the interest of the covenantees is joint, and they all die, the representative of the survivor alone can sue, and the representatives of those who died before him cannot be joined.

On the other hand, if the interest of the covenantees is several, and one of them dies, his executor may maintain a separate action on the covenant, notwithstanding the other covenantee is living. It makes no difference that the language of the covenant is joint.[60] But a joint covenant in a lease will not be regarded as several merely because the demise is to two persons as tenants in common.[61]

---

[57] *Friend* v. *Young* [1897] 2 Ch. 421, 429; *Thomas* v. *Rose* [1968] 1 W.L.R. 1797, 1805. As to "personal" contracts, see *ante*, p. 517.

[58] *Anderson* v. *Martindale* (1801) 1 East 497. See *Barford* v. *Stuckey* (1820) 2 Br. & Bing. 333.

[59] See note to *Eccleston* v. *Clipsham* (1666) 1 Saund. 154. See also *Withers* v. *Bircham* (1824) 3 B. & C. 254, 256; and *Lane* v. *Drinkwater* (1834) 1 C.M. & R. 599, where, however, the covenant was joint only.

[60] *Withers* v. *Bircham, supra* (joint covenant to pay several annuities); *cf. Eccleston* v. *Clipsham, supra.*

[61] *White* v. *Tyndall* (1888) 13 App.Cas. 263. *cf. National Society* v. *Gibbs* [1900] 2 Ch. 280.

CHAPTER 47

DEVOLUTION OF LAND

As has been explained[1] real estate now devolves in the same way as chattels real. Chattel interests which "concern or savour of" the realty[2] or which issue out of or are annexed to real estate[3] are known as chattels real. Thus all interests in land for a definite term less than a life are chattel interests[4] and have always devolved on the personal representative for they are not freehold.[5] A rentcharge is a chattel real if it issues out of leasehold land, even though it is granted to a man and his heirs, for an interest derived out of a chattel must itself be a mere chattel and devolves as such.[6] The same principle applies to an option to purchase the fee simple of demised land. If this is given to the lessee as an incident of the term it devolves as personalty on the lessee's death.[7] Having stated this general principle it is necessary to consider some special factors affecting (1) unregistered land and equitable interests and (2) registered land.

A. Unregistered Land And Equitable Interests

Entailed interests

After 1925 an interest in tail or in tail male or in tail female or in tail special may be created by way of trust in any property real or personal, but only by the like expressions as before 1926 would have created by deed a similar estate in freeholds.[8] Informal expressions which before 1926 might have created estates tail, when used after 1925, create absolute or fee simple interests only[9]; provided, however, that where personal estate is after

---

[1] See *ante*, p. 471.
[2] Co.Litt. 118 *b*.
[3] 2 Black.Comm. 386. Rights of wardship and marriage were, for example, chattels real. (Megarry and Wade, *The Law of Real Property*, 5th ed., p. 16).
[4] Estates for years have one quality of real property, namely, immobility, but want the other, namely, a sufficient legal indeterminate duration, the utmost period for which they can last being fixed and determined: 2 Black.Comm. 386.
[5] 1 Preston, *Estates*, 203. An estate of freehold may be defined to be "an estate in possession, remainder or reversion, in corporeal or incorporeal hereditaments held for life or for some uncertain interest, created by will or by some mode of conveyance, capable of transferring an estate of freehold, which may last the life of the devisee or grantee or of some other person." See Watkin on Conveyancing by Morley & Coote, 9th ed., p. 65.
[6] *Re Fraser* [1904] 1 Ch. 111, 726. See also *Butt's Case* (1600) 7 Co. 23 *a*; *Saffery* v. *Elgood* (1834) 1 A. & E. 191.
[7] *Re Adams and Kensington Vestry* (1884) 24 Ch.D. 199; 27 Ch.D. 394. But it must not exceed the limit allowed by the rule against perpetuities: *Woodall* v. *Clifton* [1905] 2 Ch. 257, *cf. L. & S.W. Ry.* v. *Gomm* (1881) 20 Ch.D. 562; *Muller* v. *Trafford* [1901] 1 Ch. 54; *Hutton* v. *Watling* [1947] 2 All E.R. 641; the Perpetuities and Accumulations Act 1964, s.9.
[8] Law of Property Act 1925, s.130(1).
[9] *Ibid.* s.130(2); and see Arts. in 6 *Cambridge Law Journal* 67–82; *ibid.* 46–55 and 185–191.

1925 directed to be enjoyed or held with, or upon trusts corresponding to trusts affecting entailed land, such direction is sufficient to create corresponding entailed interests in such personal estate.[10] By virtue of the transitional provisions of the Law of Property Act 1925, interests held in undivided shares in land became interests in personalty and entailed interests in such undivided shares became rights to corresponding entailed interests in the net proceeds of sale attributable to such shares.[11]

Where the words of limitation are not sufficient to create an entailed interest, on the death of the first taker, who will have taken an absolute interest, the property devolves on his general personal representatives. Again, if the words of limitation are sufficient to create an entailed interest and the tenant in tail in possession, under his statutory power in that behalf,[12] bequeaths the property absolutely by his will (or otherwise bars the entail) it will, on his death, devolve upon his general personal representatives.[13] However, if the entail is not barred and the tenant in tail is the estate owner (the legal estate in the term being vested in him solely upon the trusts of the settlement), then on his death such legal estate will as a general rule devolve upon the special personal representatives,[14] though his beneficial entailed interest, deemed to be an interest ceasing on his death, will not devolve on his representatives, general or special.[15]

Life interests

Life interests in land are governed by the Settled Land Act 1925 and include[16] interests which formerly would under the rule in *Shelley's Case*[17] have vested wholly in the first taker and devolved upon his personal representatives, as well as those which would formerly have been construed as interests for life only.[18] Although the life interest terminates on death, the legal estate vested in the life-tenant will pass to his general or special personal representatives as the case may be.[19]

Leasehold interests

If the deceased had a term of years, this vests in the executor or administrator, and he cannot refuse it though it is worth nothing; for the executorship or administratorship is entire, and must be renounced *in toto*, or not at

---

[10] Law of Property Act 1925, s.130(3); *Re Jones* [1934] Ch. 315.

[11] Law of Property (Entailed Interests) Act 1932, s.1, overriding (on this point) *Re Price* [1928] Ch. 579; *Re Kempthorne* [1930] 1 Ch. 268; *Re Thomas's Will Trusts* [1930] 2 Ch. 67.

[12] Law of Property Act 1925, s.176. See *Acheson* v. *Russell* [1951] Ch. 67.

[13] Administration of Estates Act 1925, ss.1, 3(2) (*post*, pp. 1113, 1115).

[14] *Ibid.* ss.1, 3(1)(ii), 22; see also Jud. Act 1925, s.162 (as amended); *ante*, p. 343.

[15] Administration of Estates Act 1925, s.3(3). See *ante*, p. 471.

[16] See the Law of Property Act 1925, s.131.

[17] (1581) 1 Co.Rep. 93(*b*.) *Threebridge* v. *Kilburne* (1751) 2 Ves.Sen. 233; *Garth* v. *Baldwin* (1755) *ibid.* 646; *Verulam* v. *Bathurst* (1843) 13 Sim. 374.

[18] See Fearne, Cont.Rem., 7th ed., pp. 490 *et seq.*; *Doe* v. *Lyde* (1787) 1 T.R. 593; *Knight* v. *Ellis* (1789) 2 Bro.C.C. 570; *Ex p. Sterne* (1807) 6 Ves. 156.

[19] See *ante*, pp. 18, 1272.

all.[20] A personal representative who is not the trustee of a settlement may however renounce his office in regard to settled land.[21]

Reversions and Remainders

Since the 1925 legislation these will arise under trusts for sale or settlements so that the legal estate is not affected by the death of the person interested in equity. The equitable interest vests in the representative of the deceased. The succession to statutory rights of reverter before 1987 is unclear and was not resolved by the Reverter of Sites Act 1987.[22] It is thought that such claims based on reverter to the "said estate"[23] would have vested initially in the heir at law but subsequently in the executors or administrators of the latest owner.[24]

Yearly interests

The death either of the lessor or lessee does not determine a tenancy from year to year, and the interest of the tenant is transmissible to his executor or administrator.[25] Therefore due notice to quit must be given to the latter before the lessor or his representative can recover possession[26]; and the executor or administrator of the lessee may maintain an action for ejectment.[27]

If the lessee has died intestate, then until letters of administration have issued, the tenancy vests in the President of the Family Division,[28] and notice to quit may be served on him.[29]

Joint tenancy

If land is held by two or more persons as joint tenants beneficially and one of the joint tenants dies, his interest accrues to the survivors, and his personal representatives take no interest.[30] The beneficial interest of the deceased however vests in the representative where there is a tenancy in

[20] *Billinghurst* v. *Speerman* (1695) 1 Salk. 297; *Ackland* v. *Pring* (1841) 2 Mann. & Gr. 937. As to liability to pay rent and perform covenants, notwithstanding there are no assets, see *ante*, pp. 573 *et seq*.
[21] See the Administration of Estates Act 1925, s.23(1) (*post*, p. 1123).
[22] See *Re Clayton* [1980] Ch. 99; *Re Rowhook* [1985] Ch. 62 and 100 L.Q.R. 528.
[23] See the ambiguous wording of s.2 of the School Sites Act 1841.
[24] See *Re Clayton* [1980] Ch. 99, 102 and 1984 L.S. Gazette 1851.
[25] *Doe* v. *Porter* (1789) 3 T.R. 13; *James* v. *Dean* (1805) 11 Ves. 383; *Abbey* v. *Barnstyn* [1930] 1 K.G. 660.
[26] *Parker* v. *Constable* (1769) 3 Wills. 25; *Rees* v. *Perrot* (1830) 4 C. & P. 230.
[27] *Doe* v. *Porter* (1789) 3 T.R. 13. And see *Doe* v. *Wood* (1845) 14 M. & W. 682.
[28] Administration of Estates Act 1925, s.9; *cf. Whitmore* v. *Lambert* [1955] 1 W.L.R. 495. See also *ante*, p. 461.
[29] See *Smith* v. *Mather* [1948] 2 K.B. 212 (overruled on another point in *Moodie* v. *Hosegood* [1952] A.C. 61); *Harrowby* v. *Snelson* [1951] 1 All E.R. 140; *Mackley* v. *Nutting* [1949] 2 K.B. 55; *Long* v. *Burgess* [1949] 2 All E.R. 484. *Ante*, p. 461.
[30] Co.Litt. 182 *a*; the Administration of Estates Act 1925, s.3(4) (*post*, p. 1115). See 140 N.L.J. 95.

common.[31] The representatives of a surviving joint tenant are deemed to convey as if the deceased were solely and beneficially entitled if the conveyance contains a statement to that effect.[32]

Assured Tenancies[33]

An assured tenancy created on or after January 15, 1989 under the Housing Act 1988 confers an interest which is personal to the tenant, continuing only so long as the tenant is in occupation or possession of the premises.[34] This was similarly the case for statutory tenancies under the Rent Act.[35]

Under section 17 of the Housing Act 1988, where the sole tenant under an assured periodic tenancy dies, and immediately before his death the tenant's spouse (a "spouse" including a person who was living with the tenant as his or her wife or husband[36]) was occupying the dwelling-house as his or her only or principal home, and the tenant was not himself a successor (as defined), then, on the death, the tenancy vests by virtue of the section in the spouse and does devolve under the tenant's will or intestacy. Thus statutory succession to an assured periodic tenancy is limited to one successor.

If the tenant is an assured tenant under an assured fixed term tenancy and he dies before the term has expired, the remainder of the term devolves under the will or intestacy.

If there is no successor to an assured period tenancy under section 17 of the 1988 Act, and it therefore devolves on whoever is entitled under the will or intestacy, the landlord may avail himself of the mandatory ground for possession contained in Schedule 2 to the 1988 Act, (ground 7) which enables him to recover possession where the tenancy is a periodic tenancy which has devolved under the will or intestacy of the deceased tenant and the proceedings for the recovery of possession are begun not later than 12 months after the death of the former tenant, or, if the court so directs after the date on which, in the opinion of the court, the landlord became aware of the former tenant's death.

The Housing Act 1988 amends the provisions of the Rent Act 1977 relating to statutory succession and these provisions operate where a protected or statutory tenant or a first successor dies after the commencement of the

---

[31] Where the trust is declared in writing the written provisions prevail unless there is a claim for rectification or rescission *Goodman* v. *Gallant* [1986] F. 106; *Turton* v. *Turton* [1988] Ch. 542.

[32] Law of Property (Joint Tenants) Act 1964, s.1(2). See also *City of London* v. *Flegg* [1988] A.C. 54.

[33] The present Act is the Housing Act 1988: for this, and the amendments made by the Housing Act 1988 to the Rent Act 1977, see generally Woodfall, *Landlord & Tenant*, 28th ed., Vol. 3.

[34] Housing Act 1988, s.1.

[35] *Keeves* v. *Dean* [1924] 1 K.B. 685; *Brown* v. *Brash and Ambrose* [1948] 2 K.B. 247; *Skinner* v. *Geary* [1931] 2 K.B. 546 and see *Hiller* v. *United Dairies Ltd.* [1934] 1 K.B. 57.

[36] Housing Act 1988, s.17(4).

Housing Act 1988 on January 15, 1989. The reader is referred to works on the law of landlord and tenant for the detail and effect of these provisions.

The representatives of a resident landlord have in general the same rights as that landlord.[37]

Estates for the life of another (pur autre vie)

For a statement of the interest taken by an executor or administrator in estates *pur autre vie* by the common law and the Statute of Frauds (29 Car. II, c. 3), s.12, and for the cases decided thereunder, the reader is referred to the eleventh or earlier editions of this work.[38] This statute was repealed by the Wills Act 1837, s.3, which enables estates *pur autre vie* to be disposed of by will, whether or not there is any special occupant thereof. By section 6 of the same statute, if no testamentary disposition is made of an estate *pur autre vie*, and if there is no special occupant thereof, it goes to the executor or administrator of the party who had the estate thereof by virtue of the grant; and if the same comes to the executor or administrator, either by reason of special occupancy, or by virtue of the Act, it is assets in his hands, and goes in the same manner as the personal estate. Devolution by special occupancy has now been abolished[39]; and in cases of death after 1925 the above rules, so far as land is concerned, only apply to the beneficial interests in estates *pur autre vie*. The tenant for the life of another has the powers of a tenant for life[40] but his interest is only equitable.[41] Upon his death, the anomalous situation may arise that the legal estate in property, which is an asset for payment of debts for which the general representative may call, will in fact vest in the Settled Land Act trustees as special representatives. The equitable interest meanwhile passes to the general representatives.[42]

Mortgages

Since 1925[43] 1925 a mortgage, whether created before 1926[44] or after 1925,[45] can only take effect at law as a term of years absolute (subject to a provision for cesser on redemption), or as a charge by deed by way of legal mortgage.[46] It follows that where the rights of the mortgagor are not barred at the death of the mortgagee, the legal estate of the mortgagee would now devolve upon his representatives independent of any statutory enactment.

[37] *Landau* v. *Sloane* [1982] A.C. 490; see also *Williams* v. *Mate* [1982] 46 P. & C.R. 43, 48.
[38] Pt. II, Bk. II, Chap. 1.
[39] Administration of Estates Act 1925, s.45(1)(*a*) *post*, p. 1137.
[40] Settled Land Act 1925, s.20.
[41] Law of Property Act 1925, s.1(1)(2)(3).
[42] Administration of Estates Act 1925, s.1(1).
[43] As to the pre-1926 position with respect to devolution of a legal interest in a mortgage, see 12th ed. of this work, pp. 436 *et seq.*
[44] See the Law of Property Act 1925, s.39(7)(8); Sched. 1, Pts. VII and VIII; and as to copyholds, the Law of Property Act 1922, Sched. 12, para. (1)(*f*).
[45] See the Law of Property Act 1925, ss.85, 86.
[46] As to which, see *ibid.* s.87.

On the death of a mortgagee intestate after 1925 there can be no competition between his heirs and next-of-kin (save in one exceptional case[47]) for the beneficial interests in the mortgage debt and security, because realty and personalty now devolve upon the same persons[48] but analogous questions may still arise where the mortgagee dies leaving a will disposing of his realty and personalty to different persons. As a general rule the interest of a mortgagee passes as personal estate,[49] unless the mortgage was of an estate in fee simple and the rights of the mortgagor were barred at the death of the mortgagee.[50]

If the mortgagee becomes entitled absolutely to the mortgaged land, as if the mortgagor's interest descends upon or is devised to him, though the two interests now devolve upon his representatives, the question may still arise whether the charge is to be kept alive or is merged. The rule in these cases was, that if it was indifferent to the party in whom this union of interest arose, whether the charge was kept on foot, or not, it was extinguished in equity upon the presumed intention, unless an act declaratory of a contrary intention, and consequently repelling such presumption, was done by him.[51] But if a purpose, beneficial to the owner, could be answered by keeping the charge on foot, so that the charge would be disposable by him, though the land would not[52]: or a beneficial use might have been made of it against a subsequent incumbrancer,[53] or the other creditors of the person from whom the party derived the burdened estate[54]: in these, and similar cases, equity would consider the charge as subsisting, notwithstanding that it might, before the Judicature Acts, have been merged at law[55]: and the rule was adopted in favour of the creditors of the person in whom these

---

[47] *i.e.* in the case of persons of unsound mind within the Administration of Estates Act 1925, s.51(2); *post*, pp. 1075.

[48] See the Administration of Estates Act 1925, Pt. IV (*post*, p. 1137).

[49] See, generally, as to devolution and bequests of the beneficial interest of a mortgagee, Coote, *Mortgages*, 9th ed., pp. 870 *et seq.*

[50] As to the realisation of freehold mortgages and the enlargement of a statute-barred mortgage term into a fee simple, see the Law of Property Act 1925, ss.88, 153(3). Property vested in trustees by way of security when discharged from the right of redemption is held by them on trust for sale; *ibid.* s.31.

[51] 2 Powell, Dev. 146, Jarman's ed.; *Grice* v. *Shaw* (1852) 10 Hare 76; *Ingle* v. *Vaughan Jenkins* [1900] 2 Ch. 368; but see *Manks* v. *Whiteley* [1912] 1 Ch. 735; reversed on appeal, *sub nom. Whiteley* v. *Delaney* [1914] A.C. 132, *ante*, p. 467. When the owner of an estate has also a charge on it, and there is some intermediate charge or estate between his own charge and his ownership in fee, it may be reasonable to say that without some special act, no presumption can be made of an intention to merge the charge in fee; for that might be against the interest of the owner by letting in the intermediate estate or incumbrance. But where the intermediate interest is created by the act of the owner himself, this reasoning has no application: *Johnson* v. *Webster* (1854) 4 De G.M. & G. 474, 488, by Lord Cranworth; and see *Re French-Brewster's Settlements* [1904] 1 Ch. 713.

[52] *Thomas* v. *Kemeys* (1696) 2 Vern. 348.

[53] *Gwillim* v. *Holland* (1741) cited 2 Ves. 263.

[54] *Forbes* v. *Moffatt* (1811) 18 Ves.Jun. 384.

[55] *Powell*, Dev., *ante*; *Byam* v. *Sutton* (1854) 19 Beav. 556. By s.185 of the Law of Property Act 1925, replacing s.25(4) of the Jud. Act 1873, there is no merger by operation of law only of any estate the beneficial interest in which would not be deemed to be merged or extinguished in equity.

interests centred.[56] It seems that these rules might still apply in appropriate cases after 1925.[57]

Advowsons

Where the deceased was entitled to present to a benefice, and died during a vacancy, the void term, which before 1926 would have been a chattel personal,[58] like rent due, or any other fruit fallen, vests in the representative[59] whether the deceased was seized of the advowson in his own right, or as a corporator sole.[60]

It seems, however, that on the death of the holder of office as an ecclesiastical corporator sole such as a bishop[61] or rector,[62] the right to present may not pass to the executor but may go in the one case to the Crown[63] and in the other to the patron of the rectory.[64]

If the testator presented, and (his clerk not being admitted before his death) then his executor presented his clerk, the Ordinary might elect which clerk he would receive.[65]

B. REGISTERED LAND[66]

Death of proprietor

A personal representative may apply for registration of the title to freehold[67] or leasehold[68] land.

On the death of one of two or more joint proprietors of any registered land or charge (for example, on the death of one of a number of trustees or partners), his name must be withdrawn from the register on proof of death, or on production of probate or letters of administration, together with such other evidence as the registrar may direct.[69]

On the death of the sole or last surviving proprietor (other than an

---

[56] *Powell* v. *Morgan* (1688) cited 2 Vern. 208; Powell, Dev., *ante*.

[57] See further, as to merger by union of the estates of mortgagor and mortgagee, Coote, *Mortgages*, 9th ed., pp. 1439 *et seq*.

[58] F.N.B. 33, P; *The Queen and Archbishop of Canterbury's Case* (1588) 4 Leo. 107. Co. Litt. 388a; Wats.C.L., 4th ed., p. 72. *Rennell* v. *Bishop of Lincoln* (1827) 7 B. & C. 113, 193. See also the 12th ed. of this work, Pt. II, Bk. II, Chap. 1, s.1 and Cripps, *Church and Clergy*, 8th ed., p. 259. The advowson itself is an incorporeal hereditament: 2 Bl.Com., 1st ed., p. 21.

[59] Administration of Estates Act 1925, s.3(5). the A.E. Act 1925, binds the Crown: *ibid*. s.57(1).

[60] *Mirehouse* v. *Rennell* (1833) 8 Bing. 490; 1 Cl. & F. 527.

[61] Roll.Abr.Presentment 345, E., pl. 4; Co.Litt. 90a; Co.Litt. 388a; Wats.C.L., 4th ed., p. 73.

[62] 2 Roll.Abr. 346, tit. Presentment, F., pl. 4; 1 Burn E.L., 8th ed., p. 139.

[63] *Ibid*. n. 58.

[64] *Ibid*. n. 59.

[65] *Smalwood* v. *Bishop of Lichfield* (1589) 1 Leo. 205; Wats.C.L., 4th ed., pp. 72, 225.

[66] On the subject of registered land generally, see Ruoff and Roper, *Registered Conveyancing* (sixth (looseleaf) ed. 1991).

[67] Land Registration Act 1925, s.4.

[68] *Ibid*. s.8.

[69] Land Registration Rules 1925, r. 172.

administrator[70] or trustee in bankruptcy[71] of any registered land or charge), his personal representative is, on production of the probate or letters of administration,[72] entitled to (but need not) be registered as proprietor in his place.[73]

Settled land

If the land was settled before the death of the proprietor (and the settlement is not determined on his death),[74] his special representatives, on production of the grant in their favour, must be registered as proprietors.[75]

Where a special or additional representative is appointed by the court[76] in reference to registered land comprised in an estate, then on production of the order, he must be registered as proprietor either jointly or solely with any of the other representatives, as the case may require, and a copy of the order must be filed at the registry.[77] A person intending to apply for such an appointment may lodge a caution against dealings.[78]

Registration of additional executor

Where a co-executor applies to be registered as proprietor jointly with another executor who has already been so registered, the registrar must, after notice to such other executor, make the necessary alteration in the register, on production by the applicant of probate obtained by him, or of a statement in writing signed by him that he has applied for probate and desires to be registered accordingly.[79]

Position of representative

Personal representatives who are registered as proprietors in place of a deceased proprietor would seem to be, as between them and their beneficiaries, in the same legal position, so far as their rights, duties, powers and discretions are concerned, as in the case of unregistered land,[80] though a purchaser from them, having in effect a statutory title, is in a stronger position than a purchaser of unregistered land, and is unconcerned with equitable interests not protected by an entry on the register. They may give

---

[70] On the death of an administrator a *de bonis non* grant would be required.

[71] See the Land Registration Rules 1925, rr. 173, 183.

[72] *Ibid.* r. 168.

[73] Land Registration Act 1925, s.41(1).

[74] See *ante*, pp. 18, 272.

[75] Land Registration Rules 1925, r. 168(2). The registration is without fee: see the Land Registration Act 1925, s.145(2). The land may be relevant property for the purposes of death duty relief. See *Finch* v. *I.R.C.* [1985] Ch. 1 and pp. 71 *et seq. ante.*

[76] See the Administration of Estates Act 1925, s.22; Jud. Act 1925, s.160; *ante*, p. 32.

[77] Land Registration Act 1925, s.41(1).

[78] *Ibid.* subs. (2).

[79] Land Registration Act 1925, r. 169.

[80] See the Land Registration Act 1925, ss.43, 44. But see the Land Registration Rules 1925, rr. 103–105.

effect to their wide powers of disposition[81] by means of the registered dealings authorised by the Land Registration Act 1925[82] and they may make an
assent in the prescribed form[83] in favour of a beneficiary. The registrar is
not concerned with the propriety of the transfer or assent,[84] and on
delivery thereof at the registry must register the person named therein as
proprietor.[85]

The representative of a deceased proprietor may transfer the land of the
deceased without himself being first registered, but it seems that a purchaser may be entitled (unreasonably) to insist on the representative procuring registration of himself before selling.[86]

Though it will in many cases be expedient, as where the period of administration is likely to be prolonged, it is not essential for a representative to
be registered as proprietor.[87] Without being so registered he may make an
appropriation[88] and transfer[89] or assent,[90] and on delivery of the transfer
or assent[91] at the registry, accompanied (if the representative is not already
registered as proprietor) by the grant of representation, the registrar must,
without being concerned with the propriety of the transfer or assent,[92]
register the person named in the instrument as proprietor.[93] An assent is
registered without fee.

Where on the death of a sole or last surviving proprietor the land
becomes[94] or remains settled land, a vesting assent must be made by the
general or special representatives, as the case may be,[95] in favour of the
tenant for life or statutory owner entitled to call for the legal estate in the
settled land and not being an infant.[96]

---

[81] As to which, see *post*, pp. 666 *et seq.* and 684 *et seq.*

[82] See the Land Registration Act 1925, ss.18, 21, 25, 31, 33 and 43.

[83] *Ibid.* s.41(4). See Forms 56 and 57.

[84] Land Registration Rules 1925, r. 170(5). *cf.* the Administration of Estates Act 1925,
s.36(7).

[85] Land Registration Rules 1925, r. 170(4). And see the Land Registration Act 1925,
s.41(4).

[86] See Ruoff and Roper, *Registered Conveyancing*, 1991 ed., 17–12, 27–15 Land Registration Act 1925, s.110(5).

[87] See Land Registration Act 1925, r. 170.

[88] For the statutory power of a personal representative to appropriate, see the Administration of Estates Act 1925, s.41; *post*, p. 685. An appropriation, whether under seal or not,
attracts stamp duty under the Stamp Act 1891, s.62, unless made under a power not requiring
consent.

[89] See the Land Registration Act 1925, ss.18(5), for the meaning of "transfer."

[90] For forms of assent, see the Land Registration Rules, Sched. Forms 56 and 57. As to
assents see *post*, pp. 1055 *et seq.*

[91] An appropriation is carried out by means of an assent.

[92] Land Registration Act 1925, r. 170(5).

[93] *Ibid.* r. 170(4). See also the Land Registration Act 1925, s.41(4).

[94] As to the duty of a personal representative to apply for restrictions where the land is
settled, see the Land Registration Rules 1925, r. 104.

[95] As a rule "special," if the land was settled before death and remains settled land;
"general," if the settlement was created or arose under the will or on the intestacy. See also
post, p. 1058.

[96] Land Registration Act 1925, s.87(1). For the form of assent, see the Land Registration
Rules, Sched. Form 57.

Where there is a minority

Where a settlement is created or arises under a will or on intestacy and an infant becomes beneficially entitled to an estate in fee simple or a term of years absolute or would, if he were of full age, be or have the powers of a tenant for life, the representatives under the will or on the intestacy must, during the minority, be registered as proprietors.[97] But after administration is completed the representatives must (unless themselves the statutory owners) thenceforth give effect on the register to the directions of the statutory owners.[98] *Semble*, this does not affect the right of the statutory owners to be registered as proprietors after administration is completed if they so wish.[99] Further, if there is a person of full age entitled jointly with an infant, that person is entitled, after administration is completed, to be registered as proprietor during the minority.[1]

Transfer subject to registered charge

A representative may, as a condition of giving an assent or making a conveyance, require security for the discharge of any duties, debts, or liabilities affecting the estate or interest disposed of by him.[2] Where the title is registered this security may consist of a registered charge under the Land Registration Act 1925, ss.25 and 37.

Inheritance tax[3]

Where it appears to the Registrar upon first registration, or upon the conversion of a registered title, that the registered land is subject to an Inland Revenue charge for inheritance tax, or where the Commissioners of Inland Revenue themselves apply for the registration of notice of such a charge, the Registrar must enter notice of such a charge on the register in the prescribed manner. A registered disposition takes effect subject to any such charge, unless (a) it is in favour of a purchaser as defined in s.272 of the Inheritance Tax Act 1984; and (b) the charge is not, at the time of registration of the disposition, protected by a notice on the register.

---

[97] Land Registration Act 1925, s.91(1).

[98] *Ibid.*; the Land Registration Rules 1925, r. 171. And see the Settled Land Act 1925, s.26; *post*, p. 689.

[99] See Land Registration Act 1925, s.87(1); the Land Registraton Rules 1925, r. 171(4).

[1] Land Registration Rules 1925, r. 171(3). And see the Settled Land Act 1925, s.19(3).

[2] See the Administration of Estates Act 1925, s.36(10). See *post*, pp. 1024, 1060.

[3] Land Registration Act 1925, s.73, as substituted by the Finance Act 1975, Sched. 12, para. 5 and amended by the Inheritance Tax Act 1984, s.276 and Sched. 8, para. 1.; the Land Registration Rules 1975, rr. 191–193, as substituted by the Land Registration (Capital Transfer Tax) Rules 1975. As to death duties in general, see *ante* pp. 71 *et seq.*, and as to the charge, see *ante*, pp. 72, 81.

CHAPTER 48

INCIDENCE OF LIABILITIES OF THE DECEASED

The law on this subject is based partly upon the characteristics which surrounded the ancient forms of action. Some forms of action, such as debt, trespass and trover, did not at common law survive against personal representatives. Others, such as detinue, replevin and assumpsit, did so survive. Further, it was often possible to substitute a form of action which survived in place of some other, and possibly more appropriate, form which did not survive.[1]

All forms of action have been abolished, and it is now material to explain the principles which have survived them, as well as the new rules which have been introduced by statute. This chapter should be read in conjunction with Chapter 46.[2] The procedures where a representative is plaintiff or defendant are considered in Chapters 62 and 63 respectively.

General rule

The general rule is that the right of action on which the deceased might have been sued in his life time survives his death and is enforceable against his representatives. This is not affected by the fact that a grant of administration may be a limited grant.[3]

Every person to whom administration is granted has, subject to the limitations contained in the grant, the same rights and liabilities as if he were the executor of the deceased.[4] If a cessate grant terminates the administrator is in the same position as an executor whose grant has been terminated by the court.[5] Thus an administrator acting under a grant during minority may get in the estate, pay debts, sell[6] and assent.[7] He could formerly retain[8] for his own debt and for debts arising from litigation even if his grant determined during the proceedings,[9] and may now exercise the rights of representative under section 10 of the Administration of Estates Act 1971.[10] The grant does not of itself break the chain of

---

[1] See *Hambly* v. *Trott* (1776) 1 Cowp. 375, by Lord Mansfield.
[2] *Ante*, p. 515.
[3] See *ante*, p. 316.
[4] Administration of Estates Act 1925, s.21. See *ante*, p. 475.
[5] *Re Thomas* [1956] 1 W.L.R. 1516.
[6] *Re Cope* (1880) 16 Ch.D. 49, 52, and see *Hewson* v. *Shelley* [1914] 2 Ch. 13.
[7] Bac.Abr.Exors.V. 1, 2; *Prince's Case* (1599) 5 Co. 29B; *Anon.* (1675) 1 Freem. K.B. 288; *Monsell* v. *Armstrong* (1872) L.R. 14 Eq. 423. See *ante*, p. 476, *post*, p. 1059.
[8] *Roskelley* v. *Godolphin* (1683) T.Raym, 483; Com.Dig.Admon.F.
[9] *Sparks* v. *Crofts* (1698) Comb. 465, by Lord Holt.
[10] See *post*, pp. 640 *et seq.*

a representation.[11] Similarly an order obtained against an administrator *ad litem* is binding on any future representative.[12]

1. CONTRACT

The general rule has been established from very early times, with respect to such personal claims as are founded upon any obligation, contract, debt, covenant, or other duty, that the right of action, on which the testator or intestate might have been sued in his lifetime, survives his death, and is enforceable against his executor or administrator.[13] And it is the duty of a representative to perform all the contracts of his testator or intestate, as the case may be, that can be enforced whether by way of specific performance or otherwise.[14]

By the Law Reform (Miscellaneous Provisions) Act 1934, s.1, it is enacted that on the death of any person after July 25, 1934, all causes of action subsisting against him shall, subject to certain qualifications mentioned later,[15] survive against his estate.[16] Therefore, it is clear that the executors or administrators are answerable, as far as they have assets, for debts of every description due from the deceased, either debts of record, as judgments, statutes, or recognisances; or debts due on special contract, as for rent[17] or on bonds, covenants and the like, under seal; or debts, on simple contract, as notes unsealed, and promises not in writing, either expressed or implied.[18]

Conveyancing chains

When the deceased dies before completing the contracts for sale and purchase of houses in a conveyancing "chain" heavy liabilities can arise.[19] The delay in completing which must result from delays in obtaining a grant may entitle other members of the chain to damages for breach of contract.[20] Where there is such a risk it will often be essential to obtain an

---

[11] Administration of Estates Act 1925, s.7(3), (*post*, p. 1116).

[12] *Davis* v. *Chanter* (1848) 2 Phil. 545; *Faulkner* v. *Daniel* (1843) 3 Hare 199, 208; *Ellice* v. *Goodson* (1845) 2 Coll. 4. See further as to the need for a general grant if a general order is required, *ante*, pp. 826, 827.

[13] Touchst. 482; 1 Saund. 216(a), n. (1) to *Wheatly* v. *Lane*; *Sollers* v. *Lawrence* (1743) Willes 413; *Phillips* v. *Homfray* (1883) 24 Ch.D. 439; *Batthyany* v. *Walford* (1887) 36 Ch.D. 269; *Concha* v. *Murrieta* (1889) 40 Ch.D. 543, 553; *Peebles* v. *The Oswaldtwistle Urban District Council* [1896] 2 Q.B. 159 (where the alleged cause of action arose out of a statutory duty); *Blackmore* v. *White* [1899] 1 Q.B. 293 (where the cause of action arose from a breach of an implied contract to discharge the customary obligation to repair a tenement according to the custom of the manor); *Flower* v. *Prechtel* (1934) 150 L.T. 491, 494.

[14] *Ahmed Angullia, etc.* v. *Estate and Trust Agencies* [1938] A.C. 624; *Youngmin* v. *Health* [1974] 1 W.L.R. 135, C.A.

[15] At pp. 557, 558 *et seq.*

[16] This principle is the complement of the survival of actions from the deceased to the personal representative. See *ante*, p. 515.

[17] See *Eaton College* v. *Beauchamp* (1669) 1 Chanc.Cas. 121. As to the power of a personal representative to escape future liability for rent, etc., see *post*, p. 655.

[18] Bac.Abr.Exors.P. 1; Com.Dig.Admon.B. 14. See *Shaw* v. *Shaw* [1954] 2 Q.B. 429.

[19] See *Rainer* v. *Miles* [1981] A.C. 1050.

[20] See 140 N.L.J. 95.

expedited grant and in some cases to insure the life in question and to cover the additional likely mortgage costs.

Land charges

When an estate owner dies having created a land charge and this charge has not been registered the person entitled to register must do so against the names of the representatives, or the President (if there is an intestacy). This creates obvious difficulties.[21]

A contract to do something uncertain

There is no difference between a promise to pay a debt certain, and a promise to do a collateral act, which is uncertain and rests only in damages. Wherever in such cases the testator himself is liable to an action, his executors are liable also.[22]

Where representatives not named

The executors or administrators so completely represent their testator or intestate, that every bond, or covenant, or contract of the deceased (not being a contract personal to the deceased) includes them, though they are not named in the terms of it,[23] for the executors or administrators of every person are implied in himself.[24]

Thus, if a person is under contract to build a house before a particular time, and dies before that time, his executors must complete the contract.[25] Again where a testator specifically devised a farm which was destroyed by fire after the date of the will and the testator had received the insurance money and contracted to effect repairs, the specific devisees were held entitled to require the executors to effect repairs at the expense of the testator's estate notwithstanding the disclaiming of the contract by the executors without protest from the builder.[26]

Carrying on deceased's business

Though, as is pointed out later,[27] representatives have no general authority in law to carry on the business of the deceased, yet in some cases they

[21] See Law Com. 184 para. 2.2, and 140 N.L.J. 95; Land Charges Act 1972, s.3(1).
[22] Bac.Abr.Exors.P. 2. See *Meredith* v. *Davey* [1960] C.L.Y. 544.
[23] Wentw.Off.Ex. c. 11, 14th ed., pp. 239, 243; *Bradbury* v. *Morgan*, 1 H. & C. 249, 255.
[24] By Lord Macclesfield in *Hyde* v. *Skinner* (1723) 2 P.Wms. 197. See also *Harwood* v. *Helyard* (1678) 2 Mod. 268 (executor liable under testator's contract, though notice given to him and not, as required by the contract, to the testator); *Kennewell* v. *Dye* [1949] Ch. 517, 521, *per* Roxburgh J.
[25] *Quick* v. *Ludborrow* (1615) 3 Bulstr. 30. See also *Marshall* v. *Broadhurst, infra*; *Flower* v. *Prechtel* (1934) 150 L.T. 491, *per* Scrutton L.J. at p. 492; and *Ahmed Angullia, etc.* v. *Estate and Trust Agencies* [1938] A.C. 624.
[26] *Re Rushbrook's Will Trusts* [1948] Ch. 421.
[27] *Post*, p. 722.

are bound to complete contracts entered into by the deceased, and to this extent to carry on his business.[28]

Bonds and Covenants

Again, a personal representative is liable on a bond which becomes due, or on a note payable, after the death of the deceased.[29] And where a person covenanted that A should serve B as an apprentice for a term of years, and died, it was held that if A departed during that term, an action lay against the executor of the covenantor.[30]

Under the Law of Property Act 1925[31] a covenant, bond or contract by deed made after December 31, 1881, binds the real estate as well as the personal estate of the covenantor unless a contrary intention is expressed.[32] This provision extends to a covenant implied by the Act.[33] As the whole real and personal estate of a person dying after 1925, to the extent of his beneficial interest therein, is liable in the hands of his representatives for the payment of his debts,[34] it would seem to make no difference that the contract is not under seal.

A person may covenant in a form binding upon his representatives, in which case they can be sued upon the covenant whatever its nature.[35]

Partners

Where partners covenant that they and their respective executors and administrators will continue partners for a certain term of years, and one of them dies before the term has expired, his representatives cannot be compelled to become partners personally, though the covenant is binding on the estate of the deceased partner in their hands.[36] Liability for covenants affecting land is considered later.[37]

Exceptions

(i) Contracts personal to the deceased. The principle that representatives are liable upon every contract of the deceased, though not named, does not

---

[28] See *Collinson* v. *Lister* (1855) 20 Beav. 356, 365, 366.

[29] Toller 463. An executrix of a surety has no equity to support an injunction to restrain an action on the bond: *Gordon* v. *Calvert* (1828) 2 Sim. 253; 4 Russ. 581.

[30] Bro. Covenant, 12 Bac.Abr.Exors. P. 1.

[31] Law of Property Act 1925, s.80(1), reproducing s.59 of the Conveyancing Act 1881 with amendments. Law of Property (Miscellaneous Provisions) Act 1989, s.1.

[32] The contrary intention must be expressed in fact: *Kirk* v. *Eustace* [1937] A.C. 491.

[33] As to these, see Law of Property Act 1925, ss.76 and 77. And as to covenants relating to land, including covenants to do some act relating to land, see *ibid.* ss.79, 80(4). Such covenants bind the successors of, and persons deriving title under, the covenantor.

[34] Administration of Estates Act 1925, s.32; *post*, pp. 587, 1127.

[35] *Powell* v. *Graham* (1817) 7 Taunt. 580; *Randall* v. *Rigby* (1838) 4 M. & W. 132; *Ex p. Tindall* (1832) 8 Bing. 402. *Perrot* v. *Austin* (1591) Cro.Eliz. 232, as explained in Wentw.Off.-Ex., 14th ed., 250, only decided that a particular form of action, *viz.* debt. would not lie against the executor. See also *Plumer* v. *Marchant* (1765) 3 Burr. 1380.

[36] *Downs* v. *Collins* (1848) 6 Hare 418, 438. See *per* James L.J. in *Baird's Case*, L.R. 5 Ch.App. 725, 733; *post*, p. 591, n. 44. As to partnership liabilities, see *post*, p. 566.

[37] See *post*, p. 573.

at common law extend to contracts personal to the deceased, as in cases of principal and agent and master and servant.[38] In such cases no liability attaches upon the representatives, unless a breach was incurred in the lifetime of the deceased,[39] or there was a stipulation, express or implied, to the contrary. Thus, if an author undertakes to compose a work, and dies before completing it, his executors are discharged from this contract; for the undertaking is merely personal in its nature, and by the intervention of the contractor's death, has become impossible to be performed.[40] So a covenant by a master for the instruction of his apprentice is personal to the master, and his executors are not liable upon it.[41] In such a case the contract is discharged by supervening impossibility of performance or frustration, for, being one which can be performed only by the promisor in person, it is subject to the implied condition that he shall be alive to perform it.[42]

On a covenant that in consideration of a weekly payment to A and his executors for a term certain A shall not exercise a particular trade, the executors of A are not bound to abstain from exercising it after his death.[43]

On the other hand, if a testator orders goods, the contract is not, as a general rule, personal to himself, so that his executors must receive and pay for the goods.[44]

Again, an underwriting contract by which A agrees to place the share capital of a company is not a contract personal to A, but is one which can be enforced against his executors.[45]

A contract personal to the deceased although not enforceable at common law against the executors may nevertheless in theory be enforceable under the Act. Formerly for this purpose the proceedings must have been pending at death or the cause of action must have arisen not earlier than six months before the death, and the proceedings have been taken within six months of the date of grant.[46] These conditions are now repealed by the Proceedings Against Estates Act 1970.

---

[38] *Farrow* v. *Wilson* (1869) L.R. 4 C.P. 744; *Campanari* v. *Woodburn* (1854) 15 C.B. 400. See *post*, p. 558 as to agency. See also *ante*, pp. 517, 528. For rights and duties under the Employment Protection (Consolidation) Act 1978, see *post*, p. 584.

[39] *Hyde* v. *The Dean of Windsor* (1579) Cro.Eliz. 552; *Siboni* v. *Kirkman* (1836) 1 M. & W. 418, 423, *per* Parke B.

[40] *Marshall* v. *Broadhurst* (1831) 1 Tyrwh. 349, by Lord Lyndhurst. In *Wentworth* v. *Cock* (1839) 10 A. & E. 45, Patterson J. said that there was a case at Liverpool where a contract to build a lighthouse was held to be personal, on the ground of its being a matter of personal skill and science.

[41] See *post*, p. 579.

[42] See Chitty, *Contracts*, 26th ed. As to the adjustment of the rights and liabilities of parties on discharge of a frustrated contract, see the Law Reform (Frustrated Contracts) Act 1934. *B.P. Exploration* v. *Hunt* (*No. 2*) [1981] 1 W.L.R. 232.

[43] *Cooke* v. *Colcraft* (1773) 2 W.Bl. 856; 3 Wils. 380.

[44] See *Wentworth* v. *Cock* (1839) 10 A. & E. 42. See also *Cooper* v. *Jarman* (1866) L.R. 3 Eq. 98; *cf. Re Day* [1898] 2 Ch. 510; *Re Rushbrook's Will Trusts* [1948] Ch. 421.

[45] *Re Worthington* [1914] 2 K.B. 299.

[46] Law Reform (Miscellaneous Provisions) Act 1934, s.1(3). See also *ante*, p. 527.

(ii) Affiliation orders.   The liability under an affiliation order has been held to be purely personal, so that if the father dies the mother cannot claim against his estate for future payments.[47] The Affiliation Proceedings Act 1957[48] gives the justices power to make an order and lays down the mode for enforcing the order. That mode of enforcement predicates the existence of the putative father and if he be dead, it has been suggested that, notwithstanding anything contained in the Law Reform (Miscellaneous Provisions) Act 1934, the claim is not enforceable against his estate.[49] However, there seems to be no provision in the 1934 Act to prevent the liability surviving against the representatives and as a matter of construction the 1957 Act seems to limit the duration of the order to a period related only to the age of the child and not to the lifetime of the putative father.[50]

The representatives of the mother of an illegitimate child are not liable for necessaries supplied to the child after her death.[51] In practice claims would now be made under the Family Provision legislation. [51a]

(iii) Contract of agency.   Since the authority of an agent is personal and is revoked by death, neither party can, generally speaking,[52] sue the executor of the other after the death of either.[53] The agency may be ratified by the representative[54] or it may be construed, as a matter of interpretation, as binding after death.[55] The death of a joint agent, or presumably of a joint principal similarly determines the agency.[56]

2. TORT

On the death of any person on or after July 25, 1934, all causes of action, "whether in contract or in tort or otherwise,"[57] subsisting against him survive against his estate, except causes of action for defamation[58] or seduction or for inducing one spouse to leave or remain apart from the other or statutory claims for damages on the ground of adultery.[59]

---

[47] *Re Harrington* [1908] 2 Ch. 687. But *quaere* as to arrears; see the Summary Jurisdiction Act 1879, s.6, and *cf. L.C.C.* v. *Betts* [1936] 1 K.B. 430, *per* du Parcq J. at p. 439.

[48] Re-enacting, by s.4 the Bastardy Laws Amendment Act 1872, s.4.

[49] See Williams, *Executors*, 14th ed., p. 1013.

[50] See *ante*, pp. 527, 528, as to the basis upon which personal contracts determine. This liability is not contractual. See also as to matrimonial causes, *post*, p. 560.

[51] *Ruttinger* v. *Temple* (1863) 4 Best & Sm. 491.

[51a] See p. 757, *post.*

[52] As to representatives acting under powers of attorney, see *post*, p. 701.

[53] See *ante*, p. 556 and Bowstead, *Agency*, 14th ed., p. 426.

[54] *Campanari* v. *Woodburn* (1854) 15 C.B. 400.

[55] *Wilson* v. *Harper* [1908] 2 Ch. 370.

[56] *Friend* v. *Young* [1897] 2 Ch. 421.

[57] This applies to penalties imposed under a taxing Act: *Att.-Gen.* v. *Canter* [1939] 1 K.B. 318.

[58] But see as to defamation of title, *ante*, p. 519.

[59] Law Reform (Miscellaneous Provisions) Act 1934, s.1(1). As to contribution between tortfeasors, see *post*, p. 569.

Before 1934 the principle *"actio personalis moritur cum persona"* applied to tortious acts of a deceased person. Personal representatives could not be sued for a wrong committed by the deceased for which unliquidated damages only were recoverable.[60]

The only cases in which, apart from breach of contract express or implied and certain statutory exceptions, a remedy for a wrongful act could be pursued against the estate of a deceased person were where property or the proceeds or value of property belonging to another had been appropriated by the deceased person and added to his own estate or money. In such cases the action, though arising out of a wrongful act, did not die with the person. This rule was limited to the recovery of specific acquisitions or their value. It did not include the recovery of damages, as such, for a wrong, though the wrong might have increased the wrongdoer's estate in the sense of being useful to him or saving him expense.[61]

Devastavit by deceased

At common law, if a person was appointed executor, and committed a *devastavit* and died, the executor of such executor was not liable for the *devastavit*,[62] but this was reversed by statute now comprised in section 29 of the Administration of Estates Act 1925.[63] Such an executor is liable to the extent of the available assets of the defaulter in the same manner as the defaulter would have been if living.[64]

Misrepresentation or negligence by company directors

Formerly an action for damages for misrepresentation[65] or negligence[66] did not survive against the representatives of a deceased director of a com-

---

[60] *Kirk* v. *Todd* (1882) 21 Ch.D. 484, 488. See *ante*, p. 518.

[61] *Phillips* v. *Homfray* (1883) 24 Ch.D. 439; *Hambly* v. *Trott* (1776) 1 Cowp. 371. But an action in tort for damage to the property of the deceased survives to the executor. See *post*, p. 518.

[62] *Sir Brian Tucke's Case* (1590) 3 Leon. 241; *Browne* v. *Collins* (1675) 1 Ventr. 292. But he was liable in equity: *Price* v. *Morgan* (1676) 2 Chanc.Cas. 215. *Cf. post*, p. 912 (judgment obtained). As to breach of trust see p. 563 *post*.

[63] See Appendix. This took the place of the Executors of Executors (Waste) Act 1678, 30 Car. 2, c. 7; explained and made permanent by the Executors (Estreats) Act 1692, 4 & 5 Will & Mary, c. 24, s.12, but replaced by the Administration of Estates Act 1925, Sched. 2, Pt. I. See 1 Saund. 216a, note to *Wheatley* v. *Lane*; *Coward* v. *Gregory* (1866) L.R. 2 C.P. 153; *Thorne* v. *Kerr* (1855) 2 K. & J. 54, 63, 64.

[64] See p. 1126 *post*.

[65] *Peek* v. *Gurney* (1873) L.R. 6 H.L. 377; *Re Duncan* [1899] 1 Ch. 387.

[66] *Overend, Gurney & Co.* v. *Gurney* (1869) L.R. 4 Ch. 701; L.R. 5 H.L. 480.

pany,[67] except in so far as the estate of the deceased director had benefited directly from the misrepresentation or negligence.[68] Nor did the liability for untrue statements made in a prospectus survive.[69]

It is clear, however, that an action for misrepresentation or negligence now survives against the representatives of the deceased director. Similarly, liability under the Financial Services Act 1986, which is a liability in tort,[70] would now survive, since the rock upon which the action against the representatives formerly foundered—the principle *actio personalis*, etc.—is now destroyed. Liability under the provisions of earlier Acts seems, however, to have been treated by the courts on rather a different footing. In *Re Feltom's Executor's Case*[71] an action based on the Act of 1862[72] against the personal representatives of the deceased director was dismissed, not on the ground that the action was a personal one which died with the director, but on the ground that the procedure was inapplicable to the case of personal representatives. It seems that an action in respect of such a cause may survive under the Law Reform (Miscellaneous Provisions) Act 1934 because that Act expressly provides for the survival of "all causes of action," but the procedure by summons may still be inappropriate.

The right of a director to recover contribution survives against the representatives of a deceased director.[73]

3. OTHER CLAIMS

Matrimonial causes

In general matrimonial suits abate on the death of the husband or wife.[74] Where damages had been assessed against a co-respondent in a divorce suit and he died within a month after the decree nisi ordering him to pay the money into court, it was held that the cause of action did not survive, and that there was no remedy against his executors in the Divorce Court.[75] But a fund lodged in court by the husband before his death as security for his

---

[67] As to the liability of the representatives of a deceased partner, see *Ellis* v. *Wadeson* [1899] 1 Q.B. 714, 718; *Phillips* v. *Homfray* (1883) 24 Ch.D. 439; *Re Shephard* (1889) 43 Ch.D. 131. But *cf. New Sombrero Phosphate Co.* v. *Erlanger* (1877) 5 Ch.D. 73, 117 (aff. 3 App.Cas. 1218).

[68] See Williams, *Executors*, 12th ed., p. 1130.

[69] *Geipel* v. *Peach* [1917] 2 Ch. 108; and see *Re British Guardian Life Ass. Co.* (1880) 14 Ch.D. 335.

[70] *Geipel* v. *Peach, ante* (decided under sections of earlier Acts replaced by the Act of 1948).

[71] (1863) L.R. 1 Eq. 219, 224; followed and applied in *Re British Guardian Life Ass. Co., ante.*

[72] s.165.

[73] *Shepheard* v. *Bray* [1906] 2 Ch. 235; [1907] 2 Ch. 571. See also as to contribution p. 569 *post.*

[74] *Maconochie* v. *Maconochie* [1916] P. 326; *Stanhope* v. *Stanhope* (1886) 11 P.D. 103; *D'Este* v. *D'Este* [1973] Fam. 55. But "abate" is not a precise term in this connection: see *Barder* v. *Caluori* [1988] A.C. 20 and p. 541 *ante.*

[75] *Brydges* v. *Brydges* [1909] P. 187; *Coleman* v. *Coleman* [1920] P. 71; and see the Law Reform (Miscellaneous Provisions) Act 1934, s.1(1).

wife's costs of the hearing was available to the wife for her costs after the husband's death and the consequent abatement of the divorce suit.[76] Where, in an action for divorce, an order has been made against the husband to secure the wife an annual sum, but no agreement has been reached before the husband's death as to the properties of the husband which should be selected as security, the wife has an enforceable claim against the husband's estate, but the court cannot at this date vary, either by way of increase or decrease, the amount of maintenance.[77] Claims for arrears of maintenance and alimony have been held not to be recoverable against the estate of a deceased husband[78] but the court will enforce a maintenance order for an ascertainable amount intended to provide for the wife after the husband's death.[79] A claim for divorce against the respondent and a claim for damages against the co-respondent are distinct causes of action, so that the latter does not abate on the death of the respondent.[80]

In practice any substantial matrimonial claims after death are now likely to be made under the Family Provision legislation.[81]

Arrears of maintenance pending suit

The only means by which a wife could enforce payment of arrears of maintenance pending suit was under section 5 of the Debtors Act 1869. This is now covered by section 22 of the Matrimonial Causes Act 1973. On the husband's death the remedy ceases to be available and so the arrears are not recoverable.[82] It has also been held that the right of a wife to maintenance is not a cause of action against the husband so as to survive against his estate.[83]

Fines

A fine is a monetary penalty due to the Crown as soon as sentence is pronounced. The executors of the person sentenced are accordingly liable for the amount of the fine as a debt of record.[84]

---

[76] *Beaumont* v. *Beaumont* [1933] P. 39.
[77] *Mosey* v. *Mosey and Barker* [1956] P. 26.
[78] See below.
[79] *Mosey* v. *Mosey and Barker* [1956] P. 26, 41; and see as to affiliation orders, *ante*, p. 558. As to provision for a former spouse under the Inheritance (Provision for Family and Dependants) Act 1975, see *post*, p. 757 *et seq.*
[80] *Monsell* v. *Monsell* [1922] P. 34.
[81] See *post*, p. 757 *et seq.*
[82] *Re Hedderwick* [1933] Ch. 669; *Re Woolgar* [1942] Ch. 318; and see *Re Bidie* [1948] Ch. 697 (arrears of maintenance under an order made under the Summary Jurisdiction (Married Women) Act 1895). Contrast *Re Stillwell* [1916] 1 Ch. 365, which was not followed in the foregoing cases and the remark of Denning L.J. (as he then was) in *Sugden* v. *Sugden* [1957] P. 120, 135. See also p. 540 *ante.*
[83] *Dipple* v. *Dipple* [1942] P. 65. *Barder* v. *Caluori* [1988] A.C. 35. See p. 541 *ante.*
[84] *Treasury* v. *Harris* [1957] 2 Q.B. 516; *R.* v. *Woolf* (1819) 2 B. & Ald. 609; *R.* v. *Rowe* [1955] 1 Q.B. 573. See article by J. E. Hall Williams, 20 M.L.R. 502.

Penalties and tax

It has been held that the right of the Crown to sue for a penalty in default of making a return of income for the purposes of taxation is a cause of action which will survive against the estate of the taxpayer.[85] If a person chargeable to tax dies, his representatives are liable for the tax chargeable on him, and may deduct any payment made in discharge of such liability out of the assets and effects of the deceased. On neglect or refusal of payment the personal representatives are liable like any other defaulter.[86] However, the general time limit of six years is for assessments on representatives shortened to three years, unless the assessment is made for the purpose of making good any loss of tax attributable to the fraud, wilful default or neglect of the deceased.[87]

Alternative claims (tort and contract)

Formerly it was held that where, although a deceased person was liable in tort he might also have been sued independently in respect of the same act on a contract express or implied, the plaintiff could waive the tort and proceed on the contract against representatives of the deceased wrongdoer. In this way the plaintiff was often enabled to evade the operation of the *actio personalis* rule. Thus, though the executor of an innkeeper could not, at common law, be sued in tort for the loss of a guest's goods, he could be sued in an action based upon an implied contract.[88]

Again, if a person dealt as agent for another without authority, his executor, though he could not be sued for the tort, might be made liable for breach of an implied warranty of authority.[89]

It seems also that an action for money had and received was maintainable against the executors of a sheriff who wrongfully retained the proceeds of an execution.[90] The distinction between actions in contract and in tort against a deceased person was formerly of importance because of the time limit imposed by section 1(3) of the Law Reform (Miscellaneous Provisions) Act 1934 on actions in tort against the estate of the deceased.[91]

---

[85] *Att.-Gen.* v. *Canter* [1939] 1 K.B. 318. As to time limits on penalty proceedings, see the Taxes Management Act 1970, s.103, and *British Tax Encyclopedia* 4–103. See also p. 583 *post.*

[86] Taxes Management Act 1970, s.74; *British Tax Encyclopedia* 4–074.

[87] Taxes Management Act 1970, ss.40, 41; reference should be made to the detailed provisions. See *British Tax Encyclopedia* 4–040 and for partnerships *Harrison* v. *Willis Brothers* [1966] Ch. 619.

[88] *Morgan* v. *Ravey* (1861) 2 Frost. & Fin. 283; 6 H. & N. 265. *Cf. Robb* v. *Green* [1895] 1 Q.B. 1; 2 Q.B. 315. And see *Wilson* v. *Tucker* (1822) 3 Stark.N.P.C. 154. See also *Dutton* v. *Taylor* (1700) 18 Hill, MS. 285; *Blyth* v. *Fladgate* [1891] 1 Ch. 337, 366.

[89] *Collen* v. *Wright* (1857) 7 E. & B. 301, *ibid.* in error, 8 E. & B. 647. *Cf. Halbot* v. *Lens* [1901] 1 Ch. 344, and *Younge* v. *Toynbee* [1910] 1 K.B. 215. A public servant acting on behalf of the Crown is not, however, liable in such a case for a breach of implied warranty of authority: *Dunn* v. *Macdonald* [1897] 1 Q.B. 401, 555; nor, therefore, could his executor be sued for such breach.

[90] See *Perkinson* v. *Gilford* (1639) Cro.Car. 539, in conjunction with *Gloucestershire Banking Co.* v. *Edwards* (1887) 20 Q.B.D. 107. See also *Packington* v. *Culliford* (1619) 1 Roll.Abr. 921, tit. Exors.H., pl. 2.

[91] See, *ante,* p. 557.

The conditions imposed by this subsection have now been repealed[92] but the distinction is still of potential importance and the topics of duty of care economic loss and limitation are still much ventilated.[93]

Breaches of trust by deceased

A representative may be liable, in his representative capacity, to equitable claims which might have been enforced against the deceased at the time of his death.[94] The representatives of a trustee who has committed a breach of trust may be charged with any consequential loss, whether or not the trustee's estate derived any benefit from the breach.[95] Thus, where a tenant for life of chattels lost or injured them, it was held that she was in the position of trustee for the remainderman, who was therefore entitled to recover from her executor the amount necessary to replace or restore the chattels.[96] And where a person accepts a benefit under a will on condition that he will discharge a certain liability (*e.g.* to repair leaseholds) and dies without having satisfied such liability, his representatives are liable to make good any damage suffered from the breach of the equitable obligation.[97]

If a trustee commits a breach of trust, whether by wilful default or by active breach of trust, and the consequences do not occur until after his death, his estate is liable, though if redress had been sought for that breach it could have been repaired in his lifetime.[98]

Ecclesiastical dilapidations

The representatives of a deceased incumbent may be liable for ecclesiastical dilapidations or the execution of various works by ecclesiastical law.[99]

Judgment debts

A representative is bound, as far as he has assets, to satisfy all judgments[1] recovered against the deceased whether or not the judgment was founded on a cause of action which would have survived his death.[2]

---

[92] See *post*, p. 904.

[93] See *e.g. D & F Estates* v. *Church Commissioners* [1989] A.C. 177 and cases there cited.

[94] See Toller, 6th ed., p. 479. As to devastavit see p. 559 *ante*.

[95] *Adair* v. *Shaw* (1803) 1 Sch. & Lef. 243; *Montfort* v. *Cadogan* (1810) 17 Ves. 485; *Walsham* v. *Stainton* (1863) 1 De G.J. & S. 678; 1 H. & M. 322. *Re Bell's Indenture* [1980] 1 W.L.R. 1217. As to the "great use" of a trustee to commit *judicious* breaches of trust see *Perrins* v. *Bellamy* [1899] 1 Ch. 797 as corrected at [1905] A.C. 376.

[96] *Re Swan* [1915] 1 Ch. 829. As to the liability of the estate of a tenant for life of a lease who, in disregard of the will, neglected to renew the lease, see *Colegrave* v. *Manby* (1826) 6 Madd. 72.

[97] *Jay* v. *Jay* [1924] 1 K.B. 826.

[98] *Devaynes* v. *Robinson* (1857) 24 Beav. 86, 95. And see *Grayburn* v. *Clarkson* (1868) L.R. 3 Ch. 605.

[99] See the Repair of Benefice Buildings Measure 1972 and generally 14 Halsbury's *Laws*, 4th ed., paras. 1164 *et seq.*

[1] Including inferior debts of record, *e.g.* fines imposed at quarter sessions: see Wentw.Off.-Ex., c. 11. p. 249; but see *Anon.*, Cro.Jac. 219.

[2] See, *e.g. Whitacres* v. *Onsley* (1572) Dyer 322a, *b* (judgment against sheriff for an escape).

Pending litigation

Where a party to an action dies, but the cause of action survives,[3] the action does not abate and where the interest or liability of that party devolves upon some other person the court may substitute that person as a party.[4] Thus a representative will normally be substituted on an *ex parte* application,[5] but this is not necessary if the death occurs after trial but before judgment.[6] If no order is made the action may be struck out as against the party who has died.[7]

Joint and several liability

If several persons are liable jointly and severally on a contract[8] and one dies, the survivors and the representatives of the deceased contractor may be sued in one action.[9] And if the action on the contract had already begun before one of the parties died, his representatives could be joined under Order 15, r. 7.

Joint liability

On the other hand, where one of several persons liable jointly on a contract[10] dies before judgment whether before or after action begun, the action does not survive against his estate. Such an action may be brought or continued against the survivors or the representatives of the last survivor, but the representatives of the contracting parties other than the last survivor cannot be made directly liable at all.[11] So a release given by the obligee to the representatives of a deceased obligor is no answer to an action against a surviving obligor.[12]

---

[3] *Eldridge* v. *Burgess* (1878) 7 Ch.D. 411; *Re Shephard* (1889) 43 Ch.D. 131.

[4] *Burstall* v. *Fearon* (1883) 24 Ch.D. 126 (plaintiff); *Duke* v. *Davis* [1893] 2 Q.B. 260 (defendant); *Andrew* v. *Aitken* (1882) 21 Ch.D. 175 (counterclaim).

[5] R.S.C., Ord. 15, r. 7.

[6] R.S.C., Ord. 35, r. 9. As to new proceedings by the plaintiff, see *Swindell* v. *Bulkeley* (1887) 18 Q.B.D. 250.

[7] R.S.C., Ord. 15, r. 9.

[8] As to what words will be sufficient to create a joint and several bond, see *Tippins* v. *Coates* (1847) 18 Beav. 401; *White* v. *Tyndall* (1888) 13 App. Cas. 263; *National Society* v. *Gibbs* [1900] 2 Ch. 280.

[9] See Ord. 15, r. 4; *Frankenburg* v. *The Great Horseless Carriage Co.* [1900] 1 Q.B. 504.

[10] If two covenant generally for themselves without any words of severance, or that they *or* one of them shall do such a thing, a joint charge is created: *White* v. *Tyndall* (1888) 13 App.-Cas. 263, 269; *Levy* v. *Sale* (1877) 37 L.T. 709; *Clarke* v. *Bickers* (1845) 14 Sim. 639; even though the covenant be contained in a demise to two as tenants in common: *White* v. *Tyndall*. *supra*.

[11] *Lampton* v. *Collingwood* (1694) 4 Mod. 314; *Godson* v. *Good* (1816) 6 Taunt. 587. See also *Slater* v. *Wheeler* (1838) 9 Sim. 156; *Richardson* v. *Horton* (1843) 6 Beav. 185. *Semble*, the action could proceed against the survivors without the necessity of obtaining any order. As to equitable rights of contribution see n. 34, *infra*.

[12] *Ashbee* v. *Pidduck* (1836) 1 M. & W. 564. Under a joint contract or a joint debt there is only one cause of action. If the action is merged in a judgment against one, the cause of action is gone as against all; see *Re Hodgson* (1886) 31 Ch.D. 177, 188.

Death between judgment and execution

As to the position after judgment has been obtained, it is provided that if any change has taken place by death in the parties liable to execution, leave must be obtained to issue execution.[13] Notice of the application for leave must be served on the representatives of the deceased judgment debtor.[14]

Where, however, judgment has been given against two or more defendants, if one (or some) of such defendants dies within six years after judgment and before execution, execution may still be issued against the estates of the survivors or survivor without obtaining any order for that purpose; though if it is desired to enforce the judgment against the estate of the deceased person (or persons), an order, under R.S.C., Ord. 46, r.2, is necessary.[15]

Death before equitable execution

Equitable execution is not "execution" within the meaning of this rule. What is commonly called equitable execution is not in fact execution, but equitable relief, which is granted because there is a hindrance in the way of execution at law. It is subject to the ordinary rule that equitable relief can be granted only when proper parties are before the court. Thus, a receiver by way of equitable execution cannot be appointed of the estate of a deceased judgment debtor in the absence of the persons on whom the estate has devolved.[16]

Charging order

The court has no power, under R.S.C., Ord. 50, rr. 2–7, to make a charging order after the death of a judgment debtor against his executor, in respect of a judgment debt of the deceased, unless in some way judgment has been first obtained against the executor.[17] An order giving leave to issue execution is not equivalent to a judgment against the executor. It dispenses with the necessity of a judgment against him, and enables the person alleging himself to be entitled to execution to issue execution against the executor without it. Consequently such an order does not satisfy the requirements of R.S.C., Ord. 50, rr. 2–7, so as to enable a charging order to be made against the executor of a deceased judgment debtor, but the creditor must bring an administration action.[18]

---

[13] See R.S.C., Ord. 46, r. 2. Apprently at common law a plaintiff could, without any order, issue execution against the goods of a sole deceased defendant if the judgment was recovered within a year before his death: *Wheatly* v. *Lane* (1669) 1 Saund. 216.

[14] *Re Shephard* (1889) 43 Ch.D. 131; see *Thompson* v. *Gill* [1903] 1 K.B. 760.

[15] Daniell's Chancery Practice, 8th ed., p. 722; and see *Davis* v. *Andrews* [1884] W.N. 94.

[16] *Re Shephard, ante; Norburn* v. *Norburn* [1894] 1 Q.B. 448.

[17] *Stewart* v. *Rhodes* [1900] 1 Ch. 386. As to when an action lies on a judgment, see *post*, p. 877, n. 85.

[18] *Ibid.* n. 85.

Continuing cause of action

In a joint action where joint liability is established the liability of the parties may be differentiated in point of time.[19] This was the established Chancery practice. So in an action against partners for encroachment on a mine, the cause of action continuing, if one of the partners died, his estate would only be accountable for the actual profits received up to his death, while the liability of the surviving partners would be quite different, and might continue till a later date.[20]

Liability of estate of deceased partner

The contractual liability of partners is joint[21] and not (as there was at one time a tendency to regard it)[22] joint and several. At common law, therefore, on the death of a partner the remedy against his representatives is extinguished. It has long been established in equity,[23] however, that the creditors of the firm may claim in the administration of the estate of a deceased partner.[24]

Remedies of creditor of partnership

Thus a creditor of a partnership firm, though not strictly a joint and several creditor, has concurrent remedies against the estate of a deceased partner and the surviving partners, and it makes no difference which remedy he pursues first.[25] He may resort to the assets of the deceased partner, leaving it to the personal representatives of the deceased partner to take proper measures for recovering what, if anything, should appear upon the partnership accounts to be due from the surviving partner to the estate of the deceased partner.[26] "It is now well established that a Court of Equity does treat the estate of a deceased partner as still liable to the partnership creditors, though at law the survivor has become solely liable. And it must now be considered as established that the partnership creditor may obtain relief against the estate of the deceased partner without having exhausted

---

[19] *O'Keeffe* v. *Walsh* [1903] 2 Ir.R. 681.

[20] *Per* Gibson J., *ibid.* p. 717. Under R.S.C., Ord. 37, r. 6, where damages are to be assessed in respect of any continuing cause of action, they shall be assessed down to the time of assessment. See *Jones* v. *Simes* (1890) 43 Ch.D. 607.

[21] See the Partnership Act 1890, s.9; *Kendall* v. *Hamilton* (1879) 4 App.Cas. 504.

[22] See *Sumner* v. *Powell* (1816) 2 Mer. 37; Turn. & R. 423. See also Glanville Williams, *Joint Obligations*, p. 68.

[23] For a short history of the equitable rule, see Glanville Williams, *Joint Obligations* p. 64, n. 1. See also Lindley, *Partnership*, 15th ed., p. 363.

[24] *Vulliamy* v. *Noble* (1817) 3 Mer. 619; *Winter* v. *Innes* (1838) 4 My. & Cr. 101; *Liverpool Borough Bank* v. *Walker* (1859) 4 De G. & J. 24 (principle applied to executors as such carrying on testator's partnership); *Brown* v. *Gordon* (1852) 16 Beav. 302; *Ridgway* v. *Clare* (1854) 19 Beav. 111 (where Romilly M.R. discussed the procedure where the partnership or the estate of the deceased partner, or both, is insolvent); *Lodge* v. *Pritchard* (1863) 4 Giff. 294; 1 De G.J. & S. 610; *Kendall* v. *Hamilton, ante*; and see *Holme* v. *Hammond* (1872) L.R. 7 Ex. 218; and n. 42 on p. 568, *post*.

[25] *Re Hodgson* (1886) 31 Ch.D. 177.

[26] *Devaynes* v. *Noble* (1816) 1 Meriv. 529; *Wilkinson* v. *Henderson* (1833) 1 K. & K. 582.

his remedy against the survivor."[27] Nor will the creditor be precluded from resorting to the assets of the deceased partner by having in the first instance obtained judgment against the surviving partners.[28]

But the surviving partners are necessary parties to a creditor's action against the assets of the deceased partner, for they are interested in the issues raised between the creditor and the executors.[29]

Partnership debts postponed to separate debts

Further, in the administration of the estate of a deceased partner the partnership debts are postponed to the separate debts of the deceased.[30] "The right of the creditor of the firm is to have the separate estate of the deceased ascertained and applied in payment of his separate debts and liabilities, and to have the surplus applied in payment of his joint liabilities."[31]

Under the Partnership Act 1890[32] every partner is liable jointly with the other partners for all debts and obligations of the firm incurred while he is a partner, and after his death his estate is also severally liable in course of administration, so far as such debts and obligations remain unsatisfied, but subject to the prior payment of his separate debts.[33]

The propositions stated above do not of course affect the rights of the partners and their representatives as between themselves which will be regulated by the partnership terms and possible rights of contribution in equity.[34]

Duration of liability of deceased partner's estate

The estate of a deceased partner is not liable for partnership debts contracted after his death.[35] But for the debts which affected him at the time of his death it continues liable until they are, in some way, fully discharged.[36] The discharge, however, may take place in various ways; not only by direct

---

[27] Per Cotton L.J. in Kendall v. Hamilton (1879) 3 C.P.D. 403, 407.

[28] Liverpool Borough Bank v. Walker (1859) 4 De G. & J. 24; Jacomb v. Harwood (1751) 2 Ves.Sen. 265.

[29] Hills v. M'Rae (1851) 9 Hare 297; Re Hodgson (1886) 31 Ch.D. 177, 192.

[30] Re Hodgson, ante. As to partnership covenants, see ante, p. 556.

[31] Lindley, Partnership, 15th ed., 747.

[32] Other relevant provisions of this Act are: ss.33(1) (dissolution of partnership by death of partner), 39 (rights of partners as to application of partnership assets on dissolution), 42 (right of estate of outgoing partner to receive share of profits or 5 per cent. on his share), 43 (retiring or deceased partner's share to be a debt accruing on dissolution or death). And see generally, Lindley, supra, and post, p. 472.

[33] A limited partner is not liable beyond the amount contributed by him: the Limited Partnership Act 1907, s.4(2).

[34] See as to subrogation in equity Re Downer Enterprises [1974] 1 W.L.R. 1460, 1468. "If A and B are liable to a creditor for the same debt in such circumstances that the ultimate liability falls on A, and if B in fact pays the debt to the creditor, then B is entitled to be reimbursed by A, and likewise to take over by subrogation any securities or rights which the creditor may have against A" (Per Pennycuick V.C.), see also post, pp. 569, 571.

[35] See the Partnership Act 1890, s.36(3).

[36] Vulliamy v. Noble (1817) 3 Meriv. 619.

payment, but also by dealings with the continuing partners operating as a payment of the joint debt, or from the creditors having agreed to take and taking the security of the surviving partners in discharge of the joint debt.[37] Or there may be an equitable bar to the remedy; for, as the right is only equitable, if the dealing of the creditor with the surviving partners has made it inequitable that he should go against the assets of the deceased partner, he will not be entitled to the benefit of the demand.[38] But the estate of the deceased partner is not discharged by the mere circumstance that the creditor, knowing of the death, continues his transactions with the surviving partners, and forbears for several years, at their request, to take any steps to enforce payment of his debt[39]; nor by his receipt of interest from them and a new partner.[40]

Joint obligation treated as several

Though a partnership liability will not generally be treated as joint and several in equity, apart from administration, yet there are cases in which a court of equity will treat a joint obligation as several. The true doctrine appears to be that, wherever a court of equity sees that in a contract joint in form, the real intention of the parties was that it should be joint and several, it will give effect to such intention. Accordingly, in certain cases, a joint bond has, in equity, been considered as several.[41] Thus a joint bond has, in equity, been considered as several where there has been a credit previously given to the different persons who have entered into the obligation, and it was not the bond which first created the liability to pay.[42] Again, in *Beresford* v. *Browning*,[43] the Court of Appeal construed a contract relating to payment and indemnity to a retiring partner, which was joint in form, as several, on the grounds that the circumstances in which the contract was made showed that there was a joint and several liability

[37] *Thompson* v. *Percival* (1834) 5 B. & Ad. 925; *Winter* v. *Innes* (1838) 4 My. & Cr. 101; *Brown* v. *Gordon* (1852) 16 Beav. 302. See also *Lee* v. *Flood* (1854) 2 Sm. & G. 250; *Blair* v. *Bromley* (1847) 5 Hare 555; *Lyth* v. *Ault* (1852) 7 Exch. 669; *Bilborough* v. *Holmes* (1876) 5 Ch.D. 255. As to discharge by proof, where there is no *locus poenitentiae*, against the estate of the continuing parties in bankruptcy, see *Scarf* v. *Jardine* (1882) 7 App.Cas. 345. See also *Simpson* v. *Henning* (1875) L.R. 10 Q.B. 406, as to the effect of the receipt of a composition of the joint debt.

[38] *Ex p. Kendall* (1811) 17 Ves. 526, by Lord Eldon.

[39] *Winter* v. *Innes* (1838) 4 My. & Cr. 101.

[40] *Harris* v. *Farwell* (1846) 13 Beav. 403. And see the Partnership Act 1890, s.14(2); *Webster* v. *Webster* (1791) 3 Swanst. 490.

[41] *Primrose* v. *Bromley* (1739) 1 Atk. 90; *Bishop* v. *Church* (1751) 2 Ves.Sen. 100, 371; *Hoare* v. *Contencin* (1779) 1 Bro.C.C. 27; *Thomas* v. *Frazer* (1797) 3 Ves. 399; *Burn* v. *Burn* (1798) 3 Ves. 573; *Ex p. Kendall* (1811) 17 Ves. 514; *Liverpool Borough Bank* v. *Walker* (1859) 4 De G. & J. 24; and *cf. National Society, etc.* v. *Gibbs* [1900] 2 Ch. 280. And see further Glanville Williams, *Joint Obligations*, pp. 70 *et seq.*

[42] In *Thorpe* v. *Jackson* (1837) 2 Y. & C.Ex. 553, it was said that the equitable remedy against the assets of a deceased contractor extends to every joint contract for a loan of money giving to the creditor the benefit of the security of several persons, whether or not the debt is a mercantile debt incurred by joint traders. But see *Slater* v. *Wheeler* (1838) 9 Sim. 157; *Other* v. *Iveson* (1855) 3 Drew 177.

[43] (1875) 1 Ch.D. 30; *cf. Wilmer* v. *Currey* (1848) 2 De G. & Sm. 347, where it was held on the fact that the deed imported a new liability.

independently of the contract, and, therefore, an intention that the continuing partners should be severally liable.

Where, however, the obligation exists only by virtue of a joint covenant or bond, the extent of its operation can be measured only by the words in which it is conceived; equity cannot give the instrument any other than its legal effect.[44] Accordingly, where a joint promissory note, signed "J. and J. Ewing—James Parr, surety," was given to a creditor of the firm of John and James Ewing, and James Parr died, John and James Ewing being both alive, one of whom afterwards became bankrupt, and the other insolvent, it was held that the promissory note could not be considered as several against James Parr the surety.[45] So where A and B were obligors in a joint bond, and A, who was alleged to be the principal debtor, died, it was held that his assets were not, in equity, liable upon the bond, but that the liability survived to B.[46]

Contribution

Although a contract may be joint and not several, so that the primary liability falls upon the survivor, the survivor may in equity have a right of contribution against the executor of his co-contractor, where the parties incurred a common demand for their common benefit.[47] Thus, though it cannot be stated as a general proposition that, in all cases where two or more jointly employ a third person, there is an implied undertaking in all to contribute rateably *inter se*, so as to bind the executors of a deceased co-contractor; yet if several persons jointly contract for a chattel, to be made or procured for the common benefit of all (for instance, the building of a ship or the furnishing of a house), and as to which the executors of any party dying before the work is completed, are by agreement to stand in the place of the party dying; in such a case, though the legal remedy of the party employed would be solely against the survivors, yet the law would certainly imply a contract on the part of the deceased co-contractor, that his executors should contribute his proportion of the price of the article to be furnished.[48]

---

[44] *Sumner* v. *Powell*, 2 Meriv. 30; *ibid.*, affirmed, Turn & R. 423; *Richardson* v. *Horton* (1843) 6 Beav. 185; *Wilmer* v. *Currey* (1848) 2 De G. & Sm. 347. See also *White* v. *Tyndall* (1888) 13 App.Cas. 263.
[45] *Rawstone* v. *Parr* (1827) 3 Russ. 424, 539; *Other* v. *Iveson* (1855) 3 Drew. 177. See also *Slater* v. *Wheeler* (1838) 9 Sim. 157.
[46] *Richardson* v. *Horton* (1843) 6 Beav. 185. And see *Clarke* v. *Bickers* (1845) 14 Sim. 639; *White* v. *Tyndall, ante.*
[47] See *Spottiswoode's Case* (1855) 6 De G.M. & G. 345, 371; *Johnson* v. *Wild* (1890) 44 Ch.D. 146; *Whitham* v. *Bullock* [1939] 2 K.B. 81, 87 and cases there cited. See also p. 567 *ante.*
[48] *Prior* v. *Hembrow* (1841) 8 M. & W. 873. See also *Batard* v. *Hawes* (1853) 2 E. & B. 287, 298, where the court seemed to think the executors liable without any special agreement. As to the principles of subrogation see also *Re Downer Enterprises Ltd.* [1974] 1 W.L.R. 1460 and *ante*, p. 567.

Liability to contribution may also arise from suretyship.[49] trusteeship,[50] company directorship[51] and joint tort.[52]

Deceased shareholder[53]

A deceased shareholder remains, that is, his estate remains, a member[54] of the company[55] till the register is altered.

In a joint stock company the presumption is that the personal representatives of a deceased shareholder if registered as members succeed to the full liability as well as to the rights of their testator or intestate. The Articles of Association must be looked at, not to see whether they impose such liability on the personal representatives, but whether they take it away or limit it.[56] If the articles of an unlimited company forbid executors from being proprietors of the shares of a deceased member, the executors are nevertheless entitled to petition for winding-up as contributories.[57]

The position of an executor is different in principle from that of trustees who take a transfer of shares in their names. Trustees have not, in any proper sense of the word, a representative character but executors have. The executors merely intimate their title as executors to a company in order to claim and exercise the rights which belong to them as the legal representatives of their testator. Having representative rights it is impossible that they should not be entitled to produce the legal evidence of them to the company without making themselves personally liable.[58] Thus the executor may, subject to the articles, be registered fully as a member and take on full rights and liabilities, or he may simply be recorded and recognised in the manner so described by Lord Cairns without submitting to personal liability. When the administration is complete the representative will normally hold as bare trustee for the beneficiaries but, subject to the articles, is not obliged to transfer or otherwise deal with the shares if the beneficiaries do not want him to do this.[59]

---

[49] See Snell, *Equity*, 29th ed., pp. 474–477.

[50] See Snell, *Equity*, 29th ed., p. 477.

[51] See *ante*, p. 559.

[52] See the Law Reform (Married Women and Tortfeasors) Act 1935, s.6. *Ronex* v. *John Laing* [1983] Q.B. 398.

[53] See generally Palmer's *Company Law*, paras. 40–31 to 40–33; Gore-Browne, *Companies*, paras. 16–20 *et seq.*, 20–4.

[54] The term "member" in the Companies Act 1948, s.287 and the Insolvency Act 1986, s.110 includes the estate of a deceased member: *Llewellyn* v. *Kasinto Rubber Estates Ltd.* [1914] Ch. 670 (decided on the corresponding section of the Act of 1908). See Companies Act 1985, ss.183, 187. *Roberts* v. *Letter "T"* [1961] A.C. 795, 804.

[55] *Baird's Case* (1870) L.R. 5 Ch. 725. As to the executors' right to vote at meetings, see *Marks* v. *Financial News* [1919] W.N. 237; the Companies Act 1948, Sched. 1, Table A, art. 32; and as to their being qualified to be directors, see *Grundy* v. *Briggs* [1910] 1 Ch. 444.

[56] *Baird's Case*, *ante*.

[57] *Re Norwich Yarn Co.* (1850) 12 Beav. 366; but as to a wider statement of this principle, see *Re Cuthbert Cooper* [1937] 1 Ch. 392, 399; *Re Westbourne Galleries* [1973] A.C. 360.

[58] *Buchan's Case* (1879) 4 App.Cas. 549 (*per* Lord Cairns).

[59] *Safeguard Investments* v. *National Westminster Bank* [1982] 1 W.L.R. 589.

Liability of estate of deceased contributory

The liability of a contributory[60] creates a specialty debt payable either when a call is made[61] or when an order is made.[62] On a contributory's death his representatives become liable.[63] The liquidator may take proceedings for administration of the estate to enforce the debt[64] or if there are no representatives he may himself take out a grant in his official name.[65] If the estate is insolvent he may prove against the estate for the estimated value of the liability and have a fund set apart to meet the liability when this has been ascertained and a call made.[66]

Personal liability of representative

As has been seen[66a] besides the liability of the estate of a deceased shareholder for shares, the executor or administrator may make himself personally liable for the same. If he has the shares transferred into his own name, without any statement that he holds the shares in a representative capacity,[67] he becomes to all intents a member of the company.[68] By adopting this course he may render himself personally liable. If shares are once put into the names of representatives individually, though offered to and accepted by them in a representative capacity, they cannot say that their liability is to be limited to the extent of the assets of the testator.[69]

On the other hand, mere notification of the grant does not authorise the company to put the name of the representative upon the register of shareholders so as to make him personally liable.[70]

In this case, though the shares are not transferred into his name, the representative has power to transfer them in the same way as the deceased shareholder could have done.[71] He ought to have a reasonable time

---

[60] See the Insolvency Act 1986, s.79. The list of contributories must distinguish between persons liable in their own right and those liable as representatives (*ibid.* s.148(3)). The liability will stem from calls upon shares not fully paid up and from orders under s.151 (*e.g.* an order upon a fully paid up contributory to repay a dividend). The word "contributory" is not confined to holders of partly-paid shares. (See *Re Aidall Ltd.* [1933] Ch. 323 as considered in *Re Consolidated Goldfields* [1953] Ch. 689.)

[61] Companies Act 1985, s.14; Insolvency Act 1986, s.80; and see *Buck v. Robson* (1870) L.R. 10 Eq. 629; *Re Muggeridge* (1870) L.R. 10 Eq. 443.

[62] *i.e.* under s.151 (see n. 60, *supra*).

[63] Insolvency Act 1986, s.81(1).

[64] *Ibid.* s.81(3).

[65] *Ibid.* s.167. Sched. 4. Act III. 11.

[66] *Re Muggeridge* (1870) L.R. 10 Eq. 443.

[66a] See p. 570, *ante.*

[67] Trusts are not to be entered on the register in England: the Companies Act 1985, s.360.

[68] *Buchan's Case* (1879) 4 App.Cas. 549, 588; *Re Jermyn Street Turkish Baths Ltd.* [1970] 1 W.L.R. 1194.

[69] See *Spence's Case* (1853) 17 Beav. 203; *Re Cheshire Banking Co., Duff's Executors' Case* (1886) 32 Ch.D. 301. See also *Re Leeds Banking Co.* (1886) L.R. 1 Ch. 231; *Jackson v. Turquand* (1869) L.R. 4 H.L. 305.

[70] *Burchan's Case, supra.*

[71] See the Companies Act 1985, s.183(3).

allowed him to sell the shares and to produce a purchaser who will take a transfer of them.[72]

However a representative may simply by his own conduct make himself personally liable. Thus, where executors paid a legacy without providing for any contingent liability[73] in respect of shares which they retained unsold, and the company was subsequently wound up and the executors placed on the list of contributories, they were held liable to pay the amount of the legacy in satisfaction of calls.[74] *Secus*, where the distribution is made under an order of the court.[75]

Executor of debenture holder

There is no obligation on executors of a debenture holder to register the probate with the company as soon as they obtain it, and delay in registration beyond the date fixed for payment off does not disentitle them to interest.[76]

Executor of shareholder under the Companies Clauses Consolidation Act 1845

This Act contains different provisions for procedure on the death of a shareholder in a company governed by that Act. Under section 18, the secretary, on receipt of the declaration required by that section, is obliged to enter in the register the name of the person entitled by transmission to the shares of the deceased member. When an executor finds that his testator has died entitled to shares in such a company, he may do one of two things. He may leave the shares alone outstanding in the name of the testator: the consequence would be that he could not transfer the shares, nor vote in respect of them, nor receive dividends on them, and, though he might be liable for calls, it would only be in his representative capacity. On the other hand, the executor may want to deal with the shares, or to receive dividends in respect of them. If so, he must avail himself of the machinery given by section 18 and procure himself to be registered as a shareholder. Once registered under it, executors clearly become shareholders, the company having nothing to do with the capacity in which they hold the shares, whether as executors or trustees.[77]

---

[72] *Buchan's Case, supra.*

[73] As to the manner in which personal representatives may protect themselves from future liabilities, see *post*, p. 654.

[74] *Taylor* v. *Taylor* (1870) L.R. 10 Eq. 477. As to the right of executors to be indemnified by the legatees, see *Jervis* v. *Wolferstan* (1874) L.R. 18 Eq. 18; *Whittaker* v. *Kershaw* (1890) 45 Ch.D. 320. As to the liability of an executor where a release given to a testator by a company had been set aside, see *Re Bewley* (1871) 24 L.T. 177; 19 W.R. 464.

[75] *Re King* [1907] 1 Ch. 72.

[76] *Fowler* v. *Midland Electric Corpn.* [1917] 1 Ch. 656.

[77] *Per* Lindley L.J. in *Barton* v. *London and North-Western Ry.* (1888) 24 Q.B.D. 77, 88.

Liabilities under covenants concerning land

It is expressly provided that the burden of every covenant (whenever made) running with the land binds the persons who succeed to the title of the covenantor.[78] Further, a covenant made after 1925 relating to any land of the covenantor or capable of being bound by him, is, unless a contrary intention is expressed, deemed to be made on behalf of himself, his successors in title, and the persons deriving title under him or them, and takes effect as if such successors and other persons were expressed.[79]

The foregoing provisions do not detract from the generality of the common law rule that all covenants made by a person are binding on his representatives unless they were personal to him.[80] In accordance with this rule, it appears that even before 1898, when real estate still devolved upon the heir and not the personal representatives, the latter were liable, so far as they had assets, for a breach of a covenant made by the deceased relating to real estate.[81] Not only are the representatives liable for breaches in the deceased's lifetime, but also for breaches in their own time. The privity of contract of the deceased is not determined by his death.[82]

Covenants in leases

Where the burden of an express covenant by a lessee runs with the land, an assignee of the term is liable for a breach of it committed while his interest lasts.[83] This, however, does not exempt the personal representatives of the original lessee from liability for breaches of covenant committed after an assignment by the deceased original lessee or by himself, and even though the lessor has accepted the assignee as his tenant.[84] An assignee of the reversion or part of it may enforce this liability.[85]

Similarly, though obligations entered into by a lessor with reference to the subject-matter of the lease may be enforced against an assignee of the reversion, or of part of the reversion,[86] yet the estate of the original lessor

---

[78] Law of Property Act 1925, s.80(2). As to devolution of real estate see p. 459, *ante*.

[79] *Ibid*. s.79. See generally Preston and Newsom, *Restrictive Covenants*.

[80] Bro.Covenant, pl. 12; Com.Dig. Covenant, C. 1; *Hyde* v. *Dean of Windsor* (1597) Cro.Eliz. 553; *Bally* v. *Wells* (1769) 3 Wils. 29.

[81] See *Thurseden* v. *Warthen* (1613) 2 Bulstr. 158 (covenant to convey copyholds); *Macartney* v. *Blundell* (1690) 2 Ridgw.P.C. 113 (covenant to renew lease).

[82] *Coghil* v. *Freelove* (1690) 3 Mod. 326; Wentw.Off.Ex., 14th ed., 251. And see F.N.B. 145, E. n. (*a*); *Hohler* v.*Aston* [1920] 2 Ch. 420; *Beswick* v. *Beswick* [1968] A.C. 58, 81.

[83] As to what covenants run with the land, see Woodfall's *Landlord and Tenant*, 28th ed., 1978. And see Law of Property Act 1925, ss.78 and 79.

[84] See *Hillier* v. *Casbard* (1665) 1 Sid. 266; *Coghil* v. *Freelove* (1690) 3 Mod. 325; *Pitcher* v. *Tovey* (1692) 4 Mod. 71, 76; 1 Saund. 241 *b*, n. (5); *Re Downer Enterprises* [1974] 1 W.L.R. 1460. But as to terms into which perpetually renewable leases have been coverted, see the Law of Property Act 1922, Sched. 15, para. 11.

[85] See the Law of Property Act 1925, s.141; 1 Wolst. & Ch., 12th ed., pp. 474–477; *Brett* v. *Cumberland* (1619) Cro.Jac. 521, 522; 1 Saund. 241 *a*, n. (5) to *Thursby* v. *Plant*. See also *Lewin* v. *American & Colonial Distributors Ltd*. [1945] Ch. 225.

[86] See the Law of Property Act 1925, s.142; 1 Wolst. & Ch., 13th ed., pp. 259–260.

remains liable for breaches of express covenants though they occur after the assignment of the reversion.[87]

Indemnity where executor assigns lease

In view of the continuing liability for express covenants of the estate of the original lessee, his executors always had a right, when assigning the lease and where the contract was silent on the subject, to require from the purchaser a covenant for indemnity against payment of rent and performance of covenants.[88] The benefit of such a covenant runs with the land.[89]

In assignments of leases made after 1925 such a covenant is generally implied[90] and when implied extends to breaches whether committed before or after a subsequent assignment, and *semble*, will bind the estate of the implied covenantor. The benefit runs with the estate or interest of the implied covenantee.[91]

Independently, however, of any covenant, express or implied, if the lessor proceeds against the executor of the original lessee, and recovers damages for a breach of covenant after assignment, the executor may sue the assignee for having neglected to perform the covenant whereby the executor sustained damage.[92] This liability in the assignee does not extend to breaches occurring after he has parted with his interest.[93] It has been suggested that the executor has the same remedy against each subsequent assignee for breaches committed during the continuance of the interest of each.[94] This point is of less importance now that there is generally an implied covenant in such a case.[95]

Covenants where deceased was assignee

Except under a covenant in the assignment, express or implied,[96] the estate of an assignee of a lease is not liable for a breach of covenant committed after a subsequent assignment. Thus, an executor of an assignee may discharge the deceased's estate from all future liability to the lessee by an assignment over, even to a pauper.[97]

There is a distinction between an express covenant and a covenant

---

[87] *Stuart* v. *Joy* [1904] 1 K.B. 362.

[88] *Staines* v. *Morris* (1812) 1 Ves. & B. 8; *Wilkins* v. *Fry* (1816) 1 Meriv. 265, 266. As to the construction of covenants by the assignee, see *Re Poole and Clark's Contract* [1904] 2 Ch. 173.

[89] Law of Property Act 1925, s.189(2).

[90] *Ibid.* s.77(1)(C)(D); 2nd Sched., Pts. IX and X; 1 Wolst. & Ch. 13th ed., pp. 158–162, 383–385.

[91] Law of Property Act 1925, s.77(5).

[92] *Burnett* v. *Lynch* (1826) 5 B. & C. 589; *Marzetti* v. *Williams* (1830) 1 B. & Ad. 424; *Moule* v. *Garrett* (1872) L.R. 5 Exch. 132; L.R. 7 Exch. 101.

[93] *Wolveridge* v. *Steward* (1833) 1 Cr. & M. 644; *Humble* v. *Langston* (1841) 7 M. & W. 517; *Rowley* v. *Adams* (1839) 4 My. & Cr. 534.

[94] *Wolveridge* v. *Steward* (1833) 1 Cr. & M. 660.

[95] See *ante*, p. 574.

[96] See *Lyons & Co. Ltd.* v. *Knowles* [1943] 1 K.B. 366.

[97] *Taylor* v. *Shum* (1797) 1 B. & P. 21. Indeed, after an offer to surrender the lease to the landlord, the executor may be guilty of a *devastavit* in neglecting to adopt this course: *Rowley* v. *Adams* (1839) 4 My. & Cr. 534; and see *Whitehead* v. *Palmer* [1908] 1 K.B. 151.

implied by law. If a covenant is only implied by law, as for instance the covenant by a lessor for quiet enjoyment implied by the use of the word "demise," the executor is not liable for breaches occurring after the death of the implied covenantor.[98]

Statutory protection of executors

Personal representatives may protect themselves from future liabilities which may arise for rents and covenants in leases,[99] but this does not extend to circumstances where they have incurred personal liability.[1]

Distress against executor of tenant

Where the lessee of land dies before the expiration of the term and his executor or administrator continues in possession during the remainder, a distress may be taken out for rent due for the whole term.[2] The executor or administrator cannot plead "administration complete" (*plene administravit*).[3] So the distress may be taken, by virtue of the Landlord and Tenant Act 1709,[4] within six months after the determination of the tenancy, if the executor or administrator continues in possession.[5]

Liability for rent in lifetime of testator

For rent and (presumably) other liabilities accrued during the lifetime of the testator the executor can only be sued in his representative capacity[6]; if judgment is given against him, it must be *de bonis testatoris*; that is, against the testator's property only.[7]

Liability for rent after death of testator

Similarly, if rent accrues after the death of the lessee, and the executor has not entered upon the demised premises, he cannot be made personally responsible for such rent.[8] He is, however, liable as executor, for he cannot waive the term so as not to be liable for the rent as far as he has assets.[9]

---

[98] *Adams* v. *Gibney* (1830) 6 Bing. 656. And see *Williams* v. *Burrell* (1845) 1 C.B. 402, for what constitutes an implied covenant within the meaning of this rule. *Semble*, it does not include the covenant of indemnity implied on an assignment of a lease by the Law of Property Act 1925, s.77(1)(C) and (D); *ante*, p. 573.

[99] See *post*, p. 655.

[1] *Re Owers* [1941] Ch. 389.

[2] Wentw.Off.Ex., 14th ed., 291; *Braithwaite* v. *Cooksey* (1790) 1 H.Black. 465.

[3] Wentw., *ante*. As to this plea see *post*, p. 892 *et seq.*

[4] 8 Anne, c. 18 ss.6 and 7.

[5] *Braithwaite* v. *Cooksey*, *ante*.

[6] As to the protection afforded to an executor by an order for the administration of the testator's estate, see *Minford* v. *Carse* [1912] 2 Ir.R. 245.

[7] 1 Roll.Abr. 603, S., pl. 9; *Fruen* v. *Porter* (1657–1670) 1 Sid. 379; for judgments against personal representatives generally, see pp. 908 *et seq.*

[8] *Wollaston* v. *Hakewill* (1841) 3 M. & Gr. 297; *ibid.*, 3 Scott N.R. 593; *Rendall* v. *Andreae* (1892) 61 L.J.Q.B. 630; *Whitehead* v. *Palmer* [1908] 1 K.B. 151. See also *Ackland* v. *Pring* (1841) 2 M. & Gr. 937; *Kearsley* v. *Oxley* (1864) 2 H. & C. 896. *cf. Nation* v. *Tozer* (1834) 1 C.M. & R. 172, 176; 4 Tyrwh. 561, 565.

[9] *Howse* v. *Webster* (1607) Yelv. 103; *Helier* v. *Casbert* (1665) 1 Lev. 127; *Youngmin* v. *Heath* [1974] 1 W.L.R. 135, see also *post*, p. 577.

On the other hand, if the executor enters upon the demised premises, and thereby becomes personally liable, by virtue of privity of estate on the covenants contained in the lease,[10] the lessor has an election either to sue the executor in his representative capacity, or to sue him personally as assignee of the term. This is so whether the action is for rent accrued,[11] or for a breach of covenant committed,[12] after the death of the lessee.

Thus, if the executor of a tenant from year to year continues in occupation of the premises he is liable in his personal character in accordance with the terms of the original demise.[13] Personal liability may also arise where an intermeddler becomes executor *de son tort* and is estopped from denying that he is an assignee of the term.[14]

Though an executor by entering renders himself personally liable, the entry of one of two executors does not make them both liable in an action for use and occupation.[15]

Plea of plene administravit

When sued in his representative capacity for rent accrued,[16] or for a breach of covenant to pay rent,[17] the executor can plead "administration complete" (*plene administravit*.)[18] It has been suggested,[19] however, that, since the executor cannot legally apply any profit arising from the land to any other purpose than the payment of rent, if the land yields any profit, he can only plead *plene administravit* less that profit. But even if this qualification is well founded, it cannot be extended beyond cases in which the lessor is suing the executors of the lessee on a covenant in the lease to pay rent.[20]

If a representative is sued as assignee for rent accrued after his entry, he cannot plead "administration complete" even though he is named in the pleadings as executor.[21] Similarly, if judgment is given against him it is

---

[10] See *Re Owers* [1941] Ch. 389, 390.

[11] Besides the cases mentioned in n. 8, *ante*, see *Boulton* v. *Canon* (1675) Freem.K.B. 337; *ibid*. Pollexf. 125; 1 Saund. 1, n. (1) to *Jevens* v. *Harridge*; *Royston* v. *Cordrye* (1677) Aleyn 42; *Hope* v. *Bague* (1802) 3 East 2; *Hargrave's Cave* (1514) 5 Co. 31; *Rich* v. *Frank* (1610) Cro.Jac. 238; *Caly* v. *Joslin* (1671) Aleyn 34. If he enters, the executor may be charged personally for the current half-year's rent which commenced before the testator died: *The Bailiffs of Ipswich* v. *Martin* (1664) Cro.Jac. 411; *Jevens* v. *Harridge* (1666) 1 Wms.Saund. 1.

[12] *Buckley* v. *Pirk* (1710) 1 Salk. 317; *Tilny* v. *Norris* (1700) 1 Raym. 553; *ibid*. 1 Salk. 309; Carth. 519; 1 Saund. 1, n. (1).

[13] *Buckworth* v. *Simpson* (1835) C.M. & R. 834; *Arden* v. *Sullivan* (1850) 14 Q.B. 832, 840.

[14] *Stratford-upon-Avon Corporation* v. *Parker* [1914] 2 K.B. 562. See *ante*, p. 93.

[15] *Nation* v. *Tozer* (1834) 1 C.M. & R. 172. *Semble*, this is not affected by the Administration of Estates Act 1925, s.2(2).

[16] *Lyddall* v. *Dunlapp* (1743) 1 Wils. 5.

[17] *Ibid*. 4; *Wilson* v. *Wigg* (1808) 10 East 315.

[18] See as to this plea *post*, pp. 892 *et seq*.

[19] The suggestion seems originally to have been made in earlier editions of this work.

[20] *Collins* v. *Crouch* (1849) 13 Q.B. 542.

[21] *Caly* v. *Joslin* (1671) Aleyn 34; *Helier* v. *Casbert* (1665) 1 Lev. 127, 128; *Sackill* v. *Evans* (1674) Freem. 171; *Buckley* v. *Pirk* (1710) 1 Salk. 317.

against his own property (*de bonis propriis*),[22] notwithstanding that in the pleadings he is alleged to have occupied as executor.[23]

Executor may limit his liability

To avoid hardship, an executor may, by proper pleading, limit his liability for rent to the letting value of the premises.[24] "If an executor is sued as assign of the lease for the rent accrued during the time in which he was in possession, he is entitled to set up by way of defence that he is only assign as executor, and that the profits or yearly value . . . of the property amount only to a sum less than the rent. Then he must pay into court the amount that he admits to be the value, and if his plea is proved, and that is the full value, he will be under no further liability in respect of the matter."[25]

The executor "is liable for the actual value of the premises during the time in which he held the premises as assign."[26] This value, however, is not confined to what he actually receives.[27] It includes the profits actually received, but it also includes the amount which he might have received by the exercise of reasonable diligence.[28] For instance, if the letting value of premises decreases because the executor has not fulfilled the repairing covenants, he can only limit his liability for rent to the letting value which would have been produced if he had properly repaired the premises.[29]

Executor liable under covenant to repair

Where an executor is sued as assignee on a covenant to repair, he is liable like any other assignee. In such a case he cannot limit his liability to the letting value of the demised premises.[30]

When executor may waive lease

Generally speaking, an executor cannot waive a lease, for he must renounce the executorship *in toto*, or not at all.[31] He may do so, however, if the value of the land is of less amount than the rent, and there is a

---

[22] Wentw.Off.Ex., 14th ed., 285, 286; 1 Saund. 1, n. (1). As to this judgment see *post*, p. 913.

[23] *Wigley* v. *Ashton* (1819) 3 B. & Ald. 101; *Atkins* v. *Humphrey* (1846) 2 C.B. 654.

[24] *Rendall* v. *Andreae* (1892) 61 L.J.Q.B. 630, 633; *Re Bowes* (1887) 37 Ch.D. 128; *Whitehead* v. *Palmer* [1908] 1 K.B. 151. And see *Billinghurst* v. *Speerman* (1695) 1 Salk. 297; *Buckley* v. *Pirk* (1709) 1 Salk. 317; 1 Saund. 1, n. (1); *Rubery* v. *Stevens* (1832) 4 B. & Ad. 241, 247; *Hopwood* v. *Whaley* (1848) 6 C.B. 744; *Re Owers* [1941] Ch. 389, 390; Toller 6th ed., p 280.

[25] *Per* North J. in *Re Bowes* (1887) 37 Ch.D. 128, 131.

[26] *Per* North J. in *Re Bowes* (1887) 37 Ch.D. 128, 134.

[27] See *Whitehead* v. *Palmer* [1908] 1 K.B. 151, 157, 158.

[28] *Ibid. Re Bowes, supra*; *Hopwood* v. *Whaley* (1848) 6 C.B. 744.

[29] See *Hornidge* v. *Wilson* (1840) 11 Ad. & E. 645.

[30] *Tremeere* v. *Morison* (1834) 1 Bing.N.C. 89; *Hornidge* v. *Wilson, supra*; *Sleap* v. *Newman* (1862) 12 C.B.(N.S.) 116; *Rendall* v. *Andreae* (1892) 61 L.J.Q.B. 630. And see *Ive* v. *Sammes* (1597) 2 Anders. 51; 2 Inst. 302. *cf. Reid* v. *Lord Tenterden* (1833) 4 Tyrwh. 118, 120. See also Woodfall 28th ed., para. 1–1824 *et seq*.

[31] See *ante*, p. 379 and *Doyle* v. *Blake* (1804) 2 Sch. & Lef. 231, 245.

deficiency of assets.[32] If there are assets to bear the yearly loss for some years, but not during the whole term, the executor must, it seems, pay the rent as long as the assets will hold out, and must then waive the possession, giving notice to the reversioner.[33]

Effect of assignment

Where a lease is assigned by the testator, his executor cannot be charged as assignee, because the lease did not pass to him. But an action may be brought against him if he is the executor of the original lessee (but not otherwise) for a breach of covenant by the lessee to pay rent, even though the lessor has accepted the assignee as his tenant.[34]

If the executor enters, and afterwards himself assigns the lease, he is personally liable as assignee for that time only during which he occupied.[35] But if he represents the original lessee he remains liable in his representative capacity for all breaches of covenant committed, or non-payment of rent accrued, after the assignment by himself.[36]

Liability on covenant to renew lease

In *Stephens* v. *Hotham*,[37] Wood V.-C., following with reluctance *Phillips* v. *Everard*,[38] made an order for specific performance of a covenant in a lease to take a renewed lease against the executors of the lessee, who had entered and admitted assets. The learned judge said that, in this case, the lease must be so framed that no personal liability should be incurred by the executors; though if the lease were a beneficial one claimed by them, they must enter into full covenants.

Liability for licensed house

The executor of a licensee of a licensed house is, until the next special sessions for licensing purposes, liable to penalties for breaches of public order on the premises.[39] He may on the other hand maintain an appeal from a refusal of the justices to renew the licence[40] and apply for the confirmation of an order for removal of an existing licence.[41]

---

[32] Wentw.Off.Ex., 14th ed., pp. 224, 290; *Wilkinson* v. *Cawood* (1797) 3 Anstr. 909, by Macdonald C.B. (cited by Wood V-C., 1 K. & J. 575). *Semble*, he must promptly offer to surrender the lease, and this will help him as to subsequent breaches of covenant. See *Reid* v. *Lord Tenterden* (1833) 4 Tyrwh. 111, 118, 120.

[33] *Wentw.Off.Ex., supra.* See also *Youngmin* v. *Heath* [1974] 1 W.L.R. 135.

[34] *Ante*, pp. 573 *et seq.*

[35] *Ante*, p. 576.

[36] *Ante*, p. 573; *Wilson* v. *Wigg* (1808) 10 East 313.

[37] (1855) 1 K. & J. 571.

[38] (1831) 5 Sim. 102.

[39] *McDonald* v. *Hughes* [1902] 1 K.B. 94.

[40] *Cooke* v. *Cooper* [1912] 2 K.B. 248. As to the liability of an executor to contribute towards repairs to a party-wall, see *Thacker* v. *Wilson* (1835) 3 A. & E. 142. And see the Law of Property Act 1925, s.38; Sched. 1, Pt. V; 1 Wolst. & Ch., 13th ed., pp. 99–100, 370–371.

[41] *R.* v. *Derby JJ., Confirming Authority, ex p. Blackshaw* [1958] 1 Q.B. 36.

Liability of executor as to articles and apprentices

On the death of the master, the agreement for service on the part of the apprentice is at an end, generally speaking.[42] Similarly, the executors of the master are discharged from all agreements and covenants for the instruction of the apprentice, for these are considered as personal to the testator, and determined by his death.[43] But the covenant on the part of the master for maintenance of the apprentice still continues in force,[44] so that the executor is liable, as far as he has assets, if he neglects to maintain him.[45] By the custom of London, the executor must put the apprentice to another master of the same trade.[46]

Where an attorney or other person, to whom a clerk or youth has been articled or apprenticed, dies before the articles expire, in the absence of an agreement to the contrary, his estate is not liable for the return of any part of the premium[47] unless there has been total failure of consideration.

Liability on deceased's arbitration agreement

An executor or administrator was not formerly bound to appoint an arbitrator where the deceased had agreed to do so if disputes arose under an agreement.[48] Where a party died pending a reference and the subject-matter of the reference was some claim or cause of action which survived his death the question whether his representatives were bound by the submission depended on its terms.[49] Subject to this the ordinary rule of law that the death of a principal revokes the authority of his agent took effect and the representatives of the deceased party were not bound.[50] It is now provided, however, by the Arbitration Act 1950, s.2(1), that an arbitration agreement shall not be discharged by the death of any party thereto, but shall be enforceable by or against the representatives of the deceased. This subsection does not apply to statutory arbitration.[51]

Husband not liable for torts, debts or contracts of his wife

The Law Reform (Married Women and Tortfeasors) Act 1935, s.3, provides that the husband shall not, by reason only of being the husband, be

---

[42] See *ante*, p. 557.

[43] *R.* v. *Peck* (1697) 1 Salk. 66; *Baxter* v. *Burfield* (1747) 2 Stra. 1266; *Wadsworth* v. *Gye* (1664) 1 Keb. 820; *ante*, p. 000. *Walker* v. *Hull* (1665) 1 Lev. 177, *contra*, was disapproved in *Baxter* v. *Burfield* (1747) 2 Stra. 1267. But see *Cooper* v. *Simmons* (1862) 7 H. & N. 707.

[44] *R.* v. *Peck* (1697) 1 Salk. 66; *ibid. nomine R.* v. *Pett* (1690) 1 Show. 405; *Baxter* v. *Burfield* (1747) 2 Stra. 1266; *Soam* v. *Bowden* (1678) Finch.Rep. 396.

[45] But an order of magistrates that the executor or administrator shall maintain and provide for the apprentice is bad, and may be quashed: *R.* v. *Pett*, 1 Show. 405; *ibid.* Carth. 231; 1 Salk. 66; 3 Salk. 41; 12 Mod. 27; *R.* v. *Chaplin* (1831) Comberb. 324.

[46] By Lord Holt in *R.* v. *Peck* (1697) 1 Salk. 66.

[47] *Whincup* v. *Hughes* (1871) L.R. 6 C.P. 78; *Ferns* v. *Carr* (1885) 28 Ch.D. 409. *Hirst* v. *Tolson* (1850) 2 M. & G. 134, must now be treated as overruled. See also *ante*, p. 528.

[48] *Re Oercuvak* (1885) 2 T.L.R. 150.

[49] *Dowse* v. *Coxe* (1825) 3 Bing. 20; *Clarke* v. *Crofts* (1827) 4 Bing. 143.

[50] *Toussaint* v. *Hartop* (1816) 7 Taunt. 571; *Cooper* v. *Johnson* (1819) 2 B. & Ald. 394.

[51] Arbitration Act 1950, s.30. As to arbitration initiated by the executor see *post*, pp. 720, 721.

liable in respect of any tort committed by his wife whether before or after the marriage, or in respect of any contract entered into or debt or obligation incurred, by her before the marriage.[52]

Where wife was husband's agent

The husband is now liable only where the wife acts as his agent, in which case, of course, the liability will survive on the husband's death. The special rules relating to a wife's agency of necessity were abolished by section 41 of the Matrimonial Proceedings and Property Act 1970.[53] A husband tacitly appoints his wife as his agent within the scope of ordinary household affairs and accounts by allowing her to act as his housekeeper.[54] He may consequently be compelled to pay for them, and so may his executors if he leaves assets. This authority, however, will be revoked by the death of the husband. In *Blades* v. *Free*,[55] a man who had for some years cohabited with a woman who passed for his wife, went abroad, leaving her and her family at his residence in this country, and died abroad. It was held that the woman might have the same authority to bind him by her contracts for necessaries as if she had been his wife, but that his executor was not bound to pay for any goods supplied to her after his death, though before information of his death had been received.[56]

Services with a view to a legacy

If a person performs services for the testator, as if a stockbroker transacts all the money concerns of the deceased, without any view to a reward, but in the expectation of a legacy, he cannot set up any demand for such services against the executor or administrator.[57]

Incomplete gift by testator

As equity will not, *inter vivos*, compel a party in the absence of consideration,[58] to complete his gift, so it will not compel the executor to complete the gift of the testator, but it seems that an executor may at times be entitled to do that which the court will not force him to do.[59] An act of bounty which has not been perfected by the testator is of no avail against

[52] For the law under the Act of 1882, see the 12th edition of Williams, *Executors*, p. 1155, n. (*h*). As to a husband's right to throw his wife's funeral expenses upon her estate, see *Rees* v. *Hughes* [1946] K.B. 517, *ante*, p. 64.
[53] See Chitty, *Contracts*, 24th ed., 1977, para. 2035.
[54] *Ibid.* para. 2036.
[55] (1829) 9 B. & C. 167.
[56] See *Smout* v. *Ilbery* (1842) 10 M. & W. 1. And *cf. Drew* v. *Nunn* (1879) 4 Q.B.D. 661, 668.
[57] *Osborn* v. *Guy's Hospital* (1726) 2 Stra. 728; *Le Sage* v. *Coussmaker* (1794) 1 Esp. 188; *Shallcross* v. *Wright* (1850) 12 Beav. 505. But contrast *Baxter* v. *Gray* (1842) 3 M. & Gr. 771. See also *Maddison* v. *Alderson* (1883) 8 App.Cas. 467.
[58] See *Meredith* v. *Davey* [1960] C.L.Y. 544.
[59] See articles by D. W. Elliott (1960) 76 L.Q.R. 100 and J. A. Hornby (1962) L.Q.R. 228.

his executor.[60] An incomplete gift may, however, be perfected by the donor appointing the donee as his executor.[61] But where a gift is complete in equity, although the legal title of the donee is not completed before the death of the donor, the executor of the donor is bound to allow the donee to complete his title. Thus where the deceased had executed a transfer of shares, by way of making a gift, the gift was complete in equity, and the donee was able to complete the legal title by registration on the books of the company after the death of the donor.[62]

Uncorroborated claim of creditor

In claims by creditors against the estate of a dead person, the court looks with suspicion upon a claim which is supported only by the uncorroborated evidence of the claimant.[63] There is, however, no rule of law which precludes a claimant from recovering against the estate of a deceased person on his own testimony without corroboration, though the court will in general require such corroboration.[64]

Verdict against deceased

A verdict against the deceased may be produced in evidence against his representatives, and binds them.[65]

Escrow of testator

If a person who has delivered a deed as an escrow, to be handed over to the party for whose use it is made upon the performance of some condition, dies before the performance of the condition, and the condition is afterwards performed, the deed is available notwithstanding such death.[66]

---

[60] *Hooper* v. *Goodwin* (1811) 1 Swanst. 485; *Cotteen* v. *Missing* (1815) 1 Madd. 176; *Meek* v. *Kettlewell* (1843) 1 Phil.C.C. 342; *Callaghan* v. *Callaghan* (1841) 8 Cl. & F. 374; *Searle* v. *Law* (1846) 15 Sim. 95; *Dillon* v. *Coppin* (1839) 4 M. & Cr. 647; *Ward* v. *Audland* (1845) 8 Beav. 201; *Cox* v. *Barnard* (1850) 8 Hare 310; *Bridge* v. *Bridge* (1852) 16 Beav. 315; *Weale* v. *Olive* (1853) 17 Beav. 252; *Beech* v. *Keep* (1854) 18 Beav. 285; *Marler* v. *Tommas* (1873) L.R. 17 Eq. 8, 12; *Re Fry* [1946] Ch. 312. An executor may be compelled to execute an agreement by the testator to grant an annuity: *Nield* v. *Smith* (1808) 14 Ves. 491.

[61] *Re Stoneham* [1919] 1 Ch. 149; and see *post*, p. 651.

[62] *Re Rose* [1949] Ch. 78; [1952] Ch. 499; *Re Paradise Motor Co.* [1968] 1 W.L.R. 1125. As to imperfect gifts, see article "Equity and the Imperfect Gift," 118 N.L.J. 769 (August 15, 1968): *Snell on Equity*, 29th ed., p. 122 *et seq.*

[63] *Hill* v. *Wilson* (1873) L.R. 8 Ch. 888; *Re Whittaker* (1882) 21 Ch.D. 657. And see *Parish* v. *Parish* (1863) 32 Beav. 207.

[64] *Re Hodgson* (1886) 31 Ch.D. 177. See also *Lovesy* v. *Smith* (1880) 15 Ch.D. 655; *Re Finch* (1882) 23 Ch.D. 267; *Re Garnett* (1885) 31 Ch.D. 1; *Re Farman* (1887) 57 L.J.Ch. 637, 639; *Rawlinson* v. *Scholes* (1898) 79 L.T. 350; *Re Cummins* [1972] Ch. 62.

[65] *R.* v. *Hebden* (1739) Andr. 389. See *Smith* v. *Smith* (1836) 3 Bing.N.C. 29, as to the admissibility of the declarations of the deceased as evidence against his representative. See also *Spiers* v. *Morris* (1833) 9 Bing. 687, as to the admissibility of entries made by a deceased executor against his interest. The provisions of the Civil Evidence Act 1968 relating to hearsay may be relevant.

[66] By Lord Ellenborough in *Copeland* v. *Stephens* (1818) 1 B. & Ald. 606, where *executor* appears to be printed by mistake for *escrow*. See also as to the nature of an *escrow*, *London Freehold and Leasehold Property Co.* v. *Baron Suffield* [1897] 2 Ch. 608.

Bills of exchange

A person who is under an obligation to indorse a bill in a representative character may indorse it in such terms as to negative personal liability.[67] Where a person signs a bill as drawer, indorser, or acceptor, and adds words indicating that he signs in a representative character, he is not personally liable; but the mere addition of words describing him as filling a representative character will not exempt him from personal liability.[68]

Death of drawee of bill

Where the drawee of a bill is dead, the holder may either present the bill for acceptance to the drawee's personal representative,[69] or treat the bill as dishonoured by non-acceptance.[70]

Where the drawee, acceptor, or maker of a bill is dead and no place of payment is specified, presentment for payment must be made to his representative, if there is one, and with the exercise of reasonable diligence he can be found.[71] If there is no representative the holder should demand payment at the house of the deceased. Delay in making presentment for payment is excused when the delay is caused by circumstances beyond the control of the holder, and not imputable to his default, misconduct, or negligence. When the cause of delay ceases to operate, presentment must be made with reasonable diligence.[72]

Where the bill is made payable at a particular place, and is presented at that place, and after the exercise of reasonable diligence no person authorised to pay or refuse payment can be found there, it is not necessary to present it also at the house of the representative.[73] If, when a bill of exchange becomes due and is dishonoured, the drawer or indorser is dead, notice of the dishonour ought to be given to his representative, if there is one, and with the exercise of reasonable diligence he can be found.[74]

Where holder appoints acceptor his executor

If the holder of a bill made the acceptor his executor and died, this, which at law[75] operated as a discharge of the debt by making the debtor executor, operated also as a discharge of the drawer and prior indorsers.[76]

---

[67] Bills of Exchange Act 1882, s.31(5).

[68] *Ibid.* s.26(1). See *King* v. *Thom* (1786) 1 T.R. 489; *Alexander* v. *Sizer* (1869) L.R. 4 Ex. 102.

[69] Bills of Exchange Act 1882, s.41(1)(*c*).

[70] *Ibid.* s.41(2)(*a*).

[71] *Ibid.* s.45(7).

[72] Bills of Exchange Act 1882, s.46(1).

[73] *Philpot* v. *Briant* (1827) 3 Carr. & P. 244. *cf.* Bills of Exchange Act 1882, s.45(5).

[74] *Ibid.* s.49(9). In America it has been held that if there are no personal representatives at the time, a notice sent to the residence of the deceased's family is sufficient: *Merchants Bank* v. *Birch* (1859) 17 Johns.R. 25; Bayley, 418, Amer. ed. *cf.* New York Negotiable Instruments Law, § 169, which reproduces s.49(9) and adds, "if there be no personal representative, notice may be sent to the last residence or last place of business of the deceased."

[75] See *post*, pp. 649 *et seq.*

[76] Chitty, *Bills*, 8th ed., p. 569.

But, *semble*, at the present time the executor would be accountable, for the rule in equity now prevails.[77]

Promissory notes

If a testator has given a promissory note in this form, "I promise for myself and my executors to pay A B or his executors, one year after my death £300, with legal interest," and no proof of the consideration can be given the note bears interest from its date, and not merely from the testator's death; for, in the absence of particular proof, it must be presumed that the note was given for value.[78]

Executor liable on deceased's guarantee

The death of the surety does not of itself operate as a revocation of a continuing guarantee,[79] and his executor may be liable for advances made after the testator's death.[80]

But upon the death of the surety, though no express notice thereof has been given by the executor, the fact that such death has come to the knowledge of the creditor will, it seems in the absence of express provision, operate as a revocation of the guarantee, and the executor will not be liable for subsequent advances made thereunder.[81]

But a guarantee, the consideration for which is given once and for all, as, for instance, where an office or employment is conferred in consideration of such a guarantee, cannot be determined by the guarantor, and does not cease on his death.[82]

Income tax

The representative within the territorial limits of the jurisdiction[83] is liable for tax chargeable on the deceased and may deduct any payments of such tax from the assets of the deceased.[84] Tax chargeable will now include

[77] See *post*, p. 650. *Semble*, this principle is not affected by the Bills of Exchange Act 1882, s.61, because of the words "in his own right."

[78] *Roffey* v. *Greenwell* (1839) 10 A. & E. 222. See also the Bills of Exchange Act 1882, s.9(3).

[79] By the Partnership Act 1890, s.18, it is enacted that: "A continuing guaranty or cautionary obligation given either to a firm or to a third person in respect of the transactions of a firm is, in the absence of agreement to the contrary, revoked as to future transactions by any change in the constitution of the firm to which, or of the firm in respect of the transactions of which, the guaranty or obligation was given."

[80] *Bradbury* v. *Morgan* (1862) 1 H. & C. 249; *Harriss* v. *Fawcett* (1873) L.R. 15 Eq. 311; L.R. 8 Ch. 866, 869, *per* Mellish L.J.; *Re Silvester* [1895] 1 Ch. 573.

[81] *Harriss* v. *Fawcett, supra*; *Coulthart* v. *Clementson* (1870) 5 Q.B.D: 42; *Re Whelan* [1897] 1 Ir.R. 575.

[82] *Gordon* v. *Calvert* (1828) 2 Sim. 253; 4 Russ. 581; *Lloyd's* v. *Harper* (1880) 16 Ch.D. 290; *Re Crace* [1902] 1 Ch. 733.

[83] See *Clark* v. *Oceanic Contractors* [1988] 2 A.C. 130, 152.

[84] Taxes Management Act 1970, s.74. And see Whiteman, *Income Tax*, 3rd ed., 1988, paras. 27–113. As to assessments for loss of tax, see *ante*, p. 562. *Kelly* v. *Rogers* [1935] 2 K.B. 446.

any "post-cessation" receipts of a discontinued trade or business.[85] There are special provisions for the recovery from a deceased wife's executors, of tax assessed on the husband,[86] for the husband's disclaimer[87] and for the effect of death on charges[88] on patent rights.[89] For the position as to tax on the income of the estate in course of administration see *post*, p. 932. It seems that where estate income accrues to an executor overseas and the estate is still in course of administration so that no beneficial interests have accrued a co-executor within the jurisdiction will not be liable for tax on such income.[90]

Where on the death of an employee sums are payable by the employer to the representatives of the employee, tax may not be payable. The question is whether such sums are paid as part of the terms of the contract of employment or in consideration of its cancellation.[91]

The first £30,000 of a payment by an employer in respect of the termination of a person's employment is exempt[92] and a payment made by an employer in respect of the termination of a person's employment by reason of that person's death is not liable to tax.[93] Subject to this, tax is payable under Schedule E on a receipts basis[94] and emoluments earned before death and paid to personal representatives are assessed and charged on the representatives.[95]

Reimbursement of tax   As to the right of reimbursement as against co-beneficiaries see *Leedale* v. *Lewis* [1982] 1 W.L.R. 1319, 1335 and under *Refunding and Tracing*, p. 1076 *post*.

Employment Protection (Consolidation) Act 1978

Section 150 and Schedule 12 to this Act contain detailed provisions relating to the effect of the death of employees and employers on their rights and duties under the Act. Reference should be made to the detailed provisions.[96]

---

[85] Income and Corporation Taxes Act 1988, ss.103, 105. And see Whiteman, *Income Tax*, 3rd ed., 1988, paras. 6–29 *et seq.*
[86] *Ibid.* s.285. (Repealed for 1990/91 and later years by the Finance Act 1988, s.48 and Sched. 4).
[87] *Ibid.* s.286. (Repealed for 1990/91 and later years by the Finance Act 1988, s.48 and Sched. 4).
[88] *Ibid.* s.524.
[89] *Ibid.* s.525.
[90] See *Dawson* v. *I.R.C.* [1988] 1 W.L.R. 930 (concerning trustees not executors).
[91] See Whiteman and Wheatcroft, *Income Tax*, 3rd ed., 1988, paras. 14–48.
[92] I.C.T.A. 1988, s.188(4).
[93] I.C.T.A. 1988, s.188(1).
[94] I.C.T.A. 1988, s.202A(1).
[95] I.C.T.A. 1988, s.202A(3).
[96] See Drake and Bercusson, *The Employment Acts 1974–1980.*

Part Six

ADMINISTRATION OF ASSETS

Chapter 49

ASSETS

HAVING obtained his grant[1] and having considered his position in relation to the property which has devolved upon him[2] the representative is concerned with the administration of the assets. Two general questions arise. First, what portion of a deceased person's estate is liable for the payment of his debts. Secondly, the order in which the various properties comprised in a deceased person's solvent estate are, as between beneficiaries,[3] liable to contribute towards the payment of such debts.

The property which will be the subject of these two inquiries is called *assets* in the hands of the executor or administrator, that is, *sufficient*, from the French *assez*, to make him chargeable to a creditor, and a legatee or party in distribution, so far as such property extends.

A. WHAT ARE ASSETS?

Statutory definition

By the Administration of Estates Act 1925, s.32(1),,[4] the real and personal estate, whether legal or equitable,[5] of a deceased person, to the extent of his beneficial interest therein, and the real and personal estate of which a deceased person in pursuance of any general power (including the statutory power to dispose of entailed interests[6]), disposes by his will, are assets for payment of his debts (whether by specialty or simple contract), and liabilities,[7] and any disposition by will inconsistent with this enactment is void as against the creditors. The court will, if necessary, administer the property for the purpose of the payment of the debts and liabilities.

The subsection takes effect without prejudice to the rights of incumbrancers.[8]

For this purpose "real estate" includes real estate held by way of mort-

---

[1] See *ante*, pp. 113–446.

[2] See *ante*, pp. 449–584.

[3] Creditors may generally resort to any portion of the estate. This gives rise to the doctrine of marshalling, *post*, pp. 997 *et seq.*

[4] See *post*, p. 1127.

[5] The definition thus includes estates *pur autre vie*.

[6] Law of Property Act 1925, s.176, authorises such a disposition.

[7] *Semble*, including all liabilities which may result out of the obligations entered into by the deceased person during his life. See *Hamer's Devisees' Case* (1852) 2 De G.M. & G. 366, a decision on the Administration of Estates Act 1833.

[8] On s.32 generally, see 5 Wolst, and Ch., 13th ed., pp. 55–38.

gage, chattels real, land in possession, remainder or reversion, and every beneficial interest[9] in or over land to which a deceased person was entitled at the time of his death.[10] This definition of assets is not exhaustive.[11] For tax purposes the word "assets" has been given a wide meaning so as to include non-assignable rights which have no market value.[12]

Property held on trust

Though property vested in a sole surviving trustee devolved, even before 1926, upon his representatives,[13] it never has been assets.[14] Despite the definition of "real estate,"[15] the words in section 32(1) "to the extent of his beneficial interest therein" exclude trust estates.

Further, representatives cannot be in a better position, with respect to the estate of the deceased, than he himself. They cannot employ as general assets property which he would have been bound to apply to a particular purpose.[16] Thus, in Hassall v. Smithers,[17] a remittance in bills and notes for a specific purpose, viz., to answer acceptances, was received by an administrator, in consequence of the death of the party to whom the remittance was made; and it was held that the special purpose operated in equity as a lien, and that the sum remitted could not be applied as general assets.

Where a person takes out a policy of assurance for and on behalf of his infant child and pays the premiums on the policy the terms of which show clearly that the assured intended to constitute himself a trustee for the infant, then on the death of the assured the policy does not form part of the assured's own estate.[18] Assets must be actually or notionally[19] realisable so that non-assignable contractual rights could not be "assets."[20]

---

[9] Including an interest in real estate of an intestate lunatic or defective within s.51(2) of the Administration of Estates Act 1923, which devolves as under the pre-1926 law by virtue of that section: see Re Gates [1930] 1 Ch. 199; and the cases mentioned, post, p. 1075.

[10] See Administration of Estates Act 1925, s.55(1)(xix), incorporating the definition in ibid, s.3 (post, p. 1149).

[11] See post, p. 590.

[12] See O'Brien v. Benson's Hosiery [1980] A.C. 562 (disposal of assets for purposes of capital gains tax). Finance Act 1963, s.22.

[13] As to real estate held upon trust, see the Administration of Estates Act 1925, Pt. I, replacing in this respect the Conveyancing Act 1883, s.30; as to this latter section, see previous editions of this work.

[14] Bac.Abr.Exors.H. 1. See also Parker v. Baylis (1800) 2 B. & P. 73; Deering v. Torrington (1704) 1 Salk. 79; cf. Byrn v. Godfrey (1798) 4 Ves. 6 (promissory note given to testator held to be assets, despite testator's declaration to his executor that he never meant to call for payment of it). And see Re Parker's Trusts [1894] 1 Ch. 707.

[15] Administration of Estates Act 1923, s.3(1)(ii).

[16] See Taylor v. Plumer (1815) 2 M. & S. 578; Ashby v. Ashby (1827) 7 B. & C. 444, 453.

[17] 12 Ves. 119. For other instances of assets in the hands of an executor which were not regarded as part of the testator's personal estate, see Parry v. Ashley (1829) 3 Sim. 97; Cruikshank v. Roberts (1821) 6 Madd. 104; Thacker v. Wilson (1835) 3 A. & E. 142; Smedley v. Philpot (1838) 3 M. & W. 573.

[18] Re Webb [1941] Ch. 225; and see Re Gordon [1940] Ch. 851. Cf. Re Engelbach's Estate [1924] 2 Ch. 348; Re Sinclair's Life Policy [1938] Ch. 799.

[19] I.R.C. v. Crossman [1937] A.C. 26.

[20] O'Brien v. Benson's Hosiery Ltd. See note 12, supra.

A term of office

Whether or not a grant for years of a term of office comes within section 32(1), it is assets in the hands of the representatives of the grantee.[21]

Property assigned in fraud of creditors

Property assigned by a deed which is set aside as defrauding creditors[22] of the deceased becomes assets in the hands of his representatives.[23]

Goodwill of partnership

In the absence of express agreement to the contrary the goodwill of a trade[24] carried on in partnership forms part of the partnership stock.[25] If, therefore, a partnership is dissolved by the death of a partner,[26] the goodwill does not, in the absence of an agreement to the contrary,[27] accrue for the benefit of the surviving partners. It must be sold for the benefit of all the partners, if any of them insist on such a sale.[28] "The executors, therefore, in the absence of a special provision in the partnership contract, would be entitled to require that the goodwill should be sold together with the other assets for the purposes of division between the executors and the surviving partner; if the surviving partner refused to carry out this implied contract, then the executors could by an action in the Chancery Division obtain an order for the sale of the goodwill under the direction of the court."[29]

Thus, independently of section 32(1), the value, or a proportionate part of the value, of the goodwill of a trade is assets in the hands of the representatives of a deceased partner.[30]

[21] *Sir George Reynel's Case* (1611) 9 Co. 97 *a*; *Schellinger* v. *Blackerby* (1769) 1 Ves.Sen. 347. (Menial office of profit in the House of Lords.)

[22] See s.423, of the Insolvency Act 1986 replacing the Law of Property Act 1925, s.172, replacing 13. Eliz. 1, c. 5. Fraudulent intent does not have to be proved: *Re Eichholz* [1959] 1 Ch. 708.

[23] *Richardson* v. *Smallwood* (1822) 1 Jac. 552; *Shear* v. *Rogers* (1832) 3 B. & Ad. 362; *Shee* v. *French* (1857) 3 Drew. 716. And see *post*, pp. 592 *et seq.*

[24] The remark in this paragraph would apply equally to the goodwill of a professional partnership. See *Smale* v. *Graves* (1850) 3 De G. & Sm. 706; *Hill* v. *Fearis* [1905] 1 Ch. 466; but *cf. Spicer* v. *James*, Rolls M.T. 1830, cited in Collyer, Partnership, p. 82; *Farr* v. *Pearce* (1818) 3 Madd. 89.

[25] *Hammond* v. *Douglas* (1800) 5 Ves. 539 (doubted in *Crawshay* v. *Collins* (1808) 15 Ves. 227, which doubt can no longer be supported); *Re David and Matthews* [1899] 1 Ch. 378; *Hill* v. *Fearis*, *ante*. See also *Featherstonhaugh* v. *Fenwick* (1810) 17 Ves. 298; *Wedderburn* v. *Wedderburn* (1856) 22 Beav. 84, 104; *Smith* v. *Everett* (1859) 27 Beav. 446; *Scott* v. *Scott* (1903) 89 L.T. 582.

[26] As to which, see *post*, p. 591, n. 44.

[27] For an example of agreement to the contrary, see *Att.-Gen* v. *Boden* [1912] 1 K.B. 539. Such an agreement can prevent a transfer of value on death of the goodwill for the purposes of capital tranfer tax: Dymond's *Capital Taxes*, paras. 7.153, 9.301.

[28] *Hill* v. *Fearis*, *ante*; *Re David and Matthews*, *ante*, Lindley and Banks on *Partnership*, 16th ed., 1990, paras. 10–161.

[29] *Per* Romer J. in *Re David and Matthews* [1899] 1 Ch. 378, 382.

[30] See *Gibblett* v. *Read* (1744) 9 Mod. 459; *Worral* v. *Hand* (1791) Peake N.P.C. 105. See also *Re Douglas* [1930] 1 Ch. 342.

Assets vesting after death

Section 32(1) does not purport to be exhaustive, and property in the hands of a representative is often regarded as assets, though it was never in the hands of the deceased. Thus, income of a testator's residuary estate accruing after the testator's death is assets.[31] So also if an executor renews a lease, he must account for the new lease, as well as the old, as assets,[32] even though the new lease comprises additional property to that included in the testator's lease, and is at an increased rent.[33] So if A covenants with B to grant him a lease of certain land by such a day, and B dies before the day, and before any lease is granted, A is bound to grant the lease to the executor of B, and the lease so granted is assets in his hands; or if A refuses to grant the lease, he is liable to make the executor a compensation in damages, which are also assets.[34] So if A promises, for valuable consideration, to deliver to B by such a day certain goods, and this is not performed in the life of B, but delivery is made to his executor, the goods will be assets in his hands, just as the money recovered in damages, for not performing, would have been.[35]

Again, chattels which were never vested in the testator in possession, but accrue to the executor by remainder,[36] will be assets in his hands.

Similarly if assets are wrongly purchased out of trust moneys a beneficiary may elect to treat the asset as trust property or as security for recoupment.[37]

Under the equitable doctrine of election[38] where a person elects under the instrument his property set free to pass under it becomes liable for the debts of the testator.[39]

Increase of assets after death

So goods which have accrued by increase since the testator's death are assets in the hands of the executor. Thus, if the sheep of the testator bear lambs after the testator's death,[40] or if the executor of a lessee for years

---

[31] *Re Tong* [1931] 1 Ch. 202.
[32] *Anon.*, 2 Ch.Cas 208; *Bromfield* v. *Chichester* (1773) Dick. 480; *James* v. *Dean* (1805) 11 Ves. 392; *Randell* v. *Russell* (1817) 3 Meriv. 190. See also *Fitzroy* v. *Howard* (1828) 3 Russ. 225; *Giddings* v. *Giddings* (1827) *ibid.* 241; *Fosbrooke* v. *Balguy* (1833) 1 M. & K. 226; *Bevan* v. *Webb* [1905] 1 Ch. 620 (purchase of reversion): *Re Thomson* [1930] 1 Ch. 203 (new lease of offices on another floor in same building).
[33] *Re Morgan* (1881) 18 Ch.D. 93.
[34] Wentw.Off.Ex. 188, 14th ed.; *Chapman* v. *Dalton* (1565) Plowd. 286; Com.Dig.Assets, C.
[35] Wentw.Off.Ex. 188, 14th ed.; Com.Dig.Assets, C.
[36] Land in remainder is within s.32(1) of the Administration of Estates Act 1925, *ante*, p. 000.
[37] *Re Tilley's Will Trusts* [1967] 1 Ch. 179.
[38] See generally *post*, pp. 879 *et seq.*
[39] See *post*, p. 981.
[40] Com.Dig.Assets, C.

enters into the tenements, the profits, over and above the rent,[41] or if an executor has a lease for years of land of the value of £20 a year, rendering rent of £10 a year,[42] these are all assets. Again, if an executor employs the testator's goods in trade, the profits are assets[43]; and whether the executor takes upon himself to carry on the testator's trade, or does so in pursuance of a provision in articles of partnership entered into by the deceased,[44] or by direction of the testator, contained in his will, or under the direction of the court, the profits of such trade are assets, for which he is accountable.[45] Thus, in *Gibblett* v. *Read*,[46] Lord Hardwicke held that a share in a news-paper should be considered as the personal property of the deceased, transmissible to his representatives, and that the profits of printing the same after his death should be distributed accordingly. And his Lordship said that there were many cases where no part of the property of a testator had been employed or made use of in carrying on the business, and yet the executor had been held accountable for the profits of the business as the testator's personal estate[47]; as in the instance of physical secrets or nos-trums, where everything was carried on with materials purchased after the testator's death, and yet the nostrum was part of the personal estate of the testator.[48] The same principle applies to copyright.[49]

Assets accruing by a condition

Again, chattels, real or personal, to which the executor becomes entitled, after the death of the testator, by force of a condition, will be assets. Thus, where a lease for years, or cattle, plate, or other chattel, was granted by the testator, upon condition that if the grantee did not pay such a sum of money, or do other acts, etc., and this condition is broken or not performed after the testator's death, the chattel will be brought back to the executor, and be assets.[50] The law is the same where the condition is that the testator shall pay money or do any other act to avoid the grant. Accord-

[41] *Buckley* v. *Pirk* (1710) 1 Salk. 79; Wentw.Off.Ex. 190, 191, 14th ed. But the profits, as far as the amount of the rent, are received by the executor as terretenant, and appropriated to the use of the lessor: 1 Salt. 79.

[42] *Body* v. *Hargrave*, Cro.Eliz. 712; Godolph. Pt. 2, c. 24, s.1.

[43] Godolph. Pt. 2, c. 24, s.4; Com.Dig.Assets, C.

[44] Subject to an agreement between the partners, the death of a partner, of itself, dissolves the partnership: *Vulliamy* v. *Noble* (1817) 3 Meriv. 614; the Partnership Act 1890, s.33(1). And even where the partners have covenanted that they and their respective executors shall continue partners for a certain time yet unexpired, the executors of the late partner are entitled to a decree for a dissolution, subject to their liability to damages recoverable in an action by the surviving partners, for a breach of the covenant: *Downs* v. *Collins* (1848) 6 Hare 418.

[45] See *Palmer* v. *Mitchell* (1809) 2 M. & K. 674n.; *Willett* v. *Blanford* (1842) 1 Hare 253; and *post*, p. 703.

[46] 9 Mod. 459. See also *Pitt* v. *Pitt* (1758) 2 Lee 508 (administratrix charged with wages earned by deceased's apprentices since his death).

[47] See also *Moseley* v. *Rendell* (1871) L.R. 6 Q.B. 338; *Abbott* v. *Parfitt* (1871) L.R. 6 Q.B. 346.

[48] As to the goodwill of a business, see *ante*, p. 589.

[49] See *ante*, p. 528. Copinger & Skone James: *Copyright*, 13 ed., para. 5–2.

[50] Wentw.Off.Ex. 181, 14th ed.

ingly, chattels, whether real or personal, mortgaged or pledged by the testator, and redeemed by the executor, are assets in the hands of the executor, for so much as they are worth beyond the sum paid on their redemption.[51] Further, a lease which belonged to an intestate, upon which the plaintiff had a lien, on account of which he retained it in his hands, was nevertheless assets in the hands of the administrator, who had the power to redeem it.[52] But if the executor redeems with his own money the goods pledged by the testator, he will be indemnified for the sum he has disbursed, out of the effects of the testator, or, if necessary, by the sale of the chattel itself; and in that case the surplus over and above such indemnity will be assets.[53]

B. PROPERTY APPOINTED UNDER A POWER OF APPOINTMENT[54]

A statement of the earlier law is necessary to an understanding of the present.[55]

Appointments of personalty before 1926

At common law, personalty appointed by will did not devolve upon the representatives of the appointor as such.[56] But if the appointment was made under a general power in favour of a volunteer,[57] creditors of the appointor could, by instituting proceedings in Chancery, satisfy their claims out of the appointed fund to the extent to which the other assets of the appointor proved insufficient for this purpose.[58] The appointee was only entitled to the surplus of the property appointed after the appointor's creditors had been satisfied,[59] for the appointor could have exercised the power in favour of his creditors, and the claims of creditors were in equity paramount to the claims of a volunteer.[60] It was inequitable that the

---

[51] Wentw.Off.Ex. 182, 14th ed.; *Hawkins* v. *Lawse* (1590) 1 Leon. 155; *Harecourt* v. *Wrenham*, or *Harwood* v. *Wraynam* (1613) Moore 858; 1 Roll.Rep. 56, pl. 32; 1 Brownl. 76; 1 Roll.Abr. 920, G. pl. 5; *Alexander and Lady Gresham's Case* (1591) 1 Leon. 224. See also *Glaholm* v. *Rowntree* (1837) 6 Ad. & Ell. 710.

[52] *Vincent* v. *Sharp* (1819) 2 Starke N.P.C. 507.

[53] Wentw.Off.Ex. 182, 14th ed.

[54] This would include a power exercisable with trustees' consent: *Re Phillips*, [1931] 1 Ch. 347. *Cf. Re Watts* [1931] 2 Ch. 302. As to modern difficulties in the classification of powers, see 26 *Conveyancer* 25, 32, and *post*, p. 596.

[55] As to the position after 1925, see *post*, p. 593.

[56] *O'Grady* v. *Wilmot* [1916] 2 A.C. 231, overruling *Re Hadley*, *post*.

[57] Including a creditor: *Beyfus* v. *Lawley* [1903] A.C. 411; *post*, p. 594.

[58] *Thompson* v. *Towne* (1694) 2 Vern. 319; *Hinton* v. *Toye* (1739) 1 Atk. 465; *Bainton* v. *Ward* (1741) 2 Atk. 172; *Townshend* v. *Windham* (1750) 2 Ves.Sen. 1, 9; *Jenney* v. *Andrews* (1882) 6 Madd. 264; *Williams* v. *Lomas* (1852) 16 Beav. 1; *Platt* v. *Routh* (1840) 6 M. & W. 789; *Fleming* v. *Buchanan* (1853) 3 De G.M. & G. 976, 979; *Re Hadley* [1909] 1 Ch. 20; *Re Pryce* [1911] 2 Ch. 286; *O'Grady* v. *Wilmot*, *ante*; *Re Khan* [1966] Ch. 567.

[59] See n. 58.

[60] This statement was quoted with approval by Maugham J. in *Re Phillips* [1931] 1 Ch. 347, 351.

appointor should confer a benefit upon a volunteer whilst his creditors remained unsatisfied.[61]

In *Townshed* v. *Windham*[62] it was decided that this right in the creditors to be preferred to volunteers was the same whether the appointment under a general power was made by will or by deed to take effect after the appointor's death.[63] It was pointed out by Lord Hardwicke that there could be no material distinction between an appointment by will and an appointment by deed, to take effect after death for otherwise "the justice intended by the court in these cases would be avoided in every instance; as then it would be putting it barely on the form of the conveyance."[64]

Appointments of realty before 1926

So far as real estate was liable at all for the payment of debts, real estate appointed by will under a general power seems to have been in the same position as a fund of personalty so appointed.[65] Thus, after 1833, when all realty had become assets, a creditor whose claims were unsatisfied by the property of the deceased debtor, had a better right to realty appointed by the will of the debtor than the volunteer in whose favour the appointment was made.[66]

As there was no distinction for this purpose between realty and personalty, realty disposed of by a deed of appointment taking effect on the death of the appointor would also have been liable, as a last resort, to the claims of creditors.

Summary of law before 1926

Thus, immediately before 1926, the rule seems to have been that property, real or personal, comprised in a general power of appointment exercised by will, or by a deed not operating to transfer the property to the appointee during the lifetime of the appointor, was available, in default of other assets, for the payment of the appointor's debts.[67]

Appointment by will after 1925

So far as real estate, including chattels real, is concerned, no difficulty should normally arise. Under Part I of the Administration of Estates Act 1925 such property devolves upon the representatives of the appointor, and so becomes assets in their hands.

[61] See the judgment of Lord Hardwicke in *Townshend* v. *Windham, ante*. See also *Re Phillips* [1931] 1 Ch. 347.

[62] (1750) 2 Ves.Sen. 1.

[63] And see *George* v. *Millbanke* (1803) 9 Ves. 190; *O'Grady* v. *Wilmot, ante*. See also *Pack* v. *Bathurst* (1745) 3 Atk. 269; *Troughton* v. *Troughton* (1748) *ibid.* 656.

[64] 2 Ves.Sen. 1.

[65] See *Fleming* v. *Buchanan* (1853) 3 De G.M. & G. 976; *O'Grady* v. *Wilmot, ante*.

[66] See n. 65.

[67] See the statement of Lord Buckmaster in *O'Grady* v. *Wilmot* [1916] 2 A.C. 231 at p. 248. See also Administration of Estates Act 1925, s.55(3). *Appendix, post*, p. 1148.

But there is nothing, either at common law,[68] or in the Act, to make a fund of pure personalty (over which a testator has exercised a general power by will) devolve upon his representatives as such. This anomaly should not, however, give rise to any great difficulty in practice. It is clearly established that, though such property does not devolve upon representatives as such, yet they can give a valid receipt for it,[69] and can, no doubt, pay creditors out of it.

One creditor cannot be preferred by appointment

The donee of a general power cannot by exercising the power by will in favour of one creditor, prefer him to other creditors. This is so even though the testator may have contracted for value to exercise the power in favour of that creditor. Having once exercised the power, he has made the property assets for the payment of all creditors. It is useless for the appointee to claim that he is not a volunteer. He is only a legatee under the will, and all legatees are in the position of volunteers.[70]

Appointment by deed after 1925

Though property appointed by deed is not specifically mentioned in section 32, there is nothing in the Administration of Estates Act 1925 to deprive a creditor of his equitable right to resort in the last instance to property appointed under a general power by a deed which purports to transfer the property to a volunteer on the appointor's death.[71] Such property, whether real or personal, did not at common law, and still does not, devolve upon the appointor's representatives.

If the property appointed by deed is pure personalty, and the property of the appointor is insufficient to pay all debts, the creditors have a right to institute proceedings to "intercept" the appointed fund.[72] The representatives could exercise this right on behalf of the creditors. Thus, if the trustees of the appointed fund were satisfied that all the appointor's debts could not be paid out of the appointor's property, they would be justified in transferring to the personal representatives of the appointor whatever portion of the fund was required for the payment of debts.[73]

If the property appointed is land, it must come within the provisions of the Settled Land Act 1925.[74] An appointment of land can only operate in equity.[75] The person in whose favour the appointment is made can call for a conveyance of the legal estate from the "estate owner" in whom it is

---

[68] O'Grady v. Wilmot, supra.

[69] Re Hoskin's Trusts (1877) 5 Ch.D. 229; 6 Ch.D. 281; Re Peacock's Settlement [1902] 1 Ch. 552; O'Grady v. Wilmot [1916] 2 A.C. 231, 250, 251.

[70] Beyfus v. Lawley [1903] A.C. 411.

[71] As to this right, see ante pp. 592–593.

[72] O'Grady v. Wilmot [1916] 2 A.C. 231, 248. And see Re Phillips [1931] 1 Ch. 347.

[73] That the personal representatives can give a valid receipt for a fund appointed by will is now settled: see ante, n. 69.

[74] See the Settled Land Act 1925, ss.1, 20(1)(ii) and (iii).

[75] Law of Property Act 1925, s.1(7).

vested.[76] But if the appointor's assets are insufficient to satisfy the demands of his creditors, the latter have a better right to the land than the volunteer appointee. They, or the representatives of the appointor on their behalf, should call upon the "estate owner" for the legal estate.[77] If their demands are justified, the "estate owner" should only convey to the appointee the legal estate in so much of the land as is not required for the payment of the appointor's debts. The best course would be for the "estate owner," by the direction of the appointee and the representatives, to convey the land to trustees for sale to pay out of the proceeds the requisite sum to the representatives and the balance to the appointee.

The above remarks apply where the appointment by deed only authorises the property to be transferred on the death of the appointor.

Purchaser for value preferred

Though the rights of creditors prevail over the right of a volunteer claiming on the death of the appointor under an appointment, whether by will or by deed, a purchaser in good faith, for valuable consideration, from the volunteer is preferred, both under the old law[78] and under the new,[79] to the creditors.

Appointment in favour of appointor

Where a person having a general power of appointment, or a special power of appointment with himself as one of the objects,[80] executes the power in his own favour, the subject-matter of the power becomes part of his estate, and is, like the rest of his estate, assets for the payment of creditors.

Voidable appointments

Again, where a deed of appointment is set aside as being in fraud of creditors,[81] or presumably where it is shown that a testator has not applied his mind to the exercise of his discretion,[82] the property appointed becomes the general assets of the appointor.[83] An appointment may be set aside as defrauding creditors, notwithstanding the fact that, if the power

---

[76] Under the Settled Land Act 1925, s.16.

[77] See n. 76.

[78] *George* v. *Milbanke* (1803) 9 Ves. 190; *Hart* v. *Middlehurst* (1746) 3 Atk. 377; Sugd. Pow., 8th ed., 477.

[79] Administration of Estates Act 1925, ss.32(2) and 38(3) (*post*, pp. 1127, 1132).

[80] See *Re Penrose* [1933] Ch. 793, and 26 *Conveyancer* 23, 32; *Edie* v. *Babington* (1854) 3 Ir.Ch. 568.

[81] See Insolvency Act 1986, s.423 replacing the Law of Property Act 1923, s.172, replacing, with amendment, 13 Eliz. 1, c. 5.

[82] See *Turner* v. *Turner* [1984] Ch. 100.

[83] See *Townshend* v. *Windham* (1730) 2 Ves.Sen. 1, 10, 11.

had not been exercised at all, the property could not have been touched by the creditors of the donee of the power.[84] But the Bankruptcy Act 1914, s.42, and section 339 of the Insolvency Act 1986 which avoid certain settlements of property against the settlor's trustee in a subsequent bankruptcy, do not apply to settlements made in exercise of a general power of appointment.[85]

Property disentailed by will

Under the Administration of Estates Act 1925, s.32, property which is disentailed and disposed of by will is made assets for the payment of the testator's debts.

Exceptions—special powers

The principles stated above do not apply to appointments under special powers[86] unless the appointor is entitled to and does appoint himself as one of the objects,[87] nor to property subject to a general power which has not been exercised and to which the appointor is not entitled in default of appointment.[88] The trusts declared by a document exercising a special power are read into the original document.[89]

Problems of classification

The distinction drawn above between general and special powers is however, as has been pointed out,[90] now demonstrably inadequate in the light of judicial recognition of a number of intermediate or "hybrid" powers such as (1) a general power exercisable by will alone,[91] (2) a general power to appoint subject to a specified exception,[92] (3) a general power to appoint by deed except to the appointor,[93] (4) a general power to appoint to anyone living at the death of the appointor,[94] (5) a special power of which the appointor is an object,[95] (6) a consent power,[96] (7) a joint power.[97]

---

[84] See n. 83.

[85] *Re Mathieson* [1927] 1 Ch. 283.

[86] *Townshend* v. *Windham*, *supra*, at p. 9.

[87] See n. 80.

[88] *Holmes* v. *Coghill* (1806) 7 Ves. 499; 12 Ves. 206.

[89] *Muir* v. *Muir* [1943] A.C. 468; *Roome* v. *Edwards* [1982] A.C. 293.

[90] See article by A. D. Hughes in 126 *Conveyancer* 25.

[91] There is no distinction between powers created by deed and powers created by will on the basis that a testator cannot delegate. See *Re Beatty* [1990] 1 W.L.R. 1503.

[92] See *Re Byron* [1891] 3 Ch. 474; *Re Hay* [1982] 1 W.L.R. 202.

[93] See *Re Park* [1932] 1 Ch. 580; *Re Beatty* [1990] 1 W.L.R. 1503, 1506.

[94] See *Re Jones* [1945] Ch. 105.

[95] See *Re Penrose* [1933] Ch. 793.

[96] See article by Prof. F. R. Crane, 18 *Conveyancer* 565, and *Re Earl of Coventry* [1974] 1 Ch. 77.

[97] See n. 96.

Delegation

Powers of appointment cannot in general be delegated[98] but this rule does not apply to an intermediate power vested in a person beneficially rather than vested in trustees as such.[99]

Summary

It would seem that the application of the principles above stated to hybrid powers would have the following results:

(a) If any power, general or special, is validly exercised in favour of the appointor, so as to take effect at or after his death, the subject property is "assets" within section 32 of the Administration of Estates Act 1925.[1]

(b) If any power is not exercised and the appointor is entitled in default the subject property is "assets.'

(c) Subject to these two propositions categories (1) (2) (3) and (4) are in substance "general" and the subject property is assets, but categories (5) (6) and (7) are in substance "special" and the subject property is not assets.[2]

C. ASSETS NOT IN THE REPRESENTATIVE'S HANDS

Liability confined to assets in his hands

The general rule has long been established, and there is nothing in the Administration of Estates Act 1925 to alter it, that a representative cannot be charged with any goods as assets other than those which come to his hands.[3] Presumably this must include property which, but for his wilful default, would have come to his hands.[4] The phrase "available assets" in section 29 of the Administration of Estates Act 1925 must therefore, it seems, include all assets which come into the hands of the representative or which would have so come but for his wilful default but must exclude assets which do not come into his hands,[5] and trust assets in which the deceased or his estate have no interest.[6]

---

[98] *Re Pilkington's Will Trusts* [1964] A.C. 612, 639.

[99] *Re Triffitt* [1958] Ch. 852; *Re Hay* [1982] 1 W.L.R. 202, 213.

[1] See *ante*, p. 596.

[2] This view appears to conflict with *Re Phillips* [1931] 1 Ch. 347 but see *Commissioner of E. & S.D. (Barbados)* v. *Bowring* [1962] A.C. 171, 185–187.

[3] *Read's Case* (1604) 5 Co.Rep. 33*b*, 34*a*; Wentw.Off.Ex. 227, 14th ed. Presumably, since the Land Transfer Act 1897, a similar rule applies to real estate. See the Administration of Estates Act 1925, s.2, Appendix, *post*, p. 1114.

[4] For the liability of an executor for property which, after coming into his possession, is lost, see p. 732, *post*.

[5] See p. 478 *ante*. As to property passing to a surviving joint tenant and thus by-passing the representative. See 1990 Law Journal Vol. 140 p. 95.

[6] Thus if the deceased had only a life interest the reversion will pass to his representatives, if at all, impressed with trusts affecting the reversion and the latter will not be "assets" of the estate.

Application of this rule

Thus, when goods of the deceased are converted by a stranger before the representative gets them into his hands, though the damages which he recovers are assets in his hands, yet, if he does not recover so much in damages as really the goods are worth, and that happens through no fault of his, he is accountable for no more than he recovers.[7]

Again, if the goods are perishable, and before any default in the executor to preserve them, or sell them at due value, they are impaired, he is not answerable for their original value.[8] And if the testator's sheep or other beast die, or if his ship perish by tempest, the executor is not chargeable with them as assets.[9]

The same rule applies in connection with claims (*things in action*). Though debts of every description due to the testator are assets, yet the executor or administrator is not to be charged with them till he has received the money.[10] So if the executor or administrator recovers any damages or compensation for any injury done to the personal estate of the testator before or since his decease, or for the breach of any covenant or contract made with the testator,[11] or with himself in his representative character,[12] all damages thus recovered are assets in his hands, the costs and charges of recovering them being deducted,[13] but he is not chargeable with them until he has reduced them into possession.[14] Thus, in *Williams* v. *Innes*,[15] in order to prove assets in the hands of the defendants, who were executors, an account rendered by them was given in evidence, in which they stated that £1,000 had been awarded as due to the testator's estate from a person who had been jointly concerned with him in underwriting policies of insurance; but Lord Ellenborough held that this was not sufficient proof of assets, as it did not show that any part of the sum awarded had been received by the executors.

Such debts or damages are, however, regarded as assets, though never, in point of fact, received, if they are released by the executor; for the release, in contemplation of law, amounts to a receipt.[16] And if the execu-

---

[7] *Jenkins* v. *Plombe* (1705) 6 Mod. 181; *ibid.*, 1 Salk. 207. See also Com.Dig.Assets, D. For power to insure, see *post*, p. 676.

[8] See n. 7.

[9] Wentw.Off.Ex. 236, 14th ed. He may be liable for failure to insure.

[10] Com.Dig.Assets, D.; Bac.Abr.Exors.H. 2.

[11] Co.Litt. 144 *a*; 1 Roll.Abr. 920, Exors.G., pl. 4, 5; Godolph. Pt. 2, c. 24, ss.1, 2; Bac. Abr.Exors.H. 2; Com.Dig.Assets, C.

[12] See *post*.

[13] Wentw.Off.Ex. 191, 14th ed. Where the testator recovered a judgment for debt and costs, and his executor sued out a *sci.fa* upon that judgment, the debt and costs due to the testator were assets when received; but the sum due for costs to the executor was only by way of indemnity to himself, and was not assets; *per* Parke B. in *Smedley* v. *Philpot* (1838) 3 M. & W. 573, 586. Present practice is to obtain leave to issue execution under R.S.C., Ord. 46, rr. 2 and 4.

[14] Godolph. Pt. 2, c. 24, s.5; *Jenkins* v. *Plombe* (1705) 1 Salk. 207; 11 Vin.Abr. 239, 240. See also *Lowe* v. *Peskett* (1855) 16 C.B. 500.

[15] 1 Campb. 364.

[16] *Cocke* v. *Jennor* (1614) Hob. 66; *Brightman* v. *Keighley* (1585) Cro.Eliz. 43.

tor takes an obligation in his own name for a debt due to the testator, he is chargeable as if he had received the money; for the new security has extinguished the old right, and is a quasi payment.[17]

D. FOREIGN ASSETS

Liability for foreign assets

It has been said[18] that "assets in any part of the world shall be assets in every part of the world"; and again, that[19] "the effects of the testator are assets wherever situated, whether at home or abroad; and such effects as are in a foreign country at the time of the testator's death, although they remain and are wholly administered there by the executor, are equally assets."

Thus it has been held[20] that assets found in a country beyond the sea which have come to the hands of the English executor are assets on a plea of *plene administravit.*

Suggested limit of liability

The above quotations, however, taken in their broad import, need some qualification.[21] As a general rule, a representative can only be liable in this country to the extent of the assets which he has, or ought to have, under his control in his capacity of English representative,[22] but it is not really possible to generalise, and if under the foreign law he is liable the English courts may well enforce such liability.

It is therefore necessary to inquire as to what foreign assets an English representative has, or ought to have, under his control. This of course implies consideration of what law applies and how far such application extends.[23]

Recovery of foreign assets

When a person has received a grant of probate or letters of administration in England he is entitled (so far as the English courts are concerned) if not obliged to take legitimate steps "to recover any property of the

[17] *Norden* v. *Leven* (1677) 2 Lev. 189; *Hosier* v. *Arundell* (1802) 3 Bos. & Pull. 7; *Partridge* v. *Court* (1818) 5 Price 412, 419–421; *Sparkes* v. *Restal* (1856) 22 Beav. 587. See also *Jenkins* v. *Plombe* (1705) 1 Salk. 207; *ibid.* 6 Mod. 181.

[18] Sheppard's *Touchstone*, p. 496.

[19] By Lord Lyndhurst in *Att.-Gen.* v. *Diamond* (1831) 1 C. & J. 370

[20] *Dowdale's Case*, 6 Co. 47 *b*; *ibid.* Cro.Jac. 55. As to this case, see Dicey & Morris, *Conflict of Laws*, 11th ed., 1987, p. 990 and Story's *Conflict*, Chap. xiii, s.514*a*.

[21] *cf.*, however, *Re Ewin* (1830) 1 C. & J. 151; *Bligh* v. *Darnley* (1731) 2 P.Wms. 619, 622; *Gardiner* v. *Fell* (1819) 1 Jac. & Walk. 22, 24.

[22] See *ante*, p. 597.

[23] Reference should be made to the leading works on private international law and conflict of laws. See, *e.g.* Dicey & Morris, *Conflict of Laws*, 11th ed., 1987, pp. 981–1001.

deceased wherever situate."[24] For such assets as he receives or, but for his default, would have received,[25] he will, no doubt, be held liable.[26]

The English grant, however, cannot of itself give him any authority to collect foreign assets, or to compel payment or delivery thereof to him.[27] Whether he is able to obtain possession of foreign assets must depend upon the law of the foreign country,[28] which may of course involve a *renvoi* back to English law. There is no general duty on an executor where foreign assets are specifically bequeathed to procure such assets for the beneficiary.[29]

Assets recovered without grant

Generally nothing which is assets can be recovered by process of law except by the representative acting under the authority issuing out of the court whose process is sought to be enforced[30]; but there are some apparent exceptions to that rule. One is that where assets have come into the jurisdiction by being remitted to the agent of a foreign administrator, the foreign administrator may sue his agent without taking out letters of administration in the country to the forum of which he is resorting. Thus, in *Eames* v. *Hacon*,[31] where an intestate died domiciled in Ireland, and letters of administration were granted in Ireland, and the Irish administratrix instructed her attorneys to procure letters of administration in India for her use and benefit, and they did so, and having received Indian assets, and paid the Indian debts, and remitted the net proceeds to their agents in England, it was said by Jessel M.R. and Baggallay L.J. that the Irish administratrix would have been entitled to sue the agents in England even if she had not had the Irish letters of administration resealed. Again in a somewhat different context it was held in *Re Macnichol*[32] that where judgment had been obtained in a foreign court by the foreign administrator of a creditor against an English debtor who had since died and whose estate was being administered in England, the foreign administrator could prove without taking out English administration to his intestate estate.

Right to ancillary grant (English domicile)

The concept of a "grant" or "probate" or "administration" is foreign to many laws and it is impossible to generalise.[33] However, it seems that in

[24] See Dicey & Morris, *Conflict of Laws*, 11th ed., 1987, p. 991.
[25] See *per* Bayley B., in *Re Ewin* (1830) 1 C. & J. 151.
[26] See Dicey & Morris, *Conflict of Laws*, 11th ed., 1987, p. 991.
[27] See *ante*, pp. 33, 8, 11; Story's *Conflict, ante.*
[28] Dicey & Morris, *Conflict of Laws*, 11th ed., 1987, p. 991.
[29] *Re Scott* [1915] 1 Ch. 592; *Re Fitzpatrick* [1952] Ch. 86. See also p. 602 *post.*
[30] *Fernandes' Executors Case* (1870) L.R. 5 Ch. 314.
[31] (1881) 18 Ch.D. 347.
[32] (1874) L.R. 19 Eq. 81.
[33] See, *e.g.* as to certificate of inheritance in German Law, E.J. Cohn, *Manual of German Law*, 2nd ed., pp. 288–290; Amos and Walton, *Introduction to French Law*, 3rd ed., pp. 323. See generally: Pugh: *The Administration of Foreign Estates* (Guernsey, Jersey, Isle of Man, France, Spain, Portugal, Italy and Florida).

most common law countries similar conceptions still prevail. In this context, if the deceased died domiciled in England the grant of administration in England is, in English law, deemed the principal or primary one. The English representative has, as a rule, a right to apply to the courts of a foreign country where there are assets for an ancillary grant for himself or his attorney.[34] But if such a grant is made, the new administration thereunder is made subservient to the rights of all creditors whose claims are recognised by the foreign law.[35] It is only the residuum of the foreign assets, after all such claims have been satisfied, which is transmissible and becomes assets in the hands of the English representative as such.[36] It is not, however, every representative who can claim a right[37] to an ancillary grant nor does it necessarily follow that his right to an ancillary grant according to English law will be recognised by the foreign courts.[38]

The liability to death duties of the representative of a person dying domiciled in England, in respect of foreign assets may be an inducement to him to obtain an ancillary grant.[39] For consideration of the double taxation conventions in relation to death duties, reference should be made to the works on that topic.[40]

Separate foreign grant

Where the foreign court makes a grant to a person other than the English representative, or his agent, in order to secure the rights of claimants in the foreign country, the foreign representative has a right to hold the foreign assets comprised in his grant as against the English representative.[41] The only mode of reaching such assets is to require their transmission or distribution after all the claims against the foreign administration have been duly ascertained or settled.[42]

Liability of ancillary representative

If the deceased died domiciled outside England, the English representative has no right as such to apply for a foreign grant. Nor can he require a foreign representative to transmit foreign assets to him. His duty, is to administer the assets under his control, and either transmit the residue to

---

[34] Dicey & Morris, *Conflict of Laws*, 11th ed., 1987, p. 993–995, *ante*, p. 000.

[35] *Ante*, pp. 11 *et seq.*; *Eames* v. *Hacon* (1881) 18 Ch.D. 347; Story's *Conflict*, Chap. xiii, s.513.

[36] See n. 35.

[37] *Ibid.*, *e.g.* a creditor obtaining administration in this country has no such privilege: *Blackwood* v. *R.* (1882) 8 App.Cas. 82, 92. See also *Burn* v. *Cole* (1762) Ambl. 415.

[38] Dicey's *Conflict*, 10th ed., 1980, p. 566.

[39] See Dicey & Morris, *Conflict of Laws*, 11th ed., 1987, p. 994.

[40] See *e.g.* British Tax Encyclopaedia.

[41] *Post*, pp. 659 *et seq.*; Story's *Conflict*, Chap. xiii, s.518. As to whether a foreign personal representative can be sued in this country for assets which he sends or brings into England, see Dicey & Morris, *Conflict of Laws*, 11th ed., 1987, p. 996.

[42] See Story's *Conflict*, *ante*.

the principal representative, or distribute it amongst the persons beneficially entitled according to the *lex domicilii*.[43]

It seems, however, that a representative, whether principal or ancillary, within the jurisdiction, may be compelled by the English courts to distribute all assets vested in him, or in his possession, or under his control, whether English or foreign, among the person beneficially entitled thereto.[44]

E. Legal and Equitable Assets

Former distinction

Formerly there was an important distinction between legal and equitable assets. This distinction is only now relevant to understand the earlier cases. Reference should be made to earlier editions of this work.[45]

There is, at the present time, no distinction between legal and equitable assets.[46]

F. Assets in the Hands of a Beneficiary

Assigneee from beneficiary protected

Section 32(2) of the Administration of Estates Act 1925[47] provides that if any person to whom a beneficial interest devolves or is given, or in whom any such interest vests, disposes of that interest in good faith before an action is brought or process is sued out against him, he shall be liable for the value of the interest so disposed of by him, but that interest shall not be liable to be taken in execution in the action or under the process.

This section applies to all property and took the place of similar provisions contained in the Debts Recovery Act 1830, ss.6 and 8, which covered only real estate.[48]

The section is designed to protect a person deriving title from a legatee, devisee, or the like, who has a beneficial interest in the estate of a deceased person. The replaced sections only protected an alienee from the heir or devisee; they in no way affected disposition made by representatives. And though the words of subsection (2) are wide enough to cover the assignee of a representative, they do not apply in such cases, because the right to follow assets is expressly reserved.[49]

In other words, the property continues to be assets in the hands of a

---

[43] *Post*, pp. 937 *et seq.*

[44] See *Ewing* v. *Orr-Ewing, post*, pp. 659–663.

[45] See 16th ed., p. 556.

[46] But see as to personalty appointed under a general power which still does not devolve upon the appointer's personal representative as such, *ante*, p. 594.

[47] See Appendix, *post*, p. 1127.

[48] For decisions on the rest of this Act, see 11th edition of this work. For decisions bearing on ss.6 and 8, see *post*, p. 603.

[49] See the Administration of Estates Act 1925, s.38, Appendix, *post*, p. 1131.

beneficiary,[50] even after an assent has been made.[51] And it would seem to follow that a creditor of the deceased could enforce his right against the property by applying to the court under section 38(2). The court, under that section, might direct a sale or other transaction, or declare the beneficiary a trustee for the creditor.[52] Whilst if the creditor succeeded in extracting payment from the representative, the latter could apply to the court under the same section as some "other person interested."

Where, however, before the creditor brings an action or sues out process against him, the beneficiary disposes of the property, or an interest therein, in good faith, though, apparently, not necessarily for value, the interest disposed of ceases to be assets and cannot be reached by the creditor. The beneficiary becomes, in such circumstances, personally liable to the creditor to the extent of the value of the interest disposed of by him.[53]

Old authorities still applicable

The present subsection is, as has already been shown, based upon the Debts Recovery Act 1830, ss.6 and 8. Under section 6 the heir, and under section 8, a devisee, were made personally liable[54] for the debts of the deceased to the extent of the value of any interest in the property devolving on them which they had bona fide alienated before action brought.[55] The principles underlying several decisions on these sections thus apply to the present subsection.[56]

On these repealed sections it was held that the liability of a devisee, who alienated the land, in respect of the unpaid debts of the testator, was such that on the alienation the debts became his own debts to the extent of the land alienated.[57] A purchaser in good faith from the heir or devisee, whether or not he had notice of the fact that the claims against the deceased's estate were not fully satisfied, need not see to the application of the purchase-money; neither he nor the property in his hands was liable for such claims.[58]

The sections applied whether the alienation (made in good faith before action brought) was of an equitable or of a legal interest. Thus, if a devisee created an equitable charge on his interest, either by deed or by a deposit

[50] Including the Crown taking the estate of the deceased at *bona vacantia*: the Administration of Estates Act 1923, ss.46(1)(vi), 57(1).

[51] A personal representative may let a beneficiary into possession before making an assent: *ibid.* s.43(1), *post*, p. 684.

[52] See *post*, p. 864; 3 Wolst. & Ch., 13th ed., pp. 48–49.

[53] See s.32(2), Appendix, *post*, p. 1127.

[54] And see *Spackman* v. *Timbrell* (1837) 8 Sim. 253; *Richardson* v. *Horton* (1843) 7 Beav. 112.

[55] The registration of an administration action as a *lis pendens* may prevent a subsequent alienation from depriving the creditors of their right against the property alienated: *Price* v. *Price* (1887) 35 Ch.D. 297.

[56] For decisions on the rest of the Act, see previous editions of the work.

[57] *Re Hedgely* (1886) 34 Ch.D. 379.

[58] See *Jones* v. *Noyes* (1858) 4 Jur.(N.S.) 1033; *Kinderley* v. *Jervis* (1856) 22 Beav. 1; *British Mutual Investment Co.* v. *Smart* (1875) L.R. 10 Ch. 567; *Re Moon* [1907] 2 Ch. 304.

of title deeds with a memorandum of charge,[59] or if a devisee only entitled under the will to an equitable interest mortgaged that interest,[60] the equitable interest taken by the mortgagee could not be reached by the testator's creditors, the devisee in each case becoming personally liable to the extent of the value of the equitable interest charged by him.

On the other hand, neither a conveyance by old to new trustees,[61] nor a covenant to settle,[62] nor a judgment entered up against the heir,[63] was a sufficient "alienation" within the sections, so as to withdraw the estate from the claim of the deceased's creditors. But in applying these authorities to the present subsection, it is important to bear in mind that the expression "disposes thereof" has a wide definition.[64]

[59] *British Mutual Investment Co.* v. *Smart, supra.*
[60] *Re Atkinson* [1908] 2 Ch. 307.
[61] *Coope* v. *Creswell* (1866) L.R. 2 Ch. 112.
[62] *Pimm* v. *Insall* (1849) 1 Mac. & G. 449; 7 Hare 193. *Secus,* if the settlement were completed: see *Spackman* v. *Timbrell* (1837) 8 Sim. 253; *Richardson* v. *Horton* (1843) 7 Beav. 112.
[63] *Kinderley* v. *Jervis* (1856) 22 Beav. 1.
[64] Administration of Estates Act 1925, s.55(1)(iii) (*post*, p. 1148).

CHAPTER 50

THE PAYMENT OF DEBTS

Having got in the estate of the deceased[1] the personal representative is concerned to ascertain the debts and liabilities[2] and arrange their payment in a due course of administration.[3] If there is any risk that the estate will prove insolvent difficult questions may arise, caution is essential, and representatives should consider administering the estate according to the principles governing the administration of insolvent estates.[4] This chapter is concerned to discuss (A) ascertainment of debts (notice of claims), (B) payment of debts where the estate is solvent, (C) payment of debts where the estate is insolvent, and (D) retainer and preference.

A. ASCERTAINMENT OF DEBTS

Liability for debts

A representative is liable, unless he is misled by the creditor,[5] for debts of which he had no notice provided there were sufficient assets to pay.[6] It is not therefore safe to rely simply upon information obtained from the will or from documents or relatives, before distributing.[7]

Advertisement for claims

A representative will escape the liability mentioned above, for debts of which he has no notice, if he advertises in accordance with section 27 of the Trustee Act 1925.[8] This requires advertisement in the *London Gazette* and in a newspaper circulating in the district in which any land is situated,[9] and

---

[1] See *post*, pp. 665–666, as to powers for this purpose.
[2] As to liabilities other than simple debts, see *ante*, p. 553.
[3] See *Re Hubback* (1885) 29 Ch.D. 934, 941.
[4] See pp. 623 *et seq.*
[5] *Re Birch* (1884) 27 Ch.D. 622; *Jewsbury* v. *Mummery* (1872) L.R. 8 C.P. 60; *Richards* v. *Browne* (1837) 3 Bing.N.C. 493; *Stroud* v. *Stroud* (1844) 7 M. & Gr. 417. Mere failure to prosecute does not, however, bar the creditor if the action is brought within the limitation period; *Re Baker* (1881) 20 Ch.D. 230; *Re Gale* (1882) 22 Ch.D. 820; *Rochefoucald* v. *Boustead* [1897] 1 Ch. 196, 210; *Re Gallard* [1897] 2 Q.B. 8. See further, *post*, p. 657.
[6] *Chelsea Waterworks* v. *Cowper* (1795) 1 Esp.N.P.C. 275; *Norman* v. *Baldry* (1834) 6 Sim. 621; *Smith* v. *Day* (1837) 2 M. & W. 684; *Knatchbull* v. *Fearnhead* (1837) 3 My. & Cr. 122; *Hill* v. *Gomme* (1839) 1 Beav. 540. As to creditors of a foreign testator, see *post*, p. 656.
[7] If distribution is delayed and the assets remain in the executor's hands, delay, advertisement or absence of notice will normally be no bar to the claim; see *Harrison* v. *Kirk* [1904] A.C. 1.
[8] As amended by Law of Property (Amendment) Act 1926, Sched. (The section reproduces s.29 of Lord St Leonard's Act (Law of Property Amendment Act 1859).) See Appendix. The section must be strictly complied with. *Re Bracken* (1889) 43 Ch.D. 1 (C.A.).
[9] *Wood* v. *Weightman* (1872) L.R. 13 Eq. 434.

such other like notices as would have been directed by the court.[10] The advertisement gives notice of the intention to convey or distribute and requires particulars of any claim within not less than two months. After this the representative is protected from claims of which he had no notice at the time of conveyance or distribution. The claimant is not, however, barred from "following" the trust property,[11] nor is the representative free from the obligation to make the searches which an intending purchaser would make or from claims known to him but not notified in answer to the advertisement.[12]

Effect of advertisement

By such advertisement the representative gets the same protection as if he had administered the estate under court order,[13] notwithstanding anything to the contrary in the will.[14] Although each case must be conducted according to its own circumstances,[15] advertisement should be prompt and was judicially regarded as late where there was a delay of five months after the death.[16] Although it has been held that an advertisement for "claims against the estate" gives protection from creditors and persons beneficially interested,[17] this is not the correct form, which should ask for "any person interested."[18]

Application to court

Where advertisement is impossible or impracticable, application may be made to the court for the protection of the representative in distributing by leave "on the footing that" all the debts had been ascertained.[19]

Quantification of debts

Debts are necessarily expressed in sterling. If there is an administration order, debts arising under another currency are quantified according to the sterling value of the debt at the date of the order.[20]

---

[10] This in practice refers to the jurisdiction of the Chancery Masters in giving directions as to advertisement. In difficult cases it is obviously desirable for the protection of the personal representatives to obtain such directions: see *Re Holden* [1935] W.N. 52; *Re Letherbrow* [1935] W.N. 34, 40, 48; *Re Gess* [1942] Ch. 37, but the practice is well settled and in a normal case it is not difficult to see what advertisements should be made. See R.S.C., Ord. 44, r. 5 (1935) 79 LawJo. 183; (1936) 81 LawJo. 163.

[11] See *post*, p. 1080.

[12] *Re Land Credit Co.* (1860) 21 W.R. 135; *Guardian Trust* v. *Public Trustee* [1942] A.C. 115, P.C.

[13] *Clegg* v. *Rowland* (1866) L.R. 3 Eq. 368; *Hunter* v. *Young* (1879) 4 Ex.D. 256.

[14] s.27(3) of the Trustee Act 1925.

[15] *Re Bracken* (1889) 43 Ch.D. 1.

[16] See *Re Kay* [1897] 2 Ch. 518, 523.

[17] *Newton* v. *Sherry* (1876) 1 C.P.D. 246; *Guardian Trust* v. *Public Trustee* [1942] A.C. 115, P.C. As to beneficial interests, see *post*, pp. 938, 1029.

[18] *Re Aldhous* [1955] 2 All E.R. 80.

[19] *Re Gess* [1942] Ch. 37, following the principle in *Re Benjamin* [1902] 1 Ch. 723; see also *Re Taylor* [1969] 2 Ch. 245. As to the procedure by originating summons, see *post*, p. 823.

[20] *Re Hawkins* [1972] Ch. 714.

B. SOLVENT ESTATES

Creditors not affected

If an estate is solvent, creditors are not concerned with the order of application of assets. Section 34(2) of the Administration of Estates Act 1925 applies. If the estate is liable to pay an annuity this liability is valued at the cost, at the date of death, of purchasing a British Government annuity of the same amount.[21] The beneficiaries may, however, be concerned as to where the ultimate liability for a debt is to fall.[22] A creditor may resort to any part of the deceased's estate which is liable for the payment of his debts.[23] If a creditor obtains payment out of assets which are not, as between the persons claiming beneficial interests in the deceased's estate, primarily liable for the deceased's debts, this apparent injustice is remedied by the doctrine of marshalling considered later.[24]

Duty to pay debts

An executor is often directed by the will to pay debts. The form of this direction is of concern to the beneficiaries but not normally to the creditors[25] who are in any event entitled to be paid with due diligence. There is no rule of law that it is the duty of executors to pay debts within a year of the death, for all the circumstances must be considered, but if debts are not paid within the year the executors must justify the delay.[26] The duty to pay with due diligence is owed to creditors and beneficiaries, and is not confined to interest-bearing debts,[27] nor does it arise only out of a duty to prevent avoidable loss.[28] If there has been a breach of duty the court may direct an inquiry as to damages.[29]

Debts charged on property (Administration of Estates Act 1925, s.35)

In considering the ultimate liability for a debt the initial question, which is frequently a matter of construction,[30] is whether the debt is charged upon or incidental to[31] the property. The same question may also arise in considering the liability to inheritance tax on death. If reduced rates of tax

---

[21] *Westminster Bank* v. *I.R.C.* [1954] 1 W.L.R. 242.
[22] As to marshalling, see *post*, p. 996.
[23] See Bro.Assets, *per* Descent, 33; *Davy* v. *Pepys* (1573) 2 Plowd. 439b; *Quarles* v. *Capell* (1561) 2 Dyer 204b; *Davies* v. *Churchman* (1684) 3 Lev. 189; *Galton* v. *Hancock* (1745) 2 Atk. 426. See also the Administration of Estates Act 1925, s.35(3).
[24] *Post*, pp. 996 *et seq.*
[25] *Re Tankard* [1942] Ch. 69, 74. See *post*, p. 934. But see as to limitation, *post*, p. 901. In so far as there is a trust to pay debts the creditors may be beneficiaries.
[26] *Ibid.* p. 69; *Grayburn* v. *Clarkson* (1868) L.R. 3 Ch. 605. See *ante*, p. 112.
[27] *Hall* v. *Hallet* (1784) 1 Cox Eq.Cas. 134. As to interest on debts see *post*, p. 1035.
[28] *Ibid.* n. 26.
[29] *Re Stevens* [1898] 1 Ch. 162, 172.
[30] See *post*, p. 609, n. 53.
[31] See *post*, p. 614.

are payable on part of the assets it may be material to decide whether or not a given debt falls on (and reduces the value of) such part.[32]

Locke King's Acts

The general principle:

The general principle is that, in the absence of an intention to the contrary, debts charged upon property must be borne, as between the persons claiming through the deceased, by the property upon which they are charged. This principle is enacted in section 35 of the Administration of Estates Act 1925 which will be found set out in the Appendix, *post*, p. 1129. Section 35 extended the principle introduced for land only by the Real Estate Charges Acts (Locke King's Acts) 1854, 1867 and 1877, now repealed.[33]

The principle applies, not only to a charge by way of legal mortgage, but also, as did Locke King's Acts, to an equitable charge, whether or not accompanied by a memorandum of charge[34]; to a lien for unpaid purchase-money[35]; to a lien upon shares for debts owed to the company by a shareholder[36]; a solicitor's lien on the title deeds to realty[37]; to a rentcharge[38]; to arrears of interest charged on property and due at the date of death; to a charge of estate duty on real estate[39]; to a statutory charge in favour of local authorities[40]; to a charge created by delivery in execution under a duly registered writ of *elegit* of land held in fee simple[41]; and to a vendor's charge for unpaid purchase-money.[42]

It was decided in *Hepworth* v. *Hill*,[43] that a general charge of debts by a testator on his real estate in case his personal estate proved insufficient, was not a charge within Locke King's Acts. *Semble*, such a charge would not come within the provisions of section 35.[44–45] But it is uncertain whether a

---

[32] See *Encyclopaedia of Capital Taxation*, paras. 1A7–03, 1A9–14 *et seq.*

[33] *Re Turner* [1938] Ch. 593.

[34] *Pembroke* v. *Friend* (1860) 1 Johns. & H. 132; *Coleby* v. *Coleby* (1866) 12 Jur.(N.S.) 496; *Davis* v. *Davis* (1876) 24 W.R. 962; *Re Hawkes* [1912] 2 Ch. 251.

[35] See the Administration of Estates Act 1925, s.35(1), expressly referring to such a lien and thereby taking the place of the Act of 1867. See also *Re Cockcroft* (1883) 24 Ch.D. 94; *Re Kidd* [1894] 3 Ch. 558; *Re Coxen* [1948] 2 All E.R. 492, 496 (where there was held not to be a lien).

[36] *Re Turner* [1938] Ch. 593.

[37] *Re Riddell* [1936] Ch. 747.

[38] *Re Fraser* [1904] 1 Ch. 111, 726.

[39] *Re Bowerman* [1908] 2 Ch. 340.

[40] *Re Hesketh* (1900) 45 S.J. 11, provided, of course, it is not defeated for want of registration under the Land Charges Act 1925, s.15 (as amended by s.18 of the Land Charges Act 1972).

[41] *Re Anthony* [1892] 1 Ch. 450. As to when such a charge arises, see the Law of Property Act 1925, s.195.

[42] *Re Birmingham* [1959] Ch. 523.

[43] (1862) 30 Beav. 476.

[44–45] The section refers to a charge "at the time of" death of the deceased, not "immediately after" his death.

charge which is not specific, such as a banker's lien, is included in the section.[46] Unlike Locke King's Acts, section 35 applies to property appointed by will under a general power.[47] It is also made to apply to an entailed interest disentailed and disposed of by the will of the tenant in tail in possession.[48]

Contribution

Where different portions of the interest charged with the payment of money are given to different persons, the donees, in the absence of a sufficient expression of a contrary intention, must contribute according to the value of their respective portions.[49]

Before 1926, the fact that one portion of realty was given specifically, whilst the other portion was merely included in a residuary gift, was not of itself a sufficient indication of a contrary intention so as to exonerate the property specifically given.[50] The reason was that a residuary devise, despite the Wills Act 1837, s.24, was in its nature specific.[51] This distinction was lost with the 1925 legislation.[52] It is now simply a matter of construction whether or not the will shows a "contrary or other intention."[53]

"Secondary" and "collateral" securities

If a person procures an advance by mortgaging two properties, one of them being only in the nature of a secondary security, this property will not be liable to bear the debt at all, except for any surplus unsatisfied by the property which was made the primary security.[54] Where, however, one of the two properties mortgaged is described as being a "collateral security," this does not necessarily mean that it is only to be a secondary security.[55] And if, in the circumstances, it is not a secondary security, the two properties are liable rateably according to their respective values.[56]

[46] See *Re Dunlop* (1882) 21 Ch.D. 583; *Hepworth* v. *Hill* (1862) 30 Beav. 476; *cf. Re Hawkes* [1912] 2 Ch. 251.

[47] See subs. (1). Such property is assets within s.32; see *ante*, p. 593.

[48] See subs. (1). For the power to dispose of entailed interests, see the Law of Property Act 1925, s.176. *Aliter* as to undisposed-of entailed interests, *post*, p. 610.

[49] *Re Newmarch* (1878) 9 Ch.D. 12. See also *Evans* v. *Wyatt* (1862) 31 Beav. 217; *Trestrail* v. *Mason* (1878) 7 Ch.D. 665; *Leonino* v. *Leonino* (1879) 10 Ch.D. 460; *Re Major* [1914] 1 Ch. 278.

[50] *Sackville* v. *Smyth* (1873) L.R. 17 Eq. 153 (not following *Brownson* v. *Lawrance* (1868) L.R. 6 Eq. 1); *Gibbins* v. *Eyden* (1869) L.R. 7 Eq. 371; *Re Smith* (1886) 33 Ch.D. 195. See also *Lipscomb* v. *Lipscomb* (1868) L.R. 7 Eq. 501; *De Rochefort* v. *Dawes* (1871) L.R. 12 Eq. 540.

[51] Besides cases in last note, see *Hensman* v. *Fryer* (1867) L.R. 2 Ch. 420.

[52] *Re Biss* [1956] Ch. 243 (overruled [1962] Ch. 643). *Re Wilson* [1967] Ch. 53, 68.

[53] *Re Neeld* [1962] Ch. 643, 693, overruling *Re Biss*, *supra*, and *Re Cohen* [1960] Ch. 179, and following remarks of Evershed M.R. in *Re Cole* [1958] Ch. 877, 898; see 78 L.Q.R. 333.

[54] See *Re Athill* (1880) 16 Ch.D. 211. See also *Bute* v. *Cunynghame* (1826) 2 Russ. 275; *Re Ritson* [1899] 1 Ch. 128. As to the ambiguity in the use of the words "primary" and "secondary" see *Re Downer Enterprises* [1974] 1 W.L.R. 1460, 1470. "Primary" may mean "direct" or it may mean "ultimate."

[55] *Re Athill*, *supra*.

[56] See n. 55.

Several charged estates to one donee

Where several estates, charged with separate incumbrances, devolve upon,[57] or are given item by item to,[58] the same person, if one of such estates is insufficient to bear its own charge the unpaid surplus must, in the absence of a contrary intention, be paid out of the deceased's general estate. But if such estates are given as one aggregate gift, the donee must take the gift as a whole, subject to the aggregate charges, in exoneration of the deceased's general estate.[59]

Limits of section 35 of the Administration of Estates Act 1925

The primary liability thrown upon property charged with the payment of a sum of money under section 35 does not impose any personal liability upon the recipient.[60] Nor does it prejudice the right of the chargee to obtain payment out of any part of the assets of the deceased.[61]

Section 35 applies "as between the different persons claiming through the deceased." These words, besides reinforcing the rights of creditors, make it clear that the section does not apply to an undisposed-of[62] entailed interest. The person taking the entailed interest on the death of the deceased claims under the settlement, not through the deceased.[63]

Semble, on the other hand, the Crown taking property on an intestacy after 1925 as *bona vacantia*[64] does claim through the deceased. In any event, where the Crown became entitled to an interest in the land of a person who died intestate before 1926, it was held that Locke King's Acts[65] applied though the Crown did not claim through the deceased.[66]

Contrary intention

The operation of section 35 may be negatived by a "contrary or other intention" shown by the deceased in a will, deed[67] or other document.[68] In subsection (2) it is expressly enacted that a "contrary or other intention" is not signified merely by a general direction to pay debts, or all debts, out of the testator's personal estate,[69] or his residuary real and personal estate,[70]

---

[57] *Re Holt* (1916) 85 L.J.Ch. 779.

[58] *Re Baron Kensington* [1902] 1 Ch. 203.

[59] See n. 58.

[60] *Syer* v. *Gladstone* (1885) 30 Ch.D. 614. For text of the section, see *post*, p. 1129.

[61] See subs. (3).

[62] *Aliter*, if disposed of by will; *ante*, p. 609.

[63] *Re Anthony* [1893] 3 Ch. 498. And see *Re Ritson* [1899] 1 Ch. 128 (charge created by partner); *Re Fison's W.T.* [1950] Ch. 394 (person to whom option to purchase is bequeathed).

[64] See the Administration of Estates Act 1925, ss.46(1)(vi) and 57(1). But see *Re Musurus* [1936] 2 All E.R. 1666 and *Ing on Bona Vacantia*, p. 59.

[65] See p. 608, *ante*.

[66] *Dacre* v. *Patrickson* (1860) 1 Dr. & Sm. 182.

[67] See, *e.g. Re Campbell* [1893] 2 Ch. 206.

[68] See *Re Birmingham* [1959] Ch. 523 (specific devisee of house left in codicil subject to unpaid purchase-money).

[69] This reproduces the Act of 1867. And see *Re Rossiter* (1879) 13 Ch.D. 355.

[70] This reproduces the Act of 1877. And see *Elliott* v. *Dearsley* (1880) 16 Ch.D. 322.

or his residuary real estate,[71] or by a charge of debts upon such property. A charge of debts on, or a general direction to pay debts out of, his real estate, though not mentioned in subsection (2), would seem to be in the same position.[72]

In all the above cases, however, a contrary intention may be shown if the testator provides that some property should be "primarily" liable, or, instead of merely referring to his debts generally, refers expressly[73] or by necessary implication,[74] to all or some part of the charge.[75] Thus a direction to pay debts, except a mortgage debt on a particular property, shows that other mortgage debts are to be paid off.[76]

It is not necessary that the testator should expressly refer to "mortgage debts," if he has sufficiently described them in some other way.[77] But in *Re Bernstein*,[78] it was held that a direction to pay, out of a particular fund, "any sums of money secured on mortgage" of certain property, did not exonerate that property from its primary liability to satisfy a vendor's lien charged thereon.

A letter written by the deceased giving notice to a mortgagee of her intention to pay off the mortgage debt does not show a contrary intention so as to exonerate the property mortgaged from its primary liability under the section to bear the mortgage debt.[79] Nor does a letter written by the deceased, or his solicitor, in which is enclosed a cheque for the payment of the balance of purchase-money, if the deceased dies before the date fixed for completion.[80]

Effect of exclusion of section 35

If the testator shows an intention that such debts as would otherwise, under section 35, be paid out of the property upon which they are charged, are to be paid out of a particular fund, then effect must be given to his intention. But the property charged is only exonerated to the extent that this special fund is available for discharging the debt, and in so far as it is inadequate the property charged remains liable.[81] And where a testator directed that a bank overdraft secured by a deposit of title deeds should be paid out of accumulations of income till the mortgage was paid, and after the testator's death the bank required his trustees to repay the overdraft (which they did with moneys raised by a new legal mortgage of the prem-

---

[71] This reproduces the Act of 1877. And see *Re Newmarch* (1878) 9 Ch.D. 12.
[72] See *Re Newmarch, ante.*
[73] See, *e.g. Re Major* [1914] 1 Ch. 278.
[74] See, *e.g. Re Pimm* [1904] 2 Ch. 345.
[75] See the words in subs. (2). And see *Nelson* v. *Page* (1868) L.R. 7 Eq. 25.
[76] *Re Valpy* [1906] 1 Ch. 531.
[77] *Re Fleck* (1888) 37 Ch.D. 677.
[78] [1925] Ch. 12.
[79] *Re Nicholson* [1923] W.N. 251.
[80] *Re Wakefield* [1943] Ch. 169.
[81] *Re Birch* [1909] 1 Ch. 787; *Re Fegan* [1928] 1 Ch. 45 (extending the principle to personalty). See also *Re Major* [1914] 1 Ch. 278.

ises) it was held that the new mortgage ought not to be discharged out of accumulations of income for that would in effect be to make "a new will for the testator to meet an event for which he had not provided."[82] On the other hand, if the testator merely negatives the operation of section 35, but shows no further intention, all his debts, whether charged on property or not, must, as a general rule, be borne by the various portions of his estate in the order specified by Part II of Schedule 1 to the Administration of Estates Act 1925.[83]

It seems, however, that this is not always the case; for there are some liabilities which, independently of Locke King's Acts, or of section 35 which replaces these Acts, must, in the absence of a contrary intention, be borne primarily by the property on which they are charged, or to which they are annexed. Thus, if a settlor of real estate covenanted for the payment of the portions of children,[84] or widow's jointure,[85] or if a person made a voluntary gift by way of charge and covenanted for the payment of the money,[86] the land was the primary fund for payment; for in these cases the charge is in its nature real, and the covenant only an additional security.[87]

Charges not created by testator

Similarly the right of the heir or devisee, before the passing of Locke King's Acts, and subject to the provisions of the testator's will, to throw the burden of a mortgage debt charged on the land descended or devised on the general personal estate,[88] applied only to incumbrances created by the ancestor or testator himself,[89] or to mortgage debts which, though not originally created by him, he had adopted and made his own by some act affording sufficient evidence of his intention so to do.[90] Thus, if a person bought an estate subject to an existing mortgage,[91] or an estate descended on him as heir-at-law,[92] or was devised to him,[93] charged with a mortgage

[82] *Re Brandon* (1932) 49 T.L.R. 48.
[83] See *post*, p. 615.
[84] See *Graves* v. *Hicks* (1833) 6 Sim. 391, 398.
[85] *Lanoy* v. *Athol* (1742) 2 Atk. 444; *Edwards* v. *Freeman* (1727) 2 P.Wms. 435; *Coventry* v. *Coventry*, *ibid.* 222; *Loosemore* v. *Knapman* (1853) Kay 123. But see *Field* v. *Moore* (1855) 7 De G.M. & G. 691, where the provision was first secured by a covenant creating a debt to which the covenant for securing the charge was manifestly auxiliary.
[86] *Wilson* v. *Darlington* (1785) 1 Cox 172; *Ex p. Digby* (1821) Jack. 235.
[87] See *Ibbetson* v. *Ibbetson* (1841) 12 Sim. 206; *Jenkinson* v. *Harcourt* (1854) Kay 688; *Re Anthony* [1893] 3 Ch. 498. *cf. Field* v. *Moore, ante.*
[88] See Coote, *Mortgages*, 9th ed., pp. 780 *et seq.*, as to exemption of personalty by expression of contrary intention.
[89] See Coote, *Mortgages*, 9th ed., pp. 784 *et seq.*
[90] See *ibid.* and the 11th edition of this work, pp. 1310 and 1311, for what is sufficient evidence of the intention of the heir, the devisee, or the purchaser to make the debt his own.
[91] Coote, *Mortgages*, 9th ed., p. 786.
[92] *Noel* v. *Lord Henley* (1819) 7 Price 241; *ibid.* in Dom. Proc., 12 Price 213; *Re Leeming* (1861) 3 De G.F. & J. 43.
[93] *Perkins* v. *Baynton* (1784) 2 P.Wms. 664; note to *Evelyn* v. *Evelyn.*

debt, and he had neither paid off the debt nor adopted it as his own, on his death the land charged would have been, independently of Locke King's Acts,[94] the primary fund for payment, and his heir or devisee could not have thrown the debt on his personal estate.[95]

And even a direct and original mortgage made by the person to whom land had descended or been devised did not, as a general rule,[96] operate to make his personal estate the primary fund for the discharge of the mortgage debt if the money had been borrowed for the purpose of paying off the debts[97] or legacies[98] of the ancestor or devisor, and the law was the same though a bond[99] or note of hand[1] was given by the heir or devisee for the payment of debts or legacies charged on the land.

Unpaid purchase-money

If the purchaser of real estate died before 1926 without having paid the purchase-money, and if he had excluded the operation of Locke King's Acts,[2] his heir, or the devisee of the land purchased, was entitled, subject to the terms of the will, to have the purchase-money paid out of the general personal estate.[3] If he paid it himself he could claim to be reimbursed.[4] Further, if the personal estate proved insufficient to perform the contract, and the agreement was in consequence rescinded, the heir or devisee was entitled, it would seem, to the personalty so far as it went. And if by reason of the complication of the testator's affairs the purchase-money could not be paid immediately, and the vendor for that reason rescinded the contract, yet on the coming in of assets, the devisee might compel the executor to lay out the purchase-money in the purchase of other estates for his benefit.[5]

On the other hand, if a title could not be made, or there was not a perfect contract, or the court considered that the contract ought not to be

---

[94] See p. 608, *ante*.

[95] *Scott* v. *Beecher* (1820) 5 Madd. 96; *Swainson* v. *Swainson* (1856) 6 De G.M. & G. 648; *Hepworth* v. *Hill* (1862) 30 Beav. 476, 484.

[96] But in this case also the person to whom the land subject to the original debt descended or was devised might have made the debt his own, *e.g.* by creating, in effect, an entirely new mortgage, in which case his personal estate would have been the primary fund for payment; see *Barham* v. *Lord Thanet* (1834) 3 M. & K. 607, followed in *Bagot* v. *Bagot* (1864) 34 Beav. 134.

[97] *Tankerville* v. *Fawcett* (1786) 1 Cox 237; *Perkins* v. *Baynton*, *supra*.

[98] *Basset* v. *Percival* (1786) 1 Cox 268; *ibid.* 2 P.Wms. 664n.

[99] *Billinghurst* v. *Walker* (1789) 2 Bro.C.C. 604; *Woods* v. *Huntingford* (1796) 3 Ves. 128, 131.

[1] *Mattheson* v. *Hardwicke* (1789) 2 P.Wms. 665n.

[2] See p. 608, *ante*.

[3] *Milner* v. *Mills* (1729) Mosely 123; *Broome* v. *Monck* (1805) 10 Ves. 597; *Hudson* v. *Cook* (1872) L.R. 13 Eq. 417. *Aliter*, if Locke King's Acts applied: see *Re Cockcroft* (1883) 24 Ch.D. 94.

[4] *Broome* v. *Monck* (1805) 10 Ves. 597, 614, 615. Also *Lord* v. *Lord* (1857) 1 Sim. 505.

[5] *Whittaker* v. *Whittaker* (1881) 4 Bro.C.C. 31; *Broome* v. *Monck*, *supra*; Sugd. V. & P., 14th ed., p. 192. And see *Lysaght* v. *Edwards* (1876) 2 Ch.D. 499, 521.

executed, the heir or devisee had no claim either to the land,[6] or to the deceased's personal estate.[7]

Semble, the same principles will apply after 1925 if section 35 is negatived, save that the purchase-money is no longer payable primarily out of general personalty, but in the order specified by the Administration of Estates Act 1925, Sched. 1, Pt. II, hereafter considered.

Conclusion

Thus if the testator does no more than negative the operation of section 35 of the Administration of Estates Act 1925, all the liabilities above described, which even before the passing of Locke King's Acts, were primarily payable out of the property on which they were charged, would remain primarily payable out of such property, unless, in the circumstances, the mere exclusion of section 35 is held to show an intention to release all property charged with the payment of money from its primary liability to bear such charge.

Charges incidental to the property

Again, though the mere exclusion of the operation of section 35 will generally entitle a specific legatee to have his legacy redeemed from charges created by the testator at the expense of the general estate,[8] yet he will have no such right, apart from a direction in the will, for charges which are incidental to the property bequeathed. The reason for this distinction is that charges of the latter nature always have, apart from any statutory enactment, been primarily payable out of the properties to which they are annexed. "In fact the distinction turns upon this, is the charge one created by the testator for what has been called a temporary purpose, that is, with the view of raising money or of making use of the property, . . . or is it from its nature a charge incident to the property, as in the case of rent on leaseholds or calls payable on railway shares? In the first case the specified legatee is entitled" (provided now that s.35 is excluded) "to have the legacy redeemed or freed from the charge. In the second case he is not so entitled, because the testator is supposed to give the thing as it is, and the charge upon it is not in strictness an incumbrance, but something incident to the nature of the thing."[9] Thus the legatees of leasehold estates must take them with the burden (*cum onere*)[10] and notwithstanding the estate of

---

[6] There is no conversion in such cases, so that on the death of the vendor the land devolves as real estate.

[7] *Green* v. *Smith* (1738) 1 Atk. 573; *Broome* v. *Monck, ante.* And see *Curre* v. *Bowyer* (1818) 5 Beav. 6, n. (*b*).

[8] See *Bothamley* v. *Sherson, post.*

[9] See *Bothamley* v. *Sherson* (1875) L.R. 20 Eq. 304, 316. For the position as to calls, see below.

[10] *Hickling* v. *Boyer* (1851) 3 Mac. & G. 635; *Fitzwilliams* v. *Kelly* (1852) 10 Ha. 266; *Armstrong* v. *Burnet* (1855) 20 Beav. 424; *Hawkins* v. *Hawkins* (1880) 13 Ch.D. 470. Hence, if the premises are dilapidated, the executors may require an indemnity against their liability in this respect from the legatee before letting him into possession: *Hickling* v. *Boyer, ante.*

the testator may remain liable to the lessor by reason of the covenants contained in the lease.[11]

Liability for breach of covenant in a lease

This liability which is incident to the relation of landlord and tenant, such as a covenant to repair, falls upon the devisee of the lease.[12] "On the other hand, if the covenant is not in its nature incident to the relation of landlord and tenant—if the thing to be done is something preparatory to the complete establishment of that relation, it would seem to be fair and in accordance with the probable wishes of the testator that the burthen of the covenant unperformed by him in his lifetime, should be borne by his estate rather than by the specific devisees."[13]

Call on shares

It was established before 1926 that, in the absence of a contrary intention, any payment necessary at the testator's death to constitute him a complete shareholder had to be borne by his estate, but that all calls made after his death were payable by the specific legatee.[14] Where, however, a testator dies after 1925, and calls are made before his death, and the company by its articles or constitution has a lien for unpaid calls, *semble*, such calls ought prima facie to be borne by the specific legacy under section 35.[15]

Statutory order of application of assets—the Schedule

Subject to what has been said about debts charged upon, or incident to, property at the death of the deceased, the present order[16] of application of assets (where the estate is solvent) for the payment of "the funeral, testamentary and administration expenses, debts and liabilities"[17] is contained in the Administration of Estates Act 1925, Sched. 1, Pt. II. The order provided by that Schedule is as follows:

"1. Property of the deceased undisposed of by will, subject to the retention thereout of a fund sufficient to meet any pecuniary legacies.

2. Property of the deceased not specifically devised or bequeathed but included (either by a specific or general description) in a residuary gift,

---

[11] As to which, see *ante*, p. 573.

[12] *Eccles* v. *Mills* [1898] A.C. 360; *Re Hughes* [1913] 2 Ch. 491; *Re Day* [1962] 1 W.L.R. 1419. cf. *Marshall* v. *Holloway* (1832) 5 Sim. 196, explained in *Fitzwilliams* v. *Kelly* (1852) 10 Hare 266, 278, and doubted in *Eccles* v. *Mills* [1898] A.C. 360, 372; see 27 *Conveyancer* 72.

[13] From the judgment of the P.C. in *Eccles* v. *Mills*, at p. 372; *Re Rushbrook* [1948] Ch. 421; see *ante*, p. 555.

[14] *Armstrong* v. *Burnet* (1855) 20 B. 424; *Moffett* v. *Bates* (1857) 3 Sm. & G. 468; *Addams* v. *Ferick* (1859) 26 Beav. 384. See also *Re Box* (1863) 1 H. & M. 552.

[15] See 5 Wolst. & Ch., 13th ed., p. 57; and see *Re Turner* [1938] Ch. 593.

[16] As to the order of application where a person died before 1926, see *post*, p. 616 and 11th ed. of Williams, *Executors and Administrators*, 11th ed., p. 1330; *Manning* v. *Spooner* (1796) 3 Ves. 114, 117. See also *post*, p. 997.

[17] Administration of Estates Act 1925, s.34(3), which incorporates the order set out in Sched. 1, Pt. II (*post*, pp. 1129, 1152).

subject to the retention out of such property of a fund sufficient to meet any pecuniary legacies, so far as not provided for as aforesaid.[18]

3. Property of the deceased specifically appropriated or devised or bequeathed (either by a specific or general description) for the payment of debts.

4. Property of the deceased charged with, or devised or bequeathed (either by a specific or general description) subject to a charge for the payment of debts.

5. The fund, if any, retained to meet pecuniary legacies.

6. Property specifically devised or bequeathed rateably according to value.

7. Property appointed by will under a general power, including the statutory powers to dispose of entailed interests, rateably according to value.

8. The following provisions shall also apply:

   (a) The order of application may be varied by the will of the deceased.

   (b) This part of this Schedule does not affect the liability of land to answer the death duty imposed thereon in exoneration of other assets."

In *Re Eve*,[19] Roxburgh J. held that property subject to an option to purchase is the last to be available for the payment of debts. It is not a specific bequest and so long as the purchase price is, with the other assets, sufficient for the payment of debts, it, and not the property, is the fund available. But if it is not sufficient the option is totally destroyed.

Order before 1926

Where a person died before 1926 his general personal estate was primarily liable for the payment of debts and legacies.[20] This primary liability could be negatived[21] if the deceased showed in his will an intention to discharge the personalty.[22] This intention might be either express or

---

[18] As to this category in particular, see *Re Wilson* [1967] Ch. 53, 67.

[19] [1956] Ch. 479.

[20] *Manning* v. *Spooner* (1796) 3 Ves. 114; *Harmood* v. *Oglander* (1803) 8 Ves. 106. This did not prejudice the right of a creditor to resort in the first instance to real estate. Where, in the course of administration in different countries, the question arises whether particular debts are properly and ultimately payable out of the personal estate, or are chargeable on the real estate of the deceased, the law of his domicile will govern in cases of intestacy, and in cases of testacy his intention: Story's *Conflict*, Chap. xiii, s. 528; Dicey and Morris, *Conflict*, 11th ed., 1987, pp. 600, 608.

[21] *Ancaster* v. *Mayer* (1785) 1 Bro.C.C. 454, 462.

[22] But circumstances *dehors* the will were inadmissible to show such an intention: *Bootle* v. *Blundell* (1815) 1 Mer. 193, 216. Also *Inchiquin* v. *French* (1744) 1 Cox 9; *Stephenson* v. *Heathcote* (1758) 1 Eden 39; *Andrews* v. *Emmot* (1787–88) 2 Bro.C.C. 297; *Standen* v. *Standen* (1795) 2 Ves. 589; *Coote* v. *Coote* (1846) 3 J. & Lat. 175; *Re Grainger* [1900] 2 Ch. 756, 763; *ibid. sub nom. Higgins* v. *Dawson* [1902] A.C. 1, 9–11.

implied.[23] It was not, however, sufficient, to remove the primary liability of personalty, that the testator should have charged his real estate with debts and legacies,[24] or that he should have directed his real estate to be sold for the payment of debts and legacies.[25] Such a charge or direction only made the real estate liable after the primary fund of personalty had been exhausted.[26] There had to be an intention shown not only to charge the real estate, but also to discharge the personal estate.[27] On the other hand, a charge of debts on a specific fund of personalty was in itself sufficient to discharge the general personalty from its primary liability.[28]

"Property"

Although there is doubt as to the application of the Schedule to legacies[29] the position is clear as to debts. The Schedule deals throughout with "property." " 'Property' includes a thing in action and any interest in real or personal property."[30] Thus funeral, testamentary and administration expenses, debts and liabilities are, subject to the provisions of the will, borne, as between the real and personal property comprised in any class of property specified by the Schedule, rateably in proportion to their respective values. This principle applies even to a beneficial interest in real estate which devolves, by reason of the Administration of Estates Act 1925, s.51(2), in accordance with the general law in force before 1926 applicable to freehold land.[31]

Condition as to payment of debts

If a legacy is given upon condition that the legatee will pay the testator's debts, and the legatee accepts the gift he may be compelled to pay all the debts though they far exceed the value of the property given to him.[32]

[23] *Bootle* v. *Blundell* (1815) 1 Mer. 193, 219, 230; *Dawes* v. *Scott* (1828) 5 Russ. 32. See also *Collis* v. *Robins* (1847) 1 De G. & Sm. 131, 141; *Kilford* v. *Blaney* (1886) 31 Ch.D. 56, 61; *Wilkinson* v. *Adam* (1813) 1 V. & B. 422, 466.
[24] *Davies* v. *Ashford* (1845) 15 Sim. 42; *Roberts* v. *Roberts* (1757) 13 Sim. 336; *Gainsford* v. *Dunn* (1874) L.R. 17 Eq. 405; *Re Boards* [1895] 1 Ch. 499. Even where the charge for payment of debts was created by deed: *French* v. *Chichester* (1706) 2 Vern. 568.
[25] *Rhodes* v. *Rudge* (1826) 1 Sim. 79, 84, 85; *Walker* v. *Hardwick* (1833) 1 M. & K. 396; *Forrest* v. *Prescott* (1870) L.R. 10 Eq. 545. See also *Re Ovey* (1886) 31 Ch.D. 113; *Poole* v. *Heron* (1873) 42 L.J.Ch. 348.
[26] See last note. And for other cases in which it was held that there was not a sufficient expression by the testator of an intention to exonerate personal estate, see 11th ed. of Williams, *Executors and Administrators*, 11th ed., pp. 1319–1321.
[27] *Bootle* v. *Blundell* (1815) 1 Mer. 193, 220, 230; *Bickham* v. *Cruttwell* (1838) 3 M. & Cr. 763; *Collis* v. *Robins* (1847) 1 De G. & Sm. 131, 141; *Trott* v. *Buchanan* (1885) 28 Ch.D. 446, 453.
[28] *Webb* v. *De Beauvoisin* (1862) 31 Beav. 573, 576; *Vernon* v. *Manvers* (1862) 31 Beav. 623; *Coventry* v. *Coventry* (1865) 2 Dr. & Sm. 470; *Trott* v. *Buchanan* (1885) 28 Ch.D. 446.
[29] See *post*, pp. 989, 993.
[30] Administration of Estates Act 1925, s.55(1)(xvii).
[31] *Re Gates* [1930] 1 Ch. 199; *post*, p. 1075.
[32] *Messenger* v. *Andrews* (1828) 4 Russ. 478. cf. *Henvell* v. *Whitaker* (1827) 3 Russ. 343; *Dover* v. *Gregory* (1839) 10 Sim. 393.

Debts fund and pecuniary legacies fund

So the first step to be taken in the administration of a solvent estate is to set aside out of undisposed of or residuary personalty (as the case may be), a fund to meet pecuniary legacies. That is the first charge, and except in so far as there are provisions to the contrary in the will, it is a charge on personalty.[33] Then a second fund consisting of realty and personalty in proportion to their respective values is to be set aside out of the undisposed of or residuary property (as the case may be) to meet debts, expenses and liabilities. This second fund has to be exhausted in meeting debts, expenses and liabilities before any part of the first fund (the pecuniary legacies fund) is touched.[34]

Application of statutory order

In construing the Schedule set out above, due attention must be paid to the order in which the various paragraphs appear. If property happens to come within more than one paragraph it should, in the absence of a contrary intention to be found in the will,[35] be liable under that paragraph which appears first in the Schedule.[36] The following considerations apply accordingly, following the numbering of the paragraphs in the Schedule.

1. *Property undisposed of*

A lapsed share of residue, since it becomes "undisposed of,"[37] is liable for debts before the shares which have not lapsed, unless there is a contrary intention to be found in the will. Where the residuary realty and personalty are given to trustees on trust for conversion, so as to create a mixed fund for the payment of debts, and subject thereto the residuary fund is to be divided into shares, all such shares, whether lapsed or not, must bear the debts proportionately.[38] On the other hand where there is merely a direction to pay funeral and testamentary expenses or debts, followed by a gift of a share of residue, and the gift lapses, the statutory order applies.[39] In the former class of cases there is an express charge of the specified items

---

[33] *Re Rowe* [1941] Ch. 343; *Re Wilson* [1967] Ch. 53.

[34] *Re Anstead* [1943] Ch. 161; *Re Ridley* [1950] Ch. 415.

[35] Administration of Estates Act 1925, s.34(3) and Sched. 1, Pt. II, para. 8(*a*); *Re Petty, infra*; *Re Atkinson* [1930] 1 Ch. 47.

[36] This mode of construction was applied by Clauson J. to the Law of Property Act 1925, Sched. 1, Pt. IV (transitional provisions dealing with undivided shares), in *Re Dawson* [1928] Ch. 421.

[37] Para. (1) deals with property "undisposed of." For the definition of "disposes of," see the Administration of Estates Act 1925, s.55(1)(iii). See also *ibid.*, s.33(1).

[38] *Greville* v. *Browne* (1859) 7 H.L.C. 690; *Re Petty* [1929] 1 Ch. 726; *Re Cruse* [1930] W.N. 206; *Re Atkinson* [1930] 1 Ch. 47; *Re Kempthorne, ibid.* 268; *Re Littlewood* [1931] 1 Ch. 443; *Re McKee* [1933] 2 Ch. 145; *Re Harland-Peck* [1941] Ch. 182; *Re Beaumont* [1950] Ch. 462; *Re Martin* [1955] Ch. 698; *Re Berrey's W.T.* [1959] 1 W.L.R. 30; *Re Feis* [1964] Ch. 106, 116; *cf. Re Midgley* [1955] Ch. 576; and see the criticism of *Re Martin* in *Re Taylor's Estate and Will Trusts* [1969] 2 Ch. 245, 251 and 27 *Conveyancer* 519.

[39] *Re Lamb* [1929] 1 Ch. 722; *Re Tong* [1931] 1 Ch. 202; *Re Worthington* [1933] Ch. 771; *Re Sanger* [1939] 1 Ch. 238.

upon the subject-matter of the gift; while in the latter class of cases there is merely a direction to pay the specified items unsupported by any charge, express or to be implied.[40]

Under the law in force before 1926 all shares in the residue, whether lapsed or not, were liable proportionately. The reason for this was that there could be no true "residue" of personalty until all debts were paid; all that lapsed was a share in the net residue after payment of debts.[41]

Before 1926 the fact that a gift lapsed[42] or failed[43] seemed not, as a rule, to affect the order in which the property, the subject-matter of the gift, was liable for the payment of debts. But if a testator expressly exonerated some portion of his estate in favour of a particular beneficiary, and the gift to the person so intended to be benefited failed, the express exoneration itself failed.

2. *Residuary gifts*

Before 1926 a residuary devise of real estate was liable for the payment of debts rateably with specific devises.[44] Under the present Schedule, however, a residuary devise falls within paragraph (2), not paragraph (6). But a gift of all a testator's real estate and the residue of his personal estate to persons in equal shares does not make the gift of real estate a residuary gift[45]; nor is a devise of "all my real estate" a residuary devise, if the will contains a later gift of residue.[46] Although before 1926 all devises were from their nature specific the subject-matter of a general gift of real estate after 1925 may be a residuary gift for purposes of administration.[47]

3. and 4. *Property appropriated for payment of debts*

Property appropriated for the payment of debts[48] is liable under paragraph (3); property charged with the payment of debts[49] under paragraph (4). The position here is substantially the same as was the position of real estate

[40] *Per curiam* in *Re Harland-Peck* [1941] Ch. 182, *ante*, at p. 190.
[41] *Trethewy* v. *Helyar* (1876) 4 Ch.D. 53; *Fenton* v. *Wills* (1877) 7 Ch.D. 33; *Blann* v. *Bell* (1877) *ibid.* 382. *cf.* as to real estate, *Scott* v. *Cumberland* (1874) L.R. 18 Eq. 578; *Trethewy* v. *Helyar*, *ante*.
[42] *Ryves* v. *Ryves* (1871) L.R. 11 Eq. 539. See also *Stead* v. *Hardaker* (1873) L.R. 15 Eq. 175. A devise of real estate subject to debts before 1926 did not exonerate the personal estate: *Re Banks* [1905] 1 Ch. 547; and a lapsed share so charged was applied in the same order as shares not lapsed: *Ryves* v. *Ryves*, *ante*.
[43] *Hurst* v. *Hurst* (1884) 28 Ch.D. 159.
[44] *Manning* v. *Spooner* (1796) 3 Ves. 114; *Hensman* v. *Fryer* (1867) L.R. 3 Ch. 420; *Lancefield* v. *Iggulden* (1874) L.R. 10 Ch. 136; *Gibbins* v. *Eyden* (1869) L.R. 7 Eq. 371. See also *Farquharson* v. *Floyer* (1876) 3 Ch.D. 109; *Tombs* v. *Roch* (1846) 2 Coll. 490; *Jackson* v. *Pease* (1874) L.R. 19 Eq. 96.
[45] *Re Rowe* [1941] Ch. 343.
[46] *Re Ridley* [1950] Ch. 415, 421.
[47] *Re Wilson* [1967] Ch. 53, 68.
[48] See *Stead* v. *Hardaker* (1873) L.R. 15 Eq. 175.
[49] As to what words were, before 1926, sufficient to charge real estate with debts and legacies, see 1 Rop.Leg. 571 *et seq.*, 3rd ed.; 2 Pow.Dev. 644 *et seq.*, Jarman's ed.; Jarman 8th ed., Chap. 41. And see below.

appropriated[50] or charged[51] before 1926. It seems somewhat anomalous that property comprised in a residuary gift should be liable before property specifically appropriated for the payment of debts. But *semble*, anything wider than a "charge" or "appropriation" would be construed as a "contrary intention" so as to make the property specified primarily liable.[52]

Property charged by implication

A testator may by implication charge part of his estate with the payment of debts, and it is conceived that property so charged would, subject to a contrary intention to be found in the will, be liable for debts under paragraph (4). As to what is sufficient indication of an intention to charge property with debts, it has been established that if there is a direction that the executors shall pay the testator's debts, followed by a gift of all his estate to them, either beneficially or on trust, all the debts will be payable out of all the estate[53] so given to them. The same rule applies whether the executors take the whole beneficial interest as in *Henvell* v. *Whitaker*,[54] or only a beneficial life interest as in *Finch* v. *Hattersley*,[55] or no beneficial interest at all as in *Hartland* v. *Murrel*.[56] But this rule seems only to apply where the entirety of the liability has been thrown on the entirety of the estate.[57] Generally the intention must be collected from the whole will,[58] and it has been said that there is an exception from the general rule where there are two or more executors to whom unequal benefits are given by the will.[59]

Realty and personalty liable rateably

Where a testator directs that his debts (and legacies) are to be paid out of part of his realty and personalty, it would seem that, in the absence of an expression of a contrary intention, the realty and personalty must prima facie contribute in proportion to their relative values.[60] This was so before 1926, even though the realty was not subject to an absolute trust for conversion, provided that the realty and personalty were thrown into one

---

[50] See *Manning* v. *Spooner* (1796) 3 Ves. 114; *Harmood* v. *Oglander* (1803) 8 Ves. 106; *Phillips* v. *Parry* (1856) 22 Beav. 279.

[51] *Harmood* v. *Oglander, ante*; *Davies* v. *Topp* (1780) 1 Bro.C.C. 524. But real estate descended, whether acquired before or after the making of the will, was liable after property appropriated for, but before property charged with, the payment of debts: *Wride* v. *Clarke* (1766) 2 Bro.C.C. 261, n.; *Harmood* v. *Oglander, ante*; *Row* v. *Row* (1869) L.R. 7 Eq. 414.

[52] See *post*, p. 622.

[53] The cases on this subject were decided in connection with real estate devised to an executor. But, *semble*, the same principle applies to all property which the executor derives under the will whether personal or real. See *Henvell* v. *Whitaker* (1827) 3 Russ. 343, 348; *Wasse* v. *Heslington, post*, n. 58.

[54] (1827) 3 Russ. 343.

[55] (1775) 3 Russ. 345.

[56] (1859) 27 Beav. 204.

[57] *Bailey* v. *Bailey* (1879) 12 Ch.D. 268.

[58] *Wasse* v. *Heslington* (1834) 3 My. & K. 495.

[59] *Harris* v. *Watkins* (1854) Kay 438; but see *Re Tanqueray-Willaume and Landau* (1882) 20 Ch.D. 465.

[60] For realty and personalty are on an equal footing throughout the Schedule.

fund,[61] and that the testator directed payment of debts (and legacies) out of that fund.[62]

"All my just debts"

The expression in a will "all my just debts" includes all the testator's debts whenever and wherever contracted, thus including a debt contracted after the making of the will in a foreign country other than that of domicile, and secured upon property in that country.[63]

5. The fund for pecuniary legacies

This fund (if any) is next in line. Similar considerations apply as apply to 3 and 4 above.

6. Specific Gifts

In Re Maddock[64] it was held that a binding secret trust is, for the purpose of payment of debts, in the same position as a specific devise or bequest. Semble, this principle still applies. Thus, if a secret trust is undertaken by a residuary devisee or legatee, only that part of the residue which is unaffected by the secret trust is within paragraph (2). The property subject to the trust is liable under paragraph (6).

7. Property appointed under general power

Property appointed by will under a general power is not liable until all other assets are exhausted.[65] In this respect the law was the same before 1926.[66] Paragraph (7), however, includes property disentailed and disposed of by the will of a tenant in tail in possession.[67]

Where, by virtue of the Wills Act 1837, s.27, a power is exercised by a general residuary devise or bequest, the subject-matter of the power is included in "a residuary gift," thus falling within paragraph (2).[68] Further, it would seem that, owing to the words "(either by a specific or general des-

---

[61] Allan v. Gott (1872) L.R. 7 Ch. 439. cf. Boughton v. Boughton (1848) 1 H.L.C. 406.

[62] Elliott v. Dearsley (1880) 16 Ch.D. 322; Re Boards [1895] 1 Ch. 499. A fortiori, this was so where the realty in the mixed fund was subject to a trust for conversion; see Roberts v. Walker (1830) 1 Russ. & M. 752, and the numerous other cases cited in n. (z) to p. 1322 of Williams, Executors, 11th ed.

[63] Maxwell v. Maxwell (1870) L.R. 4 H.L. 506.

[64] [1902] 2 Ch. 220. As to secret trusts see ante, p. 154, and Theobald, Wills, 14th ed., pp. 96–102.

[65] See para. (7) ante, p. 616.

[66] Fleming v. Buchanan (1853) 3 De G.M. & G. 976; Holmes v. Coghill (1806) 7 Ves. 499; 12 Ves. 206.

[67] Under the Law of Property Act 1925, s.176.

[68] The law remains the same in this respect as it was before 1926: see Re Hartley [1900] 1 Ch. 152. For an example of a general power held to have been exercised by virtue of s.27, see Re Harvey [1950] W.N. 112.

cription)," property disentailed and disposed of by will, but not specifically devised or bequeathed, is liable under paragraph (2).[69]

Though property appointed by deed may be made liable for the debts of the appointor,[70] it can only be resorted to where the estate is otherwise insolvent.

Appropriation does not of itself vary the order

The order mentioned in the Schedule may be varied by the will of the deceased.[71] Since undisposed of property and property comprised in residuary gifts appear first and second in the statutory order, while property appropriated and property charged with the payment of debts appear as third and fourth, it is often difficult to determine what constitutes sufficient contrary intention to amount to a variation of the statutory order. The mere fact that a testator appropriates or bequeaths certain property for, or charges it with, the payment of debts, is not in itself sufficient to vary the order.[72]

Thus, in *Re Gordon*[73] a testatrix whose estate was solvent, by her will, bequeathed a specific legacy, and also a legacy of £50 to pay thereout her debts, funeral and testamentary expenses, and to pay any balance remaining to the Rationalist Press Association. The residuary estate was undisposed of. It was held that there was nothing in the will to vary the statutory order, and the debts, funeral and testamentary expenses must therefore be paid out of the undisposed of estate.

Contrary intention

In order to vary the statutory order there must be found in the will, not only a devise or bequest of particular property for the payment of debts, but also an intention to exonerate therefrom another category of property disposed of by the will.[74] The matter is indeed one of construction of each will, whether or not the testator has varied the order of application of assets or not. Accordingly, if a testator wishes to vary the present order, his safest course is to appropriate for debts the property that he wishes to be primarily liable in exoneration of the rest of his estate, or such part of his estate as he wishes to be exonerated.

[69] An entailed interest may be disposed of under the Law of Property Act 1925, s.176, "by means of a devise or bequest referring specifically either to the property or to the instrument under which it was acquired or to entailed property generally."

[70] *Ante*, p. 594.

[71] Administration of Estates Act 1925, Sched. 1, Pt. II, para. 8(a), and see the words "subject to . . . the provisions . . . contained in his will" in *ibid.* s.34(3). See further the cases mentioned in nn. 38 and 39 on p. 618 *ante*. And see *Re James* [1947] Ch. 256.

[72] *Re Kempthorne* [1930] 1 Ch. 268, 278; *Re Gordon* [1940] Ch. 851; *Re James* [1947] Ch. 256.

[73] [1940] Ch. 769.

[74] *Re James, ante*; *Re Meldrum* [1952] Ch. 208.

Exoneration in favour of beneficiary

Before 1926 it was a general rule that, in the absence of any expression of intention to the contrary, if a testator charged his real estate, or a certain portion of his personal estate,[75] with the payment of debts in exoneration of his general personal estate, and bequeathed such general personal estate to particular individuals, he intended to exonerate his personal estate for the benefit only of those legatees. Thus, if the bequest of the general personal estate failed, whether by the death of the legatees in the lifetime of the testator or by reason of the Mortmain Acts, so that it went to persons other than those intended by the testator, those persons were not entitled to the benefit of the exoneration.

If, after 1925, a testator intends to exonerate property made primarily liable by the Schedule, he should bear this rule in mind, for, *semble*, in the absence of a contrary intention the principle of the rule will still apply.

C. INSOLVENT ESTATES

The administration of insolvent estates was formerly governed by section 34(1) and Part I of the First Schedule to the Administration of Estates Act 1925 or, where the estate was being administered in bankruptcy, by section 130 of the Bankruptcy Act 1914.[76] Those provisions have now been replaced by such of the provisions of the Insolvency Act 1986 as are adopted, modified or added by the Administration of Insolvent Estates of Deceased Persons Order 1986[77] which came into force on December 29, 1986.[78] Accordingly, where a person died after December 29, 1986, the new provisions apply to the administration of the estate whether in or out of bankruptcy.[79] However, where an order for the administration of an estate in bankruptcy was made on a petition presented before December 29, 1986, the old Bankruptcy Act 1914 will continue to apply.[80] What is less clear is whether the new or old law governs the administration of a person's estate outside bankruptcy[81] where that person died before December 29, 1986. This is not a novel problem for, in cases decided at the time when the Administration of Estates Act 1925 (*i.e.* the old law) had just come into force,[82] some judges assumed that that Act governed the administration outside bankruptcy of an estate of a person who died before that act came

[75] *Kilford* v. *Blaney* (1885) 31 Ch.D. 56. See also *Fisher* v. *Fisher* (1838) 2 Keen 610.
[76] As to which, reference should be made to the previous edition of this work.
[77] S.I. 1986 No. 1999; made pursuant to Insolvency Act 1986, s.421. References in these footnotes to "the Order" are references to this order and references to "the Act" are references to this Act. References to the Order only appear where the Act has been modified or new words substituted by Sched. I, Pt. II of the Order; but also note the substitutions set out in Sched. 1, Pt. I.
[78] The Order, Art. 1. See *Muir Hunter on Personal Insolvency*, p. 5001 (Part V).
[79] As to the methods of administration under the new provisions; see below, p. 624.
[80] See the Act, Sched. 11, para. 10 and the Order, Sched. 1, Pt. II, para. 36.
[81] *i.e.* by the representatives out of court or by the Chancery Division pursuant to an order under R.S.C., Ord. 85; see *post*, p. 624.
[82] December 31, 1925.

into force[83]; whilst others assumed that the previous law continued to apply.[84] Given the wording of the new law[85] and the fact that the old law has been repealed (save where the transitional provisions apply), it seems probable that the new law should govern; however, the contrary may be arguable.[86]

Meaning of insolvent estate

The estate of a deceased person is insolvent if the assets, when realised, will not be sufficient to meet in full all of the debts and other liabilities (including the funeral, testamentary and administration expenses[87]) to which it is subject.[88] Whether an estate is insolvent is a question of fact[89] as to which the court may direct an inquiry.[90] In determining the solvency of an estate which is charged (otherwise than by the testator's will) with the payment of an annuity, the annuitant is entitled to have his annuity valued and to treat the capital value as a debt due from the estate.[91] Where there is any doubt as to whether or not an estate is solvent, it should be administered in accordance with the rules applicable to insolvent estates until all of the expenses and debts have been paid in full.[92]

Methods of administration

There are three ways in which an insolvent estate can be administered:

(1) Administration by the representative out of court.

(2) Administration by the Chancery Division after order obtained by a creditor under R.S.C. Order 85.[93] An application may also be made by the representative provided a creditor is willing to be joined as a defendant.[94] If an administration order has been made in a beneficiary's action but insolvency supervenes, then the action can only continue if reconstituted by way of substituting a creditor for the beneficiary.[95]

(3) Administration in bankruptcy after the making of an insolvency

---

[83] *Per* Luxmoore J. in *Re Bush* [1930] 2 Ch. 202 at pp. 204–205.

[84] *Per* Clauson J. in *Re Pink* [1927] 1 Ch. 237 at pp. 240–241.

[85] *i.e.* the Order, Art. 4.

[86] But note that, even if the old law applied, an unsecured creditor (wishing to take advantage of the fewer categories of preferential creditors under the new law) could, in effect, attempt a change to the new law by presenting a petition.

[87] *Re Leng* [1895] 1 Ch. 586, 658.

[88] s.421(4) of the Act.

[89] *Re Pink, ante.*

[90] *Re Smith* (1883) 22 Ch.D. 586 at p. 592 and *George Lee & Sons (Builders) Ltd.* v. *Olink* [1972] 1 W.L.R. 214.

[91] *Ibid.* n. 89.

[92] See *Re Milan Tramways Co.* (1884) 25 Ch.D. 587; *Re Pink, ante*; *Re Hopkins* (1881) 18 Ch.D. 370 at p. 377; *Re McMurdo* [1902] 2 Ch. 684.

[93] See Supreme Court Practice para. 85/3–6/6. An annuitant whose annuity is not in arrear is not a creditor for this purpose, *Re Hargreaves* (1890) 44 Ch.D. 236.

[94] *Re Bradley* [1956] Ch. 615. For procedure see p. 625, *post.*

[95] *Re Van Oppen* [1935] W.N. 51; 179 L.T.J. 255.

administration order.[96] The following people may petition for an insolvency administration order:

(a) the representative of a deceased person[97] only on the ground that the estate is insolvent. In such a case, the court may make an order if satisfied that the estate is insolvent[98];

(b) a creditor whose debt would have been sufficient to support a bankruptcy petition against the deceased debtor had he remained alive.[99] In such a case the court may make such an order if satisfied that the debt, if payable, has neither been paid nor secured or compounded for, or, if not yet payable, has no reasonable prospect of being able to be paid when it falls due and, in either case, that there is a reasonable probability that the estate of the deceased person will be insolvent.[1] The statutory demand procedure does not apply to the insolvent estates of deceased persons;

(c) the supervisor or other person bound by a voluntary arrangement proposed by the deceased debtor and approved by his creditors[2] and

(d) the Official Petitioner (or other specified person) following the making of a criminal bankruptcy order against the deceased person.[3]

A petition for an insolvency administration order cannot be presented after proceedings for the administration of the deceased's estate have been commenced in any court.[4] However, the court hearing the proceedings for administration may, if satisfied that the estate is insolvent, transfer the proceedings to a court exercising jurisdiction in bankruptcy.[5]

A petition for an insolvency administration order must, unless the court otherwise directs, be served on the representative of the deceased and on such other persons as the court may direct.[6]

[96] For a form of insolvency administration order, see the Order, Sched. 3, Form 4.

[97] s.272(1) of the Act, as modified by the Order, Sched. 1, Pt. II, paras. 6; and s.273 of the Act, as substituted by the Order, Sched. 1, Pt. II, para. 7. See *Re Bradley, ante.*

[98] See n. 97 above.

[99] ss.264(1)(a) and 267 of the Act, as modified by the Order, Sched. 1, Pt. II, paras. 1 and 3. In general, in order to support a petition, the debt relied upon by a creditor must be clear and undisputed; for where there is a genuine triable issue as to the existence of the debt, the court will take the view that that issue should be tried in a normal action and will dismiss the petition.

[1] s.271 of the Act, as substituted by the Order, Sched. 1, Pt. II, para. 5.

[2] s.264(1)(c) of the Act, as modified by the Order, Sched. 1, Pt. II, para. 1(d).

[3] s.264(1)(d) of the Act, as modified by the Order, Sched. 1, Pt. II, para. 1(e) and s.277 of the Act. The power to make criminal bankruptcy orders has been abolished as from April 3, 1985. S.264(1)(d) only applies to existing cases and will (with other provisions relating to criminal bankruptcy orders) be repealed in due course by statutory instrument.

[4] s.271(2) of the Act, as substituted by the Order, Sched. 1, Pt. II, para. 5.

[5] s.271(3) of the Act, as substituted by the Order, Sched. 1, Pt. II, para. 5.

[6] s.266(1) of the Act, as substituted by the Order, Sched. 1, Pt. II, para. 2. The words "unless the Court otherwise directs" indicate a change from the old law where the court had no power to make an order on a petition until a representative had been appointed (see *Re A Debtor* [1939] Ch. 594).

When proceedings on a petition for an insolvency administration order are pending or an insolvency administration order has been made, any action, execution or other legal process against the deceased's estate may be stayed by the court.[7] Further, any court in which proceedings are pending against the estate may, upon proof of the presentation of a petition, stay those proceedings or allow them to continue on terms.[8] After the making of an insolvency administration order, no person who is a creditor of the deceased's estate in respect of a debt provable in the bankruptcy has any remedy against the property of the deceased in respect of that debt and, before the discharge of the bankruptcy, such person may not commence any action or other legal proceedings against the deceased's representatives except with the leave of the court and on such terms as the court may impose.[9]

The court has power to annul an insolvency administration order if it at any time appears to the court either that, on the grounds existing at the time that the order was made, the order ought not to have been made, or that the bankruptcy debts and expenses have all, since the making of the order, been paid in full or secured to the satisfaction of the court.[10]

If an insolvency administration order is made, then, until the appointment of a trustee in bankruptcy, the official receiver is the receiver and manager of the estate of the deceased[11] and the representative is obliged to deliver to him possession of the deceased's estate and of all books, papers and other records of which he has possession or control and which relate to the deceased's estate or affairs and to perform certain other duties.[12]

Upon the appointment of the trustee,[13] the deceased's estate[14] vests in the trustee.[15] The administration of the estate is carried out by the trustee according to those provisions of the Insolvency Act 1986 which are specified and, in some cases, modified by the Administration of Insolvent Estates of Deceased Persons Order 1986.[16]

Choice of methods

The same rules govern the payment of the estate's expenses and debts whichever method of administration is adopted[17]; accordingly, provided

---

[7] s.284(1) of the Act.

[8] s.285(2) of the Act.

[9] s.285(3) of the Act; but see ss.285(4) and (5) and ss.346 and 347 of the Act.

[10] s.282(1) of the Act. S.282(4) of the Act validates transactions entered into by the official receiver or trustee before the annulment and provides for the re-vesting of the bankrupt's estate in the former bankrupt.

[11] s.287 of the Act.

[12] s.291 of the Act.

[13] As to the appointment of the trustee, see ss.292–297 of the Act as modified by the Order, Sched. 1, Pt. II, para. 18.

[14] As defined by s.283 of the Act as modified by the Order, Sched. 1, para. 12. The estate comprises the deceased's property (subject to specified exceptions) as at the date of death.

[15] s.306 of the Act.

[16] *i.e.* those provisions specified (as modified) by the Order, Sched. 1. See also p. 623, n.78, *ante*.

[17] See *ante*, p. 624.

the representative is willing and competent to follow those rules, it is often preferable to administer the estate outside bankruptcy. However, as appears below, administration in bankruptcy may be preferable so as to take advantage of the more extensive remedies which may be available to a trustee in bankruptcy.

Co-ownership of property

A trustee in bankruptcy may be in a better position than representatives as regards property of which the deceased was a co-owner. For example, it may be that the making of an insolvency administration order operates to sever any beneficial joint tenancy in property to which the deceased was entitled and to vest the severed beneficial share in the trustee in bankruptcy thereby defeating any claim by another joint tenant that the right of survivorship operates.[18] Further, where a trustee in bankruptcy applies[19] for an order for sale of jointly owned property, the courts under the old law consistently held that, save in exceptional circumstances, the interests of the creditors should prevail over other interests.[20] Under the Insolvency Act 1986, whilst the spouse of a deceased debtor has some protection in respect of a dwelling house of which the spouse and the deceased were trustees for sale,[21] that protection is slight, for if the trustee in bankruptcy applies[22] for the sale of that property more than a year after the deceased's estate has vested in him, the court must assume, save in exceptional circumstances, that the interests of the creditors outweigh all other considerations.[23]

[18] See *Muir Hunter on Personal Insolvency* at para. 5–035/1. It could be argued to the contrary that, had it been intended that the deceased's interests under a joint tenancy should vest in his trustee thereby defeating the right of survivorship, s.283 (as modified by the Order, Sched. 1, Pt. II, para. 12) should have referred to the deceased's property "immediately before his death" (see, for example, the Inheritance (Provision for Family and Dependents) Act 1975, s.9 and the Inheritance Tax Act 1984, s.4) rather than to his property as at the date of his death. Further, *Muir Hunter* appears to argue that, as para. 12 deems the insolvency administration order to have been made on the date of the deceased's death, that date is also deemed to be the date when property vests in the trustee and is the date when severance occurs. However, it is not clear that this is correct. It is the vesting of property in the trustee rather than the making of the bankruptcy (or, presumably, the insolvency administration) order which operates to sever a joint tenancy (see *Re Gorman* [1990] 1 W.L.R. 616 at p. 624B *per* Vinelott J. and *Re Dennis* [1992] 3 W.L.R. 204 at p. 205G *per* Nicholls V.C.). Whereas, under the old law, the bankrupt's property vested in the official receiver as trustee upon the making of the bankruptcy order (see the Bankruptcy Act 1914, ss.18(1) and 53), under the new law, the vesting of property takes place upon the appointment of the trustee which may be some time later. Para. 12 does not affect the date of appointment; rather it provides that the property which vests in the trustee on the date of his appointment is that property which belonged to or was vested in the deceased at the date of his death.

[19] Under Matrimonial Homes Act 1983, s.1 or Law of Property Act 1925, s.30.

[20] For a review of the authorities see *Re Citro* [1991] Ch. 142. As to exceptional circumstances, see *Re Citro* at p. 157C, a case under the old law.

[21] s.336(4) of the Act.

[22] Under s.336(3) of the Act, such an application must be made to the court having jurisdiction in relation to the bankruptcy.

[23] s.336(5) of the Act. As to exceptional circumstances, see n. 20, *ante*.

Disclaiming onerous property

A trustee in bankruptcy has extensive powers to disclaim onerous property.[24]

Challenging transactions

Under the Insolvency Act 1986, a trustee in bankruptcy has certain rights to challenge dispositions of the deceased's estate. For example, under sections 339 and 340, if, at a relevant time,[25] the deceased has entered into a transaction at an undervalue[26] or has given a preference,[27] the trustee in bankruptcy may apply to the court for an order for restoring the position to what it would have been if the deceased debtor had not entered into such transaction[28] or given such preference.[29] Under section 343, the trustee may challenge extortionate credit transactions[30] entered into by the deceased debtor not more than three years before the commencement of the bankruptcy.[31] Further, as the date of the presentation of the petition and the date of the insolvency administration order are deemed, for the purposes of sections 283 to 285 of the Insolvency Act 1986, to be the date of the death of the deceased debtor,[32] any disposition of the deceased's property made between that date and the date when the deceased's property vests in the trustee is void except to the extent that it is or was made with the consent of the court or is or was subsequently ratified by the court.[33] Although there may be some protection for dispositions made in good faith by a representative in the period before the date when the insolvency administration order was actually made[34] and for third parties who acquire assets from the deceased's estate before the deceased's death and in good faith and for value,[35] the scope of this protection is uncertain.[36]

Whether or not an insolvent estate is being administered in bankruptcy,

---

[24] ss.315–321 of the Act; onerous property may be unprofitable contracts or other property which is unsaleable or which is such that it may give rise to a liability to pay money or perform some onerous act.

[25] Defined by s.341 of the Act as modified by the Order, Sched. 1, para. 27. The period specified ends with the date of the deceased's death.

[26] Defined by s.339(3) of the Act.

[27] Defined by s.340(3) of the Act, see also s.340(4) and (5) of the Act.

[28] ss.339(2) of the Act.

[29] ss.340(2) of the Act.

[30] Defined by s.343(1) and (3) of the Act.

[31] s.343(2) of the Act. The date of commencement is the date on which the insolvency administration order was made; see s.278, as modified by the Order, Sched. 1, para. 10. Since the Bankruptcy Act 1914, s.66 (which prevented a creditor proving for interest at more than 5 per cent. on his debt unless all other debts had been paid) has not been re-enacted in the Act, s.343 may be of use in challenging claims for very high rates of interest.

[32] The Order, Sched. 1, Pt. II, para. 12.

[33] s.284 of the Act, as modified by the Order, Sched. 1, Pt. II, para. 12.   ·

[34] See s.271(5) of the Act as substituted by the Order, Sched. 1, Pt. II, para. 5.

[35] See s.284(4) of the Act, as modified by the Order, Sched. 1, Pt. II, para. 12.

[36] See *Muir Hunter on Personal Insolvency* at paras. 5–035 and 5–022. The uncertainty in the case of representatives is that the relieving provision (s.271(5) of the Act, as modified) does not, on its wording, apply to give relief from the provisions of s.284 of the Act.

a transaction made by the deceased at an undervalue[37] and for the purpose of putting assets beyond the reach of or otherwise prejudicing the interests of a person who is making or who may make a claim against the deceased[38] may be challenged under sections 423 to 425 of the Insolvency Act 1986.[39] Upon such an application, the court may make such order as it thinks fit to restore the position to what it would have been if the transaction had not been entered into and to protect the interests of the victims of the transaction.[40] If an insolvency administration order has been made, an application under sections 423 to 425 can only be made by the trustee in bankruptcy, or the official receiver, or (with the leave of the court) by a victim of the transaction.[41] If no insolvency administration order has been made, the application can only be made by a victim of the transaction unless a voluntary arrangement is in place, in which case only the supervisor of that arrangement may apply.[42] The representative of the deceased has no right to make an application in his capacity as representative.

Principles governing administration

Where an estate is insolvent,[43] whether or not it is being administered in bankruptcy, the rules applicable in bankruptcy apply to the respective rights of secured and unsecured creditors, to debts and liabilities provable,[44] and liabilities provable, to the valuation of future and contingent liabilities and to the priority of debts and other liabilities.[45]

Secured creditors

A creditor is a secured creditor to the extent that he holds any security over the deceased's property whether by way of mortgage, charge, lien or other security.[46] However, a lien on books, papers or other records is not security except to the extent that those documents give a title to property and are held as such.[47]

The rights of a secured creditor are as follow:

    (i) He may rely on his security[48] and not prove for his debt.

    (ii) He may realise his security and prove for the balance of the debt.[49]

---

[37] As defined by s.423(1) of the Act.
[38] s.423(3) of the Act.
[39] ss.423–425 replaces s.172 of the Law of Property Act 1925. As to s.172, see *Re Eichholz* [1959] Ch. 708 and *Lloyd's Bank* v. *Marcan* [1973] 1 W.L.R. 1387.
[40] ss.423(2) and 425 of the Act.
[41] s.424(1)(*a*) of the Act.
[42] s.424(1)(*b*) and (*c*) of the Act.
[43] See *ante*, p. 624.
[44] As to the procedure for the proving of debts and liabilities, see s.322 of the Act and the Insolvency Rules (S.I. 1986 No. 1925) Part 6, Chapters 8 and 9.
[45] The Order, Arts. 3 and 4. See *post*, pp. 632 *et seq.*
[46] s.383(2) of the Act.
[47] s.383(4) of the Act.
[48] s.285(4) of the Act.
[49] s.322(1) of the Act; the Insolvency Rules (S.I. 1986 No. 1925) r. 6.109.

(iii) He may surrender his security for the benefit of the creditors and prove for the whole debt.[50]

(iv) He may set a value on his security and prove for the balance of his debt.[51] Care must be taken in valuing the security because a revaluation will only be allowed with the agreement of the trustee or with the leave of the court[52] and because the deceased's representative or the trustee may elect to redeem the security at the value given in the proof.[53]

Debts and liabilities provable

Since the rules applicable in bankruptcy apply to determine which debts and liabilities are provable whether or not an insolvent estate is being administered in bankruptcy,[54] a creditor may prove for any debt or liability for which the deceased was liable at the date of his death. It does not matter whether that debt or liability is present or future, certain or contingent, whether the amount is fixed or liquidated or capable of being ascertained by fixed rules or as a matter of opinion[55]; and the liability may have arisen under an enactment, for breach of trust, or in contract, tort, bailment or out of an obligation to make restitution.[56] However, by way of exception to the general rule, certain debts arising under the Financial Services Act 1986[57] or under section 49 of the Banking Act 1987[58] are not provable until all other claims of creditors have been paid in full with interest; and certain other debts are not provable at all, namely, any fine imposed for an offence[59]; any obligation arising under an order made in family or domestic proceedings[60]; any obligation arising under certain confiscation orders[61] and any debt which, under any enactment or rule of law, is not provable whether by reason of public policy or otherwise.[62]

The valuation of future and contingent liabilities

Where any provable debt or liability does not bear a certain value, because it is subject to a contingency or for some other reason, an estimate

---

[50] s.322(1) of the Act; the Insolvency Rules, r. 6.109(2).

[51] *Ibid.* r. 6.98(1)(*g*).

[52] *Ibid.* r. 6.115. Note, however, that in some circumstances the leave of the court must be obtained, see r. 6.115(2).

[53] *Ibid.* r. 6.117.

[54] See *ante*, p. 626.

[55] s.382(1) and (3) of the Act and Insolvency Rules, r. 12.3(1).

[56] s.382(4) of the Act.

[57] Insolvency Rules, r. 12.3(2A)(*a*).

[58] *Ibid.* r. 12.3(2A)(*b*).

[59] *Ibid.* r. 12.3(2)(*a*).

[60] *Ibid.* n. 58.

[61] *Ibid.*, r. 12.3(2)(*b*).

[62] *Ibid.*, r. 12.3(3); *e.g.* debts arising out of unenforceable or illegal contracts, statute barred debts etc.

must be made of its value by the trustee[63] or, on an application to the court challenging the trustee's decision, by the court.[64] An annuitant is entitled to claim for the estimated capitalised value of his annuity; thus, where a tax free annuity had been covenanted to be held on protective trusts, not only was the annuitant entitled to claim but such claim was on the same footing as if the life interest had been given to her unconditionally, that is, without liability to forfeiture; nor was any regard paid to any possible rise or fall of income tax; but the court will not treat as an unknown factor anything which has become known or can be ascertained when the valuation is made.[65]

Set-off

Where there have been mutual credits, mutual debts or other mutual dealings between the deceased and the creditor proving or attempting to prove for a debt, an account must be taken and the sum due from the one party set off against the sum due from the other, and the balance only claimed.[66]

Amount of interest provable

Section 322(2) of the Insolvency Act 1986[67] provides that, where a debt bears interest, that interest is provable as part of the debt in respect of the period up to the commencement of the bankruptcy. Unfortunately, "the commencement of the bankruptcy" is defined by the Administration of Insolvent Estates of Deceased Persons Order as being the date of the insolvency administration order. This means that, where an estate is being administered in bankruptcy, interest is provable up to the date of the order but that the question as to the date to which interest is provable where the estate is administered otherwise than in bankruptcy is left open. It is thought that, as under the old law, interest in such cases should be calculated up to the date of the death of the deceased[68–69] but it would have been preferable (as seems to have been the intention)[70] for that date to have applied in all cases.

---

[63] s.322(3) of the Act; see also, *Re Bridges* (1887) 11 Ch.D. 342, *Ex parte Neal* (1880) 14 Ch.D. 579, *Re McMahon* [1900] 1 Ch. 173 (proof by company of estimated value of liability of deceased insolvent shareholder for future calls).

[64] See ss.322(4) and 303 of the Act.

[65] *Re Rothermere* [1945] Ch. 72. As to the valuation of annuities charged on the estate see *ante*, p. 607.

[66] s.323 of the Act.

[67] The Order, Sched. 1, Pt. II, para. 23.

[68–69] Because it is a question "with respect to.....debts and liabilities provable" within the Order, Art. 4. And see *Re Bush* [1930] 2 Ch. 202; *Re Sagor* [1930] W.N. 149; *Re Whitaker* [1901] 1 Ch. 9 and *Re Theo Garvin Ltd.* [1969] 1 Ch. 624; not following *Re Wells* [1929] 2 Ch. 269 and *Re Agric. Wholesale Soc. Ltd.* [1929] 2 Ch. 261.

[70] As appears from s.328(4) of the Act, as modified by the Order, Sched. 1, Pt. II, para. 24, which is difficult to reconcile with an unmodified s.322(2). Although, in *Re Sagor*, *ante*, interest was calculated up to the date of the administration order.

The Insolvency Act has not re-enacted the provisions of the Bankruptcy Act[71] which prevented a creditor proving for interest of more than five per cent. until all other bankruptcy debts had been paid.[72]

The order of priority of expenses and debts

The order for the payment of the expenses and debts of an insolvent estate is the same whether the estate is being administered in bankruptcy or outside bankruptcy[73] and cannot be altered by the deceased.[74] The order is as follows:

(1) *Secured creditors*

It follows from what has been said above,[75] that a secured creditor by realising his security in effect takes precedence over the deceased's other creditors.[76] However, to the extent that he proves for his debt he is an unsecured creditor and is subject to the ordinary rules for priority of debts in bankruptcy.

(2) *Debts preferred by statute*

There are some debts which are given a level of priority by statute. For example, where a deed of arrangement under the Deeds of Arrangement Act 1914 or a voluntary arrangement under the Insolvency Act 1986 is avoided by reason of the debtor's bankruptcy, such expenses as the trustee under the deed or the supervisor of the arrangement may have incurred are a first charge over the estate.[77] As these are a first charge, they have, it seems, priority over the bankruptcy expenses and also over funeral, testamentary and administration expenses.

Whether other debts preferred by statute have a similar priority is more questionable and must turn on the construction of the relevant statute. For example, whilst an executor or trustee in bankruptcy is bound to account, in preference to any other debt or claim, for property belonging to a friendly society and held by the deceased as an officer of that society[78] and, whilst the Regimental Debts Act 1893[79] provides for certain debts of a deceased serviceman to be payable in preference to all other debts or liab-

---

[71] Bankruptcy Act 1914, s.66(1).

[72] For the trustee in bankruptcy's power to challenge high interest rates on debts, see s.343 of the Act and n. 31 at p. 628, *ante.*

[73] The Order, Arts. 3 and 4.

[74] See *Turner* v. *Cox* (1853) 8 Moo.P.C. 288: *Re Rothermere* [1943] 1 All E.R. 307.

[75] *See ante*, p. 629.

[76] But see *Re Turner* [1907] 2 Ch. 126, 539, where a charging order in favour of the plaintiff's solicitor under the Solicitors Act 1860, s.28, was postponed to the costs, charges and expenses of the defendant trustee.

[77] Deeds of Arrangement Act 1914, s.21 (and see *Re Green* [1971] 1 K.B. 183) and s.276(2) of the Act.

[78] Friendly Societies Act 1974, s.59. Note that this provision applies even if the deceased had ceased to be an officer of the society as at his death, *Re Eilbeck* [1910] 1 K.B. 136.

[79] s.2.

ilities, it is arguable that these provisions do not give them priority over the bankruptcy, funeral, testamentary and administration expenses but only over other debts, claims or liabilities including the preferential debts listed in Schedule 6 to the Insolvency Act 1986.[80] To some extent, these difficulties have been increased by the fact that, under the new law, the funeral, testamentary and administration expenses only have priority over the Schedule 6 preferential debts[81] (which do not include the debts preferred by statute) whereas, under the old law, they (and, therefore, the bankruptcy expenses) had "priority to all other debts,"[82] including, it would seem, the debts preferred by statute discussed in this paragraph.

(3) *Bankruptcy expenses*

If the deceased's estate is being administered in bankruptcy, next in order of priority are the bankruptcy expenses.[83] These are themselves subject to a specific order of payment as laid down by the Insolvency Rules.[84]

(4) *Funeral, testamentary and administration expenses*

If the estate is being administered in bankruptcy, the trustee in bankruptcy, provided that he has sufficient funds in hand for the purpose, must have regard to a claim by the representative or, if there is no representative, by any other person, for payment of the reasonable funeral, testamentary and administration expenses incurred in respect of the deceased's estate by such representative or other person. If a claim is made, such expenses have priority over the deceased's preferential debts listed in Schedule 6 to the Insolvency Act 1986[85] but not, it seems, over the bankruptcy expenses. However, despite this, it has been held, in a case where an estate was being administered in bankruptcy but where the representatives of the deceased still held some of the deceased's assets, that the representatives were entitled to deduct the proper costs of the deceased's funeral before handing the balance to the trustee in bankruptcy.[86] If the estate is being administered outside bankruptcy, the reasonable funeral, testamentary and administration expenses have priority over the Schedule 6 preferential debts.[87]

Although there is no express statutory provision, it has always been the

---

[80] This priority is retained by s.328(6) of the Act. As to the Schedule 6 Preferential Debts, see *post*, p. 635.
[81] s.305(5) of the Act, as added by the Order, Sched. 1, Pt. I, para. 20, and Arts. 4(2) and 5(2).
[82] Bankruptcy Act 1914, s.130(6) and see Administration of Estates Act 1925, s.34(1) and Sched. 1, Pt. I, para. 1.
[83] For a possible exception to this, see below, the text to n. 86.
[84] Insolvency Rules, r. 6.224.
[85] s.305(5), as added by the Order, Sched. 1, Pt. I, para. 20.
[86] *Re Walter* [1929] 1 Ch. 647 *per* Tomlin J. at p. 655.
[87] The Order, Art. 4(2).

rule that the reasonable funeral expenses should be paid before any other testamentary or administrative expense.[88]

There is no definition in the Order or in the Acts of the expression "testamentary and administration expenses," but, as is apparent from section 305(5) of the Insolvency Act 1986,[89] they are distinct from the bankruptcy expenses. In the construction of wills, the expressions "testamentary expenses" and "administration expenses" both denote those expenses incident to the proper performance of the duty of a representative, namely, the ascertaining and paying of the debts and liabilities of the estate and the proper distribution of its assets.[90] They include the expense of the funeral, of obtaining a grant of probate or letters of administration, the payment by the representative of debts falling due after the death of the deceased (*e.g.* rent), the costs incurred by the representative in obtaining the advice of solicitors and counsel as to the administration or distribution of the estate and the expenses incurred by the representative in protecting the deceased's estate (other than property specifically devised or bequeathed).[91] It would seem that the expression also includes the reimbursement of a beneficiary who, in circumstances where there is an equitable right of subrogation, has discharged a liability of the estate which was incurred by a representative in the course of administration.[92]

The expression "testamentary expenses" contained in a direction in a will has been held to include the costs of a successful probate action to obtain a grant of administration[93] and the costs of an administration action.[94] Whilst, in an administration action properly instituted, the costs of the plaintiff and all necessary parties are administration expenses and are a first charge thereon,[95] if the estate is insufficient to pay all such costs, the representatives are entitled to have their costs paid first.[96] Further, a

[88] See *Re Wade* (1815) 5 Price 621 *per* Richards C.B., at p. 628; *Sharp* v. *Lush* (1879) 10 Ch.D. 468 *per* Jessel M.R., at p. 472 and *Rees* v. *Hughes* [1946] K.B. 517 *per* Scott L.J. at p. 524. The funeral expenses of a wife are a charge on her estate if it is sufficient: *Rees* v. *Hughes*, *ante*. As to the executor's liability, see *post*, p. 721.

[89] As added by the Order, Sched. 1, Pt. II, para. 20.

[90] *Sharp* v. *Lush*, at p. 470; *Re Taylor* [1969] 2 Ch. 245 at p. 254.

[91] *Re Rooke* [1933] Ch. 970, not following *Sharp* v. *Lush*, *ante*. *Re Wilson* [1967] Ch. 53. As to when the expressions include Inheritance Tax see *ante*, pp. 76, 77.

[92] See *Re Downer Enterprises Ltd.* [1974] 1 W.L.R. 1460 (company liquidation).

[93] *Re Clemow* [1900] 2 Ch. 182.

[94] *Miles* v. *Harrison* (1874) L.R. 9 Ch.App. 316; *Harloe* v. *Harloe* (1875) L.R. 20 Eq. 471; *Penny* v. *Penny* (1879) 11 Ch.D. 440; *Re Buckton* [1907] 2 Ch. 406 at p. 414. The expression "legal expenses" includes the costs of an administration action: *Coventry* v. *Coventry* (1863) 2 Dr. & Sm. 470; *Row* v. *Row* (1869) L.R. 7 Eq. 414.

[95] *Loomes* v. *Stotherd* (1823) 1 Sim. & Stu. 458; *Tipping* v. *Power* (1842) 1 Hare 405 at p. 411; *Gaunt* v. *Taylor* (1843) 2 Hare 413; *Newbegin* v. *Bell* (1857) 23 Beav. 386; *Sanderson* v. *Stoddart* (1863) 32 Beav. 155.

[96] *Ibid.*, *Re Griffith* [1904] 1 Ch. 807; and see *Dodds* v. *Tuke* (1884) 25 Ch.D. 617. As to priority of executors' costs where there is no personal estate, see *Re Pearce* (1887) 56 L.T. 228; *Hibernian Bank* v. *Lauder* [1898] 1 Ir.R. 262; *Re Samson* (1907) 123 L.T.J. 86. See also *Re Spensley* (1872) L.R. 15 Eq. 16 (plaintiff in administration action obtained order of sale of real and leasehold estate; representatives' costs paid in priority to plaintiff's costs of sale). But see *Pinchard* v. *Fellows* (1874) L.R. 7 Eq. 421.

defendant executor's costs of an administration action have priority over a charging order obtained by the plaintiff's solicitors,[97] and over the costs of litigation instituted, after an administration order made by the Chancery Division notwithstanding the order of the probate judge that such costs be paid out of the estate and "have priority over all other claims on the estate."[98]

The expression "testamentary and administration expenses" does not include the plaintiff's costs in an unsuccessful action which sought to impeach the validity of a will even though the probate judge ordered the costs to be paid out of the testator's estate[99] nor does it include foreign duties or specific bequests.[1]

(5) *Preferential debts*

The preferential debts are payable after the categories of expenses, debts and liabilities referred to above have been paid in full; they rank equally between themselves and should be paid in full unless the estate is insufficient, in which case they must abate in equal proportions between themselves.[2]

The Insolvency Act 1986 has made significant changes to the old law as respects preferential debts.[3] Under the new law, preferential debts are those debts listed in the six categories contained in Schedule 6 to the Insolvency Act 1986,[4] namely:

(i) Category 1[5]:—Certain debts due to the Inland Revenue, namely, those debts due as at the date of the deceased's death,[6] either by way of income tax which the deceased was liable to deduct under the P.A.Y.E. provisions[7] from his employees' emoluments paid in the 12 months before his death or by way of deductions from payments to sub-contractors in the construction industry.[8]

(ii) Category 2[9]:—Certain debts due to Customs and Excise, namely: (a) V.A.T. referable to the period of six months before the death of the deceased; (b) car tax due at the date of death of the deceased and which became due in the 12 months before that date

---

[97] See *Re Turner* [1907] 2 Ch. 126.

[98] *Re Mayhew* (1877) 5 Ch.D. 596; *Re Price* (1886) 31 Ch.D. 485. And see *Major* v. *Major* (1854) 2 Drew. 281.

[99] *Re Prince* [1898] 2 Ch. 225; *Re Vickerstaff* [1906] 1 Ch. 762.

[1] *Re Matthews* [1961] 1 W.L.R. 1415.

[2] ss.328(1) and (2) of the Act.

[3] For example, local rates, and taxes assessed on and due from the deceased himself are no longer preferential debts; for the old law, see the 16th edition of this work at pp. 581–583.

[4] s.386 of the Act.

[5] Sched. 6 to the Act, Pt. II, paras. 1 and 2.

[6] s.387 of the Act as modified by the Order, Sched. 1, Pt. II, para. 34.

[7] The P.A.Y.E. provisions are now contained in the Income and Corporation Taxes Act 1988, s.203.

[8] The "sub-contractors" deduction provisions are now contained in the Income and Corporation Taxes Act 1988, s.559.

[9] Sched. 6 to the Act, paras. 3–5.

and (c) general betting duty or bingo duty, or general betting duty and pool betting duty recoverable from an agent collecting stakes, or gaming licence duty, due at the date of death of the deceased and which became due in the 12 months before that date.

(iii) Category 3[10]:—Certain social security contributions, namely: (a) Class 1 or Class 2 contributions which are due from the deceased at the date of his death and which became due in the 12 months before that date; (b) Class 4 contributions assessed on and due from the deceased as at the date of his death and up to April 5 next before that date, but not exceeding, in the whole, one year's assessment.

(iv) Category 4[11]:—Any sum which is owed by the deceased on account of contributions to occupational pension schemes and state scheme premiums.

(v) Category 5[12]:—(a) Any amount payable by the deceased to an employee or former employee and payable by way of remuneration[13] in respect of the whole or part of the four months before the date of the death of the deceased but not exceeding such amount as should be specified by the Secretary of State[14]; (b) an amount owed by way of accrued holiday remuneration, in respect of any period of employment before the death of the deceased, to an employee whose employment has been terminated, whether before, on or after the deceased's death; (c) so much of any sum owed in respect of money advanced and applied for the payment of any debt which, if it had not been paid, would have been a debt within (a) or (b) above; (d) any amount ordered to be paid by the deceased under the Reserve Forces (Safeguard of Employment) Act 1985 in respect of the deceased's default made before his death, but not exceeding such amount as should be specified by the Secretary of State[15];

(vi) Category 6[16]:—All sums due from the deceased as at the date of his death in respect of levies under Articles 49 and 50 of the E.C.S.C. Treaty or any surcharge for delay under Article 50(3) of that Treaty and Article 6 of the Decision of the High Authority of the Coal and Steel Community.

Where a landlord or other person has distrained upon the deceased's goods or effects within the three months before the making of the Insolvency

[10] Sched. 6 to the Act, paras. 6 and 7.
[11] Sched. 6 to the Act, para. 8.
[12] Sched. 6 to the Act, paras. 9–12.
[13] Remuneration is defined in paras. 13–15 of Sched. 6 to the Act.
[14] The amount is currently £800.
[15] *Ibid.* n.13.
[16] Sched. 6 to the Act, para. 15A, as added by the Insolvency (E.S.C.S. Levy Debts) Regulations 1987 (S.I. 1987 No. 2093).

Administration Order, the distrained goods or effects, or their proceeds of sale are charged for the benefit of the deceased's estate with the preferential debts of the deceased to the extent that the estate is insufficient to satisfy those debts.[17]

(6) *Ordinary debts*

The ordinary debts are those debts which are not within any of the above classes of debts but which are not deferred debts. These rank equally between themselves, so that, if they cannot be paid in full, they must abate in equal proportions between themselves. It should be noted that a judgment debt against the deceased or his estate is an ordinary debt[18] and also that a creditor who has issued execution against the goods or land of the deceased or has attached a debt due to the deceased, cannot retain the benefit of the execution or attachment and has, unless he has completed such execution or attachment, an ordinary debt.[19]

(7) *Interest on preferential and ordinary debts*

Any surplus remaining in the estate after the payment in full of the preferential and ordinary debts is applied to the payment, with equal priority, of interest on both preferential and ordinary debts for the period for which they have been outstanding since the date of the deceased's death.[20] The rate of the interest payable is the greater of either that specified in section 17 of the Judgments Act 1838[21] as at the deceased's death or the rate applicable to that debt apart from the bankruptcy.[22]

(8) *Deferred debts*

Next in the order of priority are the deferred debts. These include: (a) those debts owed in respect of credit provided by a person who (whether or not the deceased's spouse at the time when the credit was provided) was the deceased's spouse as at the date of the deceased's death.[23] Interest on such a debt has the same level of priority as the debt itself and is payable as from the death of the deceased[24] and (b) advances made to a partnership by way of loan bearing interest varying with the profits or sums due for the price of the goodwill of a business where such price takes the form of a share in the profits.[25]

---

[17] s.347(3) of the Act; and see *Re Caidan* [1942] Ch. 90.
[18] The legislation contains no special provision for judgment debts.
[19] s.346 of the Act.
[20] s.328(4) of the Act, as modified by the Order, Sched. 1, Pt. II, para. 24.
[21] s.328(5)(*a*) of the Act, as modified by the Order, Sched. 1, Pt. II, para. 24.
[22] s.328(5)(*b*) of the Act.
[23] s.329 of the Act, as modified by the Order, Sched. 1, Pt. II, para. 24.
[24] ss.2 and 3 Partnership Act 1890 and s.328(6) of the Act.
[25] s.329(2) of the Act, as modified by the Order, Sched. 1, Pt. II, para. 24.

(9) *Debts whose proving is deferred*

These are debts which cannot be proved until all other expenses and debts have been paid in full.[26]

Effect of payment in the wrong order

A representative who misapplies the assets of the estate commits a *devastavit*.[27] Thus, before 1926, he became answerable out of his own estate on a deficiency of assets if, having notice of a superior debt, he paid an inferior one.[28] It was otherwise if he had no such notice.[29] Similarly, if, when sued for an inferior debt, he failed to plead the existence of a superior debt of which he had notice, and that the estate did not have sufficient assets to meet both debts, he became personally liable,[30] for a failure to raise this defence amounted to an admission that the estate had assets sufficient to meet both debts.[31] Again, he did not become so liable if he had no notice of the superior debt.[32]

These principles must clearly continue to apply under the present law where a representative fails to comply with his duty to distribute the assets of the estate according to the order referred to above. So that a representative who pays a deferred debt, having notice of a preferential or an ordinary debt, will be personally liable to satisfy those superior debts of which he had notice.[33]

Despite this, a representative has some protection if he makes a payment in the wrong order. First, a representative is covered by the usual protection afforded to trustees for breaches of trust where they have acted honestly and reasonably and where they ought, fairly, to be excused for the breach.[34] Secondly, if a representative, acting in good faith, pays a debt at a time when he has no reason to believe that the estate is insolvent, then (unless he is a representative to whom letters of administration have been granted as a creditor and the debt which he has paid is his own debt), if the estate subsequently appears to be insolvent, he is protected as against other creditors of the same class of priority as the creditor whose debt he has paid[35]; he is not, however, protected against those creditors with a higher priority.

---

[26] See *ante*, pp. 632 *et seq*.

[27] See *post*, p. 730.

[28] 2 Bl.Comm. 511. But there is no *devastavit* where the executor pays the inferior debt with his own money; Com.Dig.Admon.I. 2: *Wheatly* v. *Lane* (1669) 1 Saund. 216.

[29] *Harman* v. *Harman* (1686) 2 Show. 492; provided a reasonable time had elapsed since the testatrix's death: Toller 6th ed., p. 192; see also *Re Fludyer* [1898] 2 Ch. 562.

[30] See *Britton* v. *Batthurst* (1683) 3 Lev. 114.

[31] *Rock* v. *Layton* (1700) 1 Salk. 310; 1 Saund. 33 a.n. And see *Abbis* v. *Winter* (1733) 3 Swanst. 578n.

[32] See *Davies* v. *Monkhouse* (1729) FitzGib. 76; but the absence of notice had to be pleaded: *Sawyer* v. *Mercer* (1787) 1 T.R. 690.

[33] See *Re S.P.* [1936] Ch. 735.

[34] Trustee Act 1925, s.61 (and see ss.68(1)(17) and 69(1)).

[35] Administration of Estate Act 1971, s.10(2).

Power of distress

Under section 347 of the Insolvency Act 1986,[36] a landlord (or other person) who is owed rent by the deceased's estate may only exercise his power of distress for the rent accrued due in the six months before the date of the insolvency administration order. It seems that there is no such limitation on the power of distress where the deceased's estate is being administered outside bankruptcy.[37]

Composition with creditors

If, on a composition with creditors, the estate has been administered by paying to each creditor a proportion of his debt and then some time later further assets come into the hands of the representative, such further assets must be applied in payment of the balance of the debts owed to the creditors, except insofar as their claims may have become barred by limitation. Moreover, a creditor may not be bound by an agreement to accept a smaller sum than the amount owing "in full satisfaction" of that amount unless his claim was disputed or for an unliquidated sum.[38] Where, however, the creditors agreed together a lower sum,[39] or where each creditor, in agreeing with the representative to accept a lower sum, clearly understood that he did so as part of a general settling of debts,[40] or if the lesser sum were paid by a third party, such that the creditor would be committing a fraud on the other creditors or on the third party if he claimed the full sum after agreeing to accept less,[41] then, it seems that the representative is entitled to administer any later assets which fall into the estate on the basis that those debts have been fully paid.

Debtor's death after presentation of a petition

Where a debtor against whom a bankruptcy petition has been presented dies then, unless the court orders otherwise, the bankruptcy proceedings continue as if he were still alive but subject to the modifications contained in Schedule 2 of the Administration of Insolvent Estates of Deceased Persons Order.[42] Once again, assuming that the representative or other person gives notice to the trustee, the reasonable funeral and testamentary

---

[36] As modified by the Order, Sched. 1, Part I.

[37] It was decided in Re Wells [1929] 2 Ch. 269 that the true construction of the words "commencement of bankruptcy" in Bankruptcy Act 1914, s.35 (i.e. the equivalent of s.347 of the Act) precluded the section applying in a case where an estate was being administered outside bankruptcy and that the words in the Administration of Estates Act 1925, s.34 and Sched. 1, Pt. I (i.e. the equivalent of the Order, Art. 4) made no difference to this as the power of distress was not a matter "in respect of the priority of debts and other payments"; see also Re Fryman (1888) 38 Ch.D. 468.

[38] Foakes v. Beer (1884) 9 App.Cas. 605. However, this principle is now subject to certain exceptions such as equitable estoppel. See generally Chitty on Contracts, 26th ed., Vol. 1, at paras. 226 to 243.

[39] Good v. Cheeseman (1831) 2 B. & Ad. 328.

[40] Chitty, ante, at para. 234.

[41] Hirachand Punamchand v. Temple [1911] 2 K.B. 330.

[42] The Order, Art. 5(1).

expenses have priority over the preferential debts listed in Schedule 6.[43] If the debtor died after presentation but before service of the petition, the court may order service on his representative or on such other person as it thinks fit.[44]

Partnership property

There have been considerable changes to the law relating to insolvency proceedings against members of a partnership.[45] However, the principle remains that on the death of an insolvent partner, the joint estate is applicable, in the first instance, in payment of partnership liabilities, and his separate estate is used, in the first instance, in payment of his separate liabilities. Only if one of the estates exceeds its liabilities is the balance to be used towards the payment of the liabilities of the other estate.

D. RETAINER AND PREFERENCE

Before 1972 a representative had a right to "retain" a debt due to himself from the deceased in priority to other debts of the same class and to "prefer" one creditor of the same class to another instead of paying all *pro rata*. However a creditor administrator was normally precluded from exercising such rights by the terms of his bond.[46]

These rights were abolished by section 10 of the Administration of Estates Act 1971 (when the death occurred after 1971) with the proviso following:

> "(2)   Nevertheless a personal representative—
>   (a) other than one mentioned in paragraph (b) below, who, in good faith and at a time when he has no reason to believe that the deceased's estate is insolvent, pays the debt of any person (including himself) who is a creditor of the estate;
>   (b) to whom letters of administration have been granted solely by reason of his being a creditor and who, in good faith and at such a time pays the debt of another person who is a creditor of the estate;
>
>   shall not, if it subsequently appears that the estate is insolvent, be liable to account to a creditor of the same degree as the paid creditor for the sum so paid."

The section as enacted thus preserves the distinction between creditor administrators and others: creditor administrators are not protected if they pay their own debts before those of other creditors, even though they are

---

[43] The Order, Art. 5(2).

[44] The Order, Art. 5(3).

[45] See the Insolvent Partnership Order 1986 (S.I. 1986 No. 2142) and *Muir Hunter on Personal Insolvency*, Part IV.

[46] For the law on this topic see the 15th edition of this work, pp. 701–709 and Article (1972) 122 N.L.J. 26. For an alternative use of the word "retainer" see p. 694, *post*. See also p. 935 *post* and *c.f.* the rule in *Strong* v. *Bird* p. 650, *post*, and pp. 463, 467 *ante*.

acting in good faith and have no reason to believe that the estate is insolvent, but other representatives are so protected.

The section does not enable a representative to affect priorities; he remains liable to account to creditors of a higher degree than those paid.

The protection given by the section is intended to enable representatives to pay pressing debts, of the kind that the deceased would have had to discharge with some promptitude if he had lived. Examples are gas, electricity and telephone bills, and tradesmen's accounts. If the representative did not pay these, hardship could be caused to the family of the deceased, or to debtors, or to both.

CHAPTER 51

DEBTS DUE TO AND FROM EXECUTORS AND BENEFICIARIES

THIS chapter is concerned with (1) legacies by debtors to their creditors, (2) legacies by creditors to their debtors[1] (3) appointment of debtors as executors[2] and (4) appointment of creditors as executors.[3]

1.—A LEGACY BY A DEBTOR TO HIS CREDITOR—SATISFACTION

The legacy satisfies the debt

Where a debtor bequeaths to his creditor a legacy equal to, or exceeding the amount of, his debt, it will be presumed, in the absence of any intimation of a contrary intention, that the legacy was meant by the testator as a satisfaction of the debt.[4] The presumption is not affected by the fact that the legatee was appointed executor,[5] nor by the fact that the debt carries interest whereas the legacy does not.[6]

The rule has long prevailed and is still the rule[7]; but it has met with the censure of several eminent judges; and the courts have inclined to lay hold of any minute circumstances whereupon to ground an exception to it.[8] Thus, there is no presumption of satisfaction *pro tanto* where the legacy is of less amount than the debt.[9] It has been held, however, that where there is a debt of £100, carrying 5 per cent. interest, which interest is in arrear at the testator's death, it is satisfied by a legacy of £100.[10] Again the presump-

---

[1] *Post*, p. 645.

[2] *Post*, p. 649.

[3] *Post*, p. 651.

[4] *Brown* v. *Dawson* (1705) Prec.Chance. 240; *Talbott* v. *Shrewsbury* (1714) *ibid.* 394; *Fowler* v. *Fowler* (1735) 3 P.Wms. 353; *Richardson* v. *Greese* (1743) 3 Atk. 65; *Gaynon* v. *Wood* (1759) 1 Dick. 331; *Hammond* v. *Smith* (1864) 33 Beav. 452; *Atkinson* v. *Littlewood* (1874) L.R. 18 Eq. 595; *Re Fletcher* (1888) 38 Ch.D. 373; *Re Rattenberry* [1906] 1 Ch. 667, 670. So a legacy may operate as a satisfaction of a covenant; *Wathen* v. *Smith* (1819) 4 Madd. 325; *Re Hall* [1918] 1 Ch. 562; *Re Haves* [1951] 2 All E.R. 928. But see *Cole* v. *Willard* (1858) 25 Beav. 568; *Charlton* v. *West* (1861) 30 Beav. 124; *Toller* 264. See generally Maitland's *Equity*, Lecture XV; Snell's *Equity*, 29th ed., p. 518. As to satisfaction of portions, see *post*, pp. 948 *et seq.*

[5] *Re Rattenberry* [1906] 1 Ch. 667.

[6] *Fitzgerald* v. *National Bank Ltd.* [1929] 1 K.B. 394.

[7] *Re Stibbe* (1946) 175 L.T. 198, 201.

[8] See the remarks of Clarke, M.R. in *Mathews* v. *Mathews* (1755) 2 Ves.Sen. 636, and of Lord Alvanley in *Hinchcliffe* v. *Hinchcliffe* (1797) 3 Ves. 529, and of Lord Cottenham in *Thynne* v. *Glengall* (1848) 2 H.L.C. 153; *Re Horlock* [1895] 1 Ch. 516, 518. See also *Hales* v. *Darell* (1840) 3 Beav. 324, 332; *Smith* v. *Lyne* (1843) 2 Y. & C.C.C. 345; *Hassell* v. *Hawkins* (1859) 4 Drew. 468.

[9] *Cranmar's Case* (1701) 2 Salk. 508; *Graham* v. *Graham* (1749) 1 Ves.Sen. 263; *Thynne* v. *Glengall* (1848) 2 H.L.C. 153, 154.

[10] *Fitzgerald* v. *National Bank Ltd.* [1929] 1 K.B. 394.

tion of satisfaction does not arise where the debt was not contracted till after the making of the will; for the testator could not have intended by the legacy to have satisfied a debt which did not then exist.[11] Nor does it arise where the debt is due upon a current account; for the state of the account, and on whose side the balance lay, might be unknown to the testator[12]; nor where the debt was upon a bill of exchange, or other negotiable security; for the debt might have been transferred to a stranger by the legatee passing away the instrument.[13]

Other exceptions

(i) **Legacy contingent or uncertain.** Again, where a legacy is at all contingent or uncertain, it will not be a satisfaction of a debt.[14] As where the legacy is given upon the contingency of the legatee surviving a particular person or period,[15] or where the legacy is of the whole or part of a residue[16]; for it may possibly turn out, after all the claims on the testator's estate are satisfied, that such legacy is not of equal amount to the debt.[17] So a provision by will that the legatee should have the interest of a particular fund, or other proceeds, for life, will not be a satisfaction of a sum of money which the legatee is entitled to claim absolutely from the testator.[18] The problem will increasingly be regarded as one of construction, but a contingent or uncertain legacy must as a matter of construction indicate an absence of intent to satisfy the debt by the legacy.[19]

(ii) **Legacy not payable immediately.** Another exception to the presumption exists where the legacy is not payable immediately after the death of the testator; for the debt is due at the death of the testator, and therefore the legacy must be so too.[20] Thus, in *Mathews* v. *Mathews*,[21] Clarke M.R. said that he remembered a case before Lord Hardwicke where an old lady, indebted to a servant for wages, by will gave 10 times as much as she owed, or was likely to owe; yet because the legacy was made payable in a month after her own death, the court laid hold of that circum-

---

[11] *Cranmer's Case*, *supra*; *Jeffs* v. *Wood* (1723) 2 P.Wms. 128; *Thomas* v. *Bennet* (1725) 2 P.Wms. 343; *Wiggins* v. *Horlock* (1888) 39 Ch.D. 142.

[12] *Rawlins* v. *Powel* (1718) 1 P.Wms. 299.

[13] *Carr* v. *Eastabrooke* (1797) 3 Ves. 561.

[14] *Nicholls* v. *Judson* (1742) 2 Atk. 300.

[15] *Crompton* v. *Sale* (1729) 2 P.Wms. 553.

[16] *Crichton* v. *Crichton* [1895] 2 Ch. 853.

[17] *Devese* v. *Pontet* (1785) 1 Cox 188; *Thynne* v. *Glengall*, *ante*.

[18] *Alleyn* v. *Alleyn* (1750) 2 Ves.Sen. 37; *Forsight* v. *Grant* (1791) 1 Ves. 298; and see *Re Hall* [1918] 1 Ch. 562.

[19] *Re Hall* [1918] 1 Ch. 562, 566.

[20] By Lord Hardwicke in *Clarke* v. *Sewell* (1744) 3 Atk. 96. See also *Atkinson* v. *Webb* (1704) Prec.Chanc. 236; *Nicholls* v. *Judson* (1742) 2 Atk. 300; *Mathews* v. *Mathews* (1755) 2 Ves.Sen. 635; *Haynes* v. *Micro* (1781) 1 Bro.C.C. 129; *Jeacock* v. *Falkner* (1783) 1 Bro.C.C. 295; *Adams* v. *Lavender* (1824) 1 M'Clel. & Y. 41.

[21] (1755) 2 Ves.Sen. 636.

stance to take it out of the general rule.[22] Where, however, a legacy is given generally without directions as to the time of payment or interest, the presumption of satisfaction will arise, though it is not payable until the end of a year from the death of the testator,[23] and in such a case interest is payable on the legacy from the death.[24]

(iii) Legacy and debt of different nature.

A further exception may be found where the legacy and debt are of a different nature,[25] as where the testator is indebted by bond, and bequeaths an interest in land to his creditor.[26] Thus, in *Bartlett* v. *Gillard*,[27] a leasehold estate of the testator's was subject to an annuity of £12 to Mrs. B. for her sole use, to be paid to her half-yearly, on January 27 and July 27. The testator devised all his lands, in which the leasehold was included, to G, he paying to Mrs. B. £12 per annum, by half-yearly payments, to be made on January 27 and July 27. The Lord Chancellor held that, though the amounts of the two annuities and the days of payment were precisely the same, yet as the second was charged upon the freehold as well as the leasehold property, and was payable to Mrs. B. generally and not to her separate use, this was sufficient to repel the presumption that the second annuity was intended at a satisfaction of the first, and that consequently both were payable.

Again, a legacy of a specific chattel, however great its value, will not be a satisfaction of a debt, unless the testator bequeaths it with such condition expressed, and the legatee accepts it by way of satisfaction.[28]

Question of construction

The presumption of satisfaction may be counteracted by other parts of the will; as where the legacy appears to be given with some other intention, some particular purpose being expressed as the ground of the bequest[29]; or where there is an express direction in the will for the payment of all debts and legacies,[30] or of debts alone.[31] A liability on a covenant made on mar-

---

[22] In *Richardson* v. *Greese* (1743) 3 Atk. 69, Lord Hardwicke said that legacies to servants had never been held to be in satisfaction of debts. But this case mentioned by Sir T. Clarke, and also *Chanceys Case* (1611) 1 P.Wms. 408, seems to decide that they are to be so considered, unless there are circumstances to take the case out of the general rule.

[23] *Re Rattenberry* [1906] 1 Ch. 667; *cf. Re Horlock* [1895] Ch. 516. *Secus*, it seems, in the case of annuities; *Re Dowse* (1881) 50 L.J.Ch. 285; *Re Stibbe* (1946) 175 L.T. 198; *Re Van Den Bergh's W.T.* [1948] 1 All E.R. 935.

[24] *Clark* v. *Sewell* (1744) 3 Atk. 96, 98; *Re Rattenberry* [1906] 1 Ch. 667, 671.

[25] See the observations of Lord Hardwicke in *Bellasis* v. *Uthwatt* (1737) 1 Atk. 428.

[26] *Eastwood* v. *Vinke* (1731) 2 P.Wms. 614; *Richardson* v. *Elphinstone* (1794) 2 Ves. 463.

[27] (1827) 3 Russ. 148.

[28] *Byde* v. *Byde* (1761) 1 Cox.Eq.Cas. 44, 49.

[29] *Mathews* v. *Mathews* (1755) 2 Ves.Sen. 635.

[30] *Chancey's Case* (1611) 1 P.Wms. 408, 410, 411; *Richardson* v. *Greese* (1743) 3 Atk. 65, 68; *Field* v. *Mostin* (1778) 2 Dick. 543; *Hales* v. *Darell* (1840) 3 Beav. 324; *Lethbridge* v. *Thurlow* (1851) 15 Beav. 334; *Jefferies* v. *Mitchell* (1855) 20 Beav. 15; *Wathen* v. *Smith* (1819) 4 Madd. 325, 331; *Charlton* v. *West* (1861) 30 Beav. 124.

[31] *Re Huish* (1889) 43 Ch.D. 260; *Re Manners* [1949] Ch. 613. See also *Cole* v. *Willard* (1858) 25 Beav. 568; *Glover* v. *Hartcup* (1864) 34 Beav. 74. *cf. Atkinson* v. *Littlewood* (1874) L.R. 18 Eq. 595.

riage is a debt within the meaning of a direction "to pay debts."[32] Thus a general direction by a testator to pay his just debts is prima facie sufficient to rebut the presumption that a covenant made by him during his lifetime to pay a life annuity is satisfied by a direction in his will to purchase a like annuity for the same person.[33]

A legacy given by a parent to a child is regarded, with respect to the rule in question, in the same light as a legacy to a stranger.[34] Nor is a legacy given by a husband to his wife considered upon any different footing.[35]

It is said that a legacy should in all cases be construed as a satisfaction, in case there is a deficiency of assets.[36]

Erroneous description of debt

An erroneous recital that the testator owes a legatee a sum of money, followed by a direction to pay the debt, will amount to a gift of that which is actually owed[37] unless there can be found in the will an intention to confer a bounty, when the sum mentioned by the testator will pass.[38]

2.—A LEGACY BY A CREDITOR TO HIS DEBTOR-RELEASE

The legacy does not of itself release the debt

Where a creditor bequeaths a legacy to his debtor, and either does not refer to the debt, or mentions it in such a manner as to leave his intention doubtful, and after his death the securities for the debt, if any exist, are found uncancelled among the testator's property, equity does not consider the legacy to the debtor as necessarily, or even prima facie, a release or extinguishment of the debt, but requires evidence clearly expressive of the intention to release.[39] No set formula is required for the release or forgiveness of a debt in a will; all that is required is that the testator shall have made his intention clear.[40] If such intention does not appear clearly expressed or implied on the face of the will, evidence from other sources will be admitted.[41]

Intention to release

The testator may show an intention to release the debt.[42] Thus, if he makes an absolute gift by will to a debtor, and directs that the debt is to be

---

[32] *Cole* v. *Willard, ante. cf. Re Hall* [1918] 1 Ch. 562.
[33] *Re Manners* [1949] Ch. 613. And see *Horlock* v. *Wiggins* (1888) 39 Ch.D. 142.
[34] *Tolson* v. *Collins* (1799) 4 Ves. 483.
[35] *Fowler* v. *Fowler* (1735) 3 P.Wms. 353; *Re Fletcher* (1888) 38 Ch.D. 373.
[36] Toller 6th ed., p. 265.
[37] *Wilson* v. *Morley* (1877) 5 Ch.D. 776.
[38] *Whitfield* v. *Clemment* (1816) 1 Mer 402; *Re Rowe* [1898] 1 Ch. 153.
[39] *Wilmot* v. *Woodhouse* (1793) 4 Bro.C.C. 227; *Jeffs* v. *Wood* (1723) 2 P.Wms. 128, 132.
[40] *Per* Evershed M.R. in *Re Horn* [1946] Ch. 254.
[41] *Eden* v. *Smyth* (1800) 5 Ves. 341. It is dangerous to extend the doctrine of this case; *Chester* v. *Urwick* (1856) 23 Beav. 404.
[42] See, for instance, *Hyde* v. *Neate* (1847) 15 Sim. 554.

brought into hotchpot, the debt is extinguished if the legacy exceeds the debt in amount.[43] But if the amount of the debt exceeds the value of the legacy[44] or share of the legacy,[45] or the debtor is a tenant for life of a settled share of residue and his debt is directed to be brought into hotchpot and treated as part of the settled share,[46] then, in the absence of clear words, the debt is not released. A direction that the debt is to be taken in full or part satisfaction of the legacy has been held to constitute clear words of release.[47]

If a testator bequeaths a debt to his debtor, this amounts to a release of the debt and operates merely as a legacy, so that the debt is an asset subject to the payment of the testator's debts.[48] If the debt has been repaid before the date of the will, a forgiveness may amount to a legacy of the same amount.[49]

Prima facie a bequest to a debtor of the debts due from him means the debts due from him severally, and does not include debts from a firm of which he is a member.[50]

Rule in Cherry v. Boultbee—contribution and set off

The principle of *Cherry* v. *Boultbee*,[51] has been stated[52] as follows: "*Where a person entitled to participate in a fund is also bound to make a contribution in aid of that fund, he cannot be allowed to participate unless and until he has fulfilled his duty to contribute.*"

Thus, where a legatee is indebted to the testator the executor may apply the legacy either in full or part satisfaction of the debt,[53] and the same principle applies to next-of-kin, or other persons entitled on intestacy, who owe money to the estate of the intestate.[54] Similarly, one executor can apply a legacy due to his co-executor in respect of a *devastavit* by the latter.[55]

If children are entitled under a will to the share that their father would have taken had he survived the testator, they are entitled to the whole

---

[43] See the judgments of Astbury J, in *Re Trollope* [1915] 1 Ch. 853, and *Re Barker* [1918] 1 Ch. 128.

[44] *Re Clark* [1924] W.N. 75.

[45] See *Re Horne, ante.*

[46] *Re Barker, ante.*

[47] *Re Trollope, ante.*

[48] *Rider* v. *Wager* (1725) 2 P.Wms. 328, 331.

[49] *Findlater* v. *Lowe* [1904] 1 Ir.R. 519.

[50] *Re Bennett* (1877) 5 Ch.D. 800.

[51] (1839) 2 Keen 319; affirmed on appeal, 4 M. & Cr. 442. See also *Re Rhodesia Goldfields* [1910] 1 Ch. 239, 246; *Selanger United Rubber* v. *Cradock* [1969] 1 W.L.R. 1773.

[52] *Per* Sargant J. in *Re Peruvian etc. Co.* [1915] 2 Ch. 144, 150. See also *per* Kekewich J. in *Re Akerman* [1891] 3 Ch. 212, 219.

[53] *Jeffs* v. *Wood*, 2 P.Wms. 128, 130; *Smith* v. *Smith* (1861) 3 Giff. 263; *Re Savage* [1918] 2 Ch. 146. See also *Re Melton* [1918] 1 Ch. 37 (legacy to debtor whose debt testator had guaranteed and paid).

[54] *Re Cordwell's Estate* (1875) L.R. 20 Eq. 644. The right is sometimes, but should not be, called a right of "retainer"; *Re Akerman* [1891] 3 Ch. 212, 219.

[55] *Sims* v. *Doughty* (1800) 5 Ves. 243.

share, though if the father had survived a deduction could have been made in respect of a debt due from him to the testator.[56] The effect of assignment of a legacy is considered later.[57]

Statute-barred debts

The principle of *Cherry* v. *Boultbee* enables a trustee or executor to set off a debt which is barred by the Limitation Act either against the original beneficiary,[58] or his assignee,[59] as the case may be, and is not confined to cases where the beneficiary owes a specific sum of money. Thus a beneficiary's liability for damages may be set off against his claim.[60]

On the other hand, there can be no set-off unless there was due from the beneficiary a debt for which, but for the Limitation Act, the executor or trustee could have sued.[61]

Qualification: mutual claims

Further, there is this important qualification to the rule, a qualification established in the actual case of *Cherry* v. *Boultbee*,[62] that the right, whether it is described as retainer or set-off, does not arise unless there has been a period during which the legacy or fund was payable, by the person who was entitled to receive, and to the person who was liable to pay, the debt.

Thus, if the beneficiary is an undischarged bankrupt at the time of the death or when the legacy or fund becomes payable, and he owes the testator's estate or the trust fund a debt, the whole debt cannot be set off against the legacy or share in the fund. The reason is that the beneficiary can only claim his share as agent for his trustee in bankruptcy, whilst the latter is not liable to pay the whole debt. If the debt had been proved, however, the amount of the dividends payable on the debt could be set off against the claim of the assignee in bankruptcy.[63]

Assuming, however, that the beneficiary goes bankrupt after the time when he has become entitled to receive his share, then the whole debt can as a rule be set off; for in this case there has been a time at which the beneficiary was both liable to pay the whole debt to the trustee, and entitled to

---

[56] See *Re Binns* [1929] 1 Ch. 677.

[57] See *post*, p. 1029.

[58] *Courtenay* v. *Williams* (1844) 3 Hare 539; *Rose* v. *Gould* (1852) 15 Beav. 189; *Coates* v. *Coates* (1864) 33 Beav. 249; *Campbell* v. *Graham* (1831) 1 Russ. & M. 453. See the remark of Knight Bruce V.-C. in *Harvey* v. *Palmer* (1851) 4 De G. & Sm. 427. See also *Re Cordwell's Estate* (1875) L.R. 20 Eq. 644. This principle does not enable executors to retain damages due to a debtor of the estate in respect of waste committed by the deceased in discharge of a statute-barred debt: *Dingle* v. *Coppen* [1899] 1 Ch. 726.

[59] *Doering* v. *Doering* (1889) 42 Ch.D. 203; *Re Dacre, ante.*

[60] *Re Rhodesia Goldfields* [1910] 1 Ch. 239; *Re Jewell* [1919] 2 Ch. 161.

[61] *Re Wheeler* [1904] 2 Ch. 55; *Re Bruce* [1908] 2 Ch. 682; *Re Sewell* [1909] 1 Ch. 806.

[62] (1839) 2 Keen 319; affirmed on appeal, 4 M. & Cr. 442. And see *Re Briant* (1888) 39 Ch.D. 471, 479; *Re Akerman, ante*; *Re Taylor* [1894] 1 Ch. 671.

[63] *Cherry* v. *Boultbee, supra*; *Re Hodgson* (1878) 9 Ch.D. 673; *Re Orpen* (1880) 16 Ch.D. 202; *Re Pink* [1912] 1 Ch. 498, 505; *Re Peruvian Ry.* [1915] 2 Ch. 442.

receive his share from the trustee; and the right of retainer having once attached against the beneficiary his assignee can be in no better position.[64] But if the executor or trustee should prove in the beneficiary's bankruptcy, from that time onwards only the dividends on the debt can be set off.[65] Further, if the bankrupt should obtain his discharge, as the debt is gone so is the right of retainer, or set-off.[66]

Joint debts

The beneficiary must be severally liable for the debt before it can be set off. Thus an executor cannot set off against a legatee a debt due from the firm of which the legatee was a member, for partners are only jointly liable.[67] It may be that joint and several debts are within the rule, in which case presumably the executor could set off the debt due from the firm against the estate of a deceased partner and legatee who had died after the testator, for the separate property of a deceased partner is, to a certain extent, liable for the firm's debts.[68]

Instalments of a debt

When a debt is payable by instalments, future instalments cannot be set off, for this would completely change the very nature of the debt.[69]

Specific legacy

The rule in *Cherry* v. *Boultbee*[70] applies even to a specific legatee, if the legacy is actually represented by money in the hands of the executors.[71] But there must be money payable against money payable, and the mere fact that the gift is something like money, or easily turned into money, is not enough, so that a specific bequest of stock cannot be retained.[72]

Claims in different rights

The rule is inapplicable where the right to receive and the obligation to contribute arise in different capacities, as where a legatee owes the executor a sum of money in his personal capacity, and not as executor. Indeed, where cross-demands are essentially in different rights there can never be a

---

[64] *Re Watson* [1896] 1 Ch. 925; *Re Melton* [1918] 1 Ch. 371; *Re Lennard* [1934] Ch. 235. And see *Lee* v. *Egremont* (1852) 5 De G. & Sm. 348, 368; *Bousfield* v. *Lawford*, 1 De G.J. & S. 459.

[65] *Re Watson* [1896] 1 Ch. 925, 933.

[66] *Ibid.*; *Re Sewell* [1909] Ch. 806.

[67] *Turner* v. *Turner* [1911] 1 Ch. 716; *Jackson* v. *Yates* [1912] 1 Ir.R. 267; *Re Pennington and Owen* [1925] Ch. 825.

[68] See *Turner* v. *Turner, ante,* explaining *Smith* v. *Smith* (1861) 3 Giff. 263.

[69] *Re Abrahams* [1908] 2 Ch. 69.

[70] See p. 646 *ante.*

[71] *Re Taylor* [1894] 1 Ch. 671.

[72] *Re Savage* [1918] 2 Ch. 146. "Money" here was presumably intended to mean "cash" (*cf. Perrin* v. *Morgan* [1943] A.C. 399).

right to set off one against the other, unless the right to do so is conferred by agreement, express or implied.[73]

3.—Appointment of Debtor as Executor

Release at common law

At common law an appointment by the testator of his debtor, whether he was a sole debtor or one of several joint debtors, or even one of joint and several debtors, to his executor, operated as a release or extinguishment of the debt, on the principle that a debt is merely the right to recover the amount by way of action, and as an executor could not maintain an action against himself, his appointment by the creditor to that office suspended the action for the debt; and where a personal action was once suspended by the voluntary act of the party entitled to it, it was for ever gone and discharged.[74] Thus if the obligee of a bond made the obligor his executor, this amounted at law to a release of the debt,[75] even if there were other obligors on a joint and several bond.[76]

At common law the debt was released for ever though the executor died without having proved or administered.[77] Since 1857 the debt is no longer released if the debtor who was appointed executor died without having taken out probate of the will, or was cited to take out probate of the will and did not appear to the citation, or renounced probate, for in such cases he is in the same position as if he had never been appointed executor.[78] But the mere fact that an executor does not prove does not seem to prevent the debt being released. At all events an opportunity is given him to come in and prove.[79]

As between the debtor executor and the creditors of the testator, the common law doctrine was applicable only in cases where there were assets sufficient to satisfy the testator's debts,[80] for it would have been unfair to defraud the creditors of their just debts by a release which was absolutely voluntary.[81] Thus the debt due from the executor was considered, on their behalf, as assets in his hands.[82]

---

[73] See *Freeman* v. *Lomas* (1851) 9 Hare 109.

[74] On this subject, see *Jenkins* v. *Jenkins* [1928] 2 K.B. 501. Where the executor is one of several co-debtors, and in equity is held accountable for the debt as assets, he may have a right personally to recover contributions from his co-debtors.

[75] *Nedham's Case* (1610) 8 C.Rep. 135*a*, 136*a*.

[76] *Cheetham* v. *Ward* (1797) 1 Bos. & P. 630.

[77] *Wankford* v. *Wankford* (1704) 1 Salk. 299; Wentw.Off.Ex., 14th ed., c. 2; Com.Dig. Admon.B. 5.

[78] Court of Probate Acts 1857, s.79, and 1858, s.16, reproduced by the Administration of Estates Act 1925, s.5.

[79] *Re Applebee* [1891] 3 Ch. 422.

[80] Bac.Abr.Exors.A. 10.

[81] 2 Bl.Comm 512.

[82] *Holiday* v. *Boas* (1609) 1 Roll Abr. 920, 921; Exors.G., pl. 13; *Woodward* v. *Lord Darcy* (1558) 1 Plowd. 184; *Dorchester* v. *Webb* (1634) Cro.Car. 373; Touchst. 497, 498; *Wankford* v. *Wankford*, 1 Salk. 299, 305. The author of *The Office of an Executor* seems to be of opinion that the debt would be assets in equity only: Chap. 2, 14th ed., pp. 73, 74.

Accountable in equity

The effect in equity[83] of the appointment of a debtor to the office of executor is that the debt due from the debtor executor is considered to have been paid to him by himself; and upon this supposition it is an established rule in equity that the executor should be accountable for the amount of his debt as assets.[84] *Semble*, the debt is general assets for the payment, not only of the testator's debts, but also of his legacies.[85]

There are, indeed, some authorities for considering the appointment in the light of a specific legacy to the debtor for the purpose of discharging the debt, and that, therefore, though, like all other legacies, it is not to be paid or retained till the debts are satisfied, yet the executor has a right to it exclusively of the other legatees.[86] It seems now, however, to be settled[87] that the appointment of a debtor to be executor is no more than a parting with the action, and that a trust is accordingly raised in equity, not only for a residuary legatee,[88] but even for a next-of-kin.[89]

Rule in Strong v. Bird

It is apparent then that when a debtor is appointed executor the debt is released at law, but the persons claiming through the testator, as creditors or beneficiaries, have an equity against the debtor for the debt which he has in his hands. This equity may be rebutted by showing that the testator intended to release the debt during his lifetime.[90] Evidence is admissible to prove such an intention[91]; though a document which in effect purports to release the debt after the testator's death, unless properly executed as a will, would not be admissible.[92]

The principle laid down in *Strong* v. *Bird*—"*that where a testator has expressed the intention of making a gift of personal estate belonging to him to one who upon his death becomes his executor, the intention continuing unchanged, the executor is entitled to hold the property for his own bene-*

[83] See *Re Greg* [1912] 2 Ch. 243.

[84] See *Freakley* v. *Fox* (1829) 9 B. & C. 130; *Ingle* v. *Richards* (1860) 28 Beav. 366; *Re Bourne* [1906] 1 Ch. 697.

[85] *Flud* v. *Rumcey* (1609) Yelv. 160; *Phillips* v. *Phillips* (1679) Freem.Ch. 11; *Errington* v. *Evans* (1772) 2 Dick. 456; *Carey* v. *Goodinge* (1790) 3 Bro.C.C. 111; *Berry* v. *Usher* (1805) 11 Ves. 87; *Simmons* v. *Gutteridge* (1806) 13 Ves. 262; Bac.Abr.Exors.A. 10; *Re Price* (1879) 11 Ch.D. 163. See also *Re Boddington* (1848) 6 Notes of Cas. 18; *Tomlin* v. *Tomlin* (1841) 1 Hare 236, 247.

[86] Co.Litt. 246 *b*. n. (1), by Butler; 2 Bl.Comm. 512; Toller 349. But Lord Holt in *Wankford* v. *Wankford* (1704) 1 Salt. 306 denies that making a debtor executor amounts to a legacy; and even if it did, it would seem that he would have no right of retainer against other specific legatees.

[87] See *Carey* v. *Goodinge* (1790) 23 Bro.C.C. 110; *Berry* v. *Usher* (1805) 11 Ves. 87; *Commr. of Stamp Duties* v. *Bone* [1977] A.C. 511, P.C.

[88] *Brown* v. *Selwin* (1735) Cas.Temp.Talb. 240.

[89] *Carey* v. *Goodinge, ante*; *Commr. of Stamp Duties* v. *Bone, supra*.

[90] *Strong* v. *Bird* (1874) L.R. 18 Eq. 315; *Re Griffin* [1899] 1 Ch. 408, 412; *Re Pink* [1912] 2 Ch. 528; *Jenkins* v. *Jenkins* [1928] 2 K.B. 501. As to equity and the imperfect gift, see (1968) 118 *New Law Journal* 769.

[91] *Re Applebee* [1891] 3 Ch. 422.

[92] *Re Hyslop* [1894] 3 Ch. 522; *Re Pink* [1912] 2 Ch. 528.

fit"[93]—applies not only to cases of releases of debts, but also to cases of imperfect gifts *inter vivos* which may therefore be perfected by the donor appointing the donee his executor, and it is immaterial that the donee is only one of several executors.[94] The principle has been applied to perfect an imperfect gift of real estate made by the deceased owner to the person who in due course became his administratrix,[95] but its application to administrators has recently been doubted.[96]

The principle ought not to be extended so as to apply to a gift of money which is not sufficiently identified to enable it to be separated from the rest of the testator's property.[97] Nor will it be extended so as to apply to a promise to make a gift or a mere intention to make a gift.[98] It only applies where it is clearly shown that the gift was complete in all respects except as regards the legal formalities necessary for the proper transfer of title.[99] Moreover, the intention must remain unchanged until the settlor's death, and so, where the settlor forgot the existence of a settlement, and continued to regard the settled property as her own, the rule was not applicable.[1]

4.—APPOINTMENT OF CREDITOR AS EXECUTOR

Creditor sole executor

If a debtor makes his creditor, or the executor of his creditor, his sole executor, then, if the executor has assets of the debtor, the debt is extinguished, for the person who is to receive the money is the person who ought to pay it.[2] When, however, the executor has no assets,[3] the debt is not extinguished, nor is the running of time under the Limitation Act suspended. In the case of debtors dying after 1926, it seems that any assets in possession would be sufficient, provided the debt was due to the executor in his own right.[4]

Where one of two or more joint and several debtors makes their common

[93] *Per* Neville J. in *Re Stewart* [1908] 2 Ch. 251, 254.
[94] *Re Stewart, supra*; *Re Stoneham* [1919] 1 Ch. 149, 157 and see *Re Wilson* [1933] Ir.R. 729. See n. 89 above.
[95] *Re James* [1935] Ch. 449. But contrast *Re Greene* [1949] Ch. 333, where it was held there was no gift. As to the perfection of imperfect gifts by estoppel see *Pascoe* v. *Turner* [1979] 1 W.L.R. 431.
[96] *Re Gonin* [1979] Ch. 16, 35.
[97] *Re Innes* [1910] 1 Ch. 188.
[98] *Re Innes, ante*; *Re Freeland* [1952] Ch. 110.
[99] *Re Freeland* [1952] Ch. 110.
[1] *Re Wale* [1956] 1 W.L.R. 1346. As to the limits of the principle see 1982 Conveyancer 14 "A Fresh Look . . . " by G. Kodilinge.
[2] *Woodward* v. *Lord Darcy* (1558) 1 Plowd. 184; *Fryer* v. *Gildridge* (1614) Hob. 10; *Cock* v. *Cross* (1672) 2 Lev. 73; *Wankford* v. *Wankford* (1704) 1 Salk. 299, 305.
[3] 1 Roll.Abr. 940, M. pl. 5; *Pidgeon* v. *Pitts* (1684) 2 Show. 401, pl. 273; Co.Litt. 264b, note by Butler. And see *Bowring-Hanbury's Trustee* v. *Bowring-Hanbury* [1943] Ch. 104 (where "the supposal that the executor has assets which he may retain to pay himself" did not arise on the facts). See also (1943) 6 M.L.R. 233 (G.L.W.).
[4] As to retainer generally, see *ante*, pp. 640 *et seq.*; 2 Wolst. & Ch., 12th ed., pp. 1460, 1462.

creditor his sole executor, if such executor has assets, the debt is extinct, and he cannot sue the other debtor; for having assets amounts to payment.[5]

Creditor one of several executors

Again, the same doctrine prevails where the debtor appoints his creditor to be one of several executors, if the creditor administers.[6] But if the creditor neither proves the will, not acts as executor, he may bring an action against the other executor,[7] nor is it necessary to enable him so to do, that he should renounce probate.[8] So if the debtor makes the creditor and another his executors, and the creditor does not administer, but dies, his executor has an action against the surviving executor.[9]

On the same principle, a creditor who has taken out letters of administration to his debtor can successfully sue a person who has intermeddled in the deceased's affairs as executor *de son tort*, provided he can prove that he, the creditor administrator, has no assets to satisfy his debt.[10]

[5] *Wankford* v. *Wankford* (1704) 1 Salk 299, 305.
[6] *Woodward* v. *Lord Darcy* (1558) 1 Plowd. 184; *Dorchester* v. *Webb* (1634) Cro.Car. 372.
[7] *Dorchester* v. *Webb* (1634) W.Jones 345.
[8] *Rawlinson* v. *Shaw* (1790) 3 T.R. 557.
[9] *Woodward* v. *Lord Darcy* (1558) 1 Plowd. 184. And see the Administration of Estates Act 1925, s.5.
[10] *Ashley* v. *Childers*, 1 Roll.Abr. 940, Extinguishment, M. pl. 5.

CHAPTER 52

PRIORITY OF CREDITORS OVER BENEFICIARIES

Debts preferred to legacies

As the whole real and personal estate to which the deceased was beneficially entitled for an interest not ceasing on his death is liable in the hands of the representative to the payment of the debt of the testator, the representative must take care to discharge them, before he satisfies any description of legacy or assents to any devise. The ascertainment of debts, advertisement for debts, and the liability for debts of which the representative had no notice have been previously discussed.[1] This chapter is concerned with provision for known debts.

If an executor, though acting bona fide and under a conviction that the assets are amply sufficient for the payment of the testator's debts, permits specific legatees to retain or possess themselves of the articles bequeathed to them, he will be answerable for the value of those articles, with interest,[2] if there should ultimately be a deficiency of assets, though the deficiency should be occasioned by subsequent events which he had no reason to anticipate. The court will direct an account to be taken of the value of the property so possessed by the legatees, and interest to be computed, unless it is certain that the assets will ultimately be sufficient to pay all the creditors.[3]

Even future liabilities of the estate, such as covenanted annuities, must be provided for by suitable appropriation[4] before any of the estate can properly be distributed.[5] But the court may give leave to distribute without regard to contingent liabilities.[6]

Contingent debts and liabilities

On the same principle contingent liabilities must, apart from the statutory protection to be considered,[7] be provided for[8] even though there is

---

[1] See *ante*, pp. 605 *et seq.*

[2] R.S.C., Ord. 44, r. 19. As to interest generally and deduction of tax, see *post*, p. 1035.

[3] *Spode* v. *Smith* (1827) 3 Russ. 511.

[4] As to appropriation see *post.*

[5] *Jones* v. *Powell* (1712) 1 Eq.Cas.Abr. 84, pl. 2; *Cox* v. *Barnard* (1850) 8 Hare 310; *Hales* v. *Cox* (1863) 32 Beav. 118; *Dawson* v. *Kearton* (1856) 3 Sm. & G. 186; *Re Arnold* [1942] Ch. 272 (where *Re Johnson* [1940] W.N. 195 is explained).

[6] *Re Sales* [1920] W.N. 54; *Re Clark* (unreported); *Re Johnson* [1940] W.N. 195; *Re Arnold* [1942] Ch. 272.

[7] See *post*, pp. 655 *et seq.*

[8] See *Nector* v. *Gennet* (1595) Cr.Eliz. 466; *Eeles* v. *Lambert* (1648) Style 37, 54, 73; *Hawkins* v. *Day* (1753) Ambl. 160; *Pearson* v. *Archdeaken*, 1 Alcock & Nap. 23. As to valuation in the case of an insolvent estate, see *ante*, p. 630. As to appropriation for this purpose, see *post*, p. 685.

notice of only a remotely possible liability. If no provision is made the representative will have no answer to the claim of the creditor whose contingent claim has ripened into a certain claim. Thus, where executors of a shareholder paid a legacy under his will without providing for any contingent liability on the shares which they retained unsold, they were liable to pay the amount of the legacy in satisfaction of calls.[9] As against the legatee, however, the executor may claim repayment of the capital sum which he has paid to the legatee, but without any intermediate income. This is so even though he had notice of the contingent liability at the time when he distributed the estate, but not if, at the time when the legacy was paid, the contingent liability had ripened into a debt of which the executor had notice.[10]

Indemnity

When there are contingent liabilities, an executor is not bound to part with the assets to a beneficiary without a sufficient indemnity.[11] A court of equity will not compel him to do so without such indemnity, or without impounding a sufficient part of the residuary estate for that purpose,[12] for otherwise, if the contingent covenants, etc., should afterwards be broken, the executor would be liable to answer the damages himself without any fault in him. By making an unconditional assent executors lose their right to an indemnity out of the general estate.[13]

An order of the court directing the administration of the assets is of itself a complete and perfect indemnity to the executor, provided he keeps back nothing which ought to be disclosed to the court.[14]

Liability on shares

Where there is a possible future claim for calls on shares the court may order distribution of the estate without directing the retention of assets to meet the claim, and such order will completely exonerate the executors

---

[9] *Taylor* v. *Taylor* (187;) L.R. 10 Eq. 477 *Knatchbull* v. *Fearnhead* (1837) 3 M. & C. 122; *Newcastle Banking Co.* v. *Hymers* (1856) 22 Beav. 367; *Re Bewley's Estate* (1871) 24 L.T. 177.
[10] See *Jervis* v. *Wolferstan* (1874) L.R. 18 Eq. 18; *Whittaker* v. *Kershaw* (1890) 45 Ch.D. 320; *Cf. Re West* [1909] 2 Ch. 180.
[11] See *post*, p. 1060.
[12] *Simmons* v. *Bolland* (1817) 3 Mer. 547; *Vernon* v. *Egmont* (1827) 1 Bligh (N.S.) 554; *Cochrane* v. *Robinson* (1840) 11 Sim. 378; *Fletcher* v. *Stevenson* (1844) 3 Hare 360, 370; *Dobson* v. *Carpenter* (1850) 12 Beav. 370; *Hickling* v. *Boyer* (1851) 3 Mac. & G. 635; *Dean* v. *Allen* (1855) 20 Beav. 1.
[13] *Shadbolt* v. *Woodfall* (1845) 1 Coll. 30; *Re Bennett* [1943] 1 All E.R. 467. See *Hickling* v. *Boyer* (1851) 3 M. & G. 635, 646; *Smith* v. *Smith, infra. Roome* v. *Edwards* [1932] A.C. 279, 299.
[14] *Dean* v. *Allen* (1855) 20 Beav. 1. See *Smith* v. *Smith* (1861) 1 Dr. & Sm. 384; *Dobson* v. *Sammell, ibid.* 575; *Waller* v. *Barrett* (1857) 24 Beav. 413; *Bennett* v. *Lytton* (1860) 2 J. & H. 155; *Adams* v. *Ferick* (1859) 26 Beav. 384; *Williams* v. *Headland* (1864) 4 Giff. 505; *England* v. *Tredegar* (1866) L.R. 1 Eq. 344; *Re King* [1907] 1 Ch. 72; *Re Johnson* [1940] W.N. 195.

from all liability; but, *semble*, the order can only be made in proceedings in which administration is requested.[15]

Liability under covenant for annuity

Although the court will allow distribution without making provision for future contingent liabilities, it will not do so where the liability arises under a deed of covenant executed by the deceased to pay an annuity, and this liability is not dependent on any contingency except the survival of the annuitants, for the annuitants are future creditors of an ascertained sum and have priority over the beneficiaries.[16]

Liability under leases

A lessor has no equity to apply to have a fund set apart to indemnify him for breaches of covenants given by a deceased lessee,[17] unless the property comprised in the lease did not of itself furnish a sufficient security, in which case, it was the practice of the court[18] to set apart out of the residuary estate a reasonable sum to cover any liability which might in any reasonable probability arise by reason of a future breach. Where a fund was so set aside and paid into court there is no necessity to retain the fund in court after the expiration of a period on the expiration of which any possible action by the lessors against the executors would be statute-barred. So on the expiration of such period the court will order the fund to be paid out to the beneficiaries.[19] Executors are not entitled to any indemnity out of the estate in respect of leasehold properties as to which they have already assented.[20] The effect of setting apart a fund to answer future breaches of covenant is to throw a great burden on the residuary legatee which should not be inflicted upon him unless absolutely necessary.[21]

Statutory protection

Protection is given by statute[22] to a representative or trustee, liable as such, from personal liability if in the case of a lease or rentcharge he satisfies all accrued liabilities claimed on rents, covenants, agreements or

[15] *Re King* [1907] 1 Ch. 72; *Re Johnson* [1940] W.N. 195.
[16] *Re Arnold* [1942] Ch. 272; *cf. Re Johnson, ante*, as to annuity claims on an insolvent estate, see *ante*, p. 631.
[17] *King* v. *Malcott* (1852) 9 Hare 692.
[18] See, for example, *Re Lewis* [1939] Ch. 232.
[19] *Re Lewis, ante.*
[20] *Re Bennett, ante*, p. 654.
[21] *Brewer* v. *Pocock* (1857) 23 Beav. 310; *Smith* v. *Smith, supra; Dodson* v. *Sammell, supra*; referred to in *Hardy* v. *Fothergill* (1888) 13 App.Cas. at p. 370.
[22] Trustee Act 1925, s.26 (reproducing with amendments, ss.27 and 28 of Lord St. Leonard's Act), as amended by the Law of Property (Amend.) Act 1926, Sched. See 4 Wolst. & Ch., 13th ed., pp. 33 *et seq*. This section applies to trusts, including executorships and administratorships created before or after the commencement of the Act; s.69(1).

indemnities and where necessary sets apart a sufficient fund to answer any future claim that may be made in respect of any fixed and ascertained sum which the lessee or grantee agreed to lay out. He may then convey the property to a purchaser, legatee devisee or other person entitled to call for a conveyance and distribute the estate, other than the fund to set apart, amongst the persons entitled without further provision for future liability. This protection is given without prejudice to the right of a lessor or grantor or his successors to follow the assets into the hands of the beneficiaries,[23] and it applies notwithstanding any contrary provisions of the will.[24] The words "lease" and "grant" are widely defined.[25] The section, however, deals only with the liability of the representative as such and does not protect a representative who has entered into possession of the deceased's leaseholds and thereby incurred, in addition to his liability as representative, the personal liability of an assignee of the term.[26] In such a case it is necessary to follow the old practice and set aside a fund by way of indemnity.[27]

But where there is no personal liability the court will not decree that a fund be set aside and this is normally the position where the statute applies.[28]

Creditors of foreign testator

Where the English grant is only ancillary to a grant made in a foreign country in respect of a person of foreign domicile, the representative in England is nevertheless liable to pay foreign debts. But if he does not himself distribute the assets to the persons entitled as legatees, heirs or otherwise as beneficiaries, but, after paying the English debts and advertising in England, pays over the remaining assets to the foreign administrator, he gets a good discharge, and is not liable to foreign creditors of whom he did not have notice,[29] or for claims by beneficiaries.[30] Nor is such a representative bound to advertise abroad. On the other hand the English courts will not in every case compel the English administrator to hand the assets to the foreign administrator.[31] Accordingly, the English administrator has a choice, and may pay the administered assets to the persons beneficially entitled thereto, although distribution is normally better left to the principal administrator in the country of the deceased's domicile.[32] If he does so

---

[23] See post, p. 1076.
[24] Trustee Act 1925, s.26(2).
[25] See Trustee Act 1925, s.26(3).
[26] Re Owers [1941 Ch. 389, 391; Re Bennett [1943] 1 All E.R. 467:
[27] Ibid. n. 26.
[28] Re Nixon [1904] 1 Ch. 638; Re Sales [1920] W.N. 54. See n. 6 supra and see also ante p. 654.
[29] Re Achillopoulos [1928] Ch. 433. See further as to attorney administrators, post, p. 937.
[30] Re Weiss [1962] P. 136.
[31] Re Lorillard [1922] 2 Ch. 638.
[32] Re Weiss [1962] P. 136. See also post, pp. 937–938.

administer he is liable to foreign creditors of whom he had no notice, but may presumably rely on advertisement to escape liability.

Creditor's delay—laches

The effect of delay by a creditor in notifying or claiming his debt depends upon the circumstances. If the estate is being administered out of court he will not, in the absence of wilful default,[33] be prejudiced so long as there are assets in hand.[34] If there are no such assets or no sufficient assets he may elect to sue any of the beneficiaries for the whole debt or the balance as the case may be, irrespective of the right that the person sued may have against other beneficiaries.[35] The latter remedy lies, however, only in equity[36] and the creditor may be met by the equitable defence of laches.[37]

If the estate is being administered in court a late creditor may be put upon terms which may affect his priority.[38] If a creditor does not come in till after the executor has paid away the residue under the order of the court he is not without remedy, though he is barred from the benefit of that judgment. If (having first exhausted his remedy against the representatives) he chooses to sue the legatee and bring back the fund he may do so.[39] He cannot affect the executor at all where the distribution has been under the order of the court or after advertisement under s.27 of the Trustee Act 1925; and consequently in either of these events the executor is not a proper party to any subsequent proceeding against the legatees.[40] Where a

[33] *Re Metcalfe* (1879) 13 Ch.D. 236; *Re McMurdo* [1902] 2 Ch. 684; *cf. Cattell v. Simons* (1845) 8 B. 243.

[34] *Brown v. Lake* (1847) De G. & Sm. 144. See also *ante*, p. 605, n. 5.

[35] *Davies v. Nicolson* (1858) 2 De G. & J. 693.

[36] *Harrison v. Kirk* [1904] A.C. 1, 7.

[37] *Ridgway v. Newstead* (1860) 2 Giff. 492, 501, affirmed 3 D.F. & J. 474, but see *post*, n. 40.

[38] See *Harrison v. Kirk* [1904] A.C. 1, 6. See *per* Lord Eldon in *Gillespie v. Alexander* (1826) 3 Russ. 130; *March v. Russell* (183) 3 My. & Cr. 31; *Hartwell v. Colvin* (1852) 16 Beav. 140; and the observations of Lord Lyndhurst in *Vernon v. Egmont* (1827) 1 Bligh (N.S.) 544, 570; also *Re McMurdo* [1902] 2 Ch. 684; 71 L.J.Ch. 691; *Harrison v. Kirk* [1904] A.C. 1. As to the old practice, see *Parker v. Moorley* (1839) 3 Y. & C.Ex. 720; *Lee v. Flood* (1853) 2 Sm. & G. 250.

[39] See *post*, p. 1076; *Davis v. Frowd* (1833) 1 My. & K. 200, 209, 210; *Sawyer v. Birchmore* (1837) 1 Keen. 391, 401; 2 My. & Cr. 611; *March v. Russell*, 3 My. & Cr. 31; *Underwood v. Hatton* (1842) 5 Beav. 36. Persons claiming as legatees or next-of-kin have similar rights to those established in favour of creditors by *David v. Frowd, supra*. See *Ministry of Health v. Simpson* [1951] A.C. 251. Where an intestate's estate had been distributed under a decree in an administration suit among persons found by the report to be his next-of-kin, it was held that a person claiming to be sole next-of-kin was not precluded to be his next-of-kin from filing a bill against the persons alleged to have been erroneously found to be the next-of-kin for the purpose of obtaining restitution of the fund so distributed. Acquiescence or laches may, however, disentitle such a person to maintain the action, *Mohan v. Broughton* [1899] P. 211; and see *Williams v. Evans* [1911] P. 175.

[40] *Gillespie v. Alexander* (1827) 3 Russ. 130, 136, 137; *David v. Frowd* (1833) 1 My. & K. 200, 209, 210; *Seale v. Buller* (1860) 2 Giff. 312; *Clegg v. Rowland* (1866) L.R. 3 Eq. 368; *Hunter v. Young* (1879) 4 Ex.D. 256. And see *Harrison v. Kirk, ante; Ministry of Health v. Simpson* [1951] A.C. 251.

debt is governed as to limitation by an express statutory provision there is no room for the doctrine of laches.[41]

The rule in Gillespie v. Alexander

A difficulty arises if, where there is administration by the court,[42] a creditor does not come in until some individual legatees have received their legacies in full under the sanction of the court, and there are left in court certain funds which have been directed to be appropriated to other individual legatees, who have not been paid. The question then is, whether a creditor so coming in is to be paid his whole debt by the unpaid legatees, or whether he should take from them such a proportion only of his debt as would have been borne by them if he had applied before the other legacies were paid, and that he should be left to recover the residue of it against the paid legatees. In *Gillespie* v. *Alexander*[43] (which was an administration action), after an order on further directions had sanctioned payments made by the executor in discharge of legacies and had directed the fund in court to be apportioned among the other legatees, a creditor obtained permission to prove his debt. The master subsequently reported a debt to be due to him; but in the meantime the fund had been apportioned, and part of it had been paid over, while the remainder had been carried to the account of particular legatees, who were infants. Lord Eldon held *that the creditor was entitled to receive out of the funds of the legatees so remaining in court, not the whole of the debt but only part of it, bearing the same proportion to the whole as the legacies given to those legatees bore to the whole amount of the legacies given by the will; and that he must seek the payment of the rest of his debt, in proper proportions, amongst those legatees who had been actually paid.*[44] Where a decree has been made for the administration of the estate of a deceased person, and the assets in hand have been distributed among his creditors, who have come in and proved, and at a later period further funds come in, and some only of the creditors who had proved come forward in answer to advertisements, the creditors who thus claim payment at the later period are not entitled to have the whole of the new fund applied so far as it will extend in payment of their claims, but only to receive rateable proportions of it according to the proportion which their debts bear to the total amount of the debts.

---

[41] *Re Pauling* [1964] Ch. 303, 353.
[42] The rule applies only in case of administration by the court (*Davies* v. *Nicolson* (1858) 2 De G. & J. 693).
[43] (1826) 3 Russ. 130. And see *Grieg* v. *Somerville* (1830) 1 Russ. & M. 338.
[44] See *David* v. *Frowd* (1833) 1 My. & K. 200, 210.

CHAPTER 53

ADMINISTRATION WHEN THE DECEASED WAS DOMICILED ABROAD

Grants to estates of foreigners

Hitherto it has been assumed that the intestate was, at the time of his death, domiciled in a place where the law of England is the law of the land.

A grant of letters of administration or probate or other similar authority such as issue of a certificate of inheritance or executorship may be made by the courts of the country in which the deceased person left any property, movable or immovable, irrespective of the domicile or place of death of the deceased.[1]

Administration where property situate

The administration of the estate (as distinct from the ultimate distribution amongst the persons beneficially entitled) must be in the country in which possession of it is taken and held under lawful authority, but some countries[2] will not administer assets of a non-resident foreigner until the decision of the foreign court has been obtained. Thus, by the law of England, the person to whom administration is granted by the probate court is by statute bound to administer the estate, and to pay the debts of the deceased. The letters of administration, under which he acts, direct him to do so, and he takes an oath that he will well and truly administer all the goods of the deceased, and pay his debts so far as his goods will extend, and exhibit a full and true account of his administration: and these duties remain the same, notwithstanding the intestate may have died domiciled elsewhere.[3] A guide to the probate procedures in a number of European Countries and in Florida will be found in Pugh: *Administration of Foreign States*.[4]

Again, with respect to all the property of which the intestate died pos-

---

[1] See Dicey and Morris, *Conflict of Laws*, 11th ed. 1987, pp. 981 *et seq.* Graveson, *Conflict of Laws*, 7th ed., 1974, pp. 509–527; *Campbell* v. *Beaufoy* (1859) Johns, 320, 326; 126 S.J. 634; 127 S.J. 181, 850; 123 S.J. 254. As to the as yet unadopted Hague Convention on Succession see generally p. 16 *ante*.

[2] *i.e.* Switzerland.

[3] *Preston* v. *Lord Melville* (1840–41) 8 Cl. & F. 1. See accord, *per* Lord Cranworth in *Enophin* v. *Wylie* (1862) 10 H.L.C. 1, 19. See also Lord St Leonards' observations on this case in *The Carron Iron Co.* v. *Maclaren* (1855) 5 H.L.C. 456; *Stirling-Maxwell* v. *Cartwright* (1879) 9 Ch.D. 173; 11 Ch.D. 522; *Eames* v. *Hacon* (1881) 16 Ch.D. 407; 18 Ch.D. 347; *Ewing* v. *Orr-Ewing* (1885) 9 App.Cas. 453; and *Re Bonnefoi* [1912] P. 233.

[4] This covers Guernsey, Jersey, Isle of Man, France, Italy, Spain and Portugal and includes precedents for the Administration Oath, Power of Attorney, Inland Revenue Affidavit and Deed of Entitlement.

sessed in the Queen's dominions out of England, the administrator, under the letters granted there, has a right to hold it against an administrator under a grant obtained in this country.[5] But where a foreign administrator remitted a part of the assets to England to be sold and the proceeds to be carried to the account of the intestate's estate, and came himself to this country, he was held answerable here to a next-of-kin of the deceased, who had taken out administration here, of those assets; and the court had a right to deal with them, and to appoint a receiver if there was danger of their being taken out of the jurisdiction.[6]

Lex fori governs administration

Again, the administration of the estate is carried out in accordance with the law of the country in which the grant was made.[7] Thus where assets are being administered in England the priority of creditors is governed by English law.[8] Again, a claim by a foreign creditor (and it should be noticed that foreign creditors may claim on an equal footing with English creditors in the administration of assets in England[9]) which is statute-barred by English law cannot be enforced in the English administration, although it is not statute-barred by the law of the country in which the deceased died domiciled,[10] but such a claim may be enforceable in any foreign country in which there are assets.

Assets prematurely transmitted

To this principle there is an exception. It is based on the conception that creditors should not be prejudiced by the fact that a representative has acted contrary to his duty.[11] It is the duty of every representative to satisfy the claims of creditors of the deceased in accordance with the law of the country from which he derives his authority.[12] If then, before satisfying such claims, he transmits assets to the representative in another country, the latter must, in English law, administer those assets according to the law

---

[5] *Currie* v. *Bircham* (1822) 1 Dowl. & Ryl. 75. See also *Jauncy* v. *Sealey* (1686) 1 Vern. 397; Story's *Conflict of Laws*, Chap. 13, s.518.

[6] *Hervey* v. *Fitzpatrick* (1854) Kay 421. See also *Sandilands* v. *Innes* (1829) 3 Sim. 263.

[7] *Re Lorillard* [1922] 2 Ch. 638; Dicey and Morris, *Conflict of Laws*, 11th ed., 1987, p. 993; Graveson's *Conflict*, 7th ed., 1974, p. 515.

[8] *Cook* v. *Gregson* (1856) 2 Drewr. 286; *Blackwood* v. *R.* (1882) 8 App.Cas. 82, 92; *Eames* v. *Hacon* (1881) 18 Ch.D. 347, 351; *Re Kloebe* (1884) 28 Ch.D. 175 (where *Wilson* v. *Dunsany* (1854) 18 Beav. 293, *contra*, was disapproved); *Re Lorillard*, *supra*. See *Carron Iron Co.* v. *Maclaren* (1855) 5 H.L.C. 456. See also Westlake, 7th ed., s.110.

[9] *Re Kloebe*, *supra*; *Ewing* v. *Orr-Ewing* (1885) 10 App.Cas. 453, 523; *Re Holden* [1935] W.N. 52. Where judgment has been given for the administration of an estate, the court has no power to restrain a foreign creditor from proceeding in a foreign court against the administrator; but judgment by default in the foreign court is only treated in the administration action as prima facie evidence of the debt; *Re Boyse* (1880) 15 Ch.D. 591.

[10] *Re Lorillard*, *ante*.

[11] See *Cook* v. *Gregson*, *ante*.

[12] *Ante*, p. 659.

of the country in which they were collected, and from which they have been prematurely transmitted.[13]

Powers of English representative

It follows from the rule stated above, to the effect that the administration of the estate is carried out in accordance with the *lex fori*, that the English representative has, as a general rule, the same powers as if the deceased had been domiciled in England. Thus the representative in England may exercise the power to postpone the sale of property comprised in the English grant.[14] He may also appoint a trustee of the share of the assets to which an infant may be entitled.[15] *Semble*, a trustee so appointed may exercise the power to maintain the infant conferred on him by the Trustee Act 1925, s.31.[16]

Jurisdiction of English courts

Where the deceased was domiciled abroad the English court cannot conveniently make any order as to foreign assets, unless the foreign court itself expects the English court to act. When all debts which may be proved by English law have been satisfied out of English assets, the English courts will direct the surplus of the English assets to be handed over to the principal personal representative, or distributed according to the *lex domicilii*.[17]

If representative has English and foreign assets

To this last statement there is an exception. Where the same person has vested in him English and foreign assets and is within the jurisdiction, then, whether the English administration is principal or ancillary, the English courts, if called upon so to do by a person entitled to claim in the administration, may[18] judicially administer the whole of the assets vested in him. The court may make such a general order notwithstanding the opposition of the majority of the executors.[19]

However, the court will only make such a general order so far as the ultimate distribution amongst beneficiaries is concerned. It could hardly attempt to regulate the payment of debts in a foreign country out of foreign assets.[20] Further, it may be that this exception only extends to the

---

[13] *Cook* v. *Gregson, supra.* See also Dicey and Morris, *Conflict of Laws,* 11th ed., 1987, p. 993.

[14] *Re Wilks* [1935] Ch. 645. See also *Re Goenaga* [1949] P. 367.

[15] *Re Kehr* [1952] Ch. 26.

[16] *Re Kehr, ante. Sed quaere* whether the power of maintenance should not be treated as one of distribution.

[17] *Ewing* v. *Orr-Ewing* (1885) 10 App.Cas. 453, 514; *Re Lorillard, ante.* See Graveson, *Conflict,* 7th ed., 1974, p. 141; Dicey and Morris, *Conflict of Laws,* 11th ed., 1987, p. 999.

[18] The court now has a discretion: see p. 937, n. 76.

[19] *Stirling-Maxwell* v. *Cartwright* (1879) 9 Ch.D. 173; 11 Ch.D. 522.

[20] See *Ewing* v. *Orr-Ewing* (1883) 9 App.Cas. 34, 44, 45. The power is now purely discretionary. See R.S.C. Ord. 85. The practice has therefore altered since the *Ewing* case. See also the Administration of Estates Act 1925, s.32(1).

execution of the trusts of a will, the court acting on the person of the representative not as such, but as trustee of the will.[21] Undoubtedly, this was the course pursued in *Ewing* v. *Orr-Ewing*.[22]

This exception is an illustration of the principle that equity, by acting on the person of trustees, may control property outside the jurisdiction.[23]

Where foreign proceedings adopted

Where this exception applies, the English courts, in the course of an English action, will not allow proceedings to be carried further than is convenient according to the comity of courts, and will adopt the proceedings of the courts of the country of the domicile of the deceased according to the necessities and exigencies of the case.[24] The English court could, if there was a pending suit in the courts of the country of the deceased's domicile, in which all questions which would arise in the course of the administration could be decided, stay the English action and prevent it from going on here vexatiously, and unnecessarily.[25] Where it seems, however, that a foreign judgment may have been obtained by fraud, the English court may direct an issue to be tried whatever the views of the foreign court.[26]

Courts of domicile have no exclusive jurisdiction

Despite some authority to the contrary,[27] it is settled that, in countries where domicile is the principal test, it is not necessary for the persons who have a claim to a beneficial interest in the estate to make their claim in the courts of the country where the deceased was domiciled. Stirling J. in his judgment in *Re Trufort*,[28] after quoting passages from the cases mentioned in the footnote,[29] says that the rule to be extracted from these cases appears to be this: that though the parties claiming to be entitled to the estate of a deceased person may not be bound to resort to the tribunals of the country in which he was domiciled, and though the courts of this country may be called upon to administer the estate of a deceased person domiciled abroad, and may in such a case be bound to ascertain as best they can who, according to the law of the domicile, are entitled to the estate, yet where

---

[21] *Ibid.* 10 App.Cas. 453, 499, 505, 527, 528.

[22] (1883) 9 App.Cas. 34. Ultimately, it was held (10 App.Cas. 453) that the Scottish courts had jurisdiction to sequester the trust property, which had all been transferred to Scotland, and to appoint a judicial factor in place of the existing trustees. In effect this rendered the English decree nugatory: *ibid.* 530.

[23] See, *e.g. Penn* v. *Baltimore* (1750) 1 Ves.Sem. 444.

[24] *Stirling-Maxwell* v. *Cartwright* (1879) 11 Ch.D. 522.

[25] See *per* Cotton L.J. in *Re Orr-Ewing* (1882) 22 Ch.D. 456, 469.

[26] *Jet Holdings* v. *Patel* [1990] 1 Q.B. 335. For the principles governing stages of English or Foreign proceedings see Dicey & Morris: *Conflict of Laws* 4th Cum. Supplement to the 11th ed. pp. [49]-[52].

[27] See the statement of Lord Westbury in *Enohin* v. *Wylie* (1862) 10 H.L.C. 1, 13. Dicey and Morris, *Conflict of Laws*, 11th ed., 1987, p. 1002. See also *post*, p. 937.

[28] (1887) 36 Ch.D. 600. And see *Re Ross* [1930] 1 Ch. 377, 396.

[29] *Enohin* v. *Wylie* (1862) 10 H.L.C. 1; *Ewing* v. *Orr-Ewing* (1885) 10 App.Cas. 453; *Doglioni* v. *Crispin* (1866) L.R. 1 H.L. 301. See also *Chellaram* v. *Chellaram* [1985] Ch. 409.

the title has been adjudicated upon by the courts of the domicile such adjudication is binding upon and must be followed by the courts of this country,[30] even if the judgment of the foreign court has by default of the party complaining of the judgment proceeded on a mistake as to the English law[31]; or the whole of the facts were not before the foreign tribunal[32]; for the courts of this country do not sit to hear appeals from foreign tribunals, and if the decision of the foreign tribunal is wrong recourse must be had to the mode of appeal provided in the foreign country.[33]

In many countries, however, domicile is not the test and jurisdiction is founded upon residence,[34] nationality[35] or possession of assets within the jurisdiction.

Each case must depend upon its circumstances and the only generalisation possible is that persons claiming an interest in the estate should apply first to the courts of the country in which the deceased has left assets of greatest value.

Domicile

The complex question of domicile is beyond the province of this work. Reference should be made to specialist works for this topic,[36] but it should be noted that the construction of a will is no longer affected in English law, by reason of any change in the testator's domicile after the execution of the will.[37]

---

[30] See n. 28.
[31] *Castrique* v. *Imrie* (1870) L.R. 4 H.L. 414; *Godard* v. *Gray* (1870) L.R. 6 Q.B. 139.
[32] *Re De Cosse, Brissac* v. *Rathbone* (1861) 6 H. & N. 301.
[33] *Bank of Australasia* v. *Nias* (1851) 16 Q.B. 717; *Pemberton* v. *Hughes* [1899] 1 Ch. 781. See further as to the conclusiveness of the judgments of the courts of domicile in the courts of a foreign country, *ante*, p. 12.
[34] *e.g.* France, Switzerland.
[35] *e.g.* Germany.
[36] See, *e.g.* Dicey and Morris, *Conflict of Laws*, 11th ed., 1987, pp. 116–170 and the Supplement thereto Cheshire and North, *Private International Law*, 9th ed., pp. 160–198; Graveson, *Conflict of Laws*, 7th ed., 1974, pp. 185–225; Wolff, *Private International Law*, 2nd ed., pp. 106–124. See also *Rayden on Divorce*, 13th ed., 1979, pp. 43–69.
[37] See the Wills Act 1963, s.4.

Chapter 54

POWERS OF THE REPRESENTATIVE

The powers available to an executor or administrator in the administration[1] and distribution[2] of the estate are extensive.[3] Where power is lacking, doubtful or in dispute, recourse must be had to the court[4] as a matter of last resort, but this can often be avoided by use of the power to compromise claims.[5] In general, however, the powers of a representative are derived from the Will itself, from common law or from statute and frequently from all three. However these powers are not as such exercisable after assent,[6] cannot be delegated[7] and must be exercised in good faith for the benefit of the estate.[8] Powers of appointment are considered later.[9]

The will

If there is an express power in the will there is no difficulty unless questions of public policy[10] or construction[11] arise. Reference should be made to works on wills.[12]

Common law

Although most of his powers have been superseded or codified by statute, it is a mistake to think that the powers of a representative are confined to those appearing in statute law.[13] As has been seen, his power to litigate derives from the devolution on him of the claims (choses in action) of the deceased[14] and he has at common law powers of disposition[15] and management inherent in his office.[16]

---

[1] As to issues arising on administration see pp. 587–663 *ante*.

[2] As to issues arising on distribution see pp. 961–1084 *post*.

[3] As to the history see Maitland, *Equity* pp. 193–214.

[4] See p. 821 *post*, and Trustee Act 1925, s.57.

[5] See p. 665 *post*.

[6] See p. 679 *post*.

[7] See pp. 700 *et seq*.

[8] See p. 51 *ante* and pp. 703 *post*.

[9] See p. 1025 *post*. See also *Turner* v. *Turner* [1984] Ch. 100, and cases cited therein.

[10] See as to public policy *Theobald on Wills* 14th ed. p. 624.

[11] See p. 824 *post* and R.S.C. Ord. 85.

[12] See generally *Theobald on Wills* 14th ed.; *Jarman on Wills* 8th ed.; *Williams on Wills* 6th ed.

[13] See in particular Administration of Estates Act 1925, ss.39–44; Trustee Act 1925, ss.12, 14–16, 19, 21–25, 31 and 32; (pp. 1132–1137, 1097 *et seq.*).

[14] See p. 515 *ante*.

[15] See pp. 666 *post* (sale) 669 (mortgage) 670 (lease).

[16] See pp. 681 *et seq*. Powers to appropriate and partition and to continue a *business* for a short time probably fall into this category.

Statute

Since nearly all the necessary powers are now covered by statute it is convenient, having made these distinctions, to consider the powers of the representative under general headings and without detailed analysis as to whether they apply to administration, distribution or both. After considering the general powers of a representative it is necessary to look at limitations applicable to various types of representative,[17] to joint representation[18] and to the devolution and delegation of powers.[19]

A. GENERAL POWERS

Power to compromise and compound

This in practice is probably one of the most important powers of a representative. He has the same extensive statutory power to compromise claims on behalf of the estate as a trustee[20] and as a tenant for life under the Settled Land Act 1925,[21] without obtaining the consent of the beneficiaries.[22] Provided he is acting in good faith he may, without responsibility for loss, enter into agreements, accept property in advance, apportion funds, submit to arbitration,[23] allow time for payment, and pay or allow any debt or claim on any evidence he thinks sufficient.[24] Extensive powers of compromise are also given by the common law[25] including the power for one executor to compromise the claim of another against the estate.[26]

There is, however, no power, statutory or otherwise, without sanction of the court[27] to compromise the claim of an infant, to indemnify, or to pay a statute-barred debt judicially so declared.[28]

Representatives also have extensive statutory powers to facilitate dealings with reversionary interests, to obtain valuations[29] and to deal with undivided shares.[30]

---

[17] See p. 688–689 *post*.

[18] See p. 690–694 *post*.

[19] See p. 695–702 *post*.

[20] A sole personal representative has this power even where because receipts are required, two trustees may be necessary. Trustee Act 1925, s.15 (*post*, p. 1099). See Lewin, *Trusts*, 16th ed., p. 287.

[21] Settled Land Act 1925, s.58, imported by the Law of Property Act 1925, s.28, and the Administration of Estates Act 1925, s.39.

[22] *Re Strafford* [1978] 3 W.L.R. 223.

[23] As to whether this admits assets, see *post*, p. 720.

[24] Trustee Act 1925, s.15. The power in s.15(*f*) is thought to extend to claims by beneficiaries. See *Re Warren* (1884) 53 L.J.Ch. 1016. The power to appropriate (*post*, p. 685) may sometimes conveniently be used to provide for future debts, *e.g.* a covenanted annuity. See *ante*, pp. 653–655.

[25] *Re Houghton* [1904] 1 Ch. 622, 625.

[26] *Ibid.* n. 25.

[27] As to applications for such sanctions, see *post*, pp. 821 *et seq.* For an example where a compromise was not upheld, see *De Cordova* v. *De Cordova* (1879) 4 App.Cas. 692 (P.C.).

[28] See *post*, p. 735. Even after a young person is of age the presumption of undue influence may be so strong that the compromise cannot be implemented. See *Powell* v. *Powell* [1900] 1 Ch. 243.

[29] See the Trustee Act 1925, s.22 (*post*, p. 1101) and the definitions in s.68(7). (See p. 681, n. 85, *post*).

[30] Trustee Act 1925, s.24 (*post*, p. 1104).

Power to bring actions

As a representative has the same property in the estate devolving upon him as the deceased had when living, so he has the same power to bring actions in that respect.[31] An executor *de son tort* cannot, however, bring an action in right of the deceased[32] although his possession of the goods of the deceased may give him rights against a mere wrongdoer.[33] The right to sue and distrain for rent has been discussed[34] and the details of proceedings by representatives are considered later.[35]

Power to enter house of the deceased

Before the Land Transfer Act 1897, within a convenient time after the testator's death, or the grant of administration, the executor or administrator had a right to enter the house, descended to the heir or devisee, in order to remove the goods of the deceased,[36] provided he did so without violence.[37] He had also a right to take deeds and other writings relative to the personal estate out of a chest in the house if it were unlocked, or the key were in it; but he had no right to break open even a chest. If he could not take possession of the effects without force, he must desist, and resort to his action.[38] On the other hand, if the executor or administrator, on his part, were remiss in removing the goods within a reasonable time, the heir might distrain them as causing damage (*damage feasant*).[39]

Since the Land Transfer Act 1897,[40] the real estate has all devolved on the representative, so that this situation could now, it seems only arise as between the general and special representatives of a tenant for life,[41] or as against the survivors of a beneficial joint tenancy,[42] or relatives in occupation.

Power to sell—common law

It is a general rule of law and equity that a representative has an absolute[43] power of disposition over all the personal estate of his testator or

---

[31] *Ante*, pp. 515 *et seq.*
[32] Bro.Abr. Administration, 8.
[33] See *ante*, pp. 93–103, and *post*, p. 827.
[34] *Ante*, p. 531.
[35] See *post*, pp. 821, 868.
[36] Wentw.Off.Ex., 14th ed., p. 202.
[37] *Ibid.*; Toller 6th ed., p. 255.
[38] Wentw.Off.Ex., 14th ed., pp. 81, 202.
[39] *Ibid.* 202; Plowd. 280, 281; *Stodden* v. *Harvey* (1608) Cro.Jac. 204.
[40] See *ante*, p. 460.
[41] See *ante*, p. 17.
[42] See *ante*, p. 545.
[43] He does not have the same duty as a trustee to hold the balance between the beneficiaries, *Re Hayes* [1971] 1 W.L.R. 758, 764. Even where such balance has to be held account need not be taken of merely speculative evidence of expected future increases in value: *Thomas* v. *Williams* (1883) 24 Ch.D. 558, 565.

intestate[44]; and that such estate when so disposed of cannot be followed by creditors,[45] much less by legatees, either general or specific.[46] This rule is based on the principle that the executor or administrator is, in many cases, driven to realise the assets,[47] in order to perform his duty in paying debts and distributing the estate; and no one would deal with an executor or administrator if liable afterwards to be called to account.[48]

Thus, representatives could, by virtue of their office, even at common law, dispose absolutely of terms of years vested in them as representatives,[49] and might make a good title even against a specific legatee. This common law power of disposing of chattels real now extends to real estate generally,[50] and in the exercise thereof they may sell the surface and minerals separately.[51]

Power to sell—statute

In addition to the above-mentioned powers of sale, representatives now have, "for purposes of administration, or during a minority of any beneficiary or the subsistence of any life interest, or until the period of distribution arrives," a statutory power to sell[52] or exchange the real or personal estate of the deceased, or any part thereof, or any easement, right or privilege of any kind over or in relation thereto.[53] Such sale or exchange may be made

[44] The powers of executors to dispose of a chattel specifically bequeathed seems to have been formerly questioned: *Humble* v. *Bill* (1703) 2 Vern. 444; but later became well established: *Ewer* v. *Corbet* (1723) 2 P.Wms. 149; *Burting* v. *Stonard* (1723) *ibid.* 150; *Langley* v. *Lord Oxford* (1743) Ambl. 17: though the purchaser of pure personalty specifically bequeathed might be well advised to obtain the concurrence of the specific legatee, lest an assent had already been made. As to following assets after assent (as distinct from disposal for purposes of administration) see *post*, p. 1076.

[45] Nor can it be followed by one who has paid off a debt of the testator's, or who has made advances to the executor to enable him to do so: *Haynes* v. *Forshaw* (1853) 11 Hare 93. See also *Chandler* v. *Thompson* (1619–20). Hob. 266 (sale by temporary representative). A creditor has no specific rights against any property of a deceased debtor of which the executor has taken possession. His right is to sue the executor.

[46] *Whale* v. *Booth* (1784) 4 T.R. 625, note to *Farr* v. *Newman*; *Nugent* v. *Gifford* (1738) 1 Atk. 463. Also *Spackman* v. *Timbrell* (1837) 8 Sim. 253, 260 (leaseholds settled by executor and beneficiary on marriage could not be followed as against beneficiaries under the settlement): *Dilkes* v. *Broadmead* (1860) 2 De G.F. & J. 566; *Wolverhampton Bank* v. *Marston* (1861) 7 H. & N. 148 (assignment by executrix for benefit of testator's creditors after judgment recovered against her for testator's debts, held valid against the judgment creditor). As to preservation of specific legacies, see *ante*, p. 509, *post*, p. 688 and n. 44, *supra*.

[47] See *Re Kemnal and Still* [1923] 1 Ch. 293.

[48] *Whale* v. *Booth*, *ante*.

[49] Bac.Abr. Leases, I. 7.

[50] Administration of Estates Act 1925, s.2(1) (*post*, p. 1114). A sole representative may exercise this power, see pp. 683, 691–692.

[51] *Re Cavendish and Arnold* [1912] W.N. 83; *Re Chaplin etc.* [1922] 2 Ch. 824. As to the statutory power, see *post*, n. 54.

[52] See also Trustee Act 1925, s.16, for an express power to raise money by the sale of any property in possession.

[53] Administration of Estates Act 1925, s.39(1)(iii); Law of Property Act 1925, s.28(1) (as amended); Settled Land Act 1925, s.38. As to restrictions on sale of the principal mansion house, see *ibid.* s.65. For the power to leave two-thirds of the purchase-money on loan, see the Trustee Act 1925, s.10(2). It seems probable that the Settled Land Act powers to sell or

of the surface and minerals separately[54]; and may be made in consideration of a rentcharge.[55] Further, they have power to enter into a contract to effect any such sale or exchange,[56] and such a contract will bind their successors in title.[57]

Finally, a representative may sell or concur[58] with any other person in selling all or any part of the deceased's estate, either subject to prior changes or not, and either together or in lots, by public auction or by private contract, subject to any such conditions[59] respecting title or other matters as he thinks fit, with power to vary any contract for sale, and to buy in at any auction, or to rescind any contract for sale and to resell, without being answerable for any loss.[60]

Sale of deceased's share to surviving partners

The representative of a deceased partner may sell the share of the deceased to the surviving partners, if this can be done fairly and properly. The court will, however, examine such sales closely, for in dealings between the representative of a deceased partner and the surviving partners there may be an inequality of knowledge, leading to inequitable and unfair results.[61] But a surviving partner may take over the share of a deceased partner, even though he is the executor of the deceased partner, since the conflict of interest and duty has been brought about by the testator himself,[62] provided that there is a contract of sale in the articles of partnership. Where, however, there is no agreement for sale in the articles, the conflict between interest and duty where the partner is also sole[63] executor makes it virtually impossible for the executor to enter into an arrangement which is not liable to be set aside,[64] unless the court's approval is obtained.[65]

---

lease import the conditions of s.106 of the Settled Land Act 1925 so that conditions tending to affect the exercise of these powers are void. See *Re Davies* [1932] 1 Ch. 530, 532.

[54] Settled Land Act 1925, s.50. Trustee Act 1925, s.12(2). As to the common law power, see *ante*, n. 51.

[55] Settled Land Act 1925, s.39, which contains certain general regulations as to the consideration for sales under that Act; and see s.40 for regulations as to exchanges.

[56] *Ibid.* s.90(1).

[57] *Ibid.* subs. (2). And see the Administration of Estates Act 1925, s.39(1)(iii).

[58] As to the power of a representative to concur with others in dealing with undivided shares. see *post*, p. 687.

[59] For the power to sell subject to depreciatory conditions, see the Trustee Act 1925, s.13.

[60] *Ibid.* s.12(1).

[61] *Chambers* v. *Howell* (1847) 11 Beav. 6. See Lindley & Banks, *Partnership*, 16th ed., p. 534.

[62] *Hordern* v. *Hordern* [1910] A.C. 465; *Sergeant* v. *National Westminster Bank* [1988] 59 P. & C.R. 182. And see *Re Houghton* [1904] 1 Ch. 622.

[63] If the surviving partner is not sole executor it is, of course, an easier matter to negotiate. *Re Houghton* [1904] 1 Ch. 622.

[64] Lindley & Banks, *Partnership*, 16th ed., 1990, pp. 534 *et seq.*; *Wedderburn* v. *Wedderburn* (1838) 2 Keen 722; *Cook* v. *Collingridge* (1823) Jac. 607, 621.

[65] For procedure, see *post*, pp. 823, 842.

Sale to non-proving executor, etc.

A sale is not voidable merely because, when entered upon, the purchaser may at his option become trustee of the property purchased (*e.g.* by proving a will which relates thereto), if in point of fact he never does become such. Such a purchaser is under no disability, and, in order to avoid a sale, it must be shown that he in fact used his power in such a way as to render it inequitable that the sale should be upheld.[66]

Similarly, a sale may be made by the proving executors to a person who, though appointed an executor by the will, has renounced.[67] Whether such a sale can be supported in equity must depend upon the circumstances. In *Mackintosh* v. *Barber*[68] such a sale was supported, the master having found that it would be for the benefit of the *cestuis que trust* that the contract should be completed.[69]

But a sale to an executor who has not renounced is generally voidable.[70]

Power to mortgage—common law

Even at common law, unless the will peremptorily required an absolute sale, the executor could raise any money required for administration purposes by a partial sale or mortgage of the assets vested in him.[71] The mortgage might have been either of legal or equitable assets,[72] or of a mere claim (*chose in action*)[73]; it might have been by actual assignment or by deposit,[74] and might properly have given the mortgagee a power of sale.[75] Again, the executor might pledge a part of the assets to enable him to administer the estate.[76]

These common law powers, "including power to raise money by mortgage or charge (whether or not by deposit of documents)," are now exercisable by representatives over the real and personal estate of the deceased.[77]

Power to mortgage—statute

In addition to the above-mentioned powers of mortgaging, representatives now have, "for the purposes of administration, or during a minority

---

[66] *Clark* v. *Clark* (1884) 9 App.Cas. 733; *cf. Re Boles* [1902] 1 Ch. 244.

[67] *Mackintosh* v. *Barber* (1822) 1 Bingh. 50, which may be taken to have overruled the statement to the contrary in Co.Litt. 113 *a*.

[68] (1822) 1 Bingh. 50.

[69] Sugd. on Pow., 8th ed., 125.

[70] See *Holder* v. *Holder* [1968] Ch. 353.

[71] *Mead* v. *Orrery* (1745) 3 Atk. 235, 239; *Scott* v. *Tyler* (1788) 2 Dick. 712, 725; *M'Leod* v. *Drummond* (1810) 17 Ves. 152, 154; *Child* v. *Thorley* (1880) 16 Ch.D. 151; *Re O'Donnell* [1905] 1 Ir.R. 406 (sub-mortgage); *Halley* v. *O'Brien* [1920] 1 Ir.R. 149, 330. And see Coote, *Mortgages*, 9th ed., 422.

[72] *Nugent* v. *Gifford* (1738) 1 Atk. 463; *Graham* v. *Drummond* [1896] 1 Ch. 968. There is no longer any distinction between legal and equitable assets.

[73] *Scott* v. *Tyler* (1788) 2 Dick. 712, 724; *Vane* v. *Rigden* (1870) L.R. 5 Ch. 663, 667.

[74] *Vane* v. *Rigden* (1870) L.R. 5 Ch. 663, 667, 670.

[75] *Russell* v. *Plaice* (1854) 18 Beav. 21.

[76] *Ibid.* 28, 29.

[77] Administration of Estates Act 1925, s.39(1) (*post*, p. 1132).

of any beneficiary or the subsistence of any life interest, or until the period of distribution arrives," power to raise money by legal mortgage to discharge incumbrances, or for equality of exchange, or for any one of the several other purposes indicated in section 71 of the Settled Land Act 1925.[78] Further, they have (for the same purposes) power to shift incumbrances (with the consent of the incumbrancer), and to make provisions therefor by legal mortgage or otherwise.[79] They may also (with the incumbrancer's consent) vary the provisions (including the rate of interest charged) of an instrument creating an incumbrance on the estate of the deceased, and (with the life consent) may charge that incumbrance on any part of the estate (whether already charged therewith or not) by way of additional security, or of consolidation of securities, and by way of legal mortgage or otherwise make provision accordingly.[80] And they have power to enter into a contract to effect any such mortgage, charge or other disposition authorised by the Settled Land Act 1925,[81] and such contract will bind their successors in title.[82]

Finally, a representative may, "for giving effect to beneficial interests," limit or demise land for a term, with or without impeachment for waste, to trustees on usual trusts for raising or securing money for which the land, or any part thereof, is liable.[83]

Mortgages to building societies

Unless he is authorised so to do by the will, an executor is not entitled on behalf of the estate to take shares in a building society. Where a mortgage is made by an executor to a building society to secure not only money advanced and interest, but also all money becoming due from him as shareholder, the mortgage does not bind the estate so as to charge it with the executor's liabilities as a shareholder. But if the advance is made in good faith to the executor in that capacity, and the mortgage is not merely a colourable device for securing an advance to the executor in his personal capacity, the mortgage is good and binds the estate to the extent of the money advanced and reasonable interest thereon.[84]

Power to lease—common law

The common law power of a representative to grant leases was of a somewhat limited nature. A representative upon whom a term of years had devolved might have granted an underlease thereof.[85] But such a trans-

---

[78] Settled Land Act 1925, s.71; Town and Country Planning Act 1971, s.275; Agricultural Holdings Act 1986, s.88. See also the Trustee Act 1925, s.16(1), for an express power to raise money by mortgage of property in possession.
[79] Settled Land Act 1925, s.69.
[80] *Ibid.* s.70. See also *ibid.* s.49(1)(c) (power to shift equitable charge under a settlement).
[81] *Ibid.* s.90(1).
[82] *Ibid.* subs. (2); and see the Administration of Estates Act 1925, s.39(1)(iii).
[83] Administration of Estates Act 1925, s.40; see *post*, pp. 685, 1133.
[84] *Thorne* v. *Thorne* [1893] 3 Ch. 196.
[85] Bac.Abr.Leases, 1, 7; *Re Owen* [1912] 1 Ch. 519 (where a sub-lease was made at a loss).

action was an exceptional mode of dealing with the assets, and those who accepted title in that way had to take it subject to the question whether it was the best way of administering the assets.[86] Thus it seems that a lease granted by an administrator, even at full value, to a person having notice that the beneficiaries required a sale might have been set aside.[87]

A will might expressly or by implication confer a power to lease,[88] but this could not be inferred simply from a trust for sale, so that specific performance of an underlease so granted was not allowed.[89] But an underlease which in practice amounted to a full assignment was held to be authorised by a trust for sale.[90]

At the present time, however, not only is the common law power of a representative to grant an underlease extended to the granting of leases of real estate generally,[91] but, further, a person taking a lease or underlease from a representative now receives the benefit of the statutory protection afforded to a "purchaser"[92] under the provisions hereinafter discussed.[93]

Power to lease—statute

In addition to the above-mentioned powers of leasing, a representative now has, "for the purposes of administration, or during a minority of any beneficiary or the subsistence of any life interest, or until the period of distribution arrives," by reference[94] to the Settled Land Act 1925, the following powers of leasing, namely:

(1) A power, under section 41 of that Act, of leasing the land of the deceased vested in him, or any part thereof,[95] or any easement, right or privilege of any kind over or in relation to the estate, for any purpose, whether or not involving waste, for any term not exceeding[96]:

    (i) In case of a building lease, 999 years[97];
    (ii) In case of a mining lease, 100 years[98];
    (iii) In case of a forestry lease, 999 years[99];
    (iv) In case of any other lease, 50 years.

---

[86] *Oceanic Steam Co.* v. *Sutherberry* (1880) 16 Ch.D. 236, 243; *Keating* v. *Keating* (1835) 1 L1. & G. 133. *Johnson* v. *Clarke* [1928] Ch. 847.

[87] *Drohan* v. *Drohan* (1809) 1 Ball & B. 185 (where, however, the lease was made at an undervalue).

[88] See *Re North* [1909] 1 Ch. 625.

[89] *Evans* v. *Jackson* (1836) 8 Sim. 217.

[90] *Re Judd and Poland* [1906] 1 Ch. 684.

[91] See *ante*, p. 466.

[92] "Purchaser" includes a "lessee"; Administration of Estates Act 1925, s.55(1)(xviii).

[93] See *post*, pp. 677 *et seq.*

[94] Administration of Estates Act 1925, s.39; Law of Property Act 1925, s.28(1) (as amended), introducing powers conferred by the Settled Land Act 1925.

[95] The surface and minerals may be leased separately: Settled Land Act 1925, s.50.

[96] These limits apply only to the exercise of the statutory power and can be ignored where the common law power is effectively invoked. See *ante*, p. 670.

[97] For special regulations about building leases, see *ibid.* ss.44, 46; *Re Grosvenor's S.E.* [1933] Ch. 97.

[98] For special regulations about mining leases, see the Settled Land Act 1925, ss.45–47.

[99] For special regulations about forestry leases, see *ibid.* s.48.

Provisions governing the grant of such leases are contained in section 42, and it is expressly provided by section 43 that the power of leasing extends to the grant of leases to give effect (so far as the law permits) to covenants for renewal, and to confirm void or voidable leases.

(2) A power, with or without consideration, to grant by writing an option[1] to purchase or take a lease of the land, or any part thereof, at a fixed price or rent.[2] Such option must be made exercisable within an agreed number of years, not exceeding 10.[3]

(3) A power to accept, with or without consideration, a surrender of any lease, or a regrant of any land granted in fee simple.[4]

(4) A power to enter into a contract to effect any such lease or other disposition authorised by the Settled Land Act 1925.[5] Such a contract will bind successors in title.[6]

Effect of condition against assigning or underletting

The power of a representative to assign or underlet a term of years vested in him may be restrained by the provisions contained in the lease. If a lease is made subject to a condition against, and with a proviso for reentry in the event of, any assignment or underlease made by the lessee without the lessor's licence,[7] the term will nevertheless devolve upon the lessee's representatives without breach of the condition.[8] But when the term has so devolved, if the representative is expressly named in the condition or proviso (or, as is now of common occurrence, by reason of a wide definition of the expression "lessee"), he is bound thereby.[9] Thus, where a lease was made upon condition that the lessee, his executors or assigns, should not assign without the consent of the lessor, an assignment by the

---

[1] Query whether this would include a power to grant a right of pre-emption. See generally *Pritchard* v. *Briggs* [1980] Ch. 338, 362. CA.

[2] *Ibid.* s.51(1). Although a personal representative might at common law grant an underlease, if necessary for the purposes of administration, he could not given an option to purchase: *Oceanic Steam Co.* v. *Sutherberry* (1880) 16 Ch.D. 236.

[3] Settled Land Act 1925, s.51(2).

[4] Settled Land Act 1925, s.52.

[5] *Ibid.* s.90(1).

[6] *Ibid.* subs. (2); and see the Administration of Estates Act 1925, s.39(1)(iii).

[7] Such licence must not be unreasonably withheld (Landlord and Tenant Act 1927, s.19(1)) and no fine is payable (Law of Property Act, s.144). See Woodfall, *Landlord and Tenant*, 28th ed., 1978.

[8] *Parry* v. *Harbert* (1539) Dyer 45 *b*. It has been questioned whether a bequest of a term by will to a specific legatee is not a breach of a condition not to assign: *Berry* v. *Taunton* (1594) Cro.Eliz. 331; but see *Fox* v. *Swann* (1655) Sty. 482; *Crusoe* v. *Bugby* (1771) 3 Wils. 237; *Doe* v. *Bevan* (1815) 3 M. & S. 361. In principle it would seem that the opinion of Bayley J. in *Doe* v. *Bevan*, is correct, that assignment and such like words apply only to transfer *inter vivos*, and that if the lessor desires to exclude a specific devise of the term, he must do so by express words: Woodfall, 28th ed., 1978. A covenant against assignment is not broken by an involuntary alienation—*e.g.* to the trustee in bankruptcy of the lessee.

[9] *Roe* v. *Harrison* (1788) 2 T.R. 425; see also *Doe* v. *Bevan*, 3 M. & S. 361; *Lloyd* v. *Crispe* (1813) 5 Taunt. 249; *Phillips* v. *Everard* (1831) 5 Sim. 102.

administrator of the lessee was held to be a breach of the condition, since the administrator was an assign within the condition.[10]

But it seems on principle that even without express mention of the representative a covenant or condition will now be binding because a contract made by a deceased person, unless personal to him, binds his representatives.[11]

There are, however, old authorities to the contrary raising presumptions or principles of construction sufficient for a contrary intention to be inferred from the absence of express mention in the lease.[12]

Representative may not become lessee of the estate

Since a representative is precluded from purchasing the assets of the deceased for himself[13] he cannot purchase for himself leaseholds vested in himself as representative, nor can he grant to himself a lease of property comprised in the deceased's estate.[14] On the same principle, a representative cannot obtain for his own benefit a renewal of a lease forming part of the estate, even if the lessor has refused to grant him a renewal for the beneficiaries.[15] He becomes a constructive trustee of all such purchases.[16]

Beneficial joint tenants can make a lease to one of their number,[17] and this principle was, in *Cowper* v. *Fletcher*,[18] applied to co-executors. But it seems difficult to see why the general rule,[19] which forbids a representative from purchasing any part of the property, should not apply so as to prevent him from taking a lease thereof. At any rate, if co-executors allow one of their number to take a lease at less than a fair occupation rent, they may be charged with such rent,[20] and any representative who does in fact obtain a lease from the estate will be held accountable as trustee for all profits made while bearing personally all losses.[21]

---

[10] *Sir Wm. More's Case* (1584) Cro.Eliz. 26.

[11] See the Law of Property Act 1925, ss.79, 80(2).

[12] *Anon.* (1549) Dyer 66, *a*, pl. 8; *Seers* v. *Hind* (1791) 1 Ves. 294. See also Touchst. 133, and see cases cited in n. 9, *ante*.

[13] See *post*, pp. 703–713. As to exceptions in the case of payment of debts by the executor and appropriation of chattels in compensation, see *ante*, p. 467, and as to where the testator himself has brought about a conflict of interest and duty, see *ante*, p. 668.

[14] See also *Re Thompson* [1930] 1 Ch. 203 (executor may not take for himself (in competition) a tenancy of premises on which the business of the deceased is to be conducted by his co-executors). The powers contained in s.68 of the Settled Land Act 1925 to enable the trustees of the settlement to negotiate with the tenant for life in granting leases, etc., to him do not seem to be applicable to representatives exercising the powers of a tenant for life in normal circumstances.

[15] *Keech* v. *Sandford* (1726) Sel.Ca.Ch. 61; *Re Knowles' Will Trusts* [1948] 1 All E.R. 866; *Re Biss* [1903] 2 Ch. 40; *Re Jarvis* [1958] 1 W.L.R. 815; *Industrial Development* v. *Cooley* [1972] 1 W.L.R. 443. As to the duration of the rule, see *Boardman* v. *Phipps* [1967] 2 A.C. 46, 131, and *post*, p. 704, see also [1969] 33 Conv. 161.

[16] *Re Edwards* [1981] 3 W.L.R. 15, 25.

[17] Co.Litt. 186 *a*.

[18] (1865) 34 L.J.Q.B. 187.

[19] See *post*, p. 707.

[20] *De Cordova* v. *De Cordova* (1879) 4 App.Cas. 692.

[21] *Re Jarvis* [1958] 1 W.L.R. 815 and see *post*, p. 707.

Representative may in certain circumstances purchase the reversion

A representative is only precluded from purchasing trust assets or from deriving a personal advantage from his fiduciary position, so that while he may not purchase for himself the reversion on a lease forming part of the estate, so long as there is a right or customary prospect of renewal, thus intercepting and cutting off that right or chance of renewal,[22] the strict rule against renewal of the lease for his own benefit does not apply to the purchase of the freehold reversion.[23]

This distinction, which has stood for over 160 years,[24] can be justified on the ground that in the case of renewal there is in effect a purchase of a part of the trust property,[25] whereas the reversion is something different in nature from and extraneous to the lease. This distinction is not, it is submitted, to be regarded as overruled by the Court of Appeal in *Protheroe* v. *Protheroe*,[26] where none of the relevant authorities were cited. The principle, laid down in that case, that a trustee owning the leasehold who gets in the freehold holds the latter as part of the trust property should not apply where the purchaser can show that he has neither deprived the trust or estate of any asset or obtained any advantage, either as regards the opportunity to make the purchase or the terms on which it was made, from his fiduciary position.

Exercise of option

Where a testator granted a person an option to purchase land and later appointed him his executor, the subsequent fiduciary relationship did not preclude the executor from exercising the option.[27]

Effect of administration action

The representative's power of disposal over the assets is not controlled or suspended by the mere commencement of an action, on the part of a creditor of the deceased, for the administration of his estate. The power of the representative to dispose of, and make a good title to, any part of the assets continues until there has been judgment in the action.[28]

[22] *Phillips* v. *Phillips* (1885) 29 Ch.D. 673; *Re Bias* [1903] 2 Ch. 40.
[23] *Randall* v. *Russell* (1817) 3 Mer. 190; *Longton* v. *Wilsby* (1887) 67 L.T. 770; *Bevan* v. *Webb* [1905] 1 Ch. 620.
[24] Indeed, it appears to have been accepted by Lord Hardwicke L.C. as early as *Norris* v. *Le Neve* (1743) 3 Atk. 26.
[25] *Phipps* v. *Boardman* [1964] 1 W.L.R. 993, 1009, *per* Wilberforce J.
[26] [1968] 1 W.L.R. 519; [1968] 1 All E.R. 1111. See for further discussion (1968) 84 L.Q.R. 310: "The Rationale of *Keech* v. *Sandford*" by S. Cretney 33 *Conveyancer* 161, and, as to fiduciary relationships in general, articles by L. S. Sealy in (1962) C.L.J. 69, and *ibid.* (1963) C.L.J. 119. See also D. W. M. Waters, *The Constructive Trust*.
[27] *Re Mulholland* [1949] 1 All E.R. 460.
[28] *Neeves* v. *Burrage* (1849) 14 Q.B. 504; see *post*, p. 841.

Purchaser and application of purchase-money

Even under the old law a purchaser or mortgagee, though he knew that he was dealing with a representative, was not bound to see that the purchase or mortgage money was properly applied.[29] "It is of great consequence that no rules should be laid down here, which may impede executors in their administration, or render their disposition of the testator's effects unsafe, or uncertain to the purchaser; his title is complete by sale and delivery; what becomes of the price is no concern of the purchaser: This observation applies equally to mortgages or pledges, and even to the present instance, where assignable bonds were merely pledged, without assignment."[30]

Now, under section 14 of the Trustee Act 1925 and notwithstanding anything to the contrary in the will,[31] the receipt in writing of a representative[32] for any money, securities or other personal property payable or transferable to him under any trust or power is a sufficient discharge to the person so paying or transferring, and exonerates him from seeing to, or being answerable for, the application thereof. Further, section 17 of the same Act (which applies to the duties incident to the office of a representative[33]) provides that no purchaser[34] or mortgagee[35] should be concerned to see that the money paid or advanced is wanted, or that no more than is wanted is raised, or otherwise as to the application thereof.[36]

Sale, etc., by representative for his own purpose

Formerly, at law, an executor might, in the absence of fraud to which the purchaser was a party, make a valid sale of a deceased person's property in satisfaction of his own private debt, though the purchaser knew that the goods sold were those of the deceased.[37] But in equity, generally speaking, the executor or administrator could make no valid sale or pledge of the assets ostensibly as a security for, or in payment of, his own debt, on the principle that the transaction itself gave the purchaser or mortgagee notice

---

[29] *M'Leod* v. *Drummond* (1810) 17 Ves. 152, 154.

[30] *Per* Lord Thurlow, in *Scott* v. *Tyler* (1788) Dick, 712, 725.

[31] Trustee Act 1925, s.14(3), which negatives *ibid.* s.69(2) (*post*, p. 1098).

[32] A sole personal representative, as such, can give a valid receipt even for the proceeds of land: Law of Property Act 1925, s.27(2); Administration of Estates Act 1925, s.2(1) (*post*, p. 1114).

[33] Trustee Act 1925, s.68(17).

[34] The Trustee Act 1925 contains no definition of a "purchaser," but the definition in the Administration of Estates Act 1925 includes a "lessee," see *ante*, n. 92.

[35] A mortgagee for the purpose of the Trustee Act 1925 includes a chargee by way of legal mortgage, and relates to every estate and interest regarded in equity as merely a security for money, and every person deriving title under the original mortgagee: Trustee Act 1925, s.68(17).

[36] See also the Settled Land Act 1925, s.95; Law of Property Act 1925, s.27(1).

[37] See *Whale* v. *Booth* (1784) 4 T.R. 625; *Farr* v. *Newman* (1792) *ibid.* 642, 645; *Doe* v. *Fellows* (1832) 2 Cr. & J. 481; 2 Tyrw, 460. *Semble*, if the purchaser knew the debts were unpaid there would have been sufficient fraud to vitiate the sale: *Whale* v. *Booth*, *ante cf.* the Administration of Estates Act 1925, s.36(8), *post*, pp. 678, 1062, 1079, 1130.

of the misapplication, and necessarily involved his participation in the breach of trust.[38]

Though the rule of equity now prevails,[39] it is interesting to notice that the effect of the protection afforded by the 1925 legislation to purchasers in good faith is to restore original common law principles. But a representative had no right to raise money for his own purposes or otherwise than for the purposes of administration or other authorised objects.

Position before 1926 of purchaser on such sale—principles

Where, before 1926,[40] a disposition was made by a representative not for the purposes of administration, the position of the purchaser or mortgagee may be summarised according to the following principles:

1. A representative purporting to act for administration purposes only would generally confer a good title upon a person in whose favour he made a transfer or conveyance of the legal estate.[41]

2. A representative selling or mortgaging part of the deceased's estate was presumed to be acting in discharge of the duties imposed upon him as such representative, unless there was something in the transaction showing the contrary; and the contrary was not made out merely from the fact that the conveyance or mortgage did not purport to be made by him in that capacity.[42] Further, it was not enough to impeach a mortgage of part of the assets that it was made to secure a debt originally contracted on the personal security of the executor, and without reference to the assets.[43]

3. A mortgage made by a representative, known to be such, for a purpose other than administration, would be set aside as against a mortgagee having notice of the purpose for which the money was raised.[44] Thus a mortgagee having actual notice that there were no debts, and no reason being suggested for the mortgage, was not safe in lending.[45]

4. A mortgage by deposit made by a representative, not known to be such, for a purpose other than administration, would not be supported, the

---

[38] *Bonney* v. *Ridgard* (1784) 1 Cox 145, 148; *Scott* v. *Tyler* (1788) 2 Dick. 712, 724; 2 Bro.C.C. 136; *M'Leod* v. *Drummond* (1810) 17 Ves. 152, 170; *Keane* v. *Robarts* (1819) 4 Madd. 357, 358; *Watkins* v. *Cheek* (1825) 2 Sim. & Stu. 199, 205; *Cubbidge* v. *Boatwright* (1826) 1 Russ. 549; *Wilson* v. *Moore* (1834) 1 M. & K. 337; *Eland* v. *Eland* (1839) 4 My. & Cr. 420, 427; *Pannell* v. *Hurley* (1845) 2 Coll. 241; *Haynes* v. *Forshaw* (1853) 11 Hare 93, 99; *Cole* v. *Muddle* (1852) 10 Hare 186; *Downes* v. *Power* (1814) 2 Ball. & B. 491; *Collinson* v. *Lister* (1855) 20 Beav. 356; *Re Morgan* (1881) 18 Ch.D. 93, 98; *Ricketts* v. *Lewis* (1882) 20 Ch.D. 745. See also *Nelson* v. *Arholt* [1948] 1 K.B. 339 and note 45 *post*.

[39] Supreme Court Act 1982, s.49, replacing the Judicature Act 1873, s.25(11).

[40] The position of such a purchaser before 1926 is still relevant not only in matters of title, but in following the later legislation.

[41] See, *e.g. Berry* v. *Gibbons* (1873) L.R. 8 Ch. 747.

[42] *Re Venn and Furze* [1894] 2 Ch. 101, 114; and see *Re Henson, post*.

[43] *Miles* v. *Durnford* (1852) 2 De G.M. & G. 641.

[44] See *Wilson* v. *Moore* (1834) 1 M. & K. 337.

[45] *Re Verrell* [1903] 1 Ch. 65. *Secus*, after 1925, see the Administration of Estates Act 1925, s.36(8), *infra*. And *cf. Re Henson* [1908] 2 Ch. 356 (mortgage expressed to be made for payment of legacies).

equity of the estate being prior to the equity of the mortgagee.[46] It is conceived that a legal mortgage made in such circumstances would have been supported against the equitable claim of the deceased's estate.

5. Executors by assenting, expressly or by implication, cease to hold property as executors, and though they might have held as trustees, they were precluded from making title as executors.[47] Thus, if, as trustees, they had no power of disposition, a sale by them to a person who had, or ought to have had, notice of the assent, would have been set aside.[48]

6. The last principle (here mentioned) applicable to dispositions made by representatives to purchasers before 1926, was stated by Romer J. in *Graham* v. *Drummond*[49] as follows: "I think it is settled law that, if an executor who is also residuary legatee sells or mortgages an asset of the testator for valuable consideration to a person who has no notice of the existence of unsatisfied debts of the testator, or of any ground which rendered it improper for the executor so to deal with the asset, that person's purchase or mortgage is valid against any unsatisfied creditor of the testator."

The same principle applied to a sale or mortgage by an executor, who was also a specific legatee, of the subject of the specific legacy for the satisfaction of his private debt.[50] And the purchaser from one of several executors, who was also a legatee, was not concerned to inquire whether the other creditors had given their assent.[51]

The principle applied whether or not the purchaser or mortgagee acquired the legal estate,[52] and therefore applied to both legal and equitable assets.[53] But it did not apply where either the executor or the court administering the testator's estate retained control over the asset, the purchaser in such a case taking subject to the risk of the claims of the testator's creditors.[54]

Position after 1925 of purchaser on such sale

The powers conferred upon representatives by section 2(1) of the Administration of Estates Act 1925 are not expressly made exercisable for the purposes of administration only; but being merely extensions of the common law powers they remain subject to their former limitations. On the other hand, the powers conferred by section 39 are expressed to be "for

---

[46] *Re Morgan* (1881) 18 Ch.D. 93.

[47] *Attenborough* v. *Solomon* [1913] A.C. 76. And see *post*, p. 1049.

[48] *Wise* v. *Whitburn* [1924] 1 Ch. 460. But see now the Administration of Estates Act 1925, s.36(4), (5), (6) and (7), *post*, pp. 1049 *et seq.*

[49] [1896] 1 Ch. 968, 974. And see the cases there cited.

[50] *Taylor* v. *Hawkins* (1803) 8 Ves. 209; *Hall* v. *Andrews* (1872) 27 L.T. 195; 20 W.R. 799.

[51] *Cole* v. *Miles* (1852) 10 Hare 179, 186.

[52] *Graham* v. *Drummond* [1896] 1 Ch. 968, 985. *cf. Re Morgan*, *ante*, which is however, clearly distinguishable.

[53] *Graham* v. *Drummond*, *ante*. There is now no distinction between legal and equitable assets.

[54] See *Graham* v. *Drummond*, *ante*, and the cases there cited.

purposes of administration, or during a minority of any beneficiary or the subsistence of any life interest, or until the period of distribution arrives." Representatives are not authorised to exercise their powers for their own purposes.

A purchaser from a representative after 1925, however, has greater protection than he would have received under the principles in force before 1926. The first two of those principles,[55] being in favour of a purchaser, would seem to remain applicable to dispositions made after 1925. But the third principle,[56] (relating to the effect of notice by a mortgagee of the purpose for which a personal representative is raising the money) is materially affected by section 36(8) of the Administration of Estates Act 1925, which enacts that a conveyance[57] of a legal estate by a representative to a purchaser is not invalidated by reason only that the purchaser may have notice that all the debts, liabilities, funeral, and testamentary or administration expenses, duties, and legacies of the deceased have not been discharged or provided for.

For the purposes of section 36, a "purchaser" means a lessee, mortgagee or other person who is in good faith acquires an interest in property for money or money's worth.[58]

Subsection (8) in effect enables a purchaser to refrain from making any inquiries as to the purposes for which the disposition by the representatives is being made. It is conceived, however, that if he does in fact know that the representatives, by making a disposition in his favour, are committing a direct breach of trust (as opposed to a mere inference arising from knowledge that all debts are paid), he will not be a purchaser in good faith so as to be protected under this subsection.

Sale by representative of life tenant

On the death of a tenant for life of settled land, if the land remains settled, his special representatives hold upon trust to convey, as provided by section 7 of the Settled Land Act 1925, to the person next entitled. They are, it seems,[59] thus in the position of the representatives of any other sole trustee,[60] having powers to perform the trust but no more. They do not normally require, and have no power, to sell for purposes of administration, and if a sale is necessary for raising inheritance tax a sole representa-

---

[55] The first principle relates to a disposition purporting to be made for administration purposes: the second relates to the presumption that the representative is acting in discharge of his duties. See *ante*, p. 676.

[56] *Ante*, p. 676.

[57] A conveyance in the Administration of Estates Act 1925, "includes a mortgage, charge by way of legal mortgage, lease, . . . release and every other assurance of property or of an interest therein by any instrument . . . " (s.55(1)(iii) (*post*, p. 1148).

[58] Administration of Estates Act 1925, ss.36(11), 55(1)(xviii).

[59] A contrary view was expressed in earlier editions.

[60] See *post*, p. 697, and 23 *Conveyancer* 360, Administration of Estates Act 1925, s.55(1); Settled Land Act 1925, ss.110(3), 117(1)(xviii) and see *post*, p. 689.

tive cannot give a good receipt.[61] Thus if a purchaser has actual notice that no inheritance tax is payable he does not obtain a good title.[62]

Purchaser of a legal estate in land protected by assent and indorsement

The difficulty which arose before 1926 from the fact that by making an assent (possibly unknown to himself) the representative ceased to be in a position to make a disposition as such[63] has mainly disappeared, for in order to pass a legal estate in land an assent must now in writing, signed by the representative, and naming the person in whose favour it is given.[64] Further protection is given to a purchaser[65] from a personal representative by the Administration of Estates Act 1925, s.36, which provides for indorsement of notice of the assent upon the grant[66] and enables a purchaser to rely upon a statement by the representative that he has not given or made a previous assent or conveyance,[67] and upon the assent or conveyance having been made in favour of the person entitled.[68]

Purchaser of equitable interest in land

The provisions mentioned above afford protection to purchasers of legal estates from representatives but do not apply to equitable interests or to personalty. Thus where representatives, in whom a legal estate in land is vested,[69] in *devastavit* or breach of trust make a disposition of a mere equitable interest in the land (as in the case of a mortgage by deposit) for their own purposes, the equity of the persons beneficially interested in the estate of the deceased prevails over that of the purchaser from the representatives.[70] This would appear to be so whether or not such purchaser knew that he was purchasing from representatives, so long as the representative is not beneficially entitled.[71] Thus, in view of the sixth principle mentioned above[72] a purchaser or mortgagee from an executor of an equitable interest in property, to which the executor is (subject to administration purposes) beneficially entitled, is protected from the claims of the testator's creditors, unless he had notice of the existence of unsatisfied debts of the

[61] See the Settled Land Act 1925, ss.8(3)(6), 94. See also 71 S.J. 224, 243, 262; and 171 L.T. 160.
[62] See *Wise* v. *Whitburn* [1924] 1 Ch. 460.
[63] See the fifth principle mentioned as being applicable before 1926, *ante*, p. 677 and notes thereto.
[64] Administration of Estates Act 1925, s.36(4). See *post*, pp. 1057.
[65] See n. 58; *ante*.
[66] Administration of Estates Act 1925, s.36(5).
[67] Administration of Estates Act 1925, s.36(6). See *post*, pp. 1061, 1130.
[68] Administration of Estates Act 1925, s.36(7). See *post*, pp. 1061, 1130.
[69] If the legal estate were vested in some person other than the personal representatives, the priority of the conflicting equitable claims would seem to depend upon the priority of notice given to such person: see the Law of Property Act 1925, s.137; 1 Wolst. & Ch., 13th ed., pp. 206 *et seq.*
[70] See *Re Morgan* (1881) 18 Ch.D. 93 (mortgage by deposit: mortgagee unaware that he was dealing with an executor). See also the Law of Property Act 1925, s.13.
[71] See below.
[72] See *ante*, p. 677 and *Graham* v. *Drummond* [1896] 1 Ch. 968.

testator, or of any ground which rendered it improper for the executor so to deal with the property.

Purchaser of personalty

The sixth principle would seem also to apply to a disposition of any interest, legal or equitable, in pure personalty.[73] The reason for this principle is that a purchaser should not be concerned to inquire whether or not an implied assent has been made in favour of the executor-legatee.[74] Where the executor is not beneficially interested, so that the sixth principle[75] does not apply, it seems that the purchaser of pure personalty is also fully protected[76] except possibly in the case of chattels specifically bequeathed.[77]

Fraudulent purchaser is not protected

Fraud will vitiate any transaction; nor does a purchaser, not taking in good faith, obtain statutory protection for dealings with representatives.[78] If, therefore, a person concerts with a representative and obtains the deceased's property at a nominal price, or at a fraudulent undervalue,[79] or if he concerts to apply the real value to the purchase of other property for himself, or in extinguishing the private debt of the representative, or in any other manner contrary to the duty of the representative as such, he will become liable for the full value.[80] Thus, where the person to whom an executor collusively conveys the property knows that the executor is acting in violation of his trust, and in fraud of the persons interested in the due administration of the assets, the fraud vitiates the transaction, and the attempt to transfer the property is ineffectual and void.[81]

That an executor may waste the money is not alone sufficient to invalidate the sale or mortgage; it must further appear that the purchaser or mortgagee participated in the *devastavit*, or breach of duty in the executor.[82]

Where there is collusion such as to render a dealing by a representative invalid, not only a creditor, but a legatee, whether general or specific, is

[73] s.36(8) does not apply, for "legal estate" in that subsection only applies to legal estates, charges and interests in or over land: Administration of Estates Act 1925, s.55(1)(vii).
[74] See *Cole* v. *Miles* (1852) 10 Hare 179, 186.
[75] See *ante*, p. 677.
[76] See *ante*, p. 666. The decision in *Re Morgan* (1881) 18 Ch.D. 93 does not seem to extend to pure personalty.
[77] See *ante*, p. 666.
[78] See definition of "purchaser" in the Administrative of Estates Act 1925, ss.36(11), 55(1)(xviii).
[79] *Rice* v. *Gordon* (1848) 11 Beav. 265 (sale by an administrator to his brother and co-partner at gross undervalue, set aside).
[80] *Scott* v. *Tyler* (1788) 2 Dick. 712, 725. See also the Administration of Estates Act 1925, s.28 (reproducing 43 Eliz. c. 8), as to treating a collusive purchaser as an executor *de son tort*; *ante*, pp. 93 *et seq.*
[81] *Doe* v. *Fallows* (1832) 2 Cr. & J. 481; 2 Tryw. 460.
[82] *Whale* v. *Booth* (1784) 4 Tr. 625n.

entitled to follow the assets.[83] But he must enforce his right within a reasonable time, or it may be barred by his acquiescence.[84]

Powers of investment

There is no distinction[85] between the powers of investmment conferred expressly or by statute upon trustees and those so conferred for purposes of administration upon representatives. Reference for detailed consideration of this topic should be made to the leading works on trusts[86] and to the enactments mentioned below.

The statutory power of investment is now found in the Trustee Investment Act 1961, which repeals section 1 of the Trustee Act 1925 and, subject to express powers contained in the will,[87] allows investment of half the fund in "equities," provides for the fund to be divided for that purpose and obliges representatives to obtain and consider proper advice. There is power under the Trustee Act 1925 to invest in bearer securities,[88] to deposit money in the bank, and to pay calls on shares.[89] There is power for the representative to concur in the reconstruction or amalgamation of a company.[90] There is also power for a representative to invest in land and in the other forms of investment specified in section 73 of the Settled Land Act 1925.[91]

However a power to purchase freehold land as an investment may not be construed as a power to purchase a freehold house with vacant possession as home for the tenant for life and the testator's children.[92]

Powers of management

Whilst in possession of any land forming part of the deceased's estate, representatives have the powers of management and superintendence indicated in section 102 of the Settled Land Act 1925.[93] These powers include a

[83] *Hill* v. *Simpson* (1802) 7 Ves. 152; *M'Leod* v. *Drummond* (1810) 17 Ves. 169; *Wilson* v. *Moore* (1834) M. & K. 337. And see the Administration of Estates Act 1925, s.38(1); *cf.* s.32(2). As to tracing assets, see *post*, p. 1081.

[84] *Elliot* v. *Merryman* (1740) 2 Atk. 41; *Andrew* v. *Wrigley* (1792) 4 Bro.C.C. 125; *M'Leod* v. *Drummond* (1810) 14 Ves. 353, 359, 363; *ibid.* 17 Ves. 152.

[85] Under the Trustee Act 1925, s.68(17), "trust" includes the duties incident to the office of a personal representative, and "trustee," where the context admits, includes a personal representative. This definition applies to the Trustee Investments Act 1961 (s.17(4)).

[86] See, *e.g.* Lewin, *Trusts*, 16th ed., pp. 321–384.

[87] See the Trustee Act 1925, s.69(2); Settled Land Act 1925, s.119(1)(*a*); *Re Harari* [1949] 1 All E.R. 430.

The Trustee Investment Act 1961 has been amended by the Building Societies Act 1986 to allow investment in deposits and shares of a Building Society (*ibid.* s.120 and Sched. 18, Part I) and the Financial Services Act 1986 allows investment in authorised unit trusts (*ibid.* Sched. 16).

[88] s.7.

[89] s.11.

[90] s.10(3).

[91] By virtue of the Administration of Estates Act 1925, s.39; Law of Property Act 1925, s.28(1); *Re Wellsted* [1949] Ch. 296.

[92] *Re Power* [1947] Ch. 572.

[93] Administration of Estates Act 1925, s.39(1); Law of Property Act 1925, s.28(1).

power to fell timber,[94] to erect or pull down and repair buildings,[95] to continue the working of mines and quarries,[96] to drain or otherwise improve the land,[97] to insure against loss by fire,[98] to make arrangements with tenants,[99] to determine tenancies and accept surrenders of leases,[1] and generally to deal with the land in a proper and due course of management.[2] The expenses of management are payable out of the produce of the land.[3]

The powers of management and of leasing and accepting surrenders of leases, conferred on representatives by reference to the powers of trustees for sale,[4] may be revocably delegated from time to time, by writing, signed by them, to any person of full age (not being merely an annuitant) for the time being beneficially entitled in possession to the net rents and profits of the land during his life or for any less period.[5]

Power to effect improvements

Representatives may, "for purposes of administration, or during a minority of any beneficiary or the substance of any life interest, or until the period of distribution arrives,"[6] effect certain authorised improvements[7] upon any land vested in them as such. Further, without prejudice to the beneficial interests of beneficiaries, they may pay for such improvements out of money forming part of the deceased's estate,[8] and may raise the money required by a legal mortgage.[9]

Power to enter into contracts

In addition to the powers of compromise and investment already mentioned (which are inherently contractual) representatives may contract to make any sale, exchange, mortgage, charge, lease or other disposition, or

[94] Settled Land Act 1925, s.102(2)(a); see also ibid. s.66; and as to restrictions against commission of waste: ibid. ss.66, 89. As to position of tenant for life, with respect to cutting of ripe non-timber trees, see Re Harker [1938] Ch. 323.
[95] Settled Land Act 1925, s.102(2)(b).
[96] Ibid. sub-para. (c).
[97] Ibid. sub-para. (d). As to general power to effect improvements, see below.
[98] Settled Land Act 1925, s.102(2)(e). See also the Trustee Act 1925, s.19. As to the application of the insurance money, see ibid. s.20; 4 Wolst. & Ch., 13th ed., pp. 23 et seq. And see ante, p. 538.
[99] Settled Land Act 1925, s.102(2)(f). See also ibid. ss.59 (power to vary leases and to give licences and consents) and 60 (to appropriate rents).
[1] Settled Land Act 1925, s.102(2)(g); see also ibid. s.52.
[2] Settled Land Act 1925, s.102(2)(h).
[3] Ibid. subs. (3).
[4] Administration of Estates Act 1925, s.39(1)(p. 1132).
[5] Law of Property Act 1925, s.29; and see post, p. 702.
[6] Administration of Estates Act 1925, s.39(1).
[7] Ibid.; Law of Property Act 1925, s.28(1); Settled Land Act 1925, s.83, 3rd Sched. See, on these provisions generally, 3 Wolst. & Ch., 13th ed., pp. 182–191; 261–268. See also Re Insole's S.E. [1938] Ch. 812.
[8] See the Settled Land Act 1925, ss.73(1)(iii)(iv), 84, 85. As to whether repairs or improvements should be borne by capital or income, see Re Smith [1930] 1 Ch. 88 and the other cases mentioned in 3 Wolst. & Ch., 13th ed., p. 262. See also Re Battle Abbey S.E. [1933] W.N. 215.
[9] Settled Land Act 1925, s.71(1)(ii); Trustees Act 1925, s.16 (post, p. 1099).

to do any act, which they are authorised to enter into or do by reference to the Settled Land Act 1925[10]; and such contract will bind and be enforceable by their successors in title.[11] They may also vary or rescind such a contract with or without consideration.[12]

Further, they may make any disposition which is necessary or proper for giving effect to a contract entered into by a predecessor in title, and which if made by that predecessor would have been valid as against his successors in title.[13]

Overreaching powers

Representatives may, by a conveyance of a legal estate in land to a purchaser, overreach any equitable interest or power affecting that estate, and capable of being overreached by such conveyance, as if the same affected the proceeds of sale, whether or not he has notice of such equitable interest.[14] They can also exercise the overreaching powers conferred by section 72 of the Settled Land Act 1925.[15]

Semble, representatives may overreach equitable interests, though they have not for this purpose been approved or appointed by the court.[16] An equitable interest may be overreached though the conveyance is made by a sole representative.[17]

Power to deposit documents

Representatives are empowered[18] to deposit documents with a bank or any other company whose business includes the safe custody of documents, and the cost is payable out of income.

Fire insurance

A representative may insure against loss or damage by fire any building or other insurable property (which he is not bound on request forthwith to convey absolutely to any beneficiary[19]) to any amount, including the amount of any insurance already on foot, not exceeding three-quarters of the full value thereof. He may pay the premiums for such insurance out of

---

[10] Settled Land Act 1925, s.90(1).

[11] *Ibid.* subs. (2); Administration of Estates Act 1925, s.39(1) (*post*, p. 1132).

[12] Settled Land Act 1925, s.90(1)(ii); Administration of Estates Act 1925, s.39(1)(iii).

[13] Administration of Estates Act 1925, s.39(1); Law of Property Act 1925, s.28(1); Settled Land Act 1925, s.63.

[14] Administration of Estates Act 1925, s.39(1)(ii); Law of Property Act 1925, ss.2(1), 3(1)(*b*)(i).

[15] Administration of Estates Act 1925, s.39(1)(ii); Law of Property Act 1925, s.28.

[16] Even if the restrictions contained in the Law of Property Act 1925, s.2 (as amended), apply to personal representatives (as to which, see the Administration of Estates Act 1925, s.39(1)(ii)), the grant of representation might be considered as an approval or appointment. See 5 Wolst. & Ch., 13th ed., pp. 69–70.

[17] See the Law of Property Act 1925, s.27(2) (as amended); Administration of Estates Act 1925, s.2(1) (*post*, p. 1114).

[18] Trustee Act 1925, s.21. See also s.68(17) and p. 681, n. 85, *ante*.

[19] Trustee Act 1925, s.19(2).

the income of the property so insured, or out of the income of other property subject to the same trusts, without obtaining the consent of any person wholly or partly entitled to such income.[20]

A representative may of course become entitled to the benefit of fire insurance taken out by the deceased. If the loss occurred before the deceased died, the representative will succeed to the rights of the deceased. If the loss occurred afterwards, the representative's rights are doubtful if the insurers have not consented to his taking over the policy. But if the terms of the policy extend the benefit of it to all persons to whom the interest of the insured may pass by will or operation of law, then they have consented in advance.[21]

Other miscellaneous powers

Other miscellaneous powers conferred on representatives by reference to the powers of trustees for sale,[22] but which it will rarely be necessary to exercise, are, power to impose restrictions and reservations on dispositions,[23] to grant water rights to statutory bodies,[24] to grant land for public and charitable purposes,[25] to dedicate streets and open spaces,[26] and to provide housing.[27]

Extension of powers

Where the representatives have no power by statute or otherwise, power may be given to them by agreement of the beneficiaries (being of full age) or by the court under its inherent jurisdiction or under section 57 of the Trustee Act 1925, section 64 of the Settled Land Act 1925 or the Variation of Trusts Act 1958. Reference should be made to works on the law of trusts.[28]

Power to make an assent

A representative may assent to the vesting "in any person who (whether by devise, bequest, devolution, appropriation or otherwise) may be entitled thereto" of any estate or interest in real estate which has devolved upon him.[29] The representative also has power to permit a person entitled,

---

[20] *Ibid.* s.19(1). And for a power to insure land of which he is in possession, see the Settled Land Act 1925, s.102(2)(e). As to the application of the insurance money, see the Trustee Act 1925, s.20: 4 Wolst. & Ch. 13th ed., p. 23. And see *ante*, p. 538. As to liability for failure to insure, see *post*, p. 733. As to perishable assets, see *ante*, p. 598.

[21] MacGillivray and Parkington, *Insurance Law*, 6th ed., 1975, paras. 1812 onwards. MacGillivray now in 8th ed.

[22] Administration of Estates Act 1925, s.39(1).

[23] Settled Land Act 1925, s.49.

[24] Settled Land Act 1925, s.54.

[25] Settled Land Act 1925, s.55.

[26] Settled Land Act 1925, s.56.

[27] Settled Land Act 1925, s.57.

[28] See Lewin, *Trusts*, 16th ed., pp. 728–748.

[29] Administration of Estates Act 1925, s.36(1); discussed *post*, pp. 1049 *et seq.*

to take possession of land before assent without prejudging the right of the representative to resume possession.[30] This enables the convenient post-ponement of assents in cases of difficulty especially where liabilities may later force a sale. An executor owes no duty (unless the will expressly so requires) to inform a legatee of the terms of his legacy even if there is a gift over or breach of condition in favour of the executor,[31] but this doctrine does not extend to a trustee under an express trust.[32]

Power to raise money

In addition to his powers of sale and mortgage[33] for giving effect to bene-ficial interests a representative may limit or demise land for a term of years absolute to trustees on usual trusts for raising or securing any principal sum for which the land is liable, and may limit a rentcharge to give effect to any annual or periodical sum for which the land or income thereof is liable.[34]

Power to appropriate

A power to appropriate the assets in satisfaction of legacies or to meet annuties may arise under an express provision in the will, by statute, or at common law.[35]

Where by the will of a testator, who died before 1926, a wide power of appropriation was conferred on trustees holding land upon trust for per-sons in undivided shares, and, by the operation of the Law of Property Act 1925, the entirety of the land became vested in the trustees on trust for sale, it was held that the express power of appropriation could not be exer-cised by the trustees for sale, since it was inconsistent with the statutory trust for sale.[36] It is difficult to see why it was not construed as an additional power; and, *semble*, the case does not go to the length of decid-ing that a testator cannot by a will taking effect after 1925 confer upon his representatives or trustees a power to partition or appropriate without the consents made requisite in exercise of the statutory powers in that behalf. But apart from an express provision in a will and the statutory provisions hereinafter mentioned, a representative has no power, unless authorised by the court,[37] to partition or appropriate without the consent of the per-

---

[30] Administration of Estates Act 1925, s.43(1). There is also provision for a person claiming against the representative to apply to the court (*ibid.* s.43(2)). See *post*, p. 1064.

[31] *Re Lewis* [1904] 2 Ch. 656; *Re Mackay* [1906] 1 Ch. 25.

[32] *Hawkesley* v. *May* [1956] 1 Q.B. 304, 322.

[33] See *ante*, pp. 666 *et seq.*

[34] Administration of Estates Act 1925, s.40 (*post*, p. 1133). This power does not now seem to be in common use but may sometimes assist.

[35] The exercise of the power may be forced upon the representatives, see *post*, p. 1021. As to appropriation in favour of infants, see *post*, p. 1026.

[36] *Re Thomas* [1930] 1 Ch. 194. *Semble*, this decision is inapplicable to land vested in rep-resentatives under the Law of Property Act 1925, Sched. 1, Pt. IV, para. 1(1): see the con-cluding words of that provision.

[37] See the Trustee Act 1925, s.57; Settled Land Act 1925, s.64; *Re Thomas, ante.*

sons beneficially entitled to the property. However, he may be able to accept a fair compromise under his powers to compromise claims and in this case consent of all beneficiaries may not be necessary.[38]

The statutory power to appropriate[39] enables the personal representative, with the consent of a person absolutely and beneficially entitled in possession[40] and without prejudicially affecting any specific devise or bequest, to appropriate any part of the estate in the actual condition or state of investment thereof at the time of appropriation in satisfaction of any legacy or other interest, settled or not according to the rights of the persons interested in the property of the deceased.[41] Property so appropriated is to be treated as an authorised investment.[42] Purchasers are given protection[43] and the appropriation is binding on all persons interested.[44] The representative has power for this purpose to fix values and if necessary to employ a qualified valuer.[45]

At common law representatives may, and if so required, must[46] appropriate with the consent of the beneficiary any part of the residuary estate in or towards satisfaction of a vested[47] legacy or share of residue[48] even if only payable in the future.[49] They can also safely distribute after making reasonable provision for contingent legacies, although they cannot strictly at common law appropriate a fund for this purpose.[50] This power extends to real and personal property[51] whether or not subject to a trust for conver-

---

[38] Trustee Act 1925, s.15 (post, p. 1099). Ad valorem stamp duty is payable on all appropriations in writing unless the will dispenses with the need for the beneficiary's consent. Jopling v. I.R.C. [1940] 2 L.B. 282 or the instrument is exempt under Stamp Duty Regulations 1987 (S.I. 1987 No. 516) (certificates).

[39] Under s.41 of the Administration of Estates Act 1925, replacing s.4 of the Land Transfer Act 1897. Reference should be made to the full wording of the section (post, p. 1133). As to registered land, see ante, p. 550.

[40] The consent of trustees of settled legacies, or of persons entitled to income, or of parents, guardians, committees or receivers of persons not sui juris, is sufficient (ibid. s.41(1)(ii)(b); no consent (save of a trustee) is required for persons not in existence or not found or ascertained at time of appropriation (ibid. s.41(1)(iii), but regard must be had to such rights (ibid, s.41(5)).

[41] As to contingent interests, see post, pp. 1020–1021.

[42] Administration of Estates Act 1925, s.41(2)(post, p. 1134).

[43] Ibid. s.41(7)(8).

[44] Ibid. s.41(4). The appropriation does not carry interest if interest is not otherwise payable Re Raine [1929] 1 Ch. 716.

[45] Administration of Estates Act 1925, s.41(3). Valuation is to be as at date of appropriation (Re Charteris [1917] 2 Ch. 379, 386). Re Collins [1975] 1 W.L.R. 309. A valuation once fixed cannot later be revised. See Re Abergavenny [1981] 1 W.L.R. 843.

[46] Re Marshall [1914] 1 Ch. 192; Re Sandeman [1937] 1 All E.R. 368; Re Weiner [1956] 1 W.L.R. 579. A sole executor may not appropriate in his own favour on his own term (Re Bythway (1918) 80 L.J.Ch. 246).

[47] There is at common law no power to appropriate for a contingent legacy unless it carries the intermediate income. Green v. Pigot (1781) 1 Bro.C.C. 103; Re Hall [1903] 2 Ch. 226; Webber v. Webber (1823) 1 Sim. & St. 311.

[48] See, e.g. Re Lepine [1892] 1 Ch. 210.

[49] Phipps v. Annesley (1740) 2 Stk. 58, but not where the legacy is to be raised out of real estate (Gawler v. Standerwick (1788) 2 Cox 15): see also Johnson v. Mills (1749) 1 Ves.Sen. 282; Re Hall [1903] 2 Ch. 226; Re Craven [1914] 1 Ch. 358, 372.

[50] Re Rivers [1920] 1 Ch. 320; Re Hall [1903] 2 Ch. 226. 233. (See ante, n. 47).

[51] Re Beverly [1901] 1 Ch. 681; Re Wragg [1919] 2 Ch. 58.

sion,[52] but it does not extend so far as to allow trustees of a settled legacy or share of residue to take unauthorised investments[53] except in the case of an unauthorised investment retained under a power so to retain.[54] A mere power to postpone sale does not authorise the appropriation of otherwise unauthorised investments.[55]

The duty of the representatives in exercising a power of appropriation is to consider the interests of the estate as a whole; they are not under a duty to hold the balance between the beneficiaries.[56] Where the control of a company is concerned it may be necessary to sell all the shares on the open market rather than let one beneficiary obtain a controlling balance.[57]

Power to partition

Before 1926 representatives had power to concur in a partition of property held in common by the deceased and other persons[58] but they had no power to partition the estate between the persons entitled as an incident of a power or trust for sale. A trust for sale or exchange, however, was treated as giving power to partition.[59]

The statutory power to partition[60] enables a representative,[61] where the net proceeds of sale have become absolutely vested in persons of full age in undivided shares, with consent, to partition unsold land and to provide by way of mortgage or otherwise for the payment of equality money. The power applies where the proceeds or some of them are vested in trustees[62] but not where they are only vested in life tenants. There are provisions for the protection of purchasers, the discharge of incumbrances, consents by committees or receivers and the retention of land partitioned to infants by the representatives, to be held on trust for sale.

Power to appoint trustees of infant's property

The power to appoint trustees of infants' property is considered later.[63]

Powers to maintain and advance

The power of representatives or trustees to make allowances out of the capital or income of a legacy for the advancement, maintenance, or other benefit of the legatee is mentioned later.[64]

---

[52] *Re Beverly* [1901] 1 Ch. 681; *Re Richardson* [1896] 1 Ch. 512; *Re Nickels* [1898] 1 Ch. 630.

[53] *Ibid.* n. 51.

[54] *Re Brooks* (1886) 76 L.T. 771; *Re Cook* [1913] 2 Ch. 661; *Re Wragg* [1919] 2 Ch. 58.

[55] *Re Craven* [1914] 1 Ch. 358; *Re Wragg* [1919] 2 Ch. 58.

[56] *Re Charteris* [1917] 2 Ch. 379; *Re Hayes* [1971] 1 W.L.R. 758.

[57] *Lloyd's Bank* v. *Duker* [1987] 1 W.L.R. 1324 (distinguishing *Re Weiner* [1956] 1 W.L.R. 579).

[58] *Re Kemnal and Still* [1923] 1 Ch. 293, 307.

[59] 4 Wolst. & Ch., 13th ed., p. 19.

[60] Law of Property Act 1925, s.28(3)(4) and (5).

[61] Law of Property Act 1925, s.33; Administration of Estates Act 1925, s.33, 39.

[62] *Re Brooker* [1934] Ch. 610; *Re Gorringe and Braybon's Contract* [1934] Ch. 614, note.

[63] See *post*, pp. 1025–1027.

[64] *Post*, p. 1027.

Powers to postpone sale and to continue business

As will be seen[65] a representative has powers to postpone sale and to continue the business of the deceased for the purpose of selling it to the best advantage of the estate.

B. THE POWERS OF VARIOUS TYPES OF REPRESENTATIVES

Powers of administrators

After a grant has been made to him, and subject to any restrictions contained therein, every administrator has the same powers as an executor.[66]

On the death of a person intestate as to any real or personal estate after 1925, not only have his representatives a power of sale, but under the Administration of Estates Act 1925, s.33, they are to hold his real and personal estate on trust for sale and conversion.[67] The same section, however, gives a power to postpone sale,[68] and provides that a reversionary interest[69] is not to be sold until it falls into possession, unless the representatives see special reason for sale; and that, "unless required for purposes of administration owing to want of other assets," personal chattels[70] are not to be sold except for special reason. Section 33 only applies to cases of intestacy affecting the whole interest in the estate or some part thereof and not to an intestacy as to a partial interest (such as a life or reversionary interest) in the residuary estate.[71] Further, it operates subject to the effective provisions of the deceased's will (if any).[72] So that if there is a partial intestacy affecting an interest under an express trust for sale, the express trust for sale takes the place of the provisions of section 33.[73]

Powers of executor of executor

Except in cases of a special trust or authority outside the office of executorship,[74] the executor of an executor, however remote, stands in the same position as to his estate and rights as the first and immediate executor, and

---

[65] See *post*, pp. 740.

[66] See Touchst. 474; Administration of Estates Act 1925, s.21 (*post*, p. 1122). See also *Fountain Forestry* v. *Edwards* [1975] Ch. 1.

[67] On s.33 generally, see 5 Wolst. & Ch., 13th ed., pp. 49–84. A trust estate devolves upon the representative, but is not affected by s.33 because it is not an estate as to which the deceased died intestate.

[68] See *Re Wilks* [1935] Ch. 645; *Re Kehr* [1952] Ch. 26.

[69] Moneys secured by a policy of assurance and payable by instalments or by a lump sum in the future are not a reversionary interest for the purpose of this section: *Re Fisher* [1943] Ch. 377; *Re Holliday* [1947] Ch. 402.

[70] "Personal chattels" are defined: Administration of Estates Act 1925, s.55(1)(x). See *ante*, pp. 498, 666.

[71] *Re Plowman* [1943] Ch. 269.

[72] Administration of Estates Act 1925, s.33(7); *Re Sullivan* [1930] 1 Ch. 84; *Re McKee* [1931] 2 Ch. 145; *Re Thronber* [1937] Ch. 29.

[73] *Re McKee* [1931] 2 Ch. 145. See *post*, pp. 1069, 1070.

[74] See Wentw.Off.Ex., 14th ed., c. 20, p. 462, and *Stile* v. *Tomson* (1561) Dyer 210a, as to the distinction between an interest and an authority only. And as to the devolution of powers generally, see *post*, pp. 695 *et seq.*

is liable to the extent of assets transmitted as if he were an original executor.[75]

Powers of administrators de bonis non

Similarly, an administrator *de bonis non* has the same power and authority with respect to the estate left unadministered as the original representative.[76]

Powers of limited administrators generally

For restrictions on the power and authority of limited administrators generally (*e.g.* administrators during minority or pending suit), reference should be made to Chapter 24 of this work, which discusses the constitution of such administrators.[77]

Powers of special representatives

Although it has been suggested in earlier editions that, in respect of settled land special representatives have, for the purposes of administration (*e.g.* for the purposes of raising money for the payment of death duties[78]) all the powers which are conferred on representatives generally by sections 2(1) and 39 of the Administration of Estates Act 1925, this is by no means clear.[79] Sir Lancelot Elphinstone has forcefully suggested[80] that the executor of a tenant for life has no power to sell except to raise estate duty or money secured on the land because there is no other "purpose of administration" applicable, and that an unauthorised sale would be a breach of trust giving no title to a purchaser with notice of the unauthorised purpose. On this basis the proper and only safe course is for the next tenant for life to sell after vesting assent.

Special powers during a minority

During the minority of an infant entitled in possession to settled land if the land is vested in a representative he has all the powers conferred by the

---

[75] Administration of Estates Act 1925, s.7(4). And see Wentw., *supra*. As to the chain of representation, see *ante*, p. 44.

[76] See *Catherwood* v. *Chaubaud* (1823) 1 B. & C. 150; *ante*, p. 50. Thus, if a temporary representative sells goods there is no remedy against the purchaser; *Chandler* v. *Thompson* (1619–20). Hob. 266; unless the transaction is fraudulent; *Munn* v. *Dunkin* (1677) Finch.R. 298.

[77] *Ante*, p. 316.

[78] There is also a special power for this purpose conferred by the Law of Property Act 1925, s.16(3); and see the Finance Act 1894, s.9. (See also *ante*, p. 678.)

[79] "Personal representative" includes a person deemed to be appointed executor as respects settled land: Administration of Estates Act 1925, s.55(1)(xi). See also the Settled Land Act 1925, ss.110(3), 117(1)(xviii). See *ante*, p. 678.

[80] 23 *Conveyancer* 360; 24 *Conveyancer* 43, 314.

Settled Land Act 1925 and the settlement on a tenant for life and on the trustees of the settlement.[81]

C. Powers Under a Joint Representation

As has been seen,[82] co-executors, however numerous, are regarded in law as an individual person. The same principle applies under a joint grant of administration.[83] Thus, under a joint grant of representation the act of one representative is regarded as the act of all[84] unless there is statutory provision to the contrary.[85] A release of a debt by one of several executors is valid, and binds the rest.[86] So one of several executors may settle an account with a person accountable to the estate, and, in the absence of fraud, the settlement will be binding on the others, though dissenting.[87] So also the attornment of one executor is the attornment of the other.[88] It has been said that if judgment is confessed by one executor it is as binding as if all the executors had joined[89]; but this is subject to the principle that, if executors plead different defences, that which is most for the advantage of the testator's estate will be accepted.[90] It seems that if a power is given by the will to two executors whether by virtue of their office or for personal reasons it will be regarded as exercisable jointly and severally and by the

[81] Settled Land Act 1925, s.26(1). Under s.26(2) a principal vesting instrument must, if required by the trustees, be executed and in the meantime effect must be given to the directions of the trustees.

[82] *Ante*, pp. 27, 469. As to separate representation in court, see *post*, p. 749. As to trustees see *Dawson* v. *I.R.C.* [1988] 1 W.L.R. 930. See p. 564 *ante*.

[83] *Willard* v. *Fenn*, Selw.N.P., 6th ed., p. 767, n. (*e*); *Jacomb* v. *Harwood* (1751) 2 Ves. Sen. 265; Administration of Estates Act 1925, s.21. See also Touchst. 485; *Smith* v. *Everett* (1859) 27 Beav. 446, 454. For the earlier contrary view: *Hudson* v. *Hudson* (1737) 1 Atk. 460; Dyer 339; *Stanley* v. *Bernes* (1828) 1 Hagg.Ecc. 222. In *Fountain Forestry* v. *Edwards* [1975] Ch. 1, Brightman J. took the view that there was no decisive authority on the question but was content to assume that a co-administrator is in the same position as a co-executor in this respect. See also *Wentworth* 1728 ed. 373.

[84] Touchst. 484; 3 Bac.Abr. 30, Exors.C. 1; Wentw.Off.Ex., 14th ed., p. 206; *Ex p. Rigby* (1815) 19 Ves. 463; *Owen* v. *Owen* (1738) 1 Atk. 494, 495.

[85] As to conveyances, see *post*, p. 691. As to share and stock transfers, see *post*, p. 692.

[86] *Anon.* (1536) Dyer 23 *b*, *in margine*; *Jacomb* v. *Harwood* (1751) 2 Ves.Sen. 265. Where an action was brought by two out of four executors and the two who were not joined in the action released the defendant, who pleaded the release, the court refused to set aside the plea, the plaintiffs having failed to make out a case of fraud: *Herbert* v. *Pigott* (1834) 2 Cr. & M. 384. See also *Charlton* v. *Durham* (1869) L.R. 4 Ch. 433, in which case the effective receipt of one executor (the signature of the other executor to such receipt having been forged) was held sufficient. But see *Lee* v. *Sankey* (1873) L.R. 15 Eq. 204, where the receipt of one trustee of a will (though also an executor) was held not a sufficient discharge for money received by the authority of the two trustees of the will.

[87] *Smith* v. *Everett* (1859) 29 L.J.Ch. 236; 34 L.T.O.S. 58; 27 Beav. 446.

[88] Dyer 23 *b*, *in margine*; 1 Madd. 616. So if one executor gets possession of the goods, and pays debts with his own money as far as the amount of them, this is a conversion of the goods of the testator to his own use and justifiable by this executor against his co-executor; Dyer 23 *b*, *in margine*.

[89] See Dyer 23 *b*, *in margine*; *Simpson* v. *Gutteridge* (1816) 1 Madd. 609, 616; *Lepard* v. *Vernon* (1813) 2 V. & B. 51, 54; *Warner* v. *Sampson* [1958] 1 Q.B. 404.

[90] *Elwell* v. *Quash* (1730) 1 Stra. 20; *Baldwin* v. *Church* (1716) 10 Mod. 323; *Midgley* v. *Midgley* [1893] 3 Ch. 282; *post*, p. 893.

survivor.[91] It was also held that if one of two executors delivered a bond due to the testator to a stranger in satisfaction of a debt due from him and then died, an action of detinue did not lie by the surviving executor, to recover it back.[92] But though one of several executors may, notwithstanding the dissent of his co-executors,[93] make an assignment in satisfaction of a debt due from the testator to a particular creditor, yet if the assignment is not complete at law it will not be enforced by a court having equitable jurisdiction so as to give to the particular creditor an advantage over the other executors and the general creditors.[94]

The principle that the act of one representative is the act of all applies also to the sale or gift of pure personalty.[95] The same principle was applied in *Brewer* v. *Westminster Bank*,[96] where McNair J. held that since the banker's obligation to joint executors on a joint account was a single obligation owed to them jointly, an action against the bank for unauthorised payments on cheques forged by one executor was not maintainable by the other executors, since the fraudulent executor would have to be joined as a party, and he was barred by his misconduct.

Where there is a trust for conversion and executors cannot agree to postpone, the trust prevails.[97]

Conveyances of land

Even before 1926, some, or one only, of several joint representatives could not sell or transfer real estate (not including chattels real) without the authority of the court,[98] though the concurrence of non-proving executors in the sale, transfer or disposition was rendered unnecessary by the Conveyancing Act 1911, s.12.

Since 1925 a conveyance[99] of real estate, including chattels real,[1] cannot

---

[91] *Re Beesty's Will Trusts* [1966] Ch. 223, 232 and see *post*, p. 697.

[92] *Kelsack* v. *Nicholson* (1596) Cro.Eliz. 478, 496; Dyer 23 *b*, *in margine*. If there is any fraud betwen the executor and the creditor, and there are no other assets to pay all the debts and legacies, the perhaps the other executor may have a remedy in equity against his co-executor and the creditor: Touchst. 484.

[93] But query if the debt is statute-barred: see *Midgley* v. *Midgley, supra*; *Astbury* v. *Astbury* [1898] 2 Ch. 111. 115.

[94] See *Lepard* v. *Vernon* (1813) 2 V. & B. 51 (debt due to testator assigned by one executor to particular creditor). See also *Re Ingham* [1893] 1 Ch. 352. *Cf.* now, the Law of Property Act 1925, s.136, replacing the Judicature Act 1873, s.25(6), as to assignment of things in action.

[95] Touchst. 484; *Kelsack* v. *Nicholson* (1596) Cro.Eliz. 478, 496; Dyer 23 *b*, *in margine*; *Cole* v. *Miles* (1852) 10 Hare 179; *cf. Sneesby* v. *Thorne* (1855) 7 De G.M. & G. 399.

[96] [1952] 2 All E.R. 650. After an appeal to the Court of Appeal had been opened, a settlement was reached. See 69 L.Q.R. 157.

[97] *Re Hilton* [1909] 2 Ch. 548; *Re Mayo* [1943] Ch. 302.

[98] Land Transfer Act 1897, s.2(2); *Johnson* v. *Clarke* [1928] Ch. 857. As to the grant of chattels real by one of several executors before 1897, see *Doe* v. *Wheeler* (1846) 15 M. & W. 623.

[99] Conveyance includes a mortgage, legal charge, lease, assent, vesting declaration, vesting instrument, disclaimer, release and any other assurance except a will (see the Administration of Estates Act 1925, s.55(1)(iii)). See also 41 *Conveyancer* 35.

[1] Administration of Estates Act 1925, s.3.

be made without the concurrence therein of all the representatives (still living) to whom a grant has been made in respect of the property conveyed,[2]
or without an order of the court.[3] But one representative can make a valid
contract for the sale of real estate.[4] It has been suggested that this anomaly
be corrected by requiring the concurrence of all proving representatives to
make a contract as well as to convey.[5] There is here a conflict between
property law and contract law. One of two joint contractors may at common law terminate the contract unilaterally.[6]

Transfer of shares or stock

Where representatives are registered as shareholders or stockholders a
transfer by one only is invalid under the Companies Clauses Acts[7] and
under the National Debt Act 1870[8] and will normally be invalid where the
company is governed by the Companies Acts.[9]

Where an estate has been fully administered so that the representatives
of the deceased hold shares as bare trustees for beneficiaries the trustees
will not normally be regarded as desirous of transferring such shares if the
beneficiaries do not wish this to be done. The matter is one of construction
of the Articles of Association and the desire of a testator expressed in his
will cannot be attributed to his representatives.[10]

Assent to legacy

An assent to a legacy of pure personalty by one of several executors is
sufficient[11]; and, if one of several executors is a legatee his own assent to
such legacy will vest the complete title in himself.[12] Again, if the subject is
entire, and given to all the executors, the assent of one of them to his own
proportion is sufficient.[13]

---

[2] General representatives and special representatives may act independently in conveying
property vested in them respectively: *ibid.* ss.2(2), 24; Supreme Court Act 1981, s.113 (*post*,
p. 1196). See *ante*, p. 470.

[3] Administration of Estates Act 1925, s.2(2). Denial of the landlord's title is not "conveyance" under this section and s.55. *cg. Warner* v. *Sampson* [1959] 1 Q.B. 297.

[4] Administration of Estates Act 1925, s.2(1); *Fountain Forestry Ltd.* v. *Edwards* [1975] Ch.
1. *cf. Sneesby* v. *Thorne* (1855) 7 De G.M. & G. 399, 403.

[5] See Law.Com. 184, 213.

[6] See *per* Lord Browne-Wilkinson in *Hammersmith L.B.C.* v. *Monk* [1992] A.C. 478 at p.
491.

[7] *Barton* v. *North Staffs. Railway* (1888) 38 Ch.D. 458, 464; *Barton* v. *L.N.W.R.* (1889) 24
Q.B.D. 77.

[8] See *ante*, p. 527.

[9] The articles will normally have this effect; see, *e.g.* Art. 29 in Table A of the Companies
Act 1948 and Art. 29 in Table A of the Companies Act 1985.

[10] See *Safeguard* v. *National Westminster Bank* [1982] 1 W.L.R. 589, 598.

[11] Godolph, Pt. 2, c. 30, s.8, p. 245; Wentw.Off.Ex., 14th ed., p. 413; Com.Ding.Admi-
nistration, C. 8.

[12] 1 Roll.Abr. 618, tit. Devise, B. pl. 2; *Townson* v. *Tickell* (1819) 3 B. & A. 31, 40; *Cole* v.
Miles (1852) 10 Hare 179.

[13] *Pannel* v. *Fenn* (1594) 1 Roll.Abr. 618, Devise, B. pl. 3; 1 Rop.Leg., 3rd ed., p. 734.

Acts binding on the co-representative

Again, as has already been shown,[14] the act of one of two executors, in possessing himself of the testator's property, is the act of the other, so as to entitle him to a joint interest in possession, and a joint right of action, if such property is afterwards taken away. But the act of one executor in taking possession of a chattel real or personal (and, as to deaths since 1897, of real estate[15]) of the testator, cannot create a new liability and impose a charge on his co-executor personally, and in his own individual character, which, without such act, would never have existed.[16] Thus, if one executor takes possession of and uses a personal chattel, the other is not liable to the creditors for such act of his co-executor; and if one executor enters and enjoys land demised and takes the profits beyond the rent, the other executor is not chargeable with the amount as assets to the creditors; but the one who actually received the profits is alone responsible.[17] The actual possession and use by one of two executors is not in law the possession and use by both, so as to attach a liability to the creditors upon both. Accordingly, if one of the executors takes actual possession of and enjoys land held for a term of years, that does not amount to possession and enjoyment by both, so as to render both liable to pay to the lessor compensation as joint occupiers in their own right.[18]

Again, though one of several executors may dispose of the assets, not being land, so as to bind the others, it is not to be inferred that one of several executors is the agent of the others, so as to bind them by his several contracts.[19] Where one of two executors, erroneously believing that he was acting with the authority of the others, contracted to sell a leasehold house, part of the testator's estate, it was held that the purchaser could not enforce specific performance of the contract.[20]

The admission of one of two or more representatives will not bind the others, unless it is made in the character of representative.[21]

When one executor may sue the other

Generally speaking, one executor could not at law sue or be sued by his co-executor[22]; nor, after the death of one of several executors, could his

---

[14] Ante, p. 469.

[15] Administration of Estates Act 1925, s.2(1), replacing the Land Transfer Act 1897, s.2(1)(2).

[16] As to how far a devastavit or receipt by one executor creates a liability in his co-executors, see post, p. 748.

[17] See ibid.

[18] Nation v. Tozer (1834) 1 Cr.M. & R. 172.

[19] Turner v. Hardey (1842) 9 M. & W. 770. As to acknowledgment by one of two or more executors, see post, p. 902. And as to payment of a statute-barred debt by a co-executor, see post, p. 735.

[20] Sneesby v. Thorne (1855) 7 De G.M. & G. 399; Naylor v. Goodall (1877) 47 L.J.Ch. 53; Fountain Forestry Ltd. v. Edwards [1975] Ch. 1.

[21] Fox v. Waters (1840) 12 A. & E. 43. See also Scholey v. Walton (1844) 12 M. & W. 510; Astbury v. Astbury [1898] 2 Ch. 111. cf. Re Macdonald [1897] 2 Ch. 181; see post.

[22] Wentw.Off.Ex., 14th ed., p. 75. But see Gleadow v. Atkin (1832) 2 C. & J. 548 (action on bond given as security for loan of assets made by one executor to the other).

executor be sued by the surviving co-executor for a debt due to their testator[23]; not could executors maintain an action at law in right of the deceased, upon a contract made by the deceased with the defendant jointly with one of themselves, for a person could not sue himself, either alone or jointly with others.[24] But if a debtor makes his creditor and another his executors, the creditor may bring an action against the other executor, provided he neither proves the will or acts as executor,[25] and even though he does not renounce.[26] And in equity one representative may bring an action against another.[27] Thus one of two executors may sue the other for an account and payment of money owing by such other executor to the testator at the time of his death, and the persons beneficially interested in the estate are not necessary parties.[28] Thus if one of two or more executors wishes to enforce a claim of the estate against another proving executor, he can only do so by instituting administration or other equitable proceedings.[29]

Where the survivor of two executors, who had taken out administration to the other, filed a bill to set aside a mortgage of part of the assets made by the deceased executor as having been a breach of trust, it was held that the fact of the plaintiff having taken out the administration did not disqualify him from maintaining the suit.[30]

The general question as to what executors should be joined as parties to an action is discussed later.[31]

Solicitors' retainer

A retainer by one of several executors will not in the absence of express authority bind the others, so that written instructions from all should be obtained.[32] If there is a dispute about retainer the taxing master can consider the propriety of the proceedings and the soundness of the advice given.[33]

---

[23] Wentw.Off.Ex., 14th ed., p. 75.

[24] Godolph., Pt. 12, c. 6, s.2. *Anon* v. *Adams* (1830) Younge 117; *Moffat* v. *Van Millingen* (1787) 2 Bos. & Pall. 124, n. (*c*); *Fitzgerald* v. *Boehm* (1821) 6 B.Moore 332; *Rose* v. *Poulton* (1831) 2 B. & A. 822, as explained in *Ellis* v. *Kerr* [1910] 1 Ch. 529. Under s.82 of the Law of Property Act 1925, a person may now enforce a contract with himself and others, but this does not seem to affect the principle here.

[25] *Dorchester* v. *Webb* (1634) W.Jones, 345.

[26] *Rawlinson* v. *Shaw* (1790) 3 T.R. 557.

[27] *Allen* v. *Story* (1585) Toth. 86. And see the American case of *Beall* v. *Hilliary*, 1 Maryland 186; 54 Amer.Dec. 649.

[28] *Peake* v. *Ledger* (1850) 8 Hare 313.

[29] For the effect of appointing a debtor to be executor, see *ante*, p. 649.

[30] *Miles* v. *Durnford* (1852) 2 De G.M. & G. 641.

[31] See *post*, pp. 868 *et seq.*

[32] *Wiggins* v. *Peppin* (1837) 2 Beav. 403; the same principle applies to trustees: see *Luke* v. *South Kensington Hotel* (1879) 11 Ch. D. 121.

[33] *Re Brockman* [1909] 2 Ch. 178; *Re Bracey* (1845) 8 B. 268, S.C.P. 1979, 3084, 3085.

D. THE DEVOLUTION AND DELEGATION OF POWERS

Whether a power conferred by an instrument[34] upon representatives or trustees can be exercised only by all the persons nominated as such in the instrument, or may be exercised by the survivors of them, or by the persons for the time being holding the office of representatives or trustees depends ultimately on the construction of the instrument conferring the power. The principles governing the devolution of powers of representatives cannot however be reduced simply to matters of construction. It is convenient first to consider these principles as affecting trustees and then to notice the differences for representatives.

Bare power

A "naked authority" given to two or more individuals[35] or a bare power given to representatives or trustees as individuals, can only be exercised by all the individuals so named.[36] On the other hand, subject to one qualification hereinafter mentioned,[37] a power annexed to an office might always be exercised by the persons for the time being holding the office, unless a contrary intention appeared in the instrument conferring the power.[38] Similarly, a power annexed to an interest in the donee, and originally authorised to be executed by the donee of the power and his assigns, passed with the interest to any person claiming the interest, however remotely, through the donee; and this was so whether the claimant was an assignee in fact, or an assignee in law, as an heir or executor.[39]

---

[34] As to powers conferred by law or by implication, see *post*, p. 697. As to the distinction between powers and trusts see *Re Balden* [1971] A.C. 424, 449. "Trusts and powers are often blended and the mixture may vary in its ingredients."

[35] A naked authority given to several cannot, at common law, survive: Co.Litt. 133 *a*; Sugd.Pow., 8th ed., 126, 127; Farw.Pow., 3rd ed., 498 *et seq.*

[36] *Brassey* v. *Chalmers* (1852) 16 Beav. 231; reversed, 4 De G.M. & G. 528 (power to sell real estate given to "my executors hereinafter named with the approbation of my trustees for the time being"; held by Lord Justices to be exercisable by survivor of two appointed executors). See also *Down* v. *Worrall* (1833) 1 M. & K. 561; *Forbes* v. *Forbes* (1854) 18 Beav. 552.

[37] *Post*, p. 696.

[38] *Brassey* v. *Chalmers*, *supra*; *Crawford* v. *Forshaw* [1891] 2 Ch. 261 (power of selection given to "my executors herein named" held exercisable by two proving executors alone, the third executors appointed having renounced); *Re Smith* [1904] 1 Ch. 139 (power of sale given to "may said trustees" held exercisable by the trustees for the time being). *Re De Sommery* [1912] 2 Ch. 622; *Re Symn's Will Trust*, 80 S.J. 994. See also *Keates* v. *Burton* (1808) 14 Ves. 434 (discretion as to payment of legacy given to "my said executors"; one executor died, the others renounced and were held unable to exercise discretion as they had "renounced the only character in which it was competent to them to exercise it"); *Granville* v. *M'Neile* (1849) 7 Hare 156 (power to appoint new trustees exercisable by two proving executors, the other appointed executor having renounced); *Re Boucherett* [1908] 1 Ch. 180. At common law such a power might be exercised by a sole surviving executor; see Sugd.Pow., 8th ed., 126, 128.

[39] Sugd.Pow., 8th ed., 180; *Howe* v. *Whitebank* (1679) 1 Freem. 476 (a power of leasing given to A and his assigns may be well exercised by the assignee of the executor of A's assign).

Power given to trustees

Neither the fact that a power is of a kind that indicates a personal confidence,[40] nor that the power is conferred on executors "herein named,"[41] is in itself sufficient to make it a bare power, so as to limit its exercise to the individuals to whom it was originally given. "Every power given to trustees which enables them to deal with or affect the trust property is prima facie given them *ex officio* as an incident of their office, and passes with the office to the holders or holder thereof for the time being; whether a power is so given *ex efficio* or not depends in each case on the construction of the document giving it, but the mere fact that the power is one requiring the exercise of a very wide personal discretion is not enough to exclude the prima facie presumption, and little regard is now paid to such minute differences as those between 'my trustee,' 'my trustees A and B,' and 'A and B, my trustees': the testator's reliance on the individuals to the exclusion of the holders of the office for the time being must be expressed in clear and apt language."[42]

Former limits to such power

Until the Conveyancing Act 1911, however, the person who was to execute a trust or exercise a power had to be a person who was in some way pointed out by the creator of the trust or power as a proper person to execute or exercise.[43] Thus, where a testator devised his residuary estate to four named persons, the words "and their heirs" being omitted, upon trust for sale, with power to postpone, and to demise and manage during postponement, it was held (in 1909) that the executors of the last survivor of the four named persons could not make a good title to a freehold house forming part of the residuary estate of the testator.[44] *Semble*, it would have been otherwise if the heir of the last surviving trustee had been named, for since 1881[45] the representatives of a deceased person have been deemed in law his heirs and assigns within the meaning of all trusts and powers.[46] Similarly a power conferred upon trustees, and the survivors or survivor of them, his heirs and assigns, could (before 1882) be exercised by the person to whom the trust estates had been devised by the last surviving trustee[47];

---

[40] *Re Smith* [1904] 1 Ch. 139, disapproving the principle stated by Grant M.R. in *Cole* v. *Wade* (1807) 16 Ves. 27; *ibid. nom Walter* v. *Maunde* (1815) 19 Ves. 423, as being inconsistent with *Crawford* v. *Forshaw*, *ante*.

[41] *Crawford* v. *Forshaw*, *supra*.

[42] *Per* Farwell J. in *Re Smith* [1904] 1 Ch. 139, 144.

[43] *Re Crunden and Meux* [1909] 1 Ch. 690, where many of the cases are discussed. As to the continuing relevance of these limits, see note 48 *post*.

[44] *Re Crunden and Meux*, *ante*.

[45] See the Administration of Estates Act 1925, s.1(2), replacing part of Conveyancing Act 1881, s.30, and 23 *Conveyancer* 360.

[46] *Ibid.* n. 42.

[47] *Titley* v. *Wolstenholme* (1844) 7 Beav. 425; *Hall* v. *May* (1857) 3 K. & J. 585. See also *Saloway* v. *Strawbridge* (1855) 1 K. & J. 371.

though it would have been otherwise if the word "assigns" had been omitted.[48]

Trustee Act 1925

Section 18(1) of this Act provides[49] that a power or trust given to or imposed on two or more trustees jointly may be exercised by the survivor and that until the appointment of new trustees the representative of the last surviving or continuing trustee may exercise or perform any power or trust which was given to, or capable of, being exercised by the sole or last surviving or continuing trustee.

Further, it is provided[50] that every trustee appointed under section 36 of the Trustee Act 1925[51] and every trustee appointed by a court of competent jurisdiction[52] shall (as well before as after the trust property became by law, assurance, or otherwise, vested in him) have the same powers, authorities and discretions, and may in all respects act as if he had been originally appointed a trustee by the instrument, if any, creating the trust.

The statutory powers conferred on trustees as above apply if and so far as a contrary intention is not expressed in the instrument, if any, creating the trust, and have effect subject to the terms of that instrument.[53]

There is nothing in section 18(1) to abrogate the rule[54] that a bare power, given to two or more persons by name and not annexed to an estate or office, does not survive without more. The subsection refers to powers given to two or more *trustees*, not to two or more persons.[55] Nor, *semble*, does subsection (2) have any reference to bare powers.

On the other hand, by reason of sections 18(2), 36(7) and 43, the rule[56] that a power or trust can only be exercised or executed by a person who was in some way pointed out by the creator of the power or trust no longer applies to powers and trusts given to or imposed on trustees as such.

Summary as to trustees' powers

As the law now stands every power conferred by an instrument upon trustees can be exercised by the persons or person[57] for the time being

---

[48] *Cooke* v. *Crawford*, 13 Sim. 91: *Re Crunden and Meux*, *ante.* See also *Macdonald* v. *Walker* (1851) 14 Beav. 556.

[49] Trustee Act 1925, s.18, replaces the Trustee Act 1895, s.22(1) (which in turn replaced the Conveyancing Act 1881, s.38), and s.18(2) replaces the Conveyancing Act 1911, s.8(1). See Appendix, *post*, p. 1100.

[50] Trustee Act 1925, s.36(7).

[51] This includes a foreign resident who may be so appointed *Re Whitehead* [1971] 1 W.L.R. 833.

[52] Trustee Act 1925, s.43.

[53] Trustee Act 1925, s.69(2).

[54] See *ante*, p. 695.

[55] *Re Harding* [1923] 1 Ch. 182.

[56] See *ante*, p. 696.

[57] But see the Trustee Act 1925, s.18(3), as to receipts (*post*, p. 1100).

holding that office, unless it appears from the instrument creating the power that it was given as a bare power to specified individuals, or that its exercise is in some other way expressly limited to certain persons. In such cases the former limits may apply.[58]

Powers of representative

In the majority of cases, powers given to representatives as such are also given to them as trustees, so that the principles already discussed would seem to apply thereto. But where a power is given by will to a representative as such, not being also a trustee, slightly different considerations apply. For though section 18(1) would seem to apply to powers and trusts vested in representatives,[59] it may be doubted whether subsection (2) does so apply.[60] It follows that though a power given by will to executors as such may, unless a contrary intention is expressed in the will, be exercised by the survivors or survivor of them for the time being, yet it may be argued that the power can only be exercised by a person who was in some way pointed out by the testator.[61] This argument might in some cases prevent the exercise of the power by the representatives of the last surviving executor, or by trustees subsequently appointed.[62] But in this connection it may be well to repeat that the representatives of a deceased person are deemed in law his heirs and assigns within the meaning of all trusts and powers.[63]

All powers conferred by law upon the representatives of a deceased person as incident to their office devolve upon the persons who are from time to time the representatives of the deceased persons. Thus all such powers of two or more proving executors,[64] or of two or more administrators,[65] are not determined by the death of one of them, but survive to the other or others, and devolve on all the persons in the chain of representation. *Semble*, the position is the same as to powers of representatives which arise by implication.[66] Whether or not a power expressly conferred by the will of the deceased will devolve in the same manner depends in each case upon the construction of the will.

---

[58] See p. 696 *ante.*

[59] "Trustee," where the context admits, includes a representative; Trustee Act 1925, s.68(17).

[60] The contrary view would seem to involve straining the words "until the appointment of new trustees" to mean until a grant is made to a person as representative of the original deceased. For the provisions of s.18(2), see p. 1100 *post.*

[61] *Re Crunden and Meux* [1909] 1 Ch. 690; *ante*, p. 689. See *Re Beesty's Will Trusts* [1966] Ch. 223 and p. 690 *ante.*

[62] See *Hibbard* v. *Lamb* (1756) Amb. 584.

[63] Administration of Estates Act 1925, s.1(2).

[64] Trustee Act 1925, s.18(1); *Flanders* v. *Clark* (1747) 3 Atk. 509.

[65] Trustee Act 1925, s.18(1); *Hudson* v. *Hudson* (1737) Talb. 127.

[66] An implied power of sale in executors (as to which see *ante*, p. 666) passes to the survivor; *Forbes* v. *Peacock* (1843) 11 M. & W. 630; and to the executors of such survivor, the intent being that the power should be executed by him to whose hands the money is to come; Sugd. Pow., 8th ed., 116, 118; Farw.Fow., 3rd ed., pp. 106, 521; 1 Pow.Dev. 243, Jarman's ed.

Devolution of power of selection

Where a deceased person was at the time of his death entitled out of several chattels to select one or more for his own benefit, his representatives may, in certain cases, claim to exercise this power of selection.[67] The principles to be extracted from the ancient authorities on this subject are as follows:

(1) Where a person has a right of selection once and for all on a particular occasion, the selection must be made on that occasion, and if not so made it cannot be made subsequently by his representatives.[68] But if the thing of which selection is given is annual, and to have continuance, and presumably, is not expressly confined to the donee's lifetime, the representatives may make the selection.[69]

(2) Where the gift is not completed save by the exercise of the power of selection, if the power is not exercised by the deceased it cannot be exercised by his representatives, for at the death of the deceased he had no property in the subject-matter of the selection.[70] For instance, if a person gives to A such of his horses as A and B shall choose, the selection must be made in A's lifetime.[71] Thus, where a testator bequeathed to his widow such articles (of a particular character and value) as she should within two months select, and she died within the two months without having made her selection, the representatives were not entitled, even within the two months, to make the selection.[72]

(3) Where, however, an interest vests immediately in the person given the selection, the selection may be made by his representatives.[73] If, therefore, the selection is merely as to the manner or degree in which the donee is to take the subject-matter of the gift, his representatives may make the selection.[74] Thus, if a lease is granted to A for 10 or 20 years, he shall select,[75] or if a lease is granted to A of 40 out of 60 acres,[76] the selection may be made by A's representatives.

Devolution of options to purchase

The question whether an option to purchase given by will to a named person is personal to the donee and exercisable only by him or is transmissible to his executors depends on the true construction of the will in the light

---

[67] See Toller 6th ed., p. 174. As to implied right of selection, see *post*, p. 1032. As to express right, see *Jarman on Wills*, 8th ed., 1951, p. 477.

[68] See Com.Dig., Election, B; Co.Litt. 145 *a*.

[69] See n. 68, *supra*.

[70] *Ibid.*

[71] *Morris* v. *Levesay* (1594) 1 Roll.Abr. 726, tit. Election, C, pl. 6; Com.Dig., *ante*.

[72] *Re Madge* [1928] W.N. 71.

[73] Com.Dig., *ante*. If a person gives one of his horses to A and B, after the death of A, B may choose which he will take, for an interested vested in them immediately by the gift: *ibid.*: 1 Roll.Abr. 725, tit. Election, C, pl.

[74] Com.Dig., *ante*: Co.Litt. 145 *a*.

[75] Toller 6th ed., p. 174.

[76] *Jones* v. *Cherney* (1680) 1 Freem. 530. As to uncertainty, see *Jenkins* v. *Green* (1858) 27 Beav. 437.

of any circumstances properly admissible in evidence.[77] It has been held
that an option for a lessee to purchase the fee simple of the land demised,
provided it does not infringe the perpetuity rule,[78] may be exercised by his
executor[79]; and an executor may elect to take new shares in a company
which his testator would have been entitled to have had offered to him.[80]

No delegation of discretionary powers

The general rule is that *delegatus non potest delegare*. Wherever a power
is given, if a personal trust or confidence is thereby reposed in the donee to
exercise his own judgment and discretion, he cannot refer the power to the
execution of another. Thus, where a power of sale is given to executors,
they cannot contract to sell by attorney.[81] But this extends merely to the
discretionary act, for it is not open to doubt that a trustee or representative
can execute a deed by an attorney, or that he can empower an attorney to
receive or join in receiving trust money[82] or to collect debts due to his testator.[83] But, as is pointed out elsewhere,[84] trustees and representatives
have never been bound personally to transact such business connected with
the proper duties of their office as, according to the usual mode of conducting business of a like nature, persons acting with reasonable care and prudence on their own account would ordinarily conduct through agents; and,
as Maugham J. (as he then was) observed in *Re Vickery*[85]: "It is hardly too
much to say that [section 23(1) of the Trustee Act 1925] revolutionises the
position of a trustee or an executor so far as regards the employment of
agents. He is no longer required to do any actual work himself, but he may
employ a solicitor or other agent to do it, whether there is any real necessity for the employment or not. No doubt he should use his discretion in

---

[77] *Skelton* v. *Younghouse* [1942] A.C. 571; *Re Avard* [1948] Ch. 43; *Re Cousins* (1885) 30
Ch.D. 203. *Re Zerny's Will Trusts* [1968] Ch.D. 203. *Re Zerny's Will Trusts* [1968] Ch. 415.
As to the courts jurisdiction to make an ineffective option workable, see *Re Malpass* [1985]
Ch. 42.

[78] See *Woodall* v. *Clifton* [1905] 2 Ch. 257; *Worthing Corporation* v. *Heather* [1906] 2 Ch.
532; *Hutton* v. *Watling* [1948] Ch. 26 (on appeal on another point, *ibid.* 398).

[79] *Re Adams and Kensington Vestry* (1884) 24 Ch.D. 199; 27 Ch.D. 199; 27 Ch.D. 394;
ante, p. 543.

[80] *James* v. *Buena Ventura Syn.* [1986] 1 Ch. 456. As to the personal representatives, statutory powers in relation to investments, see *ante*, p. 681.

[81] *Combe's Case* (1604) 9 Co. 75 *b*; Sugd.Pow., 8th ed., 179; *cf.* Farw.Pow., 3rd ed., pp.
498 *et seq.* And see *Green* v. *Whitehead* [1930] 1 Ch. 38.

[82] Per Lindley L.J., *Re Hetling and Merton* [1893] 3 Ch. 269, 280; and see *Green* v. *Whitehead*, *ante*.

[83] *Vane* v. *Rigden* (1870) L.R. 5 Ch. 663. A power of attorney given by an executrix to
receive, etc., all sums due to the deceased at the time of his death, and which were then due to
her as executrix, does not authorise the accepting of bills of exchange to charge her in her own
right, though for debts due from her testator; *Gardner* v. *Baillie* (1795) 6 T.R. 591; but *cf.*
Howard v. *Baillie* (1796) 2 H.Black. 618. And see *Re Vickery*, *ante*.

[84] *Post*, p. 744.

[85] [1931] 1 Ch. 572, 581. See notes by Sir William S. Holdsworth in 47 L.Q.R. 463, and
Gareth Jones in (1959) 22 M.L.R. 381. The section does not affect the principle that the
trustee is bound to conduct the business of the trust in such a way as an ordinary prudent man
of business would conduct his own. *Re Lucking* [1968] 1 W.L.R. 866.

selecting an agent, and should employ him only to do acts within the scope of the usual business of the agent."

But section 23(1) of the Trustee Act 1925, which enables trustees or representatives, instead of acting personally, to employ and pay an agent to transact any business or to do any act required to be transacted or done in the execution of the trust or the administration of the deceased's estate, does not seem to affect the old rule as to delegation of discretionary powers. For, *semble*, section 23 only authorises the delegation of any act requisite for completing the exercise of the power, and does not authorise the delegation of the discretion whether or not the power is to be exercised.[86] Similar considerations apply to subsection (3), which enables a trustee (including a representative) to appoint a solicitor as agent to receive and give a good discharge for money or property receivable by the trustee under the trust, or to appoint a solicitor or banker as agent to receive and give a good discharge for money payable to the trustee under a policy of insurance.[87]

Similarly where executors, who held shares as executors and were also directors of the company, agreed to vote always for the re-election of a particular director, it was held the agreement was *intra vires* the executors, and not a delegation of a discretion reposed in them by the testator.[88]

Delegation of powers over property abroad

On the other hand, the rule *delegatus non potest delegare* appears always to have been subject to the qualification that a trustee in England of property abroad might delegate the management of the property to an agent.[89]

Representatives are entitled by statute[90] to appoint any person as agent or attorney to deal with insurances[91] or to manage or sell property forming part of the estate of the deceased in any place outside the United Kingdom. Ancillary powers may be given at discretion and the personal representatives are not liable for loss arising only from such appointment.

Delegation while abroad

Again, the old rule prohibiting delegation is qualified by the Trustee Act 1925, s.25,[92] as amended by the Powers of Attorney Act 1971, s.9, which enables a trustee for a period not exceeding 12 months to delegate by

---

[86] See *Green* v. *Whitehead, ante.*

[87] s.23 is more fully discussed when dealing with the liability of a representative for the acts of his agent; see *post,* pp. 744 *et seq.*

[88] *Greenwell* v. *Porter* [1932] 1 Ch. 530.

[89] *Stuart* v. *Norton* (1860) 14 Moo.P.C. 17.

[90] Trustee Act 1925, s.23(2).

[91] "Insurances" is a misprint for "assurances": see *Green* v. *Whitehead* [1930] 1 Ch. 38, 45.

[92] 4 Wolst. & Ch., 13th ed., pp. 30–33. For powers of attorney generally see the Powers of Attorney Act 1971; Law of Property Act 1925, s.125(2); Enduring Powers of Attorney Act 1985.

power of attorney the exercise during his absence of any trusts vested in him.[93]

Delegation: leasing and management

Finally, the powers of and incidental to leasing, accepting surrenders of leases and management, conferred on trustees for sale,[94] may, by the Law of Property Act 1925, s.29, until the sale of the land, be revocably delegated from time to time, by writing, signed by them, to any person of full age (not being merely an annuitant) for the time being beneficially entitled in possession to the net rents and profits of the land during his life or any less period.[95] It would seem to follow that where a representative before making an assent of land allows the person beneficially entitled thereto into possession,[96] he may also delegate such powers of leasing and management to the beneficiary in possession.

The Emergency Provisions Acts 1939–48

Under the Execution of Trusts (Emergency Provisions) Act 1939, power was given to delegate during the emergency September 1, 1939 to May 31, 1948 and it was held under that Act that a trustee could delegate to two or more persons jointly and severally.[97] In the unlikely event of an issue ever turning on this Act, reference should be made to the Act itself.

---

[93] See *post* p. 1104.
[94] Trustees for sale have all the powers of a tenant for life and of trustees of a settlement conferred by the Settled Land Act 1925, including the powers of management during a minority (*ibid.* s.102): see the Law of Property Act 1925, s.28 (as amended). A representative has all these powers; Administration of Estates Act 1925, s.39, *ante*, p. 681.
[95] See *ante*, p. 682, 1 Wolst. & Ch., 13th ed., pp. 87–89.
[96] See *ante*, p. 689.
[97] *Re Earl of Feversham's Contract* [1942] Ch. 33.

CHAPTER 55

THE LIABILITY FOR AN EXECUTOR'S OWN ACTS

A—ACCOUNTABILITY

Executor's accounts

It has already been mentioned that an executor must account for all profits on the estate of the deceased which accrue in his own time[1]; and that if he carries on the trade or business of the testator the profits must be accounted for as assets.[2] Further, in common with a trustee, he must account for all profits which he makes from his office as executor. Thus, where he abandons it in favour of another for valuable consideration, he must surrender what he has received,[3] and where a sole executrix was in occupation of a house which formed part of the deceased's estate, and failed to show any tenancy, she was compelled to give up possession to the beneficiaries.[4] A representative is further bound to do everything in his power for the benefit of the estate, and is, therefore, absolutely precluded from buying the assets from himself or from his co-representatives, irrespective of undervalue or otherwise, for if he were allowed to buy he might thereby be induced to neglect his duty.[5] This rule is for the protection of the executor.[6] It stems from the rule that no one who has a duty to perform shall place himself[7] in a situation to have his interests conflicting with that duty.[8] Like all rules of equity it is flexible in the sense that it develops to meet the changing conditions of the time.[9] The rule no longer applies once the conflict between duty and interest has ceased.[10]

---

[1] See *ante*, pp. 51, and *post*, 673; *Watson* v. *Toone* (1820) 6 Madd. 153; *Smedley* v. *Varley* (1857) 23 Beav. 358. He is not entitled to deduct the tax which would have been payable but for a misappropriation. See *Re Bell* [1980] 1 W.L.R. 1217, 1238.

[2] See *ante*, p. 590. As to remuneration, see *ante*, p. 51.

[3] *Sugden* v. *Crossland* (1856) 3 Sm. & G. 192.

[4] *Davies* v. *Morgan* [1953] C.P.L. 148; [1953] C.L.Y. 3346. As to renewal of leases, etc., see *post*, p. 673.

[5] *Re Boles* [1902] 1 Ch. 244, 246; *Wright* v. *Morgan* [1926] A.C. 788. *Re Thompson* [1986] Ch. 99.

[6] *Boulting* v. *A.C.T.A.T.* [1963] 2 Q.B. 606; *Regal (Hastings) Ltd.* v. *Gulliver* [1942] 1 All E.R. 378. *Phipps* v. *Boardman* [1967] 2 A.C. 46; *Tito* v. *Waddell* (No. 2) [1977] Ch. 106, 225, 240. *Re Thompson* [1986] Ch. 99. See generally *Snell on Equity*, 27th ed., pp. 235–246, *Lewin on Trusts*, 16th ed., pp. 191–217, 693–706. See also *English* v. *Dedhamvale Properties* [1978] 1 W.L.R. 93, 107.

[7] He may, of course, be so placed by the will or by law or by the court. As to exercise of an option under the will and as to sale to a non-proving executor, see *post*, pp. 674, 669 respectively.

[8] *Per* Lord Cranworth in *Broughton* v. *Broughton* (1855) 5 De G.M. & G. 160, 164.

[9] See, n. 6 *supra*.

[10] See *per* Lord Upjohn in *Phipps* v. *Boardman* [1967] 2 A.C. 46, 131 (considering *Keech* v. *Sandford*). See *ante*, p. 673.

Administrator's accounts

The same rule applies to an administrator.[11] In particular an administrator during minority must account to the infant[12] after he has attained full age and obtained a grant,[13] or to any other later administrator including a creditor.[14] After the grant has determined and another representative has been constituted to whom he has accounted he can plead *plene administravit* to all other claims unless *devastavit* is alleged.[15] The remedy is against the later administrator in all other cases.[16]

Moneys employed in trade

An executor or trustee who employs trust money in trade or speculative transactions must account for the profit he makes by such employment or for interest at the rate payable under the equitable jurisdiction[17] at the option of the beneficiaries, or if it does not appear or cannot be made to appear what profits are attributable to such employment.

Similarly, if the executor or trustee mixes trust funds with his own money and employs them both in a trade or adventure of his own, the beneficiaries may either claim interest on the amount of trust funds employed or a proportionate share of the profits.[18] The beneficiaries, however, must elect to take either the profits for the whole period, or the interest for the whole period.[19]

This liability to account is not confined to partners who are also executors. If the other partners have notice of the fact that the employment of the assets in the business is a breach of trust, they also can be compelled to account for the profits made by them attributable to the employment of such assets or for interest thereon at 5 per cent.[20]

The above principles as to accounting for profits apply where executors employ assets in carrying on the deceased's trade for their own benefit,[21] even though they take a security for the assets in the shape of a mortgage of the real and personal property belonging to the partnership.[22]

On the other hand, where executors merely make an unauthorised loan to a partnership of which they are members, the firm, though cognisant of the breach of trust, is only bound to repay the capital with interest, as in

[11] Administration of Estates Act 1925, s.21.
[12] *Fotherby* v. *Pate* (1747) 3 Atk. 603.
[13] See the Judicature Act 1925, s.165(2).
[14] *Taylor* v. *Newton* (1752) 1 Lee 15.
[15] *Palmer* v. *Litherland* (1625–28) 1 Latch. 160; *Packman's Case* (1596) 6 Co. 18b.
[16] Bac.Abr.Exors.B. 1, 2; *Brooking* v. *Jennings* (1674) 1 Mod. 175.
[17] *Vyse* v. *Foster* (1872) L.R. 8 Ch. 309, 329; *Re Davis* [1902] 2 Ch. 314. See also *Jones* v. *Foxall* (1852) 15 Beav. 388; *Re Waterman's W.T.* [1952] 2 All E.R. 1054.
[18] *Docker* v. *Somes* (1834) 2 M. & K. 655; *Wedderburn* v. *Wedderburn* (1838) 4 M. & Cr. 41; *Willett* v. *Blanford* (1842) 1 Hare 253; *Portlock* v. *Gardner* (1842) *ibid.* 594, 603.
[19] *Heathcote* v. *Hulme* (1819) 1 J. & W. 122; *Vyse* v. *Foster* (1872) L.R. 8 Ch. 309, 334.
[20] *Flockton* v. *Bunning* (1868) L.R. 8 Ch. 323, n.
[21] *Wedderburn* v. *Wedderburn* (1856) 22 Beav. 84.
[22] *Townend* v. *Townend* (1859) 1 Giff. 201.

the case of any other loan. If the firm does not pay, the executors are liable only to the same extent.[23] The distinction is between a loan of money to, and the employment of capital in, a business.

Deceased's share in partnership

Where any member of a firm has died or ceased to be a partner, and the surviving or continuing partners carry on the business of the firm with its capital or assets without any final settlement of accounts as between the firm and the outgoing partner or his estate, then, in the absence of any agreement to the contrary, the outgoing partner or his estate is entitled at the option of himself or his representatives to such share of the profits made since the dissolution as the court may find to be attributable to the use of his share of the partnership assets, or to interest at the rate of 5 per cent. per annum on the amount of his share of the partnership assets.[24] This, however, is subject to the proviso that where by the partnership contract an option is given to surviving or continuing partners to purchase the interest of a deceased or outgoing partner, and that option is duly exercised, the estate of the deceased partner, or the outgoing partner or his estate, as the case may be, is not entitled to any further or other share of profits; but if any partner assuming to act in exercise of the option does not in all material respects comply with the terms thereof, he is liable to account under the foregoing provisions of this section.[25]

Where a deceased partner has appointed some of his co-partners to be his executors, and the business is carried on after his death without the withdrawal of his share, the liability to account for profits under section 42(1) is not confined to those partners who are also executors. The whole firm is liable to account for profits. Those partners who are also executors may, however, be made to account though the other partners are not made parties to the action.[26] But they cannot be made responsible for more profits than they received.[27]

The profits to be accounted for in all these cases must depend upon all the circumstances.[28] Accountability is confined to those profits which can be attributed to the employment of the assets in the business.[29] To the profits made from any other source, such as the skill of the surviving partners, the deceased's estate has no claim.[30]

---

[23] *Stroud* v. *Gwyer* (1860) 28 Beav. 130; *Vyse* v. *Foster* (1872) L.R. 8 Ch. 309; L.R. 7 H.L. 318.

[24] Partnership Act 1890, s.42. This was already established law: see *Crawshay* v. *Collins* (1808) 15 Ves. 218; *Brown* v. *De Tastet* (1819) Jac. 284; *Yates* v. *Finn* (1880) 13 Ch.D. 839. It has been suggested that the fixed rate of 5 per cent. ought to be increased. See *Sobell* v. *Boston* [1975] 1 W.L.R. 1587, 1593.

[25] Partnership Act 1890, s.42(2).

[26] See *McDonald* v. *Richardson* (1858) 1 Giff. 81.

[27] *Vyse* v. *Foster* (1875) L.R. 7 H.L. 318, 334.

[28] *Willett* v. *Blanford* (1842) 1 Hare 253.

[29] *Manley* v. *Sartori* [1927] 1 Ch. 157.

[30] *Simpson* v. *Chapman* (1853) 4 De G.M. & G. 154; *Wedderburn* v. *Wedderburn* (1856) 22 Beav. 84.

If the option, mentioned in section 42(2), is properly exercised, and the share of the deceased partner is ascertained, the relationship of debtor and creditor exists between the surviving partners and the deceased partner's estate.[31] Thus, if the executors allow the price payable for the deceased's share to remain outstanding for longer than is necessary, this gives no right to the deceased's estate to share in the profits of the business, but only to interest, even though the executors, or some of them, are partners in the business.[32]

But where no option is given in the partnership contract, as in *Cook* v. *Collingridge*,[33] a sale of a testator's share in a partnership trade, and the property belonging to it, made by his executors to his partners, for the purpose of being resold to one of his executors, will be set aside, and his estate held entitled to his *aliquot* proportion of the subsequent profits as if the partnership had continued.[34]

Remuneration of executor-director

An executor is qualified to be a director of a company as the registered holder of his testator's share.[35] If a trustee of shares in a company, by virtue of the control over the company which those shares give him, gets himself appointed to the post of director or managing director, then although his remuneration is not paid to him in respect of the trust holding but in respect of the work he does as director or managing director, yet, because he gains that emolument by virtue of the trust holding, he is not entitled to retain the remuneration for his own benefit,[36] unless he obtains the authority of the court,[37] on a proper application for that purpose.[38] Conversely it seems that a trustee who is already a director or shareholder is not to be penalised if he accepts appointment as executor.[39] However the court exercises the jurisdiction to increase remuneration sparingly. It will not alter the general level of remuneration unless that level is derisory, or there is

---

[31] See *ante*, p. 567.

[32] *Vyse* v. *Foster* (1872) L.R. 8 Ch. 309; L.R. 7 H.L. 318. And see *Stroud* v. *Gwyer* (1860) 28 Beav. 130.

[33] (1823) Jacob 607. See 27 Beav. 456.

[34] "One of the most firmly established rules is that persons dealing as trustees and executors must put their own interest entirely out of the question, and this is so difficult to do in a transaction in which they are dealing with themselves that the court will not inquire whether it has been done or not, but at once says that such a transaction cannot stand": by Lord Eldon, Jacob 621. See *Wedderburn* v. *Wedderburn* (1836) 2 Keen 722; 4 My. & Cr. 41; *Willett* v. *Blanford* (1842) 1 Hare 253. See also *Portlock* v. *Gardner* (1842) 1 Hare 594, 603.

[35] *Grundy* v. *Briggs* [1910] 1 Ch. 444. As to the director as trustee, see article by L. S. Sealy in [1967] C.L.J. 83.

[36] Per Jenkins J. in *Re Llewellin's Will Trusts* [1949] Ch. 225. And see *Re Francis* (1905) 74 L.J.Ch. 198; *Re Dover Coalfield Extension* [1908] 1 Ch. 65; *Re Macadam* [1946] Ch. 73; *Re Gee* [1948] Ch. 284; *Re Northcote* [1949] 1 All E.R. 442; *Re Orwell* 1982 1 W.L.R. 1337, 1341.

[37] The court has an inherent jurisdiction to authorise remuneration whether or not the appointment is made by the court. See *Re Masters* [1953] 1 W.L.R. 81 and cases there cited. See *ante*, p. 49, and *Re Codd* [1975] 1 W.L.R. 1139; *Re Duke of Norfolk* [1982] Ch. 61 C.A.; *Re Keeler* [1981] Ch. 156.

[38] *Re Barbour* [1974] 1 W.L.R. 1198, 1201B.

[39] See *Re Orwell* 1982 1 W.L.R. 1337, 1341.

agreement, or an implied promise by the beneficiaries, or it is necessary at or soon after acceptance in order to obtain the services of some particular trustee whose services are of special value to the trust, as there has been a radical change of circumstances.[40] The court also has an anticipatory jurisdiction on the same principles to allow a director-trustee to retain future remuneration for his own benefit. In *Williams* v. *Barton*[41] a stockbroker's clerk, whose salary comprised half the commission on business introduced by him, was also a trustee. He was held liable to account for the half-commission received by him in respect of trust business introduced by him to his firm. But a testator may expressly or by implication authorise the trustee to retain the remuneration,[42] and a director-trustee is entitled to recoup himself for necessary expenditure and to obtain payment for his work and skill.[43]

Executor buying assets from himself

An executor cannot properly purchase assets from himself.[44] If he does so he will have to account as trustee for any advantage which he gains in the transaction, and the transaction itself is voidable.[45] Thus, if an executor compounds debts or mortgages, and buys them in for less than is due upon them, he cannot take the benefit of it himself, but the other creditors and beneficiaries have the advantage of it.[46] Similarly, where the executor of a mortgagee for a term of years purchased the equity of redemption in fee for a small sum in his own name, and for his own benefit, it was held that he was a trustee of the fee for the benefit of the testator's estate.[47] But if an executor's acts are minimal and the reasons for the disability do not exist he may be entitled to purchase.[48]

Executor buying interests of beneficiaries

There is a distinction between an executor's dealing with himself and an executor's dealing with legatees or other beneficiaries. The latter dealings,

[40] See generally *Re Duke of Norfolk* [1979] Ch. 37, 58, and cases there cited; [1981] 2 W.L.R. 455, C.A.; *Re Keeler* [1981] Ch. 156.
[41] [1927] 2 Ch. 9.
[42] See *Re Llewellin's Will Trusts* [1949] Ch. 225. For qualifications of this proposition, see *ante*, 675, 668.
[43] *Re Macadam* [1946] Ch. 73, 82; *Phipps* v. *Boardman* [1964] 1 W.L.R. 993, 1018; [1967] 2 A.C. 46, 104, 112; *O'Sullivan* v. *Management Agency* [1985] 1 Q.B. 428, 458.
[44] See *ante*, p. 673, 674; and as to an exception, *post*, p. 467. See generally *Snell on Equity*, 27th ed., pp. 235–246; *Lewin on Trusts*, 16th ed., pp. 191–217, 93–706.
[45] *Campbell* v. *Walker*, 5 Ves. 678, 681; *Holder* v. *Holder* [1968] Ch. 353, 398. The accountability does not last indefinitely. The claim to avoid must be made within a reasonable time. See *Re Jarvis* [1958] 1 W.L.R. 815 and *post*, p. 722. It seems immaterial to the result whether the transaction is described as voidable or as creating a constructive trust as in *Re Edwards* [1982] Ch. 30.
[46] *Anon.* (1708) 1 Salk. 155; *Ex p. James* (1803) 8 Ves. 337.
[47] *Fosbrooke* v. *Balguy* (1833) 1 M. & K. 226.
[48] *Holder* v. *Holder* [1968] Ch. 353. *Re Thompson* [1986] Ch. 99, 115. See on "Fiduciary Relationships" in general articles by L. S. Sealy in [1962] C.L.J. 69 and [1963] C.L.J. 119.

although jealously watched,[49] are not invariably voidable,[50] and it is sometimes possible to justify a transaction which is formally a purchase of assets
by a trustee from himself as being in substance a justifiable purchase of a
beneficiary's interest.[51] The converse may also be true.[52]

Gains and losses on improper dealing

Again, if an executor lays out the assets on private securities, though he
is liable for all deficiencies which may be caused thereby, he must account
to the estate for all the benefit.[53] Indeed, the principle is general, that an
executor who takes upon himself to act with regard to the testator's property in any other manner than his trust requires must replace any loss,
though he cannot possibly be a gainer; any gain must accrue for the benefit
of his beneficiary.[54]

Representative charged with interest

The court has a statutory power to award simple interest at any rate, at
its discretion, in any proceedings including proceedings for summary judgment[55] for the recovery of a debt or damages.[56] This power will not, however, normally apply to questions of account in equity, where there are two
grounds on which an executor or administrator may be charged with interest: first, that he has been guilty of negligence in omitting to invest the
money for the benefit of the estate; secondly, that he himself has made use
of the money, or has committed some other *misfeasance*, to his own profit
and advantage.[57]

(1) Negligent failure to invest

First, it may sometimes be necessary and justifiable, especially during
the first year after the death of the deceased,[58] for a representative to keep
large sums in his hands to answer the exigency of the deceased's affairs.[59]
The necessity for such a course has to some extent, if not altogether, been

---

[49] *Coles* v. *Trecothick* (1804) 9 Ves. 244. See *Lewin on Trusts*, 16th ed., p. 697.
[50] *Ibid.*
[51] See *Williams* v. *Scott* [1900] A.C. 499.
[52] See *Barton* v. *Hassard* (1843) 3 Dr. & W. 461, where an executor contracted with legatees for the purchase of their legacies, which were accordingly assigned to a trustee for him, in
consideration of sums of money less in amount than the legacies, and it was admitted that the
transaction could not be sustained for the benefit of the executor; and it was also held that the
deed of assignment did not operate as a release of the estate, and could not be upheld, as
against the legatees who executed it, for the benefit of their co-legatees.
[53] *Adye* v. *Feuilleteau* (1783) 1 Cox 24.
[54] *Piety* v. *Stace* (1799) 4 Ves. 620; *Crosskill* v. *Bower* (1863) 32 Beav. 86.
[55] *Gardner Steel* v. *Sheffield Bros.* [1978] 1 W.L.R. 916.
[56] Supreme Court Act 1981, s.35A. See also S.C.P. 1993, 42/1/12, 44/9.
[57] *Rocke* v. *Hart* (1805) 11 Ves. 59, 60; *Tebbs* v. *Carpenter*, 1 Madd. 290, 306, 307; *Kildare*
v. *Hopson* (1734) 4 Bro.P.C. 550, Toml. ed.; *Lincoln* v. *Allen* (1768) *ibid.* 553; *Ashburnham*
v. *Thompson* (1807) 13 Ves. 401.
[58] See *Forbes* v. *Ross* (1788) 2 Cox Eq.Cas. 113, 115, 116.
[59] See *Dawson* v. *Massey* (1809) 1 Ball & B. 234.

removed by the power now conferred upon trustees and representatives,[60] pending the negotiation and preparation of any mortgage or charge, or during any other time while an investment is being sought for, to pay any trust money into a bank to a deposit or other account.[61] If a representative keeps money dead in his hands without any apparent reason or necessity, then it becomes negligence, and a breach of trust, and the court will charge the executor with interest.[62] The existence of outstanding demands, though based on probable grounds, is no reason why the executors should not lay the testator's money out.[63] But in order to give rise to a claim for interest there must be a clear case of improper retention of balances to a substantial amount.[64] And an executor is not chargeable with interest for a balance in his hands retained under a fair apprehension of his right to it,[65] nor does an action lie for damages for failure to take out probate.[66]

The court will not charge an executor, who has been guilty of delay in accounting, with interest on arrears of income unpaid by him.[67]

A representative "who has improperly paid away money is deemed by a Court of Equity still to have the money in his own hands."[68] "Principle and authority both require that in such a case he should be dealt with as if he had improperly retained the money in his own hands, and his liability to pay interest as well as principal is clear."[69]

But where an executor paid away money on what turned out to be an erroneous construction of the will, and the legatees had knowledge of this payment and acquiesced in the erroneous construction, the court did not make the executor pay interest.[70]

[60] Trustee Act 1925, s.68(17).

[61] *Ibid.* s.11(1).

[62] *Littlehales* v. *Gascoyne* (1790) 3 Bro.C.C. 73; *Browne* v. *Southouse, ibid.* 107; *Franklin* v. *Frith* (1792) *ibid.* 433; *Hall* v. *Hallet* (1784) 1 Cox 134; *Seers* v. *Hind* (1791) 1 Ves. 294; *Longmore* v. *Broom* (1802) 7 Ves. 124; *Ashburnham* v. *Thompson* (1807) 13 Ves. 402; *Turner* v. *Turner* (1819) 1 J. & W. 39; *Goodchild* v. *Fenton* (1829) 3 Y. & J. 481; *Stafford* v. *Fiddon* (1857) 23 Beav. 386; *Johnson* v. *Prendergast* (1860) 28 Beav. 480.

[63] *Franklin* v. *Frith* (1792) 3 Bro.C.C. 434; 1 Madd. 305. If money placed out at interest is called in by an executor without any cause, he must pay interest; *Taylor* v. *Gerst* (1728) Mosely 99; but he has an honest discretion to call in a debt bearing interest if he thinks the same is in hazard: *Newton* v. *Bennet* (1784) 1 Bro.C.C. 361; and if he immediately lays out the money in authorised investments he incurs no liability.

[64] *Jones* v. *Morrall* (1852) 2 Sim.(N.S.) 241, 252. See also *Davenport* v. *Stafford* (1851) 14 Beav. 319.

[65] *Bruere* v. *Pemberton* (1806) 12 Ves. 386. An administrator *pendente lite* was not liable to pay interest upon a blanace in his hands during the pendency of the suit in the Ecclesiastical Court: *Gallivan* v. *Evans* (1808) 1 Ball & B. 191. Nor, if an administrator complies with an order for payment into court of the balance representing payments disallowed in his accounts in the action, is he, in the absence of special circumstances, chargeable with interest thereon: *Re Jones* [1897] 2 Ch. 190.

[66] *Re Stevens* [1898] 1 Ch. 177.

[67] *Blogg* v. *Johnson* (1867) L.R. 2 Ch. 225.

[68] *Re Hulkes* (1886) 33 Ch.D. 552, 557, not following *Saltmarsh* v. *Barrett* (1861) 31 Beav. 349, as being inconsistent with the principle established by *Att.-Gen.* v. *Köhler* (1861) 9 H.L.C. 654, and *Att.-Gen.* v. *Alford* (1855) 4 De G.M. & G. 843.

[69] *Per* Lord Cranworth in *Att.-Gen.* v. *Köhler* (1861) 9 H.L.C. 654, 680.

[70] *Re Hulkes, supra.* For a compromised claim, see *Chichester Diocesan Board* v. *Simpson* [1944] A.C. 341.

Rate of interest on failure to invest

The rule is that where negligence alone[71] is imputable to a representative he should be charged with interest on the balances which he ought to have laid out, either in compliance with the express directions of the will, or from his general duty, where the will is silent on the subject.[72] The rate is that which under the equitable jurisdiction he could on evidence be expected to have earned. For many years this ranged between 3 and 5 per cent.[73] In order to induce the court to charge the executor with more than the ordinary rate, a special case, such as a direct breach of trust, is necessary.[74] The court is reluctant to alter the rate of interest since this introduces an element of uncertainty in practice and administration, but alterations will be made on evidence of changed conditions at least as constant as conditions when the rate was last considered.[75]

(2) Employing assets for own advantage

Secondly, it is established[76] that if a representative makes use of the money of the deceased, he ought to pay the interest he made,[77] on the principle that he ought not to derive any profit from the trust property. Hence, if a trustee, having trust money in his hands, knowingly applied it to his own use, or in his trade, he was chargeable with interest at the rate of 5 per cent.[78] It has already been shown[79] that if the fund is employed in trade, the beneficiaries have an option of taking either the interest, or the profits which have arisen from the trade. An executor who, being a trader, and having an account with a banker, placed the assets at his bankers in his own name, thereby increasing the balances in his favour, acquiring additional credit, and enjoying in his business the advantages naturally arising from that circumstances, was considered as having employed the

---

[71] As to whether misconduct increases the rate of interest chargeable, see *post*, pp. 710–712.

[72] *Dornford* v. *Dornford* (1806) 12 Ves. 130, n. 29, 2nd ed.; *ibid.* cited 1 Madd. 302; *Ashburnham* v. *Thompson* (1807) 13 Ves. 402; *Rocke* v. *Hart* (1805) 11 Ves. 58, 60, 61; *Tebbs* v. *Carpenter* (1816) 1 Madd. 290, 307; *Sutton* v. *Sharp* (1826) 1 Russ. 146, 151; *Melland* v. *Gray* (1845) 2 Coll. 295; *Re Hulkes* (1886) 33 Ch.D. 552.

[73] Though the rate was, for some time, reduced to 3 per cent. (*Re Barclay* [1899] 1 Ch. 674, 686) 4 per cent. was later charged: see *Re Parry* [1947] Ch. 23. For cases where 5 per cent. was charged, see *post*, pp. 1035–1037.

[74] *Tebbs* v. *Carpenter* (1816) 1 Madd. 290, 306; *Mousley* v. *Carr* (1841) 4 Beav. 49; *Hosking* v. *Nicholls* (1842) 1 Y. & C.C.C. 478, 480. See *De Cordova* v. *De Cordova* (1879) 4 App.Cas. 692; *Re Barclay* [1899] 1 Ch. 674.

[75] *Re Parry* [1947] Ch. 23, following *Re Beech* [1920] 1 Ch. 40. See generally as to the current position *post*.

[76] *Perkins* v. *Baynton* (1784) 1 Bro.C.C. 375; *Newton* v. *Bennet* (1784) 1 Bro.C.C. 361; *Forbes* v. *Ross* (1788) 2 Bro.C.C. 439; *Tebbs* v. *Carpenter* (1816) 1 Madd. 304. *Adams* v. *Gale* (1740) 2 Atk. 106; *Child* v. *Gibson*, *ibid.* 603, can no longer be supported.

[77] *Forbes* v. *Ross* (1788) 2 Cox 116; *Rocke* v. *Hart* (1805) 11 Ves. 60. And see *Burnell* v. *Brown* (1820) 1 Jac. & W. 175.

[78] *Mousley* v. *Carr* (1841) 4 Beav. 49; *Re Davis* [1902] 2 Ch. 314. As to rates of interest now see pp. 1035–1037, *post*.

[79] See *ante*, p. 51; *Burden* v. *Burden*, cited 1 J. & W. 134.

money for his own benefit, and was therefore, charged with interest at 5 per cent.[80]

Where a bank being sole executor placed a large sum of money forming part of the estate on deposit with itself, paying one-half per cent. interest thereon to the beneficiaries, it was conceded that this was a circumstance which made the bank accountable for the moneys so deposited and for interest at 5 per cent. thereon, but the court held that a charging clause in common form enabled the bank to avoid having to account for interest on the said moneys above one-half per cent.[81] There is, however, nothing rigid about the rate of 5 per cent. and in times of constant high rates of commercial interest it is thought that the courts might well make further increases on the principle as stated above.[82]

Other instances where a higher rate charged

There are many other cases where executors, who have applied the assets in direct dereliction of their duty, have been charged with 5 per cent. interest.[83] Thus, in *Mosley* v. *Ward*,[84] an executor who unnecessarily called in property held by him in trust for infants which was out upon good security at 5 per cent., and who kept large balances in his hands which he used as his own, was charged with interest at 5 per cent. and costs. In *Bick* v. *Motley*,[85] two executors had, by signing joint cheques, enabled each other to receive sums belonging to the estate of their testatrix, when they were both largely indebted to that estate. The sums so received by them were debts provable under their respective commissions, both executors having become bankrupt. Each was held chargeable with interest at 5 per cent. upon the sums which he had enabled his co-executor to receive, that interest being added to the principal sums to be proved against the bankrupts' estates respectively.[86]

In *Jones* v. *Foxall*[87] and *Williams* v. *Powell*,[88] Romilly M.R. stated the

---

[80] *Treves* v. *Townshend* (1783) 1 Bro.C.C. 385; *Rocke* v. *Hart* (1805) 11 Ves. 61; *Sutton* v. *Sharp* (1826) 1 Russ. 151, 152; *Re Jones* (1883) 49 L.T. 91. Although the will authorised the executor to invest the residue on "good private securities": *Westover* v. *Chapman* (1844) 1 Coll. 177. See also *Re Hilliard* (1790) 1 Ves. 90; *Melland* v. *Gray* (1845) 2 Coll. 295; *Williams* v. *Powell* (1852) 15 Beav. 461. But see *contra*, *Perkins* v. *Baynton* (1784) 1 Bro.C.C. 375; *Browne* v. *Southouse* (1790) 3 *ibid*. 107. See *Burdick* v. *Garrick* (1870) L.R. 5 Ch. 233, as to what is employ-ment of money in business. As to current rates of interest see pp. 1035–1037, *post*.

[81] *Re Waterman's W.T.* [1952] 2 All E.R. 1054.

[82] See *Re Parry, supra*. In exercise of the equitable jurisdiction in mortgages 7 per cent. has been allowed. See *Cityland* v. *Dabrah* [1968] Ch. 166. See also *post*, pp. 1035–1037.

[83] See *Forbes* v. *Ross* (1788) 2 Cox 113; *ibid*. 2 Bro.C.C. 430 (executors, with wide dis-cretion as to investments, made a loan to one of themselves on a bond at 4 per cent.); *Piety* v. *Stace* (1799) 4 Ves. 620 (employment of assets in executor's trade and various transactions in the public funds); *Pocock* v. *Reddington* (1801) 5 Ves. 794 (sale of stock and improper deal-ings with proceeds). See also *Bate* v. *Scales* (1806) 12 Ves. 402.

[84] (1805) 11 Ves. 581.

[85] (1835) 2 M & K. 312.

[86] See also *Munch* v. *Cockerell* (1836) 9 Sim. 339, 351; confirmed as to charging the trustees with interest at 5 per cent., 5 M. & Cr. 178, 220.

[87] (1852) 15 Beav. 388.

[88] *Ibid*. 461.

rule as established by the authorities, that if an executor has retained balances in his hands, which he ought to have invested, the court will charge him with simple interest at 4 per cent. on the balances; but if in addition to such retention he has committed a direct breach of trust, or been guilty of misconduct, he will be charged at the rate of 5 per cent.[89]

But in *Att.-Gen.* v. *Alford*,[90] Lord Cranworth C. said that the court does not assume to punish an executor in these cases by making him account for more than he has received. It merely charges him with the interest which he has received, or which the court is justly entitled to say he ought to have received, or which it is so fairly to be presumed that he did receive, that he is estopped from saying that he did not receive it.[91] This, however, does not alter the fact that a trustee, who uses the trust funds for his own purposes, may be charged with interest at 5 per cent.[92]

Instances of compound interest

As a general rule, the court orders the computation of simple interest.[93] But there are instances in which an executor has been charged with compound interest or with the actual profits made. An example of this is to be found in *Raphael* v. *Boehm*,[94] where the executor did not lay the testator's money out as directed, but kept upwards of £30,000 in his hands, and used it in his trade, so that there was a wilful violation of the will, which prohibited retainer and directed accumulation. And it is established that where there is an express trust for accumulation, the executor will be charged with compound interest.[95] Thus, in *Knott* v. *Cottee*,[96] where there was an express trust for accumulation, it was held that, though the circumstances were not such as to make it right to charge the executor with more than 4 per cent. interest on money which he had improperly invested, yet it was a case for annual rests.[97] Other instances where, in executors' accounts, interest has been given with rests, will be found in the cases cited in the footnote.[98]

---

[89] See also *Knott* v. *Cottee* (1852) 16 Beav. 77, 80; *Re Davis* [1902] 2 Ch. 314. Presumably much higher rates would be applied in times of higher general rates. See pp. 1035–1037 *post.*

[90] (1855) 4 De G.M. & G. 843, 851, 852.

[91] See also *Vyse* v. *Foster* (1872) L.R. 8 Ch.App. 309, 333.

[92] *Mayor of Berwick* v. *Murray* (1849) 7 De G.M. & G. 497, 519; *Re Hulkes* (1886) 33 Ch.D. 552; *Re Davis, ante.*

[93] *Robinson* v. *Cumming* (1742) 1 Atk. 410, *post*, p. 1037.

[94] (1807) 11 Ves. 92; 13 Ves. 407, 590; *Jones* v. *Foxall* (1852) 15 Beav. 388; *Re Davis* [1902] 2 Ch. 314; *Heathcote* v. *Hulme* (1819) 1 Jac. & Walk. 122; *Burnell* v. *Brown* (1820 1 Jac. & Walk. 175.

[95] See *Re Emmet's Estate* (1881) 17 Ch.D. 142; *Re Barclay, infra.*

[96] (1852) 16 Beav. 77; followed in *Re Barclay* [1899] 1 Ch. 674, save that the rate of interest charged was 3 per cent. only.

[97] A direction to the master "to make annual rests" amounts to a direction to charge compound interest: *Heighington* v. *Grant* (1840) 5 M. & Cr. 258.

[98] *Stacpoole* v. *Stacpoole* (1816) 4 Dow. 209; *Willson* v. *Carmichael* (1830) 2 Dow. & Cl. 58; *Walker* v. *Woodward* (1826) 1 Russ. 107; *Townend* v. *Townend*, 1 Giff. 201; *Walrond* v. *Walrond* (1861) 29 Beav. 586. See also on this subject, *Binnington* v. *Harwood* (1825) T. & R. 481; *Docker* v. *Somes* (1843) 2 M. & K. 655.

Principle for charging compound interest

As has been seen Lord Cranworth repudiated the doctrine of punishing the executor,[99] and maintained the principle, for compound as well as simple interest, that the court ought to charge him only with the interest which he has received, or which the court is justly entitled to say he ought to have received, or to presume he did receive.[1]

Thus in *Burdick* v. *Garrick*[2] where a solicitor-trustee employed trust money in his business, putting the funds to the firm's credit at the bank, the court only allowed simple interest. Lord Hatherley pointed out that in trade it may be presumed that compound interest has been earned, whilst capital used in a solicitor's business not infrequently yields no interest at all.

No interest charged

On the setting aside of a sale by a trustee of trust property to himself, and the reconveyance of the property to the beneficiaries, it is not the practice of the court to charge the trustee with interest on the rents and profits received by him since the date of the sale.[3]

Other forms of liability

Apart from his accountability, the origins of an executor's liability arising from his own acts will normally arise in tort or contract. In the latter case difficult issues arise in particular where he carries on the business of the testator.[4] He may be liable simply as executor[5] or he may incur personal liability.[6] The liability in tort can however be stated briefly. In all cases there is a distinction between his personal liability[7] and his liability as executor.[8] An executor may also now be liable for certain new offences in criminal law.[9] Procedure in civil actions by and against executors is considered in Chapters 62 and 63.

B—Liability in Tort

The representative is himself primarily liable for all tort committed in the course of his duties, but he is entitled to be indemnified out of the estate for

[99] Cf. *Crackelt* v. *Bethune* (1820) 1 J. & W. 586; *Tebbs* v. *Carpenter* (1816) 1 Madd. 290. Cf. also *Jones* v. *Foxall* (1852) 15 Beav. 388; *Williams* v. *Powell, ibid.* 461.

[1] *Att.-Gen.* v. *Alford, ante,* p. 712; *Re Barclay* [1899] 1 Ch. 674; *Wallersteiner* v. *Moir* [1975] Q.B. 373.

[2] (1870) 5 Ch.App. 233. See also *Guardian Ocean* v. *Banco do Brasil* [1992] *The Times,* March 19, 1992.

[3] *Silkstone Co.* v. *Edey* [1900] 1 Ch. 167.

[4] See *post*, pp. 722 *et seq.*

[5] See below.

[6] See p. 724, *post*.

[7] An order making him personally liable is said to be "*de bonis propriis,*" as against "*de bonis testatoris*" where he is not personally liable.

[8] An order confined to his liability as executor will uphold the plea of "*plene administravit,*" if the administration is complete.

[9] See *post*, p. 728.

all torts committed in the reasonable management of the estate, as for instance where in conducting a colliery business he lets down the adjacent land surface.[10]

C—LIABILITY OF EXECUTOR AS SUCH IN CONTRACT

It seems to have been once considered that wherever an action was brought against an executor or administrator on promises made by him after the death of the testator or intestate, he was chargeable in his own right, and not in his representative capacity.[11] Later authorities have, however, established that, in several instances, the executor may be sued, *as executor*, on a promise made by him as executor. In such cases he is liable no further than on a promise of the testator. He is said to be liable only as to the testator's assets (*de bonis testatoris*).

This is illustrated by *Dowse* v. *Coxe*.[12] Proceedings in Chancery, in which T.B. was a party, were referred to arbitration. One of the terms of submission was that in case either of the parties should die, the death was not to abate the reference. T.B. died before the making of the award. The arbitrator awarded that the executor should pay the plaintiff £225 out of the assets of T.B. Being so liable, the defendant executor promised to pay. It was held that the executor was not charged thereby personally, but as executor only, and that the judgment must be limited to the testator's assets (*bonis testatoris.*[13])

Again, in *Powell* v. *Graham*,[14] the testator promised in his lifetime that if the plaintiff would enter into his service as a nurse and housekeeper, and would continue to serve him till his death, his executor should, after his decease, pay the plaintiff £20. The defendant promised to pay the plaintiff that sum whenever he, as executor, should be requested so to do. The defendant was held not liable individually, but as executor only.

In the same case the court held that an allegation of an account stated between the plaintiff and the defendant as executor, and a promise by the defendant to pay the balance, does not charge him personally; but he may plead administration complete (*plene administravit,*)[15] and the whole judgment which can be given in favour of the plaintiff is *de bonis testatoris*.[16] It makes no difference whether the account is alleged to have been stated of

---

[10] *Re Raybould* [1900] 1 Ch. 199, following *Benett* v. *Wyndham* (1862) 4 D.F. & J. 259.

[11] See *Trewinian* v. *Howell* (1588) Cro.Eliz. 91; *Hawkes* v. *Saunders* (1860) 1 Cowp. 289; *Jennings* v. *Newman* (1791) 4 T.R. 347.

[12] (1825) 3 Bing. 20; *ibid.* 10 Moore 272.

[13] This judgment was reversed in K.B., but on a different ground, the Court of Error declining to give any opinion on this point; 6 B. & C. 255. As to the personal responsibility of an executor on a submission to arbitration, see *ante*, p. 579. As to the forms of judgment against representatives see *post*, pp. 908 *et seq.*

[14] (1817) 7 Taunt, 581; *ibid.* 1 Moore 305.

[15] As to this defence see *post*, p. 894.

[16] *Ashby* v. *Ashby* (1827) 7 B. & C. 444.

money due from the testator to the plaintiff,[17] or of money due from the defendant as executor to the plaintiff.[18]

Again, suppose two persons are jointly bound as sureties, one dies, and the survivor is sued and obliged to pay the whole debt. If the deceased had been living, the survivor might have sued him for contribution in an action for money paid; and it would therefore seem that he is entitled to sue the executor of the deceased for money paid to his use as executor.[19]

The distinguishing characteristic of the above illustrations seems to be that in all of them "the consideration for the promise of the executor was a contract or transaction with the testator."[20]

Representative acting under statutory powers

A representative has statutory powers to enter into certain contracts.[21] If he expressly contracts in exercise of these powers he is liable as executor or administrator, not personally. This does not generally prejudice existing creditors of the estate, for, as a rule, all the authorised contracts are beneficial to the estate.

Executor liable for unauthorised contracts

On the other hand, if the executor enters into some unauthorised contract, he renders himself personally liable. He cannot involve the deceased's estate in some new, burdensome and unauthorised obligation.[22]

Thus, if the executor was acting outside the scope of his powers, an allegation that he was, as executor, indebted to the plaintiff for so much money lent by the plaintiff to the defendant, as executor, and that the defendant, in consideration thereof, as executor promised to pay, charges him personally, and he cannot plead *plene administravit*. The only possible judgment is that he is personally liable (*de bonis propriis*.)[23]

Again, where the defendant, as executor, was indebted to the plaintiff for money had and received by the defendant, as executor, for the use of

[17] *Segar* v. *Atkinson* (1789) 1 H.Bl. 102; *Ellis* v. *Bowen* (1801) Forrest, Exch.Rep. 98.
[18] *Powell* v. *Graham* (1817) 7 Taunt. 580; *Ashby* v. *Ashby* (1827) 7 B. & C. 444; but see *Rose* v. *Bowler* (1789) 1 H.Bl. 108; 2 Saund. 117 *h*, note to *Coryton* v. *Lithebye*.
[19] *Ashby* v. *Ashby*, 7 B. & C. 444, 449, 451, 452. And see *Corner* v. *Shew* (1838) 3 M. & W. 350. See also *Batard* v. *Hawes* (1853) 2 E. & B. 287, 298, where these dicta were regarded as strong authority for holding that, if one of several co-contractors be compelled by suit to pay the whole debt, he may sue the executors of another of them who has died before payment, for contribution. See further Glanville Williams, *Joint Obligations*, pp. 164–165.
[20] By Mellish L.J. in *Farhall* v. *Farhall* (1871) L.R. 7 Ch. 123. 127.
[21] Administration of Estates Act 1925, s. 39 (1) (iii); *post*, p. 1007, 5 Wolst. & Ch., 13th ed., pp. 68–70.
[22] See *Farhall* v. *Farhall*, *ante*. And see *Owen* v. *Delamere* (1872) L.R. 15 Eq. 134.
[23] *Rose* v. *Bowler* (1789) 1 H.Bl. 108; *Powell* v. *Graham* (1817) 7 Taunt. 580; *Farhall* v. *Farhall* (1871) L.R. 7 Ch. 123. A person cannot, by contract with an executor acquire a right to prove against the estate, though the executor has power to give him a lien on specific assets: *ibid.*

the plaintiff, and in consideration thereof the defendant, as executor, promised to pay, he was held to be personally liable.[24]

Similarly, a claim on a promise by the defendant, as executor, for use and occupation after the death of the testator, has been held to charge the defendant personally, and not in his character of executor.[25] An allegation that the defendant, as executor, was indebted to the plaintiff for goods sold and delivered by the plaintiff to the defendant, as executor, at his request, or for work done and materials for the same used and provided by the plaintiff for the defendant, as executor, at his request, and that the defendant, as the executor, promised to pay, charges the defendant in his personal and not in his representative character[26] if he was not acting properly under his powers.

Interest on debts bearing interest

Where a judgment directs an account of the debts of a deceased person, unless the estate is insolvent[27] or it is otherwise ordered, interest is computed on such debts as to such of them as carry interest after the rate they respectively carry, and as to all others at the rate then payable on judgment debts from the date of judgment.[28]

Interest on debts not carrying interest

A creditor whose debt does not carry interest, who establishes the same under a judgment or order of the court, is entitled to interest upon his debt at the rate payable on judgment debts from the date of the judgment or order out of any assets which may remain after satisfying the costs of the cause or matter, the debts established, and the interest of such debts as by law carry interest.[29] These provisions do not, however, extend to creditors of the executors.[30]

Executor contracting as such, where no assets

In actions brought against an executor, as such, a promise by the executor is a *mere nudum pactum* if there were no assets.[31] But even under the

---

[24] *Rose* v. *Bowler* (1789) 1 H.Bl. 108; *Jennings* v. *Newman* (1791) 4 T.R. 347; *Brigden* v. *Parkes* (1801) 2 B. & P. 424; *Powell* v. *Graham* (1817) 7 Taunt. 580, 585, 586; *Ashby* v. *Ashby* (1827) 7 B. & C. 444. And see *Churchill* v. *Bertrand* (1842) 4 T.R. 568.
[25] *Wigley* v. *Ashton* (1819) 3 B. & Ald. 101. But see *Atkins* v. *Humphrey* (1846) 2 C.B. 654.
[26] *Corner* v. *Shew* (1838) M. & W. 350. See *post*, p. 721 as to charging an executor for the expenses of the funeral.
[27] See *Re Whitaker* [1904] 1 Ch. 299 and *ante*, p. 631.
[28] R.S.C., Ord. 44, r. 9. As to interest on other debts see *post*, p. 1035.
[29] R.S.C., Ord. 44, r. 9. S.L.P. 1991.42/1/12.
[30] *Re Bracey* [1936] Ch. 690.
[31] 1 Saund. 210, c. 211, n. (1) to *Forth* v. *Stanton*; *Pearson* v. *Henry* (1792) 5 T.R. 8; *Rann* v. *Hughes* (1778) 7 T.R. 350, n. (*a*).

old system of pleading it was not necessary to allege that the defendant had assets.[32]

D—PERSONAL LIABILITY OF AN EXECUTOR IN CONTRACT

A representative may however be personally liable in contract, in which case he is said to be so liable of his own assets (*de bonis propriis*.) For the validity of such a promise the common law requires that there should be a sufficient consideration to support the promise; in the absence of consideration he is only liable, as he would have been had there been no promise, to the extent of the assets in his hands.[33] Formerly, the Statute of Frauds added a still further requisite, that the promise should be evidenced by writing, but this was abolished by the Law Reform (Enforcement of Contracts) Act 1954.

Valid consideration[34]

Express forbearance

First. What is a valid consideration? If a creditor, at the request of an executor, forbears to sue him, that is considered a sufficient consideration to charge him personally on a promise to pay, whether or not he has assets at the time of the promise.[35] Thus, if A together with B is bound to C for the proper debt of B, and A pays the money, and B dies and makes D his executor, and D, in consideration that A will forbear to sue him until such a time, promises to pay him, this is sufficient consideration to support the promise.[36] So, if an executor owes £100 to J.S., who demands the money, the executor is chargeable only in respect of assets, and not otherwise; but if he promises to pay the debt at a future day, it becomes his own debt, and must be satisfied out of his own estate.[37]

Implied forbearance

Again, B having died indebted to G for work and labour done, his executors signed the following memorandum on the back of G's account: "Mr. G having consented to wait for the payment of the within account, we, as the executors of B, engage to pay Mr. G interest for the same at £5 per cent. until the same is settled." The executors were held personally

---

[32] *Powell* v. *Graham* (1817) 7 Taunt. 580; *Dowse* v. *Coxe* (1825) 3 Bingh. 20.

[33] *Reech* v. *Kennegate* (1748) 1 Ves.Sen. 123, 125.

[34] See generally Chitty, *Contracts*, 26th ed., 1990, paras. 151 *et seq.*

[35] *Johnson* v. *Witchcott* (1638) 1 Roll.Abr. 24, tit. Action sur Case, P. pl. 33; *Gardener* v. *Fenner* (1625) 1 Roll.Abr. 15, tit. Action sur Case, S, pl. 3; *Chambers* v. *Leversage* (1598) Cro.Eliz. 644; *Hawes* v. *Smith* (1675) 2 Lev. 122. But if the promisor is neither executor nor administrator at the date of the promise, *semble*, the forbearance is not sufficient consideration: *Nelson* v. *Serle* (1839) 4 M. & W. 795.

[36] *Scott* v. *Stevens* (1662) 1 Sid. 89.

[37] *Goring* v. *Goring* (1602) Yelv. 11. See *Reech* v. *Kennegate* (1748) 1 Ves.Sen. 123.

liable to pay the debt and interest.[38] Similarly, where two executors gave a promissory note to the plaintiff in the following words: "As executors to the late T.T., we severally and jointly promise to pay to N. C. the sum of £200 on demand with lawful interest for the same," they were held personally liable on the instrument. The insertion of a promise to pay interest necessarily imports a payment at a future day, and an executor promising to pay a debt at a future day makes the debt his own.[39]

Forbearance by assignee

A testator was indebted to A, who, after the testator's death, assigned the debt to the plaintiff, and appointed him to receive it to his own use. The defendant, the representative of the testator, in consideration that the plaintiff would accept the defendant as his debtor, promised to pay it to the plaintiff. It was held that this was not a sufficient consideration to support the promises so as to charge the defendant *de bonis propriis*.[40] But if the promise had been in consideration of forbearance by such assignee of the debt to sue the executor or administrator, that would have been sufficient[41]; for it is sufficient in the case of any other debtor whom the assignee of the debt forbears at his request, to sue.[42]

Forbearance by legatee

It seems also that an executor is personally liable on a promise by him to pay a legacy in consideration of a forbearance by the legatee to enforce the legacy by instituting proceedings.[43] The forbearance is a sufficient consideration provided the legatee had a right to institute such proceedings.[44]

Collateral advantage to promisor

A collateral advantage to the promisor may amount to a sufficient consideration. Thus, where the defendant's husband owed £50 to the plaintiff for beer, and died intestate, and administration was granted to the defendant, and she, in consideration that the plaintiff would deliver to her six barrels of beer, promised to pay to the plaintiff both the £50 due from the

---

[38] *Bradly* v. *Heath* (1830) 3 Sim. 543. But *cf.* now the Trustee Act 1925, s.15.

[39] *Childs* v. *Monins* (1821) 2 Brod. & Bing. 460; *ibid.* 5 Moore 281. See also *Barnard* v. *Pumfrett* (1841) 5 M. & Cr. 63, 71; *Lucas* v. *Williams* (1861) 3 Giff. 151. Also *Ridout* v. *Bristow* (1830) 1 Cr. & J. 231, where a widow had given a promissory note for "value received by my late husband": and it was held that the note was valid on the face of it. *Cf. Bowerbank* v. *Monteiro* (1813) 4 Taunt. 844.

[40] *Forth* v. *Stanton* (1699) 1 Wms.Saund. 210.

[41] *Pitt* v. *Bridgwater* (1651) 1 Roll.Abr. 20, pl. 11; *Russel* v. *Haddock* (1666) 1 Lev. 188; 1 Wms.Saund. 210, n. (1).

[42] *Reynolds* v. *Prosser* (1656) Hardr. 71; *Oble* v. *Dittlesfield* (1671) 1 Ventr. 153; 1 Wms.Saund. 210, n. (1).

[43] In *Davis* v. *Reyner* (1671) 2 Lev. 3; *ibid.*, *sub nom. Davis* v. *Wright* (1671) 1 Ventr. 120; 2 Keb. 758, the legatee forbore to sue for his legacy.

[44] See 2 Wms.Saund. 137 *d*, note to *Barber* v. *Fox*.

intestate and for the six barrels delivered to herself, the barrels were delivered, and it was held that the judgment should be for both debts *de bonis propriis*.[45]

Again, where an attorney delivered up deeds to an executor, which he was not obliged to do till the bill was paid, and these deeds were of great use to the executor in several suits which were then being carried on, it was held that this was a sufficient consideration to make the executor liable to the attorney's whole demand, whether there were assets or not.[46]

Having assets

It would seem that the having of assets is a good consideration for a promise by an executor or administrator to pay a debt of the deceased, or to answer damages out of the executor's own estate. "At law if an executor promises to pay a debt of his testator, a consideration must be alleged; as of assets come to his hands; or of forbearance; or if admission of assets is implied by the promise: otherwise it will be but *nudum pactum*, and not personally binding upon the executor."[47] In *Atkins* v. *Hill*[48] and in *Hawkes* v. *Saunders*,[49] it was held that the circumstance of the executor having assets sufficient to pay all the debts and legacies was a sufficient consideration to support a promise to pay a legacy, so as to render the executor individually liable on that promise in an action at law.[50] The doctrine of these cases, as respects the liability of an executor to be sued at law for a general legacy, has since been exploded[51]; but it would seem that their authority, on the sufficiency of the consideration in question to support a promise to pay debts, remains unimpeached. The consequence is that if an executor or administrator promises, in writing, that, in consideration of having assets, he will pay a particular debt of the testator or intestate, he may be sued on this promise in his individual capacity, and the judgment against him will be *de bonis propriis*.[52]

Debt personal to executor

Where the nature of the debt is such as necessarily to make the defendant liable personally, the judgment will be *de bonis propriis*, although he is charged as promising as executor.[53]

---

[45] *Wheeler* v. *Collier* (1595) Cro.Eliz. 406.

[46] *Hamilton* v. *Incledon* (1719) 4 Bro.P.C. 4, Toml. ed.

[47] *Per* Lord Hardwicke in *Reech* v. *Kennegate* (1748) 1 Ves.Sen. 123, 126.

[48] (1775) 1 Cowp. 284.

[49] (1782) 1 Cowp. 289.

[50] See also *Barnard* v. *Pumfrett* (1841) 5 M. & Cr. 63, 71.

[51] See *post*, p. 887.

[52] *Trewinian* v. *Howell* (1588) Cro.Eliz. 91. And see *Rann* v. *Hughes* (1778) 7 T.R. 350, n. (*a*).

[53] *Powell* v. *Graham*, 7 Taunt. 580, 585; *Wigley* v. *Ashton* (1819) 3 B. & A. 101; *Corner* v. *Shew* (1838) 3 M. & W. 350.

Arbitration as admission of assets

If a representative submits to arbitration disputes relating to the deceased's estate, and the arbitrator makes an award of a sum greater than there are assets, a question arises as to how far the representative is personally liable to make up the deficiency.[54]

If seems to be now settled that an unguarded submission to arbitration is not of itself sufficient to amount to an admission of assets.[55]

On the other hand, by submitting to arbitration without protest, the representative impliedly refers for decision the additional question as to whether or not he has sufficient assets to pay the debt.[56] Thus, if the arbitrator awards that the representative is to pay a certain sum, this amounts to a decision that he has sufficient assets, and he cannot in consequence plead a deficiency of assets.[57]

The terms of the award may, however, negative such an implied decision. Thus, where an arbitrator awarded that a certain sum was due from the intestate's estate, without awarding that the administrator was to pay it, it was held that the administrator was not thereby precluded from denying that he had assets.[58] Again, an award that the representative is to pay a sum out of the assets does not render him personally liable beyond the assets in his hands.[59]

An arbitrator is not justified in rejecting evidence offered by the representative to show that he has no assets to meet the demand upon the deceased's estate.[60]

Further, even though the representative is precluded by the award from denying assets, this does not operate as an admission of assets in any other action by any other creditor.[61]

A representative may render himself personally liable if he covenants unconditionally to pay any award that the arbitrator may make.[62]

Arbitration under statutory power

All the cases which support the above propositions were decided long before representatives received statutory power to submit disputes to arbi-

[54] The question is discussed in Russell, *Arbitration*, 19th ed., pp. 34–35, where it is assumed that the position is the same if the representative is acting under his statutory power to submit disputes to arbitration; but see *post*, p. 721.

[55] See *Pearson* v. *Henry* (1792) 5 T.R. 6, explaining *Barry* v. *Rush* (1787) 1 T.R. 691. But *cf. Robson* v. *Anon.* (1813) 2 Rose 50; *Riddell* v. *Sutton* (1828) 5 Bing. 200. And see *Wansborough* v. *Dyer* (1815) 2 Chitt.Rep. 40.

[56] *Worthington* v. *Barlow* (1797) 7 T.R. 453. And see the cases mentioned *ante*.

[57] See n. 56 *supra*.

[58] *Pearson* v. *Henry* (1792) 5 T.R. 6. And see *Worthington* v. *Barlow* (1797) 7 T.R. 453.

[59] *Love* v. *Honeybourne* (1824) 4 D. & R. 814. See also *Re Joseph and Webster* (1830) 1 Russ. & M. 496.

[60] Russell, *Arbitration*, 19th ed., p. 237, citing *Riddell* v. *Sutton* (1828) 5 Bing. 200.

[61] *Worthington* v. *Barlow*, *supra*.

[62] *Barry* v. *Rush*, *supra*.

tration.[63] A representative who acts in good faith under this statutory power incurs no personal liability.[64]

Funeral expenses

Reasonable[65] funeral expenses are a first charge on the assets.[66] Further, it seems that a representative who gives orders for the funeral, or who ratifies or adopts the acts of another party who has given such orders, may be made personally liable.[67]

In *Lucy* v. *Walrond*,[68] an administrator was successfully sued as administrator for funeral expenses incurred by the order of a third party, but sanctioned by him before he obtained letters of administration.[69] In this case the defendant, by pleading payment into court, admitted the right of the plaintiff to sue him as administrator. It was therefore not decided whether he ought not to have been sued personally.[70]

Even though the representative has neither given nor adopted directions for the burial, he may find himself personally liable for funeral expenses.[71] If no other person is liable under an express contract, an executor with assets is personally liable under an implied contract, to the person who furnishes the funeral, for the funeral expenses of his testator suitable to his degree and circumstances.[72] An executor without any assets is not personally liable; but it has been suggested[73] that an executor is so liable if he receives any assets, though such assets are not sufficient to satisfy the funeral expenses.

On the other hand, if some person other than the executor gives orders as to the funeral, and the undertaker gives credit to such person, the execu-

---

[63] Trustee Act 1925, s.15. See *post*, p. 1099; *ante*, p. 665.

[64] See *ante*, p. 715.

[65] See *ante*, p. 63.

[66] See *ante*, p. 663.

[67] *Brice* v. *Wilson* (1834) 8 A. & E. 349, n. (*c*); *Walker* v. *Taylor* (1834) 6 C. & P. 752; *Corner* v. *Shew* (1838) 3 M. & W. 350. As to the duties of an executor or administrator in respect of the funeral, see *ante*, pp. 60 *et seq*.

[68] (1837) 3 Bing.N.C. 841.

[69] As to the liability of an administrator for acts done before the letters of administration were obtained, see *ante*, pp. 90 *et seq*.

[70] See *Corner* v. *Shew* (1838) 3 M. & W. 350, 356. The estate of a deceased person is not liable on a contract made by a person, although for the benefit of the estate, unless that person, by subsequently obtaining letters of administration becomes authorised to bind the estate, and ratifies the contract: *Re Watson* (1887) 18 Q.B.D. 116; 19 Q.B.D. 234. See *ante*, pp. 90 *et seq*.

[71] *Semble*, the dictum of Lord Holt to the contrary in *Ashton* v. *Sherman* (1697) Holt 309 (and see 12 Mod. 256) can no longer be supported. As to funeral payments see *ante*, p. 497.

[72] *Tugwell* v. *Heyman* (1812) 3 Campb. 298; *Rogers* v. *Price* (1829) 3 Y. & J. 28; *Corner* v. *Shew* (1838) 3 M. & W. 350. See also *Hancock* v. *Podmore* (1830) 1 B. & A. 260; *Ambrose* v. *Kerrison* (1851) 10 C.B. 779; *Rees* v. *Hughes* [1946] K.B. 517, 524.

[73] By Jessel M.R. in *Sharp* v. *Lush* (1879) 10 Ch.D. 468, 472. This view seems to be supported by the older authorities. It is, perhaps, to be doubted whether a view imposing such a burden upon the executor would be upheld at the present time.

tor is not liable to the undertaker.[74] But if the person who gives the order for the funeral pays for it, and the payment is not made merely voluntarily and as an act of bounty,[75] he may have an action in equity against the executor for reasonable expenses.[76]

E—LIABILITY OF AN EXECUTOR CARRYING ON THE BUSINESS

No general authority

When a person engaged in trade or business dies, his trade or business descends to his representatives as part of his assets. The general rule was that the representatives have no authority in law to carry on the trade of the deceased.[77] If the trade is so carried on and proves beneficial the profits accrue for the benefit of the deceased's estate, but this benefit may be lost if the beneficiaries, being *sui juris*, fail to claim within a reasonable time. Thus a claim was barred on the ground of laches in equity when there was a delay of nearly 10 years notwithstanding difficulties of the war and of bomb damage.[78]

Authority given by will

It was said[79] that, in order to authorise executors to carry on a trade, or to permit it to be carried on with the assets, there ought to be the most distinct and positive authority and direction given by the will for that purpose.

Effect of power to postpone sale

A power to postpone the sale and conversion of the estate of a testator, or intestate,[80] authorises representatives to carry on his trade for any time, even if it is not carried on with a view to sale.[81] But when the estate of a testator becomes divisible the power to postpone sale ceases.[82] And a general power to postpone sale, with a direction to sell the business with all convenient speed, does not authorise the business to be carried on for an indefinite time.[83] Since 1925 there has been a power to postpone sale implied in every trust for sale of land unless a contrary intention appears.[84]

---

[74] *Brice* v. *Wilson* (1834) 8 A. & E. 349, n. (c), as explained in *Green* v. *Salmon* (1838) 8 A. & E. 348, 350.

[75] See *Coleby* v. *Coleby* (1866) 12 Jur.(N.S.) 496.

[76] *Green* v. *Salmon*, *ante*. cf. *Williams* v. *Williams* (1882) 20 Ch.D. 659. See also *Thomas* v. *Harris* [1947] 1 All E.R. 444. As to what is "reasonable," see *ante*, p. 63.

[77] *Barker* v. *Parker* (1786) 1 T.R. 295. As to completing contracts, see *ante*, pp. 554 *et seq.* For precedents see Brighouse, *Precedents of Wills and Life Transfers*, 11th ed., 115.

[78] See *Re Jarvis* [1958] 1 W.L.R. 815.

[79] By Lord Langdale in *Kirkman* v. *Booth* (1848) 11 Beav. 273, 280. See further, *Travis* v. *Milne* (1851) 9 Hare 141.

[80] On the death of a person wholly or partially intestate after 1925, the trust for sale imposed by the Administration of Estates Act 1925, s.33, contains a power to postpone sale; *ibid*. subs. (5); *post*, pp. 741, 1128.

[81] *Re Crowther* [1895] 2 Ch. 56; *Re Ball* [1930] W.N. 111.

[82] *Ibid*. n. 81.

[83] *Re Smith* [1896] 1 Ch. 171.

[84] Law of Property Act 1925, s.25.

This has altered the law[85] but how far is not clear. It seems that the statutory power to postpone sale lasts until the property becomes divisible[86] and that this power of itself necessitates and authorises the continuation of the business until that time.[87]

Restricted authorisation

A testator sometimes authorises his executors to carry on his business only with a specific part of the assets.[88] And it has been held that a mere direction to carry on the testator's business only authorises the employment in it of the capital left in the business by the testator at his death.[89]

Business carried on for convenient realisation

Apart from any express direction in a will, a representative was always entitled, where the business of the deceased was a valuable asset, to carry it on for such reasonable time as might be necessary to enable him to sell it to the best advantage of the estate.[90] This has been suggested to be commensurate with the executor's year or a comparatively short time beyond this year.[91]

Where beneficiaries agree to carrying on

If a representative considers it expedient to carry on the deceased's business not merely for the purpose of realisation, and there is no authority to carry on the business conferred by the will, he should take the precaution of obtaining an indemnity from the beneficiaries. If any of such beneficiaries are not *sui juris* this cannot safely be done and an application to the court will normally be advisable. Unless the estate is bordering on insolvency,[92] it will not usually be necessary to obtain the consent of the deceased's creditors.

Liability for improperly carrying on business

A representative who improperly and without authorisation, either by law or under the will, carries on the business of the deceased may be made liable to the deceased's estate or creditors[93] for losses incurred. Thus, if he improperly carries on the business and then goes bankrupt, the deceased's

---

[85] See *Re Rooke* [1953] 1 Ch. 716, 723, where Harman J. doubts the suggestion attributed to Luxmoore J. in *Re Ball* [1930] W.N. 111, 120; 74 S.J. 298 that s.25 has not altered the law.

[86] See *per* Chitty J. in *Re Crowther* [1895] 2 Ch. 56, 60.

[87] See *per* Fry L.J. in *Re Chancellor* (1884) 26 Ch.D. 42, 47.

[88] See *Cutbush* v. *Cutbush* (1839) 1 Beav. 184; *Thompson* v. *Andrews* (1832) 1 M. & K. 116.

[89] *M'Neillie* v. *Acton* (1853) 4 De G.M. & G. 744.

[90] See *Marshall* v. *Broadhurst* (1831) 1 Cr. & J. 405; *Garrett* v. *Noble* (1834) 6 Sim. 504; see also *Edwards* v. *Grace* (1836) 2 M. & W. 190; *Dakin* v. *Cope* (1827) 2 Russ. 170. See also *ante*, p. 555.

[91] *Per* Chitty J. in *Re Crowther* [1895] 2 Ch. 56.

[92] See *Re East* (1914) 111 L.T. 101, C.A.

[93] *Ibid.* n. 92.

creditors and beneficiaries will have a right to prove for such of the assets as have been wasted by him in the trade in proportion to their respective interests. Such assets as can be specifically distinguished as part of the testator's estate, since they are held *alieno jure*, will not pass to the trustee in bankruptcy of the representative.[94]

Similarly, an executor's estate is liable to the deceased's estate for assets expended in excess of his authority.[95] But laches will defeat the beneficiaries' claim[96]

No liability to beneficiaries for authorised carrying on

On the other hand, beneficiaries cannot prove in respect of assets which the executor employed in a business under the authority of the will.[97] Nor can a representative be made liable for the loss of the capital left in the business of the deceased, where the representative has properly carried on the business either for the purpose of convenient realisation, or under the statutory power.[98] He must not however, compete with the estate and if he does so he will be accountable.[99]

Power to convert the business into a company

Where executors are expressly authorised to carry on a business, they probably have power to convert the business into a private limited company having the same assets and management as the business.[1] Such a company will remain under their control and they will be in a fiduciary position as to the exercise of that control in appointments to the board of directors, alteration of articles, increase of capital and alterations in structure. Any fundamental changes would of course have to be referred for the direction of the court[2] but the mere "conversion"[3] of the business into such a company may in practice be little more than a matter of administrative convenience.

Executor liable personally for debts to trade creditors

A representative who carries on the business of the deceased, whether under the authority of the will or not, even for the purpose of convenient realisation and even though he avowedly acts as a representative makes himself personally liable for all debts which he contracts in so doing after

---

[94] *Ex p. Garland* (1804) 10 Ves. 110; Toller 487; *Ex p. Richardson* (1818) 1 Buck. 202.
[95] *Ex. p. Richardson, supra; Re Mellor* (1880) 13 Ch.D. 465.
[96] See *ante*, p. 722.
[97] *Scott* v. *Izon* (1865) 34 Beav. 434.
[98] See *ante*, p. 722.
[99] See *post*, p. 737 and *ante*, pp. 590, 591.
[1] *MacKechnie's Trustees* v. *Macadam* [1912] S.C. 1059.
[2] As to procedure, see *post*. A contrary view is expressed in Halsbury's *Laws*, 4th ed., Vol. 17, para. 1213.
[3] The technical form of the transaction would normally be the sale of the business by the executors to the company in return for shares.

the death of the deceased.[4] And it is the universal principle that a representative who carries on the trade of the deceased is personally liable for all trade debts contracted since the death of the deceased, and may be proceeded against as a bankrupt although he is only in the position of trustee.[5]

Where the testator was a partner in a business and his executors carry on the business under a power in the will and in the name of the firm, they are not partners and cannot be adjudicated bankrupt as partners, though they may probably be proceeded against as joint debtors.[6]

Executor's right to indemnity from beneficiaries

Where an executor is authorised to carry on a business (whether by the will, or for purposes of realisation or under the power to postpone sale[7]) then, although he is personally liable for the debts which he incurs, he is entitled as against the beneficiaries to be indemnified out of that part of the testator's estate which he is authorised to employ in the business.[8]

Where, however, the executor is in default to the specific trust estate which he is authorised to employ in the trade, he is only entitled to be indemnified against trade debts upon the terms of making good the default.[9] But he does not lose his right of indemnity merely by failure to account.[10] It is for those who take on such responsibilities to ensure that the right to indemnity is not valueless.[11]

Indemnity against creditors of estate

Whether the testator has or has not directed or authorised his executors to carry on his business is immaterial to the creditors of the estate.[12] The executor's right of indemnity is good as against such creditors only to the extent that he carries on the business for the time necessary to enable it to be sold as a going concern[13]; apart from this it does not apply as against such creditors unless they had knowledge that the testator's business was being carried on by the executor and have acquiesced in such trading.[14] Mere standing by with knowledge that the business is being carried on does not constitute assent by the creditors of the estate so as to entitle the execu-

---

[4] *Labouchere* v. *Tupper* (1857) 11 Moo.P.C. 198.
[5] *Ex p. Garland* (1804) 10 Ves. 110; *Wightman* v. *Townroe* (1813) 1 M. & S. 412; *Owen* v. *Delamere* (1872) L.R. 15 Eq. 134; *Fairland* v. *Percy* (1875) L.R. 3 P. & D. 217.
[6] *Re Fisher & Sons* [1912] 2 K.B. 491. See Lindley and Banks, *Partnership*, 16th ed., p. 684.
[7] See *ante*, pp. 722.
[8] *Ex p. Garland* (1804) 10 Ves. 110; *Dowse* v. *Gorton* [1891] A.C. 190; *Re Bracey* [1936] Ch. 690; *cf. Strickland* v. *Symons* (1884) 22 Ch.D. 666; 26 Ch.D. 245.
[9] *Re Johnson* (1880) 15 Ch.D. 548; *Re Evans* (1887) 34 Ch.D. 597; *Strickland* v. *Symons* (1883) 22 Ch.D. 666; (1884) 26 Ch.D. 245; *Re British Power Co.* [1910] 2 Ch. 470.
[10] *Re Kidd* (1894) 70 L.T. 648.
[11] See *Roome* v. *Edwards* [1982] A.C. 299.
[12] See *Re Oxley* [1914] 1 Ch. 604, 613.
[13] See *per* Lord Herschell [1891] A.C. at p. 199.
[14] *Dowse* v. *Gorton*, *ante*.

tor (and the trade creditors claiming through him[15]) to be indemnified against them.[16]

Position of receiver and manager

Similar principles apply where a receiver or manager has been appointed in an administration action to carry on the business in succession to the executor even where the will does not contain a power to carry on the business.[17]

Remedy of trade creditor

The remedy of a creditor of the business for a debt incurred since the death of the deceased is against the representative personally and not against the estate of the deceased.[18] Since his debt was contracted between the representative and himself he is not, strictly speaking, entitled to have the estate of the deceased administered[19]; but an order for administration has, in special circumstances, been made on the application of such a creditor.[20] Further, he is entitled to make the representative render to him an account of the assets of the deceased which have been employed in the business since the testator's death.[21]

Another consequence of the fact that the trade creditor's remedy is primarily against the representative personally is that, where an order for administration of the estate is made, the creditor is entitled to interest only from the date when the Master certifies the debt, and not from the date of the administration order.[22]

Trade creditor's right of subrogation

Though the remedy of such a creditor is against the representative personally, not against the assets, yet he is entitled to enforce his claim against the assets by subrogation to the right of indemnity of the representative where the latter is entitled to claim such an indemnity.[23] In such a case creditors whose debts have been incurred since the death of the deceased are entitled to stand in the place of the representative and to claim that the

---

[15] As to the trade creditors' remedy against the deceased's estate by subrogation to the executor's right of indemnity, see below.

[16] *Re Oxley, ante.* Mere assent by the creditors is not sufficient to constitute the executor their agent: *Re Millard* (1895) 72 L.T. 823.

[17] *Re Brooke* [1894] 2 Ch. 600. But as to this case, see *Re Oxley, ante.*

[18] *Farhall* v. *Farhall* (1871) L.R. 7 Ch. 123; *Re Evans, ante.* See also *ante*, p. 464.

[19] *Owen* v. *Delamere* (1872) L.R. 15 Eq. 134; *Strickland* v. *Symons* (1884) 26 Ch.D. 245.

[20] See *Re Shorey* (1898) 79 L.T. 349, and *post*, p. 829.

[21] *Thompson* v. *Dunn* (1870) L.R. 5 Ch. 573.

[22] *Re Bracey* [1936] Ch. 690; and see *Re Dietz*, unreported [1905] D. 273, cited *Supreme Court Practice*, See also *ante*, p. 716.

[23] See *ante*, p. 725.

fund out of which he is entitled to indemnity shall be applied in payment of their debts[24] and with the like priority.[25]

The trade creditor can, however, be in no better position than the representative through whom he claims. Thus, if the executor was only authorised to employ a certain portion of the estate in the business, so that he can only claim an indemnity out of the portion, the rest of the deceased's estate is immune from the claims of trade creditors which arose after the death of the testator.[26]

Again, if the executor is in default to the specific trust estate which he is authorised to employ in the trade, the trade creditors are only entitled to have their debts paid out of the specific assets upon the terms of making good the default.[27]

A trade creditor is not, however, prejudiced by the fact that one of several of the trustees carrying on the deceased's business is in default, for each of the trustees who has acted properly is entitled to be indemnified.[28]

Further, since an executor does not lose his right of indemnity merely by reason of his failure to account, the creditors do not lose their right to claim against the estate by reason of the failure of the executor to account.[29]

Creditors of estate have priority

In accordance with the same principle, the trade creditors of the executor will not obtain priority to the creditors of the estate unless the latter, with knowledge that the testator's business was being carried on by the executor, have acquiesced in such trading,[30] or, *semble*, unless the business was carried on merely for convenient realisation.[31]

The claims of the trade creditors are, however, preferred to the beneficiaries' claims in respect of those assets which the executor was authorised to employ in the business.[32]

Where carrying on is unauthorised

Where neither the whole nor any specific part of the estate is properly applicable to carrying on the trade, creditors of the business have no right to recover their debt out of the trust funds.[33] But they are entitled to any interest the representative may have in such trade as against the trust estate, *e.g.* the right to be repaid money he has advanced or become liable to pay in respect of the business.[34]

[24] *Ex p. Garland* (1804) 10 Ves. 110; *Ex p. Edmonds* (1862) 4 De G.F. & J. 488.
[25] *Moore* v. *M'Glynn* [1904] 1 Ir.R. 334. The same principle applies where a trustee claims a right of indemnity for a tort; see *Re Raybould* [1900] 1 Ch. 199.
[26] *Cutbush* v. *Cutbush* (1839) 1 Beav. 184; *Thompson* v. *Andrews* (1832) 1 M. & K. 116.
[27] See *ante*, p. 725.
[28] *Re Frith* [1902] 1 Ch. 342.
[29] *Re Kidd* [1894] 70 L.T. 648.
[30] *Dowse* v. *Gorton* [1891] A.C. 190; *ante*, p. 725.
[31] See n. 30 *supra*.
[32] See *ante*, p. 724.
[33] *Strickland* v. *Symons* (1884) 22 Ch.D. 666; 26 Ch.D. 245.
[34] *Re Evans* (1887) 34 Ch.D. 597.

Where beneficiaries consent to carry on

Finally, the trade creditor may be entitled, as against the beneficiaries, to obtain payment direct out of the deceased's assets where the beneficiaries have consented to the application thereof in carrying on the business. Lapse of time and an enjoyment of the testator's assets in a manner inconsistent with the trusts of the will, coupled with the consent of the beneficiaries, may raise an inference of a gift of the assets by the beneficiaries to the executor, and enable his judgment creditor to take them in execution. But when the possession and the time which has elapsed are in accordance with the trusts of the will, no such inference can arise.[35]

Executor may sue trade creditors

An executor who lawfully carries on the business of his testator can sue as executor for debts incurred to the estate in carrying on the trade since the testator's death.[36] If executors, who are by the testator's will to carry on his trade for the benefit of his family, suffer a person to conduct the trade in his own name, such person may bring actions in his own name for goods sold by him, though afterwards accountable to the executors.[37]

F—LIABILITY IN CRIMINAL LAW

The Theft Act 1968 introduced unattractively phrased amendments to the criminal law under which an executor or trustee may be liable. Under this Act theft is the dishonest appropriation of property belonging to another with the intention of permanently depriving the other of it.[38] An appropriation is any assumption by a person of the rights of an owner and includes later assumption of a right by keeping or dealing with it as owner, where the person concerned has come by the property (innocently or not) without stealing it.[39] Thus it would seem that an executor who "comes by" assets of his estate quite properly and later "assumes" a right to them will have "appropriated" them. If this appropriation is "dishonest" he will be guilty of theft. There may be cases when an appropriation is dishonest even if the representative is willing to pay for the property, or where he believes that the person to whom the property belongs cannot be discovered by taking reasonable steps.[40] From this it would seem that contrary to all previously accepted principles of executorship law, an executor may be faced with

[35] *Re Morgan* (1881) 18 Ch.D. 93; *cf. Jennings* v. *Mather* [1901] 1 K.B. 108; [1902] 1 K.B. 1. See also *Re Jarvis* [1958] 1 W.L.R. 815.
[36] *Abbott* v. *Parfitt* (1871) L.R. 6 Q.B. 346.
[37] *Wilkes* v. *Lister* (1806) 6 Esp. 78.
[38] Theft Act 1968. s.1.
[39] *Ibid.* s.3.
[40] *Ibid.* s.2(2) and 2(1)(c). As to the former beneficial interest of the executor, see *post*, p. 935.

prosecution for retaining quite trivial sums or assets even where the cost of tracing the legatee is utterly disproportionate to the value. His only safe course will be to pay into or deposit in court or to take proceedings for the direction of the court, presumably at some risk to himself or to the residuary estate in costs. In addition it appears that an executor is one of the few distinguished exceptions to the rule that a person cannot steal land.[41] He can be guilty if he appropriates land, or anything forming part of it, by dealing with it in breach of the confidence reposed in him[42] but it seems that the further test of "dishonesty" must be applied before he can be held guilty.

The property stolen

The property stolen has for the purposes of the Act to be "property belonging to another"[43] and this applies to persons having possession or control of the property or "having in it any proprietary right or interest (not being an equitable interest arising only from an agreement to transfer or grant an interest).[44] Thus it would seem, for example, to be possible for an executor to steal from a specific legatee or devisee (but only presumably after completion of administration[45]) or from the contractual assignee of such a legatee or devisee (for he would not be entitled *only* by reason of his contract) but not from a purchaser of assets of the estate (for he would have an equitable interest arising *only* from his agreement). Where property is subject to a trust, the persons to whom it belongs include any person having a right to enforce the trust and an intention to defeat the trust is an intention to deprive the persons having that right.[46] "Property belonging to another" also includes property received from or on account of another where there is an obligation to retain and deal with that property or its proceeds and property obtained by another's mistake where there is an obligation to restore.[47] This latter provision could affect an executor where for instance there is a mistake as to assets found among the belongings of the deceased which in fact belong to third parties.

Suppression of documents

The Theft Act 1968 also confirms criminal liability for the dishonest destruction, defacement or concealment of any valuable security, will or other testamentary document.[48] Such suppression has to be "with a view to gain

---

[41] Theft Act 1968, s.4(2)(*a*).
[42] See n. 41, *supra*.
[43] *Ibid.* s.1(1).
[44] *Ibid.* s.5(1).
[45] See *post*, p. 1050.
[46] Theft Act 1968, s.5(2). *Attorney-General's Reference (No. 1 of 1985)* [1986] Q.B. 491.
[47] *Ibid.* s.5(3), (4).
[48] *Ibid.* s.20(1). See the Eighth Report of the Criminal Law Revision Committee, Cmnd. 2977, p. 53.

for himself or another or with intent to cause loss to another." The wording is new and broad[49] and on a literal rendering would make it an offence for a testator "dishonestly" to destroy his own will. Since previous wills are admissible in evidence and often very relevant in Family Provision proceedings this may have been intended, but it is not thought that such a well accepted mode of revocation of wills would be changed in so apparently casual a manner.

Effect on civil proceedings

It is expressly provided[50] that the title to property shall not be affected by reason only of the conviction of an offender. Where property other than land has been stolen and a person has been convicted of an offence "with reference" to the theft, the criminal court has broad powers to order the restitution of the stolen property to the person entitled to it.[51] Such an order will only be made where the evidence is clear.[52] In civil proceedings the risk of incrimination under the Theft Act cannot be invoked to avoid answering questions or complying with orders, but such answers or compliances are not admissible in proceedings for an offence under the Act.[53] The rule in *Smith* v. *Selwyn*[54] under which civil proceedings might have to be stayed pending prosecution for felony no longer applies since the abolition, in effect, of felony.[55]

G—LIABILITY FOR WASTE

It remains to investigate what will amount to such a violation or neglect of duty by an executor or administrator, as will make him personally liable or accountable.

This species of misconduct is called in law a *devastavit*: that is, a wasting of the assets. It is defined to be *a mismanagement of the estate and effects of the deceased, in squandering and misapplying the assets contrary to the duty imposed on them, for which executors or administrators must answer out of their own pockets, as far as they had, or might have had, assets of the deceased.*[56] This topic sometimes converges with that of accountability for profits made by the executor, just considered.[57]

---

[49] *cf.* the Larceny Act 1861, ss. 27–30. See also *ante*, pp. 199 *et seq.* Presumably it could be "dishonest" to destroy a contractual will or the "mutual" will of a surviving testator.
[50] Theft Act 1968, s.31(2).
[51] Theft Act 1968, s.28; Criminal Justice Act 1977, s.6.
[52] *R.* v. *Accutt, and Varty* (1985) 7 Cr.App.R. (S.) 385.
[53] *Ibid.* s.31(1).
[54] [1941] 3 K.B. 98. The position was otherwise where the giving of information might lead to a prosecution for some other serious criminal offence. See *Rank Film Distributors* v. *Video Information Centre* [1982] A.C. 380, but this privilege is now withdrawn in the cases specified by s.72 of the Supreme Court Act 1981.
[55] See the Criminal Law Act 1967, s.1.
[56] Bac.Abr.Exors., I, 1. *Re Stevens* [1898] 1 Ch. 162, 177.
[57] pp. 703 *et seq. ante.*

Personal representatives as trustees

Representatives are for some purposes considered as trustees.[58] They are personally liable for all breaches of the ordinary trusts which arise from their office.[59]

Where property is bequeathed to executors, as trustees, if they prove the will, this is, in itself, an acceptance of the particular trusts. Thus, where the will contains express directions as to what the executors are to do, an executor who proves the will must do all that he is directed to do as executor, and he cannot say that, though executor, he is not clothed with any of those trusts.[60] Moreover, an executor-trustee of English and Foreign property cannot disclaim the trust of the English property while retaining control over the foreign property.[61]

Where a legacy is given to executors if they should prove the will and accept the trusteeship, and they prove the will, regard will be had to all the circumstances—the fact that they have proved the will, the acts done in discharge of their duties and whether they are duties as executors or duties as trustees—in determining whether they have accepted the trusteeship.[62] The office of trustee cannot be disclaimed after acceptance.[63]

Where property devolves on representatives by virtue of an intestacy and thereby becomes subject to a trust for sale and conversion, the administrators must observe the provisions of the special trusts imposed upon them.

The extent of the liability of representatives for breaches of trust is founded upon two principles: first, that in order not to deter persons from undertaking these offices, the court is extremely liberal in making every possible allowance, and cautious not to hold executors or administrators liable upon slight ground; second, that care must be taken to guard against an abuse of the trusts they have accepted.[64]

Distinction between devastavit and breach of trust

The same act may amount both to breach of trust and *devastavit*, but the strict distinction between the two, so far as material, is that *devastavit* is a

---

[58] See the definitions of "trust" and "trustee" in the Trustee Act 1925, s.68(17). As to when an executor is *functus officio* and becomes clothed with the character of a trustee, see *Re Timmis* [1902] 1 Ch. 176; *Solomon* v. *Attenborough* [1912] 1 Ch. 451, 458; [1913] A.C. 76; *Re Yerburgh* [1928] W.N. 208; *Harvell* v. *Foster* [1954] 2 Q.B. 367; *Hawkesley* v. *May* [1956] 1 Ch. 304; *Re Cockburn's Will Trusts* [1957] Ch. 438. *Re Aldhouse* [1955] 1 W.L.R. 459, 464. There is no authority for saying that once the debts are paid the residue is to be held upon an express trust; *Re Mackay* [1906] 1 Ch. 25. See *post*, p. 1049.

[59] *Re Marsden* (1884) 26 Ch.D. 783, 789; *Eastbourne Mutual B.S.* v. *Hastings Corpn.* [1965] 1 W.L.R. 861, 866; and see *post*, p. 1049.

[60] *Mucklow* v. *Fuller* (1821) Jac. 198; *Booth* v. *Booth* (1838) 1 Beav. 125; *Stiles* v. *Guy* (1832) 4 Y. & C.Ex. 571, 575; *Williams* v. *Nixon* (1840) 2 Beav. 472.

[61] *Re Lord and Fullerton's Contract* [1896] 1 Ch. 228.

[62] *Re Sharman's Will Trusts* [1942] Ch. 311; *Re Parry* [1969] 1 W.L.R. 614.

[63] *Ibid.* n. 62.

[64] *Powell* v. *Evans* (1801) 5 Ves. 839, 843; *Raphael* v. *Boehm* (1807) 13 Ves. 407, 410; *Tebbs* v. *Carpenter* (1816) 1 Madd. 290, 298.

breach of the duty of administration and may therefore arise where there is no express or implied trust at all, whereas simple breach of trust will normally occur after administration is complete when the assets are being held upon the trusts of the will or the statute.[65]

Liability to creditors and legatees

It has been suggested that there is a distinction between the liability of a representative to legatees and his liability to creditors.[66] Since legatees are bound by the terms of the will but creditors are not, there would seem to be some cases in which executors would be discharged as against legatees, though not as against creditors.[67] However it is clear that the relationship between a beneficiary and a trustee who has misappropriated the trust fund comprises that of creditor and debtor although it may be something more than that.[68] Conversely the will may create a trust for the creditors of the testator.

Waste by deliberate abuse

A representative may be guilty of a *devastavit* by a direct abuse of the effects of the deceased, as by spending or consuming, or converting them to his own use[69]; by applying the assets in payment of his own debt to a third party[70]; or by collusively selling the testator's property at an undervalue.[71]

Waste by negligence

He may also be guilty of a *devastavit* by such acts of negligence and wrongful administration as will disappoint the claimants of the assets.[72] For instance, he may be liable for a *devastavit* by misapplying the assets in undue expenses for the funeral[73]; by paying debts out of their legal order, to the prejudice of preferred creditors[74]; or by assenting to or paying a

---

[65] See *Re Marsden* (1884) 26 Ch.D. 783, which proceeds upon the basis that there is an implied trust for creditors of the estate. All breaches are not reprehensible. They may be "judicious," see *ante*, p. 563.

[66] *Churchill* v. *Hobson* (1713) 1 P.Wms. 241, 242; *Harden* v. *Parsons* (1758) 1 Eden 145, 148. But see *Sadler* v. *Hobbs* (1786) 2 Bro.C.C. 114, 117.

[67] *Doyle* v. *Blake* (1804) 2 Sch. & Lef. 231, 239, 240.

[68] *Sharp* v. *Jackson* [1899] A.C. 419, *per* Halsbury, L.C. at p. 426.

[69] It is no *devastavit* if he pays the testator's debts with his own money in such order as the law appoints; *Merchant* v. *Driver* (1669) 1 Saund. 307; Com.Dig.Admon.I. 2. No action will lie for neglect to take out probate, though such neglect has been followed by loss; *per* Vaughan Williams L.J. in *Re Stevens* [1898] 1 Ch. 162, 177.

[70] As to which, see *ante*, pp. 675 *et seq.*

[71] Wentw.Off.Ex., 14th ed., 302; *Rice* v. *Gordon* (1848) 11 Beav. 265.

[72] Bac.Abr.Exors.L. 1.

[73] As to which, see *ante*, p. 63.

[74] As to which, see *ante*, pp. 635 *et seq*. But if the executor pays the inferior debt out of his own money, this is not a *devastavit*: Com.Dig.Admon.I. 2; *Wheatly* v. *Lane* (1669) 1 Wms.Saund. 216, 218, by Pemberton, *arguendo*.

legacy when there is not a fund sufficient for creditors.[75] He can, however, avoid liability under the last two heads by taking the proper statutory precuations.[76]

If the executor (without taking reasonable consideration in money or money's worth) surrenders, or otherwise fails to preserve the residue of a term of years, where the land is of greater yearly value than the rent, it is a *devastavit*.[77] On the other hand, if the rent is greater than the yearly value of the land, and the testator was the assignee of the term, the executor may be guilty of a *devastavit* in neglecting to exonerate the estate of the testator from its liabilities under the lease by assigning it, where permissible, to some other person.[78]

Wilful default

Originally at common law a representative was liable for the loss of the deceased's assets when they had once come into his hands.[79] In equity, however, a more lenient doctrine was established.[80] Since there was a conflict between the rule at common law and the rule in equity, the equitable view now prevails.[81] "The rule, then, at law as well as in equity, now is that an executor or administrator is in the position of a gratuitous bailee, who cannot be charged with the loss of his testator's assets without wilful default."[82]

Thus, if an executor uses all reasonable care he is not liable when the testator's goods are stolen from his possession, or from the possession of a third party into whose custody he had delivered them.[83]

Similarly, if a trespasser takes goods out of the possession of an executor or administrator, though he is bound to sue a known trespasser, the executor is not answerable for more than he recovers in the action. But if he omits to sell the goods at a good price, and afterwards they are taken from him, he is liable for the value of the goods and not what he recovers, for there was a default in him.[84]

Again, an executor has been held not liable for the loss of his testator's assets by accidental fire,[85] even though the property has been left uninsured.[86] However, it seems likely that, at the present day, no executor

---

[75] As to which, see *ante*, p. 605.
[76] *i.e.* advertising for claims under the Trustee Act 1925, s.27; see *ante*, p. 605.
[77] Wentw.Off.Ex., 14th ed., 312; *Thompson* v. *Thompson* (1821) 9 Price 464, 476.
[78] *Rowley* v. *Adams* (1839) 4 M. & Cr. 534, *ante*, p. 574, n. 97.
[79] *Crosse* v. *Smith* (1806) 7 East 246, 258.
[80] See *Massey* v. *Banner* (1820) 1 Jac. & Walk. 241, 248.
[81] See the Judicature Act 1925, s.44, replacing the Judicature Act 1873, s.25(11).
[82] *Per* Jessel M.R. in *Job* v. *Job* (1877) 6 Ch.D. 562, 564; *Re Gunning* [1918] 1 Ir.R. 221.
[83] *Jones* v. *Lewis* (1751) 2 Ves.Sen. 240; *Brown* v. *Sewell* (1853) 11 Hare 52.
[84] *Jenkins* v. *Plombe* (1705) 6 Mod. 181, 182; *Wightwick* v. *Lord*, 6 H.L.C. 217, 234, 235.
[85] *Lady Croft's Executors* v. *Lyndsey & Covill* (1676) 2 Freem.Ch. 1.
[86] *Bailey* v. *Gould* (1840) 4 Y. & C.Ex. 221; *Fry* v. *Fry* (1859) 27 Beav. 144; *Re McEacharn* (1911) 103 L.T. 900. For the power for trustees to insure, see *ante*, p. 683.

would escape liability for failure to insure in any case where normal business practice would require insurance.[87]

But a representative is liable for a loss arising from his wilful default, *i.e.* if he is conscious that his act or omission is a breach of duty, or is recklessly careless on the point.[88] For instance, if through his default title deeds are lost or destroyed, he will be liable to an action to establish the contents thereof, and to make compensation for any damage done to the estate by such loss or destruction in addition to the costs of procuring attested and office copies.[89] But it would seem that the court will refuse to take into consideration the speculative damages which the title or marketable value of the estate might sustain upon any future dealing with it from the absence of the deeds.[90]

Unauthorised or unnecessary payments

An executor may be guilty of a *devastavit* if he applies the assets in payment of a claim which he is not bound to satisfy.[91] For instance, if the testator was bound in a *joint* obligation, and dies before his co-obligor, his executor is not liable on the instrument, and, if he pays a sum due under it, will be guilty of a *devastavit*.[92] In some cases, however, the estate of the deceased in liable in equity *pari passu* with the survivor; in such cases the executor is justified in applying the assets accordingly.[93]

In the early nineteenth century, an executor was held to be guilty of a *devastavit* in making disbursements in the schooling, feeding or clothing of the children of the deceased, after his decease.[94] Sections 31 and 32 of the Trustee Act 1925[95] now provide powers to apply and accumulate income and accrue capital for infant beneficiaries, but these powers only apply subject to contrary intention in the will or trust document. The test is whether on a fair reading one can say that such application would be inconsistent with the import of the document.[96] Executors must be allowed a reasonable time for breaking up a testator's domestic establishment and discharging his servants.[97]

[87] See *Garner* v. *Moore* (1855) 3 Drew. 277, where the criterion used is "sound exercise of discretion."
[88] *Re Vickery* [1931] 1 Ch. 572, 584.
[89] *Hornby* v. *Matcham* (1848) 16 Sim. 325. For forms of declarations and orders relating to lost instruments, see 3 Seton, 7th ed., p. 2226.
[90] *Brown* v. *Sewell* (1853) 11 Hare 49; and see also *Gillian and Nugent* v. *National Bank Ltd.* [1901] 2 Ir.R. 513.
[91] Com.Dig.Admon.I. 1; *Manning* v. *Purcell* (1855) 7 De G.M. & G. 55; *Vez* v. *Emery* (1799) 5 Ves. 141. *E.g.* by paying a bond *ex turpi causa: Winchcombe* v. *Winchester* (1616) Hob. 167, cited 1 Brownl. 33; *Robinson* v. *Gee* (1749) 1 Ves.Sen. 251, 254; Com.Dig.-Admon.I. 1.
[92] *Ante*, p. 564.
[93] *Ante*, pp. 568 *et seq.*
[94] *Giles* v. *Dyson* (1815) 1 Stark.N.P.C. 32.
[95] See pp. 1108–1110 *post.*
[96] See *I.R.C.* v. *Bernstein* [1961] Ch. 399, 413; *Re Rees* [1954] Ch. 202; *Re Delamere* [1984] 1 W.L.R. 813.
[97] *Field* v. *Peckett* (1861) 29 Beav. 568, 576.

An executor has been held accountable in paying for work and labour rendered voluntarily to the testator in the expectation of receiving a legacy.[98]

The fact that an executor in making unnecessary payments has acted under the best advice that he could procure does not relieve him from liability.[98a] But executors acting under advice will not readily be deprived of costs.[98b]

Debt paid in good faith

The executor's liability for making unnecesary payments is materially qualified by section 15 of the Trustee Act 1925. Under this section a representative has power to pay or allow any debt or claim on any evidence that he thinks sufficient. If he exercises this power in good faith he will incur no personal liability.[99]

Unenforceable debts

Subject to this statutory protection, a representative formerly committed a *devastavit* in paying a debt to a creditor who was prevented from enforcing it by the Statute of Frauds or by retaining such a debt due to himself.[1] Now, however, most of the requirements of writing under the Statute of Frauds have been abolished by the Law Reform (Enforcement of Contracts) Act 1954.

Statute-barred debts

The executor is, however, entitled to pay a debt which appears to be barred by the Limitation Act,[2] except, perhaps, against the declared wish of his co-executors, or unless it has been judicially declared to be statute-barred.[3] This rule is an anomaly and will not be extended.[4] It seems that the rule has no application where the estate is insolvent, since, according to the rules in bankruptcy for the payment of debts, which apply to an insolvent estate by virtue of the Administration of Insolvent Estates of Deceased Persons Order 1986.[5] A statute-barred debt is not provable.

---

[98] *Shallcross* v. *Wright* (1850) 12 Beav. 505; *ante*, p. 580.
[98a] *Doyle* v. *Blake* (1804) 2 Sch. & Ref. 231, 243; *National Trustees* v. *General Finance* [1905] A.C. 373.
[98b] *Re Buckton* [1970] 2 Ch. 406, 414.
[99] See *ante*, p. 665. See also the Settled Land Act 1925, s.58; Administration of Estates Act 1925, s.39. And as to relief granted by the court, see the Trustee Act 1925, s.61, *post*, pp. 753 *et seq.*
[1] *Re Rownson* (1885) 29 Ch.D. 358.
[2] *Norton* v. *Frecker* (1737) 1 Atk. 524, 526; *Stahlschmidt* v. *Lett* (1853) 1 Sm. & G. 415. See also *Hill* v. *Walker* (1858) 4 K. & J. 166 (retainer of statute-barred debt). See as to the Limitation Act, *post*, p. 899.
[3] *Midgley* v. *Midgley* [1893] 3 Ch. 282.
[4] *Midgley* v. *Midgley*, *supra*; see also *Re Rownson* (1885) 29 Ch.D. 358.
[5] S.I. 1986 No. 1999.

Duty to plead limitation

Again, he is not bound to plead the statute to an action commenced against him by a creditor of the testator.[6] Thus, if the surplus of the personal estate, after payment of the debts and legacies, is bequeathed to a residuary legatee, and several creditors, though barred by the Limitation Act, commence action against the executor, equity will not, on his refusal to plead the statute, compel him to plead it in favour of the residuary legatee.[7]

On the other hand, when once a judgment or order for administration has been made, the representative cannot admit or acknowledge a statute-barred debt so as to take it out of the statute,[8] nor can he exercise any discretion or do any act so as to vary the rights of the parties.[9] Thus, though he cannot be compelled to raise the defence of the Limitation Act, his mere omission to do so does not prevent that defence from being successfully raised by some other party. Such a defence can therefore be raised either by the residuary legatees[10] or by some other creditor,[11] unless the statute-barred creditor had already recovered his debt from the executor before the administration proceedings were taken.[12]

Limitation in administration action

It seems, however, that if the administration proceedings are instituted by a creditor whose debt is statute-barred, and the executor does not raise the defence of the statute against him, no other person has a right to do so.[13] But the persons interested in the estate are not thereby precluded from raising the defence as against some other creditor whose debt is also statute-barred.[14]

The same principles apply where proceedings are instituted by an originating summons under Order 85, r. 2, for such proceedings are merely a less expensive way of effecting the same thing as an administration action.[15] Where, therefore, executors took out such a summons asking for the determination, without administration of the estate, of the question whether the

---

[6] *Williamson* v. *Naylor* (1838) 3 Y. & C.Ex. 208, 211, n. (*a*). But see *contra*, Bayley J. in *M'Culloch* v. *Dawes* (1826) 9 D. & R. 43, disapproved by Wood V.-C. in *Hill* v. *Walker* (1858) 4 K. & J. 166; *Lowis* v. *Rumney* (1867) L.R. 4 Eq. 451.

[7] *Castleton* v. *Fanshaw* (1699) Prec.Ch. 100; *ibid.* 1 Eq.Cas.Abr. 305; 2 Eq.Cas.Abr. 254, 259, pl. 1.

[8] *Moodie* v. *Bannister, post*; *Blair* v. *Nugent*, 3 J. & Lat. 673; *Phillips* v. *Beal, post*; *Re Turner* [1917] 1 Ch. 422.

[9] See *Shewen* v. *Vanderhorst* (1831) 1 Russ. & M. 347; 2 *ibid.* 75; *Phillips* v. *Beal* (1862) 32 Beav. 26; *Re Fleetwood Etc. Syndicate* [1915] 1 Ch. 486, 492.

[10] *Shewen* v. *Vanderhorst, ante*; *Moodie* v. *Bannister* (1859) 4 Drew. 432.

[11] *Fuller* v. *Redman* (1859) 26 Beav. 600, 614.

[12] *Hunter* v. *Baxter* (1861) 3 Giff. 214 (where the executor was entitled to stand in place of the creditor who had recovered the debt from him).

[13] *Ex p. Dewdney* (1809) 15 Ves. 498; *Briggs* v. *Wilson* (1835) 5 De G.M. & G. 12; *Fuller* v. *Redman* (1859) 26 Beav. 600, 614, 617. The *cestuis que trust* of devised estates could do so before 1897; *Briggs* v. *Wilson, ante*. But query whether they can do so now.

[14] *Fuller* v. *Redman, ante*.

[15] See *post*, pp. 822 *et seq*.

first defendant was a creditor of the estate to any and (if so) what amount, the other defendant being the residuary legatee, it was held that the residuary legatee was entitled to insist on the statute being set up as a defence to the claim.[16]

In an administration action, the court is not bound, on behalf of an absent party beneficially interested in the estate, to disallow claims against the estate barred by the statute if the representative and such of the persons beneficially interested as are parties to the suit or have come in under the decree do not set up the statute.[17]

Competing with the estate

It is a general rule that an executor or trustee, having duties of a fiduciary nature towards the beneficiaries, is not allowed to enter into any engagement in which he has, or can have, a personal interest conflicting, or which possibly may conflict, with the interests of those whom he is bound to protect.[18] For example, it would be improper for an executor authorised to carry on a business for the benefit of the beneficiaries to set up on his own account a business in competition with the estate business.[19] It would also be wrong for the executor to renew the lease of premises upon which the deceased carried on his business in his own name and for his personal profit.[20]

Standard of duty

Such acts of negligence, or careless administration, or even acts committed in ignorance of certain material facts,[21] as defeat the rights of creditors, or legatees, or parties entitled in distribution, amount to a *devastavit*. If persons accept the office of executors they must perform it: they must use due diligence,[22] and not suffer the estate to be injured by their neglect.[23] They must, if unpaid, exercise the same care as an ordinary prudent businessman would apply to his own business affairs[24] but a higher standard is required of a paid trustee.[25] He must conduct the business of the trust with

---

[16] *Re Wenham* [1891] 3 Ch. 59.

[17] *Alston* v. *Trollope* (1866) L.R. 2 Eq. 205.

[18] *Re Thomson* [1930] 1 Ch. 203. See also pp. 703 *et seq.*, *ante* and p. 673.

[19] See n. 18.

[20] *Re Knowles* [1948] 1 All E.R. 866.

[21] See, for example, *Holland* v. *Administrator of German Property* (1937) 156 L.T. 373.

[22] See *Re Tankard* [1942] Ch. 69.

[23] *Tebbs* v. *Carpenter* (1816) 1 Madd. 290. See *Eaves* v. *Hickson* (1861) 30 Beav. 136, where trustees were held liable who had paid over the trust fund to wrong persons trusting to a forged marriage certificate. See also *Hopgood* v. *Parkin* (1870) L.R. 11 Eq. 74, where a trustee was held liable for a loss of a trust fund occasioned by the negligence of his solicitor. This case, however, was questioned in *Speight* v. *Gaunt* (1883) 22 Ch.D. 727 (C.A.); and see the Trustee Act 1925, s.30(1); *Re Vickery* [1931] 1 Ch. 572, and *post*, p. 748 as to liability for co-executor.

[24] *Re Lucking* [1968] 1 W.L.R. 866.

[25] *Bartlett* v. *Barclays Trust Co.* [1980] Ch. 515; *Steel* v. *Welcome Trustees* [1988] 1 W.L.R. 167, 171. See article, "The Liability of the Paid Trustee" by D. H. Mervyn Davis, Q.C. in 33 *Conveyancer* 179; [1989] *Conveyancer* 42.

the same care as an ordinary and prudent solicitor-trustee or trust corporation would apply to business for which he is receiving remuneration.[26] If any executor delays the payment of a debt payable on demand with interest, and suffers judgment for the principal and interest incurred after the testator's death, this is a *devastavit* for the interest, unless the executor can show that the assets were insufficient to discharge the debt immediately.[27] And where the executor permits debts carrying interest at a high rate to run on when he has in his hands a fund earning a lower or no rate with which he could pay them, he will be charged with interest on the difference.[28]

Neglect to get in debts

Again, if the executor, by his delay in commencing an action, has enabled the debtor of his testator to protect himself by pleading the Limitation Act, this amounts to a *devastavit*.[29] And where executors had suffered rent to be in arrear for several years, without taking any legal steps, by distress or otherwise, they were held liable for such arrears.[30]

Though an executor is generally liable for loss occasioned by his omission to call in debts,[31] this liability is subject to two qualifications.

In the first place, where it is the duty of an executor to obtain payment of a sum of money, he is exonerated, though he has taken no steps at all, provided he is able to prove[32] that they would have been, or there is reasonable ground for believing they would have been, ineffectual.[33]

Secondly, representatives have now wide statutory powers of compounding, compromising, releasing, etc., liabilities relating to the deceased's estate.[34] Provided they act in good faith, they can exercise these powers without incurring any personal liability. Thus, representatives and trustees

---

[26] See also the judgments of Jessel M.R. and Bowen L.J. in *Speight* v. *Gaunt* (1883) 22 Ch.D. 727, 739, 762 expressly dealing with unpaid trustees, and *Re Waterman's W.T.* [1952] 2 All E.R. 1054, *per* Harman J.; *Re Turner* [1897] 1 Ch. 536; *National Trustees Co.* v. *General Finance Co.* [1905] A.C. 373, P.C. and *Re Pauling* [1964] Ch. 303, 338. Indications of a contrary view are to be found in *Jobson* v. *Palmer* [1893] 1 Ch. 71, 76, Romer J. and *Shepherd* v. *Harris* [1905] 2 Ch. 310, 318 Farwell J.

[27] *Seaman* v. *Dee* (1672) 2 Lev. 40; Com.Dig.Admon.I. 1; Bac.Abr.Exors.L. 1. So if an executor can save the penalty of a bond by payment of the less sum specified in the condition, or by other performance of the condition, and he neglects to do so, it will be a *devastavit* in him if he has assets: (1669) 1 Wms.Saund. 333, n. (7) to *Hancocke* v. *Prowd*.

[28] *Hall* v. *Hallet* (1784) 1 Cox. 134, 138; *Dornford* v. *Dornford* (1806) 12 Ves. 130, n. (29), 2nd ed. *Re Stevens* [1898] 1 Ch. at pp. 176, 177. See also *Bate* v. *Robins* (1863) 32 Beav. 73. See *ante*, pp. 708 *et seq.*, as to charging executors with interest.

[29] *Hayward* v. *Kinsey* (1701) 12 Mod. 568, 573. But see *East* v. *East* (1846) 5 Hare 343.

[30] *Tebbs* v. *Carpenter* (1816) 1 Madd. 290. See also *ante*, p. 69.

[31] See *Lowson* v. *Copeland* (1787) 2 Bro.C.C. 156; *Re Brogden* (1888) 38 Ch.D. 546. For the liability of an executor who lends money on personal security, see *post*, p. 742.

[32] *Stiles* v. *Guy* (1832) 16 Sim. 230; 1 M. & G. 423.

[33] See *Clack* v. *Holland* (1854) 19 Beav. 262, 271. 272; *Re Brogden, supra*. Also the Trustee Act 1925, s.22 (2).

[34] See the Trustee Act 1925, s.15; Settled Land Act 1925, s.58; Administration of Estates Act 1925, s.39; *ante*, p. 665, 5 Wolst. & Ch. 18th ed., pp. 68–71.

who, in the exercise of an active discretion,[35] allow any time for the payment of any debt are protected from personal responsibility for any consequential loss, provided they acted in good faith.[36] Further, a trustee may be exonerated by the court.[37]

Neglect to call in and convert

A representative is liable for a *devastavit* for losses occasioned by his improperly neglecting to call in and convert into money the estate of the testator. Thus, if he omits to sell property when it ought to be sold,[38] or if he improperly allows money to remain in the hands of bankers,[39] he is liable for any consequential loss.[40] But he may, pending an investment, deposit money at a bank[41] and allow bearer securities to remain with his bankers for safe custody and collection of dividends.[42] Executors are also chargeable with neglect in allowing a part of the assets to remain outstanding in an improper state of investment, whether the person in whose hands it is so outstanding is a co-executor or a stranger, and notwithstanding that the will contains the usual indemnity clause.[43]

There is, however, no fixed period at which the loss is to be calculated. It depends upon the nature of the property and the evidence affecting it.[44]

Distribution in specie

It seems that it could be a *devastavit* for an executor to distribute shares in specie if such a distribution gives control to only one of a number of beneficiaries. In such a case he should sell all the shares in question on the open market to prevent unfairness.[45]

Postponement of conversion

The general principle of the executor's year has been considered.[46] An executor is not liable for any loss if he postpones the conversion in the

---

[35] See *Re Greenwood* (1911) 105 L.T. 509.
[36] Trustee Act 1925, s.15 (*e*).
[37] See *post*, pp. 753 *et seq*.
[38] *Phillips* v. *Phillips* (1679) Freem. 11 (lease for life of A, worth £100, retained by executor; A died, and executor held liable for value of lease at testator's death); *Taylor* v. *Tabrum* (1833) 6 Sim. 281; *Fry* v. *Fry* (1859) 27 Beav. 144. But see *Selby* v. *Bowie* (1863) 4 Giff. 300.
[39] *Moyle* v. *Moyle* (1831) 2 Russ. & M. 710; *Bacon* v. *Clark* (1836) 3 My. & Cr. 294; *Lowry* v. *Fulton* (1839) 9 Sim. 115. *Cf. Johnson* v. *Newton* (1853) 11 Hare 160, 168, 169.
[40] See *per* Lord Cottenham in *Clough* v. *Bond* (1838) 3 My. & Cr. 496.
[41] Trustee Act 1925, s.11.
[42] *Ibid*. s.7.
[43] *Stiles* v. *Guy* (1832) 16 Sim. 230; 1 Mac. & G. 422. See also *Mucklow* v. *Fuller* (1821) Jacob 198; *Stiles* v. *Guy* (1832) 4 Y. & C.Ex. 571; *Dix* v. *Burford* (1854) 19 Beav. 409. But see *Paddon* v. *Richardson* (1855) 7 De G.M. & G. 563; and *Re Godwin* (1918) 87 L.J.Ch. 645.
[44] See *Hughes* v. *Empson* (1856) 22 Beav. 181 (executors charged with value of shares, which had depreciated, at the end of 12 months from the death); *Moyle* v. *Moyle, ante*; *Johnson* v. *Newton, ante*; *Bullock* v. *Wheatley* (1844) 1 Coll. 130.
[45] *Lloyds Bank* v. *Duker* [1987] 1 W.L.R. 1324, 1331.
[46] See *ante*, p. 112.

honest and reasonable exercise of his discretion.[47] And *a fortiori* this is the case where the security retained is authorised by the will.[48]

Where there are two or more executors each has a right to exercise his own discretion; and one executor is not necessarily liable for the loss that may arise from his declining to comply with a demand made by another executor for an immediate conversion.[49]

It is not the duty of an executor to call in money invested on real security where no risk is apparent,[50] and, save for some special reason, he will not be liable for retaining an investment authorised by the will or by the general law.[51] Further, a representative cannot be made liable by reason only of his continuing to hold an investment which has ceased to be an investment authorised by the will or by the general law.[52]

On the other hand, executors ought not, without good reason, to permit money to remain upon personal security longer than is absolutely necessary.[53] Thus, unless they have acted in the exercise of an honest and reasonable discretion,[54] or under an express direction of the testator, they will be liable for a loss occasioned by their neglecting to call in money lent by the testator on personal security.[55]

Express power to postpone

An express power to retain existing investments takes a case out of the rule as to the conversion of perishable property.[56] Similarly, executors acting under a will by which an absolute discretion is given to them to postpone the sale and conversion of the testator's estate, are not bound to convert the property within a year, even though some of the property consists of shares in an unlimited company, or of a business carried on by the testator, nor will they be liable, in the absence of mala fides, for loss arising to the estate from the non-conversion.[57]

---

[47] See *Buxton* v. *Buxton* (1835) 1 My. & Cr. 80; *Marsden* v. *Kent* (1877) 5 Ch.D. 598. As to relief by the court, see *post* p. 753.

[48] *Re Chapman* [1896] 2 Ch. 763, 782. And see *Re Grindey* [1898] 2 Ch. 593; *Rawsthorne* v. *Rowley* [1909] 1 Ch. 409, n.

[49] *Buxton* v. *Buxton*, *ante*. See also *East* v. *East* (1846) 5 Hare 343. As to joint representation, see *ante*, p. 690.

[50] *Howe* v. *Dartmouth* (1802) 7 Ves. 137, 150; and see *Re Chapman*, *supra*.

[51] See n. 48, *supra*.

[52] Trustee Act 1925, ss.4, 68 (17). As to investments authorised by statute, see *post*, p. 742, n. 73.

[53] Query whether such loans are "investments" at all; see *Khoo Tek Keong* v. *Ch'ng Joo Tuan Neoh* [1934] A.C. 529; *Re Pecznenik's S.T.* [1964] 1 W.L.R. 720 at 723.

[54] See nn. 49 and 50, *ante*.

[55] *Powell* v. *Evans* (1801) 5 Ves. 839; *Tebbs* v. *Carpenter* (1816) 1 Madd. 290; *Rowley* v. *Adams* (1839) 4 My. & Cr. 534; *Eagleton* v. *Kingston* (1803) 8 Ves. 438, 467; *Att.-Gen.* v. *Higham* (1843) 2 Y. & C.C.C. 634. *cf. Ratcliffe* v. *Winch* (1853) 17 Beav. 217; *East* v. *East* (1846) 5 Hare 343.

[56] *Gray* v. *Siggers* (1880) 15 Ch.D. 74. This applies only if the power is exercised: see *Re Fisher* [1943] Ch. 377; *Re Hey's S.T.* [1945] Ch. 294.

[57] *Re Norrington* (1879) 13 Ch.D. 654. See also *Re Pitcairn* [1896] 2 Ch. 199; and see *ante*, p. 722.

Statutory power to postpone

Though on the death of a person after 1925 such of his property as to which he dies intestate is held on trust for sale and conversion, either under the terms of the will, if any,[58] or by the terms of the Administration of Estates Act 1925,[59] representatives have full power to postpone such sale and conversion for such a period as they think proper before the date of distribution without being accountable. Such representatives, therefore, will not be liable for loss arising from non-conversion if the have acted in good faith.[60]

Consensual postponement partnerships

In practice the power to postpone sale may be important in that it avoids the need for beneficiaries to consent to postponement. A consensual postponement especially if there are business assets can readily lead to allegations (for tax and other purposes) of partnership.

Duty to convert

It will be shown elsewhere[61] that, where personalty is bequeathed in a residuary gift to persons in succession, it is the duty of the executor, with certain exceptions, to convert it into authorised investments, the tenant for life being, in the absence of a contrary direction in the will,[62] entitled upon that principle. If the executor fails to comply with this duty, and pays to the tenant for life the whole interest which arises from the property in its existing state of investment, he incurs a personal liability to the remaindermen. He is bound to account for the actual interest which he has received less the amount which, had he converted the estate at the proper time, would have been received by the tenant for life in dividends.[63] His liability is not decreased by the fact that the value of the *corpus* has been actually increased by the postponement of the conversion.[64]

The remaindermen have, it seems, the alternative of claiming as *corpus* the value of the estate at the time that it ought to have been converted.[65] The executor must also pay interest on that sum from the death of the tenant for life to the date of payment.[66]

[58] *Re McKee* [1931] 2 Ch. 145.
[59] Administration of Estates Act 1925, s.33.
[60] For the extent to which they are entitled to carry on the deceased's business under this power to postpone sale, see *ante*, p. 722.
[61] *Post*, pp. 1039 *et seq.*
[62] As to the undisposed of property, there is a contrary direction contained in the Administration of Estates Act 1925, s.33 (5); *Re Sullivan* [1930] 1 Ch. 84. But see *Re Fisher* [1943] Ch. 377.
[63] *Dimes* v. *Scott* (1828) 4 Russ. 195. See also *Taylor* v. *Clark* (1841) 1 Ha. 161; and *cf. Re Chesterfield's Trusts* (1883) 24 Ch.D. 643 as to apportionment between tenant for life and remaindermen of unconverted reversionary interests in personal estate; and see *Re Woodhouse* [1941] Ch. 332.
[64] *Dimes* v. *Scott, ante.*
[65] See *Wightwick* v. *Lord* (1857) 6 H.L.C. 217. *cf. Baud* v. *Fardell* (1855) 7 De G.M. & G. 628, where the executrix had a discretion as to the nature of the investment.
[66] See *Mackenzie* v. *Taylor* (1844) 7 Beav. 467. As to what interest will be allowed, see *post*, pp. 1040, 1041.

Liability of trustees failing to invest

Where trustees are bound by the terms of their trust to invest money in the public funds, and instead of so doing they retain the money in their hands, the beneficiary may elect to charge them either with the amount of the money, or with the amount of the stock which they might have purchased with it.[67] Where, however, the trustees are not bound to invest the money in the public funds, or in any specific security, but by the terms of the trust have a discretion to invest it in various ways, if the trustees fail to invest as prescribed, they are merely chargeable with the whole amount of the trust fund, together with interest.[68]

Further, apart from any express direction as to the investment of money, a representative is not justified in unnecessarily keeping the deceased's money dead in his hands, and if he does so he is chargeable with interest thereon.[69] Thus, unless the exigencies of his office require otherwise, he should invest the unemployed money in investments authorised by the testator or by statute[70] for that purpose.[71] If he adopts this course he is not liable for the fall in value of the investments,[72] nor does he become liable by reason only of their ceasing to be authorised investments.[73] On the other hand, if he buys or sells without authority any loss[74] will, subject to any relief given by the court,[75] be thrown on him, though there was no bad faith on his part.[76] And if any profit arises from the unauthorised investment he is not entitled to the benefit thereof, but it accrues to the estate of the deceased.[77]

Loans on personal security

If a representative, without any authority from the will, lends money of the deceased upon bond, promissory note, or other personal security, he is

---

[67] *Shepherd* v. *Mouls*, 4 Hare 500, 503, 504; *Pride* v. *Fooks* (1840) 2 Beav. 430; *Robinson* v. *Robinson* (1851) 1 De G.M. & G. 247, 256.

[68] *Robinson* v. *Robinson*, *supra*. Also *Knott* v. *Cottee* (1852) 16 Beav. 77, 80, 81; *Brown* v. *Gellatly* (1867) L.R. 2 Ch. 751, 759; *Re Campbell* [1893] 3 Ch. 470; *Re Barclay* [1899] 1 Ch. 674. As to interest, see *ante*, pp. 710 *et seq.*

[69] See *ante*, p. 708.

[70] For investments authorised by statute, see *ante*, p. 681; *Re Warren* [1939] Ch. 684.

[71] *Holland* v. *Hughes* (1809) 16 Ves. 111, 114; *Tebbes* v. *Carpenter*, 1 Madd. 290, 306; *Norbury* v. *Norbury* (1819) 4 Madd. 191. As to the precautions which a personal representative ought to take, and the extent to which he may properly lend on mortgage, see the Trustee Act 1925, ss.8 and 9; 4 Wolst. & Ch., 13th ed., pp. 6–9.

[72] *Peat* v. *Crane* (1785) 2 Dick. 499, n.; *Franklin* v. *Frith* (1792) 3 Bro.C.C. 434; *Howe* v. *Dartmouth* (1802) 7 Ves. 137, 150; White & Tudor's L.C., 9th ed., pp. 596 *et seq.*

[73] Trustee Act 1925, s.4.

[74] Measured as at the date of judgment and without deduction of tax. The date may be different if the sale or purchase becomes later authorised when the date of authorisation will be taken. *Re Bell* [1980] 1 W.L.R. 1217.

[75] See Trustee Act 1925, s.61, *post*, pp. 753 *et seq.*

[76] *Hancom* v. *Allen* (1774) 2 Dick. 498; *Howe* v. *Dartmouth*, *supra*; *Clough* v. *Bond* (1838) 3 My. & Cr. 490. See also *Gordon* v. *Bowden* (1822) 6 Madd. 342.

[77] *Phayre* v. *Peree* (1815) 3 Dow 116, 128.

guilty of a breach of trust, and will be answerable personally if the security proves defective,[78] unless he is relieved from liability by the court.[79]

Where, however, the will authorises executors to invest in real or personal securities, they would be justified, as against legatees, using a sound discretion, in fairly and honestly lending it to a person whom they considered responsible, at a reasonable interest.[80] But, *semble*, the rule is different as against creditors.[81]

Where the will gives executors power to lend on personal security, this does not enable them, even as against legatees, to accommodate a trader with a loan on his bond.[82]

Where a testator empowers his executors to lend money on personal security, this does not authorise one executor to lend money to another. Should such a loan be made, it is a breach of trust and a misappropriation of the fund; if any mischief arises to the estate of the testator therefrom, the executors will be liable.[83]

Mixing of trust moneys

If an executor or trustee confuses trust moneys with his own money in the same account, the primary question is whether or not the trust moneys can be sufficiently distinguished and treated separately. If they cannot be separated with perfect accuracy the executor is liable for the whole.[84] If, however, they can be so separated but sums are later drawn out by cheque, the rule in *Clayton's* case,[85] attributing the first drawings out to the first payments in, does not apply, and the executor or trustee may be taken to have drawn out his own money preference to the trust money.[86] Although, if the account is in deficit and the beneficiary claims against property purchased by such drawings, this rule will not apply to protect the executor or trustee.[87] In such a case the beneficiary can choose whether to treat the

---

[78] *Terry* v. *Terry* (1708) Prec.Chanc. 273; *Ryder* v. *Bickerton* (1743) 3 Swanst. 80, n.; *ibid.* 1 Eden 149, n.; *Adye* v. *Feuilleteau* (1783) 1 Cox 24; *ibid.* 3 Swanst. 84, n.; *Holmes* v. *Dring* (1788) 1 Cox 1; *Wilkes* v. *Steward* (1801) Coop. 6; *Vigrass* v. *Binfield* (1818) 3 Madd. 62; *Walker* v. *Symonds* (1818) 3 Swanst. 1, 63, overruling *Harden* v. *Parsons* (1785) 1 Eden 145; *Bacon* v. *Clark* (1836) 3 My. & Cr. 294; *Clough* v. *Bond, ibid.* 490, 496; *Bullock* v. *Wheatley* (1844) 1 Coll. 130. *Cf. Webster* v. *Spencer* (1820) 3 B. & Ald. 360.
[79] Trustee Act 1925, s.4; but see *Khoo Tek Keong* v. *Ch'ng Joo Tuan Neoh* [1934] A.C. 529.
[80] *Forbes* v. *Ross* (1788) 2 Cox 113, 116; see *Re Godwin* (1918) 87 L.J.Ch. 645, where trustees were authorised to retain a promissory note.
[81] See *Doyle* v. *Blake* (1804) 2 Sch. & Lef. 231, 239, 240.
[82] *Langston* v. *Ollivant* (1807) G.Coop. 33.
[83] *Stickney* v. *Sewell* (1835) 1 M. & Cr. 8; *Anon.* v. *Walker* (1828) 5 Russ. 7; *Gleadow* v. *Atkin* (1833) 2 Cr. & J. 548, 555. But a bond which one gives the other to save him harmless from such a breach of trust would be valid at law; *Warwick* v. *Richardson* (1842) 10 M. & W. 284.
[84] *Lupton* v. *White* (1808) 15 Ves.Jr. 432; *Cook* v. *Addison* (1869) L.R. 7 Eq. 466, 470; *Re Tilley* [1967] Ch. 1179.
[85] (1816) 1 Meriv. 572. See further as to this rule, pp. 1083, 1084, *post.*
[86] *Re Hallett's Estate* (1880) 13 Ch.D. 696; *Re Oatway* [1903] 2 Ch. 356; *cf. Roscoe* v. *Winder* [1915] 1 Ch. 62. *Space Investments* v. *Canadian Imperial Bank* [1986] 1 W.L.R. 1072.
[87] *Re Tilley* [1967] Ch. 1179, 1185, 1189.

purchased asset wholly or partly as trust property or simply as security for recouping the trust money.[88]

Further, it seems that an executor who pays the money of the testator into his bank, mixing it with his own money, is liable for a loss sustained by the failure of the bank.[89]

Employment of agents

Independently of any statutory enactment, it has long been settled[90] that "trustees are not bound personally to transact such business connected with or arising out of the proper duties of their trust, as, according to the usual mode of conducting business of a like nature, persons acting with reasonable care and prudence on their own account would ordinarily conduct through mercantile agents; and that when, according to the usual and regular course of such business, moneys receivable or payable ought to pass through the hands of such mercantile agents, that course may properly be followed by trustees, though the moneys are trust moneys[91]; and that if, under such circumstances, and without any other[92] misconduct or default on the part of the trustees, a loss takes place through any fraud or neglect of the agents employed, the trustees are not liable to make good such loss."[93]

Accordingly, where a testator gave annuities to his executors for their trouble in the execution of his will, and died possessed of several houses, let at weekly rents, it was held that the executors were justified in paying a person to collect the rents, and did not, therefore, lose their annuities.[94] Again, where there were assets in India, the executor was allowed the expense of an agent to collect them: and the court appointed a receiver in India of a testator's assets on the application of an executor resident in England.[95]

Thus also if an executor living in London and receiving money of the tes-

---

[88] See n. 87, *supra*.
[89] *Wren* v. *Kirton* (1805) 11 Ves. 377; *Fletcher* v. *Walker* (1818) 3 Madd. 73; *Massey* v. *Banner* (1820) 4 Madd. 413; *ibid.* 1 Jac. & Walk. 241; *Robinson* v. *Ward* (1825) Ry. & Mood. 274; *ibid.* 2 C. & P. 59.
[90] See *Ex p. Belchier* (1754) Ambl. 219. See also *Rowth* v. *Howell* (1797) 3 Ves. 565; *Adams* v. *Claxton* (1801) 6 Ves. 226; *Wilks* v. *Groom* (1856) 3 Drewr. 584; *Swinfen* v. *Swinfen* (1860) 29 Beav. 211; *Johnson* v. *Newton* (1853) 11 Hare 160; *Mendes* v. *Guedalla* (1862) 2 J. & H. 259; *Fenwicke* v. *Clarke* (1862) 31 L.J.Ch. 728; *Re Bird* (1873) L.R. 16 Eq. 203.
[91] And even though the agent is a co-trustee employed under a power in the will: *Shepherd* v. *Harris* [1905] 2 Ch. 310.
[92] The word "other" conveys the impression that the proper employment of an agent is a misconduct, which, of course, it is not.
[93] *Per* Selborne L.C. in *Speight* v. *Gaunt* (1883) 9 App.Cas. 1 (affirming *ibid.* 22 Ch.D. 727) at p. 4; *Re Lucking* [1968] 1 W.L.R. 866. See *Bonithon* v. *Hockmore* (1685) 1 Vern. 316; *Davis* v. *Dendy* (1818) 3 Madd. 170. See also *Hopkinson* v. *Roe* (1838) 1 Beav. 180; *Jones* v. *Powell* (1843) 6 Beav. 488. *Cf. Weiss* v. *Dill* (1834) 3 M. & K. 26.
[94] *Wilkinson* v. *Wilkinson* (1825) 2 Sim. & Stu. 237. See also, as to an administrator, *Trezevant* v. *Fraser.* Hil.Term, 1832, before Shadwell V.-C. *Semble*, even at law an executor, under a plea of *plene administravit*, was allowed the reasonable charges of collecting the testator's debts: *Giles* v. *Dyson* (1815) 1 Stark.N.P.C. 32.
[95] *Cockburn* v. *Raphael* (1825) 2 Sim. & Stu. 453.

tator should remit to an attorney in the country to pay the debts there, and the attorney becomes insolvent, the executor will not be chargeable if the business was transacted in the ordinary manner without any circumstance to show suspicion.[96] And where executors employ an auctioneer to sell the leaseholds, or other portion of the assets, who receives the deposit and fails to pay it over, the executors will not, generally speaking, be held personally liable for the loss.[97]

A representative may be justified from the nature of the accounts in employing an accountant and the expense will in a proper case be allowed to him.[98] Under the Trustee Act 1925, s.22(4), he may cause the trust accounts to be audited or examined by an independent accountant.

The liability of a trustee for an agent's default is probably not increased by the fact that the trustee is remunerated for his services,[99] but where a paid trustee deliberately places himself in a position where as banker his own interest conflicts with his duty as a trustee, the court is slow to relieve him from liability for a breach of trust, not involving the default of an agent.[1]

Again, if a representative pays a solicitor for his trouble and attendance in the transacting and conduct of the deceased's affairs, he ought to be allowed and repaid what he so pays.[2] But an executor is not entitled to be allowed without question the amount of the bill of costs which he has paid bona fide to the solicitor to the trust; the master as an officer of the court, without regularly taxing the bill, may moderate the amount.[3] A representative will not be allowed the charges of his solicitor for doing things which he ought strictly to have done himself.[4]

On the other hand, apart from statute,[5] a trustee or representative would have been liable for the default of an agent who was employed neither from necessity nor conformably to the usage of mankind.[6] And though it may be in conformity with common usage to employ an agent to transact certain

---

[96] *Bacon* v. *Bacon*, 5 Ves. 331, 334, 335; *Castle* v. *Warland* (1863) 32 Beav. 660; *Re Lord de Clifford's Estate* [1900] 2 Ch. 707.

[97] *Edmonds* v. *Peake* (1843) 7 Beav. 239.

[98] *Henderson* v. *M'Iver* (1818) 3 Madd. 275.

[99] *Jobson* v. *Palmer* [1893] 1 Ch. 71. But see *Bartlett* v. *Barclays Trust Co.* [1980] Ch. 515 and *ante*, p. 737.

[1] *Re Pauling* [1964] 1 Ch. 303, 339. See further, *post*, p. 755. The emphasis here appears to be upon the conflict of duty and interest but it seems that the remuneration of the trustee is a factor to be taken into account. See "The Liability of the Paid Trustee" by D. H. Mervyn Davies, Q.C. in 33 *Conveyancer* 179; and *ante*, pp. 737, 739.

[2] *Macnamara* v. *Jones* (1784) Dick. 587. In *Stacpoole* v. *Stacpoole* (1816) 4 Dow. 209, an administrator was not allowed to set off a charge for poundage alleged to have been paid to his agent in the administration.

[3] *Johnson* v. *Telford* (1827) 3 Russ. 477.

[4] *Harbin* v. *Darby* (1860) 28 Beav. 325 (solicitor-executor); and see *ante*, p. 700. For the general rule as to an executor's costs, and as to his "charges and expenses," see *post*, p. 919 and for what are "just allowances," see *post*, pp. 919 *et seq*.

[5] As to the effect of the Trustee Act 1925, s.23 (1), see *post*, p. 747.

[6] See *Clough* v. *Bond* (1838) 3 My. & Cr. 490, 496, 497; *Speight* v. *Gaunt*, *infra*. And see *Darke* v. *Martyn* (1839) 1 Beav. 525; *Rehden* v. *Wesley* (1861) 29 Beav. 213.

business, that fact alone does not justify a trustee in delegating the care and custody of trust funds to that agent.[7]

Statutory protection where agent employed

The liability of trustees and representatives has been greatly decreased by statute. Under section 30 of the Trustee Act 1925[8] trustees (including representatives[9]) are not responsible for a loss occasioned by the acts or defaults of any banker, broker, or other person with whom trust money or securities may be properly[10] deposited, unless it can be shown that the loss happened through their own wilful default.[11] Once the employment is proved to have been proper, the burden of proof is on those who wish to charge the trustee to show a wilful default on his part.[12]

Further, a trustee (including a representative[13]) has a power under section 23 of the same Act to appoint a solicitor (or a banker in respect of money payable under a policy of insurance) to receive and give a discharge for money, valuable consideration or property receivable by the trustee under the trust, by permitting him to have the custody of and to produce, receipts signed by the person entitled to give the receipt.[14] Such trustee is not chargeable by reason only of his having made or concurred in making any such appointment.[15] It should be noticed, however, that a trustee who knows, or ought to know, that money has been so received,[16] is not relieved from liability if he suffers the money to remain in the hands of the solicitor or banker for longer than is reasonably necessary.[17]

There is also statutory power[18] to employ and pay an agent to transact any business or do any act required in the execution of a trust or the administration of an estate without the executor being responsible for the default of any such agent, provided he is employed in good faith. Such agent may receive and pay money[19] and is entitled to be allowed and paid all charges and expenses incurred.[20]

---

[7] See *Rowland* v. *Witherden* (1851) 3 M. & G. 568, 574; *Bostock* v. *Floyer* (1865) 35 Beav. 603, 606; L.R. 1 Eq. 26; *Speight* v. *Gaunt* (1883) 3 App.Cas. 1, 5. And see *Matthews* v. *Brise* (1845) 6 Beav. 239; *Challen* v. *Shippam* (1845) 4 Hare 555.

[8] *Post*, p. 1108.

[9] Trustee Act 1925, s.68(17).

[10] *Re Brier* (1884) 26 Ch.D. 238, 243.

[11] Trustee Act 1925, s.30(1). This subsection does not apply where trust funds are paid to the wrong person; *Re Windsor Steam Coal Co.* [1929] 1 Ch. 151.

[12] *Re Brier*, (*supra*).

[13] Trustee Act 1925, s.68(17).

[14] For the details of this power, see the Trustee Act 1925, s.23(3); 4 Wolst. & Ch., 13th ed., pp.27–30. As to appointment of a nominee of the Law Society to take a grant where the persons entitled fail to apply on a solicitor's death, see *Practice Direction* [1965] 1 W.L.R. 552.

[15] Trustee Act 1925, s.23(3).

[16] *Re Sheppard* [1911] 1 Ch. 50.

[17] Trustee Act 1925, s.23(3); *Wyman* v. *Paterson* [1900] A.C. 271.

[18] Trustee Act 1925, s.23(1).

[19] *cf. Re Flower* (1884) 27 Ch.D. 592.

[20] But, *semble*, executors must use their discretion as to the remuneration which they allow their agent: see *Re Weall* (1889) 42 Ch.D. 674.

This provision abolished the requirement that, for the protection of the trustee, the employment of the agent must be from necessity or in conformity with the usage of mankind.[21] Thus, it has been said that section 23(1) revolutionised the position of a trustee or executor. He no longer had to do any actual work himself but could employ a solicitor or other agent to do it, whether there was any real necessity for the employment or not.[22] The joint effect of sections 23 and 30 on the liability of a representative is that, where he employs an agent to receive money belonging to the estate he will not be liable for a loss of the money occasioned by the misconduct of the agent, unless the loss happens through the wilful default of the representative, using those words as implying either a consciousness of negligence or breach of duty, or a recklessness in the performance of a duty.[23]

Limits to this protection

Semble, the agent must still be employed in his ordinary course of business.[24] At any rate, the employment of a person to do some act outside the sphere of his business would tend to indicate the absence of good faith.

Though this provision enables a representative to employ an agent to receive money, *semble*, it does not relieve him from personal liability if he leaves the money in the hands of the agent for longer than is reasonably necessary for the completion of the transaction.[25]

The representative cannot under this provision delegate to an agent the discretions, powers and duties involved in the execution of his trust; he is only empowered to employ an agent to transact some business or do some act in connection with the execution of the trust.[26]

A trustee who employs a manager to manage the business of the trust or to manage the business of a company in which the trust holds shares, is unlikely to be protected by sections 23 and 30. Such a trustee ought not merely to avoid wilful default, but to conduct the business of the trust as an ordinary prudent man would conduct a business of his own.[27] He is not within the protection given by the sections because a person who is empowered by a trustee to manage a business owned by the trust is not a person with whom trust money or securities are deposited.[28]

---

[21] As was required by *Ex p. Belchier* (1754) Ambl. 218.

[22] *Re Vickery* [1931] 1 Ch. 572, 581. See 47 L.Q.R. 330, 463.

[23] *Ibid.* at p. 583; and *cf. Re City Equitable Fire Insurance Co. Ltd.* [1925] 1 Ch. 407. There may, of course, be circumstances where "wilful default" is not the test. See *per* Cross J. in *Re Lucking* [1968] 1 W.L.R. 866, 874, discussed below, and the test stated *ante*, p. 737. See also (1959) 22 M.L.R. 381 (G. H. Jones).

[24] See *Fry* v. *Tapson* (1884) 28 Ch.D. 268; *Re Vickery* [1931] 1 Ch. 572, *per* Maugham J. See also *Learoyd* v. *Whiteley* (1887) 12 App.Cas. 727, and *Wyman* v. *Paterson* [1900] A.C. 271.

[25] *cf.* the proviso to the Trustee Act 1925, s.23(3). *cf.* also the cases in n. 7, *ante*.

[26] See *ante*, p. 700. *cf. Green* v. *Whitehead, post*.

[27] *Re Lucking* [1968] 1 W.L.R. 866, 874; see also *ante*, p. 737; *Speight* v. *Gaunt* (1883) 22 Ch.D. 727, C.A.; *Bartlett* v. *Barclays Bank Trust Co. Ltd.* [1980] Ch. 515.

[28] See n. 27, *supra*.

Agent for property abroad

Trustees and representatives may, however, delegate all or any of their discretions, powers and duties, in respect of any property situated outside the United Kingdom, and are not, by reason only of their having so acted, responsible for any loss arising thereby.[29]

Trustee absent abroad

A trustee intending to remain out of the United Kingdom for more than one month may, by power of attorney, delegate the execution of his trust, whilst he is abroad, to any person except a sole co-trustee not being a trust corporation.[30] But in this case he is personally liable for the acts and defaults of his agent.[31] *Semble*, the provision would apply to a trustee permanently abroad. Doubt has been expressed whether the context admits of the expression trustee including a representative in this provision.[32]

Liability for devastavit of co-executor

The Trustee Act 1925, s.30(1),[33] provides, in effect, that a trustee[34] is only liable for his own acts, receipts, neglects and defaults. Now in all cases in which an executor has been held responsible for a loss occasioned by his co-executor it has not been because of the conduct of the co-executor, but because the executor by his own act or default has enabled an unnecessary loss to fall on the estate. Thus, section 30, and the sections which it has replaced,[35] have done no more than to put on a statutory footing the principles of equity which govern this matter.[36]

This view is strengthened by the fact that numerous cases have decided that the usual indemnity clause, exonerating an executor from all responsibility on account of the acts of his co-executors, affords no greater protection than was already given by equitable principles.[37] It should be added, however, that a will may be so drafted as to protect an executor from liability to beneficiaries for a loss occasioned by his co-executor.[38]

---

[29] See the Trustee Act 1925, s.23(2), set out *post*, p. 1103. This subsection has no application to trust property within the United Kingdom: *Green* v. *Whitehead* [1930] 1 Ch. 38, 45.

[30] Trustee Act 1925, s.25, *ante*, p. 701; *post*, p. 1104; 4 Wolst. & Ch., 13th ed., pp. 30–33. For a power for a personal representative to delegate his functions while engaged on war service, or while abroad, when it was not reasonably practicable for him to return, see Execution of Trusts (Emergency Provisions) Act 1939.

[31] Trustee Act 1925, s.25(5). For the right to delegate powers of leasing and management, see the Law of Property Act 1925, s.29; Administration of Estates Act 1925, s.39; *ante*, p. 702.

[32] See article in 80 S.J. 986.

[33] See generally on this section, 4 Wolst. & Ch., 13th ed., pp. 37–38.

[34] Which includes a personal representative: Trustee Act 1925, s.68(17).

[35] *i.e.* the Trustee Act 1893, s.24, which replaced 22 & 23 Vict. c. 35, s.31.

[36] See *Re Brier* (1884) 26 Ch.D. 238, 243; *Re Munton* [1927] 1 Ch. 262. As to joint representation, see *ante*, p. 740; [1989] *Conveyancer* 42.

[37] *Mucklow* v. *Fuller* (1821) Jacob 198. See also *Underwood* v. *Stevens* (1816) 1 Meriv. 712; *Hanbury* v. *Kirkland* (1829) 3 Sim. 265; *Williams* v. *Nixon* (1840) 2 Beav. 472; *Dix* v. *Burford* (1854) 19 Beav. 409; *Brumridge* v. *Brumridge* (1858) 27 Beav. 5; *Re Brier, supra*.

[38] See *Wilkins* v. *Hogg* (1861) 3 Giff. 116; *Pass* v. *Dundas* (1880) 43 L.T. 665; 29 W.R. 332.

While section 23(1) of the Trustee Act 1925 has made a fundamental change in the law relating to the employment of agents by an executor or administrator, it is not clear to what extent it has changed the rules relating to the liability of an executor for the acts of his co-executor. For this reason the older authorities are still important.

According to the older law a *devastavit* by one of two executors or administrators will not charge his companion[39]; provided he has not intentionally or otherwise contributed to it; for the testator's having misplaced his confidence in one should not operate to the prejudice of the other.[40]

Separate representation in court of co-executors

An executor is only entitled to the costs of separate representation when he and his co-executors are sued for breach of trust, if there is reasonable ground for severance. Such a ground exists where one defendant is in a position where his interest and his duty conflict or where one defendant could admit facts not believed by the other to be true or where separate relief or separate allegations of fraud are or may be made against one of the defendants.[41]

Co-executor negligently allowed to retain assets

On the other hand, the rule prevailing, at any rate before 1926, was that an executor who did some act whereby any part of the deceased's estate came to the hands of a co-executor was liable for any consequential loss, unless the act in question was prompted by necessity or was in conformity with a reasonable and prudent administration of the estate.[42] His liability for entrusting a co-executor with assets was the same as his liability for so entrusting a stranger.

Thus where A, B, C, D and E (D and E being married women) took out administration to an intestate, and afterwards appointed C to be the acting administrator, and directed the creditors to pay their debts to him, and C became insolvent, it was held that A, B and the husbands of D and E were responsible for C's receipts.[43]

Co-executor acting as agent

Where an executor permits a co-executor to act as agent, then it is conceived that after 1925 the liability of the executor for any default commit-

---

[39] Went.Off.Ex. 306, 14th ed.; *Anon.*, Dyer 210 *a*; *Hargthorpe* v. *Milforth* (1594) Cro.Eliz. 318; *Williams* v. *Nixon* (1840) 2 Beav. 472. See also *Re Lucking* [1968] 1 W.L.R. 866, 877.

[40] Cro.Eliz. 319.

[41] *Re Spurling* [1966] 1 W.L.R. 920, 925. See R.S.C.Ord. 62, r. 31(2). See *post*, pp. 822 *et seq.*

[42] See *Townsend* v. *Barber* (1763) 1 Dick. 356; *Macpherson* v. *Macpherson* (1852) 1 Macq.H. of L. 243; *Langford* v. *Gascoyne* (1805) 11 Ves. 333; *Hewett* v. *Foster* (1843) 6 Beav. 259; *Broadhurst* v. *Balguy* (1841) 1 Y. & C.C.C. 16; *Re Gasquoigne* [1894] 1 Ch. 470.

[43] *Lees* v. *Sanderson* (1830) 4 Sim. 28. And see *Gill* v. *Att.-Gen.* (1662) Hardr. 314; *cf. Lewis* v. *Nobbs* (1878) 8 Ch.D. 591; *Moses* v. *Levi* (1839) 3 Y. & C.Ex. 359. And see *Aplyn* v. *Brewer* (1701) Prec.Chan. 173; *Burrows* v. *Walls* (1855) 5 De G.M. & G. 233.

ted by such co-executor acting as such agent will be determined by the general rule applicable to the liability of an executor for the acts of his agent, that is to say, he will not be responsible for the default of any such co-executor if employed in good faith.[44]

As the law formerly stood, the fact that an executor did some act which enabled his co-executor to obtain control of assets on the faith of a false representation made by the latter, that he required them for proper administrative purposes, did not relieve the executor unless he exercised ordinary and reasonable diligence to inquire whether the representation of the co-executor was true.[45]

But if one executor placed the property of the testator in the hands of the other, who happened to be a banker, or in such a situation that the act was not imprudent, the executor so depositing was not charged in case of a loss; for if he had been a sole executor, and had, under the same circumstances, placed the money in a banker's hands, he would not have been liable.[46] Thus, if an executor in the country executed a power of attorney to a co-executor in town for the purpose of changing a fund of the testator, as the court would order it to be changed, the act was justifiable, being for a purpose belonging to the administration of assets; though it was not justifiable if the power was given for the purpose of changing the fund to an unauthorised investment.[47]

If an executor was merely passive, by not obstructing his co-executor from getting the assets into his possession, he was not necessarily responsible.[48] But it seems to have been settled,[49] before 1926, that an executor who unreasonably and imprudently refrained from obstructing his co-executor from getting into, or keeping in,[50] his possession assets of the testator, would incur personal liability for any consequential loss, though his conduct was merely passive.

Executor is his brother's keeper

It is the duty of all executors to watch over, and, if necessary, to correct the conduct of each other. An executor as well as a trustee, who stands by

[44] See *ante*, pp. 744 *et seq.*, discussing ss. 23 and 30 of the Trustee Act 1925. It seems from *Home* v. *Pringle* (1841) 8 Cl. & F. 264 that s.23 is wide enough to enable an executor to appoint his co-executor as his agent, but this section does not of itself authorise a co-trustee to charge: see 72 S.J. 623.

[45] *Shipbrook* v. *Lord Hinchinbrook* (1805) 11 Ves. 254; 16 Ves. 477; *Hanbury* v. *Kirkland* (1829) 3 Sim. 265; *Hewett* v. *Foster* (1843) 6 Beav. 259; *Trutch* v. *Lamprell* (1855) 20 Beav. 116; *Broadhurst* v. *Balguy* (1841) 1 Y. & C.C.C. 16.

[46] *Churchill* v. *Hobson* (1713) 1 P.Wms. 241; *Chambers* v. *Minchin* (1802) 7 Ves. 186. See also *Att.-Gen.* v. *Randall* (1734) M.S.Rep. 21; Vin.Abr. 534, tit.Trust.N.a.pl. 9. As to delegation, see *ante*, p. 700.

[47] *Chambers* v. *Minchin* (1802) 7 Ves. 186, 193. See also *Joy* v. *Campbell* (1804) 1 Sch. & Lef. 328, 341.

[48] See *Hovey* v. *Blakeman* (1799) 4 Ves. 596; *Langford* v. *Gascoyne* (1805) 11 Ves. 333; *Candler* v. *Tillett* (1855) 22 Beav. 257.

[49] See the judgment of Lord Cottenham in *Styles* v. *Guy* (1849) 1 M. & G. 422. See also *Egbert* v. *Butter* (1856) 21 Beav. 560.

[50] See *Lincoln* v. *Wright* (1841) 4 Beav. 427.

and sees a breach of trust committed by his co-trustee becomes respon-sible.[51] In *Styles* v. *Guy*,[52] where two out of three executors with the knowledge that there were unsettled accounts at the testator's death between him and their co-executor, on taking which the latter might be found to be indebted to the estate, took no effectual measures to compel him to account and pay or secure the balance for several years, at the end of which he became bankrupt, Lord Cottenham held that the solvent executors (who were unable to prove that an attempt to recover the money at an earlier period would have been fruitless) were responsible for the loss, as occasioned by their wilful neglect and default.

It is now provided that a trustee or representative is chargeable only for the money or securities actually received by him notwithstanding his sign-ing any receipts for the sake of conformity.[53]

The partners of a solicitor-trustee are not normally liable for his mis-application of trust funds as trustee.[54]

Delegation to co-executor

However, section 23(1) is not wide enough to enable a representative to delegate generally the discretions, powers and duties involved in the administration of the estate. It is suggested, therefore, that an executor who, whether by active or passive conduct, enables a co-executor to act exclusively in the administration will incur the same liabilities as he would have done before 1926.[55] This, however, does not apply where the trust estate is outside the United Kingdom.[56]

Before 1926 his liability for entrusting a co-executor with assets was the same as his liability for so entrusting a stranger.[57]

Executor cannot retire

An executor who, as executor, has taken any part in the administration of the assets cannot, by renouncing and putting the administration in the hands of a co-executor, exonerate himself from liability in respect of the assets which he has received.[58] Executors must either wholly renounce, or, if they act to a certain extent as executors and take upon them that charac-

---

[51] *Styles* v. *Guy* (1849) 1 M. & G. 422, 433; *Williams* v. *Nixon*, 2 Beav. 472, 475; *Horton* v. *Brocklehurst* (1858) 29 Beav. 504, 510; *Booth* v. *Booth* (1838) Beav. 125.

[52] 1 M. & G. 422. See also *Re Gasquoigne* [1894] 1 Ch. 470.

[53] Trustee Act 1925, s.30(1), replacing Trustee Act 1893, s.24.

[54] *Re Bell* [1980] 1 W.L.R. 1217.

[55] And see Trustee Act 1925, s.25 (*ante*, p. 701), for the liability of an executor who appoints an attorney whilst out of the United Kingdom.

[56] See *ante*, p. 701.

[57] See Mr. Cox's note to *Churchill* v. *Hobson* (1713) 1 P.Wms. 241; *Sadler* v. *Hobbs* (1786) 2 Bro.C.C. 114; *Home* v. *Pringle* (1841) 8 Cl. & F. 264, 288. See also *Toplis* v. *Hurrell* (1854) 19 Beav. 423; *Candler* v. *Tillett* (1855) 22 *ibid*. 257; *Cowell* v. *Gatcombe* (1859) 27 Beav. 568; *Ingle* v. *Partridge* (1863) 32 Beav. 661; *Re Gasquoigne* [1894] 1 Ch. 470.

[58] *Read* v. *Truelove* (1762) Ambl. 417; *Harrison* v. *Graham* (1700) 3 Hill's MS. 239; 1 P.Wms. 241, n. (*y*) to 6th ed.; *Underwood* v. *Stevens* (1816) 1 Meriv. 712; *Rogers* v. *Frank* (1827) 1 Y. & J. 409. And see *James* v. *Frearson* (1842) 1 Y. & C.C.C. 370.

ter, they can only be discharged by administering the assets themselves, or by putting the administration in the hands of the court.[59]

If an executor who renounces does not act as executor, but merely as agent for the executors who prove the will, he incurs no further liability than does any other agent.[60]

But once an executor has proved the will, he cannot renounce his representative capacity and act under another: he can do no act in regard to the estate for which he is not answerable as executor,[61] although minimal acts of administration may be disregarded.[62] A co-executor, however, who has proved but never acted, cannot be charged merely because he received a letter by post from a debtor to the estate, enclosing a bill of exchange on account of the debt which he immediately sent to the acting executor, who afterwards became insolvent.[63]

Further, an executor who has proved can act and be responsible, merely as the agent of his co-executor, in respect of some transaction which the co-executor was alone entitled to carry out.[64]

Agent's liability

An agent of trustees in possession of trust money is not accountable to the beneficiaries, if there is a breach of trust, so long as he has acted honestly and has not intermeddled in the trust by doing acts as trustee.[65] If he has so intermeddled, he may be liable as a constructive trustee[66] but his innocent partners will not be liable.[67]

Concurrence or acquiescence

As a general rule, concurrence in an act of *devastavit* on the part of the parties injured by it, or acquiescence without original concurrence, will release the executors.[68] But the court must inquire into all the circumstances which induced concurrence or acquiescence, and ascertain whether their conduct really amounts to such a previous sanction or subsequent ratification as ought to relieve the executors from responsibility.[69]

---

[59] *Doyle* v. *Blake* (1804) 2 Sch. & Lef. 231, 245. And see *Riky* v. *Kemmis*, 1 L. & G. 101; *Horton* v. *Brocklehurst* (1858) 29 Beav. 504. For a special case compromised before the court, see *Tiger* v. *Barclays Bk.* [1952] 1 All E.R. 85.

[60] *Orr* v. *Newton* (1791) 2 Cox 274; *Dove* v. *Everard* (1830) 1 Russ. & M. 231; *Lowry* v. *Fulton*, 9 Sim. 115. And see *Stacey* v. *Elph* (1833) 1 M. & K. 195.

[61] *Graham* v. *Keble* (1813) 2 Dow.P.C. 17.

[62] *Holder* v. *Holder* [1968] Ch. 353.

[63] *Balchen* v. *Scott* (1795) 2 Ves. 678.

[64] *Davis* v. *Spurling* (1829) 1 Russ. & M. 64.

[65] *Williams-Ashman* v. *Price and Williams* [1942] Ch. 219.

[66] See generally *Snell's Equity*, 29th ed. 192–197, Lewin, *Trusts*, 16th ed., 1964. pp. 15, 665.

[67] *Re Bell's Indenture* [1980] 1 W.L.R. 1217.

[68] *Griffiths* v. *Porter* (1858) 25 Beav. 236. See *Fletcher* v. *Collis* [1905] 2 Ch. 24; *Re Pauling* [1964] Ch. 303, 358.

[69] *Walker* v. *Symonds* (1818) 3 Swanst. 1; *Burrows* v. *Walls* (1855) 5 De G.M. & G. 233, 251; *Davies* v. *Hodgson* (1858) 25 Beav. 177. See also *Sleeman* v. *Wilson* (1871) L.R. 13 Eq. 36; *cf. Dixon* v. *Dixon* (1878) 9 Ch.D. 587; *Re Hulkes* (1886) 33 Ch.D. 552. And see further on the subject of *laches*, *ante*, p. 657.

Impounding beneficiaries' interest

Where a beneficiary has instigated a breach of trust, the trustee has a right in equity and by statute to impound the beneficiary's interest in order to indemnify himself. The statutory right, and it seems the equitable right, both apply to representatives. Both are based on subrogation[70] and not upon possession or retainer and both enable a former trustee to impound for breaches occurring when he was an actual trustee. Neither right, however, enables the trustee to control the investment of the trust fund for his own protection or to insist on remaining a trustee.[71]

The Trustee Act 1925, s.62 (as amended[72]), which expressly applies to representatives,[73] enables the court to impound the interest of a beneficiary who has instigated, requested, or consented in writing, to a breach of trust for the purpose of indemnifying the representative or persons claiming through him.[74]

The court only exercises a discretion under this section where the beneficiary must have been aware of the facts constituting the breach of trust.[75] He must have either instigated, requested, or consented in writing[76]; but it is not necessary that he should have derived a benefit.[77] The words "in writing" apply only to "consent," and not to "instigation" or "request."[78]

Relief by the court

The Trustee Act 1925, s.61, which expressly applies to representatives,[79] enables the court to relieve a trustee from personal liability for a breach of trust if it appears that he "has acted honestly and reasonably, and ought fairly to be excused for the breach of trust and for omitting to obtain the directions of the court in the matter in which he committed such breach."[80]

No general rules or principles can be laid down, for each case depends on its own circumstances. But it must be shown that the trustee acted reasonably as well as honestly[81] and ought fairly to be excused.[82] The onus is on a trustee who applies for relief under the section to prove that he has

---

[70] See *Raby* v. *Ridehalgh* (1855) 7 De G.M. & G. 104; *Re Pauling* [1963] Ch. 576, 584.

[71] *Re Pauling* [1963] Ch. 576, 583, 585.

[72] See the Married Women (Restraint upon Anticipation) Act 1949, s.1(4), Sched. 2.

[73] Trustee Act 1925, s.68(17).

[74] On this section generally, see 4 Wolst. & Ch., 13th ed., pp. 89–90.

[75] See *Griffith* v. *Hughes* [1892] 3 Ch. 105; *Re Somerset* [1894] 1 Ch. 231; *Mara* v. *Browne* [1895] 2 Ch. 69, reversed on facts [1896] 1 Ch. 199.

[76] *Re Somerset, ante.*

[77] *Fletcher* v. *Collis* [1905] 2 Ch. 24.

[78] *Griffith* v. *Hughes, ante.*

[79] Trustee Act 1925, s.68(17); *Re Kay* [1897] 2 Ch. 518; *Marsden* v. *Regan* [1954] 1 W.L.R. 423.

[80] On this section generally, see 4 Wolst, & Ch., 13th ed., pp. 87–89.

[81] *Re Turner* [1897] 1 Ch. 536; *Re Lord de Clifford's Estate* [1900] 2 Ch. 707; *Khoo Tek Keong* v. *Ch'ng Joo Tuan Neoh* [1934] A.C. 529; *Re Gale* [1941] Ch. 209, 218; *Re Gee* [1948] Ch. 284, 297. *Re Orwell* [1982] 1 W.L.R. 1357.

[82] *National Trustees Co.* v. *General Finance Co.* [1905] A.C. 373; *Re Windsor Steam Coal Co.* [1929] 1 Ch. 151, 164.

satisfied its requirements. One test where a trustee lends trust money may be whether he would have acted in the same way if the money had been his own. Prima facie the provisions of the Trustee Act 1925, s.8, as to loans, constitute a reasonable standard by which his conduct in such matters may be judged.[83]

The representative is not debarred from applying for relief merely because he acted in ignorance of some principle of construction or law.[84]

The section applies to an executor who has committed a *devastavit*, but in construing the section the court is bound to ascertain whether or not there has been any undue delay in advertising for claims under the statutory provisions[85] in that behalf.[86] It is not confined to cases of breach of trust, but applies to an action for a common account.[87]

Semble, It does not by implication confer jurisdiction on the court to exercise by anticipation the authority thereby conferred upon it, so as to excuse a breach of trust which is only contemplated.[88] This, however, is of less import now that the court has power to authorise dealings with the trust property which are "in the opinion of the court expedient."[89]

Instances of relief granted

Relief has been given where an executor neglected to sue for a debt,[90] where executors remitted money to their solicitors for administration purposes,[91] where an executor compromised a claim of his co-executor,[92] where by mistake money was paid to the wrong persons,[93] where too large a sum was advanced on mortgage,[94] where trustees made an unauthorised sale under a mistake of law,[95] where a spinster was allowed to enjoy testamentary benefits given to her "during her widowhood"[96] and where after an estate had been distributed, the Department of Health and Social Security made a claim for overpaid social security benefits.[97]

---

[83] *Re Stuart* [1897] 2 Ch. 583; and see *Waite* v. *Parkinson* (1901) 85 L.T. 456.

[84] *Holland* v. *Administrator of German Property* (1937) 156 L.T. 373; *Re Gale, ante*; *Re Wightwick's W.T.* [1950] Ch. 260, 266.

[85] See the Trustee Act 1925, s.27, as amended by the Law of Property (Amendment) Act 1926, Sched. See *ante*, p. 605.

[86] *Re Kay* [1897] 2 Ch. 518.

[87] *Ibid.*,; *Re Lord de Clifford's Estate* [1900] 2 Ch. 707, 716.

[88] *Re Tollemache* [1903] 1 Ch. 457, 466, 955.

[89] Trustee Act 1925, s.57 (on which see *Re Craven's Estate (No. 1)* [1937] Ch. 423); Settled Land Act 1925, s.64.

[90] *Re Roberts* (1897) 76 L.T. 479; *Re Grindley* [1898] 2 Ch. 593.

[91] *Re Mackay* [1911] 1 Ch. 300; *Re de Clifford, ante*. And see *Re Smith* (1902) 71 L.J.Ch. 411.

[92] *Re Houghton* [1904] 1 Ch. 622, 626.

[93] *Re Allsop* [1914] 1 Ch. 1; *Holland* v. *Administrator of German Property* (1937) 156 L.T. 373. cf. *National Trustees Co.* v. *General Finance Co., ante* (non-gratuitous trustee) and *Re Windsor Steam Coal Co.* [1929] 1 Ch. 151.

[94] *Palmer* v. *Emerson* [1911] 1 Ch. 758.

[95] *Perrins* v. *Bellamy* [1898] 2 Ch. 521; [1899] 1 Ch. 797.

[96] *Re Gale* [1941] Ch. 209.

[97] *Secretary of State for Social Services* v. *Blackie* [1975] C.L.Y. 3726.

Instances of relief refused

Relief was refused where trust funds were advanced on improper security,[98] on a second mortgage,[99] or on a contributory mortgage,[1] where some shares were paid without retaining sufficient to satisfy the others,[2] where a trust for conversion was postponed for 14 years,[3] where there was a neglect to get in debts,[4] where trustees omitted to seek advice,[5] where money was left with solicitors to invest,[6] where negligent reliance was placed on a fraudulent co-trustee,[7] where payment was made to an alleged co-trustee without proof of title,[8] and where a paid trustee placed himself in a position where his duty and his interest were in conflict.[9]

Professional trustees' relief

The court is less ready to grant relief to a paid trustee,[10] but the decision in *Jobson* v. *Palmer*[11] has never been cited in the cases said to support this proposition. It is clear that the fact and amount of any remuneration for the trustee are factors to be considered in the exercise of the discretion, and that no further statement of principle can be readily substantiated.[12] A suggested formula for the degree of care to be expected of a paid trustee has already been stated.[13] For this purpose a representative is in the position of a trustee.[14]

Practice

It is not necessary to plead section 61 as a defence.[15] The question whether the trustees or representatives have acted honestly and reasonably should not be heard on originating summons when the matter is disputed by the beneficiaries.[16]

---

[98] *Re Turner, ante; Re Stuart, ante; Shaw* v. *Cates* [1909] 1 Ch. 389; and see *Khoo Tek Keong* v. *Ch'ng Joo Tuan Neoh* [1934] A.C. 529, but see *Palmer* v. *Emerson, ante.*
[99] *Chapman* v. *Browne* [1902] 1 Ch. 785.
[1] *Re Dive* [1909] 1 Ch. 328.
[2] *Re Brookes* [1914] 1 Ch. 558.
[3] *Re Barker* (1898) 77 L.T. 712. cf. Law of Property Act 1925, s.25.
[4] *Re Greenwood* (1911) 105 L.T. 509.
[5] *Chapman* v. *Browne, ante; Re Houghton, ante.*
[6] *Williams* v. *Byron* (1901) 18 T.L.R. 172. And see *Wynne* v. *Tempest* [1897] W.N. 43.
[7] *Re Second East Dulwich etc.* (1899) 68 L.J.Ch. 196.
[8] *Davis* v. *Hutchings* [1907] 1 Ch. 356.
[9] *Re Pauling* [1964] Ch. 303, 339.
[10] *National Trustees Co.* v. *General Finance Co., ante; Re Windsor Steam Coal Co., ante; Re Pauling* [1964] 1 Ch. 303, 339. See *ante*, pp. 737, 745, n. 1 and 33. Conveyancer 179.
[11] [1893] 1 Ch. 71. This was not, however, a case of "relief."
[12] See *Re Pauling* [1964] Ch. 303, 328, 338.
[13] See *ante*, p. 737 and 33 *Conveyancer* 179.
[14] See *ante*, p. 753.
[15] *Re Pawson* [1971] 1 Ch. 541.
[16] *Re Dove's Will Trusts* [1939] W.N. 230. Proper pleadings and cross-examination will be needed.

Impounding of annuity

Where an executrix, in respect of her receipt as such, was considerably indebted to the estate, and had an annuity bequeathed to her by the will, the court directed that her annuity, as it became due, should be applied in payment of the debt due to the estate, with liberty to apply when that debt had been discharged.[17]

Defaulting executor bankrupt

If an executor becomes bankrupt, having wasted the assets, a proof for the *devastavit* can be taken in under the bankruptcy.[18] *Semble*, a specific legacy bequeathed to the executor is not on his bankruptcy specifically liable to make good the *devastavit*.[19] Where the bankrupt is one of two or more executors, and has before his bankruptcy received a part of the assets, the other executors may prove for that amount against his estate.[20] But an executor and trustee having committed a *devastavit*, cannot prove under his own bankruptcy without obtaining an order from the court.[21] Generally speaking, such order will be made on the application of a bankrupt who is sole executor,[22] but, if leave to prove is given, the dividends should be secured and not allowed to come into the bankrupt's hands.[23]

A defaulting executor or administrator who becomes bankrupt is protected by section 285 of the Insolvency Act 1986.[24]

Property held by a bankrupt in trust for any other person is expressly excluded from the property divisible amongst his creditors by section 283(3) of the same Act. But where the trustee has a right of indemnity in the nature of a lien upon the goods, such right will pass to the trustee in his bankruptcy, and will have priority over the rights of an execution creditor.[25]

---

[17] *Skinner* v. *Sweet* (1818) 3 Madd. 244. See also *Morris* v. *Livie* (1842) 1 Y. & C.C.C. 380; *ante*, p. 642.

[18] Toller 6th ed., p. 429.

[19] See *Geary* v. *Beaumont* (1817) 3 Mer. 431.

[20] *Ex p. Brown* (1832) 1 Dea. & Ch. 118; *Ex p. Phillips*, 2 Dea. 334.

[21] See *Ex p. Colman*, 2 Dea. & Ch. 584.

[22] *Ex p. Shaw* (1822) 1 Glyn & Jam. 127; *Ex p. Wyatt*, 2 Dea. & Ch. 211.

[23] *Ex p. Leeke* (1789) 2 Bro.C.C. 597; *Ex p. Shaw, supra*; *Ex p. Colman, ante*; *Ex p. Moody* (1816) 2 Rose 413.

[24] See *post*, p. 893.

[25] *Jennings* v. *Mather* [1902] 1 K.B. 1.

Part Seven

FAMILY PROVISION

CHAPTER 56

FAMILY PROVISION: THE RIGHT TO APPLY TO THE COURT

The Inheritance (Provision for Family and Dependants) Act 1975 (referred to hereafter as "the 1975 Act" or "the Act" according to context) replaced both the Inheritance (Family Provision) Act 1938[1] as amended ("the 1938 Act"), and sections 26, 27 and 28 of the Matrimonial Causes Act 1965[1] ("the 1965 Act"). The 1975 Act changed the old law as embodied in the 1938 and 1965 Acts substantially, so as to form a new and comprehensive code of family provision law. However, it gives the court essentially the same power as that given by the 1938 and 1965 Acts,[2] that is a discretionary power to re-write a particular will or alter the effect of the statutory rules of intestacy in a particular case, so as to make reasonable provision for members of what might be called the "family circle" of the deceased. The Act entitles certain persons,[3] who were linked to a deceased person by ties of marriage, blood or dependence, to apply to the court on the ground that the disposition of the deceased's estate effected by his will or the law relating to intestacy or a combination of the two is not such as to make reasonable financial provision for them. If the court agrees that reasonable financial provision has not been made for any such applicant, it may order what it considers reasonable financial provision to be made for that applicant out of the estate of the deceased.

Although the law recognises that the deceased may have been under a moral obligation to provide for some members of his "family circle," nevertheless his testamentary freedom is preserved, subject only to the scrutiny of the court that his dispositions should be capable of being regarded as reasonable in all the circumstances.[4]

---

[1] For the 1938 and 1965 Acts, see the 10th ed. of this work, pp. 539–550: Theobald. *The Law of Wills*, 13th ed., 1971, paras. 321–356: Tyler. *Family Provision*. This last gives a very full treatment. It is referred to hereafter as Tyler. The second edition, which states the law as at January 31, 1983, is referred to as Tyler (ed. Oughton).

[2] For this reason, decided cases under the 1938 and 1965 Acts are relevant and helpful under the 1975 Act: *Re Coventry* [1980] Ch. 461, 474. But see *Moody* v. *Stephenson* [1992] 2 W.L.R. 640.

[3] For the persons who may apply, see *post*, p. 768. The Law Reform Committee has suggested (Cmnd. 7902) that where a will is revoked by the testator's marriage and at the time of marriage he was incapable the beneficiaries should be entitled to apply to the court for reasonable financial provision if they are persons for whom he might have provided. The Law Commission has suggested that cohabitees should be given the right to apply as such (*Family Law: Distribution on Intestacy*, Law Com. 187). For applications to the Crown for ex gratia payments out of *bona vacantia*, see p. 1069, *post*.

[4] *Re Inns* [1947] Ch. 576, 581; *Re Catmull* [1943] Ch. 262, 268; *Re Joslin* [1941] Ch. 200, 202; *Re Coventry, ante* n. 2; Lord Wilberforce in *Hansard*, H.L. Vol. 358, col. 932.

This discretionary power is the means by which the English Parliament, and the legislatures of the Commonwealth, have sought to solve a set of problems common to all legal systems. These problems may be called the problems of disinheritance, which arise when a testator leaves his property away from his family.

Other legal systems have sought to solve the problems by different means.[5] Some give members of the deceased's family rights to fixed shares of his estate; Scots law gives rights of this kind. Other systems allow family members to claim a fixed share, if they wish. There are numerous variations and combinations. But English law neither specifies what the provision ought to be, nor gives a right to any provision at all; both the right and the *quantum* alike are matters of judicial discretion.

History[6]

In its medieval origins, English law was different; it did give fixed shares. However, the movement towards testamentary freedom was soon under way. The history of the subject is complicated by the distinction between real and personal property, and by differences between different parts of England and Wales. As a great over-simplification, it might be said that there was a large degree of testamentary freedom by about 1400, or at least by 1500, and that testamentary freedom was substantially complete by 1724. However, some limited restrictions lingered until later. The last of them was only removed by section 5 of the Mortmain and Charitable Uses Act 1891. In a sense, therefore, complete testamentary freedom only existed in England for some 47 years, from 1891 to 1938.[7]

The 1938 Act gave the right to apply for reasonable provision to four classes of persons: wives and husbands; daughters who had not been married, or who were, by reason of mental or physical disability, incapable of maintaining themselves; infant sons; and sons of full age who likewise were, by reason of some mental or physical disability, incapable of maintaining themselves. In its original form, the 1938 Act only applied to the estates of those who left valid wills, but by the Intestates Estates Act 1952 it was extended to the estates of persons who had died intestate. In 1958 separate legislation, the Matrimonial Causes (Property and Maintenance) Act, gave a former spouse who had not remarried the right to apply for reasonable provision; this legislation was later incorporated in the 1965 Act.

The 1975 Act was enacted after the Law Commission had produced a

---

[5] See the article at (1938) 1 M.L.R. 296; Tyler (ed. Oughton) pp. 1–3.
[6] See Megarry and Wade, *Law of Real Property*, 5th ed., 1984, pp. 539–548; Holdsworth, *History of English Law*, Vol. III, pp. 550–556, Vol. IV, pp. 438, 439, 464–466; Tyler, pp.3–5; E. S. P. Haynes, *The Lawyer*, p. 219; Tyler (ed. Oughton) gives an especially full treatment of the events leading up to the 1938 Act.
[7] Jarman, *Wills*, 8th ed., p. 74 (Albery).

working paper and a report.[8] It lays down a new and comprehensive code, but in the context of the history of the family provision jurisdiction it can be seen as making a jurisdiction which still rests upon the same general basis, the discretionary basis, yet more expansive. It does so in the following five ways:

(a) reasonable provision for a surviving spouse, in contrast to that for other applicants, is such financial provision as it would be reasonable in all the circumstances of the case for a surviving spouse to receive, whether or not the provision is required for his or her maintenance.[9] This change brings such provision closer to that which has to be made following divorce[10];

(b) the number of potential applicants is increased. Persons treated by the deceased as children of the family,[11] and persons who were (for no full valuable consideration) being wholly or partly maintained by the deceased at the date of his death,[12] are included. Moreover, such children, and true children of the deceased, may apply whatever their age or marital status;

(c) the powers of the court as to the orders it may make for provision are enlarged[13];

(d) the property available for provision is increased[14];

(e) the court is given the power to interfere with dispositions and contracts intended to defeat applications for family provision.[15]

Themes

A number of general concepts underlay both judicial decisions under, and academic discussion of, the family provision jurisdiction under the 1938 and 1965 Acts. They are likewise proving to do so under the 1975 Act. These concepts are, as it were, themes which with their expositions, developments, and variations make up the law and practice of the subject. They are important practically as well as theoretically, because they must influence almost every judicial decision in a family provision matter to a greater or lesser degree, either explicitly or implicitly. They will be mentioned in particular contexts later, but they can usefully be mentioned generally now.

[8] Law Comm. 61. The extent to which the court can look at this report to help it decide individual cases is uncertain: see *Black-Clawson International Ltd.* v. *Papierwerke Waldhof-Aschaffenburg A.G.* [1975] A.C. 591; *Wachtel* v. *Wachtel* [1973] Fam. 72, 93.

For parliamentary debates see H.L. Deb. Vol. 356, col. 1423; Vol. 358, col. 917; Vol. 361, col. 1377; H.C. Vol. 895, col. 1910.

[9] s.1(2). Under the 1938 Act the standard of provision for a surviving spouse was restricted to maintenance.

[10] See s.3(2), and pp. 782–786, *post.*

[11] s.1(1)(*d*).

[12] s.1(1)(*e*).

[13] s.2.

[14] ss.8, 9, 25.

[15] ss.10, 11.

(a) *Maintenance*

Applicants other than surviving spouses can apply only for such financial provision as it would be reasonable for them to receive for their maintenance.

The court treats this maintenance standard as imposing a substantial restriction. "Maintenance" under the 1975 Act means what it meant under the 1938 Act. It is more than just enough to enable a person to get by but does not extend beyond this to include general benefit or welfare.[16]

In *Re Christie*[17] the court adopted a different and more generous definition of maintenance in order, in effect, to implement a change in a will which a testatrix had intended but failed to make before she died. This definition of maintenance was disapproved in *Re Coventry*. The disapproval has been generally endorsed.[18]

(b) *Dependency*

The 1938 Act described the persons entitled to apply under it as "dependants," and the factual relationship of dependency, or the lack of it, could influence the court in making or refusing to make an order.[19] The 1975 Act refers to the persons entitled to apply as "applicants," and they include a separate class of dependents. How much will the factual relationship of dependency, or the lack of it, still influence the court? It is submitted that where the applicant was being maintained by the deceased in his lifetime, but the entitlement to apply is not based on this fact, the court will be more ready to look favourably on the applicant's case. Moreover, the amount of maintenance during the life of the deceased is some guide to the appropriate amount after his death.[20]

(c) *Testamentary freedom*

In some of the cases under the 1938 Act, the court was influenced by the unqualified freedom of testamentary disposition which had formerly existed in English law.[21] In these cases, the concept of testamentary freedom led the court to refuse to make orders for provision. The new Act works in the same way as the 1938 Act, in so far as it leaves the testator his testamentary freedom, subject only to the discretionary power of the court. The court may attach less importance to testamentary freedom than it did before, though in *Re Coventry*[22] Oliver J. expressly emphasised the

---

[16] *Re Coventry* [1980] Ch. 461; *Re E* [1966] 1 W.L.R. 709; *Millward* v. *Shenton* [1972] 1 W.L.R. 711; *Re Dennis* [1981] 1 All E.R. 140.

[17] [1979] Ch. 168.

[18] But consider *Re Leach* [1986] Ch. 226; *Re Callaghan* [1985] Fam. 1; *post*, p. 789.

[19] *Re Gregory* [1970] 1 W.L.R. 1455, C.A.

[20] See also, p. 779, *post*.

[21] *Re Inns* [1947] Ch. 576, 582; *Re Gregory, ante.* It has also been said that there is no prima facie right to provision, and no burden of proof one way or the other: *Re Ducksbury* [1966] 1 W.L.R. 1226.

[22] [1980] Ch. 461, 474.

Englishman's right (subject to the court's powers under the Act and to fiscal demands) "at his death to dispose of his own property in whatever way he pleases, or, if he chooses to do so, to leave that disposition to be regulated by the laws of intestate succession." Nevertheless, English law may perhaps be moving for good or ill somewhat towards a presumption in favour of at least some of those persons who qualify as applicants under the Act. The change in the standard of reasonable provision for a surviving spouse, from reasonable provision for maintenance to reasonable provision *simpliciter*, may be both an effect of this movement and a cause of further movement in the future.

(d) *Moral obligation*

It has been said that the 1938 Act rested on the basis that a deceased person might be under a moral obligation to provide for surviving dependants.[23] Much the same could be said of the 1975 Act. The question why there should be such an obligation is obviously beyond the scope of discussion here. It is not a legal question at all. The question why, granted such an obligation, the law should give effect to it, is a legal question, but it raises general issues of legal and social policy which will likewise not be considered here. For present purposes, the starting point must be that Parliament has given legal effect to some sort of moral obligation of this kind. However, one aspect of this moral obligation may usefully be considered. The obligation to provide may derive from a sentiment that family and dependants ought to be left money to live on; or it may derive from a sentiment that they have the primary right to the deceased's property. These sentiments are different, though related, and within the restraints and guidelines provided by the Act and the decided cases they will point the court in divergent directions. The sentiment that family and dependants ought to be left money to live on will point towards a somewhat restrictive exercise of the jurisdiction, emphasising the concept of maintenance. The sentiment that family and dependants have the primary right to the deceased's property will point towards a generous exercise of the jurisdiction, and towards ideas of family property.

(e) *The limits of the obligation*

The obligation discussed in the preceding section is one of those "underlying principles which most rubrics of the law disclose, almost invariably so general as to be incapable of precise definition."[24] However, under the 1938 Act the limits of the obligation were marked out by three boundary features, as it were. First, the obligation was an obligation to maintain only. Secondly, it was limited to persons who were linked to the deceased

---

[23] Williams and Mortimer, *Executors, Administrators and Probate*, 10th ed., 1970, p. 539; *Re Ducksbury* [1966] 1 W.L.R. 1226.
[24] Goff and Jones, *The Law of Restitution*, 3rd ed., p. 13.

by ties of marriage or parenthood. Thirdly, those persons were likely to be dependent upon the deceased as a matter of fact. The successive amendments to the 1938 Act, and the introduction of similar legislation relating to former spouses, did not remove these boundary features.

The 1975 Act partly removed them. The removal of the maintenance standard of provision for spouses raises rather special considerations, which will be considered later.[25] The grant of the right to apply to adult children, to children of the family, and to persons maintained by the deceased, has a more general significance. The Act gives no definite guidance as to how far and how readily the Courts ought to travel beyond the old boundaries, and make orders in favour of adult children, children of the family, and persons maintained by the deceased. Three different degrees of adventurousness, as it were, are possible for the Court on the mere language of the Act, and all three have been adopted in the reported cases. Most cautiously, the Court can refuse to travel beyond the old boundaries, unless there is some special factor or circumstance which spurs it to do so. Rather more adventurously, the Court can pass beyond the old boundary features not only if there is some special factor or circumstance, but also if the facts before it are analogous to, but not the same as, facts which would have given the applicant rights before the 1975 Act was passed, either under the old family provision legislation or under some principle of law or equity. Most adventurously, and indeed rashly, the Court can be so willing to favour an application by another child, child of the family, or person maintained by the deceased as to come closer and closer to replacing the terms of the will or the rules of intestacy by its own general ideas of fairness in the particular case.

The most cautious approach is that of Oliver J. (as he then was) in *Re Coventry*.[26] The second, somewhat more adventurous approach is the one which pays regard to analogies between *de facto* relationships and the legal relationships of husband and wife and parent and child; as in *Re McC, CA v. CC*.[27] It can also be seen, perhaps, in the way in which the reliance upon the deceased of a person maintained by him can be likened to the reliance which works an estoppel; this is hinted at by Stephenson L.J. in *Jelley v. Iliffe*.[28] The third and most adventurous approach is the one adopted in *Re Christie*,[29] and subsequently much criticised, although two later cases on applications by children of the family, *Re Callaghan*[30] and *Re Leach*[31] shows signs of its persistence.

It is submitted that the most cautious approach is the correct one, although the second approach, with its reliance on analogies, can also be

---

[25] See pp. 769, 781 *et seq.*, *post.*
[26] [1980] Ch. 461; [1979] C.L.J. 286.
[27] *The Times*, November 11, 1978; (1979) 9 Fam. Law 26; (1979) 123 Sol. Jo. 35.
[28] [1981] Fam. 128; and see p. 774, *post.*
[29] [1979] Ch. 168; [1979] C.L.J. 286.
[30] [1985] Fam. 1.
[31] [1986] Ch. 226.

appropriate and helpful in some cases. The third and most adventurous approach is simply wrong.[32]

Preliminary Requirements

Certain requirements must be satisfied before the court has jurisdiction and can exercise its powers under the 1975 Act.

Date of death

The deceased must have died after the commencement of the Act.[33] The Act came into force on April 1, 1976.[34] Therefore, the deceased must have died after the moment of midnight between March 31 and April 1, 1976.

Domicile

The deceased must have died domiciled in England and Wales.[35] In English law, a person's domicile is his permanent home, as the law understands it.[36] The burden of establishing that the deceased died domiciled in England and Wales lies on the applicant for provision,[37] although if the point is not disputed the statement to that effect in the probate or letters of administration ought to be sufficient evidence.

The requirement that the deceased must have died domiciled in England has been criticised.[38] The critics have suggested that the normal rule of English private international law ought to apply, whereby succession to movables is governed by the law of the last domicile of the deceased, and succession to immovables by the law of the place where the immovables are situate. On the other hand, the requirement has been defended on the ground that the question whether the surviving members of a deceased person's family should have a claim to an interest in his estate should be governed by his personal law, which is the law of his domicile.[39] Either basis of jurisdiction could produce anomalies, and there seems much to be said for the view of the Law Commission that the point is best left to be resolved by an international convention.

---

[32] *Re Coventry, supra*; *Re Homer, Rann.* v. *Jackson*, C.A., November 16, 1978, C.A.T. 78/723; Tyler (ed. Oughton) pp. 41–43; Sachs [1985] *Conveyancer* 258; Sachs [1990] *Conveyancer* 45 (discussions of the working of the Act); Green (1988) 51 M.L.R. 181, (a discussion of the policy of and practice under the Act; Virdi (1982) 12 Fam. Law 240, ("reasonable financial provision"). See also *Jessop* v. *Jessop, The Times*, October 16, 1991, C.A.T. 91/1034.

[33] s.1(1). If he or she died before, the 1938 and 1965 Acts apply: see s.26.

[34] s.27.

[35] s.1(1).

[36] For domicile, see Dicey and Morris, *Conflict of Laws*, 11th ed., 1987, pp. 116–170, and supplement. As to the Hague Convention on Succession, see generally p. 16 *ante* and Article 7 of the final Act.

[37] *Mastaka* v. *Midland Bank Executor and Trustee Co. Ltd.* [1941] Ch. 192; *Re Harmsworth* [1982] C.L.Y. 3388.

[38] See Tyler (ed. Oughton) p. 46.

[39] Law Comm. 61, para. 262.

Time for application

Section 4 of the Act provides that an application for an order shall not, except with the permission of the court,[40] be made[41] after the end of the period of six months from the date on which representation with respect to the estate of the deceased is first taken out. In considering when representation with respect to an estate was first taken out, a grant limited to settled land or to trust property is to be left out of account, and so is a grant limited to real estate or to personal estate unless a grant limited to the remainder of the estate has previously been made or is made at the same time.[42]

Under the 1938 Act, if a will which had already been proved in common form was subsequently proved in solemn form, a fresh period of six months did not start to run with the proof in solemn form, because such proof merely affirmed the original grant in common form.[43] But if one will was proved and another will was later discovered and proved, the six month period probably ran only from the date of proof of the later will.[44] There is now authority to this effect. In *Re Freeman*[45] a grant in common form had been revoked because the execution of the will was shown not to have been properly attested. The Court held that "representation" in section 4 means "effective" or "valid" representation, so that the six month period ran from the later grant. That later grant was in fact a grant of letters of administration on intestacy, but the principle must be the same whatever the nature of the later grant.

The existence of a grant is not a precondition of an application; an application can be made before grant.[46] It is suggested that the executors named in the unproved will, or the beneficiaries if different, should be made defendants. There will have to be a grant at a later stage, if a order is to be made. Should there be no person both entitled and willing to take out a grant, the Official Solicitor may be prepared to do so, in order to enable the claim to go forward. A grant to the Official Solicitor may also be appropriate when the applicant is the person primarily entitled to a grant, and no one else is entitled and willing to take it out.[47]

Applicants can protect themselves from being caught unawares by a grant by making use of the new "standing search" procedure.[48]

Representatives are protected if they distribute the estate of the

---

[40] The extension of time cannot affect joint property: s.9.

[41] An application is made when it is issued, not when it is served: *Re Chittenden* [1970] 1 W.L.R. 1618.

[42] s.23. It is submitted that, by analogy, other limited grants, for example those *ad colligenda bona* or *pendente lite*, do not count either: *Re Johnson* [1987] C.L.Y. 3882. *cf. Re Bidie* [1949] Ch. 121.

[43] *Re Miller* [1969] 1 W.L.R. 583.

[44] *Re Bidie* [1949] Ch. 121.

[45] [1984] 1 W.L.R. 1419.

[46] *Re Searle* [1949] Ch. 73. But see *Re McBroom* [1992] 2 F.L.R. 49.

[47] See also pp. 240–241, *ante*; s.116 of the Supreme Court Act should not be forgotten.

[48] p. 373 *ante*. The *caveat* procedure is not appropriate.

deceased after the end of the six-month period, although this does not prejudice any power to recover any part of the estate so distributed.[49] The powers referred to are presumably the powers, if any, available to recover assets wrongly paid under the principles relating to refunding and tracing.[50] Before the six-month period has expired, representatives distribute the estate at their own risk, and they ought to be prepared to resist any pressure by the beneficiaries to make anticipatory payments. However, they should not adopt a purely negative attitude. In *Re Ralphs*[51] Cross J., as he then was, after consultation with his fellow judges of the Chancery Division, gave guidance which is as useful under the 1975 Act as it was under the 1938 Act. He said that representatives: "should form their own view, with the assistance, of course, of their legal advisers, as to the payments which can properly be made, and if they are not prepared to make such payments on their own responsibility, they should ask the parties who might conceivably be affected, whether applicant or residuary legatee, for their consent. If such consent is not forthcoming the executors can apply to the court for leave to make the payment in question, and the court, if it thinks that any withholding of consent was unreasonable, could throw the costs of the application on the party to blame."

The circumstances in which representatives can safely make payments are difficult to define precisely, but it is thought that there could be little injury to the estate (or danger to the personal representatives) in paying, to an applicant who was given a benefit by the will and is asking for more, his entitlement under the will; or in paying his legacy to a legatee whose legacy is trifling in comparison with the size of the residue; or in paying his legacy to a legatee who has a high moral claim and is suffering hardship for want of money.[52]

Extension of time

Under the 1975 Act, the court's discretion to extend the six-month time limit for applications is unfettered, as it eventually was under the 1938 Act, after its amendment by the Family Provision Act 1966.[53] In *Re Ruttie*,[54] Ungoed-Thomas J. rejected the suggestion that the discretion should be exercised with the same indulgence as is exercised towards procedural time limits, where extension is granted except "when irreparable mischief would be done by acceding to a tardy application," but he considered that it would be premature to lay down any alternative guiding principles. Under

---

[49] s.20(1). On the wording of the section, personal representatives would not appear to be protected if they distribute any part of the estate after proceedings have actually been commenced.

[50] See p. 1076 *post*. Goff and Jones, *The Law of Restitution*, 3rd ed., pp. 60–81.

[51] [1968] 1 W.L.R. 1522.

[52] see *Re Ralphs, ante*.

[53] Where an extension is sought, this relief should be expressly asked for in the originating summons, and the grounds on which it is claimed should be set out in the affidavit in support: *Practice Note* [1976] 1 W.L.R. 418.

[54] [1970] 1 W.L.R. 89.

the 1975 Act courts of first instance have identified some guidelines. In *Re Salmon*[55] Megarry J. set out six considerations, "plainly not exhaustive," which should guide the court in the exercise of its discretion:

(1) The discretion is unfettered, and is thus to be exercised judicially and in accordance with what is just and proper.

(2) The onus is on the plaintiff to establish sufficient grounds for the case to be taken out of the general rule, thus depriving those who are protected by it of its benefits.

(3) It is material to consider how promptly and in what circumstances the applicant seeks the permission of the court after the time limit has expired. The whole of the circumstances have to be looked at,[56] and not least the reasons for the delay, and the promptitude with which, by letter before action or otherwise, the claimant gives warning to the defendants of the proposed application. Where there has been some error or oversight, an obvious question is whether the applicant has done all that is reasonably possible to put matters right promptly, and has kept the defendants informed.

(4) It is obviously material whether or not negotiations have been commenced within the time limit; even negotiations commenced after the time limit may aid the applicant.

(5) It is also relevant to consider whether or not the estate has been distributed before a claim under the Act has been made or notified.

(6) It is relevant to consider whether a refusal to extend the time would leave the claimant without redress against his advisers.

These guidelines are not exhaustive, and a further aid to the court is to consider whether the applicant has an arguable case by reference to the same factors as are considered when deciding whether to give leave to defend under Order 14 of the Rules of the Supreme Court.[57] The existence of a pending application by another applicant is presumably also relevant.[58]

In the two cases[59] on extension of time which have reached the Court of Appeal, that Court has not disputed the usefulness of the various guidelines. However, it has tended to emphasise the unfettered nature of the discretion, and the decision in *Re Adams* substantially reduces the significance of the sixth guideline in *Re Salmon*. Ormrod L.J. said that "it seems to me that the right approach is to consider the justice of the case as between the parties, first of all, and to take into account all the matters set out very helpfully by the Vice-Chancellor in *Re Salmon*. It is only if, having done that computation, one finds that the plaintiff on the one hand has suffered severe prejudice, and the defendant on the other hand has suffered

---

[55] [1981] Ch. 167.

[56] Including any representation made by a beneficiary: *Re John* (1967) 111 S.J. 15.

[57] *Re Stone* (1969) 114 S.J. 36; *Re Dennis* [1981] 2 All E.R. 140.

[58] See *post*, p. 796 for the relationship between s.4 and s.6 (Variation of Orders).

[59] *Re Adams*, C.A., July 22, 1981, C.A.T. 81/299; *Re Escritt*, C.A., October 15, 1981, C.A.T. 81/396. Maybe *Re Longley* [1981] C.L.Y. 2885 cannot stand with *Re Adams*.

severe prejudice, or will if the limitation period is extended, that the claim for damages against the plaintiff's solicitors becomes relevant." Dunn L.J. simply remarked that "Speaking for myself, I am not prepared to go so far as to say that the chance of the plaintiff having a remedy against his or her solicitors is a wholly irrelevant consideration under section 4."

Failure to make reasonable provision

The preliminary requirements already discussed are preconditions of jurisdiction to consider an application at all. Failure to make reasonable provision is a precondition of an order. The court has to proceed in two stages.[60] First it must be satisfied that the disposition of the deceased's estate is not such as to make reasonable financial provision. Secondly, if it is so satisfied, it may itself make reasonable provision.[61] The matters to which the court is directed to have regard at both stages are the same, but the result of considering them may be different, in the sense that, at the first stage, the court may decide that the disposition of the deceased's estate does make reasonable provision, and therefore may not proceed to the second stage, although, if it had proceeded to the second stage, it would have made somewhat different provision itself. Reasonable provision is an area rather than a point.[62] The two stages must be kept separate because the Act envisages them as separate.[63]

At the first stage, the test of whether reasonable provision has been made is objective. The question is not whether the deceased was reasonable in making the provision he did, but whether the provision actually made is reasonable. The objective nature of the test appears from the wording of the Act,[64] and is consonant with the interpretation of the test under the 1938 Act which eventually achieved general acceptance.[65]

Consistently with the objective nature of the test, the court must take into account the facts as known to it at the date of the hearing[66] (as distinct from unenforceable assurances[67]).

An objective test is the only one which can be applied when an applicant alleges that the disposition of the deceased's estate effected by the law relating to intestacy fails to make reasonable provision for him or her. The effect of the intestacy rules cannot be reasonable or unreasonable in a subjective sense. At first sight, it might appear strange that rules laid down, as the intestacy rules are, for the purpose of making reasonable provision, should need to be subject to a dispensing power in case they do not do so.

---

[60] *Re Sivyer* [1967] 1 W.L.R. 1482, 1486, 1487; *Re Coventry* [1980] Ch. 461, 469; *Williams* v. *Johns* [1988] 2 F.L.R. 475: See (1984) 14 Fam. Law 171 for a comment.

[61] s.3(1). Note that provision which is reasonable in amount may be unreasonable because of a condition to which it is subject: *Re Doring* [1955] 1 W.L.R. 1217.

[62] Jarman *Wills*, 8th ed., p. 79 (Albery); Virdi (1982) 12 Fam. Law 240.

[63] See the opening of s.3(1).

[64] See the concluding words of s.1(1).

[65] *Millward* v. *Shenton* [1972] 1 W.L.R. 711.

[66] s.3(5).

[67] *Rajabally* v. *Rajabally* [1987] 2 F.L.R. 390.

The reason is of course that general rules are inflexible and cannot produce the correct result in every case. For example, the extensive rights given to widows and widowers on intestacy operate for the best in the great majority of instances, but they can produce an unreasonable result sometimes. One instance is where the marriage to the widow or widower was a second or subsequent marriage, and the deceased left dependent children by an earlier marriage.[68]

Persons entitled to apply

The 1975 Act allows any of the following persons to apply for provision[69]:

(a) the wife[70] or husband of the deceased;

(b) a former wife or former husband of the deceased who has not remarried;

(c) a child of the deceased;

(d) any person (not being a child of the deceased) who, in the case of any marriage to which the deceased was at any time a party, was treated by the deceased as a child of the family in relation to that marriage;

(e) any person (not being a person included in the foregoing categories) who immediately before the death of the deceased was being maintained, either wholly or partly, by the deceased.

An applicant's right to apply comes to an end on his or her death, and any pending proceedings abate.[71]

There is nothing to prevent a bankrupt from applying, but he is unlikely to succeed and any lump sum award will vest in his trustee, and any award of periodical payments may be gathered in by the trustee.[72]

At common law, the rule which precluded a person who had unlawfully killed another from acquiring a benefit in consequence of the killing also

---

[68] For cases under the former legislation where the deceased died intestate, see *Re Cook* [1956] 106 L.J. 466; *Re Sivyer* [1967] 1 W.L.R. 1482; *Re Trowell* [1957] C.L.Y. 3745. For cases under the 1975 Act, see *Re Coventry, supra; Re Kozdrach* [1981] Conv. 224; *Re Kirby* (1981) 11 Fam. Law 210; *Re Wood* (1982) 79 L.S. Gaz. 774; *Harrington* v. *Gill* (1983) 4 F.L.R. 265; *Re Callaghan* [1985] Fam. 1; *Re Leach* [1986] Ch. 226.

[69] s.1(1).

[70] A wife bears the burden of proving her marriage to the deceased, so should in strictness adduce evidence of it, and should certainly do so if it may be disputed: *Re Peete* [1952] 2 All E.R. 599; *Re Watkins* [1953] 1 W.L.R. 1323. By analogy all other applicants must likewise bear the burden of proving their membership of the relevant category: *Re Wilkinson* [1978] Fam. 22; *Re Beaumont* [1980] Ch. 444.

[71] *Whytte* v. *Ticehurst* [1986] Fam. 64; *Re R.* (1986) 16 Fam. Law. 58; *Re Bramwell* [1988] 2 F.L.R. 263.

[72] Formerly under ss.38(*a*) and 51(2) of the Bankruptcy Act 1914, respectively, and now under s.307 and 310 of the Insolvency Act, 1986. See the Australian case of *Coffey* v. *Bennett* [1961] V.R. 264. The power to settle property could be used to assist a bankrupt and his family. See p. 794, *post.*

precluded him from applying for provision out of that other's estate under the family provision jurisdiction.[73] As a result of sections 3 and 5 of the Forfeiture Act 1982, it is only persons convicted of murder who are so precluded.

A wife or husband

This surviving spouse category includes a person who in good faith entered into a void marriage with the deceased, unless either (a) the marriage was dissolved or annulled during the lifetime of the deceased and the dissolution or annulment is recognised by the law of England and Wales, or (b) that person has during the lifetime of the deceased entered into a later marriage.[74] As a result of this definition, there could be more than one surviving spouse entitled to claim provision as the wife or husband of a deceased person, if the void marriage had been followed by a further marriage. The same could happen as a result of a polygamous marriage.[75] These unusual situations need create no insuperable problems because, as will be seen when the matters to be considered by the court are discussed, the provision which it is reasonable for an applicant to receive will vary with the number and weight of the claims to provision possessed by other applicants and by the existing beneficiaries under the Will or intestacy of the deceased.[76]

There is no reason why an application by a widower should be less favourably entertained than one by a widow, merely because the applicant is a widower. Early cases[77] to that effect under the 1938 Act were subsequently disapproved,[78] and the disapproval must still operate. Widowers may well apply less often than widows, and perhaps succeed less often, but that will be because they are usually more able to support themselves. It will not be merely because they are widowers.

The remarriage of a surviving spouse does not automatically terminate an order for periodical payments under the Act, although it may provide a ground for varying it.[79]

The general standard of reasonable provision for a surviving spouse is such provision as it would be reasonable in all the circumstances of the case for the surviving spouse to receive, whether or not that provision is required for his or her maintenance.[80] However, if the marriage was the subject of a decree of judicial separation and at the date of death the

---

[73] *Re Royse* [1985] Ch. 22.

[74] s.25(4). For the meaning of "remarriage," see s.25(5).

[75] Law Comm. 61, para. 29; *Re Sehota* [1978] 1 W.L.R. 1506.

[76] See pp. 776, 777, *post.*

[77] *Re Sylvester* [1941] Ch. 87; *Re Styler* [1942] Ch. 387.

[78] *Re Clayton* [1966] 1 W.L.R. 969, 972. See also *Moody* v. *Stephenson* [1992] 2 W.L.R. 640.

[79] This follows from the terms of s.2(1), s.19(2) and s.6(3); *cf.* orders made in favour of former spouses and judicially separated spouses.

[80] s.1(2); and see pp. 781–786, *post.*

decree was in force and the separation continuing, it is such provision as would be reasonable for maintenance.

A former wife or former husband

This is the former spouse category. "Former wife" or "former husband" means a person whose marriage with the deceased was during the deceased's lifetime dissolved or annulled by a decree under the Matrimonial Causes Act 1973.[81] Persons whose marriages were dissolved abroad have now the same rights to apply for provision under the 1975 Act as persons whose marriages are dissolved or annulled under the 1973 Act.[82]

The general standard of reasonable provision for former spouses is such provision as would be reasonable for maintenance.[83] A former spouse will usually have had the opportunity to apply for more under the matrimonial jurisdiction at the time of the divorce or annulment, so the restriction to reasonable provision for maintenance is sensible.[84] However, it could operate unfairly if the death of one spouse followed soon after the divorce or annulment, so that the surviving former spouse had no opportunity of obtaining an order under the matrimonial jurisdiction. For this reason, the Act provides[85] that where within 12 months from the date on which a decree of divorce or nullity has been made absolute or a decree of judicial separation has been granted, a party to the marriage dies and either (a) an application for financial provision or for property adjustment under the Matrimonial Causes Act 1973 has not been made by the surviving party, or (b) such an application has been made but the proceedings have not been determined at the time of the death of the deceased party, then, if an application under section 2 of the Act is made, the court shall have the power to treat the surviving party as if there had been no decree of divorce, nullity, or judicial separation. Therefore, financial provision can be awarded on the more generous basis, disregarding the maintenance restriction. The power only exists in a case of judicial separation if at the death of the deceased the decree of judicial separation was still in force and the separation continuing[86]; if it is not, then the maintenance restriction does not apply anyway.[87]

Four special provisions of the Act relating to the rights of former spouses should be noted. First, in matrimonial proceedings the court is empowered, on the application of either party to the marriage, to bar future appli-

---

[81] s.25(1).

[82] s.25(1) of the 1975 Act has been amended by s.25 of the Matrimonial and Family Proceedings Act 1984 which provides that a surviving former spouse whose marriage was dissolved or annulled outside England and Wales may make a claim for reasonable financial provision from the estate of the deceased former spouse under the 1975 Act as amended by s.8 of the 1984 Act.

[83] s.1(2).

[84] Law Comm. 61, para. 19 onwards. *Re Fullard* [1982] Fam. 42.

[85] s.14.

[86] s.14(2).

[87] Anecdotal evidence received by one of the editors suggests that the 12 month period is too short.

cations for family provision.[88] This provides a means whereby property arrangements on the break up of a marriage can be given the advantage of finality. Secondly, on an application under the Act by a person entitled to payments from the deceased under a secured periodical payments order made under the Matrimonial Causes Act 1973, the court is given power to vary or discharge that order.[89] Thirdly, the court has a similar power to vary or revoke a maintenance agreement, on an application under the Act by a person entitled to payments under such an agreement.[90] Fourthly, the reverse applies: where an application is made under section 31(6) of the Matrimonial Causes Act 1973 for the variation or discharge of a secured periodical payments order after the death of the payer, or under section 36(1) of the Matrimonial Causes Act 1973 for the alteration of a maintenance agreement, the court has power, in effect, to treat the application as an application under the Act and exercise its powers thereunder.[91] This does not apply, however, if future applications under the Act have been barred by an order under section 15 of the Act, as explained above.

A child of the deceased

This includes an illegitimate child, and a child *en ventre sa mère* on the death of the deceased.[92] In contrast to the 1938 Act, there is no distinction between sons and daughters, and neither age nor marriage automatically disqualifies a child of either sex as an applicant. Age and marital status are matters which the court will consider,[93] but they are not automatic bars.[94] Although there is no decision on the point, it is submitted that a child adopted by the deceased must be entitled to apply, by virtue of the Adoption Acts.[95] However a natural child of the deceased, adopted by others, is not.[96]

The standard of reasonable financial provision for children (as for all applicants other than spouses) is such financial provision as it would be reasonable for them to receive for their maintenance. However, maintenance can be provided by capital payments.[97]

If an order for periodical payments is made in favour of a child applicant,

---

[88] s.15, as amended by s.8 of the Matrimonial and Family Proceedings Act 1984; the consent of both parties was required under the original s.15. Law Comm. 61, paras. 185–188. Apart from this provision, it is submitted that public policy prevents "contracting out" of the Act. This was the law under the 1965 Act (*Re M.* [1968] P. 174), although there was no decision under the 1938 Act.

[89] s.16; Law Comm. 61, paras. 263–276.

[90] s.17.

[91] s.18.

[92] s.25.

[93] *Re Coventry* [1980] Ch. 461; *Re Homer, Rann* v. *Jackson,* C.A., November 15, 1978, C.A.T. 78/723.

[94] If a young child may need provision when he or she is older, the proceedings can be adjourned: *Re Franks* [1948] Ch. 62; and see p. 798, *post.*

[95] See especially s.38 onwards of the Adoption Act 1976.

[96] *Re Collins* [1990] Fam. 56.

[97] Note the observations in *Re Dennis* [1981] 2 All E.R. 140 at 145.

the order may provide for the payments to be made to the child's mother, on her undertaking to maintain the child.[98]

A person treated by the deceased as a child of the family

This is a new category. The concept of a "child of the family" is imported from the matrimonial law.[99] As a member of the family circle of the deceased, a child of the family who was not a natural or adopted child of the deceased is thought of as having claims upon the deceased, just as his natural or adopted children have. As with natural or adopted children, the maintenance standard of provision applies.[1]

The relevant treatment of the applicant can include events which precede or follow the period of the marriage.[2]

In deciding whether reasonable provision has been made for a person treated as a child of the family, and in deciding what provision ought to be made, the court is directed[3] to have regard:

    (a) to whether the deceased had assumed any responsibility for the child's maintenance and, if so, to the extent to which and the basis upon which the deceased assumed that responsibility, and to the length of time for which the deceased discharged that responsibility;

    (b) to whether in assuming and discharging that responsibility the deceased did so knowing that the child was not his own child; and

    (c) to the liability of any other person to maintain the child.

A person maintained by the deceased

This is another new category, made up of persons who are only entitled to apply for provision because they were being maintained by the deceased immediately before his death. The word "immediately" refers not simply to the moment of death, but to the settled basis or arrangement between the parties at that moment.[4]

The Act provides that a person shall be treated as being maintained by the deceased, either wholly or partly, if the deceased, otherwise than for full valuable consideration, was making a substantial contribution in money or money's worth towards the reasonable needs of that person.[5] The applicant must establish, first, that the deceased was making a substantial contribution in money or money's worth towards the reasonable needs

---

[98] *Re Westby* [1946] W.N. 141; see also n. 42, *post* 796.

[99] Matrimonial Causes Act 1974, s.52(1), although under that Act the child must have been treated as a child of the family by both parties to the marriage.

[1] s.1(2).

[2] *Re Leach, supra*; and see p. 789, *post*.

[3] s.3(3). Compare the Matrimonial Causes Act 1973, s.25(3).

[4] *Re Beaumont* [1980] Ch. 444, 482; *Jelley* v. *Iliffe* [1981] Fam. 128; *Kourkey* v. *Lusher* (1982) 12 Fam. Law 86. In *Re Dymott*, C.A. December 15, 1980. C.A.T. 80/942 Ormrod L.J. spoke of "the norm of this relationship" being one of no dependency.

[5] s.1(3); the subsection is a restrictive provision, and as a matter of grammar ought perhaps be read with the word "only" before "if": *Re Beaumont, supra* at p. 451.

of the applicant, and secondly, that the deceased was so doing otherwise than for full valuable consideration.[6] The reference to "full valuable consideration" was not merely intended to exclude maintenance provided under a contract.[7] In determining whether or not the deceased was making a substantial contribution the court has to take a common sense approach, avoiding fine balancing computations involving the value of the normal exchange of support in the domestic sense.[8]

The category is a very wide one. It covers both relatives by blood or marriage other than those already qualified to apply for provision, and also other persons whose sole tie with the deceased was the factual relationship of maintenance. It can include an elderly housekeeper[9] who receives food, shelter, warmth and clothing in return for purely nominal services; a nephew who is attending school at the expense of the deceased; and a widowed sister who is receiving board and lodging in the home of the deceased but making some contribution in cash to the expenses of the home.[10] It can also include a lover or a mistress, whether fairly describable as a *"de facto* spouse" or not.[11] In an appropriate case, a parent could apply, and so could a grandparent or (perhaps more likely) a grandchild. So could a former spouse who had remarried, in the most unlikely event of her still being maintained by the deceased.

At first sight, the idea underlying this category of applicant might seem to be that the maintaining of a person by the deceased during his life may have put him under an obligation to continue the maintenance after his death. This is consistent with the guideline in the Act[12] that, in considering whether reasonable financial provision has been made for an applicant in this category, and in deciding what provision (if any) to order, the Court must have regard to the extent to which, and the basis upon which, the deceased assumed responsibility for the maintenance of the applicant, and to the length of time for which he or she discharged that responsibility.

Despite the potentially restrictive effect of this guideline, the category remains a wide one. It may be thought that the mere maintenance of one person by another while both are alive creates no obligation on the person

---

[6] *Jelley* v. *Iliffe ante*; *Bishop* v. *Plumbley* [1991] 1 F.L.R. 121. *Re Wilkinson* [1978] Fam. 22. The provision of accommodation may be a substantial contribution to needs: *Jelley* v. *Iliffe*, *ante*. *Bishop* v. *Plumley*, *ante*.

[7] *Re Beaumont, supra*; *Jelley* v. *Iliffe*, *ante*; (1978) 94 L.Q.R. 175; (1978) 41 M.L.R. 352.

[8] *Bishop* v. *Plumley*, *ante*, at 126C.

[9] It was held under the 1938 Act that a deceased person did not owe a moral obligation to his housekeeper merely because she was such: *Re Preston* [1969] 1 W.L.R. 317. But this does not affect the right of a housekeeper to apply for provision as a person maintained by the deceased (if she was such) under the 1975 Act.

[10] Law Comm. 61, para. 98; see further p. 789. For claims by sisters, see *Re Wilkinson*, *ante*, and *Re Viner* [1978] C.L.Y. 3091.

[11] A lover or mistress is not necessarily a *"de facto* spouse"; in *Malone* v. *Harrison* [1979] 1 W.L.R. 1353 the deceased had both a *"de facto* spouse" and a mistress, the mistress being the applicant.

[12] s.3(4). This is the only particular guideline for applicants under section 1(1)(*e*); see p. 789, *post*.

providing the maintenance to continue it after his death. Moreover, it may be suspected that Parliament did not intend to recognise any such wide obligation, and that no one else thought that Parliament ought to or was recognising it. These suspicions are justified. The Law Commission Report and the discussion and comment preceding the 1975 Act, and also the way in which the Courts have applied the Act and the discussion and comment on its application, strongly suggest that the category is an umbrella, intended to cover three situations which are often related in fact, but are logically distinct.

The first situation is one of accidental or unintentional failure to make provision. As the Law Commission Report expressed it, ". . . where a deceased person was contributing to someone's maintenance before his death his failure to make provision for that person may have been accidental or unintentional; he may have made no will; his will may be stale; or his will may have operated in a way he did not anticipate (for example, the specific legacies may exhaust the estate and leave no residue). In these cases an order for family provision would be doing for the deceased what he might reasonably be assumed to have wished to do himself. This argument carries particular weight where the "dependant" is a person with whom the deceased has been cohabiting."[13]

The second situation is one in which the Act is required to remedy "the injustice of one, who has been put by a deceased person in a position of dependency upon him, being deprived of any financial support, either by accident or by design of the deceased, after his death," as Stephenson L.J. said in *Jelley* v. *Iliffe*.[14] Since the applicant presumably did not have to accept the maintenance when it was offered to him, unless perhaps the circumstances were very special, the words of the learned Lord Justice seem to suggest a kind of quasi-estoppel, or at least an idea related to estoppel. The applicant has changed his position as a result of his continuing receipt of maintenance, so that it would be unreasonable for him to be deprived of it.

The third situation exists when the relationship between the deceased and the applicant was similar to the relationship which would have existed between the deceased and a spouse or child of his. The paramount example here is the "*de facto* spouse."

All these three situations are capable of coming within the category, but in some cases they may not do so. For example, a "*de facto* spouse" who was self supporting or who made a contribution to the joint income which was the same as or greater than that of the deceased is not qualified to apply under the Act, however deserving on other grounds her moral claim to provision may be. On the other hand, a person whose moral claim upon the deceased's bounty may have been much less is qualified to claim if there was maintenance. For example, a woman who was maintained by the

[13] Law Comm. 61, para. 90.
[14] *Ante*, at 137, 138. Law Comm. 61, para. 88.

deceased in a relationship which had no similarity to marriage is qualified to apply.

Odd results could follow in other cases too. Suppose three elderly ladies make their home together, pooling their respective incomes in proportion, to some extent, to the size of those incomes. One owns the house in which the three of them live, but has no more income than the state pension. The second has, in addition to her state pension, a substantial private pension or income from investments. The third has no more than the state pension. Because of the pooling arrangement, the first and second ladies are not maintaining each other, but both are maintaining the third. If the first dies, leaving all her money to a charity, the other two are homeless. The second is not qualified to apply under the Act, but the third is.

In summary, the scope of section 1(1)(e) is unsatisfactory.[15]

---

[15] For interesting criticisms of the terms of section 1(1)(e), see Tyler (ed. Oughton), p. 63 onwards. See also [1980] *Conveyancer* 46, and the proposal to give cohabitees a right to apply as such, in *Family Law: Distribution on Intestacy* (Law. Com. 187).

CHAPTER 57

FAMILY PROVISION: EXERCISE OF DISCRETION

Section 3 of the Inheritance (Provision for Family and Dependants) Act 1975 specifies certain matters to which the court is to have regard both in determining whether the disposition of the deceased's estate makes reasonable provision for an applicant and, if it decides that reasonable provision has not been made, in determining what provision to order. The same matters are therefore specified for both the first and the second stages of the court's consideration of an application. The Law Commission referred to the matters as "guidelines."[1] Some of the guidelines apply to all applicants generally, and some of them to particular categories of applicant only. The guidelines are in a sense the heart of the jurisdiction, because it is they which guide the court in coming to its decisions in individual cases. They must therefore guide applicants and potential applicants in starting proceedings, and in compromising proceedings or taking them to a hearing. Conversely, they must guide the beneficiaries under wills and intestacies in deciding how far to resist applications.

The general guidelines

The general guidelines to which the court is directed to have regard are:

    (a) the financial resources and financial needs which the applicant has or is likely to have in the foreseeable future;

    (b) the financial resources and financial needs which any other applicant for an order under the Act has or is likely to have in the foreseeable future;

    (c) the financial resources and financial needs which any beneficiary[2] of the estate of the deceased has or is likely to have in the foreseeable future;

    (d) any obligations and responsibilities which the deceased had towards any applicant for an order or towards any beneficiary[3] of the estate of the deceased;

    (e) the size and nature of the net estate of the deceased;

    (f) any physical or mental disability or any applicant for an order or any beneficiary[4] of the estate of the deceased;

    (g) any other matter, including the conduct of the applicant or any

---

[1] Law Comm. 61, para. 32.

[2] Including a beneficiary under a statutory nomination or a *donatio mortis causa*: s.25(1).

[3] *Ibid.* n. 2.

[4] *Ibid.* n. 2.

other person, which in the circumstances of the case the court may consider relevant.

The guidelines resemble those laid down by statute for financial provision in the matrimonial jurisdiction,[5] and also those set out in the 1938 Act and developed by the court under it.

The balancing of claims

The first four of the general guidelines are balancing guidelines. The court has to balance the competing claims of applicants and beneficiaries by reference to their different resources and needs, and the obligations and responsibilities owed by the deceased to each of them. The first four guidelines render statutory a judicial method that was explicit[6] or implicit in many if not most cases under the 1938 Act, for under that Act large provision, small provision, or no provision at all was likewise the result of this balancing of conflicting claims by reference to the resources and needs of applicants and beneficiaries and the obligations owed to them by the deceased. Lying behind all this is, perhaps, an older image of the reasonable testator, who makes reasonable provision for the persons who have claims upon his bounty by weighing up their respective resources and his obligations to them.[7]

However, the criticism can be made that the Act gives too little guidance on the weight of the competing claims, and of the different guidelines. For example, the Act gives no indication of the direction in which the Court should move when one party has the greater need, but the deceased owed a greater obligation to another party.

Resources and needs

Section 3(6) of the Act expressly provides that, in considering the financial resources of any person, the court shall take into account his earning capacity, and in considering his financial needs, his financial obligations and responsibilities. There was authority under the 1938 Act for considering earning capacity, potential[8] as well as actual, but the second limb of the subsection is new. Can an applicant's obligations to his own family and dependants strengthen his claim as an applicant? Presumably they can, in an appropriate case. For example, a widowed daughter with young children would have a stronger claim to provision from her father's estate than

---

[5] Matrimonial Causes Act 1973, s.25(1). In both the matrimonial jurisdiction and the family provision jurisdiction, Parliament has granted the Courts great powers over the property of individual citizens, exercisable in accordance with guidelines expressed in very general terms. It is perhaps surprising that this has not given rise to criticism on grounds of constitutional propriety.

[6] *Re Joslin* [1941] Ch. 200; *Re E.* [1966] 1 W.L.R. 709; *Re Clarke* [1968] 1 W.L.R. 415. Also under the 1965 Act: *Re Eyre* [1968] 1 W.L.R. 530, and the cases were cited.

[7] See, for example, *Banks* v. *Goodfellow* (1870) L.R. 5 Q.B. 549, 565. (A case on testamentary capacity referred to at p. 159, *ante*.)

[8] *Re Ducksbury* [1966] 1 W.L.R. 1226.

a daughter who had no family or dependants.[9] On the other hand, where a woman and her child by the deceased are both applicants, an order in favour of the woman may make sufficient indirect provision for the child.[10]

The availability of State aid, for example under the National Health Service, is a factor to be taken into account in considering what provision is reasonable, by way of reducing the applicant's claim, because State aid is part of the resources of an applicant or beneficiary. However, it is only a factor, for extra comforts to be added to State provision may well be reasonable.[11]

Damages received for personal injuries are part of a person's resources.[12]

Expectations of capital in the future must, it is submitted, be considered by the court,[13] but often accretions of capital to the estate would best be dealt with after they have fallen in, on an application under section 6 of the Act for variation of the original order.[14] In order to preserve its power under section 6, the court must make an order for periodical payments on the original application, but a nominal order for a token amount would suffice for this purpose, if it is expressed in such a way that the accretion of capital is "relevant property" as defined in section 6(6).

Of all the needs of an applicant or beneficiary, the need for somewhere to live is likely to be especially important.[15]

The obligations and responsibilities of the deceased

The fourth guideline is concerned with the moral duty of the deceased to applicants and beneficiaries, rather than with their own resources and needs. There may be more moral claims on the deceased than his estate can satisfy.[16] A common instance of conflict between these claims is that between the claims of wife and mistress, but there are other instances, such as that between the claims of spouse and children (usually children of a different marriage),[17] or even between parent and spouse.[18] The weight of one of the conflicting claims will be increased if a substantial part of the estate of the deceased was derived in some way from the claimant; for example, if a wife has helped the deceased to build up a business.[19] Simi-

---

[9] *Re Goard* (1962) 106 S.J. 721 may be another example, although the facts were rather special.

[10] *Bayliss* v. *Lloyds Bank* C.A., December 9, 1977, C.A.T. 77/978A.

[11] *Re E.* [1966] 1 W.L.R. 709; *Re Pringle, The Times,* February 2, 1956; *Re Parry, The Times,* April 19, 1956; *Re Wood* (1982) 79 L.S. Gaz. 774; *Re Collins* [1990] Fam. 56.

[12] *Daubney* v. *Daubney* [1976] Fam. 267.

[13] For an example under the matrimonial jurisdiction, see *Morgan* v. *Morgan* [1977] Fam. 122. It is submitted that the court has power to settle property on conditions or contingencies; for the power to settle property, see *post,* p. 794.

[14] See *post,* p. 796.

[15] See *post,* pp. 785, 790, in connection with different categories of applicant.

[16] *Re Joslin* [1941] Ch. 200.

[17] *Re Singer* [1967] 1 W.L.R. 1482; *Re Bellman* [1963] P. 239.

[18] *Re Clarke* [1968] 1 W.L.R. 415.

[19] *Re Thornley* [1969] 1 W.L.R. 1037; for another example, see *Jelley* v. *Iliffe* [1981] Fam. 128.

larly, the children of a first marriage have a stronger claim if a substantial part of the deceased's estate came to the deceased from their other parent,[20] and the children of the family have one if it came from their natural parent.[21]

Provision of capital in the past may reduce the strength of an applicant's claim.[22] On the other hand, the fact that an applicant (otherwise entitled to apply) was being maintained by the deceased may strengthen his claim. There was authority[23] under the 1938 Act that the use of the word "dependant" in that Act was significant, so that a factual relationship of dependency strengthened the claim of an applicant. There is no reason why the introduction by section 1(1)(e) of the 1975 Act of a separate category of persons maintained should affect this in relation to applicants in the other categories, and the existence of a factual relationship of dependency remains important.[24]

If the Court decides to make an order for the maintenance of an applicant, the amount of the maintenance received by him in the period before the death of the deceased is a very important factor in deciding what provision is reasonable after the death of the deceased. If the needs and means of an applicant remain as they were before the death of the deceased, and the net estate is sufficient for the purpose (taking into account the other claims on the deceased's bounty), it may be reasonable that provision should continue at the same level[25] (although it may be appropriate to capitalise the maintenance by making a lump sum order). However, the inadequate size of the net estate, or the strength of the other claims on the deceased's bounty, may invalidate this basis of measurement.[26] In any event, the basis cannot be elevated to a general rule of measurement, because the Act requires the Court to exercise its discretion by reference to the specified guidelines, rather than to any principle that levels of maintenance must be kept up.[27]

Size and nature of the estate

The reasonableness of any provision made or not made depends not only on the number and weight of the claims on the bounty of the deceased, but also upon the size of the estate available to satisfy them. A rich man can and in an appropriate case ought to make generous provision,[28] but a poor man may be justified in making no provision to satisfy a claim which would

---

[20] *Re Styler* [1942] Ch. 387; *Re Pugh* [1943] Ch. 387; *Re Sivyer* [1967] 1 W.L.R. 1482.

[21] *Re Leach* [1986] Ch. 226; *Re Callaghan* [1985] Fam. 1.

[22] *Re E.* [1966] 1 W.L.R. 709; *Re Ducksbury* [1966] 1 W.L.R. 1226.

[23] *Re Gregory* [1970] 1 W.L.R. 1455.

[24] *Re Fullard* [1982] Fam. 42; *Williams* v. *Johns* [1988] 2 F.L.R. 475.

[25] *Re Eyre* [1968] 1 W.L.R. 530, and the cases there cited; *Malone* v. *Harrison* [1979] 1 W.L.R. 1353.

[26] *Re E.*, *ante*, at p. 713, 714; *Re Borthwick* [1949] Ch. 395.

[27] *Re Crawford* (1983) 4 F.L.R. 273.

[28] *Re Borthwick* [1949] Ch. 395; *Re Black*, *The Times*, March 25, 1953; *Re Besterman* [1984] Ch. 458.

otherwise be strong. This is especially so if the major net effect of the provision would be a reduction in the applicant's social security benefits, leaving the applicant little better off.[29] If an estate is small there is still jurisdiction and the claim must be fully considered, but it will be material to consider (1) what state aid is available, (2) how far effective provision can be made, and (3) whether the costs are disproportionate.[30]

Disability of an applicant or beneficiary

Disability may increase the need of a member of the deceased's family circle, and the obligation of the deceased towards him, so this guideline is implicit in guidelines (a) to (d). However, its inclusion as a separate guideline emphasises its importance,[31] and was also probably desirable because incapacity is not, as it was under the 1938 Act, a condition precedent to some applications.

Conduct and other matters

The concept of conduct is vague and general. Its relevance to the particular categories of spouses and children will be discussed later. At this point three aspects must be stressed. First, its very vagueness and generality. Secondly, the fact that this vagueness and generality does not create any difficulties for the Court. In appropriate cases the court takes conduct into account, and considers whether an applicant has been a good and loving wife,[32] or a dutiful child.[33] Thirdly, any reduction in the emphasis given to conduct may mean a step away from testamentary freedom, and towards the application of ideas of family property. For if conduct does not strengthen or weaken a claim for provision, then that claim must derive, to some extent at least, from the mere fact of relationship by blood, marriage, or dependency.

The 1938 Act required the court to have regard to the deceased's reasons for making the provision he did. The 1975 Act does not so require. It would fit ill with the objective nature of the test for reasonable provision. In so far as the deceased's reasons are good reasons, they will weigh with the court anyway. In so far as they are bad reasons, they will not, and may even rouse the court's hostility.[34] However, if a testator has good reasons for failing to make provision for a potential applicant, he can usefully make

---

[29] *Re E., ante.*

[30] *Re Clayton* [1966] 1 W.L.R. 969, 971.

[31] Note the somewhat surprising decision at first instance in *Millward* v. *Shenton* [1972] 1 W.L.R. 711, which perhaps suggests that an express mention of disability in the Act was desirable. An adult child's disability gives him a stronger claim; see for example *Re Debenham* [1986] 1 F.L.R. 404. However, note the view of Tyler (ed. Oughton) at p. 179 that mere disability, even if causing financial hardship, ought not to be a ground for awarding provision to adult children.

[32] *Re Morris, The Times,* April 14, 1967; *Re Snoek* (1983) 13 Fam. Law 19.

[33] *Re Andrews* [1955] 1 W.L.R. 1105; *Re Cook* [1956] 106 L.J. 466; *Williams* v. *Johns* [1988] 2 F.L.R. 475. For a lengthy discussion of conduct as a factor under the 1938 Act, see Tyler, pp. 59–64.

[34] See, for example, *Re Borthwick* [1949] Ch. 395; *Re Clarke* [1968] 1 W.L.R. 415.

a written statement of them, to be kept with his will,[35] which will be admissible in evidence.[36]

Three "other matters" are worth specific mention. First, a promise or a non-contractual agreement by the deceased to dispose of his estate in a particular way will be taken into account by the Court, although it will not necessarily be decisive.[37] Secondly, the failure of a will to have the effect that the deceased expected may be material, and encourage the Court to make an order.[38] Thirdly, the Court will take account of any evidence of the deceased's expressions of intention to make provision for the applicant, especially when the fulfilment of that intention has been frustrated by supervening circumstances[39]; although again, this evidence will not necessarily be decisive.[40]

It is respectfully suggested that the Court is right to take account of evidence of the deceased's expressions of intention to make provision for an applicant, but ought to pay especial attention to its weight. To take an extreme example, it is one thing for the Court to intervene when the deceased has died the day before he was due to visit his solicitors to execute a will in favour of the applicant[41]; but another thing entirely for the Court to be influenced by vague expressions of intention which the deceased never took any steps to implement, although he could easily have done so.

As under the 1938 Act, testamentary capacity or the lack of it is not a matter which should be investigated on an application under the Act.[42] Feebleness of mind or understanding will not weigh with the court, because the test of reasonableness is objective.

Particular guidelines: surviving spouse

Subsection 3(2) of the Act provides that, where an application is made by a spouse or former spouse, the court shall have regard to (a) the age of the applicant and the duration of the marriage; and (b) the contribution made by the applicant to the welfare of the family of the deceased, including any contribution made by looking after the home or caring for the family. Also, in the case of an application by a spouse, unless there was a continuing judicial separation, the subsection directs the court to have

[35] Earlier wills are admissible and may be relevant. As to suppression of documents, see p. 729, *ante*.

[36] s. 21, and see p. 812, *post*.

[37] *Re Styler* [1942] Ch. 387; *Re Brown* [1955] 105 L.J. 169; and see *Jelley* v. *Iliffe* [1981] Fam. 128, 138, 140.

[38] *Re Goodwin* [1969] 1 Ch. 283; *Bayliss* v. *Lloyds Bank*, C.A. December 9, 1977. C.A.T. 77, 478A; and see *Re Besterman* [1984] Ch. 458, 465.

[39] *Re Callaghan* [1984] 3 W.L.R. 1076; *Re Coventry* [1980] Ch. 461, 490, commenting upon *Re Christie* [1979] Ch. 168.

[40] *Re Brindle* (1941) 192 L.T.J. 75.

[41] As has happened.

[42] *Re Blanch* [1967] 1 W.L.R. 987. If testamentary capacity is in issue, it can be decided in a Probate action heard immediately before the family provision hearing, and by the same Chancery judge: see p. 809, *post*.

regard to the provision which the applicant might reasonably have
expected to receive if on the date on which the deceased died the marriage,
instead of being terminated by death, had been terminated by decree of
divorce.[43]

The particular guidelines and the general guidelines

The first two of these particular guidelines expressly direct the attention
of the Court to matters which have already been put before it, by implication, in the general guidelines, and especially by that in section 3(1)(d).
The age of the applicant, the duration of the marriage, and the contribution of the applicant spouse to the welfare of the family of the deceased are
all highly relevant to the obligations and responsibilities of the deceased to
the applicant. Moreover, they are matters which influenced the Court
under the 1938 and 1965 Acts.[44]

However the first two of the particular guidelines, and even more the
third of them, are intended to do more than make express some matters
which are implied by the general guidelines. They are a corollary to the
wider definition of reasonable financial provision for spouses, as stated in
section 1(2) of the Act, and in effect repeat for the purposes of family provision law guidelines (d) and (f) in section 25(1) of the Matrimonial Causes
Act 1973, (re-enacted with some modifications by the Matrimonial and
Family Proceedings Act, 1984).

Family assets

In the view of the Law Commission, the particular guidelines for surviving spouses, and the wider definition of reasonable financial provision for
spouses in section 1(2) of the Act, were intended to give the surviving
spouse a claim upon the "family assets" at least equivalent to that of a
divorced spouse.[45]

The phrase "family assets" is, or at least was, commonly used to describe
the totality of the assets acquired by one or other or both of the parties to
the marriage, with the intention that they should be continuing provision
for them and their children during their joint lives, and used for the benefit
of the family as a whole.[46]

However, the usefulness of the phrase is now doubtful, at the least.[47]
The primary task and obligation of the court in the divorce jurisdiction is to

---

[43] For financial provision on divorce, see Miller, *Family Property and Financial Provision*;
Jackson, *Matrimonial Finance and Taxation*; Cretney, *Principles of Family Law*.
[44] For examples, see *Bayliss* v. *Lloyds Bank* C.A., December 9, 1977, C.A.T. 77/478A; *Re
Clarke* [1968] 1 W.L.R. 415; *Re Sylvester* [1941] Ch. 87; *Re Thornley* [1969] 1 W.L.R. 1037.
[45] Law Comm. 61, para. 32. See also Miller (1986) 102 L.Q.R. 445 and *Moody* v. *Stephenson* [1992] 2 W.L.R. 640; *Jessop* v. *Jessop, The Times,* October 16, 1991; C.A.T. 91/1034.
[46] See *Wachtel* v. *Wachtel* [1973] Fam. 72, 93, and generally.
[47] *Daubney* v. *Daubney* [1976] Fam. 267; *P.* v. *P* [1978] 1 W.L.R. 483 at 487, *per* Ormrod
L.J.

have regard to the statutory guidelines,[48] and the position must (it is submitted) be the same in the family provision jurisdiction.

The correct approach is not to seek to put a label on particular assets. Rather ought the court to have regard to the origin of the various assets when exercising its discretion under either jurisdiction. In some cases the parties to a marriage have built up capital assets by their joint efforts (and, often, have started their married life with little or nothing but their earning capacities).[49] In such cases, the court may well in effect exercise its discretion, whether on divorce or on death, so as to award a spouse a share in the assets subject to its discretion, which recognises that spouse's contribution to the welfare of the family in both financial and non-financial ways. In a sense the spouse has earned her share (it is usually the wife), and the court's powers enable it to award that share to her.

Different are the cases where one of the spouses has brought substantial capital assets into the marriage, or has acquired such assets during the marriage by inheritance, gift or otherwise[50]; and in cases where the marriage has been short.[51] In these cases the assets have not been acquired by the joint efforts of the parties for the joint benefit and use of themselves and their children.

Different also are cases in which "fossil marriages" are before the Court.[52] If cohabitation ended some time before the death of the deceased, and the parties to the marriage had arranged their lives on the footing that the marriage had ended, the family has come to an end as a unit for practical purposes, and the assets in the legal ownership of the parties cannot be described as "family assets." Finally, there are cases which have no parallel in the divorce jurisdiction, namely those where there has been, so to say, an accidental or inadvertent failure to make reasonable provision.[53] In such a situation, the deceased intended to make reasonable provision for his spouse, but delay in making the will, or supervening circumstances, have rendered unreasonable the provision made. The size of the estate, or the nature of the assets which make it up, may have had an unforeseen effect; or the circumstances of the surviving spouse or the other beneficiaries may have changed. The Court is at least as likely to seek to repair the

---

[48] O'D v. O'D [1976] Fam. 83 at 89; and see P. v. P., ante, at 487 onwards.

[49] See for example the remark of Purchas L.J. in Stead v. Stead [1985] F.L.R. 16 at 23; "When one reviews the progress of the family wealth demonstrated from the evidence in this case . . . ."

[50] Such as O'D v. O'D, ante; for other examples under the divorce jurisdiction, see Trippas v. Trippas [1973] Fam. 134 and Calderbank v. Calderbank [1976] Fam. 93; for examples under the family provision jurisdiction, see Re Bunning [1984] Ch. 480 and Re Besterman [1984] Ch. 458.

[51] As in the divorce case of S. v. S. itself; Cumbers v. Cumbers [1974] 1 W.L.R. 1331; and Re Chatterton, C.A., November 1, 1978. C.A.T. 78/660 (a case under the 1975 Act).

[52] As in the divorce case of Krystman v. Krystman [1973] 1 W.L.R. 927. For examples of such marriages see Re Gregory [1970] 1 W.L.R. 1455 (under the 1938 Act) and Re Rowlands [1984] F.L.R. 813 (under the 1975 Act).

[53] For examples see Re Goodwin [1969] 1 Ch. 283; Re Lewis, C.A., March 13, 1980. C.A.T. 80/158 (where inflation was the supervening circumstance). See also pp. 774, 781 ante.

consequences of the accident or inadvertence than to impose its own views as to the share of the family assets which ought to pass to the surviving spouse.

Arithmetical approaches

In considering the appropriate provision for a wife on divorce, there was in the years immediately after the enactment of the Matrimonial Causes Act 1973 a tendency to adopt an arithmetical approach, taking as a flexible starting point one-third of the capital assets of the parties, and one-third of the joint earnings.[54] This was in a sense a substitute for a half-and-half division of the assets of the partnership.[55] This approach now has limited value.[56] In any event the court cannot adopt it in the family provision jurisdiction, because the deceased has no more earnings. However, there are some family provision cases in which the court has come to the conclusion, by applying the statutory guidelines to the facts, that an order which puts half the joint capital assets at the disposal of the surviving spouse, either absolutely or for life, makes reasonable financial provision. The court has then been strengthened in its view by the fact that it has reached a half and half result. That result can therefore be a useful guide or cross check in an appropriate case.[57]

The relevance of the need for maintenance

As has already been observed, the three particular guidelines were enacted to enable the courts to recognise the contribution of a surviving spouse to the welfare of the family, and to make her claim similar somewhat to that of a divorced spouse.[58] So was the wider definition of reasonable financial provision for spouses in section 1(2) of the Act. However, this does not mean that reasonable financial provision for a spouse is provision for maintenance only, should the spouse not have made such a contribution. Even if she has not earned her share, she is entitled to a reasonable finanancial provision measured by the more generous standard. This follows from the terms of the Act, whereby the wider definition of reasonable financial provision applies to all spouses. Moreover, the reported cases[59] show that the court makes awards in accordance with the

[54] *Wachtel* v. *Wachtel*, above, was the leading case.
[55] *Wachtel* v. *Wachtel*, above at 95.
[56] See generally the discussions in Miller, *Family Property and Financial Provision*; Jackson, *Matrimonial Finance and Taxation*; Cretney, *Principles of Family Law*. Also Miller, (1986) 102 L.Q.R. 445.
[57] *Re Bunning* [1984] Ch. 480 at 499; *Stead* v. *Stead* [1985] F.L.R. 16 at 27; *Re Besterman* [1984] Ch. 458 at 473 (although that was a case of a large estate, in which a half and half result was clearly inappropriate for many reasons); *Preston* v. *Preston* [1982] Fam. 17 at 25 (a matrimonial case); *Stephens* v. *Stephens* July 1, 1985, C.A.T. 85/344; *Smith* v. *Smith* [1991] 2 All. E.R. 306.
[58] See p. 782, *ante.*
[59] *Re Besterman, ante,* is the strongest authority; see also to some extent *Re Bunning, ante.*

more generous standard, even though the spouse has not made a significant direct or indirect contribution to the deceased's assets, nor any especial contribution to the welfare of the family.[60]

Although reasonable financial provision for a spouse must be measured by a more generous standard than the need for maintenance, that need is likely to loom the larger before the Court the smaller the estate. As Purchas L.J. observed in *Stead* v. *Stead*,[61] "where the estate is of more modest proportions, the margin available from which the Court is able to make provision in excess of that required for reasonable maintenance of the surviving spouse as indicated by section 1(2)(*a*) of the Act is considerably reduced." At the other end of the scale, where resources are very large, the awards required for reasonable financial provision probably begin to "level off," as in the divorce jurisdiction.[62] Reasonable financial provision for the widow of a millionaire may well be much less than one third of the capital available for distribution, unless perhaps her contribution to the welfare of the family has been very great.

Whether the estate of the deceased is large or small, the Court is likely to be especially concerned to ensure that the applicant spouse has satisfactory accommodation.[63] Also, if it makes a lump sum order, it will seek to ensure, so far as possible, that the lump sum is sufficient to make allowance for future contingencies, and for inflation.[64] When the spouse is elderly and the beneficiaries are the adult children of the deceased, it is suggested that most or all of the provision may best be made by way of a life interest.[65]

The relevance of conduct

Under the original section 25 of the Matrimonial Causes Act 1973, there was strong authority that the conduct of the parties was irrelevant to financial provision, unless it was obvious and gross.[66] Under the new section 25, enacted by section 3 of the Matrimonial and Family Proceedings Act 1984, the Divorce Court is directed to have regard to "the conduct of each of the parties, if that conduct is such that it would in the opinion of the Court be inequitable to disregard it."

Under the influence of the divorce jurisdiction, questions of conduct appear to have become less important in applications by spouses under the 1975 Act.[67] However, conduct which is obvious and gross, or such that it would in the opinion of the Court be inequitable to disregard it, will cer-

[60] For interesting criticisms of the decision of the Court of Appeal in *Re Besterman* in relation to this, see Tyler (ed. Oughton) at p. 312 onwards.
[61] [1985] F.L.R. 16, 22.
[62] *Re Besterman, ante,* citing *Preston* v. Preston [1982] Fam. 17, 28.
[63] See generally *Re Besterman, ante,* and *Re Bunning, ante.*
[64] *Re Besterman, ante,* 476.
[65] *S.* v. *S., ante; Stead* v. *Stead, ante;* see also p. 778, *ante.*
[66] *Wachtel* v. *Wachtel, ante.*
[67] See for example *Re Bunning, ante; Stead* v. *Stead, ante.*

tainly influence the Court.[68] Moreover, conduct may well have to play a somewhat larger part in the family provision jurisdiction than in the divorce jurisdiction, for two reasons. First, general guideline (d) directs the Court to consider the obligations and responsibilities of the deceased to applicants and beneficiaries. These obligations and responsibilities must be affected by the conduct of applicants and beneficiaries. Secondly, the concept of conduct in the divorce jurisdiction is a concept with a core of more or less clear and restricted meaning: that core is the conduct which provided grounds for divorce before the Divorce Reform Act 1969.[69] Indeed, the great reduction in the importance of conduct in the divorce jurisdiction derived from the change made in the grounds for divorce in that Act.[70] But outside the context of divorce proceedings, the concept of conduct loses this core of meaning. It becomes vague and general; a person's conduct is everything about the way he behaves.

A former spouse

The first and second, but not the third, of the particular guidelines for applications by spouses are also specified for former spouses. The court is to have regard to (a) the age of the former spouse and the duration of the marriage and (b) the contribution made by the former spouse to the welfare of the family of the deceased, including any contribution made by looking after the home or caring for the family.[71]

In *Re Fullard*[72] the Court of Appeal observed that the Divorce Court now has power to make appropriate adjustments as between spouses after divorce, and that therefore the number of cases in which it is possible for a former spouse to apply successfully under the 1975 Act is comparatively small. The Court of Appeal gave as examples of applications which might succeed ones in which periodical payments have been made for a long time,[73] and there is a reasonable amount of capital in the estate; and ones in which substantial capital funds are unlocked by the death of the deceased, because of insurance or pension policies.

It is difficult to think of other circumstances in which a former spouse could apply successfully. The mere fact of accretion of wealth after the dissolution of the marriage is unlikely to be sufficient of itself to justify an application.[74] Possibly concealment by the deceased of his true financial

[68] *Re Snoek* (1983) 13 Fam. Law 19.
[69] However, conduct is not restricted to this meaning: *Jones (M.A.)* v. *Jones (W.)* [1976] Fam. 8.
[70] *Wachtel* v. *Wachtel, ante.*
[71] s.3(2).
[72] [1982] Fam. 42; [1982] Conv. 75.
[73] Of course an application may not succeed, even though periodical payments have ended with the death of the deceased: *Re Talbot* [1962] 1 W.L.R. 113.
[74] *Re Fullard* at 52. For cases of accretion of wealth under the 1938 and 1965 Acts, see *Re Borthwick* [1949] Ch. 395; *Re Whittle*, C.A., March 5, 1973, C.A.T. 73/94A; *Re Eyre* [1968] 1 W.L.R. 530.

position would have some significance.[75] Just possibly the applicant's mere ignorance of an improvement in the deceased's financial circumstances would weigh with the Court; or a great disparity between the resources and needs of the former spouse and the beneficiaries; or help and support by the former spouse after the divorce.[76] However, it is suggested that only a combination of more than one of these other circumstances is at all likely to give rise to a situation in which a former spouse could apply successfully.

In *Re Eyre*[77] the Court observed that (1) an order for secured mainten-ance, made on divorce, ought not to be treated as a predetermination of what a survivor should receive after the death of a former spouse; (2) there could not be any general rule that a first wife should be accorded financial equality with a widow; (3) contrariwise, a lack of parity between the finan-cial position of a first and a second wife during the lifetime of the husband should not of itself be treated as sufficient reason for prolonging that pos-ition after his death; and (4) assuming that the former wife's needs and her means remain as they were before the husband's death, and assuming that the net estate is sufficient for the purpose, then it is reasonable that she should continue to receive the same provision as during the husband's life-time, sufficiency being determined having regard to the provision for or needs of other claimants on the husband's bounty. It is submitted that the reported cases on the 1975 Act, especially *Re Fullard*,[78] *Re Crawford*,[79] and *Re Farrow*,[80] have left the force of the first observation untouched, and have strengthened that of the second, but have weakened that of the third and especially, that of the fourth.[81]

A child or person treated as a child

These two categories can be considered together. The guideline common to them both is that the court is directed to have regard to the manner in which the applicant was being or in which he might expect to be educated or trained.[82]; Presumably some applicants might expect to receive private education,[83] others not, and in relation to this the other claims on the deceased, and the size of the estate, are obviously relevant. In relation to higher education, for which grants from central or local government might be available to an applicant, presumably the court's approach will be simi-

---

[75] In *Brill* v. *Proud* [1984] 14 Fam. Law such concealment was alleged, but the allegation was not made out. The secretiveness of the deceased about his financial affairs appears to have had some weight with the Court in *Re W* [1975] 119 Sol. Jo. 436, an application by a for-mer spouse under the 1965 Act.

[76] *Re Bellman* [1963] P. 239.

[77] [1968] 1 W.L.R. 530.

[78] [1982] Fam. 42.

[79] [1983] 4 F.L.R. 273.

[80] [1987] 1 F.L.R. 205. For change of circumstances, see *Smith* v. *Smith* [1991] 2 All E.R. 306 (a matrimonial case).

[81] See also p. 779, *ante*.

[82] s.3(3).

[83] See *Bosch* v. *Perpetual Trustee Co. Ltd.* [1938] A.C. 463; compare private medical care: *Re Sanderson* [1963] C.L.Y. 3624.

lar to that already adopted towards the government provision of social security benefits[84]: the student may be awarded money for extra comforts, but not so as merely to reduce his grant.

Under the 1938 Act, the conduct of a child could be relevant as increasing his or her claim, for instance if a daughter had made sacrifices to look after the deceased.[85] It could also reduce the claim, for example, if contact had not been close or the child had not been dependent on the deceased for some time.[86] It is submitted that conduct continues to be relevant in these respects.[87]

The Act specifies three further guidelines for applications by persons who were not children of the deceased, but were treated as such.[88] The court is to have regard (a) to whether the deceased had assumed any responsibility for the applicant's maintenance and, if so, the extent to which and the basis upon which the deceased assumed that responsibility and to the length of time for which he discharged that responsibility; (b) to whether in assuming and discharging that responsibility the deceased did so knowing that the applicant was not his own child; and (c) to the liability of any other person to maintain the applicant. These guidelines correspond with those laid down for the matrimonial jurisdiction by the Matrimonial Causes Act 1973.[89]

The introduction of the new category of persons treated as children raises the question whether their claims will be weaker than those of true children; in other words, whether the blood tie is of itself significant. It is submitted that, since the blood tie is not mentioned in the Act, it ought to have less weight than the guidelines which do appear there.[90] The claims of true children may well be stronger in most cases anyway, by reason of the operation of the specified guidelines, both general and particular.

Re Coventry[91] is authority for the proposition that, where a child or person treated as a child is an adult male in employment, and so capable of earning his own living, some special circumstance is required to render unreasonable a failure on the part of the deceased to make some financial provision for the child. The same applies where the child is an adult female capable of earning her own living.[92]

Under the 1938 Act, the Court sometimes considered that the claim on the bounty of the deceased of a child who was a beneficiary under his will was relatively stronger in relation to the claim of an applicant who was a surviving spouse (and a step-parent) if a substantial part of the estate of the

---

[84] See p. 778, ante.
[85] Re Cook (1956) 106 L.J. 466.
[86] Re Andrews [1955] 1 W.L.R. 1105; Re Ducksbury [1966] 1 W.L.R. 1226.
[87] This view is shared by J. G. Miller: see Current Law Statutes (1975), notes to s.3.
[88] s.3(3).
[89] s.25(4) of that Act, as amended.
[90] But it did apparently have some weight under the 1938 and 1965 Acts: Re Harker-Thomas [1969] P. 28, 31.
[91] [1980] Ch. 461. Contrast the position of an adult child who is not capable of earning his or her own living: Re Debenham [1986] 1 F.L.R. 404.
[92] Williams v. Johns [1988] 2 F.L.R. 475.

deceased was derived from the child's other parent.[93] In one reported case,[94] the Court was influenced in the same way in the converse situation, when the child was the applicant, and the step-parent the beneficiary. The child was only 15 years old, so the case is consistent with *Re Coventry*. However, in two cases under the 1975 Act, *Re Leach*[95] and *Re Callaghan*,[96] adults who were not in any special need applied for provision out of the estate of their step-parent, they being qualified to do so as persons treated as children of the family by the step-parent. In both cases the step-parent died intestate and collateral members of the step-parent's family were the beneficiaries. In each case, the Court made a substantial order in favour of the applicant, being strongly influenced by the fact that the deceased's estate was partly derived from the applicant's natural parent. The decisions are very understandable, because it is hard that property should pass right out of a family through the intervention of a step-parent. However, they are not easy to reconcile with *Re Coventry*.[97]

A person maintained by the deceased

This new category is potentially a very wide one. However, as has already been mentioned,[98] its operation is restricted by its one particular guideline, whereby the court is directed to have regard to the extent to which, and the basis upon which, the deceased assumed responsibility for the maintenance of the applicant, and to the length of time for which the deceased discharged that responsibility.[99] In *Re Beaumont*,[1] Megarry V.-C. held that an applicant was not entitled to apply at all unless the deceased had assumed responsibility for his or her maintenance, and that the burden of establishing such an assumption of responsibility lay upon the applicant. However in *Jelley* v. *Iliffe*[2] the Court of Appeal took a different approach, holding that the mere maintenance of the applicant by the deceased usually means that the deceased has assumed that responsibility. The Court of Appeal does not appear to have considered the question whether an express disclaimer of responsibility would automatically disqualify an applicant, or merely be a factor for the court to consider in the exercise of its discretion.

---

[93] *Re Styler* [1942] Ch. 387; *Re Pugh* [1943] Ch. 387.

[94] *Re Sivyer* [1967] 1 W.L.R. 1482.

[95] [1985] 3 W.L.R. 413.

[96] [1985] Fam. 1.

[97] The actual decision in *Re Callaghan* can be strongly defended on the ground that the deceased clearly intended to make a will in favour of the applicant, and was in effect prevented from doing so by illness, in circumstances which were very creditable to the applicant. However, the learned judge did not put this in the forefront of her reasoning.

[98] See p. 773, *ante*.

[99] s.3(4).

[1] [1980] Ch. 444; Naresh (1980) L.Q.R. 534 (a whole review article on this and other cases under s.1(1)(e)); Dewar (1982) 12 Fam. Law 158 (discussing contributions and considerations.).

[2] [1981] Fam. 128.

If the estate is sufficient, it appears that the award made to a successful applicant in this category will reflect the degree of the applicant's dependence on the deceased before his death.[3]

However, the Court is also concerned, as with applicants in other categories, to ensure that the person maintained has somewhere to live.[4] In addition, the Court may be influenced by similarities between the relationship of the deceased and the applicant and the more formal relationships of marriage and parenthood.[5] It may also be influenced by the help and comfort the applicant gave to the deceased, and their future plans together.[6]

The facts of such cases as *Re Beaumont, supra*, and *Jelley* v. *Iliffe, supra*, suggest that the guidelines in section 3 of the Act give little if any indication of the weight which should be given to the claims of a person maintained by the deceased as against the claims of beneficiaries who are close relatives of the deceased but in no great financial need, as might be, perhaps, adult children of the deceased. It is submitted that beneficiaries who are children of the deceased have a moral claim to their parents' estates, even if not themselves in need, and that the court ought to recognise their claims. Parliament surely cannot have intended that the claims of "an elderly housekeeper . . . a nephew . . . a widowed sister . . . "[7] should necessarily prevail over those of the children of the deceased, being beneficiaries under his will or intestacy, just because the children were in no great financial need.

Certainly in one case the Court has balanced the claims of an applicant against those of the daughter of the deceased, the sole beneficiary, by awarding the greater part of the provision in the form of life interests.[8]

Orders which the court can make

Under the 1975 Act the court can make any one or more of the following orders[9]:

    (a) an order for the making to the applicant out of the net estate of the deceased of such periodical payments and for such term as may be specified in the order;

    (b) an order for the payment to the applicant out of that estate of a lump sum of such amount as may be so specified;

    (c) an order for the transfer to the applicant of such property comprised in that estate as may be so specified;

[3] *Malone* v. *Harrison* [1979] 1 W.L.R. 1353; [1980] L.Q.R. 165.
[4] *Re Haig* (1979) 129 New L.J. 420; *Harrington* v. *Gill* (1983) 4 F.L.R. 265.
[5] *Re McC, C.A.* v. *C.C. The Times*, November 17, 1978; (1979) 9 Fam. Law 26; (1979) 123 S. J. 35.
[6] *Williams* v. *Roberts* (1984) Fam. Law 210.
[7] See pp. 772–775, *ante*.
[8] *Harrington* v. *Gill*, *ante*.
[9] s.6(2).

(d) an order for the settlement for the benefit of the applicant of such property comprised in that estate as may be so specified;

(e) an order for the acquisition out of property comprised in that estate of such property as may be so specified and for the transfer of the property so acquired to the applicant or for the settlement thereof for his benefit;

(f) an order varying any ante-nuptial or post-nuptial settlement (including such a settlement made by will) made on the parties to a marriage to which the deceased was one of the parties, the variation being for the benefit of the surviving party to that marriage, or any child of that marriage, or any person who was treated by the deceased as a child of the family in relation to that marriage.

Under the 1938 Act and the 1965 Act the court could only make one or both of the first two orders, an order for periodical payments or a lump sum payment. The wider powers of the court under the 1975 Act correspond with the powers to make orders given to the court in the matrimonial jurisdiction by the Matrimonial Causes Act 1973,[10] and the reported cases on the exercise of the powers in that jurisdiction are of assistance in the family provision jurisdiction.

Periodical payments

An order for periodical payments may provide for[11] (a) payment of such amount as may be specified in the order (*e.g.* £100 a month),[12] or (b) payments equal to the whole of the income of the net estate or of such portion thereof as may be so specified (*e.g.* one-third of the income of the net estate) or (c) payments equal to the whole of the income of such part of the net estate as the court may direct to be set aside or appropriated for the making, out of the income thereof, of periodical payments (*e.g.* the whole of the income of one-third of the net estate, such one-third of the net estate being appropriated). Alternatively, the order may provide for the amount of the payments or any of them to be determined in any other way the court thinks fit. It is a little difficult to envisage a way other than the three stated, but perhaps one example would be an order which provided for fluctuating payments not directly proportionate to the income of the estate; for example, one-third if the income is below a certain sum, but one-half if it rises above that sum. The retail price index could even be used in some way; but such sophisticated orders are likely to be rare.

It is expressly provided[13] that the order for periodical payments may

---

[10] ss.23(1), 24(1) of that Act.

[11] s.2(2).

[12] In an appropriate case, an order may be made for periodical payments in excess of the income of the estate: *Re F.* (1965) 109 S.J. 212.

[13] s.2(3).

direct that a specified part of the net estate shall be set aside or appropriated for the making, out of the income thereof, of the periodical payments.[14] However, no larger part of the net estate is to be set aside or appropriated than is sufficient, at the date of the order, to produce by the income thereof the amount required for the making of the payments. This provision is the nearest to the provision in the Matrimonial Causes Act 1973[15] which gives the court power to secure periodical payments. Such a power to secure is less necessary in the family provision jurisdiction because the estate of the deceased is held by personal representatives who are in a position of trusteeship.

The periodical payments are to be for a term specified in the order. Normally, no doubt, the term will begin with the death of the deceased, but this is not essential; provision could, for instance be ordered from the date of the judgment,[16] or from the end of the "executor's year" of 12 months after the death.[17] As for the end of the term, the Act itself provides that an order in favour of a former spouse shall, in so far as it provides for the making of periodical payments, cease to have effect on the remarriage of that former spouse, except in relation to any arrears.[18] The same applies in cases of judicial separation. But apart from this, no time is fixed by the Act for the ending of the term. The court must decide it when it makes the order. Therefore, for example, an order for periodical payments in favour of a surviving spouse does not automatically terminate on remarriage, although the court could in its order have made the term end on future remarriage. Likewise orders in favour of children or persons treated as children of the family will not automatically terminate on the attainment of full age or marriage, although again the court could have made any particular order so terminate. The end of the term for the periodical payments is thus, with the one exception for former spouses and judicially separated spouses, left to be fixed when the order is made. However, it is difficult if not impossible to think of a case in which it would be right for the court to order that the term should continue after the death of the applicant.

Orders for periodical payments may be subsequently varied under the power given by section 6 of the Act; this power is explained, *post*.[19] The power to vary extends to a variation of the date or event originally fixed by the court for the end of the term of the periodical payments, because the fixing of that date or event is part of the order of the court.[20] However, the power to vary does not allow the court to vary or give a dispensation from the rule that orders in favour of former spouses and judicially separated

---

[14] If real property is to be appropriated, care must be taken to get the conveyancing right. For example, the appropriation may require a trust for sale or a strict settlement to be set up.

[15] s.23(1)(*b*) of that Act.

[16] *Re Lecoche* (1967) 111 S.T. 136; *Lusternik* v. *Lusternik* [1972] Fam. 125. But see p. 875, *post*; difficulties may arise on administration if the date of judgment is chosen.

[17] See p. 816, *post*.

[18] s.19(2). This may be an important consideration in litigation and negotiation.

[19] See pp. 796–798, *post*.

[20] s.6(3).

spouses terminate on remarriage, because that rule is part of the Act itself.[21]

Lump sums

The power to award provision for maintenance by way of an order for payment of a lump sum existed under the 1938 Act and the 1965 Act. In some cases under the 1938 Act the court stressed that lump sums were to be awarded by way of maintenance,[22] and this approach ought logically to be followed in cases under the new Act where the applicants are only entitled to claim the maintenance standard of provision (that is, of course, all applicants other than surviving spouses).[23] Under the 1938 Act there was a tendency to consider lump sums more appropriate in applications relating to small estates.[24] This tendency may have derived from the original restriction of lump sum orders to cases in which the net estate did not exceed £2,000. It is submitted that the tendency will exist in so far as a small estate can most effectively make provision by means of a lump sum payment, but ought not to, and will not, prevent the award of a lump sum from a medium sized or large estate, in so far as such an award would be otherwise appropriate. This is especially so in application by surviving spouses.[25] In such applications, the practice of the court in ordering lump sums under the Matrimonial Causes Act 1973 may provide useful guidance,[26] provided as always that caution is exercised in comparing the two jurisdictions.

It appears to be permissible, and could sometimes be appropriate, to order payment of a lump sum equivalent to the whole of the net estate; for example, where the deceased died intestate, leaving a small estate, the claimant is a mistress who has lived with him as his wife for many years, and the beneficiaries are distant relatives who never knew him. In *Millward v. Shenton*[27] the Court of Appeal ordered a lump sum equivalent to eleven-twelfths of the net estate, the beneficiary being a charity, and the applicant a disabled son.

A lump sum order can provide for the payment of the lump sum by instalments.[28] The number, amounts, and dates for payment of the instalments can be varied on a subsequent application for variation; apart from this, a lump sum order cannot be varied.

Where a lump sum is awarded in lieu of maintenance the most usual practice is to begin with the figure and term appropriate for annual main-

---

[21] s.6(3).

[22] *Re Sivyer* [1967] 1 W.L.R. 1482, 1487.

[23] See *Re Besterman* [1984] Ch. 458, 465.

[24] *Re Sivyer, ante; Re Clayton* [1966] 1 W.L.R. 969.

[25] Not least because of the concept of family assets: see pp. 782, 784, *ante.*

[26] See pp. 784, *ante,* and Miller, *Family Property and Financial Provision*; Jackson, *Matrimonial Finance and Taxation* and Cretney, *Principles of Family Law.*

[27] [1972] 1 W.L.R. 711.

[28] s.7. A lump sum may also be charged on property and the enforcement of the charge deferred: *Re H.* (1975) 120 S.J. 81.

tenance and deduce from this the value of such an interest. This appears to be the only logical approach to the assessment of the appropriate sum when the applicant is only entitled to the maintenance standard of provision.[29]

Transfer of property

An order for the transfer of a specific item of property is especially useful when a lump sum order would necessitate an improvident realisation of part of the estate.

"Property" has a wide meaning. It includes a chose in action[30]; thus, presumably, an order under the Act could in effect forgive a debt owned to the deceased by a person entitled to apply for provision, by directing the debt to be transferred to him. Under the Matrimonial Causes Act 1973, "property" also includes a weekly contractual tenancy, whether granted by a private landlord or a local authority,[31] and it is submitted that the position must be the same under the family provision jurisdiction.

An order for the transfer of property cannot be varied, but such an order can be made, although not made originally, on an application to vary a previous order for periodical payments.[32]

The court can make an order which is in effect the grant of an option. In Re Kozdrach, Sobesto v. Farren[33] the applicant had been living with the deceased as his wife. His dwelling-house was worth £28,000 at the date of the hearing. The court awarded the applicant a lump sum of £18,000, and ordered that she could within 6 months apply for a transfer of the dwelling-house at a price of £9,000.

Settlement of property

An order for the settlement of property is especially appropriate when an applicant is a minor, or needs to be protected for some other reason. However, it can be useful in other situations. Care must be taken by those advising applicants and beneficiaries to see that the settlement is well drafted from the point of view of trust and tax law; it would be a pity if, for example, a settlement on a child applicant failed to take full advantage of the inheritance tax advantages provided by an accumulation and mainten-

---

[29] In Re Crawford (1983) 4 F.L.R. 273 annuity quotations were relied upon, but in Malone v. Harrison [1979] 1 W.L.R. 1353 the court used a form of personal injury calculation, with a multiplier and a multiplicand.

[30] s.25(1).

[31] Hale v. Hale [1975] 1 W.L.R. 931 (private landlord); Thompson v. Thompson [1976] Fam. 25 (local authority landlord). However, in cases where the landlord can and does refuse his consent to an assignment, the court ought not to make an order for the transfer of the tenancy. Also, the court should not make orders in respect of council tenancies which put pressure on councils or which may be rejected by councils: Regan v. Regan [1977] 1 W.L.R. 84. But quaere whether this case would be followed now that council tenants and their families have security of tenure and rights of succession under the Housing Acts.

[32] s.6(2).

[33] [1981] Conveyancer 224.

ance trust which satisfies the requirements of section 71 of the Capital Transfer (or Inheritance) Tax Act 1984.[34]

The power to order a settlement of property, together with the other powers given to the court, will authorise the creation of a charge on the property, as is the case under the matrimonial jurisdiction.[35]

An order for the settlement of property cannot be varied, nor can such an order be made on an application to vary an existing order for periodical payments.

Acquisition of property

An order for the acquisition of property, and its transfer to or settlement upon an applicant, will be useful when the applicant needs a home, for example when a surviving spouse wants to move to a smaller house.[36]

The order cannot be varied,[37] nor can such an order be made on an application to vary an order for periodical payments.

Variation of settlements

The meaning of the phrase "ante-nuptial or post-nuptial settlement" has been made tolerably clear by a series of cases under the matrimonial jurisdiction. However, it is difficult to give a short and simple explanation of the phrase, because it extends beyond settlements as understood by conveyancers, although it includes them. Briefly, it means some document or transaction (other than an absolute gift) providing for the financial benefit of one or other or both of the spouses concerned as spouses and with reference to their married state, prospective or actual. The settlement must be made in contemplation of or because of marriage and with reference to the interests of married people or their children.[38]

The court's power to vary the settlement is restricted, because the variation must be for the benefit of the surviving party to the marriage concerned, or any child of that marriage, or any person who is treated by the deceased as a child of the family in relation to that marriage.[39] Thus an applicant only entitled to apply as a dependant of the deceased cannot seek a variation of such a settlement in his or her quest for reasonable provision.

An order for the variation of an ante-nuptial or post-nuptial settlement

[34] Formerly Finance Act 1975, Sched. 6, para. 15. For Inheritance Tax, see generally Wheatcroft and Hewson, *Encyclopedia of Capital Taxation*; Dymond, *Capital Taxes*.

[35] *Hector* v. *Hector* [1973] 1 W.L.R. 1122, and see *Re H* n. 28, p. 793, *ante*.

[36] Law Comm. 61, para. 116.

[37] But if the trusts constitute a settlement under the Settled Land Act 1925 the life tenant will have the powers of a tenant for life under that Act (including the power of sale) unless the order deprives him of them. See *Re Hills* [1941] W.N. 123; *Re Mason* (1975) 5 Fam. Law 124.

[38] See generally Miller, *Family Propety and Financial Provision*, and the cases there cited, especially *Prinsep* v. *Prinsep* [1929] P. 225, 232, and *Hargreaves* v. *Hargreaves* [1926] P. 42, 45; Cretney, *Principles of Family Law*, pp. 377, 753.

[39] s.2(1)(*f*).

cannot itself be varied, nor can it be made on an application to vary a previous order for periodical payments.[40]

Burden of orders

If the court is to make an order for provision which balances the claims of applicants against those of the existing beneficiaries under the will or intestacy, and treat the members of both classes as fairly as possible, it must have power to apportion the burden of its order among the existing beneficiaries in the way it thinks right. Such an apportionment was possible under the 1938 Act and the 1965 Act, and was practised by the court.[41] Such beneficiaries will of course have to be joined as parties and this can often raise problems as to whether in particular mere pecuniary legatees should be made defendants.[42] Apportionment now receives statutory authority. The order may contain such consequential and supplemental provisions as the court thinks necessary or expedient for giving effect to the order or securing that the order operates fairly as between one beneficiary of the estate and another, and may, in particular, (a) order any person who holds any property which forms part of the net estate of the deceased to make such payment or transfer such property as may be specified in the order[43]; (b) vary the disposition of the deceased's estate effected by the will or the intestacy rules, or both will and intestacy rules, as the court thinks fair and reasonable having regard to the provisions of the order and all the circumstances of the case; and (c) confer on the trustees of any property which is the subject of an order such powers as appear to the court to be necessary or expedient.[44]

Variation of orders

Section 6 of the Act gives a limited power to vary existing orders.[45] The essence of the power is that, if an order for periodical payments has been made, the court can on a subsequent application either make a new order for periodical payments payable out of the property out of which the existing periodical payments are payable; or order a lump sum payment out of that property[46]; or order a transfer of the property, or part of it. Thus the property out of which provision has to be made—called in the section "rel-

---

[40] As a matter of general law a settlement can of course be varied by agreement if all parties are of full capacity, and if not, then maybe under the Variation of Trusts Act 1958.

[41] Re Westby [1946] W.N. 141; and see post p. 812.

[42] Re Preston [1969] 1 W.L.R. 317. In Re Lidington [1940] Ch. 927, an order was made in favour of a surviving spouse on terms that she maintained her children by the deceased, who were beneficiaries under his will.

[43] It is submitted that the court could order a specific legatee of the shares in a company to make a money payment to the applicant.

[44] s.2(4). See also n. 28, p. 793, ante.

[45] Including orders (other than interim orders) made under the 1938 and 1965 Acts: see s.26(4).

[46] Presumably, even if a lump sum order, as well as the periodical payments order, had benn made on the original application.

evant property"—cannot be increased.[47] To some extent this preserves the advantages of finality, in the sense that the variation of an order already made cannot take more property out of the estate, which would make administration impossible. By contrast, the right to apply is not restricted to existing successful applicants. It extends to (a) any person originally entitled to apply; (b) the personal representatives of the deceased; (c) the trustees of any "relevant property"; and (d) any beneficiary of the estate.[48] Moreover, the power to vary can be exercised repeatedly.[49] The power to vary can only affect property which is applicable for the making of periodical payments. Thus it cannot affect a dwelling-house in which the applicant is allowed to live under the terms of the original order.[50]

The right to apply for a variation lasts for six months after the periodical payments have terminated under the original order, but there is no power to vary an order for periodical payments so as to extend them beyond the remarriage of a former spouse (as distinct from the remarriage of a surviving spouse).[51]

The power to vary could have strange results if one application against an estate is made within the six-month time limit imposed by section 4 of the Act, and another application is made by a different applicant outside the time limit. If the second applicant is not given an extension of time, he cannot apply while the first application is pending. But if and when an order for periodical payments is made at the hearing of the first application, the second applicant can then apply for its variation. Perhaps the practical answer to the problem is that, when one application is already pending, further applicants will be given extensions of time if their applications have any chance of success.

When the court varies an order for periodical payments, it must have regard to all the circumstances of the case, including any change in circumstances which would alter the effect of the general guidelines or any relevant particular guidelines.[52]

As already mentioned, orders for the settlement of property, the acquisition of property, or the variation of an ante-nuptial or post-nuptial settlement cannot be made on an application to vary an order for periodical payments.[53] Nor can orders be made affecting property held on joint tenancy, nor can orders be made under the powers[54] to counteract transactions intended to defeat applications under the Act.[55]

In addition to its power to vary orders for periodical payments made

---

[47] s.6(6).

[48] s.6(5). Conditions as to notifying the trustees of changes in circumstances may be included in the order: *Re Hills* [1941] W.N. 123.

[49] s.6(4).

[50] *Re Fricker* (1982) 3 F.L.R. 228.

[51] s.6(3).

[52] s.6(7). An applicant will not normally be penalised for thrift: *Re Gale* [1966] Ch. 236.

[53] s.6(9); *ante*, p. 796.

[54] ss.10 and 11.

[55] s.6(9).

under the Act, the court has power under the Act to vary secured periodical payment orders made under the Matrimonial Causes Act 1973, and to
vary the terms of maintenance agreements.[56]

It should be noted that, under the 1938 Act, if an applicant, for example
a young child, had a good claim to maintenance in the future the court
could adjourn the proceedings.[57] Presumably this can be done under the
1975 Act.

Interim orders

If an applicant is suffering hardship pending the hearing of the application, it is possible for representatives of the deceased to pay and the
beneficiaries under the will or intestacy to consent to the payment of something "on account" of the provision which will eventually be agreed by the
parties, or awarded by the court.[58] If they will not do so, then the applicant
can apply for an interim order, which may be made if it appears to the
court (a) that the applicant is in immediate need of financial assistance, but
it is not yet possible to determine what final order (if any) should be made;
and (b) that property forming part of the net estate of the deceased is or
can be made available to meet the needs of the applicant.[59] Interim relief is
not restricted to periodical payments, but may be by way of a lump sum.
However, presumably periodical payments will be more suitable than a
lump sum in most cases. So far as the urgency of the case admits, the court
must in making an interim order have regard to the guidelines prescribed
for orders generally,[60] and the court has its general powers as to the form
of orders and the burden of orders.[61] It is unlikely that applications for
interim orders will be frequent. The court will be unlikely to consider such
an application until all parties have had an opportunity of filing evidence;
by then the court will be in a position to deal with the substantive application, if necessary on an expedited hearing.[62] An interim order is most
likely to be made where, because of difficulties in administration, there is
expected to be delay in ascertaining the amount of the estate.

Representatives and beneficiaries will naturally be reluctant to agree to
interim payments unless the applicant's claim is a strong one, because the
money so paid will probably be lost for ever to the estate. On the other
hand, the possibility of such loss is implicit in the court's power to make
interim orders.[63] Perhaps the practical answer is that an applicant who is in

---

[56] ss.16, 17. These have already been mentioned: see *ante*, p. 771.

[57] *Re Franks* [1948] Ch. 62; *Re Bateman* (1941) 85 S.J. 454.

[58] Personal representatives would be unwise to make any such payment without the consent
of all the beneficiaries or an indemnity.

[59] s.5(1).

[60] s.5(3).

[61] s.5(2).

[62] Appeals from interim orders are strongly discouraged: *Re Pitkin*, C.A., January 18,
1980, C.A.T. 80/19.

[63] Note the protection for personal representatives in s.20(2). Maybe "conditions or restrictions" as mentioned in s.5(1), can give some protection to the beneficiaries.

immediate need of financial assistance will usually have a strong claim.[64] Certainly the possibility of loss to the beneficiaries as a result of a successful applicant for an interim order having received nothing on the final hearing of his or her application does not seem to have caused trouble under the 1938 Act.

The court has power under the general law to make interim orders of other kinds, if appropriate. Examples would be orders for the preservation of property in its existing state,[65] or *Mareva* injunctions.[66] However there is a county court decision to the effect that non-molestation and ouster injunction are not available as interlocutory relief under the Act.[67]

---

[64] Any interim payments ordered by the court may be treated by a final order as paid on account of the provision ordered by that final order: s.5(4).

[65] *Re Kozdrach*, C.A., November 9, 1979, C.A.T. 79/755.

[66] See as such injunctions the notes to Order 29 in the *Supreme Court Practice* (1993 ed.).

[67] *Andrew* v. *Andrew* [1990] 2 F.L.R. 366.

CHAPTER 58

PROPERTY AVAILABLE FOR PROVISION

The basic principle is that provision is ordered out of the "net estate" of the deceased. This is defined in the first instance[1] as (a) all property of which the deceased had power to dispose by his will[2] (otherwise than by virtue of a special power of appointment) less the amount of his funeral, testamentary and administration expenses, debts and liabilities, including any capital transfer tax payable out of his estate on his death. However, the definition is extended[3] to include (b) any property in respect of which the deceased held a general power of appointment (not being a power exercisable by will) which has not been exercised; (c) money or property passing by statutory nomination or *donatio mortis causa*; (d) property held on a joint tenancy; and (e) money or property made available as a result of the exercise by the court of its powers to set aside dispositions and contracts intended to defeat an application for family provision (these powers are discussed in the section on anti-avoidance provisions).[4]

Property of which the deceased had power to dispose

This alone was the net estate for the purposes of the 1938 Act and the 1965 Act. As part of their normal duties, the personal representatives of the deceased will have to ascertain what property the deceased owned, and any doubts must be resolved by finding out the relevant facts and applying the relevant principles of the general law. However, two problems of ownership can usefully be mentioned in connection with applications for family provision. First, there may be an item or items of property of which the deceased was the undoubted legal owner, but in which some other person claims rights of beneficial ownership under a trust. It should be comparatively easy to find out whether an express trust exists, but problems will arise if the alleged trust is a resulting or constructive trust,[5] created by alleged contributions made towards the purchase price or cost of repair or improvement of the item of property.[6] Secondly, there may be an item of property—for example, the home of the deceased—in respect of which a

---

[1] s.25(1) "net estate" (*a*).
[2] The fact that the property passes as *bona vacantia* on the death of the deceased intestate is irrelevant: s.24. So is the fact that the deceased lacked the capacity to make a valid will: s.25(2). For *bona vacantia* see pp. 265, 266 *ante*, and pp. 1068, 1069 *post*.
[3] s.25(1) "net estate" (*b*) to (*e*).
[4] See *post*, pp. 805–808.
[5] Sometimes called an implied or imputed trust.
[6] For such trusts see Snell, *Equity*, 29th ed., pp. 184–190.

person may assert a contractual claim, usually based upon a contract to make a will.[7]

These problems of ownership can arise when there is no application for family provision, but they are especially relevant to such applications because an applicant may make a claim by way of contract or resulting trust in addition to or in the alternative to an application for family provision. Also a beneficiary, faced with an application for family provision, may seek to reduce the net estate by making such a claim. An obvious example of the latter situation would be the mistress who asserts that she helped to pay for the house in which she lived with the deceased. Claims must be assessed on their individual merits, but those based on contract will be subject to the anti-avoidance provisions discussed below.[8]

Powers of appointment

Since a general power of appointment *inter vivos* or by will allows the donee to appoint to himself, property subject to it is property of which he could dispose by will, and as such is within the net estate of the donee. However, a general power may be restricted to exercise *inter vivos*, and the Act provides that property in respect of which the deceased held such a power, which he had not exercised, also forms part of his net estate.[9]

Special powers of appointment enable the donee to appoint property among a limited group or class of persons only. Property in respect of which the deceased had such a power does not form part of his net estate for the purposes of the Act. The deceased could never have made such property his own, therefore it was never something out of which he was under any sort of obligation to make provision of the kind with which the jurisdiction is concerned.

Statutory nominations

Some statutes and statutory instruments authorise persons who own or are entitled to certain kinds of property to dispose of it by nominations made during their lifetime but taking effect on their death.[10] The property concerned is mostly either the remuneration of public servants, or savings in public securities such as National Savings Certificates. The value of property which can be nominated in this way is restricted, usually (but not always) to a comparatively low level. The Act treats property so nominated as part of the net estate of the deceased, to the extent of its value at the

---

[7] For such contracts, see Theobald, *Wills*, 14th ed., pp. 92–95. *Wakeham* v. *Mackenzie* [1968] 1 W.L.R. 1175; *Re Gonin* [1979] Ch. 16. A claim might also be based on proprietary estoppel: Snell, pp. 573–579, and the cases there cited, especially *Jones* (*A.E.*) v. *Jones* (*F.W.*) [1977] 1 W.L.R. 438; *Grant* v. *Edwards* [1986] Ch. 638; *Re Basham* [1986] 1 W.L.R. 1498.

[8] See *post*, pp. 805–808.

[9] s.25(1) "net estate" (*b*).

[10] See *post*, p. 802.

death of the deceased, and after the deduction of any inheritance tax payable in respect of it.[11]

The Act provides that no person shall be liable for having paid the sum or transferred the property nominated to the persons named in the nomination in accordance with the directions given in the nomination.[12] This measure of protection for the holder of the nominated fund, usually some sort of public office, may on the wording of the Act apply even after an order has been made, but it need not affect the result of the court order as between beneficiaries and applicants. It is submitted that successful applicants would have an equity to trace.[13]

Other nominations made by the deceased, for example under the terms of his or her employer's pension scheme, are not covered; these nominations are discussed, *post*.[14]

Donationes mortis causa[15]

The Act treats property so given as part of the net estate of the deceased, on the same terms as to inheritance[16] and otherwise as property subject to a statutory nomination.[17]

Property held on joint tenancy

The deceased's share in property of which he was a beneficial joint tenant will accrue to the other joint tenant or tenants on his death, and will accordingly not be property of which he or she could dispose by his or her will.[18] The Law Commission felt that this could create an unsatisfactory situation in cases where a major asset of the deceased, for example his or her dwelling-house, was held jointly.[19] The Act therefore enables the court to treat the deceased's share in such property as part of his or her estate at its value immediately before his or her death.[20] For the purposes of the Act, it is made clear that there can be a joint tenancy of a chose in action,[21] for example, the asset represented by a credit balance in a joint bank account.

In contrast with the provisions relating to statutory nominations and *donationes mortis causa,* the deceased's share under a joint tenancy is not automatically treated as part of his estate for the purpose of the Act; the

[11] s.8(1).
[12] s.8(1).
[13] See *post*, p. 803.
[14] See p. 804.
[15] See *ante*, pp. 478 *et seq*.
[16] s.8(2).
[17] See s.8(3).
[18] Megarry and Wade, *The Law of Real Property*, 5th ed., 1984, pp. 417, 432; contrast property held by beneficial tenants in common.
[19] Law Comm. 61, para. 138.
[20] s.9; for some conveyancing aspects, see [1980] *Conveyancer* 60.
[21] s.9(4).

court has to make an order to that effect. Moreover, the application for provision under which the order is made must have been commenced before the expiry of the general six-month time limit for applications. The court's discretion to extend this general time limit does not allow it to dispense with this requirement in relation to property held on a joint tenancy.[22]

In determining the extent to which the deceased's beneficial share is to be treated as part of the net estate, the court is directed to have regard to any inheritance tax payable in respect of that share.[23]

If the court does make an order treating the share as part of the net estate, the share will not be treated differently from the rest of the net estate, merely because it is joint property.[24]

When the court makes an order treating the share as part of the net estate, nobody is made liable for anything done before the order was made.[25] Thus a bank can safely pay the balance in a joint bank account to the survivor of the joint holders. Moreover, the surviving joint tenant must himself, it is submitted, be able to dispose of the property without incurring any liability. In that event, the applicant would presumably have the right to trace the property or its proceeds in equity.[26]

Property available as a result of the anti-avoidance provisions in the act

The anti-avoidance provisions are considered as a whole in the section, *post*.[27] If money or property is recovered under these provisions, then by that very fact it becomes available for provision.

Property not available: insurance policies

The deceased may have insured his life for the benefit of himself or his estate, creating no trust of the proceeds of the policy. In that event the proceeds of the policy will be part of his estate when he dies, and liable to be made the subject of an order under the Act. If the deceased created a trust of the policy, for example for the benefit of his wife, the proceeds of the policy will not fall into his estate.[28] The Act leaves this situation untouched, although the payment by the deceased of the premium or premiums under a policy of either kind is capable of being a disposition

---

[22] s.9(1).

[23] s.9(2).

[24] *Re Crawford* (1983) 4 F.L.R. 273. See also *Jessop* v. *Jessop, The Times*, October 16, 1991; C.A.T. D1/1034.

[25] s.9(3).

[26] See pp. 1081 *et seq., post*. Snell, *Equity*, 29th ed., 1990, pp. 297–305. Goff and Jones, *The Law of Restitution*, 3rd. ed., pp. 63 *et. seq*. For a comment on the problems that can arise, see [1980] Conv. 60.

[27] See pp. 805 *et seq., post*.

[28] See s.11 of the Married Women's Property Act 1882.

intended to defeat an application for provision, and is therefore subject to the anti-avoidance provisions.[29]

If an applicant for provision or a beneficiary of the estate is also the beneficiary under a trust policy, then the benefit under the policy will be part of the financial resources of that applicant or beneficiary, and thereby fall to be considered by the court under the general guidelines, so as to affect the order made on an application.[30]

Property not available: non statutory nominations

The major source of provision for the family of a deceased person may be neither the property he owns, nor the benefits he has himself arranged with an independent insurance company, but the benefits payable under a pension scheme run by his employers. The benefits under a scheme may under the rules of the scheme fall automatically into the estate of the deceased employee, in which case they will be property of which he or she was competent to dispose, and as such be part of the net estate available for provision under the Act. Alternatively, they may, under the rules of the scheme, be automatically payable to another person or persons, for example a surviving spouse, in which case they will not be part of the net estate of the deceased. However, schemes commonly give the employee a power of nomination, under which the employee can name the person he wishes to take the benefit payable under the scheme. The legal nature and effect of such nominations have not been fully worked out.[31] A nomination may be binding on the trustees of the scheme, or (as is more usual) it may merely take effect as a request; this will depend upon the true interpretation of the scheme, but in either case the money which is paid under the scheme would seem to be no part of the net estate of the deceased as defined in the Act. Even if the nomination is binding on the trustees, the money payable under it is unlikely to be "property of which the deceased had power to dispose *by his will.*"[32]

As with insurance policies subject to a trust, if an applicant for provision or a beneficiary of the estate is also the beneficiary under a nomination, then the benefit must be part of the financial resources of the person concerned, which falls to be considered by the court under the general guidelines.[33]

---

[29] See the section on anti-avoidance provisions, pp. 805 *et seq., post.* The report of the Law Commission appears to assume that the act of creating a trust of a policy is not a disposition of property within s.10. See Law Comm. 61, paras. 203–206. It is not clear why it should not be, especially if the policy existed before the trust was created.

[30] See *Re Charman* [1951] 2 T.L.R. 1095, and *Re Lecoche* (1967) 111 S.J. 136; and see p. 778 *ante.*

[31] *Re Danish Bacon Co. Ltd. Staff Pension Fund Trusts* [1971] 1 W.L.R. 248; *Baird* v. *Baird* [1990] 2 A.C. 548; Samuels (1967) 31 *Conveyancer* (N.S.) 85.

[32] s.25(1) "net estate" (*a*); *Re Cairnes* (1982) 12 Fam.Law. 177.

[33] *Re Lecoche, ante.* See further *Family Provision: Law and Practice* (Ross Martyn), pp. 60–61.

Anti-avoidance provisions

One of the main criticisms, if not the main criticism, of the 1938 Act was the ease with which it could be avoided.[34]

The 1975 Act includes anti-avoidance provisions. There are two sets of them, those in section 10 relating to dispositions, and those in section 11 relating to contracts to leave property by will; sections 12 and 13 contain supplementary provisions for both. The sections do not operate in quite the same way; nor do they operate in the same manner as the anti-avoidance section (s.37) of the Matrimonial Causes Act 1973, although their objective is similar. The sections do not enable the court to set aside dispositions and contracts directly. Instead they enable it to order a person who has benefited under certain dispositions and contracts made by the deceased to help provide the resources from which claims to family provision can be satisfied. Such a person will of course have to be made a defendant in the proceedings.[35]

It should be noted that the powers which the sections give are only available when an application is made for provision, and not, for example, when an application is made to vary an existing order for periodical payments.[36]

Dispositions

The court is given power to order a donee, whether or not he still holds any interest in the property disposed of to him, to provide for the purposes of making financial provision such sum of money, or other property, as may be specified in the order. Before exercising this power, the court must be satisfied (a) that, less than six years before the death of the deceased, he made a disposition with the intention of defeating an application for financial provision under the Act; (b) that full valuable consideration[37] was not given for the disposition; and (c) that the exercise of the power would facilitate the making of financial provision for the applicant.[38] The requirement of intention is satisfied if the court is of the opinion that, on a balance of probabilities, the intention of the deceased, though not necessarily his sole intention, was to impede an order for financial provision under the Act.[39] In deciding whether and how to exercise its powers under the section, the court is directed to have regard to the circumstances in which the

---

[34] Tyler, pp. 24–28.

[35] For contracts to make a will, see n. 7 on p. 801, *ante*. The Privy Council cases of *Schaefer* v. *Schuhmann* [1972] A.C. 572 and *Dillon* v. *Public Trustee of New Zealand* [1941] A.C. 294 (disapproved in *Schaefer* v. *Schuhmann*) and *Cadogan* v. *Cadogan* [1977] 1 W.L.R. 1041 may be relevant to questions of avoidance when ss.10 and 11 of the new Act do not apply. For a discussion of the desirability of anti-avoidance provisions, see *Family Provision: Law and Practice* (Ross Martyn) at pp. 66–68.

[36] s.6(9).

[37] This does not include marriage or a promise of marriage: s.25(1).

[38] s.10(2). For cases on s.10, see *Re Dawkins* [1986] 2 F.L.R. 360; *Clifford* v. *Tanner* C.A., June 10, 1986, C.A.T. 86/616.

[39] s.12(1); *Re Kennedy* [1980] C.L.Y. 2820, County Court.

disposition was made, any valuable consideration given for the disposition, the relationship (if any) of the donee to the deceased, the conduct and financial resources of the donee, and all the other circumstances of the case.[40]

For the purposes of this section, "disposition" includes any payment of money (including an assurance premium) and any conveyance, assurance, appointment or gift of property of any description, whether made by an instrument or otherwise. However, there are expressly excluded (a) any provision in a will, any statutory nomination, and any *donatio mortis causa* and (b) any appointment of property made, otherwise than by will, in the exercise of a special power of appointment.[41] The section does not apply to any disposition made before the commencement of the Act.[42]

The donee is given a measure of protection, in two ways. First, he can operate a kind of third party procedure, whereby if the disposition to him is challenged he can himself challenge other dispositions.[43] Secondly, if he was given money, he cannot be ordered to provide more in money or the value of property than the money he received; and if he was given property, he cannot be ordered to provide more than the value of that property at the death of the deceased (or, if he had already disposed of the property by that time, its value when he disposed of it).[44]

The section appears to imply that an order can be made against a donee for the benefit of an applicant even if the disposition to that donee was made with the intention of defeating an application by some other person. Thus, if the donee is a mistress, and the disposition to her was made to defeat an application by a wife, the court could make an order against her for the benefit of the deceased's children.

Contracts

The provisions as to contracts are necessarily somewhat different, although the approach is the same. The court has to be satisfied on four points: (a) that the deceased made a contract by which he agreed to leave or transfer money or property by will; (b) that the contract was made with the intention of defeating an application for financial provision under the Act; (c) that full valuable consideration[45] was not given or promised by the donee or anyone else and (d) that the exercise of the court's powers under the section would facilitate the making of financial provision for the applicant.[46] If the court is so satisfied, it may, if money has been paid or prop-

---

[40] s.10(6); for s.10 generally, see [1978] *Conveyancer* 13.
[41] s.10(7). The release of a covenant may be a disposition: *Clifford* v. *Tanner*, *ante*.
[42] s.10(8).
[43] s.10(5). The same subsection gives similar rights to any applicant for an order under s.2 of the Act. It is not clear what this adds to the rights already conferred on such persons by s.10(1) and (2).
[44] s.10(3), (4). Allowance is made for any inheritance tax paid by the donee.
[45] This does not include marriage or a promise of marriage: s.25(1).
[46] s.11(2).

erty transferred under the contract, direct the donee to provide money or other property for the purpose of making financial provision. If and in so far as money has not been paid or property has not been transferred, the court may direct the personal representatives not to pay or transfer it.[47]

The intention of the deceased under point (b) is a matter of the balance of probabilities, but if there was no valuable consideration for the contract, the intention is presumed until the contrary is shown.[48]

As with dispositions, the powers relating to contracts are discretionary; even if the court is satisfied on the four points, it may nevertheless refuse to make an order. In deciding whether to make an order, and in deciding what kind of order to make, the court is directed, as with dispositions, to have regard to the circumstances in which the contract was made, the relationship of the donee to the deceased, the conduct and financial resources of the donee and all the circumstances of the case.[49] The donee is protected by a provision that the court shall exercise its powers only to the extent that the money or the value of the property given exceeds the value of any valuable consideration for the contract.[50]

Contracts made before the commencement of the Act are not caught.[51]

It should be noted that a contract can be the subject of an order under section 11 however long before the death of the deceased it was made; there is no time limit, as there is for dispositions. The reason for this distinction is that the deceased will generally have retained enjoyment of the money or property subject to the contract up until the time of his death.[52]

Representatives

The anti-avoidance provisions in sections 10 and 11 are available against the representatives of the donee as they are against the donee, but once the donee's property has been distributed by his representatives it is no longer subject to the provisions.[53] Moreover, representatives are not liable if they distribute any of the donee's property without notice of the making of an application under sections 10 or 11.[54]

Trustees

If the disposition or contract involves the payment of money or transfer of property to a trustee, any order made against the trustee cannot take from him more than the money, or the value of the property, that he has at

---

[47] s.11(2).
[48] s.12(1), (2).
[49] s.11(4).
[50] s.11(3).
[51] s.11(6), April 1, 1976.
[52] Law Comm. 61, para. 237.
[53] s.12(4).
[54] s.13(1). But they are allowed to anticipate the making of an application and delay the performance of a contract which may be the subject of an order under s.11: see s.20(3).

the date of the order.[55] In addition, the trustee cannot be made liable for distributing money or property on the ground that he ought to have taken into account the possibility of an application under sections 10 or 11 being made.[56]

---

[55] s.13(1). Note the terms of the subsection—property which is derived from the money and property transferred is caught.
[56] s.13(2).

CHAPTER 59

PROCEDURE

An application for an order for family provision under the Act may be made in the Chancery Division of the High Court, the Family Division of the High Court, or the county court.

Choice of division

The procedure on an application under the Act in the High Court is regulated by Order 99 of the Rules of the Supreme Court. This order allows the applicant to bring proceedings either in the Chancery Division or the Family Division, at his option. It is submitted that this dual jurisdiction is desirable, because some applications are more suitable for the Chancery Division, and some for the Family Division. The Law Commission has given[1] the following examples of those more suitable for the Chancery Division:

(a) applications in which it is necessary for a Chancery judge to decide in a probate action on the validity of the will which is alleged not to make reasonable provision for the applicant. In such cases the probate action can be heard immediately before the family provision application, and by the same judge, thus saving time and expense;

(b) applications in which a Chancery judge must first decide the true meaning of the will on a construction summons.[2] In these cases also the construction summons can be heard immediately before the family provision application and by the same judge;

(c) those in which problems arise in the administration of the estate of the deceased either as a result of or independently of the application for family provision;

(d) those in which preliminary orders are required to ascertain or safeguard the assets of the estate. In connection with the safeguarding of the assets, the speed of the interlocutory Chancery procedure on motion, which brings a matter before the judge in open court after only two clear days' notice, may be especially valuable;

(e) those in which complicated accounts have to be taken;

(f) those in which an order for family provision might have important

---

[1] See Law Comm. 61, para. 253.
[2] Other documents may have to be construed: *Re Lidington* [1940] Ch. 927.

tax implications; this particularly applies, of course, to applications against the larger estates.

To these must be added applications in which a Chancery Judge is asked to rectify a will[3] and the rectification, if granted, will affect the application for family provision.

On the other hand, some cases are more suitable for the Family Division, for example, perhaps, those in which there has already been an order under the Matrimonial Causes Act 1973 or its predecessors.[4]

High Court procedure

The procedure on an application in the High Court is the same in the Chancery Division as in the Family Division. Perhaps the most significant feature of the procedure is that masters of the Chancery Division, district judges of the Principal Registry of the Family Division, and other district judges hear applications, and make final orders for disposing of them. This is the effect of rule 8 of Order 99. No doubt masters and district judges will exercise their discretion so as to refer to a High Court judge any case which is likely to involve a difficult, long or complex issue of fact or law[5] or a question of jurisdiction, but no doubt also they can be the effective tribunal of decision in many if not most cases. This saves time and expense. There is a power to transfer applications to the county court (r. 11), but this may be seldom exercised.[6]

The application has to be made by originating summons in the expedited form (Form No. 10 in App. A to the Rules of the Supreme Court), supported by an affidavit (r. 3).[7] If an extension of time for making the application is sought under section 4, this should be expressly asked for in the originating summons, and the grounds on which it is claimed should be set out in the affidavit in support.[8] Though it is not required by any rule or practice direction, it is also desirable to ask expressly in the originating summons for any provision claimed out of property treated as part of the net estate by virtue of sections 8 and 9,[9] or any relief sought under the anti-avoidance provisions.[10] Rule 3(3) states that the affidavit should be lodged with the court, and should exhibit an official copy of the grant of representation to the deceased's estate and of every testamentary document admitted to proof. In some cases, the applicant may not have these documents, but it should be possible to obtain them from the Probate Registry. Indeed, the applicant may not have time to prepare his affidavit before the six months' time limit under section 4 of the Act has expired. In these situ-

---

[3] Under s.20 of the Administration of Justice Act 1982.
[4] See *Practice Note* [1976] 1 W.L.R. 418. Details of such proceedings should be given in the affidavit in support of the summons.
[5] See *Re Beaumont* [1980] Ch. 444.
[6] See the discussion of the county court jurisdiction, *post,* pp. 817–818.
[7] For the position if there is no grant, see p. 764. *ante.*
[8] *Practice Note* [1976] 1 W.L.R. 418.
[9] See pp. 801–803, *ante.*
[10] ss.10–13, *supra,* pp. 803, 805–808.

ations, it is suggested that the applicant should issue the summons and leave the lodging of the affidavit until it is ready. If necessary, the affidavit will have to explain why copies cannot be exhibited as required by the rule. A copy of the applicant's affidavit must be served on every defendant, with the summons (r. 3(3)).

The affidavit lodged on behalf of the applicant should contain full information about the applicant and about such of the circumstances of the case as are relevant to the statutory guidelines. In particular the affidavit should state the effect of the deceased's will (or of the intestacy rules) and the resources and needs of the applicant. This statement of resources and needs can conveniently be made as a "budget," showing income and outgoings (and also the capital possessed by the applicant, if any).[11]

Rule 5 provides that within 21 days any defendant who is a representative must, and any other defendant may, lodge an affidavit in answer. By rule 5(2), the affidavit in answer lodged by a representative must state, to the best of his ability: (a) full particulars of the value of the deceased's net estate; (b) the person or classes of persons beneficially interested in the estate, giving the names and (in the case of those who are not already parties) the addresses of all living beneficiaries, and the value of their interests so far as ascertained; (c) if such be the case, that any living beneficiary (naming him) is a minor or a patient within the meaning of Order 80, r. 1 of the Rules of the Supreme Court; and (d) any facts known to the representative which might affect the exercise of the court's powers under the Act.[12] Every defendant who lodges an affidavit must serve copies of it on the other parties (except those represented by the same solicitor as himself) (r. 5(3)).

The defendants or any of them are entitled to apply to strike out an application either under Order 18, rule 19 of the Rules of the Supreme Court, or under the inherent jurisdiction of the Court, on the ground that it discloses no reasonable cause of action; or it is scandalous, frivolous or vexatious; or is otherwise an abuse of the process of the Court. In appropriate cases, such an application may be a convenient way of deciding a preliminary question which has no connection with the merits of the application, for example a question as to domicile or parentage. However, applications to strike out are unlikely to save time or costs for defendants on the question whether an applicant under paragraph (e) was maintained by the deceased. In this connection the Court of Appeal has expressed the view that claims under the Act ought to be dealt with immediately on the merits, and time and money not spent on applications to strike out.[13]

---

[11] If necessary, the affidavit should also adduce evidence of the relationship which entitles the applicant to apply (see n. 70 on p. 768, *ante*), and the grounds of any claim under ss.8 and 9, or under the anti-avoidance provisions (ss.10–13).

[12] A personal representative who is also a beneficiary need not disclose his means: *Re Clark* [1981] C.L.Y. 2884.

[13] *Re Dymott* C.A., December 12, 1980; C.A.T. 80/942. See also *Re Beaumont* [1980] Ch. 444 and *Jelley* v. *Iliffe* [1981] Fam. 128.

Parties

Once an application has been made, further parties may have to be added. The court has its general powers as to parties under Order 15 of the Rules of the Supreme Court, and by rule 4(2) of Order 99 its power to make representation orders under Order 15, r. 13, is extended to applications under the Act. In addition, without prejudice to its general powers under Order 15, the court has power to add a person as a party or to direct that notice of the proceedings be served on him (r. 4(1)). There is also provision for the separate representation of joint applicants (r. 6), although the old practice whereby different plaintiffs were made into defendants may well be followed by the court. These procedural matters will be decided by the master or district judge at the preliminary hearings of the summons.

Because there may be argument over how the burden of any order is to be borne between existing beneficiaries,[14] it is not considered appropriate for the personal representatives to represent the beneficiaries under Order 15, r. 14. Unless there are grounds for seeking a representation order, the applicant should generally at the outset join as defendants, in addition to the personal representatives, all beneficiaries and other persons likely to be affected: this would not normally include legatees for small sums. It is likely to cause extra expense and delay if further parties have to be joined on the direction of the court, and the costs thrown away may have to be borne by the applicant. However, consideration should alternatively be given to service of a notice under Order 15, r. 13A of the Rules of the Supreme Court.

Hearsay evidence

The general rules relating to hearsay evidence apply to proceedings under the Act as they do to all other legal proceedings. Under the Civil Evidence Act 1968, oral or written statements made by a person can be admitted as evidence of any fact of which direct oral evidence by him would be admissible. There is some doubt whether this rule is apt to render statements of a deceased person admissible in proceedings which by their nature could only be brought after his death, so section 21 of the Act expressly provides that such statements by the deceased against whose estate the application is made are admissible under the Civil Evidence Act.

Compromise

Neither the Act nor Order 99 provides specifically for the compromise of applications but in all cases the possibility of compromising the application should be considered.[15] Although unjustified claims will no doubt be

---

[14] See *ante*, p. 796.

[15] For compromise generally, see *Atkin's* Court Forms, Vol. 12 *Compromise and Settlement*; Foskett, *the Law and Practice of Compromise*.

resisted by the beneficiaries and their advisers, it is difficult to say with certainty that any claim is unjustified, at least until all the evidence is lodged.[16] The saving in costs that a compromise can bring should always be borne in mind, especially when the estate is small. In negotiating a compromise, care must be taken to use tax law to the best advantage; the most obvious example is the total inheritance tax exemption given to surviving spouses, which can be used to reduce the net cost of provision for a surviving spouse, and thus facilitate a compromise.

If an application under the 1938 Act was compromised, and all the parties, being of full age and capacity, embodied the compromise in a "Tomlin Order," that order was not an order made under the Act.[17] The position is the same under the 1975 Act, at least in the Chancery Division, but all orders are now endorsed[18] and treated as orders under the Act so the distinction has lost significance. Formerly, it might have been important because there was doubt whether a consent order modified the dispositions made by the will for the purposes of inheritance tax, as an order not made by consent clearly did: see section 19(1) of the 1975 Act, and section 122 of the Finance Act 1976. However, section 146(8) of the Capital Transfer (or Inheritance) Tax Act 1984[19] now provides that, where an order is made staying or dismissing proceedings under the Act on terms set out in or scheduled to the order, section 146 has effect as if any of the terms which could have been included in an order under section 2 or section 10 of the Act were provisions of such an order.

If a charity is a beneficiary, the Attorney-General can authorise the charity to compromise an application, or the court or the Attorney-General can authorise an ex-gratia payment by the charity.[20] The Charity Commission can authorise a compromise also.[21]

Persons under disability: minors and patients[22]

An applicant or a beneficiary may be under disability as a minor or a mental patient. In accordance with the general rule, such a person will sue by his next friend and defend by his guardian *ad litem*. Next friends and guardians *ad litem* have a heavy responsibility, and if a compromise is proposed they must seriously consider whether it is for the benefit of the per-

---

[16] The affidavit procedure is of course helpful to and encourages compromise because the relevant evidence is available on oath before trial.

[17] Direction of Farwell J. dated April 23, 1942.

[18] *Practice Direction* [1979] 1 W.L.R. 1, which provides that memoranda of consent orders must nevertheless be endorsed, see *post*, p. 815.

[19] Re-enacting s.122(7A) of the Finance Act 1976, which was itself inserted in s.122 by s.92 of the Finance Act 1980.

[20] *Re Snowden* [1970] Ch. 700.

[21] Charities Act 1960, ss.23(1), (2).

[22] The Court of Protection may be involved; its function is to protect and control the administration of the property and affairs of persons who, through mental disorder, are incapable of managing their own affairs. See Heywood and Massey, *Court of Protection Practice*, 12th ed., 1991, *Hoggett: Mental Health Law*, 3rd ed., pp. 343, 345, 355 *et seq.*

sons they have to protect.[23] Their legal advisers must consider carefully whether it is, and advise them accordingly.[24]

Order 80, r. 10 of the Rules of the Supreme Court provides that, where in any proceedings money is claimed by or on behalf of a person under disability, no settlement, compromise or payment and no acceptance of money paid into Court, whenever entered into or made, shall so far as it relates to that person's claim be valid without the approval of the Court. This rule is commonly assumed to apply to applications by minors or patients under the 1975 Act. Certainly the author of this book has never known or heard of a case in which the relevance of Order 80 has been challenged, still less of one in which a Master, Registrar or Judge has declined jurisdiction to approve the compromise of an application by a minor or patient. However, it is arguable that in strictness Order 80, rule 10 does not apply, because claims under the legislation are not claims for the payment of money, but claims to be put in the position of a legatee.[25]

Apart from Order 80, r. 10, it is submitted that the Court has an inherent jurisdiction to approve a compromise of any kind on behalf of a minor or patient,[26] possibly by virtue of the *parens patriae* of the Crown. Certainly Court approval is desirable or in practice essential in the great majority of cases involving minors or patients, for the protection of other parties, and for the protection of the next friend or guardian *ad litem*, because minors and patients cannot fully bind themselves by contract. The distinction is one between a positive provision of the Rules of the Supreme Court, and the availability of an inherent jurisdiction which must usually be invoked to cure an incapacity at common law.

In the great majority of cases the distinction has no significance. However, it may have some significance in the class of case in which the estate is small, and a minor or patient is a party to, but is not playing the leading part in, the litigation. An example might be a claim by a former wife in which her children, the step-children of the deceased, are also claiming as children of the family under paragraph (*d*) of subsection 1(1). If their claim is obviously secondary to that of their mother, and a quick and simple compromise can be achieved between their mother and the beneficiaries, the compromise could include a small payment to them, and Court approval dispensed with on terms that their mother gives the executors and beneficiaries an indemnity against any future claims of theirs. If Order 80, rule 10 does not apply, an arrangement of this kind is probably less vulnerable than it would be if the rule does apply. For example, the childrens' mother cannot subsequently argue that the rule invalidates her indemnity.

When the Court approves a compromise it will require to have before it an affidavit by the next friend or guardian *ad litem*, deposing that he considers the proposed compromise to be for the benefit of his minor or patient, and

[23] *Re Whittall* [1973] 1 W.L.R. 1027.
[24] *Re Barbour's Settlement Trusts* [1974] 1 W.L.R. 1198.
[25] *Re Jennery* [1967] Ch. 280.
[26] *Chapman* v. *Chapman* [1954] A.C. 429, 445.

exhibiting his solicitor's case to counsel and counsel's opinion in favour of the proposed compromise.[27]

A court order approving a compromise affecting a minor or patient is an order under the Act; and a memorandum of the order must be endorsed on the grant of representation.

The substantive hearing

After the preliminary hearings of the summons, usually two in number, before the master or district judge, the summons will be adjourned to the substantive hearing.

This hearing will follow the normal course of the substantive hearing of an originating summons, whether it is in chambers or in court. The applicant's advocate will open his case. The affidavits will be read, and then there will be cross-examination, if orders for cross-examination have been made.[28] Independent personal representatives, if there are such, will be represented. It is their duty to take up a neutral position, and to assist the court generally. After the evidence, there will be final speeches and judgment.

If the hearing was before a master or district judge sitting in chambers, a dissatisfied party can appeal to the judge.[29] An appeal lies from the judge to the Court of Appeal in the normal way. If the initial hearing was before the judge or before a master or district judge sitting in open court under Order 36, r. 11, then an appeal lies to the court of Appeal.[30]

The Order

Order 99, r. 7 provides that the representatives must produce to the court the grant of representation to the deceased's estate, and, if an order is made under the Act, the grant must remain in the custody of the court until a memorandum of the order has been endorsed on or permanently annexed to the grant. It is now the practice, both in the Chancery Division and the Family Division, to endorse a memorandum of all consent orders, whether or not strictly speaking made under the Act.[31] Section 19(3) of the Act provides for the endorsement or annexation of the memorandum, and by section 19(1) the order has effect as from the deceased's death for all purposes, including the purposes of inheritance tax.[32]

---

[27] *Supreme Court Practice*, notes to rr. 10 and 11 of Ord. 80.

[28] There must be cross-examination if the court is to make findings on disputed questions of fact: *Re Singer* [1967] 1 W.L.R. 1482, 1485. Any necessary orders for cross-examination should be made at the preliminary hearings of the summons. See *Practice Direction* [1969] 1 W.L.R. 983.

[29] Under Ord. 58 there is an appeal to the judge in the Chancery Division, and not an adjournment to the judge. The personal representatives may not wish to appear on the appeal, in order to save costs. In that event, it is suggested that they seek the agreement of the other parties or the directions of the lower court.

[30] For the approach of the Court of Appeal, see p. 818 *post.*

[31] *Practice Direction* [1979] 1 W.L.R. 1.

[32] See also Capital Transfer (or Inheritance) Tax Act 1984, s.146.

The order is not an order for the payment of money, but puts the successful applicant in the position of a beneficiary, who can enforce the order by starting on administration action.[33] It is desirable that the provisions of the order should themselves be designed to take effect either as at death or as from 12 months after death (the end of the "executor's year"), otherwise difficulties may arise on administration for which the order makes no provision.

If, after an order has been made, there is a further application in respect of the same estate, that application has to be made by a summons in the original proceedings (r. 9).

Costs

Neither the Act nor Order 99 makes provision for the costs of an application. They are in the court's discretion. In the past, when an application under the 1938 Act or the 1965 Act succeeded, the practice was to order the costs of the parties generally on the common fund basis to be paid out of the estate.[34] Where an application failed, there was no consistent practice. Sometimes the normal rule in adverse litigation was followed, and the unsuccessful applicant had to pay the costs of the other parties,[35] sometimes no order for costs was made,[36] and sometimes, even, the applicant was awarded his costs out of the estate.[37]

There is no reason why the practice as to costs should not remain the same under the 1975 Act, and the authors have no reason to suppose that it is proving to be different.[38] Where an application is successful, the costs of all parties will usually come out of the estate, taxed if not agreed (on the indemnity basis for the executors and the standard basis for the other parties). If an application is unsuccessful the applicant will be very lucky indeed if he gets his costs out of the estate.[39] However, he may avoid having to pay the costs of the other parties if his application has some merit. The degree of merit required will depend on all the circumstances, and especially, it is submitted, upon the effect of the costs of the application on the beneficiaries. The Court will be less likely to make an unsuccessful applicant pay the defendants' costs if the burden of those costs is small in relation to the value of the estate, or possibly the means of the beneficiaries generally. However in all cases the court has a discretion under Order 62. Thus, a clearly unworthy defence by one of several residuary beneficiaries might attract an award of costs against him rather than against residue.

---

[33] *Re Jennery* [1967] Ch. 280.

[34] In the absence of misconduct, trustees and personal representatives were awarded their costs on the indemnity basis appropriate to trustees as they still are: see p. 921, *post.*

[35] *Re Joslin* [1941] Ch. 200; *Re E.* [1966] 1 W.L.R. 709, 716.

[36] *Re Pugh* [1943] Ch. 387; *Re Gregory* [1970] 1 W.L.R. 1455.

[37] *Re Inns* [1947] Ch. 576; *Re MacLagen, The Times,* March 12, 1953.

[38] For a contrary view, see Tyler (ed. Oughton) at pp. 264–266. As to trustees' and executors' costs see *Supreme Court Practice* 1993, paras. 62/14 *et seq.,* and 62/A4/20 *et seq.*

[39] *Re Fullard* [1982] Fam. 42, 46.

There is no provision for payment into court, but the discretion of the court as to costs may often be influenced by an offer of settlement made by one party. Such an offer may be especially useful when an applicant may have a strong claim to something more than he has been given by the will or under the intestacy, but not to as much as he is claiming. An offer by the beneficiaries may help them on the question of costs, if the court awards the applicant nothing, or even if it awards him no more than he was offered. To have an effect on costs, the offer must either be made as an open offer, or as an offer which is expressly stated to be made without prejudice to the issue as to the application but reserving the right to refer to it on the issue of costs.[40]

It should be noted that an award under the Act is a protected payment for legal aid purposes, so that any interim payment under section 5 of the Act and the first £2,500 of money or property passing to a successful applicant under a final order, is not subject to the statutory charge for the money expended by the Legal Aid Fund on the applicant's behalf.[41] The extent to which legal aid gives an advantage to applicants under the Act, as against beneficiaries who may be only a little more affluent, cannot be discussed here at any length, although it often has to be borne in mind by those advising beneficiaries. Small payments may have to be made to unmeritorious applicants in order to save costs, a predicament which Parliament cannot have intended. However, the Court of Appeal has emphasised the duty of practitioners to inform the Legal Aid authorities of the likely effect of costs on the estate,[42] and the solicitors acting for the representatives or for the beneficiaries are entitled to give information to those authorities with a view to persuading them to discharge, amend or revoke an applicant's Legal Aid Certificate.[43]

An order for security for costs can be obtained in appropriate circumstances, even against a party who is legally aided.[44]

The county court

The High Court and County Court Jurisdiction Order 1991 (S.I. 1991 No. 724 (L.5)), which came into force on the July 1, 1991, gives the county court unlimited jurisdiction under the 1975 Act.[45] However, the guidelines for the allocation of proceedings, contained in paragraphs 7 and 9 of the Order, point towards claims worth less than £25,000 being tried in the county court, and claims worth £50,000 or more being tried in the High Court. The figures refer to "the amount of money which the plaintiff or

---

[40] As to the latter, see *Calderbank* v. *Calderbank* [1976] Fam. 93, 106; *Cutts* v. *Head* [1984] Ch. 290; R.S.C. Ord. 22, r. 14; Ord. 62, r. 9.
[41] Legal Aid Act 1988, ss.16(6); Civil Legal Aid (General) Regulations 1989, reg. 94.
[42] *Brill* v. *Proud* [1984] Fam. Law 59; C.A.T. 83/369.
[43] Matthews and Oulton, *Legal Aid and Advice*, p. 245.
[44] *Re Nobbs*, C.A., June 9, 1980, C.A.T. 80/372.
[45] By reference to the County Courts Act 1984, s.25.

applicant could reasonably state to be the financial worth of the claim to him" (paragraph 9), and not to the size of the estate.

Because masters and district judges can hear and decide applications under 'the Act, the new unlimited jurisdiction, and the guidelines, are likely to have less importance than might appear. The important questions for the practitioner will probably be, first, what kind of judge ought to hear the case, and secondly, which forum will be quickest and cheapest? The answers to these questions are not necessarily obvious when proceedings are started. Unless the application is obviously a simple and modest one, the best policy may be to start in the High Court, but be alert to the possibility of an order for trial in the county court if time and money will thereby be saved.

Procedure in the county court is governed by Order 48 of the County Court Rules. The proceedings are begun by originating application. Order 48 is similar to Order 99 of the Rules of the Supreme Court, although the contents of the Originating Application are prescribed, and every defendant, and not just the representatives, must file an answer. The jurisdiction of each individual court has a geographical limitation.

Appeals

Appeals lie to the Court of Appeal from the High Court and the county court, but questions under the Act are eminently a matter for the discretion of the judge at first instance, especially where there has been cross-examination and oral evidence. The Court of Appeal has repeatedly deprecated appeals in family provision cases, especially where the estate is small.[46] A party who loses an appeal is therefore more at risk for the costs in the Court of Appeal than for those at first instance.[47]

---

[46] *Re Gregory* [1970] 1 W.L.R. 1455; *Re Coventry* [1980] Ch. 461; *Re Portt*, C.A., March 25, 1980; C.A.T. 80/289; *Brill* v. *Proud* [1984] Fam. Law 59. As to review of the exercise of a discretion see *Ward* v. *James* [1966] 1 Q.B. 273, 293.

[47] See for example *Milward* v. *Shenton* [1972] 1 W.L.R. 711.

Part Eight

ADMINISTRATION AND OTHER ACTIONS

CHAPTER 60

ADMINISTRATION PROCEEDINGS

Where problems or disputes[1] arise in the course of administration as between creditors,[2] beneficiaries or representatives, the court[3] will normally be approached by writ or originating summons, for the purpose of resolving the difficulties and getting the estate properly administered. Such proceedings are known as administration proceedings and are to be distinguished from litigation adverse to the estate in which the personal representatives are involved as plaintiffs or defendants representing the deceased.[4] The latter proceedings will invariably be contentious, whereas the former will often take the form of a non-contentious application for the guidance or decision of the court on matters which cannot be decided by agreement because, for instance, some of the persons concerned are under disability or are missing. A representative is always entitled to the guidance of the court in matters of difficulty and will normally be protected in costs both in obtaining such guidance and in its implementation. In such cases separate counsel may be instructed to represent the different interests in court but the family solicitor often acts and instructs all such counsel for all parties without the need for separate solicitors.[5] Since the executor or trustee is surrendering his discretion to the court, the court must be provided with all the information it needs before it can act.[6]

The procedure and its history

Procedure is governed by Order 85,[7] which defines an "administration action" as an action[8] for the administration under the direction of the court

---

[1] As to the effect of a condition in the will against disputing the will, see *post*, p. 837.

[2] Where there is a creditor's claim and the dispute turns on questions of fact pleadings are usual but the matter may be determined in administration proceedings (by summons or writ) where the issue is one of law. See *Re Powers* (1885) 30 Ch.D. 296; *Re Royle* (1889) 43 Ch.D. 18, *post*, p. 822. If facts and issues are clear an Originating Summons may be issued.

[3] *i.e.* the Chancery Division of the High Court. As to proceedings out of London see *Practice Direction* [1988] 1 W.L.R. 630. As to proceedings in the county court see *post*, p. 841. It is important to choose the correct court—see *post*, p. 841.

[4] See *post*, pp. 868 *et seq.* and *Marley* v. *Mutual Security* [1991] 3 All E.R. 198. This distinction cannot always effectively be made. The court has a statutory duty where administration proceedings are pending to make provision for tax. See Inheritance Tax Act 1984, s.232.

[5] In sanctioning a compromise the court has to act in the same way as any trustee on the balance of possibilities and apparent advantages (*Re Ezekiel* [1942] Ch. 230). See further *post*, p. 842. *Re Strafford* [1980] Ch. 28.

[6] *Marley* v. *Mutual Security* [1991] 3 All E.R. 198.

[7] See *post*, p. 1260.

[8] This term includes proceedings begun by originating summons which is a prescribed method of beginning proceedings under Ord. 5, r. 1. See the Supreme Court Act 1981, s.151 and *Re Vardon* (1885) 55 L.J.Ch. 259. The term "administration action" is sometimes used for applications under Ord. 85, r. 2, but on the wording of Ord. 85 as a whole is more properly

of the estate of a deceased person or for the execution of a trust.[9] When the relief needed is less than a general order for the administration of the whole estate such an order need not be asked for and the court can and will normally decide questions or grant the relief needed without an order for administration by virtue of rules 2 and 5 of Order 85. However there is no jurisdiction under this procedure to decide questions which could not have been decided in an administration action.[10]

When the Court of Chancery first developed its jurisdiction in the administration of estates, it proceeded by taking over the administration of the whole estate and making a general administration order.[11] In many cases neither the plaintiff nor any other party needed such an order, but merely wanted the determination by the court of a specific question which had arisen in the administration of the estate, for example a question as to the rights of a particular beneficiary; or the grant of specific relief, such as an order requiring the representatives to do a particular act. A practice therefore grew up whereby such a plaintiff started an action for general administration, raised the particular point by his pleadings, obtained a determination or order on that point and then stayed further proceedings in the action.[12] Rules of Court subsequently made express provision for the determination of specific questions and the grant of specific relief, and rule 2 of Order 85 is their successor.

Choice between writ and originating summons

Procedure by writ is designed for contentious litigation likely to involve conflict of evidence and cross-examination of witnesses. It tends to be more costly, but is essential in proceedings involving fraud or damages for breach of duty (*i.e.* in this context *devastavit* or breach of trust).[13]

Proceedings by writ are nearly always in open court, and there are usually pleadings. Proceedings by originating summons are often in chambers, without pleadings in the ordinary sense of the word, for an originating summons is itself a pleading. An originating summons may be adjourned into open court, but such an adjournment is merely a continua-

---

restricted to actions seeking general administration: see further p. 822, *post.* In this book, we have sought to use the term "administration proceedings" to cover both.

[9] Ord. 85, r. 1 (*post*, p. 1260).

[10] *Re Royle* (1890) 43 Ch.D. 18; *Re Bridge* (1887) 56 L.J.Ch. 779; *Re Gladstone* [1888] W.N. 185; *Re Carlyon* (1886) 56 L.J.Ch. 219; *Re Davies* (1888) 38 Ch.D. 210; *Re Ellis* (1888) 37 W.R. 91. Claims by creditors of the deceased may be decided in administration proceedings (Ord. 85, r. 2(c)), but other claims adverse to the estate may not. Objection to the jurisdiction will not be entertained if first raised on appeal (*Re Turcan* (1888) 58 L.J.Ch. 101).

[11] For what constitutes a general administration order, see *Re Alpha Co. Ltd., Ward* v. *Alpha & Co.* [1903] 1 Ch. 203 and S.C.P. 1991 85/3–6/5. For the form of such orders, see Chancery Master's Practice Forms, Nos. 10 and 11 and for their effect see *post*, p. 841.

[12] *Re Medland* (1889) 41 Ch.D. 476, 492.

[13] See Ord. 5, r. 2; *Re Weall* (1889) 37 W.R. 779; *Dowse* v. *Gorton* [1891] A.C. 190; *Re Dove* [1939] W.N. 230; *Re Giles* (1890) 43 Ch.D. 391. But see n. 17 below.

tion of the hearing in chambers.[14] The costs in the adjournment follow the same rule as the costs in chambers.[15]

The relief required under an originating summons will normally be listed in the form of questions or requests for declarations and it is usual to ask for full administration "if and so far as necessary." The summons must be intituled "In the matter of . . . " the estate or will trusts in question and if statutory jurisdiction is invoked a reference to the Act will appear at the foot of the summons. An originating summons is appropriate for proceedings where the principal question is of law or of the interpretation of an Act or document, or where there is unlikely to be a substantial dispute of fact,[16] or for an account.[17] The choice between the two procedures, although in theory difficult to make, is in practice not normally difficult. It is usually desirable for proceedings of a contentious nature involving disputed evidence to be begun by writ,[18] although Order 85, r. 4 now enables the court to grant relief for breach of trust, wilful default or other misconduct notwithstanding that the action was begun by originating summons. If there is doubt it may be wiser to choose an originating summons because this can, if necessary, be treated as a writ[19] and if a writ is chosen in proceedings found to be appropriate to the originating summons procedure any additional costs may be thrown upon the plaintiff. However, the costs of proceeding by writ are not invariably greater and may be less. As many orders can only be made by the judge in person[20] and most important matters are adjourned to him, both time and expense can often be saved by proceeding by writ, and the judge can, and will, upon application by motion and with the consent of the parties, make the required order at once.

The difficulty or importance of the question involved is no reason for refusing to hear it on originating summons, but in matters of special difficulty or where large amounts are involved, the court has in the past looked with indulgence on proceedings by writ.[21]

Originating summons

As has been seen, a representative is entitled to the guidance of the court in matters of dispute or difficulty. In such cases he applies as plaintiff by

[14] *Leeds* v. *Lewis* (1857) 3 Jur.(N.S.) 1290. An objection to jurisdiction should be taken in chambers on pain of costs of the adjournment into court (*Re Davies* (1888) 38 Ch.D. 210).

[15] *Dicken* v. *Hamer* (1860) 2 L.T. 276.

[16] See Ord. 5, r. 4. A writ is, however, desirable if summary judgment may be required under Ord. 14 or 86.

[17] An originating summons may be appropriate to a claim involving a question of breach of trust where the executor would be found liable simply on the common account for moneys come into his hands. See *per* Stirling J. in *Re Stuart* (1896) 74 L.T. 546; *Re Newland* [1904] W.N. 181.

[18] *Re Sir Lindsay Parkinson & Co. Ltd.* [1965] 1 W.L.R. 372. See also *ante*, p. 821, n. 2.

[19] See Ord. 85, r. 4, and Ord. 28, r. 8. In any event the personal representative will normally be allowed costs out of the estate where a bona fide mistake has occurred: *Re Jellard* [1888] W.N. 42.

[20] See Ord. 32, r. 14. As to the master's powers, see [1990] 1 W.L.R. 52.

[21] See *Bond* v. *Walford* (1886) 54 L.T. 672. As to appeals, see *post*, p. 836.

originating summons and makes the beneficiaries or creditors defendants. His affidavit evidence will place the full relevant[22] facts before the court and thereafter the argument will proceed as between the defendants.[23] Difficulties, however, can arise where an executor requires guidance as to whether he should bring or defend proceedings and one of the beneficiaries is, or is likely to be, a party to such proceedings. In such cases the practice is for the executor to exhibit to his affidavit instructions to, and the opinion of, counsel as to the merits of the proceedings in question, but this evidence is not in general made available to such a beneficiary nor is such a beneficiary entitled to be present in chambers when the matter is debated[24] although the court will adapt its practice so far as practicable to do justice in all the circumstances.[25] Difficulties can arise on an originating summons where questions are raised which are exclusively entrusted to another jurisdiction (as for instance tax). If this is the sole or main issue the summons will be struck out but it seems that if the conflict is seriously delaying the administration or distribution of the estate the court would use its inherent jurisdiction to force the issue.[26]

Interpretation or construction of wills

Where problems arise as to the testator's intention as expressed in a will the normal procedure will be by "construction summons," that is to say an originating summons asking the court to construe the will. For the general rules of construction reference should be made to the principal works on wills. However as a result of the recommendations of the Law Reform Committee[27] the Administration of Justice Act 1982 introduced provisions amending the Wills Act 1837[28] and then proceeded to allow for rectification[29] the admission of additional evidence[30] and the interpretation of

---

[22] Direct evidence of intention is not of course admissible but the affidavit should set out the surrounding circumstances (*e.g.* of "the Jewish faith" as practised by the testator's family.) See *Re Tepper* [1987] Ch. 358 at 377).

[23] Copies of affidavits should be supplied to the other parties as soon as possible (and in any event at least four clear days before the first hearing by the master) and be lodged with the Chancery Registry at least two days before hearing. Parties on whom copy affidavits have been served should be prepared to inform the master what time they need to answer. A solicitor should leave with the Registry a note of names and telephone numbers of all solicitors known to be concerned in the case. (See for details *Practice Direction* [1983] 1 W.L.R. 791. As to communications with Chancery Chambers by post or telephone, see [1983] 1 W.L.R. 791 and as to such communications with the central office of the Supreme Court, see [1976] 1 W.L.R. 489 and [1980] 3 All E.R. 822. For Directions Index see [1987] 1 W.L.R. 93; [1990] 1 W.L.R. 52.

[24] *Re Moritz* [1960] Ch. 251, distinguishing *Re Kay* [1939] Ch. 329 (where there was no dispute as to the evidence in question) and *Re Hinchliffe* [1895] 1 Ch. 117, C.A. (where the general rule is stated that a person entitled to a copy affidavit is entitled to the exhibits).

[25] *Re Eaton* [1964] 1 W.L.R. 1269. As to Ord. 85, r. 2, see *post*, p. 841.

[26] See *Argosan Finance* v. *Oxby* [1965] Ch. 390, 423; *Vandervell* v. *White* [1971] A.C. 912; *Balenvirc* [1978] 52 T.C. 406; *Beecham Group* v. *I.R.C.* [1992] *The Times*, December 1, 1992.

[27] 1973 Cmnd. 5301.

[28] See ss.17 and 18.

[29] Administration of Justice Act 1982, s.20. See p. 1203, appendix, *post*.

[30] Administration of Justice Act 1982, s.21. See p. 1204, appendix, *post*.

gifts to spouses.[31] The following paraphrases should be checked against the actual words of the Act.

Rectification

The court may now[32] rectify a will if satisfied that the will is so expressed that it fails to carry out the testator's intentions in consequence of a clerical error or of a failure to understand his instructions.[33] The application to rectify must be made within six months of the date of the grant after which period the executor is under no liability for distributing the assets without taking into account the possibility of rectification.

Admission of evidence

Extrinsic evidence of the testator's intention may now be admitted to the extent that any part of the will is meaningless or ambiguous on the face of it[34] or in so far as evidence other than evidence of intention shows that the language is ambiguous in the light of surrounding circumstances.[35]

Gifts to spouses

There is[36] a presumption that a testator who makes a gift to his spouse in terms of an absolute interest and then gives his issue an interest in the same property intends to give his spouse an absolute interest.

Counsel's opinion

Where representatives or trustees have taken the opinion of Counsel of at least 10 years' standing the court may make an order authorising them to act on the opinion as provided in the Order.[37] Application is by ex parte originating summons[38] supported by affidavit exhibiting instructions, opinion, minutes of order required and details of persons affected, relevant and admissible circumstances, Counsel's experience, value of fund and whether a dispute exists.[39]

Declaratory judgments

The court, including a county court where the matter is within its jurisdiction,[40] has power to make declaratory judgments or orders[41] but the

---

[31] Administration of Justice Act 1982, s.22. See p. 1204, appendix, *post.*
[32] For all deaths after 1982.
[33] See *ante*, n. 27.
[34] See *Re Williams* [1985] 1 W.L.R. 905.
[35] See *ante*, n. 29.
[36] See *ante*, n. 30.
[37] Administration of Justice Act 1985, s.48.
[38] R.S.C. Order 93, r. 21.
[39] *Practice Direction* [1987] 1 W.L.R. 251.
[40] See *post*, p. 841.
[41] See R.S.C. Ord. 15, r. 16, *Mellstrom* v. *Garner* [1970] 1 W.L.R. 603.

power is discretionary and is exercised with great caution.[42] In particular declarations affecting future questions will not normally be made when all the parties interested are not ascertained.[43] But the court will make declarations affecting future issues if all the parties are of age and ready to argue[44] or where matters of title are in issue between vendor and purchaser.[45]

In all other cases the court will refuse to make declarations simply because the parties have chosen to admit something. The court declares what it has found to be the law after proper argument. There are usually no declarations without argument.[46] By section 47 of the Administration of Justice Act 1985 rules of court may be made for judgments to be binding on persons who would not otherwise be bound but have been given notice. This applies only to actions relating to the estates of deceased persons or to trusts specified by such rules.[47]

Parties

All the representatives or trustees of the trust must be parties to administration proceedings and where the action is brought by executors, administrators or trustees, any of them who do not consent to being joined as plaintiffs must be made defendants.[48] All the beneficiaries, however, need not be joined[49] despite the rule which normally requires all persons entitled to relief to be joined. The plaintiff may make parties such beneficiaries as he thinks fit having regard to the nature of the relief claimed,[50] but he should ensure that there is before the court at least one party to argue each different interest. Where the Inland Revenue Commissioners are concerned with the outcome of the proceedings it is often convenient to add them as defendants, but this can only be done under rule 15 of the Rules of the Supreme Court with their consent or on[51] their application to be added. Where however questions arise on all originating summons which are not exclusively entrusted to the Commissioners the court has jurisdic-

---

[42] *Guaranty Trust Co.* v. *Hannay* [1915] 2 K.B. 536; *Mellstrom* v. *Garner* [1970] 1 W.L.R. 603.

[43] *Curtis* v. *Sheffield* (1882) 21 Ch.D. 1.

[44] *Curtis* v. *Sheffield* (1882) 21 Ch.D. 1; *Re Staples* [1916] 1 Ch. 322, 326.

[45] *Re Freme's Contract* [1895] 2 Ch. 256, 778.

[46] *Metzger* v. *D.H.S.S.* [1977] 3 A.E.R. 444, 451. But see *Patten* v. *Burke Publishing Co. Ltd.* [1991] 1 W.L.R. 541.

[47] See R.S.C. Ord. 15, r. 13A. As to the effect of a grant of probate see p. 87, *ante.*

[48] Ord. 85, r. 3(1) (*post,* p. 1261). See *Lowry* v. *Fulton* (1839) 9 Sim. 115; *Dowdeswell* v. *Dowdeswell* (1878) 9 Ch.D. 294; *Re a Debtor* [1939] Ch. 594. Ord. 15, r. 15, which allows the court to proceed in the absence of a representative, has no application to this case; see *Silver* v. *Stein* (1852) 1 Drew, 295.

[49] Ord. 85, r. 3(2). In many cases all the potential beneficiaries are not ascertained and the court will make a representation order to bind them. See *post*, pp. 833–835.

[50] *Ibid.*

[51] See R.S.C. Ord. 77, r. 8A, and *Re Vandervell* [1971] A.C. 912, P.C. The court has a duty to provide for tax. (Inheritance Tax Act 1984, s.232.)

tion to determine issues as between the parties and the Inland Revenue Commissioners.[52]

Executor as plaintiff

A plaintiff executor cannot obtain an order before he has proved the will although he may initiate proceedings before probate. However, where a temporary grant has been obtained the court has no jurisdiction at the instance of the executor until that grant has been revoked.[53] Thus the court has no jurisdiction to entertain questions arising out of a will, where the executors appointed by the will, not having obtained probate, are before the court as administrators *pendente lite*, not as executors.[54]

Where representatives seek the directions of the court it is their duty to remain impartial and to lay before the court all the facts which may assist the just determination of the issues.[55] If further facts come to their knowledge after hearing, which should have been brought to the attention of the court, they must raise these matters either in the Court of Appeal or in a further application in administration proceedings.[56]

Representative of deceased executor

Where there are two or more representatives, and one dies, it is not necessary in administration proceedings to join the representatives of the deceased representative, if it is not sought to charge his estate, or an account against it is waived,[57] but only if a claim is made against the deceased representative personally, for example, for an account on the footing of wilful default.[58]

Representatives under limited grants

A representative appointed during minority is generally a necessary party.[59] Where general administration is required, neither the administrator of a deceased executor,[60] nor an administrator *ad litem*,[61] nor, *sem-*

---

[52] *Argosam Finance* v. *Oxby* [1965] Ch. 300, 423. See also note 26 and text *ante*.

[53] Administration of Estates Act 1925, s.15 (*post*, p. 1120).

[54] *Re West* [1947] W.N. 2.

[55] *Re Burton* [1901] W.N. 202. Counsel for the plaintiff executor cannot appear also for an interested beneficiary, but he does in principle represent the interests of absent or unascertained beneficiaries.

[56] *Re Herwin* [1953] Ch. 701. As to appeals, see *post*, p. 836.

[57] *Masters* v. *Barnes, supra*; *Re Harrison* [1891] 2 Ch. 349. As to joinder, see Ord. 15, r. 6. Also *post*, p. 887.

[58] See *Holland* v. *Prior* (1834) 1 M. & K. 237; *Hall* v. *Austin* (1846) 2 Coll. 570; but see *Masters* v. *Barnes* 2 Y. & C.C.C. 616; *Re Harrison, post*; *Coppard* v. *Allen* (1864) 2 De G.J. & S. 173.

[59] See *Glass* v. *Oxenham* (1740) 2 Atk. 121.

[60] *Barber* v. *Walker* (1867) 15 W.R. 728.

[61] *Dowdeswell* v. *Dowdeswell* (1878) 9 Ch.D. 294; but see *Re Toleman* [1897] 1 Ch. 866; *Re Mastelloui* [1917] W.N. 243.

ble, an executor *de son tort*,[62] is alone sufficient to represent the estate of the deceased.

Foreign representatives

Where the executor or administrator is required to be made a party, it is not sufficient that he is such by the authority and appointment of a foreign state[63]; he must obtain his right to represent the estate from the Probate Court in this country.[64]

Beneficiary as plaintiff[65]

After administration is complete

Where an executor or administrator has so administered a fund that by reason of such dealing it has ceased to bear the character of a legacy or share of residue, and has assumed the character of a trust fund, of a status different from that when the executor or administrator held it—thus if it has been taken out of the estate of the testator, and appropriated to, or made the property of, the beneficiary—it may not be necessary that the beneficiary should bring before the court the representative of the testator in a suit to recover that part of the estate.[66]

Before administration is complete

Since an executor is supposed to remain impartial, his proper course is himself to bring before the court any problem affecting his beneficiaries. If he does not do this any one of the beneficiaries may initiate proceedings, but, of course, at such beneficiary's own risk as to costs. A plaintiff beneficiary will make the representatives defendants since they must be before the court in administration proceedings[67] though not necessarily in other forms of proceeding.[68] Where there are no representatives a beneficiary

---

[62] *Penny* v. *Watts* (1846) 2 Phil.C.C. 149, 152; *Rowsell* v. *Morris* (1873) L.R. 17 Eq. 20. And *Creasor* v. *Robinson* (1851) 14 Beav. 589 (action for account). But see *contra*, *Re Lovett* (1876) 3 Ch.D. 198; *Rayner* v. *Koehler* (1872) L.R. 14 Eq. 262; *Coote* v. *Whittington* (1873) L.R. 16 Eq. 534; *Blewitt* v. *Blewitt* (1832) Yo. 541.

[63] See also *post*, p. 888.

[64] *Tyler* v. *Bell* (1837) 2 M. & Cr. 89, 110; *Maclean* v. *Dawson* (1859) 27 Beav. 21; *Flood* v. *Patterson* (1861) 29 Beav. 295; *Re Macnichol* (1874) L.R. 19 Eq. 81. See also *Re Lovett* (1876) 3 Ch.D. 198. See p. 370 *et seq.*, *ante*, as to resealing of a foreign grant.

[65] As to the appointment of a judicial trustee in place of a recalcitrant executor see *ante*, p. 24.

[66] *Bond* v. *Graham* (1842) 1 Hare 482, 484. See also *Arthur* v. *Hughes* (1841) 4 Beav. 506; *Penny* v. *Watts* (1846) 2 Phil.C.C. 149, 153, 154. But see *Rayner* v. *Koehler* (1872) L.R. 14 Eq. 262; *Coote* v. *Whittington* (1873) L.R. 16 Eq. 534.

[67] *Penny* v. *Watts* (1846) 2 Phil.C.C. 149, 153; *Cary* v. *Hills* (1872) 15 Eq. 79; *Rowsell* v. *Morris* (1873) 17 Eq. 20.

[68] *Rayner* v. *Koehler* (1872) 14 Eq. 262; *Coote* v. *Whittington* (1873) 16 Eq. 534; *Re Lovett* (1876) 3 Ch.D. 198; *Re Chalmers* [1921] W.N. 129.

may thus be impelled himself to obtain a grant and administer.[69] He cannot join as defendant an executor who has not proved the will.[70] It will not normally be necessary to join other beneficiaries or creditors in proceedings for an account[71] (against the representation) unless there are special circumstances,[72] but in other cases beneficiaries with interests in conflict with those of the plaintiff will be added as defendants. A defendant executor should of course, so far as possible remain impartial and must be represented separately from defendant beneficiaries or others.

Creditor as plaintiff

Similar considerations apply where a creditor is plaintiff. He may proceed by originating summons if the dispute arises as a matter of law, but will normally issue a writ if facts are in dispute.[73] In this case administration proceedings will often be inappropriate and his claim should be against the representatives as representing the estate of the deceased.

A general administration order has been obtained by a creditor whose debt was incurred by the executors in carrying on the deceased's business under an authority in the will, though the testator himself had incurred no debts which remained unpaid.[74] But the proper remedy of such a creditor is to bring an action against the representative personally.[75]

In *Re Bradley*[76] the plaintiff, the widow and executrix where the husband's estate was believed to be insolvent, applied by originating summons for an order for the administration of the estate. A substantial creditor was unwilling to be either plaintiff or defendant in the proposed action, and the question was whether the action was properly constituted and could proceed. The court held that it could not insist on an action proceeding against the creditor. The plaintiff would be protected if she petitioned for the estate to be administered in bankruptcy. However the plaintiff could have asked for a declaration against the claimed creditor, rather than an administration order.

A person to whom arrears of maintenance pending suit are due under an order of the Family Division in a divorce is not a creditor of the deceased after his death and cannot maintain administration proceedings[77] nor is an annuitant under a covenant made by the deceased in his lifetime if the annuity is not in arrear.[78]

---

[69] *Re Sutcliffe* [1942] Ch. 453.
[70] *Re Leask* [1891] W.N. 159; *Re West* [1947] W.N. 2; *Re Sutcliffe* [1942] Ch. 453.
[71] *Brown* v. *Dowthwaite* (1816) 1 Madd. 446.
[72] *Hertford* v. *De Zichi* (1845) 9 Beav. 11.
[73] *Re Powers* (1885) 30 Ch.D. 291.
[74] *Re Shorey* (1898) 79 L.T. 349.
[75] *Owen* v. *Delamere* (1872) L.R. 15 Eq. 134; *Strickland* v. *Symons* (1884) 26 Ch.D. 245. And see *ante*, p. 726.
[76] [1956] Ch. 615.
[77] *Re Woolgar* [1942] Ch. 318; see *ante*, p. 561.
[78] *Re Hargreaves* (1890) 44 Ch.D. 236; see also *Re Beeman* [1896] 1 Ch. 48; *Re Pink* [1927] 1 Ch. 237, 238.

Creditor on behalf of all creditors: costs

A creditor has always been allowed to sue on behalf of himself and all other creditors.[79] Upon such an application the court directs a general account of the estate and debts to be taken, or, if assets are admitted, and the debt admitted or proved, makes an immediate order for payment.[80] But there is no actual necessity for a creditor to sue on behalf of himself and all other creditors.[81]

A creditor who sued on behalf of himself and all other creditors was entitled, where the estate proved insufficient for payment of debts, to costs on the "common fund" basis.[82] The reason for the rule is thus stated by Kindersley V.-C.: "If a creditor files a bill on behalf of himself and all the other creditors, and it turns out that the estate applicable to the payment of debts is insufficient, the estate belongs to the creditors exclusively; and therefore if a creditor has for the benefit of all the other creditors instituted a suit, in which he has recovered a fund, it is extremely unreasonable that the fund which would be divisible among the creditors *pro rata* should be applied in the payment of debts without recouping that creditor what he has properly expended in recovering the fund, and he is clearly entitled to his costs as between solicitor and client, and not as between party and party only."[83]

R.S.C. Ord. 6, r. 3 requires the writ to be endorsed (at its foot) with a statement as to the plaintiff's representative capacity.

The rule applies equally to the case of a creditor who obtains the conduct of an action originally commenced by a legatee or next-of-kin.[84]

The rule has been extended to the case of a separate creditor suing on behalf of himself and all other creditors of the testator, though all separate creditors of the testator were paid in full, the trading firm of the testator being insolvent.[85]

Documents: discovery

There is no standard procedure for discovery of documents on an originating summons. The parties simply exhibit to affidavits those documents

[79] Mitf.Pl., 5th ed., 193; and see the judgment of Upjohn J. in *Re Bradley, supra.* A creditor having *debitum in praesenti solvendum in futuro* may maintain such a suit: *Whitmore* v. *Oxborrow* (1842) 2 Y. & C.C.C. 13. And so may a creditor under a voluntary covenant; *Watson* v. *Parker* (1843) 6 Beav. 283, n. (*n*).

[80] *Woodgate* v. *Field* (1842) 2 Hare 211.

[81] *Re Greaves* (1881) 18 Ch.D. at p. 554; *Re Blount* (1879) 27 W.R. 865; *Re James* [1911] 2 Ch. 348.

[82] This was the equivalent of the former "solicitor and client" basis. See R.S.C. Ord. 62, r. 28, and *Re Richardson* (1880) 14 Ch.D. 611; *Re Roby* [1916] W.N. 37. See also as to costs of a creditor, *post*, p. 839. On this reasoning such a creditor would now be entitled to costs on an indemnity basis. As to the present bases for taxation of costs see pp. 921–922, *post.*

[83] *Thomas* v. *Jones* (1860) 1 Dr. & Sm. 134, 136; approved by Kay J. in *Re McRea* (1886) 32 Ch.D. 613, 615.

[84] *Re Richardson, ante.*

[85] *Re McRea, ante.*

they consider to be relevant, but discovery may be specifically ordered.[86] A grant of representation proves itself and may be accepted as proof of death for procedural purposes[87] (but not for title).

Defence of Statute of Frauds

Although there are not strictly any pleadings in an originating summons, notice should be given of an intention to invoke the Statute of Frauds or the Limitation Acts. This can be done in the affidavit or by open letter to the other parties.[88]

Cross-examination as between co-defendants

Where there is an issue between the co-defendants[89] there is a right to cross-examine,[90] but this will not be allowed if it amounts to a right for counsel to cross-examine his own client. On the other hand it has been said that it is contrary to natural justice that the evidence of one party should be received as evidence against another party, without the latter having an opportunity to test by cross-examination the truthfulness of that evidence.[91]

The General Administration Order

As has been seen[92] the court may on originating summons or in an action by writ decide questions or grant relief without making a general order for administration. However, no order short of a general administration order will prevent a creditor from suing for a debt[93] or an executor from preferring a creditor.[94] The need for a general administration order will therefore depend upon the circumstances of each case.[95]

One ground on which the court directs a general administration is that without it the personal representative cannot be adequately protected. For instance, where a testator had up to his death been engaged in the business of a merchant, shipbroker, insurance broker, and farmer, and was also the managing owner of six steamers, the proprietor of a colliery, and a partner in two other collieries, and he was also the sole defendant in a partnership action relating to one of the collieries, in which heavy claims were made against him by the partners, questions arose whether any and which of his

---

[86] See R.S.C. Ord. 24, rr. 3, 6(3). As to trustees' or executors' documents, see p. 854, *post.*
[87] *Practice Direction* [1970] 1 W.L.R. 520.
[88] *Re Shearman* (1886) 2 T.L.R. 236.
[89] *Re Wagstaff* (1907) 96, L.T. 605.
[90] *Lord* v. *Colvin* (1855) 3 Dr. 222; *Re Baden* [1967] 1 W.L.R. 1457, 1462. (Affirmed on appeal but not on this point [1969] Ch. 388.)
[91] *Allen* v. *Allen and Bell* [1894] P. 248.
[92] *Ante*, p. 823.
[93] *Re Mills* [1884] W.N. 21. Conduct of an order for sale is normally given to the personal representatives. See Ord. 85, r. 6 (*post*, p. 1262).
[94] *Re Barrett* (1890) 43 Ch.D. 70. As to the abolition of preference by right, see p. 640, *ante.*
[95] See *Re Wilson* (1885) 28 Ch.D. 457; *Re Gyhon* (1885) 29 Ch.D. 834.

businesses ought to be carried on, and what ought to be done by his executors as to the defence of the pending action, and how and when his property ought to be realised. On these facts, Chitty J. directed a general administration, and in addition directed special inquiries with regard to the testator's businesses and shares in ships.[96]

The fact that the testator has by his will directed his trustees to commence an action for administration does not deprive the court of its discretion to refuse to make an order for general administration. The court used to give weight to such a direction in considering whether the order should, or should not, be made[97]; the smallness of the assets was a material circumstance to decide the court against making such an order.[98]

It was not uncommon for testators to make such directions in the nineteenth century in order to protect the estate from incompetent or dishonest trustees, but the practice is now obsolete.

A master may make an order for general administration whether the estate is solvent or not.

Order for administration with proviso

Where a representative either has proceedings commenced against him in respect of debts due from the deceased, or is threatened with such proceedings, it may sometimes be important that an order for general administration of the estate should be obtained, so as to protect it for the general body of creditors, or to give time to realise it properly. Where such a course is necessary there is power for the court or a judge (including a county court judge where the administration proceedings are instituted in the county court[99]) to make the usual judgment or order for administration, with a proviso that no proceedings are to be taken under such judgment or order, or under any particular account or inquiry directed, without leave of the judge in person.

There is express power[1] to make such an order where the application for administration is by a creditor or a beneficiary, and where no accounts or insufficient accounts have been rendered. The court has an inherent power to make such an order where the application is by a representative.[2]

Order for stay until accounts delivered

In the same way, upon an application for administration or execution of trusts by a creditor or a beneficiary where the plaintiff alleges that no or insufficient accounts have been furnished the court[3] may order that proceedings be stayed for a period specified in the order and that the execu-

---

[96] *Re Dickinson* [1884] W.N. 199.
[97] *Re Stocken* (1888) 38 Ch.D. 319.
[98] *Re Jennings* (1884) 28 S.J. 477.
[99] County Courts Act 1984, s.23; C.C.R., Order 23.
[1] Ord. 85, r. 5(2)(*b*); C.C.R., Ord. 29, r. 20.
[2] See the order in *Re Johnson* [1940] W.N. 195.
[3] Including the county court where there is jurisdiction (C.C.R., Ord. 23).

tors, administrators or trustees, as the case may be shall within that period furnish the plaintiff with proper accounts.[4] The normal effect of this order will be that if accounts are not furnished in time the executor will be penalised in costs. If and when they are furnished the other parties then have an opportunity to examine them, and, if they are dissatisfied, to continue with the action.

Absent persons not bound by order

It has been the practice of the court in administration proceedings to entertain actions by creditors, legatees and parties entitled in distribution, on behalf of themselves and all others, and to exonerate the representative for payment of assets pursuant to its order. However, such an order is not absolutely binding upon the absent beneficiaries or creditors who have had no opportunity of proving and presenting their claims,[5] and have been guilty of no laches,[6] unless either a representation order has been made under Order 15, r. 12 or 13, or the absent beneficiaries have been served with notice of the administration order pursuant to Order 44, r. 2; or they have failed to respond to a notice served under Order 15, r. 13A; or the court has ordered pursuant to Order 44, r. 2(2), that they should be bound by the administration order to the same extent as if they had been served with such notice. Such creditors have no remedy against the personal representative, but, unless one of these courses has been taken, they would have a right to assert the claim against the beneficiaries or creditors who have received assets or payment.[7]

Effect of order made on originating summons

If an order is made on an originating summons asking for construction of a document and consequent questions, but not asking for general administration, the summons will not be kept alive unless the order so provides. If, therefore, further questions arise, a fresh summons will be required.[8]

Binding absent parties

It is important to understand how the interests of persons affected by an account or inquiry directed in administration proceedings may be bound when they are not actually parties to the action.

There seem to be six ways in which such interests will be bound:

1. The court may, under Order 44, r. 2, direct that such persons shall be served with notice of the judgment or order.

After such notice the persons served are bound by the proceedings, in

[4] Ord. 85, r. 5(2)(a) (post, p. 1262).
[5] David v. Frowd (1833) 1 My. & K. 200. See Anon. (1821) 9 Price 210.
[6] Sawyer v. Birchmore (1837) 1 Keen 391; ibid. (1837) 2 M. & Cr. 611. See also Cattell v. Simons (1843) 8 Beav. 243.
[7] Story on Equity Plead, Chap. iv, s.106. As to tracing and following, see p. 1081.
[8] Re Pattman [1965] 1 W.L.R. 728.

the same manner as if they had originally been parties, and are at liberty to attend the proceedings[9] after acknowledging service. Any person so served may, within one month after such service and without acknowledging service, apply to the court or a judge to discharge, vary or add to the judgment or order.[10]

2. The court may, under Order 44, r. 2(2), dispense with service of such notice and direct that a person, with regard to whom service has been dispensed, shall be bound by the judgment to the same extent as if he had been served with notice thereof, and he will then be bound accordingly, except where the judgment has been obtained by fraud or non-disclosure of material facts.

3. Where there are numerous parties having the same interest one or more of such persons may sue or be sued, or may be authorised by the court or a judge to defend in such cause or matter, on behalf or for the benefit, of all persons so interested under Order 15, rule 12.[11] If an order made in such an action is intended to bind absent parties the court will make a "representation order" in the form "it appearing that the residuary legatees (or whatever the class may be) are numerous, and that A is one of such class, order that A do defend in the cause (or matter) on behalf and for the benefit of all persons so interested."[12]

4. The court has power, under Order 15, r. 13, in any proceedings concerning the administration of the estate of a deceased person, or property subject to a trust, or the construction of a written instrument, to appoint one or more persons to represent any person or any class of persons (including an unborn person), who is interested, or may be interested, in the proceedings. Such a representative may be appointed where the person interested in the proceedings cannot be ascertained, or readily ascertained, or, although ascertained, cannot be found. A representative may also be appointed where although the person or the class and the members thereof can be ascertained and found, it appears to the court expedient (regard being had to all the circumstances, including the amount at stake and the degree of difficulty of the point to be determined) to exercise the power for the purpose of saving expense. The judgment or order of the court in the presence of the persons so appointed is binding on the persons represented. The relief granted in such a representative action will normally be declaratory relief.[13]

Costs on the indemnity basis may be awarded though the parties are not actually before the court, but only by reason of a representation order.[14]

5. Executors may sue and be sued as representing the estate of the

---

[9] Ord. 44, r. 2(5).

[10] Ord. 44, r. 2(4).

[11] For the power of the court to approve a compromise and order it to be binding on absent parties whose interest is represented before the court, see Ord. 15, r. 13(4) and *Re Tame* [1956] 2 All E.R. 293; *Re Archibald* [1974] C.L.Y. 1592.

[12] See *May* v. *Newton* (1887) 34 Ch.D. 347.

[13] See *Prudential Assurance* v. *Newman* [1981] Ch. 229, 254.

[14] *Re Davies* [1891] W.N. 104.

deceased, without joining any of the persons beneficially interested therein; but the court may, at any stage of the proceedings, order any of such persons to be made parties, either in addition to or in lieu of the previously existing parties.[15]

Where, however, the representatives are the accounting parties, and the question is one of accounts, it would not be a proper case for them to represent the interests of the absent beneficiaries.[16]

There is now provision (designed to remedy to some extent the reluctance of the courts to make declaratory judgments under R.S.C. Ord. 15, r. 16[17]) rules of court to make judgments binding on persons who are or may be affected.[18] These provisions are limited to actions in the High Court relating to trusts for the estates of deceased persons, and appear to enable orders made on admissions or by consent to be made binding on non-parties.

Plaintiff is dominus litis

Until an order for administration has been made the plaintiff is *dominus litis*, so that he may deal with the action as he pleases. He may settle the matter with the executor, by the latter paying the debt and costs of the action, and compromise the action and relinquish proceedings.[19] Indeed, the court will compel the creditor to accept payment of his debt if the executor offers to pay it with the costs of the action.[20]

All creditors may come in under order

On the other hand, after the usual judgment or order for general administration has been obtained every creditor has an interest in the action,[21] and is in a sense, deemed to be before the court.[22] The practice is to allow all creditors to come in under the order, whose debts have become due before the date of the master's certificate.[23] And it seems that where an account of debts has been ordered to be taken all persons having demands upon the estate, whether certain or contingent, should send in claims.[24]

Where, however, after an order for general administration has been

[15] Ord. 15, r. 14. As to estoppel by record, see *Pople* v. *Evans* [1969] 2 Ch. 255.

[16] See *May* v. *Newton* (1887) 34 Ch.D. 347, 349.

[17] See *e.g. ET 24 ER* v. *D.H.S.S.* [1978] 1 W.L.R. 1046.

[18] Administration of Justice Act 1985, s.47. R.S.C., Order 15, r.13A. In practice the assessment of who is or may be affected remains a question of degree and of the actual risks involved.

[19] *Woodgate* v. *Field* (1842) 2 Hare 211, 213; *Wood* v. *Westall* (1831) Younge 305.

[20] *Woodgate* v. *Field, ante; Pemberton* v. *Topham* (1838) 1 Beav. 316; *Holden* v. *Kynaston* (1840) 2 Beav. 204.

[21] *Sterndale* v. *Hankinson* (1827) 1 Sim. 393, 399, 400; *Cook* v. *Bolton* (1828) 5 Russ. 282; *Brown* v. *Lake* (1846) 2 Coll. 620; *Smith* v. *Guy* (1846) 2 Phil.C.C. 159; *Harpur* v. *Buchanan* [1919] 1 Ir.R. 1. But see *Re Greaves* (1881) 18 Ch.D. 551.

[22] This may be important to prevent the limitation period from running as against such creditors.

[23] *Thomas* v. *Griffith* (1860) 2 De G.F. & J. 555, 564. Now order R.S.C. Ord. 44, r. 11.

[24] Dan.Ch.Pr., 8th ed., 897.

made and upon valuing the accounts the estate is found to be insolvent, the beneficiaries are no longer interested in the estate which, under the altered circumstances, belongs to the creditors. The proceedings must be reconstituted and must be carried on by the creditors as plaintiffs, the executors becoming defendants along with the beneficiaries. The beneficiaries are entitled to remain before the court so that the question of their costs may be determined. New accounts and inquiries must be substituted for those directed by the original order.[25]

Claims by non-parties

In administration proceedings *no party* other than the executor may, except by leave of the court, appear either in court or in chambers on the claim of any person not a party to the action. The court may, however, direct or give liberty to any other party to the action to appear, either in addition to or in place of the executor, upon such terms as to costs or otherwise as it thinks fit.[26]

Appeals

Where an executor is merely seeking the guidance or protection of the court he will be protected by the court order and it is not for him to appeal.[27] A beneficiary may of course appeal and so may an executor beneficiary in his character of beneficiary[28] and of course very different considerations apply where a beneficiary is impeaching the validity of an executor's actions. Difficulties may also arise on appeal as to the right to be heard and as to costs.[29] The general principle is that a respondent is not entitled to support an appellant on appeal.[30] However the modern practice in the Court of Appeal seems to be to hear all parties and allow all costs out of the estate[31] and in view of doubts as to whether a party who does not appeal or appear can take advantage of an order on appeal, the tendency is for all parties to participate.[32]

Appeal can in some cases be direct from the High Court to the House of Lords.[33]

---

[25] *Re Van Oppen* [1935] W.N. 51; see the form of the order in that case. As to insolvent estates, see *ante*, p. 623. See also C.M. Practice Form 22.

[26] Ord. 44, r. 13. See *Re Schwebacher* [1907] 1 Ch. 719. The court has a duty to provide for tax (Inheritance Tax Act 1984, s.231).

[27] *Re Londonderry* [1965] Ch. 918. See also *post*, p. 928.

[28] *Ibid.*

[29] See *post*, p. 928.

[30] *Re Marquis of Allesbury* [1892] 1 Ch. 506, 526; *Re Mellor* [1922] 1 Ch. 312, 321. Daniell's Chancery Practice, 8th ed., p. 1140; 30 *Halsbury's Laws* 3rd ed., p. 466.

[31] See *e.g. Re Petrie* [1962] Ch. 355; *Re Neeld* [1962] Ch. 643; *Re Jebb* [1966] Ch. 666; *Re Allsop* [1968] Ch. 39. *Re Stuart* [1940] 4 All E.R. 80, C.A. See also p. 928, *post*.

[32] See *Elliott* v. *Joicey* [1935] A.C. 209, 235, *per* Lord Russell of Killowen, and *cf. Perrin* v. *Morgan* [1943] A.C. 399, 424, *per* Lord Thankerton.

[33] See *Practice Direction* [1970] 1 W.L.R. 97.

Condition not to dispute the will

A condition that the legatee should not dispute the will is valid at law,[34] unless it is so worded as to prohibit the legatee from taking any legal proceedings necessary for the protection of his rights.[35] Such conditions are considered, however, as merely *in terrorem*, and no forfeiture will be incurred by reason of the legatee's having disputed the validity[36] or effect[37] of the will, unless there is a gift over to another legatee should there be a breach of the condition.[38] A condition purporting to make the determination of the will trustees conclusive and binding on all persons interested under the will has been held void as repugnant, and contrary to public policy.[39]

Similarly a condition in the will attempting to impose the costs of proceedings upon a beneficiary who initiates such proceedings would normally be disregarded, for the court's discretion cannot rightly be supplanted. Thus a condition that if administration proceedings should be commenced by any beneficiary as plaintiff the costs of all parties should be paid out of the plaintiff's share, does not apply to an action based on wilful default, and if applicable would be void for repugnancy.[40]

Stay of other proceedings when order made

Where administration proceedings have already been commenced there is nothing to prevent other creditors or beneficiaries from instituting further administration proceedings; and as it is possible that, before the order, the litigating creditor may stop his action, the court permits the actions to go on together until an order in one of them is obtained.[41] But when the usual order for general administration has been obtained in one of such actions, if another action is instituted praying no further relief than might be had in the former action, the parties to such former action ought to apply to have the proceedings in the latter action transferred if necessary to the Master[42] before whom the proceedings under the order are pending, and thereafter to have the second action stayed; otherwise the costs of it may be dealt with as costs in their action.[43]

On the application to stay the proceedings, the question is, whether the

---

[34] *Cooke* v. *Turner* (1846) 14 Sim. 493.

[35] *Rhodes* v. *Muswell Hill Land Co.* (1861) 29 Beav. 560; *Re Williams* [1912] 1 Ch. 399.

[36] *Powell* v. *Morgan* (1688) 2 Vern. 90; *Loyd* v. *Spillet* (1734) 3 P.Wms. 344.

[37] *Morris* v. *Burroughs* (1737) 1 Atk. 399, 404.

[38] *Cleaver* v. *Spurling* (1729) 2 P.Wms. 528; *Cooke* v. *Turner, ante.*

[39] *Re Raven* [1915] 1 Ch. 673; *Re Wynn* [1952] Ch. 271. *cf. Dundee General Hospitals Board* v. *Walker* [1912] 1 All E.R. 896.

[40] *Re Williams* [1912] 1 Ch. 399. See *post,* p. 915.

[41] *Woodgate* v. *Field* (1842) 2 Hare 211, 214. As to staying proceedings in the other suits, see *Hawkes* v. *Barrett* (1820) 5 Madd. 17; *Turner* v. *Dorgan* (1842) 12 Sim. 504; *Reid* v. *Territt* (1844) 1 Coll. 1; *Dryden* v. *Foster* (1843) 6 Beav. 146; *Frowd* v. *Baker* (1841) 4 Beav. 76; *Portarlington* v. *Damer* (1847) 2 Phil.C.C. 262; *Duffort* v. *Arrowsmith* (1857) 7 De G.M. & G. 434; *Harris* v. *Gandy* (1859) 1 De G.F. & J. 13.

[42] See Ord. 4, r. 1.

[43] *Therrey* v. *Henderson* (1842) 1 Y. & C.C.C. 481.

action which is sought to be stayed asks something more than could be obtained under the existing order,[44] as where more complete and beneficial relief is sought or can be obtained in the second proceedings,[45] or further questions are raised, such as wilful default or breaches of trust.[46] Even where the second proceedings go further than the first, proceedings in the second proceedings have been stayed on the executor undertaking not to object to any additions to the order in the first proceedings which the court may think fit to add.[47]

Later proceedings stayed

The ordinary practice is to allow the proceedings in which an order has first been obtained to proceed and to stay the other proceedings.[48]

But if the order first obtained has been "snapped," or unfairly obtained,[49] or if the second proceedings in which the order is first obtained have been improperly instituted,[50] the court will either not stay the other proceedings or will give the conduct of the proceedings in which the order has been made, to the plaintiff in the other proceedings.[51]

Where first proceedings stayed

Where the first proceedings are stayed because an order has been made in later proceedings, the conduct of the second proceedings will usually be given to the plaintiff in the first proceedings.[52] The court will, however, depart from this rule where there are special circumstances; for instance, where the court comes to the conclusion that the object of the plaintiff in the first proceedings is not the bona fide administration of the estate,[53] or where he is a creditor whose claim is bona fide disputed.[54]

In some cases the first proceedings will be partially stayed, and liberty given to the plaintiff in the first proceedings to prove in the second proceedings for what he may eventually establish in the first.[55]

---

[44] *Rigby* v. *Strangways* (1846) 2 Phil.C.C. 175; *Rump* v. *Greenhill* (1854) 20 Beav. 519; *Plunkett* v. *Lewis* (1840) 11 Sim. 379. See also *Suisse* v. *Lowther* (1843) 2 Hare 424; *Gwyer* v. *Peterson* (1858) 26 Beav. 83; *Hoskins* v. *Campbell* (1864) 2 H. & M. 42; *Belcher* v. *Belcher* (1865) 2 Dr. & Sm. 444.

[45] *Re McRae* (1883) 25 Ch.D. 16; *Budgen* v. *Sage* (1838) 3 M. & Cr. 683; *Taylor* v. *Southgate* (1839) 4 M. & Cr. 203; *Underwood* v. *Jee* (1849) 1 M. & G. 276; *Pickford* v. *Hunter* (1831) 5 Sim. 122.

[46] *Zambaco* v. *Cassavetti* (1871) L.R. 11 Eq. 439.

[47] *Gwyer* v. *Peterson* (1858) 26 Beav. 83; *Matthews* v. *Palmer* (1863) 11 W.R. 610; *Van Bunan* v. *Piffard* (1865) 13 W.R. 425.

[48] Dan.Ch.Pr., 8th ed., 1645.

[49] *Harris* v. *Gandy* (1859) 1 De G.F. & J. 13.

[50] *Frost* v. *Ward* (1864) 2 De G.J. & S. 70.

[51] *Rhodes* v. *Barret* (1871) L.R. 12 Eq. 479. R.S.C. Ord. 15, r. 17.

[52] *Zambaco* v. *Cassavetti* (1871) L.R. 11 Eq. 439; *Kenyon* v. *Kenyon* (1866) 35 Beav. 300; *Belcher* v. *Belcher* (1865) 2 Dr. & Sm. 444; *Frost* v. *Ward, supra.*

[53] *Re Swire* (1882) 21 Ch.D. 647.

[54] *Re Ross* [1907] 1 Ch. 482.

[55] *Dryden* v. *Foster* (1843) 6 Beav. 146; *Re Smith's Estate* (1876) 33 L.T. 804; *Crowie* v. *Russell* (1878) 4 C.P.D. 186.

Right of creditor to costs

The old practice was that a plaintiff at law was entitled, unless his claim proved unfounded,[56] upon the injunction to stay being granted for general administration, to his costs of the action up to the time when he had notice of the decree.[57] And if the creditor commenced his action at law before bill for the decree filed, and then discontinued it, and came in under the decree, he would be entitled to prove his costs at law, in addition to his debt.[58] He was also entitled to the costs of the motion to injunct him from suing at law.[59] But he was not allowed the costs of further proceedings at law after actual notice of the decree[60] nor in such case his costs of the motion to injunct his proceedings.[61] If, however, the executor took any steps in the action after the plaintiff at law had notice of the decree, the latter would be allowed all his costs at law and also those of the motion for the injunction.[62] The practice with regard to the costs of a creditor whose proceedings are transferred would seem to be substantially the same as before the Judicature Acts.[63] It was observed by Lord Lyndhurst[64] that any delay in the application before judgment would, in most cases, properly resolve itself into a mere question of costs.

Execution by creditor after general administration order

It has just been shown that the practice of restraining proceedings by injunction has given way to that of transferring the action to the judge making the general administration order. Where, however, a creditor has obtained judgment *de bonis testatoris* against a representative,[65] and subsequently an order for general administration is made, so that the assets are taken from the representative and administered by the court, it seems that the court may restrain the creditor from proceeding further upon the

---

[56] *King* v. *King* (1864) 34 Beav. 10.

[57] *Dyer* v. *Kearsley* (1816) 2 Meriv. 483, note to *Terrewest* v. *Featherby*; *Paxton* v. *Douglas* (1803) 8 Ves. 520; *Ratcliffe* v. *Winch* (1853) 16 Beav. 576. In *Drewry* v. *Thacker* (1819) 3 Sw. 529, 541, Lord Eldon said that the usual form in which the order for the injunction was drawn (*i.e.* "on payment of costs") was improper, inasmuch as the parties entitled to the injunction, if they were required to pay costs as a preliminary, might from the situation of the assets, be unable to obtain it in time. See also as to a creditor's costs *ante*, p. 830.

[58] *Goate* v. *Fryer* (1789) 3 Bro.C.C. 23.

[59] *Jones* v. *Jones* (1835) 5 Sim. 678. But see *Anon.* (1825) 2 Sim. & Stu. 424.

[60] *Paxton* v. *Douglas* (1803) 8 Ves. 521; *Curre* v. *Bowyer* (1818) 3 Madd. 456; *Jones* v. *Brain* (1843) 2 Y. & C.C.C. 170.

[61] *Curre* v. *Bowyer*, *supra*; *Jones* v. *Brain*, *supra*. See *Hayward* v. *Constable* (1836) 2 Y. & C.Ex. 43; *Moore* v. *Prior*, *bid.* 375. He might be ordered to pay these costs if, after bringing in his claim under the decree, he proceeded with his own suit: *Beauchamp* v. *Huntley* (1822) Jacob 546; *Gardner* v. *Barrett* (1855) 20 Beav. 469; notwithstanding the suit was in a foreign court; *Graham* v. *Maxwell* (1849) 1 M. & G. 71. He might set off such costs against his costs incurred before notice of the decree: *Gardner* v. *Garrett*, *supra*.

[62] *Turner* v. *Connor* (1847) 15 Sim. 630.

[63] Dan.Ch.Pr., 8th ed., 1645.

[64] *Rouse* v. *Jones* (1844) 1 Phil.C.C. 462, 464.

[65] As to forms of judgment against personal representatives, see *post*, p. 908.

verdict or judgment obtained by him.[66] But it will not restrain proceedings where the creditor has obtained a judgment by which the representative is liable *de bonis propriis*.[67]

The court will not restrain an action merely because the representative has been restrained by injunction from disposing of the deceased's estate.[68]

Injunction against persons proceeding in a foreign court

The Chancery Division has power to restrain proceedings in a foreign court against a representative by persons within the jurisdiction,[69] by the exercise of its jurisdiction *in personam* against such persons. It will do so where proceedings are improperly or vexatiously instituted or prosecuted in the foreign court to determine questions which ought to be adjudicated upon in this country.[70] This jurisdiction can be exercised whether or not an administration order has been made.[71] But proceedings in a foreign court will not be restrained on the ground of mere hardship or inconvenience.

Transfer to Bankruptcy Court

Where proceedings have been commenced in any court for the administration of the estate of a deceased debtor, such court may, on proof that the estate is insolvent, transfer the proceedings to the Court of Bankruptcy.[72]

Semble, a creditor must have proved his debt before applying for the transfer of an insolvent estate into bankruptcy.[73]

The transfer will be ordered even after an order for general administration has been made,[74] unless there are difficult questions of law to be determined or the proceedings are far advanced.[75]

The exercise of this power of transfer is discretionary.[76] In one case, the

---

[66] *Brook* v. *Skinner* (1816) 2 Meriv. 48in.; *Clarke* v. *Ormonde* (1821) 1 Jacob 108; *Drewry* v. *Thacker* (1819) 3 Sw. 529, 542, 543, 547, 548; and see *Terrewest* v. *Featherby* (1817) 2 Meriv. 480; *Gaunt* v. *Taylor* (1843) 2 Hare 413.

[67] See *Etheridge* v. *Womersley* (1885) 29 Ch.D. 557, and cases cited in last note. As to forms of judgment against personal representatives see *post*, p. 908.

[68] See *Davis* v. *Salter* (1832) 2 Cr. & J. 466.

[69] The court has no such jurisdiction if the persons sought to be restrained are not within the jurisdiction: *Re Boyse* (1880) 15 Ch.D. 591.

[70] *Bushby* v. *Munday* (1821) 5 Madd. 297; *Baillie* v. *Baillie* (1867) L.R. 5 Eq. 175; *Bunbury* v. *Bunbury* (1839) 1 Beav. 318, 336; *Cood* v. *Cood* (1863) 33 Beav. 314.

[71] The general jurisdiction to stay proceedings with a foreign element is outside the scope of this work. Reference should be made to the *Supreme Court Practice 1991*, especially at para. 11/1/7, and Dicey and Morris, *The Conflict of Laws*, 11th ed., 1987, pp. 389 *et seq*, and 4th Supplement.

[72] Bankruptcy Act 1914, s.130(3), repealed by the Administration of Estates Act 1925, Sched. 2, Pt. I, but restored by the Expiring Laws Act 1925. See now Insolvency Act 1986, ss.272, 421 and S.I. 1986 No. 1999, Sched. I, Pt. II para. 5(3).

[73] *Re Weaver* (1885) 29 Ch.D. 236.

[74] *Re York* (1887) 36 Ch.D. 233; *Senhouse* v. *Mawson* (1885) 52 L.T. 745; *Re Briggs* (1891) 7 T.L.R. 572.

[75] *Re Kenward* (1906) 94 L.T. 277. The matter is one of convenience but on balance the bankruptcy jurisdiction will be chosen.

[76] *Re Baker* (1890) 44 Ch.D. 262; *Re Weaver, ante*.

mere fact that the executor had a right of retainer and a liberty not to plead the Limitation Act to a debt, which rights would have been recognised in the Chancery Division but might have been taken away by a transfer to the Bankruptcy Court, was held to be no ground for the transfer.[77]

Administration in county court

The whole question of the allocation of proceedings between the High Court and the county courts has been altered radically by the Courts and Legal Services Act 1990. The "value of the claim" is no longer the determinative factor. The nature of the proceedings, the parties to the proceedings, the degree of complexity likely to be involved and the importance of any question likely to be raised are additional factors to be taken into account when orders are made by the Lord Chancellor under the Act. The question of transfer to and from the county court is now governed by section 2 of the Courts and Legal Services Act 1990 and any order made thereunder. Before commencing proceedings, therefore, reference should be made to the rules as claims wrongly made may be struck out or penalised in costs. Up to date information can usually be found in the current County Court Practice or the current Supreme Court Practice.

Effect of administration proceedings

The issue of a summons under Order 85, r. 2,[78] does not interfere with or control any power or discretion vested in any executor, administrator, or trustee,[79] except so far as such interference or control may necessarily be involved in the particular relief sought.[80] However, where an order has been made for general administration, the powers of the representatives to administer the assets of the estate cannot be exercised without obtaining the sanction of the court.[81] This will readily be given if the court is satisfied that the proposed transaction is a proper one. This rule prevails even if the accounts and inquiries ordered are not proceeded with except with the leave of the judge in person.[82] Where an administration action has been heard on further consideration and no subsequent further consideration has been reserved but general liberty to apply has been given, representatives may exercise their power without obtaining the sanction of the court.[83]

---

[77] Re Baker, ante. But see Re York, supra. And see Re Rhoades [1899] 2 Q.B. 347.
[78] As to which, see ante, pp. 821–822.
[79] See also ante, p. 674.
[80] This still appears to be the position although the former Ord. 55, r. 12, has not been replaced in the 1965 Rules of Court. See also Re Allen-Meyrick [1966] 1 W.L.R. 499.
[81] Re Furness [1943] Ch. 415, following Bethell v. Abraham (1873) L.R. 17 Eq. 24, and distinguishing Berry v. Gibbons (1873) L.R. 8 Ch.App. 747. Also Minors v. Battison (1876) 1 App.Cas. 428, H.L.
[82] Ibid.
[83] Lewin on Trusts, 16th ed., 1964, p. 290; Re Furness [1943] Ch. 415, 421.

Exercise of power by trustees

Where a testator has given a pure discretion to trustees as to the exercise of a power, the court will not enforce the exercise of the power against the wish of the trustees or one of them, if such one reasonably entertains a different opinion from that of his co-trustees as to the desirability of exercising it in the particular manner proposed, but it will prevent them from exercising it improperly[84]; and even where the power is coupled with a trust or duty, the court will enforce the proper and timely exercise of the power, but will not interfere with the discretion of the trustees as to the particular time or manner of their bona fide exercise of it.[85]

Other methods of obtaining the directions of the court

Although the application is almost invariably made by originating summons under Order 85, r. 2,[86] mention should be made of other methods whereby the directions of the court may be obtained.

1. Order 33, r. 3 provides that the court may order any question or issue arising in a cause or matter whether of fact or law or partly of fact and partly of law, and whether raised by the pleadings or otherwise, to be tried before, at or after the trial, and may give directions as to the manner in which the question or issue shall be stated.

2. Where the facts can be agreed on between the parties they can be stated in the plaintiff's statement of claim, and the action brought on for hearing on the facts so stated. In an action so instituted, the court has full jurisdiction over the whole matter, and can make binding orders, whether or not any consequential relief is or could be claimed.[87]

3. Under Order 18, r. 21 questions may be raised on issues of fact without pleadings. As this method presents no special advantage to executors or administrators, no further mention need be made of it.

Procedure under Order 85, r. 2, favoured by court

In cases falling within Order 85, r. 2, a representative, where there is any doubt or difficulty, should issue an originating summons and have the matter decided by the court, and not rely on the advice of a solicitor or the opinion of counsel, which, according to the circumstances, may or may not afford him some indemnity.[88] The tendency of the court seems rather to encourage than to discourage applications by representatives under this

[84] *Tempest* v. *Lord Camoys* (1882) 21 Ch.D. 571. As to this general principle in trust law see further *Cowan* v. *Scargill* [1985] Ch. 270.
[85] *Re Burrage* (1890) 62 L.T. 752; *Re Allen-Meyrick* [1966] 1 W.L.R. 499. Where trustees for sale refuse to exercise powers, see Law of Property Act 1925, s.30; *post*, p. 863.
[86] As to which, see *ante*, p. 821, *post*, p. 1260.
[87] See Ord. 15, r. 16. Administration of Justice Act 1985, s.47. See p. 825, *ante*.
[88] See *Re Beddoe* [1989] 1 Ch. 547, 557. *Re Dallaway* [1982] 1 W.L.R. 756. *Re Evans* [1986] 1 W.L.R. 101 (C.A.). For the liability of a representative who, acting bona fide, distributes the estate on what turns out to be an erroneous construction of the will, see *ante*, p. 709.

rule.[89] They are entitled to the fullest possible protection which the court can give them, and on applying to the court under advice, though it may appear to be unsound, they will not readily be treated as not acting with propriety and be deprived of costs.[90]

The jurisdiction of the court to authorise transactions not already authorised by law or by the will on the application of representatives has already been considered.[91]

Judicial trustees

The appointment of a judicial trustee is in effect a form of relief which can be sought by a beneficiary in place of an order for general administration, when the beneficiary does not wish to put the estate to the expense of a general administration by the court, but the administration of the estate by the ordinary representative has broken down generally,[92] so that an application for a specific direction under Order 85, r. 2 is inappropriate.

Payment into court

Representatives may obtain relief from some of the responsibilities incident to their office by paying money into court. Section 63 of the Trustee Act 1925 enables a representative[93] to pay trust money or securities into court. In this respect the wishes of the majority in number prevail and the receipt of the proper officer gives a sufficient discharge.[94]

Similarly, funds may, under the County Court Rules, Order 49, r. 20, be paid by the trustees, executors, etc., into the county court.

Executors holding assets on charitable trusts are entitled to pay trust money into court without the sanction of the Charity Commissioners[95] but there should be reasonable grounds before this is done[96] and they should in practice always consult first with the Charity Commissioners who have extensive jurisdiction and powers to assist.[97] After charity trustees have

---

[89] See, *e.g.*, Stirling J. in *Re Partington* (1887) 57 L.T. 654, 660; *ante*, pp. 821, 823–824; *post*, p. 927.

[90] *Re Buckton* [1907] 2 Ch. 406, 414. In the case of small estates where the costs of an originating summons seem unjustified it is sometimes convenient to give a dissident beneficiary with an arguable case a time limit in which to issue a summons himself, after which the personal representative will administer or distribute as advised. Alternatively the cost of proper insurance may be a reasonable expense.

[91] See the Trustee Act 1925, s.57; Settled Land Act 1925, s.64; *ante*, p. 684.

[92] *Re Ridsdel* [1947] Ch. 597, 605. For Judicial Trustees, see *ante*, p. 24. For replacement of a representative under s.50 of the Administration of Justice Act 1985, see p. 34.

[93] Trustee Act 1925, s.68(17). See further, *post*, p. 849.

[94] On this section generally, see 4 Wolst. & Ch., 13th ed., pp. 90–91. By the payment into court, trustees are not exonerated from liability for past breaches of trust: *Att.-Gen.* v. *Alford* (1855) 4 De G.M. & G. 843. As to lodgment under this section, see Ord. 92, r. 2.

[95] *Re Poplar & Blackwall Free School* (1878) 8 Ch.D. 543; Ord. 92, r. 2. Tudor, *Charities*, 7th ed., 343.

[96] *Re Giles* (1886) 34 W.R. 712.

[97] See Tudor, *Charities*, 7th ed. pp.308–311 and Charities Act 1960, s.18.

paid into court their functions cease and further initiative lies with the Attorney-General.[98]

Payment into court to be avoided if possible

The payment of funds into court, and the subsequent application for payment out of court, are expensive processes, which ought to be avoided in the interests of *cestuis que trust* where any other reasonable and safe course is open.

A trustee paying money into court in a proper case is entitled to his costs of payment in and of his appearance on the summons for payment out.[99] But the court has a discretion to deprive him of his costs if he pays the money in vexatiously,[1] or where there is no reasonable doubt as to the persons entitled to it,[2] or where he could have had the matter settled by originating summons.[3] In view of the wide scope of Order 85,[4] and of the various indemnities given to trustees,[5] there will not be many occasions upon which it will be proper for trustees to pay money into court.

Where the representative has properly paid money into court, the costs of payment in ought to be borne by the general estate,[6] unless the fund paid in has already been completely severed from the general estate, and appropriated, when the costs of payment in ought to come out of the fund itself.[7]

Costs of payment out

The costs of paying the fund out of court generally fall upon the fund itself,[8] but the court may, on a proper application, order them to be paid by the general estate, where such general estate remains in the hands of the representative.[9]

Upon the application for payment out, the jurisdiction of the court is limited to the fund which has actually been brought into court: it cannot order repayment by the trustees of costs and expenses deducted by them on payment in; but if it can be shown that the costs and expenses have been improperly retained, separate proceedings must be taken against the trustees to recover the amount.[10]

---

[98] *Ibid.*

[99] See *Re Jenkins* (1864) 3 N.R. 408; *Re Bendyshe* (1857) 26 L.J.Ch. 814; *Re Headington* (1857) 27 L.J.Ch. 175; *Re Jones* (1857) 3 Drew. 679; *Re Davies* (1915) 59 S.J. 234.

[1] *Re Woodburn* (1857) 1 De G. & J. 333; *Re Cater* (1858) 25 Beav. 361.

[2] *Re Knight* (1859) 27 Beav. 45; *Re Elliot's Trusts* (1873) L.R. 15 Eq. 194.

[3] *Re Giles* (1886) 55 L.J.Ch. 695.

[4] As to which, see *ante*, p. 821.

[5] See the Trustee Act 1925, ss.26–28, 30, and the Administration of Estates Act 1925, s.42.

[6] *Re Cawthorne* (1848) 12 Beav. 56; *Re Jones* (1857) 3 Drew. 679.

[7] *Re Lorimer* (1850) 12 Beav. 521.

[8] *Re Dickson* (1850) 1 Sim.(N.S.) 37; *Re Ross, ibid.* 196; *Re Jones, ante*; *Re Robertson* (1858) 6 W.R. 405; *Re Wilson* (1866) 14 W.R. 161.

[9] *Re Trick's Trusts* (1869) L.R. 5 Ch.App. 170; *Re Birkett* (1878(9 Ch.D. 576; and *Re Gibbons' Will* (1887) 36 Ch.D. 486. *cf. Re Parker's Will* (1888) 39 Ch.D. 303.

[10] *Re Parker's Will, ante.*

Procedure

How applications for payment in or out of court should be made is considered hereafter.[11]

In *Re Hood's Trusts*,[12] North J. on an executor's petition ordered the payment out to him of funds paid in (before discovery of a will) by the administrator.

[11] *Post*, p. 853.
[12] [1896] 1 Ch. 270.

CHAPTER 61

OTHER PROCEEDINGS IN ADMINISTRATION

In this chapter consideration is given to applications in the Chancery Division for: (1) Appointment of Receivers; (2) Payment into Court: Attachment; (3) Production of Documents: Accounts: Accounting for Wilful Default: Immediate Order for Payment: Admission of Assets; (4) Vesting and Similar Orders; (5) Writ Ne Exeat Regno; (6) Mareva Injunctions

A.—APPOINTMENT OF RECEIVER OR JUDICIAL TRUSTEE

Appointment pending grant of administration

The Chancery Division may, before probate or letters of administration have been granted, interfere on behalf of a creditor or beneficiary in case of need to protect the estate of the deceased by the appointment of a receiver or manager, or both.[1]

It had been held that an application for the appointment of a receiver pending probate should not be made to the Chancery Division unless there were special circumstances, such as danger to assets, requiring the appointment[2]; that such applications being on the way to probate proceedings were properly made in the Probate Division,[3] and if made elsewhere would not be encouraged.[4] But the Chancery Division came to entertain these applications in administration actions where by the writ[5] there was a claim for the appointment of a receiver pending the grant of probate or letters of administration.[6] The person named as executor, or the person with a right to take out administration, was commonly made defendant.

Now that contentious probate proceedings are assigned to the Chancery Division, there would appear to be no ground for objecting to this practice. "If there are proceedings on foot an application should be made in them for the appointment of an administrator, but if there is no such suit then an

---

[1] *Steer* v. *Steer* (1864) 2 Dr. & Sm. 311; *Nothard* v. *Proctor* (1875) 1 Ch.D. 4; *Blackett* v. *Blackett* (1871) 24 L.T. 276. See Kerr, *Receivers*, 17th ed., p. 18. After a grant has been made, the relief usually sought is the appointment of a judicial trustee. Supreme Court Practice 1993, para. 30/1/12. As to the appointment of a substituted personal representative, see p. 34 *ante*.

[2] *Re Henderson* (1886) 2 T.L.R. 322; *Re Pryse* [1904] P. 301; but see *Re Oakes* [1917] 1 Ch. 230, where there was no jeopardy and *ante*, p. 22, as to bankruptcy.

[3] As to the appointment of an administrator or receiver *pendente lite*, see *ante*, pp. 333 *et seq*.

[4] *Re Henderson, ante*; *Re Parker* (1885) 54 L.J.Ch. 694; *Re Moore* (1888) 13 P.D. 36.

[5] The proceedings had to be by writ and not by originating summons: *Re Sutcliffe* [1942] Ch. 453; and the creditor had to undertake, if necessary, to take steps to procure a grant to be made to himself: *ibid*.

[6] *Re Wenge* [1911] W.N. 129; *Re Oakes, ante*. And see further, *ante*, p. 334.

administration action should be commenced asking for the appointment of a receiver."[7] The Family Division still has jurisdiction to appoint, and has done so in the last ten years.

The addition of a claim for administration of the estate to a claim for its protection until the appointment of a legal representative has been held to be irregular.[8] But when administration proceedings have begun, after grant, whether by writ or originating summons, the Chancery Division has jurisdiction to appoint a receiver.[9]

Grounds for appointment

Where any misconduct, waste or improper disposition of assets by the representative was shown, the Chancery Division would instantly interfere and appoint a receiver,[10] though since the Judicial Trustees Act 1896 it is more usual in such circumstances to appoint a Judicial Trustee.[11] The bankruptcy of a sole executor and trustee has been held to be a ground for such an appointment,[12] and a receiver has been appointed where the husband of an executrix was in bad circumstances.[13] In *Hervey* v. *Fitzpatrick*[14] the court, on the application of the English administrator, appointed a receiver against a foreign administrator who had brought assets into the jurisdiction, but intended to depart with them.

But administration is not to be taken from a representative on slight grounds, as, for instance, merely on the ground of his poverty.[15] The fact that the executor declined to admit assets, and that consequently, if a receiver were not appointed, the executor might prefer one creditor to another, was not sufficient ground for application to the court.[16] The court would not appoint a receiver merely for the purpose of depriving the executor of his right of preference,[17] nor would it interfere with an executor's right of retainer by appointing a receiver in a creditor's administration action, merely because he would probably exercise his right to the prejudice of the general body of creditors. The court will not appoint a receiver unless it is shown that assets are being wasted.[18]

---

[7] *S.C.P.* 1991, para. 30/1/13.

[8] *Overington* v. *Ward* (1865) 34 Beav. 175; *Rawlings* v. *Lambert* (1860) 1 J. & H. 458; but see last note.

[9] *Re Francke* (1888) 58 L.T. 305; but see *Re Sutcliffe, ante.*

[10] *Anon.* (1806) 12 Ves. 4; *Middleton* v. *Dodswell* (1806) 13 Ves. 266, 268. Also *Havers* v. *Havers* (1740) Barn.Ch. 22; *Richards* v. *Perkins* (1838) 3 Y. & C.Ex. 299.

[11] See p. 24.

[12] *Re Johnson* (1866) L.R. 1 Ch.App. 325. The fact of the assignees not being before the court is not a sufficient ground for refusing to appoint a receiver. *cf. Re Hopkins* (1881) 19 Ch.D. 61; and see *Bowen* v. *Phillips* [1897] 1 Ch. 174; Dan.Ch.Pr., 8th ed., 1458.

[13] *Taylor* v. *Allen* (1741) 2 Atk. 213; *Scott* v. *Becher* (1817) 4 Pri. 346.

[14] Kay 421.

[15] *Middleton* v. *Dodswell, supra*; *Anon.* (1806) 12 Ves. 4; *Howard* v. *Papera* (1815) 1 Madd. 142; *Manners* v. *Furze* (1847) 11 Beav. 30, 31. See also *Smith* v. *Smith* (1836) 2 Y. & C.Ex. 353; *Whitworth* v. *Whyddon* (1850) 2 M. & G. 52; Dan.Ch.Pr., 8th ed., 1458.

[16] *Philips* v. *Jones* (1884) 28 S.J. 360.

[17] *Per Chitty* L.J. in *Re Stevens* [1898] 1 Ch. 162, 173, 174.

[18] *Re Wells* (1890) 45 Ch.D. 569; *Re Stevens, ante.*

A receiver appointed in a creditor's action begun before grant of representation should, where security[19] is not ordered, be required to lodge his first account within 14 days after the expiration of his receivership, or three months from the date of the order by which he is appointed, whichever period is the shorter.[20]

Receiver's accounts

The court has no jurisdiction to order, in a summary way, the executor of a deceased receiver to bring in and pass his testator's accounts, and pay the balance to be found due out of the assets.[21] The proper course, in such a case, if the balance is not ascertained so that the recognisances may be put in suit, is to bring an action against the executor for an account. But this course may be avoided if the executor will consent to an order to pass the receiver's accounts and to pay the balance.[22]

Procedure

In the Chancery Division an application for appointment of a receiver may be made by motion in court or summons before the master.[23] Applications for the appointment of a judicial trustee are normally made to the master in the first instance, as are applications for the appointment of an administrator *pendente lite* in a probate action.[24]

The appointment of a receiver in an administration action operates to prevent a return of *nulla bona* to a writ of *fi. fa.* issued on a judgment against representatives from constituting a presumption of *devastavit*.[25]

Judicial trustee

It is often convenient to appoint a judicial trustee rather than a receiver.[26] A judicial trustee may ask the court to give him directions at any time[27] but this does not deprive the judicial trustee of his power to compromise under section 15 of the Trustee Act 1925.[28] A bank has been appointed a judicial trustee,[29] when its memorandum gives it power so to act. This may be convenient when there are problems with regard to secur-

---

[19] For form of order on re-appointment of receiver after lapse, see *Practice Note* [1943] W.N. 71.

[20] *Re Sutcliffe* [1942] Ch. 453, in which case the plaintiff had to give an undertaking that, if no grant of administration had been made within three calendar months he would apply to the court for directions, and would, if so directed, take all necessary steps to procure a grant to be made to himself.

[21] *Jenkins* v. *Briant* (1834) 7 Sim. 171.

[22] Dan.Ch.Pr., 8th ed., 1495.

[23] *Re Francke*, 58 L.T. 305; and see *Supreme Court Practice* 1993, Ord. 30 and notes thereto, 30/1/2. Kerr, *Receivers*, 17th ed., p. 114. *Practice Direction* [1988] 1 W.L.R. 632.

[24] Judicial Trustee Rules 1972, r. 4; Ord. 76, r. 14.

[25] *Batchelor* v. *Evans* [1939] Ch. 1007.

[26] As to such appointment see pp. 24, 843 *ante*.

[27] Judicial Trustee Rules 1983, s.8.

[28] *Re Ridsdel* [1947] Ch. 597.

[29] *Re Cohen* [1918] W.N. 77.

ity or when the estate is involved in complex investment or accounting situations.[30]

B.—PAYMENT INTO COURT: COMMITTAL

Payment into court on admission of assets

The court will order payment into court if it appears that assets in the hands of a representative are at risk, though this is usually only done as a last resort, and only if the assets cannot be adequately safeguarded in any other way because of the additional expense and inconvenience it causes. A different view seems to have prevailed in the past. In earlier editions it has been stated that the court will, as a rule, immediately upon an admission of assets by a personal representative, order so much as he admits to have in his hands to be paid into court; though it was formerly thought necessary for the plaintiff to show that the personal representative had abused his trust, or that the fund was in danger from his insolvent circumstances.[31] In any event it was stated that this rule is not absolute, but that where a creditor is suing for his own debt only, or where the application is by persons interested in reversion subject to a tenancy for life, some reasonable ground, such as danger to the fund, ought to be made out.[32]

Money admitted by the executor to be in the hands of his partner has been regarded as in his own hands for the purpose of being paid into court.[33]

Probate suit pending

Though the Chancery Division used to appoint a receiver when a probate action was pending in the Probate Division, about the validity of a will, it would not, on that account alone, order the person named as executor to pay into court money in his hands belonging to the deceased's estate.[34] As mentioned above, it would now be normal in such circumstances to appoint an administrator pending suit.

Where executor has not paid all debts

Semble, any balance which is admitted to be in the executor's hands used as a general rule to be ordered into court, notwithstanding that there were

---

[30] See also J.J. Rules 1983, r. 13.

[31] *Strange* v. *Harris* (1791) 3 Bro.C.C. 365; *Blake* v. *Blake* (1804) 2 Scho. & Lef. 26; *Robertson* v. *Scott* (1866) 14 L.T. 187.

[32] Dan.Ch.Pr., 8th ed., 1516; *Reeve* v. *Goodwin* (1846) 10 Jur. 1050; *Re Braithwaite* (1882) 21 Ch.D. 121.

[33] *Johnson* v. *Aston* (1822) 1 Sim. & Stu. 73; *White* v. *Barton* (1854) 18 B. 192.

[34] See *Reed* v. *Harris* (1836) 7 Sim. 639; *Edwards* v. *Edwards* (1853) 10 Hare, App. II, lxiii.

demands on it to which the executor was liable.[35] Thus, in *Yare* v. *Harrison*,[36] an executor, having admitted a large balance of the personal estate to be in his hands, was ordered to pay the whole into court, although he stated that an action at law was pending against him for a debt to a considerable amount due from the testator; but with liberty, in case the plaintiff in the action should recover, to apply to the court to have a sufficient sum paid out again. The plaintiff in the action did recover, and the court ordered the amount to be paid out to the plaintiff in the action, and not to the executor.[37]

Where executor admits himself a debtor

Where the executor admits himself to have been a debtor to the testator at the time of his death, that has always been held a clear admission of assets in his hand to the amount of the debt, and he is compellable to pay it into court accordingly.[38] In this case, the person to pay and the person to receive being the same, the court assumes that what ought to have been done has been done, and orders the payment, not as of a debt by a debtor, but as of money realised in the hands of the executor.[39]

The court, in making an order of this kind, used to adhere strictly to the rule of acting on the executor's admission only, and would refuse to proceed upon its knowledge derived from any other source.[40]

The practice of the Court of Chancery originally was to order a defendant to pay money into court upon an interlocutory motion, only when he had by his answer admitted that the sum was in his hands. An admission that the sum in question was due from him to the plaintiff was not sufficient; he must have admitted that it was actually in his hands. The practice was afterwards extended to admissions made by a defendant in affidavits,[41] and a still further extension was made by Jessel M.R., in *Freeman* v. *Cox*,[42] by ordering a defendant to pay money upon an affidavit of the plaintiff, which the defendant had not answered, that he had a sum of money in his hands; but such orders ought to be made only when it is made out to the satisfaction of the court that the defendant has the sum claimed

---

[35] *Betagh* v. *Concannon* (1830) 2 Moll. 559; Dan.Ch.Pr., 8th ed., 1516. But see *Blake* v. *Blake* (1804) 2 Scho. & Lef. 26, *contra*. If an executor admits that all the testator's debts, etc., have been paid, the court will, on motion, order the income of a balance paid in by the executor to be paid to the person entitled to the residue: *Dando* v. *Dando* (1827) 1 Sim. 510. But see *Abby* v. *Gilford* (1847) 11 Beav. 28.

[36] (1793) 2 Cox. 377.

[37] As to the power to transfer actions pending in other Divisions, see Ord. 4, rr. 3, 4 and 5.

[38] *Mortlock* v. *Leathes* (1817) 2 Meriv. 491; *Rothwell* v. *Rothwell* (1825) 2 Sim. & Stu. 218; *Costeker* v. *Horrox* (1839) 3 Y. & C.Ex. 530; *Toulmin* v. *Copland, ibid.* 625; *White* v. *Barton* (1854) 18 Beav. 192.

[39] *Richardson* v. *Bank of England* (1838) 4 M. & Cr. 165, 174, 175; Dan.Ch.Pr., 8th ed., 1517.

[40] *Richardson* v. *Bank of England, ante*; *Meyer* v. *Montriou* (1841) 4 Beav. 343; *Scott* v. *Wheeler* (1850) 12 Beav. 366.

[41] *Jervis* v. *White* (1802) 6 Ves. 738.

[42] (1878) 8 Ch.D. 148.

in his hands, and that he has no real defence to the plaintiff's demand.[43] The defendant, however, should state, not merely that no part of the money is in his hands, but further, that it is not in his power or under his control.[44]

Order 85, r. 2(3), applies where assets in hand

Order 85, r. 2(3), which provides[45] for an order being made for the payment into court of money held by a person in his capacity as executor, administrator or trustee, applies only to money actually in the hands of the trustee, executor, or administrator, and if it is not in his hands, although he is responsible for it and ought to have it, that rule does not apply.[46]

How representative may discharge himself

Where an executor admits that a certain amount of assets has come to his possession, he may discharge himself from the payment of it into court, wholly or partially, by taking credit for sums which he shows a right to have allowed him.[47] Where an executor admitted that he had received a certain sum belonging to the testator's estate, but added that he had made payments, the amounts of which he did not specify, the court allowed him to verify the amount of his payments, by affidavit, and ordered him, on motion, to pay the balance into court.[48]

But when there is a sufficient admission by the executor of assets once come to his hands, he cannot relieve himself from paying them into court by showing any unauthorised application of them, or any investment or disposition of them which in substance amounts to a breach of his duty as executor.[49] Clearly, the defendant would not escape an order being made against him by stating that he paid the money away to someone to whom he had no right to pay it, and who had no title to receive it.[50]

In *Roy* v. *Gibbon*,[51] it was said by Wigram V.-C. that the practice was that "where a party charged himself with the receipt of a fund, he was bound by that charge until he had relieved himself from it by showing a proper application of the money. It was not enough for a party, whose duty it was to know the truth and be ready with information, to leave the appli-

---

[43] *Neville* v. *Matthewman* [1894] 3 Ch. 345.
[44] *Re Benson* [1899] 1 Ch. 39.
[45] See *ante*, p. 821, *post*, p. 1260.
[46] *Nutter* v. *Holland* [1894] 3 Ch. 408, disapproving *Re Chapman* (1886) 54 L.T. 13.
[47] *Roy* v. *Gibbon* (1844) 4 Hare 65.
[48] *Anon.* (1831) 4 Sim. 359. See also *Proudfoot* v. *Hume* (1841) 4 Beav. 477; *Crompton and Evans' Union Bank* v. *Burton, post.*
[49] *Wyatt* v. *Sharratt* (1840) 3 Beav. 498; *Hinde* v. *Blake* (1842) 4 Beav. 597; *Score* v. *Ford* (1844) 7 Beav. 333; *Roy* v. *Gibbon* (1844) 4 Hare 65; *Ingle* v. *Partridge* (1863) 32 Beav. 661.
[50] See *Crompton and Evans' Union Bank* v. *Burton* [1895] 2 Ch. 711, 714. And see *Lord* v. *Purchase* (1853) 17 Beav. 171.
[51] (1844) 4 Hare 65. Contrast *Freeman* v. *Fairlie* (1812) 3 Mer. 39.

cation in doubt, by merely expressing ignorance with regard to the charges to which the fund was liable."[52]

Time allowed for payment into court

If there is no danger of the property being lost, from the executor being insolvent or otherwise, a reasonable time will be allowed for bringing the fund into court; and a longer time will be allowed when the money is in a foreign country.[53] If the assets appear to have been invested on an improper security, time will be allowed (which may, in a proper case, be extended from time to time) to enable the executor to realise the security.[54] In fixing the day for payment, time will be allowed for the trustee, if he desires it, to show that no reason exists for calling the money into court.[55]

Payment does not affect him

An executor who has by order paid money into court is not thereby deprived of his lien on the fund for his costs.[56]

Who may apply for payment in

The general rule as to payment of money into court is that the plaintiffs must be solely entitled, or have such an interest jointly with others as to entitle them, on behalf of themselves and of those others, to have the fund secured.[57] Where part of a residuary estate has been invested on an improper security, and the defendant has an interest therein, the court, on being satisfied that there is no existing claim on the estate, sometimes confines the amount to be paid into court to the share of the plaintiff.[58]

Where the only creditor of a deceased debtor had obtained in an administration action a personal order against the executor for payment of his certified debt, the fiduciary relationship which previously existed between the creditor and executor was determined, and the creditor could not subsequently pursue any remedy depending on the continued existence of this fiduciary relationship. He was not entitled, therefore, to an order against the executor for payment into court of money in his hands as such executor, nor to the subsequent committal of the executor under the punitive jurisdiction reserved to the court under the third exception to section 4 of

---

[52] See also *Hinde* v. *Blake* (1842) 4 Beav. 597.
[53] *Roy* v. *Gibbon* (1844) 4 Hare 65.
[54] *Score* v. *Ford* (1844) 7 Beav. 333; *Wyatt* v. *Sharratt* (1840) 3 Beav. 498; *Hinde* v. *Blake* (1842) 4 Beav. 597.
[55] *Hinde* v. *Blake* (1842) 4 Beav. 597.
[56] *Blenkinsop* v. *Foster* (1838) 3 Y. & C.Ex. 205.
[57] *Freeman* v. *Fairlie* (1812) 3 Mer. 29.
[58] *Score* v. *Ford* (1844) 7 Beav. 333.

the Debtors Act 1869.[59] This was because the relationship had changed to that of judgment creditor and debtor.

Committal on failure to pay in

If failure to comply with an order for payment of money into court is a case for committal, it must be because it falls within the third exception to section 4 of the Debtors Act 1869, which is in these terms: "*Default by a trustee or person acting in a fiduciary capacity and ordered to pay by a court of equity any sum in his possession or under his control.*" In order to bring a case within that exception it must be proved that the money ordered to be paid into court is, or has been, in the actual possession or control of the person sought to be committed. Mere constructive receipt by an agent or solicitor on his behalf, who may never have accounted, is not enough.[60]

A judgment in the form that the plaintiff do recover money from a defaulting executor, made before October 1, 1966 could not be enforced by a supplemental four-day order for payment by the defendant, so as to found a right to apply for an order of committal of the defendant in default of payment within the stipulated time.[61] Now where a judgment or order does not specify a time-limit the court has power subsequently to make an order imposing a time-limit.[62]

A defaulting executor or administrator who becomes bankrupt is protected from committal by section 285(1) of the Insolvency Act 1986 and if he becomes bankrupt after committal he may be released.[63]

But that section does not take away the jurisdiction of the court under the Debtors Act 1869, s.4(3), to order the committal of a defaulting executor against whom a receiving order has been made,[64] and he cannot evade the Debtors Act by denuding himself of the assets and filing a petition in bankruptcy with the object of escaping payment.[65]

Procedure by motion or summons

Applications for the bringing of money or securities into court before judgment are made by motion or summons. If opposed, the summons may be adjourned into court.[66]

On interlocutory proceedings the relief will be confined to the payment of money into court, and the court will not direct any permanent relief,

---

[59] *Re Thomas* [1912] 2 Ch. 348. See p. 463 *ante*.
[60] *Re Fewster* [1901] 1 Ch. 447; followed by Buckley J. in *Re Wilkins* [1901] W.N. 203, but stating that he would not express any opinion of his own.
[61] *Re Oddy* [1906] 1 Ch. 93. *Supreme Court Practice 1993*, Ord. 45. See para. 45/6/1.
[62] See Ord. 45, r. 6(2).
[63] *Re Manning* (1885) 30 Ch.D. 480.
[64] *Re Smith* [1893] 2 Ch. 1.
[65] *Re Bourne* [1906] 1 Ch. 697.
[66] Dan.Ch.Pr., 8th ed., 1525.

such as the repurchase of stock which had been sold by the executor; for that can be done only at the hearing of the cause.[67]

The ordinary method of application for payment or transfer out of a fund in court is by summons,[68] supported by an affidavit of entitlement.

Small estates

Where the estate of an intestate is entitled to a fund in court and the assets do not exceed £5,000 including such fund, the court may allow payment out without requiring the issue of a grant.[69]

Payment out to representative

As a general rule funds in court belonging to the estate of a deceased person are not, after the expiration of 10 years from his death, paid to his legal representative without notice to beneficiaries; but if a trust exists and the trustees still have duties to perform, payment may be made to the trustees without notice to beneficiaries, notwithstanding that the testator has been dead more than 10 years.[70]

C.—Documents: Accounts: Accounting for Wilful Default: Immediate Order for Payment: Admission of Assets

Deposit of documents and valuables

A representative may be ordered to deposit documents relating to the estate, for the benefit of the parties interested, in the Central Office,[71] unless there are other purposes which require that he should retain them in his own hands.[72] Such an order may be made at the instance of persons only entitled in reversion.[73]

A representative may also be ordered to deposit valuables or securities at the Bank of England[74] or to preserve property.[75]

Production of documents

Where the production of documents is required, the application for it must in all cases be made by summons in chambers, and the party required

---

[67] *Futter* v. *Jackson* (1843) 6 Beav. 424 for procedure on interlocutory motions. *Practice Direction* [1988] 1 W.L.R. 632.

[68] See Ord. 92, r. 5. Unless the application is made in a pending cause or matter an originating summons will be appropriate.

[69] Ord. 22, r. 11; S.C.F.R. 1987, r. 43(2)–(3).

[70] *Practice note* [1964] W.N. 135; and see *Gordon* v. *Smith* [1913] W.N. 161.

[71] See Ord. 63, r. 5. The place for deposit is the Filing Department, Room 81, Royal Courts of Justice.

[72] *Freeman* v. *Fairlie* (1812) 3 Mer. 30.

[73] *Re Dartnall* [1895] 1 Ch. 474.

[74] See S.C.F.R. 1975, r. 23.

[75] See Ord. 29, r. 2, and notes thereto in the S.C.P.

to produce will then be ordered to file an affidavit, stating what documents he has, or has had, in his possession or power relating to the matters in question, and to produce them (excepting such as he may by his affidavit object to produce) to the party requiring production.[76] An executor is not entitled to avoid discovery on the ground that he is sued in a representative capacity only. He must discover and produce all documents in both his representative and his individual capacity.[77]

Prima facie evidence in support of a claim will entitle a creditor in an administration action to an order directing the executors to file an affidavit as to their possession of documents relating to the claim, or any item in it.[78]

The old practice was for the party producing the documents to leave them at the Record or Writ Clerk's Office (now the Central Office[79]). It is now the ordinary practice to produce them at his solicitor's office.[80]

Grounds for objection to produce documents

Apart from objections on practical grounds of convenience or otherwise there may be legal grounds for disputing an order. Thus there is no right for beneficiaries to inspect communications between individual trustees and appointors, or letters to or from an individual beneficiary, nor need the agenda and minutes of meetings be disclosed so far as these concern matters on which the trustees need not disclose reasons for their decisions, as for instance the exercise of a discretionary power.[81] Apart from these legal grounds, the general rule is that beneficiaries *sui juris* are entitled to see all trust documents in the power of the trustes.[82]

Accounts

An action for an account is not based on allegations of breach of trust. It arises from the fiduciary relationship of the trustee and beneficiary.[83]

It is the duty of a representative to keep clear up to date and distinct accounts of the property which he is bound to administer. If he chooses to mix the accounts with those of his own trading concerns, he cannot thereby protect himself from producing the original books in which any part of those accounts may be inserted. If his partners in trade have *permitted* him to mix the accounts, it seems they cannot afterwards object to the production: and clearly they cannot do so where the representative has admitted

---

[76] See Ord. 24, rr. 11–14. As to discovery on originating summons, see *ante*, p. 830.

[77] *Buchanan-Michaelson* v. *Rubinstein* [1965] Ch. 258. See also *ante*, p. 506.

[78] *Re M'Veagh* (1863) 1 De G.J. & S. 399.

[79] See now R.S.C. Ord. 24, r. 11A.

[80] This would appear to be authorised by Ord. 24, rr. 9, 10 and 11, but was formerly said to be a matter of indulgence and convenience only. *Prestney* v. *Corporation of Colchester* (1883) 24 Ch.D. 376; and see *Leslie* v. *Cave* [1886] W.N. 162, where the documents were ordered to be deposited in court.

[81] *Re Londonderry* [1965] Ch. 918. For a consideration of this and earlier cases and the debatability of this rule of equity, see (1964) 80 L.Q.R. 875 and (1965) 81 L.Q.R. 192.

[82] See *Re Londonderry* [1965] Ch. 918.

[83] *Att.-Gen.* v. *Cocke* [1988] Ch. 414. Hence s.23 of the Limitation Act 1980 may not apply.

that he lent to his firm part of the trust property and that the firm has been dealing with it.[84]

In *Freeman* v. *Fairlie*,[85] an executor in India, coming to England, and, after 21 years, being called upon to account, alleged that he left his books, etc., behind him in India; but he was nevertheless ordered to produce copies of all entries in such books, etc., within six months, though it was impossible for him to do so, in order that the court might have an opportunity from time to time of seeing that he had used proper diligence.

Costs of furnishing accounts

Trustees can, where they are required to furnish accounts in respect of their trust estate, demand to be paid or to be guaranteed the costs of doing so, before complying: it makes no difference that one of the trustees is a solicitor.[86]

Usual accounts

Under the usual administration order obtained on a writ or originating summons, an executor or administrator can only be charged for actual receipt by himself, or his agent, not for a default of his co-trustee.[87] The practice is to make representatives account only for the money they themselves have received, not for what they might have received but for their own default.[88] To make them account on the latter footing, wilful default must be pleaded.[89] That is to say, the plaintiff must plead that assets might have been received but for the default of the representatives; to plead this is technically termed "to plead wilful default." The plaintiff must allege and prove at least one act of wilful default.[90]

Where one or more breaches of trust are proved or admitted a general account on the footing of wilful default will be ordered if the past conduct of the trustees is such as to give rise to a reasonable inference that other breaches of trust not yet known to the plaintiff or the court have occurred.[91]

In an action for an account as distinct from an action for breach of trust,

---

[84] *Freeman* v. *Fairlie* (1812) 3 Mer. 29, 43, 44. The court, however, will not order a defendant, who has a joint possession of a document with someone else not before the court, to produce the document itself: *Taylor* v. *Rundell* (1841) Cr. & Ph. 104, 111; Dan.Ch.Pr., 8th ed., 632.

[85] (1812) 3 Mer. 44.

[86] *Re Bosworth* (1889) 58 L.J.Ch. 432.

[87] *Re Fryer* (1857) 3 K. & J. 317; *Blakely* v. *Blakely* (1855) 1 Jur.(N.S.) 368.

[88] *Shepherd* v. *Towgood* (1823) T. & R. 379, 388; *Pybus* v. *Smith* (1790) 1 Ves. 189, 193; *Barber* v. *Mackrell* (1879) 12 Ch.D. 534; *Re Stevens* [1897] 1 Ch. 422; [1898] 1 Ch. 162. But see *Bulstrode* v. *Bradley* (1747) 3 Atk. 582. *Semble*, a claim for compound interest on balances retained by trustees (see *ante*, p. 712, 713) does not, for this purpose, involve a charge of wilful default: see *Re Barclay* [1899] 1 Ch. 674.

[89] *Ibid.*

[90] *Sleight* v. *Lawson* (1857) 3 K. & J. 292; *Re Youngs* (1885) 30 Ch.D. 421; *Re Stevens* [1897] 1 Ch. 422, 432, *per* North J. See article by H. G. Hanbury in (1936) 52 L.Q.R. 365.

[91] *Re Tebbs* [1976] 1 W.L.R. 924, disapproving the interpretation of *Wildes* v. *Dudlom* [1870] W.N. 251 in the previous edition of this work.

a plaintiff beneficiary who does not allege wilful default is entitled to an order for an account as of right.[92]

In actions in which there are no pleadings a charge of wilful default can be raised by affidavit.[93]

An administrator during minority,[94] after such administration is determined, may be compelled to account to the infant[95] after he has attained full age and has obtained a grant,[96] or, it seems, to any other person, including a creditor,[97] who has obtained a subsequent grant.

Where the administrator during minority has duly administered the assets, and has paid over the surplus to the person who has obtained a subsequent grant, the remedy of a creditor is against the executor or subsequent administrator.[98] In such circumstances, the administrator during minority, if sued by a creditor,[99] may plead *plene administravit*,[1] except, possibly, where he has committed a *devastavit*.[2] But as the court would allow a party to follow assets into any hands, if it were shown that he had not accounted to the person who subsequently obtained a grant, but fraudulently and by collusion had detained any part, in such a case an action might be maintained against the administrator during minority without joining the executor or subsequent administrator.[3]

Account on footing of wilful default

Where wilful default has been alleged and a case is made for it on the pleadings, an account on the footing of wilful default can be directed either at the hearing or trial of the action, or at any subsequent stage.[4] Conversely a plaintiff who alleges breach of trust but at trial accepts a common form administration judgment cannot later charge the trustees with further breaches.[5]

If the statement of claim alleges wilful default, but the judgment at the trial gives no relief on that footing, but does not dismiss the claim for that

---

[92] *Re Wells* [1962] 1 W.L.R. 874. No particulars need be given by the plaintiff.

[93] See *Barber* v. *Mackrell, ante.* Ord. 85, r. 4.

[94] See p. 323 *ante.*

[95] See *Fotherby* v. *Pate* (1747) 3 Atk. 603.

[96] See Supreme Court Act 1981, s.118.

[97] *Taylor* v. *Newton* (1752) 1 Lee 15.

[98] See Bac.Abr.Exors. B. 1, 2. See also *Fotherby* v. *Pate, supra,* and *Brooking* v. *Jennings* (1674) 1 Mod. 175.

[99] A creditor cannot sue such an administrator as an executor *de son tort: Palmer* v. *Litherland* (1662) Latch. 160; *Lawson* v. *Crofts* (1659) 1 Sid. 57.

[1] *Anon.* (1674) 1 Freem. 150. See also *Brooking* v. *Jennings, supra.*

[2] Bull.N.P. 145, citing *Palmer* v. *Litherland, ante; Packman's Case* (1596) 6 Co. 19b; and it has been said, even though he should have obtained a release from the minor on attaining full age: *Anon.* (1674) 1 Freem. 150; Com.Dig.Admon.F. But *quaere.* See the Trustee Act 1925, ss. 14, 15 (*post,* p. 982).

[3] See *Fotherby* v. *Pate* (1747) 3 Atk. 603.

[4] *Job* v. *Job* (1877) 6 Ch.D. 562, as explained in *Mayer* v. *Murray* (1878) 87 Ch.D. 424; *Barber* v. *Mackrell* (1879) 12 Ch.D. 534; *Re Symons, post.* As to the power of the court to direct any necessary accounts to be taken at any stage of the proceedings, see Ord. 43, rr. 1, 2. This rule does not dispense with the necessity for the pleading of wilful default.

[5] *Re Wrightson* [1908] 1 Ch. 789.

relief, the court can, at any subsequent stage of the proceedings, upon evidence of wilful default, direct further accounts and inquiries on that footing.[6]

But where a common administration order has been made against a defendant, the leave of the court must be obtained before continuing the action against him on the footing of wilful default.[7] In *Laming* v. *Gee*[8] proof was required that the information on which the fresh action was founded was not acquired in time to be utilised in the first action. But leave was given in a subsequent case[9] without such proof being required, upon the plaintiff, an undischarged bankrupt, giving security for the executor's costs of the fresh action.

Proof of wilful default

Where the plaintiff by his statement of claim alleges wilful default, he must be prepared to support his allegations at the hearing; he has no right to insist on the question of wilful default being left for decision at some subsequent stage of the action.[10]

The burden of proof is on the party alleging wilful default, and he must show not only a loss, but a loss under such circumstances as to show default on the part of the executor or administrator,[11] or, where there are no pleadings, in the affidavit alleging wilful default.

Particulars of the allegations of wilful default should be given in the pleading.[12] Accounts on the footing of wilful default cannot be obtained on application for accounts under Order 43.[13]

Order for payment without accounts

If the plaintiff's claim is uncontested or proved, and the executor admits assets, the plaintiff is entitled at the hearing to an immediate order for payment without taking the accounts.[14] The same doctrine prevails though the executor denies assets in hand at the time of filing his answer, if he also discloses that he had at one time sufficient assets, but that he has since misapplied them.[15] An admission of assets for the payment of a legacy is an admission of assets for the purposes of the suit, and extends to costs, if the court thinks fit to give them.[16]

---

[6] *Re Symons* (1882) 21 Ch.D. 757.
[7] *Laming* v. *Gee* (1878) 10 Ch.D. 715.
[8] *Supra.*
[9] *Re Kurtz* (1904) 90 L.T. 12.
[10] *Smith* v. *Armitage* (1883) 24 Ch.D. 727. *Re Wells* [1962] 1 W.L.R. 874.
[11] *Re Brier* (1884) 26 Ch.D. 238. *Re Stevens* [1898] 1 Ch. 162, 175.
[12] *Re Anstice* (1885) 54 L.J.Ch. 1104. See also Ord. 18, r. 8 and r. 12.
[13] *Re Bowen* (1882) 20 Ch.D. 538.
[14] *Woodgate* v. *Field* (1842) 2 Hare 211. Where the answer admitted assets, but insisted that, under the circumstances stated, the legacy sought to be recovered had been paid, it was held that the plaintiff had a right to read the passage admitting the assets without reading that as to the payment of the legacy: *Connop* v. *Hayward* (1841) 1 Y. & C.C.C. 33.
[15] *Rogers* v. *Soutten* (1839) 2 Keen 598.
[16] *Philanthropic Society* v. *Hobson* (1833) 2 M. & K. 357.

If it is alleged that the executor has rendered himself personally liable to pay the plaintiff's debt or legacy by an admission of assets made before suit, or by any other means, and the plaintiff can sustain this allegation, he will entitle himself to an order for payment at once.[17]

The admission of assets by an executor will not preclude creditors from coming on a fund specifically appropriated for their benefit, although that fund may have been disposed of to a purchaser.[18]

Admission of assets

A representative "admits assets," that is to say admits that he has in his hands assets of the deceased for which he is accountable, either by express acknowledgment to that effect or by some conduct exclusively referable to the existence of such assets in his hands. Thus where the deceased gave money out on mortgage to a charity in Ireland, and his executrix by her own will attempted to provide other means for payment of that legacy, and stated as a reason that his personal estate was out on mortgage, she thereby admitted assets of her testator.[19]

Executors having invested an infant's legacy in their partnership concern, it was held that the entry by them in the partnership books of the amount of the legacy to the credit of the legatee was a sufficient admission of assets, there being no evidence that the entries were mistaken, and the course of conduct observed being consistent with them.[20]

An acknowledgment by executors of their indebtedness for principal and interest due on a legacy may amount to an admission of assets.[21]

Payment of interest on a legacy by the executor, from time to time, will be evidence of assets, though a single instance of payment of interest will not.[22] Payment of the interest of a specific or demonstrative legacy, when that payment is clearly not made out of the general assets, nor referable to the general assets, is not an admission of general assets.[23]

Inland Revenue accounts

Query whether accounts delivered to the Inland Revenue are admissible as tending to prove the existence of assets. It appears that the obsolete inventory at one time exhibited in the Court of Probate was admissible, but

[17] *Barnard* v. *Pumfrett* (1841) 5 M. & Cr. 63; *Dinsdale* v. *Dudding* (1842) 1 Y. & C.C.C. 265. See *Re Marvin* [1905] 2 Ch. 490.
[18] *Curtis* v. *Blow* (1831) 2 B. & Ad. 426.
[19] *Campbell* v. *Earl of Radnor* (1783) 1 Bro.C.C. 271; *Barnard* v. *Pumfrett* (1841) 5 M. & Cr. 63, 70. See also *Elliot* v. *Holwell* (1754) 1 Lee 574.
[20] *Townend* v. *Townend* (1859) 1 Giff. 201. Contrast *Hutton* v. *Rossiter* (1855) 7 De G.M. & G. 9.
[21] See *Holland* v. *Clark* (1843) 2 Y. & C.C.C. 319; *cf. Stephens* v. *Venables* (*No.* 2) (1862) 31 Beav. 124.
[22] *Corporation of Clergymen's Sons* v. *Swainson* (1748) 1 Ves.Sen. 75; *Barnard* v. *Pumfrett* (1841) 5 M. & Cr. 63, 70; *Whittle* v. *Henning* (1840) 2 Beav. 396; *Att.-Gen.* v. *Chapman* (1840) 3 Beav. 255; *Att.-Gen.* v. *Higham* (1843) 2 Y. & C.C.C. 634.
[23] *Severs* v. *Severs* (1853) 1 Sm. & G. 400.

that it was only prima facie evidence of assets.[24] And, *semble*, an inventory exhibited by one representative was not even prima facie evidence against another.[25]

Payment of probate duty was presumptive evidence of an admission, but not an absolute admission, of assets to the extent covered by the amount of duty paid.[26] The payment of legacy duty seemed to have a somewhat similar result; but the effect of such a payment really depended upon the circumstances in which it was paid.[27] Presumably payments of Inheritance tax would be considered in the light of these authorities.

Acknowledgment of debt

An executor does not admit assets by paying interest on a bond due from the testator[28]; nor by an admission that a debt is a just debt, nor by a promise to pay a debt as soon as he can.[29]

Admission by third party

If an executor refers a party to a third person for information about the effects of the testator, an admission of assets by such third person may bind the executor.[30]

The admission of assets in an action against a representative by his failing to plead *plene administravit* is considered later.[31]

Admission retracted or explained

The general rule is that an admission of assets can never be retracted unless a case of mistake is most clearly established.[32] But an admission is always susceptible of explanation,[33] and if a strong case is made out this may enable the court to relieve the executor from the admission.[34] But he must clearly prove the mistake, and show that the circumstance on which he built his admission failed.[35]

An admission of assets by the executor's answer was waived by the plain-

---

[24] *Giles* v. *Dyson* (1815) 1 Stark. N.P.C. 32. See also *Shelly's Case* (1693) 1 Salk. 296; *Young* v. *Cawdrey* (1819) 8 Taunt. 734. See *ante*, pp. 64–69.

[25] See *Stearn* v. *Mills* (1833) 4 B. & Ad. 657.

[26] *Lazonby* v. *Rawson* (1854) 4 De G.M. & G. 556. See also *Stearn* v. *Mills*, *supra*; *Mann* v. *Lang* (1835) 3 Ad. & E. 699.

[27] See *Lazonby* v. *Rawson*, *ante*; cf. *Hutton* v. *Rossiter* (1855) 7 De G.M. & G. 9. See also *Whittle* v. *Henning* (1840) 2 Beav. 396.

[28] *Cleverly* v. *Brett*, cited by Buller J. (1772) 5 T.R. 8; 2 Phill.Ev., 6th ed., 348.

[29] *Hindsley* v. *Russell* (1810) 12 East 232, 235; 2 Phill., *ante*. But as to an admission by compounding with creditors, see *post*, p. 895.

[30] *Williams* v. *Innes* (1808) 1 Camp. 364.

[31] *Post*, p. 894.

[32] *Drewry* v. *Thacker* (1819) 3 Sw. 529, 548; *Roberts* v. *Roberts*, cited (1780) 1 Bro.C.C. 487.

[33] *Payne* v. *Little* (1856) 22 Beav. 69. See also *Cadbury* v. *Smith* (1869) L.R. 9 Eq. 37, 41.

[34] See *Foster* v. *Foster* (1789) 2 Bro.C.C. 616; *Young* v. *Walter* (1804) 9 Ves. 365.

[35] *Horsley* v. *Chaloner* (1750) 2 Ves.Sen. 83.

tiff's going on to an account of assets, and procuring a receiver to be appointed.[36]

Admission by co-executor

If there are two or more executors and one or more of them admits assets, an account may be decreed against the rest.[37]

Admission to one, admission to all

The general rule is that an admission of assets by the executor to one claimant on them is an admission to all.[38] But the circumstances may be such that an admission of assets to pay, or the payment of one legacy, will not be treated by the court as amounting to an admission of assets to pay other legacies,[39] or even the claims of creditors.[40]

D.—VESTING AND SIMILAR ORDERS[41]

Realty

For the purposes of the Trustee Act 1925, "trustee" includes, where the context admits, a personal representative.[42] By section 44 of that Act[43] the court[44] is authorised to make a vesting order vesting land or any interest therein in such person, in such manner, and for such estate or interest as the court may direct[45] in any of the circumstances there described.[46]

These include briefly[47]: upon appointment under an express or statutory power and cases where a trustee is under disability,[48] out of the jurisdiction, cannot be found, or being a corporation has been dissolved, and cases of uncertainty or refusal to act or where it appears to the court to be expedient. By section 47 the court may, if it thinks expedient, for the pur-

---

[36] *Wall* v. *Bushby* (1785) 1 Bro.C.C. 484.

[37] *Norton* v. *Turvill* (1723) 2 P.Wms. 145. Where, in an examination put in by two executors, it was stated that their receipts had been joint, but it appeared by affidavit that that statement was made through mistake and inadvertence, and that one of the executors had, in fact, received nothing, liberty was given to him to put in a supplemental affidavit to correct the mistake: *Hewes* v. *Hewes* (1830) 4 Sim. 1.

[38] *Cook* v. *Martyn* (1737) 2 Atk. 2; *Barnard* v. *Pumfrett* (1841) 5 M. & Cr. 63, 70.

[39] See *Postlethwaite* v. *Mounsey* (1842) 6 Hare 33, n. (*a*); *Cadbury* v. *Smith, supra; Re Schneider* (1906) 22 T.L.R. 223.

[40] See *Savage* v. *Lane* (1847) 6 Hare 32. And see *Re Brogden* (1888) 38 Ch.D. 546.

[41] See, for detailed treatment, Lewin, *Trusts*, 16th ed., 1964, pp. 436–445.

[42] See *ante*, pp. 18, 43.

[43] See 2 Wolst. & Ch., 12th ed., pp. 1351 *et seq.*

[44] Trustee Act 1925, s.67. For the concurrent jurisdiction of the Court of Protection, see *ibid.* s.54 (as amended by s.148 of Sched. 4 to the Mental Health Act 1983). See Heywood and Massey, *Court of Protection Practice*, 12th ed., 1991.

[45] For the effect of a vesting order, see the Trustee Act 1925, s.49. See also the Law of Property Act 1925, s.9.

[46] See Lewin, *Trusts*, 16th ed., 1964, pp. 436–438, and the Trustee Act 1925, s.44. As to the court's inability to appoint an executor or administrator under the Trustee Act 1925, see *ante*, p. 17.

[47] Reference should be made to the full text of the section.

[48] See *ante* n. 44.

pose of giving effect to a judgment or order directing a sale or mortgage of any land, make an order vesting the land or any part thereof for such estate or interest as the court thinks fit in the purchaser or mortgagee or in any other person.[49]

Appointment of person to convey

In any of the above cases the court may, if it is more convenient, appoint a person to convey the land or any interest therein, and a conveyance by such a person has the same effect as if a vesting order had been made.[50]

Personalty

Section 51 of the same Act[51] authorises the court to make an order vesting the right to transfer or call for a transfer of stock, or to receive the dividends or income thereof, or to sue for or recover a thing in action, in any such person and in such manner[52] as the court may direct[53] in any of the circumstances there described.

These include briefly[54]: upon appointment under an express or statutory power and cases where a trustee is under disability,[55] out of the jurisdiction, cannot be found, or being a corporation has been dissolved, and cases of uncertainty, refusal to act or where it appears to the court to be expedient.

In such cases the court may, if it is more convenient, appoint some proper officer of the bank, or the company or society whose stock is to be transferred, to make or join in making the transfer.[56]

"Stock"

For the purposes of section 51 "stock" includes fully paid shares, and any fund, annuity or security transferable in books kept by any company or society, or by instrument of transfer either alone or accompanied by other formalities, and any share or interest therein.[57] Section 51 also applies to

---

[49] See also the Trustee Act 1925, s.48.

[50] Trustee Act 1925, s.50. And see the Law of Property Act 1925, s.9(3). See, generally, 4 Wolst. & Ch., 13th ed., pp. 77–78. As to execution of instruments by order of the court, see Supreme Court Act 1981, s.39, and note thereto in *Supreme Court Practice*. This procedure can be useful in avoiding a direct refusal resulting in contempt of court.

[51] On s.51 generally, see 4 Wolst. & Ch., 13th ed., pp. 78–81 and Lewin, *Trusts*, 16th ed., 1964, p. 441.

[52] See the Trustee Act 1925, s.51(5).

[53] For the effect of the order, see *ibid.* subss. (3) and (4).

[54] Reference should be made to the full text of the section, which is in differing terms from s.44.

[55] See the Trustee Act 1925, s.54, as amended by s.149 of and Sched. 7 to the Mental Health Act 1959, and Heywood and Massey, *Court of Protection Practice*, 10th ed., 1978, pp. 203 *et seq.*

[56] Trustee Act 1925, s.51(2). And see n. 50, *ante*.

[57] *Ibid.* s.68(14); see 4 Wolst. & Ch., 13th ed., p. 96.

shares in ships registered under the Acts relating to merchant shipping as if they were stock.[58]

Jurisdiction as to vesting orders

The powers of the court to make vesting orders under the Trustee Act 1925 extend to all property in any part of Her Majesty's dominions except Scotland.[59]

Trustees for sale refusing to sell

By section 30 of the Law of Property Act 1925, if trustees for sale including a representative holding land on trust for sale,[60] refuse to sell or to exercise any of the powers conferred by section 28 (which brings into operation the Settled Land Act powers,[61] and enables trustees for sale to partition with certain consents)[62] or by section 29 (which enables trustees for sale to delegate their powers of leasing and management[63]) of that Act, or any requisite consent cannot be obtained,[63a] any person interested may apply to the court[64] for a vesting or other order directing the trustees to give effect thereto, and the court may make such order (for example, for a trustee refusing to sell to concur in a sale) as it thinks fit.[65]

Settled land

Where any representative or other person in whom is vested settled land wrongly refuses or neglects to execute the requisite conveyance, vesting deed or vesting assent,[66] or is outside the United Kingdom or cannot be found, or it is not known whether he is alive or dead, or for any reason the court is satisfied that the requisite conveyance, vesting deed or vesting assent cannot be executed, either at all or without undue delay or expense, the court may, on the application of any person interested, make an order vesting the settled land in the person entitled to call for the legal estate in the same.[67] No stamp duty is payable on a vesting order made in place of a vesting or other assent.[68]

---

[58] Trustee Act 1925, s.51(6).

[59] *Ibid.* s.56.

[60] Law of Property Act 1925, s.205(1)(xxix).

[61] See *post*, p. 665.

[62] See *Re Beale's Settlement Trusts* [1932] 2 Ch. 15.

[63] See *ante*, p. 702.

[63a] *Ante*, n. 62.

[64] Law of Property Act 1925, s.203(3).

[65] For the effect of such order, see *ibid.* s.9. The court may appoint some person to convey in accordance with the provisions of the Trustee Act 1925: see the Law of Property Act 1925, s.9(3). For the court's exercise of its discretion under s.30 see generally 1 Wolst. & Ch., 13th ed., pp. 89–90; Megarry and Wade, *The Law of Real Property*, 5th ed., p. 441; *Jones v. Challenger* [1961] 1 Q.B. 176; *Re Evers* [1980] 1 W.L.R. 1327.

[66] For the procedure on change of ownership, see Settled Land Act 1925, ss.7 and 8.

[67] *Ibid.* s.12. The provisions of the Trustee Act 1925, as to vesting orders apply in such a case: see Settled Land Act 1925, s.113(9).

[68] Settled Land Act 1925, s.12(2). See also S.I. 1987 No. 516, Schedule (Stamp Duty Exempt Investments) Regulations.

Equitable interests

Further powers are given to the court to make vesting orders transferring or creating a legal estate in land for the purpose of giving effect to equitable interests.[69]

Vesting orders after assent

Notwithstanding any assent or conveyance by a representative to a person other than a purchaser the court may, under the Administration of Estates Act 1925, s.38(2), whenever the testator or intestate died,[70] but without prejudice to the rights of a purchaser or a person deriving title under him[71] on the application of a creditor or other person interested (a) order a sale, exchange, mortgage, charge, lease, payment, transfer or other transaction to be carried out which the court considers requisite for the purpose of giving effect to the rights of the persons interested; or (b) declare that the person, not being a purchaser, in whom the property is vested is a trustee for those purposes; or (c) give directions respecting the preparation and execution of any conveyance or other instrument or as to any other matter required for giving effect to the order; or (d) make any vesting order, or appoint a person to convey in accordance with the provisions of the Trustee Act 1925.

Vesting order as against representative

Further, the Administration of Estates Act 1925, s.43(2), which also applies whether the testator or intestate died before or after the commencement of the Act,[72] enables the court to make vesting orders, to which the provisions of the Trustee Act apply, against representatives, on the application of persons claiming possession of real estate or the appointment of a receiver, or a conveyance, assent or registration as proprietor thereof under the Land Registration Act 1925.[73]

Other similar orders

Similar orders include the power of the court to vest land or release it from contingent rights in unborn persons[74] or in infant mortgagees[75] and to vest land in consequence of orders for sale of mortgaged land[76] or of orders for

---

[69] See the Law of Property Act 1925, s.3(5); Settled Land Act 1925, s.16(7). For other instances of vesting orders, see 4 Wolst. & Ch., 13th ed., p. 75.

[70] Administration of Estates Act 1925, s.38(3). See *post*, p. 1132.

[71] *Ibid.*

[72] *Ibid.* s.43(3).

[73] Vesting orders have been made under this subsection against a recalcitrant executor without a formal order to assent being first made.

[74] Trustee Act 1925, s.45; Lewin, *Trusts*, 16th ed., 1974, p. 438.

[75] *Ibid.*, p. 438.

[76] *Ibid.*, p. 438.

specific performance.[77] There are also vesting powers in relation to charity property[78] and the maintenance of infants.[79]

E.—WRIT NE EXEAT REGNO

Limited application of writ

The writ *ne exeat regno* is a sort of mesne process until final judgment to apprehend a person and so prevent him from leaving the realm, unless he has given security for the amount of his debt.[80] Although not much used the procedure is not obsolete.[81]

The jurisdiction was not abolished by the Debtors Act 1869[82] and it is not limited to cases where the plaintiff wishes to call the defendant as his witness.[83] It is confined to cases within section 6 of that Act,[84] which provides that a person shall not be arrested upon mesne process in any action. Where the plaintiff in any action in which, if brought before the commencement of the Act, the defendant would have been liable to arrest, proves at any time before final judgment by evidence on oath, to the satisfaction of a judge, that the plaintiff has good cause of action against the defendant to the amount of £50 or upwards, and that there is probable cause for believing that the defendant is about to quit England unless he be apprehended, and that the absence of the defendant from England will materially prejudice the plaintiff in the prosecution of his action, such judge may in the prescribed manner order such defendant to be arrested and imprisoned for a period not exceeding six months, unless and until he has sooner given the prescribed security, not exceeding the amount claimed in the action, that he will not go out of England without the leave of the court. Where the action is for a penalty or sum in the nature of a penalty other than a penalty in respect of any contract, it is not necessary to prove that the absence of the defendant from England will materially prejudice the plaintiff in the prosecution of his action, and the security given (instead of being that the defendant will not go out of England) is to the effect that any sum recovered against the defendant in the action shall be paid, or that the defendant shall be arrested and imprisoned. The exercise of the power of arrest under section 6 is discretionary.[85] Where the

---

[77] *Ibid.*, p. 439.

[78] *Ibid.*, p. 443 and Tudor, *Charities*, 7th ed., 1984, p. 384.

[79] Trustee Act 1925, s.53; Lewin, *Trusts*, 16th ed., 1974, p. 303.

[80] Seton's *Judgments and Orders*, 7th ed., 504–506; form of order, *ibid.* 504; form of writ, Dan.C.F., p. 758.

[81] *Felton* v. *Callis* [1969] 1 Q.B. 200, in which the earlier authorities are examined. See also S.C.P. 1993 para. 45/1/37 and *Al Nahkel for Contracting and Trading Ltd.* v. *Lowe* [1986] Q.B. 235 and *Allied Arab Bank Ltd.* v. *Hajjal* [1988] Q.B. 787.

[82] 32 & 33 Vict. c. 62.

[83] See *ante* n. 81.

[84] See *Drover* v. *Beyer* (1879) 13 Ch.D. 242; *Hands* v. *Hands* (1881) 43 L.T. 750; *Felton* v. *Callis*, *supra*.

[85] *Hasluck* v. *Lehman* (1890) 6 T.L.R. 435.

defendant is arrested under it, he can only be kept in prison until final judgment.[86]

Practice: equitable claims only

The application is made *ex parte* on affidavit.[87] The usual practice is to require the plaintiff to give an undertaking as to damages and to accept short notice of motion. The defendant may at any time after arrest apply to the court or a judge to rescind or vary the order or to be discharged from custody, or for such relief as may be just.[88]

The writ of *ne exeat regno* has been considered as in the nature of equitable bail,[89] and a court of equity proceeded by analogy to the proceedings at law in cases of legal bail.[90] It is only applicable to claims such as before the Judicature Acts could have been brought forward in Chancery.[91]

The object is to obtain security from a person intending to leave the country, when the other party has no legal remedy, and cannot hold him to bail.[92] But it was settled, that, though a plaintiff, swearing to the balance of an account, might have bail at law, yet the Court of Chancery holding a concurrent jurisdiction upon the head of account, the plaintiff might also have the writ of *ne exeat regno*; and that when a creditor filed a bill for an account and administration of the assets, if there was a clear affidavit of assets received, the Court of Chancery would grant the writ.[93]

Proof required

Generally speaking, the affidavit, on which the application for a *ne exeat regno* is grounded, "must be as positive as to the equitable debt, as an affidavit of a legal debt, to hold to bail"[94]; but in the case of partners and executors, information and belief is sufficient.[95] The affidavit ought to swear, or allege to the best of the knowledge and belief of the deponent, that assets have come to the hands of the executor or administrator[96]; and

---

[86] *Hume* v. *Druyff* (1873) L.R. 8 Ex. 214. As to attachment under the Debtors Act 1869, s.4(3), see *ante*, pp. 852 *et seq.*

[87] The procedure was regulated by former Ord. 69, which is not contained in R.S.C. 1965.

[88] As to discharging the writ *ne exeat regno*, see Dan.Ch.Pr., 8th ed., 1446.

[89] *Haffey* v. *Haffey* (1807) 14 Ves. 261. And see *Sobey* v. *Sobey* (1873) L.R. 15 Eq. 200. For practice, see Dan.Ch.Pr., 8th ed., pp. 1441 *et seq.*

[90] *Pannell* v. *Tayler* (1823) Turn. & R. 96, 103. See *Jenkins* v. *Parkinson* (1833) 2 M. & K. 5.

[91] *Drover* v. *Beyer* (1879) 13 Ch.D. 242.

[92] *Swift* v. *Swift* (1810) 1 Ball & B. 326.

[93] *Jones* v. *Alephsin* (1810) 16 Ves. 471. But a residuary legatee cannot have a writ of *ne exeat regno* against a debtor of the testator on the ground that he colludes with the executor: *Graves* v. *Griffith* (1820) 1 Jac. & Walk. 646; *Colverson* v. *Bloomfield* (1885) 29 Ch.D. 341.

[94] *Jackson* v. *Petrie* (1804) 10 Ves. 164; *Amsinck* v. *Barklay* (1803) 8 Ves. 597.

[95] *Jackson* v. *Petrie, supra*; *Rico* v. *Gualtier* (1747) 3 Atk. 501. An affidavit founded on information and belief, which, under Ord. 41, r. 5 is admissible on interlocutory applications, must state the sources and grounds of such belief. See the rule itself, and *Re J. L. Young Manufacturing Co.* [1900] 2 Ch. 753.

[96] *Anon.* (1752) 2 Ves.Sen. 489; and see *Re Underwood* (1903) 51 W.R. 335. A present vested interest, though capable of being divested, is a sufficient interest to support a writ of *ne exeat regno*: *Howkins* v. *Howkins* (1860) 1 Dr. & Sm. 75, 78.

it should appear distinctly that he has a present intention to leave the country.[97]

The debt must be actually due and payable and for an ascertained amount.[98] The evidence of the debt must be positive and clear,[99] as also must the defendant's intention to leave the country.[1] The plaintiff must also clearly prove that he will be materially prejudiced in the prosecution of his claim by the defendant leaving the kingdom.[2]

If the court is satisfied that the defendant is going abroad to evade payment, it can make an order of *ne exeat*, although an order for payment has been made but the time for payment has not arrived.[3]

F.—MAREVA INJUNCTION AND ANTON PILLER ORDERS

It is submitted that there is no reason why a *Mareva* injunction or an *Anton Piller* order should not be granted in administration proceedings.[4] *Mareva* injunctions are granted, most commonly in commercial cases, to restrain a defendant from removing assets from the jurisdiction of the English courts or from dissipating assets pending the final determination of proceedings.[5] However, the injunction must be part of the substantive relief to which the plaintiff seeking it is entitled by his cause of action.[6] *Anton Piller* orders are granted where there is a real risk that property or evidence will be destroyed or hidden so as to defeat the ends of justice.[6a] Application is made to the Court *ex parte*, and the Court will sit *in camera*. The order does not (as is commonly thought) authorise the applicant and his solicitor to search the defendant's premises, but rather is an order *in personam* requiring the defendant to permit such a search and the removal of property and documents covered by the order.

The law and practice[7] relating to *Mareva* injunctions and *Anton Piller* orders is of general application to all High Court proceedings and is developing rapidly. Reference should accordingly be made to the current edition of the Supreme Court Practice.[8]

[97] *Darley* v. *Nicholson* (1842) 1 Dr. & W. 66; *Perry* v. *Dorset* (1871) 19 W.R. 1048.
[98] *Colverson* v. *Bloomfield* (1885) 29 Ch.D. 341; *Anon.* (1865) 5 N.R. 358; *Flack* v. *Holm* (1820) 1 J. & W. 405. *cf. Whitehouse* v. *Partridge* (1818) 3 Sw. 365.
[99] *Perry* v. *Dorset* (1871) 19 W.R. 1048.
[1] *Perry* v. *Dorset, ante*; and see *Re Underwood, ante.*
[2] *Drover* v. *Beyer* (1879) 13 Ch.D. 242.
[3] *Sobey* v. *Sobey* (1873) L.R. 15 Eq. 200; *Whitehouse* v. *Partridge* (1818) 3 Sw. 365. But see *Colverson* v. *Bloomfield* (1885) 29 Ch.D. 341, where the order was not served.
[4] *Rahman* (*Prince Abdul*) *bin Turki al Sudairy* v. *Abu-Taha* [1980] 1 W.L.R. 1268; *Barclay-Johnson* v. *Yuill* [1980] 1 W.L.R. 1259. For general principles see *Ninemia* v. *Trave* [1983] 1 W.L.R. 1412 (C.A.).
[5] *Rasu Maritima S.A.* v. *Perusahaan Pertambangan Minyak Dan Gas Bumi Negara* [1978] 1 Q.B. 644; *Mareva Compania Naviera S.A.* v. *International Bulkcarriers S.A.* [1975] 2 Lloyd's Rep. 509.
[6] *Siskina* v. *Distos Compania Naviera S.A.* [1979] A.C. 210.
[6a] See *Anton Pillerking* v. *Manufacturing Processes Ltd.* [1976] Ch. 55.
[7] Guidelines for applicants are stated in *Third Chandris Shipping Corporation* v. *Unimarine S.A.* [1979] Q.B. 645.
[8] *Supreme Court Practice 1993* notes to Order 29 (29/1/20) and (29/2–3/6) *et seq.*

CHAPTER 62

THE REPRESENTATIVE AS PLAINTIFF AND OTHER PARTIES

An executor may be involved in two quite different types of litigation. If difficulties arise in the administration of the estate as to the rights *inter se* of creditors or beneficiaries or as to the meaning of the will or relevant legislation then administration proceedings are appropriate. These have been considered.[1] It remains to consider the second type of litigation, namely contentious litigation by or against the representatives. This will be considered in three sections, namely (1) actions begun by the deceased; (2) actions accruing after death; and (3) procedure.

A. ACTIONS BEGUN BY THE DECEASED IN HIS LIFETIME

Procedure on death of a party

Where the cause of action survives[2] the action does not abate by reason of the death of a party.[3] The representative or other party applies *ex parte* and the court will then join the representative and order the proceedings to carry on, if it thinks this necessary, to ensure that all matters in dispute may be effectually and completely determined.[4] The order must be served on all parties, who have 14 days, after such service, in which to apply to discharge or vary the order.

Administrator ad litem

It was always possible to obtain a grant of administration, limited to commencing or substantiating proceedings in the Court of Chancery.[5] Now it is possible, by virtue of the Supreme Court Act 1981, s.116, as amended, to obtain a grant limited to commencing, defending or carrying on proceedings in any Division of the High Court, or in any other court. Thus a

[1] See *ante*, p. 821. Administration proceedings are frequently non-contentious in that the parties are not hostile, frequently instruct the same solicitor for all parties, and simply require the court's decision for the protection of the personal representatives and to bind persons not *sui juris*.

[2] See *ante*, pp. 515 *et seq*. A writ issued after death but before grant of administration is a nullity: *Finnegan* v. *Cementation Ltd.* [1953] 1 Q.B. 688; unless R.S.C. Ord. 15, r. 6A is followed.

[3] R.S.C. Ord. 15, r. 7(1). If the cause of action does not survive there will be abatement and no order can be made: *Kirk* v. *Todd* (1882) 21 Ch.D. 484; *Phillips* v. *Homfray* (1883) 24 Ch.D. 439.

[4] R.S.C. Ord. 15, r. 7(2). There is provision for a person already a party to be joined in a different capacity or removed from one side of the record (*ibid*. r. 7(3)). There is a wide discretion: *Re Tate* [1959] Ch. 615.

[5] *Woolley* v. *Green* (1820) 3 Pill. 314; *Maclean* v. *Dawson* (1859) 1 Sw. & Tr. 425; *Re Dodgson* (1859) 1 Sw. & Tr. 259; *Burdon* v. *Morgan* (1872) L.R. 2 P. & D. 371. See *ante*.

grant was made under this section where it was intended to sue the estate of the deceased in the King's Bench Division under the provisions of the Law Reform (Miscellaneous Provisions) Act 1934, s.1, for negligence in a motor accident in which the deceased had met his death, and the next-of-kin of the deceased, who died intestate, declined to take out a grant.[6] In such cases the grant may be made to a nominee of the intending plaintiff. But no grant may be made in favour of a person who is not willing to act.[7] In such cases the court will not grant a general administration, but only an administration limited for the purposes of substantiating and carrying on the proceedings.[8]

If the grantee of such limited letters is made a party to the suit, the estate of the deceased is properly represented, so as to enable the court to proceed in the cause[9]; and an order obtained against such an administrator will be binding on any future grantee of general letters of administration.[10]

The appointment of an administrator *ad litem* is in many cases unnecessary, since the court has power where any deceased person interested in the matter in question has no representative, to proceed in the absence of such representative, or to appoint some person to represent the estate for the purposes of the proceedings. Any order made in the proceedings binds the estate of the deceased person to the same extent as if his representative had been a party to them.[11]

Mode of application on death of a party

The application for an order to carry on under Order 15, r. 7 is made to the master, supported by affidavit evidence to show the nature of the proceedings, the stage reached, the fact and date of death and of grant of representation (if any), the interest or liability of the deceased party and of the person on whom this has devolved, the survival of the cause of action and the form of order desired.[13] The court will adapt the procedure to the circumstances in any cases to which the Rule does not apply.[12]

---

[6] *Re Simpson* [1936] P. 40; *Re Knight* [1939] 3 All E.R. 928.

[7] *Pratt* v. *L. P. T. Board* [1937] 1 All E.R. 473.

[8] *Re Chanter*(1844) 1 Robert. 273.

[9] *Davis* v. *Chanter* (1848) 2 Phil.C.C. 545, overriding *ibid.* 14 Sim. 212; and see *Brant* v. *King*, cited in 2 Ph. 551.

[10] See *Faulkner* v. *Daniel* (1843) 3 Hare 199, 208; *Ellice* v. *Goodson* (1845) 2 Coll. 4. That is to say, it binds the general administrator, when appointed, as to the particular question involved in the action, but, if the relief sought for is general administration, a general administrator has always been required: see *Dowdeswell* v. *Dowdeswell* (1878) 9 Ch.D. 294; *Re Mastelloui* [1917] W.N. 243; and *ante*, p. 827. In *Shipton* v. *Rawlings* (1845) 4 De G. & Sm. 477, it was held that an *administrator ad litem* of a married woman did not sufficiently represent her separate estate to enable the court to decide how far that estate was liable in respect of her acts as trustee.

[11] Ord. 15, rr. 6A, 15; *post*, pp. 889–891.

[12] See the notes to Ord. 15, r. 7 in the *Supreme Court Practice 1993*.

[13] *Hemming* v. *Williams* (1871) L.R. 6 C.P. 480; *Canning* v. *Farren* [1907] 2 Ir.R. 486; *Smith* v. *Williams* [1922] 1 K.B. 158 (death of respondent before case stated by Income Tax Commissioners for purposes of appeal had been signed and filed: held that the proceedings had not abated by the death and that the court could mould procedure for continuing appeal: order made for respondent's executor to be added as respondent).

Death pending appeal

The same procedure applies if the death occurs pending appeal[14] save that the order may be made by the Court of Appeal, and similarly the Court of Appeal may make the order where there is an appeal to the House of Lords.[15]

Death of plaintiff

If a sole plaintiff dies his representatives will normally obtain an order to carry on as above described.[16] If a joint plaintiff dies and the action is joint the survivors may continue without an order[17] but in any other case an order is necessary.[18]

Death of defendant

If a sole defendant dies the action cannot continue until his representative has been added as a party by an order to carry on, applied for either by the plaintiff or by such personal representative.[19] If there are several defendants jointly liable the liability continues in the survivors so that the representatives of a deceased defendant need not be joined,[20] but they will normally be joined if there is several liability.[21] If the deceased defendant has no representative the court may appoint a person to represent the estate in order to enable the plaintiff to continue.[22]

Failure to proceed

If, after the death of the plaintiff or the defendant in any action in which the cause of action survives, no order to carry on is made under Order 15, r. 7, the court may order that unless the action is proceeded with within a specified time it shall be struck out as against the deceased party. Where it is the plaintiff who has died, notice of the application must be given to his representatives (if any), and to any other interested parties.[23] The cessation of the solicitor's authority on the death of his client must, however, be remembered. This is considered later.[24]

---

[14] *Ranson* v. *Patton* (1881) 17 Ch.D. 767; *Smith* v. *Williams* [1922] 1 K.B. 148.
[15] *London, Tilbury Ry. Co.* v. *Paterson* [1912] W.N. 261.
[16] See *Burstall* v. *Fearon* (1883) 24 Ch.D. 126; *Re Atkins* (1875) 1 Ch.D. 82.
[17] *Smith* v. *L.N.W.R.* (1853) 2 E. & B. 69.
[18] See *Arnison* v. *Smith* (1889) 40 Ch.D. 567.
[19] *Duke* v. *Davis* [1893] 2 Q.B. 260. If there is a counterclaim such personal representatives must obtain an order on their own application to carry on the counterclaim: *Andrew* v. *Aitken* (1882) 21 Ch.D. 175.
[20] See *Ashby* v. *Day* (1886) 45 L.T. 408.
[21] *Ellis* v. *Wadeson* [1899] 1 Q.B. 714, 718.
[22] *Re Simpson* [1936] P. 40. As to consent of such person, see p. 890 *post*. See generally R.S.C., Ord. 15, r. 15, and the notes thereto in the *Supreme Court Practice*.
[23] R.S.C., Ord. 15, r. 9.
[24] See *post*, p. 873.

Abatement

Where the cause of action does not survive, the action abates and the claim will be struck out,[25] or the defendant may get an order staying the action.[26]

Liability for costs

An executor who has obtained an order to continue an action, even after judgment,[27] becomes liable for costs *ab initio* in the same manner as if the action had been commenced by him, though without prejudice to an indemnity out of the estate.[28]

Death of plaintiff between verdict and judgment

Whether or not the cause of action survives, if the plaintiff dies between verdict and judgment, judgment may be entered notwithstanding the death,[29] but before giving judgment the judge may make an order to carry on substituting his representatives under R.S.C., Order 15, r. 7(2).[30]

Entry of judgment retrospectively

The power for the court or judge to order judgment to be entered *nunc pro tunc* is confirmed by Order 42, r. 3, which provides that a judgment takes effect from the day of its date and is dated as of the day on which it is given unless the court orders it to be dated as of some earlier or later day.[31]

Death of plaintiff after judgment: execution

Where the deceased plaintiff has obtained judgment, his representatives may apply to the court or judge, under Order 46, r. 2, for leave to issue execution. The court or judge, if satisfied that the party so applying is entitled to issue execution, may make an order to that effect, or may order an issue to be tried.[32] Where, after judgment, the plaintiff died, having made a will appointing executors, an application by them to the court *ex parte* for leave to issue execution was granted on production of the pro-

---

[25] *Eldridge* v. *Burgess* (1878) 7 Ch.D. 411.

[26] *Warder* v. *Saunders* (1878) 10 Q.B.D. 114.

[27] *Boynton* v. *Boynton* (1879) 4 App.Cas. 733 (order obtained after notice of appeal against judgment in deceased's favour).

[28] *Ibid.*; see also *Re London Drapery Stores* [1898] 2 Ch. 684, where the same principle was applied on a company liquidation.

[29] R.S.C., Ord. 35, r. 9.

[30] See *ante*, p. 868.

[31] Where between the trial of the action and the delivery of judgment one of the defendants died, the judgment was dated as of the last day of the trial: *Ecroyd* v. *Coulthard* [1897] 2 Ch. 554; and see *Bond* v. *Nottingham Corporation* [1940] Ch. 429.

[32] As to matrimonial proceedings, see *Coleman* v. *Coleman* [1920] P. 71 (death of husband who had been ordered to pay wife's taxed costs in divorce proceedings: court could not enforce payment against his representatives). For procedure in general, see Ord. 46, r. 4, and see Chapter 48, *ante*.

bate.[33] Unless the executor has obtained such leave he is not entitled to issue a bankruptcy notice.[34]

Semble, this rule applies where one of two or more plaintiffs dies after judgment and before execution.[35]

Attachment of debt

Originally the representative was not entitled to attach a debt due to the judgment debtor until he had made himself a party to the judgment.[36] This is no longer necessary.[37]

Writ of fi. fa.

If the plaintiff dies after a *fieri facias*[38] has been sent out, the writ may, notwithstanding, be executed, and his representative is entitled to the money; or if there is no executor, and administration has not been granted, the money should be brought into court, and there deposited until some person appears to claim it as representative of the deceased.[39]

New trial before administration granted

It would seem that no motion for a new trial can be made where the plaintiff has died since the trial, until probate or administration to the deceased has been obtained,[40] unless the court exercises its discretion to proceed in the absence of a person representing the estate or appoints a person for this purpose.[41] *Semble* this would be rare in the case of the death of a plaintiff.

Arbitrator's authority

The authority of an arbitrator is not revoked by the death of either party before award made.[42] Further, an arbitration agreement is not discharged by the death of any party thereto, either as respects the deceased or any other party, but is enforceable by or against the representative of the

---

[33] See *Re Woodall, post*. The executor need no longer revive the judgment.

[34] *Re Woodall* (1884) 13 Q.B.D. 479; see *Re Bagley* [1911] 1 K.B. 317.

[35] Formerly the survivors might, within a year after judgment in a personal action, issue execution without reviving the judgment: but execution had to be taken out in the joint names of all the plaintiffs: *Davis* v. *Andrews* [1884] W.N. 94.

[36] Common Law Procedure Act 1854 (17 & 18 Vict. c. 125), s.61.

[37] *Re Bagley* [1911] 1 K.B. 317.

[38] As to this writ, see R.S.C., Ord. 47.

[39] *Clerk* v. *Withers* (1704) 2 Ld.Raym. 1072; 1 Chit.Archb. 881, 14th ed. See also *Ellis* v. *Griffith* (1846) 16 M. & W. 106 (writ of *capias ad satisfaciendum*). A writ of sequestration, however, is suspended by the death of the person at whose instance it issued, until it is revived: *Wharram* v. *Broughton* (1748) 1 Ves.Sen. 183. As to the writ of sequestration, see R.S.C., Ord. 46, r. 5.

[40] *Lloyd* v. *Ogleby* (1859) 5 C.B.(N.S.) 667.

[41] See R.S.C., Ord. 15, r. 15.

[42] Arbitration Act 1950, s.2(2).

deceased.[43] This does not apply to statutory arbitrations.[44] And where the reference to arbitration is by court order, it may be desirable to provide expressly that, in the case of the death of either of the parties before the making of the award,[45] it shall be delivered to their representatives. Where such a clause is inserted in the order an award made after the death of either party appears to be valid and would be for or against the personal representatives.[46] This, however, must be understood as limited to an action in which the cause of action survives for or against the representatives of the deceased party.[47] *Secus*, where the cause of action has been determined and the damages only are referred to an arbitrator for assessment.[48]

In an action where the cause of action survives for, and against, representatives, if either party dies *after* the award is made under an order of *nisi prius* (where a verdict has been taken subject to the award), judgment may be entered notwithstanding the death, under the provisions of Order 35, r. 9. The power of the court to order judgment to be entered retrospectively has been already referred to.[49]

Solicitor's authority

The authority of a solicitor in an action is determined by the death of his client. Consequently, when, after a verdict for the plaintiff, and pending a rule for a new trial, the plaintiff died, no cause could be shown against the rule until there was a representative.[50] Cause could not be shown on behalf of the solicitor who claimed a lien on the verdict for his costs.[51] So where money was paid into court by a defendant who died before verdict or interlocutory judgment, and the suit abated, the money could be paid out of court only to the representatives of the defendant; and an application on the part of his solicitor would not be entertained.[52] Now, if the cause of

---

[43] Arbitration Act 1950, s.2(1).

[44] Arbitration Act 1950, s.31.

[45] See the observations of Abbott C.J. in *Cooper* v. *Johnson* (1819) 2 2 B. & A. 395.

[46] *Tyler* v. *Jones* (1824) 3 B. & C. 144; *Clarke* v. *Crofts* (1827) 4 Bing. 143; *Macdougall* v. *Robertson*, 2 Y. & Jerv. 11; *Rogers* v. *Stanton* (1816) 7 Taunt. 575 (n). But it cannot be enforced by committal against the representative of a deceased party: *Newton* v. *Walker* (1741) Willes 315, 3 B. & C. 146.

[47] *Bowker* v. *Evans* (1885) 15 Q.B.D. 565; see also Arbitration Act 1950, s.2(3).

[48] *Chapman* v. *Day* (1883) 48 L.T. 907. See *Re Donovan and Burke* [1908] 2 Ir.R. 143.

[49] *Ante*, p. 871.

[50] *Shoman* v. *Allen* (1838) 1 Man. & Gr. 96, n. (c). But where after a verdict for the defendant, he died, and then the plaintiff obtained a rule for new trial calling on the "legal representatives of the defendant or their attorneys," to show cause, and it was served on the latter, it was held that cause might be shown by counsel instructed by the attorneys acting for the executors named in the will, though they had not proved it. The court distinguished *Shoman* v. *Allen*, on the ground that in that case there was no person who could be served with the rule, whereas in the present case there was: *Thomas* v. *Dunn* (1845) 1 C.B. 139. The distinction is unconvincing and appears contrary to principle.

[51] *Shoman* v. *Allen* (1838) 1 M. & Gr. 96, n. (c).

[52] *Palmer* v. *Reiffenstein* (1840) 1 Man. & Gr. 94.

action survives, the action does not abate,[53] but the solicitor's authority is determined nonetheless.

B. ACTIONS ACCRUING AFTER THE DEATH

Tort

If an injury is done, after the death of a testator or intestate, to any property forming part of his estate, the executor or administrator may bring an action for damages for the tort. In such circumstances, he has his option, either to sue in his representative capacity, and plead as executor or administrator, or to bring the action in his own name, and in his individual character. If, however, he sues in his representative capacity the indorsement of claim must, under Order 6, r. 3, show in what capacity he sues.[54]

The executor or administrator has this right of action, and the option as to the form in which it may be brought, whether or not he has ever had actual possession of the property.[55] It is a rule of law, that the ownership of personal chattels draws to it the possession[56]; and on the death of the testator or intestate, his executors or administrators are, in point of law, the owners of the goods which belonged to him. Consequently, representatives, whether or not in actual possession of such goods before the tort committed, may plead, as any other persons may, in right of their own property, when wrongfully damaged by another.[57]

Thus, under the old procedure, the underlying principles of which are still applicable, executors or administrators might maintain trespass for taking away the goods of the testator or intestate after his death, either in their own name, or in their representative character, whether they were ever actually possessed of them or not.[58] If they sued as executors or administrators, they might either declare that the deceased was possessed of the goods and the trespass committed after his death to the damage of the executors or administrators[59]; or, as the property in the goods draws to it the possession in law, they might declare on their own possession as executors.[60] So with trover, if the goods of the testator were taken and converted after his death, and before the executor had obtained possession of them, he might either bring an action in his own name without alleging himself executor,[61] or he might sue as executor, and either declare that the testator was possessed of the goods and that the defendant after his death

---

[53] R.S.C., Ord. 15, r. 7(1).
[54] See also *post*, p. 892.
[55] *Bollard* v. *Spencer* (1797) 7 T.R. 358; *Hollis* v. *Smith* (1808) 10 East 294; *Grimstead* v. *Shirley* (1809) 2 Taunt. 116.
[56] Bro. Trespass 303; *Hudson* v. *Hudson* (1678) Latch. 214.
[57] *Hollis* v. *Smith* (1808) 10 East 295.
[58] *Adams* v. *Cheverel* (1606) Cr.Jac. 113.
[59] Cro.Jac. 113.
[60] 2 Saund. 47n., note to *Wilbraham* v. *Snow*.
[61] *Hole* v. *King* (1709) Com.Rep. 163; *Jenkins* v. *Plombe* (1704) 6 Mod. 181.

converted them,[62] or that he himself was possessed as executor, and that the defendant converted them.[63]

It has already appeared that an executor or administrator may sue in such circumstances, though the injury was done before probate or administration granted.[64]

Contract

It has been decided, in a variety of cases, that an executor or administrator may sue *as such*, as well as in his own name, upon a contract made with him in his representative character. The indorsement of claim must, however, show the capacity in which he sues.[65] He may sue as such, not only in cases where the consideration flows from the deceased, but also in cases where the consideration flows directly from himself as executor. Thus an executor may plead as such, not only on an account stated with him as executor concerning money due to the testator from the defendant, but also on an account stated with him as executor concerning money due to him as executor.[66] Again, a representative has been held entitled to sue,[67] as such, for money lent by him as representative[68]; for money had and received to his use as representative after the death of the deceased[69]; to recover money paid as representative to the use of the defendant[70]; to recover money which he had been compelled to pay by reason of the deceased having become surety; to recover money paid by him in his representative capacity and which he ought not to have paid[71]; and for goods sold and delivered after the death of the deceased.[72]

In *Marshall* v. *Broadhurst*,[73] the testator had agreed to do certain work, and died before the work was begun and the executors did the work, using the materials of the testator, and then brought an action, in their representative character, for work and labour done, materials found, and goods sold and delivered by the plaintiffs as executors. It was held that they might recover the value of the materials; and the court seemed to be of opinion

[62] *Hudson* v. *Hudson* (1678) Latch. 214.

[63] *Anon.* (1697) Comberb. 451; 2 Saund. 47n., note to *Wilbraham* v. *Snow*. And see *Fraser* v. *Swansea Canal Co.* (1834) 1 A. & E. 354 (action of trover by administrator of deceased mortgages of colliery, machinery, barges, etc., for illegal seizure by defendant company of barges, etc., from possession of lessee or mortgagor).

[64] *Ante*, pp. 553 *et seq.*

[65] R.S.C., Ord. 6, r. 3. See *post* p. 892.

[66] *Needham* v. *Croke* (1681) 1 Freem. 538; *Thompson* v. *Stent* (1808) 1 Taunt. 322.

[67] In all these cases the form of action was in *assumpsit*.

[68] *Webster* v. *Spencer* (1820) 3 B. & A. 360.

[69] *Foxwist* v. *Tremain* (1670) 2 Saund. 202.

[70] *Ord.* v. *Fenwick* (1802) 3 East 104.

[71] *Clark* v. *Hougham* (1823) 2 B. & C. 149, 155. But in *Munt* v. *Stokes* (1792) 4 T.R. 561, the testator had borrowed money on a *respondentia* contract, prohibited by the laws of this country, and his executors refunded the money to the lenders. The court held that the executors could not recover back this money, since, knowing the whole transaction, and being bound to know the law, they had paid it voluntarily, and there was nothing contrary to conscience in the lenders receiving the money which they had advanced.

[72] *Cowell* v. *Watts* (1805) 6 East 405.

[73] (1831) 1 Cr. & J. 403.

that they might recover also for the work and labour as executors. It was afterwards expressly decided in *Edwards* v. *Gracc*,[74] that an executor might sue, as such, for work done by him as executor. So in *Aspinall* v. *Wake*,[75] where the plaintiffs, being executors, had continued to work the leasehold quarries of their testator and had shipped off for the defendant, from time to time, cargoes of stone, dug partly before, and partly after the testator's death, and the defendant had accepted bills for the price of some of the cargoes, drawn by the plaintiffs as executors, it was held that they might well sue, as executors, for the price of the remainder of the cargoes. Lastly, in *Werner* v. *Humphreys*,[76] a coat had been ordered by the defendant of a tailor, and had been cut out of the tailor's own cloth, tacked together and tried on in his lifetime, but was finished and delivered after his death by his administratrix. It was held that she could not sue for the price, as for goods sold and delivered by the intestate, but that the proper form of action was for goods sold and delivered by her as administratrix.

If a bill of exchange is indorsed to A and B as executors, they may plead as such in an action against the acceptor.[77] Thus, in *Partridge* v. *Court*,[78] it was held that an administrator may sue, as such, on a promissory note given to him as administrator since the death of the intestate. And a representative may sue on a bill of exchange indorsed to the deceased after, and in ignorance of, his death.[79] Further, in *Catherwood* v. *Chabaud*,[80] it was held that where the cause of action is such that the original administrator may sue in his representative character, the right of action devolves on an administrator *de bonis non*.

General rule

The rule may now be regarded as firmly established,[81] that *where the money recovered will be assets, the executor may sue for it, and sue in his representative character.*[82]

Where, however, the executor or administrator took a bond from a simple contract debtor to the estate of the deceased, though it was given to him as executor or administrator, it was held that he could not sue on it in his representative capacity, because the effect of the bond was to

[74] (1836) 2 M. & W. 190.
[75] (1833) 10 Bing. 51.
[76] (1841) 2 M. & G. 853; *Moseley* v. *Rendell* (1871) L.R. 6 Q.B. 338.
[77] *King* v. *Thom* (1786) 1 T.R. 487, recognised by Tindal C.J. in *Aspinall* v. *Wake* (1833) 10 Bing. 55.
[78] (1818) 5 Price 412, confirmed 7 Price 591.
[79] *Murray* v. *E. I. Co.* (1821) 5 B. & A. 204. And see the Bills of Exchange Act 1882, ss.7(3), 34(3).
[80] (1823) 1 B. & C. 150; see and *cf. ante*, p. 50.
[81] In some of the earlier cases, contracts (especially in the instance of negotiable instruments) made with a personal representative were considered personal to him, and enforceable by him only in his own right.
[82] *Cowell* v. *Watts* (1805) 6 East 410, 411, 412; *Heath* v. *Chilton* (1844) 12 M. & W. 637, *per* Parke B.; *Abbott* v. *Parfitt* (1871) L.R. 6 Q.B. 346, distinguishing *Bolingbroke* v. *Kerr*, L.R. 1 Ex. 222, in which case the business was not carried on for the benefit of the estate.

extinguish the simple contract debt, creating a new and personal obligation of a higher nature.[83]

Where some of several executors contract

Further, if there are two or more executors, it does not follow that in all cases where the money recovered would be assets, all the executors may join in suing in their representative character on a contract, if they did not all make the contract. Thus, in *Heath* v. *Chilton*,[84] two out of three executors (who had alone proved the will) authorised an attorney to receive rents due to the estate of the testator, and to give receipts in their names, and the rents were received, and receipts given accordingly. It was held that the three executors could not jointly sue the attorney for the money, unless it was found by the jury, that the two who had contracted with him did so on account of themselves and the other co-executor, or generally on account of the estate, with a view to the interference of the co-executor, in case he should choose to take part in the management of it.

Action on judgment

A representative may sue, either in his representative character, or in his own name, on a judgment recovered by him as representative,[85] for whenever there is a final order or judgment for payment of a sum of money an action will lie thereon[86] even if the final order is that of a foreign court.[87] Exceptions to this principle existed in the case of decrees in equity for there was no implied promise to pay a mere equitable debt.[88] Exceptions may also exist where the order is based upon a statutory remedy.[89] In particular no action can be brought in the county court on a judgment of the High Court.[90]

Joinder of causes of action

Claims by or against an executor or administrator as such, may be joined with claims by or against him personally, provided the last-mentioned

---

[83] *Hosier* v. *Lord Arundell* (1802) 3 Bos. & Pull. 7; *Partridge* v. *Court* (1818) 5 Price 419, 420, 421; *Price* v. *Moulton* (1851) 10 C.B. 561, considered in *Commissioners of Stamps* v. *Hope* [1891] A.C. 476, where it is stated that their Lordships would hesitate to assent to a proposition that the reported language of the court in some places is to be understood as importing that a merger of a simple contract debt in a debt of a higher nature is effected by law, merely by the existence of an identical covenant, and notwithstanding the plain intention of the parties to the contrary.

[84] (1844) 12 M. & W. 632. This accords with the decision in *Fountain Forestry* v. *Edwards* [1975] Ch. 1. See p. 690 *ante*.

[85] *Crawford* v. *Whittal* (1773) 1 Dougl. 4, n. (1).

[86] *Hutchinson* v. *Gillespie* (1856) 11 Ex. 798.

[87] *Grant* v. *Easton* (1883) 13 Q.B.D. 302; *Nouvion* v. *Freeman* (1889) 15 App.Cas. 1; *Beatty* v. *Beatty* [1924] 1 K.B. 807.

[88] See n. 86.

[89] See *Bailey* v. *Bailey* (1884) 13 Q.B.D. 855; *Robins* v. *Robins* [1907] 2 K.B. 13; *Beatty* v. *Beatty* [1924] 1 K.B. 807.

[90] County Courts Act 1984, s.36; *Cheetham* v. *Hollingsworth* (1914) 136 L.T.J. 348.

claims are alleged to arise with reference to the estate in respect of which the plaintiff or defendant sues or is sued as executor or administrator,[91] and there is a proper indorsement as to capacity.[92]

Suits accruing on contracts made with testator

In the above cases of contract, the promise sued upon by the representative was expressly or impliedly made to himself in his representative character; but in many cases an action on which the deceased himself could not have sued may accrue to the executor or administrator upon a contract made with the deceased in his lifetime.

It has already appeared that, where a cause of action accrued in the lifetime of the testator on a contract made with him, without naming his executors, or to him and his assigns, such *chose in action*, generally speaking, is transmitted to the executor.[93] The executor will be entitled to sue on such a contract, though the action does not accrue till after the death of the testator. Thus, if A covenants with B to grant him a lease of certain land by such a day, and B dies before the day, and before any lease made, if A refuses to grant the lease, when the day arrives, to the executor of B, the executor will have an action as such on the covenant.[94]

In *Husband* v. *Pollard*,[95] a covenant to renew a lease, entered into for the benefit of the covenantee, his executors, administrators and assigns, was held enforceable at the suit of the representatives of the covenantee. Similarly, a covenant to grant a lease to A and his assigns by a particular day,[96] or a contract to deliver a chattel on a given day to A or his assigns,[97] may, if A dies before the specified day, be enforced by his executors, who, for this purpose, are his assigns in law.[98]

If, however, A should, in his lifetime, have appointed some person to take the chattel, that person would be his assignee in deed.[99] And where X is only to pay £20 to such person as B shall by will appoint, and B by his will appoints executors, but no person to whom £20 is to be paid, the executors, not being assignees in fact, are not entitled to the payment.[1] For where an assignee in fact is indicated, the law will not seek out an assignee in law.[2]

A suit may accrue in the time of the executor or administrator by reason

---

[91] Ord. 15, r. 1; *Tredegar* v. *Roberts* [1914] 1 K.B. 283; *Re Pimm* [1916] W.N. 202. This rule also applies to counterclaims: Ord. 15, r. 2; *Re Richardson* [1933] W.N. 90; overruling *Macdonald* v. *Carington* (1878) 4 C.P.D. 28.

[92] See Ord. 6, r. 3.

[93] *Ante*, pp. 515 *et seq.*

[94] *Chapman* v. *Dalton* (1565) 1 Plowd. 284; Wentw.Off.Ex., 14th ed., p. 188.

[95] Cited in *Randal* v. *Randal* (1728) 2 P.Wms. 467.

[96] Wentw.Off.Ex., 14th ed., p. 215; Vin.Abr.Executors, X, pl. 10.

[97] *Chapman* v. *Dalton* (1565) Plowd. 288.

[98] *Ibid.*, Bro.Abr., tit. Deputy. See also *Anon.* (1589) 1 Leon. 316 (arbitrators'award that party should pay before a certain day a sum to A or his assigns: A's administrator held an assignee for this purpose: but, *per* Gawdy J., it would have been the same if the word "assignee" had been omitted).

[99] *Chapman* v. *Dalton, ante.*

[1] See *ante*, p. 517.

[2] *Goodall's Case* (1597) 5 Co. 97 *a*; but see *Chapman* v. *Dalton, supra.*

of a condition made to the deceased. Thus, cattle, plate, or other chattels may have been granted by the testator upon condition that if A did not pay such a sum of money, or do some other act as the testator appointed, etc. If this condition is not duly performed after the testator's death, the chattel comes back to his executor, and he may maintain an action in respect of it. So where the condition is that the testator or his executors shall pay the money to avoid the grant (*e.g.* where he pledges a jewel or a piece of plate) and before the day limited for payment the testator dies, his executor is entitled to redeem at the day and place appointed.[3]

If no time is set for the redemption of the pledge, the pledgor has his whole life to redeem, unless he is called upon to redeem by the pledgee; and if the pledgor dies without such a demand having been made, his representative may redeem.[4] If the pledgee dies, the tender should be to the executor of the pledgee.[5]

Payment out of court

Where money has been paid into court in an action, and the action has come to an end by reason of the death of the plaintiff or defendant, the court has jurisdiction on the application of the representatives of the deceased party to order payment out to them on their showing such grounds as the deceased would have had to show if he had been alive.[6]

Presentment of bill of exchange

If the holder of a bill of exchange is dead, and his executor has not yet proved the will, it is said that the bill must nevertheless be presented for payment at the regular time. But, *semble*, the drawers and indorsers would not be discharged if the presentment were made, and notice given of the dishonour, by the representative within a reasonable time.[7]

Cheques

Where a person draws a cheque, and dies before the holder presents it for payment, the authority of the banker to pay the cheque is determined by notice of the customer's death.[8] If the holder of the cheque has received it by way of gift from the deceased drawer, he cannot successfully sue the drawer's executors because he is not a holder for value.

The executor is entitled to receive any balance standing to the deceased's credit in his banking account, but proof of his authority depends upon the

---

[3] Wentw.Off.Ex., 14th ed., p. 181; Toller 164; Bac.Abr., Bailment, B.

[4] Com.Dig., tit. Mortgage, B. and Story, *Equity*, 12th ed. (1877), § 1032. *Semble, Ratcliff* v. *Davis* (1610) 1 Bulstr. 29, *contra* (referred to in *Kemp* v. *Westbrook* (1749) 1 Ves.Sen. 278), would not now be sustained. See *Vanderzee* v. *Willis* (1789) 3 Bro.C.C. 21, and other cases of redemption in equity referred to in *Story on Bailments*, § 348.

[5] 1 Bulstr. 29; Cro.Jac. 244; 3 Salk. 267; Bac.Abr., Bailment, B.

[6] *Brown* v. *Feeney* [1906] 1 K.B. 563; *Maxwell* v. *Wolseley* [1907] 1 K.B. 274.

[7] See the Bills of Exchange Act 1882, s.46(1). *cf.* Byles, *Bills*, 26th ed., p. 118.

[8] Bills of Exchange Act 1882, s.75(2). *Re Swinburne* [1926] Ch. 38.

probate or (in the case of an administrator) his letters of administration, and the banker is entitled to require the production of these before making payment.[9]

C. PROCEDURE

Legal aid

Where an application for legal aid is made by a person who is concerned in the proceedings only in a representative, fiduciary or official capacity, then, for the purpose of determining whether legal aid is available or the amount of any contribution to be made to the legal aid fund, the personal resources of the applicant are disregarded.[10] But such an application may be refused if the Area Director having taken into account the value of the property or estate or amount of the fund out of which the applicant is entitled to be indemnified and the resources of the persons, if any, who might benefit from the outcome of the proceedings, has concluded that such refusal will not cause hardship.[11]

Which executors should join as plaintiffs

If there are two or more executors, all those who are of full age[12] and have proved the will should join as plaintiffs in an action.[13] Unless they have acted,[14] executors who have not proved should not be joined,[15] even though they have not renounced.[16] Nor is an absconding executor a necessary party.[17]

It seems, however, that where one of two or more executors sells goods[18] of the testator, he alone may maintain an action for the price.[19] The same principle seems to apply where goods are taken out of the possession of one executor.[20] And if one executor contracts on his own account alone, he must sue on such contract though the money recovered will be assets.[21]

---

[9] *Tarn* v. *Commercial Bank of Sydney* (1884) 12 Q.B.D. 294.
[10] Civil Legal Aid (General) Regulations 1989, reg. 33.
[11] *Ibid.*
[12] See the Supreme Court Act 1981, s.118. Before 1926, even an infant executor had to be joined: *Smith* v. *Smith* (1609) Yelv. 130; 16 Vin.Abr. 251, tit. Parties, B, pl. 20.
[13] Bro.Exors 88; *Latch* v. *Latch* (1875) L.R. 10 Ch. 464. As to one of two or more executors making an application to the court, see *Re Bunting*, 2 A. & E. 467. See also R.S.C. Ord. 15, r. 4 and *Supreme Court Practice 1993* 15/14/11.
[14] *Vickers* v. *Bell* (1864) 4 De G.J. & S. 274; *Re Lovett* (1876) 3 Ch.D. 198.
[15] See the Administration of Estates Act 1925, ss.5 and 8; *Dyson* v. *Morris* (1842) 1 Ha. 413.
[16] *Davies* v. *Williams* (1826) 1 Sim. 5; Administration of Estates Act 1925, ss.5 and 8.
[17] *Drage* v. *Hartopp* (1885) 28 Ch.D. 414.
[18] One of two or more proving executors can no longer dispose of realty, including leaseholds, without the others: Administration of Estates Act 1925, s.2(2).
[19] Godolph. Pt. 2, c. 16, s.1; Wentw.Off.Ex., 14th ed., 224; *Brassington* v. *Ault* (1824) 2 Bing. 177.
[20] *Ibid.*
[21] *Heath* v. *Chilton* (1844) 12 M. & W. 632.

Joinder of co-administrators

Presumably the position is the same with regard to the joinder of persons to whom letters of administration have been granted. Moreover, since an administrator (other than an administrator with the will annexed[22]) has no cause of action as such, until he obtains a grant of letters of administration, a writ issued by him before such a grant is a nullity.[23]

Misjoinder of parties

No cause or matter is defeated by reason of the misjoinder or non-joinder of parties. The court has power, of its own motion or on application, to order that the names of parties improperly joined should be struck out, or the names of parties who ought to have been joined should be added.[24] But no person may be added as a plaintiff without his written consent.[25] The only objection which a defendant can take to the non-joinder of one of two or more executors as plaintiff is to take out a summons to have him joined as plaintiff.[26] The necessary facts and interest should be shown by affidavit in support of the application.

Executor refusing to join

Where one of two or more executors refuses to join as plaintiff or is unable to join as having an interest in the subject-matter inconsistent with his position as plaintiff, the other or others can still bring the action, making the executor who refuses to join a defendant.[27] If all the executors refuse to sue or are unable, a beneficiary may, it seems, himself sue, adding the executors as defendants,[28] or may apply to the court for leave to sue in the name of the executors. Now Order 15, r. 13A makes it possible to bind a potential plaintiff or defendant.

Death of executor plaintiff

Where one of two or more executor-plaintiffs dies, the action may be continued without the necessity for any order, since the interest of the deceased executor devolves upon the survivors.[29]

Beneficiaries not necessary parties

A representative may sue on behalf of or as representing the estate without joining any of the persons beneficially interested therein; but the court

---

[22] See *ante*, p. 83.
[23] *Ingall* v. *Moran* [1944] 1 K.B. 160.
[24] Ord. 15, rr. 6, 8. The Inland Revenue may only be joined with consent. See *ante*, p. 826.
[25] See n. 24.
[26] *Werderman* v. *Société Générale d'Electricité* (1881) 19 Ch.D. 246. ·
[27] *Luke* v. *S. Kensington Hotel* (1879) 11 Ch.D. 121; *Gandy* v. *Gandy* (1885) 30 Ch.D. 57. Ord. 15, r. 4(2).
[28] See n. 27.
[29] See Toller 6th ed., p. 285.

may at any stage of the proceedings order any of them to be made parties.[30] Where beneficiaries are neither parties nor represented the trustees prima facie represent them whether they are unascertained or not; and it is the duty of the trustees' counsel to put before the court any consideration which may affect the interests of any of them.[31] The judgment resulting will then be binding upon the beneficiaries who will be estopped by the record.[32]

Where no representative exists

In addition to its power to appoint a person to represent persons who are not ascertained or not found or in other case for saving expense,[33] the court may, where a deceased person interested in the matter in question has no personal representative, proceed in the absence of a person representing the estate or make a "representation order" appointing a person to represent that estate for the purposes of the proceedings.[34]

What claims may be joined

By Order 15, r. 1, a plaintiff may in one action (subject to questions of embarrassment, delay or inconvenience[35]) claim relief for more than one cause of action if the plaintiff claims or the defendant is alleged to be liable as executor or administrator in one or more causes and in his personal capacity with reference to the same estate.[36]

Whether representative should claim as such

Every action brought by a representative, where the cause of action accrued in the time of the deceased, must be brought in his representative capacity.[37] But where the cause of action accrues after the death of the testator or intestate, the executor or administrator may sue as such, or not, at his option.[38]

Where the plaintiff claims in trespass or trover on his constructive possession as representative, he should sue as such. But were he has been in actual possession of the property which is the subject of the suit, it is not

---

[30] Ord. 15, rr. 6, 14.

[31] cf. Mellor v. Daintree (1886) 33 Ch.D. 198, 205; Re Brown's Will (1884) 27 Ch.D. 179, 186.

[32] See Pople v. Evans [1969] 2 Ch. 255 and cases there cited as to estoppel by record in general. Ord. 15, r. 14. See also post, p. 888, and ante, p. 365.

[33] Ord. 15, r. 13.

[34] Ord. 15, r. 15. See further post, p. 891.

[35] See Ord. 15, r. 5.

[36] The rule will be strictly construed; it is not a question of convenience: Tredegar v. Roberts [1914] 1 K.B. 283; Re Pimm [1916] W.N. 202; Whitworth v. Darbishire (1893) 68 L.T. 216. It applies also to counterclaims: Re Richardson [1933] W.N. 90.

[37] 1 Wms.Saund. 112, n. to Dean of Bristol v. Guyse; Com.Dig. Pleader, 2 D. 1; Gallant v. Bouteflower (1781) 3 Dougl. 36.

[38] Ibid. And see ante, pp. 874 et seq.

necessary for him to claim or give evidence of his title as representative in an action against a wrongdoer.[39]

If he sues in a representative capacity, the indorsement of claim on the writ of summons must show in what capacity he sues,[40] and this may of course be challenged on the pleadings.

Proof of plaintiff as representative

Though an executor derives his title from the will by which he is appointed, and not from the probate of the will, yet it is the probate alone which authenticates his right, and the probate, or something tantamount thereto, such as an official certificate of the grant[41] or an office copy of the record from the Probate Registry,[42] is the only legitimate evidence that the property is vested in an executor, or of the executor's appointment.[43] The original will cannot be read in evidence for that purpose, though produced by an officer of the Probate Division,[44] unless it bears the seal of the court, or some other mark of authentication.[45] The seal of the court on the probate proves itself.[46]

The old rule was that the title of two or more plaintiffs, claiming as executors, was well evidenced by probate granted to one only of the will appointing them all.[47] The rule was the same whether they sued in their representative character or not[48]; for probate granted to one of two or more executors enured to the benefit of all.[49] This principle no longer applies because since 1925 an executor who does not prove the will must either have died, failed to appear to a citation, renounced, or had power reserved, in all of which cases the executors who actually prove are, until further grant, in the position of the only executors.[50]

The title of the plaintiff, as administrator, may be proved by the production of the letters of administration, or by an office copy of the record from the Probate Registry,[51] or by an official certificate of the grant.[52]

The title of an administrator *de bonis non* is sufficiently proved by the letters of administration *de bonis non*, without those granted to the first executor or administrator.[53]

---

[39] See *ante*, pp. 874 *et seq.*
[40] Ord. 6, r. 3.
[41] See the Supreme Court Act 1981, s.125.
[42] See Ord. 38, r. 10.
[43] *Ante*, p. 9; *Hamilton* v.*Aston* (1845) 1 Carr. & Kirw. 679.
[44] *cf. Gorton* v. *Dyson* (1819) 1 Brod. & Bing. 219.
[45] *R.* v. *Barnes* (1816) 1 Stark.N.P.C. 243; *Pinney* v. *Pinney* (1828) 8 B. & C. 335. Nor is a copy of the will evidence: Bull.N.P. 246.
[46] Supreme Court Act 1981, s.132.
[47] *Walters* v. *Pfeil* (1829) 1 Mood. & Malk. 362; *Scott* v. *Briant* (1836) 6 Nev. & M. 381.
[48] See n. 47.
[49] *Watkins* v. *Brent* (1835) 7 Sim. 512; *Cummins* v. *Cummins*, 3 J. & Lat. 64.
[50] See the Administration of Estates Act 1925, ss.5 and 8.
[51] See Ord. 38, r. 10.
[52] See the Supreme Court Act 1981, s.125.
[53] *Catherwood* v. *Chabaud* (1823) 1 B. & C. 150. See also *Gradell* v. *Tyson* (1726) 2 Stra. 716. See p. 50 *ante*.

Where an executor or administrator produced the probate or letters in proof of his representative character, and his case showed that he sued for a greater value than was covered by the probate or administration stamp, he could not recover.[54] But it seems doubtful whether this is so under the present practice, at any rate where the value of the property had altered since the date of the grant.

The effect of a grant has already been considered.[55]

An administrator during minority[56] must as plaintiff prove the minority of the infant because this is a matter within his cognisance and part of his "title."[57] For the same reason the plaintiff need not establish the infant's minority when suing such an administrator.[58]

Revocation of probate after judgment

If an executor or administrator obtained judgment, and then the probate or letters of administration was revoked, the regular mode for the defendant to obtain relief was by an *audita querela*[59]; but this procedure was abolished and the proper course now is to apply for a stay of execution on the ground of matters which have occurred (*sic*) since the date of the judgment or order.[60]

Set-off

Debts which accrue due before the death of a person cannot be set off against debts which accrue due after his death, and vice versa.[61] Thus, where a representative sues, either personally[62] or in his representative capacity,[63] a debt which accrued due from the defendant to the deceased's estate after his death, the defendant cannot set off a debt which accrued due to him from the deceased in his lifetime.

This doctrine does not, however, apply where the estate is being administered in bankruptcy.[64]

Another principle is that the debts sued for and intended to be set off must be mutual,[65] and in the same right.[66] Thus, a defendant cannot set off

---

[54] *Hunt* v. *Stevens* (1810) 3 Taunt. 113; *Carr* v. *Roberts* (1831) 2 B. & Ad. 905.

[55] *Ante*, pp. 449 *et seq*. And see the Administration of Estates Act 1925, s.15.

[56] See *ante*, p. 475.

[57] *Piggot's Case* (1614) 5 Co.Rep. 29a.

[58] *Beal* v. *Simpson* (1698) 1 Ld.Raym. 409.

[59] *Turner* v. *Davies* (1670) 2 Saund. 148.

[60] Ord. 45, r. 11.

[61] The defence of set-off is governed by R.S.C., Ord. 18, r. 17.

[62] *Shipman* v. *Thompson* (1738) Willes 103; *Tegetmeyer* v. *Lumley* (1785) 25 G. 3, B.R., reported in Durnford's note to *Hutchinson* v. *Sturges* (1741) Willes 264; *Lambarde* v. *Older* (1851) 17 Beav. 542; cf. *Wrout* v. *Dawes* (1858) 25 Beav. 369.

[63] *Rees* v. *Watts*, 11 Exch. 410, affirming *ibid.* 9 Exch. 696; *Newell* v. *N. P. Bank* (1876) 1 C.P.D. 496; *Hallett* v. *Hallett* (1879) 13 Ch.D. 232; *Re Gregson* (1887) 36 Ch.D. 223. See also *Wilkinson* v. *Cawood* (1797) 3 Anstr. 905; *Henderson* v. *Henderson* (1844) 6 Q.B. 288.

[64] *Watkins* v. *Lindsay & Co.* (1898) 67 L.J.Q.B. 362.

[65] As to the meaning of "mutual debts," see *Bennett* v. *White* [1910] 2 K.B. 643.

[66] *Bishop* v. *Church* (1751) 3 Atk. 691; *Gale* v. *Luttrell* (1826) 1 Y. & J. 180. cf. *Blakesley* v. *Smallwood* (1846) 8 Q.B. 538.

a debt due to him from the plaintiff personally where the latter is suing in a representative character.[67] And conversely, a defendant sued as executor or administrator cannot set off a debt due to him personally,[68] nor, if sued for his own debt, can he set off what is due to him as executor or administrator.[69]

Set-off of debt due to trustee

Though the debts sued for and intended to be set off must be in the same right, the interposition of a trustee for a beneficial owner does not prevent the right of set-off. A debt due from a person can be set off against a debt due to the trustee of that person.[70] The court looks to the actual beneficial interests.

Thus, though as a general rule a person having a personal account and also an account as executor at the same bank, cannot set off a sum due from him to the bank on his own account against a sum due from the bank on the executorship account, yet he could do so where he had already paid, as executor, all debts, etc., and merely holds the ascertained residue on trust for himself beneficially as residuary legatee.[71]

This equitable right of set-off has always been confined to cases where there has been a plain and distinct admission or evidence of a simple liquidated and ascertained trust fund. The court will not take an account in order to ascertain how much of the fund standing in the name of the trustee will ultimately turn out to belong to him beneficially.[72]

In answer to a set-off, a representative may give in evidence the advance of money by him as representative to the defendant.[73]

Counterclaim

A counterclaim is on a different footing. It is in the nature of a cross-action and the defendant's counterclaim need not be an action of the same nature as the original action or even analogous thereto.[74] Consequently a counterclaim may be brought against the plaintiff in a character other than that in which he sued.[75] The court has the discretion to order separate trials in case of potential embarrassment, delay or inconvenience.[76]

---

[67] *Stumore* v. *Campbell* [1892] 1 Q.B. 314.
[68] *Re Dickinson* [1888] W.N. 94; *Phillips* v. *Howell* [1901] 2 Ch. 773.
[69] *Nelson* v. *Roberts* (1893) 69 L.T. 352.
[70] *Cochrane* v. *Green* (1860) 9 C.B.(N.S.) 448.
[71] See *Ex p. Morier* (1879) 12 Ch.D. 491. See also *Baillie* v. *Edwards* (1848) 2 H.L.C. 74; *Bridges* v. *Smyth* (1831) 8 Bing. 29.
[72] *Ex p. Morier, supra.*
[73] *Gallant* v. *Bouteflower* (1781) 3 Dougl. 34.
[74] *Beddall* v. *Maitland* (1881) 17 Ch.D. 174, 181, *per* Fry J.
[75] *Re Richardson* [1933] W.N. 90.
[76] Ord. 15, r. 5.

CHAPTER 63

THE REPRESENTATIVE AS DEFENDANT

In this chapter consideration is given to (1) the actions which may be brought against the representative, (2) parties to such actions, and (3) some of the defences available.

A—WHAT ACTIONS MAY BE BROUGHT AGAINST PERSONAL REPRESENTATIVES

Actions by creditors and beneficiaries

Though the usual procedure used to be to commence an administration action in the Chancery Division,[1] it is also possible, and now more common, not only for creditors,[2] but also in some cases for legatees, to recover their individual claims by an action in debt against the deceased's representatives.

However any prospective plaintiff in proceedings against representatives should carefully consider whether or not his claim should take the form of a claim in an administration action[3] by writ. In general a simple claim against the representatives as representing the whole estate should not take administration form, but where there are complications, where the courts' powers in administration are likely to be needed or where there are obvious complications or duplication of claims against defendants in differing capacities an administration action by writ will be more appropriate.

A person entitled to a share of a sum of money, which is due as a debt from the deceased, must sue on behalf of himself and all other parties interested in the debt, or make those other persons parties to the action.[4]

Though a representative is not bound to distribute the estate of the deceased before the expiration of one year from the death,[5] he is liable to be sued for debts immediately after the death.[6]

A creditor cannot, however, sue a person named in the will as executor unless he has administered or obtained a grant of probate.[7] But a receiver may be appointed to protect the estate pending the grant of administration.[8]

---

[1] As to which, see *ante*, pp. 821 *et seq.*
[2] See the Civil Procedure Act 1833 (3 & 4 Will. 4, c. 42) s. 14 (the old action of debt), and the Administration of Justice Act 1705 (4 & 5 Anne, c. 3) (Ruff. c. 16), s. 27 (the old action of account).
[3] See p. 829 *ante.*
[4] *Alexander* v. *Mullins* (1830) 2 Russ. & M. 568, Ord. 15, r.4 (2).
[5] Administration of Estates Act 1925, s.44.
[6] *Nicholls* v. *Judson* (1742) 2 Atk. 301. See also *Re Tankard* [1942] Ch. 69.
[7] *Mohamidu Mohideen Hadjiar* v. *Pitchey* [1894] A.C 437.
[8] See *ante*, p. 846.

Creditor may obtain summary judgment

A creditor may obtain summary judgment under Order 14 against a representative who does not set up a defence of *plene administravit*, though a representative can obtain leave to defend more readily than the deceased could have done. If the representative successfully pleads *plene administravit*, the plaintiff is entitled to judgment with costs against future assets *quando acciderint*, but the representative is entitled to costs of the action as against the plaintiff.[9]

Action at law by legatee

An action does not lie against a representative for a general legacy,[10] nor for a distributive share of an intestate's estate,[11] even though he may have expressly, though without consideration, promised to pay.[12]

But a legatee of leaseholds,[13] or of any other specific legacy,[14] may bring an action at law for the recovery of the legacy after an assent has been made by the executor; and the same principle would now apply to a devisee of real estate.[15]

Further, if an executor has, by arrangement with the legatee, ceased to hold money bequeathed in his character of executor, so that he has become a debtor to the legatee, he may be sued at law by the legatee.[16] Thus, where executors had accounted to and taken a release from all the residuary legatees, including the plaintiff, but had not paid the latter his share, he having consented to allow it to remain in their hands, it was held that the plaintiff might recover the money retained in an action at law.[17]

B—PARTIES IN ACTION AGAINST PERSONAL REPRESENTATIVES

All representatives should be joined

The general rule is that if there are two or more representatives, all[18] who are alive[19] and who have administered[20] should be joined as defendants.[21]

---

[9] *Millar* v. *Keane* (1889) 24 L.R. Ir. 49; *Cockle* v. *Treacy* [1896] 2 Ir. R. 267.

[10] *Deeks* v. *Strutt* (1794) 5 T.R. 690.

[11] *Holland* v. *Clark* (1842) 1 Y. & C.C.C. 151, 167. See also *Johnson* v. *Johnson* (1802) 3 B. & P. 162, 169.

[12] *Jones* v. *Tanner* (1827) 7 B & C. 542. As to an action for a legacy charged on land, see *Braithwaite* v. *Skinner* (1839) 5 M. & W. 313.

[13] *Doe* v. *Guy* (1802) 3 East 120. See also *Re Culverhouse* [1896] 2 Ch. 251.

[14] *Williams* v. *Lee* (1745) 3 Atk. 223.

[15] See also the Administration of Estates Act 1925, s. 43 (2)

[16] See *Gregory* v. *Harman* (1828) 1 Moo. & P. 209; *Hart* v. *Minors* (1834) 2 Cr. & M. 700. See also *Gorton* v. *Dyson* (1819) 1 Brod & Bing. 219; *Moert* v. *Moessard* (1827) 1 Moo. & P. 8; *Rose* v. *Savory* (1835) 2 Bing.N.C. 145; *Wasney* v. *Earnshaw* (1834) 4 Tyrwh. 806; *Roper* v. *Holland* (1835) 3 A. & E. 99; *Edwards* v. *Bates* (1844) 7 M. & 590; *Bartlett* v. *Dimond* (1845) 14 M. & W. 49, 56; *Pardoe* v. *Price* (1847) 16 M & W. 451; *Bond* v. *Nurse* (1847) 10 Q.B. 244; *Edwards* v. *Lowndes* (1852) 1 E. & B. 81; *Topham* v. *Morecroft* (1858) 8 E. & B. 972.

[17] *Gregory* v. *Harman, ante.*

[18] *Scurry* v. *Morse* (1724) 9 Mod. 89; see also *Ashurst* v. *Eyre* (1740) 2 Atk. 51 (insolvent administrator); *Smithby* v. *Hinton* (1681) 1 Vern. 31 (releasing executor). Service on one of two co–executors in possession of land was sufficient service in an action for the recovery thereof: *Doe d. Strickland* v. *Roe* (1847) 4 D. & L. 431.

[19] See *Hilbert* v. *Lewis* (1679) 1 Freem. 268

[20] Bro. Exors. 20, 88; Wentw. Off. Ex., 14th ed., 208; *Swallow* v. *Emberson* (1665) 1 Lev. 161, as to actions at law; *Brown* v. *Pitman* (1710) Gilb.Ch. 75; *Strickland* v. *Strickland* (1842) 12 Sim. 463; *Dyson* v. *Morris* (1842) 1 Hare 413, as to suits in equity.

[21] This appears to be unaffected by the Civil Liability (Contribution) Act 1978.

If one of two executors dies the action should be brought against the survivor alone and not against the survivor and the executor of the deceased executor, unless the latter administers with the survivor.[22]

Minor executor

A minor appointed executor should no longer[23] be joined as a party as executor. Though he can be appointed executor, the appointment transfers no interest to him, and he cannot obtain probate[24] or letters of administration,[25] until he is of full age; nor is he liable if he wastes assets which come to him as executor *de son tort*.[26]

Foreign representatives

Unless he can be sued as executor *de son tort*,[27] or unless he has obtained a grant of probate or letters of administration in this country, a foreign representative cannot be sued in his official character in this country.[28]

When beneficiaries necessary parties

Though one of two executors or trustees could sue the other executor or trustee without making the beneficiaries parties to the action, yet where such beneficiaries had participated in the breach of trust they were necessary parties.[29] This may, however, be affected by the Civil Liability (Contribution) Act 1978.

As a general rule, however, in actions brought against representatives as representing the estate, beneficiaries should not be joined as parties.[30]

Where, however, a plaintiff to an action also happens to be the representative of an estate which it is required to make a defendant to the action, he should not be joined as such defendant, for the general rule is that one person cannot appear on both sides of the record; either another representative, or a beneficiary, must be joined to represent the estate.[31]

When debtor or creditor to estate should be joined

Again, persons who have possessed themselves of the property of the deceased, or debtors to the estate generally, cannot, as a rule, be made parties to an action against the representative. But if there is collusion, or some special case, or the executor is insolvent, the action may be brought

---

[22] 1 Roll. Abr. 928, tit. Exors. Z. cf. the position in an administration action: see *Re Harrison* [1891] 2 Ch. 349; *ante*, p. 827.

[23] Originally minors had to be joined: see 16 Vin. Abr. 251, tit. Party, B., pl. 20.

[24] Supreme Court Act 1981, s.118.

[25] See *ante*, p. 324.

[26] *Stott* v. *Meanock* (1862) 31 L.J. Ch. 746.

[27] See *Att.-Gen.* v. *New York Breweries Co.* [1898] 1 Q.B. 205; [1899] A.C. 62. *I.R.C.* v. *Stype* [1982] Ch. 456 at 474.

[28] Story's *Conflict*, s. 513; Dicey & Morris 11th ed. 999; *Tyler* v. *Bell* (1837) 1 Keen 826, 829; *Flood* v. *Patterson* (1861) 29 Beav. 295.

[29] *Jesse* v. *Bennett* (1856) 6 De G.M. & G. 609.

[30] Ord. 15. r. 14.

[31] *Re Phillips* [1931] W.N. 271.

both against the debtor and the executor.[32] The special circumstances which will authorise making the debtor a party are not confined to collusion or insolvency.[33] But the mere refusal of a representative to sue for the recovery of outstanding assets is not, in the absence of special circumstances, sufficient to justify a beneficiary in suing the representatives and the alleged debtor to the estate.[34]

The same principles apply as to the joinder of a creditor who has been overpaid by the executor.[35] A creditor, however, cannot be joined as a party against his will.[36]

Surviving partners of deceased

It has been held[37] that the surviving partners of the deceased might be joined as parties with the executor in an action against them for an account of partnership transactions, even in the absence of special circumstances. But such a wide proposition cannot be supported.[38] "The cases,[39] I think, may fairly be considered to go this extent,—that such a bill may be supported in all cases where the relation between the executors and the surviving partners is such as to present a substantial impediment to the prosecution by the executors of the rights of the parties interested in the estate against the surviving partners."[40]

Where no personal representative and no existing proceedings

It may happen that the deceased has no representative who can be sued. In such circumstances the most convenient course is to take advantage of R.S.C. Order 15, r. 6A which enables an intended plaintiff to bring proceedings against the estate of the deceased defendant.[41] In the heading to such proceedings, the defendants should be described as "the personal rep-

[32] *Doran* v. *Simpson* (1799) 4 Ves. 651; *Troughton* v. *Binkes* (1801) 6 Ves. 573; *Alsager* v. *Rowley* (1802) 6 Ves 748; *Burroughs* v. *Elton* (1805) 11 Ves. 29; *Consett* v. *Bell* (1842) 1 Y. & C.C.C. 569; *Lancaster* v. *Evors* (1841) 4 Beav.158; *Baddeley* v. *Curwen* (1845) 2 Coll. 151; *Baker* v. *Birch* (1847) 1 De G. & Sm. 376

[33] *Meldrum* v. *Scorer* (1887) 56 L.T. 471; *Consett* v. *Bell* (1842) 1 Y. & C.C.C. 569; *Stainton* v. *Carron Co.* (1854) 18 Beav. 146; *Saunders* v. *Druce* (1855) 3 Drew. 140. And see *Travis* v. *Milne* (1851) 9 Hare 141, 150.

[34] *Yeatman* v. *Yeatman* (1877) 7 Ch.D. 210; *Hayim* v. *Citibank* [1987] A.C. 730.

[35] *Alsager* v. *Rowley* (1802) 6 Ves. 748. For refunding, see p. 1065.

[36] *Re Bradley* [1956] Ch. 615.

[37] *Bowsher* v. *Watkins* (1830) 1 Russ. & M. 277. And see *Newland* v. *Champion* (1748) 1 Ves. Sen. 106.

[38] See *Davies* v. *Davies, post; Law* v. *Law, post; Cropper* v. *Knapman* (1836) 2 Y. & C.Ex. 338.

[39] *Bowsher* v. *Watkins, ante; Gedge* v. *Traill* (1823) 1 Russ. & M. 281; *Davies* v. *Davies* (1837) 2 Keen 534; *Law* v. *Law* (1845) 2 Coll. 41; *Cropper* v. *Knapman, supra,* commented on in *Yeatman* v. *Yeatman, supra; Beningfield* v. *Baxter* (1886) 12 App.Cas. 167; *Hayim* v. *Citibank* [1987] A.C. 730.

[40] *Travis* v. *Milne* (1851) 9 Hare 141, 150, *per* Turner V. -C. and see *Re Greaves* [1904] 2 K.B. 493.

[41] Order 15, r. 6A(1) was originally introduced under section 2 of the Proceedings Against Estates Act 1970. Amendments to the rule were provided for by section 27 of the Administration of Justice Act 1977 and the power to make the rule is now in section 87(2) of the Supreme Court Act 1981.

resentatives of A.B. deceased".[42] The rule also validates proceedings commenced against a deceased defendant whether or not a grant of probate or administration has been made in his estate by treating such proceedings as proceedings against the estate of the deceased defendant.[43]

The rule further provides that, during the period of the validity for service of the writ or originating summons, the plaintiff has to apply to the court for an order appointing a person to represent the deceased's estate for the purposes of the proceedings or, if a grant of probate or administration has been made, for an order that the personal representative be made a party. The court may at any stage of the proceedings make either kind of order, allow such amendments to be made, and make such other order as it thinks necessary, in order to ensure that all matters in dispute in the proceedings may be effectually and completely determined and adjudicated upon. Before making any order the court may require notice to be given to any insurer of the deceased who has an interest in the proceedings and to such if any of the persons having an interest in the estate as the court thinks fit. The court may appoint the Official Solicitor to represent the deceased's estate but he is not compellable and such appointment must be limited to his accepting service of the writ or originating summons unless the court with the consent of the Official Solicitor directs that the appointment shall extend to taking further steps in the proceedings. Otherwise if no other legal person has been made a defendant the action cannot be continued,[44] the proceedings are a nullity and no estoppel can operate.[45]

Where deceased defendant is a personal representative

The wording of R.S.C. Order 15, r. 6A is such as to make it inapplicable in cases where the deceased defendant is a representative. It also is clearly inapplicable in, for example, administration actions or proceedings under the Inheritance (Family Provision) Act 1975, since such proceedings did not lie against the deceased defendant when he was alive.

In such cases it seems that if the chain of representation applies on the death of the deceased representative, R.S.C. Order 15, r. 7 will apply because the liability of the deceased will "devolve" on his executor, who accordingly will become the new defendant under that order.

If, on the other hand the chain of representation is not applicable, it is thought R.S.C., Order 15, r. 15 may empower the court, where valid proceedings are on foot to add a defendant in place of the deceased representative, but possibly only if the deceased representative was himself beneficially interested in the estate.[46]

---

[42] Order 15, r. 6A(2).
[43] Order 15, r. 6A(3).
[44] See *Re Amirteymour* [1979] 1 W.L.R. 63 and 140 N.L.J. 95.
[45] *Foster* v. *Turnbull* (1990) *The Times*, May 22, 1990.
[46] The words "and that he has no personal representative" in Order 15, r. 15 suggest that the "interest" of the deceased person must be one which will accrue for the benefit of his estate and not to him in a representative capacity.

When the chain of representation is not applicable, and no new grant is taken out in the deceased representative's estate, the safest course is for the plaintiff to apply to the Probate Registrar[47] for a grant of administration *ad litem* to a nominated person.[48]

Where no personal representatives and proceedings already on foot

Rule 15 of Order 15 provides that, where in any proceedings it appears to the court that a deceased person was interested in the matter in question in the proceedings and that he has no personal representative, the court may, on the application of any party to the proceedings proceed in the absence of a person representing the estate, or may by Order appoint a person to represent the estate for the purposes of the proceedings.

The court's power to make a representation order under Order 15 has been mentioned.[49]

The Chancery Procedure Act 1852, s.44, from which Order 15, r. 15, was taken, was held in *Silver v. Stein*[50] not to apply where the estate to which it is desired to appoint a representative is an estate being administered by the court.

In *Wingrove v. Thompson*,[51] where a sole plaintiff died insolvent, the court, on the application of the sole defendant, appointed a person to represent the deceased plaintiff's estate, so as to enable the defendant to have an opportunity of moving to dismiss the action for want of due prosecution.[52] This would now no longer be necessary, in view of the terms of the present Order 15, r.9.[53] The rule is not confined to the representation of the estate of a party to the litigation; and, accordingly, an appointment has been made of a representative to the estate of a deceased person, for the purpose of enabling third–party proceedings to be taken against the estate.[54]

---

[47] N.C.P.R. 1987, rule 52.

[48] See Tristram and Coote: *Probate Practice* 27th ed. pp. 385–6.

[49] See *ante*, p. 882.

[50] 1 Drew. 295; see *Moore* v. *Morris* (1871) L.R. 13 Eq. 139, 149, for further suggested limitations. See also *Groves* v. *Levi* (1852) 9 Hare, App. xlvii; *cf. Chaffers* v. *Headlam ibid.* xlvi.

[51] (1879) 11 Ch.D. 419.

[52] For instances of the exercise of this jurisdiction, see *Mortimer* v. *Mortimer* (1863) 11 W. R. 740; *Crossley* v. *City of Glasgow Assurance Co.* (1876) 4 Ch.D. 421; *Webster* v. *British Empire Co.* (1880) 15 Ch.D. 169; *Curtius* v. *Caledonian etc. Insurance Co.* (1881) 19 Ch.D. 534; *Re Silder* [1920] W.N. 77. This rule has been made use of where a mortgagor has no personal representative, as in *Peat* v. *Gott* [1885] W.N. 46; *Neal* v. *Barratt* [1887] W.N. 88. But contrast *Aylward* v. *Lewis* [1891] 2 Ch. 81, where a foreclosure order absolute was refused in the absence of a properly constituted legal representative of the mortgagor's estate. The rule cannot be used to enable an equitable mortgagee, who has no legal estate in the mortgaged property, to obtain a vesting order when the mortgager has died intestate, and no personal representative has been constituted: *Re Deans* [1954] 1 W.L.R. 332

[53] See *ante*, p. 870.

[54] *Lean* v. *Alston* [1947] K.B. 467.

No person will be appointed under this rule unless his consent is first obtained.[55]

Misjoinder of parties

As has been seen, an action is no longer defeated by the misjoinder or non-joinder of parties,[56] but failure to join the right parties in the right capacity may lead to defeat under the Limitation Act 1980.[57]

Indorsement of writ

In an action against a representative, as such, the indorsement of the writ must show in what capacity he is sued,[58] but failure to comply with this rule does not enable a representative to draw the distinction between his capacities for all purposes. He may be required to discover documents in his possession in a case where he is sued in a representative capacity and has parted with documents to himself in an individual capacity.[59]

Joinder of claims

Formerly, a plaintiff could not bring an action against a person charging him as executor and also in his own right, the judgment in the latter being *de bonis propriis*, and in the former *de bonis testatoris*.[60] At the present time, however, claims against a representative as such may be joined with claims against him personally, provided the last–mentioned claims are alleged to arise with reference to the estate in respect of which the defendant is sued as representative.[61]

C—DEFENCES WHICH MAY BE RAISED BY PERSONAL REPRESENTATIVES

Defences generally

In an action against an executor or administrator, the defendant may plead any matter which the testator or intestate might have pleaded.[62] In addition to such defences he may specifically deny the character in which he is sued, pleading that he never was a representative. This is the old plea of "*ne unques executor or administrator.*" Or he may admit this and deny

---

[55] *Pratt* v. *L.P.T.B.* [1937] 1 All E.R. 473.

[56] Ord. 15, rr. 6, 8; *ante*, p. 881.

[57] Ord. 6, r. 3. See also *ante*, p. 463. Claims against a defendant as an individual will not normally arise out of the same or substantially the same facts as a claim against him as executor because death and probate will not normally be material to the former claim. The words "in issue on" in s.35 (5) of the Limitation Act 1980 mean "material to". See *Fannon* v. *Backhouse* (1987), *The Times*, August 22, 1987.

[58] See n. 57 *supra*.

[59] *Buchanan-Michaelson* v. *Rubinstein* [1965] Ch. 258.

[60] *Dean of Bristol* v. *Guyes* (1667) 1 Saund. 112 *a*; *Rann* v. *Hughes* (1778) 4 Bro.P.C. 27, Toml. ed.; Com.Dig.Abatement, F. 20; *ibid.* Pleader, 2 D. 2, *ante*, p. 713, n. 7.

[61] Ord. 15, r. 1.

[62] Com.Dig. Pleader. 2 D 8.

that he has assets left in his hands. This is the old plea of *"plene administra-vit"* which may be elaborated to admit only certain assets so as to become *"plene administravit praeter . . . "* and to claim that these are insufficient or that debts are due to other creditors of superior degree.[63]

Unless *a devastavit* is suggested, a representative cannot plead his own bankruptcy, for the proceedings in bankruptcy would not bind any effects, upon which, if the plaintiff obtained judgment and execution, the sheriff would have a right to levy under a *fi. fa.*[64]

There appears to be nothing in the Judicature Acts altering the ancient rule that if there are two or more executors, they may plead different pleas; and that which is most to the testator's advantage is received.[65]

Plea ne unques executor

If the defendant intends to deny his being executor or administrator, he must plead such denial specifically[66]; otherwise he will admit his representative character. If this specific denial is traversed by the plaintiff, the burden of proof is on him to prove affirmatively that the defendant is executor or administrator.

For the purpose of introducing formal and documentary evidence that the defendant is an executor or administrator, it is always prudent, and in some cases absolutely necessary, to give notice to the defendant to produce at the trial the probate of the will, or the letters of administration.[67] But in order to let in secondary evidence, it is not also necessary to prove that the probate or letters are in the defendant's possession; for if he has been duly appointed executor or administrator, they must necessarily be presumed to be in his possession.[68] Some evidence of the identity of the party, namely, that the person, described in the documentary evidence as executor or administrator, is the party sued, may be required.[69] Formerly if there were two executors and one proved the will in the name of both, even against the will of the other, that other could not plead *ne unques executor*,[70] but this would not now be possible since each applicant for the grant must swear the oath required by Rule 8 of the Non–Contentious Probate Rules 1987. Further proof that the defendant has intermeddled with the property, so as to make himself executor *de son tort*, is sufficient proof that he is executor.[71]

---

[63] Tidd. 644, 9th ed. As to the present order of precedence of debts, see *ante*, pp. 632 *et seq.* As to such defences by an executor *de son tort* see *ante*, p. 99.

[64] See *Serle* v. *Bradshaw* (1833) 2 Cr. & M. 148; *ante*, p. 464.

[65] *Midgley* v. *Midgley* [1893] 3 Ch. 282, 298, 302. As to the costs where defendants sever in their pleadings, see *Stumm* v. *Dixon* (1889) 22 Q.B.D. 99; *ibid.* 529. See also *ante*, p. 690.

[66] Ord. 18, r. 13.

[67] 2 Phill.Ev. 346, 6th ed.

[68] 2 Phill.Ev. 347, 6th ed.

[69] See n. 685, *supra*.

[70] See Com.Dig.Pleader, 2 D. 7. See also Wentw.Off.Ex. c. 15, p. 339, 14th ed.

[71] *Keble* v. *Osbaston* (1614) Hob. 49; Com.Dig. Pleader, 2 D 7; and see *Kellow* v. *West-combe* (1673) 1 Freem. 122; *Hinde* v. *Skelton* (1865) 34 L.J.Ch. 378; 2 H. & M. 690.

Plea of revocation of grant

If the defendant, being sued as administrator, pleads that before the date of the writ, his administration was revoked and granted to another, he ought to allege that he has fully administered all the goods in his hands, or else that he has delivered them over to the new administrator.[72] For he may be made liable for wasting assets before the second administration was granted.[73]

Plea of plene administravit

If a representative has not assets to satisfy the claim upon which an action is brought against him, he must take care to plead *plene administravit* or *plene administravit praeter*, etc.[74] For it seems that, even under the present system of pleading,[75] if a representative fails to plead that he has fully administered the assets, or that with the exception of certain assets he has fully administered, and the judgment, whether by default or otherwise,[76] is given for the plaintiff, this amounts to a conclusive admission that he has assets to satisfy such judgment.[77]

On the other hand, if, after pleading either a general or special *plene administravit*, judgment is given against him, this only amounts to an admission of assets to the extent of assets proved to be in his hands.[78]

When *plene administravit* is pleaded, the burden of proof lies on the plaintiff to show that assets existed, or ought to have existed, in the hands of the defendant[79] at the time that the writ was issued.[80] But if he wishes to give evidence that assets have been received after the issue of the writ, he must plead this matter specifically.[81]

In order to prove assets, the plaintiff may give in evidence some conduct

---

[72] *Garter* v. *Dee* (1671) 1 Freem. 13, *ante*, p. 366. These goods as in the case of goods possessed by an executor *de son tort*, are not assets in the hands of the new administrator until they come to his possession: *ibid.*; *Keble* v. *Osbaston* (1614) Hob. 49.

[73] See *Packman's Case* (1596) 6 Co. 18 *b*.

[74] See *Re Marvin* [1905] 2 Ch. 490. For forms of these pleadings, see *Bullen and Leake*, 12th ed., 1975, pp. 1058 *et seq.*

[75] *Thompson* v. *Clarke* (1901) 17 T.L.R. 455; and see *Lacons* v. *Warmoll* [1907] 2 K.B. at p.360.

[76] See *Rock* v. *Layton* (1700) 1 Salk 310; *ibid.* admitted 3 T.R. 685; *Leonard* v. *Simpson* (1835) 2 Bing.N.C. 176. See also *Batchelor* v. *Evans* [1939] Ch. 1007. Whether judgment by default will be *de bonis propriis*, see *post*, p. 911.

[77] Wms.Saund. 219, n. 8 to *Wheatly* v. *Lane; Ramsden* v. *Jackson* (1737) 1 Atk. 292; *Erving* v. *Peters* (1790) 3 T.R. 686; *Midland Bank Trust Co. Ltd.* v. *Green* (*No.* 2) [1979] 1 W.L.R. 460. As to the plea which should be raised by the executor of an executor, see *Wells* v. *Fydell* (1808) 10 East 315.

[78] Wms.Saund. 219, n. 8; *Cousins* v. *Paddon* (1835) 2 Cr.M & R. 547; *Re Higgins' Trusts* (1861) 2 Giff. 562.

[79] As to what assets are considered as coming to the hands of a personal representative, see *ante*, pp. 597 *et seq.* See also *Britton* v. *Jones* (1837) 3 Bing.N.C. 676; *Stroud* v. *Dandridge* (1844) 1 Car. & K. 445.

[80] *Mara* v. *Quin* (1794) 6 T.R. 10; *Webster* v. *Blackman* (1861) 2 Fost. & F. 490.

[81] *Mara* v. *Quin* (1794) 6 T.R. 11; 2 Phill.Ev., 6th ed., 347; Roscoe, *Ev. in Civil Actions*, 20th ed., 1165.

of the defendant which amounts to an admission of assets. What conduct is sufficient to amount to an admission of assets is discussed elsewhere.[82]

If the plaintiff proves that the defendant has been guilty of a *devastavit*, which has caused a failure of assets, it must be found that the defendant has assets to that amount.[83]

If an executor compounds with the creditors, and afterwards, at the suit of any of them, pleads *plene administravit*, proof of the composition would be conclusive proof of assets, and the court would not allow him to give evidence of no assets.[84]

Semble, even at the present time a representative, who has merely pleaded *plene administravit*,[85] may, in answer to the proof of assets show that he has exhausted the assets,[86] by discharging other demands upon the estate, not inferior in their nature to that of the plaintiff,[87] or even by the payment of debts of inferior degree, without notice of the plaintiff's demand.[88] Again, he may show that he has disbursed the assets in the expenses of the funeral, or of probate, or administration, or in the reasonable charges of collecting the debts of the deceased.[89]

Preference and retainer

The following principles applied before the abolition of preference and retainer by section 10 of the Administration of Estates Act 1971, and similar provisions will likewise apply, it is submitted, when representatives exercise their new rights under that section.[90]

(1) Where, before the Judicature Acts, a representative had retained assets for a debt due to himself,[91] or for the funeral[92] or administration[93] expenses, or to reimburse himself for paying out of his own pocket, and before the issuing of the writ, a debt not inferior to the debt of the plaintiff,[94] he had an option either to give evidence of such retainer under a plea of *plene administravit* or to plead the retainer specifically. *Semble*, all such

---

[82] *Ante*, pp. 859, *et seq.*

[83] Wentw.Off.Ex., 14th ed., c. 13, p. 312. And see *Reeves* v. *Ward* (1835) 2 Bing.N.C. 235; *ibid.* 2 Scott 296. As to whether the court should find the defendant had committed *devastavit* by swearing the property above its value and so incurring a greater stamp duty, see *Jackson* v. *Bowley* (1841) Carr. & M. 97.

[84] Bull.N.P. 145.

[85] See *Reeves* v. *Ward*, *supra*.

[86] As to the replication of judgment by fraud to a plea of no assets *ultra* a judgment, see the 11th edition of this work pp. 1568, 1569.

[87] See *ante*, pp. 583, 584. For another replication, see *Marston* v. *Downes* (1834) 1 A. & E. 31.

[88] *The Governors of Chelsea Waterworks* v. *Cowper* (1795) 1 Esp.N.P.C. 277; but according to the judgment of Lawrence J. in *Hickey* v. *Hayter* (1795) 6 T.R. 388, these payments without notice must be pleaded.

[89] *Giles* v. *Dyson* (1815) 1 Stark.N.P.C. 32.

[90] See *ante*, p. 640.

[91] 1 Wms.Saund. 333, n. (6); *Re Marvin* [1905] 2 Ch. 490. As to the executor's right of retainer, see *ante*, pp. 640 *et seq.*

[92] See *R.* v. *Wade* (1818) 5 Price 621.

[93] *Gillies* v. *Smither* (1819) 2 Stark.N.P.C. 528.

[94] Co.Litt. 283 *a*; Bull.N.P. 140.

defences should have been specifically pleaded, otherwise an amendment[95] might have been necessary[96]

(2) If the defendant wished to give evidence of the retainer of assets for the payment of a debt of higher degree than that on which the action is brought, he had to plead specifically the existence of such a debt.[97] If he omitted to do so, and judgment was given against him, this was an admission of assets to satisfy the judgment.[98]

(3) After a writ had been issued by one creditor, a representative might pay, or suffer judgement to be recovered by, another creditor. The fact that, after deducting such payment or judgment, there were not sufficient assets to satisfy the plaintiff's claim afforded a good defence if specifically pleaded.[99] A plea of this description, arising after action brought, had to be raised under Order 18, r. 9, in the defence, or as a further defence.[1] The plaintiff might confess such defence and sign judgment for his costs up to the time of the pleading of the defence, *Semble*, he could also sign judgment for the debt *quando acciderint*, *i.e.* in respect of any assets which may subsequently come to the hands of the defendant.[2]

Complaint of insufficient assets precluded

If, in the distribution of assets, a creditor misleads an executor, either by laches or express authority, so as thereby to induce him to pursue a course he would not otherwise have pursued, the creditor is precluded from complaining of an insufficiency of assets.[3] Thus, where a party entitled to a legacy under a will has a claim against the testator, which he conceals from the executors till after he has received his legacy, he cannot afterwards, in an action against the executors, object that the amount of the legacy was not paid in a due course of administration.[4]

[95] As to amendment of pleadings, see Ord. 20.
[96] See Ord. 18, r. 7.
[97] Bull.N.P. 141; Wms.Saund. 333 *a*, n. (8); *ante*, p. 638.
[98] *Rock* v. *Layton* (1700) 1 Salk. 310; *Earle* v. *Hinton* (1726) 2 Stra. 732.
[99] As in *Vibart* v. *Coles* (1890) 24 Q.B.D. 364, following *Re Radcliffe* (1878) 7 Ch.D. 733. But not otherwise: see *Nightingale* v. *Lee* (1673) 1 Freem. 110. Judgment against one of two or more defendants and no assets *ultra* may be pleaded by the others: *Further* v. *Further* (1596) Cro.Eliz. 471.
[1] As to when leave is required, see Ord. 20 and notes thereto in the *Supreme Court Practice*.
[2] As to this form of judgment, see *post*, pp. 908–914 *et seq.*
[3] *Richards* v. *Browne* (1837) g.N.C. 499, by Tindal C.J. This subject is discussed *ante*; pp. 605–606, 657.
[4] *Stroud* v. *Stroud* (1844) 7 M. & Gr. 417.

CHAPTER 64

LIMITATION OF ACTIONS

THE Limitation Act 1980[1] (in this chapter referred to as appropriate as "the Act" or "the 1980 Act") affects representatives, both as to claims made by them and as to claims made against them. This chapter considers both categories in this order, so far as special considerations affecting a representative may arise.

A. CLAIMS BY PERSONAL REPRESENTATIVES

The running of time

Where an action accruing before the death of a person is commenced by representatives,[2] the defendant may plead the Act in the same way as if there had been no death intervening. In computing the period of limitation no allowance is made for the interval between death and the grant of probate or letters of administration.[3]

The same rule applies where the cause of action accrues on death, *e.g.* in an action under the Law Reform (Miscellaneous Provisons) Act 1934,[4] since the grant of probate or letters of administration relates back to the death.[5] A beneficiary cannot normally establish adverse possession to enable time to run against a representative.[6]

Land—general rule

Further, if the representatives bring an action to recover any land of the deceased or to recover moneys due under a rentcharge created by the deceased's will or taking effect upon his death and in either case the deceased was in possession of the land or the land subject to the rentcharge at the date of his death, then time begins to run from the date of the deceased's death.[7]

---

[1] Consolidating the Limitation Act 1939, the Limitation Act 1963, the Limitation Act 1975, the Limitation Act 1979, and the Limitation Amendment Act 1980.

[2] The action may only be brought by the personal representatives: *Hughes* v. *Griffin* [1969] 1 W.L.R. 23. As to accrual of the right of action, see *post*, p. 907.

[3] *Penny* v. *Brice* (1865) 18 C.B.(N.S.) 393; *Rhodes* v. *Smethurst* (1840) 6 M. & W. 351; *Freake* v. *Cranefeldt* (1838) 3 My. & Cr. 499; and see the Limitation Act 1980, s.26, and see *ante*, p. 461.

[4] As to this Act, see *ante*, p. 515 *et seq.*

[5] *Ingall* v. *Moran* [1944] K.B. 160; *Hilton* v. *Sutton Steam Laundry* [1946] K.B. 65.

[6] See the Limitation Act 1980, Sched. I para 9. and, for possible exceptions, an article by M. J. Goodman (1965) 29 Conv.(N.S.) 356.

[7] Limitation Act 1980, Sched. I para 2. For the definition of "land," see the Limitation Act 1980, s.38(1). As to accruer of the cause of action, see also, *post*, p. 907.

Personalty—exception

There is, however, one notable exception to the general rule that no allowance is made for the interval between the death and the grant. Although the Act provides that in actions for the recovery of land and advowsons by an administrator, the administrator shall be treated as claiming as if there had been no interval of time between the death of the deceased and the grant of letters of administration,[8] it is clear that the old law applies to actions for the recovery of property other than land and advowsons. Under that law, *time does not begin to run in actions for the recovery of personalty by an administrator until a grant of letters of administration has been obtained.*[9] The reason for this exception is that in the absence of statutory provision, the administrator has no title until he has obtained a grant.[10]

This exception can be well illustrated by the case of a debt payable on a certain date. If that date occurs before the death of the creditor intestate, time will run from that date and no allowance will be made under the general rule mentioned above for the interval between the death and the grant. If, however, the date occurs after the death of the creditor intestate, time will not begin to run until the grant has been taken out. If there is no evidence to show whether the debt became payable or the death occurred first, time will not begin to run until the grant has been obtained.[11]

Other claims

In an action for a partnership account, where probate had been granted (so that in the normal course of events the general rule mentioned above would have been applied) but subsequently probate had been revoked and letters of administration granted, it was held that time did not begin to run until the letters of administration had been granted.[12]

It should be noted that where the action is based on fraud or mistake or any fact relevant to the plaintiff's right of action has been deliberately concealed from him by the defendant time does not begin to run to bar proceedings for the property or its value[13] until the fraud, concealment or mistake has been discovered or could with reasonable diligence have been discovered.[14] Also, in actions to recover reversionary property, time does not begin to run until the reversionary interest falls into possession.[15]

---

[8] Limitation Act 1980, s.26; see *Re Williams* (1886) 34 Ch.D. 558, a decision under s.6 of the Real Property Limitation Act 1833.

[9] *Cary* v. *Stephenson* (1694) 2 Salk. 421; *Murray* v. *East India Company* (1821) 2 B. & A. 204; *Meyappa Chetty* v. *Supramanian Chetty* [1916] 1 A.C. 603, 608, 609.

[10] The executor's title, of course, dates from the death. An administrator with will annexed may be in a similar position to an executor. See *ante*, p. 83.

[11] *Atkinson* v. *Bradford Third Equitable Building Society* (1890) 25 Q.B.D. 377, 381.

[12] *Chan Kit San* v. *Ho Fung* [1902] A.C. 257.

[13] *Eddis* v. *Chichester Constable* [1969] 2 Ch. 345, 358. Limitation Act 1980, s.32.

[14] Limitation Act 1980, s.32. *Eddis* v. *Chichester Constable* [1969] 2 Ch. 345.

[15] Limitation Act 1980, Sched. I para. 4. As to accrual see *post*, p. 907.

The limitation periods

The same limitation periods apply to actions by representatives as are applied to individuals. An interesting question arises, however, when the Crown or its nominee obtains a grant of letters of administration in pursuance of its claim to an intestate's *bona vacantia*. The Crown's claim to land is normally barred after 30 years.[16] However, where the Crown or its nominee claims land in the course of administration of a deceased person's estate, the position is governed by section 30 of the Administration of Estates Act 1925. The limitation period applicable to an action by the nominee of the Crown, who has obtained a grant of letters of administration, to recover land forming part of an intestate's estate is 12 years, for the effect of the Administration of Estates Act 1925 is to put the nominee in the same position as the subject for limitation purposes.[17] However, if the nominee has completed the administration and handed over the assets of the intestate which he has collected in the course of administration, or, *semble*, if no grant has been taken out by the nominee, it would appear that the relevant period for limitation purposes as against the Crown itself is 30 years.[18] This view must be considered to be open to doubt, however, for, if correct, a person in adverse possession of an intestate's land would be able to claim good possessory title against the next-of-kin taking out a grant more than 12 years after the intestate's death, but might, nevertheless, be unable to establish good possessory title against the Crown claiming *bona vacantia* until the expiry of the 30-year period.

It should be noted that, although the period of limitation in actions for personal injuries is three years from the cause of action accruing, the date of death, or the date of the plaintiff's "knowledge" (as defined in s.14 of the Act),[19] whichever is the later, the court has power to override these time limits if it appears equitable to do so.[20]

B. CLAIMS AGAINST PERSONAL REPRESENTATIVES

The running of time

A representative, including an executor *de son tort*,[21] may plead the Limitation Act to a claim by any person in respect of any cause of action which accrued during the lifetime of the deceased. The same rule applies to claims against representatives as applies to claims by representatives,

---

[16] Limitation Act 1980, Sched. I para. 10.

[17] Limitation Act 1980, Sched. I para. 10.

[18] Administration of Estates Act 1925, s.30(2), as amended by the Limitation Act 1939, s.34(4) and Schedule. As to the distinction between s.30(1) and s.30(2) of the Administration of Estates Act 1925, see *Re Blake* [1932] 1 Ch. 54 and *Re Mason* [1929] 1 Ch. 1.

[19] As to "knowledge" see *Halford* v. *Brookes* [1991] 1 W.L.R. 428 and *Iron Trade Mutual Insurance Co. Ltd.* v. *J. K. Buckenham* [1990] 1 All. E.R. 808. In proceedings under the Fatal Accidents Act 1846 the "date of knowledge" of the person for whose benefit the action is brought may also be relevant; see the Limitation Act 1980, s.12.

[20] Limitation Act 1980, ss.11, 12, 13, 14, 33. *Halford* v. *Brookes*, *supra*.

[21] *Doyle* v. *Foley* [1903] 2 I.R. 95.

namely, that once time has begun to run, it continues to run whatever happens. No allowance is made for the interval between death and grant.[22] The rule applies even where the creditor becomes executor of the debtor.[23] Formerly it appeared that the rule did not apply and the running of time was suspended when the debtor became the administrator of the creditor.[24] However, section 21A of the Administration of Estates Act 1925, inserted in that Act by section 10 of the Limitation Amendment Act 1980, now provides as follows:

"21.—(1) Subject to subsection (2) of this section, where a debtor becomes his deceased creditor's executor by representation or administrator—

> (a) his debt shall thereupon be extinguished; but
> (b) he shall be accountable for the amount of the debt as part of the creditor's estate in any case where he would be so accountable if he had been appointed as an executor by the creditor's will.

(2) Subsection (1) of this section does not apply where the debtor's authority to act as executor or administrator is limited to part only of the creditor's estate which does not include the debt; and a debtor whose debt is extinguished by virtue of paragraph (a) shall not be accountable for its amount by virtue of paragraph (b) of that subsection in any case where the debt was barred by the Limitation Act 1939[25] before be became the creditor's executor or administrator.

(3) In this section 'debt' includes any liability, and 'debtor' and 'creditor' shall be construed accordingly."

It seems that time will not run against a creditor whose debt was payable after the debtor's death, until a grant of letters of administration has been taken out to the debtor's estate,[26] or where the debtor dies testate, until his executor, begins to administer.[27]

The limitation periods

The limitation periods applicable to actions against representatives are the same as those applied to individuals. Thus, actions founded on contract and tort are limited to a period of six years, subject to the special rules mentioned above concerning actions for personal injuries, but an action on

---

[22] *Rhodes* v. *Smethurst* (1840) 6 M. & W. 351; *Freake* v. *Cranefeldt* (1838) 3 My. & Cr. 4?9; *Boatwright* v. *Boatwright* (1873) 17 Eq. 71. As to the right of the executor to pay statute-barred debts, see *ante*, p. 735.

[23] *Bowring-Hanbury's Trustee* v. *Bowring-Hanbury* [1943] Ch. 104.

[24] *Seagram* v. *Knight* (1867) L.R. 2 Ch.App. 628 and see discussion of that case in *Bowring-Hanbury's Trustee* v. *Bowring-Hanbury, supra.*

[25] Including the 1980 Act, see Sched. 3, to that Act.

[26] *Jollife* v. *Pitt* (1715) 2 Vern. 694.

[27] *Webster* v. *Webster* (1804) 10 Ves.93; *Flood* v. *Patterson* (1861) 29 Ves.295. As to acts before or without grant see Chap. 8, *ante.*

a specialty debt or for the recovery of money secured by a mortgage or charge is limited to a period of 12 years, as is also an action on a judgment.[28] Actions to recover the legal estate or an equitable interest in land are limited to 12 years.[29] The limitation period applicable to actions against the Crown or its nominee when a grant has been taken out in pursuance of the Crown's claim to *bona vacantia* is laid down by the Administration of Estates Act 1925.[30]

Creditor's claims—charge or trust

A difficult question can arise as to whether a testator, in providing for the payment of his debts, has merely directed payment or has created a *charge or trust* for payment. In the former case, the limitation period will be six years[31] and in the latter, 12 years.[32]

Before the Land Transfer Act 1897, a testator's debts were payable out of his personalty only. It was held in *Scott* v. *Jones*[33] that *a provision for payment of a testator's debts out of personalty was nugatory, as it added nothing to the executor's obligations or creditor's rights in law and that consequently no charge was created and the six-year period applied.* Conversely, it was said that provision for the payment of debts out of realty altered the creditor's rights in law and created a charge on the realty which enlarged the creditor's limitation period to 12 years.[34] Where provision was made for the payment of debts out of a mixed fund of realty and personalty held upon trust for sale, it was held that the provision created a charge on the realty within the fund.[35] *Re Raggi*[36] is often cited as authority for the proposition that provision for the payment of debts out of a mixed fund creates a charge on both the realty and the personalty in the fund. Warrington J. appears, however, to have decided in the special circumstances of that case that the provision created a charge exclusively on realty and that, consistently with earlier decisions, the 12-year period could be properly applied.[37]

The Land Transfer Act 1897 made realty liable for the payment of debts, but it was nevertheless held that a provision for payment of debts out of realty created a charge on the realty, so as to extend the limitation period to 12 years.[38] The reason given was that such a provision affected the pre-

---

[28] Limitation Act 1980, ss.8, 24.
[29] Limitation Act 1980, s.5, 15, 18. For the meaning of land, see s.38 (1).
[30] Administration of Estates Act 1925, s.30 (1) and s.30 (2) as amended by the Limitation Act 1939, s.34 (4) and Schedule; Limitation Act 1980, s.15 (1), Sched. 2, Part II; see also *ante*, p. 899.
[31] Limitation Act 1980, s.5.
[32] Limitation Act 1980, s.20 (1). As to a trust see *post*, p. 902.
[33] (1838) 4 Cl. & Fin. 382.
[34] *Ibid.* at p. 397; *Re Stephens* (1889) 43 Ch.D. 39, 45.
[35] *Re Stephens, supra.*
[36] [1913] 2 Ch. 206.
[37] [1913] 2 Ch. 206, 209–210.
[38] *Re Balls* [1909] 1 Ch. 791; see *Re Kempster* [1906] 1 Ch. 446.

1925 order of application of assets in discharge of debts and could not be considered to be nugatory[39] within the principle in *Scott* v. *Jones*.[40]

Since 1925 realty and personalty are equally available for the payment of debts.[41] There can, thus, be no justification for any distinction. Consequently it is suggested that the principle in *Scott* v. *Jones*, which has always been upheld, should be adhered to in the present day and that provision in a will for the payment of debts out of realty or out of a mixed fund of realty and personalty should be considered to be nugatory, so that no charge on the realty is created and so that, unless express words are used in the will charging particular assets with the payment of debts, the six-year period will apply.

If the testator creates an express *trust* for the benefit of his creditors, however, it seems probable that section 21 of the 1980 Act will apply and the creditors will become beneficiaries for the purpose of that section.[42]

Acknowledgment

When the defence of the Act is pleaded, the creditor may rely on an acknowledgment of liability[43] to pay the debt made by the representative within the last six years.[44]

An executor's affidavit for probate which includes in the list of the testator's debts a statute-barred debt does not operate as an acknowledgment of the debt so as to take it out of the statute.[45]

An acknowledgment need not be made during the six years, but must be in writing, signed by the person making the acknowledgment, or by his agent, and must be made to the person whose claim is being acknowledged or his agent.[46]

Where there has within six years been an account stated, it is not necessary to rely on an acknowledgment.[47]

An acknowledgment given by one representative, as such, is as sufficient as an acknowledgment given by all of them to keep the debt alive as against the deceased's estate.[48] Thus, even though the representative who gave the acknowledgment has died, an order may be made in an administration

---

[39] *Ibid.* at p. 794. *Re Balls* [1909] 1 Ch. 791, 794.

[40] (1838) 4 Cl. & Fin. 382, and see *supra*.

[41] Administration of Estates Act 1925, s.34(3) and Sched. 1, Part II (*post*, pp. 1129, 1152).

[42] See, however, *Re Blow, Governors of St. Bartholomew's Hospital* v. *Cambden* [1914] 1 Ch. 233 (creditor not a "beneficiary" for the purposes of s.8(1) (*b*) of the Trustee Act 1888). As to beneficiaries' rights, see *post*, p. 904.

[43] Mere acknowledgment of facts is not enough. *Re Flynn (No. 2)* [1969] 2 Ch. 403.

[44] Limitation Act 1980, s.29(5), (6).

[45] *Bowring-Hanbury's Trustee* v. *Bowring-Hanbury* [1943] Ch. 104; Limitation Act 1980, s.29(5), (6), as to the effect of an acknowledgment contained in the will of a debtor, see *Howard* v. *Hennessey* [1947] I.R. 336.

[46] Limitation Act 1980, s.30; *Re Edwards' Will Trusts* [1937] Ch. 553.

[47] *Smith* v. *Forty* (1829) 4 Garr. & P. 126; *Ashby* v. *James* (1843) 11 M. & W. 542.

[48] Limitation Act 1980, s.31(8); *Re Macdonald* [1897] 2 Ch. 181; *cf. Astbury* v. *Astbury* [1898] 2 Ch. 111 (acknowledgment given by one of two executors in his character of trustee of real estate, against wishes of co-trustee, not the valid act of both). See *ante*, p. 693.

action for payment of the debt out of the assets remaining unadministered in the hands or under the control of the surviving representatives.[49]

Where the deceased was a joint debtor, no acknowledgment by his co-debtor, whenever made, will bind the estate of the deceased.[50]

An acknowledgment only operates where the plaintiff seeks to recover a debt or other liquidated money claim, or makes a claim to the personal estate of a deceased person or any share or interest therein.[51] In other actions acknowledgment does not cause a re-accrual of the right of action.

Payment

A payment operates in similar manner to an acknowledgment, and in the same types of proceeding, that is, claims for liquidated sums or for personal estate.[52]

A payment made at any time by one of several representatives, as such, is sufficient to keep the debt alive as against the deceased's estate.[53] Moreover, if the deceased was a joint debtor, a payment made by his co-debtor will bind his estate.[54]

Judgment

A judgment in a full administration action by a creditor within the six-year period prevents time running against the other creditors of the deceased, but the commencement of administration proceedings is not sufficient for this purpose.[56] Similarly, there may be an obligation to satisfy a foreign judgment, even if the original claim would be statute-barred and this obligation will prevent time running.[57]

Action for devastavit

Where a representative has committed a *devastavit* by parting with assets without providing for payment of a debt, the creditor's claim on such *devastavit* against the representative is barred after six years from the date of such distribution[58]; the same period applies where the creditor claims an account.[59]

---

[49] *Re Macdonald, supra.*
[50] Limitation Act 1980, s.31(6).
[51] Limitation Act 1980, s.20(5).
[52] See n. 51.
[53] *Ibid.* s.31(8).
[54] *Ibid.* s.31(6).
[55] *Ibid.* s.25(6), proviso.
[56] *Re Greaves, Bray* v. *Tofield* (1881) 18 Ch.D. 551.
[57] *Re Flynn (No. 2)* [1969] 2 Ch. 403.
[58] *Re Blow, Governors of St. Bartholomew's Hospital* v. *Cambden* [1914] 1 Ch. 233; *Re Lewis* [1939] Ch. 232.
[59] Limitation Act 1980, s.23. As to a beneficiary's claim for an account, see p. 906 *post.*

Claims in tort

An action in tort[60] is subject to the rules of limitation laid down by the Limitation Act and, subject to the special rules mentioned above concerning actions for personal injuries, is prima facie barred after six years after the right of action accrued.[61] The ordinary rules of limitation now apply to such an action brought against the estate of a deceased person.[62]

Beneficiaries' claims

It remains to consider the right of a representative to plead the Act as against the claims of beneficiaries, bearing in mind that the equitable defence of laches can only be raised where there is no express statutory provision,[63] but that the Act is expressed[64] as not affecting "any equitable jurisdiction to refuse relief on the ground of acquiescence or otherwise."

The provisions of the Act as to claims brought by beneficiaries against representatives must be read subject to section 21(1),[65] which provides that in case of fraud by the trustee, or of any action to recover trust property in the possession of the trustee, or converted by the trustee to his use, no period of limitation prescribed by the Act shall apply.[66] In other actions by a beneficiary to recover trust property, the limitation period is six years; but section 32 provides that where the action is based on the fraud of the defendant, or there has been deliberate concealment by the defendant, or the action is for relief from the consequences of a mistake, the period of limitation shall not begin to run until the plaintiff has discovered the fraud, concealment or mistake, or could with reasonable diligence have discovered it.

Personalty

Subject to the foregoing provisions, no action in respect of any claim to the personal estate[67] of a deceased person or to any share or interest in such estate, whether under a will or on an intestacy, may be brought after 12 years from the date when the right to receive the share or interest accrued.[68] Further, it is provided that no action to recover arrears of interest in respect of any legacy, or damages in respect of such arrears, shall be brought after six years from the date on which the interest became due.[69]

---

[60] A penalty under a taxing Act is not a claim in tort and no time limit applies: *Att.-Gen.* v. *Canter* [1939] 1 K.B. 318. As to claims against insolvent estates, see *ante*, p. 630.

[61] Limitation Act 1980, ss.11, 12, 13, 14, 33.

[62] Proceedings against Estates Act 1970, ss.1, 3(2), repealing the Law Reform (Miscellaneous Provisions) Act 1934 1(3), and the Law Reform (Limitation of Actions etc.) Act 1954, ss.4, 7(2). For the old law, reference should be made to previous editions of this work.

[63] See *Re Pauling's Settlement Trusts* 1962] 1 W.L.R. 86, 115; [1964] Ch. 303, 353.

[64] Limitation Act 1980, s.36(2).

[65] See *post*, pp. 905, 906.

[66] See *post*, p. 906.

[67] Excluding chattels real; Limitation Act 1980, s.38 (1).

[68] Limitation Act 1980, s.22.

[69] *Ibid.*

The 12-year period applies not only to actions by a beneficiary against a representative, but also to an action brought by an underpaid beneficiary against an overpaid beneficiary as an equitable claim *in personam*.[70]

The same provisions for the extension of the 12-year period in case of payment or acknowledgment apply as in the case of claims by creditors.[71]

Time begins to run from the date when the right to receive the share or interest accrued. Though, in the case of a legacy, the "right to receive" generally accrues at the death of the deceased,[72] section 22 of the Act will not bar the claim of a residuary legatee[73] to assets only reduced into possession by the representative within 12 years of the commencement of the proceedings.[74] Where a legacy is payable out of a reversionary interest to which the deceased is entitled, time does not begin to run until the interest falls into possession.[75]

Where a legacy or other sum of money, charged upon or payable out of any land or rent, is secured by an express trust, proceedings against the beneficial owner of the land, either by the legatee or trustee, must still be brought within the 12-year period provided by section 20.[76]

Land

Where a beneficiary sues the representative to recover land, the period of limitation which applies is 12 years from the date on which the right of action accrued.[77] "Land" is defined as including corporeal hereditaments, and rentcharges, and any legal or equitable estate or interest in land, including an interest in the proceeds of sale of land held upon trust for sale, but save as aforesaid does not include any incorporeal hereditament.[78]

It is thought, however, that in the majority of cases arising in practice the beneficiary's action will not be barred, since it will fall under the provisions of section 21(1) of the Act just referred to.

It is provided by section 18 that the provisions of the Act apply to equitable interests in land, including interests in the proceeds of sale of land held upon trust for sale, in like manner as they apply to legal estates. More detailed rules for the application of this principle are set out in the four subsections of section 18.

Under section 20(5), the recovery of arrears of interest payable on any sum of money charged on land is limited to six years from the date when

---

[70] *Re Diplock* [1948] Ch. 465; affd.*sub. nom. Ministry of Health* v. *Simpson* [1951] A.C. 251.

[71] See *ante*, p. 902.

[72] *Waddell* v. *Harshaw* [1905] 1 Ir.R. 416.

[73] *Adams* v. *Barry* (1845) 2 Coll. 285; *Re Johnson* (1885) 29 Ch.D. 964.

[74] See further, as to the "right to receive," *Bright* v. *Larcher* (1859) 27 Beav. 130; *Re Welch* [1916] 1 Ch. 375; *Ravenscroft* v. *Frisby* (1844) 1 Coll. 16; *Faulkner* v. *Daniel* (1843) 3 Hare 199, 212.

[75] *Re Ludlam, Ludlam* v. *Ludlam* (1890) 63 L.T. 330; *Re Pauling's Settlement Trusts* [1964] Ch. 303; Limitation Act 1980, s.21 (3).

[76] This follows from the wording of s.22.

[77] Limitation Act 1980, s.15 (1).

[78] *Ibid.* s.38 (1).

such interest became due. The same period applies to the recovery of arrears of rent.[79]

Account

A simple claim to an account and nothing more is based on a fiduciary relationship only and is not barred by any period of limitation.[80]

Where no limitation exists

Although an action for a legacy or a share in personal residue falls within section 22, that section is expressed to be subject to the provisions of sub-section (1) and (2) of the previous section of the Act which provides that no period of limitation is to apply to an action by a beneficiary under a trust in respect of any fraud[81] or fraudulent breach of trust to which the trustee was a party or privy or to recover from the trustee trust property or the proceeds thereof in the possession of the trustee, or previously received by the trustee and converted to his use.[82]

"Trustee" is defined by reference to the Trustee Act 1925 so as to include an implied or constructive trustee and a personal representative.[83] The result is that the 12-year period applies to claims against a representative unless he is guilty of fraud, or retains the legacy or share of the estate, or the proceeds thereof.[84] In these cases the doctrine of laches may apply.[85] Section 32 of the Act may also be relevant.[86]

If a trustee who is also a beneficiary honestly and reasonably distributes the trust property among those whom he believes are entitled to it, and, after the relevant limitation period has expired, he is sued by a "late-comer" beneficiary who was mistakenly excluded from the distribution, the liability of the trustee is limited to the excess over the trustee's proper share.[87]

[79] Limitation Act 1980, s.19.

[80] Att.-Gen. v. Cocke [1988] Ch. 414, 421; Tito v. Waddell [1977] Ch. at p. 251. See also Preston & Newsom: Limitation of Actions, 4th ed., p. 54.

[81] As to the meaning of "fraud" in the Limitation Act 1939, s.26, see Beaman v. A.R.T.S. Ltd. [1949] 1 K.B. 550, 567; see also Collings v. Wade [1896] 1 Ir.R. 340 and Re Sale Hotel and Botanical Gardens Ltd. (1897) 77 L.T. 681; Eddis v. Chichester Constable [1969] 2 Ch. 345; Applegate v. Moss [1971] 1 Q.B. 406; King v. Victor Parsons & Co. [1973] 1 W.L.R. 29. A new s.26 of the 1939 Act was inserted by s.7 of the Limitation Amendment Act 1980 as a result of these decisions. See now s.32 of the 1980 Act.

[82] Limitation Act 1980, s.21 (1).

[83] Limitation Act 1980, s.38 (1); Trustee Act 1925, s.68(17); see also Re Landi [1939] Ch. 828; Re Milking Pail Farm Trusts [1940] Ch. 996.

[84] As to the effect of the Limitation Act 1939, s.19(1), see Lewin, Trusts, 16th ed., 1964, p. 707.

[85] See ante, n. 63, p. 904.

[86] See ante, p. 904.

[87] Limitation Act 1939, ss.19(1A), now s.21(2) of the 1980 Act inserted by the Limitation Amendment Act 1980, s.5, giving effect to the recommendation made by the Law Reform Committee in para. 3.84 of its 21st Report (Cmnd. 6923). Previously the trustee would have been liable for the whole of the latecomer's share, and would have been prevented by s.19(1) from raising any defence of limitation, but he would have been unable to recoup any of the overpayment from the other beneficiaries, because they would be able to plead limitation against him.

Executor functus officio

A point of difficulty arises from section 21(3), which provides, subject to the provisions of sections 21(1) and (2), that an action by a beneficiary to recover trust property or in respect of any breach of trust, not being an action for which a period of limitation is prescribed by any other provisions of the Act, is barred after six years from the date on which the right of action accrued.[88] Although a trustee is defined (by reference to the Trustee Act) as including a personal representative, this subsection does not extend to representatives as such, since its operation is clearly limited to cases not covered by section 22.[89] The six-year period provided by this subsection may nevertheless apply where a representative has completed the administration of the estate and is thus *functus officio* and no longer fills the role of a representative.[90] It would also seem to apply where an executor becomes liable under the chain of representation for the default of an earlier executor or life tenant of settled assets, for in such a case the latest executor will normally be primarily in the position of a trustee of the "available assets."[91]

Where a testatrix gave her residue to her executors upon trust for sale and to hold the proceeds, subject to an annuity to X, for six named persons, and, some eight years after the death of X, the six persons sued the executors for an account of the fund set aside to secure the annuity, it was held that the six-year period applicable to trustees was the relevant period.[92] But, though an executor may be a trustee for sale of residue, he is not thereby a trustee of a legacy payable on the determination of an annuity.[93]

Accrual

It has to be remembered that time does not begin to run until the right of action has accrued. On this topic reference should be made to the general law on limitation.[94] Where under a settlement or trust for sale of land there is a remainder, vested or contingent, or other future interest, the remainder-man's right of action is not accelerated by the barring of a prior interest and does not accrue until his interest falls into possession.[95] In such cases the title of a representative or trustee is not extinguished under section 16[96] nor is his right of action barred[97] until all the rights of remaindermen have been barred under the Act.

---

[88] As to the effect of the Limitation Act 1939, s.19(2), see Lewin (*op. cit.*) at p. 709.

[89] The distinction between s.21(3) and s.22 is similar to that which existed between the Real Property Limitation Act 1874, s.8, and the Trustee Act 1888, s.8(1) (*b*).

[90] *Re Swain* [1891] 3 Ch. 233; *Re Timmis* [1902] 1 Ch. 176; and see *post*, p. 1049.

[91] See *Re Swan* [1915] 1 Ch. 829. See p. 731 *ante*.

[92] *Re Oliver* [1927] 2 Ch. 323; *Re Richardson* [1920] 1 Ch. 423.

[93] *Re Barker* [1892] 2 Ch. 491.

[94] See, *e.g.* Preston and Newsom, *Limitation of Actions*, 3rd ed., pp. 132 *et seq.* and *ante*, p. 86;

[95] Limitation Act 1980, Sched. I para. 4.

[96] *Ibid.* s.18(3).

[97] *Ibid.* s.18(4); *Preston and Newsom*, p. 143.

CHAPTER 65

JUDGMENTS AGAINST REPRESENTATIVES

The form of judgment against a representative depends on whether or not he is to be held personally liable.[1] If he is not personally liable the judgment is *"de bonis testatoris."* If he is personally liable it is *"de bonis propriis."* Thus if he admits that, apart from a release to himself, he has acted as representative the judgment against him must be that the plaintiff do recover the debt and costs to be levied out of the assets of the testator, if the defendant have so much; but if not, then the costs[2] out of the defendant's own goods.[3] So where the executor pleads *plene administravit*, and it is found against him, the judgment is *de bonis testatoris, et si non,* etc., then the costs *de bonis propriis.*[4]

Where a defendant pleads he never was executor (ne unques executor)

It was formerly held that where the defendant pleaded that he had never been a representative, *ne unques executor* or *administrator*, or a release to himself, and it was found against him, the judgment was that the plaintiff do recover both the debt and costs, in the first place, *de bonis testatoris, si,* etc., and *si non,* etc., *de bonis propriis.*[5] The reason alleged was that the representative must have known that these were false pleas. But the same reason seems equally to apply to other pleas where the judgment was different.[6] And this probably would no longer be held to be the law, especially as the rule was rather a pleading result, deduced from pleading admissions, which the court would not let the defendant remedy by amendment, than a punishment inflicted by the court, which had indeed no jurisdiction to inflict such a punishment.

---

[1] As to the status of the personal representative, see p. 713, 714, *ante.*
[2] As to costs generally, see post, pp. 915 *et seq.*
[3] 1 Wms.Saund. 336, n. (10) to *Hancocke* v.*Prowd*; *Gorton* v. *Gregory* (1962) 3 B. & S. 90. The court refused, after a lapse of six years, to allow a judgment for the debt *de bonis testatoris*, and for the costs *de bonis testatoris et si non de bonis propriis*, to be altered to a judgment generally *de bonis testatoris et si non de bonis propriis*, even if the latter were clearly the judgment to which the plaintiff was entitled: the distinction being between an alteration to discharge, and one to fix, the personal liability of the executor; *Burroughs* v. *Stevens* (1814) 5 Taunt. 556.
[4] 1 Roll.Abr. 931, D. pl. 3; Wentw.Off.Ex. 244, 14th ed.; see *Marshall* v. *Willder* (1829) 9 B.& C.655, 658; *ante*, p. 713, n. 7.
[5] Bros.Exors. 34; 1 Roll.Abr., p. 930, C.pl. 2, 8, p. 933, pl. 15; *Bull* v.*Wheeler* (1622) Cro. Jac.648; Wentw.Off.Ex. 338, 340, 14th ed.; 1 Saund. 336 *b*, n. (10); *Hooper* v. *Summersett* (1810) Wightw. 20, *per curiam.*
[6] 1 Wms.Saund. 336, n. (10).

Judgment where plene administravit pleaded (administration completed)

Where the representative pleads that he has completed the administration or completed with specified exceptions that is to say either a general or special *plene administravit*, he is liable only for the amount of the assets proved to be in his hands.[7] Thus, in *Harrison* v. *Beccles*,[8] the plaintiff, having proved a debt of £80, and having proved £25 assets unadministered, took a verdict on the *plene administravit* for £25, and judgment for assets which might accrue in the future[9] (*quando acciderint*) for the rest of the debt.[10]

When two or more executors plead *plene administravit* severally, and the jury finds that one of them only has assets, judgment should be given against that one only.[11] And in *Parsons* v. *Hancocke*,[12] where in an action against several executors they all pleaded jointly that they had fully administered, etc., and the plaintiff proved assets in the hands of some only of the defendants, Parke J. directed the jury to find a verdict for the plaintiff against the latter, and, as to the other executors, to find a verdict for the defendants.[13]

Judgment of future assets (quando acciderint)

In an action against a representative, if the defendant pleads *Plene administravit*, and it cannot be proved that he has assets in hand, the plaintiff may admit this defence, and take judgment immediately of assets *quando acciderint*, or, as it is sometimes called, judgment of assets *in futuro*.[14] But under the former practice if the plaintiff took issue on the general or special plea of *plene administravit*, and it was found against him he could not have judgment of assets *quando*, etc.[15] *Quaere* whether under the present practice it would be necessary for the plaintiff in such circumstances to obtain leave to amend his pleadings in order to obtain such a judgment.

By taking judgment of assets which might accrue in the future (*quando*)

---

[7] Wms.Saund. 219, n. (8) to *Wheatly* v. *Lane* (1669) 85 E.R. 228, 235; *Jackson* v. *Bowley* (1841) Carr. & M. 97. And see *ante* p. 894.

[8] Cited 3 T.R. 688.

[9] For this form of judgment, see *infra*.

[10] *Hancock* v. *Podmore* (1830) 1 B. & Ad. 265; *per* Bayley J. And see the form of judgment in Serjt. Williams's note in Sir E.V. Williams's edition, 1 Wms.Saund. 608, 609.

[11] *Bellew* v. *Juckleden* (1639) 1 Roll.Abr. 929, B. pl. 5.

[12] 1 Mood. & Malk. 330.

[13] See also the remarks of the same learned judge in *Cousins* v. *Paddon* (1835) 2 C.M. & R. 547, 558

[14] *Mary Shipley's Case* (1611) 8 Co. 134a; *Noell* v. *Nelson* (1670) 2 Saund. 214; *Parker* v. *Dee* (1674) 3 Swanst, 532, note to *Drewry* v. *Thacker*. See the form of such judgment, 2 Wms.Saund. 216, 217.

[15] 1 Roll.Abr. 929, B. pl. 2; 2 Wms.Saund. 217, n. (1) to *Noell* v. *Nelson; Lucas* v. *Jenner* (1833) 2 Dowl. 64, *per* Bayley B. But see *Hindsley* v. *Russell* (1810) 12 East 232. The same consequence does not seem to follow where *plene administravit* is pleaded: *Harris* v. *Goodwyn* (1841) 2 M. & Gr. 414, 415, *per* Tindal C.J.

the plaintiff admits that the defendant has fully administered to that time.[16] Accordingly, the terms of the judgment are that the plaintiff do recover his debt to be levied of the assets of the testator which shall thereafter come to the hands of the executor.[17] But, *semble*, such a judgment includes assets received between writ and judgment.[18]

When a representative pleads that he has fully administered, or that there are other judgments outstanding which have not been met and that he has fully administered with certain exceptions, and the plaintiff accepts the plea and takes judgment for future assets the representative is not personally liable to pay the costs[19]: nor does he seem liable thereto when he pleads *plene administravit praeter*, and the plaintiff takes judgment of the assets admitted in part, and for the residue, of assets *quando* etc.[20] But, *semble*, though a representative, in such case, is not personally liable to pay costs, yet judgment may be entered for them, to be recovered *de bonis testatoris, quando acciderint.*[21]

Judgment for testator's devastavit

Judgment against an executor for a *devastavit* committed by his testator must always be *de bonis testatoris.*[22]

Proceedings by attachment (garnishee proceedings)

A creditor who has obtained judgment *de bonis testatoris* may enforce it by attaching a debt due to the estate of the deceased.[23] Formerly, the court would not restrain such proceedings on the ground that an order for administration had been made, where such order was made after the recovery of the judgment.[24] In *Burton Finance Ltd.* v. *Godfrey*[25] the Court of Appeal reviewed the divergent authorities on garnishee orders and charging orders. It was held that similar principles applied to both, and that the court's discretion whether or not to make such orders absolute had to be exercised in the light of all relevant circumstances, which might include events occurring both before and after the order *nisi* and that the order would not be made absolute if it would be inequitable to do so. A gar-

[16] 2 Wms.Saund. 219, n. (2); *Parker* v. *Dee* (1674) 3 Swanst.532, note to *Drewry* v. *Thacker.*

[17] *Taylor* v. *Holman* (1764) Bull.N.P. 169; 2 Wms.Saund. 219 *a*, n. (2); *Mara* v. *Quin* (1794) 6 T.R. 1.

[18] See 8th ed. of this work, pp. 1964, 1992.

[19] 1 Wms.Saund. 336, n. (10); Tidd, 980, 9th ed.

[20] Tidd, 980, 9th ed. But where other pleas are unsuccessful, see *Squire* v. *Arnison* (1884) 1 T.L.R. 67.

[21] *De Tastet* v. *Andrade* (1817) 1 Chitt.Rep. 629, 630, *in notis*; *Cox* v. *Peacock* (1835) 4 Dowl. 134.

[22] 1 Wms.Saund. 219, *e, f,* n. (8) to *Wheatly* v. *Lane* (1669) 85 E.R. 228, 238; *Coward* v. *Gregory* (1866) L.R. 2 C.P. 153, 157.

[23] See Ord. 49.

[24] *Fowler* v. *Roberts* (1860) 2 Giff. 226; *Burton* v. *Roberts* (1860) 6 H. & N. 93.

[25] [1976] 1 W.L.R. 719. See also S.C.P. 1991. 62/2/58.

nishee order does not normally operate to cause forfeiture under a protective trust in a will[26] nor is a trustee a debtor beyond the sums actually in his hands due to the beneficiaries.[27]

Return of nulla bona (no assets)

It seems that, even at the present time, where a judgment has been obtained against a representative *de bonis testatoris* execution cannot be levied against his own goods until the plaintiff has obtained a second judgment. The plaintiff must bring an action for the recovery of the debt on the first judgment, and in this second action he suggests a *devastavit*. This process was substituted in lieu of the proceedings by *scire fieri* inquiry.[28] The foundation of this second action is the first judgment obtained against the executor, which, as there has been already occasion to show,[29] is conclusive upon him to show that he has assets to satisfy such judgment. If, therefore, upon a *fi. fa. de bonis testatoris*, on a judgment obtained against an executor, either no goods can be found which were the testator's, or not sufficient to satisfy the demand (or, which is the same thing, if the executor will not expose them to the execution), that is evidence of a *devastavit*, for which the executor is personally liable and chargeable *de bonis propriis*.[30] A return of *nulla bona*, is, however, only prima facie evidence of a *devastavit* and it is open to the executor to show why the assets are no longer in his hands and that that is not due to any *devastavit* committed by him.[31] Thus, the presumption was held rebutted by proof that, after the judgment, and long before the writ of *fi. fa.*, an order had been made by the court appointing a receiver and making an administration order, and that the receiver had been ordered to get in the assets of the deceased.[32]

The second action may be brought upon the judgment against the executor upon a bare suggestion of a *devastavit* without any writ of *fi. fa.* first taken out upon the judgment.[33] But the usual course is, first to sue out a *fi. fa.* upon the judgment, and upon the sheriff's return of *nulla bona* to bring the action, and state the judgment, the writ, and return, in the statement of claim; and, on the trial, the record of the judgment, the *fi. fa.*, and the return, will be sufficient evidence to prove the case.[34] *Semble*, if the sheriff cannot find any assets, he may, if he pleases, return a *devastavit* as well as

---

[26] *Re Greenwood* [1901] 1 Ch. 887.

[27] *Webb* v. *Stenton* (1883) 11 Q.B.D. 518.

[28] *Berwick* v. *Andrews* (1704) 2 Lord Raym. 971. As to the obsolete process of *scire fieri* inquiry, see the 11th ed. of this work, pp. 1578–1580.

[29] *Ante*, p. 894.

[30] 1 Wms. Saund. 219, n. (8) to *Wheatley* v. *Lane*; *Blackmor* v. *Mercer* (1672) 2 Wms.Saund. 402; *Erving* v. *Peters* (1790) 3 T.R. 686; *Farr* v. *Newman* (1792) 4 T.R. 621.

[31] *Batchelor* v. *Evans* [1939] Ch. 1007.

[32] See n. 30.

[33] *Wheatly* v. *Lane* (1669) 1 Sid. 397; 1 Wms.Saund. 219, n. (8).

[34] *Challoner* v. *Challoner*, cited in *Skelton* v. *Hawling* (1749) 1 Wils. 259; *Erving* v. *Peters* (1790) 3 T.R. 685; 1 Saund. 219c; *Sine prole*, where an irregular *testatum fi. fa.* had been issued and returned *nulla bona*: *Leonard* v. *Simpson* (1835) 2 Bing.N.C. 176.

nulla bona, to the writ of *fi. fa.*, and in that case the plaintiff may apply for leave to issue execution against the representative personally.[35]

In this form of action the judgment is *de bonis propriis*.[36] The representative may in his pleadings deny the *devastavit*. He can then give in evidence that there were goods of the testator which might have been taken in execution, and that he showed them to the sheriff.[37] But he cannot successfully plead *plene administravit*, or any other plea which puts his defence upon want of assets. This would be contrary to what was admitted by the first judgment. And if the truth were that he had no assets, he should have set it up as a defence to the original action, and having neglected to do so, he cannot successfully say so afterwards.[38] Again, if he had pleaded *plene administravit* to the original action, and the judgment was had upon a verdict finding that he had assets, he cannot now successfully plead that he had no assets.[39] And, for the same reason, he cannot give in evidence the want of assets on the trial of the *devastavit*.[40]

Judgment by default is admission of assets

If a representative allows judgment by default to go against him, this is an admission of assets, but it does not justify a judgment *de bonis propriis* against him, for no such judgment can be entered unless a *devastavit* is proved or is alleged and remains unanswered. The judgment in default against an executor is therefore in form *de bonis testatoris* as regards the debt and costs, and as to the costs only, *et si non de bonis propriis*. But after a return of *nulla bona testatoris* the plaintiff may bring a second action for the debt, for such a return raises a presumption of *devastavit*. The presumption may, however, be rebutted if any explanation is forthcoming.[41] If the presumption is not rebutted, the defendant is estopped by the first judgment from denying assets; and judgment in the second action, if the defendant again makes default, will then be *de bonis testatoris et si non de bonis propriis* as to both debt and costs.[42]

Where either party died after first judgment

Under the old practice, if a person obtained judgment against a representative, and died, his executor might bring an action upon the judgment against the representative, suggesting a *devastavit*; for such an action was brought against the same person against whom the judgment was had,

---

[35] *Wheatly* v. *Lane* (1669) 1 Wms.Saund. 216, n. (8).

[36] *Warren* v. *Consett* (1704) 2 Lord Raym. 1502.

[37] 1 Wms.Saund. 219, n. (8) to *Wheatly* v. *Lane; Midland Bank Trust Co. Ltd.* v. *Green (No. 2) The Times* July 5, 1978; [1978] C.L.Y. 1439.

[38] See n. 37.

[39] *Erving* v. *Peters* (1790) 3 T.R. 685, 693.

[40] *Rock* v. *Layton* (1700) 1 Salk. 310.

[41] *Batchelor* v. *Evans* [1939] Ch. 1007; *Marsden* v. *Regan* [1954] 1 W.L.R. 423.

[42] *Ibid.; Leonard* v. *Simpson, ante; Thompson* v. *Clarke* (1901) 17 T.L.R. 455; *Lacons* v. *Warmoll* [1907] 2 K.B.350,360.

and by that judgment assets were admitted.[43] Conversely, if a judgment[44] was had against an executor, who afterwards died, an action might[45] be brought against his executor or administrator, upon the judgment, suggesting a *devastavit* by the first executor, and the judgment was as conclusive upon the representative of the executor as it was upon the executor himself. Therefore, if an action of debt, suggesting a *devastavit* by the first executor in his lifetime, was brought against his executor or administrator, the second executor could not have pleaded that the first executor fully administered the goods of the first testator, or any other plea, purporting that he (that is, the first executor) had no assets to satisfy the judgment, any more than the executor himself could have done.[46] But the executor or administrator of the executor might plead that he, the defendant, had fully administered all the estate of his own testator or intestate.[47] Moreover, the judgment in the action, when brought against the executor or administrator of the executor, against whom the judgment was obtained, was *de bonis testatoris,* or *intestati.*[48]

Semble the same course must be adopted even under the present practice. Under Order 46, r. 2, where any change has taken place by death or otherwise in the parties entitled or liable to execution, a writ of execution may not issue without the leave of the court. But in the cases now under consideration no person or his estate is either entitled or liable to execution *de bonis propriis* until a second judgment is obtained.[49] It is conceived that Order 46, r. 2 would apply, however, when the sheriff returns a *devastavit* as well as *nulla bona,* for in that case no second action seems to be necessary.[50]

Even under the old practice, where an executor died after judgment obtained against him, it was impossible to bring a second action against his representative suggesting a *devastavit* by him without first reviving the judgment against him. He was not a party to the original judgment and so was not bound by the admission of assets.[51]

Since a judgment can no longer be revived,[52] and since Order 46, r. 2. has been shown to be inapplicable, *semble* the only way in such a case in which the second executor could be made personally liable for wasting the assets of his testator would be by an administration action.[53]

---

[43] *Berwick* v. *Andrews* (1704) 2 Lord Raym. 971; *ibid.* 1 Salk. 314.

[44] *cf. ante*, p. 559 as to the position where no judgment has been obtained.

[45] See Administration of Estates Act 1925, s.29, replacing 30 Car. 2, c. 7; as to which, see *ante* p. 559.

[46] *Skelton* v. *Hawling* (1749) 1 Wils. 258.

[47] 1 Wms.Saund. 219, *e*, n.

[48] See n. 47.

[49] In previous editions of this work it appears to have been assumed that the former Ord. 42, r. 23, would apply.

[50] *Supra*, p. 911.

[51] 1 Wms.Saund. 219, n. (8) to *Wheatly* v. *Lane* (1669) 85 E.R. 235; *Crosby* v. *Geering*, cited in *Berwick* v. *Andrews* (1704) 2 Ld.Raym. 972.

[52] Judgment used to be revived under the Common Law Procedure Act 1852, ss. 129–131, which were repealed by the Statute Law Revision and Civil Procedure Act 1883, s.3.

[53] See the remarks of Lindley M.R. in *Stewart* v. *Rhodes* [1900] 1 Ch. 386, 402 and 403.

Judgment of future assets

If a judgment of assets *quando acciderint* has been entered against a representative, the plaintiff cannot have execution until some assets come into the hands of the defendant.

If assets come to the hands of the representative the plaintiff can apply for leave to issue execution under Order 46, r. 2(1) (c), which provides for such leave where the judgment or order is against the assets of a deceased person coming to the hands of his executors or administrators after the date of the judgment or order, and it is sought to issue execution against such assets.[54]

Revenue claims

Where a taxing statute imposes an original personal liability on the representative[55] he becomes a Crown debtor and cannot claim immunity because he is ordinarily resident outside the jurisdiction. The Crown is entitled to an order *de bonis propriis*.[56]

---

[54] See on this rule, *Stewart* v. *Rhodes, ante.* For procedure, see Ord. 46, r. 4.

[55] See Finance Act 1894, s.6; *Berry* v. *Gaukroger* [1903] 2 Ch. 116; Finance Act 1975, s.25; Inheritance Tax Act 1984, s.200.

[56] *I.R.C* v. *Stannard* [1984] 1 Wil. R. 1039.

CHAPTER 66

COSTS IN ADMINISTRATION ACTIONS

In hostile litigation the representative will normally be in the position of any other litigant. The costs are in the discretion of the court and will usually follow the event.[1] No special problem initially arises here, but later as a matter of administration it becomes necessary to decide whether and how far costs are to be borne by the estate of the deceased and sometimes out of what part of the estate are they to be paid.[2]

The basis for taxation of costs was "rationalised" in 1986[3] by reducing the former party and common fund bases to "standard" and "indemnity"[4] only. It is only in exceptional circumstances that the successful party in hostile litigation is entitled to costs on the indemnity basis.[5] Thus the standard basis always applies unless the indemnity basis is specified in the order of the court.[6] The one exception to this proposition is that the representative is entitled without any order to his costs out of the estate on the indemnity basis.

Representatives costs out of the estate

Since an executor can only be deprived of this right for misconduct, he has a right to appeal from any order refusing him his costs.[7] The measure of these costs (including costs, charges and expenses) was as between solicitor and client (later known as "common fund"[8]) but now there is a complete indemnity.[9] If the assets are insufficient to pay the creditors of the deceased, these costs, and any other costs, charges, and expenses properly incurred by the representative are a first charge or lien[10] on the estate.[11] Although there is no need for an order to provide for a representative's costs if it does so provide the taxation will be on the indemnity basis[12] unless such costs were incurred contrary to his duty as a representative.[13] Costs as between solicitor and client were not usually given to a rep-

---

[1] See Dan.Ch.Pr., 8th ed., 1028. As to costs in probate actions, see *ante*, pp. 398 *et seq.*, and 437 *et seq.* As to costs generally, see Ord. 62.

[2] See *post*, p. 926.

[3] See R.S.C. Ord. 62, r. 3(4) and S.I. 1986 No. 632.

[4] R.S.C. Ord. 62, r. 12.

[5] *Bowen-Jones* v. *Bowen-Jones* [1986] 3 All. E.R. 163. See R.S.C. Ord. 62 & 12(3).

[6] R.S.C. Ord. 62, r. 3(4).

[7] *Cotterell* v. *Stratton* (1872) L.R. 8 Ch. 295. See also *post*, pp. 916, 921, 922.

[8] *Re Love* (1885) 29 Ch.D. 348; see also *Re Knight's Will* (1884) 26 Ch.D. 82; *Re Robertson* [1949] W.N. 224; and *Practice Direction* [1953] 1 W.L.R. 1365, 1452.

[9] *Post*, p. 921.

[10] See *Re Bourne* [1906] 2 Ch.427.

[11] See *ante*, p. 634.

[12] See Ord. 62, r. 14(1).

[13] See Ord. 62, r. 14(2).

resentative out of real estate, but where he had properly accounted for all the personal estate he might be paid his costs, charges and expenses out of the realty to the extent of the personal estate so accounted for, but the balance was only payable out of real estate as between party and party.[14]

Costs of third party out of estate

A representative fairly instituting an action for the direction of the court, about the trust, will be entitled to his own costs, and any person made a party to the suit, for the protection of the representative, will also have his costs out of the estate.[15] Where the Public Trustee appeared on a construction summons in one capacity as trustee and in another capacity as agent for a beneficiary, he was held entitled to his costs in both capacities.[16]

Representative guilty of misconduct

Once misconduct is proved, the court has a discretion as to the costs of a representative in an administration action.[17] In cases marked by fraud, evasion, or neglect of duty, the court will not merely refuse to allow him his costs out of the assets, but will order him to pay the costs of the action, or of so much of the action as is attributable to the breach of duty on his part.[18]

It is impossible to define exactly what will amount to such misconduct as to justify the judge in depriving a representative of his costs. Mere negligence is not sufficient.[19] An administrator is entitled to costs, even though the action was caused by a claim by him for certain payments disallowed in his accounts, provided the claim was made under an honest mistake, and was neither fraudulent nor monstrous.[20] On the other hand, where executors first withheld accounts and then rendered incorrect ones, they were ordered to pay the costs of the action.[21] Mere non-feasance has been held to amount to such misconduct, as in *Re Weall*,[22] where executors allowed their solicitor to retain and pay himself some costs which the court held to be unnecessary, and other costs which should have been charged against *corpus* but which the executors had improperly charged against income.

In *Re Chapman*[23] a barrister trustee who developed an honest delusion

---

[14] *Re Harrys* [1900] W.N.147.
[15] Dan.Ch.Pr., 8th ed., 1056, *Re Cutcliffe's Estate* [1959] P. 6. As to conditions as to costs in the will, see *ante* p. 837.
[16] *Re Abercrombie's Will Trusts* [[1931] W.N. 109.
[17] For a list of cases in which trustees and personal representatives were deprived of costs, see *Supreme Court Practice* 1982 notes to Ord. 62, r. 31(5). *cf. Holding* v. *Property Trust* [1989] 1 W.L.R. 1324.
[18] *Heighington* v. *Grant* (1845) 1 Phil.C.C. 600; *Hide* v. *Haywood* (1741) 2 Atk. 126; *Hewett* v. *Foster* (1844) 7 Beav. 348; *Re Skinner* [1904] 1 Ch. 289; *Re England* [1918] 1 Ch. 24; *Re Holton* [1918] W.N. 78; Dan.Ch.Pr., 8th ed., 1060.
[19] *Travers* v *Townsend* (1828) 1 Moll. 496; but see *Re Skinner, ante.*
[20] *Re Jones* [1897] 2 Ch. 190.
[21] *Re Radclyffe* (1881) 50 L.J.Ch. 317.
[22] (1889) 42 Ch.D. 674.
[23] [1895] 72 L.T. 66.

that the tenant for life was an imposter, and refused to pay her the trust income, was ordered to pay her costs personally as between solicitor and client. "A trustee may be honest, and yet, from over-caution or some other cause, he may act unreasonably; and if his conduct is so unreasonable as to be vexatious, oppressive or otherwise wholly unjustifiable and he thereby causes his *cestuis que trust* expense . . . the trustee must bear such expense" (*per* Lindley L.J.).

In *Re Cabburn*,[24] Bacon V.-C. ordered the plaintiff, who was executor and trustee of the will, personally to pay the costs of an administration action which was held to be unnecessary. The estate in that case was a very small one, and the defendant beneficiaries had offered to concur in a special case to settle any point of doubt or difficulty arising under the will.

Appeal from order refusing costs

A representative or trustee deprived of his costs may always appeal,[25] as he can only be deprived of them on the ground of misconduct, and the question of misconduct or no misconduct is a matter on which an appeal lies.[26] But if the judge fairly exercises his discretion as to costs of an executor, administrator or trustee, no appeal will lie from his order without the leave of the court or judge making the order.[27] If, however, the judge has merely applied some rule which in fact excluded his discretion, an appeal will lie without leave.[28]

Creditor successfully sues for debt

If a representative is sued by a creditor for a debt of the deceased, and the creditor succeeds in establishing his demand, the court will direct the payment of the amount due to the creditor, together with his costs, out of the estate[29]; but unless the estate is insufficient, no order is made for the costs of the representative, since he is entitled to reimburse himself out of the assets; so that if there is no further fund out of which he may reimburse himself, the costs must come out of his own pocket.[30]

Executor also debtor to estate

It is a clear rule that no costs are given to an executor or trustee who is a debtor to the estate until his debt is paid, or until he has complied with an

[24] (1882) 46 L.T. 848. As to an unnecessary action by a legatee, see *post*, p. 924.
[25] Dan.Ch.Pr., 8th ed., 1115, where the cases will be found conveniently cited; *Supreme Court Practice* 1993 para. 62/2/30.
[26] *Re Love (1885)* 29 Ch.D. 348. See also *Re Knight's Will* (1884) 26 Ch.D. 82. As to when the Court of Appeal may interfere in other cases, see *Smith* v. *Middleton* [1986] 1 W.L.R. 598.
[27] Supreme Court Act 1981, s.18(1)(*f*). *Bank of America* v. *Nock* [1988] A.C.1002.
[28] *The City of Manchester* (1880) 5 P.D. 221; *Bew* v. *Bew* [1899] 2 Ch. 467, disapproving *Charles* v. *Jones* (1886) 33 Ch.D. 80, on this point.
[29] Dan.Ch.Pr., 8th ed., 1065.
[30] See n. 29.

order to bring in money, and his solicitor is in no better position.[31] If one of two executors is a debtor to the estate, his co-executor is entitled to act by a separate solicitor, and if he does so he will be entitled to his costs.[32] If two executors employ one solicitor, and one of the two executors is a debtor to the estate, the taxing master on taxation finds what is the fair amount of costs to be attributed to the executor who is a debtor to the estate. This amount is deducted from the total costs of the two, and the balance after making such deduction is the amount allowed as costs of the other executor.[33]

The principle seems to be that the costs due to the executor who is indebted to the estate are set off against his debt, and the proper form of order appears to be to order payment of the costs due to him from the estate, and for the order also to provide that such costs are not to be paid until he makes good the money due from him to the estate[34]; it makes no difference for this purpose whether the debt arises from a default of the executor or trustee, or is simply a debt due from him to the testator's estate.

Executor debtor becomes bankrupt

If an executor who is indebted to the estate becomes bankrupt his costs incurred before the bankruptcy are set off against the debt.[35] Further, if the debt due to the estate was incurred by a fraudulent breach of trust it is not discharged by an order of discharge from the bankruptcy,[36] so that the executor cannot even claim his costs incurred after his bankruptcy until he satisfies the debt. But in other cases, where the bankruptcy operates to discharge the debt, the costs incurred after the bankruptcy are not set off against the debt.[37]

Costs due to a trustee who has become bankrupt, whether incurred before or after bankruptcy, are payable to the trustee in bankruptcy, unless the solicitor of the trustee obtains a charging order in his favour.[38]

Where an executor is the sole plaintiff or defendant, and the court considers that the assistance rendered by his solicitor was essential to enable the account to be properly taken and vouched, costs have in some cases been allowed though the executor was a debtor to the estate: this principle has been applied where the executor was bankrupt.[39] Where the estate was insolvent and the executor was represented by a solicitor at the express

---

[31] *Re O'Kean* [1907] 1 Ir.R. 223.

[32] *Per* Jessel M.R. in *Smith* v. *Dale* (1881) 18 Ch.D. at p. 518.

[33] *Smith* v. *Dale* (1881) 18 Ch.D. 516. See also *McEwan* v. *Crombie* (1883) 25 Ch.D. 175.

[34] *Lewis* v. *Trask* (1882) 21 Ch.D. 862; *Re Basham* (1883) 23 Ch.D. 195.

[35] *Smith* v. *Dale, ante*; *Re Basham, ante*; *Re Vowles* (1886) 32 Ch.D. 243.

[36] Bankruptcy Act 1914. s.28; Williams and Muir Hunter, *The Law and Practice in Bankruptcy*, 19th ed., p. 141; Insolvency Act 1986, s.281 *Muir Hunter on Personal Insolvency*, para. 3–132 *et seq*.

[37] *Lewis* v. *Trask, ante*; *Re Basham, ante*; *McEwan* v. *Crombie, ante*; *Re Vowles, ante*, *Clare* v. *Clare* (1882) 21 Ch.D. 865, *contra*, can no longer be supported.

[38] *Baker* v. *Abbott* [1897] W.N. 38.

[39] See remarks of Chitty J. in *Re Basham, ante*.

request of the Master, a lump sum was allowed the solicitor.[40] Where possible, the sanction of the beneficiaries or creditors should be obtained before the executor's solicitor acts in such circumstances.

Trustee making good his default

A trustee who has not been guilty of dishonesty, and who has made good to the estate the deficiency arising from an improper investment made by him, will not normally be ordered to pay costs.[41]

Costs of representative of defaulting trustee

The representative of a defaulting trustee, who accounts fairly for the assets come to his hands, is entitled to deduct his costs of the action out of the assets of his testator or intestate, even though they may be insufficient to repair the breach of trust.[42]

In *Re Griffiths*,[43] an action was brought against the executor of a deceased executor for the administration of the estate of the original testator. The defendant properly accounted for all assets which had come to his hands. A balance was found due from the estate of the original executor to the estate of the original testator, which balance the estate of the original executor was insufficient to pay. Cotton L.J. said that the strict order would be to allow the defendant out of the estate of the original testator all the costs incurred solely with reference to the original testator's estate, but as to the costs incurred by the defendant solely as representative of his own testator, the defaulting executor, he ought to be allowed them solely out of the estate of the defaulting executor. Fry L.J. in the same case pointed out that there was a third class of costs, coming under neither of the above heads, and they ought to be divided between the two funds.[44]

Charges not taxed as costs—accounts

It was previously held that representatives were not entitled to their charges and expenses on taxation without an express direction that they were to be included in the taxation, as they were presumed to retain them out of the estate.[45] However the general form of order now used includes the charges and expenses "of and incidental to" the application.[46]

Just allowances

In taking any account directed by any judgment or order, all "just allowances" are made without any direction for that purpose.[47] The question

---

[40] *Re Wells* (unrep.), *coram* Bennett J., in chambers, *reg. lib.* 1928 W. 3709.
[41] *Peacock* v. *Colling* (1885) 54 L.J.Ch. 743.
[42] *Haldenby* v. *Spofforth* (1846) 9 Beav. 195; *Horne* v. *Shepherd* (1857) 3 Jur.(N.S.) 806.
[43] (1884) 26 Ch.D. 465.
[44] See also *Palmer* v. *Jones* (1874) 43 L.J.Ch. 349; *Re Kitto* (1879) 28 W.R. 411.
[45] *Humphrys* v. *Moore* (1740) 2 Atk. 108.
[46] See *post*, pp. 920–921.
[47] Ord. 43, r. 6. See also *ante*, pp. 54, 706.

what are just allowances is usually left to be decided on the taking of the account.[48]

What are just allowances depends very much upon the circumstances of each case. It is, however, the settled rule that whatever a trustee or representative has expended in the fair execution of his trust may be allowed him in passing his accounts.[49] For instance, an executor was allowed money which he had paid to his solicitor on a misrepresentation by the solicitor, and which the latter had misappropriated.[50]

Under the head of "just allowances," money which has been reasonably expended in taking opinions and procuring directions,[51] payments by executors in discharge of legacies,[52] expenses of managing and carrying on a partnership business,[53] and a mortgagee's expenses of seizing and holding possession of a ship, advertising it for sale, and effecting insurances upon it,[54] have been allowed.

Reasonable expenses of representative

The rule is that a representative is entitled to be allowed all reasonable expenses which have been incurred in the conduct of his office,[55] except those which arise from his own default.[56] Thus an executor is allowed the expenses of keeping up the testator's domestic establishment for a reasonable time after his death[57]; but not the cost of an action against him, as executor, which he ought never to have defended.[58]

Representatives and trustees can protect themselves from personal liability for the costs of litigation by seeking the directions of the court under Order 85, r. 2.[59]

Former practice on taxation—"solicitor and client"

The ordinary practice for a long time was to allow personal representatives their costs of action (out of the estate) as between solicitor and client[60] (later common fund) together with any charges and expenses, properly incurred relating to the trust, beyond costs of action, on the suggestion of counsel. The case had to be supported before the taxing mas-

---

[48] *Brown* v. *De Tastet* (1819) Jac. 284, 294.

[49] Dan.Ch.Pr., 8th ed., 1085; and see *Re Smith's Estate* [1937] Ch. 636; *Re Roberts* [1946] Ch. 1.

[50] *Re Bird* (1873) L.R. 16 Eq. 203.

[51] *Fearns* v. *Young* (1804) 10 Ves. 184; and see *Re Robertson* [1949] 1 All E.R. 1042.

[52] *Nightingale* v. *Lawson* (1784) 1 Cox 23.

[53] *Brown* v. *De Tastet* (1819) Jac. 284, 299; *Cook* v. *Collingridge* (1823) Jac. 607, 621.

[54] *Wilkes* v. *Saunion* (1877) 7 Ch.D. 188.

[55] *Potts* v. *Leighton* (1808) 15 Ves. 273; *Hide* v. *Haywood* (1741) 2 Atk. 126; Trustee Act 1925, s.30(2).

[56] *Pannel* v. *Fenn* (1594) Cro.Eliz. 348.

[57] *Field* v. *Peckett* (*No. 3*) (1861) 29 Beav. 576 (two months held reasonable).

[58] *Chambers* v. *Smith* (1847) 2 Coll. 742; *Smith* v. *Chambers* (1847) 2 Phil.C.C.221.

[59] See *ante*, pp. 842 *post*, p. 922 and *Re Beddoe* [1893] 1 Ch. 54.

[60] *Re Robertson* [1949] W.N. 225; 1 All E.R. 1042. The costs of a construction summons properly includes a fee for counsel for the executor of the same amount as the fees of counsel for the beneficiaries: *Re Bennett* [1950] 1 All E.R. 435n.

ter; it was not the practice in taking the account in chambers to allow the charges and expenses incurred since the action, but they were provided for on further consideration.[61]

Present practice on taxation—"indemnity"

Since the 1986 "rationalisation" reducing the former bases to "standardised" and "indemnity"[62] the practice on taxation is governed by Order 62, r. 14 of the Rules of the Supreme Court. The history of the earlier practice and bases of taxation will be found in earlier editions of this work.[63] If a trustee submits to having his costs taxed he is entitled to his costs as so taxed and nothing more. He is not entitled to take the taxing master through his bill and then when the taxing master disallows certain items to go away and say; "That does not matter, I know I have wasted the taxing master's time, but I do not care about that. . . . I will help myself to whatever he has disallowed."[64]

The costs of a trustee or personal representative are taxed on an indemnity basis but are presumed to have been unreasonably incurred if they were incurred contrary to the duty of the trustee or representative as such.[65]

Application of "indemnity" basis

Executors or trustees who act in good faith and incur expenditure on behalf of the estate are entitled to this indemnity. Thus, so long as there is nothing improper in their actions, they are entitled to be repaid the fees of counsel and the taxing master is not entitled to tax down such fees because he thinks counsel might have been paid a smaller sum.[66] The propriety of the payment must be considered in relation to the complexity of the questions of law and fact involved, the amount at stake, the payments for interlocutory work and the standing of counsel concerned.[67]

What are costs, charges and expenses

The charges and expenses of a representative do not include funeral and probate expenses,[68] nor the costs of other actions unless specially provided for.[69]

---

[61] Seton, 7th ed., 1127.
[62] See p. 915 *ante*.
[63] See 16th ed., p. 827 and *Practice Note* of Vaisey J. at [1953] 1 W.L.R. 1452; *Re Dargie* [1954] Ch. 16.
[64] See [1953] 1 W.L.R. 1452. There is no need, so to submit, see p. 915, *ante*.
[65] R.S.C. Ord. 62, r. 14. This appears to be the same text as that of "propriety." See below.
[66] *Re Grimthorpe* [1958] 1 W.L.R. 381. The question is not one of "generosity" but of whether the payment was "proper or improper," *per* Danckwerts J. See also *Carver* v. *Duncan* [1983] 1 W.L.R. 494 at 502.
[67] *Re Whitley* [1962] 1 W.L.R. 922.
[68] *Collis* v. *Robins* (1847) 1 De G. & S. 131. These will normally be testamentary expenses. See *ante*, p. 634.
[69] *Payne* v. *Little* (1859) 27 Beav. 83.

The following payments have been held to be included in costs, charges and expenses: costs of proceedings by an administrator against a defaulting solicitor, taken bona fide for the benefit of the estate[70]; the costs of an action properly defended by a trustee[71]; costs of a sale rightly made by trustees under a power[72]; costs of former trustees paid to the executor of the survivor in consideration of his transferring the trust property.[73]

Appeal as to costs, charges and expenses

An order giving trustees their costs, charges and expenses covers something more than costs only and can therefore be appealed from. But trustees cannot, without the leave of the court or judge making the order, appeal as to costs only[74] if there is nothing wrong with the order as to charges and expenses.[75]

Professional executor

It is a general rule that unless the will makes special provision[76] an executor, administrator[77] or trustee, acting as solicitor or other professional adviser to the trust, is only entitled to costs out of pocket.[78] In a proper case, the court may direct remuneration to be paid, even as against creditors, but it is a jurisdiction which will only be exercised in exceptional cases.[79] This rule applies though there is no express trust.[80] In general it makes no difference that the business is done by one of the partners who is not a trustee[81] but a solicitor-trustee may employ his partner to act as solicitor for himself and his co-trustees with reference to the trust affairs, and

---

[70] Re Davis (1887) 57 L.T. 755.

[71] Walters v. Woodbridge (1878) 7 Ch.D. 504; Re Llewellin (1887) 37 Ch.D. 317, 327. Cf. Re Dunn [1904] 1 Ch. 648, where an administrator was disallowed costs of defending an action which was not for the benefit of the estate. See also Re Beddoe [1893] 1 Ch. 547, 557; ante, pp. 842, 920.

[72] Re Mansel (1885) 54 L.J.Ch. 883.

[73] Harvey v. Oliver (1887) 57 L.T. 239.

[74] See the Judicature Act 1925, s.31(1)(b).

[75] Bew v. Bew [1899] 2 Ch. 467, 472, following Charles v. Jones (1886) 33 Ch.D. 80; not following Re Chennell (1878) 8 Ch.D. 492. See also ante, p. 915.

[76] See ante, p. 52.

[77] A professional administrator will normally be acting at the request of those interested under the will or intestacy. He should therefore agree the terms of his remuneration before obtaining the grant.

[78] New v. Jones (1833) 1 M. & G 668, n.; Moore v. Frowd (1837) 3 M. & Cr.45; Fraser v. Palmer (1841) 4 Y. & C.Ex. 515; Collins v. Carey (1839) 2 Beav. 128; Re Sherwood (1840) 3 Beav. 338; Bainbrigge v. Blair (1845) 8 Beav. 588; Todd v. Wilson (1846) 9 Beav. 486; Re Corsellis (1887) 34 Ch.D. 675. See also Wilson v Carmichael (1830) 2 Dow & Cl. 51; Nicholson v. Tutin (No. 2) (1857) 3 K. & J. 1, and, for the court's jurisdiction to award remuneration to trustees generally, see Re Duke of Norfolk's Settlement Trusts [1982] Ch. 61. Taxing masters, under an order to tax costs on the common fund basis or generally, took notice that the solicitor was also a trustee, and apply the rule: Cradock v. Piper (1850) 1 M. & G. 664. As to the appointment of solicitors' partnerships to be executors and trustees, see generally articles by R.T. Oerton in 64 Law Society's Gazette 244, 343 and ante, p. 20. See also post, p. 977.

[79] Re Worthington [1954] 1 W.L.R. 526. Re Keeler [1981] Ch.156.

[80] Pollard v. Doyle (1860) 1 Dr. & Sm. 319.

[81] Christophers v. White (1847) 10 Beav. 523.

may pay him the usual charges, provided that it has been expressly agreed between himself and his partner that he himself shall not participate in the profits or derive any benefit from the charges.[82] In other words he must make the partner *quoad* the business in question an independent solicitor.[83] Thus in *Re Gates*[84] Clauson J. refused to allow profit costs where a solicitor-trustee appointed his firm (including himself) to act as solicitors to the trust, even though there was an agreement that the solicitor-trustee should have no share in the profits. This rule is subject to certain modifications.[85]

Town agent's costs

In the first place, it does not preclude an executor who acts as solicitor in a cause in which he is a party in his representative character, from being allowed, as against the estate, that proportion of the whole costs which his town agent is entitled to receive.[86]

Litigation costs

Secondly, the rule does not apply to the costs incurred in a suit where the solicitor acts in the suit for himself and his co-trustees. In such a case he is allowed the full costs which would be properly chargeable by a stranger to the trust, except in so far as they are increased by his being one of the parties.[87] This exception applies not only to proceedings in a hostile suit, but also to friendly proceedings in chambers, such as an application for maintenance of an infant.[88] It does not, however, extend to a case where a solicitor, who is a trustee, acts in a suit for himself alone, or by his partner for himself alone[89]; nor to a case of a solicitor being a trustee and acting as solicitor for himself and his co-trustees in the administration of the trust out of court.[90] Further, a solicitor cannot come within this exception unless he is actually the solicitor on the record. He cannot stipulate for a commission with a firm of solicitors to whom he introduces the trust business.[91]

Plaintiff's costs out of estate—"standard"

After the costs of a representative are satisfied the next claim on the estate is that of the plaintiff in the action for his costs incurred in it if

---

[82] *Clack* v. *Carlon* (1861) 30 L.J.Ch. 639; *Re Doody* [1893] 1 Ch. 129, 134.

[83] *Re Hill* [1934] Ch. 623, 631; and cases cited in n. 26, *ante.*

[84] [1933] Ch. 913; approved *obiter* in *Re Hill, ante.*

[85] Compensation may, in special cases, be made, under the authority of the court, to the solicitor-trustee, though not by allowing him to make the usual professional charges: *Bainbrigge* v. *Blair* (1845) 8 Beav. 588.

[86] *Burge* v. *Brutton* (1843) 2 Hare 373. *cf. Re Corsellis, post.*

[87] *Cradock* v. *Piper* (1850) 17 Sim. 41; (1850) 1 M. & G. 664. See also *Broughton* v. *Broughton* (1855) 5 De G.M. & G. 163–165; *Re Barber* (1886) 34 Ch.D. 77; *Re Corsellis* (1887) 34 Ch.D. 675.

[88] *Re Corsellis, ante.*

[89] *Lyon* v. *Baker* (1852) 5 De G. & Sm. 622; *Re Corsellis, ante.*

[90] *Lincoln* v. *Windsor* (1851) 9 Hare 158.

[91] *Vipont* v. *Butler* [1893] W.N. 64.

allowed out of the estate.[92] Such costs will normally be allowed on the standard basis.

One consequence of this right of the plaintiff to his costs of the action appears to be that if the representative, after the judgment or order, pays a debt relying on his right to be reimbursed out of the fund in court, since this right is postponed to the plaintiff's claim to costs, he must run the risk that the fund will not be sufficient to pay the costs and also to reimburse him. Again, if the action has been properly instituted and there are either assets in court or outstanding assets to be administered, it seems to have been held that the plaintiff's costs must be paid out of those assets, notwithstanding this may result in hardship on a representative who has, before suit, paid other creditors of the estate with his own money.[93]

The representative's right of retainer for his own debt prevailed against the plaintiff's right to his costs.

Costs of plaintiff

The costs of a person (beneficiary or creditor) bringing proceedings against a representative are now always in the discretion of the court, and an order refusing a beneficiary or creditor plaintiff his costs in an administration action, or making him pay costs, is an order within the discretion of the judge and cannot be appealed from[94] without leave of the court or judge making the order.[95]

Beneficiary

Where the proceedings brought by a legatee are unnecessary or improper, he will not be allowed his costs out of the estate, as, for instance, where the plaintiff, a residuary legatee, suing by his next friend, sought to charge the defendant with costs on the ground of misconduct and failed in making out the misconduct[96]; and the legatee will be ordered to pay the costs of such improper proceedings, as for instance, the costs of taking unnecessary accounts,[97] or an abortive attempt to remove a trustee[98]; the court will not permit the costs occasioned by improper litigation or by negligent conduct of administration proceedings to be paid out of the estate.[99]

Where on a construction summons three parties interested in residue were joined at the suggestion of the Master, and all appeared by separate counsel, although their interest was already represented by a defendant

---

[92] *Hearn v. Wells* (1844) 1 Coll. 323.
[93] *Hearn v. Wells* (1844) 1 Coll. 323, 332, 333.
[94] *Re McClellan* (1885) 29 Ch.D. 495.
[95] Supreme Court Act 1981, s.18(1)(f). See p. 922 *ante*.
[96] *Williams v. Jones* (1886) 34 Ch.D. 120.
[97] *Croggan v. Allen* (1882) 22 Ch.D. 101; *Re Blake* (1885) 29 Ch.D. 913.
[98] *Fane v. Fane* (1879) 13 Ch.D. 228.
[99] *Brown v. Burdett* (1888) 40 Ch.D. 244.

who had been a party all along, the court refused to allow costs out of the estate to the three added parties.[1]

In *Ackers* v. *Ackers*[2] North J. ordered a useless administration action to be stayed, the plaintiff to pay the costs of the action, and the defendant to be at liberty to take out of the estate any costs in default.

Where a beneficiary claims adversely to other beneficiaries, and by originating summons gets a question determined which but for this procedure would be the subject of an action commenced by writ, the unsuccessful party must pay the costs of all whom he has brought before the court, with the possible exception of the trustees.[3]

In *Re Watson*[4] a residuary legatee who brought an action to establish his identity was allowed costs out of the estate.

Where a beneficiary has mortgaged his legacy or share, one set of costs only is allowed to him and his incumbrancer attending the proceedings: that set of costs is payable to the incumbrancer so far as may be necessary to satisfy the incumbrancer's costs of action, and after such payment the balance of costs is payable to the beneficiary.[5]

A plaintiff in a legatee's administration action is entitled to costs only where the estate is sufficient to pay debts but insufficient to pay legacies in full[6]; and it makes no difference that there has been a contest between the plaintiff and another legatee as to the proper mode of dividing the fund.[7]

Creditor

If a creditor plaintiff brings an action after he has been correctly informed that there are no assets applicable to the payment of his debt, he will be ordered to pay the costs, either wholly or from the time he receives the information.[8] In *Robinson* v. *Elliott*[9] a creditor filed a bill against an executrix, and she stated, by her answer, that there were no assets for the payment of his debt; he, however, persisted in the suit. The result of the account in the Master's office was that there were no assets unadministered, though the executrix was charged with more than she had admitted. The bill was dismissed without costs as against the executrix.

The right of a creditor in an administration action, suing on behalf of himself and other creditors, to his costs has already been considered.[10]

---

[1] *Re Amory* [1951] 2 All E.R. 947.
[2] [1884] W.N. 82. See also *Re Ormston* (1887) 58 L.T. 74; affirmed (1888) 59 L.T. 594.
[3] *Re Buckton* [1907] 2 Ch. 406, 415; *Re Halston* [1912] 1 Ch. 435; *Re Fletlaer* [1918] W.N. 278. *Supreme Court Practice* 1993, 62/2/75.
[4] (1884) 53 L.J.Ch. 305.
[5] For form of order, see Seton, 7th ed., 1433. See also *Re Goss* [1884] W.N. 192.
[6] *Re Harvey* (1884) 26 Ch.D. 179.
[7] *Re Wilkins* (1884) 27 Ch.D. 703. See also *Henderson* v. *Dodds* (1866) L.R. 2 Eq. 532, where the action was to administer the realty, there being no personalty.
[8] *Bluett* v. *Jessop* (1821) Jacob 240; *King* v. *Bryant* (1841) Beav. 460, 462; *Fuller* v. *Green* (1857) 24 Beav. 217.
[9] (1826) 1 Russ. 599. See Dan.Ch.Pr., 8th ed., 1068.
[10] *Ante*, p. 830.

Costs of creditors coming in under a judgment

Where a person claiming to be a creditor seeks to establish his claim to a debt under any judgment or order in accordance with the provisions for proceedings under judgments and orders in the Chancery Division,[11] he is entitled, if his claim succeeds, to his costs incurred in establishing it, unless the court otherwise directs, and, if his claim fails, he may be ordered to pay the costs of any person opposing his claim.

Fund out of which costs payable

Where the creditor fails to establish his debt, he may be ordered to pay the costs of the inquiry consequent upon his claim, though he is not a party to the action.[12]

The question out of what particular fund costs are to be paid scarcely comes within the scope of this work. In general the costs of administration fall on the general estate, but the costs of distribution fall on the gift in question. Thus, the costs of inquiries to ascertain the person entitled to any legacy, money, or share, or otherwise in relation thereto, are normally paid out of such legacy, money, or share.[13] A direction in the will that testamentary expenses are to be paid out of residue does not in itself throw such costs on the residue.[14] Where, however, the difficulty is occasioned by the ambiguous language or conduct of the testator, or where the difficulty is not in ascertaining the facts but in applying the law, the costs are costs of administration payable out of residue.[15]

If the costs of an administration action are increased by its being also an action for the execution of the trusts of a settlement, the additional costs must be borne by the settlement fund.[16]

Before 1926 it was the settled practice of the Chancery Division that the costs of an administration action, so far as they had been increased by the administration of real estate, were to be borne by that estate.[17] This practice was not altered by the Land Transfer Act 1897,[18] even though the will contained a general direction to pay testatmentary expenses out of personal estate.[19] All costs of administration, including the costs of administering real estate, should now be borne by the deceased's property

---

[11] See Ord. 44.

[12] *Hatch* v. *Searles* (1854) 2 Sm. & G. 147; *Yeomans* v. *Haynes* (1857) 24 Beav. 127. It appears that a special summons must be taken out to obtain payment: Dan.Ch.Pr., 8th ed., 908.

[13] See *Re Vincent* [1909] 1 Ch. 810; *Re Whitaker* [1911] 1 Ch. 214; *Re Phillips* [1938] 4 All E.R. 483.

[14] *Re Phillips, supra.*

[15] *Re Hall-Dare* [1916] 1 Ch. 272. See also *Re Groom* [1897] 2 Ch. 407; *Re Flecher* [1918] W.N. 278; *Re Wernher* (1918) 117 L.T. 801.

[16] *Irby* v. *Irby* (1875) 24 Beav. 525; *Skirrow* v. *Skirrow* (1869) 17 W.R. 759.

[17] *Re Middleton* (1882) 19 Ch.D. 552; *Patching* v. *Barnett* (1881) 51 L.J.Ch. 74; *Re Roper* (1890) 45 Ch.D. 126; *Re Copland* [1895] W.N. 137. As to costs of selling real estate under an order in an administration action, see *Barnwell* v. *Iremonger* (1860) 1 Dr. & Sm. 242, 255.

[18] *Re Jones* [1902] 1 Ch. 92; *Re Betts* [1907] 2 Ch. 149.

[19] *Re Betts, ante.*

generally in the order and manner specified by the Administration of Estates Act 1925, Sched. 1 Pt. II.[20]

Costs under Order 85

Even though no estate or fund is sought to be administered the court has the same jurisdiction on summons under Order 85 as in an ordinary administration action to deal with costs, so long as the proper parties are before it.[21]

Costs under Inheritance Act

No particular provision as to costs has been made for claims by dependants under the Inheritance (Provision for Family and Dependants) Act 1975 and accordingly they rest in the discretion of the court.[22]

Costs under the Variation of Trusts Act 1958

Executors or trustees should not normally be the applicants under this Act for it is the duty of the trustees to assist the court and to be the watchdog of (for example) unborn interests.[23] In particular the trustees should not be applicants because they are thought more likely to get their costs. On the other hand they must not take a merely passive role and they will be justified in applying if satisfied that (a) the proposals are beneficial, (b) likely to be approved and (c) no other person is likely to make the application.[24] It is arguable that the trustees should submit anything which supports the maintenance of the trusts set out by their settlor. Their stance is therefore that of defendants.

Security for costs

Plaintiffs who live out of the jurisdiction of the court may be compelled to give security for costs, though such plaintiffs sue as executors.[25] But an administrator to whom letters of administration were granted as the attorney of a principal abroad was not, even though he was an agent and insolvent, ordered to give security.[26] *Semble* this is because an attorney administrator is regarded as a principal. And in an action by two executors, one of whom was out of the jurisdiction and the other insolvent, the defendant was not entitled to a stay of proceedings until they gave security for costs.[27]

---

[20] See *ante*, pp. 615 *et seq.*
[21] *Re Medland* (1889) 41 Ch.D. 476.
[22] See *ante*, pp. 826, 842 *et seq.*
[23] *Re Druce* [1962] 1 W.L.R. 363, 370.
[24] *Ibid*, p. 371.
[25] *Chevalier* v. *Finnis* (1819) 1 Bro. & Bingh. 277; *Chamberlain* v. *Chamberlain* (1832) 1 Dowl. 366; *Knight* v. *De Blaquière* (1838) Sau. & Sc. 658.
[26] *Rainbow* v. *Kittoe* [1916] 1 Ch. 313.
[27] *Sykes* v. *Sykes* (1869) L.R. 4 C.P. 645. On security for costs generally, see Ord. 23, and notes thereto in *Supreme Court Practice*.

Costs on appeal parties

The strict rule on appeal is that a respondent is not allowed to be heard in support of an appeal[28] even if notice is given to that effect.[29] Thus if there is an appeal by a defendant from a decision on originating summons the plaintiff (normally the executor or trustee) and other defendants will all be respondents and ought between them only to incur one set of costs. However, the rule has often been relaxed for convenience to enable the trustee to be heard[30] and he will then be allowed his costs. His prudent course is, however, to take advice and if necessary the guidance of the court,[31] otherwise his indemnity is at risk.[32]

Other parties should appeal[33] but cannot be heard.[34] However, these strict rules appear to have been often ignored and multiplicity of parties is not uncommon on appeal, with all costs allowed out of the estate.[35] If there is an important and debatable legal issue leading to differences of judicial opinion the costs of appeal are allowed out of the estate.[36]

Taxation under Solicitors Act

Upon the application of the party or the representative[37] of the party chargeable with a solicitor's bill of costs, the bill and the solicitor's, or his personal representative's or assignee's demand thereon may, under the Solicitors Act 1974, s. 70, be referred to be taxed. Reference should be made to the text of the section for its detailed provisions.

If a solicitor's bill against a testator should be referred to taxation after the latter's death, questions of difficulty may arise as to the effect of the order for payment by the representative of the sum found due. Where justice requires that the order for taxation should be made, but it appears probable that, by reason of a deficiency of assets or otherwise, payment of the amount due ought not to be made without further investigation, the court making the order for taxation ought, it would seem, to abstain from adding the usual order for payment or the delivery up of deeds.[38]

If a solicitor dies pending an order for taxation, the proceedings may be

[28] *Re Marquis of Ailesbury* [1892] 1 Ch. 506, 526 D.C.P. 1140.
[29] *Re Mellor* [1922] 1 Ch. 312, 321 (where the difficulty was overcome by instructing counsel for such respondent to appear for the appellant).
[30] *e.g. Re Marquis of Ailesbury* [1892] 1 Ch. 506, 526, 548 (where different trustees each took a different view and each was allowed separate costs); *Ganapathy Chettiar* v. *Periakruppan Chettiar* [1962] 1 W.L.R. 279, 290.
[31] See *ante*, p. 836.
[32] *Ganapathy Chettiar* v. *Periakruppan Chettiar* [1962] 1 W.L.R. 279, 290.
[33] *Elliot* v. *Joicey* [1935] A.C. 209, 235 appears to be in direct conflict with *Perrin* v. *Morgan* [1943] A.C. 399, 424 on this point.
[34] See n. 28.
[35] See, *e.g. Re Petrie* [1962] Ch. 355; *Re Neeld* [1962] Ch. 643; *Re Jubb* [1966] Ch. 666; *Re Allsop* [1967] 2 All E.R. 1056.
[36] See *per* Birkenhead L.C. in *Boyce* v. *Wasborough* [1922] 1 A.C. 425, 435.
[37] *Jefferson* v. *Warrington* (1840) 7 M. & W. 137. And see *Re Dalby, post.* For procedure, see Ord. 106.
[38] See *Re Dalby* (1845) 8 Beav. 469.

revived by the client against the solicitor's representatives,[39] and vice versa,[40] by an *ex parte* order.

A payment of estate duty or inheritance tax made by a solicitor for the purpose of obtaining probate is not a disbursement within section 70 and ought not to be included as such in the solicitor's bill of costs.[41]

Where any person, not the party chargeable, is liable to pay or has paid the bill, he or his representative may apply, under section 71, to have it taxed just as if the application were made by the party chargeable. This section is apt to meet the case of a beneficiary who wishes to tax the bill of the executor's solicitor.

Except in special cases no order will be made for the taxation of a bill which has already been taxed.[42]

Procedure

Orders under section 70 are made on summons, and not *ex parte*, save that in the Chancery Division such an order may be made by petition of course, without any hearing, if the applicant is entitled as of right to the order the application is made by the party chargeable within one month from delivery of the bill, the procedure by petition is cheaper.[43] The taxation is as between solicitor and own client, but subject to this[44] limitation, that a solicitor cannot charge against a trust estate anything not necessary for the administration thereof, though expressly directed by the trustee, but must look for payment of such charges to the trustee personally.[45] The amount allowed by a taxing master as between the client and his solicitor is not conclusive of the amount which the court will allow out of the estate.[46]

Reference to taxation after 12 months

The court has no power under the Solicitors Act to order taxation on an application made by the party chargeable after the expiration of 12 months from payment of the bill.[47] Nevertheless there is inherent jurisidiction to order a taxation in an exceptional case, even after the 12 months have expired.[48] Furthermore, as between the representative who paid the bill and the beneficiaries the bill may still be sent to the taxing master not for taxation but to inquire whether any items objected to are fair and proper to

---

[39] R.S.C., Ord. 15, r. 7.
[40] *Ibid.*
[41] *Re Kingdom and Wilson* [1902] 2 Ch. 242.
[42] s.71(6) and see *Re Welborne* [1901] 1 Ch. 312.
[43] R.S.C., Ord. 106, rr. 3, 4; Solicitors Act 1974, s.70(1).
[44] R.S.C., Ord. 62, r. 29.
[45] See *Re Brown* (1867) L.R. 4 Eq. 464; *Re Negus* [1895] 1 Ch. 73, 80; *Re Gray* [1901] 1 Ch. 239; *Re Longbotham & Sons* [1904] 2 Ch. 152, all of which were, however, decisions on s.38 of the Solicitors Act 1843.
[46] *Brown* v. *Burdett* (1888) 40 Ch.D. 244.
[47] Solicitors Act 1974, s.70(4).
[48] *Re A Solicitor* [1961] 1 Ch. 491.

be allowed in the representative's accounts, and to what extent.[49] The fact that a bill is not disputed or referred for taxation within the time allowed for the latter purpose by the Solicitors Act is prima facie, but not conclusive, evidence of the reasonableness of the bill. Thus, the representative is not estopped from disputing the reasonableness of items in the bill, and in an administration action the bill may still be referred to the taxing master, upon this basis.[50]

[49] *Allen* v. *Jarvis* (1869) L.R. 4 Ch. 616 (solicitor-executor paid himself: his executor was called upon to account). Now, an application would probably be made by the beneficiary under s.71.
[50] *Re Park* (1889) 41 Ch.D. 326.

Part Nine

DISTRIBUTION OF ASSETS

CHAPTER 67

PROBLEMS OF DISTRIBUTION

Alteration of dispositions

As has already been mentioned in discussing Inheritance Tax it is open to beneficiaries to agree within two years of the death on a variation of dispositions taking effect under the will or intestacy or otherwise.[1] Since considerable saving in tax may ultimately result from such variations or disclaimers or the implementation of a testator's non-binding 'wishes' the possibility of such agreed variations should always be seriously considered.

Completion of administration

Having administered the estate in the sense of getting in the assets and paying or providing for payment of debt[2] and inheritance tax[3] and claims for family provision[4] the executor or administrator has performed his functions as such and logic demands the termination at this stage of any work on executors. However, the leading works on trusts and wills have never totally assumed responsibility for the problems of the executor-trustee distributing the assets of the estate, or taken any interest in the question of intestate distribution.[5] As trustee the representative now becomes concerned with the problems of distribution of the administered estate among the persons entitled. If there is a will, these problems may turn largely upon the interpretation of the will or upon rules of construction or other considerations more appropriate to a work on wills.[6] If there is no will or if a will is only partially effective the enactments governing total or partial intestacy become relevant.[7]

Preliminary considerations

Before consideration of the relevant directions for distribution, two preliminary questions may arise. First, there may be undisclosed or secret trusts which affect the distribution, whether testate or intestate.[8] Secondly, the doctrine of election may apply.[8a] In the first case problems of great diffi-

---

[1] See I.H.T. Act 1984, ss.142, 143. *British Tax Encyclopaedia* 3–5141, 5142.
[2] *Ante*, Part 6, p. 587.
[3] See *ante*, p. 72.
[4] See *ante*, pp. 757 *et seq.*
[5] But see now *The Law and Practice of Intestate Succession*, by Sherrin and Bonehill (1987).
[6] See, *e.g.* Jarman, *Wills*, 8th ed., 1951; Theobald, *Wills*, 14th ed.; Halsbury's *Laws*, 4th ed. Vol. 50.
[7] See *post*, pp. 1065 *et seq.*
[8] See Jarman, *Wills*, 8th ed. 1951, pp. 907–913. Theobald, *Wills* (14th ed. 96–102; 135 N.L.J. 1073; [1985] Conveyancer 248; as to mutual wills, see 138 N.L.J. 351.
[8a] See *post* p. 979.

culty can arise, but reference should be made to textbooks on wills.[9] In the second case the distribution may be seriously affected by the equitable doctrine.[10]

Creditor and debtor beneficiaries

The line between administration in the narrow sense, and distribution, may be crossed where a beneficiary under the testator's will is a debtor or creditor of the testator. This topic has been previously discussed.[11]

Income tax

Since a beneficiary under a will or a person entitled on intestacy has only an inchoate right until administration is complete,[12] special tax provisions apply to estates in course of administration.[13] Reference should be made to textbooks on taxation,[14] but the general effect is to attribute a notional income to the beneficiary which is taxed subject to adjustment on completion of the administration. If the interest is "absolute"[15] the notional income is based upon the "residuary income" of the estate.[16] If the interest is "limited"[17] the notional income is based upon actual payments made to the beneficiary in the course of administration.[18] In the latter case, therefore, payments made in the course of administration whether intended to be made in the form of income or advances of capital, must be treated as income for tax purposes, and have serious tax repercussions, subject only to the final adjustment on completion of the administration.[19] No charge of income tax in respect of income which arose before death can give rise to an assessment beyond the end of the third year next following the year of assessment of the death.[20] After the administration is complete the representative is a trustee and the tax position is as for any other trust.[21]

Capital gains tax

For purposes of capital gains tax on the death of an individual after March 30, 1971, all the assets of which he was competent to dispose are deemed to be acquired on his death by the representative or other person

[9] See n. 8.
[10] See *post*, p. 979.
[11] See *ante*, p. 642.
[12] See *post*, p. 1050.
[13] See the Income and Corporation Taxes Act 1988, ss.695–702 and 78 *Taxation*, pp. 277, 294, 312. British Tax Encyclopaedia 1–1708 *et seq. Whiteman on Income Tax*, 3rd ed., pp. 20–26 *et seq.*
[14] See *e.g. British Tax Encyclopaedia*; and *Whiteman on Income Tax*, 3rd ed.
[15] Income and the Corporation Taxes Act 1988, s.696.
[16] *Ibid.*, s.695.
[17] *Ibid.*, ss.695, 701.
[18] *Ibid.*, s.695.
[19] *Ibid.* ss.695, 700. See *British Tax Encyclopaedia* 1–1708 *et seq.*
[20] Taxes Management Act 1970, s.40. See *Harrison* v. *Willis Bros.* [1966] Ch. 619, C.A. *British Tax Encyclopaedia* 4–040. As to liability of the personal representative, see *post*, pp. 553 *et seq.* As to deduction of tax from interest payable on the legacies, see *post*, p. 1035.
[21] As to the executor's liability for tax chargeable on the the deceased, see *post*, pp. 459, 583.

on whom they devolve for a consideration equal to their market value at that date but are not deemed to be disposed of by him on his death, so that no capital gains tax is payable.[22] Further reference should be made to text-books on taxation.[23] Subsequent re-arrangements where the beneficial entitlement remains substantially the same do not constitute disposals.[24] Where a residuary legatee raised money by mortgage to enable the executor to convey real property to him which would otherwise have had to be sold off, the residuary legatee was held not to be entitled to add the value of the mortgage money to the balance of value in estimating capital gains tax on a subsequent sale[25] but the exercise of a power may constitute a deemed disposal for this purpose.[26]

Where assets have increased in value since the date of the death it is sometimes advantageous to distribute such assets to the beneficiaries in specie rather than to sell and distribute the proceeds of sale, for the beneficiaries may be able to take advantage of allowances not available to the representatives.

Corporation tax

For purposes of corporation tax an executor may be an "associate" of himself as a director and a "participator."[27]

Reimbursement of tax

As to the reimbursement of tax paid as between co-beneficiaries see *Lee-dale* v. *Lewis* [1982] 1 W.L.R. at p. 1335 and under Refunding and Tracing p. 1076 *post*.

Other problems of distribution

It is convenient at this point to list some of the problems arising on distribution which demand lengthier consideration. These include in addition to questions of election,[28] ademption and satisfaction,[29] capacity to take,[30] the incidence of taxation as between the persons entitled,[31] abatement,[32] marshalling,[33] order of[34] and time for distribution,[35] future legacies,[36] to

---

[22] Capital Gains Tax Act 1979, s.49; Taxation of Chargeable Gains Act 1992, s.62 (for 1992 and later). See British Tax Encyclopaedia, 3–056A.

[23] *British Tax Encyclopaedia* 1–1106. *Whiteman on Capital Gains Tax*, 4th ed., Chp. 28.

[24] *Jenkins* v. *Brown* [1989] 1 W.L.R. 1163.

[25] *Assant* v. *Jackson* [1960] S.T.C. 164.

[26] *Hart* v. *Briscoe* [1979] Ch. 1.

[27] *Willingale* v. *Islington* [1972] 1 W.L.R. 1533; I.C.T.A. 1988, s.417, and see generally Bramwell, *Taxation of Companies* 2nd ed. para. 10–03. As to loans see *ibid*. para. 11–04.

[28] See *post*, p. 979.

[29] See *post*, p. 941.

[30] See *post*, p. 972.

[31] See Jarman, *Wills*, 8th ed. 1951, p. 1806; 17 Halsbury's *Laws*, 4th ed. paras. 1304–1313. The question is in principle one of construction of the will in question.

[32] See *post*, pp. 1000 *et seq*.

[33] See *post*, p. 996.

[34] See *post*, p. 989.

[35] See *ante* p. 112.

[36] See *post*, p. 1019.

whom legacies are payable,[37] interest on legacies,[38] election,[39] payment or delivery,[40] assents,[41] and refunding.[42] Distribution on intestacy or partial intestacy is not covered in the works on wills, and is therefore fully considered in this part.[43]

Obligation to distribute

Subject to these problems a representative is bound (subject to any disclaimer[44]) after administration[45] to pay the legacies and distribute the residue to the persons entitled, or assent, as the case may be. Unless there is a direction in the will requiring conversion into money or such conversion is necessary in the course of administration, or for distribution, the actual residue should be conveyed in its unconverted state,[46] but where investments are retained upon trust there is power to sell and reinvest and vary investment within the range of authorised investment,[47] unless the will prohibits this.[48] If the will directs conversion this should take place within the executor's year[49] unless there is power to postpone.[50] The powers to appropriate and partition have been previously considered.[51]

Date of valuations

Where a testator has by his will given his personal estate to be divided in shares among his children or issue and has directed the beneficiaries to bring any advances made to them into hotchpot, it is a general rule of administration, whether in court or out of court, settled by long practice, that, in the absence of an express direction to the contrary in the will, the distributable assets are to be valued at the date of the distribution, and not at the date of the testator's death, and that advanced beneficiaries are to be debited with interest on the amount of their advances to the date of distribution.[52]

[37] See *post*, p. 1024.
[38] See *post*, p. 1034.
[39] See *post*, p. 979.
[40] See *post*, p. 1030.
[41] See *post*, p. 1049.
[42] See *post*, p. 1076.
[43] See *post*, p. 1065.
[44] See *post*, p. 940.
[45] As to the executor's year, see *ante*, p. 112.
[46] See *per* Lord Cairns in *Cooper* v. *Cooper* (1874) L.R. 7 H.L. 53; *Wightwick* v. *Lord* (1857) 6 H.L.C. 217, 226. *Re Norwood and Blake* [1917] 1 I.R. 472; *Blake* v. *Bayne* [1908] A.C. 371.
[47] *Re Pratt* [1943] 1 Ch. 326. See further Lewin, *Trusts*, 16th ed. 1964, pp. 322–355.
[48] *Ovey* v. *Ovey* [1900] 2 Ch. 524. As to conversion of assets in general and its effects, see Jarman, *Wills*, 8th ed., 1951, pp. 739–786, 1207–1232.
[49] *Grayburn* v. *Clarkson* (1868) L.R. 3 Ch.App. 605; *Hughes* v. *Empson* (1856) 22 Beav. 181; *Bate* v. *Hooper* (1855) 5 De G.M. & G. 338; *Re Norrington* (1879) 13 Ch.D. 655; *Re Rooke* [1954] Ch. 716 (criticising *Re Ball* [1930] W.N. 111).
[50] See, *e.g.* the Law of Property Act 1925, s.25; *Re Tankard* [1943] Ch. 69.
[51] See *ante*, pp. 685–687.
[52] *Re Tod* [1916] 1 Ch. 567; *Re Wills* [1939] Ch. 705; *Re Hillas-Drake* [1944] Ch. 235, where *Re Mansel* [1930] 1 Ch. 352, *Re Gunther's Will Trusts* [1939] Ch. 985, and *Re Oram* [1940] Ch. 1001, were dissented from as "out of line with authority and inconsistent with long-established

Beneficial interest of executor

The former presumption, that an executor was intended to take beneficially all personal property not disposed of by the will, was abolished by the Executors Act 1830, now replaced by section 49 of the Administration of Estates Act 1925. The question is now primarily one of construction of the will and is discussed in works on wills.[53] If the will is construed against the executor he will hold the undisposed property in trust for the persons entitled on intestacy, including in the last resort the Crown.[54] The executors of a donor to charity are not "persons interested" so as to entitle them to bring proceedings under section 28 of the Charities Act 1960.[55]

Problems where deceased died domiciled abroad

(1) *Administration*

Further problems of distribution may arise where an English representative is concerned with the administration of the estate of a person who died domiciled abroad. Problems of administration in such circumstances have already been considered.[56]

(2) *Distribution of or succession to immovables*

After payment of debts, etc., the distribution of the residue of immovables is governed by the *lex situs, i.e.* so far as English law is concerned, according to the law which would be applied in the particular circumstances of the case by the courts of the country where the immovables are situated.[57] Thus land, including leaseholds,[58] rentcharges on land,[59] mortgages secured on land[60] situated in England, and capital money arising under the Settled Land Acts,[61] devolves in accordance with the rules of devolution established by English law.

principle and practice." See also *Re Slee* [1962] 1 W.L.R. 496 and (1962) 26 *Conveyancer* 239. As to rates of interest see *post,* p. 1035.

[53] See Jarman, *Wills,* 8th ed., 1951, pp. 511–515, 724–728; Theobald, *Wills,* 14th ed. 780, 784. As to the effect on an executor's powers, see *ante,* p. 84.

[54] See *Re Skeats* [1936] Ch. 683, Administration of Estates Act 1925, s.46, and article in 120 S.J. 236. The executor may now be criminally liable for "appropriating" assets. See *ante,* p. 728.

[55] *Bradshaw* v. *University College Of Wales* [1988] 1 W.L.R. 190.

[56] See *ante,* p. 659 and the Hague Convention on Succession p. 16 *ante.*

[57] *Ante,* p. 15 *Re Ross* [1930] 1 Ch. 377; *Dicey's Conflict,* 11th ed., 1987, p. 1007. For a criticism of this rule, see Dr. J. H. C. Morris's article in (1969) 85 L.Q.R. 339. and *Re Collens* [1986] Ch. 505.

[58] *Freke* v. *Lord Carbery* (1873) L.R. 16 Eq. 461; *Duncan* v. *Lawson* (1889) 41 Ch.D. 394. See also *Re Gentili* (1875) Ir.Rep. 9 Eq. 541; *Re Moses* [1908] 2 Ch. 235; *De Fogassieras* v. *Duport* (1881) 11 L.R.Ir. 123; *Pepin* v. *Bruyère* [1900] 2 Ch. 504; [1902] 1 Ch. 24; *Leslie* v. *Baillie* (1843) 2 Y. & C.C.C. 91. Scottish "heritable bonds" are regarded as immovables: *Re Fitzgerald* [1904] 1 Ch. 573.

[59] *Chatfield* v. *Berchtoldt* (1870) L.R. 7 Ch.App. 192.

[60] *Re Holes* [1911] 1 Ch. 179.

[61] *Re Cutcliffe's Will Trusts* [1940] Ch. 565.

The doctrine of conversion has no relation to the question whether property is movable or immovable. Land held on trust for sale and not yet sold, though for some purposes considered as money, devolves as immovable property.[62]

(3) *Distribution of or succession to movables*

Whether particular property is to be considered as movable or immovable is governed (in general) by the *lex situs*.[63] On the other hand, the ultimate distribution of the residue of movables is regulated by the *lex domicilii*.[64] Thus, if a person dies intestate domiciled in England, his movables, no matter where they are situated, should be distributed according to English law.[65] Conversely, if a person domiciled abroad dies intestate, his movables in this country should be distributed according to the laws of the country where he was so domiciled. For it is part of the law of England that movable property should be distributed according to the law of the country in which the deceased died domiciled.[66] This principle has been applied to recognise the validity of a polygamous Hindu marriage in a case where a Hindu, domiciled in India, left personal property in England. The succession to this property was governed by Indian law and this involved recognition of the marriage.[67]

(4) *Bona vacantia*

Although English law applies the *lex domicilii* in order to determine the succession to movables, it will not do so where the movables pass, not by any succession, but as *bona vacantia*, or ownerless things. Thus where an Austrian illegitimate who was entitled to a fund in court in this country died in Vienna intestate and without heirs, the Austrian Government having claimed the fund, it was held that as the right claimed was not in the nature of a succession the maxim *"mobilia sequuntur personam"* did not apply, and that the Crown, by the law of England, was entitled to the fund as *bona vacantia*.[68]

Where, however, a government claims not upon a "confiscatory" but on a "succession" basis, as would be the case under many modern civil codes, English law will apply the relevant law of succession.[69]

---

[62] *Re Berchtoldt* [1923] 1 Ch. 192; *Re Cutcliffe's Will Trusts, ante.* Dicey, *Conflict*, 11th ed., 1987 p. 904.

[63] *Ibid.* n. 62.

[64] *Enohin* v. *Wylie* (1862) 10 H.L.C. 1; *Doglioni* v. *Crispin* L.R. 1 H.L. 301; *Re Trufort* (1887) 36 Ch.D. 600; Dicey's *Conflict of Laws*, 11th ed., 1987, p. 1003.

[65] *Thorne* v. *Watkins* (1750) 2 Ves.Sen. 35; *Re Ewin* (1830) 1 Cr. & J. 156.

[66] See *per* Abbott C.J. in *Doe* v. *Vardill* (1826) 5 B. & C. 438, 451, 452, 2 Cl. & F. 571; *ibid. sub nom. Birtwhistle* v. *Vardill* (1835) 7 Cl. & F. 895.

[67] *Baindail* v. *Baindail* [1946] P. 122.

[68] *Re Barnett's Trusts* [1902] 1 Ch. 847. See also *Re Musurus* [1936] 2 All E.R. 1666.

[69] *Re Maldonado* [1954] P. 223.

(5) *Distribution of movables by attorney-administrator*

It follows that a representative who has obtained a grant of probate or letters of administration in this country in respect of the estate of a person dying domiciled elsewhere, after paying all debts recognised by English law, must see to the distribution of the residue of the movables under his control in accordance with the *lex domicilii*[70] He may be justified in some cases in handing over the surplus to the principal representative[71] but where there is any doubt or where he elects to distribute the property himself he will be well advised to obtain the direction of the English court,[72] which is often the only proper course.

The remedy against an attorney-administrator who is in breach of duty was formerly an action for assignment of the administrator's bond.[73] Since the abolition of administration bonds by the Administration of Estates Act 1971, the remedy would appear to be an action against the surety, if any.

If the representative applies to the court, of if an administration action has been brought in England, the court will either direct the surplus to be handed over to the principal representative, or, after ascertaining the law of devolution in the country of domicile, distribute, or direct the English representative to distribute, in accordance therewith.[74-75]

At one time it was suggested that the only course open to the English courts was to direct the surplus to be handed over to the principal representative.[76] This view can no longer be maintained.[77] And it may be said, by way of anticipation, that English courts are not compelled to adopt this course, even though there are creditors whose claims are enforceable by the law of the country where the deceased died domiciled, but not by English law.[78] By directing a distribution the English courts are, in such circumstances, preferring beneficiaries to a class of creditors in the country of domicile. But this course is of little use where the beneficiaries are resident

---

[70] For the duty and responsibility of the attorney-administrator of a principal domiciled abroad, see *Re Achillopoulos* [1928] Ch. 433; *ante*, pp. 319 *et seq*; *Re Weiss* [1962] P. 136.

[71] See *Eames* v. *Hacon* (1881) 16 Ch.D. 407; (1881) 18 Ch.D. 347; *Re Achillopoulos*; *supra*.

[72] See *Re Lorillard* [1922] 2 Ch. 638; *Re Manifold* [1962] Ch. 1. And see Dicey's *Conflict*, 11th ed., 1987 p. 995.

[73] See, *e.g. Re Weiss* [1962] P. 136. Such assignment was refused in a case where the attorney, on the direction of his principal, made payment to a third party; *Re Weiss, supra*. But it is not clear that all the cases on this topic (see, *e.g. Re Achillopoulos* [1928] Ch. 433; *Re Lorillard* [1922] 2 Ch. 638; *Re Manifold* [1962] Ch.D. pay sufficient attention to the principles (a) that an attorney-administrator is a full administrator in his own right (*Re Dewell* (1858) 4 Drew, 269, 222; *Re Rendell* [1901] 1 Ch. 230, and see *ante*, p. 321; or (b) that his liabilities can continue after the estate has been "cleared" (*Harvell* v. *Foster* [1954] 2 Q.B. 367, 383).

[74-75] See *Preston* v. *The Carron Iron Co.* v. *Maclaren* (1855) 5 H.L.C. 456; *Re Lorillard, ante*.

[76] The statement to this effect by Lord Westbury in *Enohin* v. *Wylie* (1862) 10 H.L.C. 1, 13, was disapproved in *Ewing* v. *Orr-Ewing, supra*, and can no longer be taken in its entirety as a correct exposition of the law: *Re Trufort* (1887) 36 Ch.D. 600, 609. The statement in question was relied upon by Fry J. in *Eames* v. *Hacon* (1881) 16 Ch.D. 407, but not by the Court of Appeal in *ibid*. 18 Ch.D. 347. And see *ante*, p. 662.

[77] See *ante*, p. 662.

[78] *Re Lorillard* [1922] 2 Ch. 638.

in the country of the deceased's domicile. The creditors, whose claims are recognised in that country, can immediately claim payment of their debts out of the assets transmitted to the beneficiaries.

Missing persons

A common problem of distribution, whether under a will or an intestacy, is the tracing of beneficiaries. Advertisements and the procedure for obtaining the court's directions have been considered,[79] but it may also be mentioned that government departments can often assist even if the person concerned is not receiving a pension. Letters in sealed envelopes will be forwarded to third parties but the Ministry in question will normally take no responsibility for the contents of such a letter.[80] Arrangements for the Court to obtain in disclosure are of addresses are set out in *Practice Directions* of the Family Division.[81]

A "Benjamin" Order

It may happen that distribution is held up because the representatives cannot be sure who is entitled. Thus a person's right to share in the estate may turn on the question whether another predeceased the testator, or predeceased him without issue, and it may be uncertain on the facts whether this happened. In these circumstances, the representatives may apply to the court for a "Benjamin" order,[82] that is, an order permitting them to distribute the estate on the footing that certain events have or have not happened. The effect of such an order is to relieve the representatives of liability in their capacity as representatives should the hypothesis on which they are to be permitted to distribute turn out to be wrong. Thus, where a beneficiary who was thought to have predeceased a testator subsequently appears, he will not be entitled to bring a claim against the representatives for his share of the estate. He may, however, be entitled to claim in equity against the beneficiaries who have been wrongly paid or perhaps bring a tracing action against the recipients of the share.[83]

The basis of the jurisdiction is simply that the court will be prepared in suitable circumstances to relieve a trustee of the consequences of a potential breach of trust. Various expressions have been used to describe the cir-

---

[79] See *ante*, p. 605.

[80] The Joint Parliamentary Secretary stated in the House of Commons on July 4, 1956, that the Ministry was prepared to send on letters to third parties if they were sent in sealed envelopes addressed to the Liaison Officer, Records Branch, of the Ministry (now the Department of Health and Social Security) at Newcastle-on-Tyne. (Parliamentary Debates, H.C., Vol. 555, Col. 1516.) As to advertisement, see *ante*, p. 605.

[81] 1988] 1 W.L.R. 648; [1989] 1 W.L.R. 219.

[82] After *In Re Benjamin* [1902] 1 Ch. 723. Originally, such an order would only be made after a full kin inquiry, but in suitable cases this will be dispensed with. See *Re Beattie*, discussed in (1926) L.J. News 163. Consideration should always be given to the alternative course of distributing with the protection of insurance.

[83] See, *e.g.*, *Re Diplock* [1951] A.C. 251. The claim against wrongly paid beneficiaries will be statute barred after 12 years unless the beneficiaries were also the representatives. See ss.22 and 21(1) of the Limitation Act 1980.

cumstances in which the jurisdiction will be exercised. It has been said, for example, that an order will be made where the proposed distribution reflects the practical probabilities of what has happened[84] or is based on the probable inferences,[85] or where there is satisfactory prima facie evidence of practical impossibility of proof of the facts or events in question[86] or where every reasonable step has been taken to trace the individuals in question and it was most improbable that any such individual would ever establish a claim.[87] Where there remains a theoretical possibility of beneficiaries appearing despite their long absence, the court will consider whether it is just that the enjoyment by the known beneficiaries of their apparent interests should be further postponed.[88]

In cases where a possible beneficiary has not been heard of for many years and seems likely to have predeceased the testator, the application has many similarities to an application for a declaration that a person should be presumed to be dead.[89] The jurisdiction, however, is distinct.[90] Thus it is possible that a court would give leave to distribute on the footing that a person has died where it would not have been prepared to make a declaration of death. Further, the *Benjamin* jurisdiction is far more extensive. For example, leave can be given to distribute on the basis that a person died without issue and without having married[91] or on the basis that all debts and liabilities have been ascertained[92] or, where an original settlement has been lost, on the basis that the will trusts are those established by secondary evidence.[93]

Practice

The representatives should make the application by originating summons under Order 85 of the Rules of the Supreme Court. The persons to whom distribution is proposed to be made should be joined as defendants. It is not the practice in straightforward cases to appoint a person to represent the interests of the "missing" beneficiaries. The application should be supported by an affidavit setting out the investigations which have so far been made. At the first hearing the Master may direct that further inquiries be made or advertisements placed. When satisfied as to the evidence, the Master will make the order sought or adjourn the Originating Summons into court.

[84] *Re Green's Will Trusts* [1985] 3 All E.R. 455, 462.
[85] *Hansell* v. *Spink* [1943] Ch. 396, 399.
[86] *In Re Gess* [1942] Ch. 37, 39.
[87] *In Re Lowe's Will Trusts* [1973] 1 W.L.R. 882, 887.
[88] *Re Green's Will Trusts*, *supra*, 462.
[89] For the principles involved, see *Chard* v. *Chard* [1956] P. 259.
[90] In practice, however, the applications are often combined. In *Re Green's Will Trusts* [1985] 3 All E.R. 455, Nourse J. left open the question of what distinctions may exist between the two jurisdictions, commenting that the modern practice is to make a Benjamin order where there is no need to make a declaration.
[91] As in: *Re Benjamin*, *supra* and *Re Green's Will Trusts*, *supra*.
[92] *In Re Gess* [1942] Ch. 37.
[93] *Hansell* v. *Spink* [1943] Ch. 396.

Disclaimer

Finally a beneficiary under a will[94] can totally or partially[95] refuse or renounce the gift to him. "The law certainly is not so absurd as to force a man to take an estate against his will."[96] There is no authority to the effect that the disclaimer must take place in a court of record; it may be made by deed,[97] or even by conduct[98] but it must be total.[99] Prima facie, the disclaimer operates from the time of the testator's death and makes the gift void for certain purposes *ab initio*.[1] If successive interests in property are limited to beneficiaries and there is a disclaimer of a prior absolute interest, the subsequent interests are accelerated unless the testator has shown a contrary intention.[2] Joint interests can also be disclaimed if all joint tenants concur.[3] A disclaimer of a legacy can, before the legacy is otherwise dealt with, be retracted by the legatee.[4]

In certain circumstances, disclaimer can be used to save inheritance tax, under the provisions in the legislation relating to the alteration of dispositions taking effect on death.[5] Only one such alteration can be made.[6]

[94] It is doubtful an interest on intestacy can be disclaimed except so as to benefit the Crown. The point was not argued in *Re Scott* [1975] 1 W.L.R. 1260. See generally to 40 Conveyancer 292 (1978); 41 Conveyancer 260 (1977) and [1978] Conveyancer 213. See p. 1065 *post*.

[95] Partial disclaimer of an onerous legacy is not possible. See p. 981 *post*. It is probably a matter of interpretation of the will to decide whether partial disclaimer is allowable where the gift is not onerous.

[96] *Per* Abbott C.J. in *Townson* v. *Tickell* (1819) 3 B. & Ald. 31, 36.

[97] *Townson* v. *Tickell, supra*; see also *Peppercorn* v. *Wayman* (1852) 5 De G. & Sm. 230; *Mallott* v. *Wilson* [1903] 2 Ch. 494; *Re Wimperis* [1914] 1 Ch. 502.

[98] See *Re Clout & Frewer's Contract* [1924] 2 Ch. 230.

[99] See p. 981 *post*.

[1] See n. 97, *supra*.

[2] *Re Hodge* [1943] Ch. 300; *Re Taylor* [1957] 1 W.L.R. 1043.

[3] *Re Schar* [1951] Ch. 280.

[4] *Re Young* [1913] 1 Ch. 272; *Re Cranstown* [1949] Ch. 523.

[5] Inheritance Tax Act 1984, s.142. *British Tax Encyclopaedia* 3–5141. But see *Re Strattons Disclaimer* [1958] Ch. 42 as to earlier legislation.

[6] *Russell* v. *I.R.C.* [1988] 1 W.L.R. 834.

Chapter 68

ADEMPTION AND SATISFACTION

Meanings

A specific gift is "lost" or "withdrawn" when the subject-matter does not exist or has fundamentally changed its character at the date of the testator's death. A form of statutory *ademption* may also now arise where a will contains a gift to a former spouse. Subject to a contrary intention appearing in the will, where a marriage has been dissolved after the date of the will in question any devise or request to the former spouse will lapse.[1] This principle is known by the technical word "ademption" and it can give rise to a number of problems.

Conversely questions of *satisfaction* arise where a legacy is given to a creditor,[2] where a portion has been given to a legatee[3] and where a legacy has been given to a person entitled to a portion.[4] The word ademption is, however, sometimes used to describe the satisfaction of a legacy by a portion[5] and satisfaction to describe the questions of construction which arise when two legacies are given to the same person and it has to be decided if they are substitutional or cumulative.[6] The two topics are therefore considered together in this chapter. Satisfaction may also arise on intestacy.[7]

Ademption by change in nature of legacy

The general rule is that, in order to complete the right of a specific legatee[8] to receive his legacy, the thing bequeathed must, at the testator's death, remain *in specie* as described in the will: otherwise the legacy is adeemed.[9] For instance, if the legacy is of a specified chattel in possession, as of a gold chain, or a bale of wool, or a piece of cloth, the legacy is adeemed, not only by the testator's selling or otherwise disposing of the subject in his lifetime, but also if he changes its form so as to alter the specification of it. Thus, if he converts the gold chain into a cup, or the wool into

---

[1] Administration of Justice Act 1982 Wills Act 1837, see p. 770 *ante*.

[2] See *ante*, p. 642.

[3] See *post*, p. 953.

[4] See *post*, p. 637.

[5] See n. 3.

[6] See Theobald, *Wills*, 14th ed., 236, 746.

[7] See *Hardy* v. *Shaw* [1976] Ch. 82 and p. 1071 *post*.

[8] As to types of legacy, see *post*, p. 1000. As to whether a legacy of the inchoate rights of a beneficiary during administration is subject to ademption, see note on *Re Leigh* [1970] Ch. 277 by P. V. Baker in (1970) 86 L.Q.R. 20. See also *ante*, pp. 250, 251.

[9] If the thing bequeathed has in fact changed its character before the date of the will the question is, of course, one of description and not of ademption.

cloth, or makes the piece of cloth into a garment, the legacy is adeemed.[10] The law is that where you find a change in the thing bequeathed ademption will follow, unless it can be shown that the thing is changed in name or form only and remains substantially the same.[11]

Intention not the test

The rule operates quite independently of the testator's intention. It is the legal consequence of the change of form, unless the change is due to the unauthorised act of a third party.[12] Thus where the testator bequeathed a mortgage of £200 and the debt was later paid off the bequest was adeemed even though the testator had placed the redemption money in a separate account and given the legatee the pass-book.[13]

The same rule applies to a specific devise of realty. If, after making the will, and devising specific realty to A, the testator sells the realty, there is ademption, and A will receive nothing.[14]

Ademption by change effected by statute or act of third parties

Where there is a change of property effected by virtue even of an Act of Parliament, ademption will follow unless it is shown that the property is changed in name or form only and remains substantially the same.[15] Accordingly where a testator bequeathed the interest arising from "money invested in the Lambeth Waterworks Company," and after the date of the will the testator's stock was converted into stock of the Metropolitan Water Board, it was held that the bequest of the stock had been adeemed.[16] But the statute which effects the conversion may expressly preclude the operation of ademption.[17] Thus, a bequest of G. E. Railway Stock passed L. N. E. Railway Stock, into which the former had been converted. This bequest, however, did not pass L. N. E. Railway Stock purchased after the execution of the will.[18]

In *Re Clifford*,[19] where there was a specific bequest of "23 of the shares

---

[10] *Ashburner* v. *MacGuire* (1786) 2 Bro.C.C. 108. So where the testator took the goods bequeathed with him on a voyage, and the ship was lost at sea and the goods perished, and he was drowned, it was held, that as it could not be shown that the testator died before the goods perished, the legatee had no interest in them, and no claim on the money for which they had been insured: *Durrant* v. *Friend* (1852) 5 De G. & Sm. 343.

[11] *Re Slater* [1907] 1 Ch. 655; *Re Kuypers* [1925] Ch. 244.

[12] *Shaftsbury* v. *Shaftsbury* (1716) 2 Vern. 747; *Basan* v. *Brandon* (1836) 8 Sim. 171; *Harrison* v. *Asher* (1848) 2 De G. & Sm. 436.

[13] *Re Bridle* (1879) 4 C.P.D. 336.

[14] *Re Edwards* [1958] Ch. 168, where ademption prevented any question of election arising.

[15] *Re Slater* [1907] 1 Ch. 665; *Re Galway's Will Trusts* [1950] Ch. 1. See also *Oakes* v. *Oakes* (1852) 9 Hare 66.

[16] See n. 15.

[17] *Re Macartney* (1920) 36 T.L.R. 394; *Re Jenkins* [1931] 2 Ch. 218. See also *Re Gage* [1934] Ch. 536, where Clauson J. held that a holding of 5 per cent. War Loan remained a holding of the same stock, though some of the incidents of the stock were modified as a result of a statutory conversion under the Finance (No. 2) Act 1931, Pt. III.

[18] *Re Anderson* [1928] W.N. 46.

[19] [1912] 1 Ch. 29; and see *Re Leeming* [1912] 1 Ch. 828; *cf. Re Gillins* [1909] 1 Ch. 345.

belonging to me" in a certain company, and the original shares of £80 each had been sub-divided into four new £20 shares, it was held that the original shares though changed in form were substantially the same, and that there was no ademption. But additional shares issued to compensate share-holders for a loss incurred by the change in form of their original shares will not pass under a bequest of the original shares,[20] and it has been held that bonus shares do not pass.[21] However, the position may not be as simple as this authority indicates and there is other authority for saying that if the totality of a shareholder's rights remain the same a mere alteration in nomenclature is not material.[22]

It has been held that there was no ademption where the stock had been transferred to another fund without the knowledge or authority of the tes-tator.[23] Nor was there ademption where the stock was merely transferred, with the testator's consent, from the name of his trustee into his own.[24] And where a legacy was bequeathed of certain securities ("or the invest-ments representing the same at my death if they shall have been converted into other holdings"), the redemption of one of the securities and the plac-ing of the redemption money on deposit at a bank with the A. & N. Stores Ltd. did not cause an ademption of the legacy as the deposits could be regarded as investments.[25]

In *Re Heilbronner*[26] there was a bequest of "my bank deposit at the M. Bank." The testator had a current account but no deposit account, and shortly before his death he withdrew the whole of his current account balance and transferred it temporarily to one of his executors. It was held that "bank deposit" included both current account and deposit account, and that since the withdrawal was only for a temporary purpose, there was no ademption, and the bequest extended to the amount of the current account balance in the hands of the executor.

Demonstrative legacies

The rule of ademption does not apply to demonstrative legacies,[27] for, though the particular fund out of which the legacy is directed to be paid is not in existence at the testator's death, the legatees will be entitled to satis-faction out of the general estate.[28]

---

[20] *Re Kuypers* [1925] Ch. 244.
[21] See *Att.-Gen.* v. *Oldham* [1940] 1 K.B. 599; 2 K.B, 485. *Re Tetsall* [1961] 1 W.L.R. 938.
[22] See *per* Scott L.J. in *Re Payne* [1940] Ch. 576 and *Richards* v. *Patteson* (1847) 15 Sim. 501; *Sampson* v. *Sampson* (1869) 8 Eq. 479; *Re Leeming* [1912] 1 Ch. 828.
[23] *Shaftsbury* v. *Shaftsury* (1716) 2 Vern. 747; *Basan* v. *Brandon* (1836) 8 Sim. 171. So where the subject of a specific legacy was sold during the testator's lunacy by his son, it was held by Stuart V.-C. that there was no ademption: *Jenkins* v. *Jones* (1866) L.R. 2 Eq. 323.
[24] *Dingwell* v. *Askew* (1788) 1 Cox 427. See also *Re Johnstone's Settlement* (1880) 14 Ch.D. 162; *post*, p. 944 n. 36.
[25] *Re Lewis's Will Trusts* [1937] Ch. 118.
[26] [1953] 1 W.L.R. 1254.
[27] See n. 8.
[28] *Post*, p. 1001.

Legacy of a debt

If a debt specifically bequeathed is received by the testator, the legacy is adeemed. The subject is extinguished, and nothing remains to which the words of the will can apply.[29] Thus, in *Rider* v. *Wager*,[30] the testator specifically bequeathed to A part of a debt due to him from B, and the remainder to C. The testator called in the money. The legacy was held to be extinguished. In the same case, the testator having bequeathed to D a debt which D owed him, this legacy was held to be adeemed by payment of the money in his lifetime. So partial receipt by the testator of the debt specifically bequeathed will operate as an ademption *pro tanto*.[31]

A specific legacy of a debt is adeemed whether the debt is paid voluntarily or under compulsion. "The only rule to be adhered to is to see whether the subject of the specific bequest remained *in specie* at the time of the testator's death; for if it did not, then there must be an end of the bequest: and the idea of discussing what were the particular motives and intention of the testator in each case, in destroying the subject of the bequest, would be productive of endless uncertainty and confusion."[32]

Legacy of a fund

When a gift is made of a fund, or of the proceeds of the fund however invested, there is no ademption by an alteration in the nature of the fund, provided the proceeds of the fund can be traced.[33] Thus, a gift of "all the real and personal estate which I am or shall or may be entitled to under the will of my late uncle" was held not adeemed by an alteration in the investment of such property by the testator.[34] Whether a legacy is of a particular form of property, such as an outstanding debt, or merely of the money which happens to be so invested at the date of the will, must in each case depend upon the construction of the will.[35]

Powers

The doctrine of ademption applies to an appointment by will, whether made under a general or under a special power, and such an appointment fails when at the death of the testator the object or the subject of the appointment no longer exists.[36]

[29] *Badrick* v. *Stevens* (1792) 3 Bro.C.C. 431.
[30] 2 P.Wms. 329, 330; *Stanley* v. *Potter* (1789) 2 Cox 180; *Sidney* v. *Sidney* (1873) L.R. 17 Eq. 65. See also *Gardner* v. *Hatton* (1833) 6 Sim. 93; *cf. Re Brindle* (1879) 4 C.P.D. 336.
[31] *Ashburner* v. *MacGuire*, 2 Bro.C.C. 108. *cf. Fryer* v. *Morris* (1804) 9 Ves. 360.
[32] *Per* Lord Thurlow in *Humpheys* v. *Humphreys* (1789) 2 Cox 184. And see *Jones* v. *Southall* (1862) 32 Beav. 31. For an instance of a receipt which does not amount to an ademption, see *Graves* v. *Hughes* (1819) 4 Madd. 381.
[33] *Moore* v. *Moore* (1860) 29 Beav. 496; *Morgan* v. *Thomas* (1877) 6 Ch.D. 176.
[34] *Morgan* v. *Thomas, ante*; *Re Bythway* (1911) 80 L.J.Ch. 246. *cf. Re Bridle* (1879) 4 C.P.D. 336.
[35] See *Harrison* v. *Jackson* (1877) 7 Ch.D. 339, and *Manton* v. *Tabois* (1885) 30 Ch.D. 92, disapproving *Le Grice* v. *Finch* (1817) 3 Mer. 50, and *Clark* v. *Browne* (1854) 2 Sm. & G. 524.
[36] *Re Dowsett* [1901] 1 Ch. 398; *Re Moses* [1902] 1 Ch. 100, aff. *sub nom. Beddington* v. *Baumann* [1903] A.C. 13. *cf. Re Johnstone's Settlement* (1880) 14 Ch.D. 162, in which case

Contracts

A binding contract for the sale of property if specifically enforceable,[37] entered into after the date of the will, but not completed until after the testator's death, has the like effect to a sale in bringing about an ademption.[38]

Options

If a testator, having specifically bequeathed property by his will, then creates an option to purchase the property, the exercise of the option after the testator's death adeems the legacy.[39]

Stock

When stock is specifically bequeathed, and it has ceased to exist, either totally or in part, at the testator's death, as where the testator has sold the stock,[40] the legacy will be either totally or partially adeemed, as the case may be. Thus, where a testator gave "all my debentures," and subsequently, in exercise of an option given by the company, he converted his debentures into debenture stock, the latter were held not to pass.[41]

It is said that the legacy is irretrievably adeemed by the sale of the stock and will not be revived by a new purchase of similar stock by the testator.[42] Ademption is not based upon any presumed intention on the part of the testator.

Share in partnership

Where a testator, having made his will bequeathing his business of a solicitor, etc., to B, made B his partner in the business, giving him one-half of the profits, the bequest of the business was construed as that of his share and interest therein and was not adeemed.[43] And if a partner, under articles providing for the renewal of the partnership, specifically bequeaths his share of the profits (naming the amount), and upon the expiration of

there was held to be no ademption by a change in investment of the appointment fund made under a power to vary investments.

[37] *Re Thomas* (1866) 34 Ch.D. 166.

[38] *Watts* v. *Watts* (1873) 17 Eq. 217; and see *Re Galway's Will Trusts* [1950] Ch. 1; *Re Edwards* [1958] Ch. 168.

[39] *Weeding* v. *Weeding* (1861) 1 J. & H. 424, applying *Lawes* v. *Bennett* (1785) 1 Cox 167; *Re Currington* [1932] 1 Ch. 1; *Re Rose* [1949] Ch. 78.

[40] See *Ashburner* v. *MacGuire* (1786) 2 Bro.C.C. 108; and *Re Rose, infra.* It sometimes happens that a gift held not to be specific, but general, fails through the non-existence of a standard of value; for instance, a gift of so much money as will buy 50 shares in a company which at the death of the testator had been reconstructed and had ceased to exist: *Re Gray* (1887) 36 Ch.D. 205.

[41] *Re Lane* (1880) 14 Ch.D. 856. But see *Re Herring* [1908] 2 Ch. 493; and *cf. Re Nottage* [1895] 2 Ch. 657; *Re Weeding* [1896] 2 Ch. 364.

[42] See *Pattison* v. *Pattison* (1832) 1 M. & K. 12. But *cf.* the dicta of Lord Talbot in *Partridge* v. *Partridge* (1736) Cas.temp.Talb. 227; of Lord Hardwicke in *Avelyn* v. *Ward* (1749) 1 Ves. Sen. 426; and of Sir Thomas Clarke in *Drinkwater* v. *Falconer* (1755) 2 Ves.Sen. 625.

[43] *Re Rhagg* [1938] Ch. 828. *cf. Re Quilbell's Will Trusts* [1956] 3 All E.R. 679.

the old, new articles are entered into, by which his share of the profits is altered, the legacy will not be adeemed.[44]

Goods

Where there is a specific legacy of goods but the disposition of the subject is not absolute, the legacy will not be adeemed. Where a testator pawns or pledges an article specifically bequeathed, a right of redemption is left in him, and passes to the legatee at his death, so as to enable him to call on the executor to redeem and deliver it to him.[45] However, the legatee will have to bear the cost of redemption, unless a contrary intention is signified in the will.[46]

The ademption of a specific legacy of goods will sometimes be effected by the mere removal of them. Thus, where the bequest was of all the testator's household goods, plate, linen, china, etc., which should be in or about his dwelling-house at B at the time of his death, and he afterwards took another house, into which he removed the greater part of the furniture from the house at B, this removal was held an ademption.[47] Again, where the testator bequeathed to his wife the lease of his house in Baker Street, and the household furniture, plate, pictures and certain other articles therein, and the lease having expired in his lifetime, part of the furniture was sold, and the remainder, together with the plate, pictures and other articles, was removed to a house which the testator took in Edward Street, it was held that the legacy was adeemed; because it was clear that the testator made the bequest of the furniture, etc., with reference to giving the lease, and that he had in contemplation an enjoyment of the house with the furniture, etc., and, consequently, that the bequest had totally failed by the change of circumstances.[48]

But no ademption by removal, it would seem, will take place where the goods are temporarily removed for their preservation, as to save them from fire[49]; or from damage by enemy action[50]; or where they are temporarily sent abroad for exhibition[51]; or where they are removed by fraud, or without the testator's knowledge or authority[52]; or where, by the nature of the place described, it is clear that their locality was not referred to as essential to the bequest, as in the case of a specific legacy of goods in a ship[53]; or where the testator has two houses, in which he lives alternately, and being possessed of one set of furniture only, which he removes with

[44] *Backwell* v. *Child* (1755) Ambl. 260.
[45] *Ashburner* v. *MacGuire* (1786) 2 Bro.C.C. 108, by Lord Thurlow.
[46] Administration of Estates Act 1925, s.35, extending the principle of Locke King's Acts to personalty. See *ante*, pp. 607 *et seq.*
[47] *Heseltine* v. *Heseltine* (1818) 3 Madd. 276. See also *Spencer* v. *Spencer* (1856) 21 Beav. 548.
[48] *Colleton* v. *Garth* (1833) 6 Sim. 19.
[49] *Chapman* v. *Hart* (1749) 1 Ves.Sen. 271, 273; *Re Johnston* (1884) 26 Ch.D. 538, 553.
[50] *Re Eumorfopoulos* [1944] Ch. 133.
[51] See n. 50.
[52] *Shaftsbury* v. *Shaftsbury* (1716) 2 Vern. 747.
[53] *Chapman* v. *Hart* (1749) 1 Ves.Sen. 271, 273.

himself to each house, bequeaths, while residing in one of them, all his furniture in that house.[54]

In *Cunningham* v. *Ross*,[55] a testator bequeathed all his bills, bonds, etc., belonging to him, lying in the lodgings he possessed in the house belonging to S. At his death the testator had no effects in the house of S. It was contended that the legacy failed, on the authority of *Shaftsbury* v. *Shaftsbury*,[56] in which case the testator devised to his wife all his goods that should be in his house, and before his death he removed all the goods from the said house, and the devise was held void. But Sir George Lee was of opinion that the present case differed from that; for there the testator devised all his goods that should be in his house, which implied, that should be there at his death; but in the present case the words were only descriptive of what the testator meant to bequeath; and therefore it was immaterial whether they remained at S's house at the time of his death or not. If goods are destroyed a gift of such goods is adeemed.[57]

Leaseholds

When the testator expresses himself in the present tense, and all the words directly refer to a lease of which he was then possessed, a specific legacy of such lease will be adeemed by a surrender; and a new term, acquired by the testator upon a renewal of the surrendered lease, will not pass to the specific legatee.[58] But such an ademption will, it appears, be effected only when the testator has the legal estate in the term specifically bequeathed; for where the testator is merely a *cestui que trust*, and the equitable interest only is bequeathed, the court will not permit a mere surrender of the old lease by the testator and his trustee to defeat the specific legacy, but will consider the intention of the testator appearing upon the will.[59]

A surrender of a lease will not, however, operate as an ademption where the bequest is not specific, as where the testator devises "all and singular my leasehold estate, goods, chattels, and personal estate whatsoever."[60]

A will speaks from death

Under the Wills Act 1837, a will speaks with reference to property (but not for all purposes) as if it had been executed immediately before the tes-

---

[54] *Land* v. *Devaynes* (1794) 4 Bro.C.C. 537; *Rawlinson* v. *Rawlinson* (1876) 3 Ch.D. 302.
[55] 2 Lee 272. *cf. Green* v. *Symonds* (1730) 1 Bro.C.C. 129, in note. And see *Norris* v. *Norris* (1846) 2 Coll. 719.
[56] (1716) 2 Vern. 747.
[57] *Re Mercer* (1944) 60 T.L.R. 487 (war damage).
[58] *Abney* v. *Miller* (1743) 2 Atk. 593, 597. See also *Rudstone* v. *Anderson* (1752) 2 Ves.Sen. 418; *Hone* v. *Medcraft* (1783) 1 Bro.C.C. 261; *Porter* v. *Smith* (1848) 16 Sim. 251; *Cooper* v. *Mantell* (1856) 22 Beav. 223. But see s.24 of the Wills Act. As to the effect of this section see *Re Portal and Lamb* (1885) 30 Ch. 50, p. 55; *Re Evans* [1909] 1 Ch. 784.
[59] *Carte* v. *Carte* (1744) 3 Atk. 174; *Slatter* v. *Noton* (1809) 16 Ves. 197, 201.
[60] *Stirling* v. *Lydiard* (1744) 3 Atk. 199; *Digby* v. *Legard* (1774) 2 Dick. 500. But see *James* v. *Dean* (1805) 11 Ves. 392.

tator's death[61] and acts performed after the execution of the will cannot prevent its operation as to property of which the testator has power to dispose at his death.[62]

Cases in which it was formerly held that a will was revoked by an alteration of the testator's estate do not apply, and a will can only be revoked by marriage, by a properly executed declaration in writing, or by burning, etc.[63] Where a testator bequeathed to his wife all his term and interest in a leasehold house in which he then resided, and after the date of the will purchased the freehold, the wife was held entitled to the freehold.[64]

On the other hand, where a testator who had specifically devised a freehold[65] or leasehold[66] interest, sold the property, but took a reconveyance from the purchaser to secure part of the purchase-money, his rights as mortgagee were not a sufficient "estate or interest" in the subject-matter of the gift so as to entitle the specific devisee to the mortgage debt. It is conceived that since 1925 this principle will be applied in similar circumstances to the interest which would now be taken by the mortgagee, whether that interest be a legal charge, a term of years of a sub-term. Similarly, a bequest of a rentcharge issuing out of a freehold house, which becomes merged by a purchase of the freehold by the testator will not pass the freehold house.[67] Finally, if a testator devises real estate and afterwards sells it, and the purchase is not completed till after his death, the devisee is not entitled to the purchase-money. The right to receive the purchase-money is not an "estate or interest" in the real estate.[68] Where a testator makes a devise of real estate, the devise may be adeemed under the doctrine of conversion.[69]

Adeemed legacy not restored

A legacy which has been once adeemed will not be restored by a subsequent confirmation of the will by a codicil.[70]

The presumption of satisfaction

Where a parent is under obligation by articles or settlement to provide portions for his children and he afterwards makes provision for them in his

[61] Wills Act 1837, s.24. The limitation to property is not always remembered.
[62] *Ibid.* s.23.
[63] *Ford* v. *De Pontes* (1859) 30 Beav. 572, 593. As to divorce see p. 194 *ante*.
[64] *Saxton* v. *Saxton* (1879) 13 Ch.D. 359; *Re Fleming* [1974] 1 W.L.R. 1552. *cf. Re Knight* (1887) 34 Ch.D. 518.
[65] *Re Clowes* [1893] 1 Ch. 214. See also *Re Newman* [1930] Ch. 409.
[66] *Re Richards* [1921] 1 Ch. 513.
[67] *Re Bick* [1920] 1 Ch. 488.
[68] *Farrar* v. *Winterton* (1842) 5 Beav. 1; *Moor* v. *Raisbeck* (1841) 12 Sim. 123. See *Gale* v. *Gale* (1856) 21 Beav. 349; *Blake* v. *Blake* (1880) 15 Ch.D. 481; *Re Lloyd* (1884) 9 P.D. 65.
[69] As to the equitable doctine of conversion, see Snell's *Equity*, 29th ed., 1990 pp. 483–498 and Jarman, *Wills*, 8th ed., 1951, pp. 755 *et seq.* See also *ante* p. 945.
[70] *Drinkwater* v. *Falconer* (1755) 2 Ves.Sen. 622, applied in *Powys* v. *Mansfield* (1837) 3 My. & Cr. 359; *Hopwood* v. *Hopwood* (1859) 7 H.L.C. 728; *Re Galway's Will Trusts* [1950] Ch. 1. And see *Re Warren* [1932] Ch. 42. 51.

will this provision is prima facie presumed to satisfy the obligation.[71] The strong inclination of the courts against double portions has caused this rule to be applied without much relaxation.[72] The fact that the will directed certain sums advanced to the legatee before the date of the will to be brought into hotchpot did not rebut the presumption that a legacy to the legatee is a satisfaction of her interest under the settlement.[73]

The rule is often stated to be applicable to provision made by a *parent*, but in strictness it was formerly held to apply only to provision made by a father, on the ground that it is only on him that the duty in equity to make provision for a child fell.[74] It extends, however, to a person who is *in loco parentis* to another.[75]

If the testator, in the will, declares that the legacy is to be taken in satisfaction of the portion, or is not to be so taken, this expression of intention prevails, but difficulties of construction have arisen upon the question whether the words used by the testator are sufficient to rebut the presumption. It is clear, for example, that a direction in the will to pay debts is insufficient.[76]

Partial satisfaction

If the bequests are less in amount than the portions, or payable at different periods, such legacies will, notwithstanding, be considered satisfactions, either in full or in part according to circumstances.[77] So though a gift of a whole or part of a residue cannot be considered as a satisfaction of a debt,[78] yet it may be a satisfaction of a portion altogether, or *pro tanto* according to the amount.[79]

A provision by will may satisfy one part of a covenant to settle without satisfying the other parts of it: for instance, if a father on the marriage of his daughter should settle £1,000 on her for life with remainder to her children, a bequest of £1,000 to the daughter would satisfy her life interest but would not satisfy the interests of her children.[80] The principle of satisfac-

[71] *Bruen* v. *Bruen* (1702) 2 Vern. 439; *Copley* v. *Copley* (1711) 1 P.Wms. 147; *Moulson* v. *Moulson* (1780) 1 Bro.C.C. 82; *Ackworth* v. *Ackworth* (1773) 1 Bro.C.C. 307n.; *Weall* v. *Rice* (1831) 2 Russ. & M. 251; *Papillon* v. *Papillon* (1841) 11 Sim. 642; *Thynne* v. *Glengall* (1848) 2 H.L.C. 131; *Bennett* v. *Houldsworth* (1877) 6 Ch.D. 671; *Montagu* v. *Earl of Sandwich* (1886) 32 Ch.D. 525. See also *ante*, p. 479. As to satisfaction of debts, see *ante*, pp. 642 *et seq.*
[72] See also *infra*, as to the ademption of legacies given as portions.
[73] *Re Blundell* [1906] 2 Ch. 222.
[74] *Per* Stirling J. in *Re Ashton* [1897] 2 Ch. 574. There must now be considerable doubt about this proposition. See *Bennet* v. *Bennet* (1879) 10 Ch.D. 474.
[75] See p. 954, *post.*
[76] *Chichester* v. *Coventry* (1867) L.R. 2 H.L. 71; *Bennett* v. *Houldsworth* (1877) 6 Ch.D. 671. And see *Montagu* v. *Earl of Sandwich* (1886) 32 Ch.D. 525.
[77] *Jesson* v. *Jesson* (1691) 2 Vern. 255; *Byde* v. *Byde* (1761) 1 Cox 44; *Warren* v. *Warren* (1783) 1 Bro.C.C. 305; *Finch* v. *Finch* (1792) 1 Ves. 534; *Thynne* v. *Glengall* (1848) 2 H.L.C. 153, 154. See *Fazakerly* v. *Gillibrand* (1834) 6 Sim. 592.
[78] *Ante*, p. 643.
[79] *Thynne* v. *Glengall* (1848) 2 H.L.C. 131, 154; *Dawson* v. *Dawson* (1867) L.R. 4 Eq. 504; *Nevin* v. *Drysdale* (1867) L.R. 4 Eq. 517.
[80] *Re Blundell* [1906] 2 Ch. 22.

tion does not apply where the covenantee takes no direct interest under the will, but only a derivative interest by reason of some disposition by the legatee.[81]

Similar provisions

The presumption may be repelled or fortified by intrinsic evidence derived from the nature of the two provisions. Where the two provisions are of the same nature, or there are but slight differences,[82] the two instruments afford intrinsic evidence against a double provision. "It is not possible to define what are to be considered as slight differences between two provisions. Slight differences are such as, in the opinion of the judge, leave the two provisions substantially of the same nature; and every judge must decide that question for himself."[83]

Different provisions

Where, however, the two provisions are of a different nature, the two instruments afford intrinsic evidence in favour of a double provision.[84] And great differences in the nature of the benefits given, and in the limitations of the trusts on which they are directed to be held, will be taken as indications that the gift in the will was not meant in satisfaction of the covenant.[85] Thus, where the legacy is contingent,[86] or expressed to be given from some inconsistent motive,[87] it will not be considered a satisfaction of the portion. So also where the legacy is of an annuity which is unsecured and made subject to the testator's debts, whereas the debt consists of an annuity which is secured and not so subject to debts.[88] Again, where the gift by will is not to the child, but to trustees to pay debts and legacies, and then to pay the residue to the child, the form of the gift will be taken as an indication that the debts due under the settlement must be satisfied before the residue is declared,[89] unless the liability under the settlement is of such a nature that it cannot be described as a debt.[90] Where the portion is of land, and the legacy of money, or vice versa, there is no presumption, this being regarded as sufficiently negatived by the difference in the nature of the property.[91]

[81] See n. 80.
[82] Per Turner L.J. in Coventry v. Chichester (1864) 2 H. & M. 149; Chichester v. Coventry (1867) L.R. 2 H.L. 71; Campbell v. Campbell (1866) L.R. 1 Eq. 383; Russell v. St. Aubyn (1876) 2 Ch.D. 398.
[83] Per Leach M.R. in Weall v. Rice (1831) 2 Russ. & M. 268; McCarogher v. Whieldon (1866) L.R. 3 Eq. 236; Re Tussaud (1878) 9 Ch.D. 363.
[84] Chichester v. Coventry, ante; Weall v. Rice, supra; Paget v. Grenfell (1868) L.R. 6 Eq. 7; Re Tussaud, ante; Montagu v. Earl of Sandwich (1886) 32 Ch.D. 525; Re Vernon (1906) 95 L.T. 48.
[85] Ibid.
[86] Bellasis v. Uthwatt (1737) 1 Atk. 426; Hanbury v. Hanbury (1788) 2 Bro.C.C. 352.
[87] Foster v. Evans (1833) 6 Sim. 15; Glover v. Hartcup (1864) 34 Beav. 74.
[88] Re Stibbe (1946) 175 L.T. 198.
[89] Chichester v. Coventry (1867) L.R. 2 H.L. 71.
[90] Bennett v. Houldsworth (1877) 6 Ch.D. 671.
[91] Bellasis v. Uthwatt (1737) 1 Atk. 426; Grave v. Earl of Salisbury (1784) 1 Bro.C.C. 425.

Conflict of laws

Semble, the question, whether a testamentary disposition is to be taken in satisfaction of a portion or not, is one of construction of the will and is therefore governed prima facie by the law of the domicile of the testator when the will was made but this is subject to indications pointing to a contrary intention on the part of the testator. In *Campbell* v. *Campbell*,[92] where the testator, being of English domicile, had covenanted in a Scottish settlement made upon the marriage of his daughter with a Scotsman, to pay certain sums to the trustees, it was held that the English doctrine of satisfaction, unknown to Scots law, should apply, since the testator gave a large bequest to his daughter by his will.

Satisfaction (or ademption) of legacies

When a legacy is given for the benefit of a person for whom the testator was already liable to provide by settlement, the presumption arises, as has been shown, that the legacy was given with the intention of satisfying that liability. Similarly, when a legacy is given, and subsequently the testator pays to the legatee a sum of money as a portion, in certain cases[93] the presumption arises that this payment was intended to satisfy or be in substitution for, the legacy, although this is not truly "satisfaction" because there is no obligation where a legacy is contained in the will of a living person. Hence the word ademption is sometimes used in this context. In either case the presumption may be rebutted by intrinsic evidence; but using this terminology the presumption of "ademption" is more difficult to repel than that of "satisfaction"; for, in the former case, the first gift is made by will, which may be revoked or altered at the testator's pleasure, whereas in the latter case the beneficiaries under the settlement are in the position of purchasers.[94] Moreover, when the presumption of "satisfaction" arises, the beneficiaries cannot be thus arbitrarily deprived of their rights under the settlement, and may elect whether they will claim under the settlement or take the legacy instead.[95]

Debt to child not a portion

A legacy by a father to a child is not a satisfaction of a debt due to the child, or of money owing to the child in the nature of a debt, in any other way than a debt due to a stranger would be satisfied by a legacy[96]: and therefore circumstances of difference, such as there has already been

---

[92] (1866) L.R. 1 Eq. 383. Dicey's *Conflict* 11th ed., 1987 pp. 1022–1028. Also the Hague Convention on Succession see p. 15 *ante*.

[93] See *post*, pp. 953 *et seq.*

[94] *Chichester* v. *Coventry*, *supra*; *Dawson* v. *Dawson* (1867) L.R. 4 Eq. 504; *Cooper* v. *Macdonald* (1873) L.R. 16 Eq. 258; *Stevenson* v. *Masson* (1873) L.R. 17 Eq. 78.

[95] *Chichester* v. *Coventry*, *supra*; *Re Blundell* [1906] 2 Ch. 222.

[96] *Ante*, p. 644.

occasion to point out,[97] will be laid hold of by the court to prevent the application of the rule of satisfaction.[98]

Rebuttal by parol evidence

The presumption of satisfaction may be rebutted or confirmed by the application of parol evidence of a different intention on the part of the testator,[99] even though there may be intrinsic evidence in favour of or against the presumption.[1] Where evidence is admissible for that purpose, counter-evidence is also admissible, even of declarations of intention by the testator.[2] It was held by Leach M.R. in *Booker* v. *Allen*,[3] that if it be proved by parol evidence that the testator intended the provision made by the settlement to be in lieu of the legacy left by the will, the settlement will be held in satisfaction of the legacy, though the two provisions differ so much from each other, that they cannot be considered substantially the same.[4] Parol evidence is only properly admissible in such cases for the purpose of showing what the testator meant by the act subsequent to the will.[5]

The law on this subject was fully considered by Wigram V.-C. in *Kirk* v. *Eddowes*.[6] A testator bequeathed the sum of £3,000 to his daughter for her separate use for life, with remainder to her children as she should appoint, and, in default of appointment, to her children equally, with provisions for survivorship, advancement, and for the substitution of their issue; and subject to an annuity, and to his debts, he devised and bequeathed all the residue of his real and personal estate (naming securities for money) to his son absolutely. After the date of the will, the testator gave to his daughter and her husband a promissory note for £500 then due to the testator. In an action by the children of the daughter against the son, claiming to have the legacy of £3,000 invested and secured for their benefit, the defendant tendered parol evidence that, after the date of the will, the testator was requested by his daughter to confer some benefit on her husband, and that, thereupon, the testator gave her the promissory note, declaring that it was to be in part satisfaction of the legacy of £3,000; and that the testator was advised by his solicitor that it was not necessary to alter his will to give it

---

[97] *Ante*, pp. 642 *et seq.*

[98] *Tolson* v. *Collins* (1799) 4 Ves. 483; *Stocken* v. *Stocken* (1831) 4 Sim. 152. See *Plume* v. *Plume* (1802) 7 Ves. 258; and *Hall* v. *Hill* (1841) 1 Dr. & Warr. 94.

[99] *Trimmer* v. *Bayne* (1802) 7 Ves. 508; *Powys* v. *Mansfield* (1837) 3 My. & Cr. 359; *Hopwood* v. *Hopwood* (1859) 7 H.L.C. 728; *Phillips* v. *Phillips* (1864) 34 Beav. 19, 21; *Re Tussaud's Estate* (1878) 9 Ch.D. 363; *Fowkes* v. *Pascoe* (1875) L.R. 10 Ch. 343; *Re Scott* [1903] 1 Ch. 1. The test of intention is subjective: *Hardy* v. *Shaw* [1976] Ch. 82.

[1] *Weall* v. *Rice* (1831) 2 Russ. & M. 251; *Glengall* v. *Barnard* (1836) 1 Keen 769, 793; *Wallace* v. *Pomfret* (1805) 11 Ves. 542, but see *Hall* v. *Hill* (1841) 1 Dr. & Warr. 94.

[2] *Powys* v. *Mansfield* (1837) 3 My. & Cr. 359, 374.

[3] (1831) 2 Russ. & M. 270.

[4] See also *Lloyd* v. *Harvey* (1832) 2 Russ. & M. 310.

[5] *Hall* v. *Hill* (1841) 1 Dr. & W. 94, 116–119, 131, 132.

[6] (1844) 3 Hare 509, explained in *Re Shields* [1912] 1 Ch. 591; *cf. Smith* v. *Conder* (1878) 9 Ch.D. 170; *Re Lacon* [1891] 2 Ch. 482.

that effect. This evidence was admissible as constituting an essential part of a transaction subsequent to, and independent of, the will, of which subsequent transaction there was no evidence in writing; the parol evidence was not receivable as evidence of revocation or alteration of any part of the will, but as evidence of a transaction whereby the legatee had received part of her legacy by anticipation[7]; and, the advance to the daughter and her husband was an ademption *pro tanto* of the legacy bequeathed by the will for the benefit of the daughter and her children, which was in the nature of a portion. It might have been otherwise if the children had been all living at the date of the will, and been named therein individually, and not merely described as a class.

But evidence of the testator's intention cannot be admitted for the purpose of construing the will where there is no presumption against the apparent intention of the testator,[8] because a presumption in favour of the apparent intention of the testator is really a rule of construction.[9] Parol evidence of the circumstances in which the testator made the will is, however, on general principles, admissible to enable the court to construe the will by placing itself in the testator's position, but this must not be done to show the testator's actual intention.[10]

Satisfaction of legacy given as portion

The rule is that where a parent gives a legacy to a child, it must be understood as a portion, though not so described in the will, because it is a provision by a parent for his child[11]; and if the parent afterwards advances a portion for that child, as upon marriage, it will be a complete satisfaction (or ademption) of the legacy, not only in cases where the advancements are larger than, or equal to, the testamentary portions,[12] but also where the sums advanced are less than the sums bequeathed.[13] But where the portion

---

[7] The Vice-Chancellor disclaimed holding that declarations of the testator made at any other time than contemporaneously with the advance would be admissible. See also *M'Clure* v. *Evans* (1861) 29 Beav. 422.

[8] See *Lee* v. *Pain* (1845) 4 Hare 201, 216. *cf.* the evidence admissible to rebut the presumption of "ademption," *post*, p. 957.

[9] *Hurst* v. *Beach* (1820) 5 Madd. 351.

[10] *Guy* v. *Sharp* (1833) 1 My. & K. 589; *Martin* v. *Drinkwater* (1840) 2 Beav. 215; *Wilson* v. *O'Leary* (1872) 7 Ch.App. 448. See generally on admission of extrinsic evidence. *Higgins* v. *Dawson* [1902] A.C. 1, *per* Lord Davey.

[11] By Lord Eldon in *Ex p. Pye* (1811) 18 Ves. 153. See also *Suisse* v. *Lowther* (1843) 2 Hare 434 *et seq.*; *Re Lacon* [1891] 2 Ch. 482; *Re Scott* [1903] 1 Ch. 1. The rule is not confined to gifts by a father, see *post*, p. 954.

[12] *Ward* v. *Lant* (1701) Prec.Chanc. 182; *Jenkins* v. *Powell* (1689) 2 Vern. 115; *Upton* v. *Prince* (1735) Cas.temp.Talb. 71; *Scotton* v. *Scotton* (1719) 1 Stra. 236; *Watson* v. *Lincoln* (*Earl*) (1756) Ambl. 325; *Grave* v. *Salisbury* (1784) 1 Bro.C.C. 425; *Carver* v. *Bowles* (1831) 2 Russ. & M. 301; *Montague* v. *Montague* (1852) 15 Beav. 565; *Hopwood* v. *Hopwood* (1856) 22 Beav. 488; (1859) 7 H.L.C. 728; *Re Scott, ante.*

[13] *Hartop* v. *Whitmore* (1720) 1 P.Wms. 681; *Clarke* v. *Burgoine* (1767) 1 Dick. 353; *Ex p. Pye* (1811) 18 Ves. 140, 153. Where a sum is secured by a settlement on the marriage of the child, it is not necessary that it should be paid in order to operate as an ademption of a previous legacy: *Hopwood* v. *Hopwood, ante.*

is less than the legacy, it operates only as an ademption *pro tanto*. The sum advanced must be brought into account.[14] The legacy will not be set up by a codicil, made after the settlement, ratifying and confirming the will, and all the devises and bequests therein contained.[15] A similar principle applies by statute on intestacy.[16]

A sum expended by a father in paying his son's debts is not necessarily an advance to the son by way of portion, but may be regarded as a temporary assistance.[17]

In deciding whether a sum paid to or on behalf of a child amounts to such an advance the largeness of the sum is material[18] as is the age of the child.[19] It has been suggested[20] that a threefold test ought to be the criterion: (1) if the sum is too small it cannot be an advancement; (2) if the sum is really substantial it must be an advancement; (3) if the sum is large enough to be an advancement but not so large as to exclude doubt it becomes relevant to consider surrounding circumstances, including the relative size of the estate and age of the child.

Where the testator is *in loco parentis* to the legatee the legacy will be considered as a portion, and will be adeemed by a subsequent advancement in all cases where it would be so if made by the actual parent.[21]

Parental authority

The question, who is *in loco parentis* is one of considerable difficulty,[22] which must in a great degree depend upon the individual circumstances of each particular case. The proper definition of a person *in loco parentis* to a child is a person who assumes the situation of the lawful parent of the child,

---

[14] *Pym* v. *Lockyer* (1841) 5 M. & C. 29; *Re Pollock* (1885) 28 Ch.D. 552, 556. See *Kirk* v. *Eddowes* (1844) 3 Hare 509, 515; *Re Blundell* [1906] 2 Ch. 222. Where the advance is a gift of stock, its value must be ascertained as at the time of the gift; *Watson* v. *Watson* (1864) 33 Beav. 574, 576; *Re Crocker* [1916] 1 Ch. 25.

[15] *Booker* v. *Allen* (1831) 2 Russ. & M. 270; *Powys* v. *Mansfield* (1831) 3 My. & Cr. 359; *Montague* v. *Montague* (1852) 15 Beav. 565; *Hopwood* v. *Hopwood* (1859) 7 H.L.C. 728; and see *Re Warren* [1932 and 79 Law Society's Gazette 785] 1 Ch. 42, 51; *Re Galway's Will Trusts* [1950] Ch. 1.

[16] See *post*, p. 1071. As to the nature of an advancement, see also *post* p. 1071.

[17] *Taylor* v. *Taylor* (1875) L.R. 20 Eq. 155; *Re Scott* [1903] 1 Ch. 1 (overruling in effect, *Boyd* v. *Boyd* (1867) L.R. 4 Eq. 305, and *Re Blockley* (1885) 29 Ch.D. 250); *Re Lacon* [1891] 2 Ch. 482; *Re Hayward* [1957] Ch. 528; *Hardy* v. *Shaw* [1976] Ch. 82 (Intestacy).

[18] *Taylor* v. *Taylor* (1875) L.R. 20 Eq. 155; *Re Lacon* [1891] 2 Ch. 482; *Re Scott* [1903] 1 Ch. 1; *Re Hayward* [1957] Ch. 528 (not following *Re Livesey* [1953] 1 W.L.R. 1114).

[19] *Re Hayward* [1957] Ch. 528; *Hardy* v. *Shaw* [1976] Ch. 82 (a case on s.47(1)(iii) of the Administration of Estates Act 1925).

[20] See notes by R. E. Megarry, Q.C. (as he then was) in (1957) 73 L.Q.R. 22, 302.

[21] *Monck* v. *Monck* (1810) 1 Ball. & Beat. 298; *Trimmer* v. *Bayne* (1802) 7 Ves. 508; *Booker* v. *Allen* (1831) 2 Russ. & M. 270; *Powys* v. *Mansfield* (1837) 3 My. & Cr. 359; *Twining* v. *Powell* (1845) 2 Coll. 263; *Fowkes* v. *Pascoe* (1875) L.R. 10 Ch. 343.

[22] See the remarks of Lord Eldon in *ex p. Pye* (1811) 18 Ves. 150; *Bennet* v. *Bennet* (1879) 10 Ch.D. 474, 477. The relation must exist at the time of the will: *Watson* v. *Watson* (1864) 33 Beav. 574.

with reference to the parent's office and duty of making a provision for the child.[23]

Mothers,[24] great uncles,[25] uncles,[26] grandfathers or grandmothers,[27] or putative fathers,[28] are not considered *in loco parentum* unless they have intended to assume the office and duty of a parent. But a person may stand *in loco parentis* to a child though the child resides with, and is maintained by, his father.[29] And when the testator's assumption of the office of a parent is established, his legacy will be considered a portion, and accordingly prima facie adeemed by a subsequent advancement, not only in cases where he is collaterally related to, or the putative father of, the legatee, but also where no relationship of any kind subsists between them.[30]

Parol evidence is admissible to prove that the testator was *in loco parentis* to the legatee; and as the fact to be tried is the intention of the party, his declarations, as well as his acts, must be admissible for that purpose.[31]

Effect of adoption order

It is suggested that an adoption order will put an adopting father or mother in the same position as a natural parent for the purposes of ademption and satisfaction.[32]

Ademption of legacy given to a child for a purpose

Where the testator stands neither in the natural nor assumed relation of parent to the legatee, the legacy will be considered as a bounty, and will not be adeemed by a subsequent advancement,[33] unless the legacy is given for a particular purpose, and the testator advances money for the same

[23] *Powys* v. *Mansfield* (1837) 3 My. & Cr. 359. See *Rogers* v. *Soutten* (1838–9) 2 Keen 598; *Tucker* v. *Burrow* (1865) 2 H. & M. 519; *Campbell* v. *Campbell* (1866) L.R. 1 Eq. 383; *ex p. Pye* (1811) 18 Ves. 140, 154.

[24] *Bennet* v. *Bennet* (1879) 10 Ch.D. 474; *Re De Visme* (1863) 2 De G.J. & S. 17; *Sayre* v. *Hughes* (1868) L.R. 5 Eq. 376; *Re Ashton* [1897] 2 Ch. 574. It seems unlikely that in modern conditions a mother would be held not in *loco parentis*. See, *e.g. Pettit* v. *Pettit* [1970] A.C. 777, 795, 811, 824.

[25] *Shudal* v. *Jekyll* (1743) 2 Atk. 516, 518.

[26] See *Powel* v. *Cleaver* (1789) 2 Bro.C.C. 517, 518.

[27] *Roome* v. *Roome* (1744) 3 Atk. 181, 183; *Perry* v. *Whitehead* (1801) 6 Ves. 544, 547; *Lyddon* v. *Ellison* (1854) 19 Beav. 565; *Re Dawson* [1919] 1 Ch. 102.

[28] *Grave* v. *Salisbury* (1784) 1 Bro.C.C. 425, cited (1801) 6 Ves. 547.

[29] *Powys* v. *Mansfield* (1837) 3 My. & Cr. 359; overruling *ibid.* 6 Sim. 528.

[30] *Re Pollock* (1885) 28 Ch.D. 552, 556. The reader is referred to 1 *Roper on Legacies*, 3rd ed., p. 384, as to what circumstances are sufficient to invest the testator with the assumed relation of parent to the legatee, and whether parol evidence is admissible to show that the legacy by a testator, who is not actually a parent, was intended for a portion.

[31] *Powys* v. *Mansfield* (1837) 3 My. & Cr. 359, 370. And see n. 22. See also the Civil Evidence Act 1968.

[32] Children Act 1975, s.8, and Sched. 1. An adoption order may be made for purposes other than the welfare of the child during infancy: *Re D* (1991) *The Times*, January 23, 1991.

[33] *Wetherby* v. *Dixon* (1815) 19 Ves. 407; *Fowkes* v. *Pascoe, ante.*

purpose,[34] or unless the intention otherwise legally appears that the advancement was made with a view to ademption.[35]

A particular purpose may consist in the fulfilment of a moral obligation.[36] In such a case a reference to any special application of the money by or on behalf of the legatee is unnecessary.[37] It seems, however, that a reference to the moral obligation must appear on the face of the will. In *Re Fletcher*,[38] a legacy was given to a creditor of the exact amount of the debt due. Hence the presumption of satisfaction arose,[39] *i.e.* that the legacy was given for the particular purpose of paying the debt. It was held that a subsequent payment of the debt by the testator adeemed the legacy under this rule. A legacy to the trustees of an endowment fund of a hospital is within the rule, and is therefore adeemed by a gift of the same amount to the same trustees in the testator's lifetime.[40] On the other hand, a legacy to a trustee for the benefit of an infant, to whom the testator is not *in loco parentis*, is not given for a particular purpose within the above rule.[41]

Residuary bequest adeemed by portion

Despite earlier decisions to the contrary,[42] it is now settled law that a residuary bequest may be adeemed by a portion.[43] Where, however, the residuary bequest is to children and a stranger,[44] the latter cannot benefit by the ademption. The advances brought into account must be shared between the children alone.[45]

Presumption of ademption stronger than satisfaction

If the limitations of the portion under the will are widely different from the limitations under the settlement the principle of ademption will still apply.[46] Where, therefore, a father makes an absolute gift by will to his child, and afterwards, on the marriage of that child, settles a like sum on

---

[34] *Debeze* v. *Mann* (1789) 2 Bro.C.C. 166; *Monck* v. *Monck*, 1 Ball. & Beat. 298, 303; *Re Pollock* (1885) 28 Ch.D. 552, 556; *Re Ashton* [1897] 2 Ch. 574; *Re Jupp* [1922] 2 Ch. 359. In the following cases the legacy was held not to be adeemed by reason of the non-correspondence of the purposes of the legacy and the advancement: *Roome* v. *Roome* (1744) 3 Atk. 181; *Spinks* v. *Robins* (1742) 2 Atk. 491; *Re Aynsley* [1915] 1 Ch. 172.

[35] *Pankhurst* v. *Howell* (1870) L.R. 6 Ch. 136; *Re Ashton* [1898] 1 Ch. 142; *Re Eardley's Will* [1920] 1 Ch. 397; *Re Ware* [1926] W.N. 163.

[36] *Re Pollock*, *ante*.

[37] *Re Jupp*, *ante*.

[38] (1888) 38 Ch.D. 373.

[39] As to this presumption, see *ante*, p. 642.

[40] *Re Corbett* [1903] 2 Ch. 326; *cf. Re Aynsley*, *ante*.

[41] *Re Smythies* [1903] 1 Ch. 259.

[42] See *Farnham* v. *Phillips* (1741) 2 Atk. 215.

[43] *Montefiore* v. *Guedalla* (1859) 1 De G.F. & J. 93. See also *Schofield* v. *Heap* (1858) 27 Beav. 93; *Beckton* v. *Barton* (1859) 27 Beav. 99; *Re George's Will Trusts* [1949] Ch. 154.

[44] A grandchild is a stranger for this purpose: *Re Dawson* [1919] 1 Ch. 102.

[45] *Meinertzagen* v. *Walters* (1872) L.R. 7 Ch. 670; *Re Heather* [1906] 2 Ch. 230.

[46] *Trimmer* v. *Bayne* (1802) 7 Ves. 508, 515; *Ex p. Pye* (1811) 18 Ves. 140, 153; *Hartopp* v. *Hartopp* (1810) 17 Ves. 184; *Sheffield* v. *Coventry* (1833) 2 Russ. & M. 317; *Platt* v. *Platt* (1830) 3 Sim. 503; *Phillips* v. *Phillips* (1864) 34 Beav. 19; *Dawson* v. *Dawson* (1867) L.R. 4 Eq. 504; *Re George's Will Trusts*, *supra*.

the husband and wife and their children, the settlement is an ademption of the legacy.[47] Again, where a legacy is given to M with a contingent limitation over to N, in the event of M dying without children, and the legacy to M is adeemed by a subsequent gift to M in the lifetime of the testatrix, to which no limitation in favour of N is attached, the legacy is not merely adeemed as to M, but extinguished as to N.[48]

This doctrine was settled by the decision of the House of Lords in *Durham* v. *Wharton*.[49] In this respect there is a distinction between the principle of the ademption of legacies given as portions, and that of the satisfaction of debts or portions by legacies.[50] In the latter case, as has already been shown,[51] anything greater than a "slight difference" repels the presumption.

Where presumption rebutted

The presumption of ademption, however, will not prevail where the testamentary portion and subsequent advancement are not *ejusdem generis*[52]; nor where the subsequent advancement depends upon a contingency, and the testamentary portion is certain[53]; nor where a legacy or advancement is not merely given as a portion, but is expressed to be made in lieu of, or as compensation for, an interest to which the child was entitled[54]; nor where the testator has not in his will made any definite provision for his children but has left it to the trustees of his will to distribute the residue of his estate for the benefit of his children or grandchildren.[55] It seems also that the principle does not extend to devises of real estate.[56]

[THE NEXT PAGE IS 961.]

---

[47] *Barry* v. *Harding* (1844) 1 J. & Lat. 475.

[48] *Twining* v. *Powell* (1845) 2 Coll. 262; see *Garner* v. *Holmes*, Dru.temp. Napier 132; *Phillips* v. *Phillips* (1864) 34 Beav. 19; *McCarogher* v. *Whieldon* (1866) L.R. 3 Eq. 236.

[49] (1836) 10 Bligh 526; 3 Cl. & Fin. 146.

[50] *Monck* v. *Monck* (1810) 1 Ball. & Beat. 298; *Durham* v. *Wharton* (1836) 10 Bligh 526, 545.

[51] See *ante*, p. 951, on this point, and generally as to the fact that it is easier to rebut the presumption of "satisfaction" than that of "ademption," see Snell's *Equity*, 29th ed., 1990, pp. 528–9.

[52] *Holmes* v. *Holmes* (1783) 1 Bro.C.C. 555; *Davys* v. *Boucher* (1839) 3 Y. & C.Ex. 397, 411. A gift of a sum of money to the husband of a daughter by her father, *simpliciter*, after marriage, is not an ademption of a legacy given by him to his daughter: *Ravenscroft* v. *Jones* (1864) 32 Beav. 669. Nor is an advance to the daughter herself of a sum for her marriage outfit: *ibid*. Nor occasional small gifts, nor an annual allowance of a small sum: *Watson* v. *Watson* (1864) 33 Beav. 574; *Schofield* v. *Heap* (1858) 27 Beav. 93.

[53] *Spinks* v. *Robins* (1742) 2 Atk. 491. See further *Crompton* v. *Sale* (1729) 2 P.Wms. 553. But see also the observations of Lord Cottenham in *Powys* v. *Mansfield* (1837) 3 My. & Cr. 359, 374, 375.

[54] *Baugh* v. *Read* (1790) 1 Ves. 257. But see the observations of Lord Lyndhurst in *Durham* v. *Wharton* (1836) 10 Bligh 526, 546.

[55] *Re Vaux* [1939] Ch. 465, 477.

[56] *Davys* v. *Boucher* (1839) 3 Y. & C.Ex. 397.

CHAPTER 69

DESCRIPTION

In this chapter consideration is given to four types of description of a legatee. The description of legatees is in general a topic for works on wills to
which reference should be made. This chapter is confined to the descriptions "heirs," "next-of-kin," "executors" and "representatives." The
question is always one of construction of the particular will but previous
usage and case-law is of at least illustrative assistance.

"Heirs"

Where, before 1926, personal estate was limited to the heirs of a person,
and the word "heirs" was used to denote succession or substitution (*e.g.* to
"A or his heirs"),[1] it generally meant such persons as would on an intestacy
legally succeed to the property according to its nature and quality.[2] These
would be, in the case of personal estate, the persons entitled under the
Statute of Distributions, as ascertained at the death of the person whose
heirs were mentioned, or if he predeceased the testator, at the death of the
latter.[3] A widow, therefore, was included, whilst a husband was excluded.[4]

Where, however, the word was used, not to denote succession or substitution, but to describe a legatee, and there was no context to explain it
otherwise,[5] the person to take was the heir in the ordinary sense of the
term.[6] For instance, where a testatrix by her will devised her real estate to
a person not her heir, and by a codicil gave a pecuniary legacy "to my
heir," the heir and not the next-of-kin took the legacy.[7] This was *a fortiori*

---

[1] *Gittings* v. *M'Dermott* (1834) 2 M. & K. 69; *Doody* v. *Higgins* (1856) 2 K. & J. 729. So,
again, a direction for distribution amongst heirs is an indication that the testator by "heirs"
meant next-of-kin: *Low* v. *Smith* (1856) 2 Jur. 344; *Re Steeven's Trusts* (1872) L.R. 15 Eq.
110.

[2] *cf. Powell* v. *Boggis* (1866) 35 Beav. 535.

[3] *Vaux* v. *Henderson* (1806) 1 Jac. & Walk. 388, n. (*c*); *Holloway* v. *Holloway* (1800) 5 Ves.
399; *Re Newton's Trusts* (1867) L.R. 4 Eq. 171; *Re Philps' Will* (1868) L.R. 7 Eq. 151; *Finla-
son* v. *Tatlock* (1870) L.R. 9 Eq. 258; *Re Steeven's Trusts* (1872) L.R. 15 Eq. 110; *cf. Re Dixon*
(1878) 4 P.D. 81. See also *Wingfield* v. *Wingfield* (1878) 9 Ch.D. 658; *Keay* v. *Boulton* (1883)
25 Ch.D. 212. See Hawkins, and Ryder on *The Construction of Wills*, pp. 121–124.

[4] *Doody* v. *Higgins* (1856) 2 K. & J. 729, 738; *Re Porter's Trusts* (1857) 4 *ibid.* 188; *Parsons*
v. *Parsons* (1868) L.R. 8 Eq. 260; *Re Boyer* [1935] Ch. 382; *cf.* also *Re Bromby* [1900] W.N.
187. The heirs took as tenants in common in the proportion fixed by the statute: *Jacobs* v.
Jacobs (1853) 16 Beav. 557; *Re Porter's Trusts, supra.*

[5] See, for example, *Lightfoot* v. *Maybery* [1914] A.C. 782 ("nearest male heir" construed
nearest male relative).

[6] So the words "next lawful heir" in an ultimate gift of real and personal estate were construed in their strict sense: *De Beauvoir* v. *De Beauvoir* (1846) 3 H.L.C. 524, 557; *Haslewood*
v. *Green* (1859) 28 Beav. 1; *Smith* v. *Butcher* (1878) 10 Ch.D. 113; *Re Dixon* (1878) 4 P.D. 81.

[7] *Mounsey* v. *Blamire* (1828) 4 Russ. 384. The reported disapproval of this case by Jessel
M.R. in *Smith* v. *Butcher* (1878) 10 Ch.D. 113, 114, if correct, clearly does not go to the authority of the decision as a whole.

the case when the testator exhibited such an intention,[8] as by blending the
realty and personalty in one gift. In each case the question was whether
there was anything to control the ordinary meaning of the word "heir" so
as to prevent him from taking the personalty as a *persona designata*, and to
raise the inference that the next-of-kin were to take in substitution or in
succession.[9]

In wills of personal estate coming into operation after 1925, where a testator refers to an "heir" as a *persona designata*, the person who would have
answered the description of heir of freeholds according to the general law
in force before 1926 will take by purchase.[10] Apart from this, however, the
word is construed to denote the persons entitled on intestacy. These persons take as under the intestacy provisions[11] if there is express reference in
the will to the relevant statute, but if there is no such reference they take
together simply as joint tenants.[12]

Before 1926 a legacy "to my next-of-kin or heir-at-law, whom I appoint
my executor," was void for uncertainty,[13] though a bequest "to the *heirs* or
next-of-kin of A" was held to be a gift to A's next-of-kin under the statute.[14] By the same reasoning it would seem that the effect of such a provision in post-1925 wills will be to benefit the persons now entitled on an
intestacy, unless the testator referred to his next-of-kin and heir as *personae designatae*, when the gift would be void for uncertainty.

In one case[15] it was argued that the rule "*nemo est haeres viventis*" precluded a gift "to such person or persons as at the death of the testator's
wife should be the testator's heir or heirs at law absolutely" from taking
effect in favour of the person who would have been the testator's heir had
he died at the same time as his wife (who in fact predeceased the testator).
The majority of the Court of Appeal, however, refused to accept this argument and upheld the gift in favour of the person who would have been the
testator's heir in the circumstances indicated.

Although for conveyancing purposes[16] in tracing a legal estate the heir at
law now has no significance there still remain problems as to the rights of

---

[8] *Gwynne* v. *Muddock* (1808) 14 Ves. 488; *De Beauvoir* v. *De Beauvoir* (1846) 3 H.L.C.
524.

[9] On this ground *Smith* v. *Butcher*, *supra*, can be reconciled with *Wingfield* v. *Wingfield*,
supra.

[10] Law of Property Act 1925, s.132, and the Administration of Estates Act 1925, s.51(1);
see *Re Bourke* [1980] 1 W.L.R. 539, 548; *Re Cossentine* [1933] Ch. 119. *cf. Macleay* v. *Tread-
well* [1937] A.C. 626.

[11] As to these, see Administration of Estates Act 1925, Pt. IV. See also *post*, Chap. 79,
p. 1065.

[12] *Re Kilvert* [1957] Ch. 388 (applying *Re Gansloser's W.T.* [1952] Ch. 30). *Re Balls, Smith*
v. *Balls* (1978) unreported. In cases where there are words of severance so that the interests
are several and not joint, it is an open question whether infants take absolutely or contingently on attaining their majorities. See *Re Bridgen* [1938] Ch. 205.

[13] *Lowndes* v. *Stone* (1799) 4 Ves. 649. For the effect of a purported gift before 1926 to "my
own right heirs" (other than S. and his issue), see *Re Smith* [1933] Ch. 847, where the matter
was referred to but it was not necessary to decide it.

[14] *Re Thompson's Trusts* (1878) 9 Ch.D. 607.

[15] *Re Hooper* [1936] Ch. 442.

[16] See pp. 550, 551, *ante*.

such an heir in other respects. For instance it remains an open question whether the heir or the personal representatives are interested under burial law[17] and in some cases of reverter.[18]

"Next-of-kin"

A man's "kindred," means persons related to him by blood.[19] The words "relations" or "relatives" do not necessarily mean "next-of-kin."[20] Relations by marriage are generally incapable of bringing themselves within the description of "next-of-kin" in a will; and before 1926 neither husband nor wife could, as a rule, be entitled under a bequest to the "next-of-kin" of either of them.[21] But it was observed by Lord Eldon, in *Garrick* v. *Lord Camden*,[22] that it was competent to, and required from, the court, to look through the whole will, and to see whether, from the whole, an intention was manifested to include the wife among those who were to be taken more strictly as next-of-kin, a description prima facie excluding her.[23]

Persons related to the testator by the half-blood were before 1926 equally of "kin" to him with those of the whole-blood, and equally entitled, with respect to the description of "nearest of kin" in a will, to every preference over the more remote kindred of the testator.[24]

If there is nothing to show that the testator had reference to the Statute of Distribution, or to a division as in case of intestacy, only the nearest of kin are entitled under the description of "next-of-kin"[25] or "next-of-kin in blood."[26] Hence, a surviving brother of the intestate will be entitled, in exclusion of the children of a deceased brother or sister.[27] *A fortiori*, the nearest of kin will be alone entitled under a bequest to "next-of-kin in equal degree."[28]

---

[17] *Ante* pp. 60–62.

[18] See, *e.g.* questions raised in argument in *Re Clayton* [1980] Ch. 99 at p. 102; *Re Rowhook* [1985] Ch. 62.

[19] It includes after 1969 all illegitimate relationships, see the Family Law Reform Act, s.15; 1981 *Conveyancer* 343.

[20] *Re Poulton* [1987] 1 W.L.R. 795 not following *Re Deakin* [1987] 1 W.L.R. 795.

[21] *Nichols* v. *Savage*, cited in *Bailey* v. *Wright* (1811) 18 Ves. 50; *Garrick* v. *Lord Camden* (1807) 14 Ves. 382. But see *post*, p. 964.

[22] 14 Ves. 382.

[23] See also *MacLeroth* v. *Bacon* (1799) 5 Ves. 159, for an instance where a relation *by marriage* may be included in the word "family." Where some of the testator's children are illegitimate the context may show an intention that by next-of-kin those who would have been next-of-kin if the testator's children had been legitimate should take: *Re Wood* [1902] 2 Ch. 542; distinguished in *Re Cullum* [1924] 1 Ch. 540.

[24] *Collingwood* v. *Pace* (1664) 1 Vent. 424; *Brown* v. *Wood* (1647) Aleyn 36.

[25] *Smith* v. *Campbell* (1815) 19 Ves. 404; see *Re Richards* [1910] 2 Ch. 74. *Philips* v. *Garth*, 3 Bro.C.C. 64, which was in favour of those entitled under the statute, has been overruled: *Elmsley* v. *Young* (1835) 2 M. & K. 780; *Withy* v. *Mangles* (1843) 10 Cl. & F. 215; *Rook* v. *Att.-Gen.* (1862) 31 Beav. 313; *Avison* v. *Simpson* (1859) Johns. 43.

[26] *Halton* v. *Foster* (1868) L.R. 3 Ch. 505; *Re Gryll's Trust* (1868) L.R. 6 Eq. 589; *Re Gray's Settlement* [1896] 2 Ch. 802. See further, *Nichols* v. *Haviland* (1855) 1 Kay & J. 504. Under a devise of land "to my nearest of kin by way of heirship," it was held that the heir was entitled, though not next-of-kin: *Williams* v. *Ashton* (1860) 1 J. & H. 115.

[27] See *Brandon* v. *Brandon* (1819) 3 Swanst. 312; *Elmsley* v. *Young* (1835) 2 M. & K. 780.

[28] *Wimbles* v. *Pitcher* (1806) 12 Ves. 433.

Accordingly, where by the marriage settlement of E. M., the ultimate limitation of a sum of £10,000, which her father thereby covenanted to pay, was to "such person or persons as at the time of her death should be her next-of-kin," and she died leaving her husband and a child of the marriage and her own father and mother surviving, it was held by the House of Lords in *Withy* v. *Mangles*,[29] that her father, mother and child were entitled, under the limitation, to the £10,000 in joint tenancy; for the words "next-of-kin" used *simpliciter* must be construed in their natural meaning of nearest in proximity of blood, and, by the law of England, the child and the parent are equal in degree of proximity, *i.e.* both are in the first degree, though the child (and the lineal descendants of the child) is preferred in the succession to property,[30] and consequent grant of administration.[31]

Again, where a testator bequeathed the residue of his effects to his wife for life, remainder to his daughter absolutely, but if his wife survived his daughter, then at his wife's death, one-third of the capital was to go according to her will, and the other two-thirds were to be paid "to my other the next-of-kin of my paternal line," it was held that, on the death of his wife who had survived the daughter, his grandchildren and brothers took the two-thirds of the capital as joint tenants.[32]

A sister of the testator has been held entitled in preference to the son of the testator's paternal uncle under a bequest to the "nearest of kin in the male line in preference to the female line."[33]

Statutory next-of-kin

Of course, if the testator clearly showed that by next-of-kin he meant the persons entitled under the Statutes of Distribution or if the gift might otherwise fail for uncertainty,[34] such persons would take. If he also showed that they were to take according to the title given by the statutes they took as tenants in common,[35] but otherwise as joint tenants.[36] A wife was entitled under a bequest "to such persons as would have been entitled under the statutes in case of an intestacy,"[37] though not as the next-of-kin of her husband according to the statutes.[38] On the other hand, a husband was held not entitled under a limitation "to such persons as would be

---

[29] (1843) 10 Cl. & F. 215, affirming the decree of Lord Langdale (1841) 4 Beav. 358.
[30] See *post*, p. 1075.
[31] *Ante*, p. 258.
[32] *Cooper* v. *Denison* (1843) 13 Sim. 290 (though grandchilren would have been preferred under the Statute of Distribution, and brothers and sisters under the Canon Law).
[33] *Boys* v. *Bradley* (1853) 10 Hare 389; 4 De G.M. & G. 58; *ibid.* 5 H.L.C. 873, *nomine Sayer* v. *Bradly.*
[34] See Jarman, *Wills*, 8th ed., 1951, p. 1621; *Re Gansloser* [1952] Ch. 30, 46–47; *Re Barlow* [1979] 1 W.L.R. 278, 283; *Re Poulton* [1987] 1 W.L.R. 795.
[35] *Downes* v. *Bullock* (1858) 25 Beav. 54; *Bullock* v. *Downes* (1860) 9 H.L.C. 1; *Re Nightingale* [1909] 1 Ch. 385.
[36] *Lucas* v. *Brandreth* (1860) 28 Beav. 274; *Re Greenwood's Will* (1861) 3 Giff. 390; *Re Kilvert* [1957] Ch. 388.
[37] *Jenkins* v. *Gower* (1846) 2 Coll. 537; and see *Ash* v. *Ash* (1863) 33 Beav. 187; *Starr* v. *Newberry* (1857) 23 Beav. 436.
[38] *Cholmondeley* v. *Lord Ashburton* (1843) 6 Beav. 86.

entitled, as next-of-kin or otherwise, under the statutes" to the personal estate of his wife, for the husband had no title under the statutes.[39] Where the bequest was to the persons who would have been entitled under the statutes to the personal estate of a wife, had she died intestate and a spinster, the husband was excluded, but not the children of the marriage.[40]

The expression "Statutes of Distribution" contained in a deed made, or a will coming into operation, before 1926, is, unless the contrary thereby appears,[41] construed to refer to the enactments, other than the Intestates' Estates Act 1890,[42] in force before 1926 relating to the distribution of effects of intestates.[43]

In wills (and instruments *inter vivos*) coming into operation after 1925 a reference to any Statute of Distribution is construed as meaning Part IV of the Administration of Estates Act 1925 and a reference to statutory next-of-kin as meaning the persons entitled under sections 45 to 49 of that Act (as amended by the Intestates' Estates Act 1952, the Family Provision Act, 1966, and the Family Law Reform Act, 1969) unless the context otherwise requires.[44] This includes the surviving spouse.[45]

Time of ascertaining next-of-kin

The natural and ordinary meaning of the phrase "next-of-kin" is next-of-kin at the death of the persons whose next-of-kin is spoken of, whether the will speaks of the testator's own next-of-kin or of the next-of-kin of some other person, unless the context demonstrates that such a construction would counteract the apparent intention of the testator.[46] The rule is not varied by the fact that the bequest is contingent on an event which may or may not happen.[47] Nor is it varied when the bequest to the next-of-kin is preceded by a life estate,[48] and even though the will goes on to provide, expressly or in effect, that the fund should go to the persons who should then be his next-of-kin; for the context may justify the construction of the

[39] *Milne* v. *Gilbart* (1875) 2 De G.M. & G. 715; 5 De G.M. & G. 510.
[40] *Norman's Trust* (1853) 3 De G.M. & G. 965, *Pratt* v. *Mathew* (1856) 22 Beav. 328; 8 De G.M. & G. 522; see further, Jarman, 8th ed., 1951, p. 1599. After 1969 illegitimate children are included (Family Law Reform Act 1969, s.14).
[41] See, for example, *Re Vander Byl* [1931] 1 Ch. 216; but contrast *Re Sutton* [1934] Ch. 209.
[42] *Re Morgan* [1920] 1 Ch. 196.
[43] Administration of Estates Act 1925, s.50(2) (*post*, p. 1146); *Re Sutcliffe* [1929] 1 Ch. 123; *Re Sutton, supra; Re Jackson* (1944) 113 L.J. Ch. 78; and see *Re Hooper's Settlement* [1943] Ch. 116.
[44] Administration of Estates Act 1925, s.50(1) (*post*, p. 1146); Family Law Reform Act 1969, s.14(6); *Re Krawitz* [1959] 1 W.L.R. 1192; see also *Re Bridgen* [1938] Ch. 205; *Re Hart's Will Trusts* [1950] Ch. 84. For an example of a contrary intention, see *Re Walsh* [1936] 1 All E.R. 327.
[45] See *Re Gilligan* [1950] P. 32, 37; *Re Krawitz* [1959] 1 W.L.R. 1192.
[46] *Gundry* v. *Pinniger* (1852) 1 De G.M. & G. 505, 506; *Downes* v. *Bullock* (1858) 25 Beav. 54; *Bullock* v. *Downes* (1860) 9 H.L.C. 1; *Holloway* v. *Radcliffe* (1857) 23 Beav. 163; *Eagles* v. *Le Breton* (1873) L.R. 15 Eq. 149; *Mortimore* v. *Mortimore* (1879) 4 App.Cas. 448. See *Re Rees* (1890) 44 Ch.D. 484; and *cf. Hood* v. *Murray* (1888) 14 App.Cas. 124; *Re Soper* [1912] 2 Ch. 467; *Re Gansloser* [1952] Ch. 30; *Re Krawitz* [1959] 1 W.L.R. 1192.
[47] *Bird* v. *Luckie* (1850) 8 Hare 301.
[48] *cf. Hood* v. *Murray* (1888) 14 App.Cas. 124.

word "then" as an adverb referring to the event (*i.e.* equivalent to "in the event of") and not the time, or as an adverb of time, but referring to the time at which the next-of-kin are to take, and not the time at which their class is to be ascertained. Each will, however, must be construed according to the apparent intention of the testator, and in some cases the word "then," or the like, has been construed so as to create an artificial class, composed of those persons who would have been next-of-kin if the person whose next-of-kin are referred to had died intestate at the time of the death of the tenant for life.[49]

Further, even though the tenant for life happens to be one of the next-of-kin, or even the sole next-of-kin, he is not on that account to be excluded from the gift in remainder,[50] though at one time it was thought that in this case the rule was varied. But, again, it is the testator's intention which is the true test.[51]

A bequest to the next-of-kin of a person who is dead at the date of the will must, under ordinary circumstances, receive an interpretation analogous to that adopted in the cases of a bequest to the testator's own next-of-kin, and if there is nothing in the context to make the words applicable to a class to be ascertained at any other time than that of the testator's death, those who at the testator's death are the next-of-kin of the deceased person named in the will would naturally be the persons to take.[52] A gift by a widow "to such person or persons as would have become entitled to my said husband's personal estate under or by virtue of the Statutes of Distribution had he died intestate and without leaving a widow him surviving," was, however, held by Stirling J., by virtue of the concluding words, to be a

---

[49] See *Hutchinson* v. *National Refuges, etc.* [1920] A.C. 794, where all the relevant cases are collected and discussed. *cf. Lucas-Tooth* v. *Lucas-Tooth* [1921] 1 A.C. 594. See *Moss* v. *Dunlop* (1858) John. 490, as to the effect of the words "for the time being." *Re Krawitz* [1959] 1 W.L.R. 1192.

[50] *Holloway* v. *Holloway* (1800) 5 Ves. 399; *Doe* v. *Lawson* (1803) 3 East 278; *Pearce* v. *Vincent* (1836) 1 Cr. & M. 598; 2 Bing. N.C. 328; 2 Keen 230; *Stert* v. *Platel* (1839) 5 Bing. N.C. 434; *Elmsley* v. *Young* (1835) 2 M. & K. 780; *Jennings* v. *Newman* (1839) 10 Sim. 219; *Smith* v. *Smith* (1841) 12 Sim. 317; *Urquhart* v. *Urquhart* (1844) 13 Sim. 613; *Withy* v. *Mangles* (1843) 4 Beav. 358; 10 Cl. & F. 215; *Nicholson* v. *Wilson* (1845) 14 Sim. 549; *Jenkins* v. *Gower* (1846) 2 Coll. 537; *Wilkinson* v. *Garrett, ibid.* 643; *Allen* v. *Thorp* (1843) 7 Beav. 72, 75; *Lasbury* v. *Newport* (1835) 9 Beav. 376; *Seifferth* v. *Badham* (1846) 9 Beav. 370; *Say* v. *Creed* (1847) 5 Hare 580, 587; *Baldwin* v. *Rogers* (1853) 3 De G.M. & G. 649, 656, 657; *Re Barber* (1852) 1 Sm. & G. 118; *Gorbell* v. *Davison* (1854) 18 Beav. 556; *Lee* v. *Lee* (1860) 1 Dr. & Sm. 85. See *Clarke* v. *Hayne* (1889) 42 Ch.D. 529.

[51] *Briden* v. *Hewlett* (1831) 2 M. & K. 90; *Butler* v. *Bushnell* (1834) 3 M. & K. 232; *Booth* v. *Vicars* (1844) 1 Coll. 6; *Bird* v. *Wood* (1825) 2 Sim. & Stu. 400 (as explained in *Elmsley* v. *Young* (1833) 2 M. & K. 82, 89; *Urquhart* v. *Urquhart* (1844) 13 Sim. 627); *Clapton* v. *Bulmer* (1840) 10 Sim. 426; 5 M. & Cr. 108; *Minter* v. *Wraith* (1842) 13 Sim. 52; *Cooper* v. *Denison* (1843) 13 Sim. 290; *Say* v. *Creed* (1847) 5 Hare 590; *Pinder* v. *Pinder* (1860) 28 Beav. 44; *Chalmers* v. *North* (1860) 28 Beav. 175; *Re Greenwood's Will* (1861) 3 Giff. 390; *Lees* v. *Massey* (1861) 3 De G.F. & J. 113; *Re Mellish* [1916] 1 Ch. 562. See also *Tiffin* v. *Longman* (1852) 15 Beav. 275. It has been doubted whether *Jones* v. *Colbeck* (1802) 8 Ves. 38, which was decided upon this principle, was properly within it. And the current of later authorities (*supra*, n. 46) seems to justify the extension of this doubt to some of the cases above cited).

[52] *Wharton* v. *Barker* (1858) 4 K. & J. 483, 502. See also *Philps* v. *Evans* (1850) 4 De G. & Sm. 188; *Vaux* v. *Henderson* (1806) 1 Jac. & W. 388n.; *Re Philps' Will* (1868) L.R. 7 Eq. 151.

gift to the next-of-kin of the husband at his death and not to that of the testatrix.[53]

A gift to the nearest of kin of a deceased husband and wife is a gift to the nearest of kin of each of them at the death of the testator, and not a gift to the nearest of kin of them both jointly.[54]

"Executors" and "representatives"

The expressions "legal representatives," "personal representatives," "legal personal representatives," or "representatives"[55] are to be understood, in a will of personalty, in the ordinary sense of executors or administrators, unless controlled by the context of the will.[56] This is equally so whether the bequest is direct to the representative of another, or to the testator's own representatives.[57] Further, it seems, despite earlier decisions to the contrary, that the meaning of these expressions is the same in a bequest to a person or his representatives, although the bequest is not preceded by a life estate.[58]

The ordinary sense of these expressions, however, may be controlled by a different intention appearing upon the whole instrument.[59] Hence, in the following cases "representatives," etc., were construed to mean next-of-kin and not executors or administrators[60]: (i) Where a husband was appointed trustee of a fund, on trust to pay the interest to the wife for life, remainder as she should by will appoint, and in default of appointment to her "personal representatives"; for the husband was made legatee merely as trustee to pay it over, if his wife died in his lifetime, and not to retain it[61]: (ii) Where, after a life estate to M, the personalty was given "to or amongst such person or persons as would be the personal representatives of" M[62]: (iii) Similarly, in a gift to "legal personal representatives, share and share alike"[63]: (iv) Where a testator gave £450 to trustees, their execu-

---

[53] *Re Rees* (1890) 44 Ch.D. 484.

[54] *Re Soper* [1912] 2 Ch. 467.

[55] *Re Crawford's Trusts* (1854) 2 Drew. 230; *Corbyn* v. *French* (1799) 4 Ves. 418; *Re Turner* (1865) 2 Dr. & Sm. 501, 508; *Chapman* v. *Chapman* (1864) 33 Beav. 556; *Alger* v. *Parrott* (1865) L.R. 3 Eq. 328; *Re Best's Settlements* (1874) L.R. 18 Eq. 686; *Re Brooks* [1928] Ch. 214.

[56] See *Stockdale* v. *Nicholson* (1867) L.R. 4 Eq. 359.

[57] Prima facie they take *qua* executors, not beneficially: *Mackenzie* v. *Mackenzie* (1849) 3 Mac. & G. 559; *Morris* v. *Howes* (1845) 4 Hare 599; *Long* v. *Watkinson* (1852) 17 Beav. 471; *Trethewy* v. *Helyar* (1876) 4 Ch.D. 53. cf. *Lord Advocate* v. *Bogie* [1894] A.C. 83; *Re Bosanquet* (1915) 85 L.J.Ch. 14. See also *Smith* v. *Barneby* (1846) 2 Coll. 728, 736; *Re Crawford's Trusts*, supra, and *post*, p. 970.

[58] See *Re Brooks* [1928] Ch. 214.

[59] See *Styth* v. *Monro* (1834) 6 Sim. 49; *Horsepool* v. *Watson* (1797) 3 Ves. 383. In *Briggs* v. *Upton* (1872) L.R. 7 Ch. 376, where, in a settlement, the words "to pay to legal representatives in a due course of administration" were held to amount to a direction to pay to next-of-kin, and not to executors and administrators. cf. *Re Gryll's Trusts* (1868) L.R. 6 Eq. 589. See also *Minter* v. *Wraith* (1842) 13 Sim. 52.

[60] See *Re Horner* (1887) 37 Ch.D. 695.

[61] *Robinson* v. *Smith* (1833) 6 Sim. 47.

[62] *Baines* v. *Ottey* (1832) 1 M. & K. 465.

[63] *King* v. *Cleaveland* (1859) 4 De G. & J. 477; 26 Beav. 26, 166.

tors, etc., in trust for his son for life, and, after his son's decease, to pay
two legacies of £100, and to pay the residue to the son's "legal representatives," and he gave the residue of his personal estate to his son's executors,
etc.; for the testator had clearly differentiated between executors and representatives, and, further, the ordinary construction would have made the
son residuary legatee of the £450, and also general residuary legatee of the
testator's personal estate.[64]

The ordinary sense even of the express words "executors and administrators" is controllable by the plain intent collected from the whole instrument. Thus in *Bulmer* v. *Jay*,[65] there was a trust in a marriage settlement to
raise a sum of money out of the settled estate of the husband, at the end of
12 months from the decease of the survivor of the husband and wife, and to
pay the same to the "executors or administrators" of the wife. The wife
died in the husband's lifetime, and her next-of-kin were held entitled to the
money. Again, in *Smith* v. *Dudley*,[66] where in a marriage settlement, the
ultimate trust of the wife's chattels was for the executors or administrators
of the wife *of her own family*, and the ultimate trust of the husband's chattels was for his executors or administrators *of his own family*, Shadwell
V.-C. held that, though the same words were used, *mutatis mutandis*, in
both limitations, yet the court was justified in holding that, for the wife's
chattels, they meant her next-of-kin at the death, and, for the husband's
chattels, his executors or administrators simply.

In *Daniel* v. *Dudley*,[67] Lord Cottenham said: "Legal or personal representatives may mean next-of-kin, but executors or administrators cannot. Therefore, none of those cases in which next-of-kin have been held to
take, *ex vi termini*, by the description of legal or personal representatives,
have any application to the present. The limitation in this case being to the
executors or administrators, it seems to me that it cannot signify whether
these words are construed as words of limitation or words of purchase;
because, on either supposition, the persons answering that description take
in their representative character, and then the fund is to be applied and
administered in the same manner as any other assets that come to them in
that character. That is the doctrine of all the cases that have been cited,
except that of *Bulmer* v. *Jay*, which stands alone." In a subsequent case,[68]
however, he qualified these remarks by saying that cases *might* exist where

---

[64] *Walter* v. *Makin* (1833) 6 Sim. 148. See also *Nicholson* v. *Wilson* (1845) 14 Sim. 549;
Smith v. *Palmer* (1849) 7 Hare 225; *Walker* v. *Camden (Marquis)* (1848) 16 Sim. 329; *Jennings*
v. *Gallimore* (1796) 3 Ves. 146 ("legal representatives according to the course of administration" held to mean next-of-kin); *Long* v. *Blackall* (1797) 3 Ves. 486; *Holloway* v. *Holloway*
(1800) 5 Ves. 401, 402. And see *Styth* v. *Monro* (1834) 6 Sim. 49 ("representatives" construed
as "descendants"); *Atherton* v. *Crowther* (1854) 19 Beav. 448.
[65] (1834) 4 Sim. 48; 3 M. & K. 197.
[66] (1738) 9 Sim. 125.
[67] (1841) 1 Phill.C.C. 1. This opinion was recognised in *Allen* v. *Thorp* (1843) 7 Beav. 72.
Also *Morris* v. *Howes* (1846) 4 Hare 599, 605, and *Att.-Gen.* v. *Malkin* (1846) 2 Phill.C.C. 64.
See also *Page* v. *Soper* (1853) 11 Hare 321, in which case Wood V.-C. thought himself justified in disregarding *Bulmer* v. *Jay*. See also *Seymour's Trusts* (1859) Johns. 472.
[68] *Att.-Gen.* v. *Malkin* (1846) 2 Phill.C.C. 64, 68.

the next-of-kin would be entitled under a gift to executors and administrators upon evidence of an intention derived from peculiar terms and provisions of the instrument controlling the ordinary and legal sense of the word used; but that such evidence ought to be very strong to justify such a construction. Undoubtedly cases have occurred in which the words "executors and administrators" have been construed as meaning next-of-kin, but it seems that "executors, administrators *and assigns*" are not capable of this interpretation.[69]

When, before 1926, the expressions "representatives," etc., were not construed in the ordinary sense, it was not strictly the next-of-kin, but the persons entitled on intestacy under the Statutes of Distribution to which they referred.[70] These persons took *per stirpes*.[71]

It seems that in wills coming into operation after 1925, "representatives," etc., will be construed, in such cases, to mean the persons entitled under Part IV of the Administration of Estates Act 1925.[72]

If there is a bequest to A, "his executors and administrators,"[73] or to A and "his legal personal representatives,"[74] the law and the testator's intention concur in transferring the absolute interest in the legacy to A[75]; and if A dies before the testator, the legacy will lapse, and cannot be claimed by the executors or administrators.[76]

Where a fund is bequeathed to A for life (or as one of several tenants for life[77]), remainder as he shall appoint, and in default of appointment to his executors, etc., the latter, in default of appointment, take the fund as part of the personal estate of A,[78] so that, in effect, it confers on A an absolute interest, subject to the power (and to the other life estates). A can, therefore, without executing any formal appointment, require an immediate transfer of the corpus of the fund,[79] and can assign the fund absolutely.[80] So where a gift, under a will, subject to a life estate to the testator's widow,

[69] *Grafftey* v. *Humpage* (1838) 1 Beav. 52. And see *Webb* v. *Sadler* (1873) L.R. 8 Ch. 419.

[70] *Cotton* v. *Cotton* (1839) 2 Beav. 67 (overruled, as to another part of the decision, in *Re Brooks* [1928] Ch. 214); thus apparently including a widow: see *Price* v. *Strange* (1820) 6 Madd. 162; but excluding a husband: *Horsepool* v. *Watson* (1797) 3 Ves. 383.

[71] *Booth* v. *Vicars* (1844) 1 Coll. 6; *Martin* v. *Glover* (1844) 1 Coll. 269; *Kilner* v. *Leech* (1847) 10 Beav. 362; *Fielden* v. *Ashworth* (1875) L.R. 20 Eq. 410; *Re Gryll's Trusts* (1868) L.R. 6 Eq. 589; *Re Richards* [1910] 2 Ch. 74. Where the bequest was to the "nearest personal representatives," it was held that the testator's nearest of kin took as joint tenants: *Stockdale* v. *Nicholson* (1867) L.R. 4 Eq. 359.

[72] Compare the meaning of the word "relations" after 1925, Theobald, *Wills*, 13th ed., 1971, paras. 963–968.

[73] *Anderson* v. *Dawson* (1808) 15 Ves. 537.

[74] *Taylor* v. *Beverley* (1844) 1 Coll. 108, 116; *Appleton* v. *Rowley* (1869) L.R. 8 Eq. 139.

[75] *Price* v. *Strange* (1820) 6 Madd. 159, was decided on these grounds, but *quaere* where in that case "legal representatives" should not have been construed as the persons entitled under the Statutes of Distribution: see Jarman, 8th ed., 1951, p. 1611.

[76] See Theobald, *Wills*, 13th ed., 1971, para. 1231.

[77] *Daniel* v. *Dudley* (1841) 1 Phill.C.C. 1; *Att.-Gen.* v. *Malkin* (1846) 2 Phill.C.C. 64. See also *Howell* v. *Gayler* (1842) 5 Beav. 157.

[78] See *Allen* v. *Thorp* (1843) 7 Beav. 72.

[79] *Holloway* v. *Clarkson* (1843) 2 Hare 521.

[80] *Kirkpatrick* v. *Capel*, MS. Sugd.Pow., 8th ed., p. 75. See *Cherry* v. *Boultbee* (1839) 2 Keen 319; *Grafftey* v. *Humpage* (1838) 1 Beav. 52.

and to a life estate to his daughter and her husband and the survivor, with power of appointment to the daughter which was not executed, was in trust to pay the fund "to and for the benefit of her executors or administrators," and the daughter died first, and then the husband, and then the testator's widow, it was held that the daughter's husband, on her death, became entitled to the reversionary interest in the fund as part of her estate.[81] *Secus*, where the trust in default of appointment was in favour of the tenant for life's next-of-kin according to the Statutes of Distribution.[82]

If there is a limitation of a fund to the executors of A, after the death of B and C, it does not fail by the death of B and C in the lifetime of A,[83] and the executors of A at his death are entitled to the fund as part of his residuary personal estate.[84]

Where a testator makes a limitation in favour of personal representatives, *e.g.* as substitutes for legatees who might have predeceased him, they (provided, of course, they survive the testator[85]) take in the character of representatives, and not beneficially.[86] In one case[87] a gift of residue to executors to be disposed of as they should think fit was construed as not being a gift to the executors as individuals but as a gift on trust for the testatrix's next-of-kin.[88]

It is, however, competent to a testator, if he thinks fit, to limit any interest to such persons as shall, at a particular time named by him, sustain a particular character, so that the expressions of the will may clearly entitle the executors or administrators to a beneficial interest, even though the limitation to them should be preceded by a life estate in their testator or intestate.[89]

However, in *Marshall* v. *Collett*,[90] where the trust was for the executors or administrators to and for their own use and benefit, and in *Stocks* v.

---

[81] *Att.-Gen.* v. *Malkin* (1846) 2 Phill.C.C. 64.

[82] *Hansen* v. *Miller* (1844) 14 Sim. 22.

[83] *Horseman* v. *Abbey* (1819) 1 Jac. & W. 381.

[84] *Morris* v. *Howes* (1846) 4 Hare 599. See also *Howell* v. *Gayler* (1842) 5 Beav. 157.

[85] *Re Cousen's Will Trusts* [1937] Ch. 381.

[86] *Ripley* v. *Waterworth* (1802) 7 Ves. 438; *Milner* v. *Harewood* (1811) 18 Ves. 273; *Re Cousen's Will Trusts, supra*; *Re Wray* [1951] Ch. 425. The case of *Evans* v. *Charles* (1795) 1 Anstr. 128, an express decision to the contrary, is no longer good law: *Marshall* v. *Collett* (1835) 1 Y. & C. Ex. 239; *Palin* v. *Hills* (1834) 1 M. & K. 470; *Long* v. *Watkinson* (1852) 17 Beav. 473. See also *Re Henderson* (1860) 28 Beav. 656; *Webb* v. *Sadler* (1873) L.R. 8 Ch. 419, 429, where James L.J. says: "For some time there was an opinion entertained by the courts that the words 'executors and administrators' following a gift for life were to be considered next-of-kin, or that the executors were to take beneficially as '*personae designatae*.' That was acted on in *Palin* v. *Hills* (1834) 1 M. & K. 470, before Lord Brougham, where he reversed a decision of the Master of the Rolls; and for many years there has been no question that 'executors and administrators' mean executors and administrators, and nothing else." And see *ante*, p. 967, n. 57.

[87] *Re Carville* [1937] 4 All E.R. 464.

[88] Contrast *Re Stirling* [1954] 1 W.L.R. 763, where the legacy to the personal representatives was expressly stated not to create a trust and *Re Beatty* [1990] 1 W.L.R. 1508 where there was a fiduciary power.

[89] *Holloway* v. *Holloway* (1800) 5 Ves. 401; *Sanders* v. *Franks* (1817) 2 Madd. 147; *Wallis* v. *Taylor* (1836) 8 Sim. 241. See also the Administration of Estates Act 1925, s.49(*b*).

[90] 1 Y. & C.Ex. 232.

Dodsley,[91] where the trust was for the executors and administrators *absolutely*, it was held that the executor did not take a beneficial interest. And in *Hames* v. *Hames*,[92] it was held, upon the construction of a marriage settlement, that under a limitation to the executors, administrators, or assigns of the settlor, to and for his and their own use and benefit, his executors were not entitled beneficially.[93]

[91] 1 Keen 325.
[92] 2 Keen 646.
[93] See also *Wood* v. *Cox* (1837) 2 M. & Cr. 684; *Stubbs* v. *Sargon* (1837) 3 My. & Cr. 507; *Meryon* v. *Collett* (1845) 8 Beav. 386.

CHAPTER 70

INCAPACITY TO TAKE

The general principle is that on distribution, whether testate or intestate, every person, natural or corporate, is capable of taking under a will, intestacy or partial intestacy except those expressly forbidden.[1] An alien may take on distribution.[2] The categories of persons so forbidden are now considered. This topic is of course linked with the probate jurisdiction to refuse a grant in certain cases.[3]

Bankrupt

A bankrupt takes on distribution but where an interest belongs to or is vested in a bankrupt at the commencement of his bankruptcy, it vests in the trustee in his bankruptcy immediately on the trustee's appointment taking effect and is divisible amongst his creditors.[4] Any property which has been acquired by or devolves upon the bankrupt since the commencement of the bankruptcy may be claimed for the bankrupt's estate by the trustee by notice in writing.[5]

Homicide

There is a general principle that a man is not allowed to have recourse to a Court of Justice to claim a benefit from his crime whether under contract or gift.[6] Thus as a matter of public policy a person guilty of killing another cannot take a benefit under that persons will[7] or intestacy[8] or in any other way arising from the crime.[9] On the other hand the executors of a person who has effected life insurance on his life for the benefit of his wife have a good claim to the moneys forfeited by the wife.[10] Evidence of conviction in a criminal court is admissible in civil proceedings.[11] There thus seems to be no justification for confining the principle to "felonious killing" even

---

[1] *Ante*, p. 19.

[2] See the status of Aliens Act 1914, s.17, as amended by the British Nationality Act 1948, Sched. 4.

[3] See *ante*, pp. 17–24.

[4] Insolvency Act 1986, s.306.

[5] Insolvency Act 1986, s.307.

[6] *Beresford* v. *Royal Insurance* [1938] A.C. 586 at 598 (*per* Lord Atkin) *Davitt* v. *Titcumb* [1990] 2 W.L.R. 168.

[7] *Re Hall* [1914] P. 1; *Re Pitts* [1931] 1 Ch. 546; *Re G.* [1946] P. 183; *Re Giles* [1972] Ch. 544 at 550. *Re K.* [1985] Ch. 85; *Re Royse* [1985] Ch. 22.

[8] *Re Crippen* [1911] P. 108 at 112 (refusal of grant); *Re Sigsworth* [1935] Ch. 89 (not following *Re Houghton* [1915] 2 Ch. 173 at 177); *Re Pollock* [1941] Ch. 219.

[9] *Gray* v. *Barr* [1971] 2 Q.B. 554 (insurance); *Beresford* v. *Royal Insurance* [1938] A.C. 588 (suicide/increase) *Reg* v. *Chief N.I. Commissioner* [1981] 1 Q.B. 758 (widow's allowance).

[10] *Cleaver* v. *Mutual Reserve Fund* [1892] 1 Q.B. 147.

[11] *Re Crippen* [1911] P. 108. Civil Evidence Act 1968, s.11.

before the abolition of felony.[12] This abolition does not affect the position, for section 1 of the Criminal Law Act 1967 abolishes the distinction between felony and misdemeanour but does not affect the crime itself.[13] Conversely suicide ceases under the Suicide Act 1961 to be a crime at all.[14]

The principle stated by Lord Atkin[15] seems wide enough to cover the principles adopted in the contemporary civil law systems which deprive a man of benefits if he (a) intentionally causes or attempts to cause the death if the testator, (b) deprives him of the opportunity to make a will, (c) by fraud, compulsion or threats prevents a disposition *mortis causa*, or (d) invalidates a will in circumstances where it cannot be renewed.[16] The presence or absence of moral culpability is irrelevant.[17]

There is no disability in the case of a non-criminal killing[18] or it seems if the testator confirms his intention by making or re-publishing his will after the injury in question.[19] The burden is on the claimant to show that the killing was not criminal.[20]

The effect of the principle upon a joint tenancy has not been decided by an English court but there is strong Commonwealth authority that the joint tenancy is severed in equity.[21] Only in this way can the criminal survivor be prevented from benefiting from his crime without depriving him, or his estate, of property which by severance he could have made his own at any time.

The destination of the property whose disposition is defeated by the principle passes as if the interest has lapsed.[22] It is not forfeited to the Crown nor does it pass direct to the Crown as *bona vacantia*.[23] It will pass

---

[12] *cf. Re Pollock* [1941] Ch. 222; *Re Callaway* [1956] Ch. 559 at 562. As to grants to criminals see p. 22 *ante*. In *Re Dudman* [1925] Ch. 553 the reference is not to felony but to an act of criminal origin. (Russell J.).

[13] *Re Giles* [1972] Ch. 552.

[14] The publication of "a guide to self deliverance" is not of itself criminal. See *Att-Gen* v. *Able* [1984] Q.B. 795.

[15] See n. 6.

[16] Details differ: see French Code Civil, arts. 727 *et seq.*; German BGB, ss.2339 *et seq.*; Austrian ABGB, arts. 540 *et seq.*; Swiss ZGB, arts. 540 *et seq.*; It. Cod. Civ., arts. 463 *et seq.* Roman law provided for many additional grounds, see Windscheid. *Pandekten*, Vol. 3, 9th ed., ss.670–673.

[17] *Re Giles* [1972] Ch. 544.

[18] *Re Houghton* [1915] 2 Ch. 173; *Re pitts* [1931] 1 Ch. 546 (insanity); *Re Pollock* [1914] Ch. 219 (sanity is presumed in the absence of evidence); *Felstead* v. *The King* [1914] A.C. 534.

[19] See (1914) 30 L.Q.R. 211, article by J. Chadwick. In many civil laws there is no disability if the testator in any way condones the injury, see German BGB, s.2343: Swiss ZGB, art. 540(2): Austrian ABGB, art. 540. The Roman sources do not mention condonation and French and Italian law do not recognise it.

[20] *Re Pollock* [1941] Ch. 219. The burden is, however, to the civil and not the criminal standard of proof. See *Hornal* v. *Neuberger* [1957] 1 Q.B. 247 (fraud in civil proceedings). *Cf. Halford* v. *Brookes* [1991] 1 W.L.R. 428.

[21] *Schobelt* v. *Barber* [1967] 10 R. 349; *Rasmanis* v. *Jurewitsch* (1969) 70 S.R.(N.S.W.) 407; *Re Pechar* [1969] N.Z.L.R. 574; *Re Gore* [1972] I.O.R. 550. The question was not raised in *Re K.* [1985] Ch. 85.

[22] *Cleaver* v. *Mutual Reserve Fund* [1892] 1 Q.B. 147; *Re Callaway* [1956] Ch. 559. *Davitt* v. *Titcumb* [1990] 2 W.L.R. 168.

[23] *Re Callaway* [1956] Ch. 559. But see *per* Walton J. in *Rescott* [1975] 1 W.L.R. 1270 at 1271.

according to the ordinary rules of interpretation and distribution testate or intestate as the case may be,[24] but there is no automatic vesting of the estate and it will be restored to a pardoned criminal.[25]

The Forfeiture Act 1982

This Act enables the Court to modify the operation of the forfeiture rule[26] in cases other than murder[27] where the "justice of the case" requires it.[28] Proceedings have to be brought within three months of the conviction.[29] The forfeiture rule does not preclude an application for family provision.[30] The Act also confers a discretion on the Social Security Commissioner.[31] Although the court may not make an order affecting interests acquired before July 13, 1982 this does not include property held by an executor pending administration of the estate.[32]

Unincorporated group[33]

A gift may be made validly to or in trust for an unincorporated group of persons unless the constitution or rules governing the purposes for which the group may use the fund prevent the members from dealing with it, both capital and income, in any way they please.[34] Difficulty in interpreting the constitution or rules does not affect the validity of the gift itself.[35]

Where, however, the rules of the unincorporated body prevent the members from dealing with the capital of the legacy a gift to the body may be void, on the ground that it is thereby rendered inalienable in perpetuity,[36] although in Re Taylor,[37] Farwell J. said: "if the members of the body defined therein—(that is, in the rules)—are entitled to put an end to the association and to direct the company to divide the funds in its hands among all the members there is nothing which can, in my opinion, render this gift invalid."

---

[24] Re Peacock [1957] Ch. 310.

[25] Doe'd Evans v. Evans (1826) 5 B. & C. 584; Hales Pleas of the Crown, Vol 1.360.

[26] This is defined as the rule of public policy . . . which precludes a person who has unlawfully killed another from acquiring a benefit in consequence of the killing. (s.1(1)).

[27] Forfeiture Act 1982, s.5.

[28] Forfeiture Act 1982, s.2(2).

[29] Forfeiture Act 1982, s.2(3) Re Royse [1985] Ch. 22.

[30] Forfeiture Act 1982, s.3. cf. Re Royse [1985] Ch. 22 at 27.

[31] Forfeiture Act 1982, s.4.

[32] Re K. [1986] Ch. 180 (C.A.).

[33] For more extensive treatment of this topic generally, see Tudor, Charities, 6th ed., 1967, pp. 150 onwards; Morris and Leach, The Rule against Perpetuities, 2nd ed., 1962.

[34] Re Wightwick's Will Trusts [1950] Ch. 260; Re Taylor [1940] Ch. 481, compromised on appeal [1940] Ch. 834; see also Carne v. Long (1860) 2 De G.F. & J. 75; Cocks v. Manners (1871) L.R. 12 Eq. 574; Re Clarke [1901] 2 Ch. 110; Re Prevost [1930] 2 Ch. 383; Re Price [1943] Ch. 422; Leahy v. Att.-Gen. for New South Wales [1959] A.C. 487; Neville Estates Ltd. v. Madden [1962] Ch. 832. Re Lipinski [1976] Ch. 235. See also 87 L.Q.R. 31; Re Grant [1980] 1 W.L.R. 360.

[35] Re Taylor, ante.

[36] Carne v. Long, ante.

[37] [1940] Ch. 481.

Uncertainty

The question whether the gift is void for uncertainty has sometimes arisen. It is now established that the gift is valid if it can be said with certainty that any given individual is or is not a member of the group or class.[38]

A gift be valid even where it is expressed to be for a specific purpose and there is no person or persons named as legatee, or where the person named must, by the terms of the will, hold the gift for some specific purpose; and this is so, even if the purpose stated in the will is not charitable,[39] provided the purpose is sufficiently defined. But where the testator expresses his intention vaguely and in effect leaves it to another to make a will for him, the gift is void for uncertainty,[40] unless it amounts to a fiduciary power of appointment.[41] A gift of a large income to trustees on trust to apply it to maintain the horses and hounds of the testator, together with their stables, kennels and buildings, for a period of 50 years, was held to be valid.[42] A gift of £1,000 to a trustee, to be applied in such manner as he should in his absolute discretion think fit, towards the promotion and furthering of fox-hunting was also held to be valid.[43] Similarly, gifts have regularly been held valid, for the erection of tombs and monuments, where there is no question of uncertainty or perpetuity[44]; likewise a gift for the erection of a Masonic temple.[45] Such gifts are valid although there is no person named as beneficiary or *cestui que trust*, but in so far as gifts by way of trust are concerned, they are regarded as exceptional, and the class of objects to be benefited will not be extended.[46]

Subscribing witness

Where an attesting witness is deprived of his interest under the Will[47] the interest may pass to the next person entitled on the basis of acceleration or there may be a partial intestacy. In one case a testator left by will all his real and personal estate to his wife for life, and after her death to be equally divided between such of his children as should be living at her death, and in the event of any of his daughters being married at his wife's

[38] *Re Gulbenkian* [1970] A.C. 508; McPhail v. *Doulton* [1971] A.C. 424 (*Re Baden* in the courts below); *Re Baden* (*No. 2*) [1972] Ch. 607.

[39] *Re Dean* (1889) 41 Ch.D. 552; *Re Thompson* [1934] Ch. 342. But see *Re Wood* [1949] Ch. 498; *Re Astor's Settlement Trusts* [1952] Ch. 534, and Theobald, *Wills*, 14th ed., p. 143.

[40] *Houston* v. *Burns* [1918] A.C. 337, 342; *Chichester Diocesan Fund* v. *Simpson* [1944] A.C. 341, 371.

[41] *Re Park* [1932] 1 Ch. 580; *Re Abraham* [1969] 1 Ch. 463; *Re Beatty* [1990] 1 W.L.R. 1503.

[42] *Re Dean, ante.*

[43] *Re Thompson* [1934] Ch. 342.

[44] *Trimmer* v. *Danby* (1856) 25 L.J.Ch. 424; *Musset* v. *Bingle* [1876] W.N. 170; *Masters* v. *Masters* (1718) 1 P.Wms. 421.

[45] *Re Turkington* [1937] 4 All E.R. 501.

[46] *Re Astor* [1952] Ch. 534. As to the distinction between trusts and powers, see 26 *Conveyancer* 92; 87 L.Q.R. 31.

[47] The word "will" extends to a codicil, and to an appointment by will. See s.1 of Wills Act 1837. See also Theobald, *Wills*, 13th ed., 1971, paras. 396, 405, 14th ed., p. 139, and *ante*, pp. 124, 134.

decease such proportion as they might be entitled to should be left to them
and their children exclusively, and should in no way be controlled by their
husbands. At the death of the testator's widow one of his daughters was living and had several children. Her husband had been one of the attesting
witnesses of the will. It was held that the gift to the daughter was void
under this section, but that her children were not to be disappointed by her
disability, but took an immediate interest in her share as tenants in common,[48] on the basis of "acceleration."

Section 15 of the Wills Act, though avoiding a devise to the wife of an
attesting witness, *quoad* her interest, does not strike the devise out of the
will. The will must therefore be construed before section 15 is applied.[49]
The donee has no right to a grant in the capacity of beneficiary.[50]

In *Re Taylor, decd.*,[51] Upjohn J. said: "It is, I think, made clear by the
observations of Chitty J. in *Re Townsend's Estate*[52] that if at the time of the
prior estate, whether it be by disclaimer, or witnessing the will, or for some
other reason, the gifts following on that estate are still contingent, there
can be no acceleration[53] for the reason that, the gifts being still contingent,
you cannot tell whether they will take effect. Income cannot be accumulated pending the contingency, for by giving away the life estate the
testator has evinced an intention against acceleration, and therefore
necessarily the income must remain as on a partial intestacy undisposed of,
at all events until the contingency following on the life interest takes
effect."

Section 15 does not extend to wills intended to be and in fact made as
informal wills of soldiers and sailors.[54] A solicitor who fails to advise the
testator of the possible effects of s.15 may be liable in negligence to the
deprived beneficiary,[55] but it is possible for such beneficiary to take if
the doctrine of conditional revocation applies.[56]

Where witness trustee

Section 15 only applies so as to render void beneficial interests given to
witnesses. Thus, where an attesting witness was made universal legatee in
trust for the testator's widow, the bequest was not rendered void under the

---

[48] *Re Clark* (1885) 31 Ch.D. 72; *cf. Jull* v. *Jacobs* (1876) 3 Ch.D. 703; *Re Townsend's Estate*
(1886) 34 Ch.D. 357; but see *Aplin* v. *Stone, post.* See also *Re Priest* [1944] Ch. 58, and *Re
Davies* [1957] 1 W.L.R. 922.
[49] *Re Townsend's Estate, ante*; *Aplin* v. *Stone* [1904] 1 Ch. 543.
[50] See N.C.P.R. 1987, r. 21 (*post*, p. 1231).
[51] [1957] 1 W.L.R. 1043. See also *Re Flower's Settlement Trust* [1957] 1 W.L.R. 401; *Re
Davies, ante*; *Re Scott* [1975] 1 W.L.R. 1260.
[52] *Ante.*
[53] See *Re Scott, supra*, at p. 1266, *per* Walton J.
[54] *Re Limond* [1915] 2 Ch. 240; and see *Re Priest* [1944] Ch. 58.
[55] *Ross* v. *Caunters* [1979] 3 W.L.R. 605. There is no liability in cases where the defendant
solicitor's "contemplation of the plaintiff" was not actual nominate and direct. See *Clarke* v.
Bruce Lance [1988] 1 W.L.R. 881.
[56] See p. 211 *ante.*

statute[57]; and a gift to an abbess to swell a community fund to be administered for the benefit of the community was held not to be invalidated in consequence of the attestation of the will by two nuns, members of the community.[58]

Secret trusts

This principle would seem logically to extend to a secret trust so that if it is established that a witness apparently entitled beneficially in fact holds as trustee upon a secret trust, such trust will not be defeated. Conversely it has been established that a witness entitled beneficially under a secret trust will not be disqualified[59] for his rights are derived from the trust and not the will.

Professional charging clause

A clause in a will enabling a solicitor-executor to charge for all professional business done by him under the will, in the same manner as he might have done had he not been the executor counts as investment income[60] and, is in effect a legacy of profit costs. It cannot be enforced if the solicitor has attested the will.[61] But it is otherwise if a solicitor who attests a will is appointed a trustee thereof *after* the testator's death.[62]

Codicils

Only a gift made by the same instrument as is attested by the legatee is rendered void. Thus, a bequest of a legacy by a will is not void because the legatee attests a codicil which gives him nothing; nor does a residuary legatee of a share of a residue lose it by attesting a codicil which, by revoking legacies, increases the residuary share.[63] A legacy to a person who attests a will may be made operative by a codicil attested by other witnesses, which has the effect of republishing and incorporating the will.[64]

Later marriage

The marriage after attestation of a will of a devisee to one of the attesting witnesses does not affect the validity of the devise.[65] Such supervening

---

[57] *In the Goods of Ryder* (1843) Prerog. 2 Notes of Cas. 462; *Cresswell* v. *Cresswell* (1868) L.R. 6 Eq. 69.

[58] *Re Ray's Will Trusts* [1936] Ch. 520. See also *Kelly* v. *Walsh* [1948] Ir.R. 388 (gift to priest for Masses not invalidated by priest being an attesting witness).

[59] *Re Young* [1951] Ch. 344; and see Theobald, *Wills*, 14th ed., p. 142. As to secret trusts, see article by J. A. Andrews in 27 *Conveyancer* 92.

[60] *Dale* v. *I.R.C.* [1952] Ch. 704.

[61] *Re Barber* (1885) 31 Ch.D. 665; *Re Pooley* (1888) 40 Ch.D. 1.

[62] *Re Royce's Will Trusts* [1959] Ch. 626.

[63] *Gurney* v. *Gurney* (1885) 3 Drewr. 208; *Tempest* v. *Tempest* (1856) 2 K. & J. 635; *Re Marcus* (1887) 57 L.T. 399; *Re Trotter* [1899] 1 Ch. 764.

[64] *Anderson* v. *Anderson* (1872) L.R. 13 Eq. 318. See also *Re Trotter, ante*; and *cf. Re Elcom* [1894] 1 Ch. 303.

[65] *Thorpe* v. *Bestwick* (1881) 6 Q.B.D. 311.

invalidity would not forward the policy of section 15, which is for the protection of testators.[66]

Superfluous witness

A gift to an attesting witness was formerly void even though the will was sufficiently attested by other witness.[67] But where a will had been executed in the presence of two witnesses, and in addition to their signatures the signature of a third person who was also a legatee appeared at the foot of the will, the court received evidence as to why such signature was written, and if satisfied as a question of fact on the evidence that it was not written with the intention of attesting the testator's signature, it ordered it to be omitted from the probate. In this case the validity of the legacy was not affected.[68]

[66] *Re Royce, supra.*

[67] See *Doe* v. *Mills* (1833) 1 Mood. & Rob. 288, a decision on 25 Geo. 2, c. 6, which was followed almost verbatim by s.15 of the Wills Act. *Re Bravda* [1968] 1 W.L.R. 479. Theobald, *Wills*, 14th ed., p. 45.

[68] *Re Sharman* (1869) L.R. 1 P. & D. 661; *Randfield* v. *Randfield* (1860) 8 H.L.C. 225, 228, n. (*c*); *cf. Wigan* v. *Rowland* (1853) 11 Hare 157; *Re Bravda* [1968] 1 W.L.R. 479. See now Wills Act 1968.

CHAPTER 71

ELECTION
(APPROBATION AND REPROBATION[1])

This is conveniently considered under three heads, namely, (1) *Meaning of the doctrine*, (2) *Conditions for the operation of the doctrine* and (3) *What constitutes an election.*

A. MEANING OF THE DOCTRINE

It is a principle of equity[2] that *a person who accepts a benefit under an instrument must adopt the whole, giving full effect to its provisions, and renouncing every right inconsistent with it.*[3] It follows that "if a testator gives property by design or by mistake[4] which is not his to give, and gives at the same time to the real owner of it other property, such real owner cannot take both."[5] In such a case the real owner is put to his election. He may elect to take either under or against the instrument. Where a testator disposes of property in two different countries by two separate wills, the two wills together form one "instrument" for the purposes of this doctrine.[6]

A similar situation may also arise on an intestacy where a child must account for advancements[7] before he can benefit. This principle of "statutory satisfaction"[8] may force a child to elect against his rights on intestacy.

It has been said by Lord Maugham that the doctrine of election corresponds with the doctrine of Scots law that a person cannot approbate and reprobate[9]; and it follows that Scottish decisions on that doctrine are entitled to the highest respect in the English courts.[10]

---

[1] See *Houldsworth* v. *City of Glasgow Bank* (1880) 5 App.Cas. at p. 325.

[2] See further Snell. *Equity*, 28th ed., 495; Maitland's *Equity*, Lecture XIX.

[3] See *Re Macartney* [1918] 1 Ch. 300; *Re Sullivan* [1917] 1 Ir.R. 38.

[4] The majority of cases to which the doctrine is applicable are cases of mistake by the testator. See *Re Mengel* [1962] Ch. 791, 797.

[5] *Per* James V.-C. in *Wollaston* v. *King* (1869) L.R. 8 Eq. 165, 173. The foundation of election is that no one shall claim under and in opposition to the same instrument: Sug. on *Powers*, 8th ed., 576; *cf. per* Chitty J. in *Re Chesham*, 31 Ch.D. at p. 743. See notes to the case of *Dillon* v. *Parker* (1818) 1 Swanst. 396 *et seq.*, and the cases collected in 2 Rop.Leg., 3rd ed., 482 *et seq.*

[6] *Douglas-Menzies* v. *Umphelby* [1908] A.C. 224. There seems to be an implicit application of this doctrine in *Re Berger* [1990] Ch. 118 C.A. For an example of a will expressly and consciously forcing a legatee to elect see *Re Burton's Settlement* [1955] Ch. 82, 101.

[7] As to what is an advancement, see *ante*, p. 953, *post*, p. 1071.

[8] See *post*, p. 1071 and 79 L.S. Gazette 785.

[9] See *Lissenden* v. *C.A.V. Bosch Ltd.* [1940] A.C. 412, 417; see also *Pitman* v. *Crum-Ewing* [1911] A.C. 217, 229.

[10] See n. 1 *ante*.

Basis of the doctrine

The doctrine of election is not based on presumed intention, but "on a rule of equity founded on the highest principles of equity, and as to which the court does not occupy itself in finding out whether the rule was present or was not present to the mind of the party making the will."[11] It was explained by Lord Hatherley in *Cooper* v. *Cooper*[12] as follows:

> "The equitable duty which the law imposes on a person claiming under an instrument, of giving full effect to it, as far as it would be otherwise ineffective, except through his concurrence, is simply this: the law inquires on the death of the testator, when the will comes into operation, what is his intention, as expressed in the whole will, with reference to the disposition of that which he considers to be his property; and it being found clearly and distinctly (for it must be clearly and distinctly found) that he has expressed his intention of disposing of what belongs to another—when once that is ascertained completely, there is nothing else which the law implies, with regard to his intention, beyond the ordinary intent implied in every man who affects by a legal instrument to dispose of property, that he intends all that he has expressed, and, among other things, that he intends to dispose of property as to which he has expressed an intention, though it really does not belong to him. When once that intention is ascertained there is nothing else remaining to be done, with reference to election, than to see who is in possession and who is the real owner of the property; and if you can find him who is the real owner of the property at the same time taking a benefit under the will which has erroneously endeavoured to dispose of his property, then he must give effect to that intention, though founded in error, and give it full effect by either abandoning all his interest under the will, or making compensation to the extent of the value of the disappointed intention of the testator."

Election against the instrument

If the real owner elects to retain his own property he takes against the instrument. He is entitled to take the benefit of the gift made to him by the instrument, but out of such gift he is bound to compensate for their loss the persons to whom his own property was given.[13] The result of election against the instrument is compensation, not forfeiture.[14] *Secus*, where the

---

[11] *Cooper* v. *Cooper* (1874) L.R. 7 H.L. 53, 57, *per* Lord Cairns: *Brown* v. *Gregson* [1920] A.C. 861, 868; *Re Edwards* [1958] Ch. 168; *Re Mengel* [1962] Ch. 791, 796; *Re Gordon* [1978] Ch. 145.

[12] (1874) L.R. 7 H.L. 53, 70.

[13] See note to 1 Swanst. 442. And see *Pickersgill* v. *Rodger* (1876) 5 Ch.D. 163. *Cf. Greenwood* v. *Penny* (1850) 12 Beav. 403.

[14] For the former dispute on this matter, see Mr. Swanston's note to *Gretton* v. *Haward* (1819) 1 Swanst. 433; and that of Mr. Jacob in his edition of Rop. Husb. & Wife, Vol. 1, p. 556.

gift made by the instrument is given upon an express condition that the donee should release some of his property.[15]

The persons disappointed by an election against the instrument are entitled to compensation out of the benefits given by the instrument to the party so electing, in proportion to the value of the interests in respect of which they are disappointed.[16] The amount of the compensation payable must be ascertained as at the testator's death, not at the date of election.[17] If the person electing against the will has been in possession of the property bequeathed to him by the will, there must be an account of rents and profits.[18]

A person electing to take against a will is not thereby precluded from claiming compensation from another person who, by making a similar election, deprives him of benefits given by the will.[19]

Election under the instrument

A person electing to take under the instrument must confirm, so far as he is able, the whole instrument. Thus, if he can, he must release that part of his own property which is disposed of by the will.

Where by reason of an election to take under the instrument property is set free to pass under the instrument, that property becomes subject to all the incidents to which it would have been subject had it been throughout the property of the donor.[17] Thus it becomes liable for the debts of the testator.[20]

Disclaimer of an onerous legacy

The doctrine of election must not be confused with the right of a legatee to disclaim an onerous legacy.[21] Where a testator makes two distinct bequests in the same will to the same person, one of which happens to be onerous and the other beneficial, prima facie the legatee is entitled to disclaim the onerous legacy and to take the other.[22] But, it is a question of the intention of the testator to be gathered from the will, whether the legatee must elect to take all, or none, of the gifts in the will, or whether he may accept the beneficial gifts, and repudiate that which is burdensome.[23] In cases, however, where onerous and beneficial property are included in the

---

[15] See, *e.g. Robinson* v. *Wheelwright* (1856) 21 Beav. 214; 6 De G.M. & G. 535; *Boughton* v. *Boughton* (1750) 2 Ves.Sen. 12.

[16] *Howells* v. *Jenkins* (1863) 1 De. G.J. & S. 617; *Rogers* v. *Jones* (1876) 3 Ch.D. 688.

[17] *Re Hancock* [1905] 1 Ch. 16.

[18] See n. 17.

[19] *Re Booth* [1906] 2 Ch. 321.

[20] *Re Williams* [1915] 1 Ch. 450.

[21] See *ante*, p. 940. A disclaimer does not in general constitute a transfer of value for death duties if made within two years of the testator's death. See *Encyclopedia of Capital Taxation*, para. 1A7–18; Finance Act 1975, s.47 as amended.

[22] *Guthrie* v. *Walrond* (1883) 22 Ch.D. 573; *Syer* v. *Gladstone* (1885) 30 Ch.D. 614; *Re Loom* [1910] 2 Ch. 230; *Re Lysons* (1912) 107 L.T. 146.

[23] *Talbot* v. *Radnor* (1834) 3 M. & K. 254; *Warren* v. *Rudall* (1858) 1 J. & H. 1; *Guthrie* v. *Walrond. ante*. See also art. in 82 S.J. 772.

same gift, the legatee cannot disclaim the onerous and accept the beneficial unless the will manifests a sufficient intention of the testator to the contrary. Thus, a bequest of a leasehold house "together with its contents" is a single gift and not two separate gifts, and the legatee may not disclaim the gift of the house and retain its contents.[24] The gifts may be in substance distinct, though given by one sentence in the will.[25]

A disclaimer of a legacy can, before the property is otherwise applied, be retracted by the legatee.[26] A legacy may be disclaimed by conduct.[27]

Ademption

There is no room for the doctrine of election if the gift has been adeemed. Thus where property was devised specifically to seven named persons and subsequently sold under a specifically enforceable contract to one of them it was held by the Court of Appeal that the gift having been adeemed the "purchaser" beneficiary did not have to elect.[28] The gift was inoperative for all purposes.

B. OPERATION OF THE DOCTRINE

A case of election arises although the testator proceeded on an erroneous supposition that both the subjects of bequests were absolutely at his own disposal,[29] but not if it appears that the testator meant only to dispose of the property provided he had power to do so.[30] The intention of the testator, to dispose of the property which is not his own, should be clear: the intention must appear by demonstration plain, by necessary implication.[31] "A person is not, without strong indications of such an intent, to be understood as dealing with what does not belong to him."[32] Thus it is difficult to raise a case of election on general words only[33]; and where the devise is by

[24] *Re Joel* [1943] Ch. 311, 323, not following dicta of Cotton and Lindley L.JJ. in *Re Hotchkys* 32 Ch.D. 408 at pp. 418, 419, commenting on *Syer* v. *Gladstone* (1885) 30 Ch.D. 614. But see *Re Lysons* (1912) 107 L.T. 146.

[25] *Re Hotchkys, ante; Guthrie* v. *Walrond, ante.* See also *Honywood* v. *Honywood* [1902] 1 Ch. 347; and *cf. Re Holt*, 85 L.J.Ch. 779.

[26] *Re Young* [1913] 1 Ch. 272; *Re Cranstoun* [1949] Ch. 523.

[27] See *Re Clout and Frewer's Contract* [1924] 2 Ch. 230.

[28] *Re Edwards* [1958] Ch. 168.

[29] *Whistler* v. *Webster* (1794) 2 Ves. 370; *Thellusson* v. *Woodford* (1799) 4 Ves. 227; *Welby* v. *Welby*, 2 Ves. & B. 187, 199; *Nayler* v. *Wetherell* (1831) 4 Sim. 114; *Re Brooksbank* (1886) 34 Ch.D. 160.

[30] *Church* v. *Kemble* (1832) 5 Sim, 525.

[31] *Rancliffe* v. *Parkins* (1818) 6 Dow 149, by Lord Eldon; *Johnson* v. *Telford* (1830) 1 Russ. & M. 244; *Crabb* v. *Crabb* (1834) 1 M. & K. 511; *Dillon* v. *Parker* (1833) in Dom.Proc. 7 Bligh (N.S.) 325; *ibid.* 1 Cl. & F. 303; *Clementson* v. *Gandy* (1836) 1 Keen 309. See also *Langslow* v. *Langslow* (1856) 21 Beav. 552; *Tomkyns* v. *Blane* (1860) 28 Beav. 422; *Honywood* v. *Forster* (1861) 30 Beav. 14; *Re Fowler's Trust* (1859) 27 Beav. 362; *Maddison* v. *Chapman* (1861) 1 Johns. & H. 470; *Stephens* v. *Stephens* (1857) 3 Drew. 697; 1 De G. & J. 62; *Wintour* v. *Clifton* (1856) 8 De G.M. & G. 641; *Box* v. *Barrett* (1866) L.R. 3 Eq. 244; *Cooper* v. *Cooper* (1874) L.R. 6 Ch. 15; L.R. 7 H.L. 53; *Orrell* v. *Orrell* (1877) L.R. 6 Ch. 302; *Wilkinson* v. *Dent* (1871) L.R. 6 Ch. 339; *Synge* v. *Synge* (1874) L.R. 9 Ch. 128.

[32] *Dummer* v. *Pitcher* (1832) 5 Sim. 35.

[33] *Re Harris* [1909] 2 Ch. 206; *Re Allen's Estate* [1945] 2 All E.R. 264, 267.

general words, such as "all my lands and hereditaments" or the like, no case for election arises, where there is other property of the testator's sufficient to satisfy the devise itself.[34] Further, the intention to dispose of property not belonging to the testator must appear upon the face of the will, for it seems now to be established that parol evidence is inadmissible for the purpose of showing it.[35]

The property must not be inalienable

Election means free choice, and where the circumstances do not give to the legatee a choice whether he will take under the instrument or against it, he is not put to this election. Thus, where a will purported to bequeath for the benefit of the testator's younger sons chattels which were in fact already settled as heirlooms so that the eldest son had a life interest in them, and then bequeathed the residue to the eldest son, it was held that no question of election arose; for the eldest son, having no power to alienate the chattels,[36] could not have chosen to take under the will.[36]

This principle was formerly applied where the legacy was subject to a restraint on anticipation,[37] and has later been applied where the legacy was given on protective trusts.[38]

Part interests

However, if the person who should be called upon to elect has only a part interest in the property which the testator directs to be transferred, he must nevertheless elect and must do all in his power to make the disposition effective. Suppose, for example, "A testator gives Blackacre or the proceeds of its sale to A. Blackacre in fact belongs to B, C and D as joint tenants and the testator gives legacies to each of these persons. Each of them has a separate and individual right and obligation to elect for or against the will, notwithstanding that the gift to A can only take full effect according to its terms if B, C and D all elect in favour of the will. In other words, a class is not exempted from the principle of election merely

---

[34] *Padbury* v. *Clark* (1850) 2 Mac. & G. 298; *Fitzsimmons* v. *Fitzsimmons* (1860) 28 Beav. 417; *Whitley* v. *Whitley* (1862) 31 Beav. 173; *Howells* v. *Jenkins* (1863) 2 Johns. & H. 706; *Miller* v. *Thurgood* (1864) 33 Beav. 496.

[35] *Stratton* v. *Best* (1791) 1 Ves. 285; *Doe* v. *Chichester* (1816) 4 Dow 65, 76, 78, 89; *Clementson* v. *Gandy* (1836) 1 Keen 309. See the cases, *contra*, collected in the notes to *Dillon* v. *Parker* (1818) 1 Swanst. 402, 403; *Pickersgill* v. *Rodger* (1876) 5 Ch.D. 163, 171, in which case, however, *Clementson* v. *Gandy* and the other authorities to the same effect were not cited.

[36] *Re Chesham* (1886) 31 Ch.D. 466; *Douglas* v. *Douglas* (1854) 24 D. 1191, 1208; *Brown* v. *Gregson* [1920] A.C. 860; *Re Hargrove* [1915] 1 Ch. 398.

[37] *Re Vardon's Trusts* (1885) 31 Ch.D. 275; see also *Re Wheatley* (1884) 27 Ch.D. 606; *Smith* v. *Lucas* (1881) 18 Ch.D. 531.

[38] *Re Gordon* [1978] Ch. 145. Contrast the "election" which can arise under the doctrine of satisfaction, as to which see *MacGarogner* v. *Wieldon* (1866) L.R. 3 Eq. 236, as explained in *Re Gordon, supra*.

because each can contribute only a part of the total subject matter of the gift which the testator has purported to effect."[39]

The doctrine of election is applicable to all interests that are alienable, whether immediate, remote, contingent, of value or not of value.[40]

Exercise of special powers

If the testator under a special power appoints in favour of persons who are not objects of that power, the gift is ineffectual, but if he also benefits the person entitled in default of appointment the latter must elect.[41] He may either claim in default of appointment, compensating the persons in whose favour the appointment was made out of the property given to him by the testator, or he may give up any claim to the property wrongly appointed, and take the full benefit of the testator's gift.

It is the person entitled in default of appointment, not the proper objects of the power, who is put to his election. There must, therefore, be a gift of the testator's own property to him.[42] This gift of the testator's property, if a case of election is ever to arise, must be of his own freely disposable property. An appointment under a special power is not such a gift, for the donor of the power is the real donor of the gift.[43]

If the testator appoints in favour of an object of the special power, but superadds trusts in favour of strangers to the power, the superadded trusts are disregarded, the appointment is treated as valid, and no case of election arises.[44]

An appointment which is *ex facie* void as transgressing some positive rule of English law will be completely disregarded, and no case of election arises.[45] Thus there is no case of election where a testator makes an appointment which is void as contravening the perpetuity rule,[46] although at the same time he gives the persons entitled in default of appointment property of his own.

The properties must devolve together

If the person entitled to elect dies before election and the properties do not devolve upon the same persons beneficially the doctrine cannot apply and the parties will be treated as if there had been an election against the

---

[39] *Re Dicey* [1957] Ch. 145.

[40] *Wilson* v. *Townshend* (1795) 2 Ves. 693, by Lord Loughborough; *Webb* v. *Lord Shaftesbury* (1802) 7 Ves. 480, 481.

[41] *Whistler* v. *Webster* (1794) 2 Ves. 370; *Reid* v. *Reid* (1858) 25 Beav. 469; *Pitmans* v. *Crum-Ewing* [1911] A.C. 217.

[42] *Bristow* v. *Warde* (1794) 2 Ves. 336.

[43] *Re Fowler's Trust* (1859) 27 Beav. 362.

[44] *Carver* v. *Bowles* (1831) 2 Russ. & My. 301; *Churchill* v. *Churchill* (1867) L.R. 5 Eq. 44; *Wollaston* v. *King* (1869) L.R. 8 Eq. 165, 174. But see *Re Neave* [1938] Ch. 793.

[45] *Re Warren's Trusts* (1884) 26 Ch.D. 208. *cf. Re Booksbank* (1886) 34 Ch.D. 160.

[46] See *Re Oliver's Settlement* [1905] 1 Ch. 191; *Re Beales' Settlement, ibid.* 256; *Re Wright* [1906] 2 Ch. 288; *Re Nash* [1910] 1 Ch. 1.

will.[47] Similarly, the doctrine of election does not preclude a party claiming under the will from enjoying an interest which he has derived by operation of law from a person who acquired it by taking in opposition to the will, for no case of election arose at the date of the testator's death.[48]

Creditors are not affected

Nor is the doctrine applicable as against creditors taking the benefit of a devise for payment of debts, and also enforcing their legal claim upon other funds disposed by the will.[49] It has, however, been held that a legacy to a creditor whose claim is statute-barred is bounty, so as to put him to his election under the will.[50]

Election and conflict of laws

Although an English heir was not, in cases which might have arisen before 1926, bound to give effect to a devise by the doctrine of election,[51] this exemption from the obligation to elect did not extend to an heir of foreign land, even though the devise of the foreign land was void under some positive rule of foreign law, and not merely for lack of formality.[52] It has already been shown,[53] however, that no person will be compelled to elect unless it is clear that the testator intended to dispose of his property. Thus, where a testator domiciled in England devised "all his real and personal estates, whatsoever and wheresoever," and had Scottish heritable bonds, which did not pass by the will, for want of certain formalities required by Scots law, the Scottish heir was not put to his election, but was allowed to claim English property under the will without giving up the bonds; for the devise was held to refer only to such property as was capable of being given by such a will.[54]

There does not appear to be any good reason why the exemption formerly enjoyed by the English heir should be extended for the benefit of the persons entitled to share in the distribution of the estate of an intestate under the Administration of Estates Act 1925.

There is some doubt whether the doctrine of election is a matter of the material validity of a will, or of construction, but the better view is that it is the former. Since election is independent of the actual or presumed inten-

---

[47] See *Rogers* v. *Jones* (1876) 3 Ch.D. 688; *Pickersgill* v. *Rodger* (1876) 5 Ch.D. 163; *Re Macartney* [1918] 1 Ch. 300; and see *post*, p. 986.

[48] See, *e.g. Grissell* v. *Swinhoe* (1869) L.R. 7 Eq. 291.

[49] *Kidney* v. *Coussmaker* (1806) 12 Ves. 136; 1 Swanst. 408n.; 1 Pow.Dev. 437, Jarman's ed.

[50] *Re Fletcher's Settlement Trusts* [1936] 2 All E.R. 236.

[51] See 12th ed. of this work, at p. 982; *Re De Virte* [1915] 1 Ch. 920.

[52] *Re Ogilvie* [1918] 1 Ch. 492. See also *Brown* v. *Gregson* [1920] A.C. 860, and, as to the Hague Convention on Succession, p. 16 *ante*.

[53] *Ante*, p. 983.

[54] *Allen* v. *Anderson* (1846) 5 Hare 163; *Maxwell* v. *Maxwell* (1852) 16 Beav. 106; 2 De G.M. & G. 705.

tion of the testator,[55] it is not a question of construing the will to seek out that intention; the will need only be construed in order to ascertain whether the testator intended to make a gift of the property in question.[56] It has been said also[57] that election is a doctrine which fastens on the conscience and refuses to allow a person to take the benefit except on certain conditions.

Two gifts in same will

It has been said that election is only applicable as between a gift under a will and a claim *dehors* the will and adverse to it, not as between one clause in a will and another clause in the same will.[58] For if a testator gives two properties to A, and by another clause gives one of those properties to B, the proper destination of the property will ordinarily be determined as a matter of construction.[59] However special circumstances may occasionally warrant the application of the doctrine of election as between two clauses in the same will.[60] But the proposition stated above is not readily intelligible in the light of other cases and the authority in question can be explained on the ground that the power in question was void for perpetuity and the persons claiming to be objects of the power had no interest in the property.[61]

Death before electing

If a testator devises realty to A, and purports to bequeath some of A's personalty to B, A, as we have seen, is put to his election. If A dies without electing, and all his property devolves upon the same person, that person must elect.[62] If all A's property is shared by several persons, each of those persons has an independent right of election.[63]

On the other hand, if the realty and personalty devolve upon different persons the right of election virtually ceases. The claimants to A's personalty cannot be compelled to release their rights. Thus the realty devised to A will devolve upon the persons entitled to A's realty, but charged with the payment of compensation to B for the loss of A's personalty. This seems to

[55] *Ante*, p. 979.
[56] It is submitted that *Re Allen* [1945] 2 All E.R. 264, which is to the contrary, is wrong: see Dicey and Morris, *Conflict of Laws*, 11th ed., p. 1029.
[57] See *per* Buckley J. in *Re Mengel* [1962] Ch. 791 at 797 commenting on a passage to this effect in Williams 14th ed p. 854.
[58] *Woolaston* v. *King* (1869) L.R. 8 Eq. 165.
[59] See *Wallinger* v. *Wallinger* (1869) L.R. 9 Eq. 301; *Burton* v. *Newbery* (1875) 1 Ch.D. 234; *Bizzey* v. *Flight* (1876) 3 Ch.D. 269. Where a will has the effect of confirming an incomplete settlement the latter becomes a testamentary instrument and is construed as such. (*Ibid. per* Hall V.-C. at p. 274.
[60] As in *Re Macartney* [1918] 1 Ch. 300.
[61] See *Wollaston* v. *King* (1869) 8 Eq. 165, 173.
[62] See *Cooper* v. *Cooper* (1874) L.R. 7 H.L. 53.
[63] *Fytche* v. *Fytche* (1868) L.R. 7 Eq. 494; *Re Dicey* [1957] Ch. 145.

follow from *Pickersgill* v. *Rodger*,[64] in which case A predeceased the testatrix, but, being her son, was deemed to have survived her under section 33 of the Wills Act.[65]

C. WHAT CONSTITUTES AN ELECTION

The inquiry, as to what acts or acquiescence constitute an actual or implied election, must be decided rather by the circumstances of each case than by any general principle. The questions are, whether the parties acting or acquiescing were aware of their rights; whether they intended election; whether they can restore the individuals affected by their claim to the same situation as if the acts had never been performed; or whether these inquiries are precluded by lapse of time.[66]

Right to valuation

A party bound to elect is entitled first to ascertain the value of the funds, and for that purpose may sustain an action to have all necessary accounts taken.[67] An election made under a misconception of the extent of claims on the fund elected is not conclusive.[68]

Irrevocable or final election

The principle determining whether or not an election is final has been stated[69] as follows: "Where a party in his own mind has thought that he would choose one of two remedies, even though he has written it on a memorandum or has indicated it in some other way, that alone will not bind him; but as soon as he has not only determined to follow one of his remedies but has communicated it to the other side in such a way as to lead the opposite party to believe that he has made that choice, he has completed his election and can go no further; and whether he intended it or not, if he has done an unequivocal act . . . an act which would be justifiable if he had elected one way and could not be justified if he had elected the other way—the fact of his having done that unequivocal act to the knowledge of the persons concerned is an election." Hence where two letters declaring a determination to elect in a particular way were not sent to persons who were concerned with or affected by such determination, there was held not to be an irrevocable election.[70]

---

[64] (1876) 5 Ch.D. 163.
[65] See p. 246 *ante*.
[66] See Mr. Swanston's note to *Dillon* v. *Parker* (1818) 1 Swanst. at p. 382 and the cases there collected; *Grissell* v. *Swinhoe* (1869) L.R. 7 Eq. 291; *Cooper* v. *Cooper* (1874) L.R. 6 Ch. 15; L.R. 7 H.L. 53.
[67] 1 Swanst. 382n; *Pigott* v. *Bagley* (1825) M'Clel. & Y. 576, *per* Alexander C.B.
[68] 1 Swanst. 382n.
[69] *Per* Lord Blackburn in *Scarf* v. *Jardine* (1882) 7 App.Cas. 345, 360–361.
[70] In *Re Shepherd* [1943] Ch.8.

Election by infant

Where infants are put to their election, the court may elect for them,[71] and for this purpose will if necessary direct inquiries.[72] But in some cases the infant has been allowed to postpone his election until he comes of age.[73]

[71] *Blunt* v. *Lack* (1856) 26 L.J.Ch. 148; *Lamb* v. *Lamb* (1857) 5 W.R. 772; *Re Chesham* (1886) 31 Ch.D. 466, 472.
[72] *Brown* v. *Brown* (1866) L.R. 2 Eq. 481.
[73] Jarman, *Wills*, 8th ed., 1951, p. 563.

CHAPTER 72

PAYMENT OF LEGACIES—MARSHALLING

The order in which assets are to be applied in payment of debts has been considered as a question of administration.[1] The separate but parallel question of the order in which the estate should be applied in payment of legacies[2] is a matter of distribution and is to be distinguished also from the inter-related question of abatement.[3] In the former case the incidence of the legacies as between other beneficiaries is the main question.[4] In the latter case the estate is insufficient to meet the interests of all beneficiaries and the question is how the deficiency is to be borne. The incidence of pecuniary legacies under the 1925 legislation remains a matter of substantial conflict and difficulty, but it must be remembered that the overriding factor is the interpretation of the will (if any).[5] The topic is best approached in historical sequence.

Order for pecuniary legacies before 1926—rule in *Greville* v. *Browne*[6]

Before 1926, pecuniary legacies, like debts, were payable only out of personalty not specifically bequeathed unless a contrary intention, express or implied, appeared in the will.[7] If the property thus made available was insufficient to satisfy all the legacies in full they abated proportionately. While a contrary intention would be implied, under the rule in *Greville* v. *Browne*,[8] where the residue of the real and personal estate was given in one mass, such an implication operated to charge the realty only if and in so far as the personalty was insufficient. If such a mixed fund was specifically charged with the payment of legacies, the real and personal property comprised in it would be proportionately liable to satisfy the claims of the pecuniary legatees,[9] but realty was only available in priority to personalty

---

[1] See *ante*, pp. 605 *et seq*.
[2] Defined for the purposes of the Administration of Estates Act 1925, by s.55(1)(ix). See *post*, Appendix, p. 1149.
[3] See *post*, p. 1000.
[4] See Ryder, "The Incidence of General Pecuniary Legacies" [1956] C.L.J. 80; also notes by M. J. Albery, Q.C. (1969) 85 L.Q.R. 464, C. H. Sherrin, 120 N.L.J. 352.
[5] See generally Brighouse, *Precedents of Wills and Life Transfers*.
[6] (1859) 7 H.L.C. 689.
[7] *Robertson* v. *Broadbent* (1883) 8 App.Cas. 812.
[8] (1859) 7 H.L.C. 689.
[9] *Roberts* v. *Walker* (1830) 1 R. & My. 752. The same was true if the testator directed payment of the legacies out of the mixed fund. For definition of "pecuniary legacy," see *post*, p. 994.

if the testator showed an intention not only to charge the realty with payment of the legacies but also to exonerate the personalty.

Alterations in 1925

The extent to which these rules were altered by the Administration of
Estates Act 1925 is even now, in some respects, a matter of doubt. Section
33 of the Act imposes a trust for sale on any property as to which the
deceased has died intestate and then provides for the payment out of the
proceeds and out of the ready money of the deceased of the funeral, testamentary expenses and debts, and for a fund to be set aside out of what is
left for the pecuniary legacies. The section applies to any assets undisposed
of by the will other than any which are subject to an express trust for sale[10]
or which consist of a partial interest only in an item of property some other
interest in which has been effectively disposed of.[11] In all such cases the
representatives must clearly set aside out of any surplus after payment of
debts a fund sufficient for the payment of any pecuniary legacies[12] and
must use the fund for that purpose.[13]

If, however, the words "the ready money of the deceased" which appear
in section 33(2) are construed as including the proceeds of an express trust
for sale this could substantially affect the application of section 34(3) which
applies the order of application in Part II of Schedule 1 to the Act.[14]

The main problem; extent of the alterations

The problem which has caused the main difficulty is the impact on the
pre-1926 rules of section 34(3) and Part II of Schedule 1. Although, by the
terms of section 34(3) the statutory order deals with the application of
assets for the payment of funeral, testamentary and administration
expenses, debts and liabilities, none of which terms is apt to include pecuniary legacies, it does concern both pecuniary legatees and other beneficiaries in so far as it lays down the order in which they will be deprived of the
property given to them by the will in order to discharge the liabilities of the
estate. What is still unsettled is whether or not the phrase "subject to the
retention thereout of a fund sufficient to meet any pecuniary legacies" in
paragraphs 1 and 2 of Schedule 1, Part II, amounts to a mandatory direction to the representatives to use as much as is necessary of the property

---

[10] Except, presumably, where there is a total failure of conversion. For text see *post*,
p. 1127.

[11] *Re McKee* [1931] 2 Ch. 145; *Re Beaumont's W.T.s* [1950] Ch. 462; *Re Taylor's Estate &
W.T.s* [1969] 2 Ch. 245. See also *post*, p. 1069.

[12] s.33(2); unless, of course, this is varied by the terms of the will; s.33(7).

[13] *Re Worthington* [1933] Ch. 771: although the C.A. here based its decision on s.34(3) as
well as s.33(2), the absence of any other purpose for which the fund could be used appears to
make the implication that it must be used for payment of the legacies a necessary one. See
also *Re Taylor's Estate, supra*, at p. 251.

[14] See the note by M. J. Albery, Q.C., in (1969) 85 L.Q.R. 464.

undisposed of, and, in so far as this is insufficient, the residuary estate (whether these classes of assets consist of real or personal property or both) in providing a pecuniary legacy fund. If this phrase is mandatory it alters by a side-wind the basic principles in force before the Act.[15]

Conflicts in the case law on pecuniary legacies since 1925

In a series of cases after 1925, almost all of them concerned with whether on partial intestacy property undisposed of by the will[16] was available for the provision of pecuniary legacies before that comprised in an effective residuary gift, the courts have assumed[17] that the statutory order provides an order for the application of assets for payment of legacies as well as debts.[18] The first definite decision to this effect came in *Re Worthington*[19] where section 33, which in the circumstances produced the same results, was applicable and indeed relied on by the Court of Appeal, although *Re Gillett's Will Trusts*,[20] where the statutory order was conceded to apply unless varied by the will, contained an express trust for sale and thus cannot be explained on the same basis. The origin of the contrary line of authority lies in *Re Thompson*,[21] where the view that Part II of Schedule 1 covered the incidence of pecuniary legacies was firmly rejected. In *Re Beaumont's Will Trusts*,[22] Danckwerts J., deriving assistance from the reasoning in *Re Thompson*, held that where section 33 was excluded[23] the incidence of pecuniary legacies was governed by the rules laid down before the 1925 legislation, so that the whole residuary estate, and not merely a lapsed share of residue, was liable for the provision of those legacies.[24]

Somewhat surprisingly, the same learned judge, in the later case of *Re Martin*,[25] came to a directly opposite conclusion, holding that the statutory order operated to charge pecuniary legacies on undisposed of realty in

---

[15] Another question which has given rise to difficulty in relation to payment of both legacies and debts is that of how the statutory order can be effectively varied; see *ante*, pp. 608 *et seq.*

[16] Including a lapsed or revoked share of residue; *Re Lamb* [1929] 1 Ch. 722; *Re Tong* [1931] 1 Ch. 202; *Re Taylor* [1969] 2 Ch. 245.

[17] Probably because, before the Act, debts and legacies were governed by a single set of rules.

[18] *Re Lamb, supra*; *Re Kempthorne* [1930] 1 Ch. 268, *per* Lawrence L.J. at p. 298; *Re Harland-Peck* [1941] Ch. 182. See also *Re Feis* [1964] Ch. 106. All these cases could have been decided in the same way on the basis that s.33(2), rather than s.34(3) applied.

[19] [1933] Ch. 771.

[20] [1950] Ch. 462.

[21] [1936] Ch. 676; although as the question in issue was whether realty and personalty given in one mass were liable proportionately, and the decision that they were not is not incompatible with the application of Sched. 1, Part II, the view that it had no application was strictly *obiter*: see *Re Martin* [1955] Ch. 698.

[22] [1950] Ch. 462. *Re Gillett's W.T.s* was not cited.

[23] As it was in that case by an express trust for sale.

[24] The decision in *Re Thompson, supra*, was followed in *Re Rowe* [1941] Ch. 343 and *Re Anstead* [1943] Ch. 161, but both proceeded on the assumption that Sched. 1, Part II, was applicable.

[25] [1955] Ch. 698.

priority to residuary personalty, while, in the same year, in *Re Midgley*,[26] Harman J. also regarded section 34(3) as applicable and Schedule 1, Part II, as mandatory in that the representatives are required both to set aside a fund for the payment of the pecuniary legacies from undisposed of, and, if that is insufficient, residuary, property, and to use the fund for that purpose. The authorities were thus left in an unsatisfactory state, with *Re Gillett's Will Trusts*[27] and *Re Midgley*[28] irreconcilable with, and the reasoning in *Re Worthington*[29] and *Re Martin*[30] inconsistent with, the decision in *Re Beaumont*.[31]

For several years, little fresh light was thrown on the problem,[32] but the issue arose once more in 1969 in *Re Taylor's Estate and Will Trusts*,[33] where, after reviewing the more important authorities, Salt Q.C. Ch. decided to follow *Re Beaumont* and, as section 33 was excluded, to apply the pre-1926 law. His main reasons apart from the wording of section 34(3) itself appear to have been that to construe section 34(3) as governing the incidence of pecuniary legacies would make it inconsistent with section 33(2), under which such legacies are to be paid out of the surplus remaining after the debts and other liabilities had been discharged, and would substitute for the pre-1926 law a new conception for the provision of pecuniary legacies, favouring them, in the case of property undisposed of by the will, above the debts. So far as the wording of the statutory order itself is concerned, "subject to the retention thereout" in paragraphs (1) and (2) may be regarded as a curious formula if the legislature intended to impose, as in section 33(2), an obligation to retain a pecuniary legacy fund, while paragraph (5), dealing with the fund "if any" retained to meet pecuniary legacies, seems to contemplate that in some cases pecuniary legacies may be given, but no fund retained for their payment.[34] While it is considered that

---

[26] [1955] Ch. 576.

[27] [1950] Ch. 462.

[28] In which, while he doubted the reasoning in *Re Beaumont's W.T.s*, *supra*, Harman J. did not finally refuse to follow it, apparently distinguishing it on the ground (surely untenable in view of decisions such as *Re Tong*, *supra*) that the position might be different where, as in *Re Beaumont*, the intestacy was not apparent on the face of the will. See article by Ryder [1956] C.L.J. 80, 96.

[29] [1933] Ch. 771.

[30] Which, like *Re Worthington*, but unlike *Re Midgley*, where there was an express trust for sale, could have been decided in the same way on the basis of s.33: see the criticism of that decision in *Re Taylor's Estate* at p. 251.

[31] [1950] Ch. 462.

[32] The question was discussed, *obiter*, in *Re Berrey's W.T.s* [1959] 1 W.L.R. 30 (see also (1959) 23 Conv.(N.S.) 139), and in *Re Feis*, *supra*, and *Re Wilson* [1967] Ch. 53 the statutory order was assumed to apply. By 1969 the reported cases in which the statutory order had been applied were more numerous than those in which it had been rejected.

[33] [1969] 2 Ch. 245. For a criticism of this decision, see the article by Mr. M. J. Albery, Q.C., in (1969) 85 L.Q.R. 464.

[34] *Quaere* whether this last point does not read rather too much into the drafting of the Act. Another point taken by Professor Ryder, at p. 83, is that if the statutory order is varied so as to exonerate the undisposed-of and residuary estate, paras. (1) and (2) must in any case be inapplicable and the pre-1926 rules on pecuniary legacies apply. It would be odd if the fact that even a small part of the debts were payable out of the property dealt with by those paras. made so great a change in the position of legatees.

this is the correct view,[35] and that section 34(3) should not be used to effect, by a side-wind, a radical change in the existing rules on a question on which it neither purported nor was intended to legislate, it is open to doubt whether the interpretation of paragraphs (1) and (2) of Schedule 1, Part II, accepted by Salt Q.C. Ch, is wholly satisfactory. While he was apparently prepared to read into paragraph 1 following the phrase "subject to setting aside a fund to meet pecuniary legacies" some such words as "where appropriate" or "at the discretion of the personal representatives," the better approach, and that which his own view of the law shows he intended, is to insert instead into paragraphs (1) and (2) words charging the fund used to pay the pecuniary legacies on such property, but such property only, as was available for that purpose under the rules in force before the Act.[36]

A further problem—realty and personalty

The other and related problem has been the extent to which the Act has, where both real and personal property are available for the payment of pecuniary legacies, altered the basic rule that the latter is the primary fund. The problem may arise where, under section 33, undisposed of realty and personalty are both, after payment of the debts, made subject to a charge for provision of a pecuniary legacy fund, and, applying the reasoning used in the cases cited below, the view might be taken that the Act alters the pre-existing law only to the extent of making realty available if personalty is insufficient.[37] Likewise, where there is real and personal property, whether undisposed of or comprised in a residuary gift,[38] to which section 33 does not apply, the better view[39] appears to be that the pre-1926 law still applies, and that personalty alone is available save in so far as the will provides to the contrary, either expressly or by implication under the rule in *Greville* v. *Browne*.[40] Even in the latter case, or in one where, contrary to the conclusions reached above, the statutory order is regarded as making realty available where it would not otherwise have been, the personalty

[35] Contrary to the view taken in *Re Martin* and *Re Midgley* that there would be no point in directing retention of the fund in paras. (1) and (2) unless it was to be used to pay the pecuniary legacies, such a fund was necessary, as part of the scheme for application of assets for discharge of the debts, but in any case this question leaves untouched the central issue of whether the statutory order prescribes the assets from which the fund is to be set aside.
[36] This was suggested in earlier editions of this work, see 13th ed., p. 981; Ryder, p. 84.
[37] *cf.* Ryder at p. 97, who argues in effect that where the whole real and personal residuary estate is undisposed of, s.33 produces a situation which should be treated in the same way as that where the testator directs payment of legacies out of a mixed fund.
[38] While cases such as *Re Rowe, supra,* and *Re Ridley* [1950] Ch. 415 were at one time thought to show that even after 1925 a residuary gift of realty was impossible, the contrary decision was reached in *Re Wilson, supra.*
[39] Accepted in *Re Thompson* and *Re Rowe*; *Re Anstead*, which is apparently to the contrary, is a case where *Greville* v. *Browne* would apply. *cf. Re Harland-Peck, supra*, which considered that s.32 placed real and personal property on an equal footing for payment of both debts and legacies.
[40] Decisions such as that of Vaisey J. in *Re Timson* [1953] 1 W.L.R. 1361 suggest that the court will somewhat readily see in the will indications of intention to treat the realty and personalty as a single fund for this purpose.

should, it seems, remain the primary fund unless the will contains provisions which before 1926 would have made realty liable proportionately or in priority.

Charge of pecuniary legacies does not apply to specific gifts

It may here be mentioned that a general charge of pecuniary legacies upon the whole real and personal estate will not, in the absence of an intention to the contrary,[41] be allowed to operate as a charge in derogation of specific devises or bequests.[42]

Fund for pecuniary legacies

The retention of a fund under paragraphs (1) and (2) of Schedule 1, Part II, to the Administration of Estates Act 1925[43] to meet pecuniary legacies operates so as to make pecuniary legacies abate[44] rateably under paragraph (5). The liability of pecuniary legacies is thus substantially the same as it was before 1926.[45]

Care should be taken lest the operation of the provisions for the retention of a fund be unintentionally negatived. Indeed it seems inexpedient in drafting a will to provide for legacies to be paid out of residue. If such a trust should be construed to negative the provisions in paragraphs (1) and (2), this may operate to the prejudice of the legatees. Where a pecuniary legacy is not given generally, but only out of a particular fund the legatee can have recourse only to that fund.[46] Thus, if upon the construction of the will the legatees or portioners are only entitled to payment out of the residue, if the residue is exhausted the legatees will receive nothing. This would be an unnecessary loss if the debts were not also sufficient to exhaust property appropriated for, or charged with, debts under paragraphs (3) and (4).

Definition of "pecuniary legacies"

A "pecuniary legacy" includes an annuity, a general legacy, and any other direction by a testator for the payment of money, including all death duties free from which any devise, bequest or payment is made to take effect.[47]

[41] See *Bank of Ireland* v. *McCarthy* [1898] A.C. 181, 185.
[42] *Spong* v. *Spong* (1829) 1 Dow & C. 365; *Conron* v. *Conron* (1858) 7 H.L.C. 168. See also *Mannox* v. *Greener* (1872) L.R. 14 Eq. 456.
[43] See *post*, pp. 998, 1152 and *ante*, p. 618.
[44] Interest on legacies does not abate; it is not a legacy, nor a bounty of the testator: *Re Wyles* [1938] Ch. 313.
[45] *Clifton* v. *Burt* (1720) 1 P.Wms. 678, 680; *Re Salt* [1895] 2 Ch. 203.
[46] *Kirke* v. *Kirke* (1828) 4 Russ. 435, 449. See *Spurway* v. *Glynn* (1804) 9 Ves. 483, *Hancox* v. *Abbey* (1805) 11 Ves. 179; *Gittins* v. *Steele* (1818) 1 Swanst. 24; *Rickets* v. *Ladley* (1826) 3 Russ. 418; *Roberts* v. *Roberts* (1843) 13 Sim. 336; *Dickin* v. *Edwards* (1844) 4 Hare 273, 276; *Fream* v. *Dowling* (1855) 20 Beav. 624; *Ion* v. *Ashton* (1860) 28 Beav. 379; *Sinnett* v. *Herbert* (1871) L.R. 12 Eq. 201. *cf. Mann* v. *Copland* (1817) 2 Madd. 223 and Williams, *Executors*, 14th ed., p. 593, n. 16.
[47] Administration of Estates Act 1925, s.55(1)(ix). As to gifts "free of duty," see *ante*, pp. 78 *et seq.*

It also includes a demonstrative legacy so far as it is not discharged out of the designated property.[48] But to the extent that it is so discharged it is a specific legacy, and comes within paragraph (6).[49]

Specific gifts liable rateably

Property specifically devised or bequeathed is liable rateably according to value under paragraph (6). For the purpose of ascertaining the value of property, an incumbrance charged upon the property at the death of the deceased so as to come within section 35[50] must be deducted from the value of the property,[51] as assessed for probate and not as at the date of distribution.[52]

On the other hand, it is submitted that the value of a legacy or portion charged on the property specifically devised or bequeathed will not, as a general rule, be so deducted. A legacy generally has priority to the property on which it is charged, and should not be reduced unless the property charged, after payment of debts, is insufficient to bear the whole legacy. Thus, while the property charged will abate according to its gross value (less incumbrances), the legacy itself will not abate at all.[53] This would seem to be so whether the legacy is charged on property specifically given in exoneration of the rest of the estate, or whether it is merely a charge in aid of the fund comprised in paragraph (5).[54]

It may be apparent from the words of the will, however, that the testator intended the legacy and the property on which it is charged to abate rateably.[55] If so effect can only be given to the testator's intention by making the legacy and the property charged, less the value of the legacy, abate rateably under paragraph (6) with other property specifically devised or bequeathed.

Controlled election

It is a general principle of equity that, if a claimant has two funds to which he may resort, a person having an interest in one only has a right to compel the former to resort to the other, if that is necessary for the satisfaction of both.[56] This principle is not confined to the estate of a deceased person, but applies wherever the election of a party having two funds will

---

[48] Administration of Estates Act 1925, s.55(1)(ix).
[49] See *Sellon* v. *Watts* (1861) 9 W.R. 847.
[50] *Ante*, pp. 607 *et seq.*
[51] *Re Cohen* [1960] Ch. 179.
[52] *Re John* [1933] Ch. 370.
[53] See *Raikes* v. *Boulton* (1860) 29 Beav. 41; *Re Saunders-Davies* (1887) 34 Ch.D. 482; *Re Bawden* [1894] 1 Ch. 693. As to abatement, see *post*, p. 1000.
[54] For Sched. 1, Pt. II, of the Administration of Estates Act 1925, see *post*, p. 1152, and *ante*, p. 615.
[55] See *Re Saunders-Davies* (1887) 34 Ch.D. 482, 493.
[56] *Aldrich* v. *Cooper*, 8 Ves. 382, 388; *Tidd* v. *Lister* (1853) 3 De G.M. & G. 857, 872; *Haynes* v. *Forshaw* (1853) 11 Hare 93; *Legh* v. *Legh* (1846) 15 Sim. 135; *Finch* v. *Shaw* (1854) 19 Beav. 500; *Gibson* v. *Seagrim* (1855) 20 Beav. 614; *South* v. *Bloxham* (1865) 2 H. & M. 457.

disappoint the claimant having the single fund. Accordingly, a Court of
Equity will, if necessary, control that election, and compel the one to
resort to that fund which the other cannot reach.[57]

Marshalling

As between creditors—subrogation[58]

The more general practice, however, is to protect the claimant on the
single fund by marshalling the assets. The claimant on both funds (A and
B) may satisfy his claim as he pleases. But to the extent to which he prejudices the claimant on the single fund (A), by resorting to that fund, the
claimant on the single fund (A) is subrogated[59] to his rights over what
remains of the other fund (B).

The practical importance of the doctrine of marshalling assets has much
diminished since the passing of the Administration of Estates Act 1925. If
the estate of a testator is solvent all creditors have a right to resort to any
property of the deceased subject to the rights of incumbrancers.[60] Incumbrancers may rest upon or realise their securities; but they have the
alternative of satisfying their claims, like all other creditors, out of the
general assets. If an incumbrancer adopts this alternative, to the extent
that his claim is cleared, his charge decreases. Thus, as the charge
decreases, the value of the property charged, available for the payment of
creditors generally, increases. The unsecured creditors are not prejudiced
and no question of marshalling arises.

On the other hand, if the estate is insolvent the bankruptcy rules apply.[61]
Under these rules a secured creditor is not allowed to prove for the whole
of his debt without releasing his security. If he relies on his security he can
only prove *pari passu* with other creditors for the balance of his debt over
and above the value or the proceeds of his security.[62]

However, in the administration of an estate (whether solvent or insolvent) or otherwise, a case of marshalling may still arise as between secured
creditors where one debt is secured on two properties, the other on only
one of such properties.[63]

As between beneficiaries

A similar equity extends in favour of beneficiaries. Before 1926, unless
the testator expressed an intention to the contrary, his general personalty
was primarily liable for the payment of debts[64] not coming within the pro-

[57] See Fonbl.Treat.Eq.B. 3, c. 2, s.6, n. (*i*).
[58] As to subrogation see also p. 726, *ante*.
[59] See n. 58.
[60] See *ante*, p. 607.
[61] Administration of Estates Act 1925, s.34(1); Sched. 1, Pt. I.
[62] See the Insolvency Rules 1986 (S.I. 1986 No. 1925), r. 109(1). *Re Hopkins* (1881) 18
Ch.D. 370.
[63] See *South* v. *Bloxham* (1865) 2 H. & M. 457.
[64] *Manning* v. *Spooner* (1796) 3 Ves. 114, 117; and Williams, *Executors*, 11th ed., p. 1330.

visions of Locke King's Acts.[65] This, however, did not prejudice the right of any creditor to proceed against the realty. The creditor having both realty and personalty to resort to, the heir having only the realty, a case of marshalling arose. If the creditor resorted to the common fund of realty, the heir could stand in the place of the creditor and recoup his losses out of the general personal estate not specifically bequeathed, exonerated or exempted.[66] The right to marshal against personal assets extended not only to the heir, but also to a general[67] or particular devisee.[68]

Conversely, the creditor might proceed against and exhaust the personalty, in which case a pecuniary legatee, who had no claim in the first instance against the real estate, could stand in the place of the creditor and so satisfy his legacy out of the real estate descended.[69]

Again, where land was primarily liable under Locke King's Acts[70] to bear an incumbrance charged thereon, if the incumbrancer proceeded against other property, the persons beneficially interested in such property, whether as specific,[71] pecuniary or residuary legatees, next-of-kin, or otherwise, could marshal against the land charged. Indeed, it appears that, even though the operation of Locke King's Acts was negatived, a pecuniary legatee was preferred to, and could therefore marshal against, the devisee of the land incumbered, unless the testator showed an intention to the contrary.[72]

The principle underlying this form of marshalling is that "the choice of the creditors shall not determine, whether the legatees shall be paid, or not."[73]

Prior claims not prejudiced by marshalling

The right of a beneficiary to marshal, however, was not allowed to prejudice any person, whether creditor[74] or beneficiary,[75] having a prior claim to be satisfied. Thus the specific or residuary[76] devisee could marshal against

---

[65] For these Acts, see *ante*, pp. 608 *et seq.*

[66] *Manning* v. *Spooner* (1796) 3 Ves. 114, 117; *Harmood* v. *Oglander* (1803) 8 Ves. 106, 124. Including personalty appointed by will under a general power: *Re Hartley* [1900] 1 Ch. 152.

[67] *Lutkins* v. *Leigh* (1734) Cas.temp.Talb. 54.

[68] *Popley* v. *Popley*, 2 Chanc.Cas. 84; *Galton* v. *Hancock* (1745) 2 Atk. 427, 436. Or rentchargee: *Re Fry* [1912] 2 Ch. 86.

[69] *Bowman* v. *Reeve* (1721) Prec.Chanc. 578; *Lutkins* v. *Leigh* (1734) Cas.temp.Talb. 54; *Hanby* v. *Roberts* (1751) Ambl. 128. See also *Binns* v. *Nichols* (1866) L.R. 2 Eq. 256.

[70] As to which, see *ante*, p. 608.

[71] *e.g.* a specific legatee of a mortgaged leasehold has no contribution towards his mortgage from other specific legatees of leasehold: *Halliwell* v. *Tanner* (1830) 1 Russ. & M. 633; *Wythe* v. *Henniker* (1833) 2 M. & K. 635; *Johnson* v. *Child* (1844) 4 Hare 87; unless that is the testator's intention: *Middleton* v. *Middleton* (1852) 15 Beav. 450.

[72] *Lutkins* v. *Leigh*, *ante*; *Re Smith* [1899] 1 Ch. 365.

[73] By Lord Eldon in *Aldrich* v. *Cooper* (1803) 8 Ves. 382, 396; *Re Cohen* [1960] Ch. 179. *cf.* *Leedale* v. *Lewis* [1982] 1 W.L.R. 1319 at 1335.

[74] *Bartholomew* v. *May* (1737) 1 Atk. 487.

[75] *Oneal* v. *Mead* (1720) 1 P.Wms. 693; *Tipping* v. *Tipping*, *ibid.* 729, 736.

[76] See *Hensman* v. *Fryer* (1867) L.R. 3 Ch. 420; *Lancefield* v. *Iggulden* (1874) L.R. 10 Ch. 136; *Gibbins* v. *Eyden* (1869) L.R. 7 Eq. 371.

a residuary or pecuniary legatee, but could only marshal against a specific legatee so as to make the latter contribute rateably to the payment of debts.[77] The specific legatee had a corresponding right to make specific and residuary devisees contribute.[78] A pecuniary legatee, though he could marshal against real estate appropriated to,[79] or charged with[80] the payment of debts, could not marshal against a specific[81] or residuary[82] devisee in respect of property not so appropriated or charged, unless such realty was primarily liable for the discharge of the debt under Locke King's Acts.[83]

In other words, this form of marshalling was the method of adjustment whereby the order of liability of the assets of a deceased person, to bear his debts,[84] was ultimately enforced as between persons beneficially interested in the estate. If the testator by his will varied this order, the consequential rights of the beneficiaries to marshal varied accordingly.[85]

How rights affected by the Administration of Estates Act 1925

This right to marshal is not affected by the Administration of Estates Act 1925,[86] save that the order of application of assets has been altered.[87] For instance, a residuary devisee can no longer marshal against a pecuniary legatee,[88] a pecuniary legatee can now marshal against a residuary devisee.[89] But specific devisees and legatees must still contribute rateably for the payment of debts.[90]

---

[77] *Tombs* v. *Roch* (1846) 2 Coll. 490; *Gervis* v. *Gervis* (1847) 14 Sim. 654; for specific and residuary devises and specific legacies were liable *pro rata* before 1926: *Manning* v. *Spooner* (1796) 3 Ves. 117; *Farquharson* v. *Floyer* (1876) 3 Ch.D. 109; *Jackson* v. *Pease* (1874) L.R. 19 Eq. 96.

[78] *Long* v. *Short* (1717) 1 P.Wms. 403; *Tombs* v. *Roch, ante*; *Gervis* v. *Gervis, supra*; unless there was an intention to the contrary: *Bateman* v. *Hotchkin* (1847) 10 Beav. 426.

[79] *Manning* v. *Spooner, ante*; *Phillips* v. *Parry* (1856) 22 Beav. 279.

[80] *Foster* v. *Cook* (1791) 3 Bro.C.C. 347; *Paterson* v. *Scott* (1852) 1 De G.M. & G. 531; *Surtees* v. *Parkin* (1854) 19 Beav. 406; *Re Stokes* (1892) 67 L.T. 223. This was not affected by the Land Transfer Act 1897: *Re Kempster* [1906] 1 Ch. 446; *Re Balls* [1909] 1 Ch. 791. Nor is it affected by the Administration of Estates Act 1925, *ante*, p. 995.

[81] *Clifton* v. *Burt* (1720) 1 P.Wms. 679; *Scott* v. *Scott* (1759) Ambl. 383; *Hanby* v. *Roberts* (1741) Ambl. 128; *Keeling* v. *Brown* (1800) 5 Ves. 359; *Aldrich* v. *Cooper* (1803) 8 Ves. 382, 397.

[82] *Mirehouse* v. *Scaife* (1837) 2 M. & Cr. 695. *Hensman* v. *Fryer* (1867) L.R. 3 Ch. 420, in which Lord Chelmsford decided that residuary realty and pecuniary legacies contributed rateably, has not been followed: *Collins* v. *Lewis* (1869) L.R. 8 Eq. 708; *Dugdale* v. *Dugdale* (1872) L.R. 14 Eq. 234; *Tomkins* v. *Colthurst* (1875) 1 Ch.D. 626; *Farquharson* v. *Floyer* (1876) 3 Ch.D. 109.

[83] See *ante*, p. 608.

[84] As to the order of application of the solvent estate of a person dying before 1926, see the 11th ed. of this work, p. 1330.

[85] See, *e.g. Bateman* v. *Hotchkin* (1847) 10 Beav. 426; *Raikes* v. *Boulton* (1860) 29 Beav. 41; *Re Saunders-Davies* (1887) 34 Ch.D. 482; *Re Bawden* [1894] 1 Ch. 693.

[86] See the Administration of Estates Act 1925, s.2(3)(*a*) (*post*, p. 1114).

[87] *Ibid.* ss.34(3), 35, and Sched. 1, Pt. II (*post*, pp. 1128, 1129, 1152).

[88] For a residuary devise is liable under para. (2), a pecuniary legacy under para. (5) of *ibid.* Sched. 1, Pt. II, *Secus*, before 1926, *ante*, p. 997.

[89] See n. 88.

[90] They are liable under *ibid.* para. (6); this was also their position before 1925: see above; p. 995; *Re Cohen* [1960] Ch. 179.

Again, the extension of the principle of Locke King's Acts to property generally,[91] and the corresponding assimilation of the rules affecting realty and personalty to be found in the new order of application of assets,[92] has altered the rights of beneficiaries to marshal.

If the testator varies the order of application of assets for the payment of his debts, the rights of beneficiaries to marshal will vary accordingly.[93]

Where special fund is exhausted

If a testator sets apart a special fund for the payment of liabilities, some of which would otherwise have been payable out of specific gifts, some out of residue, and the fund proves insufficient, all the liabilities are payable out of the fund rateably. The specific devisees and legatees have no right, by marshalling or otherwise, to insist upon the fund being first applied in discharging their liabilities so as to cast upon the residue the remaining unsatisfied liabilities.[94]

Legacy charged on realty

Another instance of marshalling the assets in favour of legatees occurs where one or more legacies are charged on the real estate, and there is another legacy which is not so charged. There the legatee, whose legacy is not so charged, may stand in the place of the former legatees, to be satisfied out of the real estate.[95]

---

[91] *Ibid.* s.35; *ante*, p. 608.
[92] In *ibid.* Sched. 1, Pt. II, "property" is dealt with throughout.
[93] See n. 85, *supra*.
[94] *Re Townley* [1922] 1 Ch. 154.
[95] *Bligh* v. *Lord Darnley* (1731) 2 P.Wms. 620; *Bonner* v. *Bonner* (1807) 13 Ves. 379; 2 M. & Cr. 700. There is no distinction between the case of a class of legacies and a case of individual legacies; for the court presumes that the testator's intention in charging the land is that all the legacies shall be paid in full: *Scales* v. *Collins* (1853) 9 Hare 656.

CHAPTER 73

ABATEMENT

Before considering the abatement of legacies and annuities it is necessary to consider the different categories of legacy and annuity. These will be found in the works on Wills.[1] So far as legacies are concerned the topic is here confined to a brief study of specific, general, demonstrative and pecuniary legacies. A specific legacy is a bequest of a specified part of the testator's personal estate which is so distinguished.[2] A general legacy is a bequest of some thing or money, not necessarily part of the estate and not distinguished from all others of the same kind. a demonstrative legacy is a legacy given with reference to a particular source from which it is to be met. A pecuniary legacy is a legacy of money.[3] Categorisation is a matter partly of construction and partly of evidence.[4]

Specific legacies

A gift of general residue does not become specific because a specific part of the personalty is excepted out of it.[5] Thus, for example, "I give a diamond ring" is a general legacy, which may be fulfilled by the delivery of any ring of that kind; while "I give the diamond ring presented to me by A" is a specific legacy, which can only be satisfied by the delivery of the identical subject. Again, if the testator, having many brooches or horses, bequeathed "a brooch" or "a horse" to B, the legacy is general.[6] But a bequest of "such part of my stock of horses which A shall select, to be fairly appraised, to the vale of £800,"[7] or of "all the horses which I may have in my stable at the time of my death,"[8] is specific.

---

[1] See Jarman, *Wills*, 8th ed., 1951, pp. 1034 *et seq.*; Theobald, *Wills*, 14th ed. 227 *et seq.* For precedents, see Brighouse's *Precedents of Wills and Life Transfers*.

[2] For further definitions of specific legacies, see *Bothamley* v. *Sherson* (1875) L.R. 20 Eq. 304, 308, 309, *per* Jessel M.R.; *Giles* v. *Melsom* (1873) L.R. 6 H.L. 24, 29, *per* Lord Selborne; *Robertson* v. *Broadbent* (1883) 8 App.Cas. 812, 815 *per* Lord Selborne.

[3] For definition, see *ante*, p. 994.

[4] Evidence of circumstances (but not of actual intention) is admissible. See *Att.Gen.* v. *Grote* (1827) 2 Russ. & M. 699; *Re Hawkins* [1922] 2 Ch. 569; *Boys* v. *Williams* (1831) 2 Russ. & M. 689; 3 Sim. 563.

[5] *Re Overy* (1882) 20 Ch.D. 676; affirmed, *sub nom. Robertson* v. *Broadbent* (1883) 8 App.Cas. 812.

[6] A legacy of 50 shares of the York Union Banking Co. was held equivalent to a legacy of the value of the shares at the testator's death; *Re Gray* (1887) 36 Ch.D. 205; *Re Gage* [1934] Ch. 536; *cf.* also *Macdonald* v. *Irvine* (1878) 8 Ch.D. 102, where a legacy of 500 Egyptian Nine per cent. Bonds was held not to be specific, though the testator had such bonds at the time; and *Re Borne* [1944] Ch. 190 (a legacy of "all my personal effects and £300 Union of South Africa Stock" held, as to the stock, to be a general legacy).

[7] *Richards* v. *Richards* (1821) 9 Price 219.

[8] *Fontaine* v. *Tyler* (1821) 9 Price 98. See also *Stephenson* v. *Dowson* (1840) 3 Beav. 342, 349.

General legacies

Normally the effect of a general legacy of a sum of particular stock amounts to a direction to the executors either to buy such stock for the legatee or to pay him the value thereof.[9] If for any reason the stock cannot be bought, or if the legatee has a choice in the matter and says he would rather not have the stock, he will then take the amount of the money which would have had to be expended in buying them; for the court will do its utmost to maintain the legacy.[10]

Distinction

The distinction between general and specific legacies is of the greatest importance; for, if there is a deficiency of assets, a specific legacy will not be liable to abate with the general legacies. If a specific legacy is given to a peron *in esse*, it carries any income from the date of the testator's death.[11] While, on the other hand, if the specific legacy fails by the ademption or inadequacy of its subject, the legatee will not be entitled to any recompense or satisfaction out of the general personal estate. So that, though specific legacies have in some respects the advantage of those that are general, yet in other respects they are distinguished from them to their disadvantage.[12]

Again, if there is a specific bequest of a thing described as already in existence, and no such thing ever did exist among the testator's effects, the legacy fails. Thus, although a gift of "my grey horse" will pass a black horse, which is not strictly grey, if it is found to have been the testator's intention that it should pass by that description; yet if the testator had no horse, the executor is not to buy a grey one.[13] On the other hand, if the bequest is of "a horse," and no horse is found in the testator's possession at the time of his death, the executor is bound, provided the state of the assets will allow him, to procure a horse for the legatee.[14]

It seems to have been once considered as the criterion of a specific legacy, that it is liable to ademption.[15] But this has since been repeatedly denied.[16] Further, a legacy may be specific, notwithstanding the testator expressly provides that it "shall not be deemed specific, so as to be capable of ademption."[17]

---

[9] *Per* Vaisey J. in *Re Borne* [1944] Ch. 190; and see *per* Kay J. in *Re Gray* (1887) 36 Ch.D. 205, 211.

[10] *Re Gray, ante*; and see *Re Borne, ante*.

[11] *Re Compton* [1914] 2 Ch. 119. *cf. Re Buxton* [1930] 1 Ch. 648.

[12] *Ashton* v. *Ashton* (1735) 3 P.Wms. 384.

[13] *Evans* v. *Tripp* (1821) 6 Madd. 92.

[14] See *Bronsdon* v. *Winter* (1738) Ambl. 57.

[15] *Parrott* v. *Worsfold* (1820) 1 Jac. & Walk, 594, 601. See observations on this case by Jessel M.R. in *Bothamley* v. *Sherson* (1875) L.R. 20 Eq. 304, 309, 310.

[16] See *Stephenson* v. *Dowson, supra*, and Theobald, 14th ed., p. 231.

[17] *Jacques* v. *Chambers* (1846) 2 Coll. 435; but see *Re Compton* [1914] 2 Ch. 119.

Demonstrative legacies

A legacy of quantity is ordinarily a general legacy; but there are legacies of quantity in the nature of specific legacies, as of so much money, with reference to a particular fund for payment. This kind of legacy is called a demonstrative legacy[18]: the testator, after making a positive gift, points out the particular fund which he desires to have first applied, and which he supposes to be adequate for the purpose. If the fund indicated is not adequate, the gift is intended to take effect nevertheless out of some other property of the testator. Such a legacy is general in that if the fund is called in or fails the legatee will not be deprived of his legacy, but will be permitted to receive it out of the general assets[19]: it is specific in that it will not be liable to abate with general legacies upon a deficiency of assets,[20] provided the fund from which it is primarily to be taken is not exhausted.

Specific legacies not favoured

The courts in general are averse from construing legacies to be specific; and the intention of the testator, with reference to the thing bequeathed, must be clear.[21] Legacies, though in fact specific, may be treated by the testator as general legacies, in which case they will be treated as general legacies for the purposes of administration.[22]

Pecuniary legacies

In some circumstances, even pecuniary legacies are specific; as of a certain sum of money in a certain bag or chest,[23] or in the hands of A[24]; or of £200, the balance due to the testator from his partner on the last settlement between them, if the testator did not draw such money out of the trade before he died.[25] But a legacy of "£400 to be paid to A in cash" is a general

---

[18] "If the testator doe divise tenne quarter of corne coming of the corne which shall growe in such a soyle, or two tunnes of wine of his grapes in such a vineyard, or tenne lambs of such a flocke, though so much corne, or wine, or so many lambs doe not arise of the things above-said, yet the heire or executor is compellable by law to make them good *integraliter*: because he may seem to have mentioned the soyle, the vineyard, and the flocke, rather by way of *demonstration* than by way of consition": Fullbecke's *Parallele*, p. 37, edition 1618.

[19] *Mann* v. *Copland* (1817) 2 Madd. 223; *Fowler* v. *Willoughby* (1825) 2 Sim. & Stu. 354; *Willox* v. Rhodes (1826) 2 Russ. 452; *Creed* v. *Creed* (1844) 11 Cl. & F. 491, 509; *Tempest* v. *Tempest* (1857) 7 De G.M. & G. 470, 473.

[20] *Livesay* v. *Redfern* (1836) 2 Y. & C.Ex. 90; *Robinson* v. *Geldard* (1852) 3 Mac. & G. 735, 744, 745; *Tempest*, 7 de G.M. & G. 470; *Mullins* v. *Smith* (1860) 1 Dr. & Sm. 204. See also, further instances of demonstrative legacies, *Williams* v. *Hughes* (1857(24 Beav. 474; *Paget* v. *Huish* (1863) 1 Hemm. & M. 663; *Jones* v. *Southall* (1862) 32 Beav. 31; *Bevan* v. *Att.-Gen.* (1836) 4 Giff. 361; *Disney* v. *Crosse* (1866) L.R. 2 Eq. 592; *Hodges* v. *Grant* (1867) L.R. 4 Eq. 140; *Re Webster* (1937) 156 L.T. 128. *cf. Boyd* v. *Boyd* [1928] N. Ir. 14.

[21] *Kirby* v. *Potter* (1799) 4 Ves. 748; *Innes* v. *Johnson* (1799) 4 Ves. 568; *Re O'Connor* [1948] Ch. 628; *Re Rose* [1949] Ch. 78.

[22] *Re Compton* [1914] 2 Ch. 119.

[23] *Lawson* v. *Stitch* (1738) 1 Atk. 508.

[24] *Crockat* v. *Crockat* (1723) 2 P. Wms. 164.

[25] *Ellis* v. *Walker* (1756) Ambl. 310.

legacy.[26] So is a legacy of money to procure a specified object for the legatee, as of a sum to buy a ring,[27] or to purchase lands[28] or government securities[29] for the legatee; and a bequest of an annuity out of, or charged on, the personal estate is a general legacy.[30]

A money legacy will not be rendered specific by postponement of its payment until a particular investment of a fund takes place. Thus where there is a bequest to A and B of £1,000 each, "which legacies I direct to be paid so soon as my property in India shall be realised in England,"[31] the legatees are entitled to satisfaction, though all the property in India belonging to the testator should have been transmitted to England in his lifetime. So where sums of money are bequeathed by a testator, who has property in England and India, to persons resident in each place, with a direction that they shall be paid out of the assets in the respective countries, such a direction will not constitute the legacies specific.[32]

General legacies abate before specific

Where the assets are sufficient to answer the debts and specific legacies, but not the general legacies, the latter are subject to abatement, unless the will clearly indicates the contrary.

This abatement must take place among all the general legatees in equal proportions.[33] The value of general legacies of stock is taken for abatement as at the end of one year next after the testator's death.[34] An executor had no power to give himself a preference in regard to his own legacy, as he had with his own debt.[35]

Generally speaking, nothing will, in such cases, be abated from the specific legacies.[36] But if the testator bequeaths specific legacies, and also general pecuniary legacies, and directs by his will that such pecuniary legacies should come out of all his personal estate, or words tantamount, then, if there is no other personal estate than the specific legacies, they must be intended to be subject to those which are pecuniary; otherwise the words of the bequest to the pecuniary legatees would be nugatory.[37]

---

[26] *Richards* v. *Richards* (1821) 9 Price 219, 226.

[27] *Apreece* v. *Apreece* (1813) 1 Ves. & Beam. 364.

[28] *Hinton* v. *Pinke* [1719] 1 P. Wms. 539.

[29] *Lawson* v. *Stitch* (1738) 1 Atk. 507. So a direction to invest so much money as will produce a certain amount of stock is a pecuniary legacy: *Edwards* v. *Hall* (1853) 11 Hare 1, 23.

[30] *Alton* v. *Medlicott* , cited in *Lewin* v. *Lewin* (1752) 2 Ves.Sen. 417; *Creed* v. *Creed* (1844) 11 Cl. & F. 491, 508.

[31] *Sadler* v. *Turner* (1803) 8 Ves. 617; *Raymond* v. *Brodbelt* (1800) 5 Ves. 199.

[32] *Kirkpatrick* v. *Kirkpatrick* , cited in *Roberts* v. *Pocock* (1798) 4 Ves. 158.

[33] Treat. Eq.Bk. 4, Pt. 1, Chap. 2, s.5. General legacy includes an annuity.

[34] *Blackshaw* v. *Rogers*, cited *per curiam* in *Simmons* v. *Vallance* (1793) 4 Bro. C.C. 349; *Auther* v. *Auther* (1843) 13 Sim. 422, 440. For the purpose of abatement, the capital sum required to satisfy a contingent legacy must be ascertained on the basis of investment in Consols: *Re Hollins* [1918] 1 Ch. 503.

[35] Toller 6th ed., p. 347; for the abolition of preference and retainer see *ante* , p. 640.

[36] Treat.Eq.Bk. 4, Pt. 1, Chap. 2, s.5; *Clifton* v.*Burt* (1720) 1 P.Wms. 678; 2 Bl.Comm. 513; Toller 6th ed., p. 339.

[37] *Sayer* v. *Sayer* (1714) Prec. Chanc. 393; Treat.Eq.Bk. 4, Pt. 1, Chap. 2, s.5.

Residue goes first

A residuary legatee has no right to call upon any general legatees to abate. All property not specifically bequeathed must be exhausted before those legatees can be obliged to contribute anything out of their bequests.[38]

But where a testator disposes of an estate which he assumes will produce a given sum, or of an ascertained fund, giving a portion to A and the "residue" to B, if the estate or fund does not come up to his expectations the legacies to A and B will abate proportionately. The gift to B in such a case is in realty a specific legacy of an aliquot share in the estate of the fund.[39]

Legacies for consideration

Formerly, the rules of abatement were subject to an exception in that a legacy given to a widow in consideration of her right to dower was entitled to preference of payment over the other general legacies.[40]

It has been said[41] that the above exception was based upon a distinction between legacies which were mere bounties, and legacies given for valuable consideration. If this is correct, it follows that a legacy given in consideration of the release of a debt owed to the legatee should have preference. This conclusion receives some support from *Davies* v. *Bush*.[42] In that case a testator had bequeathed a legacy to a person, between whom and himself accounts had subsisted for some time, on condition of his executing to the testator's executors a general release of all claims and demands which the legatee had on the testator. The legatee executed the release, but the assets were insufficient for the payment of all the legacies. It did not appear whether the legatee had any legal claim or demand on the testator. Lord Lyndhurst C.B. was of opinion that if there was not a debt actually due to the legatee, he could not be considered as a purchaser of the legacy, so as to avoid an abatement with the other legatees; and that if no debt were due, and the release was required merely for the sake of peace, then, unquestionably, the legatee could not be treated as a purchaser. In *Re Wedmore*,[43] however, it was decided that a legacy given in satisfaction of an ascertained debt was not to be preferred. Kekewich J. observed that *Davies* v. *Bush* was not a direct authority on the point. He regarded the case of a legacy given in consideration of a release of dower as anomalous.

---

[38] *Purse* v. *Snablin* (1738) 1 Atk. 414, 418; *Fonnereau* v. *Poyntz* (1785) 1 Bro.C.C. 472, 478. See *Harley* v. *Moon* (1861) 1 Dr. & Sm. 623; *Baker* v. *Farmer* (1868) L.R. 3 Ch.App. 537.

[39] *Page* v. *Leapingwell* (1812) 18 Ves. 463; *Miller* v. *Huddlestone* (1868) L.R. 6 Eq. 65; *Wright* v. *Weston* (1859) 26 Beav. 429; *Elwes* v. *Causton* (1862) 30 Beav. 554 *cf. Petre* v. *Petre* (1851) 14 Beav. 197; *Harley* v. *Moon* (1861) 1 Dr. & Sm. 623; *De Lisle* v. *Hodges* (1874) L.R. 17 Eq. 440.

[40] *Burridge* v. *Bradyl* (1710) 1 P. Wms. 127; *Norcott* v. *Gordon* (1844) 14 Sim. 258. And see Treat.Eq.Bk. 4, Pt. 1, Chap. 2, s.5.

[41] *Inter alia*, in previous editions of this book and in Theobald, *Wills*.

[42] (1831) 1 Younge 341, explained in *Re Whitehead* [1913] 2 Ch. 56.

[43] [1907] 2 Ch. 277, observed upon in *Re Whitehead* [1913] 2 Ch. 56.

Whether *Re Wedmore* is right or wrong, it is at any rate certain that a legacy given in consideration of the legatee releasing an annuity due to him from a third party must abate with other general legacies.[44] Again, general legacies, bequeathed to creditors whose debts have been previously liquidated by composition at less than their real amounts, are merely voluntary, and therefore not exempt from abatement together with other general legacies upon a deficiency of assets.[45] So where the testator bequeaths money to pay the debts of a relation or friend, such legacies must be considered as bounties, and in no better condition than other general legacies.[46]

General legacies priority

A general legacy given to a volunteer will not be entitled to any exemption from abatement, merely because it is to be applied to any particular object or purpose. Thus legacies of a certain sum each to executors for their care and trouble,[47] or of profit costs to a solicitor trustee,[48] or of sums of money for mourning rings,[49] or to servants,[50] or to charities,[51] are not to be preferred to other general legacies. So also a bequest made in favour of a wife or child of the testator, even though directed to be paid immediately, must, unless specific priority is given, abate with the rest of the general legacies.[52]

If by the express words or fair construction of the will the intent of the testator is clearly manifest to give one general legatee a priority to the others, that intention must be carried into effect,[53] as where the testator gave legacies to his two sons and his daughter, with a proviso that if the assets should fall short for the satisfaction of those legacies, his daughter notwithstanding should be paid her full legacy, and the abatement be borne proportionately by the legacies of the sons only.[54] Again, where a testator gave £1,000 to trustees upon trust to pay the interest to his wife during her life, and after her decease he declared his will to be that the

---

[44] *Re Whitehead* [1913] 2 Ch. 56.

[45] *Coppin* v. *Coppin* (1725) 2 P. Wms. 291. See *Turner* v. *Martin* (1857) 7 De G.M. & G. 429.

[46] *Shirt* v. *Westby* (1808) 16 Ves. 393, 396.

[47] *Duncan* v. *Watts* (1852) 16 Beav. 204. See also *Re White* [1898] 2 Ch. 217.

[48] *Re Brown* [1918] W.N. 118; *O'Higgins* v. *Walsh* [1918] 1 Ir.R. 126.

[49] *Apreece* v. *Apreece* (1813) 1 V. & B. 364. In *Masters* v. *Masters* (1717) 1 P.Wms. 423, Lord Parker exempted a legacy of a certain sum for building a monument to the memory of a relation from abating with the general legacies; but this decision has been doubted on strong grounds: see *Blackshaw* v. *Rogers*, cited 4 Bro. C.C. 349.

[50] *Att.-Gen.* v. *Robins* (1722) 2 P.Wms. 23.

[51] *Att.-Gen.* v. *Hudson* (1720) 1 P.Wms. 675; *Bishop of Peterborough* v. *Mortlock* (1784) 1 Bro.C.C. 566; *Re Brown, supra.*

[52] *Blower* v. Morret (1752) 2 Ves.Sen. 420; *Re Hardy* (1881) 17 Ch.D. 798, to the contrary, was disapproved in *Re Schweder's Estate* [1891] 3 Ch. 44. And see *Roper* v. *Roper* (1876) 3 Ch.D. 714, 720.

[53] *Lewin* v. *Lewin* (1752) 2 Ves.Sen. 415; *Re Hardy* (1881) 17 Ch.D. 798, 803; *Re Backhouse* [1916] 1 Ch. 65; and see *Re Cox* [1938] Ch. 556.

[54] *Marsh* v. *Evans* (1720) 1 P. Wms. 668; and see *Att.-Gen.* v. *Robins* (1722) 2 P.Wms. 23. See also *Stammers* v. *Halliley* (1841) 12 Sim. 42; *Re Backhouse* [1916] 1 Ch. 65.

£1,000 should become part of his personal estate, and applicable to the trusts or payment of the legacies given by his will, and he gave a legacy of £500, in trust for N.M. and his wife, in nearly the same words, it was held that a priority was given to these two legacies.[55]

Priorities

The testator, in the absence of plain proof to the contrary, must have considered that his estate would be sufficient to answer the purposes to which he has devoted it, and consequently not to have thought it necessary to provide against a deficiency, by giving a priority, in case of a deficiency, to some of the objects of his bounty. It follows that the onus lies on the party seeking priority to make out that such priority was intended by the testator, and the proof of this must be clear and conclusive.[56] Where the expressions are ambiguous, and do not mark with certainty the testator's intention, no priority can be allowed. For example, it is not sufficient that the testator gives a direction as to a general legacy to his wife, that it should be paid immediately after his death out of the first money that should be received by the executors.[57] So if the words are "in the first place, I give £1,000 to A," this will not give a priority over other general legatees.[58] In *Beeston* v. *Booth*,[59] the testator gave his personal estate to executors, in the first place, to pay debts, funeral and testamentary expenses, and in the next place, to pay three legacies to B, C and D, with interest from three months after his death, and afterwards to raise and set apart three sums of money to be applied as therein mentioned. The court declared that none of the legacies was entitled to priority of payment, and that all of them must abate proportionately, according to the general rule.[60]

Legacies free of tax

Where legacies are given free of tax and the estate is insufficient, the tax on each legacy is to be regarded as an additional legacy, and added to the

[55] *Brown* v. *Brown* (1836) 1 Keen 275. See, for further examples of preference of general legatees in payment, in consequence of the intention of the testator, not expressed in terms, but sufficiently apparent from the whole contents of the will, *Lewin* v. *Lewin* (1752) 2 Ves.-Sen. 415; *Beeston* v. *Booth* (1819) 4 Medd. 161, 170; *Pepper* v. *Bloomfield* (1843) 3 Dr. & W. 499; *Haynes* v. *Haynes* (1853) 3 De G.M. & G. 590; *Gyett* v. *Williams* (1862) 2 Johns. & H. 429.
[56] *Miller* v. *Huddlestone* (1851) 3 Mac. & G. 513.
[57] *Blower* v. *Morret* (1752) 2 Ves.Sen. 420; *Re Schweder's Estate* [1891] 3 Ch. 44. And see n.52 above.
[58] *Brown* v. *Allen* (1681) 1 Vern. 31.
[59] (1819) 4 Madd. 161.
[60] See also *Thwaites* v. *Foreman* (1844) 1 Coll. 409; *Creed* v. *Creed* (1844) 1 Dr. & W. 416; 11 Cl. & F. 491; *Ashburnham* v. *Ashburnham* (1848) 16 Sim. 186; *Miller* v. *Huddlestone* (1851) 17 Sim. 71; 3 Mac. & G. 513; *Lord Dunboyne* v. *Brander* (1854) 18 Beav. 313; *Eavestaff* v. *Austin* (1854) 19 Beav. 591; *Haynes* v. *Haynes* (1853) 3 De G. M. & G. 591; *Coore* v. *Todd* (1856) 23 Beav. 92; 7 De G. M. & G. 520; *Wright* v. *Weston* (1859) 26 Beav. 429; *Haslewood* v. *Green* (1860) 28 Beav. 1; *Elwes* v. *Causton* (1862) 30 Beav. 554; *Re Harris* [1912] 2 Ch. 241.

original legacy, and then such legacies must abate rateably.[61] Interest on legacies is not an additional legacy so as to abate.[62]

Abatement of specific legacies

It has appeared that so long as any of the assets, not specifically bequeathed, remain, such as are specifically bequeathed are not to be applied in payment of debts,[63] although to the complete disappointment of the general legacies.[64] But when the assets, not specifically bequeathed, are insufficient to pay all the debts, then the specific legacies must abate, in proportion to the value of their individual legacies.[65]

Abatement of demonstrative legacies

For the purpose of abatement, a demonstrative legacy,[66] whilst it remains such, is in the same position as, and abates with, specific legacies. The testator, in referring to specific parts of his estate for the payment of particular legacies, is presumed to have intended those legacies as a preference to others which he has not so secured.[67] When, however, the fund or estate out of which the demonstrative legacy was to be paid is exhausted, that legacy is not adeemed, as a specific legacy would be, but must abate proportionately with the other general legacies.[68]

Abatement resulting from devastavit—connivance

A difficult question arises where there are pecuniary legatees and a residuary legatee, and by reason of the *devastavit*[69] of the executor the estate becomes insufficient to pay all the pecuniary legacies. In *Dyose* v. *Dyose*,[70] it was decided that as there was a residue at the testator's death, the residuary legatee must be entitled to something. The wreck of the estate was therefore divided amongst all the legatees according to the proportion of their legacies, allowing the residuary legatee to claim as a legatee of the amount of the residue as it stood at the death of the testator. It seems clear,

---

[61] *Re Turnbull* [1905] 1 Ch. 726; *Re Snape* [1915] 2 Ch. 179. For the incidence of duty generally, see *ante*, pp. 71 *et seq.* The only relevant duty at the present time would be capital transfer tax.

[62] *Re Wyles* [1938] Ch. 313.

[63] Or of costs, when a suit has been instituted: *Barton* v. *Cooke* (1800) 5 Ves. 461. But see *Newbegin* v. *Bell* (1857) 23 Beav. 386; *Re M'Morren* [1917] 1 Ir.R. 278.

[64] See now the Administration of Estates Act 1925, Sched. 1, Pt. II, set out *post*, p. 1152.

[65] *Sleech* v. *Thorington* (1754) 2 Ves.Sen. 561, 564; *Clifton* v. *Burt* (1720) 1 P.Wms. 678; *Duke of Devon* v. *Atkins* (1726) 2 *ibid.* 382, 383; 2 Fonbl. Treat.Eq.Bk. 4, Pt. I, c.2, s.5, n. (*q*). See *Fielding* v. *Preston* (1857) 1 De G. & J. 438; *Re Cohen* [1960] Ch. 179.

[66] As to which, see *ante*, p. 1002.

[67] *Roberts* v. *Pocock* (1798) 4 Ves. 150; *Lambert* v. *Lambert* (1806) 11 Ves. 607; *Robinson* v. *Geldard* (1851) 3 M. & G. 735, 745; *Acton* v. *Acton* (1816) 1 Mer. 178; *Creed* v. *Creed* (1845) 11 cl. & F. & 491, 509; *Tempest* v. *Tempest* (1844) 2 K. & J. 635; affd. 26 L.J. Ch. 501.

[68] See *Paget* v. *Huish* (1863) 1 H. & M. 663; *Robinson* v. *Geldard* (1851) 3 Mac. & G. 735; *Mullins* v. *Smith* (1860) 1 Dr. & Sm. 204, 210.

[69] For *devastavit* see *ante*, pp. 730 *et seq.*

[70] (1715) 1 P.Wms. 305.

however, that this decision can no longer be supported,[71] and that even in the case of a *devastavit* the residuary legatee has no claim till all the general legacies are satisfied.

To this rule there are exceptions. Thus, if an executor makes payments to a legatee in person, or to a trustee for a legatee, or makes such appropriation as is equivalent to payment, the other persons entitled under the will (including the residuary legatee) are not to be called upon to contribute for any loss which may afterwards happen to the fund so paid or appropriated.[72] But the ordinary rule applies if there has been no such payment or appropriation,[73] or if there has been no consent of the legatees to the special appropriation of the fund out of which their legacies are payable,[74] unless, it is conceived, such consent is rendered unnecessary by the will or by statute.[75]

A further exception is established by *Ex p. Chadwin*.[76] This case is an authority to show that a legatee, entitled to a priority, may have so dealt, in respect to his legacy, with an executor guilty of a *devastavit*, as to lose all priority, and to render it just that the estate should be divided as if no *devastavit* had taken place.

The result in this case was the same in *Dyose* v. *Dyose*, but it was arrived at upon a totally different principle. *Ex p. Chadwin* cannot be considered as confirmatory of the decision in *Dyose* v. *Dyose*.

Income gifts and annuities

Gifts of income or annuities necessarily give rise to difficulties in abatement. The difficulties again vary according to the nature of the gift. Thus there may be a simple gift of the income of a fund which will normally be variable in amount or there may be a gift of an annuity or fixed annual sum payable out of certain property. In the latter case, the annuity may be for a fixed term, for life,[77] or perpetual, and it may be payable out of income only, out of accumulated income, or charged upon capital.

Where the "interest" or "produce" of a fund is bequeathed to a legatee, or in trust for him,[78] *without any limitation as to continuance, the principal will*

---

[71] *Fonnereau* v. *Poyvtz* (1785) 1 Bro.C.C. 478; *Humphreys* v. *Humphreys* (1789) 2 Cox 184; *Page* v. *Leapingwell* (1812) 18 Ves. 466; *Baker* v. *Farmer* (1868) L.R. 3 Ch. 537.

[72] See *Willmott* v. *Jenkins* (1838) 1 Beav. 401. And see *Morris* v. *Livie* (1842) 1 Y. & C.C.C. 380. If no appropriation has been made, the residuary legatee may be compelled to refund: see *post*, Chap. 80, p. 1076.

[73] See n. 72.

[74] *Baker* v. *Farmer, ante*; *Harley* v. *Moon* (1861) 1 Dr. & Sm. 623.

[75] See the Administration of Estates Act 1925, s.41, set out *post*, p. 1133, and see *ante*, p. 685.

[76] 3 Swanst, 380.

[77] This is, of course, the normal meaning: see *Blewitt* v. *Roberts* (1841) 1 Cr. & Ph. 274, 280.

[78] A bequest to a woman of a fund, with the interest thereon, to be vested in trustees, the income arising therefrom to be for her sole use and benefit, was held to vest the capital in her for her separate use: *Adamson* v. *Armitage* (1815) 19 Ves. 416. See also *Humphrey* v. *Humphrey* (1851) 1 Sim. (N.S.) 536. It is a question of construction whether the *corpus* passes

be regarded as bequeathed also.[79] Thus, an indefinite gift of the dividends gives the absolute property of the stock,[80] and, on the same principle, a gift of rent passes the land itself.[81] But as to funds this rule is not a very strong one, and in each case the court must find out the meaning from the context.[82] Further, though applicable to shares in a limited company, it does not apply to a share in a partnership.[83] But where there is a limitation, so that the rule does not apply, the person entitled to income does not have the precedence on abatement which is accorded to an annuity.[84] It is not always easy to determine whether the legacy is of an annuity or of the income of a fund.[85] The mere fact that the gift of an annuity is followed by a direction to set apart a fund to secure it, will not cut down the right of an annuitant to a right to receive only the income of the fund.[86] A provision that the fund out of which the annuity is directed to be paid shall fall into residue on the death of the annuitant, is an indication that the testator intended to bequeath an annuity.[87] Again, where there is a gift of an annuity payable out of income, and "subject thereto" the fund is given

where the testator makes a gift of income only to a person during his minority and there is no gift of residue in the will: *Re Arnould* [1955] 1 W.L.R. 539.

[79] *Elton* v. *Sheppard* (1781) 1 Bro.C.C. 532; *Philipps* v. *Chamberlaine* (1798) 4 Ves. 51; *Rawlings* v. *Jennings* (1806) 13 Ves. 39; *Adamson* v. *Armitage* (1815) 19 Ves. 418; *ibid.* Cooper 283, 284; *Stretch* v. *Watkins* (1816) 1 Madd. 253; *Clough* v. *Wynnet* (1817) 2 Madd. 188; *Haig* v. *Swiney* (1823) 1 Sim. & Stu. 487; *Hawkins* v. *Hawkins* (1834) 7 Sim. 173; *Clarke* v. *Gould, ibid.* 197; *Humphrey* v. *Humphrey* (1851) 1 Sim.(N.S.) 536; *Jenings* v. *Baily* (1853) 17 Beav. 118; but see *Cooke* v. *Bowler* (1836) 2 Keen 54; *M'Donald* v. *Bryce, ibid.* 517. See also Jarman, 8th ed., 1951, p. 1172. This is the converse of the principle in *Saunders* v. *Vautier* (1841) Cr.& Ph. 240; 4 Beav. 115 (see *post*), p. 1019). Where the entire fund or the entire interest of a fund is given for a particular purpose which fails, the court holds the donee entitled to the whole fund, treating the purpose merely as the motive for the gift. *Secus*, where the gift is of the whole *or any part* of the fund: *Re Sanderson's Trusts* (1857) 3 Kay & J. 497; *Re Andrew's Trust* [1905] 2 Ch. 48; *Re Osoba* [1979] 1 W.L.R. 247.

[80] *Page* v. *Leapingwell* (1812) 18 Ves. 463; *Haig* v. *Swiney* (1823) 1 Sim. & Stu. 487, 490; *Southouse* v. *Bate* (1852) 16 Beav. 132.

[81] *Ashton* v. *Adamson* (1841) 1 Dr. & W. 198; Jarman, *Wills*, 8th ed., 1951, p. 1280.

[82] *Blann* v. *Bell* (1852) 5 De G. & Sm. 658, 663; *Wetherell* v. *Wetherell* (1862) 4 Giff. 51; 1 De G.J. & S. 134; *Page* v. *Young* (1875) L.R. 19 Eq. 501.

[83] *Re Lawes-Wittewronge* [1915] 1 Ch. 408.

[84] *Croly* v. *Weld* (1853) 3 De G.M. & G. 993; *Baker* v. *Baker* (1858) 6 H.L.C. 616; *May* v. *Bennett* (1826) 1 Russ. 370; *Carmichael* v. *Gee* (1880) 5 App.Cas. 588; *Re Carew* [1939] Ch. 794; *Scott* v. *Salmond* (1833) 1 M. & K. 363.

[85] The following are cases in which annuities have been held payable out of the *corpus* or capital of the testator's estate: *Wright* v. *Callender, infra; Miller* v. *Huddlestone* (1851) 17 Sim. 17; *Haynes* v. *Haynes* (1853) 3 De G.M. & G. 590; *Croly* v. *Weld, ibid.* 993; *Miner* v. *Baldwin* (1853) 1 Sim. & G. 522; *Hickman* v. *Upsall* (1860) 2 Giff. 124; *Howarth* v. *Rothwell* (1862) 30 Beav. 516, where the earlier cases are given; *Bright* v. *Larcher* (1858) 3 De G. & J. 148; *Upton* v. *Vanner* (1861) 1 Dr. & Sm. 594; *Phillips* v. *Gutteridge* (1862) 32 L.J.Ch. 1; *Birch* v. *Sherratt* (1867) L.R. 2 Ch. 644; *Pearson* v. *Helliwell* (1874) L.R. 18 Eq. 411; *Re Hedges' Trust* (1874) L.R. 18 Eq. 419; *Michell* v. *Wilton* (1875) L.R. 20 Eq. 269; *Re Mason* (1878) 8 Ch.D. 411; *Carmichael* v. *Gee, supra; Re Tucker* [1893] 2 Ch. 323. The following are cases in which they were held payable out of income: *Tarbottom* v. *Earle* (1863) 11 W.R. 680; *Bague* v. *Dumergue* (1853) 10 Hare 462; *Hindle* v. *Taylor* (1855) 20 Beav. 105, 109; *Baker* v. *Baker,* 6 H.L.C. 616; *Stelfox* v. *Sugden* (1859), Johns. 234; *Booth* v. *Coulton* (1870) L.R. 5 Ch. 684; *Wormaid* v. *Muzeen* (1881) 45 L.T. 115; *Re Boden* [1907] 1 Ch. 132.

[86] *Re Mason* (1878) 8 Ch.D. 411.

[87] *May* v. *Bennett, supra; Wright* v. *Callender, infra; Re Cottrell* [1910] 1 Ch. 402; *Re Richardson* [1915] 1 Ch. 353.

over, there is an annuity prima facie charged on corpus.[88] On the other hand, a provision for the destination of surplus income during the life of the annuitant goes to show that the annuity is payable out of or a charge on income only.[89]

Precedence of annuity

The principle that general legacies are not reduced before residuary legacies are exhausted is of great importance when applied to gifts of annuities. An annuity, strictly speaking, is an annual payment charged upon corpus.[90] If there is a gift of an annuity, and a residuary gift, the annuity takes precedence. The annuitant must be paid in full before the residuary legatee takes anything from the estate or fund on which the annuity is charged.[91] This rule is subject to a direction to the contrary contained in the will.[92]

Types of annuity

Before considering how an annuity is to be valued for abatement, it may be necessary to consider, often as a matter of construction of the will or other document creating the annuity, precisely what rights are given. Thus, it has long been held that where an annuity is charged on corpus, and capital is in fact paid out to meet the annuity the tenant for life of residue cannot be forced to recoup such capital,[93] nor can recoupment be demanded if there is a continuing charge on income and it cannot be shown that over the years there will be a deficiency in the total income available to meet the total charge.[94] Similarly, an annuity may amount simply to a debt and be apportionable under the rule in *Allhusen* v. *Whittell*.[95] It was long thought that income retained to meet future deficiencies was to be treated as accumulated income and was therefore subject to section 164 of the Law of Property Act 1925, but this is not so.[96] If payment of an annuity is of necessity deferred, no interest is payable.[97]

An annuity is not necessarily charged on income or corpus.[98] This will be

---

[88] *Re Howarth* [1909] 2 Ch. 19; *Re Watkins* [1911] 1 Ch. 1; *Re Young* [1912] 2 Ch. 479; *Re Chance* [1962] Ch. 593, 598, 601.

[89] *Wormald* v. *Muzeen* (1881) 50 L.J.Ch. 776; reversing *ibid*. 17 Ch.D. 167; *Stelfox* v. *Sugden* (1859) Johns. 234; and see *Re Coller's Deed Trusts* [1939] Ch. 277; *Re Griffiths* [1945] 1 All E.R. 610; *Re Cameron* [1955] 1 W.L.R. 140.

[90] But see below, n. 98.

[91] *Croly* v. *Weld* (1853) 3 De G.M. & G. 993; *May* v. *Bennett* (1826) 1 Russ. 370; *Wright* v. *Callender* (1852) 2 De G.M. & G. 652; *Carmichael* v. *Gee* (1880) 5 App.Cas. 588; *Re Hill* [1944] Ch. 270, 275.

[92] *Farmer* v. *Mills* (1827) 4 Russ. 86. *Cf. Re Lyne's Estate* (1869) L.R. 8 Eq. 482.

[93] *Re Croxon* [1915] 2 Ch. 290; *Re Berkeley* [1968] Ch. 744.

[94] *Re Warwick* [1937] Ch. 561.

[95] See *post*, *Re Perkins* [1907] 2 Ch. 596; *Re Berkeley* [1968] Ch. 744, 754.

[96] See *Re Berkeley* [1968] Ch. 744, overruling *Re Robb* [1953] Ch. 459 and *Re Nash* [1965] 1 W.L.R. 221. See also *Baird* v. *Lord Advocate* [1979] A.C. 666 at 675.

[97] *Re Berkeley* [1968] Ch. 744, 761.

[98] *Stelfox* v. *Sugden* (1859) Johnson 234; *Re Coller's Deed Trusts* [1939] Ch. 277, 282 (where the different species of annuity are discussed).

the position where, for instance, surplus income in any given year is specifically disposed of. Where, however, the annuity is charged on income the surplus should normally be paid over to those entitled to the surplus even where it seems there may later be a deficiency.[99]

The types of annuity have been classified as fourfold,[1] namely: (1) annuities payable solely out of the income of that year (absolutely non-cumulative); (2) annuities payable out of income down to some defined date (cumulative to a limited extent); (3) annuities payable out of income generally (indefinitely cumulative); (4) annuities ultimately charged on and payable out of capital. Types (3) and (4) are now virtually indistinguishable.[2] Type (1) is only an interpretation adopted in the case of clear and definite language to that effect.[3] Type (4) requires some language in the ultimate gift of capital which does not merely refer to the prior gift out of income but in itself charges or recognises a charge on capital.[4] An example of type (2) occurred in the decision of Wilberforce J. in *Re Chance*.[5]

Duration of annuities

A simple gift of an annuity to A does not give an annuity beyond the life of A.[6] Thus, "if one gives by will an annuity . . . to A, A shall have it only for life; for if A might give it to his executors it might go on from executors to executors for ever.[7]

To make an annuity created by will perpetual there must be express words in the will so describing it, or the testator must by some language in the will indicate an intention to that effect.[8] Thus, if an annuity is given to one for life, and after his death to another simply, the latter does not necessarily take an absolute interest in the annuity.[9] The fact of the first interest being expressly limited to life does not afford an argument that the second interest is not so limited on the principle of the maxim "*expressio unius est exclusio alterius*," for the duration of the life of the first taker is expressed not for the purpose of limiting the gift of the first taker, but of

---

[99] *Re Platt* [1916] 2 Ch. 563; *Re Coller's Deed Trusts* [1939] Ch. 277, 284; *Re Chance* [1962] Ch. 593.

[1] *Re Rose* (1915) 113 L.T. 142; *Re Chance* [1962] Ch. 593, 599.

[2] See *per* Greene M.R. in *Re Coller's Deed Trusts* [1939] Ch. 277, 279; *Re Watkins* [1911] 1 Ch. 1; *Re Young* [1912] 2 Ch. 479, 482, 486.

[3] See *per* Sargant J. in *Re Rose* (1915) 113 L.T. 142. See also n. 98, *supra*.

[4] See n. 3.

[5] [1962] Ch. 593, 601, applying a dictum in *Re Platt* [1916] 2 Ch. 563.

[6] *Kerr* v. *Middlesex Hosp.* (1852) 2 De G.M. & G. 576, 583; *Blewitt* v. *Roberts* (1841) 1 Cr. & Ph. 274; *Potter* v. *Baker* (1851) 13 Beav. 273; *Re Groves' Trust* (1859) 1 Giff. 74; *Blight* v. *Hartnoll* (1881) 19 Ch.D. 294, 296; *Re Morgan* [1893] 3 Ch. 222.

[7] *Per* Lord Hardwicke L.C. in *Savery* v. *Dyer* (1752) Amb. 139, 140. See also *Wilson* v. *Maddison* (1843) 2 Y. & C.C.C. 372; and *Reid* v. *Coggans (or Reid)* [1944] A.C. 91.

[8] *Lett* v. *Randall* (1861) 2 De G.F. & J. 388, 392. *Re Wynn* [1984] 1 W.L.R. 237.

[9] *Blewitt* v. *Roberts* (1841) 10 Sim. 491; 1 Cr. & Ph. 274; *Lett* v. *Randall, supra*; *Blight* v. *Hartnoll* (1881) 19 Ch.D. 294; *Re Morgan* [1893] 3 Ch. 222; *Kirby* v. *Phillips* [1948] Ch. 109. The decision in *Evans* v. *Walker* (1876) 3 Ch.D. 211, was disapproved in *Blight* v. *Hartnoll, ante*.

limiting the commencement of the gift to the second.[10] But there may be other circumstances affecting the construction which are sufficient to show an intention to give the annuity indefinitely.[11]

Where, in effect, the bequest is a gift of property which will produce the amount of the annuity, or, in other words, where the will dedicates the corpus of a fund to the purchase of the annuity, it is a gift in perpetuity.[12] So, where the will deals with the annuity as being in existence and operative beyond the period of the life of him who is first to enjoy it, and no other period can be fixed for such further duration short of making it perpetual,[13] the annuity must be considered as given in perpetuity; that is to say, it is a bequest of so much property as will produce the income which the testator prescribes as the amount of the gift he intends for the legatee.

Again, where there is a direction by the testator to segregate and appropriate a portion of his property from the interest or profits of which an annuity is to be paid, such an annuity is perpetual and the corpus so appropriated passes under the bequest.[14] But an appropriation of property to meet an annuity does not have this effect.[15] Nor does a direction to the executors as to the best way of providing the annuity.[16] The distinction between these cases seems to depend upon what appears from the words of the will to be the subject-matter of the bequest.[17] If the testator is dealing primarily with an annuity, then the mere incident that he charges the annuity on a fund is not sufficient to transfer the corpus or give to a second taker more than a life interest. If, however, the testator is dealing primarily with a gift of the produce or a part of the procedure of a fund the mere incident that he gives a life estate to one person is not sufficient to prevent the second taker from taking the corpus of the fund as the taker of an unlimited gift of income.

Annuities for lives

A gift of an annuity for a term of *pur autre vie* is a gift to the annuitant and his representatives during the term, or the life of the *cestui que vie*, and is not limited to the life of the annuitant.[18] And a gift of the income to arise from a fund during the life of A to B for his maintenance is an absolute gift

---

[10] *Blight* v. *Hartnoll* (1881) 19 Ch.D. 294, 297.

[11] *Potter* v. *Baker* (1851) 13 Beav. 273; 15 Beav. 489. See also *Pawson* v. *Pawson* (1854) 19 Beav. 146.

[12] *Stokes* v. *Heron* (1845) 12 Cl. & F. 161; *Kerr* v. *Middlesex Hospital* (1852) 2 De G.M. & G. 577, 584; *Hill* v. *Rattey* (1862) 2 J. & H. 634; *Hedges* v. *Harpur* (1858) 3 De G. & J. 129; *Ross* v. *Borer* (1862) 2 J. & H. k469; *Bent* v. *Cullen* (1871) L.R. 6 Ch. 235; *Hicks* v. *Ross* (1872) L.R. 14 Eq. 141; *Evans* v. *Walker* (1876) 3 Ch.D. 211. See, however, the observations on *Bent* v. *Cullen*, *ante*, in *Re Morgan* [1893] 3 Ch. 222.

[13] *Stokes* v. *Heron* (1845) 12 Cl. & F. 161, 194; *Robinson* v. *Hunt* (1841) 4 Beav. 451.

[14] *Lett* v. *Randall*, *ante*.

[15] *Innes* v. *Mitchell* (1803) 9 Ves. 212; *Re Morgan*, *ante*.

[16] *Re Jackson* [1946] 1 All E.R. 327.

[17] The distinction does not turn upon the use of the word "annuity": *Bent* v. *Cullen* (1871) L.R. 6 Ch. 235. But see the comments on this case in *Re Morgan*, *ante*.

[18] *Re Ord* (1835) 9 Ch.D. 667; 12 Ch.D. 22; *Re Cannon* [1915] W.N. 344.

to B, his executors and administrators during the life of A, and is not confined to the joint lives of A and B.[19]

A bequest of an annuity to several persons during their lives without words of survivorship is a bequest to each of them of a separate annuity, and upon the death of each his separate annuity ceases.[20]

Under a gift of an annuity to A and B to be equally divided between them for their lives with a gift over after the death of both, or after the death of the survivor, the survivor takes the whole for life.[21]

Bequest to purchase annuity

Where a sum of money is bequeathed to be laid out in the purchase of an annuity for the life of the legatee, if the legatee survives the testator he is entitled to take the sum,[22] or to have it laid out in an annuity.[23] If the bequest simply directs the purchase of an annuity the annuitant is entitled to a government annuity or the price of it.[24] If the executors are given a discretion as between "government or any public company" the annuitant cannot insist on a government annuity[25] unless the executors have abandoned their discretion.[26] But, though it has been held that a restraint upon anticipation does not prevent the legatee from claiming the sum,[27] yet where there is a gift over of the annuity if the legatee assigns or incumbers his interest, he cannot claim the capital sum; for clearly he was only intended to receive the income, and his representatives in such a case could make no claim.[28] A direction that the annuitant shall not be entitled to have the value of his annuity, and that if he shall sell his annuity the same should cease and form part of the testator's residuary estate, is inconsistent with the gift itself, and the annuitant is absolutely entitled.[29]

If the legatee dies before the sum has been laid out, or before the will is proved, or even before the fund is available, as during the life of the person

---

[19] *Attwood* v. *Alford* (1866) L.R. 2 Eq. 479. And see *Re Jackson, ante* (gift of life annuity to be applied for maintenance until annuitant attained 21).

[20] *Re Evans* (1908) 77 L.J.Ch. 583.

[21] See Theobald, *Wills*, 14th ed., p. 537, and see *Re Ragdale* [1934] Ch. 352. See also *Re Riall* [1939] 3 All E.R. 657 (where the same principle was applied to shares of residue given to persons for life and after the death of the survivor the whole residue given to certain charities); *Re Pringle* [1946] Ch. 124; *Re Foster* [1946] Ch. 135.

[22] *Stokes* v. *Cheek* (1860) 28 Beav. 620.

[23] *Dawson* v. *Hearn* (1831) 1 Russ. & M. 606, 608; *Kerr* v. *Middlesex Hospital* (1852) 2 De G.M. & G. 576; *Ford* v. *Batley* (1853) 17 Beav. 303; *Stokes* v. *Cheek, supra*; *Re Robbins* [1907] 2 Ch. 8; *Re Castle, supra.* As to the valuation of annuities as liabilities of the estate see *Westminster Bank* v. *I.R.C.* [1954] 1 W.L.R. 242 and *ante*, pp. 607, 631.

[24] *Re Castle* [1916] W.N. 195; *Westminster Bank* v. *I.R.C.* [1954] 1 W.L.R. 242.

[25] *Re Smith* [1923] W.N. 92.

[26] *Ford* v. *Batley* (1853) 17 Beavan 303.

[27] *Woodmeston* v. *Walker* (1831) 2 Russ. & M. 197; *cf. Re Ross* [1900] 1 Ch. 162.

[28] *Re Draper* (1888) 57 L.J.Ch. 942; *Power* v. *Hayne* (1869) L.R. 8 Eq. 262, not following *Day* v. *Day* (1853) 1 Drewr. 569.

[29] *Hunt-Foulston* v. *Furber* (1876) 3 Ch.D. 285; *Re Mabbett* [1891] 1 Ch. 707. *Roper* v. *Roper* (1876) 3 Ch.D. 714 (purporting to distinguish *Hatton* v. *May* (1876) 3 Ch.D. 148).

after whose death the investment is to be made, the legacy vests at the testator's death, and the sum belongs to the representatives of the legatee.[30]

Annuity as a general legacy

An annuity charged on the personal estate is a general legacy.[31] As between annuitants and legatees, in the absence of a direction in the will to the contrary,[32] there is no priority where there is a deficient estate, but both must abate proportionately. Whether an annuity is to commence immediately on the death of the testator or at a future period, this principle will equally apply. As annuities abate with reference to other legacies, they must, of course, abate between themselves.[33]

Value of annuities

Where an annuitant entitled to a perpetual annuity, adequately secured, is willing to receive a present payment of cash in lieu of his annuity, the amount of such cash payment ought to be such a sum as at the price of the day will purchase Government Stock sufficient to produce the annuity, excluding any charge for brokerage.[34]

Where one of the liabilities of the testator's estate is a life annuity, the annuitant is not, in the administration of the estate, entitled to the value of the annuity as a gross sum.[35]

In all other cases the value of an annuity must be ascertained on an actuarial basis.[36] The rights of the annuitant have to be considered separately in relation to (1) the residuary legatee and (2) the pecuniary legatee.

(1) *Annuitant and residuary legatee*

Where there is a simple gift of an annuity with a direction to set aside a fund to answer it, the annuity being charged on capital as well as income, and there being a gift over of the residue of the estate, the right of the annuitant and the other persons interested is to have the directions of the testator carried into effect; and, if the income of the estate is not sufficient to pay the annuitant in full, he is entitled to have the deficiency made up

---

[30] *Bayley* v. *Bishop* (1803) 9 Ves. 6. See also *Yates* v. *Compton* (1725) 2 P.Wms. 309; *Barnes* v. *Rowley* (1797) 3 Ves. 305; *Palmer* v. *Craufurd* (1819) 3 Swanst. 483; *Re Mabbett* [1891] 1 Ch. 707; *Re Robbins* [1907] 2 Ch. 8.

[31] *Innes* v. *Mitchell* (1846) 1 Ph. 716; *Miller* v. *Huddlestone* (1851) 3 Mac. & G. 513. But if annuities are given as specific gifts of interest in the real estate, they will not abate with legacies charged generally on the real estate: *Creed* v. *Creed* (1844) 11 Cl. & F. 491 (overruling the decision of Sugden C. of Ireland, 1 Dr. & W. 416).

[32] See, for example, *Re Cox* [1938] Ch. 556; *Re Nicholson* [1938] 3 All E.R. 270.

[33] See *Innes* v. *Mitchell* (1847) 2 Ph. 346, reversing in part *ibid.* 1 Ph. 710.

[34] *Hicks* v. *Ross* [1891] 3 Ch. 499; *Re Jones* [1950] 2 All E.R. 239. *Westminster Bank Ltd.* v. *I.R.C.* [1954] 1 W.L.R. 242.

[35] *Yates* v. *Yates* (1860) 28 Beav. 637. As to whether, in the construction of the word "legacies" in a will, annuities bequeathed are to be included, see *Cornfield* v. *Wyndham* (1846) 2 Coll. 184; *Bromley* v. *Wright* (1849) 7 Hare 334; *Heath* v. *Weston* (1853) 3 De G.M. & G. 601; *Gaskin* v. *Rogers* (1866) L.R. 2 Eq. 284; *Re Feather* [1945] Ch. 343.

[36] See *Re Bradberry and Re Fry* [1943] Ch. 35 and *post,* p. 1017.

out of capital, but he is not entitled (except with the consent of the persons entitled to the residue) to have the value of the annuity paid over to him.[37] This is the position where the question is simply between the annuitant and the residuary legatees.[38]

(2) *Annuitant and pecuniary legatee—Rule in Re Cottrell*[39]

Where there are pecuniary legacies and annuities, which cannot be paid in full, the rule in *Re Cottrell* applies. This was explained by Simonds J. in *Re Cox*[40] as follows: "*As between pecuniary legatees and annuitants*, the rule of administration is clear: that where the estate is inadequate to provide for the payment of both in full it is necessary to have a valuation of the annuities, *and the pecuniary legatees and the annuitants are entitled to have paid to them their legacies and the amount of the valuation of the annuities pari passu*. It is also clear that where the contest is not between pecuniary legatees and annuitants, but between and annuitant and the residue, the annuitant is not entitled to have his annuity valued and the amount of the valuation paid to him. The reason is obvious. The annuitant is entitled, as between himself and the residuary legatee, to have the whole income and, so far as is necessary, the corpus applied in payment of the annuity: the residuary legatee can get nothing until the annuity is paid in full."

(3) *Annuitant and pecuniary and residuary legatees*

In *Re Hill*[41] the Court of Appeal considered whether the rule applicable where there were legacies and annuities was a rule of law, and therefore of universal application, or not. In that case, there were pecuniary legacies, and several annuities payable out of income and capital, and although the residue was initially insufficient to pay all of them, there was no commercial risk that the annuities would not be paid in full. In fact, when any of the annuities, even the smallest, ceased, the income of the estate would be sufficient to pay the remainder. In these circumstances, Lord Greene M.R. (delivering the judgment of the Court of Appeal) observed: "There is an intermediate case where, although the estate is insufficient to pay pecuniary legacies in full and to set aside a fund sufficient by its income to answer the annuities, the estate is sufficient to pay the pecuniary legacies and the full value of the annuities and even to leave a surplus for residue, and in such a case it is usual to apply the rule[42]; but it would seem that there is no

---

[37] *Wright* v. *Callender* (1852) 2 De G.M. & G. 652.

[38] *Re Hill* [1944] Ch. 270, 275. *cf. Re De Chassiron* [1939] Ch. 934, where the testatrix directed this procedure to be followed.

[39] [1938] Ch. 556; *Wroughton* v. *Colquhoun* (1847) 1 De G. & Sm. 357; *Wright* v. *Callender, ante. Re Cox*, however, was a case in which there was no competition between annuitant and pecuniary legatee as the testator had provided that the pecuniary legacies had priority.

[40] See n. 39.

[41] [1944] Ch. 270.

[42] *i.e.* that applicable to the payment of legacies and annuities, as stated by Simonds J. in *Re Cox, ante.*

reason to do so if there is no competition between the legatees and annuitants or do so if there is no competition between the legatees and annuitants or between the annuitants *inter se*; for example, in a case like the
present where the pecuniary legatees can be paid in full at once, and it is
plain on the evidence that the residue will be more than sufficient to pay all
the annuities in full as and when they fall due. It was argued that the
decision in *Re Cottrell*[43] laid it down that the rule was of universal application, and ought to be applied, even in cases where it is certain that a testator's directions with regard to the payment in full of legacies will be
fulfilled to the last penny, although the direction to set aside a fund sufficient by its income to provide the annuities cannot be satisfied. We are
unable to agree that the direction goes to any such length. The facts in *Re
Cottrell*[44] would appear to leave little doubt but that the residue of the
estate after payment of the legacies was in all circumstances sufficient by its
income and capital to ensure that the annuity would be paid in full and that
the residue would not be exhausted unless the annuitant lived for a period
far beyond the expectancy of human life, but no reference was made to this
either in argument or by the judge. In that case, as in the general run of
cases, the direction to appropriate a sum to provide by its income for an
annuity is, properly speaking, a provision for convenience of administration and is really ancillary to the gift of the annuity if it be charged on capital, and it is plain from *Wright* v. *Callender* that, if there be no competing
legacy, such a direction would be ignored. It seems to follow that if an
estate, after payment in full of the legacies bequeathed, can be said to be
sufficient to answer out of income supplemented by capital an annuity (if
only one be given) or a number of annuities the direction to set aside
should also be ignored."

"The reason for the application of the rule in *Re Cottrell*[45] is, we think;
correctly stated by Simonds J. in *Re Cox*,[46] as follows, 'The reason (for the
application of the rule) is clear from a hypothetical example. Suppose an
annuity of £100 is bequeathed to one annuitant, A. who is nineteen years
of age, and a similar annuity to another, B, who is nineteen years of age
and suppose that the whole estate available for satisfaction of the annuities
is only £1,000. If both the income and the capital of that sum are applied
year by year until it is exhausted in payment of the two annuities, A will
probably get his annuity paid in full for the whole of his life, but B will not
do so. There is thus an inequality in this treatment which the testator is presumed not to have intended. The only fair way dealing with annuities, as
between annuitants of different ages, is to make an actuarial valuation of
the annuities and to pay the value of each so ascertained to the annuitants.' "

"The reason so stated has obviously no application to a case like the

[43] [1910] 1 Ch. 402.
[44] See n. 43.
[45] [1910] 1 Ch. 402.
[46] [1938] Ch. 556, 563.

present where it is plain that the available estate is more than sufficient to provide for the payment in full of the annuities out of income and capital as directed by the testator unless a series of events should transpire entirely outside the scope of human expectation, namely, the joint survival of all the annuitants for a period of time of impossible length having regard to their respective ages at the time the matter is to be considered."

"Although Uthwatt J. obviously felt the hardship on the residuary legatees that would be caused by so doing, he applied the rule, because he thought it was one of universal application, and that to refuse to do so would create confusion in the administration of other estates. But the rule is not a rule of law. It is one of convenience. As Uthwatt J. himself said in *Re Bradberry*[47]:"

"'Matters of administration are settled by practice which reflects common sense or, what is to my mind the same thing, reason tempered by convenience.'"

"It would be contrary to common sense to apply the so-called rule to a case where there is no proper ground for its application, and when by so doing the testator's directions are interfered with unnecessarily and an inequitable result is achieved. No confusion can be caused if the court refuses to apply the rule where is is clear on the evidence that all the annuities can properly be satisfied in full out of the estate and there is no commercial risk of any insufficiency."

In *Re Hill*,[48] therefore, the rule was not applied, and the declaration was made that the annuities ought to be paid out of income of the testator's estate, and, so far as the income was insufficient, out of capital.[49]

Actuarial Valuation

Where annuities have to be valued the valuation will normally be made as at the date of the order.[50] If the annuitant has died before the date of the order, his estate is only entitled to the amount of his annuity which has accrued due at that date.[51] But if the annuitant has died after the date of the order his estate is entitled to the value of the annuity.[52] This is a rule of convenience; but it cannot be disregarded merely because it operates unfairly in particular cases.[53]

The valuation should be an actuarial valuation; and facts such as the health of the annuitant or the risks attendant to his vocation are to be disre-

---

[47] [1943] Ch. 35, 40.
[48] [1944] Ch. 270.
[49] See also *Re Vardon* (1938) 159 L.T. 455; *Re Farmer* [1939] Ch. 573; *Re Nicholson* [1938] 3 All E.R 270; *Re Wilson* [1940] Ch. 966.
[50] *Re Bradberry and Re Fry* [1943] Ch. 35. And see 60 L.Q.R. 383.
[51] *Todd* v. *Bielby* (1859) 27 Beav. 353; *Potts* v. *Smith* (1869) L.R. 8 Eq. 683; *Re Ellis* [1935] Ch. 193; *Re Cox, ante; Re Ball* [1940] 4 All E.R. 245; *Re Twiss* [1941] Ch. 141; *Re Bradberry and Re Fry, ante.*
[52] *Re Ross* [1900] 1 Ch. 162.
[53] *Per* Simonds J. in *Re Twiss, ante,* at p. 145.

garded.[54] It is to be made, whenever possible, by reference to the sum which is required to purchase a government annuity of the amount specified by the testator.

Annuitant may choose

If the annuitant is absolutely entitled to the annuity, then he can choose whether he will take the abated value or will have the value laid out in the purchase of an annuity. If he is an infant, the capital value ought to be laid out in the purchase of an annuity.[55]

Instructions to valuer

Where, in the course of administration, it becomes necessary for purposes of division of the estate to place a value on annuities it is within the competence of the representatives to do what the court would order to be done, for the case is not one where judicial discretion has to be exercised; but executors who feel a difficulty about the course they should pursue are entitled to take the court's directions.[56] A mere intention on the part of the executors to administer the estate on a basis which is correct at the time of such intention is not enough to conclude the position of the annuitants under the will although an actual distribution following such intention is enough.[57]

Annuities subject to conditions

The capital sum should in no case be paid directly to the annuitant if the annuity given by the testator was made liable to be determined in some event before the death of the annuitant.[58] In such a case the court usually directs the purchase, with this sum, of a government annuity on the life of the annuitant. The government annuity will then be subject to the same conditions as the original annuity would have been, had the assets been sufficient to provide for it in full.[59]

---

[54] *Re Bradberry and Re Fry* [1943] Ch. 35, 40.

[55] *Re Twiss, ante; Re Ross, ante; Re Ellis, ante;* and see *Re Dempster* [1915] 1 Ch. 795.

[56] *Re Bradberry and Re Fry, ante,* at p. 39.

[57] See n. 56.

[58] *Carr* v. *Ingleby* (1831) 1 De G. & Sm. 362; *Re Richardson* [1915] 1 Ir.R. 39; *Re Dempster* [1915] 1 Ch. 795. *Cf. Re Sinclair* [1897] 1 Ch. 921, explained in *Re Dempster, ante; Re Rothermere* [1945] Ch. 72.

[59] For general provisions relative to annuities, see Stat. Will Forms 1925, Form 5. As to appropriation for annuities, see *post,* p. 1021.

CHAPTER 74

FUTURE LEGACIES

Future legacies to infants[1]

If a legacy is given to A to be paid at 18 and the intermediate interest is not given, and A dies before that period, his representative will have to wait for the money until A, if living, would have attained 18.[2] Where, however, interest is given during the minority, and the legatee dies under age, his executors or administrators will be entitled immediately on his death.[3]

Again, where a legacy is given to A at 18 and if he dies before that period, then to B, and A dies before he attains his age, B is entitled immediately; for he does not claim under A, the bequest being a distinct substantive bequest to take effect on the contingency of A dying during his minority.[4]

Where a testator gives a legatee an absolute vested interest in a defined fund, so that, according to the ordinary rule, he will be entitled to receive it on attaining 18, but, by the terms of the will payment is postponed to a subsequent period, *e.g.* till the legatee attains the age of 25, the court will nevertheless, order payment on his attaining 18; for at that age he has the power of charging or selling, or assigning it, and the court will not subject him to the disadvantage of raising money by these means, when the thing is absolutely his own.[5] Thus, though a legacy is directed to accumulate for a certain period,[6] *e.g.* until the legatee attains the age of 30, yet if he has an absolute indefeasible interest in the legacy, so that no other person has an interest in the direction to accumulate, he did require payment the moment he is competent to give a valid discharge,[7] having attained 18. The position

---

[1] Receipts for legacies to infants are discussed *post*, p. 1024.

[2] *Crickett* v. *Dolby* (1795) 3 Ves. 10. *Garthshore* v. *Chalie* (1804) 10 Ves. 1; *Collins* v. *Macpherson* (1827) 2 Sim. 87; Swinb. Pt. 7, s.23, pl. 9; Godolph Pt. 3, c. 24, s.25; *Shrimpton* v. *Shrimpton* (1862) 31 Beav. 425; *Re Couturier* [1907] 1 Ch. 470.

[3] *Cloberry* v. *Lampen* (1677) 2 Freem. 25; *Crickett* v. *Dolby* (1795) 3 Ves. 10. *Aliter*, if the legacy is payable out of land; *Gawler* v. *Standerwick* (1788) 2 Cox 15.

[4] *Laundy* v. *Williams* (1728) 2 P.Wms. 478. See also *Moore* v. *Godrey* (1708) 2 Vern. 620. See also, as to a legacy charged on land, *Feltham* v. *Feltham* (1725) 2 P.Wms. 271.

[5] *Curtis* v. *Lukin* (1842) 5 Beav. 147, 155, 156; *Rocke* v. *Rocke* (1845) 9 Beav. 66; *Re Young's Settlement* (1853) 18 Beav. 199.

[6] For the periods allowed by law for accumulation of interest, see the Law of Property Act 1925, ss. 164–166; 1 Wolst. & Ch., 13th ed., pp. 294–300. Perpetuities and Accumulations Act 1964.

[7] *Josselyn* v. *Josselyn* (1837) 9 Sim. 63; *Saunders* v. *Vautier* (1841) 4 Beav. 115; Cr. & Ph. 240; *Greet* v. *Greet* (1842) 5 Beav. 123; *Re Colson's Trusts* (1853) Kay 133, 141; *Re Jacob's Will* (1861) 29 Beav. 402; *Gosling* v. *Gosling* (1859) Johns. 265; *Coventry* v. *Coventry* (1865) 2 Dr. & Sm. 470; *Holloway* v. *Webber* (1868) L.R. 6 Eq. 523; *Re Wrey* (1865) 30 Ch.D. 507; *Gott* v. *Nairne* (1876) 3 Ch.D. 278; *Hurbin* v. *Masterman* [1894] 2 Ch. 184; *Wharton* v. *Masterman* [1895] A.C. 186, where the legatee was a charity; *Re Couturier* [1907] 1 Ch. 470; *Re Nunburnholme* [1912] 1 Ch. 489, *Re Knapp* [1929] 1 Ch. 341.

is, of course, different where the legacy is given conditionally upon the legatee attaining the age of 30.[8]

The law before 1970 was the same save that the age of 21 must be substituted for 18.[9]

Neglect to invest legacies

Where the court orders the payment of legacies which by the will are directed to be invested in stock, it is immaterial whether the executor might or might not have been able, with reasonable diligence, to provide for the legacies at an earlier period, in order to fix him with such amount of stock as at the earlier period might have been purchased with the legacy. Probably the reason is that the difficulty and expense which would attend such an inquiry in the case of an executor, make it more convenient in practice that the legacy should be provided for in money at the time of the administration by the court, without reference to the price of stocks. Where, however, a legacy is given by a will to a trustee who is not an executor, and he is directed to invest it immediately upon receiving it in the purchase of stock, and he receives it from the executor, and instead of investing it keeps it in his own hands, his conduct is a plain breach of trust, and he is clearly answerable to his beneficiaries for any loss by a subsequent rise in the price of stock. There is in such a case no difficulty or inconvenience in ascertaining the extent of the loss. Thus, when an executor, who happens also to be named a trustee of a legacy to be laid out in stock, has fully administered the estate, and assented to the legacy, and retains the legacy in his hands, not as assets of the testator, but as trustee of the legacy, then the principles which would apply to any other trustee must apply to him. He is no longer clothed with the character of executor, but is, as to the legacy, a mere trustee.[10]

Appropriation

As has been seen,[11] since January 1, 1926, there have been statutory powers to appropriate and partition. The power to appropriate extends to interest to which a person is not absolutely entitled in possession at the date of appropriation and thus applies to contingent and vested future interests.[12]

Although a legatee is not entitled in any case to receive his legacy before the day of payment arrives, yet he may, quite apart from any statutory provision, where the legacy is vested although payable *in futuro*, require a sufficient sum to be set aside to answer the legacy when it becomes due.[13] It

---

[8] See *Re Turner* [1937] Ch. 15.
[9] See Family Law Reform Act 1969.
[10] *Byrchall* v. *Bradford* (1822) 6 Madd. 13; *ibid.* 235, 240: See, as to when an executor is *functus officio* and becomes a trustee, *post*, p. 1049.
[11] See *ante*, pp. 685 *et seq.* As to infants, see *post*, p. 1024.
[12] Administration of Estates Act 1925, s.41(8) (*post*, p. 1135).
[13] By Lord Hardwicke in *Phipps* v. *Annesley* (1740) 2 Atk. 58. *Secus*, where the legacy is to be raised out of real estate: *Gawler* v. *Standerwick* (1788) 2 Cox. 15.

follows that an executor may, apart from statute, appropriate, with the consent of the legatee, a fund in satisfaction of a vested legacy payable *in futuro*.[14] The same rules apply where a contingent legacy carries the intermediate income.[15]

Where, however, a contingent legacy does not carry the intermediate income there is, apart from statute, no power to appropriate since the legatee cannot require the executor to set aside a sum to answer the contingency.[16] It seems, however, that an executor, apart from statute, can safely distribute the residue if he has made reasonable arrangements for securing the contingent legacy; thus although he cannot definitely appropriate a fund, he can set it aside for his own convenience as a reasonable arrangement, and thus distribute the residue.[17]

When the appropriation is made under a proper direction of the court,[18] or where the representative properly exercises a power of appropriation,[19] the legatee must bear any losses, and will enjoy any accretions which the fluctuation in the value of the appropriated property may cause. On the other hand, if an executor makes an improper appropriation, this does not prejudice the right of the legatee to the actual sum bequeathed to him. Thus, where an executor, before 1926, appropriated a fund in satisfaction of a contingent pecuniary legacy, but the legatee was not entitled to the intermediate interest, the executor was compelled to make good the loss caused to the legatee by a depreciation in the value of the fund.[20]

Where a valid appropriation has been made but it satisfies only part of the ulimate entitlement of the benficiary in question, account is taken of the property so appropriated at its cash value at the date of appropriation.[21]

Appropriation to secure annuity

When a testator bequeaths legacies and annuities, and then gives the residue of his property, after payment of his debts, funeral and testamentary expenses, legacies and annuities, the annuitants are not entitled as a matter of right to have the estate converted, and a sum sufficient to answer the annuity invested in such securities as the court would approve for the

---

[14] *Johnson* v. *Mills* (1749) 1 Ves.Sen. 282; *Re Hall* [1903] 2 Ch. 226. See *Re Craven* [1914] 1 Ch. 358.

[15] *Green* v. *Pigot* (1781) 1 Bro.C.C. 103; *Re Hall, ante.*

[16] *Re Hall, ante,* at p. 235; see, too, *Webber* v. *Webber* (1823) 1 Sim. & St. 311.

[17] *Re Hall, ante,* at p. 233. See also *Re Rivers* [1920] 1 Ch. 320.

[18] *Green* v. *Pigot* (1781) 1 Bro.C.C. 105, 106; *Burgess* v. *Robinson* (1817) 3 Meriv. 7. See also *Rock* v. *Hardman* (1819) 4 Madd. 254; *Kimberley* v. *Tew* (1843) 4 Dr. & W. 139; *cf. Re Oswald* [1920] W.N. 22.

[19] *Re Lepine* [1892] 1 Ch. 210; *Re Richardson* [1896] 1 Ch. 512; *Re Hall* [1903] 2 Ch. 226; *Re Street* [1922] W.N. 291.

[20] *Re Hall, ante.* See also *Re Salaman* [1907] 2 Ch. 46; *Re Kirkley,* 87 L.J.Ch. 247; *Re Rivers* [1920] 1 Ch. 320; *Re Salomons* [1920] 1 Ch. 290.

[21] *Re Richardson* [1896] 1 Ch. 512; *Re Gollin* [1969] 1 W.L.R. 1858; *Re Leigh* [1981] C.L.Y. 2453.

investment of funds under its control; but they are entitled to have the annuities sufficiently secured, for instance, by a mortgage of real estate of the testator,[22] or by the grant of a rentcharge.[23]

Effect on annuitant

The annuitant is bound only if the appropriation is a proper one.

When a fund has been approriated for the payment of an annuity given by will, a question may arise whether the legatee is to suffer the loss conse-quent of the partial failure of the fund. Where the annuity is a charge upon the whole personal estate, it seems clear that the executor cannot affect the legatee's right to the entire annuity by any purported appropriation.[24] Thus in *May* v. *Bennett*[25] a testator having directed his executors to lay out, in what government security they pleased, as much money as would pro-duce a certain annual interest, and having given that annual interest to his wife during her life, the executors invested in the 5 per cents. a sum which yielded dividends exactly equal to the specified income. Those dividends were afterwards diminished by the conversion of the 5 per cents. into 4 per cents. The widow was held entitled to have the deficiency made good, either by the sale from time to time of portions of the appropriated stock, or out of any other part of the residue which could be made available.[26]

But it is otherwise where the appropriation is made in certain stock by the executor in conformity with the direction of the testator, so that the bequest may be regarded as a gift of the interest of the particular stock. In this case, if the dividends from the stock specified by the testator decrease in value, the legatee is not entitled to make good the consequential loss by claiming against the residuary estate.[27] And, *semble*, if the legatee of the annuity consents to the appropriation of some particular fund for the pay-ment of it, the failure thereof, whether partial or total, would be at his risk,[28] though such consent must be clearly established.[29] Presumably an appropriation made under section 41 of the Administration of Estates Act 1925, subsection (9) of which authorises the setting apart of a fund to answer an annuity by means of the income of that fund, or otherwise, would similarly bind the annuitant.

---

[22] *Re Parry*, 42 Ch.D. 570; *Harbin* v. *Masterman* [1896] 1 Ch. 351. As to annuities, see *ante*, p. 1010.

[23] Administration of Estates Act 1925, s.40 (*post*, p. 1133).

[24] *Gordon* v. *Bowden* (1822) 6 Madd. 342. As to the right of trustees to retain surplus income to meet a possible deficiency of an annuity in future years, see *Re Platt* [1916] 2 Ch. 563; *cf. Re Strict* (1922) 67 S.J. 79, and see *ante*, p. 1010.

[25] (1826) 1 Russ. 370. And this was adopted in the case of *Carmichael* v. *Gee* (1880) 5 App. Cas. 588. *cf. Harbin* v. *Masterman* [1896] 1 Ch. 351.

[26] See also *Davies* v. *Wattier* (1823) 1 Sim. & Stu. 463; *Boyd* v. *Buckle* (1840) 10 Sim. 595.

[27] *Kendall* v. *Russell* (1830) 3 Sim. 424. See also *Bague* v. *Dumergue* (1853) 10 Hare 462; *Baker* v. *Baker* (1858) 6 H.L.C. 616, 628; *Hickman* v. *Upsall* (1860) 2 Giff. 124; *Re Strict, supra.*

[28] See Lumley, *Annuities*, p. 298.

[29] *Arundell* v. *Arundell* (1833) 1 M. & K. 316.

Devastavit by executor-legatee

Where, although the requisite amount of stock has been appropriated in the name of the executor, he afterwards sells it and wrongfully applies the proceeds to his own use, he and all those who may stand in his place, including a claimant by assignment from him for valuable consideration, even when made before the *devastavit*, of his share in the testator's residuary estate, are of course precluded from contending that due provision was made for the annuity; and consequently the deficiency caused by the executor's *devastavit* must be supplied out of his share of the residue.[30]

Appropriation where debts unascertained

Where the existence and amount of a testator's debts are contingent, and depend upon the result of legal proceedings before a foreign tribunal, which are not likely to be speedily settled, the court, in administering his assets, will not be induced by that circumstance to direct an appropriation of the fund in court to answer pecuniary legacies subject to such demands as creditors may eventually establish.[31]

---

[30] *Morris* v. *Livie* (1842) 1 Y. & C.C.C. 380; *Burnett* v. *Sheffield* (1852) 1 De G.M. & G. 371; *Doering* v. *Doering* (1889) 42 Ch.D. 203; *Re Dacre* [1916] 1 Ch. 344. As real estate now vests in the representative, there would seem to be no difference, so long as the real estate continues so vested, between a person deriving title under a residuary legatee and a person deriving title under a residuary devisee in this respect. *cf. Fox* v. *Buckley* (1876) 3 Ch.D. 508; *Re Brown* (1886) 32 Ch.D. 597.

[31] *Thomas* v. *Montgomery* (1830) 1 Russ. & M. 729; *ante*, p. 113.

CHAPTER 75

PAYMENT AND RECEIPT

A representative must of course be careful to pay legacies only to those who have authority to receive them. Two problems may arise here. In the first place there may be doubt as to the person intended to be benefited, and secondly such person may be incapacitated and therefore unable to give the representative a valid receipt. If there is doubt as to the person intended this will normally be a matter of construction which must be referred to the court.[1] For a discussion of the construction of wills reference should be made to the textbooks on wills.[2] This chapter is concerned with cases where the legatee is incapacitated, missing, or has assigned his legacy.

Right to receipt or discharge by deed

A representative is entitled to a receipt on payment, but only in exceptional circumstances to a release by deed.[3] To obtain an effective discharge he is, therefore, concerned to obtain a valid receipt from the proper recipient of the legacy or interest in question. The receipt of residuary legatees will normally be given by signing the residuary accounts.

Infant legatees

An executor is not discharged by paying a legacy to a minor, for a minor cannot give a valid receipt, unless the will expressly so provides.[4] After 1925, however, a married minor may give valid receipts for income, including statutory accumulations of income made during the minority.[5] Even where for any reason a minor can give a good discharge this does not entitle him to demand payment, for the representative and the court have a discretion to decide whether payment is for the infant's benefit.[6]

Nor is the executor justified, without the sanction of the court or the will or the authority of statute (*e.g.* for maintenance under the Trustee Act 1925, s.31), in paying the legacy to the minor's parents or other relations.[7]

---

[1] See the procedure explained *ante*, p. 823. As to conditional assets, see p. 1060 *post*.

[2] See *ante*, p. 931, n. 6.

[3] *Re Roberts* (1869) 38 L.J.Ch. 708. A deed is, of course, necessary if the terms of the will are being varied by agreement and in cases of complexity in administration.

[4] *Re Somech* [1957] Ch. 165.

[5] See the Law of Property Act 1925, s.21; Trustee Act 1925, s.31(2)(i).

[6] See n. 4.

[7] *Dagley* v. *Tolferry* (1715) 1 P.Wms. 285; *ibid. nomine Doyley* v. *Tolferry* (1715) 1 Eq. Cas.Abr. 300, pl. 2; *ibid. nomine Dowley* v. *Ballfrey* (1715) Gilb.Eq.Rep. 103. A contrary doctrine was acted upon in the early case of *Holloway* v. *Collins* (1675) 1 Chan.Cas. 245; *ibid.* 1 Eq.Cas.Abr. 303, pl. 1. In *Walsh* v. *Walsh* (1852) 1 Drewr. 64 Kindersley V.-C., in special circumstances, ordered a minor's legacy of small amount to be paid to the father. *M'Creight* v.

If he does so he makes himself liable to pay it over again to the legatee on his coming of age,[8] unless the legatee, on attaining majority, has by some clear and unequivocal act shown his intention to ratify the former application of his legacy.[9] If a legatee has attained majority, payment to the father is not good, unless it is made by the consent of the legatee, or confirmed by his subsequent ratification.[10]

Foreign domicile

Where the legatee is of foreign domicile,[11] and has attained majority either by the law of the place of domicile or by English law, he may give a valid receipt for a legacy.[12] But if the legatee, being a minor by English law is also a minor by the law of the place of domicile, the legacy must be paid according to English law, even if the law of domicile permits it to be paid to a parent or guardian of the minor.[13]

Courses open to executor

An executor has the following choices open to him when a minor is entitled and the will make no special provision:

(a) He may pay the legacy into court.
(b) He may appropriate and retain the legacy until a valid receipt is obtainable.
(c) He may appoint trustees who can then give him a good discharge.

Payment into court

Before 1926, in order to free both himself and the residue from liability, the executor's only safe course, short of an administration action, was to pay the legacy into court under statute,[14] after deducting the charges due thereon.[15] This course is still open to an executor. The receipt or certificate of the proper officer of the court is a sufficient discharge to the executor for the money paid in.[16] This amounts to "payment" so that if interest is given to the legatee until payment, interest under the will ceases to run from the

---

M'Creight (1849) 13 Ir.Eq. 314, in which testamentary guardians were held entitled to give a discharge for the general personal estate of minors under the Irish stat. 15 Car. 2, c. 19 (Ir.), is not an authority enabling an executor in England to pay a legacy with safety to a testamentary guardian: *Re Cresswell* (1881) 45 L.T. 468.

[8] *Toller* 314; *Dagley v. Tolferry, ante.*

[9] 1 Rop.Leg., 3rd ed., 771; *Dagley v. Tolferry, supra*; *Cooper v. Thornton* (1790) 3 Bro.C.C. 97; *Lee v. Brown* (1798) 4 Ves. 362.

[10] *Cooper v. Thornton, supra*, by Lord Alvanley.

[11] As to the administration of foreign estates see generally Pugh on this topic.

[12] *Re Hellman* (1866) L.R. 2 Eq. 363; *Re Schnapper* [1928] Ch. 420.

[13] *Re Hellman, supra; Re Wilks* [1935] Ch. 645. See also Consular Conventions Act 1949, s.2(1) for the powers of a consular officer to give receipts for a foreign national.

[14] Trustee Act 1893, s.42, replaced by the Trustee Act 1925, s.63(1). As to county courts, see C.C.R. Ord. 49, r. 20.

[15] *Re Salomons* [1920] 1 Ch. 290. As to the retrospective protection given in 1925, see the Administration of Estates Act, s.42(2) (*post*, p. 1136).

[16] Trustee Act 1925, s.63(2). R.S.C., Ord. 92, r. 2.

time that the money is paid into court.[17] The executor would be ill-advised to commence a suit to secure the legacy. He would have to pay the costs thereof, since all he need do is to pay the legacy into court.[18]

Appropriation

Since 1925 a representative has a discretionary power to appropriate any part of the deceased's property, not specifically devised or bequeathed, in or towards satisfaction of the legacy, or other interest devised or bequeathed to the minor.[19]

A statutory appropriation in favour of a minor absolutely and beneficially entitled in possession can only be made with the consent of the minor's parents or parent, testamentary or other guardian, or if there are no such persons, by the court on the application of the minor's next friend. When the minor is entitled to a settled legacy, share or interest, which includes any interest to which he is not entitled in possession at the date of the appropriation, the consent of the trustee thereof, other than the representative, is necessary. But if there is no such trustee, and the property appropriated is an investment authorised by law or by the will, then no consent is required. This power of appropriation must be exercised according to the respective rights of the persons interested in the deceased's estate, but when properly exercised, and with the necessary consents, binds all parties concerned.[20] After appropriation the representative holds as trustee and will have the usual powers of maintenance and advancement under the Trustee Act 1925, ss.31 and 32),[21] subject to the terms of the will.[22]

Appointment of trustees

A representative on completing the administration can always assent in his own favour as trustee for sale and thereupon appoint new trustees of the whole[23] or part[24] of the trust property. There is no legal bar to the appointment of a foreign resident as trustee of an English trust.[25] However, a representative has also a more limited power,[26] where a minor is absolutely entitled and the property is not given to trustees for the minor,

---

[17] *Re Salaman* [1907] 2 Ch. 46. The money then earns its own interest. See R.S.C., Ord. 22, r. 13; *Practice Direction* [1970] 1 W.L.R. 470; *Maxwell* v. *Wettenhall* (1722) 2 P.Wms. 26.

[18] *Whopham* v. *Wingfield* (1799) 4 Ves. 630. And see *Wells* v. *Malbon* (1862) 31 Beav. 48.

[19] See *ante*, p. 685. As to future legacies, see *ante*, p. 1020.

[20] See the Administration of Estates Act 1925, s.41(1); 5 Wolst. & Ch., 13th ed., pp. 72–76 and *ante*, p. 685; *post*, p. 1133.

[21] See p. 1135 *post*.

[22] See *Re Delamere* [1984] 1 W.L.R. 813.

[23] Trustee Act 1925, s.36. See *post*, p. 1057.

[24] Trustee Act 1925, s.37.

[25] *Re Whitehead* [1971] 1 W.L.R. 833.

[26] Administration of Estates Act 1925, s.42. See *Re Wilks* [1935] Ch. 645, 650. The section deals expressly with settled land, see *post*, p. 1135.

to appoint a trust corporation[27] or two or more individuals not exceeding four (whether or not including the representatives or one or more of the representatives), to be the trustee or trustees of the property for the minor. This can be done before completion of administration and gives the representatives a discharge from all further liability. Although the section[28] is expressed to apply on intestacy it is confined to absolute interests and cannot, therefore, apply to an intestacy since 1925, because a minor's interests under such an intestacy are contingent and not absolute.[29] It therefore seems that the section[30] will apply on intestacy only in cases where the minor has married under 21[31] or where the infant is absolutely entitled under foreign law to English personalty. In the latter case an attorney administrator in England has been held entitled under this section to appoint trustees.[32]

Payment to trustee for minor

When the bequest has not been made to the minor direct but to someone for him, the executor is justified in paying the money to the person so appointed.[33] Hence, if the testator orders the sum to be paid to the father, he will be a trustee for his child, and entitled to receive the money; and his receipt will be a good discharge to the executor.[34] The direction for payment to the trustee must appear upon the face of the will, and cannot be proved by parol evidence.[35]

Bankrupt legatees

The bankrupt's estate for the purposes of distribution under the Insolvency Act 1986[36] comprises, *inter alia*, all property belonging to or vested in the bankrupt at the commencement of the bankruptcy, that is to say, the day on which the bankruptcy order is made.[37] It includes money, goods, things in action, land and every description of property wherever situated and also obligations and every description of interest, whether present or future or vested or contingent, arising out of, or incidental to, property.[38] Such property automatically vests in the trustee in bankruptcy[39] who can give a good receipt.[40] Where at any time after the commencement of the

---

[27] The section does not authorise the payment of remuneration to a trust corporation, not being the Public Trustee.

[28] See n. 26.

[29] Administration of Estates Act 1925, s.47. See *Re Yerburgh* [1928] W.N. 208.

[30] See n. 26.

[31] See n. 29.

[32] *Re Kehr* [1952] Ch. 26. Such trustees will have the statutory powers of maintenance and advancement. See *post*, p. 1108 and Lewin, *Trusts*, 16th ed., 1964, pp. 292 *et seq.*

[33] 1 Rop.Leg., 3rd ed., 771.

[34] *Cooper* v. *Thornton* (1790) 3 Bro.C.C. 96; *Robinson* v. *Tickell* (1803) 8 Ves. 142.

[35] *Cooper* v. *Thornton* (1790) 3 Bro.C.C. 97.

[36] Insolvency Act 1986, s.283(1), (2).

[37] *Ibid.* s.278.

[38] *Ibid.* s.346.

[39] *Ibid.* s.306(1).

[40] Insolvency Act 1986, Sched. 5, Part II, para. 10.

bankruptcy any property devolves upon the bankrupt, the bankrupt is under a duty within 21 days of his becoming aware of the relevant facts, to give the trustee notice of such property.[41] Subject to certain excluded property the trustee may by notice in writing claim such property for the bankrupt's estate.[42] The property vests in the trustee upon service of such notice on the bankrupt.[43] Where, whether before or after service of such notice a person acquires property in good faith, for value and without notice of the bankruptcy, the trustee is not in respect of that property entitled by virtue of this statutory claim to the property to any remedy against that person.[44] This provides protection to the representative who has no knowledge of the bankruptcy and makes payment to an undischarged bankrupt in good faith.[45]

Mental patients

If a receiver has been appointed for a patient under the Mental Health Act 1983[46] the representative can normally obtain a good receipt from the receiver. If a receiver has not been appointed and doubts arise as to the capacity of a legatee, but there is no relative able and willing to apply for appointment of a receiver, a representative as trustee of a trust in which the patient is interested can apply for appointment of a receiver.[47] Alternatively the legacy can be paid into court.[48]

Protective trusts

The income of legacies may be settled for the benefit of any person on "protective trusts." In such a case, even if the income is variable and uncertain, as, for instance, income paid under the discretionary trust,[49] section 33 of the Trustee Act 1925 applies, subject to any variation contained in the will, if the direction is for the period of the person's life or any less period. Where income is held upon protective trusts then, without prejudice to any prior interest, it is the duty of the trustees to hold the income (1) for the principal beneficiary either for the trust period (*i.e.* for life or any lesser period) or until he does or attempts to do any act or thing, or until any event happens, other than an advance under a statutory or express power, whereby he would have been deprived of his right to

---

[41] *Ibid.* s.333(2) and the Insolvency Rules 1986, r. 6.200(1).

[42] *Ibid.* s.307(1), (2).

[43] *Ibid.* s.307(3).

[44] *Ibid.* s.307(4) The release of a right is 'value.' *Re Pope* [1908] 2 K.B. 169.

[45] This protection is based on the Bankruptcy Act 1914, s.47 which gave statutory effect to the rule in *Cohen* v. *Mitchell* (1890) 25 Q.B.D. 262 C.A. See also *Herbert* v. *Sayer* (1844) 5 Q.B. 965 and *Re Ball* [1899] 2 Ir.R. 322. The bankrupt is not the "slave of the trustee"; *per* Lord Mansfield (see 25 Q.B.D. 268). He can in some circumstances maintain proceedings. *United Telephone Co.* v. *Bassano* (1886) 31 Ch.D. 630.

[46] See s.99 and Hoggett, *Mental Health Law* 2nd ed., p. 336.

[47] See Heywood and Massey, *Court of Protection Practice*, Mental Health Act 1983, ss.93–113, Hoggett, *Mental Health Law* 2nd ed., pp. 331–337.

[48] See *ante*, p. 1025, and *Re Parker* (1888) 39 Ch.D. 303.

[49] *Re Isaacs* (1948) 92 Sol.J. 336.

receive the income or any part thereof[50]: and (2) if this interest fails or determines during the trust period, the income is to be applied at the trustees' discretion for the maintenance or support, or otherwise for the benefit of the principal beneficiary and his or her wife or husband, if any, and his or her children or remoter issue, or if there is no wife, husband or issue of the principal beneficiary, then for the principal beneficiary and the persons who would, if he were dead, be entitled to the trust property, or the income thereof.

A representative will as such be concerned with protective trusts only where these arise under the terms of his testator's will or where such a will directs to be held upon protective trusts under a settlement already in existence. In both cases the problems which may arise are appropriate to the problems of trustees rather than of executors.[51]

Absent or missing legatees

A difficulty may occur where a legacy is given to a legatee who has been abroad, and not heard of for a long time. In one case, a legatee, having been abroad 28 years and not heard of for 27, was presumed dead.[52] And the same presumption was made in a subsequent case,[53] after an absence, without any tidings, of 16 years. But in some cases the court has required that the parties entitled to the legacies in the event of the death of the legatees should give security to refund, in case the legatee should return.[54] However, the executor may avoid all responsibility by paying the legacy into court[55]; an executor may also obtain a valid receipt from a consular officer for a foreign national resident abroad.[56]

Assignee of legacy

When an executor receives notice[57] that a legatee[58] has assigned or charged his legacy in favour of a stranger, the executor is bound to with-

---

[50] See *Re Baring's Settlement Trusts* [1940] Ch. 737; *Re Dennis' Settlement* [1942] Ch. 283; *Re Pozot* [1952] 1 All E.R. 1107; *Re Richardson's Will Trusts* [1958] Ch. 504; *Re Allsopp's Marriage Settlement* [1959] Ch. 81. See *post*, p. 1111.

[51] The topic is considered in Lewin, *Trusts*, 16th ed., 1964, pp. 99–106, Snell, *Equity*, 28th ed., 139–141. As to the exemptions afforded protective trusts for purposes of inheritance tax see the Inheritance Tax Act 1984, s.73; *Encyclopedia of Capital Taxation*, 3–5072; and pp. 71 *et seq. ante.*

[52] *Dixon* v. *Dixon* (1792) 3 Bro.C.C. 510. See also *Re Hutton* (1847) 1 Curt. 595; *Re Lewes' Trust* (1871) L.R. 11 Eq. 356; L.R. 6 Ch.App. 356. As to advertisements, see *ante*, p. 605. See also *ante*, p. 938, n. 80.

[53] *Mainwaring* v. *Baxter* (1800) 5 Ves. 458.

[54] *Norris* v. *Norris* (1679) Finch R. 419; *Bailey* v. *Hammond* (1802) 7 Ves. 590; *Dowley* v. *Winfield* (1844) 14 Sim. 277; *Cuthbert* v. *Purrier* (1822) 2 Phil.C.C. 199.

[55] See *ante*, p. 1025.

[56] Consular Conventions Act 1949, s.1(2).

[57] As to notice under the rule in *Dearle* v. *Hall* (1832) 3 Russ. 1 and s.137 of the Law of Property Act 1925, see Lewin, *Trusts*, 16th ed., 1964, pp. 599–612.

[58] The rule in *Dearle* v. *Hall*, *supra*, applies only where the assignor is beneficially interested. See *B. S. Lyle Ltd.* v. *Rosher* [1959] 1 W.L.R. 8.

hold all further payments unless made with the consent of the assignee.[59] All rights of set-off and adjustment of equities between the legatee and the executor already existing at the date of the notice have priority[60] and may properly be deducted from the amount coming to the assignee; but executors can create no new charge or right of set-off after that time.[61] Where, however, an executor who is himself beneficially interested assigns his interest under the will the assignee takes subject to the equities which attach to the executor. The assignee must therefore make good even a *devastavit* committed by the executor after the assignment[62] but not a breach of trust committed by the assignor as trustee of a separate trust although under the same will.[63]

Currency for payment[64]

The intention of the testator, as apparent from the construction of the will, determines the currency in which legacies are to be paid.[65] Where legacies are given generally, it will be presumed that the testator intended that they should be paid in the money of the country in which he was domiciled and the will was made, without regard to the currency of the place where the legatees reside.[66] Thus, if a testator, domiciled in England, charges his lands abroad with legacies generally, without mentioning whether they are to be paid in sterling money or in currency, they will be payable in sterling money of England.[67]

Payment of pecuniary legacies: exchange rate

Where a legacy is given in a foreign country and coin, as in Sicca rupees, by a will of a testator domiciled in India, the payment, if made by remittance to this country, must be according to the current value of the rupee in

[59] The silence or conduct of the assignee may in equity be regarded as such consent and deprive the assignee of his priority; *Re Pain* [1919] 1 Ch. 38, 49.

[60] See *ante*, p. 646. *Cherry* v. *Boultbee* (1839) 2 Keen 319; *Ward* v. *Duncombe* [1893] A.C. 369; *Re Harrald* (1884) 51 L.T. 441; *Re Knapman* (1880) 18 Ch.D. 300.

[61] See *per* Romilly M.R. in *Stephens* v. *Venables* (1862) 30 Beav. 625, 627; *Re Pain* [1919] 1 Ch. 38. The costs of proceedings pending at the date of assignment are deductible as against an assignee (*Re Knapman* (1880) 18 Ch.D. 300).

[62] *Morris* v. *Livie* (1842) 1 Y. & C.C. 380, 388; *Re Dacre* [1916] 1 Ch. 344; *Re Pain* [1919] 1 Ch. 38. See Lewin, *Trusts*, 16th ed., 1964, pp. 595–599.

[63] *Re Towndrow* [1911] 1 Ch. 662. As to the distinction between *devastavit* and breach of trust, see *ante*, p. 731.

[64] See generally Dicey and Morris, *Conflict of Laws*, 10th ed., 1980, pp. 629–632. As to Court orders in terms of foreign currencies see *Miliangos* v. *Frank* [1976] A.C. 443; *Re Scandinavian Bank* [1988] Ch. 87.

[65] *Lansdowne* v. *Lansdowne* (1820) 2 Bligh 91; *Yates* v. *Maddan* (1849) 16 Sim. 613.

[66] *Saunders* v. *Drake* (1742) 2 Atk. 466; *Pierson* v. *Garnet* (1786) 2 Bro.C.C. 38; *Malcolm* v. *Martin* (1790) 3 Bo.C.C. 50; *Lansdowne* v. *Lansdowne* (1820) 2 Bligh 91; *Yates* v. *Maddan* (1849) 16 Sim. 613.

[67] *Phipps* v. *Lord Anglesea* (1721) 5 Vin.Abr. 209, pl. 8; (1721) 1 P.Wms. 696; *Wallis* v. *Brightwell* (1722) 2 P.Wms. 88, 89; *Lansdowne* v. *Lansdowne* (1820) 2 Bligh 91. See also *Noel* v. *Rochfort* (1836) 10 Bligh (N.S.) 483; (1836) 4 Cl. & F. 158.

India, without regard to the expense of remittance. The same rule applies to other countries.[68] But in *Campbell* v. *Graham*,[69] where legacies, given by a testator domiciled in Jamaica, were ultimately payable in England out of assets in England, it was held that as there could be no expense of remittance, their value was to be computed according to the standard par of exchange between Jamaican and British currency, and not according to the actual rate at the time of payment.

Where a legacy was given in dollars or the equivalent in sterling at the current rate exchange, it was held that the rate of exchange from dollars into sterling must be ascertained on the first anniversary of the testatrix's death or other due date of payment.[70]

The English courts will now make orders in terms of a foreign currency at least in cases of contract.[71]

Specific legacies: increase after will or death

For the purpose of ascertaining what is comprised in a devise or bequest, a will is to be construed to speak and take effect as if it had been executed immediately before the death of the testator, unless a contrary intention appears in the will.[72] Thus, in the absence of such contrary intention,[73] a legatee is entitled to any increase which may have happened to the subject of the legacy between the date of the will and the death of the testator.[74]

If the testator bequeaths to a specific legatee a certain quantity of bank stock, for example, £5,000, standing in his name, and a bonus is given by the bank in the interval between the date of the will and the testator's death, the additional capital will not normally pass to the legatee.[75] But in *Matthews* v. *Maude*,[76] a testatrix had power to dispose by will of property, which she enjoyed under the residuary gift of her brother; a part of this property consisted of £7,000 bank stock which after the brother's death was increased by a bonus to £8,750. The testatrix in her will, made shortly after the bonus was declared, described the bank stock as consisting of £7,000. It was held that £8,750 passed by force of general expressions, which plainly manifested an intention to bequeath all that the testatrix derived from her brother.[77] Bonuses which accrue after the death of the testator, upon

---

[68] *Cockerell* v. *Barber* (1810) 16 Ves. 461. See *Scott* v. *Bevan* (1831) 2 B. & A. 78; *Manners* v. *Pearson* [1898] 1 Ch. 581.

[69] (1831) 1 Russ. & M. 453.

[70] *Re Eighmie (No. 1)* [1935] Ch. 524.

[71] See *Miliangos* v. *George Frank* [1976] A.C. 443; *Re Scandinavian Bank* [1988] Ch. 87.

[72] See the Wills Act 1837, s.24 and *ante*, p. 947.

[73] As to what amounts to a sufficient "contrary intention," see Jarman, *Wills*, 8th ed., 1951, pp. 426 *et seq.*; Theobald, *Wills*, 14th ed., 209, 219–226, 230.

[74] And see *Harcourt* v. *Morgan* (1838) 2 Keen 274, where arrears of interest accrued on a bond before the testator's death were held to pass.

[75] *Norris* v. *Harrison* (1817) 2 Madd. 268; *Loscombe* v. *Wintringham* (1849) 12 Beav. 46; *Courtney* v. *Ferrers* (1827) 1 Sim. 137, 145.

[76] (1830) 1 Russ. & M. 397.

[77] See also *Carver* v. *Bowles* (1831) 2 Russ. & M. 301, 304.

shares specifically bequeathed to him, belong to the specific legatee.[78] As has been seen,[79] specific legacies ought, if possible, to be preserved.

Cost of transferring legacies

There was formerly a conflict of opinion as to whether the costs of packing and transferring specific legacies should be borne out of the general estate or by the specific legatee.[80] But the more recent authorities indicate that the specific legatee must bear such costs.[81] Accordingly, where the deceased was domiciled in England but resided in Monaco, it was held that the expenses incurred by the executors in arranging for the carriage and insurance of specifically devised chattels from Monaco to England, where the specific legatee lived, should be borne by the specific legatee.[82] The same rule applies to foreign duties on the chattels specifically bequeathed.[83]

It appears that all costs incurred in the upkeep, care and preservation of chattels specifically bequeathed from the testator's death until the executor's assent, must be paid by the specific legatees.[84] Indeed it is difficult to explain on what principle the profits in such a case ought to be paid to the legatee, if he is not also to be made liable for the preservation and upkeep of the legacy.[85] But if the legatees merely have a right of selection, the profits accruing before selection fall into residue, and the expenses of preservation until selection fall upon residue.[86]

All costs and duties incurred by the trustees of a will in connection with a specific legacy, after an asset has been made or, it seems, could or should have been made, must come out of the property specifically bequeathed.[87]

Implied right of selection in legatee

If a testator, dying solvent, bequeaths to A a given number of articles forming part of a stock of articles of the same description, as, for instance, if he has 20 horses in his stable and bequeaths six of them, the legatee, and not the executor, has the right of selection.[88] This right of selection is

---

[78] See *Maclaren* v. *Stainton* (1859) 27 Beav. 460, 462; *reversed* (1861) 3 De G.F. & J. 202. See *post*, p. 1034.

[79] See *ante*, pp. 509, 667, 688.

[80] *Perry* v. *Meddowcroft* (1841) 4 Beav. 197, 204; *Re Hewett* [1920] W.N. 366; but see *Re De Sommery* [1912] 2 Ch. 622; *Re Scott* [1915] 1 Ch. 592, 607.

[81] *Re De Sommery, ante*; *Re Grosvenor* [1916] 2 Ch. 375; *Re Sivewright* [1922] W.N. 338; *Re Leach* [1923] 1 Ch. 161; *Re Fitzpatrick* [1952] Ch. 86.

[82] *Re Fitzpatrick, ante*.

[83] *Re Scott* [1914] 1 Ch. 847; [1915] 1 Ch. 592; *Re Cunliffe-Owen* [1951] Ch. 964.

[84] *Re Pearce* [1909] 1 Ch. 819; *Re Rooke* [1933] Ch. 970; *Re Wilson* [1967] Ch. 53, 65.

[85] *Re Rooke, ante* at p. 974.

[86] *Re Collins* [1971] 1 W.L.R. 37.

[87] *Re De Sommery, ante*; *Re Grosvenor* [1916] 2 Ch. 375. And see *Stinson* v. *Crozier* [1936] N.I. 203. *Re Cockburn* [1957] Ch. 438, 440.

[88] *Tapley* v. *Eagleton* (1879) 12 Ch.D. 683. As to express right of selection, see Jarman, *Wills*, 8th ed., 1951, p. 477; Theobald, *Wills*, 14th ed., 266.

generally personal to the legatee,[89] but it may in some circumstances devolve upon his personal representatives.[90]

However, if a testator has several properties answering the description in the will, and it is impossible to say, either from the will itself or from extrinsic evidence, which of these several properties the testator referred to, the gift fails for uncertainty, and the court cannot, to avoid an intestacy, construe the will as giving the legatee the option of selecting which property he will take.[91] But where a testatrix gave "one house to each of my nephews and nieces and on to N. H. One to F. R. One to my sister. One to my brother."—it was held that the gift was not void for uncertainty, but that a choice had been given to the several devisees in the order in which they were named and that if the nephews and nieces could not agree, the choice among them was to be determined by lot in accordance with the analogy of Roman law.[92]

Gift of unopened packet

If a testator directs his executor to deliver a specified packet, part of the property of the deceased, to a particular legatee unopened, the executor cannot, consistently with his duty, comply with this direction.[93]

---

[89] *Re Madge* [1928] W.N. 71; approved in *Skelton* v. *Younghouse* [1942] A.C. 571, where it was held, however, that it is a matter of construction in each case, whether an option bequeathed by a will may be exercised by the executor of the legatee.

[90] See *ante*, p. 699.

[91] *Asten* v. *Asten* [1894] 3 Ch. 260; *Re Cheadle* [1900] 2 Ch. 620.

[92] *Re Knapton* [1941] Ch. 428.

[93] See *Pelham* v. *Newton* (1754) 2 Lee 46. The direction conflicts with the duty to prepare an inventory if demanded. See *ante*, p. 64.

CHAPTER 76

INCOME, INTEREST AND ANNUITIES

A representative about to distribute the estate is frequently confronted with difficulties affecting income and interest and the provision for annuities. These are properly topics for consideration under "Wills"[1] but the main issues which may arise during the executor's year are usefully summarised at this point. The question whether expenditure is attributable to income or capital depends, subject to the terms of the will, on whether or not the expenditure is intended to be for the benefit of capital.[2] The general principle as to interest, to which the exceptions are numerous, is that in the absence of express directions in the will,[3] interest begins to run in favour of creditors and beneficiaries from the end of the executor's year.[4] But of course the representatives remain liable to pay the interest which would have been payable by the deceased in his lifetime where they are concerned with an interest bearing debt. Income or other accretions earned by the estate in the course of the executor's year, if not otherwise disposed of, pass to the residuary legatee.[5] Conversely an annuity runs from the date of death.[6] Thus interest on a general legacy,[7] even if payable "as soon as possible,"[8] interest secured on proceeds of sale of realty directed to be sold immediately after the death of the testator,[9] interest on a legacy for life[10] and interest on a postponed legacy directed to be paid "with interest,"[11] will in each case begin to run only after the end of the executor's year.

A. INCOME

Income and accretions[12] pass as from the date of the testator's death, in the absence of other directions, to a specific legatee or devisee, even if his

---

[1] See Jarman, *Wills*, 8th ed., 1951, pp. 1079–1090; Theobald, *Wills*, 14th ed. 247–259, 515–532. As to the executor's year, see *ante*, p. 112.

[2] *Carver* v. *Duncan* [1985] A.C. 1082 at 1099.

[3] See, *e.g. Re Riddell* [1936] Ch. 747; *Re Pollock* [1943] Ch. 338.

[4] See *ante*, p. 112.

[5] *Wyndham* v. *Wyndham* (1789) 3 Bro.C.C. 58; *Shawe* v. *Cunliffe* (1792) 4 Bro.C.C. 144; *Guthrie* v. *Walrond* (1883) 22 Ch.D. 573. As to interest on money in court, see *ante*, p. 1025.

[6] See *ante*, p. 114.

[7] *Wood* v. *Penoyre* (1807) 13 Ves. 325; *Walford* v. *Walford* [1912] A.C. 658; *Re Wyles* [1938] Ch. 313, 316.

[8] *Webster* v. *Hale* (1803) 8 Ves. 410, 413; *Benson* v. *Maude* (1821) 6 Madd. 15.

[9] *Turner* v. *Buck* (1874) 18 Eq. 301. It is otherwise if the trust for sale is postponed to a life estate in the unconverted realty. See *Re Waters* (1889) 42 Ch.D. 517.

[10] See *ante*, p. 115.

[11] *Knight* v. *Knight* (1826) 2 Sim. & Stu. 490; *Re Palfreeman* [1914] 1 Ch. 877.

[12] *Re Buxton* [1930] 1 Ch. 648. Accumulations during infancy are such accretions: Trustee Act 1925, s.31(2). Income is defined to include rents and profits. Administration of Estates Act 1925, s.55(1)(v) (*post*, p. 1148).

interest is contingent or future,[13] but not if it is merely pecuniary[14] or there are protective trusts.[15] Similarly a specific or contingent residuary devise of realty[16] and a gift of residuary personalty[17] carry the income and accretions from the date of death. The income of a contingent residuary gift is accumulated[18] and passes as an accretion, but a future gift which is not contingent does not carry the income. Such income is undisposed of.[19] If a testator makes a complete disposition of settled property so that each successive interest arises on the cesser of the prior interest, the income is expressly disposed of within the terms of section 175 of the Law of Property Act 1925[20] which provide for contingent and future testamentary gifts to carry intermediate income in the absence of such express disposition.

B. Interest

Until the implementation of section 15 of the Administration of Justice Act 1982, the courts had no jurisdiction to award interest on claims or debts other than judgment debts. There is now a wide discretion subject to rules of court.[21]

The rate of interest on judgment debts is regulated by statutory instrument under section 44 of the Administration of Justice Act 1970[22] and in the case of county courts under section 74 of the County Courts Act 1984. Where an estate is being administered in the High Court it is thought that the court would now act by analogy to these statutory rates and that therefore representatives acting in an administration out of court should follow the same or similar rates[23] or the rate received under the courts' short term

---

[13] Law of Property Act 1925, s.175; *Sleech* v. *Thorington* (1754) 2 Ves.Sen. 560; *Barrington* v. *Tristam* (1801) 6 Ves. 345; *Bristow* v. *Bristow* (1842) 5 Beav. 289; *Clive* v. *Clive* (1854) Kay 600.

[14] *Re Raine* [1929] 1 Ch. 716; *Re Reade-Revell* [1930] 1 Ch. 52.

[15] *Re Spencer* [1935] Ch. 533. As to protective trusts, see *ante*, p. 1028; *post*, p. 1111.

[16] Law of Property Act 1925, s.175. In so far as residue is unascertainable during administration it cannot have ascertainable income. When residue is ascertained the income content can only be notional, so these provisions are scarcely intelligible.

[17] *Nicholls* v. *Osborn* (1727) 2 P.Wms. 419, 421; *Re Gillett* [1950] Ch. 102. See the question as stated *ibid.* at p. 110.

[18] *Green* v. *Ekins* (1742) 2 Atk. 473; *Bective* v. *Hodgson* (1864) 10 H.L.C. 656; *Re Taylor* [1901] 2 Ch. 134; *Glanvill* v. *Glanvill* (1816) 2 Mer. 38.

[19] *Re Gillett* [1950] Ch. 102; *Re Wragg* [1959] 1 W.L.R. 922; *Re Geering* [1964] Ch. 136; and see 23 *Conveyancer* 400 and 27 *Conveyancer* 73.

[20] *Re Hatfeild* [1958] Ch. 469. Tax is normally deductible at source.

[21] Administration of Justice Act 1982, s.15 inserting a new s.35A into the Supreme Court Act 1981 and s.97A into the County Courts Act 1959.

[22] See R.S.C. Ord. 44, r. 9 (In 1985 this was set at 15 per cent. under S.I. 1985 No. 437.) Interest on the widow's statutory legacy is fixed by Order under section 28 of the Administration of Justice Act 1977. (See *Sherrin & Bonehill on Intestate Succession* p. 206.) An order for payment of costs is a judgment debt. *Hunt* v. *Douglas* [1990] A.C. 398. A claim to interest should be specifically pleaded (R.S.C. Ord. 18 r. 8(4)). See also the Administration of Justice Act 1982, s.15.

[23] It is now provided by R.S.C. Ord. 44, r. 10 that subject to court order or directions in the will interest is allowed on legacies at the rate of 6 per cent. p.a. as from the expiration of one year after the testator's death. This applies strictly to accounts directed by a judgment only but should obviously be followed in administrations out of court.

investment account.[24] However there is a general equitable jurisdiction to fix the rate. This was last reported at 4 per cent.[25] where Romer J. quoted Eve J. in *Re Beech*.[26] "A departure from a salutary rule in matters of this kind—introducing as it does an element of uncertainty in practice and administration—can only be justified if the changed conditions on which it is founded continue at least as constant as those upon which the rule was itself framed." However there are a number of rates fixed by statute and the whole question remains ripe for legislation although it could perhaps be remedied by practice direction so far as the equity jurisdiction is concerned.[27] Where large amounts are in issue the proper course under current conditions must be for the executor to obtain the directions of the court. Subject to what is said above, simple[28] interest at 6 per cent.[29] is normally allowed on a pecuniary legacy, but the principle is to allow the rate of interest which could reasonably be earned[30] in England.[31] A higher rate may be payable as against an executor in default.[32] Interest is payable as from the death, in the absence of express provision in the will, where a legacy is charged on realty,[33] where it is given in satisfaction of a debt,[34] where the will directs immediate segregation of the legacy from the general estate,[35] even if the legacy is only payable in the future,[36] where the legacy is an immediate legacy[37] in favour of[38] a legitimate[39] infant[40] child of whom

[24] See *Bartlett* v. *Barclays Trust Co.* [1980] Ch. 515, 547.

[25] [1947] Ch. 23, p. 46. In mortgage proceedings an equity rate of 7 per cent. was fixed, on evidence, in *City Land* v. *Dabrah* [1968] Ch. 166, 182.

[26] [1920] 2 Ch. 40. See also *post*, p. 1040. Snell *Equity* 29th ed. p. 229. As to "guidelines" set by the courts see *Wright* v. *B.R.* [1983] A.C. 773. See also *President of India* v. *La Pintada* [1985] A.C. 104, 117.

[27] See *per* Kekewich J. in *Re Goodenough* [1895] 2 Ch. 537, and see *post*, p. 1040.

[28] *Perkyns* v. *Baynton* (1784) 1 Bro.C.C. 574; *Crackelt* v. *Bethune* (1820) 1 Jac. & W. 586. Compound interest may be allowed where there has been failure to comply with an obligation to accumulate; *Raphael* v. *Boehm* (1803) 11 Ves. 92; 13 Ves. 590; *Dornford* v. *Dornford* (1806) 12 Ves. 127; *Jones* v. *Foxall* (1852) 15 Beav. 388, 461; *Knott* v. *Cottee* (1852) 16 Beav. 77; *Arnold* v. *Arnold* (1835) 2 M. & K. 365. see *ante*, p. 712.

[29] See R.S.C., Ord. 44, r. 10 *Re Campbell* [1893] 3 Ch. 468, 472; *Re Davy* [1908] 1 Ch. 61. As to rates of interest, see *post*, p. 1040. As to deduction of tax, see above n. 20.

[30] *Malcolm* v. *Martin* (1790) 3 Bro.C.C. 50.

[31] *Hamilton* v. *Dallas* (1878) 38 L.T. 215; *Bourke* v. *Ricketts* (1804) 10 Ves. 330; *Stapleton* v. *Conway* (1750) 1 Ves.Sen. 427.

[32] See *ante*, p. 711.

[33] *Pearson* v. *Pearson* (1833) 1 Sch. & Lef. 11; *Spurway* v. *Glynn* (1804) 9 Ves. 483.

[34] *Clark* v. *Sewell* (1744) 3 Atk. 96; *Shirt* v. *Westby* (1808) 16 Ves. 393.

[35] *Re Inman* [1893] 3 Ch. 518; *Re George* (1877) 5 Ch.D. 837; *Re Judkin* (1884) 25 Ch.D. 743; *Re Dickson* (1885) 29 Ch.D. 331, 336; *Re Medlock* (1886) 55 L.J.Ch. 738; *Festing* v. *Allen* (1844) 5 Hare 573; *Re Clements* [1894] 1 Ch. 665; *Re Woodin* [1895] 2 Ch. 309; *Re Eyre* [1917] 1 Ch. 351; *Re Boulter* [1918] 2 Ch. 40.

[36] *Re Inman, supra; Dundas* v. *Wolfe Murray* (1863) 1 H. & M. 425; *Re Snaith* (1894) 71 L.T. 318; *Re Eyre, supra*.

[37] A legacy to trustees for a child carries interest only from the end of the executor's year; *Re Pollock* [1943] Ch. 338.

[38] Including a condition requiring maintenance: *Re Ramsay* [1917] 2 Ch. 64.

[39] *Lowndes* v. *Lowndes* (1808) 15 Ves. 301; but *cf.* text and n. 00 below.

[40] *Raven* v. *Waite* (1818) 1 Swan. 553; *Wall* v. *Wall* (1847) 15 Sim. 513; *Re Crane* [1908] 1 Ch. 379.

the testator is parent or at the time of the will[41] *in loco parentis*[42] and for whom the testator has made no other express provision for maintenance,[43] where the testator has shown an intention that any[44] legatee should be maintained out of the legacy[45] or educated out of it,[46] where it can be inferred from the fact that two legacies carry interest from the death that a third was to be treated in the same way,[47] and where a legacy is given to an infant on his accepting office as an executor.[48] Where a child is *en ventre* at the date of death interest runs from date of birth.[49]

Compound Interest

It is only in cases of breach of fiduciary duty that compound interest may be payable since interest cannot normally be charged on interest.[50] In equity compound interest can be charged where profits made in breach of a fiduciary duty have been used in trade.[51]

Appropriation of payments to interest

Interest payable on a legacy is not a bounty conferred by the testator[52] but a sum given in course of administration to the legatee because justice requires that the failure to pay his legacy in due time should be made good to him. Hence the interest will not abate with legacies; and where payment in full of legacies is postponed because it is impossible to realise a testator's estate, the rule of administration, subject to any directions to the contrary by the testator, is that each payment made to legatees on account of principal and interest must be appropriated first to interest and then to the principal.[53]

---

[41] *Watson* v. *Watson* (1864) 33 Beav. 574.

[42] *Wilson* v. *Maddison* (1843) 2 Y. & C.C.C. 372. As to this term, which is a question of intent and fact, see *Ex p. Pye* (1811) 18 Ves. 140; *Bennet* v. *Bennet* (1879) 10 Ch.D. 474; *Re Ashton* [1897] 2 Ch. 574; *Re Dawson* [1919] 1 Ch. 102.

[43] *Beckford* v. *Tobin* (1749) 1 Ves.Sen. 308; *Crickett* v. *Dolby* (1795) 3 Ves. 10, 13; *Ackerley* v. *Wheeler and Vernon* (1721) 1 P.Wms. 783; *Hill* v. *Hill* (1814) 3 V. & B. 183; *Mills* v. *Robarts* (1830) 1 Russ. & M. 555; *Re West* [1913] 2 Ch. 45. A contingent legacy may not carry such interest: *Re Abrahams* [1911] 1 Ch. 108; *Re Jones* [1932] 1 Ch. 642.

[44] This analogous exception from the general principle is not confined to children of the testator or to legitimate children or even, *semble*, to infants. See *Newman* v. *Bateson* (1786) 3 Swan. 689; *Dowling* v. *Tyrell* (1831) 2 Russ. & M. 343; *Re Churchill* [1909] 2 Ch. 431.

[45] *Re Richards* (1869) L.R. 8 Eq. 119; *Re Stokes* [1928] Ch. 716; *Chambers* v. *Goldwin* (1805) 11 Ves. 2; *Martin* v. *Martin* (1866) L.R. 1 Eq. 369.

[46] *Re Selby-Walker* [1949] 2 All E.R. 178.

[47] *Re Stokes* [1928] Ch. 716.

[48] Since the minor cannot accept office before he reaches majority the legacy will not carry interest from the death: *Re Gardner* (1892) 67 L.T. 552.

[49] *Rawlins* v. *Rawlins* (1796) 2 Cox 425.

[50] See Law Reform (Miscellaneous Provisions) Act 1934, s.3(1).

[51] *O'Sullivan* v. *Management Agency and Music Limited* [1985] 1 Q.B. 428 at 461. "He must disgorge the profits he has made." *Ibid.* p. 474. For an instance of interest payable on a costs order see *Walton* v. *Egan* [1982] 1 Q.B. 1232. As to compound interest under the rules of equitable apportionment see p. 1044 *post*. See also as to principles for charging compound interest in commercial circumstances, p. 713 *ante*.

[52] *Re Wyles* [1938] Ch. 313.

[53] *Re Morley's Estate* [1937] Ch. 491.

Rule in Bower v. Marris—Appropriation of payments on account

The rule that, *if a payer of a sum of money is a debtor and the payee a creditor, the payee has the right to treat any sum paid to him without appropriation in respect of the debt primarily as a payment of interest due,*[54] applies when the payer is an executor and the payee a legatee.[55] Accordingly where there are insufficient funds to pay legacies when due, and interest thereon becomes payable, the legatees are entitled, when payments are made on account at a later date and there is no appropriation between principal and interest, to appropriate such payments *pro tanto* as payments of interest due to them at the time of payment on account of such legacies.[56]

C. ANNUITIES

As has been seen[57] an annuity bequeathed without mentioning any time of payment is considered as commencing from the death of the testator, and the first payment as due at the expiration of one year,[58] from which latter period interest may be claimed in cases where it is allowed at all. But, generally speaking, the court has refused applications for interest upon the arrears of annuities given by will,[59] except where the person charged with the payment of the annuity has at law incurred a forfeiture by non-payment of the annuity, against which he is obliged to seek relief in equity. There no assistance will be given him by the court, except upon terms of doing equity, *viz.* by consenting to pay the grantee of the annuity the arrears due, with interest.[60] The court has also allowed interest on arrears where the annuitant held some legal security which, but for the interference of the court, he might have made available for the payment of interest, or where the accumulation of arrears has been occasioned by the misconduct of the party bound to pay.[61] Difficulties also arise on the valuation of annuities for abatement,[62] appropriation to secure annuities[63] and the security for the annuity, whether charged upon income or capital.[64]

---

[54] *Bower* v. *Marris* (1841) Cr. & Ph. 351.
[55] *Re Prince* (1935) 51 T.L.R. 526.
[56] See n. 55.
[57] *Ante*, p. 114.
[58] See *ante*, p. 114.
[59] *Torre* v. *Browne* (1855) 5 H.L.C. 555; *Booth* v. *Coulton* (1861) 2 Giff. 514; *Re Berkeley* [1968] Ch. 744, 747, 761, C.A.
[60] *Ferrers* v. *Ferrers* (1733) Cas.temp.Talb. 2; 2 Rop.Leg., 3rd ed., 309.
[61] *Torre* v. *Browne* (1855) 5 H.L.C. 578 (*per* Lord Cranworth).
[62] See *ante*, p. 1008.
[63] See *ante*, p. 1021.
[64] See *ante*, p. 1010.

CHAPTER 77

EQUITABLE APPORTIONMENT

In addition to the rule in *Allhusen* v. *Whittell*[1] affecting the amount of income to be regarded as attributable to residue when residue has ultimately been ascertained, there are rules developed by equity[2] to ensure fairness as between the tenant for life and the remaindermen. These rules are sometimes referred to collectively as the rule in *Howe* v. *Lord Dartmouth*[3] but since the rule in *Howe* v. *Lord Dartmouth* forms in effect only one of the three relevant major rules these are better described as the rules of equitable apportionment.[4] Although these rules are really matters appropriate to works on wills or trusts they are of frequent concern to a representative and are therefore considered here.

Equitable apportionment regulates only residue left by will, and then only that part of such residue as consists of personalty. It applies whether or not the residuary personalty is bequeathed subject to an express trust for conversion. It may be excluded by the terms of the will.[5]

The principles are set out under the three major rules:

(1) Apportionment of the income of unauthorised wasting residue, where there is an express trust for conversion: this was formulated in *Dimes* v. *Scott*[6];

(2) apportionment of reversionary property where there is an express trust for conversion: this is known as the rule in *Re Chesterfield's Trusts*[7];

(3) the implication of a trust for sale and conversion, where none is expressed, in order to bring the foregoing rules into operation: this is properly called the rule in *Howe* v. *Lord Dartmouth*.[8]

The rule in Dimes v. Scott

Where a testator expressly directs that the whole, or a part, of the residue of his personal estate is to be converted, the rule in *Dimes* v. *Scott*

---

[1] See *ante*, p. 115.

[2] As to legal apportionment by statute, see *ante*, p. 538.

[3] (1802) 7 Ves. 137. The rule is discussed in 7 Conv.(N.S.) 128.

[4] Many will forms expressly exclude these rules. This can be sensible in an estate of normal simplicity and size but could lead to serious problems in large complex estates, where a large vacuum might arise in consequence of the exclusion.

[5] *Re Chance* [1962] Ch. 593, 608.

[6] (1828) 4 Russ. 195. See also *Gibson* v. *Bott* (1802) 7 Ves. 89, 97. The rules no longer apply to long leaseholds which are not authorised investments (*Re Gough* [1957] Ch. 323. See *post*, p. 1044).

[7] (1883) 24 Ch.D. 643.

[8] (1802) 7 Ves. 137.

applies,[9] even if there is a power to postpone sale.[10] The effect is that, *as securities which are not authorised by the will should be sold within a year, the tenant for life is not entitled, if they are retained, to the actual income arising therefrom.* The court, acting upon a general rule, feigns the property to be converted, as directed by the testator, at the end of one year from his death, and as from the death of the testator[11] *gives to the tenant for life, by way of income, interest at a rate equivalent to the income that would have resulted had conversion occurred[12] from the testator's death till realisation, on the value taken one year after the testator's death.*[13]

In *Dimes* v. *Scott*,[14] the tenant for life of residuary personalty directed to be converted into money and the proceeds invested in government or real securities, was held not to be entitled to the actual income arising from an unconverted unauthorised security, but only to the dividends as from the testator's death of so much 3 per cent. stock as would have been purchased with the proceeds of the unauthorised security at the end of a year from the testator's death.

Later application of Dimes v. Scott

But the later practice was generally to give to the tenant for life interest at 4 per cent. upon the capital value of the unauthorised investments[15] taken as one aggregate. This figure of 4 per cent. was consistently followed without much question until 1961,[16] but there is the authority of the Privy Council[17] for saying that no fixed rule as to rates of interest should be laid down and that the proper criterion is that of the "fair equivalent" stated above.[18] In the case of unauthorised investments realised during the year following the death of the testator, the tenant for life is entitled to receive interest on the net proceeds of realisation from the date of the death.[19] Any excess of income from unauthorised investments beyond the interest payable to the tenant for life should be invested in authorised investments,

[9] (1828) 4 Russ. 195. See *Morgan* v. *Morgan* (1851) 14 Beav. 72; *Holgate* v. *Jennings* (1857) 24 Beav. 623; *Brown* v. *Gellatly* (1867) L.R. 2 Ch.App. 751 (third point decided); *Porter* v. *Baddeley* (1877) 5 Ch.D. 542; *Re Parry* [1947] Ch. 23.

[10] *Re Berry* [1962] Ch. 97, 107 (where Pennycuick J. refused to follow the contrary proposition of Bennett J. in *Re Fisher* [1943] Ch. 377). See also (1961) 77 L.Q.R. 164 (P.V.B.). The purpose of the power to postpone may, however, be material.

[11] See the order made in *Brown* v. *Gellatly* (1867) L.R. 2 Ch.App. 751, 760.

[12] *Wentworth* v. *Wentworth* [1900] A.C. 163, 171. See also *ante*, pp. 710, 1035.

[13] *Re Fawcess* [1940] Ch. 402.

[14] (1828) 4 Russ. 195.

[15] *Re Fawcett* [1940] Ch. 402, 407; *Re Parry* [1947] Ch. 23; *Re Berry* [1962] Ch. 97.

[16] See *Re Berry* [1962] Ch. 97 (where *Wentworth* v. *Wentworth* was not cited and no more than 4 per cent. was apparently claimed). See also *per* Lord Reid in *Taylor* v. *O'Connor* [1971] A.C. 115.

[17] See n. 12.

[18] See text to n. 12 above. Presumably higher rates could have been justified in recent times of high bank rate and high minimum lending rate. See also *ante*, p. 1035.

[19] *Re Fawcett, ante*. In this case Farwell J. discusses fully the rights of the persons interested respectively in capital and income where there is no express power to postpone the sale of unauthorised investments.

the subsequent income of this invested excess being payable as income.[20] Where the aggregated unauthorised investments fail to yield the rate allowed in any one year, the deficit is carried forward, and may be made up out of excess income in subsequent years or out of the proceeds of sale of unauthorised investments, when they are finally sold.[21] Accounts are made on the anniversary of death.

Though, for the purpose of determining the amount of income to which the tenant for life is entitled, the property must be feigned to be in a proper state of investment at the date of valuation, it does not follow that he can demand payment of income to that amount, until the property in respect of which is is payable has been got in.[22]

Where rule inapplicable

This principle of notional conversion does not apply to securities authorised by the will,[23] or directed not to be sold.[24] The tenant for life in these cases is entitled to the actual income produced. Nor does the principle extend to cases where trustees have invested money in authorised securities after the testator's death. In this case also, provided the trustees replace the original capital, the tenant for life is entitled to the whole income, though it may have been increased[25] by such investment.[26]

Date for valuation

The rule applies whether there is an express or statutory trust for conversion, or whether the trust for conversion arises under the rule in *Howe* v. *Lord Dartmouth*.[27] A distinction has, however, long existed as to the date at which the unauthorised investments are to be valued for the purpose of assessing the interest to which the tenant for life is entitled. Where the trust for conversion is implied, or where there is no express power to postpone, the unauthorised investments are valued one year after the death of the testator, and the tenant for life is entitled to an income at a percentage of that valuation from the date of death until the investments are sold.[28] But if the investments are in fact sold during the executor's year, the price they fetch is taken as the proper valuation.[29] Where, however, there is an

---

[20] See n. 19.

[21] See n. 19.

[22] *Taylor* v. *Clark* (1841) 1 Hare 161, 170.

[23] *Brown* v. *Gellatly, supra* (second point decided): *Re Gough* [1957] Ch. 323.

[24] *Green* v. *Britten* (1863) 1 De G.J. & S. 649. *Cf. Caldecott* v. *Caldecott* (1842) 1 Y. & C.C.C. 312.

[25] But where a loss is incurred, see *Re Bird* [1901] 1 Ch. 916 for the method of apportioning it between tenant for life and remaiderman. As to the method of apportioning a loss caused by an investment in an authorised security, see *Re Atkinson* [1904] 2 Ch. 160.

[26] *Stroud* v. *Gwyer* (1860) 28 Beav. 130; *Slade* v. *Chaine* [1908] 1 Ch. 522; *Re Hoyles* [1912] 1 Ch. 67.

[27] (1802) 7 Ves. 137; *post,* p. 1045. For the modern application of this rule, see *Re Fawcett* [1940] Ch. 402.

[28] *Dimes* v. *Scott* (1828) 4 Russ. 195; *Re Fawcett, ante.*

[29] *Re Fawcett, ante.*

express trust for conversion, but the testator gives his trustees a discretionary power to postpone conversion, and the power is given and exercised for
the benefit of the estate generally, the unauthorised securities must be
valued as at the time of the testator's death.[30] From that date the tenant for
life of the residue is entitled to receive interest on that value. The surplus
interest, if any, arising from the unauthorised securities must be accumulated and invested. The income from such accumulated investments
belongs to the tenant for life; the *corpus* to the remainderman.[31] The basis
of this rule is that the respective interests of tenant for life and remainderman should not be altered by a discretion in the trustees not expressly
given to them in the will. It therefore applies to unauthorised securities,
whether of a wasting character or not.[32]

Apportionment excluded—Rule in Rowlls v. Bebb[33]

The rules of apportionment do not apply where the power to postpone
actual conversion, instead of being given for the benefit and more convenient administration of the estate generally, is inserted for the benefit of
the tenant for life, or where the income of unconverted investments is
given in specific words.[34] The person entitled to income is then entitled to
receive the whole income which actually accrues before conversion.[35]

Further, if it appears from the will[36] that the testator intended the tenant
for life to receive the whole income until actual conversion, the latter is
entitled to that income until conversion,[37] or, at any rate, until the property might have been converted but for improper delay.[38] A direction
excluding apportionment in respect of wasting interests, that is, a direction
that the tenant for life is to receive the whole income until conversion, also
excludes apportionment for reversionary interests, that is to say, it extends
to property not producing income (such as a reversionary interest), as well

---

[30] *Meyer* v. *Simonsen* (1852) 5 De G. & S. 723 (third division); *Brown* v. *Gellatly*, *supra*
(first point decided); *Wentworth* v. *Wentworth* [1900] A.C. 163; *Re Woods* [1904] 2 Ch. 4; *Re
Chaytor* [1905] 1 Ch. 233; *Re Owen* [1912] 1 Ch. 519; *Re Beech* [1920] 1 Ch. 40; *Re Parry*
[1947] Ch. 23.
[31] See however the remarks of Brightman L.J. in *Bartlett* v. *Barclays* [1980] Ch. 515 at 547:
"to some extent the high interest rates payable on money lent reflect and compensate for the
continual erosion of the value of money by reason of galloping inflation. It seems to me arguable therefore that if a high rate of interest is payable in such circumstances a proportion of
that interest should be added to capital."
[32] *Re Chaytor*, *ante*; *Re Owen*, *ante*.
[33] [1900] 2 Ch. 107.
[34] *Re Thomas* [1891] 3 Ch. 482; *Re Chaytor* [1905] 1 Ch. 233; *Re Inman* [1915] 1 Ch. 187; *Re
Chance* [1962] Ch. 593, 609.
[35] *Re Inman* [1915] 1 Ch. 187.
[36] See Stat. Will Forms 1925, Form 8.
[37] *Wrey* v. *Smith* (1844) 14 Sim. 202; *Mackie* v. *Mackie* (1848) 5 Hare 70; *Sparling* v. *Parker*
(1846) 9 Beav. 524; *Re Chancellor* (1884) 26 Ch.D. 42. And see *Re Crowther* [1895] 2 Ch. 56,
as to profits of business pending sale; *Re Elford* [1910] 1 Ch. 814.
[38] *Rowlls* v. *Bebb* [1900] 2 Ch. 107; *Re Hey's Settlement Trusts* [1945] Ch. 294. See as to
intestacy p. 1074 *post*.

as to property of a wasting character.[39] But where there is an express trust to convert and a discretion to postpone conversion followed by an express clause excluding the rule, such clause will only operate if the executors, in proper exercise of the power, determine to postpone conversion of the asset.[40] A clause in a will excluding apportionment does not necessarily exclude the rule in *Allhusen* v. *Whittell*.[41]

No apportionment of realty

The rules of apportionment do not apply to realty. Where real estate is directed to be sold, and the proceeds held on trust for a tenant for life with remainders over, and the sale is without impropriety postponed, the tenant for life is entitled, in the absence of a contrary intention in the will, to the rents and profits of the realty until conversion.[42] Similarly, where a mixed fund of the proceeds of realty and personalty is given on such trusts, the tenant for life should receive, so far as the realty is concerned, the rents and profits until sale.[43] On the other hand a tenant for life of residuary realty does not become entitled to income from a reversionary interest forming part of such residue which, in the interests of the proper management of the estate as a whole, is not immediately realised.[44]

Income disposed of

Again, the claim of the tenant for life to any income at all during the year may, of course, be controlled by an opposite disposition of the income before investment. Thus, where a residue is directed to be laid out in land, to be settled on a person for life, with remainder over, and the interest to accumulate until the money is so laid out, the accumulation should cease at the end of the year from the testator's death, and from that period the legatee for life will be entitled to the interest.[45]

Leaseholds

Before 1926 leaseholds were on the same footing as other forms of residuary personalty directed to be converted. But since 1925 the tenant for life is entitled, in the absence of direction to the contrary, to the rents and

---

[39] *Mackie* v. *Mackie* (1845) 5 Hare 70; *Rowlls* v. *Bebb, ante,* at p. 114.

[40] *Rowells* v. *Bebb, ante,* at pp. 115–116; *Rey Hey's Settlement Trusts* [1945] Ch. 294.

[41] *Re Ullswater* [1952] Ch. 105. See *ante,* p. 000.

[42] *Yates* v. *Yates* (1860) 28 Beav. 637; *Re Searle* [1900] 2 Ch. 829.

[43] *Re Darnley* [1907] 1 Ch. 159; *Re Oliver* [1908] 2 Ch. 74.

[44] *Re Woodhouse* [1941] Ch. 332.

[45] *Sitwell* v. *Bernard* (1801) 6 Ves. 520; *Stair* v. *Macgill* (1827) 1 Bligh. (N.S.) 662; *Vigor* v. *Harwood* (1841) 12 Sim. 172; *Tucker* v. *Boswell* (1843) 5 Beav. 607; *Macpherson* v. *Macpherson* (1852) 1 Macq.H. of L. 243; *Vickers* v. *Scott* (1834) 3 M & K. 500. See also *Parry* v. *Warrington* (1820) 6 Madd. 155; *Greisley* v. *Lord Chesterfield* (1851) 13 Beav. 288, as to which case see, however, *Marshall* v. *Crowther* (1874) 2 Ch.D. 199. As to the allocation of profits to interest and capital under a partnership deed, and the effect on the interest of a tenant for life, see *Straker* v. *Wilson* (1871) L.R. 6 Ch.App. 503.

profits until sale of leaseholds whether comprised in an express[46] or in a statutory[47] trust for sale.[48]

In *Re Gough, decd.*,[49] Vaisey J. held that the rule in *Howe* v. *Lord Dartmouth*[50] no longer applied to long leaseholds since they were authorised investments under section 73(1)(xi) of the Settled Land Act 1925, and the long leasehold was settled land.

The rule in Re Chesterfield's Trusts

The second of the three rules of equitable apportionment relates to property of a future or reversionary nature, which produces no income.[51] Where such property is included in a gift of residuary personalty, it should, by the application of the rule in *Howe* v. *Lord Dartmouth*,[52] be sold, whether or not there is a trust for conversion expressed in the will. Where, however, sale is postponed until the property falls into possession, the tenant for life would, apart from apportionment, lose the income that would have been produced by authorised investments bought with the proceeds of sale of the reversionary property.

There can be no apportionment until the reversionary property falls in. When it falls in it is *apportioned as between capital and income by ascertaining the sum which would, together with accumulations, have produced on the day of falling in the amount actually received. The accumulations are calculated on the basis that the sum is put out at interest*[53] *on the day of the testator's death and the interest accumulated compound with yearly rests by adding the annual income after payment of income tax at the current rates.*[54] *The sum so ascertained should be treated as capital, the accumulations as*

---

[46] *Re Brooker* [1926] W.N. 93. This decision is based upon the statutory directions as to the trusts of rents and profits until sale of land held on trust for sale: Law of Property Act 1925, s.28(2). The principle of it seems to apply equally, so as to exclude the rules in *Dimes* v. *Scott*, *Meyer* v. *Simonsen*, and *Howe* v. *Lord Dartmouth* (*infra*). The case is reported as negativing the rule in *Howe* v. *Lord Dartmouth*, but from the facts given it would seem that, but for the Law of Property Act 1925, s.28(2) the rule to apply would have been that established in *Meyer* v. *Simonsen*. (See n. 30, *supra*.)

[47] *Re Berton* [1939] Ch. 200.

[48] As to apportionment between capital and income of value payments under the War Damage Act for settled leaseholds, see *Re Scholfield* [1949] Ch. 341.

[49] [1957] Ch. 323.

[50] (1802) 7 Ves. 137.

[51] The rule applies only where no income is produced or where the income or interest is indefinite or does not accrue from day to day so that no method of legal apportionment can be applied. See *Re Lewis* [1907] 2 Ch. 296, as explained in *Re Chance* [1962] Ch. 593, 610, 613.

[52] *Post*, p. 1045.

[53] For rates of interest, see *ante*, pp. 1035 *et seq*. *Re Parry* [1947] Ch. 23; *Re Fawcett* [1940] Ch. 402.

[54] Thus if the value of property when it falls in after five years is £10,000, and interest is taken at 15 per cent. and tax at 30 per cent. it is necessary first to deduct 30 per cent., from the interest rate. This gives 10·5 per cent. per annum. Since interest is to be compounded at yearly intervals the denomination becomes $1·105,^5$ thus

$$\frac{£10,000}{1·105^5} = \frac{£10,000}{1·6474} = £6,070$$

The accumulations are £10,000 − £6,070 = £3,930.

income.[55] The capital must then be invested in authorised investments and the remainder treated as income paid to the tenant for life or other person entitled to the income since the death of the testator.

Periodical payments

The rule in *Chesterfield's Trusts* applies to reversionary interests forming part of the residue. It has no application to realty.[56] It has been held to apply only to those reversionary interests which are non-income-bearing; where, therefore, the testator was entitled under a settlement to an immediate interest, subject to a proviso that the trustees should pay out of the income such annual sums to a third party during her lifetime as they might think fit, and the trustees in fact paid the whole income to that third party, it was held that the interest of the testator under the settlement was not reversionary, so as to be subject to apportionment, when it reverted to the testator's estate on the death of the third party.[57]

Periodical sums payable to the estate of the testator under a policy of insurance or an agreement made by the deceased[58] are treated as capital,[59] and are therefore to be apportioned according to the rule in *Re Chesterfield's Trusts*.

Rule in Howe v. Lord Dartmouth

Where there are no express directions in the will as to conversion, there frequently arises an implied trust to convert under the rule in *Howe* v. *Lord Dartmouth*.[60] The rule is that *where there is a residuary bequest of personal estate to be enjoyed by several persons in succession, a court of equity, in the absence of any evidence of a contrary intention, will assume that it was the intention of the testator that his legatees should enjoy the same thing in succession, and, as the only means of giving effect to such intention, will direct the conversion into permanent investments of a recognised character of all such parts of the estate as are of a wasting or reversionary character, and also all such other existing investments as are not of the recognised character, and are consequently deemed to be more or less hazardous.*[61]

It is upon this principle that the tenant for life is entitled,[62] so that should the trustees fail to convert unauthorised securities which might be converted immediately without sacrificing the interests of the tenant for life

---

[55] *Re Chesterfield's Trusts* (1883) 24 Ch.D. 643; *Re Hollebone* [1919] 2 Ch. 93. See also *Re Woodhouse* [1941] Ch. 332.

[56] *Re Woodhouse, ante.*

[57] *Re Holliday* [1947] Ch. 402.

[58] *Re Fisher* [1943] Ch. 377; *Re Payne* (1943) 60 T.L.R. 49.

[59] *Re Fisher, ante; Re Payne, ante; Re Hey's Settlement Trusts* [1945] Ch. 294, following *Crawley* v. *Crawley* (1835) 7 Sim. 427.

[60] (1802) 7 Ves. 137 *a; Wightwick* v. *Lord* (1857) 6 H.L.C. 217, 228; see also *Fearns* v. *Young* (1804) 9 Ves. 549, 552.

[61] *Macdonald* v. *Irvine* (1876) 8 Ch.D. 101, 112, *per* Baggallay L.J. And see *Meyer* v. *Simonsen* (1852) 5 De G. & S. 723 (second division recognised by Parker V.-C.). *Lloyds Bank* v. *Duker* [1987] 1 W.L.R. 1324 and see p. 740 *ante.*

[62] See n. 60.

and remainderman, the former is entitled only, so far as these unauthorised securities in one aggregate are concerned, to an income from the testator's death equal to what would have been obtained after conversion upon the capital value (at the end of the first year after the testator's death) of the unauthorised investments.[63]

Practice-valuation

Where the property is so laid out as to be secure and to produce a large annual income, but is not capable of immediate conversion without loss and damage to the estate,[64] the practice has always been *to set a value upon it, and to give the tenant for life interest on such value, and the residue of the income must then be invested and the income of the investment paid to the tenant for life, but the corpus must be secured for the remainderman.*[65]

Rule excluded by contrary intention or express trusts

Since the rule is based on the presumed intention of the testator it may be excluded by a contrary intention in the will. Accordingly, where the bequest to the tenant for life is specific, the legatee in remainder is not entitled to have the property converted, even if it is a decreasing fund and the legacies over may altogether fail.[66] So where the bequest is not specific, in the strict sense of the expression, yet if the court finds in the will an intention that the property is to be enjoyed in its existing state, that intention must be carried into effect, and the property will be so enjoyed.[67] The

---

[63] *Meyer* v. *Simonsen* (1852) 5 De G. & Sm. 723 (second division recognised by Parker V.-C.); *Brown* v. *Gellatly* (1867) L.R. 2 Ch.App. 751; *Re Fawcett* [1940] Ch. 402. See *ante* p. 1040.

[64] As in *Gibson* v. *Bott* (1802) 7 Ves. 89; *Caldecott* v. *Caldecott* (1842) 1 Y. & C.C.C. 312; and *Re Llewellyn's Trust* (1861) 29 Beav. 171.

[65] *Meyer* v. *Simonsen* (1852) 5 De G. & S. 723 (third division recognised by Parker V.-C.).

[66] *Vincent* v. *Newcombe* (1832) Younge 599; *Lord* v. *Godfrey* (1819) 4 Madd. 455; *Cockran* v. *Cockran* (1844) 14 Sim. 248; *Bethune* v. *Kennedy* (1835) 1 My. & Cr. 114. And see *post*, p. 1048. Where there is a specific legacy of investments, the personal representatives have a power to sell the investments and invest the proceeds: *Re Pratt* [1943] Ch. 326; but there is no trust for sale, unless expressed.

[67] *Collins* v. *Collins* (1833) 2 M. & K. 703; *Alcock* v. *Sloper* (1833) 2 M. & K. 699; *Pickering* v. *Pickering* (1839) 4 M. & Cr. 289; *Vaughan* v. *Buck* (1841) 1 Phil.C.C. 75; *Harvey* v. *Harvey* (1842) 5 Beav. 134; *Daniel* v. *Warren* (1845) 2 Y. & C.C.C. 290; *Hinves* v. *Hinves* (1844) 3 Hare 609; *Cafe* v. *Bent* (1847) 5 Hare 24; *Hubbard* v. *Young* (1847) 10 Beav. 203; *Hunt* v. *Scott* (1847) 1 De G. & Sm. 219; *Burton* v. *Mount* (1848) 2 De G. & Sm. 383; *Neville* v. *Fortescue* (1848) 16 Sim. 333; *Harris* v. *Poyner* (1852) 1 Drew. 174; *Marshall* v. *Bremner* (1854) 2 Sm. & G. 237; *Hind* v. *Selby* (1856) 22 Beav. 373; *Green* v. *Britten* (1863) 1 De G.J. & S. 649; *Wilday* v. *Sandys* (1869) L.R. 7 Eq. 455; *Re Sewell's Estate* (1870) L.R. 11 Eq. 80; *Thursby* v. *Thursby* (1875) L.R. 19 Eq. 395; *Gray* v. *Siggers* (1880) 15 Ch.D. 74; *Re Chancellor* (1884) 26 Ch.D. 42; *Re Sheldon* (1888) 39 Ch.D. 50; *Re Wilson* [1907] 1 Ch. 394; *Re Nicholson* [1909] 2 Ch. 111. For cases where the court has *not* been able to find such intention, see *Lichfield* v. *Baker* (1840) 13 Beav. 447; (see also 2 Beav. 481); *Benn* v. *Dixon* (1840) 10 Sim. 636; *Caldecott* v. *Caldecott* (1842) 1 Y. & C.C.C. 312; *Sutherland* v. *Cooke* (1844) 1 Coll. 498; *Johnson* v. *Johnson* (1846) 2 Coll. 441; *Chambers* v. *Chambers* (1846) 15 Sim. 183; *Morgan* v. *Morgan* (1851) 14 Beav. 72; *Thornton* v. *Ellis* (1852) 15 Beav. 193; *Blann* v. *Bell* (1852) 2 De G.M. & G. 775; *Murton* v. *Markby* (1854) 18 Beav. 196; *Hood* v. *Clapham* (1854) 19 Beav. 90; *Jebb* v. *Tugwell* (1855) 20 Beav. 84; *Brown* v. *Gellatly* (1867) L.R. 2 Ch.App. 751; *Tickner* v. *Old*

court will find such an intention much more easily where the gift is an absolute one followed by an executory limitation.[68] There is no distinction for the purposes of the rule between unauthorised securities of a wasting and those of a permanent nature.[69]

The rule has been held to be excluded where the will directed that specific parts of the residue should be sold after the death of the tenant for life,[70] for an express limited trust for sale must be supposed to negative any implied trust for sale; or where the residue has been disposed of after the death of the tenant for life by reference to specific assets forming part of it.[71] Where the gift to the tenant for life is of all "property yielding income," the rule is excluded[72]; similarly where the gift is of the "rents" of leasehold property,[73] and there are no freeholds, or where there is a trust for sale with the consent of the life-tenant.[74] The rule has also been excluded where the residue was to be sold and divided into several shares on the death of the life-tenant,[75] although a direction to divide is in itself not sufficient to exclude the rule.[76]

Rule inapplicable

The rule in *Howe* v. *Lord Dartmouth*[77] does not apply to investments authorised by law[78] for the investment of trust property, the tenant for life being entitled as from the testator's death to the whole income arising therefrom.[79] The rule has never applied to realty, nor to any form of property limited to persons in succession by settlement *inter vivos*.[80] Further, where the unauthorised and hazardous security and the parties entitled thereto are out of jurisdiction, the rule cannot be applied until the parties come within jurisdiction.[81]

Farming stock, implements of husbandry,[82] and stock-in-trade[83] are not things *quae ipso usu consumuntur* within this rule. A gift for life of such property generally confers only a life interest. The tenant for life is bound

---

(1874) L.R. 18 Eq. 422; *Porter* v. *Baddeley* (1877) 5 Ch.D. 542; *Macdonald* v. *Irvine* (1876) 8 Ch.D. 101; *Re Game* [1897] 1 Ch. 881; *Re Wareham* [1912] 2 Ch. 312; *Re Evans' Will Trusts* [1921] 2 Ch. 309.

[68] *Re Bland* [1899] 2 Ch. 336.

[69] *Re Nicholson* [1909] 2 Ch. 111.

[70] *Skirving* v. *Williams* (1857) 24 Beav. 275; *Rowe* v. *Rowe* (1861) 29 Beav. 276.

[71] *Holgate* v. *Jennings* (1857) 24 Beav. 623.

[72] *Boys* v. *Boys* (1860) 28 Beav. 436.

[73] *Goodenough* v. *Tremamondo* (1840) 2 Beav. 512. *cf. Re Game* [1897] 1 Ch. 881; *Re Wareham* [1912] 2 Ch. 312.

[74] *Re Rogers* [1915] 2 Ch. 437.

[75] *Collins* v. *Collins, ante*; *Pickering* v. *Pickering, ante*; *Re Barratt* [1925] Ch. 550.

[76] *Re Evans' Will Trusts* [1921] 2 Ch. 309.

[77] (1802) 7 Ves. 137.

[78] As to which, see the Trustee Act 1925, Pt. 1. See *ante*, pp. 681 *et seq.*

[79] *Meyer* v. *Simonsen, ante* (first division recognised by Parker V.-C.).

[80] *Re Van Straubenzee* [1901] 2 Ch. 779.

[81] See *Holland* v. *Hughes* (1809) 16 Ves. 111.

[82] *Groves* v. *Wright* (1856) 2 K. & J. 347; *Myers* v. *Washbrook* [1901] 1 K.B. 360.

[83] *Phillips* v. *Beal* (1862) 32 Beav. 25.

to keep up the value of such stock for the benefit of the remainderman,[84] though only to the extent of its value at the testator's death.[85] Where, however, this implied obligation is expressly negatived by the testator, the tenant for life, who is not bound to replace consumed articles, takes the property absolutely.[86]

Sale of investments

Although, as we have seen, the rule in *Howe* v. *Lord Dartmouth*[87] never applies to specific legacies, the effect of the Trustee Act 1925, s. 1, is to confer on representatives a power to sell investments specifically bequeathed and to invest the proceeds in authorised investments.[88]

Income of contingent legacies

If contingent legacies do not carry the intermediate income, the tenant for life of the residuary estate is entitled to the intermediate income of the fund set apart to meet them. That fund is residue until it is wanted.[89]

---

[84] *Groves* v. *Wright, supra*; *Cockayne* v. *Harrison* (1872) L.R. 13 Eq. 432; *Paine* v. *Warwick* [1914] 2 K.B. 486.
[85] *Re Powell* [1921] 1 Ch. 178.
[86] *Breton* v. *Mockett* (1878) 9 Ch.D. 95.
[87] *Ante*, p. 1045.
[88] *Re Pratt* [1943] Ch. 326.
[89] *Allhusen* v. *Whittell* (1867) L.R. 4 Eq. 295. *cf. Re Whitehead* [1894] 1 Ch. 678.

CHAPTER 78

ASSENTS

It has been shown[1] that all real and personal property to which a deceased person was entitled for an interest not ceasing on his death, now devolves upon his representatives. They are responsible for the satisfaction of the deceased's debts to the extent of the whole estate, even though the testator may have directed that a portion of it should be applied to other purposes.[2] In view of this liability they should not distribute any portion of the deceased's estate until satisfied that such debts have been actually paid or are adequately secured,[3] or can be paid without recourse to that portion of the estate.[4] In this respect they are protected, for the title of claimants to the deceased's property, whether devisees, legatees or persons entitled on intestacy, is not completed except by some act of the representatives themselves. This act, according to the circumstances, consists in either an assent or a conveyance, and until it has taken place the administration continues.[5]

Executorship and trusteeship (beneficiaries)[6]

Before considering the operation of an assent it is essential to consider the position of the representative and the beneficiary before assent. The general principle seems to be that neither an executor nor an administrator is *ipso facto* a trustee and that the expression "personal representatives" does not include trustees.[7] A representative is, of course, in a fiduciary position as to assets coming to him in right of his office and he is for certain limited purposes treated as a trustee,[8] but this does not give a beneficial interest to legatees during the course of administration.[9] Representatives will be fully in the position of trustees (a) when the will so directs and (b) when on intestacy distribution is postponed by reason of minority or life interests.[10] However, when administration is complete the repesentative

---

[1] *Ante*, p. 471.

[2] *Ante*, p. 602.

[3] See the Administration of Estates Act 1925, s.36(10); *post*, p. 1061.

[4] But they incur no risk in permitting a beneficiary to take possession of land under the Administration of Estates Act 1925, s.43(1), see *post*, p. 1050.

[5] The question whether or not the administration is complete is a question of fact. *Re Tankard* [1942] Ch. 69.

[6] As to trusteeship for creditors see p. 607, *ante*.

[7] *Re Trollope's Will Trusts* [1927] 1 Ch. 596; *Re Spencer & Hauser's Contract* [1928] Ch. 598. See also *ante*, pp. 449, 710.

[8] *Re Marsden* (1884) 26 Ch.D. 783, 789; *Commr. of Stamp Duties* v. *Livingston* [1965] A.C. 694, 707; *Re Hayes* [1971] 1 W.L.R. 758; *Ayerst* v. *C. & K.* [1976] A.C. 167 at 177.

[9] *Eastbourne B.S.* v. *Hastings* [1965] 1 W.L.R. 861, 867, and see *post*, p. 1050.

[10] Administration of Estates Act 1925, ss.33, 39. See also as to the history in limitation matters Preston and Newsom, *Limitation of Actions*, 3rd ed., p. 187. *Re Smith* (1889) 42 Ch.D. 302.

becomes a trustee of the net residue for the persons beneficially interested.[11] This does not necessarily and automatically discharge him from his
obligations as representative.[12] Although his statutory powers of management may cease, he retains his character of representative for all time or
until the termination of the grant.[13]

Tax

It seems that where one of a number of joint executors is resident in the
United Kingdom but the others are abroad and the persons interested in
the estate are also abroad the Inland Revenue could not assess the resident
executor to tax any more than it could assess a trustee in a similar situation.[14] If, however, after assent a beneficiary obtains an absolute vested
interest, or the trustee has a beneficial interest or there has been a transfer
of assets designed to avoid tax the position is different.[15]

Right of beneficiary before assent

Until assent or conveyance, a person interested under the will or intestacy has an inchoate right transmissible to his own representatives.[16] He
cannot, however, without the authority of the representatives,[17] take possession of the property, even though the testator expressly directs that he
shall do so; otherwise a testator might appoint all his effects to be taken in
fraud of creditors.[18] Should he go into possession the representatives may
sue him in ejectment, trespass or trover, according to the circumstances.
Thus, although he is actually in possession of property specifically
bequeathed, and the assets are fully adequate to the payment of debts, he
has no right to retain it in opposition to the representatives, by whom, in
such a case, an action will lie to recover it.[19]

A residuary legatee has no interest in a defined part of the estate until
the residue is ascertained, nor can income be ascribed to unascertained

[11] *Eaton* v. *Daines* [1894] W.N. 32; *Re Ponder* [1921] 2 Ch. 59; *Re Pitt* (1928) 44 T.L.R.
371. It would seem that failure to execute an assent in his own favour as trustee could not prevent the trusts arising: *Re Cockburn* [1957] Ch. 438. See also *post*, p. 1057. As to the meaning
of the phrase "trustees as such" in the Rent Acts see *Williams* v. *Mate* (1982) 46 P. & C.R. 51.
For an example of completion of the administration and its consequences, see *Lilley* v. *Public
Trustee* [1981] A.C. 839; (1984) *Conveyancer* 423.
[12] *Harvell* v. *Foster* [1954] 2 Q.B. 367, 383. As to attorney administrators, see *ante*, p. 937.
See also as to purchasers before 1926, *ante*, p. 677.
[13] *Re Timmis* [1902] 1 Ch. 176, 183; *Solomon* v. *Attenborough* [1912] 1 Ch. 451, 458; *Re
Grosvenor* [1916] 2 Ch. 375. But see as to executorial duties, *per* Romilly M.R. in *Brougham*
v. *Poulett* (1855) 19 Beav. 119, 134 and p. 721 *ante*.
[14] See *Dawson* v. *I.R.C.* [1988] 1 W.L.R. 930.
[15] *Per* Nicholls L.J. in *Dawson* v. *I.R.C.* [1988] 1 W.L.R. 930 at p. 936.
[16] Wentw.Off.Ex., 14th ed., 69; and see *Re Parsons* [1943] Ch. 12; *Re Leigh's Will Trusts*
[1970] Ch. 277 and article by P. V. Baker in 86 L.Q.R. 20. As to intestacy, see *post*, p. 1065.
As to beneficiaries in possession, see *ante*, p. 460.
[17] Personal representatives may permit a beneficiary to take possession of land: Administration of Estates Act 1925, s.43(1), *ante*, pp. 460, 684, 685.
[18] Went.Off.Ex., 14th ed., 409.
[19] *Mead* v. *Orrery* (1745) 3 Atk. 235, 239; Com.Dig.Admon.C. 5; Bac.Abr.Exors.L. 3.

residue.[20] His right, which is of course transmissible,[21] is to have the estate properly administered and applied for his benefit when the administration is complete.[22] The right of a beneficiary claiming on a total intestacy is similar, except that he takes under a statutory trust for sale and conversion.[23] However, it has been suggested[24] that the interest on intestacy of a person dying within the year is vested.[25]

Operation of assents

Before 1926 an assent did not need to be in writing but could only be made in favour of some person entitled under the will of the deceased. The beneficiary derived title from the will, but the will did not operate in his favour until the executor had done some act which showed, or was presumed to show, that he intended the disposition in the will to become operative.[26]

Assent in favour of executor

Where a legacy is bequeathed to the executor, his assent to his own legacy may, as well as his assent to that of another legatee, be either express or implied.[27] He may not only, in positive terms, announce his election to take it as a bequest, but such election may also be implied from his language or his conduct.[28] The rule as to the latter is that "if an executor, in his manner of administering the property, does any act which shows that he has assented to the legacy, that shall be taken as evidence of his assent to the legacy, but if his acts are referable to his character of executor, they are not evidence of an assent to the legacy."[29]

Therefore, if the executor says that he will have the legacy according to the will, this will amount to an assent to take it as legatee. Again, an assent to take part as a residuary legatee is an assent also to take the whole residue in the same character.[30] On the other hand, if the executor merely says that the testator "left all to me,"[31] this will not amount to an election to

---

[20] *Barnardo's Homes* v. *I.R.C.* [1921] 2 A.C. 1; *I.R.C.* v. *Smith* [1930] 1 K.B. 713; *Corbett* v. *I.R.C.* [1938] 1 K.B. 567; *Sudeley* v. *Att.-Gen.* [1897] A.C. 11; *Re Neeld* [1962] Ch. 643, 689; *Commr. of Stamp Duties* v. *Livingston* [1965] A.C. 694; *Eastbourne Mutual B.S.* v. *Hastings* [1965] 1 W.L.R. 861 (intestacy); *Lall* v. *Lall* [1965] 1 W.L.R. 1249. See also *Barclay* v. *Barclay* [1970] 3 W.L.R. 82. As to the statutory attribution of a notional income to the estate for tax purposes see *ante*, p. 932.
[21] Such a right is a chose in action and can itself be the object of a trust. *cf. Lord Strathcona Steamship Co.* v. *Dominion Coal Co.* [1926] A.C. 108 at 124.
[22] See n. 20.
[23] See the Administration of Estates Act 1925, s.33. *Cooper* v. *Cooper* (1874) L.R. 7 H.L. 53.
[24] See 14th ed., p. 868.
[25] *Brown* v. *Farndell* (1688) Carth 51, 52. Bac.Abr.Exors. I, 4.
[26] *Attenborough* v. *Solomon* [1913] A.C. 76.
[27] As to assents to the vesting of land since 1925, see *post*, pp. 1055 *et seq.*
[28] Toller 6th ed., p. 345; *Fenton* v. *Clegg* (1854) 9 Exch. 680.
[29] *Per* Gibbs C.J. in *Doe* v. *Sturges* (1816) 7 Taunt. 223.
[30] *Hinson* v. *Button* (1620) 2 Roll.Rep. 158.
[31] 1 Roll.Abr. 620, Devise, D.pl. 6; Com.Dig.Admon.C. 7.

take as legatee. Before 1926, if the whole interest in some leasehold property was bequeathed to an executor, he would have impliedly assented in his own favour by taking possession of that property. Where, however, a life interest in leasehold property was given to an executor, mere entry into possession would no have been sufficient to amount to an assent. The law required clear evidence that the possession of the executor was intended by him to be beneficial possession,[32] since an assent to a life interest would amount to an assent to the interest in remainder,[33] and thereby prevent the executor from availing himself of the interest in remainder for the purpose of paying the liabilities of the estate. A similar rule applies in the case of personal chattels bequeathed in succession.[34]

Forgiveness of debt

The forgiveness of a debt due to the testator from a particular person is a form of, and has characteristics of, a specific legacy. It is, indeed, subject to the rules which affect all legacies.[35] Thus it may be adeemed[36]; it will lapse[37] by the death of the debtor in the lifetime of the testator,[38] unless an intention "specifically penned" is shown to release the debt whether the debtor survives or not.[39] The debt is not discharged until the executor has assented to the release.[40]

Pure personalty

At common law the title of a legatee of pure personalty was not complete until the executor had assented orally, by conduct, or in writing to the legacy.[41] This was so even though the legatee was himself an executor.[42] The assent might be either express or implied. If an executor refused his assent without cause he could be compelled by the court to give it.[43] All this is good law at the present time. Whether or not the residue is ascer-

---

[32] *Doe* v. *Sturges* (1816) 7 Taunt. 217; *Doe* v. *Tatchell* (1832) 3 B. & Ad. 675; *Young* v. *Holmes* (1913) 1 Stra. 70; *Richards* v. *Browne* (1837) 3 Bing.N.C. 493; *Att.-Gen.* v. *Potter* (1844) 5 Beav. 164; see also *Trail* v. *Bull* (1853) 22 L.J.Ch. 1082. As to the position since 1926, see *post*, p. 1055.

[33] *Stevenson* v. *Mayor of Liverpool* (1874) L.R. 10 Q.B. 81; *Wise* v. *Whitburn* [1924] 1 Ch. 460.

[34] *Richards* v. *Browne, supra.*

[35] *Re Wedmore* [1907] 2 Ch. 277; *Commr. of Stamp Duties* v. *Bone* [1971] A.C. 511, 519, P.C.

[36] *Rider* v. *Wager* (1725) 2 P.Wms. 328, 332.

[37] As to the meaning of "lapse" see *Re Sinclair* [1985] Ch. 446 at 450.

[38] *Toplis* v. *Baker* (1787) 2 Cox 118; *Elliott* v. *Davenport* (1705) 1 P.Wms. 83; *Maitland* v. *Adair* (1796) 3 Ves. 231; *Izon* v. *Butler* (1815) 2 Price 34.

[39] *Sibthorp* v. *Moxom* (1747) 3 Atk. 580; *South* v. *Williams* (1842) 12 Sim. 566.

[40] Wentw.Off.Ex., 14th ed., 72.

[41] Swinb.Pt. 1, s.6, pl. 5; s.7, pl. 1; 1 Saund. 278, n. (5) to *Duppa* v. *Mayo*; *Re West* [1909] 2 Ch. 180. An administrator could not assent. See *post*, p. 1056.

[42] Toller, 6th ed, p. 345; Wentw.Off.Ex., 14th ed., 67, 68.

[43] Com.Dig.Admon.C. 8; *Martin* v. *Wilson* [1913] 1 Ir.R. 470. See also the Administration of Estates Act 1925, ss.38(2), 43(2); *ante*, pp. 684, 685.

tained so as to enable an assent to be made is a question of fact. The existence of an outstanding mortgage does not necessarily prevent the residue from being ascertained.[44] And whether or not there has been an assent may involve questions of law, but it is generally a question of fact.[45] An act or expression, however, which is ambiguous is no evidence of an assent.[46] The executor may in direct terms authorise the legatee to take possession of his legacy, or his concurrence may be inferred either from direct expressions or particular acts; and such constructive permission will be equally available.[47] So where the interest of a bequest is directed to be applied for the maintenance of the legatee during minority, if the executor commences so to apply it, his consent to the principal will be presumed,[48] though an assent would not convert a contingent or defeasible interest into an absolute interest. So also if the legacy is subject to a charge, which is paid by the executor, the assent to the charge is assent to the disposition of the fund out of which it is to be satisfied.[49] Again, when the executor informs a legatee that he intends him to have the legacy according to the devise,[50] or that the legacy is ready for him whenever he will call for it,[51] such declarations clearly amount to a good assent to the bequest.

Further, in certain cases the assent of the executor may be presumed, upon the principle that, in the absence of evidence, the executors should be taken to have acted in conformity with their duty; as when executors die after the debts and duties are paid, but before the legacies are satisfied.[52] And *semble*, the assent of an executor may be concluded from the legatee's possessing himself of the subject bequeathed, and retaining it for some considerable time without complaint by the executor.[53]

An assent is not necessarily to be implied from payments of income made by the executor to a tenant for life of investments,[54] but if the whole of the income, or all the income so far received, is accounted for to the tenant for life an assent will be implied.[55]

An assent to a life interest is an assent to the interest in remainder, and

---

[44] *I.R.C.* v. *Smith* [1930] 1 K.B. 713. *I.R.C.* v. *Pilkington* (1941) 24 T.C. 160.

[45] *Elliott* v. *Elliott* (1841) 9 M. & W. 23; *Mason* v. *Farnell* (1844) 12 M. & W. 674. *Wall* v. *I.R.C.* (1933) 17 T.C. 744.

[46] *Doe* v. *Harris* (1847) 16 M. & W. 517.

[47] Com.Dig.Admon.C. 6; Toller 308, 309. Wentw.Off.Ex., 14th ed., 414.

[48] *Paramour* v. *Yardley* (1579) 2 Plowd. 539. As to assents implied in this manner with respect to leaseholds before 1926, see *Doe* d. *Mabberley* v. *Mabberley* (1833) 6 C. & P. 126; cf. *Thorne* v. *Thorne* [1893] 3 Ch. 196. As to assents relating to land after 1925, see *post*, pp. 1055 *et seq.*

[49] *Young* v. *Holmes* (1717) 1 Stra. 70.

[50] Touchst. 456; *Barnard* v. *Pumfrett* (1841) 5 M. & Cr. 70, *per* Lord Cottenham.

[51] *Hawkes* v. *Saunders* (1782) 1 Cowp. 289, 293; *Barnard* v. *Pumfrett, ante.*

[52] See *Cray* v. *Willis* (1729) 2 P.Wms. 531, 532.

[53] Matthews, *Presumptions*, 267; 3 Preston, Abstr., 2nd ed., 145; *Cole* v. *Miles* (1852) 10 Hare 179. *Carlish* v. *I.R.C.* (1958) 38 T.C. 37 and compare *Daw* v. *I.R.C.* (1928) 14 T.C. 58. This appears to be a question for the jury: *Richardson* v. *Gifford* (1834) 1 A. & E. 52.

[54] *Thorne* v. *Thorne* [1893] 3 Ch. 196; and see *Cunard's Trustees* v. *I.R.C.* [1946] 1 All E.R. 159.

[55] *Doe* d. *Mabberley* v. *Mabberley* (1833) 6 C. & P. 126.

conversely an assent to an interest in remainder enures for the benefit of the tenant for life.[56]

Choses in action

In general a chose in action is not susceptible of a simple assent alone as is the case with pure personalty.[57] For instance, the share or other interests of any member in a company are transferable in manner provided by the articles of the company.[58] The articles of a company cannot, however, bypass the representatives. If they purport themselves to operate a transfer they are invalid to this extent.[59] The title of a legatee of stocks, shares and debentures is not generally completed until he is registered as a member of the company.[60] The name of an assignee, including a legatee, of stock in the public funds must be entered in the prescribed manner in the books of the Bank of England.[61] Where a person dies solely entitled to stocks and shares, his representatives may, subject to the provisions of the articles of association, require their names to be registered in any order they may choose as shareholders or stockholders.[62] But they may, as a general rule, assign such property without themselves being registered as shareholders or stockholders.[63]

The usual practice is to send the probate or grant to the secretary of each company in which the deceased had an interest, when the secretary will endorse notice of its production and charge the usual fee.

Leaseholds

The law governing the assent by an executor to a bequest of leaseholds was, before 1926, the same as in the case of pure personalty.[64] The assent might be either express or implied.[65]

New leaseholds are, for all practical purposes,[66] so far as assents are con-

---

[56] *Stevenson* v. *Mayor of Liverpool* (1874) L.R. 10 Q.B. 81; *Wise* v. *Whitburn* [1924] 1 Ch. 460; *Re Swan* [1915] 1 Ch. 829.

[57] As to transfers of mortgage debts, see *post*, p. 1057. As to registered land, see *ante*, pp. 550–551.

[58] Companies Act 1985, s.182.

[59] *Re Greene* [1949] Ch. 333. Companies Act 1985, s.187.

[60] See Companies Act 1985, s.8, and Table A. Arts. 23–28.

[61] See the National Debt Act 1870, ss.22 and 23; *ante*, p. 527.

[62] *Re T. H. Saunders & Co. Ltd.* [1908] 1 Ch. 415; *Scott* v. *Frank F. Scott (London) Ltd.* [1940] Ch. 794; see also *Edwards* v. *Ransomes & Rapier Ltd.* [1930] W.N. 180 (executor and beneficiary entitled to be registered in his own name as a debenture-holder). See also the Companies Act 1985, ss.183, 187. *Re Paradise Motor Co.* [1968] 1 W.L.R. 1125; *Re Jermyn Street Turkish Baths Ltd.* [1970] 1 W.L.R. 1194, 1205.

[63] See the Companies Act 1985, s.183(3).

[64] Swinb., Pt. 1, s.6, pl. 5; s.7, pl. 1; 1 Saund. 275, n. (5) to *Duppa* v. *Mayo*; *Re Culverhouse* [1896] 2 Ch. 251.

[65] See *ante*, p. 1053 as to implied or presumed assents.

[66] There can still be an implied assent of an equitable interest in leaseholds, as to which, see *post*, p. 1056. As to mortgage debts, see *post*, p. 1057.

cerned, on the same footing as realty.[67] Under the old law an assent, express or implied, to a bequest of leaseholds to a person for his life operated as an assent in favour of the remainderman, and vice versa.[68] After 1925, however, the whole legal estate in the leaseholds should be conveyed by a vesting assent to the tenant for life or "statutory owners,"[69] or by an absolute assent to trustees for sale, as the case may require.[70] Under a vesting assent the tenant for life becomes the "estate owner,"[71] and will hold the leaseholds on trust for himself and the remainderman successively. No assent should be made of the equitable remainder. After an assent has been made of the legal estate the persons entitled to equitable interests are no longer concerned with the representatives, but with the "estate owner," or, on his death, his representatives, or with the trustees for sale in whom the and has been vested, as the case may be.[72]

It is probably still true to say that an assent to a term of years amounts by implication to an assent in respect to rent, or to a condition or contingency issuing out of or annexed to the land,[73] though the converse proposition can no longer be maintained.[74]

Realty

An assent to real estate (including leaseholds[75]) has now to be in writing. Section 36 of the Administration of Estates Act 1925 provided that a representative[76] may assent to the vesting, in any person who (whether by devise, bequest, devolution, appropriation or otherwise)[77] may be entitled thereto, either beneficially or as a trustee or personal representative, of any estate or interest in real estate to which the testator or intestate was entitled or over which he exercised a general power of appointment by his

---

[67] See the Administration of Estates Act 1925, s.36.

[68] *Stevenson* v. *Mayor of Liverpool* (1874) L.R. 10 Q.B. 81; *Wise* v. *Whitburn* [1924] 1 Ch. 460.

[69] See the Settled Land Act 1925, ss.23, 26, 117(1)(xxvi).

[70] Or other person entitled to the legal estate under the Settled Land Act 1925. See *ibid.* ss.6, 7, 8, 19, 20; 3 Wolst. & Ch., 13th ed., p. 40 *et seq.*

[71] *i.e.* the owner of the legal estate: the Settled Land Act 1925, s.117(1)(xi).

[72] See 5 Wolst. & Ch., 13th ed., pp. 61–63.

[73] See *Goffe* v. *Haywood* (1616) 1 Roll.Rep. 620, tit. Devise, E. pl. 2; *ibid.* pl. 3; Com.Dig.Admon.C. 6.

[74] For an assent relating to land must now be in writing; *post*, p. 1055.

[75] Administration of Estates Act 1925, s.55(1)(xix), (*post*, p. 1149).

[76] An executor *de son tort* is not, for this purpose, included in the definition of personal representative: *ibid.* s.55(1)(xi). For the precise words of this section, see Appendix, *post*, p. 1149. As to registered land, see *ante*, pp. 550–551.

[77] There is some doubt whether the words "or otherwise" allow an executor to make an assent in favour of a purchaser from a beneficiary. Until the doubt has been resolved it will be better to complete the transaction by a conveyance in any case where the person entitled claims otherwise than directly under the will or intestacy (*i.e.* if there is any intervening step in his title). This difficulty is not clearly met by the overreaching provisions of s.36(6) (7) because in practice such a purchaser is unlikely often to make title without the will trusts or intestacy being apparent. In such a case, the assent of itself may not be "sufficient," but see 35 M.L.R. 206, 207; 140 N.L.J. 96.

will, including the statutory power to dispose of entailed interests,[78] and which devolved upon the representative.[79]

Before the Land Transfer Act 1897 realty did not (with the exception of trust and mortgage estates[80]) vest in representatives. By section 3 (1) of that Act the personal representatives could make an assent in favour of a devisee in respect of real estate which vested in them.[81] The operation of the assent was not to convey the property to the devisee, but to perfect an interest which until then had been inchoate. An assent of realty, as in the case of personalty, might have been either express or implied.

Equitable interests

There can still be an implied assent of an equitable interest in property, including land.[82] The fact that a representative has been given a power to allow a beneficiary to take possession of land, including receipt of rents and profits, before an assent is made,[83] will no doubt detract from the force that authorised possession used to have in implying an assent.

On the death of a person in whom is vested an equitable interest in land, not ceasing on his death (*e.g.* an estate *pur autre vie*), but who is not the "estate owner" (*e.g.* where the legal estate is vested in "statutory owners"[85]), an assent to the vesting of the equitable interest in the person entitled thereto will be necessary. But where the deceased was the "estate owner," and an assent in writing is made vesting the legal estate in the person next entitled thereto, an assent (express or implied) in respect of an equitable interest in the same land will be unnecessary. The person in whom is vested the legal estate will always hold the land on trust for the persons entitled to equitable interests therein. Thus, after an assent in respect of the legal estate, the owners of the equities will look to the "estate owner," not to the representatives.[86]

Extension to administrators

The power to assent under section 36 of the Administration of Estates Act 1925 is conferred on the representatives, that is, on administrators as

[78] As to this power, see the Law of Property Act, s.176.

[79] As it is a condition that the property should be property to which the deceased was entitled and which devolved upon the personal representative, there is doubt whether an assent is applicable in the case of property which falls into the deceased's estate after his death and is conveyed to the personal representative to hold as part of his estate. It seems wiser to effect any further disposition by means of a conveyance to the person entitled. See *Re Stirrup's Contract* [1961] 1 W.L.R. 449. See also (1961) 25 Conv.(N.S.) 490. As to mortgage debts, see *post*, p. 1057.

[80] This exception was introduced by the Conveyancing Act 1881, s.30. Both this Act and the Land Transfer Act are replaced by the Administration of Estates Act 1925, ss.1 and 3.

[81] A devisee could not insist on a conveyance in preference to an assent: *Re Pix* [1901] W.N. 165.

[82] *Re Edwards* [1981] 3 W.L.R. 15, 24.

[83] *Ibid.* s. 43(1). See *ante*, pp. 460, 684.

[84] *i.e.* the owner of the legal estate; Settled Land Act 1925, s.117(1)(xi).

[85] See *ibid.* ss. 23, 26, 117(1)(xxvi).

[86] See 5 Wolst. & Ch., 13th ed., pp. 61–63.

well as executors.[87] The above provision, however, is limited to estates or interests in real estate, and does not enable an administrator to assent to the vesting of pure personalty in a person entitled on intestacy. This is generally immaterial, because in the case of stocks, shares and debentures (not being bearer securities) a transfer is requisite, and in the case of personal chattels and bearer securities delivery is sufficient.

A mortgage debt is not an "estate or interest in real estate." Hence an administrator cannot assent to the vesting of such a debt in the statutory next-of-kin of an intestate. So it should be assigned, not assented, to a person entitled on intestacy. This is preferable even if the person entitled is a legatee under a will, though a written assent by an executor would seem to be sufficient to assign the debt in that case.[88]

Before 1926 where there was an intestacy, the representatives had to convey personalty and realty to the next-of-kin or the heir in order to complete his title.

Form of assent

An assent to the vesting of a legal estate in land must be in writing, signed by the representative, and name the person in whose favour it is made.[89] Such an assent will operate to vest the legal estate in the person so named.[90] Apart from this provision, no particular form of assent is prescribed, save in the case of registered land.[91] It will help to remove possible disputes, however, if assents even of pure personalty, are made or recorded in writing. An assent need not be under seal[92]; and if not under seal and not in favour of a purchaser or made pursuant to an exercise of the statutory power of appropriation,[93] it need not be stamped[94] notwithstanding that it contains provisions (such as an acknowledgment of a right to the production of the grant) incidental to the assent. A mere misdescription of the document used, as for instance the description of a conveyance as an assent, is immaterial if the intention is clear and formalities, such as the requirement of a seal, are complied with.[95]

Assent in favour of representative

While it is clearly desirable for a representative, who is entitled beneficially or as trustee, to make an assent in his own favour after completion

---

[87] See the Administration of Estates Act 1925, s.55(1)(xi) (*post*, p. 1149).

[88] See the Law of Property Act 1925, s.136. See also article in 68 L.J. 364.

[89] Administration of Estates Act 1925, s.36(4) (*post*, p. 1130).

[90] Administration of Estates Act 1925, s.36(4). As to the passing of the benefit of a restrictive covenant, where there is an assent in writing in respect of the land for the benefit of which it exists, see *Newton Abbot C.W.S.* v. *Williamson and Treadgold* [1952] Ch. 286.

[91] See the Land Registration Act 1925, s.41; Land Registration Rules, r. 170; *ibid.* Sched., Form 56; and *ante*, pp. 550–551.

[92] An assent is excepted from the requirement that a conveyance of a legal estate in land must be by deed (Law of Property Act 1925, s.52). See p. 43.

[93] *G.H.R. Co. Ltd.* v. *I.R.C.* [1943] K.B. 303; and see *Jopling* v. *I.R.C.* [1940] 2 K.B. 282. See also (1943) 6 M.L.R. 238.

[94] *Kemp* v. *I.R.C.* [1905] 1 K.B. 581; Administration of Estates Act 1925, s.36(11).

[95] *Re Stirrup's Contract* [1961] 1 W.L.R. 449 (assent under seal upheld as a conveyance).

of administration,[96] the view was taken that despite the provisions of section 36(4) of the Administration of Estates Act 1925 requiring an assent in writing to effectuate the passing of the legal estate, a written assent was not strictly necessary as there was no passing of the legal estate but merely a change in the character in which it was held.[97] This view has been held incorrect in a decision where the relevant authorities were not all cited.[98] In future a representative will never safely be able to terminate his character of representative in his own favour otherwise than by a written assent and if the chain of representation has been broken without assent being made, it will be necessary, although the administration is at an end, to obtain a grant of administration *de bonis non* to put the title in order. While this is the only safe view to take, its correctness must be doubted in the light of the authorities here[99] and on p. 1049, *ante*.

Vesting assents—land already settled

Where land is limited within the provisions of the Settled Land Act 1925,[1] the whole legal estate therein (which must be either a fee simple absolute in possession or a term of years absolute[2]) is vested in some person or persons known as an "estate owner."[3] On the death of that person, or the survivor of those persons, the legal estate will devolve on his representatives.[4] If the land remains settled land[5] the representatives will hold it, if satisfied that death duties are properly paid or will be paid[6] on trust, if and when so required, to convey the legal estate to the person next entitled as estate owner.[7] The conveyance should be by a vesting assent.[8] This must contain all the statements and particulars required for a vesting deed.[9]

On the other hand, if the land ceases to be settled land on the death of an estate owner, a *vesting* assent is inappropriate. If the settlement comes to an end because the next person entitled is of full age and will hold the land absolutely and beneficially free from all charges created under the settle-

---

[96] *Re Yerburgh, Yerburgh* v. *Yerburgh* [1928] W.N. 208. As to trusts, see *ante*, p. 1049.

[97] *Re Hodge, Hodge* v. *Griffiths* [1940] 1 Ch. 260; *Re Cockburn's Will Trusts* [1957] Ch. 438. See also *Phillipo* v. *Munninags* (1837) 2 X & Cr. 309; *Dix* v. *Burford* (1854) 19 Bevan 409. *Re Smith* (1889) 42 Ch.D. 302.

[98] *Re King's Will Trusts, Assheton* v. *Boyne* [1964] Ch. 542. See also (1964) 28 Conv.(N.S.) 298; (1895) 64 *Law Journal* 401; (1964) 108 *Solicitors' Journal* 698, 719; (1964) 80 L.Q.R. 328; Farrand, *Contract and Conveyance*, 2nd ed., p. 111 *et seq.*; *Re Edwards* [1981] 3 W.L.R. 15; 140 N.L.J. 96.

[99] See n. 97.

[1] Settled Land Act 1925, s.1.

[2] Law of Property Act 1925, s.1(1).

[3] Settled Land Act 1925, s.117(1)(xi). This person will be the tenant for life of full age in possession: s.19; if none, a person given the powers of a tenant for life under ss.20, 21; if none, the "statutory owners" under s.23 or 26.

[4] Administration of Estates Act 1925, ss.1(1) and 3(1)(ii) (*post*, pp. 1113, 1115).

[5] Settled Land Act 1925, s.3.

[6] *Ibid.* s.8(3)(*b*).

[7] *Ibid.* s.7(1). As to who will be so entitled, see n. 3.

[8] Settled Land Act 1925, s.8(1), (4)(*b*). For an appropriate form, see *ibid.* Sched. 1, Form 5.

[9] See n. 8.

ment[10] there should be an ordinary written assent made in his favour.[11] Should the land, on the death of an estate owner, become subject to an "immediate binding trust for sale,"[12] so that the Settled Land Act 1925 ceases to apply to it,[13] the representatives should assent to the trustees on trust for sale.[14] Again, if the persons entitled are representatives, the assent should be made in their favour as such.

It may be added that the beneficial equitable interests of persons entitled to successive interests in land will only devolve on their representatives if the interest does not cease on death.[15] And even if their interest does so survive, no assent should be made in respect thereto if the legal estate also was vested in the deceased. The assent to the vesting of the legal estate in the proper person is all that is required.[16]

Vesting assents—land settled by the testator's will

Where the testator's will itself creates a settlement the will is for the purposes of the Settled Land Act 1925 a trust instrument and the representatives of the testator hold the settled land on trust if and when required to do so, to convey it to the person who under the will is the life tenant or statutory owner and if more than one as joint tenants.[17] This may be done by vesting assent.

A right of or condition as to residence may create a settlement within the Settled Land Act 1925,[18] and if it does the condition itself may be void under section 106 of the Settled Land Act 1925 as tending to affect the statutory powers of the tenant for life.[19]

Who may assent

An executor, who derives title from the will, not the probate, may assent to a legacy before he proves the will. The assent is effectual even though he dies without taking out probate.[20] Though, *semble*, this rule now applies equally to devises of realty,[21] assents relating to a legal estate in land should, after 1925, only be made after grant of probate, so that notices of assents may be indorsed on the probate.[22]

---

[10] See n. 5.

[11] For an appropriate form, see the Law of Property Act 1925, Sched. 5, Form 8.

[12] For the meaning of this expression, see *Re Parker's S.E.* [1928] 1 Ch. 247; *Re Norton* [1929] 1 Ch. 84; *Re Sharpe's Deed of Release* [1939] Ch. 51. Megarry and Wade, *Law of Real Property*, 4th ed., 1975, pp. 359 onwards and further references therein.

[13] Settled Land Act 1925, ss.1(7), 117(1)(xxx).

[14] For an appropriate form, see the Law of Property Act 1925, Sched. 5, Form 9.

[15] Administration of Estates Act 1925, ss.1(1), 3(1).

[16] See *ante*, p. 1058.

[17] Settled Land Act 1925, s.6.

[18] See *Ungurian* v. *Lesnoff* [1990] Ch. 206 and cases there cited.

[19] See also pp. 666, 667, *ante*. *Theobald on Wills*, 14th ed., 635.

[20] *Ante*, p. 85. *Semble*, the Administration of Estates Act 1925, s.5(i), does not alter this. See *post*, p. 1116.

[21] See the Administration of Estates Act 1925, s.2(1).

[22] See the Administration of Estates Act 1925, s.36(5); *post*, p. 1061.

An administrator[23] can make an assent of real estate.[24] This assent, however, cannot be made before he has obtained letters of administration, for he derives title solely from the grant.[25]

Assent by one executor

An assent or conveyance of pure personalty maybe made by any one or more of the executors appointed.[26] Hence if one of two or more executors is a legatee, his single assent to his own legacy will vest the complete title in him.[27] But if an executor legatee renounces probate, or if he is cited to take out probate of the will and does not appear to the citation,[28] his assent to his own legacy will be ineffectual. If he takes the thing bequeathed without the permission of one of the proving executors, or of the administrator with the will annexed, he will incur the same liabilities as any other legatee so acting.[29]

On the other hand, an assent or conveyance of real estate, including, after 1925, chattels real,[30] must be made with the concurrence of all the surviving representatives who obtain probate or letters of administration, or under an order of the court.[31] The concurrence of executors who have not proved the will is unnecessary.[32]

There is one exception to this rule. Where a separate grant of representation has been made of a trust estate,[33] including settled land,[34] the concurrence of the representatives of the trust estate is unnecessary in a disposition of the general estate, and vice versa.[35]

Conditional assent

An assent which does not relate to an estate or interest in land[36] may be given upon a condition precedent. For instance, an executor might tell a legatee that he will pay the legacy, provided the assets are sufficient to answer all demands.[37] But an assent will be considered absolute if the executor attempts to annex a condition which he has no authority to impose. Such a condition might be that the legatee should do something for

---

[23] As to the efficacy of an assent by an administrator during minority, see *ante*, p. 553.

[24] See *ante*, p. 1056.

[25] See *ante*, p. 90.

[26] See *ante*, p. 692.

[27] Roll Abr. 618, Devise, B. pl. 2, 3; Perk. s.572; Com.Dig.Admon.C. 8; *Townson* v. *Tickell* (1819) 3 B. & A. 31, 40.

[28] See the Administration of Estates Act 1925, s.5 (*post*, p. 1116). As to the effect of death of an executor before proving, see *ante*, p. 85.

[29] Administration of Estates Act 1925, s.5; and *Broker* v. *Charter* (1590) Cro.Eliz. 92.

[30] Administration of Estates Act 1925, s.3(1) (*post*, p. 1115).

[31] *Ibid.* s.2(2). See also s.8.

[32] *Ibid.* s.2(2), replacing Conveyancing Act 1911, s.12.

[33] See the Supreme Court Act 1981, s.113.

[34] See the Administration of Estates Act 1925, s.24 (*post*, p. 1124).

[35] *Ibid.* ss.2(2) and 24; and the Supreme Court Act 1981, s.113.

[36] Before 1926 these remarks applied equally to chattels real. As to the right of indemnity, see *ante*, p. 654.

[37] Wentw.Off.Ex., 14th ed., 429.

the executor's personal benefit.[38] Further, a condition subsequent cannot be imposed. Thus, a condition that a legatee will pay the executor a certain sum annually is void, and failure to perform it will not divest the legatee of his legacy.[39]

Semble, an assent to the vesting of an estate or interest in land can only be subject to the condition authorised by section 36(10) of the Administration of Estates Act 1925.[40] That subsection provides that a representative may, as a condition of giving an assent or making a conveyance, require security for the discharge of any duties, debts or liability to which the estate or interest is subject, but is not entitled to postpone the giving of an assent merely by reason of the subsistence of any such duties, debt or liability if reasonable arrangements have been made for discharging the same; and an assent may be given subject to any legal charge or charge by way of legal mortgage.[41]

Right of beneficiary after assent

The beneficiary is entitled to assume that the executors have properly administered the estate. If he receives assets or money believing himself in good faith entitled he does not have the heavy burden of trusteeship imposed upon him.[42]

After an assent by an executor to a specific legacy, the interest in the chattel bequeathed vests in the legatee.[43] He may bring an action to recover it,[44] even against the executor himself.

If there is a specific bequest to the executor himself on trust, and he assents to it, the thing bequeathed thereupon ceases to be part of the testator's assets, and the executor becomes a trustee of it for those who are beneficially interested.[45] He is thereupon precluded from dealing with it or making title as executor.[46]

An assent or conveyance of a legal estate is sufficient, but not conclusive, evidence that the person in whose favour it is made is the person entitled to have the legal estate conveyed to him, unless notice[47] of a previous assent or conveyance affecting that legal estate has been placed on or annexed to

---

[38] *Elliott* v. *Elliott* (1841) 9 M. & W. 23. See also *ante*, p. 522; *post*, p. 1129.

[39] See n. 37.

[40] See 5 Wolst. & Ch., 13th ed., pp. 65–66.

[41] See *Williams* v. *Holland* [1965] 1 W.L.R. 739. Under the Settled Land Act 1925, s.8(6), a personal representative may reserve a term of years to himself to keep himself indemnified against unpaid duties; see 3 Wolst. & Ch., 13th ed., p. 46.

[42] *Re Diplock* [1948] Ch. 465 at 478; *Re Montago* [1987] Ch. 264 at 279.

[43] *Doe* v. *Guy* (1802) 3 East 120. See, as to leaseholds, *Re Culverhouse* [1896] 2 Ch. 251. As to the desirability of sale after assent rather than by the special executors of a deceased life tenant, see *ante*.

[44] *Doe* v. *Guy, ante*; *Williams* v. *Lee* (1745) 3 Atk. 223.

[45] *Dix* v. *Burford* (1854) 19 Beav. 409.

[46] *Attenborough* v. *Solomon* [1913] A.C. 76; *Wise* v. *Whitburn* [1924] 1 Ch. 460.

[47] A person in whose favour a conveyance has been made may require notice of such conveyance to be indorsed on the probate or letters of administration: Administration of Estates Act 1925, s.36(5).

the probate or letters of administration.[48] Thus a purchaser[49] when investigating a title may safely accept an assent as evidence that the person in whose favour it has been made was the person entitled to have the legal estate conveyed to him, unless and until, upon a proper investigation by him of the vendor's title, facts come to his knowledge which indicate the contrary. When that happens, the assent cannot be accepted as sufficient evidence of something which the purchaser knows or has reason for believing to be contrary to the facts.[50] Thus a purchaser who discovers that the assent has been made in favour of a purchaser from a legatee rather than the legatee himself may be in difficulty.[51] This provision does not, however, prejudice the claim of any person rightfully entitled to the estate so conveyed.[52]

A conveyance by a representative of a legal estate in land to a purchaser[53] accepted on the faith of a statement in writing by the representative that he has not previously made an assent or conveyance of that estate, will operate to pass that estate, unless it has already passed to a prior purchaser claiming mediately or immediately through the representative, or unless notice of a previous assent or conveyance has been indorsed on the probate or grant.[54] If the representative makes a false statement in writing he is liable as if the statement had been contained in a statutory declaration.[55]

Assent not retractable

An executor may not retract an assent once implemented,[56] and notwithstanding a subsequent dissent, a specific legatee has a right to take the legacy, and has a lien on the assets for that specific part, and may follow them.[57] If the assent has not been completed by payment, in the case of a general legacy, or possession, in that of a specific one, and its recall is not attended with injury to a third person, as to a purchaser in good faith from the legatee on the faith of such assent. The executor may have the power of retracting it; for example, where he assents upon a reasonable ground for considering that the assets are sufficient to answer all demands, but

---

[48] Administration of Estates Act 1925, s.36(7); *Re Duce and Boots', etc., post.*

[49] Purchaser means only a purchaser for money or money's worth: Administration of Estates Act 1925, s.36(11).

[50] *Re Duce and Boots', etc., Contract* [1937] Ch. 642. See *ante*, p. 675.

[51] See *ante*, p. 1055, n. 77.

[52] Administration of Estates Act 1925, s.36(7).

[53] See the Administration of Estates Act 1925, ss.36(11), 55(1)(xviii).

[54] *Ibid.* s.36(6); but see Williams, *The Law Relating to Assents*, Appendix V.

[55] See the Administration of Estates Act 1925, s.36(5), (6). See also subs. (7) for position of purchaser from assentee. And see 5 Wolst. & Ch., 13th ed., pp. 63–65.

[56] *Noell* v. *Robinson* (1686) 2 Vent. 358; Wentw.Off.Ex., 14th ed., 415; Com.Dig. Admon.C. 8. So if executors have set apart and appropriated assets to meet a legacy, and have admitted to the legatee that such appropriation has been made, they cannot retain or impound any part of such appropriated assets to meet a debt from the legatee to the general estate of the testator: *Ballard* v. *Marsden* (1880) 14 Ch.D. 374.

[57] *Mead* v. *Orrery* (1745) 3 Atk. 235; Toller 6th ed., p. 311.

unknown debts are unexpectedly claimed, thus occasioning a deficiency.[58] However, if the assent has been completed by a payment or possession and cannot be retracted the executor is still entitled to compel the legatee to refund when debts appear of which the executor had no previous notice.[59]

An assent relating to land is not made expressly irrevocable by the Administration of Estates Act 1925, but is so by implication.[60] An assent or conveyance given or made by a representative does not, except in favour of a purchaser[61] of a legal estate, prejudice the right of the representative or any other person to recover the estate or interest to which the assent or conveyance relates, or to be indemnified out of such estate or interest against any duties, debt, or liability to which such estate or interest would have been subject if there had not been any assent or conveyance.[62]

Relation back of assent

At common law the assent of an executor relates back to the time of the testator's death,[63] so as to confirm intermediate dealing.[64] Thus such an assent confirms an intermediate grant by the legatee of his legacy.[65] An assent to a residuary bequest, however, does not relate back to the testator's death, for the legatee has no interest in any defined portion of the estate until the residue is ascertained.[66] An assent to the vesting of an estate or interest in land made after 1925 by an executor or administrator relates back to the death of the testator or intestate, unless a contrary intention appears.[67]

Assent to wrong person

The assent can only operate in favour of the legatee to whom the legacy is given. If a legacy, to which an assent has been made, is revoked by a codicil subsequently discovered and given to another, the latter can recover the legacy and mesne profits from the first legatee, on the ground that the assent operated to vest the right to sue for the legacy in the person

---

[58] See 1 Rop.Leg., 3rd ed., 855, 856.

[59] See *post*, p. 1077; *Doe* v. *Guy* (1802) 3 East 120, 123.

[60] But there can now be a provisional assent, see the Administration of Estates Act 1925, s.43 (*post*, p. 1136).

[61] *i.e.* purchaser for money or money's worth: *ibid.* subs. (11).

[62] Administration of Estates Act 1925, ss.36(9) and 38(1) (*post*, p. 1131).

[63] *I.R.C.* v. *Hawley* [1928] 1 K.B. 578. As to relation back in connection with the acts of an administrator, other than his assent to the vesting of an estate or interest in land (which is considered here), see *ante*, pp. 90 *et seq.*

[64] See Wentw.Off.Ex., 14th ed., 445, 446; *Saunders' Case* (1599) 5 Co. 12*a*, in which references were made to tithes, advowsons and rents, all of which when legal interests in land, would now fall within the Administration of Estates Act 1925, s.36(2).

[65] Toller 6th ed., p. 311. But see Wentw.Off.Ex., 14th ed., 445; and *Doe* v. *Sgurges* (1816) 7 Taunt. 223, *per* Gibbs C.J. *dubitante.*

[66] *Barnardo's Homes* v. *I.R.C.* [1921] 2 A.C. 1; *Corbett* v. *I.R.C.* [1938] 1 K.B. 567. The Income and Corporation Taxes Act 1970, Part XV, though affecting the incidence of income tax on residuary estates of deceased persons, does not affect the nature of the beneficiaries' interest in the residue.

[67] Administration of Estates Act 1925, s.36(2). See Appendix, *post*, p. 1129.

properly entitled thereto, even though his identity was mistaken.[68] But an assent required to be in writing under the Administration of Estates Act 1925, must name the person in whose favour it is given, and it will pass the legal estate to that person whether he is properly entitled under the will or not.[69] The extent to which an assent may safely be accepted by a purchaser has been discussed.[70]

As has been seen[71] an assent or conveyance does not prejudice the right of the representative or any other person to recover the property to which the assent or conveyance related or any property representing the same, where for example a devise to which an assent has been made is revoked by a codicil subsequently discovered.

Cost of transfer

Once an executor has assented to a specific bequest of shares or mortgages, all costs of transfer, including those of the executor in connection therewith, must be borne by the specific legatee[72]; but the costs of an assent in relation to settled land are payable out of the trust estate.[73]

Applications in court

The court may, on the application of any creditor or other person interested, and notwithstanding an assent or conveyance by representatives, make necessary orders in respect of the property, save, however, as against a purchaser.[74]

---

[68] *Re West* [1909] 2 Ch. 180. As to refunding, see *post*, p. 1077.
[69] Administration of Estates Act 1925, s.36(2), (4). The position in equity will remain unaffected.
[70] See *ante*, p. 1061.
[71] See n. 62, *supra*.
[72] *Re Grosvenor* [1916] 2 Ch. 375. As to the cost of transferring specific legacies generally, see *ante*, p. 1032.
[73] See the Settled Land Act 1925, s.8(2).
[74] See *ibid.* ss.38(2), 43(2) (Appendix *post*).

CHAPTER 79

DISTRIBUTION ON INTESTACY

The rights of the next of kin of an intestate have already necessarily been considered for the purposes of Chapter 19,[1] which is concerned with the right to a grant of administration. This chapter therefore refers back for many purposes to Chapter 19. The difficult question of disclaimer on intestacy is referred to on p. 940. It must also be remembered[2] that the right of those entitled on intestacy is a right which can only be asserted by calling upon the administrator to perform his duty.[3]

Statutory distribution[4]

The rules for distribution of the estate where the deceased has died totally or partially intestate are prescribed by statute. The old rules were varied in 1925,[5] 1952,[6] 1966[7] (only as to the interest of a surviving spouse) and in 1969 (as to illegitimate children). These changes took effect in the case of deaths on and after January 1, 1926, 1952, 1967 and 1970 respectively.[8] It has been held that the statutory rules do not "dispose" of the intestate's property but simply provide how so much of it as was undisposed of should be administered. The powers of administrators on intestacy have already been considered.[9]

Residuary estate

The residuary estate of the intestate[10] is the residue of the net money arising from the sale and conversion of real and personal estate after payment of testamentary expenses and liabilities and after setting aside a fund to provide for any pecuniary legacies, together with any unsold invest-

---

[1] See *ante*, p. 253. As to the well-known presumption against intestacy see *Theobald on Wills*, 14th ed., 785 and *Re Harrison* (1885) 30 Ch.D. 390, 393: "when a testator has executed a will in solemn form you must assume that he did not intend to make it a solemn farce." As to title on death see (1990) *Conveyancer* 358.

[2] See p. 1050 *ante*.

[3] *Cooper* v. *Cooper* (1824) L.R. 7 H.L. 53 at 65.

[4] For table of distribution, see p. 1138. As to advertisement for claims, see *ante*, p. 605.

[5] Administration of Estates Act 1925, ss.46, 49 (*post*, pp. 1137, 1145). See *Re Bridgen* [1938] Ch. 205, 209 as to the effect of the changes in 1925. For distribution under the Statutes of Distribution see earlier editions, and Sherrin and Bonehill *Intestate Succession* pp. 24–39.

[6] Intestates' Estates Act 1952, ss.1, 3. See Appendix, *post*.

[7] Family Provision Act 1966, s.1. *Re Buttle's Will Trusts* [1977] 1 W.L.R. 1200, 1211.

[8] See p. 1075 *post*.

[9] See *ante*, p. 688 trust for sale and conversion: p. 685, appropriation.

[10] Administration of Estates Act, 1925, s.33(4).

ments not required for administration and any ready money of the deceased. This residuary estate is distributed in the manner or held upon the trusts mentioned in section 46 of the Administration of Estates Act 1925, as amended. Since the right to a grant of administration follows in substance the beneficial interests on distribution, the rules of distribution on a total intestacy have in effect already been considered.[11] It is here only necessary to refer to the exact wording of the statutes,[12] to consider a number of ancillary matters, and to discuss partial intestacy. A table of distribution will be found in Appendix 1 for easy reference.[13]

Nature of the rights on intestacy

Although it seems to have been suggested that the next-of-kin take a vested interest[14] upon the death of an intestate, it is doubtful whether they can take more than the inchoate right pending administration and assent, which is the only right of the legatee.[15] This would seem to be no more than a right to apply for a grant in accordance with the practice of the Family Division, or to force the representative to administer properly or obtain an administration order in the Chancery Division. But whatever the nature of this right, it has been held that the court will not defeat it by retrospectively avoiding the dissolution of a company which would have been entitled if in existence at the date of death.[16]

The surviving spouse

The surviving spouse has, under an intestacy, three rights which require primary consideration. These are (1) the statutory legacy or fixed net sum[17] (2) the right to purchase or redeem the life interest[18] and (3) the right to acquire the matrimonial home.

The statutory legacy

This is varied from time to time by order of the Lord Chancellor and at present stands at £85,000.[19]

---

[11] See *ante*, pp. 258 *et seq.* and tables of distribution, *post*, p. 1138. As to the meaning of personal chattels, see *ante*, p. 498.

[12] See Appendix, *post*, p. 1137.

[13] See n. 11.

[14] See *Re Servers of the Blind* [1960] 1 W.L.R. 564. Under the statutory trusts which arise when the residuary estate is ascertained beneficiaries do not obtain a vested interest until they attain majority or marry under that age. See *ante*, p. 262.

[15] See *ante*, p. 1050 and *Eastbourne Mutual B.S.* v. *Hastings* [1965] 1 W.L.R. 861; *Lall* v. *Lall* [1965] 1 W.L.R. 1249.

[16] *Re Servers of the Blind League* [1960] 1 W.L.R. 564.

[17] See generally Sherrin & Bonehill, *Intestate Succession*, pp. 204–211, and pp. 259 *et seq. ante* and 1066 *post*.

[18] See n. 20.

[19] See n. 17.

Right of the surviving spouse to purchase or redeem the life interest

The life interest of the surviving spouse[20] may at the election of such spouse be purchased or redeemed by the representative,[21] and the residuary estate may then be distributed free from the life interest.

The capital value of the life interest is reckoned in accordance with the rules and tables extant in the Intestate Succession (Interest and Capitalisation) Order 1977.[22]

An election to take a capital sum in lieu of a life interest may only be exercised if at the time of election the whole of the part of the residuary estate consists of property in possession, but a life interest in property partly in possession and partly not in possession is treated as comprising two separate life interests in those respective parts of the property.

If the tenant for life dies after electing, but before the election takes effect, the date of redemption is the date immediately before the death of the tenant for life. Election must occur, however, within 12 months of the date when representation to the estate is first taken out, but the court may extend the period in special circumstances. The mode of election is by notice to the representatives in writing. Once given, notification may not be revoked, except with the consent of the representatives. Where the tenant for life is the sole representative, written notice must be given to the principal probate registrar. An infant may make a binding election, but the representative must not pay him the capital sum, but hold it on the statutory trusts.[23]

Apart from their power of appropriation,[24] the representatives have power[25] to raise the whole or any part of this capital sum, or the fixed net sum payable to the surviving spouse or any part thereof and the interest thereon, and, in either case, the proper costs of the transaction, on the security of the whole or any part of the residuary estate (other than the "personal chattels"[26]).

Matrimonial home

The surviving spouse may acquire from the representatives by way of appropriation any matrimonial home owned by the deceased, in which the spouse was living at the death of the intestate.[27] But this right does not give

[20] See *ante*, pp. 259, 359: 102 L.Q.R. 445.
[21] See s.47A of the Administration of Estates Act 1925 (*post*, p. 1142), inserted by s.2 of the Intestates' Estates Act 1952, and amended by s.28 of the Administration of Justice Act 1977. For a review of the practical considerations to be taken into account when such an election arises, see the article by J. H. George, LL.B., in (1968) 32 Conv.(N.S.) 246.
[22] Printed, *post*, p. 1270.
[23] Administration of Estates Act 1925, s.47A, as set out in the Intestates' Estates Act 1952, s.2 (*post*, p. 1142).
[24] See *ante*, p. 685.
[25] Administration of Estates Act 1925, s.48(2) (*post*, p. 1144).
[26] Administration of Estates Act 1925, s.55(1)(x) and p. 498 *ante*.
[27] Intestates' Estates Act 1952, s.5 and Sched. II; note especially the provisions in para. 5 of Sched. II.

a surviving spouse the right to defend a claim for possession[28] if she has not taken out a grant.

Any valuation must be taken as at the date of the appropriation, and not as at the date of death.[29] If the value of the matrimonial home is greater than the value of the surviving spouse's interest the appropriation will be partly in satisfaction of that interest and partly for a money payment reflecting the difference.[30]

Rights of issue, parents and of the Crown

The rights of issue and parents in the residuary estate[31] have already been discussed[32] together with the rights of the Crown to *bona vacantia*.[33] Conflicts may, however, arise between the Crown nominee and next-of-kin who come forward after the grant. For this purpose it is provided that any legal proceeding by or against that nominee are to be of the same character and to be carried on in the same manner as if the administration had been granted to the nominee as one of the persons interested in the estate.[34] The nominee is thus in the position of any other administrator[35] but he has been held not to be an "express trustee" for limitation purposes.[36] If the next-of-kin succeed against the nominee they are entitled to interest[37] but interest cannot be obtained as against the Crown if there has been no grant on the Crown's behalf.[38]

Practice where Crown entitled

Where it appears that the Crown, the Duchy of Lancaster or the Duke of Cornwall may be entitled to claim *bona vacantia* the facts should be referred as soon as possible to the Treasury Solicitor or the Solicitor to the Duchy concerned. It is for such Solicitor to make any necessary inquiries and issue advertisements before applying for the grant. He has no special powers either before or after grant. He will not intervene if the estate is insolvent and may renounce if a creditor wishes to administer. He is not entitled to undertake an administration where there are in existence kin of

[28] *Lall* v. *Lall* [1965] 1 W.L.R. 1249. The charge conferred by the Matrimonial Homes Act 1967 determines on death, *ibid.* s.2(2)(*a*).

[29] *Re Collins* [1975] 1 W.L.R. 309.

[30] *Re Phelps* [1980] Ch. 275.

[31] See *ante*, p. 1065.

[32] See *ante*, pp. 261, 263, and tables of distribution, *post*, p. 1138.

[33] See *ante*, pp. 265.

[34] Administration of Estates Act 1925, s.30(1), replacing the Intestates' Estates Act 1884, s.2 (*post*, p. 1126).

[35] See also the Administration of Estates Act 1925, s.30(2); *Att.-Gen.* v. *Kohler* (1861) 9 H.L.C. 654, discussed in *Re Mason* [1928] Ch. 385, 395; affirmed on appeal on another point [1929] 1 Ch. 1; *Re Dewell* (1858) 4 Dr. 269; *Re Gosman* (1881) 17 Ch.D. 771. Informations and petitions of right (mentioned in s.30) were abolished by the Crown Proceedings Act 1947, Sched. 1.

[36] *Re Blake* [1932] 1 Ch. 54, 62. There appear to have been no decisions on the effect of the Crown Proceedings Act 1947 or the Limitation Act 1939 upon the cases cited above.

[37] *Partington* v. *Att.-Gen.* (1869) 4 H.L. 100.

[38] *Re Gosman* (1881) 17 Ch.D. 771. C.A.

the deceased who are entitled but decline to take a grant. There are variations of practice between the Crown and the Duchies.[39]

Discretionary provision for dependants and other persons out of bona vacantia

It is open to anyone who considers he is a person for whom the intestate might reasonably have been expected to make provision to apply to the Treasury Solicitor or the Solicitor to the Duchy, as the case may be, for an *ex gratia* payment to be made to him from the estate. There are differences of practice between the Crown and the Duchies. The Treasury Solicitor and the Solicitors to the Duchies will advise on correct procedure. Payments are made by reference to the practice referred to in section 46(1)(vi) of the Administration of Estates Act 1925 (as amended) and on a number of grounds. Common grounds are the performance of essential services for the intestate by the applicant; failure by the testator to comply with the attestation rules; the absence of a will where the expressed wishes of a testator are known; and remoteness of relationship, *e.g.* where the applicant is related but outside the immediate classes otherwise entitled. Where the intestate was of illegitimate birth, grants were frequently made to the persons who would have been entitled by the law of intestacy to share in the estate apart from the illegitimacy.

Partial intestacy

Total intestacy arises where the deceased has made no effective disposition of any of his property, even though there may be a will.[40] On intestacy the assets are administered under Part 3 of the Administration of Estates Act 1925,[41] and the distribution is governed by Part 4.[42] Where, however, a person dies leaving a will effectively disposing of part of his property, the will is the controlling instrument.[43] Sections 33, 46, 47 and 48 of the Administration of Estates Act 1925 are only applied so far as they can be applied consistently in all respects with the terms of the will.[44] Thus, as has been seen,[45] an express trust for sale in the will excludes the statutory trusts for sale under section 33, for there cannot be two subsisting trusts for conversion, but neither the express trust nor the statutory trust will normally be construed as applying to reversionary interests created by the will, but undisposed of.[46] Such interests are not to be sold, nor are the

---

[39] There was formerly some doubt as to the Duchy rights in Cornwall. See *Solicitor of Duchy of Cornwall* v. *Canning* (1880) 5 P.D. 114, but see now the Administration of Estates Act, 1925, s.46(1)(vi); 84 L.S. Gazette 3315.

[40] *Re Ford* [1902] 2 Ch. 605; *Re Cuffe* [1908] 2 Ch. 500; *Re Skeats* [1936] Ch. 683.

[41] ss.32–44 (*post*, pp. 1127 *et seq.*).

[42] ss.45–52. See also the Family Law Reform Act 1969 as to illegitimate children.

[43] A will may exclude a person from benefiting on intestacy and if it so provides will be construed as operating a gift by implication to next of kin not excluded. *Re Wynn* [1984] 1 W.L.R. 232.

[44] *Re McKee* [1931] 2 Ch. 145, 148; *Re Plowman* [1943] Ch. 269; *Re Taylor* [1969] 2 W.L.R. 1371; Administration of Estates Act 1925, s.49 (1969) 85 L.Q.R. 464, and see *ante*, p. 990.

[45] See *ante*, p. 688.

[46] See n. 44.

testamentary expenses payable out of such interests, nor can the next-of-kin claim immediate payment.[47] However, if a widow has a life interest under the will, but the reversionary interest arising after her death is undisposed of, she can claim payment of her capital sum forthwith, because the life interest merges in it.[48] She is now accountable, however, for interests taken under the Will.[49]

The court will ignore or set aside provisions attempting to govern the interests which are undisposed of, as for instance directions to accumulate income in favour of non-existent children.[50] Where both the will and the statute are silent the old law applies.[51]

Trust for sale

Where there is an immediate partial intestacy an immediate express trust for sale will apply,[52] but if there is no express trust for sale in the will it seems doubtful if section 33 (which is in Part 3) can strictly operate because section 49 only applies Part 4 of the Act to the partial intestacy.[53]

Modifications of the will

Section 49, as amended, provides that where any person dies leaving a will disposing of part of his property, Part 4 of the Act has effect as respects the part of the property not so disposed of subject to the provisions contained in the will and subject to two modifications. First in all cases of partial intestacy property, including beneficial interests in property abroad,[54] acquired by issue under the will[55] must be brought into account and the representative is a trustee for the next-of-kin.[56] Further, since 1953 beneficial interests taken by a spouse under the will are deducted from the lump sum payments to such spouse.[57] It has, however, been questioned whether it is always necessary in applying section 49 to keep to the provisions of section 47(1)(iii) in so far as they require the value to be reckoned as at the death of the intestate.[58] Secondly the representative is, subject to his rights and powers for the purposes of administration, a trustee for the persons

---

[47] See n. 44.

[48] *Re Bowen-Buscarlet* [1972] Ch. 463. The assumption to the contrary in *Re KcKee* [1931] Ch.145 is incorrect.

[49] A.E.A. 1925, s.49(1)(*aa*). See *Re Bowen-Buscarlet* [1972] Ch. 463 at 469.

[50] *Re Thornber* [1937] Ch. 39; and see *Re Sullivan [1930] 1 Ch. 84.*

[51] *Re Taylor* [1969] 2 Ch. 245, 249, 250.

[52] *Per* Maugham J. [1931] 2 Ch. 149.

[53] *Per* Hanworth M.R. [1931] 2 Ch. 159. *Re Douglas* [1959] 1 W.L.R. 744, seems insupportable on this point.

[54] *Re Osoba* [1978] 1 W.L.R. 791, 797, *per* Megarry V.-C.

[55] Including interests received under the exercise of a general but not a special power of appointment by the will. See Intestates' Estates Act 1952, s.3(3). As to the surviving spouse see note 49 *ante*.

[56] Administration of Estates Act 1925, s.49; *Re Young* [1951] Ch. 185. Life interests are accounted for on an actuarial valuation. See *Re Morton* [1956] Ch. 644. *Re Grover* [1971] Ch. 168.

[57] Intestates' Estates Act 1952, s.3(2).

[58] See *per* Pennycuick J. in *Re Grover* [1971] Ch. 168, 179.

entitled under Part 4 unless it appears by the will that he is entitled to take beneficially.

Issue must account for advancements

Where the property is divisible into shares under total or partial intestacy, because two or more children or their issue survive the intestate, a statutory satisfaction (inaccurately in this case called "hotchpot") provision applies.[59] In the absence of a contrary intention, expressed or appearing in the circumstances, a child[60] must bring into account at a valuation, the value to be reckoned at the intestate's death,[61] any money or property, including a life or less interest, which, by way of advancement[62] or on the marriage of the child, has been paid or settled, or covenanted to be paid or settled,[63] by the intestate for the benefit of the child. It seems that where an intestate has during his lifetime made a settlement on any child and the child's spouse and issue, the sum to be brought into account is not the value of that child's interest under the settlement, but the value of the whole amount settled.[64] Funds transferred by the trustees of a marriage settlement to a son in pursuance of an appointment in his favour made by his father in exercise of a special power of appointment amongst his children and of a surrender of the father's life interest, have been held not to be money or property paid by way of advancement to the son by the father within the meaning of "statutory provision."[65] The statutory rules for hotchpot on intestacy may differ from those which apply in equity.[66] Where a life interest falls to be valued for purposes of hotchpot it seems that, unlike an annuity,[67] it has to be valued at its actuarial value regardless of the actual period of survival.[68]

Nature of advancement

The word "advancement" is used in two senses. First, there is the typical gift by way of advancement for establishing a child in life. Secondly, there

---

[59] Administration of Estates Act 1925, s. 47 (1) (iii). For the position on testacy, see *ante*, p. 953.

[60] Under a total intestacy children only have to account. Issue account only in respect of the parent for whom they are substituted. Under a partial intestacy all issue must account for property acquired under the will, but are otherwise in the same position as issue under a total intestacy.

[61] As to circumstances in which it may be necessary to depart from this provision see *ante*, n. 58, p. 1070.

[62] As to what is an advancement, see *infra*, and *ante*, p. 953.

[63] For the covenant will be satisfied under *ibid.*, s.33, before distribution. See also *Hardy* v. *Shaw* [1976] Ch. 82, 87.

[64] *Re Reeve* [1935] Ch. 110.

[65] See n. 64.

[66] See article "Hotchpot on Intestacy" by J. T. Farrand in (1961) 25 Conv. (N.S.) 468. A close analysis of the wording of s.47 may indicate the differences.

[67] See *ante*, p. 631.

[68] *Re Thomson* [1953] Ch. 414.

is the advancement or anticipation of the interest or portion to be taken under the will or intestacy.[69] Under section 5 of the Statutes of Distribution 1670 any child of the intestate had to bring into account any "estate by settlement" and anything advanced by portion. Section 47(1)(iii) of the Administration of Estates Act 1925 is narrower and provides only for "money or property which, by way of advancement or on the marriage of a child of the intestate" has been paid, but decisions on the old Act are, generally speaking, applicable to the new.[70]

In general it is a question of fact whether a benefit given to a child is an "advancement" within the section. Not every "settlement" is now an advancement, nor is the relative value of the sum advanced in relation to the size of the estate conclusive, if such sum is insufficient to constitute a permanent provision. The age of the child, the size of the sum and the number of payments are all relevant factors.[71]

Other relatives do not account

Persons other than children and issue who take a distributive share under section 46 do not, in the absence of an express provision, have to account for property, whether advanced to them by the intestate during his lifetime or given to them by his will.[72]

Subject to this, the "statutory trusts" in favour of relatives correspond with those in favour of children and the issue of deceased children, as if references to the members or member of the class (*e.g.* of brothers and sisters) were substituted for references to the children or child of the intestate.[73]

Election

The next-of-kin do not of course have to claim and may elect on a partial intestacy to take under the will and abandon their rights on intestacy, as was recognised under the old statutes.[74]

Failure of "statutory trusts"

The "statutory trusts," either in favour of children or any other class of relatives, must fail if all the objects thereof die without attaining a vested

---

[69] See *per*Jenkins L.J. in *Re Hayward* [1957] Ch. 528, 540; and (1957) 73 L.Q.R. 22, 302. The strength of the presumption of advancement is now much diminished. *per* Lord Reid in *Petit* v. *Petit* [1970] A.C. 737 at 793.

[70] [1957] Ch. 535. See *post*, p. 1075.

[71] *Re Hayward* [1957] Ch. 528; *Hardy* v. *Shaw*, *supra*.

[72] *Ibid.* ss.47(3) and 49(1)(*a*); and see *Re McKee* [1931] 2 Ch. 145, 153. Since 1958 a surviving spouse must under partial intestacy deduct any interest under the will from the lump sum due to such spouse. See *ante*, p. 1070.

[73] *Ibid.* s.47(3) (*post*, p. 1142).

[74] *Re Sullivan* [1930] 1 Ch. 84.

interest, *i.e.* under the age of majority and unmarried. In such circumstances, the residuary estate, and the income and accumulations of income not already applied (*e.g.* by way of advancement or maintenance[75]), are distributed as if none of the objects of the defunct class in question had survived the intestate.[76]

Infant's freeholds

There is an exception to the rules of distribution stated above, where an infant dies intestate.[77] In this case his personal estate is distributed as stated above, but a legal estate in freehold land cannot be vested in an infant.[78] A deed, will or other instrument in his favour will operate either as a settlement[79] or as an agreement to settle.[80] In either case his beneficial interest, if he dies intestate and unmarried, is deemed to be an entailed interest and the settlement is construed accordingly.[81] This means that his beneficial interest will revert to the settlor, or, if the settlement was created by will, to the residuary estate of the testator, or, if the infant was entitled under a pre-1926 intestacy, to the next heir of the intestate.[82]

Estate pur autre vie

If a testator disposed of his estate by will only after the death of A, this would leave an estate *pur autre vie* undisposed of. If A were the widow, it is conceived that she could not get more than the income undisposed of. But if A were not the widow, clearly the widow would be entitled to require her capital sum with interest to be raised by a sale of the estate *pur autre vie*. After paying to the widow the capital sum with any interest due, the representatives should invest the balance of the proceeds in authorised investments.[83] The income arising from one-half[84] of such investments would be paid to the widow, and the income of the other half and the capital thereof would devolve on the widow, issue or other persons entitled under section 46 to the "residuary estate of the intestate." Exactly the same rules apply when the surviving spouse is the husband.

---

[75] *Ante*, p. 1027, n. 32.

[76] Administration of Estates Act 1925, s.47(2)(*a*) (*post*, p. 1142).

[77] An infant cannot in general make a will. See the Wills Act 1837, s.7.

[78] Law of Property Act 1925, s.1(6). It is conceived that an infant cannot disentail and dispose of personalty entailed by s.51(3) (by virtue of the Law of Property Act 1925, s.176) even by making a valid will under the Wills (Soldier and Sailors) Act 1918, s.1.

[79] Settled Land Act 1925, s.1(1)(ii)(*d*). A settlement in favour of the infant is "deemed" if he is entitled on intestacy (*ibid.* s.1(2)), but since 1925 he cannot take a "vested estate" until majority of marriage.

[80] Settled Land Act 1925, s.27.

[81] Administration of Estates Act 1925, s.51(3) (*post*, p. 1147).

[82] *Re Taylor* [1931] 2 Ch. 243.

[83] See the Administration of Estates Act 1925, s.33(3) (*post*, p. 1128).

[84] See the Administration of Estates Act 1925, ss.46(1)(i) and 47(2), and the Intestates' Estates Act 1952 (*post*, pp. 1137, 1142 *et seq*).

Homicide

The disability which prevents a person from benefiting under the will of a testator he has by his own criminal act[85] killed and from being the personal representative of such a person[86] applies on intestacy.[87]

Effect of trusts: foreign beneficiaries

Where an estate is held upon trusts, whether arising from the intestacy provisions or otherwise and some or all of the beneficiaries are domiciled abroad so that income suffers additional taxation the court may, under the Variation of Trusts Act 1958, substitute other arrangements.[88]

Apportionment on intestacy

Where a person dies after 1925 intestate, the property passing on intestacy is held by his representatives upon trust for sale with power to postpone sale[89]; and if the deceased leaves a spouse surviving, interests in succession may arise in such property.

It is established that (subject to the effective provisions of the will, if any, though without regard to provisions which have become inoperative by disclaimer or lapse[90]) the rules of apportionment are excluded if the representatives, exercising their discretion, have postponed the sale and conversion of an unauthorised wasting asset.[91] And where reversionary interests form part of the estate, the rules of apportionment are excluded, since reversionary interests are expressly excluded from the statutory trust for sale until they fall into possession.[92] "Reversionary interests" in this context does not include future non-income-bearing property which has not yet fallen into possession[93]; accordingly such property is held upon trust for sale.

Where property is subject to the statutory trust for sale, and is retained otherwise than by a proper exercise of the discretion to retain, it has been held[94] that, notwithstanding the provisions of the Administration of Estates Act 1925, equitable apportionment must take place according to

---

[85] See *ante*, p. 22, as to the abolition of the distinction between felony and misdemeanour.
[86] See *ante*, p. 348.
[87] See p. 972 *ante*.
[88] See *Re Seale* [1961] Ch. 574, and as to an earlier example, *Re Liddiard* (1880) 14 Ch.D. 310. See note in (1961) 77 L.Q.R. 473. See also *Re Weston* [1969] 1 Ch. 223; *Re Windeatt's Will Trusts* [1969] 1 W.L.R. 692; Harris, *Variation of Trusts*. See also *Re Whitehead* [1971] 1 W.L.R. 833.
[89] Administration of Estates Act 1925, s.33(1) (*post*, p. 1127).
[90] *Re Sullivan* [1930] 1 Ch. 84.
[91] *Re Trollope's Will Trusts* [1927] 1 Ch. 596, 604; *Re Sullivan, ante*; *Re Fisher* [1943] Ch. 377, 381. As to statutory apportionment see *ante*, p. 533. As to equitable apportionment see *ante*, p. 1039.
[92] *Re Fisher* [1943] Ch. 377; Administration of Estates Act 1925, s.33(1).
[93] *Re Fisher, ante*.
[94] *Re Fisher, ante; cf. Re Hey's Settlement Trusts* [1945] Ch. 294.

the rules in *Dimes* v. *Scott*[95] and *Re Chesterfield's Trusts*.[96] If this decision is supported, it means that the rule in *Rowlls* v. *Bebb*[97] applies to intestacies as well as to wills; it is difficult to see, however, what meaning can be given to the Administration of Estates Act 1925, s.33(5). It is submitted that the true effect of subsections (1), (4) and (5) of the Administration of Estates Act 1925, s.33, is to exclude the rules of apportionment on an intestacy whether the power to postpone is exercised or not.[98]

Funds in court

Where a person entitled dies intestate and the assets of his estate, including the value of his interest in a fund in court, do not exceed £5,000 in value, the court may order payment or transfer to the person who would have the prior right to a grant.[99]

The Statutes of Distribution (1670)

The intestacy rules which applied to deaths before 1926[1] can still be relevant in matters of title and in the following (now rare) cases:

1. Where reversionary or other interests fall into the estate of a person who died before 1926.
2. Where there is an entail[2] or one is deemed to arise.[3]
3. Where a person of unsound mind living and of full age on January 1, 1926 dies intestate without having recovered testamentary capacity.[4]
4. To ascertain the heir by purchase.[5]

For the old rules and their operation reference should be made to earlier editions of this work.[6]

---

[95] (1828) 4 Russ. 195.
[96] (1885) 24 Ch.D. 643.
[97] (1900) 2 Ch.D. 107. See *ante*, p. 1042.
[98] See the 12th ed. of this work, at p. 919.
[99] See Ord. 22, r. 11, for precise terms. As to grants for small estates, see *ante*, p. 106.
[1] The Statutes of Distribution 1670 applied to personalty. The 1925 legislation assimilated the provisions for distribution on intestacy of realty and personalty.
[2] L.P.A. 1925, s.130(4).
[3] Where an unmarried infant dies equitably entitled to freeholds or property settled to devolve therewith an entail is deemed to arise. A.E.A. 1925, S.5(iii). See p. 1116 *post.*
[4] A.E.A. 1925, S.51(2).
[5] A.E.A. 1925, s.51(1). See p. 1146 *post.*
[6] See also Sherrin and Bonehill, *Intestate Succession* pp. 24–39.

CHAPTER 80

REFUNDING AND TRACING

Beneficiaries[1] may be bound in equity[2] to refund assets together with costs charges and expenses incurred[3] or a rateable part of them, either to the executor, or to a creditor, or to another beneficiary. The rights to compel legatees or next-of-kin to refund in the two latter cases, however, are not strictly within the scope of this treatise. The distinction between the claim *in personam* to a refund and the claim *in rem* by way of tracing is mentioned below.[4] Where a beneficiary pays tax attributable to a whole fund, it seems to be reasonably clear that there is a right of reimbursement so far as is necessary to give an equitable balance between those interested in the fund.[5]

Law and equity

There is a distinction between the claim at common law for money had and received under a *mistake of fact*[6] and the claim in equity based on a *fiduciary duty* arising from the administration or distribution of an estate or otherwise.[7] In particular the equitable claim is not qualified by the condition that the wrongful payment must not have been made under a *mistake of law*.[8] This distinction does not seem always to have been made in the past so that there are cases where the executor's claim has failed on the footing that it was based on mistake of law[9] although it was held that he could deduct sums overpaid from future payments due to the beneficiary.[10] The equitable right is based on a constructive trust[11] and specific assets may be refunded[12] but what relationships are sufficient to create the trust

---

[1] This term is used here to cover legatees devisees and next-of-kin.
[2] See *Salih* v. *Atchi* [1961] A.C. 778, 793 as to the equitable nature of this duty. For the general principles see Goff and Jones, *The Law of Restitution*, 2nd ed., 1978, pp. 89, 450–453 and *Chase Manhattan Bank* v. *Israel-British Bank* [1981] Ch. 105. For the relevance of the principles to Family Provision see pp. 764, 765, 801, 802.
[3] *Whittaker* v. *Kershaw* (1890) 45 Ch.D. 320.
[4] See *post*, pp. 1080–1081.
[5] *Re Latham* [1962] Ch. 616, 641; *Leedale* v. *Lewis* [1982] 1 W.L.R. 1319 at 1335.
[6] See *Re Robinson* [1911] 1 Ch. 502 as discussed in *Re Diplock* [1948] Ch. 465, 498; [1951] A.C. 272.
[7] See Goff and Jones; *The Law of Restitution* 2nd ed., 1978, p. 450 *Agip (Africa)* v. *Jackson* [1991] Ch. 547.
[8] *Ministry of Health* v. *Simpson* [1951] A.C. 251, 273. As to equitable defences see *post*, p. 1079.
[9] *Re Hatch* [1919] 1 Ch. 351, 356.
[10] *Dibbs* v. *Goren* (1849) 11 Beav. 483; *Re Musgrave* [1916] 2 Ch. 417.
[11] *Chase Manhattan* v. *Israel British Bank* [1981] Ch. 105, 118, 119. *Eagle Trust P.L.C.* v. *S.B.C. Securities Limited* (*The Times*, February 14, 1991).
[12] *Crooksbank* v. *Smith* (1836) 2 Y. & C. 58.

or the fiduciary relationship have still not been precisely laid down.[13] An initial fiduciary relationship is necessary and this will normally be present where an executor has been concerned. It is clear however that the fund to be claimed need not have been the subject of fiduciary obligations before it got into the wrong hands.[14]

The executor's right to refund

The executor's right may depend on whether the payment was made voluntarily or involuntarily. If it was made *under compulsion of proceedings*, he is entitled to compel the beneficiary to refund if there is a deficiency of assets.[15] If, however, an executor pays a legacy *voluntarily*, the presumption is that he has sufficient assets to pay all legacies. Consequently, *he can only compel a legatee to refund if, after the payment of the legacy, liabilities appear of which he had no previous notice.*[16]

Thus, an executor cannot compel residuary legatees to refund if he has paid over the assets with notice of a debt.[17] A notice, however, of a possible remote contingent liability (such as future calls on shares) is not sufficient to disable an executor from recovering back the assets when it afterwards ripens into a debt.[18]

It is not the practice for beneficiaries to give security to the executor to refund if the assets should prove insufficient.[19] "It has been in my opinion the practice of the Court, when administering an estate of a deceased person in cases where trustees have under an honest mistake overpaid one beneficiary, in the adjustment of the accounts between the trustees and the *Cestui que trust*, to make allowance for the mistake in order that the trustee may so far as possible be recouped the money which he has inadvisedly paid."[20] Thus, where an executrix, by mistake, made payments to a legatee in respect of his annuity for two years before the annuity became payable, she was allowed to retain that amount out of the future payments of the annuity.[21] Again, where executors inadvertently paid legacy duty on a life interest out of capital, they were allowed to retain the amount out of future payments of income.[22]

---

[13] *Re Diplock* [1948] Ch. 465, 540; *Chase Mahattan v. Israel-British Bank* [1981] Ch. 105, 119.

[14] See n. 11.

[15] *Newman v. Barton* (1690) 2 Vern. 205; *Noell v. Robinson* (1686) 2 Ventr. 358, 368.

[16] *Jervis v. Wolferstan* (1874) L.R. 18 Eq. 18; *Nelthrop v. Hill* (1669) 1 Chanc.Cas. 136; *Davis v. Davis* (1718) 8 Vin.Abr. 423, tit. Devise, Q.d.pl. 35; 1 Rop. Leg. 3rd ed., 398; *Doe v. Guy* (1802) 3 East 120, 123. See also *Orr v. Kaines* (1750) 2 Ves.Sen. 194; *Coppin v. Coppin* (1725) 2 P.Wms. 291, 296; *Re Horne* [1905] 1 Ch. 76; but see *Re Ainsworth, post.*

[17] *Jervis v. Wolferstan, ante.*

[18] *Jervis v. Wolferstan, ante*; *Whittaker v Kershaw* (1890) 45 Ch.D. 320.

[19] For the old practice, see *Chamberlain v. Chamberlain* (1675) 1 Ch.Cas. 257; *March v. Russell* (1837) 3 M. & Cr. 31. Later the court ceased to require such security: *Anon* (1738) 1 Atk. 491.

[20] *Livesey v. Livesey* (1827) 3 Russ. 287. See also *Cooper v. Pitcher* (1845) 4 Hare 485.

[21] *Per* Neville J. in *Re Musgrave* [1916] 2 Ch. 417, 423.

[22] *Re Ainsworth* [1915] 2 Ch. 96; and see *Re Musgrave, ante*; *Re Wooldridge* [1920] W.N. 78, where trustees paid annuities without deducting income tax.

Effect of assent

An assent or conveyance given or made after 1925 by a representative does not, except in favour of a purchaser of a legal estate, prejudice the right of the representative or any other person to recover the estate or interest to which the assent or conveyance related.[23]

Further, a representative may now, as a condition of giving an assent or making a conveyance, require security for the discharge of any duties, debts or liabilities to which the subject-matter of the assent or conveyance would have been subject if there had been no such assent or conveyance.[24]

The creditor's right to refund

An unsatisfied creditor, even though he may also be the executor,[25] can compel a satisfied beneficiary to refund, whether the executor acted voluntarily or by compulsion.[26] The basis of the chancery jurisdiction in such a case, the evil to be avoided and its remedy have been described[27] as follows: *"The Court of Chancery, in order to do justice and to avoid the evil of allowing one man to retain what is really and legally applicable to the payment of another man, devised a remedy by which, where the estate had been distributed either out of court or in court without regard to the rights of a creditor, it has allowed the creditor to recover back what has been paid to the beneficiaries or the next-of-kin who derive title from the deceased testator or intestate."*

The unsatisfied creditor has this right whether the testator's estate at the time of his death was,[28] or was not,[29] sufficient to satisfy both debts and legacies; and though the assets were handed over to the legatee by the representative in ignorance of the creditor's demand.[30] So where a bankrupt effected policies on his life and died intestate, and his administrator distributed the policy money among the next-of-kin, it was held that the administrator was not personally liable, but that the next-of-kin must refund

---

[23] See the Admistration of Estates Act 1925, ss.36(9), 38, and *ante*, p. 1063; Appendix, *post*, p. 1131.

[24] Administration of Estates Act 1925, s.36(10) (*post*, p. 1131).

[25] *Jervis* v. *Wolfersan*, *ante*.

[26] *Hodges* v. *Waddington* (1683) 2 Ventr. 360; *Noell* v. *Robinson* (1686) 1 Vern. 90; *Anon.* (1683) 1 Vern. 162; *Newman* v. *Barton* (1680) 2 Vern. 205; *March* v. *Russell* (1837) 3 M. & Cr. 31; *Noble* v. *Brett* (1858) 24 Beav. 499; *Gillespie* v. *Alexander* (1827) 3 Russ. 130, 137 (*ante*, p. 603). If in an action against executors for a legacy the executors admit assets, and judgment is given for payment of the legacy *de bonis propriis*, *quaere* whether an unpaid creditor can call upon the legatee to refund the legacy. *Semble*, the creditor could recover the legacy in such a case if it was in fact paid out of the testator's assets, but not if it was paid by the executors *de bonis propriis*; *Re Brogden* (1888) 38 Ch.D. 546.

[27] By Lord Davey in *Harrison* v. *Kirk* [1904] A.C. 1, 7, quoted by Lord Simonds in *Ministry of Health* v. *Simpson* [1951] A.C.251, 266. See *Hawkins* v. *Day* (1753) Amb. 804; *March* v. *Russell* (1837) 3 M. & Cr. 31, 42.

[28] *Hodges* v. *Waddington*, *ante*; *Thomas* v. *Griffith* (1860) 2 Giff. 555.

[29] See cases mentioned in n. 26.

[30] *March* v. *Russell* (1837) 3 M. & Cr. 31.

money even though paid and received in good faith and without notice of the bankruptcy.[31]

Executor need not be joined

Semble, in an action by a creditor to refund a legacy, the executor need not be joined as a party if he had no notice of the creditor's claim when he paid the legacy. At any rate this is so if the executor has shielded himself by advertising for claims.[32]

Equitable defences as a bar

The right of a creditor to follow the testator's assets, which is expressly preserved by the sections just mentioned,[33] may be lost by laches, acquiescence, or such a course of dealing as would render the assertion of such right inequitable.[34] Thus, the mortgagees of real estate, whose security proves insufficient, will not be allowed to come against the residuary legatees of the estate of the mortgagor, if it would be inequitable for them to do so.[35] But mere delay is not in itself sufficient to deprive a creditor of this right.[36]

Valuable consideration as a bar

Further, the right extends only as against beneficiaries and volunteers claiming through them. If an executor who is also residuary legatee sells or mortgages an asset of the testator for valuable consideration[37] to a person who has no notice of the existence of unsatisfied debts of the testator,[38] or of any ground which rendered it improper for the executor so to deal with the asset, that person's purchase or mortgage is valid against any unsatisfied creditor of the testator.[39] The case of an executor who is residuary legatee dealing with an asset is the same in principle as the case of a legatee who is not an executor, but whose legacy has been assented to by the executor, and who deals with his legacy for valuable consideration. In this last case unsatisfied creditors have the right to follow the legacy as against the legatee or volunteers claiming through him, but not as against purchasers[40] from the legatee for valuable consideration; and the immunity of

---

[31] *Re Bennett* [1907] 1 K.B. 149.

[32] *Hunter* v. *Young* (1879) 4 Ex.D. 256; see *ante*, p. 605.

[33] See n. 23 *ante*.

[34] *Ridgway* v. *Newstead* (1861) 2 Giff. 492; *ibid.* on appeal, 30 L.J.Ch. 889; *Salih* v. *Atchi* [1961] A.C. 778 at 793.

[35] *Blake* v. *Gale* (1886) 32 Ch.D. 571.

[36] *Re Eustace* [1912] 1 Ch. 561.

[37] Marriage consideration is sufficient to bar the creditor's right: *Salih* v. *Atchi* [1961] A.C. 778 (P.C.); *Dilkes* v. *Broadmead* (1860) 2 Giff. 113; *Spackman* v. *Timbrell* (1837) 8 Sim. 253.

[38] Such notice is not, of itself, sufficient to invalidate a conveyance to a purchaser of a legal estate by a personal representative: Administration of Estates Act 1925, s.36(8). See *ante*, p. 675.

[39] See *Ministry of Health* v. *Simpson* [1951] A.C. 251.

[40] The vendor beneficiary however, remains liable for the value of the interest so disposed of: see the Administration of Estates Act 1925, s.32(2), (*post*, p. 1127).

the purchasers is not limited to legal assets or to cases where the purchasers have obtained the legal estate or its equivalent.[41] There is no such immunity however where the executor or the court administering the testator's estate still retains control over the assets.[42]

Beneficiary's right to refund

If the assets were not originally sufficient to pay all the beneficiaries[43] and one receives payment in full, the unsatisfied beneficiaries may compel the one so paid to refund.[44] *Secus*, if the assets were originally sufficient, but afterwards there is a deficiency, either by the *devastavit* of the executor, or, *a fortiori*, from merely accidental circumstances.[45]

Similarly, where the representative by a mistake of fact or law overpays a beneficiary, or pays assets to a person not entitled, the unsatisfied beneficiaries may compel the person improperly paid to refund.[46]

Where an executor makes an unauthorised payment and the payee knows or ought to know of the want of authority the payee is liable to refund.[47]

Remedy primarily against executor

The remedy, however, is, in the first place, against the executor. This can result in unfairness, since the liability to refund of persons who have obtained assets to which they are not entitled depends upon the amount which can be extracted from the executor on *devastavit* or otherwise. A converse rule would seem to be more sensible so that the executor would be liable only to the extent that the fund was not recovered from the person who had unjustifiably benefited.[48] The present rule depends on "blame." "Since the original wrong payment was attributable to the blunder of the representatives, the right of the unpaid beneficiary is in the first instance against the wrongdoing executor or administrator, and the beneficiary's direct claim in equity against those overpaid or wrongly paid should be limited to the amount which he cannot recover from the party respon-

[41] *Per* Romer J. in *Graham* v. *Drummond* [1896] 1 Ch. 968. See also *Dilkes* v. *Broadmead* (1860) 2 Giff. 113.

[42] *Noble* v. *Brett* (1858) 24 Beav. 499; and *Hooper* v. *Smart* (1875) 1 Ch.D. 90.

[43] *i.e.* legatees, devisees or next-of-kin.

[44] *Anon.* (1718) 1 P.Wms. 495; *Walcott* v. *Hall* (1788) 2 Bro.C.C. 305. See also *Noell* v. *Robinson* (1686) 1 Vern. 90, 93. And see n. (1) by Mr. Cox; *ibid.* 2 Bro.C.C. 305. See also the observations in *Gillespie* v. *Alexander* (1827) 3 Russ. 133, and *David* v. *Frowd* (1833) 1 M. & K. 200. See also for the general principle *Duncan Fox* v. *North and South Wales Bank* (1880) 6 App.Cas. 1. H.L.

[45] *Fenwicke* v. *Clarke* (1862) 31 L.J.Ch. 728.

[46] *Re Diplock* [1948] Ch. 465; affd., *Ministry of Health* v. *Simpson* [1951] A.C. 251.

[47] *Nelson* v. *Larholt* [1948] 1 K.B. 339. The basis of the claim is simply that the defendant has received some share of the estate to which he was not entitled. (*Re Diplock* [1948] Ch. 465 at 503). *Eagle Trust p.l.c.* v. *S.B.C. Securities Limited* (*The Times*, February 14, 1991).

[48] *Orr* v. *Kaines* (1750) 2 Ves.Sen. 194; 1 Rop.Leg., 3rd ed., 399; *Re Diplock, ante*; *Ministry of Health* v. *Simpson, ante*. For critism of this rule, see Goff and Jones, *The Law of Restitution*, 2nd ed., 1978, pp. 59, 60, 450. It is not clear whether this thinking is implicit in the decision of Denning J. in *Nelson* v. *Larholt* [1948] 1. K.B. 339.

sible."[49] In some cases the amount will be the whole amount of the payment wrongly made, *e.g.* where the executor or adminsitrator is shown to be wholly without assets or is protected from attack by having acted under an order of the court.

Where the estate of a testator or of an intestate is decreased by wasting, one of several beneficiaries can only be compelled to refund in favour of the others who are disappointed if the wasting occurred before he received his share. The burden of proof lies on those who call upon the residuary legatee or next-of-kin to refund, to show that the wasting took place before the share was paid over.[50]

It seems, however, that a specific legatee can always compel the residuary legatees to refund, if his legacy has not already been paid or appropriated,[51] and provided he has not, by his own conduct, lost the right to priority.[52] Further, in an action by a residuary legatee for the administration of the testator's estate, the court has jurisdiction to compel the residuary legatee to refund assets paid to him before the action, for the purpose of paying the legacy of a legatee who is not a party to the action.[53]

Where representatives acting under a mistaken belief that a residuary disposition was valid, distributed the residuary estate, the next-of-kin were held to have a direct claim in equity against the persons to whom such residue had been wrongfully distributed, subject, however, to the qualification that they must first have exhausted their remedy against the representatives.[54]

Tracing the assets

In addition to the action already mentioned, which is an action *in personam* in equity, a legatee has also a proprietary right in the legacy, which enables him to trace the assets representing the legacy, or the proceeds of such assets, into the hands of a third party, other than a purchaser for value without notice.[55] Tracing at common law depends upon receipt by the defendant of identifiable assets of the plaintiff and the right to trace at law remains while the assets are in an identifiable form. In equity however, where there is a fiduciary relationship money can be traced into a mixed fund.[56] The remedy of the legatee is, however, somewhat limited where the third party, although a volunteer, has no notice that the payment to

---

[49] *Re Diplock, ante,* at p. 503 *per* Lord Greene M.R.

[50] *Peterson* v. *Peterson* (1866) L.R. 3 Eq. 11.

[51] See *Re Rivers* [1920] 1 Ch. 320; *ante,* pp. 1007, 1020.

[52] *Prowse* v. *Spurgin* (1868) L.R. 5 Eq. 99.

[53] This seems to follow from what is said *ante* at p. 1004.

[54] *Ministry of Health* v. *Simpson* [1951] A.C. 251. See also *Re Leslie Engineers* [1976] 1 W.L.R. 292, 299.

[55] *Re Diplock* [1948] Ch. 465; affd., *Ministry of Health* v. *Simpson, ante*; see also the Trustee Act 1925, s.26(2). *Re Hallett* (1879) 13 Ch.D. 696; *Pennell* v. *Deffell* (1853) De G.M. & G 372, 388; *Re Oatway* [1903] 2 Ch. 356; *Re Tilley's Will Trusts* [1967] Ch. 1179. *Nelson* v. *Larholt* [1948] 1 K.B. 339.

[56] *Agip Ltd. (Africa)* v. *Jackson* [1991] Ch. 547, 563, 566.

himself or receipt of chattels[57] is wrongful; for where an innocent volunteer mixes "moneys" of his own with "moneys" which in equity belong to the legatee, the legatee cannot claim a charge on the mass superior to the claim of the volunteer; but the legatee is entitled to a charge ranking *pari passu* with the claim of the volunteer.[58] The notice which is relevant in the doctrine of a purchaser without notice is different from the knowledge that suffices for the imposition of a constructive trust.[59]

Charge on mixed fund

Subject to this, *if property is purchased partly with trust funds and partly with the trustee's own money, or if the trustee mixes trust money with his own, the persons entitled to the trust fund have a primary charge on the whole for the amount of the trust fund so expended or mixed.*[60] The judgment of the Court of Appeal in *Re Diplock*[61] (which, on the question of tracing assets, was not modified by the House of Lords[62]) pointed out that the right was not confined to cases such as *Re Hallett's Estate*,[63] where the right was asserted against the original "mixer" who was in a fiduciary relationship to the claimant. It is one illustration of a wider principle (of which *Sinclair* v. *Brougham*[64] is another), which is, that one whose money has been mixed with that of another or others may trace his money into a mixed fund (or assets acquired in place of that fund) though the fund be held, and even though the mixing was done, by an innocent volunteer, provided that (a) there was originally such a fiduciary or quasi-fiduciary relationship between the claimant and the recipient of the money as to give rise to an equitable proprietary interest in the claimant; (b) the claimant's money is fairly identifiable; and (c) the equitable remedy available, *i.e.* the charge on the mixed fund, does not work injustice.

Thus:

(a) Where the defendant is in a fiduciary relation to the claimant, and has mixed the claimant's money with his own, the claimant takes priority. The same result follows if the defendant had notice that the money was in equity the claimant's.

(b) Where the contest is between two claimants to a mixed fund consisting of moneys belonging to both and therefore held on behalf of both, they share *pari passu*.

(c) Where a claimant's moneys are handed by way of transfer to a person who takes for value without notice of the claimant's

---

[57] *Re Montagu* [1987] Ch. 264 at 279.

[58] *Re Diplock, ante*, p. 524.

[59] See n. 55 *ante*.

[60] *Re Hallett's Estate* (1879) 13 Ch.D. 696. *Space Investments* v. *Canadian Imperial Bank* [1986] 1 W.L.R. 1072.

[61] [1948] Ch. 465; *Chesworth* v. *Farrar* [1967] 1 Q.B. 407.

[62] *Ministry of Health* v. *Simpson* [1951] A.C. 251.

[63] See n. 60.

[64] [1914] A.C. 398.

equity, the claim (like all equitable claims in like circumstances) is extinguished.

(d) Where a volunteer takes without notice (*e.g.* by way of gift from the fiduciary agent), if there is no question of mixing, he holds the money on behalf of the true owner, whose equitable right to the money still persists as against him.

(e) But if the volunteer innocently mixes the money with money of his own, or receives it mixed with his own money from a fiduciary agent, he must admit the claim of the true owner, but is not precluded from setting up his own claim in respect of the moneys which he has contributed to the mixed fund, the result being that they share *pari passu*, neither being entitled to priority.

In *Re Diplock*, the executors had wrongly distributed the residuary estate, amounting to over £260,000, amongst a large number of hospitals, when in reality the next-of-kin was entitled to it. The action against the executors personally was compromised, and the remaining question was the extent of the rights of the next-of-kin to recover against the charities to whom the money had been wrongly paid. There were two distinct heads of claim: (1) against the legatees *in personam*, which the House of Lords fully recognised, and (2) against the legatees *in rem*, by way of tracing. It was to this branch of the claims that the principles explained by the Court of Appeal, and mentioned above, were applicable. It therefore followed that where there had been a mixing of trust money with charity money (or where it had been paid into a special account and remained unmixed) the next-of-kin were entitled to recover *pari passu* with the charity in the case of mixed funds (subject to a rateable reduction in respect of the amounts recovered from the executors under the compromise). But *where the moneys received by the charity had not been mixed with moneys of the charity but had been expended on the alteration or improvement of their own assets, e.g. by erecting buildings on their own land, or in discharging secured or unsecured debts of the charity, the trust money could not be disentangled, the equitable remedy of a charge would work an injustice, and the claim of the next-of-kin was no longer available.*

Finally, where the trust money had been paid into an active bank account of the charity, prima facie the rule in *Clayton's Case*[65] was applicable.

Rule in Clayton's case

If a person who holds money in a fiduciary capacity pays it into his account at his bankers, and mixes it with his own money, and afterwards draws out cheques in the ordinary way, *the rule in Clayton's Case,*[66] *attributing the first drawings out to the first payments in*, does not apply. The drawer must be taken to have drawn out his own money in preference to

[65] (1816) 1 Mer. 572. See also p. 743 *ante*.
[66] See n. 65.

the trust money.[67] But where an innocent volunteer pays moneys representing trust property into an account so as to be mixed with moneys of his own, and afterwards draws out cheques, the rule in *Clayton's Case* applies; and the innocent volunteer is entitled to a charge on the mass, ranking *pari passu* with the claim of the beneficiary under the trust.[68] The rule also probably applies in the same way as between beneficiaries of the same trustee under different trusts.[69]

The rule is one of convenience and it is not applied if impractical or if it would result in injustice where there was a preferable alternative. It will not be applied where the express or presumed intention was to the contrary.[70]

Interest[71]

It remains to be considered in what cases beneficiaries who are compelled to refund must do so with interest. On this point Lord Eldon stated[72] the rule to be: "*If a legacy has been erroneously paid to a legatee who has no further property in the estate, in recalling that payment I apprehend that the rule of the court is not to charge interest; but if the legatee is entitled to another fund making interest in the hands of the court, justice must be done out of his share.*"

It has been held that where a specific legacy had been assented to and paid, and by a codicil subsequently discovered it was found to be revoked and given to another, the latter could recover from the former both the legacy and the mesne income.[73]

The claim to interest was rejected by the House of Lords in the *Diplock* case, but as has been explained, the speeches seem to have been primarily concerned with the claim *in personam*.[74]

---

[67] *Re Hallett's Estate* (1879) 13 Ch.D. 696.
[68] Re Diplock [1948] Ch. 465; affd., *Ministry of Health* v. *Simpson* [1951] A.C. 251.
[69] *Re Hallett's Estate* (1879) 13 Ch.D. 696, 670; *Hancock* v. *Smith* (1889) 41 Ch.D. 456; *Re Stenning* [1895] 2 Ch. 433.
[70] *Vaughan* v. *Barlow Clowes International Ltd.* [1992] *The Times*, March 6, 1992.
[71] As to rates of interest under the equitable jurisdiction, see *ante*, p. 1035.
[72] *Gittins* v. *Steele* (1818) 1 Swanst. 200; *Jervis* v. *Wolferstan* (1874) L.R. 18 Eq. 18; and see *Re Diplock* [1948] Ch. 465; 506, 507, *per* Lord Greene M.R.
[73] *Re West* [1909] 2 Ch. 180.
[74] *Ministry of Health* v. *Simpson, ante.*

Appendix One

STATUTES

Appendix One

STATUTES

WILLS ACT 1837

(7 Will. 4 and 1 Vict, c. 26)

ARRANGEMENT OF SECTIONS

*   *   *   *

Meaning of certain words in this Act

1. The words and expressions hereinafter mentioned, which in their ordinary signification have a more confined or a different meaning, shall in this Act, except where the nature of the provision or the context of the Act shall exclude such construction, be interpreted as follows; (that is to say,) the word "will" shall extend to a testament, and to a codicil, and to an appointment by will or by writing in the nature of a will in exercise of a power, and also to a disposition by will and testament or devise of the custody and tuition of any child, . . . and to any other testamentary disposition; and the words "real estate" shall extend to manors, advowsons, messuages, lands, tithes, rents, and hereditaments, . . . whether corporeal, incorporeal, or personal, and to any undivided share thereof, and to any estate, right, or interest (other than a chattel interest) therein; and the words "personal estate" shall extend to leasehold estates and other chattels real, and also to monies, shares of government and other funds, securities for money (not being real estates), debts, choses in action, rights, credits, goods, and all other property whatsoever which by law devolves upon the executor or administrator, and to any share or interest therein; and every word importing the singular number only shall extend and be applied to several persons or things as well as one person or thing; and every word importing the masculine gender only shall extend and be applied to a female as well as a male.

2. [*(Repealed by the Statute Law Reform Act 1874)*].

All property may be disposed of by will

3. It shall be lawful for every person to devise, bequeath, or dispose of, by his will executed in manner hereinafter required, all real estate and all personal estate which he shall be entitled to, either at law or in equity, at the time of his death, and which, if not so devised, bequeathed, and disposed of, would devolve . . . upon his executor or administrator; and . . . the power hereby given shall extend . . . to all contingent, executory or other future interests in any real or personal estate, whether the testator may or may not be ascertained as the person or one of the persons in whom the same respectively may become vested, and whether he may be entitled thereto under the instrument by which the same respectively were created, or under any disposition thereof by deed or will; and also to all rights of entry for conditions broken, and other rights of entry; and also to such of the same estates, interests, and rights respectively, and other real and personal estate, as the testator may be entitled to at the time of his death, notwithstanding that he may become entitled to the same subsequently to the execution of his will.

4–6. [*Repealed by the Statute Law Reform Act 1969*].

No will of a person under age valid

7. No will made by any person under the age of [eighteen years] shall be valid.

8. [*Repealed by the Statute Law Reform Act 1969*].

Signing and attestation of wills

9. No will shall be valid unless—

(*a*) it is in writing, and signed by the testator, or by some other person in his presence and by his direction; and

(*b*) it appears that the testator intended by his signature to give effect to the will; and

(*c*) the signature is made or acknowledged by the testator in the presence of two or more witnesses present at the same time; and

(*d*) each witness either—

(i) attests and signs the will; or

(ii) acknowledges his signature,

in the presence of the testator (but not necessarily in the presence of any other witness),

but no form of attestation shall be necessary.

AMENDMENT

As to deaths before January 1, 1983 see section 1 of the Wills Act Amendment Act 1852. The present form of this section derives from section 17 of the Administration of Justice Act 1982.

Appointments by will to be executed like other wills, and to be valid, although other required solemnities are not observed

10. No appointment made by will, in exercise of any power, shall be valid, unless the same be executed in manner herein-before required; and every will executed in manner herein-before required shall, so far as respects the execution and attestation thereof, be a valid execution of a power of appointment by will, notwithstanding it shall have been expressly required that a will made in exercise of such power should be executed with some additional or other form of execution of solemnity.

Soldiers and mariners wills excepted

11. Provided always, . . . that any soldier being in actual military service, or any mariner or seaman being at sea, may dispose of his personal estate as he might have done before the making of this Act.

12. [*Repealed by the Admiralty, &c Acts Repeal Act 1865, s.1*].

Publication not to be requisite

13. Every will executed in manner herein-before required shall be valid without any other publication thereof.

Will not to be void on account of incompetency of attesting witness

14. If any person who shall attest the execution of a will shall at the time of the execution thereof or at any time afterwards be incompetent to be admitted a witness to prove the execution thereof, such will shall not on that account be invalid.

Gifts to an attesting witness to be void

15. If any person shall attest the execution of any will to whom or to whose wife or husband any beneficial devise, legacy, estate, interest, gift, or appointment, of or affecting any real or personal estate (other than and except charges and directions for the payment of any debt or debts), shall be thereby given or made, such devise, legacy, estate, interest, gift, or appointment shall, so far only as concerns such person attesting the execution of such will, or the wife or husband of such person, or any person claiming under such person or wife or husband, be utterly null and void, and such person so attesting shall be admitted as a witness to prove the execution of such will, or to prove the validity or invalidity thereof, not-withstanding such devise, legacy, estate, interest, gift, or appointment mentioned in such will.

Creditor attesting to be admitted a witness

16. In case by any will any real or personal estate shall be charged with any debt or debts, and any creditor, or the wife or husband of any creditor, whose debt is so charged, shall attest the execution of such will, such credi-tor notwithstanding such charge shall be admitted a witness to prove the execution of such will, or to prove the validity or invalidity thereof.

Executor to be admitted a witness

17. No person shall, on account of his being an executor of a will, be incompetent to be admitted a witness to prove the execution of such will, or a witness to prove the validity or invalidity thereof.

Will to be revoked by marriage

18.—(1) Subject to subsections (2) and (4) below, a will shall be revoked by the testator's marriage.

(2) A disposition in a will in exercise of a power of appointment shall take effect notwithstanding the testator's subsequent marriage unless the property so appointed would in default of appointment pass to his personal representatives.

(3) Where it appears from a will that at the time it was made the testator was expecting to be married to a particular person and that he intended

that the will should not be revoked by the marriage, the will shall not be revoked by his marriage to that person.

(4) Where it appears from a will that at the time it was made the testator was expecting to be married to a particular person and that he intended that a disposition in the will should not be revoked by his marriage to that person,—

(*a*) that disposition shall take effect notwithstanding the marriage; and

(*b*) any other disposition in the will shall take effect also, unless it appears from the will that the testator intended the disposition to be revoked by the marriage.

AMENDMENT

This wording was substituted for the original section 18 by section 18 of the Administration of Justice Act 1982. It applies only to wills made after 1982, but the date of death is irrelevant if the will was made before 1983. In that case the old wording applies.

Effect of dissolution or annulment of marriage on wills

18A.—(1) Where, after a testator has made a will, a decree of a court [of civil jurisdiction in England and Wales] dissolves or annuls his marriage [or his marriage is dissolved or annulled and the divorce or annulment is entitled to recognition in England and Wales by virtue of Part II of the Family Law Act 1986],—

(*a*) the will shall take effect as if any appointment of the former spouse as an executor or as the executor and trustee of the will were omitted; and

(*b*) any devise or bequest to the former spouse shall lapse,

except in so far as a contrary intention appears by the will.

(2) Subsection (1)(*b*) above is without prejudice to any right of the former spouse to apply for financial provision under the Inheritance (Provision for Family and Dependants) Act 1975.

(3) Where—

(*a*) by the terms of a will an interest in remainder is subject to a life interest; and

(*b*) the life interest lapses by virtue of subsection (1)(*b*) above,

the interest in remainder shall be treated as if it had not been subject to the life interest and, if it was contingent upon the termination of the life interest, as if it had not been so contingent.

AMENDMENT

This section was inserted by section 18 of the Administration of Justice Act 1982 and applies to deaths after 1982.

No will to be revoked by presumption

19. No will shall be revoked by any presumption of an intention on the ground of an alteration in circumstances.

No will to be revoked by another will or codicil, or by a writing executed like a will, or by destruction

20. No will or codicil, or any part thereof, shall be revoked otherwise than as aforesaid, or by another will or codicil executed in manner hereinbefore required, or by some writing declaring an intention to revoke the same and executed in the manner in which a will is hereinbefore required to be executed, or by the burning, tearing, or otherwise destroying the same by the testator, or by some person in his presence and by his direction, with the intention of revoking the same.

No alteration in a will shall have any effect unless executed as a will

21. No obliteration, interlineation, or other alteration made in any will after the execution thereof shall be valid or have any effect, except so far as the words or effect of the will before such alteration shall not be apparent, unless such alteration shall be executed in like manner as hereinbefore is required for the execution of the will; but the will, with such alteration as part thereof, shall be deemed to be duly executed if the signature of the testator and the subscription of the witnesses be made in the margin or on some other part of the will opposite or near to such alteration, or at the foot or end of or opposite to a memorandum referring to such alteration, and written at the end or some other part of the will.

No will revoked to be revived otherwise than by re-execution or a codicil to revive it

22. No will or codicil, or any part thereof, which shall be in any manner revoked, shall be revived otherwise than by the re-execution thereof or by a codicil executed in manner hereinbefore required and showing an intention to revive the same; and when any will or codicil which shall be partly revoked, and afterwards wholly revoked, shall be revived, such revival shall not extend to so much thereof as shall have been revoked before the revocation of the whole thereof, unless an intention to the contrary shall be shown.

A devise not to be rendered inoperative by any subsequent conveyance or act

23. No conveyance or other act made or done subsequently to the execution of a will of or relating to any real or personal estate therein comprised, except an act by which such will shall be revoked as aforesaid, shall prevent the operation of the will with respect to such estate or interest in such real or personal estate as the testator shall have power to dispose of by will at the time of his death.

A will shall be construed to speak from the death of the testator

24. Every will shall be construed, with reference to the real estate and personal estate comprised in it, to speak and take effect as if it had been executed immediately before the death of the testator, unless a contrary intention shall appear by the will.

A residuary devise shall include estates comprised in lapsed and void devises

25. Unless a contrary intention shall appear by the will, such real estate or interest therein as shall be comprised or intended to be comprised in any devise in such will contained, which shall fail or be void by reason of the death of the devisee in the lifetime of the testator, or by reason of such devise being contrary to law or otherwise incapable of taking effect shall be included in the residuary devise (if any) contained in such will.

A general devise of the testator's lands shall include copyhold and leasehold as well as freehold lands

26. A devise of the land of the testator, or of the land of the testator in any place or in the occupation of any person mentioned in his will, or otherwise described in a general manner, and any other general devise which would describe a . . . leasehold estate if the testator had no freehold estate which could be described by it, shall be construed to include the . . . leasehold estates of the testator, or his . . . leasehold estates, or any of them, to which such description shall extend, as the case may be, as well as freehold estates, unless a contrary intention shall appear by the will.

A general gift shall include estates over which the testator has a general power of appointment

27. A general devise of the real estate of the testator, or of the real estate of the testator in any place or in the occupation of any person mentioned in his will, or otherwise described in a general manner, shall be construed to include any real estate, or any real estate to which such description shall extend (as the case may be), which he may have power to appoint in any manner he may think proper, and shall operate as an execution of such power, unless a contrary intention shall appear by the will; and in like manner a bequest of the personal estate of the testator, or any bequest of personal property described in a general manner, shall be construed to include any personal estate, or any personal estate to which such description shall extend (as the case may be), which he may have power to appoint in any manner he may think proper, and shall operate as an execution of such power, unless a contrary intention shall appear by the will.

A devise without any words of limitation shall be construed to pass the fee

28. Where any real estate shall be devised to any person without any words of limitation, such devise shall be construed to pass the fee simple, or other the whole estate or interest which the testator had power to dispose of by will in such real estate, unless a contrary intention shall appear by the will.

The words "die without issue," or "die without leaving issue," shall be construed to mean die without issue living at the death

29. In any devise or bequest of real or personal estate the words "die without issue" or "die without leaving issue," or "have no issue," or any other words which may import either a want or failure of issue of any person in his lifetime or at the time of his death, or an indefinite failure of his issue, shall be construed to mean a want or failure of issue in the lifetime or at the time of the death of such person, and not an indefinite failure of his issue, unless a contrary intention shall appear by the will, by reason of such person having a prior estate tail, or of a preceding gift, being, without any implication arising from such words, a limitation of an estate tail to such person or issue, or otherwise: Provided, that this Act shall not extend to cases where such words as aforesaid import if no issue described in a preceding gift shall be born, or if there shall be no issue who shall live to attain the age or otherwise answer the description required for obtaining a vested estate by a preceding gift to such issue.

No devise to trustees or executors, except for a term or a presentation to a church, shall pass a chattel interest

30. Where any real estate (other than or not being a presentation to a church) shall be devised to any trustee or executor, such devise shall be construed to pass the fee simple or other the whole estate or interest which the testator had power to dispose of by will in such real estate, unless a definite term of years, absolute or determinable, or an estate of freehold, shall thereby be given to him expressly or by implication.

Trustees under an unlimited devise, where the trust may endure beyond the life of a person beneficially entitled for life, shall take the fee

31. Where any real estate shall be devised to a trustee, without any express limitation of the estate to be taken by such trustee, and the beneficial interest in such real estate, or in the surplus rents and profits thereof, shall not be given to any person for life, or such beneficial interest shall be given to any person for life, but the purposes of the trust may continue beyond the life of such person, such devise shall be construed to vest in such trustee the fee simple, or other the whole legal estate which the testator had power to dispose of by will in such real estate, and not an estate determinable when the purposes of the trust shall be satisfied.

Devises of estates tail shall not lapse

32. Where any person to whom any real estate shall be devised for an estate tail or an estate in quasi entail shall die in the lifetime of the testator leaving issue who would be heritable under such entail, and any such issue shall be living at the time of the death of the testator, such devise shall not lapse, but shall take effect as if the death of such person had happened immediately after the death of the testator, unless a contrary intention shall appear by the will.

Gifts to children or other issue who leave issue living at the testator's death shall not lapse

33.—(1) Where—

    (*a*) a will contains a devise or bequest to a child or remoter descendant of the testator; and

    (*b*) the intended beneficiary dies before the testator, leaving issue; and

    (*c*) issue of the intended beneficiary are living at the testator's death,

then, unless a contrary intention appears by the will, the devise or bequest shall take effect as a devise or bequest to the issue living at the testator's death.

(2) Where—

    (*a*) a will contains a devise or bequest to a class of person consisting of children or remoter descendants of the testator; and

    (*b*) a member of the class dies before the testator, leaving issue, and

    (*c*) issue of that member are living at the testator's death,

then, unless a contrary intention appears by the will, the devise or bequest shall take effect as if the class included the issue of its deceased member living at the testator's death.

(3) Issue shall take under this section through all degrees, according to their stock, in equal shares if more than one, any gift or share which their parent would have taken and so that no issue shall take whose parent is living at the testator's death and that no issue shall take whose parent is living at the testator's death and so capable of taking.

(4) For the purposes of this section—

    (*a*) the illegitimacy of any person is to be disregarded; and

    (*b*) a person conceived before the testator's death and born living thereafter is to be taken to have been living at the testator's death.

AMENDMENT

This wording was substituted by section 19 of the Administration of Justice Act 1982 and applies to deaths after 1982.

Act not to extend to wills made before 1838, or to estates pur autre vie of persons who die before 1838

34. This Act shall not extend to any will made before the first day of January one thousand eight hundred and thirty-eight; and every will re-executed or republished, or revived by any codicil, shall for the purposes of this Act be deemed to have been made at the time at which the same shall be so re-executed, republished or revived; and this Act shall not extend to any estate pur autre vie of any person who shall die before the first day of January one thousand eight hundred and thirty-eight.

Act not to extend to Scotland

35. This Act shall not extend to Scotland.

TRUSTEE ACT 1925

(15 & 16 Geo. 5, c. 19)

ARRANGEMENT OF SECTIONS

Part II

GENERAL POWERS OF TRUSTEES AND PERSONAL REPRESENTATIVES

General Powers

*   *   *   *

Part II

GENERAL POWERS OF TRUSTEES AND PERSONAL REPRESENTATIVES

General Powers

Power of trustees for sale to sell by auction, &c.

12.—(1) Where a trust for sale or a power of sale of property is vested in a trustee, he may sell or concur with any other person in selling all or any part of the property, either subject to prior charges or not, and either together or in lots, by public auction or by private contract, subject to any such conditions respecting title or evidence of title or other matter as the trustee thinks fit, with power to vary any contract for sale, and to buy in at any auction, or to rescind any contract for sale and to re-sell, without being answerable for any loss.

(2) A trust or power to sell or dispose of land includes a trust or power to sell or dispose of part thereof, whether the division is horizontal, vertical, or made in any other way.

(3) This section does not enable an express power to sell settled land to be exercised where the power is not vested in the tenant for life or statutory owner.

Power to sell subject to depreciatory conditions

13.—(1) No sale made by a trustee shall be impeached by any beneficiary upon the ground that any of the conditions subject to which the sale was made may have been unnecessarily depreciatory, unless it also appears that the consideration for the sale was thereby rendered inadequate.

(2) No sale made by a trustee shall, after the execution of the conveyance, be impeached as against the purchaser upon the ground that any of the conditions subject to which the sale was made may have been unnecessarily depreciatory, unless it appears that the purchaser was acting in collusion with the trustee at the time when the contract for sale was made.

(3) No purchaser, upon any sale made by a trustee, shall be at liberty to make any objection against the title upon any of the grounds aforesaid.

(4) This section applies to sales made before or after the commencement of this Act.

Power of trustees to give receipts

14.—(1) The receipt in writing of a trustee for any money, securities, or other personal property or effects payable, transferable, or deliverable to him under any trust or power shall be a sufficient discharge to the person paying, transferring, or delivering the same and shall effectually exonerate him from seeing to the application or being answerable for any loss or misapplication thereof.

(2) This section does not, except where the trustee is a trust corporation, enable a sole trustee to give a valid receipt for—

   (a) the proceeds of sale or other capital money arising under a [. . .] trust for sale of land;

   (b) capital money arising under the Settled Land Act 1925.

(3) This section applies notwithstanding anything to the contrary in the instrument, if any, creating the trust.

AMENDMENT

In subsection (2)(a) the words omitted were repealed by the Law of Property (Amendment) Act 1926.

Power to compound liabilities

15. A personal representative, or two or more trustees acting together, or, subject to the restrictions imposed in regard to receipts by a sole trustee not being a trust corporation, a sole acting trustee where by the instrument, if any, creating the trust, or by statute, a sole trustee is authorised to execute the trusts and powers reposed in him, may, if and as he or they think fit—

> (*a*) accept any property, real or personal, before the time at which it is made transferable or payable; or
> (*b*) sever and apportion any blended trust funds or property; or
> (*c*) pay or allow any debt or claim on any evidence that he or they think sufficient; or
> (*d*) accept any composition or any security, real or personal, for any debt or for any property, real or personal, claimed; or
> (*e*) allow any time of payment of any debt; or
> (*f*) compromise, compound, abandon, submit to arbitration, or otherwise settle any debt, account, claim, or thing whatever relating to the testator's or intestate's estate or to the trust;

and for any of those purposes may enter into, give, execute, and do such agreements, instruments of composition or arrangement, releases, and other things as to him or them seem expedient, without being responsible for any loss occasioned by any act or thing so done by him or them in good faith.

Power to raise money by sale, mortgage, &c.

16.—(1) Where trustees are authorised by the instrument, if any, creating the trust or by law to pay or apply capital money subject to the trust for any purpose or in any manner, they shall have and shall be deemed always to have had power to raise the money required by sale, conversion, calling in, or mortgage of all or any part of the trust property for the time being in possession.

(2) This section applies notwithstanding anything to the contrary contained in the instrument, if any, creating the trust, but does not apply to trustees of property held for charitable purposes, or to trustees of a settlement for the purposes of the Settled Land Act 1925, not being also the statutory owners.

Protection to purchasers and mortgagees dealing with trustees

17. No purchaser or mortgagee, paying or advancing money on a sale or mortgage purporting to be made under any trust or power vested in trustees, shall be concerned to see that such money is wanted, or that no more than is wanted is raised, or otherwise as to the application thereof.

Devolution of powers or trusts

18.—(1) Where a power or trust is given to or imposed on two or more trustees jointly, the same may be exercised or performed by the survivors or survivor of them for the time being.

(2) Until the appointment of new trustees, the personal representatives or representative for the time being of a sole trustee, or, where there were two or more trustees of the last surviving or continuing trustee, shall be capable of exercising or performing any power or trust which was given to, or capable of being exercised by, the sole or last surviving or continuing trustee, or other the trustees or trustee for the time being of the trust.

(3) This section takes effect subject to the restrictions imposed in regard to receipts by a sole trustee, not being a trust corporation.

(4) In this section "personal representative" does not include an executor who has renounced or has not proved.

Power to insure

19.—(1) A trustee may insure against loss or damage by fire any building or other insurable property to any amount, including the amount of any insurance already on foot, not exceeding three fourth parts of the full value of the building or property, and pay the premiums for such insurance out of the income thereof or out of the income of any other property subject to the same trusts without obtaining the consent of any person who may be entitled wholly or partly to such income.

(2) This section does not apply to any building or property which a trustee is bound forthwith to convey absolutely to any beneficiary upon being requested to do so.

Application of insurance money where policy kept up under any trust, power or obligation

20.—(1) Money receivable by trustees or any beneficiary under a policy of insurance against the loss or damage of any property subject to a trust or to a settlement within the meaning of the Settled Land Act 1925, whether by fire or otherwise, shall, where the policy has been kept up under any trust in that behalf or under any power statutory or otherwise, or in performance of any covenant or of any obligation statutory or otherwise, or by a tenant for life impeachable for waste, be capital money for the purposes of the trust or settlement, as the case may be.

(2) If any such money is receivable by any person, other than the trustees of the trust or settlement, that person shall use his best endeavours to recover and receive the money, and shall pay the net residue thereof, after discharging any costs of recovering and receiving it, to the trustees of the trust or settlement, or, if there are no trustees capable of giving a discharge therefore, into court.

(3) Any such money—

    (*a*) if it was receivable in respect of settled land within the meaning of the Settled Land Act 1925, or any building or works thereon, shall be deemed to be capital money arising under that Act from the settled land, and shall be invested or applied by the trustees, or, if in court, under the direction of the court, accordingly;

(*b*) if it was receivable in respect of personal chattels settled as heirlooms within the meaning of the Settled Land Act 1925, shall be deemed to be capital money arising under that Act, and shall be applicable by the trustees, or, if in court, under the direction of the court, in like manner as provided by that Act with respect to money arising by a sale of chattels settled as heirlooms as aforesaid;

(*c*) if it was receivable in respect of property held upon trust for sale, shall be held upon the trusts and subject to the powers and provisions applicable to money arising by a sale under such trust;

(*d*) in any other case, shall be held upon trusts corresponding as nearly as may be with the trusts affecting the property in respect of which it was payable.

(4) Such money, or any part thereof, may also be applied by the trustees, or, if in court, under the direction of the court, in rebuilding, reinstating, replacing, or repairing the property lost or damaged, but any such application by the trustees shall be subject to the consent of any person whose consent is required by the instrument, if any, creating the trust to the investment of money subject to the trust, and, in the case of money which is deemed to be capital money arising under the Settled Land Act 1925, be subject to the provisions of that Act with respect to the application of capital money by the trustees of the settlement.

(5) Nothing contained in this section prejudices or affects the right of any person to require any such money or any part thereof to be applied in rebuilding, reinstating, or repairing the property lost or damaged, or the rights of any mortgagee, lessor, or lessee, whether under any statute or otherwise.

(6) This section applies to policies effected either before or after the commencement of this Act, but only to money received after such commencement.

Deposit of documents for safe custody

21. Trustees may deposit any documents held by them relating to the trust, or to the trust property, with any banker or banking company or any other company whose business includes the undertaking of the safe custody of documents, and any sum payable in respect of such deposit shall be paid out of the income of the trust property.

Reversionary interests, valuations, and audit

22.—(1) Where trust property includes any share or interest in property not vested in the trustees, or the proceeds of the sale of any such property,

or any other thing in action, the trustees on the same falling into possession, or becoming payable or transferable may—

    (*a*) agree or ascertain the amount or value thereof or any part thereof
        in such manner as they may think fit;

    (*b*) accept in or towards satisfaction thereof, at the market or current
        value, or upon any valuation or estimate of value which they may
        think fit, any authorised investments;

    (*c*) allow any deductions for duties, costs, charges and expenses
        which they may think proper or reasonable;

    (*d*) execute any release in respect of the premises so as effectually to
        discharge all accountable parties from all liability in respect of any
        matters coming within the scope of such release;

without being responsible in any such case for any loss occasioned by any
act or thing so done by them in good faith.

(2) The trustees shall not be under any obligation and shall not be
chargeable with any breach of trust by reason of any omission—

    (*a*) to place any distringas notice or apply for any stop or other like
        order upon any securities or other property out of or on which
        such share or interest or other thing in action as aforesaid is
        derived, payable or charged; or

    (*b*) to take any proceedings on account of any act, default, or neglect
        on the part of the persons in whom such securities or other prop-
        erty or any of them or any part thereof are for the time being, or
        had at any time been, vested;

unless and until required in writing so to do by some person, or the guardian of some person, beneficially interested under the trust, and unless also
due provision is made to their satisfaction for payment of the costs of any
proceedings required to be taken:

Provided that nothing in this subsection shall relieve the trustees of the
obligation to get in and obtain payment or transfer of such share or interest
or other thing in action on the same falling into possession.

(3) Trustees may, for the purpose of giving effect to the trust, or any of
the provisions of the instrument, if any, creating the trust or of any statute,
from time to time (by duly qualified agents) ascertain and fix the value of
any trust property in such manner as they think proper, and any valuation
so made in good faith shall be binding upon all persons interested under
the trust.

(4) Trustees may, in their absolute discretion, from time to time, but not
more than once in every three years unless the nature of the trust or any
special dealings with the trust property make a more frequent exercise of
the right reasonable, cause the accounts of the trust property to be examined or audited by an independent accountant, and shall, for that purpose,
produce such vouchers and give such information to him as he may require;
and the costs of such examination or audit, including the fee of the auditor,

shall be paid out of the capital or income of the trust property, or partly in one way and partly in the other, as the trustees, in their absolute discretion, think fit, but, in default of any direction by the trustees to the contrary in any special case, costs attributable to capital shall be borne by capital and those attributable to income by income.

Power to employ agents

23.—(1) Trustees or personal representatives may, instead of acting personally, employ and pay an agent, whether a solicitor, banker, stockbroker, or other person, to transact any business or do any act required to be transacted or done in the execution of the trust, or the administration of the testator's or intestate's estate, including the receipt and payment of money, and shall be entitled to be allowed and paid all charges and expenses so incurred, and shall not be responsible for the default of any such agent if employed in good faith.

(2) Trustees or personal representatives may appoint any person to act as their agent or attorney for the purpose of selling, converting, collecting, getting in, and executing and perfecting insurances of, or managing or cultivating, or otherwise administering any property, real or personal, moveable or immoveable, subject to the trust or forming part of the testator's or intestate's estate, in any place outside the United Kingdom or executing or exercising any discretion or trust or power vested in them in relation to any such property, with such ancillary powers, and with and subject to such provisions and restrictions as they may think fit, including a power to appoint substitutes, and shall not, by reason only of their having made such appointment, be responsible for any loss arising thereby.

(3) Without prejudice to such general power of appointing agents as aforesaid—

(a) A trustee may appoint a solicitor to be his agent to receive and give a discharge for any money or valuable consideration or property receivable by the trustee under the trust, by permitting the solicitor to have the custody of, and to produce, a deed having in the body thereof or endorsed thereon a receipt for such money or valuable consideration or property, the deed being executed, or the endorsed receipt being signed, by the person entitled to give a receipt for that consideration;

(b) A trustee shall not be chargeable with breach of trust by reason only of his having made or concurred in making any such appointment; and the production of any such deed by the solicitor shall have the same statutory validity and effect as if the person appointing the solicitor had not been a trustee;

(c) A trustee may appoint a banker or solicitor to be his agent to receive and give a discharge for any money payable to the trustee under or by virtue of a policy of insurance, by permitting the banker or solicitor to have the custody of and to produce the policy of insurance with a receipt signed by the trustee, and a trustee shall not be chargeable with a breach of trust by reason only of his having made or concurred in making any such appointment:

Provided that nothing in this subsection shall exempt a trustee from any liability which he would have incurred if this Act and any enactment replaced by this Act had not been passed, in case he permits any such money, valuable consideration, or property to remain in the hands or under the control of the banker or solicitor for a period longer than is reasonably necessary to enable the banker or solicitor, as the case may be, to pay or transfer the same to the trustee.

This subsection applies whether the money or valuable consideration or property was or is received before or after the commencement of this Act.

Power to concur with others

24. Where an undivided share in the proceeds of sale of land directed to be sold, or in any other property, is subject to a trust, or forms part of the estate of a testator or intestate, the trustees or personal representatives may (without prejudice to the trust for sale affecting the entirety of the land and the powers of the trustees for sale in reference thereto) execute or exercise any trust or power vested in them in relation to such share in conjunction with the persons entitled to or having power in that behalf over the other share or shares, and notwithstanding that any one or more of the trustees or personal representatives may be entitled to or interested in any such other share, either in his or their own right or in a fiduciary capacity.

Power to delegate trusts during absence abroad

25.—(1) Notwithstanding any rule of law or equity to the contrary, a trustee may, by power of attorney, delegate for a period not exceeding 12 months the execution or exercise of all or any of the trusts, powers and discretions vested in him as trustee either alone or jointly with any other person or persons.

(2) The persons who may be donees of a power of attorney under this section include a trust corporation but not (unless a trust corporation) the only other co-trustee of the donor of the power.

(3) An instrument creating a power of attorney under this section shall be attested by at least one witness.

(4) Before or within seven days after giving a power of attorney under this section the donor shall give written notice thereof (specifying the date on which the power comes into operation and its duration, the donee of the power, the reason why the power is given and, where some only are delegated, the trusts, powers and discretions delegated) to—

(a) each person (other than himself) if any, who under any instrument creating the trust has power (whether alone or jointly) to appoint a new trustee; and

(b) each of the other trustees, if any;

but failure to comply with this subsection shall not, in favour of a person dealing with the donee of the power, invalidate any act done or instrument executed by the donee.

(5) The donor of a power of attorney given under this section shall be liable for the acts of defaults of the donee in the same manner as if they were the acts of defaults of the donor.

(6) For the purpose of executing or exercising the trusts or powers delegated to him, the donee may exercise any of the powers conferred on the donor as trustee by statute or by the instrument creating the trust, including power, for the purpose of the transfer of any inscribed stock, himself to delegate to an attorney power to transfer but not including the power of delegation conferred by this section.

(7) The fact that it appears from any power of attorney given under this section, or from any evidence required for the purposes of any such power of attorney or otherwise, that in dealing with any stock the donee of the power is acting in the execution of a trust shall not be deemed for any purpose to affect any person in whose books the stock is inscribed or registered with any notice of the trust.

(8) This section applies to a personal representative, tenant for life and statutory owner as it applies to a trustee except that subsection (4) shall apply as if it required the notice there mentioned to be given—

(a) in the case of a personal representative, to each of the other personal representatives, if any, except any executor who has renounced probate;

(b) in the case of a tenant for life, to the trustees of the settlement an to each person, if any, who together with the person giving the notice constitutes the tenant for life;

(c) in the case of a statutory owner, to each of the persons, if any, who together with the person giving the notice constitute the statutory owner and, in the case of a statutory owner by virtue of section 23(1)(a) of the Settled Land Act 1925, to the trustees of the settlement.

AMENDMENT

This section is printed as substantially amended by the Powers of Attorney Act 1971, s.9.

Indemnities

Protection against liability in respect of rents and covenants

26.—(1) Where a personal representative or trustee liable as such for—

(a) any rent, covenant, or agreement reserved by or contained in any lease; or

(b) any rent, covenant or agreement payable under or contained in any grant made in consideration of a rentcharge; or

(c) any indemnity given in respect of any rent, covenant or agreement referred to in either of the foregoing paragraphs;

satisfies all liabilities under the lease or grant [which may have accrued and been claimed] up to the date of the conveyance hereinafter mentioned, and, where necessary, sets apart a sufficient fund to answer any future claim that may be made in respect of any fixed and ascertained sum which the lessee or grantee agreed to lay out on the property demised or granted, although the period for laying out the same may not have arrived, then and in any such case the personal representative or trustee may convey the property demised or granted to a purchaser, legatee, devisee, or other person entitled to call for a conveyance thereof and thereafter—

(i) he may distribute the residuary real and personal estate of the deceased testator or intestate, or, as the case may be, the trust estate (other than the fund, if any, set apart as aforesaid) to or amongst the persons entitled thereto, wihout appropriating any part, or any further part, as the case may be, of the estate of the deceased or of the trust estate to meet any future liability under the said lease or grant;

(ii) notwithstanding such distribution, he shall not be personally liable in respect of any subsequent claim under the said lease or grant.

(2) This section operates without prejudice to the right of the lessor or grantor, or the persons deriving title under the lessor or grantor, to follow the assets of the decreased or the trust property into the hands of the persons amongst whom the same may have been respectively distributed, and applies notwithstanding anything to the contrary in the will or other instrument, if any, creating the trust.

(3) In this section "lease" includes an underlease and an agreement for a lease or underlease and any instrument giving any such indemnity as aforesaid or varying the liabilities under the lease; "grant" applies to a grant whether the rent is created by limitation, grant, reservation, or otherwise, and includes an agreement for a grant and any instrument giving any such indemnity as aforesaid or varying the liabilities under the grant; "lessee" and "grantee" include persons respectively deriving title under them.

AMENDMENT

In subsection (1) the words in square brackets were substituted by the Law of Property (Amendment) Act 1926.

Protection by means of advertisement

27.—(1) With a view to the conveyance to or distribution among the persons entitled to any real or personal property, the trustees of a settlement or of a disposition on trust for sale or personal representatives, may give notice by advertisement in the Gazette, and [in a newspaper circulating in the district in which the land is situated] and such other like notices, including notices elsewhere than in England and Wales, as would, in any special case, have been directed by a court of competent jurisdiction in any action for administration, of their intention to make such conveyance or distribution as aforesaid, and requiring any person interested to send to the trustees or personal representatives within the time, not being less than two months, fixed in the notice or, where more than one notice is given, in the last of the notices, particulars of his claim in respect of the property or any part thereof to which the notice relates.

(2) At the expiration of the time fixed by the notice the trustees or personal representatives may convey or distribute the property or any part thereof to which the notice relates to or among the persons entitled thereto, having regard only to the claims, whether formal or not, of which the trustees or personal representatives then had notice and shall not, as respects the property so conveyed or distributed, be liable to any person of whose claim the trustees or personal representatives have not had notice at the time of conveyance or distribution; but nothing in this section—

    (*a*) prejudices the right of any person to follow the property, or any property representing the same, into the hands of any person, other than a purchaser, who may have received it; or

    (*b*) frees the trustees or personal representatives from any obligation to make searches or obtain official certificates of search similar to those which an intending purchaser would be advised to make or obtain.

(3) This section applies notwithstanding anything to the contrary in the will or other instrument, if any, creating the trust.

AMENDMENT

The words in square brackets in subsection (1) were substituted by the Law of Property (Amendment) Act 1926.

GENERAL NOTES

The provisions of this section are excluded in respect of certain claims by the Land Commission: Land Commission Act 1967, Sched. 12, para. 9(4).

Protection in regard to notice

28. A trustee or personal representative acting for the purposes of more than one trust or estate shall not, in the absence of fraud, be affected by notice of any instrument, matter, fact or thing in relation to any particular trust or estate if he has obtained notice thereof merely by reason of his acting or having acted for the purposes of another trust or estate.

29. [*Repealed by the Powers of Attorney Act* 1971, *s*.11(2) *and Sched.* 2.]

Implied indemnity of trustees

30.—(1) A trustee shall be chargeable only for money and securities actually received by him notwithstanding his signing any receipt for the sake of conformity, and shall be answerable and accountable only for his own act, receipts, neglects, or defaults, and not for those of any other trustee, nor for any banker, broker, or other person with whom any trust money or securities may be deposited, nor for the insufficiency or deficiency of any securities, nor for any other loss, unless the same happens through his own wilful default.

(2) A trustee may reimburse himself or pay or discharge out of the trust premises all expenses incurred in or about the execution of the trusts or powers.

Maintenance, Advancement and Protective Trusts

Power to apply income for maintenance and to accumulate surplus income during a minority

31.—(1) Where any property is held by trustees in trust for any person for any interest whatsoever, whether vested or contingent, then, subject to any prior interests or charges affecting that property—

>   (i) during the infancy of any such person, if his interest so long continues, the trustees may, at their sole discretion, pay to his parent or guardian, if any, or otherwise apply for or towards his maintenance, education, or benefit, the whole or such part, if any, of the income of that property as may, in all the circumstances, be reasonable, whether or not there is—
>   (*a*) any other fund applicable to the same purpose; or
>   (*b*) any person bound by law to provide for his maintenance or education; and
>   (ii) if such person on attaining the age of 18 years has not a vested interest in such income, the trustees shall thenceforth pay the income of that property and of any accretion thereto under subsection (2) of this section to him, until he either attains a vested interest therein or dies, or until failure of his interest:

Provided that, in deciding whether the whole or any part of the income of the property is during a minority to be paid or applied for the purposes aforesaid, the trustees shall have regard to the age of the infant and his requirements and generally to the circumstances of the case, and in particular to what other income, if any, is applicable for the same purposes: and where trustees have notice that the income of more than one fund is applicable for those purposes then, so far as practicable, unless the entire income of the funds is paid or applied as aforesaid or the court otherwise directs, a proportionate part only of the income of each fund shall be so paid or applied.

(2) During the infancy of any such person, if his interest so long continues, the trustees shall accumulate all the residue of that income in the way of compound interest by investing the same as the resulting income thereof from time to time in authorised investments, and shall hold those accumulations as follows:—

    (i) If any such person—
        (*a*) attains the age of 18 years, or marries under that age, and his interest in such income during his infancy or until his marriage is a vested interest: or
        (*b*) on attaining the age of 18 years or on marriage under that age becomes entitled to the property from which such income arose in fee simple, absolute or determinable, or absolutely, or for an entailed interest;
      the trustees shall hold the accumulations in trust for such person absolutely, but without prejudice to any provision with respect thereto contained in any settlement by him made under any statutory powers during his infancy, and so that the receipt of such person after marriage, and though still an infant, shall be a good discharge; and
    (ii) In any other case the trustees shall, notwithstanding that such person had a vested interest in such income, hold the accumulations as an accretion to the capital of the property from which such accumulations arose, and as one fund with such capital for all purposes, and so that, if such property is settled land, such accumulations shall be held upon the same trusts as if the same were capital money arising therefrom;

but the trustees may, at any time during the infancy of such person if his interest so long continues, apply those accumulations, or any part thereof, as if they were income arising in the then current year.

(3) This section applies in the case of a contingent interest only if the limitation or trust carries the intermediate income of the property, but it applies to a future or contingent legacy by the parent of, or a person standing in loco parentis to, the legatee, if and for such period as, under the general law, the legacy carries interest for the maintenance of the legatee, and in any such case as last aforesaid the rate of interest shall (if the income available is sufficient, and subject to any rules of court to the contrary) be five pounds per centum per annum.

(4) This section applies to a vested annuity in like manner as if the annuity were the income of property held by trustees in trust to pay the income thereof to the annuitant for the same period for which the annuity is payable, save that in any case accumulations made during the infancy of

the annuitant shall be held in trust for the annuitant or his personal representatives absolutely.

(5) This section does not apply where the instrument, if any, under which the interest arises came into operation before the commencement of this Act.

GENERAL NOTE

The age of 18 was substituted for that of 21 by the Family Law Reform Act 1969, Sched. 1.

Power of advancement

32.—(1) Trustees may at any time or times pay or apply any capital money subject to a trust, for the advancement or benefit, in such manner as they may, in their absolute discretion, think fit, of any person entitled to the capital of the trust property or of any share thereof, whether absolutely or contingently on his attaining any specified age or on the occurrence of any other event, or subject to a gift over on his death under any specified age or on the occurrence of any other event, and whether in possession or in remainder or reversion, and such payment of application may be made notwithstanding that the interest of such person is liable to be defeated by the exercise of a power of appointment or revocation, or to be diminished by the increase of the class to which he belongs:

Provided that—

(*a*) the money so paid or applied for the advancement or benefit of any person shall not exceed altogether in amount one-half of the presumptive or vested share or interest of that person in the trust property; and

(*b*) if that person is or becomes absolutely and indefeasibly entitled to a share in the trust property the money so paid or applied shall be brought into account as part of such share; and

(*c*) no such payment of application shall be made so as to prejudice any person entitled to any prior life or other interest, whether vested or contingent, in the money paid or applied unless such person is in existence and of full age and consents in writing to such payment or application.

(2) This section applies only where the trust property consists of money or securities or of property held upon trust for sale calling in and conversion, and such money or securities, or the proceeds of such sale calling in and conversion are not by statute or in equity considered as land, or applicable as capital money for the purposes of the Settled Land Act 1925.

(3) This section does not apply to trusts constituted or created before the commencement of this Act.

Protective trusts

33.—(1) Where any income, including an annuity or other periodical income payment, is directed to be held on protective trusts for the benefit of any person (in this section called "the principal beneficiary") for the period of his life or for any less period, then, during that period (in this section called the "trust period") the said income shall, without prejudice to any prior interest, be held on the following trusts, namely:—

(i) Upon trust for the principal beneficiary during the trust period or until he, whether before or after the termination of any prior interest, does or attempts to do or suffers any act or thing, or until any event happens, other than an advance under any statutory or express power, whereby, if the said income were payable during the trust period to the principal beneficiary absolutely during that period, he would be deprived of the right to receive the same or any part thereof, in any of which cases, as well as on the termination of the trust period, whichever first happens, this trust of the said income shall fail or determine;

(ii) If the trust aforesaid fails or determines during the subsistence of the trust period, then, during the residue of that period, the said income shall be held upon trust for the application thereof for the maintenance or support, or otherwise for the benefit, of all or any one or more exclusively of the other or others of the following persons (that is to say)—

(a) the principal beneficiary and his or her wife or husband, if any, and his or her children or more remote issue, if any; or

(b) if there is no wife or husband or issue of the principal beneficiary in existence, the principal beneficiary and the persons who would, if he were actually dead, be entitled to the trust property or the income thereof or to the annuity fund, if any, or arrears of the annuity, as the case may be;

as the trustees in their absolute discretion, without being liable to account for the exercise of such discretion, think fit.

(2) This section does not apply to trusts coming into operation before the commencement of this Act, and has effect subject to any variation of the implied trusts aforesaid contained in the instrument creating the trust.

(3) Nothing in this section operates to validate any trust which would, if contained in the instrument creating the trust be liable to be set aside.

(4) In relation to the dispositions mentioned in section 19(1) of the Family Law Reform Act 1987, this section shall have effect as if any reference (however expressed) to any relationship between two persons were construed in accordance with section 1 of that Act.

AMENDMENT

Subsection (4) was added by the Family Law Reform Act 1987.

ADMINISTRATION OF ESTATES ACT 1925

(15 & GEO. 5, C. 23)

ARRANGEMENT OF SECTION

PART I

DEVOLUTION OF REAL ESTATE

PART II

EXECUTORS AND ADMINISTRATORS

General Provisions

Special provisions as to Settled Land

Duties, Rights and Obligations

PART III

ADMINISTRATION OF ASSETS

PART IV

DISTRIBUTION OF RESIDUARY ESTATE

PART V

SUPPLEMENTAL

An Act to consolidate enactments relating to the administration of the estates of deceased persons.

[April 9, 1925.]

*   *   *   *

PART 1

DEVOLUTION OF REAL ESTATE

Devolution of real estate on personal representative

1.—(1) Real estate to which a deceased person was entitled for an interest not ceasing on his death shall on his death, and notwithstanding any testamentary disposition thereof, devolve from time to time on the personal representative of the deceased, in like manner as before the commencement of this Act chattels real devolved on the personal representative from time to time of a deceased person.

(2) The personal representatives for the time being of a deceased person are deemed in law his heirs and assigns within the meaning of all trusts and powers.

(3) The personal representatives shall be the representative of the deceased in regard to his real estate to which he was entitled for an interest not ceasing on his death as well as in regard to his personal estate.

Application to real estate of law affecting chattels real

2.—(1) Subject to the provisions of this Act, all enactments and rules of law, and all jurisdiction of any court with respect to the appointment of administrators or to probate or letters of administration, or to dealings before probate in the case of chattels real, and with respect to costs and other matters in the administration of personal estate, in force before the commencement of this Act, and all powers, duties, rights, equities, obligations, and liabilities of a personal representative in force at the commencement of this Act with respect to chattels real, shall apply and attach to the personal representative and shall have effect with respect to real estate vested in him, and in particular all such powers of disposition and dealing as were before the commencement of this Act exercisable as respects chattels real by the survivor or survivors of two or more personal representatives, as well as by a single personal representative, or by all the personal representatives together, shall be exercisable by the personal representatives or representative of the deceased with respect to his real estate.

(2) Where as respects real estate there are two or more personal representatives a conveyance of real estate devolving under this Part of this Act shall not, save as otherwise provided as respects trust estates including settled land, be made without the concurrence therein of all such representatives or an order of the court, but where probate is granted to one or some of two or more persons named as executors, whether or not power is reserved to the other or others to prove, any conveyance of the real estate may be made by the proving executor or executors for the time being, without an order of the court, and shall be as effectual as if all the persons named as executors had concurred therein.

(3) Without prejudice to the rights and powers of a personal representative, the appointment of a personal representative in regard to real estate shall not, save as hereinafter provided, affect—

(*a*) any rule as to marshalling or as to administration of assets;
(*b*) the beneficial interest in real estate under any testamentary disposition;

(c) any mode of dealing with any beneficial interest in real estate, or the proceeds of sale thereof;

(d) the right of any person claiming to be interested in the real estate to take proceedings for the protection or recovery thereof against any person other than the personal representative.

Interpretation of Part I

3.—(1) In this Part of this Act "real estate" includes—

(i) Chattels real, and land in possession, remainder, or reversion, and every interest in or over land to which a deceased person was entitled at the time of his death; and

(ii) Real estate held on trust (including settled land) or by way of mortgage or security, but not money to arise under a trust for sale of land, nor money secured or charged on land.

(2) A testator shall be deemed to have been entitled at his death to any interest in real estate passing under any gift contained in his will which operates as an appointment under a general power to appoint by will, or operates under the testamentary power conferred by statute to dispose of an entailed interest.

(3) An entailed interest of a deceased person shall (unless disposed of under the testamentary power conferred by statute) be deemed an interest ceasing on his death, but any further or other interest of the deceased in the same property in remainder or reversion which is capable of being disposed of by his will shall not be deemed to be an interest so ceasing.

(4) The interest of a deceased person under a joint tenancy where another tenant survives the deceased is an interest ceasing on his death.

(5) On the death of a corporator sole his interest in the corporation's real and personal estate shall be deemed to be an interest ceasing on his death and shall devolve to his successor.

This subsection applies on the demise of the Crown as respects all property, real and personal, vested in the Crown as a corporation sole.

PART II

EXECUTORS AND ADMINISTRATORS

General Provisions

4. [*Repealed by the Supreme Court of Judicature (Consolidation) Act 1925 (c. 49), Sched. 6 and now replaced by the following section*]:

[Summons of executor to prove or renounce

112. The High Court may summon any person named as executor in a will to prove, or renounce probate of, the will, and to do such other things

concerning the will as the court had power to order such a person to do immediately before the commencement of this Act].

GENERAL NOTE

This section of the Supreme Court Act 1981 supersedes section 4 of the Administration of Estates Act 1925 and section 159 of the Supreme Court of Judicature (Consolidation) Act 1925, which was repealed by the 1981 Act, Sched. 7.

Cesser of right of executor to prove

5. Where a person appointed executor by a will—

(i) survives the testator but dies without having taken out probate of the will; or

(ii) is cited to take out probate of the will and does not appear to the citation; or

(iii) renounces probate of the will;

his rights in respect of the executorship shall wholly cease, and the representation to the testator and the administration of his real and personal estate shall devolve and be committed in like manner as if that person had not been appointed executor.

Withdrawal of renunciation

6.—(1) Where an executor who has renounced probate has been permitted, whether before or after the commencement of this Act, to withdraw the renunciation and prove the will, the probate shall take effect and be deemed always to have taken effect without prejudice to the previous acts and dealings of and notices to any other personal representative who has previously proved the will or taken out letters of administration, and a memorandum of the subsequent probate shall be endorsed on the original probate or letters of administration.

(2) This section applies whether the testator died before or after the commencement of this Act.

Executor of executor represents original testator

7.—(1) An executor of a sole or last surviving executor of a testator is the executor of that testator.

This provision shall not apply to an executor who does not prove the will of his testator, and, in the case of an executor who on his death leaves surviving him some other executor of his testator who afterwards proved the will of that testator, it shall cease to apply on such probate being granted.

(2) So long as the chain of such representation is unbroken, the last executor in the chain is the executor of every preceding testator.

(3) The chain of such representation is broken by—

(*a*) an intestacy; or

(b) the failure of a testator to appoint an executor; or

(c) the failure to obtain probate of a will;

but is not broken by a temporary grant of administration if probate is subsequently granted.

(4) Every person in the chain of representation to a testator—

(a) has the same rights in respect of the real and personal estate of that testator as the original executor would have had if living; and

(b) is, to the extent to which the estate whether real or personal of that testator has come to his hands, answerable as if he were an original executor.

Right of proving executors to exercise powers

8.—(1) Where probate is granted to one or some of two or more persons named as executors, whether or not power is reserved to the others or other to prove, all the powers which are by law conferred on the personal representative may be exercised by the proving executor or executors for the time being and shall be as effectual as if all the persons named as executors had concurred therein.

(2) This section applies whether the testator died before or after the commencement of this Act.

Vesting of estate of intestate between death and grant of administration

9. Where a person dies intestate, his real and personal estate, until administration is granted in respect thereof, shall vest in the Probate Judge in the same manner and to the same extent as formerly in the case of personal estate it vested in the ordinary.

GENERAL NOTE

For the effect of this section on hire-purchase agreements, and conditional sale agreements, see the Hire-Purchase Act 1965, s.26(2)(a). This section is excluded for certain purposes by the Companies Act 1967, s.33(4)(c).

10–14 [*Repealed by the Supreme Court of Judicature (Consolidation) Act 1925, (c. 49), Sched. 6 and now replaced by the following sections*]:

[Power of court to pass over prior claims to grant

116. (1) If by reason of any special circumstances it appears to the High Court to be necessary or expedient to appoint as administrator some person other than the person who, but for this section, would in accordance with probate rules have been entitled to the grant, the court may in its discretion appoint as administrator such person as it thinks expedient.

(2) Any grant of administration under this section may be limited in any way the court thinks fit.]

General Note

This section of the Supreme Court Act 1981 supersedes section 10 of the Administration of Estates Act 1925 and section 162 of the Supreme Court of Judicature (Consolidation) Act 1925, which was repealed by the 1981 Act, Sched. 7. As to its effect on section 164 of the Judicature Act 1925, see p. 331.

[Power to require administrators to produce sureties

120.—(1) As a condition of granting administration to any person the High Court may, subject to the following provisions of this section and subject to and in accordance with probate rules, require one or more sureties to guarantee that they will make good, within any limit imposed by the court on the total liability of the surety or sureties, any loss which any person interested in the administration of the estate of the deceased may suffer in consequence of a breach by the administrator of his duties as such.

(2) A guarantee given in pursuance of any such requirement shall ensure for the benefit of every person interested in the administration of the estate of the deceased as if contained in a contract under seal made by the surety or sureties with every such person and, where there are two or more sureties, as if they had bound themselves jointly and severally.

(3) No action shall be brought on any such guarantee without the leave of the High Court.

(4) Stamp duty shall not be chargeable on any such guarantee.

(5) This section does not apply where administration is granted to the Treasury Solicitor, The Official Solicitor, the Public Trustee, the Solicitor for the affairs of the Duchy of Lancaster or the Duchy of Cornwall or the Crown Solicitor for Northern Ireland, or to the consular officer of a foreign state to which section 1 of the Consular Conventions Act 1949 applies, or in such other cases as may be prescribed.]

General Note

This section of the Supreme Court Act 1981 supersedes section 11 of the Administration of Estates Act 1925, as substituted by the Administration of Estates Act 1971, section 8 and section 167 of the Supreme Court of Judicature (Consolidation) Act 1925 which was repealed by the 1981 Act, Sched. 7.

[Number of personal representatives

114.—(1) Probate or administration shall not be granted by the High Court to more than four persons in respect of the same part of the estate of a deceased person.

(2) Where under a will or intestacy any beneficiary is a minor or a life interest arises, any grant of administration by the High Court shall be made either to a trust corporation (with or without an individual) or not less than two individuals, unless it appears to the court to be expedient in all the circumstances to appoint an individual as sole administrator.

(3) For the purpose of determining whether a minority or life interest

arises in any particular case, the court may act on such evidence as may be prescribed.

(4) If at any time during the minority of a beneficiary or the subsistence of a life interest under a will or intestacy there is only one personal representative (not being a trust corporation), the High Court may, on the application of any person interested or the guardian or receiver of any such person, and in accordance with probate rules, appoint one or more additional personal representatives to act while the minority or life interest subsists and until the estate is fully administered.

(5) An appointment of an additional personal representative under subsection (4) to act with an executor shall not have the effect of including him in any chain of representation.]

GENERAL NOTE

This section of the Supreme Court Act 1981 supersedes 12 of the Administration of Estates Act 1925 and section 160 of the Supreme Court of Judicature (Consolidation) Act 1925, which was repealed by the 1981 Act, Sched. 7.

[Power of court to sever grant

113.—(1) Subject to subsection (2), the High Court may grant probate or administration in respect of any part of the estate of a deceased person, limited in any way the court thinks fit.

(2) Where the estate of a deceased person is known to be insolvent, the grant of representation to it shall not be severed under subsection (1) except as regards a trust estate in which he had no beneficial interest.]

GENERAL NOTE

This section of the Supreme Court Act 1981 supersedes section 13 of the Administration of Estates Act 1925 and section 155 of the Supreme Court of Judicature (Consolidation) Act 1925, which was repealed by the 1981 Act, Sched. 7.

[Grants to trust corporations

115.—(1) The High Court may—

(a) where a trust corporation is named in a will as executor, grant probate to the corporation either solely or jointly with any other person named in the will as executor, as the case may require; or

(b) grant administration to a trust corporation, either solely or jointly with another person,

and the corporation may act accordingly as executor or administrator as the case may be.

(2) Probate or administration shall not be granted to any person as nominee of a trust corporation.

(3) Any officer authorised for the purpose by a trust corporation or its directors or governing body may, on behalf of the corporation, swear affi-

davits, give security and do any other act which the court may require with a view to the grant to the corporation of probate or administration; and the acts of an officer so authorised shall be binding on the corporation.

(4) Subsections (1) to (3) shall also apply in relation to any body which is exempt from the provisions of section 23(1) of the Solicitors Act 1974 (unqualified persons not to prepare papers for probate etc.) by virtue of any of paragraphs (e) to (h) of subsection (2) of that section.

GENERAL NOTE

This section of the Supreme Court Act 1981 supersedes section 14 of the Administration of Estates Act 1925 and section 161 of the Supreme Court of Judicature (Consolidation) Act 1925, which was repealed by the 1981 Act, Sched. 7.
Subsection (4) was added by the Courts and Legal Services Act 1990, s.54.

Executor not to act while administration is in force

15. Where administration has been granted in respect of any real or personal estate of a deceased person, no person shall have power to bring any action or otherwise act as executor of the deceased person in respect of the estate in or affected by the grant until the grant has been recalled or revoked.

16. [*Repealed by the Supreme Court of Judicature (Consolidation) Act 1925 (15 & 16 Geo 5, c. 49), Sched. 6, and now replaced by the following section*]:

[Administration pending suit

117.—(1) Where any legal proceedings concerning the validity of the will of a deceased person, or for obtaining, recalling or revoking any grant, are pending, the High Court may grant administration of the estate of the deceased person in question to an administrator pending suit, who shall, subject to subsection (2), have all the rights, duties and powers of a general administrator.

(2) An administrator pending suit shall be subject to the immediate control of the court and act under its direction; and, except in such circumstances as may be prescribed, no distribution of the estate, or any part of the estate, of the deceased person in question shall be made by such an administrator without the leave of the court.

(3) The court may, out of the estate of the deceased, assign an administrator pending suit such reasonable remuneration as it thinks fit.]

GENERAL NOTE

This section of the Supreme Court Act 1981 supersedes section 16 of the Administration of Estates Act 1925 and section 163 of the Supreme Court of Judicature (Consolidation) Act 1925, which was repealed by the 1981 Act, Sched. 7.

Continuance of legal proceedings after revocation of temporary administration

17.—(1) If, while any legal proceeding is pending in any court by or against an administrator to whom a temporary administration has been granted, that administration is revoked, that court may order that the proceeding be continued by or against the new personal representative in like manner as if the same had been originally commenced by or against him, but subject to such conditions and variations, if any, as that court directs.

(2) The county court has jurisdiction under this section where the proceedings are pending in that court.

AMENDMENT

Subsection (2) was added by the County Courts Act 1984, Sched. 2.

GENERAL ACT

The county court shall have jurisdiction: County Courts Act 1959, Sched. 1.

18. [*Repealed by the Supreme Court of Judicature (Consolidation) Act 1925 which was itself repealed by the Supreme Court Act 1981. The terms of this section are now covered by the 1981 Act, s.116; above, p. 1117*].

19–20. [*Repealed by the Supreme Court of Judicature (Consolidation) Act 1925 (15 & 16 Geo. 5, c. 49), Sched. 6, and replaced by the following sections*]:

[Administration with will annexed

119.—(1) Administration with the will annexed shall be granted, subject to and in accordance with probate rules, in every class of case in which the High Court had power to make such a grant immediately before the commencement of this Act.

(2) Where administration with the will annexed is granted, the will of the deceased shall be performed and observed in the same manner as if probate of it had been granted to an executor.]

GENERAL NOTE

This section of the Supreme Court Act 1981 supersedes section 19 of the Administration of Estates Act 1925 and section 166 of the Supreme Court of Judicature (Consolidation) Act 1925, which was repealed by the 1981 Act, Sched. 7.

[Effect of appointment of minor as executor

118. Where a testator by his will appoints a minor to be an executor, the appointment shall not operate to vest in the minor, the estate, or any part of the estate, of the testator, or to constitute him a personal representative in respect of the settled land, and a special or additional personal representative for any purpose, unless and until probate is granted to him in accordance with probate rules.]

This section of the Supreme Court Act 1981 supersedes section 20 of the Administration of Estates Act 1925 and section 165 of the Supreme Court of Judicatue (Consolidation) Act 1925, which was repealed by the 1981 Act, Sched. 7.

Rights and liabilities of administrator

21. Every person to whom administration of the real and personal estate of a deceased person is granted, shall, subject to the limitations contained in the grant, have the same rights and liabilities and be accountable in like manner as if he were the executor of the deceased.

Debtor who becomes creditor's executor by representation or administrator to account for debt to estate

21A.—(1) Subject to subsection (2) of this section, where a debtor becomes his deceased creditor's executor by representation or administrator—

(a) his debt shall thereupon be extinguished; but

(b) he shall be acountable for the amount of the debt as part of the creditor's estate in any case where he would be so accountable if he had been appointed as an executor by the creditor's will.

(2) Subsection (1) of this section does not apply where the debtor's authority to act as executor or administrator is limited to part only of the creditor's estate which does not include the debt; and a debtor whose debt is extinguished by virtue of paragraph (a) shall not be accountable for its amount by virtue of paragraph (b) of that subsection in any case where the debt was barred by the Limitation Act 1939 before he became the credtor's executor or administrator.

(3) In this section "debt" includes any liability, and "debtor" and "creditor" shall be construed accordingly.

Section 21A was added by the Limitation Amendment Act 1980.
The reference in section 21A(2) to the Limitation Act 1939, is construed as referring also to the Limitation Act 1980.—(amended by Limitation Act 1980, Sched. 3).

Special Provisions as to Settled Land

Special executors as respects settled land

22.—(1) A testator may appoint, and in default of such express appointment shall be deemed to have appointed, as his special executors in regard to settled land, the persons, if any, who are at his death the trustees of the settlement thereof, and probate may be granted to such trustees specially limited to the settled land.

In the subsection "settled land" means land vested in the testator which was settled previously to his death and not by his will.

(2) A testator may appoint other persons either with or without such trustees as aforesaid or any of them to be his general executors in regard to his other property and assets.

Provisions where, as respects settled land, representation is not granted to the trustess of the settlement

23.—(1) Where settled land becomes vested in a personal representative, not being a trustee of the settlement, upon trust to convey the land to or assent to the vesting thereof in the tenant for life or statutory owner in order to give effect to a settlement created before the death of the deceased and not by his will, or would, on the grant of representation to him, have become so vested, such representative may—

(*a*) before representation has been granted, renounce his office in regard only to such settled land without renouncing it in regard to other property;

(*b*) after representation has been granted, apply to the court for revocation of the grant in regard to the settled land without applying in regard to other property.

(2) Whether such renunciation or revocation is made or not, the trustees of the settlement, or any person beneficially interested thereunder, may apply to the High Court for an order appointing a special or additional personal representative in respect of the settled land, and a special or additional personal representative, if and when appointed under the order, shall be in the same position as if representation had originally been granted to him alone in place of the original personal representative, if any, or to him jointly with the original personal representative, as the case may be, limited to the settled land, but without prejudice to the previous acts and dealings, if any, of the personal representative originally constituted or the effect of notices given to such personal representative.

(3) The court may make such order as aforesaid subject to such security, if any, being given by or on behalf of the special or additional personal representative, as the court may direct, and shall, unless the court considers that special considerations apply, appoint such persons as may be necessary to secure that the persons to act as representatives in respect of the settled land shall, if willing to act, be the same persons as are the trustees of the settlement, and an office copy of the order when made shall be furnished to the [principal registry of the Family Division of the High Court] for entry, and a memorandum of the order shall be endorsed on the probate or administration.

(4) The person applying for the appointment of a special or additional personal representative shall give notice of the application to the [principal registry of the Family Division of the High Court] in the manner prescribed.

(5) Rules of court may be made for prescribing for all matters required for giving effect to the provisions of this section, and in particular—

(a) for notice of any application being given to the proper officer;
(b) for production of orders, probates, and administration to the registry;
(c) for the endorsement on a probate or administration of a memorandum of an order, subject or not to any exceptions;
(d) for the manner in which the costs are to be borne;
(e) for protecting purchasers and trustees and other persons in a fiduciary position, dealing in good faith with or giving notices to a personal representative before notice of any order has been endorsed on the probate or administration or a pending action has been registered in respect of the proceedings.

AMENDMENT

In subsections (3) and (4) the words in square brackets were substituted by the Administration of Justice Act 1970, s.1. Sched. 2.

Power for special personal representatives to dispose of settled land

24.—(1) The special personal representatives may dispose of the settled land without the concurrence of the general personal representatives, who may likewise dispose of the other property and assets of the deceased without the concurrence of the special personal representatives.

(2) In this section the expression "special personal representatives" means the representatives appointed to act for the purposes of settled land and includes any original personal representative who is to act with an additional personal representative for those purposes.

Duties, Rights, and Obligations

[Duty of personal representatives

25. The personal representative of a deceased person shall be under a duty to—

(a) collect and get in the real and personal estate of the deceased and administer it according to law;
(b) when required to do so by the court, exhibit on oath in the court a full inventory of the estate and when so required render an account of the administration of the estate to the court;
(c) when required to do so by the High Court, deliver up the grant of probate or administration to that court.]

AMENDMENT

This section was substituted by the Administration of Estates Act 1971, s.9.

Rights of action by and against personal representative

26.—(1) and (2) [*Repealed by the Law Reform (Miscellaneous Provisions) Act* 1934 (24 & 25 *Geo.* 5, *c.* 41), *s.*1(7)].

(3) A personal representative may distrain for arrears of a rentcharge due or accruing to the deceased in his lifetime on the land affected or charged therewith, so long as the land remains in the possession of the person liable to pay the rentcharge or of the persons deriving title under him, and in like manner as the deceased might have done had he been living.

(4) A personal representative may distrain upon land for arrears of rent due or accruing to the deceased in like manner as the deceased might have done had he been living.

Such arrears may be distrained for after the termination of the lease or tenancy as if the term or interest had not determined, if the distress is made—

    (*a*) within six months after the termination of the lease or tenancy;

    (*b*) during the continuance of the possession of the lessee or tenant from whom the arrears were due.

The statutory enactments relating to distress for rent apply to any distress made pursuant to this subsection.

(5) and (6) [*Repealed by the Law Reform (Miscellaneous Provisions) Act* 1934 (24 & 25 *Geo.* 5, *c.* 41) *s.*1(7)].

Protection of persons acting on probate or administration

27.—(1) Every person making or permitting to be made any payment or disposition in good faith under a representation shall be indemnified and protected in so doing, notwithstanding any defect or circumstance whatsoever affecting the validity of the representation.

(2) Where a representation is revoked, all payments and dispositions made in good faith to a personal representative under the representation before the revocation thereof are a valid discharge to the person making the same; and the personal representative who acted under the revoked representation may retain and reimburse himself in respect of any payments or dispositions made by him which the person to whom representation is afterwards granted might have properly made.

Liability of person fraudulently obtaining or retaining estate of deceased

28. If any person, to the defrauding of creditors or without full valuable consideration, obtains, receives or holds any real or personal estate of a deceased person or effects the release of any debt or liability due to the estate of the deceased, he shall be charged as executor in his own wrong to the extent of the real and personal estate received or coming to his hands, or the debt or liability released, after deducting—

    (*a*) any debt for valuable consideration and without fraud due to him from the deceased person at the time of his death; and

    (*b*) any payment made by him which might properly be made by a personal representative.

Liability of estate of personal representative

29. Where a person as personal representative of a deceased person (including an executor in his own wrong) wastes or converts to his own use any part of the real or personal estate of the deceased, and dies, his personal representative shall to the extent of the available assets of the defaulter be liable and chargeable in respect of such waste or conversion in the same manner as the defaulter would have been in living.

Provisions applicable where administration granted to nominee of the Crown

30.—(1) Where the administration of the real and personal estate of any deceased person is granted to a nominee of the Crown (whether the Treasury Solicitor, or a person nominated by the Treasury Solicitor, or any other person), any legal proceeding by or against that nominee for the recovery of the real or personal estate, or any part or share thereof, shall be of the same character, and be instituted and carried on in the same manner, and be subject to the same rules of law and equity (including, except as otherwise provided by this Act, the rules of limitation under the statutes of limitation or otherwise), in all respects as if the administration had been granted to such nominee as one of the persons interested under this Act in the estate of the deceased.

(2) An information or other proceeding on the part of His Majesty shall not be filed or instituted, and a petition of right shall not be presented, in respect of the real or personal estate of any deceased person or any part or share thereof, or any claim thereon, except [. . .] subject to the same rules of law and equity within and subject to which a proceeding for the life purposes might be instituted by or against a subject.

(3) The Treasury Solicitor shall not be required, when applying for or obtaining administration of the estate of a deceased person for the use or benefit of His Majesty, to deliver, nor shall the Probate, Divorce and Admiralty Division of the High Court or the Commissioners of Inland Revenue be entitled to receive in connexion with any such application or grant of administration, and affidavit, statutory declaration, account, certificate, or other statement verified on oath; but the Treasury Solicitor shall deliver and the said Division and Commissioners respectively shall accept, in lieu thereof, an account or particulars of the estate of the deceased signed by or on behalf of the Treasury Solicitor.

(4) References in section two, four, [. . .] and seven of the Treasury

Solicitor Act 1876 and in subsection (3) of section three of the Duchy of Lancaster Act 1920 to "personal estate" shall include real estate.

AMENDMENTS

In Subsection (2) the words omitted were repealed by the Limitation Act 1939 and in subs. (4) the words omitted were repealed by the Statue Law Repeals Act 1981.

Power to make rules

31. Provision may be made by rules of court for giving effect to the provisions of this part of this Act so far as relates to real estate and in particular for adapting the procedure and practice on the grant of letters of administration to the case of real estate.

PART III

ADMINISTRATION OF ASSETS

Real and personal estate of deceased are assets for payment of debts

32.—(1) The real and personal estate, whether legal or equitable, of a deceased person, to the extent of his beneficial interest therein, and the real and personal estate of which a deceased person in pursuance of any general power (including the statutory power to dispose of entailed interests) disposes by his will, are assets for payments of his debts (whether by speciality or simple contract) and liabilities, and any disposition by will inconsistent with this enactment is void as against the creditors, and the court shall, if necessary, administer the property for the purpose of the payment of the debts and liabilities.

This subsection takes effect without the prejudice to the rights of incumbrancers.

(2) If any person to whom any such beneficial interest devolves or is given, or in whom any such interest vests, disposes thereof in good faith before an action is brought or process is sued out against him, he shall be personally liable for the value of the interest so disposed of by him, but that interest shall not be liable to be taken in execution in the action or under the process.

Trust for sale

33.—(1) On the death of a person intestate as to any real or personal estate, such estate shall be held by his personal representatives—

(a) as to the real estate upon trust to sell the same; and
(b) as to the personal estate upon trust to call in sell and convert into money such part thereof as may not consist of money,

with power to postpone such sale and conversion for such a period as the personal representatives, without being liable to account, may think proper, and so that any reversionary interest be not sold until it falls into possession, unless the personal representative see special reason for sale, and so also that, unless required for purposes of administration owing to want of other assets, personal chattels be not sold except for special reason.

(2) Out of the net money to arise from the sale and conversion of such real and personal estate (after payment of costs), and out of the ready money of the deceased (so far as not disposed of by his will, if any), the personal representative shall pay all such funeral, testamentary and admin- istration expenses, debts and other liabilities as are properly payable there- out having regard to the rules of administration contained in this Part of this Act, and out of the residue of the said money the personal representa- tive shall set aside a fund sufficient to provide for any pecuniary legacies bequeathed by the will (if any) of the deceased.

(3) During the minority of any beneficiary or the subsistence of any life interest and pending the distribution of the whole or any part of the estate of the deceased, the personal representatives may invest the residue of the said money, or so much thereof as may not have been distributed, in any investments for the time being authorised by statute for the investment of trust money, with power, at the discretion of the personal representatives, to change such investments for others of a like nature.

(4) The residue of the said money and any investments for the time being representing the same, including (but without prejudice to the trust for sale) any part of the estate of the deceased which may be retained unsold and is not required for the administration purposes aforesaid, is in this Act referred to as "the residuary estate of the intestate."

(5) The income (including net rents and profits of real estate and chattels real after payment of rates, taxes, rent, costs of insurance, repairs and other outgoings properly attributable to income) of so much of the real and personal estate of the deceased as may not be disposed of by his will, if any, or may not be required for the administration purposes aforesaid, may, however such estate is invested, as from the death of the deceased, be treated and applied as income, and for that purpose any necessary apportionment may be made between tenant for life and remainderman.

(6) Nothing in this section affects the rights of any creditor of the deceased or the rights of the Crown in respect of death duties.

(7) Where the deceased leaves a will, this section has effect subject to the provisions contained in the will.

Administration of assets

34.—(1) Where the estate of a deceased person is insolvent, his real and personal estate shall be administered in accordance with the rules set out in Part I of the First Schedule to this Act.

(2) [*Repealed by the Administration of Estates Act* 1971, *ss.* 10, 12(2), (6), *Sched.* 2 *Pt.* II].

(3) Where the estate of a deceased person is solvent his real and personal estate shall, subject to rules of court and the provisions hereinafter contained as to charges on property of the deceased, and to the provisions, if any, contained in his will, be applicable towards the discharge of the funeral, testamentary and administration expenses, debts and liabilities payable thereout in the order mentioned in Part II of the First Schedule to this Act.

Charges on property of deceased to be paid primarily out of the property charged

35.—(1) Where a person dies possessed of, or entitled to, or, under a general power of appointment (including the statutory power to dispose of entailed interests) by his will disposes of, an interest in property, which at the time of his death is charged with the payment of money, whether by way of legal mortgage, equitable charge or otherwise (including a lien for unpaid purchase money), and the deceased has not by will deed or other document signified a contrary or other intention, the interest so charged shall, as between the different persons claiming through the deceased, be primarily liable for the payment of the charge; and every part of the said interest, according to its value, shall bear a proportionate part of the charge on the whole thereof.

(2) Such contrary or other intention shall not be deemed to be signified—

(*a*) by a general direction for the payment of debts or of all the debts of the testator out of his personal estate, or his residuary real and personal estate, or his residuary real estate; or

(*b*) by a charge of debts upon any such estate;

unless such intention is further signified by words expressly or by necessary implication referring to all or some part of the charge.

(3) Nothing in this section affects the right of a person entitled to the charge to obtain payment or satisfaction thereof either out of the other assets of the deceased or otherwise.

Effect of assent or conveyance by personal representative

36.—(1) A personal representative may assent to the vesting, in any person who (whether by devise, bequest, devolution, appropriation or otherwise) may be entitled thereto, either beneficially or as a trustee or personal representative, of any estate or interest in real estate to which the testator or intestate was entitled or over which he exercised a general power of appointment by his will, including the statutory power to dispose of entailed interests, and which devolved upon the personal representative.

(2) The assent shall operate to vest in that person the estate or interest to which the assent relates, and, unless a contrary intention appears, the assent shall relate back to the death of the deceased.

(3) The statutory covenants implied by a person being expressed to convey as personal representative, may be implied in an assent in like manner as in a conveyance by deed.

(4) An assent to the vesting of a legal estate shall be in writing, signed by the personal representative, and shall name the person in whose favour it is given and shall operate to vest in that person the legal estate to which it relates; and an assent not in writing or not in favour of a named person shall not be effectual to pass a legal estate.

(5) Any person in whose favour an assent or conveyance of a legal estate is made by a personal representative may require that notice of the assent or conveyance be written or endorsed on or permanently annexed to the probate or letters of administration, at the cost of the estate of the deceased, and the probate or letters of administration be produced, at the like cost, to prove that the notice has been placed thereon or annexed thereto.

(6) A statement in writing by a personal representative that he has not given or made an assent or conveyance in respect of a legal estate, shall, in favour of a purchaser, but without prejudice to any previous disposition made in favour of another purchaser deriving title mediately or immediately under the personal representative, be sufficient evidence that an assent or conveyance has not been given or made in respect of the legal estate to which the statement relates, unless notice of a previous assent or conveyance affecting that estate has been placed on or annexed to the probate or administration.

A conveyance by a personal representative of a legal estate to a purchaser accepted on the faith of such a statement shall (without prejudice as aforesaid and unless notice of a previous assent or conveyance affecting that estate has been placed on or annexed to the probate or administration) operate to transfer or create the legal estate expressed to be conveyed in like manner as if no previous assent or conveyance had been made by the personal representative.

A personal representative making a false statement, in regard to any such matter, shall be liable in like manner as if the statement had been contained in a statutory declaration.

(7) An assent or conveyance by a personal representative in respect of a legal estate shall, in favour of a purchaser, unless notice of a previous assent or conveyance affecting that legal estate has been placed on or annexed to the probate or administration, be taken as sufficient evidence that the persons in whose favour the assent or conveyance is given or made is the person entitled to have the legal estate conveyed to him, and upon the proper trusts, if any, but shall not otherwise prejudicially affect the claim of any person rightfully entitled to the estate vested or conveyed or any charge thereon.

(8) A conveyance of a legal estate by a personal representative to a purchaser shall not be invalidated by reason only that the purchaser may have notice that all the debts, liabilities, funeral, and testamentary or adminis-

tration expenses, duties, and legacies of the deceased have been discharged or provided for.

(9) An assent or conveyance given or made by a personal representative shall not, except in favour of a purchaser of a legal estate, prejudice the right of the personal representative or any other person to recover the estate or interest to which the assent or conveyance relates, or to be indemnified out of such estate or interest against any duties debt, or liability to which such estate or interest would have been subject if there had not been any assent or conveyance.

(10) A personal representative may, as a condition of giving an assent or making a conveyance, require security for the discharge of any such duties, debt, or liability, but shall not be entitled to postpone the giving of an assent merely by reason of the subsistence of any such duties, debt or liability if reasonable arrangements have been made for discharging the same; and an assent may be given subject to any legal estate or charge by way of legal mortgage.

(11) This section shall not operate to impose any stamp duty in respect of an assent, and in this section "purchaser" means a purchaser for money or money's worth.

(12) This section applies to assents and conveyances made after the commencement of this Act, whether the testator or intestate died before or after such commencement.

Validity of conveyance not affected by revocation of representation

37.—(1) All conveyances of any interest in real or personal estate made to a purchaser either before or after the commencement of this Act by a person to whom probate or letters of administration have been granted are valid, notwithstanding any subsequent revocation or variation, either before or after the commencement of this Act, of the probate or administration.

(2) This section takes effect without prejudice to any order of the court made before the commmencement of this Act, and applies whether the testator or intestate died before or after such commencment.

Right to follow property and powers of the court in relation thereto

38.—(1) An assent or conveyance by a personal representative to a person other than a purchaser does not prejudice the rights of any person to follow the property to which the assent or conveyance relates, or any property representing the same, into the hands of the person in whom it is vested by the assent or conveyance, or of any other person (not being a purchaser) who may have received the same or in whom it may be vested.

(2) Notwithstanding any such assent or conveyance the court may, on the application of any creditor or other person interested,—

(*a*) order a sale, exchange, mortgage, charge, lease, payment, transfer or other transaction to be carried out which the court considers requisite for the purpose of giving effect to the rights of the persons interested;

(*b*) declare that the person, not being a purchaser, in whom the property is vested is a trustee for those purposes;

(*c*) give directions respecting the preparation and execution of any conveyance or other instrument or as to any other matter required for giving effect to the order;

(*d*) make any vesting order, or appoint a person to convey in accordance with the provisions of the Trustee Act 1925.

(3) This section does not prejudice the rights of a purchaser or a person deriving title under him, but applies whether the testator or intestate died before or after the commencement of this Act.

"(4) The county court has jurisdiction under this section where the estate in respect of which the application is made does not exceed in amount or value the county court limit."

AMENDMENT

Subsection (4) was added by the County Courts Act 1984, Sched. 2.

GENERAL NOTE

For cases where the county court has jurisdiction, see sections 15–45 of the County Courts Act 1984.

Powers of management

39.—(1) In dealing with the real and personal estate of the deceased his personal representatives shall, for purposes of administration, or during a minority of any beneficiary or the subsistence of any life interest, or until the period of distribution arrives, have—

(i) the same powers and discretions, including power to raise money by mortgage or charge (whether or not by deposit of documents), as a personal representative had before the commencement of this Act, with respect to personal estate vested in him, and such power of raising money by mortgage may in the case of land be exercised by way of legal mortgage; and

(ii) all the powers, discretions and duties conferred or imposed by law on trustees holding land upon an effectual trust for sale (including power to overreach equitable interests and powers as if the same affected the proceeds of sale); and

(iii) all the powers conferred by statute on trustees for sale, and so that every contract entered into by a personal representative shall be binding on and be enforceable against and by the personal representative for the time being of the deceased, and may be carried into effect, or be varied or rescinded by him, and, in the case of a contract entered into by a predecessor, as if it had been entered into by himself.

(2) Nothing in this section shall affect the right of any person to require an assent or conveyance to be made.

(3) This section applies whether the testator or intestate died before or after the commencement of this Act.

Powers of personal representative for raising money, &c.

40.—(1) For giving effect to beneficial interests the personal representative may limit or demise land for a term of years absolute, with or without impeachment for waste, to trustees on usual trusts for raising or securing any principal sum and the interest thereon for which the land, or any part thereof, is liable, and may limit or grant a rentcharge for giving effect to any annual or periodical sum for which the land or the income thereof or any part thereof is liable.

(2) This section applies whether the testator or intestate died before or after the commencement of this Act.

Powers of personal representative as to appropriation

41.—(1) The personal representative may appropriate any part of the real or personal estate, including things in action, of the deceased in the actual condition or state of investment thereof at the time of appropriation in or towards satisfaction of any legacy bequeathed by the deceased, or of any other interest or share in his property, whether settled or not, as to the personal representative may seem just and reasonable, according to the respective rights of the persons interested in the property of the deceased:
Provided that—

   (i) an appropriation shall not be made under this section so as to affect prejudicially an specific devise or bequest;

   (ii) an appropriation of property, whether or not being an investment authorised by law or by the will, if any, of the deceased for the investment of money subject to the trust, shall not (save as hereinafter mentioned) be made under this section except with the following consents:

   (*a*) when made for the benefit of a person absolutely and beneficially entitled in possession, the consent of that person;

   (*b*) when made in respect of any settled legacy share or interest, the consent of either the trustee thereof, if any (not being also the personal representative), or the person who may for the time being be entitled to the income:

If the person whose consent is so required as aforesaid is an infant or [is incapable, by reason of mental disorder within the meaning of the Mental Health Act 1983 of managing and administering his property and affairs], the consent shall be given on his behalf by his parents or parent, testamentary or other guardian, [. . .] or receiver, or if, in the case of an infant, there is no such parent or guardian, by the court on the application of his next friend;

(iii) no consent (save of such trustee as aforesaid) shall be required on behalf of a person who may come into existence after the time of appropriation, or who cannot be found or ascertained at that time;

(iv) if no [receiver is acting for a person suffering from mental disorder], then, if the appropriation is of an investment authorised by law or by the will, if any, of the deceased for the investment of money subject to the trust, no consent shall be required on behalf of the [said person];

(v) if, independently of the personal representative, there is no trustee of a settled legacy share or interest, and no person of full age and capacity entitled to the income thereof, no consent shall be required to an appropriation in respect of such legacy share or interest, provided that the appropriation is of an investment authorised as aforesaid.

"(1A) The county court has jurisdiction under proviso (ii) to subsection (1) of this section where the estate in respect of which the application is made does not exceed in amount or value the county court limit."

(2) Any property duly appropriated under the powers conferred by this section shall thereafter be treated as an authorised investment, and may be retained or dealt with accordingly.

(3) For the purposes of such appropriation, the personal representative may ascertain and fix the value of the respective parts of the real and personal estate and the liabilities of the deceased as he may think fit, and shall for that purpose employ a duly qualified valuer in any case where such employment may be necessary; and may make any conveyance (including an assent) which may be requisite for giving effect to the appropriation.

(4) An appropriation made pursuant to this section shall bind all persons interested in the property of the deceased whose consent is not hereby made requisite.

(5) The personal representative shall, in making the appropriation, have regard to the rights of any person who may thereafter come into existence, or who cannot be found or ascertained at the time of appropriation, and of any other person whose consent is not required by this section.

(6) This section does not prejudice any other power of appropriation conferred by law or by the will (if any) of the deceased, and takes effect with any extended powers conferred by the will (if any) of the deceased, and where an appropriation is made under this section, in respect of a

settled legacy, share or interest, the property appropriated shall remain subject to all trusts for sale and powers of leasing, disposition, and management or varying investments which would have been applicable thereto or to the legacy, share or interest in respect of which the appropriation is made, if no such appropriation had been made.

(7) If after any real estate has been appropriated in purported exercise of the powers conferred by this section, the person to whom it was conveyed disposes of it or any interest therein, then, in favour of a purchaser, the appropriation shall be deemed to have been made in accordance with the requirements of this section and after all requisite consents, if any, had been given.

(8) In this section, a settled legacy, share or interest includes any legacy, share or interest to which a person is not absolutely entitled in possession at the date of the appropriation, also an annuity, and "purchaser' means a purchaser for money or money's worth.

(9) This section applies whether the deceased died intestate or not, and whether before or after the commencement of this Act, and extends to property over which a testator exercises a general power of appointment, including the statutory power to dispose of entailed interests, and authorises the setting apart of a fund to answer an annuity by means of the income of that fund or otherwise.

AMENDMENTS

Subsection (1A) was added by the County Courts Act 1984, Sched. 2.
In subsection (1)(ii) the words in square brackets were substituted, and the words omitted were repealed by the Mental Health Act 1959. Sched. 7, Pt. I.
In subsection (1)(iv) the words in square brackets were substituted by the same provision.

GENERAL NOTE

This section is excluded in respect of requirements or consents made under the Intestates' Estates Act 1952, Sched. 2.
In subsection (1)(ii) for cases where the county court has jurisdiction, see the County Courts Act 1984, ss.15–45.
In subsection (5), for the rights of the surviving spouse as respects the matrimonial home, see the Intestates' Estates Act 1952, Sched. 2, para. 1(3), as amended by the Leasehold Reform Act 1967, s.7(8).

Power to appoint trustees of infants' property

42.—(1) Where an infant is absolutely entitled under the will or on the intestacy of a person dying before or after the commencement of this Act (in this subsection called "the deceased") to a devise or legacy, or to the residue of the estate of the deceased, or any share therein, and such devise, legacy, residue or share is not under the will, if any, of the deceased, devised or bequeathed to trustees for the infant, the personal representatives of the deceased may appoint a trust corporation or two or more individuals not exceeding four (whether or not including the personal representatives or one or more of the personal representatives), to be the trustee or trustees of such devise, legacy, residue or share for the infant, and to be trustees of any land devised or any land being or forming part of such residue or share for the purposes of the Settled Land Act 1925 and of the statutory provisions relating to the management of land during a minority, and may execute or do any assurance or thing requisite for vesting such devise, legacy, residue or share in the trustee or trustees so appointed.

On such appointment the person representatives, as such, shall be discharged from all further liability in respect of such devise, legacy, residue, or share, and the same may be retained in its existing condition or state of investment, or may be converted into money, and such money may be invested in any authorised investment.

(2) Where a personal representative has before the commencement of this Act retained or sold any such devise, legacy, residue or share, and invested the same or the proceeds thereof in any investments in which he was authorised to invest money subject to the trust, then, subject to any order of the court made before such commencement, he shall not be deemed to have incurred any liability on that account, or by reason of not having paid or transferred the money or property into court.

Obligations of personal representative as to giving possession of land and powers of the court

43.—(1) A personal representative, before giving an assent or making a conveyance in favour of any person entitled, may permit that person to take possession of the land, and such possession shall not prejudicially affect the right of the personal representative to take or resume possession nor his power to convey the land as if he were in possession thereof, but subject to the interest of any lessee, tenant or occupier in possession or in actual occupation of the land.

(2) Any person who as against the personal representative claims possession of real estate, or the appointment of a receiver thereof, or a conveyance thereof, or an assent to the vesting thereof, or to be registered as proprietor thereof under the Land Registration Act 1925 may apply to the court for directions with reference thereto, and the court may make such vesting or other order as may be deemed proper, and the provisions of the Trustee Act 1925, relating to vesting orders and to the appointment of a person to convey, shall apply.

(3) This section applies whether the testator or intestate died before or after the commencement of this Act.

GENERAL NOTE

In subsection (2), for cases where the county court has jurisdiction, see, the County Courts Act 1959, Sched. 1.

Power to postpone distribution

44. Subject to the foregoing provisions of this Act, a personal representative is not bound to distribute the estate of the deceased before the expiration of one year from the death.

PART IV

DISTRIBUTION OF RESIDUARY ESTATE

Abolition of descent to heir, curtesy, dower and escheat

45.—(1) With regard to the real estate and personal inheritance of every person dying after the commencement of this Act, there shall be abolished—

(a) All existing modes rules and canons of descent, and of devolution by special occupancy or otherwise, of real estate, or of a personal inheritance, whether operating by the general law or by the custom of gavelkind or borough English or by any other custom of any county, locality, or manor, or otherwise howsoever; and

(b) Tenancy by the curtesy and every other estate and interest of a husband in real estate as to which his wife dies intestate, whether arising under the general law or by custom or otherwise; and

(c) Dower and freebench an every other estate and interest of a wife in real estate as to which her husband dies intestate, whether arising under the general law or by custom or otherwise: Provided that where a right (if any) to freebench or other like right has attached before the commencement of this Act which cannot be barred by a testamentary or other disposition made by the husband, such right shall, unless released, remain in force as an equitable interest; and

(d) Escheat to the Crown or the Duchy of Lancaster or the Duke of Cornwall or to a mesne lord for want of heirs.

(2) Nothing in this section affects the descent or devolution of an entailed interest.

Succession to real and personal estate on intestacy

46.—(1) The residuary estate of an intestate shall be distributed in the manner or be held on the trusts mentioned in this section, namely:—

(i) [If the intestate leaves a husband or wife, then in accordance with the following Table:

TABLE

If the intestate—	

(1) leaves—
    (*a*) no issue, and
    (*b*) no parent, or brother or sister of the whole blood, or issue of a brother or sister of the whole blood
	the residuary estate shall be held in trust for the surviving husband or wife absolutely.

(2) leaves issue (whether or not persons mentioned in subparagraph (*b*) above also survive)	the surviving husband or wife shall take the personal chattels absolutely and, in addition, the residuary estate of the intestate (other than the personal chattels) shall stand charged with the payment of a [fixed net sum], free of death duties and costs, to the surviving husband or wife with interest thereon from the date of the death at [such rate as the Lord Chancellor may specify by order] until paid or appropriate, and, subject to providing for that sum and the interest thereon, the residuary estate (other than the personal chattels) shall be held—
	    (*a*) as to one half upon trust for the surviving husband or wife during his or her life, and, subject to such life interest, on the statutory trusts for the issue of the intestate, and
	    (*b*) as to the other half, on the statutory trusts for the issue of the intestate.

(3) leaves one or more of the following, that is to say, a parent, a brother or sister of the whole blood, or issue of a brother or sister of the whole blood, but leaves no issue	the surviving husband or wife shall take the personal chattels absolutely and, in addition, the residuary estate of the intestate (other than the personal chattels) shall stand charged with the payment of a [fixed net sum], free of death duties and costs, to the surviving husband or wife with interest thereon from the date of the death at [such rate as the Lord Chancellor may specify by order] until paid or appropriated, and, subject to providing for that sum and the interest thereon, the residuary estate (other than the personal chattels) shall be held—

(a) as to one half in trust for the surviving husband or wife absolutely, and

(b) as to the other half—

   (i) where the intestate leaves one parent or both parents (whether or not brothers or sisters of the intestate or their issue also survive) in trust for the parent absolutely or, as the case may be, for the two parents in equal shares absolutely

   (ii) where the intestate leaves no parent, on the statutory trusts for the brothers and sisters of the whole blood of the intestate.]

[The fixed sums referred to in paragraphs (2) and (3) of this Table shall be of the amounts provided by or under section 1 of the Family Provision Act 1966.]

(ii) If the intestate leaves issue but no husband or wife, the residuary estate of the intestate shall be held on the statutory trusts for the issue of the intestate;

(iii) If the intestate leaves [no husband or wife and] no issue but both parents, then [. . .] the residuary estate of the intestate shall be held in trust for the father and mother in equal shares abolutely;

(iv) If the intestate leaves [no husband or wife and] no issue but one parent, then [. . .] the residuary estate of the intestate shall be held in trust for the surviving father or mother absolutely;

(v) If the intestate leaves no [husband or wife and no issue and no] parent, then, [. . .] the residuary estate of the intestate shall be held in trust for the following persons living at the death of the intestate, and in the following order and manner, namely:

First, on the statutory trusts for the brothers and sisters of the whole blood of the intestate; but if no person takes an absolutely vested interest under such trusts; then

Secondly, on the statutory trusts for the brothers and sisters of the half blood of the intestate; but if no person takes an absolutely vested interest under such trusts; then

Thirdly, for the grandparents of the intestate and, if more

than one survive the intestate, in equal shares; but if there is no member of this class; then

Fourthly, on the statutory trusts for the uncles and aunts of the intestate (being brothers or sisters of the whole blood of a parent of the intestate); but if no person takes an absolutely vested interest under such trusts; then

Fifthly, on the statutory trusts for the uncles and aunts of the intestate (being brothers or sisters of the half blood of a parent of the intestate); [. . .]

(vi) In default of any person taking an absolute interest under the foregoing provisions, the residuary estate of the intestate shall belong to the Crown or to the Duchy of Lancaster or to the Duke of Cornwall for the time being, as the case may be, as bona vacantia, and in lieu of any right to escheat.

The Crown or the said Duchy or the said Duke may (without prejudice to the powers reserved by section nine of the Civil List Act 1910, or any other powers), out of the whole or any part of the property devolving on them respectively, provide, in accordance with the existing practice, for dependants, whether kindred or not, of the intestate, and other persons for whom the intestate might reasonably have been expected to make provision.

[(1A) The power to make orders under subsection (1) above shall be exercisable by statutory instrument subject to annulment in pursuance of a resolution of either House of Parliament; and any such order may be varied or revoked by a subsequent order made under the power.]

(2) A husband and wife shall for all purposes of distribution or division under the foregoing provisions of this section be treated as two persons.

[(3) Where the intestate and the intestate's husband or wife have died in circumstances rendering it uncertain which of them survived the other and the intestate's husband or wife is by virtue of section one hundred and eighty-four of the Law of Property Act 1925 deemed to have survived the intestate, this section shall, nevertheless, have effect as respects the intestate as if the husband or wife had not survived the intestate.

(4) The interest payable on the [fixed net sum] payable to a surviving husband or wife shall be primarily payable out of income.]

AMENDMENTS

Subsection (1)(i) was substituted by the Intestates' Estates Act 1952, s.1(2), except for the final paragraph which was added by the Family Provision Act 1966, s.1(2)(a). The words "fixed net sum" wherever they occur in square brackets were substituted by the latter provision. The words "such rate as the Lord Chancellor may specify by order" wherever they occur in square brackets were substituted by the Administration of Justice Act 1977, s.28(1).

In subsection (1)(iii) and (iv) the words in square brackets were added by the Intestates' Estates Act 1952, s.1(3). The words omitted were repealed by the same provision.

In subs. (1)(iv) and (v) the words omitted were repealed by the same provision. In subsection (1)(v) the words in square brackets were substituted by the same provision.

Subsections (1)(1A) was added by the Administration of Justice Act 1977, s.28(1).

Subsection (1), (3) and (4) were added by the Intestates' Estates Act 1952, s.1(4). The words "fixed net sum" in square brackets were substituted by the Family Provision Act 1966, s.1(2)(*b*).

GENERAL NOTE

The amendments to this section have effect as respects a person dying intestate after January 1, 1953. After 1969 issue includes illegitimate issue (Family Law Reform Act 1969).

Statutory trusts in favour of issue and other classes of relatives of intestate

47.—(1) Where under this Part of this Act the residuary estate of an intestate, or any part thereof, is directed to be held on the statutory trusts for the issue of the intestate, the same shall be held upon the following trusts, namely:—

(i) In trust, in equal shares, if more than one, for all or any of the children or child of the intestate, living at the death of the intestate, who attain the age of 21 years or marry under that age, and for all or any of the issue living at the death of the intestate who attain the age of 21 years or marry under that age of any child of the intestate who predeceases the intestate, such issue to take through all degrees, according to their stocks, in equal shares if more than one, the share which their parent would have taken if living at the death of the intestate, and so that no issue shall take whose parent is living at the death of the intestate and so capable of taking;

(ii) The statutory power of advancement, and the statutory provisions which relate to maintenance and accumulation of surplus income, shall apply, but when an infant marries such infant shall be entitled to give valid receipts for the income of the infant's share or interest;

(iii) Where the property held on the statutory trusts for issue is divisible into shares, then any money or property which, by way of advancement or on the marriage of a child of the intestate, has been paid to such child by the intestate or settled by the intestate for the benefit of such child (including any life or less interest and including property covenanted to be paid or settled) shall, subject to any contrary intention expressed or appearing from the circumstances of the case, be taken as being so paid or settled in or towards satisfaction of the share of such child or the share which such child would have taken if living at the death of the intestate, and shall be brought into account, at a valuation (the value to be reckoned as at the death of the intestate), in accordance with the requirements of the personal representatives;

(iv) The personal representatives may permit any infant contingently interested to have the use and enjoyment of any personal chattels in such manner and subject to such conditions (if any) as the personal representatives may consider reasonable, and without being liable to account for any consequential loss.

(2) If the trusts in favour of the issue of the intestate fail by reason of no child or other issue attaining an absolutely vested interest—

(a) the residuary estate of the intestate and the income thereof and all statutory accumulations, if any, of the income thereof, or so much thereof as may not have been paid or applied under any power affecting the same, shall go, devolve and be held under the provisions of this Part of this Act as if the intestate had died without leaving issue living at the death of the intestate;

(b) References in this Part of this Act to the intestate "leaving no issue" shall be construed as "leaving no issue who attain an absolutely vested interest";

(c) References in this Part of this Act to the intestate "leaving issue" or "leaving a child or other issue" shall be construed as "leaving issue who attain an absolutely vested interest."

(3) Where under this Part of this Act the residuary estate of an intestate or any part thereof is directed to be held on the statutory trusts for any class of relatives of the intestate, other than issue of the intestate, the same shall be held on trust corresponding to the statutory trusts for the issue of the intestate (other than the provision for bringing any money or property into account) as if such trusts (other than as aforesaid) were repeated with the substitution of references to the members or member of that class for references to the children or child of the intestate.

[(4) References in paragraph (i) of subsection (1) of the last foregoing section to the intestate leaving, or not leaving, a member of the class consisting of brothers or sisters of the whole blood of the intestate and issue of brothers or sisters of the whole blood of intestate shall be construed as references to the intestate leaving, or not leaving, a member of that class who attains an absolutely vested interest.

(5) [Repealed by the Family Provision Act 1966, s.9, Sched. 2]].

[Right of surviving spouse to have life interest redeemed

47A.—(1) Where a surviving husband or wife is entitled to a life interest in part of the residuary estate, and so elects, the personal representative shall purchase of redeem the life interest by paying the capital value thereof to the tenant for life, or the persons deriving title under the tenant for life, and the costs of the transaction; and thereupon the residuary estate of the intestate may be dealt with and distributed free from the life interest.

(2) [Repealed by the Administration of Justice Act 1977, s.28(2)].

(3) An election under this section shall only be exercisable if at the time of the election the whole of the said part of the residuary estate consists of

property in possession, but, for the purposes of this section, a life interest in property partly in possession and partly not in possession shall be treated as consisting of two separate life interests in those respective parts of the property.

[(3A) The capital value shall be reckoned in such manner as the Lord Chancellor may by order direct, and an order under this subsection may include transitional provisions.

(3B) The power to make orders under subsection (3A) above shall be exercisable by statutory instrument subject to annulment in pursuance of a resolution of either House of Parliament; and any such order may be varied or revoked by a subsequent order made under the power].

(4) [*This section was repealed by the Administration of Justice Act 1977, s.28(3)*].

(5) An election under this section shall be exercisable only within the period of 12 months from the date on which representation with respect to the estate of the intestate is first taken out:

Provided that if the surviving husband or wife satisfies the court that the limitation to the said period of 12 months will operate unfairly—

(a)   in consequence of the representation first taken out being probate of a will subsequently revoked on the ground that the will was invalid, or

(b)   in consequence of a question whether a person had an interest in the estate, or as to the nature of an interest in the estate, not having been determined at the time when representation was first taken out, or

(c)   in consequence of some other circumstances affecting the administration or distribution of the estate,

the court may extend the said period.

(6) An election under this section shall be exercisable, except where the tenant for life is the sole personal representative, by notifying the personal representative (or, where there are two or more personal representatives of whom one is the tenant for life, all of them except the tenant for life) in writing; and a notification in writing under this subsection shall not be revocable except with the consent of the personal representative.

(7) Where the tenant for life is the sole personal representative an election under this section shall not be effective unless written notice thereof is given to the Senior Registrar within the period within which it must be made; and provision may be made by probate rules for keeping a record of such notices and making that record available to the public.

In this subsection the expression "probate rules" means rules of court made under section 127 of the Supreme Court Act 1981.

(8) An election under this section by a tenant for life who is an infant shall be as valid and binding as it would be if the tenant for life were of age; but the personal representative shall, instead of paying the capital value of the life interest to the tenant for life, deal with it in the same manner as

with any other part of the residuary estate to which the tenant for life is absolutely entitled.

(9) In considering for the purposes of the foregoing provisions of this section the question when representation was first taken out, a grant limited to settled land or to trust property shall be left out of account and a grant limited to real estate or to personal estate shall be left out of account unless a grant limited to the remainder of the estate has previously been made or is made at the same time.]

AMENDMENTS

Subsection 47A was added by the Intestates' Estates Act 1952, s.2(*b*). Subsections (2) and (4) were repealed by the Administration of Justice Act 1977, s.28(2), and subsections (3A) and (3b) were added by the same provision.
Subsection (7) was amended by the Supreme Court Act 1981, Sched. 5.

GENERAL NOTE

The amendments to this section have effect as regards a person dying intestate after January 1, 1953. After 1969 issue includes illegitimate issue (Family Law Reform Act 1969).
For the new rules regarding the calculation of capital value, see the Intestate Succession (Interest and Capitalisation) Order 1977, S.I. 1977 No. 1491, p. 1270 post.

Powers of personal representative in respect of interests of surviving spouse

48.—(1) [*Repealed by the Intestates' Estates Act 1952 (15 & 16 Geo. 6 & 1 Eliz. 2, c. 64), s.2(a)*].

(2) The personal representatives may raise—

(*a*) [the fixed net sum] or any part thereof and the interest thereon payable to the surviving husband or wife of the intestate on the security of the whole or any part of the residuary estate of the intestate (other than the personal chattels), so far as that estate may be sufficient for the purpose or the said sum and interest may not have been satisfied by an appropriation under the statutory power available in that behalf; and

(*b*) in like manner the capital sum, if any, required for the purchase or redemption of the life interest of the surviving husband or wife of the intestate, or any part thereof not satisfied by the application for that purpose of any part of the residuary estate of the intestate;

and in either case the amount, if any, properly required for the payment of the costs of the transaction.

AMENDMENT

The words in square brackets were substituted by the Family Provision Act 1966, s.1(2)(*b*).

GENERAL NOTE

The amendments to this section have effect as regards a person dying intestate after January 1, 1953. After 1969 issue includes illegitimate issue (Family Law Reform Act 1969).

Application to cases of partial intestacy

49.—(1) Where any person dies leaving a will effectively disposing of part of his property, this Part of this Act shall have effect as respects the part of his property not so disposed of subject to the provisions contained in the will and subject to the following modifications:—

[(*aa*) where the deceased leaves a husband or wife who acquires any beneficial interests under the will of the deceased (other than personal chattels specifically bequeathed) the references in this Part of this Act to the [fixed net sum] payable to a surviving husband or wife, and to interest on that sum, shall be taken as references to the said sum diminished by the value at the date of death of the said beneficial interests, and to interest on that sum as so diminished, and, accordingly, where the said value exceeds the said sum, this Part of this Act shall have effect as if references to the said sum, and interest thereon, were omitted].

(*a*) The requirements [of section 47 of this Act] as to bringing property into account shall apply to any beneficial interests acquired by any issue of the deceased under the will of the deceased, but not to beneficial interests so acquired by any other persons:

(*b*) the personal representative shall, subject to his rights and powers for the purposes of administration, be a trustee for the persons entitled under this Part of this Act in respect of the part of the estate not expressly disposed of unless it appears by the will that the personal representative is intended to take such part beneficially.

[(2) References in the foregoing provisions of this section to beneficial interests acquired under a will shall be construed as including a reference to a beneficial interest acquired by virtue of the exercise by the will of a general power of appointment (including the statutory power to dispose of entailed interests), but not of a special power of appointment.

(3) For the purposes of paragraph (*aa*) in the foregoing provisions of this section the personal representative shall employ a duly qualified valuer in any case where such employment may be necessary.

(4) The references in subsection (3) of section 47A of this Act to property are references to property comprised in the residuary estate and, accordingly, where a will of the deceased creates a life interest in property in possession, and the remaining interest in that property forms part of the residuary estate, the said references are references to that remaining interest (which, until the life interest determines, is property not in possession)].

Subsection 1(*aa*) was added by the Intestates' Estates Act 1952, s.3(2). In it, the words in square brackets were substituted by the Family Provision Act 1966, s.1(2)(*b*).

In subsection (1) (*a*) the words in square brackets were added by the same provision. Subsections (2), (3) and (4) were added by the same Act, s.3(3).

GENERAL NOTE

The amendments to this section have effect as regards a person dying intestate after January 1, 1953. After 1969 issue includes illegitimate issue (Family Law Reform Act 1969).

Construction of documents

50.—(1) References to any Statutes of Distribution in an instrument inter vivos made or in a will coming into operation after the commencement of this Act, shall be construed as references to this Part of this Act; and references in such an instrument or will to statutory next of kin shall be construed, unless the context otherwise requires, as referring to the persons who would take beneficially on an intestacy under the foregoing provisions of this Part of this Act.

(2) Trusts declared in an instrument inter vivos made, or in a will coming into operation, before the commencement of this Act by reference to the Statutes of Distribution, shall, unless the contrary thereby appears, be construed as referring to the enactments (other than the Intestates' Estates Act 1890) relating to te distribution of effects of intestates which were in force immediately before the commencement of this Act.

"(3) In subsection (1) of this section the reference to this Part of this Act, or the foregoing provisions of this Part of this Act, shall in relation to an instrument inter vivos made, or a will or codicil coming into operation, after the coming into force of section 18 of the Family Law Reform Act 1987 (but not in relation to instruments inter vivos made or wills or codicils coming into operation earlier) be construed as including references to that section."

AMENDMENT

Subsection (3) was added by the Family Law Reform Act 1987, Sched. 2.

GENERAL NOTE

References to this Part of this Act shall in relation to instruments made or instruments coming into operation after the commencement of the Intestates' Estates Act 1952 include references to Part I of that Act: *ibid.*, s.6(2).

Savings

51.—(1) Nothing in this Part of this Act affects the right of any person to take beneficially, by purchase as heir either general or special.

(2) The foregoing provisions of this Part of this Act do not apply to any beneficial interest in real estate (not including chattels real) to which a

lunatic or defective living and of full age at the commencement of this Act, and unable, by reason of his incapacity, to make a will, who thereafter dies intestate in respect of such interest without having recovered his testamentary capacity, was entitled at his death, and any such beneficial interest (not being an interest ceasing on his death) shall, without prejudice to any will of the deceased, devolve in accordance with the general law in force before the commencement of this Act applicable to freehold land, and that law shall, notwithstanding any repeal, apply to the case.

For the purposes of this subsection, a lunatic or defective who dies intestate as respects any beneficial interest in real estate shall not be deemed to have recovered his testamentary capacity unless his [. . .] receiver has been discharged.

(3) Where an infant dies after the commencement of this Act without having been married, and independently of this subsection he would, at his death, have been equitably entitled under a settlement (including a will) to a vested estate in fee simple or absolute interest in freehold land, or in any property settled to devolve therewith or as freehold land, such infant shall be deemed to have had an entailed interest, and the settlement shall be construed accordingly.

(4) This Part of this Act does not affect the devolution of an entailed interest as an equitable interest.

AMENDMENT

The words omitted were repealed by the Mental Health Act 1959, Sched. 8, Pt. I.

Interpretation of Part IV

52. In this Part of this Act "real and personal estate" means every beneficial interest (including rights of entry and reverter) of the intestate in real and personal estate which (otherwise than in right of a power of appointment or of the testamentary power conferred by statute to dispose of entailed interests) he could, if of full age and capacity, have disposed of by his will and references (however expressed) to any relationship between two persons shall be construed in accordance with section 1 of the Family Law Reform Act 1987.

AMENDMENT

Section 52 is printed as amended by the Family Law Reform Act 1987, Sched. 2.

PART V

SUPPLEMENTAL

General Savings

53.—(1) Nothing in this Act shall derogate from the powers of the High Court which exist independently of this Act or alter the distribution of business between the several divisions of the High Court, or operate to transfer any jurisdiction from the High Court to any other court.

(2) Nothing in this Act shall affect any unrepealed enactment in a public general Act dispensing with probate or administration as respects personal estate not including chattels real.

(3) [*Repealed by the Finance Act* 1975, *s.59 and Sched.* 13.]

Application of Act

54. Save as otherwise expressly provided, this Act does not apply in any case where the death occurred before the commencement of this Act.

Definitions

55.—(1) In this Act, unless the context otherwise requires, the following expressions have the meanings hereby assigned to them respectively, that is to say:—

   (i) "Administration" means, with reference to the real and personal estate of a deceased person, letters of administration, whether general or limited, or with the will annexed or otherwise:

  (ii) "Administrator" means a person to whom administration is granted:

 (iii) "Conveyance" includes a mortgage, charge by way of legal mortgage, lease, assent, vesting declaration, vesting instrument, disclaimer, release and every other assurance of property or of an interest therein by any instrument, except a will, and "convey" has a corresponding meaning, and "disposition" includes a "conveyance" also a devise bequest and an appointment of property contained in a will, and "dispose of" has a corresponding meaning:

"(iiiA) 'the County Court limit,' in relation to any enactment contained in this Act, means the amount for the time being specified by an Order in Council under section 145 of the County Courts Act 1984 as the county court limit for the purposes of that enactment (or, where no such Order in Council has been made, the corresponding limit specified by Order in Council under section 192 of the County Courts Act 1959);".

 (iv) "the Court" means the High Court, and also the county court, where that court has jurisdiction [. . .]

  (v) "Income" includes rents and profits:

 (vi) "Intestate," includes a person who leaves a will but dies intestate as to some beneficial interest in his real or personal estate:

(vii) "Legal estates" mean the estates charges and interests in or over land (subsisting or created at law) which are by statute authorised to subsist or to be created at law; and "equitable interests" mean all other interests and charges in or over land or in the proceeds of sale thereof:

(viii) "Lunatic" includes a lunatic whether so found or not, and in relation to a lunatic not so found [. . .] and "defective" includes every person affected by the provisions of section one hundred and sixteen of the Lunacy Act 1890 as extended by section sixty-four of the Mental Deficiency Act 1913 and for whose benefit a receiver has been appointed:

(ix) "Pecuniary legacy" includes an annuity, a general legacy, a demonstrative legacy so far as it is not discharged out of the designated property, and any other general direction by a testator for the payment of money, including all death duties free from which any devise, bequest, or payment is made to take effect:

(x) "Personal chattels" mean carriages, horses, stable furniture and effects (not used for business purposes), motor cars and accessories (not used for business purposes), garden effects, domestic animals, plate, plated articles, linen, china, glass, books, pictures. prints, furniture, jewellery, articles of household or personal use or ornament, musical and scientific instruments and apparatus, wines, liquors and consumable stores, but do not include any chattels used at the death of the intestate for business purposes nor money or securities for money:

(xi) "Personal representative" means the executor, original or by representation, or administrator for the time being of a deceased person, and as regards any liability for the payment of death duties includes any person who takes possession of or intermeddles with the property of a deceased person without the authority of the personal representatives or the court, and "executor" includes a person deemed to be appointed executor as respects settled land:

(xii) "Possession" includes the receipt of rents and profits or the right to receive the same, if any:

(xiii) "Prescribed" means prescribed by rules of court [. . .]

(xiv) "Probate" means the probate of a will:

(xv) "Probate judge" means the President of the [Family] Division of the High Court:

(xvi) [*Repealed by the Supreme Court Act* 1981, *s.*152(4); *Sched.* 7].

(xvii) "Property" includes a thing in action and any interest in real or personal property:

(xviii) "Purchaser" means a lessee, mortgagee or other person who in good faith acquires an interest in property for valuable consideration, also an intending purchaser and "valuable consideration" includes marriage, but does not include a nominal consideration in money:

(xix) "Real estate" save as provided in Part IV of this Act means real estate, including chattels real, which by virtue of Part I of this Act devolves on the personal representative of a deceased person:

(xx) "Representation" means the probate of a will and administration, and the expression "taking out representation" refers to the obtaining of the probate of a will or of the grant of administration:

(xxi) "Rent" includes a rent service or a rent-charge, or other rent, toll, duty, or annual or periodical payment in money or money's worth, issuing out of or charged upon land, but does not include mortgage interest; and "rentcharge" includes a fee farm rent:

(xxii) [*Repealed by the Supreme Court Act* 1981, *s.*152(4); *Sched.* 7].

(xxiii) "Securities" include stocks, funds, or shares:

(xxiv) "Tenant for life," "statutory owner," "land," "settled land," "settlement," "trustees of the settlement," "term of years absolute," "death duties," and "legal mortgage," have the same meanings as in the Settled Land Act 1925 and "entailed interest" and "charge by way of legal mortgage" have the same meanings as in the Law of Property Act 1925:

(xxv) "Treasury solicitor" means the solicitor for the affairs of His Majesty's Treasury, and includes the solicitor for the affairs of the Duchy of Lancaster:

(xxvi) "Trust corporation" means the public trustee or a corporation either appointed by the court in any particular case to be a trustee or entitled by rules made under subsection (3) of section four of the Public Trustee Act 1906 to act as custodian trustee:

(xxvii) "Trust for sale," in relation to land, means an immediate binding trust for sale, whether or not exercisable at the request or with the consent of any person, and with or without a power at discretion to postpone the sale; and "power to postpone a sale" means power to postpone in the exercise of a discretion:

(xxviii) "Will" includes codicil:

(2) References to a child or issue living at the death of any person include a child or issue en ventre sa mere at the death.

(3) References to the estate of a deceased person include property over which the deceased exercises a general power of appointment (including the statutory power to dispose of entailed interests) by his will.

AMENDMENTS

In subsection (1)(iv) the words omitted were repealed by the Courts Act 1971, s.56, Sched. 2.

In subsection (1)(viii) the words omitted were repealed by the Mental Health Act 1959, Sched. 8, Pt. I.

In subsection (1)(xiii) the words omitted were repealed by the Supreme Court Act 1981, Sched. 7.

In subsection (1)(xv) the word in square brackets was substituted by the Administration of Justice Act 1970, s.1.

Subsection (1)(iiiA) was added by the County Courts Act 1984, Sched. 2.

In subsection (1)(xxv), for the extension of "treasury solicitor", see the Law of Property (Amendment) Act 1926, s.3(2).
In subsection (1)(xxvi), for the extension of "trust corporation." see *ibid.*, s.3 (1), the Japanese Treaty of Peace Order 1952 (No. 862), Art. 5(2); and the Clergy Pensions Measure 1961, s.31.

Repeal

56. The Acts mentioned in the Second Schedule to this Act are hereby repealed to the extent specified in the third column of that Schedule, but as respects the Acts mentioned in Part I of that Schedule only so far as they apply to deaths occurring after the commencement of this Act.

Application to Crown

57.—(1) The provisions of this Act bind the Crown and the Duchy of Lancaster, and the Duke of Cornwall for the time being, as respects the estates of persons dying after the commencement of this Act, but not so as to affect the time within which proceedings for the recovery of real or personal estate vesting in or devolving on His Majesty in right of His Crown, or His Duchy of Lancaster, or on the Duke of Cornwall, may be instituted.

(2) Nothing in this Act in any manner affects or alters the descent or devolution of any property for the time being vested in His Majesty either in right of the Crown or of the Duchy of Lancaster or of any property for the time being belonging to the Duchy of Cornwall.

Short title, commencement and extent

58.—(1) This Act may be cited as the Administration of Estates Act 1925.

(2) [*Repealed*].

(3) This Act extends to England and Wales only.

Subsection (2) was repealed by the Statute Law Reform Act 1950.

SCHEDULES

Section 34

FIRST SCHEDULE
PART I
RULES AS TO PAYMENT OF DEBTS WHERE THE ESTATE IS INSOLVENT

1. The funeral, testamentary, and administration expenses have priority.

2. Subject as aforesaid, the same rules shall prevail and be observed as to the respective rights of secured and unsecured creditors and as to debts and

liabilities provable and as to the valuation of annuities and future and contingent liabilities respectively, and as to the priorities of debts and liabilities as may be in force for the time being under the law of bankruptcy with respect to the assets of persons adjudged bankrupt.

PART II
ORDER OF APPLICATION OF ASSETS WHERE THE ESTATE IS SOLVENT

1. Property of the deceased undisposed of by will, subject to the retention thereout of a fund sufficient to meet any pecuniary legacies.

2. Property of the deceased not specifically devised or bequeathed but included (either by a specific or general description) in a residuary gift, subject to the retention out of such property of a fund sufficient to meet any pecuniary legacies, so far as not provided for as aforesaid.

3. Property of the deceased specifically appropriated or devised or bequeathed (either by a specific or general description) for the payment of debts.

4. Property of the deceased charged with, or devised or bequeathed (either by a specific or general description) subject to a charge for the payment of debts.

5. The fund, if any, retained to meet pecuniary legacies.

6. Property specifically devised or bequeathed, rateably according to value.

7. Property appointed by will under a geeral power, including the statutory power to dispose of entailed interests, rateably according to value.

8. The following provisions shall also apply—

(a) The order of applicaton may be varied by the will of the deceased.
(b) This part of this Schedule does not affect the liability of land to answer the death duty imposed thereon in exoneration of other assets.

Section 56   SECOND SCHEDULE

[*Repealed by S.L.R. Act* 1950 (14 *Geo.* 6, *c.* 6)].

FAMILY LAW REFORM ACT 1969

(1969, c. 46)

*   *   *   *

14.—[*Repealed by the Family Law Reform Act 1987, Sched. 4*].

15.—[*Repealed by the Family Law Reform Act 1987, Sched. 4*].

16.—[*Repealed by the Administration of Justice Act 1982, s.75(1), Sched. 9, Part I.*]

17.—[*Repealed by the Family Law Reform Act 1987, s.20, Sched. 4*].

18.—[*Repealed by the Inheritance (Provision for Family and Dependants) Act 1975, s.26(2), Sched.*]

19. Policies of assurance and property in industrial and provident societies

(1) In section 11 of the Married Women's Property Act 1882 (policies of assurance effected for the benefit of children) the expression "children" shall include illegitimate children.

(2) [. . .]

(3) Subsection (1) of this section does not affect the operation of the said Acts of 1882 and 1880 in relation to a policy effected before the coming into force of that subsection; [. . .]

ADMINISTRATION OF ESTATES ACT 1971

(1971, c.25)

ARRANGEMENT OF SECTIONS

An Act to provide for the recognition, without resealing, of certain grants of administration and confirmations throughout the United Kingdom; to allow for the inclusion of real estate in any part of the United Kingdom in the inventory of the estate of a person dying domiciled in Scotland; to amend the law with respect to the grant of administration by the High Court and resealing by that Court of administration granted outside the United Kingdom and to exempt from stamp duty guarantees given under the law so amended; to make provision with respect to the duties and rights of personal representatives; and for connected purposes.

[May 12, 1971]

Reciprocal Recognition of grants

Recognition in England and Wales of Scottish confirmations and Northern Irish grants of representation

1.—(1) Where a person dies domiciled in Scotland—

(a) a confirmation granted in respect of all or part of his estate and noting his Scottish domicile, and

(b) a certificate of confirmation noting his Scottish domicile and relating to one or more items of his estate,

shall, without being resealed, be treated for the purposes of the law of England and Wales as a grant of representation (in accordance with subsection (2) below) to the executors named in the confirmation or certificate in respect of the property of the deceased of which according to the terms of the confirmation they are executors or, as the case may be, in respect of the item or items of property specified in the certificate of confirmation.

(2) Where by virtue of subsection (1) above a confirmation or certificate of confirmation is treated for the purposes of the law of England and Wales as a grant of representation to the executors named therein then, subject to subsections (3) and (5) below, the grant shall be treated—

> (*a*) as a grant of probate where it appears from the confirmation or certificate that the executors so named are executors nominate; and
>
> (*b*) in any other case, as a grant of letters of administration.

(3) Section 7 of the Administration of Estates Act 1925 (executor of executor represents original testator) shall not, by virtue of subsection (2)(*a*) above, apply on the death of an executor named in a confirmation or certificate of confirmation.

(4) Subject to subsection (5) below, where a person dies domiciled in Northern Ireland a grant of probate of his will or letters of administration in respect of his estate (or any part of it) made by the High Court in Northern Ireland and noting his domicile there shall, without being resealed, be treated for the purposes of the law of England and Wales as if it had been originally made by the High Court in England and Wales.

(5) Notwithstanding anything in the preceding provisions of this section, a person who is a personal representative according to the law of England and Wales by virtue only of those provisions may not be required, under section 25 of the Administration of Estates Act 1925, to deliver up his grant to the High Court.

(6) This section applies in relation to confirmations, probates and letters of administration granted before as well as after the commencement of this Act, and in relation to a confirmation, probate or letters of administration granted before the commencement of this Act, this section shall have effect as if it had come into force immediately before the grant was made.

(7) In this section "confirmation" includes an additional confirmation, and the term "executors," where used in relation to a confirmation or certificate of confirmation, shall be construed according to the law of Scotland.

Recognition in Northern Ireland of English grants of representation and Scottish confirmations

2.—(1) Where a person dies domiciled in England and Wales a grant of probate of his will or letters of administration in respect of his estate (or any part of it) made by the High Court in England and Wales and noting his domicile there shall, without being resealed, be treated for the purposes of the law of Northern Ireland as if it had been originally made by the High Court in Northern Ireland.

(2) Where a person dies domiciled in Scotland—

(*a*) a confirmation granted in respect of all or part of his estate and noting his Scottish domicile, and

(*b*) a certificate of confirmation noting his Scottish domicile and relating to one or more items of his estate,

shall, without being resealed, be treated for the purposes of the law of Northern Ireland as a grant of representation (in accordance with subsection (3) below) to the executors named in the confirmation or certificate in respect of the property of the deceased of which according to the terms of the confirmation they are executors or, as the case may be, in respect of the item or items of property specified in the certificate of confirmation.

(3) Where by virtue of subsection (2) above a confirmation or certificate of confirmation is treated for the purposes of the law of Northern Ireland as a grant of representation to the executors named therein then, subject to subsection (4) below, the grant shall be treated—

(*a*) as a grant of probate where it appears from the confirmation or certificate that the executors so named are executors nominate; and

(*b*) in any other case, as a grant of letters of administration.

(4) Notwithstanding anything in any enactment or rule of law, subsection (3)(*a*) above shall not operate to entitle an executor of a sole or last surviving executor of a testator, whose will has been proved in Scotland only, to act as the executor of that testator.

(5) This section applies in relation to probates, letters of administration and confirmations granted before as well as after the commencement of this Act, and—

(*a*) in relation to a probate, letters of administration or confirmation granted, and resealed in Northern Ireland, before the commencement of this Act, this section shall have effect as if it had come into force immediately before the grant was so resealed; and

(*b*) a probate, letters of administration or confirmation granted but not resealed in Northern Ireland before the commencement of this Act shall, for the purposes of this section, be treated as having been granted at the commencement of this Act.

(6) In this section "confirmation" includes an additional confirmation, and the term "executors," where used in relation to a confirmation or certificate of confirmation shall be construed according to the law of Scotland.

Recognition in Scotland of English and Northern Irish grants of representation

3.—(1) Where a person dies domiciled in England and Wales or in Northern Ireland a grant of probate or letters of administration.

(*a*) from the High Court in England and Wales and noting his domicile there, or

(b) from the High Court in Northern ireland and noting his domicile there

shall, without being resealed, be of the like force and effect and have the same operation in relation to property in Scotland as a confirmation given under the seal of office of the Commissariot of Edinburgh to the executor or administrator named in the probate or letters of administration.

(2) This section applies in relation to probates and letters of administration granted before as well as after the commencement of this Act, and in relation to a probate or letters of administration granted before the commencement of this Act, this section shall have effect as if it had come into force immediately before the grant was made.

Evidence of grants

4.—(1) In England and Wales and in Northern Ireland—

(a) a document purporting to be a confirmation, additional confirmation or certificate of confirmation given under the seal of office of any commissariot in Scotland shall, except where the contrary is proved, be taken to be such a confirmation, additional confirmation or certificate of confirmation without further proof; and

(b) a document purporting to be a duplicate of such a confirmation or additional confirmation and to be given under such a seal shall be receivable in evidence in like manner and for the like purposes as the confirmation or additional confirmation of which it purports to be a duplicate.

(2) In England and Wales and in Scotland—

(a) a document purporting to be a grant of probate or of letters of administration issued under the seal of the High Court in Northern Ireland or of the principal or district probate registry there shall, except where the contrary is proved, be taken to be such a grant without further proof; and

(b) a document purporting to be a copy of such a grant and to be sealed with such a seal shall be receivable in evidence in like manner and for the like purposes as the grant of which it purports to be a copy.

(3) In Scotland and in Northern Ireland—

(a) a document purporting to be a grant of probate or of letters of administration issued under the seal of the High Court in England and Wales or of the principal or a district probate registry there shall, except where the contrary is proved, be taken to be such a grant without further proof; and

(b) a document purporting to be a copy of such a grant and to be sealed with such a seal shall be receivable in evidence in like manner and for the like purposes as the grant of which it purports to be a copy.

Property outside Scotland of which deceased was trustee

5.—(1) A confirmation or additional confirmation granted in respect of property situated in Scotland of a person who died domiciled there, which notes that domicile, may contain or have appended thereto and signed by the sheriff clerk a note or statement of property in England and Wales or in Northern Ireland held by the deceased in trust, being a note or statement which has been set forth in any inventory recorded in the books of the court of which the sheriff clerk is clerk.

(2) Section 1 or, as the case may be, section 2 of this Act shall apply in relation to property specified in such a note or statement as is mentioned in subsection (1) above as it applies in relation to property specified in the confirmation or additional confirmation concerned.

Inventory of Scottish estate may include real estate in any part of the United Kingdom

6.—(1) It shall be competent to include in the inventory of the estate of any person who dies domiciled in Scotland any real estate of the deceased situated in England and Wales or Northern Ireland, and accordingly in section 9 of the Confirmation of Executors (Scotland) Act 1858 the word "personal" wherever it occurs is hereby repealed.

(2) Section 14(2) of the Succession (Scotland) Act 1964 (act of sederunt to provide for description of heritable property) shall apply in relation to such real estate as aforesaid as it applies in relation to heritable property in Scotland.

Consequential amendments

7. Schedule 1 to this Act, which contains amendments consequential on the preceding provisions of this Act, shall have effect.

8. [*Repealed by the Supreme Court Act* 1981, *Sched.* 7].

Rights and duties of personal representatives in England and Wales

Duties of personal representatives

9. For section 25 of the Administration of Estates Act 1925 (duty of personal representatives as to inventory and account) there shall be substituted the following section:—
[See *ante*, p. 1124.]

Retainer, preference and the payment of debts by personal representatives

10.—(1) The right of retainer of a personal representative and his right to prefer creditors are hereby abolished.

(2) Nevertheless a personal representative—

    (*a*) other than one mentioned in paragraph (*b*) below, who, in good

faith and at a time when he has no reason to believe that the
deceased's estate is insolvent, pays the debt of any person (including himself) who is a creditor of the estate; or

(b) to whom letters of administration had been granted solely by
reason of his being a creditor and who, in good faith and at such a
time pays the debt of another person who is a creditor of the
estate;

shall not, if it subsequently appears that the estate is insolvent, be liable to
account to a creditor of the same degree as the paid creditor for the sum so
paid.

Miscellaneous and supplemental

Sealing of Commonwealth and Colonial grants

11.—(1) The following provisions of section 2 of the Colonial Probates
Act 1892, that is to say—

(a) subsection (2)(b) (which makes it a condition precedent to sealing
in the United Kingdom letters of administration granted in certain overseas countries and territories that a sufficient security has
been given to cover property in the United Kingdom); and

(b) subsection (3) (power of the court in the United Kingdom to
require that adequate security is given for the payment of debts
due to creditors residing in the United Kingdom);

shall not apply to the sealing of letters of administration by the High Court
in England and Wales under that section, and the following provisions of
this section shall apply instead.

(2) A person to whom letters of administration have been granted in a
country or territory to which the said Act of 1892 applies shall on their
being sealed by the High Court in England and Wales under the said section 2 have the like duties with respect to the estate of the deceased which
is situated in England and Wales and the debts of the deceased which fall to
be paid there as are imposed by section 25(a) and (b) of the Administration
of Estates Act 1925 on a person to whom a grant of administration has
been made by that court.

(3) As a condition of sealing letters of administration granted in any such
country or territory, the High Court in England and Wales may, in cases to
which section 120 of the Supreme Court Act 1981 (power to require administrators to produce sureties) applies and subject to the following provisions of this section and subject to and in accordance with probate rules
[. . .] require one or more sureties, in such amount as the court thinks fit,
to guarantee that they will make good, within any limit imposed by the
court on the total liability of the surety or sureties, any loss which any person interested in the administration of the estate of the deceased in England and Wales may suffer in consequence of a breach by the administrator
of his duties in administering it there.

(4) A guarantee given in pursuance of any such requirement shall enure for the benefit of every person interested in the administration of the estate in England and Wales as if contained in a contract under seal made by the surety or sureties with every such person and, where there are two or more sureties, as if they had bound themselves jointly or severally.

(5) No action shall be brought on any such guarantee without the leave of the High Court.

(6) Stamp duty shall not be chargeable on any such guarantee.

(7) Subsections (2) to (6) above apply to the sealing by the High Court in England and Wales of letters of administration granted by a British court in a foreign country as they apply to the sealing of letters of administration granted in a country or territory to which the Colonial Probates Act 1892 applies.

(8) In this section—

> "letters of administration" and "British court in a foreign country" have the same meaning as in the Colonial Probates Act 1892; and "probate rules" means rules of the court made under section 127 of the Supreme Court Act 1981.

AMENDMENT

In subsection (3) the words omitted were repealed by the Supreme Court Act 1981, Sched. 7.

Subsection (3) is printed as amended by the Supreme Court Act 1981, Sched. 5.
Subsection (8) is printed as amended by the Supreme Court Act 1981, Sched. 5.

Repeals and savings

12.—(1) The enactments specified in Part I of Schedule 2 to this Act (which include an enactment of the Parliament of Northern Ireland) are hereby repealed to the extent specified in the third column of that Schedule and the Government of Ireland (Re-sealing of Probates etc.) Order 1923 is hereby revoked.

(2) So far as they relate to England and Wales only, the enactments specified in Part II of Schedule 2 to this Act are hereby repealed to the extent specified in the third column of that Schedule.

(3) Nothing in this Act shall affect the liability of any person for, or alter the incidence of, estate duty, including estate duty payable under the law for the time being in force in Northern Ireland.

(4) The following provisions of this Act, that is to say—

> (a) [. . .]
> (b) section 11 (other than subsection (2)); and
> (c) the repeals specified in Part II of Schedule 2 to this Act, other than the repeal of section 34(2) of the Administration of Estates Act 1925;

shall not apply in relation to grants of administration made by the High Court before the commencement of this Act or to sealing by that court before the commencement of this Act of administration granted in any country or territory outside the United Kingdom.

(5) Any administration bond given before the commencement of this Act [. . .] under the Colonial Probates Act 1892 may be enforced and assigned as if this Act had not been passed.

(6) Section 10 of this Act and the appeal by this section of section 34(2) of the Administration of Estates Act 1925 shall not apply in relation to the estates of persons dying before the commencement of this Act.

AMENDMENTS

Subsection (4) (*a*) and the words omitted from subs. (5) were repealed by the Supreme Court Act 1981, Sched. 7.

Extension of powers of Parliament of Northern Ireland

13.—[*Repealed by the Northern Ireland Constitution Act 1973, Sched. 6*].

Short title commencement and extent

14.—(1) This Act may be cited as the Administration of Estates Act 1971.

(2) Section 13 of this Act and this section shall come into force on the passing of this Act and the remaining provisions of this Act shall come into force on January 1, 1972; and, notwithstanding anything in section 36 of the Interpretation Act 1889, any reference in this Act, or in any Act passed after the passing of this Act, to the commencement of this Act shall be construed as a reference to January 1, 1972.

(3) Sections 1 and 9 to 11 of this Act and subsections (2) and (4) to (6) of section 12 of this Act extend to England and Wales only.

(4) Sections 3 and 6 of this Act extend to Scotland only.

(5) Section 2 of this Act extends to Northern Ireland only.

AMENDMENT

Subsection (3) was amended by the Supreme Court Act 1981, Sched. 5.

SCHEDULES

SCHEDULE 1

Amendments consequential on ss. 1–6

Section 12 ## SCHEDULE 2

Enactments repealed

INHERITANCE (PROVISION FOR FAMILY AND DEPENDANTS) ACT 1975

(1975, c. 63)

ARRANGEMENT OF SECTIONS

Powers of court to order financial provision from deceased's estate

Property available for financial provision

Powers of court in relation to transactions intended to defeat applications for financial provision

Special provisions relating to cases of divorce, separation etc.

Miscellaneous and supplementary provisions

An Act to make fresh provision for empowering the court to make orders for the making out of the estate of a deceased person of provision for the spouse, former spouse, child, child of the family or dependant of that person; and for matters connected therewith.

[November 12, 1975]

Application for financial provision from deceased's estate

1.—(1) Where after the commencement of this Act a person dies domiciled in England and Wales and is survived by any of the following persons:—

(a) the wife or husband of the deceased;
(b) a former wife or former husband of the deceased who has not remarried;
(c) a child of the deceased;
(d) any person (not being a child of the deceased) who, in the case of any marriage to which the deceased was at any time a party, was treated by the deceased as a child of the family in relation to that marriage;
(e) any person (not being a person included in the foregoing paragraphs of this subsection) who immediately before the death of the deceased was being maintained, either wholly or partly, by the deceased;

that person may apply to the court for an order under section 2 of this Act on the ground that the disposition of the deceased's estate effected by his will or the law relating to intestacy, or the combination of his will and that law, is not such as to make reasonable financial provision for the applicant.

(2) In this Act "reasonable financial provision"—

(a) in the case of an application made by virtue of subsection (1)(a) above by the husband or wife of the deceased (except where the marriage with the deceased was the subject of a decree of judicial separation and at the date of death the decree was in force and the separation was continuing), means such financial provision as it would be reasonable in all the circumstances of the case for a husband or wife to receive, whether or not that provision is required for his or her maintenance;
(b) in the case of any other application made by virtue of subsection (1) above, means such financial provision as it would be reasonable in all the circumstances of the case for the applicant to receive for his maintenance.

(3) For the purposes of subsection (1)(e) above, a person shall be treated as being maintained by the deceased, either wholly or partly, as the case may be, if the deceased, otherwise than for full valuable consideration, was

making a substantial contribution in money or money's worth towards the reasonable needs of that person.

GENERAL NOTE

This section states the persons entitled to apply for provision, and prescribes the different standards of provision for surviving spouses and other applicants.

Powers of court to make orders

2.—(1) Subject to the provisions of this Act, where an application is made for an order under this section, the court may, if it is satisfied that the disposition of the deceased's estate effected by his will or the law relating to intestacy, or the combination of his will and that law, is not such as to make reasonable financial provision for the applicant, make any one or more of the following orders:—

> (a) an order for the making to the applicant out of the net estate of the deceased of such periodical payments and for such term as may be specified in the order;
>
> (b) an order for the payment to the applicant out of that estate of a lump sum of such amount as may be so specified;
>
> (c) an order for the transfer to the applicant of such property comprised in that estate as may be so specified;
>
> (d) an order for the settlement for the benefit of the applicant of such property comprised in that estate as may be so specified;
>
> (e) an order for the acquisition out of property comprised in that estate of such property as may be so specified and for the transfer of the property so acquired to the applicant or for the settlement thereof for his benefit;
>
> (f) an order varying any ante-nuptial or post-nuptial settlement (including such a settlement made by will) made on the parties to a marriage to which the deceased was one of the parties, the variation being for the benefit of the surviving party to that marriage, or any child of that marriage, or any person who was treated by the deceased as a child of the family in relation to that marriage.

(2) An order under subsection (1)(a) above providing for the making out of the net estate of the deceased of periodical payments may provide for—

> (a) payments of such amount as may be specified in the order,
>
> (b) payments equal to the whole of the income of the net estate or of such portion thereof as may be so specified,
>
> (c) payments equal to the whole of the income of such part of the net estate as the court may direct to be set aside or appropriated for the making out the income thereof of payments under this section,

or may provide for the amount of the payments or any of them to be determined in any other way the court thinks fit.

(3) Where an order under subsection (1)(*a*) above provides for the making of payments of an amount specified in the order, the order may direct that such part of the net estate as may be so specified shall be set aside or appropriated for the making out of the income thereof of those payments; but no larger part of the net estate shall be so set aside or appropriated than is sufficient, at the date of the order, to produce by the income thereof the amount required for the making of those payments.

(4) An order under this section may contain such consequential and supplemental provisions as the court thinks necessary or expedient for the purpose of giving effect to the order or for the purpose of securing that the order operates fairly as between one beneficiary of the estate of the deceased and another and may, in particular, but without prejudice to the generality of this subsection—

    (*a*) order any person who holds any property which forms part of the net estate of the deceased to make such payment or transfer such property as may be specified in the order;

    (*b*) vary the disposition of the deceased's estate effected by the will or the law relating to intestacy, or by both the will and the law relating to intestacy, in such manner as the court thinks fair and reasonable having regard to the provisions of the order and all the circumstances of the case;

    (*c*) confer on the trustees of any property which is the subject of an order under this section such powers as appear to the court to be necessary or expedient.

GENERAL NOTE

    This section specifies the orders which the court can make. Note especially the wide scope of subsection (4). Compare Matrimonial Causes Act 1973, ss.23 and 24.

Matters to which court is to have regard in exercising powers under s.2

3.—(1) Where an application is made for an order under section 2 of this Act, the court shall, in determining whether the disposition of the deceased's estate effected by his will or the law relating to intestacy, or the combination of his will and that law, is such as to make reasonable financial provision for the applicant and, if the court considers that reasonable financial provision has not been made, in determining whether and in what manner it shall exercise its powers under that section, have regard to the following matters, that is to say—

    (*a*) the financial resources and financial needs which the applicant has or is likely to have in the foreseeable future;

    (*b*) the financial resources and financial needs which any other applicant for an order under section 2 of this Act has or is likely to have in the foreseeable future;

    (*c*) the financial resources and financial needs which any beneficiary

of the estate of the deceased has or is likely to have in the foreseeable future;

(*d*) any obligations and responsibilities which the deceased had
towards any applicant for an order under the said section 2 or
towards any beneficiary of the estate of the deceased;

(*e*) the size and nature of the net estate of the deceased;

(*f*) any physical or mental disability of any applicant for an order
under the said section 2 or any beneficiary of the estate of the
deceased;

(*g*) any other matter, including the conduct of the applicant or any
other person, which in the circumstances of the case the court
may consider relevant.

(2) Without prejudice to the generality of paragraph (*g*) of subsection (1)
above, where an application for an order under section 2 of this Act is
made by virtue of section 1(1)(*a*) or 1(*b*) of this Act, the court shall, in
addition to the matters specifically mentioned in paragraphs (*a*) to (*f*) of
that subsection, have regard to—

(*a*) the age of the applicant and the duration of the marriage;

(*b*) the contribution made by the applicant to the welfare of the
family of the deceased, including any contribution made by looking after the home or caring for the family;

and, in the case of an application by the wife or husband of the deceased,
the court shall also, unless at the date of death a decree of judicial separation was in force and the separation was continuing, have regard to the
provision which the applicant might reasonably have expected to receive if
on the day on which the deceased died the marriage, instead of being terminated by death, had been terminated by a decree of divorce.

(3) Without prejudice to the generality of paragraph (*g*) of subsection (1)
above, where an application for an order under section 2 of this Act is
made by virtue of section (1)(*c*) or 1(1)(*d*) of this Act, the court shall, in
addition to the matters specifically mentioned in paragraphs (*a*) to (*f*) of
that subsection, have regard to the manner in which the applicant was
being or in which he might expect to be educated or trained, and where the
application is made by virtue of section 1(1)(*d*) the court shall also have
regard—

(*a*) to whether the deceased has assumed any responsibility for the
applicant's maintenance and, if so, to the extent to which and the
basis upon which the deceased assumed that responsibility and to
the length of time for which the deceased discharged that responsibility;

(*b*) to whether in assuming and discharging that responsibility the
deceased did so knowing that the applicant was not his own child;

(*c*) to the liability of any person to maintain the applicant.

(4) Without prejudice to the generality of paragraph (*g*) of subsection (1)

above, where an application for an order under section 2 of this Act is made by virtue of section 1(1)(*e*) of this Act, the court shall, in addition to the matters specifically mentioned in paragraphs (*a*) to (*f*) of that subsection, have regard to the extent to which and the basis upon which the deceased assumed responsibility for the maintenance of the applicant and to the length of time for which the deceased discharged that responsibility.

(5) In considering the matters to which the court is required to have regard under this section, the court shall take into account the facts as known to the court at the date of the hearing.

(6) In considering the financial resources of any person for the purposes of this section the court shall take into account his earning capacity and in considering the financial needs of any person for the purposes of this section the court shall take into account his financial obligations and responsibilities.

This section gives the guidelines to which the court is directed to have regard. Some guidelines apply to all applicants, others only to particular categories of applicant.

Subsection (2) gives the particular guidelines for surviving spouses and former spouses. Compare the Matrimonial Causes Act 1973, s.25(1).

Subsection (3) gives the particular guidelines for children and persons treated as children. Compare Matrimonial Causes Act 1973, s.25(2).

Subsection (4) gives the particular guidelines for the new category of dependants.

Time-limit for applications

4. An application for an order under section 2 of this Act shall not, except with the permission of the court, be made after the end of the period of six months from the date on which representation with respect to the estate of the deceased is first taken out.

GENERAL NOTE

See also section 23.

Interim orders

5.—(1) Where on an application for an order under section 2 of this Act it appears to the court—

(*a*) that the applicant is in immediate need of financial assistance, but it is not yet possible to determine what order (if any) should be made under that section; and

(*b*) that property forming part of the net estate of the deceased is or can be made available to meet the need of the applicant;

the court may order that, subject to such conditions or restrictions, if any, as the court may impose and to any further order of the court, there shall be paid to the applicant out of the net estate of the deceased such sum or sums and (if more than one) at such intervals as the court thinks reasonable; and the court may order that, subject to the provisions of this Act, such payments are to be made until such date as the court may specify, not being later than the date on which the court either makes an order under the said section 2 or decides not to exercise its powers under that section.

(2) Subsections (2), (3) and (4) of section 2 of this Act shall apply in relation to an order under this section as they apply in relation to an order under that section.

(3) In determining what order, if any, should be made under this section the court shall, so far as the urgency of the case admits, have regard to the same matters as those to which the court is required to have regard under section 3 of this Act.

(4) An order made under section 2 of this Act may provide that any sum paid to the applicant by virtue of this section shall be treated to such an extent and in such manner as may be provided by that order as having been paid on account of any payment provided for by that order.

Variation, discharge etc. of orders for periodical payments

6.—(1) Subject to the provisions of this Act, where the court has made an order under section 2(1)(a) of this Act (in this section referred to as "the original order") for the making of periodical payments to any person (in this section referred to as "the original recipient"), the court, on an application under this section, shall have power by order to vary or discharge the original order or to suspend any provision of it temporarily and to revive the operation of any provision so suspended.

(2) Without prejudice to the generality of subsection (1) above, an order made on an application for the variation of the original order may—

(a) provide for the making out of any relevant property of such periodical payments and for such term as may be specified in the order to any person who has applied, or would but for section 4 of this Act be entitled to apply, for an order under section 2 of this Act (whether or not, in the case of any application, an order was made in favour of the applicant);

(b) provide for the payment out of any relevant property of a lump sum of such amount as may be so specified to the original recipient or to any such person as is mentioned in paragraph (a) above;

(c) provide for the transfer of the relevant property, or such part thereof as may be so specified, to the original recipient or to any such person as is so mentioned.

(3) Where the original order provides that any periodical payments payable thereunder to the original recipient are to cease on the occurrence of an event specified in the order (other than the remarriage of a former wife or former husband) or on the expiration of a period so specified, then, if, before the end of the period of six months from the date of the occurrence of that event or of the expiration of that period, an application is made for

an order under this section, the court shall have power to make any order which it would have had power to make if the application had been made before that date (whether in favour of the original recipient or any such person as is mentioned in subsection (2)(*a*) above and whether having effect from that date or from such later date as the court may specify).

(4) Any reference in this section to the original order shall include a reference to an order made under this section and any reference in this section to the original recipient shall include a reference to any person to whom periodical payments are required to be made by virtue of an order under this section.

(5) An application under this section may be made by any of the following persons, that is to say—

(*a*) any person who by virtue of section 1(1) of this Act has applied, or would be but for section 4 of this Act be entitled to apply, for an order under section 2 of this Act,

(*b*) the personal representatives of the deceased,

(*c*) the trustees of any relevant property, and

(*d*) any beneficiary of the estate of the deceased.

(6) An order under this section may only affect—

(*a*) property the income of which is at the date of the order applicable wholly or in part for the making of periodical payments to any person who has applied for an order under this Act, or

(*b*) in the case of an application under subsection (3) above in respect of payments which have ceased to be payable on the occurrence of an event or the expiration of a period, property the income of which was so applicable immediately before the occurrence of that event or the expiration of that period, as the case may be,

and any such property as is mentioned in paragraph (*a*)) or (*b*) above is in subsections (2) and (5) above referred to as "relevant property."

(7) In exercising the powers conferred by this section the court shall have regard to all the circumstances of the case, including any change in any of the matters to which the court was required to have regard when making the order to which the application relates.

(8) Where the court makes an order under this section, it may give such consequential directions as it thinks necessary or expedient having regard to the provisions of the order.

(9) No such order as is mentioned in sections 2(1)(*d*), (*e*) or (*f*), 9, 10 or 11 of this Act shall be made on an application under this section.

(10) For the avoidance of doubt it is hereby declared that, in relation to an order which provides for the making of periodical payments which are to cease on the occurrence of an event specified in the order (other than the remarriage of a former wife or former husband) or on the expiration of a period so specified, the power to vary an order includes power to provide

for the making of periodical payments after the expiration of that period or
the occurrence of that event.

GENERAL NOTE

This power to vary only applies to orders for periodical payments. An application to vary
cannot affect a part of the estate not already subject to the order for periodical payments, but
it may be made by an applicant who did not apply on the occasion of the original application,
and by certain other persons.

Payment of lump sums by instalments

7.—(1) An order under section 2(1)(*b*) or 6(2)(*b*) of this Act for the payment of a lump sum may provide for the payment of that sum by instalments of such amount as may be specified in the order.

(2) Where an order is made by virtue of subsection (1) above, the court
shall have power, on an application made by the person to whom the lump
sum is payable, by the personal representatives of the deceased or by the
trustees of the property out of which the lump sum is payable, to vary that
order by varying the number of instalments payable, the amount of any
instalment and the date on which any instalment becomes payable.

Property available for financial provision

Property treated as part of "net estate"

8.—(1) Where a deceased person has in accordance with the provisions
of any enactment nominated any person to receive any sum of money or
other property on his death and that nomination is in force at the time of
this death, that sum of money, after deducting therefrom any capital
transfer tax payable in respect thereof, or that other property, to the extent
of the value thereof at the date of the death of the deceased after deducting
therefrom any capital transfer tax payable thereon, or that other propety,
to the extent of the value thereof at the date of the death of the deceased
after deducting therefrom any capital transfer tax payable thereon, or that
other property, to the extent of the value thereof at the date of the death of
the discussed after deducting therefrom any capital transfer tax so payable,
shall be treated for the purposes of this Act as part of the net estate of the
deceased; but this subsection shall not render any person liable for having
paid that sum or transferred that other property to the person named in the
nomination in accordance with the directions given in the nomination.

(2) Where any sum of money or other property is received by any person
as a donatio mortis causa made by a deceased person, that sum of money,
after deducting therefrom any capital transfer tax payable thereon, or that
other property, to the extent of the value thereof at the date of the death of
the deceased after deducting therefrom any capital transfer tax so payable,
shall be treated for the purposes of this Act as part of the net estate of the
deceased; but this subsection shall not tender any person liable for having
paid that sum or transferred that other property in order to give effect to
that donatio mortis causa.

(3) The amount of capital transfer tax to be deducted for the purposes of this section shall not exceed the amount of that tax which has been borne by the person nominated by the deceased or, as the case may be, the person who has received a sum of money or other property as a donatio mortis causa.

GENERAL NOTE

This section brings property which the deceased has nominated to a beneficiary under the provisions of a statute and property of which he had made a *donatio mortis causa* within the definition of his net estate out of which provision may be ordered.

Property held on a joint tenancy

9.—(1) Where a deceased person was immediately before his death beneficially entitled to a joint tenancy of any property, then, if, before the end of the period of six months from the date on which representation with respect to the estate of the deceased was first taken out, an application is made for an order under section 2 of this Act, the court for the purpose of facilitating the making of financial provision for the applicant under this Act may order that the deceased's severable share of that property, at the value thereof immediately before his death, shall, to such extent as appears to the court to be just in all the circumstance of the case, be treated for the purposes of this Act as part of the net estate of the deceased.

(2) In determining the extent to which any severable share it to be treated as part of the net estate of the deceased by virtue of an order under subsection (1) above, the court shall have regard to any capital transfer tax payable in respect of that severable share.

(3) Where an order is made under subsection (1) above, the provisions of this section shall not render any person liable for anything done by him before the order was made.

(4) For the avoidance of doubt it is hereby declared that for the purposes of this section there may be a joint tenancy of a chose in action.

GENERAL NOTE

This section enables the court to bring the deceased's beneficial share in any property held on a joint tenancy within his net estate for the purposes of provision.

Powers of court in relation to transactions intended to defeat applications for financial provision

Dispositions intended to defeat applications for financial provision

10.—(1) Where an application is made to the court for an order under section 2 of this Act, the applicant may, in the proceedings on that application, apply to the court for an order under subsection (2) below.

(2) Where on an application under subsection (1) above the court is satisfied—

(*a*) that, less than six years before the date of the death of the deceased, the deceased with the intention of defeating an application for financial provision under this Act made a disposition, and

(*b*) that full valuable consideration for the disposition was not given by the person to whom or for the benefit of whom the disposition was made (in this section referred to as "the donee") or by any other person, and

(*c*) that the exercise of the powers conferred by this section would facilitate the making of financial provision for the applicant under this Act,

then, subject to the provisions of this section and of sections 12 and 13 of this Act, the court may order the donee (whether or not at the date of the order he holds any interest in the property disposed of to him or for his benefit by the deceased) to provide, for the purpose of the making of that financial provision, such sum of money or other property as may be specified in the order.

(3) Where an order is made under subsection (2) above as respects any disposition made by the deceased which consisted of the payment of money to or for the benefit of the donee, the amount of any sum of money or the value of any property ordered to be provided under that subsection shall not exceed the amount of the payment made by the deceased after deducting therefrom any capital transfer tax borne by the donee in respect of the payment.

(4) Where an order is made under subsection (2) above as respects any disposition made by the deceased which consisted of the transfer of property (other than a sum of money) to or for the benefit of the donee, the amount of any sum of money or the value of any property ordered to be provided under that subsection shall not exceed the value at the date of the death of the deceased of the property disposed of by him to or for the benefit of the donee (or if that property has been disposed of by the person to whom it was transferred by the deceased, the value at the date of that disposal thereof) after deducting therefrom any capital transfer tax borne by the donee in respect of the transfer of that property by the deceased.

(5) Where an application (in this subsection referred to as "the original application") is made for an order under subsection (2) above in relation to any disposition, then, if on an application under this subsection by the donee or by any applicant for an order under section 2 of this Act the court is satisfied—

(*a*) that, less than six years before the date of the death of the deceased, the deceased with the intention of defeating an application for financial provision under this Act made a disposition other than the disposition which is the subject of the original application, and

(*b*) that full valuable consideration for that other disposition was not given by the person to whom or for the benefit of whom that other disposition was made of by any other person,

the court may exercise in relation to the person to whom or for the benefit of whom that other disposition was made the powers which the court would have had under subsection (2) above if the original application had been made in respect of that other disposition and the court had been satisfied as to the matters set out in paragraphs (*a*), (*b*) and (*c*) of that subsection; and where any application is made under this subsection, any reference in this section (except in subsection (2)(*b*)) to the donee shall include a reference to the person to whom or for the benefit of whom that other disposition was made.

(6) In determining whether and in what manner to exercise its powers under this section, the court shall have regard to the circumstances in which any disposition was made and any valuable consideration which was given therefor, the relationship, if any, of the donee to the deceased, the conduct and financial resources of the donee and all the other circumstances of the case.

(7) In this section "disposition" does not include—

(*a*) any provision in a will, any such nomination as is mentioned in section 8(1) of this Act of any donatio mortis causa, or

(*b*) any appointment of property made, otherwise than by will, in the exercise of a special power of appointment,

but, subject to these exceptions, includes any payment of money (including the payment of a premium under a policy of assurance) and any conveyance, assurance, appointment or gift of property of any description, whether made by an instrument or otherwise.

(8) The provisions of this section do not apply to any disposition made before the commencement of this Act.

GENERAL NOTE

This is a section which is designed to nullify, or at least reduce, the effect of dispositions of money or other property made with the intention of defeating applications for provision under the Act. Contrast Matrimonial Causes Act 1973, s.37.

Contracts to leave property by will

11.—(1) Where an application is made to a court for an order under section 2 of this Act, the applicant may, in the proceedings on that application, apply to the court for an order under this section.

(2) Where on an application under subsection (1) above the court is satisfied—

(*a*) that the deceased made a contract by which he agreed to leave by his will a sum of money or other property to any person or by which he agreed that a sum of money or other property would be paid or transferred to any person out of his estate, and

(b) that the deceased made that contract with the intention of defeating an application for financial provision under this Act, and

(c) that when the contract was made full valuable consideration for that contract was not given or promised by the person with whom or for the benefit of whom the contract was made (in this section referred to as "the donee") or by any other person, and

(d) that the exercise of the powers conferred by this section would facilitate the making of financial provision for the applicant under this Act,

then, subject to the provisions of this section and of sections 12 and 13 of this Act, the court may make any one or more of the following orders, that is to say—

(i) if any money has been paid or any other property has been transferred to or for the benefit of the donee in accordance with the contract, an order directing the donee to provide, for the purpose of the making of that financial provision, such sum of money or other property as may be specified in the order;

(ii) if the money or all the money has not been paid or the property or all the property has not been transferred in accordance with the contract, an order directing the personal representatives not to make any payment or transfer any property, or not to make any further payment or transfer any further property, as the case may be, in accordance therewith or directing the personal representatives only to make such payment or transfer such property as may be specified in the order.

(3) Notwithstanding anything in subsection (2) above, the court may exercise its powers thereunder in relation to any contract made by the deceased only to the extent that the court considers that the amount of any sum of money paid or to be paid or the value of any property transferred or to be transferred in accordance with the contract exceeds the value of any valuable consideration given or to be given for that contract, and for this purpose the court shall have regard to the value of property at the date of the hearing.

(4) In determining whether and in what manner to exercise its powers under this section, the court shall have regard to the circumstances in which the contract was made; the relationship, if any, of the donee to the deceased, the conduct and financial resources of the donee and all the other circumstances of the case.

(5) Where an order has been made under subsection (2) above in relation to any contract, the rights of any person to enforce that contract or to recover damages or to obtain other relief for the breach thereof shall be subject to any adjustment made by the court under section 12(3) of this Act and shall survive to such extent only as is consistent with giving effect to the terms of that order.

(6) The provisions of this section do not apply to a contract made before the commencement of this Act.

GENERAL NOTE

This is a section which is designed to nullify, or at least reduce, the effect of contracts made with the intention of defeating applications for provision under the Act.

Provisions supplementary to ss.10 and 11

12.—(1) Where the exercise of any of the powers conferred by section 10 or 11 of this Act is conditional on the court being satisfied that a disposition or contract was made by a deceased person with the intention of defeating an application for financial provision under this Act, that condition shall be fulfilled if the court is of the opinion that, on a balance of probabilities, the intention of the deceased (though not necessarily his sole intention) in making the disposition or contract was to prevent an order for financial provision being made under this Act or to reduce the amount of the provision which might otherwise be granted by an order thereunder.

(2) Where an application is made under section 11 of this Act with respect to any contract made by the deceased and no valuable consideration was given or promised by any person for that contract then, notwithstanding anything in subsection (1) above, it shall be presumed, unless the contrary is shown, that the deceased made that contract with the intention of defeating an application for financial provision under this Act.

(3) Where the court makes an order under section 10 or 11 of this Act it may give such consequential directions as it thinks fit (including directions requiring the making of any payment or the transfer of any property) for giving effect to the order or for securing a fair adjustment of the rights of the persons affected thereby.

(4) Any power conferred on the court by the said section 10 or 11 to order the donee, in relation to any disposition or contract, to provide any sum of money or other property shall be exercisable in like manner in relation to the personal representative of the donee, and—

(a) any reference in section 10(4) to the disposal of property by the donee shall include a reference to disposal by the personal representative of the donee, and

(b) any reference in section 10(5) to an application by the donee under that subsection shall include a reference to an application by the personal representative of the donee;

but the court shall not have power under the said section 10 or 11 to make an order in respect of any property forming part of the estate of the donee which has been distributed by the personal representative; and the personal representative shall not be liable for having distributed any such property before he has notice of the making of an application under the said section 10 or 11 on the ground that he ought to have taken into account the possibility that such an application would be made.

GENERAL NOTE

This section contains provisions supplementary to the powers given to the court by sections 10 and 11, *ante*. The burden of proof is prescribed, and a presumption created for contracts which had no valuable consideration. It is made clear that the powers given by sections 10 and 11 may be exercised in relation to the personal representatives of the donee.

Provisions as to trustees in relation to ss.10 and 11

13.—(1) Where an application is made for—

(*a*) an order under section 10 of this Act in respect of a disposition made by the deceased to any person as a trustee, or

(*b*) an order under section 11 of this Act in respect of any payment made or property transferred, in accordance with a contract made by the deceased, to any person as a trustee,

the powers of the court under the said section 10 or 11 to order that trustee to provide a sum of money or other property shall be subject to the following limitation (in addition, in a case of an application under section 10, to any provision regarding the deduction of capital transfer tax) namely, that the amount of any sum of money or the value of any property ordered to be provided—

(i) in the case of an application in respect of a disposition which consisted of the payment of money or an application in respect of the payment of money in accordance with a contract, shall not exceed the aggregate of so much of that money as is at the date of the order in the hands of the trustee and the value at that date of any property which represents that money or is derived therefrom and is at that date in the hands of the trustee;

(ii) in the case of an application in respect of a disposition which consisted of the transfer of property (other than a sum of money) or an application in respect of the transfer of property (other than a sum of money) in accordance with a contract, shall not exceed the aggregate of the value at the date of the order of so much of that property as is at that date in the hands of the trustee and the value at that date of any property which represents the first-mentioned property or is derived therefrom and is at that date in the hands of the trustee.

(2) Where any such application is made in respect of a disposition made to any person as a trustee or in respect of any payment made or property transferred in pursuance of a contract to any person as a trustee, the trustee shall not be liable for having distributed any money or other property on the ground that he ought to have taken into account the possibility that such an application would be made.

(3) Where any such application is made in respect of a disposition made to any person as a trustee or in respect of any payment made or property

transferred in accordance with a contract to any person as a trustee, any reference in the said section 10 or 11 to the donee shall be construed as including a reference to the trustee or trustees for the time being of the trust in question and any reference in subsection (1) or (2) above to a trustee shall be construed in the same way.

GENERAL NOTE

This section limits the liabilities to which trustees may be subjected as a result of an application under sections 10 and 11, *ante*.

Special provisions relating to cases of divorce, separation etc.

Provision as to cases where no financial relief was granted in divorce proceedings etc.

14.—(1) Where, within 12 months from the date on which a decree of divorce or nullity of marriage has been made absolute or a decree of judicial separation has been granted, a party to the marriage dies and—

(*a*) an application for a financial provision order under section 23 of the Matrimonial Causes Act 1973 or a property adjustment order under section 24 of that Act has not been made by the other party to that marriage, or

(*b*) such an application has been made but the proceedings thereon have not been determined at the time of the death of the deceased,

then, if an application for an order under section 2 of this Act is made by that other party, the court shall, notwithstanding anything in section 1 or section 3 of this Act, have power, if it thinks it just to do so, to treat that party for the purposes of that application as if the decree of divorce or nullity of marriage had not been made absolute or the decree of judicial separation had not been granted, as the case may be.

(2) This section shall not apply in relation to a decree of judicial separation unless at the date of the death of the deceased the decree was in force and the separation was continuing.

GENERAL NOTE

This section enables the court to treat a former spouse as a surviving spouse when the other party to the marriage died within 12 months of the dissolution of the marriage and an order for provision has not been made in the matrimonial proceedings.

Restriction imposed in divorce proceedings etc. on application under this Act

15.—"(1) On the grant of a decree of divorce, a decree of nullity of marriage or a decree of judicial separation or at any time thereafter the court, if it considers it just to do so, may, on the application of either party to the marriage, order that the other party to the marriage shall not on the death of the applicant be entitled to apply for an order under section 2 of this Act.

(2) In the case of a decree of divorce or nullity of marriage an order may be made under subsection (1) above before or after the decree is made absolute, but if it is made before the decree is made absolute it shall not take effect unless the decree is made absolute.

(3) Where an order made under subsection (1) above on the grant of a decree of divorce or nullity of marriage has come into force with respect to a party to a marriage, then, on the death of the other party to that marriage, the court shall not entertain any application for an order under section 2 of this Act made by the first-mentioned party.

(4) Where an order made under subsection (1) above on the grant of a degree of judicial separation has come into force with respect to any party to a marriage, then, if the other party to that marriage dies while the decree is in force and the separation is continuing, the court shall not entertain any application for an order under section 2 of this Act made by the first-mentioned party.

Restriction imposed in proceedings under Matrimonial and Family Proceedings Act 1984 on application under this Act

15A.—(1) On making an order under section 17 of the Matrimonial and Family Proceedings Act 1984 (orders for financial provision and property adjustment following overseas divorces, etc.) the court, if it considers it just to do so, may, on the application of either party to the marriage, order that the other party to the marriage shall not on the death of the applicant be entitled to apply for an order under section 2 of this Act.

In this subsection 'the court' means the High Court or, where a county court has jurisdiction by virtue of Part V of the Matrimonial and Family Proceedings Act 1984, a county court.

(2) Where an order under subsection (1) above has been made with respect to a party to a marriage which has been dissolved or annulled, then, on the death of the other party to that marriage, the court shall not entertain an application under section 2 of this Act made by the first mentioned party.

(3) Where an order under subsection (1) above has been made with respect to a party to a marriage the parties to which have been legally separated, then, if the other party to the marriage dies while the legal separation is in force, the court shall not entertain an application under section 2 of this Act made by the first-mentioned party."

AMENDMENTS

Subsection (1) was substituted by the Matrimonial and Family Proceedings Act 1984, s.8.
Section 15A was added by the Matrimonial and Family Proceedings Act 1984, s.25.

This section enables the court in matrimonial proceedings to prevent a future application for financial provision under the Act, if the parties to the marriage agree.

Variation and discharge of secured periodical payments orders made under Matrimonial Causes Act 1973

16.—(1) Where an application for an order under section 2 of this Act is made to the court by any person who was at the time of the death of the deceased entitled to payments from the deceased under a secured periodical payments order made under the Matrimonial Causes Act 1973, then, in the proceedings on that application, the court shall have power, if an application is made under this section by that person or by the personal representative of the deceased, to vary or discharge that periodical payments order or to revive the operation of any provision thereof which has been suspended under section 31 of that Act.

(2) In exercising the powers conferred by this section the court shall have regard to all the circumstances of the case, including any order which the court proposes to make under section 2 or section 5 of this Act and any change (whether resulting from the death of the deceased or otherwise) in any of the matters to which the court was required to have regard when making the secured periodical payments order.

(3) The powers exercisable by the court under this section in relation to an order shall be exercisable also in relation to any instrument executed in pursuance of the order.

This section enables the court in family provision proceedings to vary or discharge secured periodical payment orders made under the Matrimonial Causes Act 1973. See sections 23 and 31 of that Act.

Variation and revocation of maintenance agreements

17.—(1) Where an application for an order under section 2 of this Act is made to the court by any person who was at the time of the death of the deceased entitled to payments from the deceased under a maintenance agreement which provided for the continuation of payments under the agreement after the death of the deceased, then, in the proceedings on that application, the court shall have power, if an application is made under this section by that person or by the personal representative of the deceased, to vary or revoke that agreement.

(2) In exercising the powers conferred by this section the court shall have regard to all the circumstances of the case, including any order which the court proposes to make under section 2 or section 5 of this Act and any change (whether resulting from the death of the deceased or otherwise) in any of the circumstances in the light of which the agreement was made.

(3) If a maintenance agreement is varied by the court under this section the like consequences shall ensue as if the variation had been made immediately before the death of the deceased by agreement between the parties and for valuable consideration.

(4) In this section "maintenance agreement," in relation to a deceased person, means any agreement made, whether in writing or not and whether before or after the commencement of this Act, by the deceased with any person with whom he entered into a marriage, being an agreement which contained provisions governing the rights and liabilities towards one another when living separately of the parties to that marriage (whether or not the marriage has been dissolved or annulled) in respect of the making or securing of payments or the disposition or use of any property, including such rights and liabilities with respect to the maintenance or education of any child, whether or not a child of the deceased or a person who was treated by the deceased as a child of the family in relation to that marriage.

GENERAL NOTE

This section enables the court in family provision proceedings to vary or revoke mainten-ance agreements. Compare section 36 of the Matrimonial Causes Act 1973.

Availability of court's powers under this Act in applications under ss.31 and 36 of the Matrimonial Causes Act 1973

18.—(1) Where—

(a) a person against whom a secured periodical payments order was made under the Matrimonial Causes Act 1973 has died and an application is made under section 31(6) of that Act for the vari-ation or discharge of that order or for the revival of the operation of any provision thereof which has been suspended, or

(b) a party to a maintenance agreement within the meaning of section 34 of that Act has died, the agreement being one which provides for the continuation of payments thereunder after the death of one of the parties, and an application is made under section 36(1) of that Act for the alteration of the agreement under section 35 thereof,

the court shall have power to direct that the application made under the said section 31(6) or 36(1) shall be deemed to have been accompanied by an application for an order under section 2 of this Act.

(2) Where the court gives a direction under subsection (1) above it shall have power, in the proceedings on the application under the said section 31(6) or 36(1), to make any order which the court would have had power to make under the provisions of this Act if the application under the said sec-tion 31(6) or 36(1), as the case may be, had been made jointly with an application for an order under the said section 2; and the court shall have

power to give such consequential direction as may be necessary for enabling the court to exercise any of the powers available to the court under this Act in the case of an application for an order under section 2.

(3) Where an order made under section 15(1) of this Act is in force with respect to a party to a marriage, the court shall not give a direction under subsection (1) above with respect to any application made under the said section 31(6) or 36(1) by that party on the death of the other party.

GENERAL NOTE

When an application is made under the Matrimonial Causes Act 1973 for the variation, discharge or revocation of a secured periodical payments order or a maintenance agreement after a death, this section makes available to the court the powers given by this Act, not least the power to avoid dispositions. Contrast section 37 of the Matrimonial Causes Act 1973.

Miscellaneous and supplementary provisions

Effect, duration and form of orders

19.—(1) Where an order is made under section 2 of this Act then for all purposes, including the purposes of the enactments relating to capital transfer tax, the will or the law relating to intestacy, or both the will and the law relating to intestacy, as the case may be, shall have effect and be deemed to have had effect as from the deceased's death subject to the provisions of the order.

(2) Any order made under section 2 or 5 of this Act in favour of—

(*a*) an applicant who was the former husband or former wife of the deceased, or

(*b*) an applicant who was the husband or wife of the deceased in a case where the marriage with the deceased was the subject of a decree of judicial separation and at the date of death the decree was in force and the separation was continuing,

shall, in so far as it provides for the making of periodical payments, cease to have effect on the remarriage of the applicant, except in relation to any arrears due under the order on the date of the remarriage.

(3) A copy of every order made under this Act other than an order made under section 15(1) of this Act shall be sent to the principal registry of the Family Division for entry and filing, and a memorandum of the order shall be endorsed on, or permanently annexed to, the probate or letters of administration under which the estate is being administered.

AMENDMENT

Subsection (3) is printed as amended by the Administration of Justice Act 1982, s.52.

GENERAL NOTE

Subsection (1) provides in effect that the order is read into the will or the intestacy rules.
Subsection (2) makes periodical payment orders in favour of former spouses and judicially separated spouses terminate on their remarriage.

Provisions as to personal representatives

20.—(1) The provisions of this Act shall not render the personal representative of a deceased person liable for having distributed any part of the estate of the deceased, after the end of the period of six months from the date on which representation with respect to the estate of the deceased is first taken out, on the ground that he ought to have taken into account the possibility—

    (*a*) that the court might permit the making of an application for an order under section 2 of this Act after the end of that period, or

    (*b*) that, where an order has been made under the said section 2, the court might exercise in relation thereto the powers conferred on it by section 6 of this Act,

but this subsection shall not prejudice any power to recover, by reason of the making of an order under this Act, any part of the estate so distributed.

(2) Where the personal representative of a deceased person pays any sum directed by an order under section 5 of this Act to be paid out of the deceased's net estate, he shall not be under any liability by reason of that estate not being sufficient to make the payment, unless at the time of making the payment he has reasonable cause to believe that the estate is not sufficient.

(3) Where a deceased person entered into a contract by which he agreed to leave by his will any sum of money or other property to any person or by which he agreed that a sum of money or other property would be paid or transferred to any person out of his estate, then, if the personal representative of the deceased has reason to believe that the deceased entered into the contract with the intention of defeating an application for financial provision under this Act, he may, notwithstanding anything in that contract, postpone the payment of that sum of money or the transfer of that property until the expiration of the period of six months from the date on which representation with respect to the estate of the deceased is first taken out or, if during that period an application is made for an order under section 2 of this Act, until the determination of the proceedings on that application.

GENERAL NOTE

This section contains various provisions protecting personal representatives.

Admissibility as evidence of statements made by deceased

21. In any proceedings under this Act a statement made by the deceased, whether orally or in a document or otherwise, shall be admissible under section 2 of the Civil Evidence Act 1968 as evidence of any fact stated therein in like manner as if the statement were a statement falling within section 2(1) of that Act; and any reference in that Act to a statement admissible, or given or proposed to be given, in evidence under section 2 thereof or to the admissibility or the giving in evidence of a statement by virtue of that section or to any statement falling within section 2(1) of that Act shall be construed accordingly.

GENERAL NOTE

This section makes it clear that the provisions of the Civil Evidence Act 1968 rendering hearsay evidence admissible apply to statements made by a deceased person against whose estate an application is made.

Jurisdiction of county courts

22.—[Repealed by the Administration of Justice Act 1982, Sched. 9].

Determination of date on which representation was first taken out

23. In considering for the purposes of this Act when representation with respect to the estate of a deceased person was first taken out, a grant limited to settled land or to trust property shall be left out of account, and a grant limited to real estate or to personal estate shall be left out of account unless a grant limited to the remainder of the estate has previously been made or is made at the same time.

GENERAL NOTE

This section clarifies the date when representation is taken out for the purposes of section 4.

Effect of this Act on s.46(1)(vi) of Administration of Estates Act 1925

24. Section 46(1)(vi) of the Administration of Estates Act 1925, in so far as it provides for the devolution of property on the Crown, the Duchy of Lancaster or the Duke of Cornwall as bona vacantia, shall have effect subject to the provisions of this Act.

GENERAL NOTE

This section makes it clear that the property of the deceased passing as *bona vacantia* can be made the subject of an order under the Act.

Interpretation

25.—(1) In this Act:—

"beneficiary," in relation to the estate of a deceased person, means:—
  (a) a person who under the will of the deceased or under the law relating to intestacy is beneficially interested in the estate or would be so interested if an order had not been made under this Act, and

(*b*) a person who has received any sum of money or other property which by virtue of section 8(1) or 8(2) of this Act is treated as part of the net estate of the deceased or would have received that sum or other property if an order had not been made under this Act;

"child" includes an illegitimate child and a child en ventre sa mère at the death of the deceased;

"the court" means the High Court, or where a county court has jurisdiction by virtue of section 22 of this Act, a county court;

" 'former wife' or 'former husband' means a person whose marriage with the deceased was during the lifetime of the deceased either—

(*a*) dissolved or annulled by a decree of divorce or a decree of nullity of marriage granted under the law of any part of the British Islands, or

(*b*) dissolved or annulled in any country or territory outside the British Islands by a divorce or annulment which is entitled to be recognised as valid by the law of England and Wales;".

"net estate," in relation to a deceased person, means:—

(*a*) all property of which the deceased had power to dispose by his will (otherwise than by virtue of a special power of appointment) less the amount of his funeral, testamentary and administration expenses, debts and liabilities, including any capital transfer tax payable out of his estate on his death;

(*b*) any property in respect of which the deceased held a general power of appointment (not being a power exercisable by will) which has not been exercised;

(*c*) any sum of money or other property which is treated for the purposes of this Act as part of the net estate of the deceased by virtue of section 8(1) or (2) of this Act;

(*d*) any property which is treated for the purposes of this Act as part of the net estate of the deceased by virtue of an order made under section 9 of the Act;

(*e*) any sum of money or other property which is, by reason of a disposition or contract made by the deceased, ordered under section 10 or 11 of this Act to be provided for the purposes of the making of financial provision under this Act;

"property" includes any chose in action;

"reasonable financial provision" has the meaning assigned to it by section 1 of this Act;

"valuable consideration" does not include marriage or a promise of marriage;

"will" includes codicil.

(2) For the purposes of paragraph (*a*) of the definition of "net estate" in subsection (1) above a person who is not of full age and capacity shall be treated as having power to dispose by a will of all property of which he

would have had power to dispose by will if he had been of full age and capacity.

(3) Any reference in this Act to provision out of the net estate of a deceased person includes a reference to provision extending to the whole of that estate.

(4) For the purposes of this Act any reference to a wife or husband shall be treated as including a reference to a person who in good faith entered into a void marriage with the deceased unless either:—

(a) the marriage of the deceased and that person was dissolved or annulled during the lifetime of the deceased and the dissolution or annulment is recognised by the law of England and Wales, or

(b) that person has during the lifetime of the deceased entered into a later marriage.

(5) Any reference in this Act to remarriage or to a person who has remarried includes a reference to a marriage which is by law void or voidable or to a person who has entered into such a marriage, as the case may be, and a marriage shall be treated for the purposes of this Act as a remarriage, in relation to any party thereto, notwithstanding that the previous marriage of that party was void or voidable.

(6) Any reference in this Act to an order or decree made under the Matrimonial Causes Act 1973 or under any section of that Act shall be construed as including a reference to an order or decree which is deemed to have been made under that Act or under that section thereof, as the case may be.

(7) Any reference in this Act to any enactment is a reference to that enactment as amended by or under any subsequent enactment.

AMENDMENT

In subsection (1) the definitions of "former wife" or "former husband" were substituted (Matrimonial and Family Proceedings Act 1984, s.25).

GENERAL NOTE

This is the definition section. All of it is important, but note especially the definitions of "beneficiary," "child," "former wife" and "former husband," "net estate," and "valuable consideration"; also the explanations of references to a wife or husband in subsection (4), and to remarriage in subsection (5).

Consequential amendments, repeals and transitional provisions

26.—(1) Section 36 of the Matrimonial Causes Act 1973 (which provides for the alteration of maintenance agreements by the High Court or a county court after the death of one of the parties) shall have effect subject to the following amendments (being amendments consequential on this Act), that is to say—

> (a) in subsection (3) for the words "section 7 of the Family Provision Act 1966" there shall be substituted the words "section 22 of the Inheritance (Provision for Family and Dependants) Act 1975," for the words from "the Inheritance (Family Provision) Act" to "net estate" there shall be substituted the words "that Act if the value of the property mentioned in that section" and for the words "section 26 of the Matrimonial Causes Act 1965 (application for maintenance out of deceased's estate by former spouse)" there shall be substituted the words "section 2 of that Act";
>
> (b) in subsection (7) for the words from "section 7" to "subsection (5)" there shall be substituted the words "section 22 of the Inheritance (Provision for Family and Dependants) Act 1975 (which enables rules of court to provide for the transfer from a county court to the High Court or from the High Court to a county court of proceedings for an order under section 2 of that Act) and paragraphs (a) and (b) of subsection (4)" and for the words "any such proceedings as are referred to in subsection (1) of that section" there shall be substituted the words "proceedings for an order under section 2 of that Act."

(2) Subject to the provisions of this section, the enactments specified in the Schedule to this Act are hereby repealed to the extent specified in the third column of the Schedule; and in paragraph 5(2) of Schedule 2 to the Matrimonial Causes Act 1973 for the words "that Act" there shall be substituted the words "the Matrimonial Causes Act 1965."

(3) The repeal of the said enactments shall not affect their operation in relation to any application made thereunder (whether before or after the commencement of this Act) with reference to the death of any person who died before the commencement of this Act.

(4) Without prejudice to the provisions of section 38 of the Interpretation Act 1889 (which relates to the effect of repeals) nothing in any repeal made by this Act shall affect any order made or direction given under any enactment repealed by this Act, and, subject to the provisions of this Act, every such order or direction (other than an order made under section 4A of the Inheritance Family Provision Act 1938 or section 28A of the Matrimonial Causes Act 1965) shall, if it is in force at the commencement of this Act or is made by virtue of subsection (3) above, continue in force as if it had been made under section 2(1)(a) of this Act, and for the purposes of section 6(7) of this Act the court in exercising its powers under that section in relation to an order continued in force by this subsection shall be required to have regard to any change in any of the circumstances to which the court would have been required to have regard when making that order

if the order had been made with reference to the death of any person who died after the commencement of this Act.

GENERAL NOTE

Note especially subsection (3), which preserves the 1938 and the 1965 Acts for deaths before the commencement of the new Act, and subsection (4), which makes clear that the power of variation in section 6 applies to orders made under the old Acts.

Short title, commencement and extent

27.—(1) This Act may be cited as the Inheritance (Provision for Family and Dependants) Act 1975.

(2) This Act does not extend to Scotland or Northern Ireland.

(3) This Act shall come into force on April 1, 1976.

Chapter	Short Title	Extent of Repeal
1938 c. 72.	The Inheritance (Family Provision) Act 1938.	The whole Act.
1952 c. 64.	The Intestates' Estates Act 1952.	Section 7 and Schedule 3.
1965 c. 72.	The Matrimonial Causes Act 1965.	Sections 26 to 28A and section 25(4) and (4) as applied by section 28(2).
1966 c. 35.	The Family Provision Act 1966.	The whole Act, except section 1 and sub-sections (1) and (3) of section 10.
1969 s. 46.	The Family Law Reform Act 1969.	Sections 5(1) and 18.
1979 c. 31.	The Administration of Justice Act 1970.	In Schedule 2, paragraph 16.
1970 c. 33.	The Law Reform (Miscellaneous Provisions) Act 1970.	Section 6.
1970 c. 45.	The Matrimonial Proceedings and Property Act 1970.	Section 6.
1971 c. 23.	The Courts Act 1971.	Section 45(1)(a).
1973 c. 18.	The Matrimonial Causes Act 1973.	In section 50, in subsection (1)(a) the words from "and sections 26" to the end of the paragraph, in subsection (1)(d) the words "or sections 26 to 28A of the Matrimonial Causes Act 1965" and in subsection (2)(a) the words "or under section 26 or 27 of the Matrimonial Causes Act 1965".

Chapter	Short Title	Extent of Repeal
1975 c. 7.	The Finance Act 1975.	In Schedule 2, paragraph 5(1) and in paragraph 12 the words "(*a*) sections 26 to 28A of the Matrimonial Causes Act 1965." In Schedule 12, paragraph 6.

ADOPTION ACT 1976

(1976, c. 36)

ARRANGEMENT OF SECTIONS

Part IV

STATUS OF ADOPTED CHILDREN

* * * *

Part IV

Status conferred by adoption

39.—(1) An adopted child shall be treated in law—

(*a*) where the adopters are a married couple, as if he had been born as a child of the marriage (whether or not he was in fact born after the marriage was solemnised);

(*b*) in any other case, as if he had been born to the adopter in wedlock (but not as a child of any actual marriage of the adopter).

(2) An adopted child shall, subject to subsection (3), be treated in law as if he were not the child of any person other than the adopters or adopter.

(3) In the case of a child adopted by one of its natural parents as sole adoptive parent, subsection (2) has no effect as respects entitlement to property depending on relationship to that parent, or as respects anything else depending on that relationship.

(4) It is hereby declared that this section prevents an adopted child from being illegitimate.

(5) This section has effect—

(*a*) in the case of an adoption before January 1, 1976, from that date, and

(*b*) in the case of any other adoption, from the date of the adoption.

(6) Subject to the provisions of this Part, this section—

(*a*) applies for the construction of enactments or instruments passed or made before the adoption or later, and so applies subject to any contrary indication; and

(*b*) has effect as respects things done, or events occurring, after the adoption, or after December 31, 1975, whichever is the later.

40. [*Repealed by the British Nationality Act 1981, s.52(8) Sched. 9*].

Adoptive relatives

41.—(1) A relationship existing by virtue of section 39 may be referred to as an adoptive relationship, and—

    (*a*) a male adopter may be referred to as the adoptive father;

    (*b*) a female adopter may be referred to as the adoptive mother;

    (*c*) any other relative of any degree under an adoptive relationship may be referred to as an adoptive relative of that degree,

but this section does not prevent the term "parent," or any other term not qualified by the word "adoptive" being treated as including an adoptive relative.

Rules of construction for instruments concerning property

42.—(1) Subject to any contrary indication, the rules of constuction contained in this section apply to any instrument other than an existing instrument, so far as it contains a disposition of property.

(2) In applying section 39(1) to a disposition which depends on the date of birth of a child or children of the adoptive parent or parents, the disposition shall be construed as if—

    (*a*) the adopted child had been born on the date of adoption,

    (*b*) two or more children adopted on the same date had been born on that date in the order of their actual births,

but this does not affect any reference to the age of a child.

(3) Examples of phrases in wills on which subsection (2) can operate are—

    1. Children of A "living at my death or born afterwards."

    2. Children of A "living at my death or born afterwards before any one of such children for the time being in existence attains a vested interest and who attain the age of 21 years."

    3. As in example 1 or 2, but referring to grandchildren of A instead of children of A.

    4. A for life "until he has a child," and then to his child or children.

Note. Subsection (2) will not affect the reference to the age of 21 years in example 2.

(4) Section 39(2) does not prejudice any interest vested in possession in the adopted child before the adoption, or any interest expectant (whether immediately or not) upon an interest so vested.

(5) Where it is necessary to determine for the purposes of a disposition of property effected by an instrument whether a woman can have a child, it shall be presumed that once a woman has attained the age of 55 years she

will not adopt a child after execution of the instrument, and, notwithstanding section 39, if she does so that child shall not be treated as her child or as the child of her spouse (if any) for the purposes of the instrument.

(6) In this section, "instrument" includes a private Act settling property, but not any other enactment.

Dispositions depending on date of birth

43.—(1) Where a disposition depends on the date of birth of a child who was born illegitimate and who is adopted by one of the natural parents as sole adoptive parent, section 42(2) does not affect entitlement under Part II of the Family Law Reform Act 1969 (illegitimate children).

(2) Subsection (1) applies for example where—

- (*a*) a testator dies in 1976 bequeathing a legacy to his eldest grandchild living at a specified time,
- (*b*) his daughter has an illegitimate child in 1977 who is the first grandchild,
- (*c*) his married son has a child in 1978,
- (*d*) subsequently the illegitimate child is adopted by the mother as sole adoptive parent,

and in all those cases the daughter's child remains the eldest grandchild of the testator throughout.

Property devolving with peerages etc.

44.—(1) An adoption does not affect the descent of any peerage or dignity or title of honour.

(2) An adoption shall not affect the devolution of any property limited (expressly or not) to devolve (as nearly as the law permits) along with any peerage or dignity or title of honour.

(3) Subsection (2) applies only if and so far as a contrary intention is not expressed in the instrument, and shall have effect subject to the instrument, and shall have effect subject to the terms of the instrument.

Protection of trustees and personal representatives

45.—(1) A trustee or personal representative is not under a duty, by virtue of the law relating to trusts or the administration of estates, to enquire, before conveying or distributing any property, whether any adoption has been effected or revoked if that fact could affect entitlement to the property.

(2) A trustee or personal representative shall not be liable to any person by reason of a conveyance or distribution of the property made without regard to any such fact if he has not received notice of the fact before the conveyance or distribution.

(3) This section does not prejudice the right of a person to follow the

property, or any property representing it, into the hands of another person, other than a purchaser, who has received it.

Meaning of "disposition"

46.—(1) In this Part, unless the context otherwise requires,—

"disposition" includes the conferring of a power of appointment and any other disposition of an interest in or right over property;
"power of appointment" includes any discretionary power to transfer a beneficial interest in property without the furnishing of valuable consideration.

(2) This Part applies to an oral disposition as if contained in an instrument made when the disposition was made.

(3) For the purposes of this Part, the death of the testator is the date at which a will or codicil is to be regarded as made.

(4) For the purposes of this Part, provisions of the law of intestate succession applicable to the estate of a deceased person shall be treated as if contained in an instrument executed by him (while of full capacity) immediately before his death.

(5) It is hereby declared that references in this Part to dispositions of property include references to a disposition by the creation of an entailed interest.

SUPREME COURT ACT 1981

(1981, c. 54)

ARRANGEMENT OF SECTIONS

*   *   *   *

PART V

PROBATE CAUSES AND MATTERS

Procedure in probate registries in relation to grants of representation

Powers of Court in relation to personal representatives

Revocation of grants and cancellation of resealing at instance of court

Ancillary powers of court

Provisions as to documents

Probate rules

Interpretation of Part V and other probate provisions

Part V

PROBATE CAUSES AND MATTERS

Procedure in probate registries in relation to grants of representation

Applications

105. Applications for grants of probate or administration and for the revocation of grants may be made to—

> (*a*) the Principal Registry of the Family Division (in this Part referred to as "the Principal Registry"); or
> (*b*) a district probate registry.

Grants by district probate registrars

106.—(1) Any grant made by a district probate registrar shall be made in the name of the High Court under the seal used in the registry.

(2) No grant shall be made by a district probate registrar—

> (*a*) in any case where there is contention, until the contention is disposed of; or
> (*b*) in any case where it appears to him either—
>> (i) that a grant ought not to be made without the directions of the High Court under subsection (4), or
>> (ii) that a grant ought not to be made until any particular matter relating to the grant, or to an application for it, has been determined by the High Court otherwise than under that subsection.

(3) In any case where subsection (2)(*b*)(i) applies, the district probate registrar shall send a statement of the matter in question to the Principal Registry for the directions of the court.

(4) Where its directions are sought under subsection (3), the High Court may either direct the district probate registrar to proceed with the matter in accordance with such instructions as it may think necessary, or direct him to take no further action in relation to the matter.

No grant where conflicting applications

107. Subject to probate rules, no grant in respect of the estate, or part of the estate, of a deceased person shall be made out of the Principal Registry or any district probate registry on any application if, at any time before the making of a grant, it appears to the registrar concerned that some other application has been made in respect of that estate or, as the case may be, that part of it and has not been either refused or withdrawn.

Caveats

108.—(1) A caveat against a grant of probate or administration may be entered in the Principal Registry or in any district probate registry.

(2) On a caveat being entered in a district probate registry, the district probate registrar shall immediately send a copy of it to the Principal Registry to be entered among the caveats in that Registry.

Refusal of grant where capital transfer tax unpaid

109.—(1) Subject to subsections (2) and (3), no grant shall be made, and no grant made outside the United Kingdom shall be resealed, except on the production of an account prepared in pursuance of [the Capital Transfer Tax Act 1984] showing by means of such receipt or certification as may be prescribed by the Commissioners of Inland Revenue (in this and the following section referred to as "the Commissioners") either—

(*a*) that the capital transfer tax payable on the delivery of the account has been paid; or

(*b*) that no such tax is so payable.

(2) Arrangements may be made between the President of the Family Division and the Commissioners providing for the purposes of this section in such cases as may be specified in the arrangements that the receipt or certification of an account may be dispensed with or that some other document may be substituted for the account required by [the Capital Transfer Tax Act 1984].

(3) Nothing in subsection (1) applies in relation to a case where the delivery of the account required by that Part of that Act has for the time being been dispensed with by any regulations under [section 256(1)(*a*) of the Capital Transfer Tax Act 1984].

AMENDMENT

The words in square brackets were substituted by the Capital Transfer Tax Act 1984, s.276, Sched. 8, para. 20.

Documents to be delivered to Commissioners of Inland Revenue

110. Subject to any arrangements which may from time to time be made between the President of the Family Division and the Commissioners, the Principal Registry and every district probate registry shall, within such period after a grant as the President may direct, deliver to the Commissioners or their proper officer the following documents—

(*a*) in the case of a grant of probate or of administration with the will annexed, a copy of the will;

(*b*) in every case, such certificate or note of the grant as the Commissioners may require.

Records of grants

111.—(1) There shall continue to be kept records of all grants which are made in the Principal Registry or in any district probate registry.

(2) Those records shall be in such form, and shall contain such particulars, as the President of the Family Division may direct.

Powers of Court in relation to personal representatives

Summons to executor to prove or renounce [See also under section 4 of the Administration of Estates Act 1925].

112. The High Court may summon any person named as executor in a will to prove, or renounce probate of, the will, and to do such other things concerning the will as the court had power to order such a person to do immediately before the commencement of this Act.

Power of court to sever grant [See under sections 10–14 of the Administration of Estates Act 1925].

113.—(1) Subject to subsection (2), the High Court may grant probate or administration in respect of any part of the estate of a deceased person, limited in any way the court thinks fit.

(2) Where the estate of a deceased person is known to be insolvent, the grant of representation to it shall not be severed under subsection (1) except as regards a trust estate in which he had no beneficial interest.

Number of personal representatives [See also under sections 10–14 of the Administration of Estates Act 1925].

114.—(1) Probate or administration shall not be granted by the High Court to more than four persons in respect of the same part of the estate of a deceased person.

(2) Where under a will or intestacy any beneficiary is a minor or a life interest arises, any grant of administration by the High Court shall be made either to a trust corporation (with or without an individual) or to not less than two individuals, unless it appears to the court to be expedient in all the circumstances to appoint an individual as sole administrator.

(3) For the purpose of determining whether a minority or life interest arises in any particular case, the court may act on such evidence as may be prescribed.

(4) If at any time during the minority of a beneficiary or the subsistence of a life interest under a will or intestacy there is only one personal representative (not being a trust corporation), the High Court may, on the application of any person interested or the guardian or receiver of any such person, and in accordance with probate rules, appoint one or more additional personal representatives to act while the minority or life interest subsists and until the estate is fully administered.

(5) An appointment of an additional personal representative under subsection (4) to act with an executor shall not have the effect of including him in any chain of representation.

Grants to trust corporations [See also under sections 10–14 of the Administration of Estates Act 1925].

115.—(1) The High Court may—

> (a) where a trust corporation is named in a will as executor, grant probate to the corporation either solely or jointly with any other person named in the will as executor, as the case may require; or
>
> (b) grant administration to a trust corporation, either solely or jointly with another person;

and the corporation may act accordingly as executor or administrator, as the case may be.

(2) Probate or administration shall not be granted to any person as nominee of a trust corporation.

(3) Any officer authorised for the purpose by a trust corporation or its directors or governing body may, on behalf of the corporation, swear affidavits, give security and do any other act which the court may require with a view to the grant to the corporation of probate or administration; and the acts of an officer so authorised shall be binding on the corporation.

(4) Subsections (1) to (3) shall also apply in relation to any body which is exempt from the provisions of section 23(1) of the Solicitors Act 1974 (unqualified persons not to prepare papers for probate etc.) by virtue of any of paragraphs (e) to (h) of subsection (2) of that section.

AMENDMENT

Subsection (4) was added by the Courts and Legal Services Act 1990, s.54.

Power of court to pass over prior claims to grant [See also under sections 10–14 of the Administration of Estates Act 1925].

116.—(1) If by reason of any special circumstances it appears to the High Court to be necessary or expedient to appoint as administrator some person other than the person who, but for this section, would in accordance with probate rules have been entitled to the grant, the court may in its discretion appoint as administrator such a person as it thinks expedient.

(2) Any grant of administration under this section may be limited in any way the court thinks fit.

Administration pending suit [See also under section 16 of the Administration of Estates Act 1925].

117.—(1) Where any legal proceedings concerning the validity of the will of a deceased person, or for obtaining, recalling or revoking any grant, are pending, the High Court may grant administration of the estate of the deceased person in question to an administrator pending suit, who shall, subject to subsection (2), have all the rights, duties and powers of a general administrator.

(2) An administrator pending suit shall be subject to the immediate control of the court and act under its direction; and, except in such circumstances as may be prescribed, no distribution of the estate, or any part of the estate, of the deceased person in question shall be made by such an administrator without the leave of the court.

(3) The court may, out of the estate of the deceased, assign an administrator pending suit such reasonable remuneration as it thinks fit.

Effect of appointment of minor as executor [See also under sections 19–20 of the Administration of Estates Act 1925].

118. Where a testator by his will appoints a minor to be an executor, the appointment shall not operate to vest in the minor the estate, or any part of the estate, of the testator, or to constitute him a personal representative for any purpose, unless and until probate is granted to him in accordance with probate rules.

Administration with will annexed [See also under sections 19–20 of the Administration of Estates Act 1925].

119.—(1) Administration with the will annexed shall be granted, subject to and in accordance with probate rules, in every class of case in which the High Court had power to make such a grant immediately before the commencement of this Act.

(2) Where administration with the will annexed is granted, the will of the deceased shall be performed and observed in the same manner as if probate of it had been granted to an executor.

Power to require administrators to produce sureties [See also under sections 10–14 of the Administration of Estates Act 1925].

120.—(1) As a condition of granting administration to any person the High Court may, subject to the following provisions of this section and subject to and in accordance with probate rules, require one or more sureties to guarantee that they will make good, within any limit imposed by the court on the total liability of the surety or sureties, any loss which any person interested in the administration of the estate of the deceased may suffer in consequence of a breach by the administrator of his duties as such.

(2) A guarantee given in pursuance of any such requirement shall enure for the benefit of every person interested in the administration of the estate of the deceased as if contained in a contract under seal made by the surety or sureties with every such person and, where there are two or more sureties, as if they had bound themselves jointly and severally.

(3) No action shall be brought on any such guarantee without the leave of the High Court.

(4) Stamp duty shall not be chargeable on any such guarantee.

(5) This section does not apply where administration is granted to the Treasury Solicitor, the Official Solicitor, the Public Trustee, the Solicitor for the affairs of the Duchy of Lancaster or the Duchy of Cornwall or the Crown Solicitor for Northern Ireland, or to the consular officer of a foreign state to which section 1 of the Consular Conventions Act 1949 applies, or in such other cases as may be prescribed.

Revocation of grants and cancellation of resealing at instance of court

Revocation of grants and cancellation of resealing at instance of court

121.—(1) Where it appears to the High Court that a grant either ought not to have been made or contains an error, the court may call in the grant and, if satisfied that it would be revoked at the instance of a party interested, may revoke it.

(2) A grant may be revoked under subsection (1) without being called in, if it cannot be called in.

(3) Where it appears to the High Court that a grant released under the Colonial Probates Acts 1892 and 1927 ought not to have been resealed, the court may call in the relevant document and, if satisfied that the resealing would be cancelled at the instance of a party interested, may cancel the resealing.

In this and the following subsection "the relevant document" means the original grant or, where some other document was sealed by the court under those Acts, that document.

(4) A resealing may be cancelled under subsection (3) without the relevant document being called in, if it cannot be called in.

Ancillary powers of court

Examination of person with knowledge of testamentary document

122.—(1) Where it appears that there are reasonable grounds for believing that any person has knowledge of any document which is or purports to be a testamentary document, and the High Court may, whether or not any legal proceedings are pending, order him to attend for the purpose of being examined in open court.

(2) The court may—

    (*a*) require any person who is before it in compliance with an order under subsection (1) to answer any question relating to the document concerned; and

(b) if appropriate, order him to bring in the document in such manner as the court may direct.

(3) Any person who, having been required by the court to do so under this section, fails to attend for examination, answer any question or bring in any document shall be guilty of contempt of court.

Subpoena to bring in testamentary document

123. Where it appears that any person has in his possession, custody or power any document which is or purports to be a testamentary document, the High Court may, whether or not any legal proceedings are pending, issue a subpoena requiring him to bring in the document in such manner as the court may in the subpoena direct.

Provisions as to documents

Place for deposit of original wills and other documents

124. All original wills and other documents which are under the control of the High Court in the Principal Registry or in any district probate registry shall be deposited and preserved in such places as the Lord Chancellor may direct; and any wills or other documents so deposited shall, subject to the control of the High Court and to probate rules, be open to inspection.

Copies of wills and grants

125. An office copy, or a sealed and certified copy, of any will or part of a will open to inspection under section 124 or of any grant may, on payment of the prescribed fee, be obtained—

(a) from the registry in which in accordance with section 124 the will or documents relating to the grant are preserved; or

(b) where in accordance with that section the will or such documents are preserved in some place other than a registry, from the Principal Registry; or

(c) subject to the approval of the Senior Registrar of the Family Division, from the Principal Registry in any case where the will was proved in or the grant was issued from a district probate registry.

Depositories for wills of living persons

126.—[*Repealed by the Administration of Justice Act* 1982, *Sched.* 9].

Probate rules

Probate rules

127.—(1) The President of the Family Division may, with the concurrence of the Lord Chancellor, make rules of court (in this Part referred to as "probate rules") for regulating and prescribing the practice and procedure of the High Court with respect to non-contentious or common form probate business.

(2) Without prejudice to the generality of subsection (1), probate rules may make provision for regulating the classes of persons entitled to grants of probate or administration in particular circumstances and the relative priorities of their claims thereto.

(3) Probate rules shall be made by statutory instrument to annulment in pursuance of a resolution of either House of Parliament; and the Statutory Instruments Act 1946 shall apply to a statutory instrument containing probate rules in like manner as if they had been made by a Minister of the Crown.

Interpretation of Part V and other probate provisions

Interpretation of Part V and other probate provisions

128. In this Part, and in the other provisions of this Act relating to probate causes and matters, unless the context otherwise requires—

"administration" includes all letters of administration of the effects of deceased persons, whether with or without a will annexed, and whether granted for general, special or limited purposes;

"estate" means real and personal estate, and "real estate" includes—

(*a*) chattels real and land in possession, remainder or reversion and every interest in or over land to which the deceased person was entitled at the time of his death, and

(*b*) real estate held on trust or by way of mortgage or security, but not money to arise under a trust for sale of land, nor money secured or charged on land;

"grant" means a grant of probate or administration;

"non-contentious or common form probate business" means the business of obtaining probate and administration where there is no contention as to the right thereto, including—

(*a*) the passing of probates and administrations through the High Court in contentious cases where the contest has been terminated,

(*b*) all business of a non-contentious nature in matters of testacy and intestacy not being proceedings in any action, and

(*c*) the business of lodging caveats against the grant of probate or administration;

"Principal Registry" means the Principal Registry of the Family Division;

"probate rules" means the Public Trustee or a corporation either appointed by the court in any particular case to be a trustee or authorised by rules made under section 4(3) of the Public Trustee Act 1906 to act as a custodian trustee;

"will" includes a nuncupative will and any testamentary document of which probate may be granted.

ADMINISTRATION OF JUSTICE ACT 1982

(1982, c. 53)

ARRANGEMENT OF SECTIONS

*   *   *   *

PART IV

WILLS

Rectification and interpretation of wills

Registration of wills

International wills

*   *   *   *

Rectification and interpretation of wills

Rectification

20.—(1) If a court is satisfied that a will is so expressed that it fails to carry out the testator's intentions, in consequence—

    (*a*) of a clerical error; or

    (*b*) of a failure to understand his instructions,

it may order that the will shall be rectified so as to carry out his intentions.

(2) An application for an order under this section shall not, except with the permission of the court, be made after the end of the period of six months from the date on which representation with respect to the estate of the deceased is first taken out.

(3) The provisions of this section shall not render the personal representatives of a deceased person liable for having distributed any part of the estate of the deceased, after the end of the period of six months from the date on which representation with respect to the estate of the deceased is first taken out, on the ground that they ought to have taken into account the possibility that the court might permit the making of an application for an order under this section after the end of that period; but this subsection

shall not prejudice any power to recover, by reason of the making of an order under this section, any part of the estate so distributed.

(4) In considering for the purposes of this section when representation with respect to the estate of a deceased person was first taken out, a grant limited to settled land or to trust property shall be left out of account, and a grant limited to real estate or to personal estate shall be left out of account unless a grant limited to the remainder of the estate has previously been made or is made at the same time.

Interpretation of wills—general rules as to evidence

21.—(1) This section applies to a will—

    (*a*) in so far as any part of it is meaningless;

    (*b*) in so far as the language used in any part of it is ambiguous on the face of it;

    (*c*) in so far as evidence, other than evidence of the testator's intention, shows that the language used in any part of it is ambiguous in the light of surrounding circumstances.

(2) In so far as this section applies to a will extrinsic evidence, including evidence of the testator's intention, may be admitted to assist in its interpretation.

Presumption as to effect of gifts to spouses

22. Except where a contrary intention is shown it shall be presumed that if a testator devises or bequeaths property to his spouse in terms which in themselves would give an absolute interest to the spouse, but by the same instrument purports to give his issue an interest in the same property, the gift to the spouse is absolute notwithstanding the purported gift to the issue.

Registration of wills

Deposit and registration of wills of living persons

23.—(1) The following, namely—

    (*a*) the Principal Registry of the Family Division of the High Court of Justice;

    (*b*) (*applies to Scotland only*); and

    (*c*) the Probate and Matrimonial Office of the Supreme Court of Northern Ireland,

shall be registering authorities for the purposes of this section.

(2) Each registering authority shall provide and maintain safe and convenient depositories for the custody of the wills of living persons.

(3) Any person may deposit his will in such a depository in accordance with regulations under section 25 below and on payment of the prescribed fee.

(4) It shall be the duty of a registering authority to register in accordance with regulations under section 25 below—

   (*a*) any will deposited in a depository maintained by the authority; and
   (*b*) any other will whose registration is requested under Article 6 of the Registration Convention.

(5) A will deposited in a depository provided—

   (*a*) under section 172 of the Supreme Court of Judicature (Consolidation) Act 1925 or section 126 of the Supreme Court Act 1981; or
   (*b*) under Article 27 of the Administration of Estates (Northern Ireland) Order 1979,

shall be treated for the purposes of this section as if it had been deposited under this section.

(6) In this section "prescribed" means—

   (*a*) in the application of this section to England and Wales, prescribed by an order under section 130 of the Supreme Court Act 1981;
   (*b*) (*applies to Scotland only*); and
   (*c*) in its application to Northern Ireland, prescribed by an order under section 116 of the Judicature (Northern Ireland) Act 1978.

Designation of Principal Registry as national body under Registration Convention

24.—(1) The Principal Registry of the Family Division of the High Court of Justice shall be the national body for the purposes of the Registration Convention, and shall accordingly have the functions assigned to the national body by the Registration Convention including, without prejudice to the general application of the Convention to the Principal Registry by virtue of this section, the functions—

   (*a*) of arranging for the registration of wills in other Contracting States as provided for in Article 6 of the Convention;
   (*b*) of receiving and answering requests for information arising from the national bodies of other Contracting States.

(2) In this Part of this Act "the Registration Convention" means the Convention on the Establishment of a Scheme of Registration of Wills concluded at Basle on May 16, 1972.

Regulations as to deposit and registration of wills etc.

25.—(1) Regulations may make provision—

   (*a*) as to the conditions for the deposit of a will;

(*b*) as to the manner of and procedure for—
   (i) the deposit and registration of a will; and
   (ii) the withdrawal of a will which has been deposited; and
   (iii) the cancellation of the registration of a will; and
(*c*) as to the manner in which the Principal Registry of the Family Division is to perform its functions as the national body under the Registration Convention.

(2) Regulations under this section may contain such incidental or supplementary provisions as the authority making the regulations considers appropriate.

(3) Any such regulations are to be made—

(*a*) for England and Wales, by the President of the Family Division of the High Court of Justice, with the concurrence of the Lord Chancellor;
(*b*) (*applies to Scotland only*); and
(*c*) for Northern Ireland, by the Northern Ireland Supreme Court Rules Committee, with the concurrence of the Lord Chancellor.

(4) Regulations made by virtue of subsection (1)(*c*) above shall be made by the Lord Chancellor.

(5) Subject to subsection (6) below, regulations under this section shall be made by statutory instrument and shall be laid before Parliament after being made.

(6) Regulations for Northern Ireland shall be statutory rules for the purposes of the Statutory Rules (Northern Ireland) Order 1979; and any such statutory rule shall be laid before Parliament after being made in like manner as a statutory instrument and section 4 of the Statutory Instruments Act 1946 shall apply accordingly.

(7) The Statutory Instruments Act 1946 shall apply to a statutory instrument containing regulations made in accordance with subsection (3)(*a*) or (*c*) above as if the regulations had been made by a Minister of the Crown.

(8) Any regulations made under section 172 of the Supreme Court of Judicature (Consolidation) Act 1925 or section 126 of the Supreme Court Act 1981 shall have effect for the purposes of this Part of this Act as they have effect for the purposes of the enactment under which they were made.

26. (*Applies to Scotland only*).

International wills

The form of an international will

27.—(1) The Annex to the Convention on International Wills shall have the force of law in the United Kingdom.

(2) The Annex is set out in Schedule 2 to this Act.

(3) In this Part of this Act—

"international will" means a will made in accordance with the requirements of the Annex, as set out in Schedule 2 to this Act; and

"the Convention on International Wills" means the Convention providing a Uniform Law on the Form of an International Will concluded at Washington on October 26, 1973.

International wills—procedure

28.—(1) The persons authorised to act in the United Kingdom in connection with international wills are—

(*a*) solicitors; and

(*b*) notaries public.

(2) A person who is authorised under section 6(1) of the Commissioners for Oaths Act 1889 to do notarial acts in any foreign country or place is authorised to act there in connection with international wills.

(3) An international will certified by virtue of subsection (1) or (2) above may be deposited in a depository provided under section 23 above.

(4) Section 23 above shall accordingly have effect in relation to such international wills.

(5) Subject to subsection (6) below, regulations under section 25 above shall have effect in relation to such international wills as they have effect in relation to wills deposited under section 23 above.

(6) Without prejudice to the generality of section 25 above, regulations under that section may make special provision with regard to such international wills.

(7) In section 10 of the Consular Relations Act 1968 (by virtue of which diplomatic agents and consular officials may administer oaths and do notarial acts in certain cases)—

(*a*) at the end of subsection (1)(*b*) there shall be added the words "or (*c*) in connection with an international will."; and

(*b*) at the end of subsection (4) there shall be added the words "and 'international will' has the meaning assigned to it by section 27 of the Administration of Justice Act 1982."

FORFEITURE ACT 1982

(1982, c. 34)

*   *   *   *

The "forfeiture rule"

1.—(1) In this Act, the "forfeiture rule" means the rule of public policy which in certain circumstances precludes a person who has unlawfully killed another from acquiring a benefit in consequence of the killing.

(2) References in this Act to a person who has unlawfully killed another include a reference to a person who has unlawfully aided, abetted, counselled or procured the death of that other and references in this Act to unlawful killing shall be interpreted accordingly.

Power to modify the rule

2.—(1) Where a court determines that the forfeiture rule has precluded a person (in this section referred to as "the offender") who has unlawfully killed another from acquiring any interest in property mentioned in subsection (4) below, the court may make an order under this section modifying the effect of that rule.

(2) The court shall not make an order under this section modifying the effect of the forfeiture rule in any case unless it is satisfied that, having regard to the conduct of the offender and of the deceased and to such other circumstances as appear to the court to be material, the justice of the case requires the effect of the rule to be so modified in that case.

(3) In any case where a person stands convicted of an offence of which unlawful killing is an element, the court shall not make an order under this section modifying the effect of the forfeiture rule in that case unless proceedings for the purpose are brought before the expiry of the period of three months beginning with his conviction.

(4) The interests in property referred to in subsection (1) above are—

    (*a*) any beneficial interest in property which (apart from the forfeiture rule) the offender would have acquired—

        (i) under the deceased's will (including, as respects Scotland,

any writing having testamentary effect) or the law relating to
intestacy or by way of ius relicti, ius relictae or legitim;

(ii) on the nomination or the deceased in accordance with the
provisions of any enactment;

(iii) as a donatio mortis causa made by the deceased; or

(iv) under a special destination (whether relating to heritable or
moveable property); or

(b) any beneficial interest in property which (apart from the forfeiture rule) the offender would have acquired in consequence of
the death of the deceased, being property which, before the
death, was held on trust for any person.

(5) An order under this section may modify the effect of the forfeiture
rule in respect of any interest in property to which the determination
referred to in subsection (1) above relates and may do so in either or both
of the following ways, that is—

(a) where there is more than one such interest, by excluding the
application of the rule in respect of any (but not all) of those
interests; and

(b) in the case of any such interest in property, by excluding the
application of the rule in respect of part of the property.

(6) On the making of an order under this section, the forfeiture rule
shall have effect for all purposes (including purposes relating to anything
done before the order is made) subject to the modifications made by the
order.

(7) The court shall not make an order under this section modifying the
effect of the forfeiture rule in respect of any interest in property which, in
consequence of the rule, has been acquired before the coming into force of
this section by a person other than the offender or a person claiming
through him.

(8) In this section—

"property" includes any chose in action or incorporeal moveable
property; and
"will" includes codicil.

Application for financial provision not affected by the rule

3.—(1) The forfeiture rule shall not be taken to preclude any person
from making any application under a provision mentioned in subsection (2)
below or the making of any order on the application.

(2) The provision referred to in subsection (1) above are—

(a) any provision of the Inheritance (Provision for Family and
Dependants) Act 1975; and

(b) sections 31(6) (variation etc. of periodical payments orders)
and 36(1) (variation of maintenance agreements) of the Matri-

monial Causes Act 1973 and section 5(4) of the Divorce (Scotland) Act 1976 (variation etc. of periodical allowances).

Commissioner to decide whether rule applies to social security benefits

4.—(1) Where a question arises as to whether, if a person were otherwise entitled to or eligible for any benefit or advantage under a relevant enactment, he would be precluded by virtue of the forfeiture rule from receiving the whole or part of the benefit or advantage, that question shall (notwithstanding anything in any relevant enactment) be determined by a Commissioner.

"(1A) Where a Commissioner determines that the forfeiture rule has precluded a person (in this section referred to as 'the offender') who has unlawfully killed another from receiving the whole or part of any such benefit or advantage, the Commissioner may make a decision under this subsection modifying the effect of that rule and may do so whether the unlawful killing occurred before or after the coming into force of this subsection.

(1B) The Commissioner shall not make a decision under subsection (1A) above modifying the effect of the forfeiture rule in any case unless he is satisfied that, having regard to the conduct of the offender and of the deceased and to such other circumstances as appear to the Commissioner to be material, the justice of the case requires the effect of the rule to be so modified in that case.

(1C) Subject to subsection (1D) below, a decision under subsection (1A) above may modify the effect of the forfeiture rule in either or both of the following ways—

    (*a*) so that it applies only in respect of a specified proportion of the benefit or advantage;

    (*b*) so that it applies in respect of the benefit or advantage only for a specified period of time.

(1D) Such a decision may not modify the effect of the forfeiture rule so as to allow any person to receive the whole or any part of a benefit or advantage in respect of any period before the commencement of this subsection.

(1E) If the Commissioner thinks it expedient to do so, he may direct that his decision shall apply to any future claim for a benefit or advantage under a relevant enactment, on which a question such as is mentioned in subsection (1) above arises by reason of the same unlawful killing.

(1F) It is immaterial for the purposes of subsection (1E) above whether the claim is in respect of the same or a different benefit or advantage.

(1G) For the purpose of obtaining a decision whether the forfeiture rule should be modified the Secretary of State may refer to a Commissioner for review any determination of a question such as is mentioned in subsection (1) above that was made before the commencement of subsections (1A) to

(1F) above (whether by a Commissioner or not) and shall do so if the offender requests him to refer such a determination.

(1H) Subsections (1A) to (1F) above shall have effect on a reference under subsection (1G) above as if in subsection (1A) the words 'it has been determined' were substituted for the words 'a Commissioner determines.' "

(2) Regulations under this section may make such provision as appears to the Secretary of State to be necessary or expedient for carrying this section into effect; and (without prejudice to the generality of that) the regulations may, in relation to the question mentioned in subsection (1) above or any determination under that subsection [or any decision under subsection (1A) above]—

> (a) apply any provision of any relevant enactment, with or without modifications, or exclude or contain provision corresponding to any such provision; and
> (b) make provision for purposes corresponding to those for which provision may be made by regulations under section 115 of the Social Security Act 1975 (matters relating to adjudication).

(3) The power to make regulations under this section shall be exercisable by statutory instrument which shall be subject to annulment in pursuance of a resolution of either House of Parliament.

(4) Section 166(2) [to (3A)] of the Social Security Act 1975 (provision about extent of power to make regulations) shall apply to the power to make regulations conferred by this section as it applies to the power to make regulations conferred by that Act, but as if for references to that Act there were substituted references to this section.

(5) In this section—

> "Commissioner" has the same meaning as in the Social Security Act 1975; and
> "relevant enactment" means any provision of the following and any instrument made by virtue of such a provision:
> > the Personal Injuries (Emergency Provisions) Act 1939,
> > the Pensions (Navy, Army, Air Force and Mercantile Marine) Act 1939,
> > the Polish Resettlement Act 1947,
> > [the Child Benefit Act 1975,
> > the Social Security Acts 1975 to 1986,]

and any other enactment relating to pensions or social security prescribed by regulations under this section.

AMENDMENTS

Subsections (1A)–(1H) were added by the Social Security Act 1986, s.76.
Subsection (2) was amended by the Social Security Act 1986, s.76(3).

Exclusion of murderers

5. Nothing in this Act or in any order made under section 2 or referred to in section 3(1) of this Act [or in any decision made under section 4(1A) of this Act] shall affect the application of the forfeiture rule in the case of a person who stands convicted of murder.

AMENDMENT

The words in square brackets were added by the Social Security Act 1986, s.76(4).

Corresponding provision for Northern Ireland

6. An Order in Council under paragraph 1(1)(*b*) of Schedule 1 to the Northern Ireland Act 1974 (legislation for Northern Ireland in the interim period) which contains a statement that it is made only for purposes corresponding to the purposes of this Act—

(*a*) shall not be subject to paragraph 1(4) and (5) of that Schedule (affirmative resolution of both Houses of Parliament); but

(*b*) shall be subject to annulment in pursuance of a resolution of either House.

Short title, etc.

7.—(1) This Act may be cited as the Forfeiture Act 1982.

(2) Section 4 of this Act shall come into force on such day as the Secretary of State may appoint by order made by statutory instrument; and sections 1 to 3 and 5 of this Act shall come into force on the expiry of the period of three months beginning with the day on which it is passed.

(3) This Act, except section 6, does not extend to Northern Ireland.

(4) Subject to section 2(7) of this Act, an order under section 2 of this Act or an order referred to in section 3(1) of this Act and made in respect of a person who has unlawfully killed another may be made whether the unlawful killing occurred before or after the coming into force of those sections.

ADMINISTRATION OF JUSTICE ACT 1985

(1985, c. 61)

ARRANGEMENT OF SECTIONS

*   *   *   *

PART IV

THE SUPREME COURT AND COUNTY COURTS

Proceedings relating to estates of deceased persons and trusts

*   *   *   *

PART IV

THE SUPREME COURT AND COUNTY COURTS

Proceedings relating to estates of deceased persons and trusts

Power of High Court to make judgments binding on persons who are not parties

47.—(1) This section applies to actions in the High Court relating to the estates of deceased persons or to trusts and falling within any description specified in rules of court.

(2) Rules of court may make provision for enabling any judgment given in an action to which this section applies to be made binding on persons who—

(*a*) are or may be affected by the judgment and would not otherwise be bound by it; but

(*b*) have in accordance with the rules been given notice of the action and of such matters connected with it as the rules may require.

(3) Different provision may be made under this section in relation to actions of different descriptions.

Power of High Court to authorise action to be taken in reliance on counsel's opinion

48.—(1) Where—

(*a*) any question of construction has arisen out of the terms of a will or a trust; and

(*b*) an opinion in writing given by a [person who has a 10 year High

Court qualification, within the meaning of section 71 of the Courts and Legal Services Act 1990] has been obtained on that question by the personal representatives or trustees under the will or trust,

the High Court may, on the application of the personal representatives or trustees and without hearing argument, make an order authorising those persons to take such steps in reliance on the said opinion as are specified in the order.

(2) The High Court shall not make an order under subsection (1) if it appears to the court that a dispute exists which would make it inappropriate for the court to make the order without hearing argument.

Powers of High Court on compromise of probate action

49.—(1) Where on a compromise of a probate action in the High Court—

>   (a) the court is invited to pronounce for the validity of one or more wills, or against the validity of one or more wills, or for the validity of one or more wills and against the validity of one or more other wills; and
>   (b) the court is satisfied that consent to the making of the pronouncement or, as the case may be, each of the pronouncements in question has been given by or on behalf of every relevant beneficiary,

the court may without more pronounce accordingly.

(2) In this section—

> "probate action" means an action for the grant of probate of the will, or letters of administration of the estate, of a deceased person or for the revocation of such a grant or for a decree pronouncing for or against the validity of an alleged will, not being an action which is non-contentious or common form probate business; and
> "relevant beneficiary," in relation to a pronouncement relating to any will or wills of a deceased person, means—
>   (a) a person who under any such will is beneficially interested in the deceased's estate; and
>   (b) where the effect of the pronouncement would be to cause the estate to devolve as on an intestacy (or partial intestacy), or to prevent it from so devolving, a person who under the law relating to intestacy is beneficially interested in the estate.

Power of High Court to appoint substitute for, or to remove, personal representative

50.—(1) Where an application relating to the estate of a deceased person is made to the High Court under this subsection by or on behalf of a personal representative of the deceased or a beneficiary of the estate, the court may in its discretion—

(a) appoint a person (in this section called a substituted personal representative) to act as personal representative of the deceased in place of the existing personal representative or representatives of the deceased or any of them; or

(b) if there are two or more existing personal representatives of the deceased, terminate the appointment of one or more, but not all, of those persons.

(2) Where the court appoints a person to act as a substituted personal representative of a deceased person, then—

(a) if that person is appointed to act with an executor or executors the appointment shall (except for the purpose of including him in any chain of representation) constitute him executor of the deceased as from the date of the appointment; and

(b) in any other case the appointment shall constitute that person administrator of the deceased's estate as from the date of the appointment.

(3) The court may authorise a person appointed as a substituted personal representative to charge remuneration for his services as such, on such terms (whether or not involving the submission of bills of charges for taxation by the court) as the court may think fit.

(4) Where an application relating to the estate of a deceased person is made to the court under subsection (1), the court may, if it thinks fit, proceed as if the application were, or included, an application for the appointment under the Judicial Trustees Act 1896 of a judicial trustee in relation to that estate.

(5) In this section "beneficiary," in relation to the estate of a deceased person, means a person who under the will of the deceased or under the law relating to intestacy is beneficially interested in the estate.

(6) In section 1 of the Judicial Trustees Act 1896, after subsection (6) there shall be added—

"(7) Where an application relating to the estate of a deceased person is made to the court under this section, the court may, if it thinks fit, proceed as if the application were, or included, an application under section 50 of the Administration of Justice Act 1985 (power of High Court to appoint substitute for, or to remove, personal representative)."

Amendments relating to jurisdiction of county courts and district probate registrars in probate proceedings

51.—(1) [Substitutes the County Court Act 1984, s.32].

(2) In section 106 of the Supreme Court Act 1981 (grants by district probate registrars), subsections (2) to (4) shall be omitted.

FAMILY LAW REFORM ACT 1987

(1987, c. 42)

ARRANGEMENT OF SECTIONS

PART I

GENERAL PRINCIPLE

*   *   *   *

PART III

PROPERTY RIGHTS

*   *   *   *

PART I

GENERAL PRINCIPLE

General Principle

1.—(1) In this Act and enactments passed and instruments made after the coming into force of this section, references (however expressed) to any relationship between two persons shall, unless the contrary intention appears, be construed without regard to whether or not the father and mother of either of them, or the father and mother of any person through whom the relationship is deduced, have or had been married to each other at any time.

(2) In this Act and enactments passed after the coming into force of this section, unless the contrary intention appears—

(*a*) references to a person whose father and mother were married to each other at the time of his birth include; and

(*b*) references to a person whose father and mother were not married to each other at the time of his birth do not include,

references to any person to whom subsection (3) below applies, and cognate references shall be construed accordingly.

(3) This subsection applies to any person who—

(*a*) is treated as legitimate by virtue of section 1 of the Legitimacy Act 1976;

(*b*) is a legitimated person within the meaning of section 10 of that Act;

(*c*) is an adopted child within the meaning of Part IV of the Adoption Act 1976; or

(*d*) is otherwise treated in law as legitimate.

(4) For the purpose of construing references falling within subsection (2) above, the time of a person's birth shall be taken to include any time during the period beginning with—

> (a) the insemination resulting in his birth; or
> (b) where there was no such insemination, his conception,

and (in either case) ending with his birth.

*   *   *   *

Part III

PROPERTY RIGHTS

Succession on intestacy

18.—(1) In Part IV of the Administration of Estates Act 1925 (which deals with the distribution of the estate of an intestate), references (however expressed) to any relationship between two persons shall be construed in accordance with section 1 above.

(2) For the purposes of subsection (1) above and that Part of that Act, a person whose father and mother were not married to each other at the time of his birth shall be presumed not to have been survived by his father, or by any person related to him only through his father, unless the contrary is shown.

(3) In section 50(1) of that Act (which relates to the construction of documents), the reference to Part IV of that Act, or to the foregoing provisions of that Part, shall in relation to an instrument inter vivos made, or a will or codicil coming into operation, after the coming into force of this section (but not in relation to instruments inter vivos made or wills or codicils coming into operation earlier) be construed as including references to this section.

(4) This section does not affect any rights under the intestacy of a person dying before the coming into force of this section.

Dispositions of property

19.—(1) In the following dispositions, namely—

> (a) dispositions inter vivos made on or after the date on which this section comes into force; and
> (b) dispositions by will or codicil where the will or codicil is made on or after that date,

references (whether express or implied) to any relationship between two persons shall be construed in accordance with section 1 above.

(2) It is hereby declared that the use, without more, of the word "heir" or "heirs" or any expression which is used to create an entailed interest in real or personal property does not show a contrary intention for the purposes of section 1 as applied by subsection (1) above.

(3) In relation to the dispositions mentioned in subsection (1) above, section 33 of the Trustee Act 1925 (which specifies the trust implied by a direction that income is to be held on protective trusts for the benefit of any person)

shall have effect as if any reference (however expressed) to any relationship between two persons were construed in accordance with section 1 above.

(4) Where under any disposition of real or personal property, any interest in such property is limited (whether subject to any preceding limitation or charge or not) in such a way that it would, apart from this section, devolve (as nearly as the law permits) along with a dignity or title of honour, then—

(*a*) whether or not the disposition contains an express reference to the dignity or title of honour; and

(*b*) whether or not the property or some interest in the property may in some event become severed from it,

nothing in this section shall operate to sever the property or any interest in it from the dignity or title, but the property or interest shall devolve in all respects as if this section had not been enacted.

(5) This section is without prejudice to section 42 of the Adoption Act 1976 (construction of dispositions in cases of adoption).

(6) In this section "disposition" means a disposition, including an oral disposition, of real or personal property whether inter vivos or by will or codicil.

(7) Notwithstanding any rule of law, a disposition made by will or codicil executed before the date on which this section comes into force shall not be treated for the purposes of this section as made on or after that date by reason only that the will or codicil is confirmed by a codicil executed on or after that date.

No special protection for trustees and personal representatives

20. Section 17 of the Family Law Reform Act 1969 (which enables trustees and personal representatives to distribute property without having ascertained that no person whose parents were not married to each other at the time of his birth, or who claims through such a person, is or may be entitled to an interest in the property) shall cease to have effect.

Entitlement to grant of probate etc.

21.—(1) For the purpose of determining the person or persons who would in accordance with probate rules be entitled to a grant of probate or administration in respect of the estate of a deceased person, the deceased shall be presumed, unless the contrary is shown, not to have been survived—

(*a*) by any person related to him whose father and mother were not married to each other at the time of his birth; or

(*b*) by any person whose relationship with him is deduced through such a person as is mentioned in paragraph (*a*) above.

(2) In this section "probate rules" means rules of court made under section 127 of the Supreme Court Act 1981.

(3) This section does not apply in relation to the estate of a person dying before the coming into force of this section.

INTESTATES' ESTATES ACT 1952
(15 & 16 Geo. 6 & 1 Eliz. 2, c. 64)

PART I

1–4. [*These sections amend the Administration of Estates Act 1925, ss. 46–49, ante, pp. 1011–1017.*]

Rights of surviving spouse as respects the matrimonial home
5. The Second Schedule to this Act shall have effect for enabling the surviving husband or wife of a person dying intestate after the commencement of this Act to acquire the matrimonial home.

6. [*Interpretation and construction.*]

PART III

Short title and commencement
9.—(1) This Act may be cited as the Intestates' Estates Act 1952.

(2) This Act shall come into operation on the first day of January, 1953.

FIRST SCHEDULE

[*This Schedule sets out ss. 46–49 of the Administration of Estates Act 1925, ante, pp. 1011–1017, as amended by Part I of this Act.*]

Section 5   SECOND SCHEDULE

Rights of Surviving Spouse as respects the Matrimonial Home

1.—(1) Subject to the provisions of this Schedule, where the residuary estate of the intestate comprises an interest in a dwelling-house in which the surviving husband or wife was resident at the time of the intestate's death, the surviving husband or wife may require the personal representative, in exercise of the power conferred by section forty-one of the principal Act (and with due regard to the requirements of that section as to valuation) to appropriate the said interest in the dwelling-house in or towards satisfaction of any absolute interest of the surviving husband or wife in the real and personal estate of the intestate.

(2) The right conferred by this paragraph shall not be exercisable where the interest is—
  (*a*) a tenancy which at the date of the death of the intestate was a tenancy which would determine within the period of two years from that date; or
  (*b*) a tenancy which the landlord by notice given after that date could determine within the remainder of that period.

(3) Nothing in subsection (5) of section 41 of the principal Act (which requires the personal representative, in making an appropriation to any person under that section, to have regard to the rights of others) shall prevent the personal representative from giving effect to the right conferred by this paragraph.

(4) The reference in this paragraph to an absolute interest in the real and personal estate of the intestate includes a reference to the capital value of a life interest which the surviving husband or wife has under this Act elected to have redeemed.

(5) Where part of a building was, at the date of the death of the intestate, occupied as a separate dwelling, that dwelling shall for the purposes of this Schedule be treated as a dwelling-house.

2. Where—
  (*a*) the dwelling-house forms part of a building and an interest in the whole of the building is comprised in the residuary estate; or
  (*b*) the dwelling-house is held with agricultural land and an interest in the agricultural land is comprised in the residuary estate; or
  (*c*) the whole or a part of the dwelling-house was at the time of the intestate's death used as a hotel or lodging house; or
  (*d*) a part of the dwelling-house was at the time of the intestate's death used for purposes other than domestic purposes.
the right conferred by paragraph 1 of this Schedule shall not be exercisable unless the court, on being satisfied that the exercise of that right is not likely to diminish the value of assets in the residuary estate (other than the said interest in the dwelling-house) or make them more difficult to dispose of, so orders.

GENERAL NOTE

Sub-para. (2) does not apply in certain cases: Leasehold Reform Act 1967 (c.88), s.7(8).

3.—(1) The right conferred by paragraph 1 of this Schedule—

(a) shall not be exercisable after the expiration of 12 months from the first taking out of representation with respect to the intestate's estate;

(b) shall not be exercisable after the death of the surviving husband or wife;

(c) shall be exercisable, except where the surviving husband or wife is the sole personal representative, by notifying the personal representative (or, where there are two or more personal representatives of whom one is the surviving husband or wife, all of them except the surviving husband or wife) in writing.

(2) A notification in writing under paragraph (c) of the foregoing sub-paragraph shall not be revocable except with the consent of the personal representative; but the surviving husband or wife may require the personal representative to have the said interest in the dwelling-house valued in accordance with section 41 of the principal Act and to inform him or her of the result of that valuation before he or she decides whether to exercise the right.

(3) Subsection (9) of the section 47 A added to the principal Act by section 2 of this Act shall apply for the purposes of the construction of the reference in this paragraph to the first taking out of representation, and the proviso to subsection (5) of that section shall apply for the purpose of enabling the surviving husband or wife to apply for an extension of the period of 12 months mentioned in this paragraph.

4.—(1) During the period of 12 months mentioned in paragraph 3 of this Schedule the personal representative shall not without the written consent of the surviving husband or wife sell or otherwise dispose of the said interest in the dwelling-house except in the course of administration owing to want of other assets.

(2) An application to the court under paragraph 2 of this Schedule may be made by the personal representative as well as by the surviving husband or wife, and if, on an application under that paragraph, the court does not order that the right conferred by paragraph 1 of this Schedule shall be exercisable by the surviving husband or wife, the court may authorise the personal representative to dispose of the said interest in the dwelling-house within the said period of 12 months.

(3) Where the court under sub-paragraph (3) of paragraph 3 of this Schedule extends the said period of twelve months, the court may direct that this paragraph shall apply in relation to the extended period as it applied in relation to the original period of twelve months.

(4) This paragraph shall not apply where the surviving husband or wife is the sole personal representative or one of two or more personal representatives.

(5) Nothing in this paragraph shall confer any right on the surviving husband or wife as against a purchaser from the personal representative.

5.—(1) Where the surviving husband or wife is one of two or more personal representatives, the rule that a trustee may not be a purchaser of trust property shall not prevent the surviving husband or wife from purchasing out of the estate of the intestate an interest in a dwelling-house in which the surviving husband or wife was resident at the time of the intestate's death.

(2) The power of appropriation under section 41 of the principal Act shall include power to appropriate an interest in a dwelling-house in which the surviving husband or wife was resident at the time of the intestate's death partly in satisfaction of an interest of the surviving husband or wife in the real and personal estate of the intestate and partly in return for a payment of money by the surviving husband or wife to the personal representative.

6.—(1) Where the surviving husband or wife is a person of unsound mind or a defective, a requirement or consent under this Schedule may be made or given on his or her behalf by the committee or receiver, if any, or, where there is no committee or receiver, by the court.

(2) A requirement or consent made or given under this Schedule by a surviving husband or wife who is an infant shall be as valid and binding as it would be if he or she were of age; and, as respects an appropriation in pursuance of paragraph 1 of this Schedule, the provisions of section 41 of the principal Act as to obtaining the consent of the infant's parent or guardian, or of the court on behalf of the infant, shall not apply.

7.—(1) Except where the context otherwise requires, references in this Schedule to a dwelling-house include references to any garden or portion of ground attached to and usually occupied with the dwelling-house or otherwise required for the amenity or convenience of the dwelling-house.

(2) This Schedule shall be construed as one with Part IV of the principal Act.

THIRD SCHEDULE

[*This Schedule amended the Inheritance (Family Provision) Act 1938.*]

FOURTH SCHEDULE

[*Repealed by the Family Provision Act 1966, Sched. 2.*]

Appendix Two

RULES AND ORDERS

NON-CONTENTIOUS PROBATE RULES 1987

(S.I. 1987 No. 2024 (L.10))
(As amended by S.I. 1991 No. 1876 (c. 26))

ARRANGEMENT OF RULES

SCHEDULES

The President of the Family Division, in exercise of the powers conferred upon him by section 127 of the Supreme Court Act 1981, and section 2(5) of the Colonial Probates Act 1892, and with the concurrence of the Lord Chancellor, hereby makes the following Rules:

Citation and commencement

1. These Rules may be cited as the Non-Contentious Probate Rules 1987 and shall come into force on January 1, 1988.

Interpretation

2.—(1) In these Rules, unless the context otherwise requires—

"the Act" means the Supreme Court Act 1981;
"Authorised officer" means any officer of a registry who is for the time being authorised by the President to administer any oath or to take any affidavit required for any purpose connected with his duties;
"the Crown" includes the Crown in right of the Duchy of the Lancaster and the Duke of Cornwall for the time being;
"district judge" means a district judge of the Principal Registry;
"grant" means a grant of probate or administration and includes, where the context so admits, the resealing of such a grant under the Colonial Probates Acts 1892 and 1927;
"gross value" in relation to any estate means the value of the estate without deduction for debts, incumbrances, funeral expenses or inheritance tax (or other capital tax payable out of the estate);

"judge" means a judge of the High Court;

"oath" means the oath required by rule 8 to be sworn by every applicant for a grant;

"personal applicant" means a person other than a trust corporation who seeks to obtain a grant without employing a solicitor, and "personal application" has a corresponding meaning;

"registrar" means the district probate registrar of the district probate registry—

(i) to which an application for a grant is made or proposed to be made;

(ii) in rules 26, 40, 41 and 61(2) from which the grant issued, and

(iii) in rules 46, 47 and 48 from which the citation has issued or is proposed to be issued;

the registrar of that district probate registry;

"registry" means the Principal Registry or a district probate registry;

"the senior district judge" means the Senior District Judge of the Family Division or, in his absence, the senior of the district judges in attendance at the Principal Registry;

"the Treasury Solicitor" means the solicitor for the affairs of Her Majesty's Treasury and includes the solicitor for the affairs of the Duchy of Lancaster and the solicitor of the Duchy of Cornwall;

"trust corporation" means a corporation within the meaning of section 128 of the Act as extended by section 3 of the Law of Property (Amendment) Act 1926.

(2) A form referred to by number means the form so numbered in the First Schedule; and such forms shall be used wherever applicable, with such variation as a registrar may in any particular case direct or approve.

Application of other rules

3. Subject to the provisions of these Rules and to any enactment, the Rules of the Supreme Court 1965 shall apply, with the necessary modifications, to non-contentious probate matters, save that nothing in Order 3 shall prevent time from running in the Long Vacation.

Application for grants through solicitors

4.—(1) A person applying for a grant through a solicitor may apply at any registry or sub-registry.

(2) Every solicitor through whom an application for a grant is made shall give the address of his place of business within England and Wales.

Personal applications

5.—(1) A personal applicant may apply for a grant at any registry or sub-registry.

(2) Save as provided for by rule 39 a personal applicant may not apply

through an agent, whether paid or unpaid, and may not be attended by any person acting or appearing to act as his adviser.

(3) No personal application shall be proceeded with if—

(a) it becomes necessary to bring the matter before the court by action or summons;

(b) an application has already been made by a solicitor on behalf of the applicant and has not been withdrawn; or

(c) the district judge or registrar so directs.

(4) After a will has been deposited in a registry by a personal applicant, it may not be delivered to the applicant or to any other person unless in special circumstances the district judge or registrar so directs.

(5) A personal applicant shall produce a certificate of the death of the deceased or such other evidence of the death as the district judge or registrar may approve.

(6) A personal applicant shall supply all information necessary to enable the papers leading to the grant to be prepared in the registry.

(7) Unless the district judge or registrar otherwise directs, every oath or affidavit required on a personal application shall be sworn or executed by all the deponents before an authorised officer.

(8) No legal advice shall be given to a personal applicant by an officer of a registry and every such officer shall be responsible only for embodying in proper form the applicant's instructions for the grant.

Duty of district judge or registrar on receiving application for grant

6.—(1) A district judge or registrar shall not allow any grant to issue until all inquiries which he may see fit to make have been answered to his satisfaction.

(2) Except with the leave of a district judge or registrar, no grant of probate or of administration with the will annexed shall issue within seven days of the death of the deceased and no grant of administration shall issue within fourteen days thereof.

Grants by registrars

7.—(1) No grant shall be made by a registrar—

(a) in any case in which there is contention, until the contention is disposed of; or

(b) in any case in which it appears to him that a grant ought not to be made without the directions of a judge or a district judge.

(2) In any case in which paragraph (1)(b) applies, the registrar shall send a statement of the matter in question to the Principal Registry for directions.

(3) A district judge may either confirm that the matter be referred to a

judge and give directions accordingly or may direct the registrar to proceed with the matter in accordance with such instructions as are deemed necessary, which may include a direction to take no further action in relation to the matter.

Oath in support of grant

8.—(1) Every application for a grant other than one to which rule 39 applies shall be supported by an oath by the applicant in the form applicable to the circumstances of the case, and by such other papers as the district judge or registrar may require.

(2) Unless otherwise directed by a district judge or registrar, the oath shall state where the deceased died domiciled.

(3) Where the deceased died on or after January 1, 1926, the oath shall state whether or not, to the best of the applicant's knowledge, information and belief, there was land vested in the deceased which was settled previously to his death and not by his will and which remained settled land notwithstanding his death.

(4) On an application for a grant of administration the oath shall state in what manner all persons having a prior right to a grant have been cleared off and whether any minority or life interest arises under the will or intestacy.

Grant in additional name

9. Where it is sought to describe the deceased in a grant by some name in addition to his true name, the applicant shall depose to the true name of the deceased and shall specify some part of the estate which was held in the other name, or give any other reason for the inclusion of the other name in the grant.

Marking of wills

10. —(1) Subject to paragraph (2) below, every will in respect of which an application for a grant is made—

(*a*) shall be marked by the signatures of the applicant and the person before whom the oath is sworn; and

(*b*) shall be exhibited to any affidavit which may be required under these Rules as to the validity, terms, condition or date of execution of the will.

(2) The district judge or registrar may allow a facsimile copy of a will to be marked or exhibited in lieu of the original document.

Engrossments for purposes of record

11.—(1) Where the district judge or registrar considers that in any particular case a facsimile copy of the original will would not be satisfactory for purposes of record, he may require an engrossment suitable for facsimile reproduction to be lodged.

(2) Where a will—

    (*a*) contains alterations which are not to be admitted to proof; or

    (*b*) has been ordered to be rectified by virtue of section 20(1) of the Administration of Justice Act 1982,

there shall be lodged an engrossment of the will in the form in which it is to be proved.

(3) Any engrossment lodged under this rule shall reproduce the punctuation, spacing and division into paragraphs of the will and shall follow continuously from page to page on both sides of the paper.

Evidence as to due execution of will

12.—(1) Subject to paragraphs (2) and (3) below, where a will contains no attestation clause or the attestation clause is insufficient, or where it appears to the district judge or registrar that there is doubt about the due execution of the will, he shall before admitting it to proof require an affidavit as to due execution from one or more of the attesting witnesses or, if no attesting witness is conveniently available, from any other person who was present when the will was executed; and if the district judge or registrar, after considering the evidence, is satisfied that the will was not duly executed, he shall refuse probate and mark the will accordingly.

(2) If no affidavit can be obtained in accordance with paragraph (1) above, the district judge or registrar may accept evidence on affidavit from any person he may think fit to show that the signature on the will is in the handwriting of the deceased, or of any other matter which may raise a presumption in favour of due execution of the will, and may if he thinks fit require that notice of the application be given to any person who may be prejudiced by the will.

(3) A district judge or registrar may accept a will for proof without evidence as aforesaid if he is satisfied that the distribution of the estate is not thereby affected.

Execution of will of blind or illiterate testator

13. Before admitting to proof a will which appears to have been signed by a blind or illiterate testator or by another person by direction of the testator, or which for any other reason raises doubt as to the testator having had knowledge of the contents of the will at the time of its execution, the district judge or registrar shall satisfy himself that the testator had such knowledge.

Evidence as to terms, condition and date of execution of will

14.—(1) Subject to paragraph (2) below, where there appears in a will any obliteration, interlineation, or other alteration which is not authenticated in the manner prescribed by section 21 of the Wills Act 1837, or by the re-execution of the will or by the execution of a codicil, the district judge or registrar shall require evidence to show whether the alteration was present at the time the will was executed and shall give directions as to the form in which the will is to be proved.

(2) The provisions of paragraph (1) above shall not apply to any alteration which appears to the district judge or registrar to be of no practical importance.

(3) If a will contains any reference to another document in such terms as to suggest that it ought to be incorporated in the will, the district judge or registrar shall require the document to be produced and may call for such evidence in regard to the incorporation of the document as he may think fit.

(4) Where there is a doubt as to the date on which a will was executed, district judge the registrar may require such evidence as he thinks necessary to establish the date.

Attempted revocation of will

15. Any appearance of attempted revocation of a will by burning, tearing, or otherwise destroying and every other circumstance leading to a presumption of revocation by the testator, shall be accounted for to the district judge or registrar's satisfaction.

Affidavit as to due execution, terms, etc., of will

16. A district judge or registrar may require an affidavit from any person he may think fit for the purpose of satisfying himself as to any of the matters referred to in rules 13, 14 and 15, and in any such affidavit sworn by an attesting witness or other person present at the time of the execution of a will the deponent shall depose to the manner in which the will was executed.

Wills proved otherwise than under section 9 of the Wills Act 1837

17.—(1) Rules 12 to 15 shall apply only to a will that is to be established by reference to section 9 of the Wills Act 1837 (signing and attestation of wills).

(2) A will that is to be established otherwise than as described in paragraph (1) of this rule may be so established upon the district judge or registrar being satisfied as to its terms and validity, and includes (without prejudice to the generality of the foregoing)—

(a) any will to which rule 18 applies; and
(b) any will which, by virtue of the Wills Act 1963, is to be treated as properly executed if executed according to the internal law of the territory or state referred to in section 1 of that Act.

Wills of persons on military service and seamen

18. Where the deceased died domiciled in England and Wales and it appears to the registrar that there is prima facie evidence that a will is one to which section 11 of the Wills Act 1837 applies, the will may be admitted to proof if the district judge or registrar is satisfied that it was signed by the testator or, if unsigned, that it is in the testator's handwriting.

Evidence of foreign law

19. Where evidence as to the law of any country or territory outside England and Wales is required on any application for a grant, the registrar may accept—

(*a*) an affidavit from any person whom, having regard to the particulars of his knowledge or experience given in the affidavit, he regards as suitably qualified to give expert evidence of the law in question; or

(*b*) a certificate by, or an act before, a notary practising in the country or territory concerned.

Order of priority for grant where deceased left a will

20. Where the deceased died on or after January 1, 1926 the person or persons entitled to a grant in respect of a will shall be determined in accordance with the following order of priority, namely—

(*a*) the executor (but subject to rule 36(4)(*d*) below);

(*b*) any residuary legatee or devisee holding in trust for any other person;

(*c*) any other residuary legatee or devisee (including one for life) or where the residue is not wholly disposed of by the will, any person entitled to share in the undisposed of residue (including the Treasury Solicitor when claiming bona vacantia on behalf of the Crown), provided that—

(i) unless a district judge or registrar otherwise directs, a residuary legatee or devisee whose legacy or devise is vested in interest shall be preferred to one entitled on the happening of a contingency, and

(ii) where the residue is not in terms wholly disposed of, the district judge or registrar may, if he is satisfied that the testator has nevertheless disposed of the whole or substantially the whole of the known estate, allow a grant to be made to any legatee or devisee entitled to, or to share in, the estate so disposed of, without regard to the persons entitled to share in any residue not disposed of by the will;

(*d*) the personal representative of any residuary legatee or devisee (but not one for life, or one holding in trust for any other person), or of any person entitled to share in any residue not disposed of by the will;

(e) any other legatee or devisee (including one for life or one holding in trust for any other person) or any creditor of the deceased, provided that, unless a district judge or registrar otherwise directs, a legatee or devisee whose legacy or devise is vested in interest shall be preferred to one entitled on the happening of a contingency;

(f) the personal representative of any other legatee or devisee (but not one for life or one holding in trust for any other person) or of any creditor of the deceased.

Grants to attesting witnesses, etc.

21. Where a gift to any person fails by reason of section 15 of the Wills Act 1837, such person shall not have any right to a grant as a beneficiary named in the will, without prejudice to his right to a grant in any other capacity.

Order of priority for grant in case of intestacy

22.—(1) Where the deceased died on or after January 1, 1926, wholly intestate, the person or persons having a beneficial interest in the estate shall be entitled to a grant of administration in the following classes in order of priority, namely—

(a) the surviving husband or wife;

(b) the children of the deceased and the issue of any deceased child who died before the deceased;

(c) the father and mother of the deceased;

(d) brothers and sisters of the whole blood and the issue of any deceased brother or sister of the whole blood who died before the deceased;

(e) brothers and sisters of the half blood and the issue of any deceased brother or sister of the half blood who died before the deceased;

(f) grandparents;

(g) uncles and aunts of the whole blood and the issue of any deceased uncle or aunt of the whole blood who died before the deceased;

(h) uncles and aunts of the half blood and the issue of any deceased uncle or aunt of the half blood who died before the deceased.

(2) In default of any person having a beneficial interest in the estate, the Treasury Solicitor shall be entitled to a grant if he claims bona vacantia on behalf of the Crown.

(3) If all persons entitled to a grant under the foregoing provisions of this rule have been cleared off, a grant may be made to a creditor of the deceased or to any person who, notwithstanding that he has no immediate beneficial interest in the estate, may have a beneficial interest in the event of an accretion thereto.

(4) Subject to paragraph (5) of rule 27, the personal representative of a person in any of the classes mentioned in paragraph (1) of this rule or the personal representative of a creditor of the deceased shall have the same right to a grant as the person whom he represents provided that the persons mentioned in sub-paragraphs (*b*) or (*h*) of paragraph (1) above shall be preferred to the personal representative of a spouse who has died without taking a beneficial interest in the whole estate of the deceased as ascertained at the time of the application for the grant.

Order of priority for grant to pre-1926 cases

23. Where the deceased died before January 1, 1926, the person or persons entitled to a grant shall, subject to the provisions of any enactment, be determined in accordance with the principles and rules under which the court would have acted at the date of death.

Right of assignee to a grant

24.—(1) Where all the persons entitled to the estate of the deceased (whether under a will or on intestacy) have assigned their whole interest in the estate to one or more persons, the assignee or assignees shall replace, in the order of priority for a grant of administration, the assignor or, if there are two or more assignors, the assignor with the highest priority.

(2) Where there are two or more assignees, administration may be granted with the consent of the others to any one or more (not exceeding four) of them.

(3) In any case where administration is applied for by an assignee the original instrument of assignment shall be produced and a copy of the same lodged in the registry.

Joinder of administrator

25.—(1) A person entitled in priority to a grant of administration may, without leave, apply for a grant with a person entitled in a lower degree, provided that there is no other person entitled in a higher degree to the person to be joined, unless every other such person has renounced.

(2) Subject to paragraph (3) below, an application for leave to join with a person entitled in priority to a grant of administration a person having no right or no immediate right thereto shall be made to a district judge or registrar, and shall be supported by an affidavit by the person entitled in priority, the consent of the person proposed to be joined as administrator and such other evidence as the district judge or registrar may direct.

(3) Unless a district judge or registrar otherwise directs, there may without any such application be joined with a person entitled in priority to administration—

    (*a*) any person who is nominated under paragraph (3) of rule 32 or paragraph (3) of rule 35;

    (*b*) a trust corporation.

Additional personal representatives

26.—(1) An application under section 114(4) of the Act to add a personal representative shall be made to a district judge or registrar and shall be supported by an affidavit by the applicant, the consent of the person proposed to be added as personal representative and such other evidence as the registrar may require.

(2) On any such application the district judge or registrar may direct that a note shall be made on the original grant of the addition of a further personal representative, or he may impound or revoke the grant or make such other order as the circumstances of the case may require.

Grants where two or more persons entitled in same degree

27.—(1) Subject to paragraphs (1A), (2) and (3) below, where, on an application for probate, power to apply for a like grant is to be reserved to such other of the executors as have not renounced probate, notice of the application shall be given to the executor or executors to whom power is to be reserved; and unless the district judge or registrar otherwise directs, the oath shall state that such notice has been given.

(1A) Where power is to be reserved to executors who are appointed by reference to their being partners in a firm, and not by their names, notice need not be given to them under paragraph (1) above if probate is applied for by another partner in that firm.

(2) Where power is to be reserved to partners of a firm, notice for the purposes of paragraph (1) above may be given to the partners by sending it to the firm at its principal or last known place of business.

(3) A district judge or registrar may dispense with the giving of notice under paragraph (1) above if he is satisfied that the giving of such a notice is impracticable or would result in unreasonable delay or expense.

(4) A grant of administration may be made to any person entitled thereto without notice to other persons entitled in the same degree.

(5) Unless a district judge or registrar otherwise directs, administration shall be granted to a person of full age entitled thereto in preference to a guardian of a minor, and to a living person entitled thereto in preference to the personal representative of a deceased person.

(6) A dispute between persons entitled to a grant in the same degree shall be brought by summons before a district judge or registrar.

(7) The issue of a summons under this rule in the Principal Registry or a district probate registry shall be notified forthwith to the registry in which the index of pending grant applications is maintained.

(8) If the issue of a summons under this rule is known to the district judge or registrar, he shall not allow any grant to be sealed until such summons is finally disposed of.

Exceptions to rules as to priority

28.—(1) Any person to whom a grant may or is required to be made under any enactment shall not be prevented from obtaining such a grant notwithstanding the operation of rules 20, 22, 25 or 27.

(2) Where the deceased died domiciled outside England and Wales rules 20, 22, 25 or 27 shall not apply except in a case to which paragraph (3) of rule 30 applies.

Grants in respect of settled land

29.—(1) In this rule "settled land" means land vested in the deceased which was settled previously to his death and not by his will and which remained settled land notwithstanding his death.

(2) The person or persons entitled to a grant of administration limited to settled land shall be determined in accordance with the following order of priority:

    (i) the special executors in regard to settled land constituted by section 22 of the Administration of Estates Act 1925;

    (ii) the trustees of the settlement at the time of the application for the grant; and

    (iii) the personal representatives of the deceased.

(3) Where there is settled land and a grant is made in respect of the free estate only, the grant shall expressly exclude the settled land.

Grants where deceased died domiciled outside England and Wales

30.—(1) Subject to paragraph (3) below, where the deceased died domiciled outside England and Wales, a district judge or registrar may order that a grant do issue limited in such a way as the district judge or registrar may direct to any of the following persons—

    (*a*) to the person entrusted with the administration of the estate by the court having jurisdiction at the place where the deceased died domiciled; or

    (*b*) where there is no person so entrusted, to the person beneficially entitled to the estate by the law of the place where the deceased died domiciled or, if there is more than one person so entitled, to such of them as the district judge or registrar may direct; or

    (*c*) if in the opinion of the registrar the circumstances so require, to such person as the district judge or registrar may direct.

(2) A grant made under paragraph (1)(*a*) or (*b*) above may be issued jointly with such person as the district judge or registrar may direct if the grant is required to be made to not less than two administrators.

(3) Without any order made under paragraph (1) above—

    (*a*) probate of any will which is admissible to proof may be granted—

(i) if the will is in the English or Welsh language, to the executor named therein; or

(ii) if the will describes the duties of a named person in terms sufficient to constitute him executor according to the tenor of the will, to that person; and

(b) where the whole or substantially the whole of the estate in England and Wales consists of immovable property, a grant in respect of the whole estate may be made in accordance with the law which would have been applicable if the deceased had died domiciled in England and Wales.

Grants to attorneys

31.—(1) Subject to paragraphs (2) and (3) below, the lawfully constituted attorney of a person entitled to a grant may apply for administration for the use and benefit of the donor, and such grant shall be limited until further representation be granted, or in such other way as the district judge or registrar may direct.

(2) Where the donor referred to in paragraph (1) above is an executor, notice of the application shall be given to any other executor unless such notice is dispensed with by the district judge or registrar.

(3) Where the donor referred to in paragraph (1) above is mentally incapable and the attorney is acting under an enduring power of attorney, the application shall be made in accordance with rule 35.

Grants on behalf of minors

32.—(1) Where a person to whom a grant would otherwise be made is a minor, administration for his use and benefit, limited until he attains the age of eighteen years, shall, unless otherwise directed, and subject to paragraph (2) of this rule, be granted to—

(a) a parent of the minor who has, or is deemed to have, parental responsibility for him in accordance with—
  (i) section 2(1), 2(2) or 4 of the Children Act 1989;
  (ii) paragraph 4 or 6 of Schedule 14 to that Act, or
  (iii) an adoption order within the meaning of section 12(1) of the Adoption Act 1976, or

(b) a guardian of the minor who is appointed, or deemed to have been appointed, or deemed to have been appointed, in accordance with section 5 of the Children Act 1989 or in accordance with paragraph 12, 13 or 14 of Schedule 14 to that Act,

provided that where the minor is sole executor and has no interest in the residuary estate of the deceased, administration for the use and benefit of the minor limited as aforesaid, shall, unless a district judge or registrar otherwise directs, be granted to the person entitled to the residuary estate.

(2) A district judge or registrar may by order appoint a person to obtain administration for the use and benefit of the minor, limited as aforesaid, in default of, or jointly with, or to the exclusion of, any person mentioned in paragraph (1) of this rule; and the intended shall file an affidavit in support of his application to be appointed.

(3) Where there is only one person competent and willing to take a grant under the foregoing provisions of this rule, such person may, unless a district judge or registrar otherwise directs, nominate any fit and proper person to act jointly with him in taking the grant.

Grants where a minor is a co-executor

33.—(1) Where a minor is appointed executor jointly with one or more other executors, probate may be granted to the executor or executors not under disability with power reserved to the minor executor, and the minor executor shall be entitled to apply for probate on attaining the age of eighteen years.

(2) Administration for the use and benefit of a minor executor until he attains the age of eighteen years may be granted under rule 32 if, and only if, the executors who are not under disability renounce or, on being cited to accept or refuse a grant, fail to make an effective application therefor.

Renunciation of the right of a minor to a grant

34.—(1) The right of a minor executor to probate on attaining the age of eighteen years may not be renounced by any person on his behalf.

(2) The right of a minor to administration may be renounced only by a person appointed under paragraph (2) of rule 32, and authorised by the district judge or registrar to renounce on behalf of the minor.

Grants in case of mental incapacity

35.—(1) Unless a district judge or registrar otherwise directs, no grant shall be made under this rule unless all persons entitled in the same degree as the incapable person referred to in paragraph (2) below have been cleared off.

(2) Where a district judge or registrar is satisfied that a person entitled to a grant is by reason of mental incapacity incapable of managing his affairs, administration for his use and benefit, limited until further representation be granted or in such other way as the district judge or registrar may direct, may be granted in the following order of priority—

    (*a*) to the person authorised by the Court of Protection to apply for a grant;

    (*b*) where there is no person so authorised, to the lawful attorney of the incapable person acting under a registered enduring power of attorney;

    (*c*) where there is no such attorney entitled to act, or if the attorney shall renounce administration for the use and benefit of the incapable person, to the person entitled to the residuary estate of the deceased.

(3) Where a grant is required to be made to not less than two administrators, and there is only one person competent and willing to take a grant under the foregoing provisions of this rule, administration may, unless a district judge or registrar otherwise directs, be granted to such person jointly with any other person nominated by him.

(4) Notwithstanding the foregoing provisions of this rule, administration for the use and benefit of the incapable person may be granted to such two or more other persons as the district judge or registrar may by order direct.

(5) Notice of an intended application under this rule shall be given to the Court of Protection.

Grants to trust corporations and other corporate bodies

36.—(1) An application for a grant to a trust corporation shall be made through one of its officers, and such officer shall depose in the oath that the corporation is a trust corporation as defined by these Rules and that it has power to accept a grant.

(2)(*a*) Where the trust corporation is the holder of an official position, any officer whose name is included on a list filed with the Senior District Judge of persons authorised to make affidavits and sign documents on behalf of the office holder may act as the officer through whom the holder of that official position applies for the grant.

(*b*) In all other cases a certified copy of the resolution of the trust corporation authorising the officer to make the application shall be lodged, or it shall be deposed in the oath that such certified copy has been filed with the Senior District Judge, that the officer is therein identified by the position he holds, and that such resolution is still in force.

(3) A trust corporation may apply for administration otherwise than as a beneficiary or the attorney of some person, and on any such application there shall be lodged the consents of all persons entitled to a grant and of all persons interested in the residuary estate of the deceased save that the district judge or registrar may dispense with any such consents as aforesaid on such terms, if any, as he may think fit.

(4)(*a*) Subject to sub-paragraph (*d*) below, where a corporate body would, if an individual, be entitled to a grant but is not a trust corporation as defined by these Rules, administration for its use and benefit, limited until further representation be granted, may be made to its nominee or to its lawfully constituted attorney.

(*b*) A copy of the resolution appointing the nominee or the power of attorney (whichever is appropriate) shall be lodged, and such resolution or power of attorney shall be sealed by the corporate body, or be otherwise authenticated to the district judge's registrar's satisfaction.

(c) The nominee or attorney shall depose in the oath that the corporate body is not a trust corporation as defined by these Rules.

(d) The provisions of paragraph (4)(a) above shall not apply where a corporate body is appointed executor jointly with an individual unless the right of the individual has been cleared off.

Renunciation of probate and administration

37.—(1) Renunciation of probate by an executor shall not operate as renunciation of any right which he may have to a grant of administration in some other capacity unless he expressly renounces such right.

(2) Unless a district judge or registrar otherwise directs, no person who has renounced administration in one capacity may obtain a grant thereof in some other capacity.

(3) A renunciation of probate or administration may be retracted at any time with the leave of a district judge or registrar; provided that only in exceptional circumstances may leave be given to an executor to retract a renunciation of probate after a grant has been made to some other person entitled in a lower degree.

(4) A direction or order giving leave under this rule may be made either by the registrar of a district probate registry where the renunciation is filed or by a district judge.

Notice to Crown of intended application for grant

38. In any case in which it appears that the Crown is or may be beneficially interested in the estate of a deceased person, notice of intended application for a grant shall be given by the applicant to the Treasury Solicitor, and the district judge or registrar may direct that no grant shall issue within 28 days after the notice has been given.

Resealing under Colonial Probates Acts 1892 and 1927

39.—(1) An application under the Colonial Probates Acts 1892 and 1927 for the resealing of probate or administration granted by the court of a country to which those Acts apply may be made by the person to whom the grant was made or by any person authorised in writing to apply on his behalf.

(2) On any such application an Inland Revenue affidavit or account shall be lodged.

(3) Except by leave of a district judge or registrar, no grant shall be resealed unless it was made to such a person as is mentioned in sub-para-

graph (*a*) or (*b*) of paragraph (1) of rule 30 or to a person to whom a grant could be made under sub-paragraph (*a*) of paragraph (3) of that rule.

(4) No limited or temporary grant shall be resealed except by leave of a district judge or registrar.

(5) Every grant lodged for resealing shall include a copy of any will to which the grant relates or shall be accompanied by a copy thereof certified as correct by or under the authority of the court by which the grant was made, and where the copy of the grant required to be deposited under sub-section (1) of section 2 of the Colonial Probates Act 1892 does not include a copy of the will, a copy thereof shall be deposited in the registry before the grant is resealed.

(6) The district registry registrar shall send notice of the resealing to the court which made the grant.

(7) Where notice is received in the Principal Registry of the resealing of a grant issued in England and Wales, notice of any amendment or revocation of the grant shall be sent to the court by which it was resealed.

Application for leave to sue on guarantee

40. An application for leave under section 120(3) of the Act or under section 11(5) of the Administration of Estates Act 1971 to sue a surety on a guarantee given for the purposes of either of those sections shall, unless the district judge or registrar otherwise directs under rule 61, be made by summons to a district judge or registrar and notice of the application shall be served on the administrator, the surety and any co-surety.

Amendment and revocation of grant

41.—(1) Subject to paragraph (2) below, if a district judge or registrar is satisfied that a grant should be amended or revoked he may make an order accordingly.

(2) Except on the application or with the consent of the person to whom the grant was made, the power conferred in paragraph (1) above shall be exercised only in exceptional circumstances.

Certificate of delivery of Inland Revenue affidavit

42. Where the deceased died before March 13, 1975 the certificate of delivery of an Inland Revenue affidavit required by section 30 of the Customs and Inland Revenue Act 1881 to be borne by every grant shall be in Form 1.

Standing searches

43.—(1) Any person who wishes to be notified of the issue of a grant may enter a standing search for the grant by lodging at, or sending by post to any registry or sub-registry, a notice in Form 2.

(2) A person who has entered a standing search will be sent an office

copy of any grant which corresponds with the particulars given on the completed Form 2 and which—

    (*a*) issued not more than twelve months before the entry of the standing search; or

    (*b*) issues within a period of six months after the entry of the standing search.

    (3)(*a*) Where an applicant wishes to extend the said period of six months, he or his solicitor may lodge at, or send by post to, the registry or sub-registry at which the standing search was entered written application for extension.

      (*b*) An application for extension as aforesaid must be lodged, or received by post, within the last month of the said period of six months, and the standing search shall thereupon be effective for an additional period of six months from the date on which it was due to expire.

      (*c*) A standing search which has been extended as above may be further extended by the filing of a further application for extension subject to the same conditions as set out in sub-paragraph (*b*) above.

Caveats

44.—(1) Any person who wishes to show cause against the sealing of a grant may enter a caveat in any registry or sub-registry, and the district judge or registrar shall not allow any grant to be sealed (other than a grant ad colligenda bona or a grant under section 117 of the Act) if he has knowledge of an effective caveat; provided that no caveat shall prevent the sealing of a grant on the day on which the caveat is entered.

(2) Any person wishing to enter a caveat (in these Rules called "the caveator"), or a solicitor on his behalf, may effect entry of a caveat—

    (*a*) by completing Form 3 in the appropriate book at any registry or sub-registry; or

    (*b*) by sending by post at his own risk a notice in Form 3 to any registry or sub-registry and the proper officer shall provide an acknowledgment of the entry of the caveat.

    (3)(*a*) Except as otherwise provided by this rule or by rules 45 or 46, a caveat shall be effective for a period of six months from the date of entry thereof, and where a caveator wishes to extend the said period of six months, he or his solicitor may lodge at, or send by post to, the registry or sub-registry at which the caveat was entered a written application for extension.

      (*b*) An application for extension as aforesaid must be lodged, or received by post, within the last month of the said period of six

months, and the caveat shall thereupon (save as otherwise provided by this rule) be effective for an additional period of six
months from the date on which it was due to expire.

(c) A caveat which has been extended as above may be further
extended by the filing of a further application for extension subject to the same conditions as set out in sub-paragraph (b)
above.

(4) An index of caveats entered in any registry or sub-registry shall be
maintained at the same registry in which the index of pending grant applications is maintained, and a search of the caveat index shall be made—

(a) on receipt of an application for a grant at that registry; and
(b) on receipt of a notice of an application for a grant made in any
other registry,

and the appropriate district judge or registrar shall be notified of the entry
of a caveat against the sealing of a grant for which application has been
made in that other registry.

(5) Any person claiming to have an interest in the estate may cause to be
issued from the registry in which the caveat index is maintained a warning
in Form 4 against the caveat, and the person warning shall state his interest
in the estate of the deceased and shall require the caveator to give particulars of any contrary interest in the estate; and the warning or a copy thereof
shall be served on the caveator forthwith.

(6) A caveator who has no interest contrary to that of the person warning, but who wishes to show cause against the sealing of a grant to that person, may within eight days of service of the warning upon him (inclusive of
the day of such service), or at any time thereafter if no affidavit has been
filed under paragraph (12) below, issue and serve a summons for directions.

(7) On the hearing of any summons for directions under paragraph (6)
above the district judge or registrar may give a direction for the caveat to
cease to have effect.

(8) Any caveat in force when a summons for directions is issued shall
remain in force until the summons has been disposed of unless a direction
has been given under paragraph (7) above.

(9) The issue of a summons under this rule shall be notified forthwith to
the registry in which the caveat index is maintained.

(10) A caveator having an interest contrary to that of the person warning
may within eight days of service of the warning upon him (inclusive of the
day of such service) or at any time thereafter if no affidavit has been filed
under paragraph (12) below, enter an appearance in the registry in which
the caveat index is maintained by filing Form 5; and he shall serve forthwith on the person warning a copy of Form 5 sealed with the seal of the
court.

(11) A caveator who has not entered an appearance to a warning may at
any time withdraw his caveat by giving notice at the registry or sub-registry

at which it was entered, and the caveat shall thereupon cease to have effect; and, where the caveat has been so withdrawn, the caveator shall forthwith give notice of withdrawal to the person warning.

(12) If no appearance has been entered by the caveator or no summons has been issued by him under paragraph (6) of this rule, the person warning may at any time after eight days of service of the warning upon the caveator (inclusive of the day of such service) file an affidavit in the registry in which the caveat index is maintained as to such service and the caveat shall thereupon cease to have effect provided that there is no pending summons under paragraph (6) of this rule.

(13) Unless a district judge or where application to discontinue a caveat is made by consent, a registrar by order made on summons otherwise directs, any caveat in respect of which an appearance to a warning has been entered shall remain in force until the commencement of a probate action.

(14) Except with the leave of a district judge, no further caveat may be entered by or on behalf of any caveator whose caveat is either in force or has ceased to have effect under paragraphs (7) or (12) of this rule or under rule 45(4) or rule 46(3).

Probate actions

45.—(1) Upon being advised by the court concerned of the commencement of a probate action the Senior Registrar shall give notice of the action to every caveator other than the plaintiff in the action in respect of each caveat that is in force.

(2) In respect of any caveat entered subsequent to the commencement of a probate action the Senior Registrar shall give notice to that caveator of the existence of the action.

(3) Unless a registrar of the Principal Registry by order made on summons otherwise directs, the commencement of a probate action shall operate to prevent the sealing of a grant (other than a grant under section 117 of the Act) until application for a grant is made by the person shown to be entitled thereto by the decision of the court in such action.

(4) Upon such application for a grant, any caveat entered by the plaintiff in the action, and any caveat in respect of which notice of the action has been given, shall cease to have effect.

Citations

46.—(1) Any citation may issue from the Principal Registry or a district probate registry and shall be settled by a district judge or registrar before being issued.

(2) Every averment in a citation, and such other information as the district judge or registrar may require, shall be verified by an affidavit sworn by the person issuing the citation (in these Rules called the "citor"), provided that the district judge or registrar may in special circumstances accept an affidavit sworn by the citor's solicitor.

(3) The citor shall enter a caveat before issuing a citation and, unless a district judge by order made on summons otherwise directs, any caveat in force at the commencement of the citation proceedings shall, unless withdrawn pursuant to paragraph (11) of rule 44, remain in force until application for a grant is made by the person shown to be entitled thereto by the decision of the court in such proceedings, and upon such application any caveat entered by a party who had notice of the proceedings shall cease to have effect.

(4) Every citation shall be served personally on the person cited unless the district judge or registrar, on cause shown by affidavit, directs some other mode of service, which may include notice by advertisement.

(5) Every will referred to in a citation shall be lodged in a registry before the citation is issued, except where the will is not in the citor's possession and the district judge or registrar is satisfied that it is impracticable to require it to be lodged.

(6) A person who has been cited to appear may, within eight days of service of the citation upon him (inclusive of the day of such service), or at any time thereafter if no application has been made by the citor under paragraph (5) of rule 47 or paragraph (2) of rule 48, enter an appearance in the registry from which the citation issued by filing Form 5 and shall forthwith thereafter serve on the citor a copy of Form 5 sealed with the seal of the registry.

Citation to accept or refuse or to take a grant

47.—(1) A citation to accept or refuse a grant may be issued at the instance of any person who would himself be entitled to a grant in the event of the person cited renouncing his right thereto.

(2) Where power to make a grant to an executor has been reserved, a citation calling on him to accept or refuse a grant may be issued at the instance of the executors who have proved the will or the survivor of them or of the executors of the last survivor of deceased executors who have proved.

(3) A citation calling on an executor who has intermeddled in the estate of the deceased to show cause why he should not be ordered to take a grant may be issued at the instance of any person interested in the estate at any time after the expiration of six months from the death of the deceased, provided that no citation to take a grant shall issue while proceedings as to the validity of the will are pending.

(4) A person cited who is willing to accept or take a grant may, after entering an appearance, apply ex parte by affidavit to a district judge or registrar for an order for a grant to himself.

(5) If the time limited for appearance has expired and the person cited has not entered an appearance, the citor may—

    (a) in the case of a citation under paragraph (1) of this rule, apply to a district judge or registrar for an order for a grant to himself;

(b) in the case of a citation under paragraph (2) of this rule, apply to a district judge or registrar for an order that a note be made on the grant that the executor in respect of whom power was reserved has been duly cited and has not appeared and that all his rights in respect of the executorship have wholly ceased; or

(c) in the case of a citation under paragraph (3) of this rule, apply to a district judge or registrar by summons (which shall be served on the person cited) for an order requiring such person to take a grant within a specified time or for a grant to himself or to some other person specified in the summons.

(6) An application under the last foregoing paragraph shall be supported by an affidavit showing that the citation was duly served.

(7) If the person cited has entered an appearance but has not applied for a grant under paragraph (4) of this rule, or has failed to prosecute his application with reasonable diligence, the citor may—

(a) in the case of a citation under paragraph (1) of this rule, apply by summons to a district judge or registrar for an order for a grant to himself;

(b) in the case of a citation under paragraph (2) of this rule, apply by summons to a district judge or registrar for an order striking out the appearance and for the endorsement on the grant of such a note as is mentioned in sub-paragraph (b) of paragraph (5) of this rule; or

(c) in the case of a citation under paragraph (3) of this rule, apply by summons to a district judge or registrar for an order requiring the person cited to take a grant within a specified time or for a grant to himself or to some other person specified in the summons;

and the summons shall be served on the person cited.

Citation to propound a will

48.—(1) A citation to propound a will shall be directed to the executors named in the will and to all persons interested thereunder, and may be issued at the instance of any citor having an interest contrary to that of the executors or such other persons.

(2) If the time limited for appearance has expired, the citor may—

(a) in the case where no person has entered an appearance, apply to a district judge or registrar for an order for a grant as if the will were invalid and such application shall be supported by an affidavit showing that the citation was duly served; or

(b) in the case where no person who has entered an appearance proceeds with reasonable diligence to propound the will, apply to a district judge or registrar by summons, which shall be served on every person cited who has entered an appearance, for such an order as is mentioned in paragraph (a) above.

Address for service

49. All caveats, citations, warnings and appearances shall contain an address for service in England and Wales.

Application for order to attend for examination or for subpoena to bring in a will

50.—(1) An application under section 122 of the Act for an order requiring a person to attend for examination may, unless a probate action has been commenced, be made to a district judge or registrar by summons which shall be served on every such person as aforesaid.

(2) An application under section 123 of the Act for the issue by a district judge or registrar of a subpoena to bring in a will shall be supported by an affidavit setting out the grounds of the application, and if any person served with the subpoena denies that the will is in his possession or control he may file an affidavit to that effect on the registry from which the subpoena issued.

Grants to part of an estate under section 113 of the Act

51. An application for an order for a grant under section 113 of the Act to part of an estate may be made to a district judge or registrar, and shall be supported by an affidavit setting out the grounds of the application, and

- (*a*) stating whether the estate of the deceased is known to be insolvent; and
- (*b*) showing how any person entitled to a grant in respect of the whole estate in priority to the applicant has been cleared off.

Grants of administration under discretionary powers of court, and grants ad colligenda bona

52. An application for an order for—

- (*a*) a grant of administration under section 116 of the Act; or
- (*b*) a grant of administration ad colligenda bona,

may be made to a district judge or registrar and shall be supported by an affidavit setting out the grounds of the application.

Applications for leave to swear to death

53. An application for leave to swear to the death of a person in whose estate a grant is sought may be made to a district judge or registrar, and shall be supported by an affidavit setting out the grounds of the application and containing particulars of any policies of insurance effected on the life of the presumed deceased together with such further evidence as the district judge or registrar may require.

Grants in respect of nuncupative wills and copies of wills

54.—(1) Subject to paragraph (2) below, an application for an order admitting to proof a nuncupative will, or a will contained in a copy or reconstruction thereof where the original is not available, shall be made to a district judge or registrar.

(2) In any case where a will is not available owing to its being retained in the custody of a foreign court or official, a duly authenticated copy of the will may be admitted to proof without the order referred to in paragraph (1) above.

(3) An application under paragraph (1) above shall be supported by an affidavit setting out the grounds of the application, and by such evidence on affidavit as the applicant can adduce as to—

(a) the will's existence after the death of the testator or, where there is no such evidence, the facts on which the applicant relies to rebut the presumption that the will has been revoked by destruction;

(b) in respect of a nuncupative will, the contents of that will; and

(c) in respect of a reconstruction of a will, the accuracy of that reconstruction.

(4) The district judge or registrar may require additional evidence in the circumstances of a particular case as to due execution of the will or as to the accuracy of the copy will, and may direct that notice be given to persons who would be prejudiced by the application.

Application for rectification of a will

55.—(1) An application for an order that a will be rectified by virtue of section 20(1) of the Administration of Justice Act 1982 may be made to a district judge or registrar, unless a probate action has been commenced.

(2) The application shall be supported by an affidavit, setting out the grounds of the application, together with such evidence as can be adduced as to the testator's intentions and as to whichever of the following matters as are in issue:—

(a) in what respects the testator's intentions were not understood; or

(b) the nature of any alleged clerical error.

(3) Unless otherwise directed, notice of the application shall be given to every person having an interest under the will whose interest might be prejudiced by the rectification applied for and any comments in writing by any such person shall be exhibited to the affidavit in support of the application.

(4) If the district judge or registrar is satisfied that, subject to any direction to the contrary, notice has been given to every person mentioned in paragraph (3) above, and that the application is unopposed, he may order that the will be rectified accordingly.

Notice of election by surviving spouse to redeem life interest

56.—(1) Where a surviving spouse who is the sole or sole surviving personal representative of the deceased is entitled to a life interest in part of the residuary estate and elects under section 47A of the Administration of Estates Act 1925 to have the life interest redeemed, he may give written notice of the election to the Senior District Judge in pursuance of subsection (7) of that section by filing a notice in Form 6 in the Principal Registry or in the district probate registry from which the grant issued.

(2) Where the grant issued from a district probate registry, the notice shall be filed in duplicate.

(3) A notice filed under this rule shall be noted on the grant and the record and shall be open to inspection.

Index of grant applications

57.—(1) The Senior District Judge shall maintain an index of every pending application for a grant made in any registry.

(2) Notice of every application for a grant shall be sent by the registry in which the application is made to the registry in which the index is maintained and shall be in the form of a document stating the full name of the deceased and the date of his death.

(3) On receipt of the notice referred to in paragraph (2) above, the registry shall search its current index and shall give a certificate as to the result of that search to the registry which sent the notice.

(4) The requirements of paragraph (2) above shall not apply in any case in which the application for a grant is made in the registry in which the index is maintained.

(5) In this rule "registry" includes a sub-registry.

Inspection of copies of original wills and other documents

58. An original will or other document referred to in section 124 of the Act shall not be open to inspection if, in the opinion of a district judge registrar, such inspection would be undesirable or otherwise inappropriate.

Issue of copies of original wills and other documents

59. Where copies are required of original wills or other documents deposited under section 124 of the Act, such copies may be facsimile copies sealed with the seal of the court and issued either as office copies or certified under the hand of a district judge or registrar to be true copies.

Taxation of costs

60. Every bill of costs, other than a bill delivered by a solicitor to his client which falls to be taxed under the Solicitors Act 1974, shall be referred for taxation—

   (a) where the order for taxation was made by a district judge, to a

district judge, or to a taxing officer of the Principal Registry authorised to tax costs in accordance with Order 62, rule 19 of the
Rules of the Supreme Court 1965;

(*b*) where the order for taxation was made by a registrar, to that
registrar.

Power to require applications to be made by summons

61.—(1) Subject to rule 7(2) a district judge or registrar may require any
application to be made by summons to a registrar in chambers or a judge in
chambers or open court.

(2) An application for an inventory and account shall be made by summons to a district judge or registrar.

(3) A summons for hearing by a district judge or registrar shall be issued
out of the registry in which it is to be heard.

(4) A summons to be heard by a judge shall be issued out of the Principal
Registry.

Transfer of applications

62. A district judge or registrar to whom any application is made under
these Rules may order the transfer of the application to another district
judge or registrar having jurisdiction.

Power to make orders for costs

63. On any application dealt with by him on summons, the registrar shall
have full power to determine by whom and to what extent the costs are to
be paid.

Exercise of powers of judge during Long Vacation

64. All powers exercisable under these Rules by a judge in chambers
may be exercised during the Long Vacation by a district judge.

Appeals from district judges or registrars

65.—(1) An appeal against a decision or requirement of a district judge
or registrar shall be made by summons to a judge.

(2) If, in the case of an appeal under the last foregoing paragraph, any
person besides the appellant appeared or was represented before the district judge or registrar from whose decision or requirement the appeal is
brought, the summons shall be issued within seven days thereof for hearing
on the first available day and shall be served on every such person as aforesaid.

Service of summons

66.—(1) A judge or district judge or, where the application is to be made
to a registrar, that registrar, may direct that a summons for the service of

which no other provision is made by these Rules shall be served on such person or persons as the judge, district judge or registrar may direct.

(2) Where by these Rules or by any direction given under the last foregoing paragraph a summons is required to be served on any person, it shall be served not less than two clear days before the day appointed for the hearing, unless a judge, district judge or registrar at or before the hearing dispenses with service on such terms, if any, as he may think fit.

Notices, etc.

67. Unless a district judge or registrar otherwise directs or these Rules otherwise provide, any notice or other document required to be given to or served on any person may be given or served in the manner prescribed by Order 65 Rule 5 of the Rules of the Supreme Court 1965.

Application to pending proceedings

68. Subject in any particular case to any direction given by a judge or registrar, these Rules shall apply to any proceedings which are pending on the date on which they come into force as well as to any proceedings commenced on or after that date.

Revocation of previous rules

69.—(1) Subject to paragraph (2) below, the rules set out in the Second Schedule are hereby revoked.

(2) The rules set out in the Second Schedule shall continue to apply to such extent as may be necessary for giving effect to a direction under rule 68.

FIRST SCHEDULE   Rule 2(2)

FORMS

FORM 1   Rule 42

Certificate of Delivery of Inland Revenue Affidavit

And it is hereby certified that an Inland Revenue af amounts to £ .... and that the net value of the estate amounts to £ ....

And it is further certified that it appears by a receipt signed by an Inland Revenue officer on the said affidavit that £ .... on account of estate duty and interest on such duty has been paid.

FORM 2 Rule 43(1)

Standing Search

In the High Court of Justice

Family Division

The Principal Registry

I/We apply for the entry of a standing search so that there shall be sent to me/us an office copy of every grant of representation in England and Wales in the estate of—

Full name of deceased: ....

Full address: ....

Alternative or alias names: ....

Exact date to death: ....

which either has issued not more than 12 months before the entry of this application or issues within 6 months thereafter.

Signed ....

Name in block letters ....

Full address ....

Reference No. (if any) ....

FORM 3 Rule 44(2)

Caveat

In the High Court of Justice

Family Division

The Principal [*or* .... District Probate] Registry.

Let no grant be sealed in the estate of (*full name and address*) deceased, who died on the ....

day of .... 19 ...... without notice to (*name of party by whom or on whosebehalf the caveat is entered*).

Dated this .... day of .... 19 ....

(*Signed*)   (*to be signed by the caveator's solicitor or by the caveator if acting in person*)

whose address for service is: ....

Solicitor for the said ....
(*If the caveator is acting in person, substitute "In person".*)

Rule 44(5)   FORM 4

Warning to Caveator

In the High Court of Justice

Family Division

[*The Registry in which the caveat index is maintained*]

To .... of .... a party who has entered a caveat in

the estate of .... deceased.

   You have eight days (starting with the day on which this warning was served on you):
   (i) to enter an appearance either in person or by your solicitor, at the [*name and address of the registry in which the caveat index is maintained*] setting out what interest you have in the estate of the above-named .... of .... deceased contrary to that of the party at . whose instance this warning is issued; or
   (ii) if you have no contrary interest but wish to show cause against the sealing of a grant to such party, to issue and serve a summons for directions by a registrar of the Principal Registry or a district probate registry.

If you fail to do either of these, the court may proceed to issue a grant of probate or administration in the said estate notwithstanding your caveat.

Dated the .... day of .... 19 ....

Issued at the instance of ....

[*Here set out the name and interest
(including the date of the will, if any,
under which the interest arises) of
the party warning, the name of his
solicitor and the address for service.
If the party warning is acting in per-
son, this must be stated.*]   Registrar

Rules 44(10), 46(6)   FORM 5

Appearance to Warning or Citation

In the High Court of Justice

Family Division

The Principal [*or* .... District Probate] Registry

Caveat No. .... dated the .... day of .... 19 .....

[Citation dated the .... day of .... 19 .....]

Full name and address of deceased: ....

Full name and address of person warning [*or* citor]: ....
(*Here set out the interest of the person warning, or citor, as shown in warning or citation.*)

Full name and address of caveator [or person cited].
(*Here set out the interest of the caveator or person cited, stating the date of
the will (if any) under which such interest arises.*)

Enter a appearance for the above-named caveator [*or* person cited] in this
matter.

Dated the .... day of .... 19 ..... .

(*Signed*)

whose address for service is:
                              Solicitor (*or* "In person").

FORM 6   Rule 56

Notice of Election to Redeem Life Interest

In the High Court of Justice

Family Division

The Principal [*or* .... District Probate] Registry

In the estate of .... deceased.

Whereas .... of .... died on the .... day
of .... 19 ...... wholly/partially intestate leaving his/her/lawful
wife/husband and .... lawful issue of the said deceased;
   And whereas Probate/Letters of Administration of the estate of the said
.... were granted to me, the said .... [and to
.... of ....] at the Probate Registry on the .... day
of .... 19 .....;
   And whereas [the said .... has ceased to be a personal
representative because ....] and I am [now] the sole
personal representative;
   Now I, the said .... hereby give notice in accordance with
section 47A of the Administration of Estate Act 1925 that I elect to redeem
the life interest to which I am entitled in the estate of the late ....
by retaining £ .... its capital value, and £ ....
the costs of the transaction.

Dated the .... day of .... 19 ....
(Signed)
To the Senior Registrar of the Family Division.

SECOND SCHEDULE   Rule 69

REVOCATIONS

Rules revoked	References
The Non-Contentious Probate Rules 1954	S.I. 1954/796
The Non-Contentious Probate (Amendment) Rules 1961	S.I. 1961/72
The Non-Contentious Probate (Amendment) Rules 1962	S.I. 1962/2653
The Non-Contentious Probate (Amendment) Rules 1967	S.I. 1967/748
The Non-Contentious Probate (Amendment) Rules 1968	S.I. 1968/1675
The Non-Contentious Probate (Amendment) Rules 1969	S.I. 1969/1689
The Non-Contentious Probate (Amendment) Rules 1971	S.I. 1971/1977
The Non-Contentious Probate (Amendment) Rules 1974	S.I. 1974/597
The Non-Contentious Probate (Amendment) Rules 1976	S.I. 1976/1362
The Non-Contentious Probate (Amendment) Rules 1982	S.I. 1982/446
The Non-Contentious Probate (Amendment) Rules 1983	S.I. 1983/623
The Non-Contentious Probate (Amendment) Rules 1985	S.I. 1985/1232

RULES OF THE SUPREME COURT

ORDER 76

CONTENTIOUS PROBATE PROCEEDINGS

Application and interpretation (O. 76, r. 1)

1.—(1) This Order applies to probate causes and matters, and the other provisions of these rules apply to those causes and matters including applications for the rectification of a will subject to the provisions of this Order.

(2) In these rules "probate action" means an action for the grant of probate of the will, or letters of administration of the estate, of a deceased person or for the revocation of such a grant or for a decree pronouncing for or against the validity of an alleged will, not being an action which is non-contentious or common form probate business.

(3) In this Order, "will" includes a codicil.

AMENDMENT

Rule 1 was amended by R.S.C. (Amendment No. 3) 1982 (S.I. 1982 No. 1786).

Requirements in connection with issue of writ (O. 76, r. 2)

2.—(1) A probate action must be begun by writ, and the writ must be issued out of the Chancery Chambers.

(2) Before a writ beginning a probate action is issued it must be indorsed with a statement of the nature of the interest of the plaintiff and of the defendant in the estate of the deceased to which the action relates.

AMENDMENT
Rule 2 was substituted by R.S.C. (Amendment No. 2) 1984 (S.I. 1984 No. 1051).

Parties to action to revocation of grant (O. 76, r. 3)

3. Every person who is entitled or claims to be entitled to administer the estate of a deceased person under or by virtue of an unrevoked grant of probate of his will or letters of administration of his grant shall be made a party to any action for revocation of the grant.

Lodgment of grant in action for revocation (O. 76, r. 4)

4.—(1) Where, at the commencement of an action for the revocation of a grant of probate of the will or letters of administration of the estate of a deceased person, the probate or letters of administration as the case may be, have not been lodged in court, then—

    (*a*) if the action is commenced by a person to whom the grant was made, he shall lodge the probate or letters of administration in Chancery Chambers within seven days after the issue of the writ;

(b) if any defendant to the action has the probate or letters of administration in his possession or under this control, he shall lodge it or them in Chancery Chambers within 14 days after the service of the writ upon him.

In this paragraph "court" includes the principal registry of the Family Division or a district probate registry.

(2) Any person who fails to comply with paragraph (1) may, on the application of any party to the action, be ordered by the Court to lodge the probate or letters of administration in Chancery Chambers within a specified time; and any person against whom such an order is made shall not be entitled to take any step in the action without the leave of the Court until he has complied with the order.

AMENDMENT

This rule was amended by R.S.C. (Amendment No. 2) 1982 (S.I. 1982 No. 1111).

Affidavit of testamentary scripts (O. 76, r. 5)

5.—(1) Unless the Court otherwise directs, the plaintiff and every defendant who has acknowledged service of the writ in a probate action must swear an affidavit—

(a) describing any testamentary script of the deceased person, whose estate is the subject of the action, of which he has any knowledge or, if such be the case, stating that he knows of no such script, and

(b) if any such script of which he has knowledge is not in his possession or under his control, giving the name and address of the person in whose possession or under whose control it is or, if such be the case, stating that he does not know the name or address of that person.

(2) Any affidavit required by this rule must be filed, and any testamentary script referred to therein which is in the possession or under the control of the deponent must be lodged in Chancery Chambers, within 14 days after the acknowledgment of service by a defendant to the action or, if no defendant acknowledges service and the Court does not otherwise direct, before an order is made for the trial of the action.

(3) Where any testamentary script required by this rule to be lodged in Chancery Chambers or any part thereof is written in pencil, then, unless the Court otherwise directs, a facsimile copy of that script, or of the page or pages thereof containing the part written in pencil, must also be lodged in Chancery Chambers and the words which appear in pencil in the original must be underlined in red ink in the copy.

(4) Except with the leave of the Court, a party to a probate action shall not be allowed to inspect an affidavit filed, or any testamentary script lodged by any other party to the action under this rule, unless and until an

affidavit sworn by him containing the information referred to in paragraph
(1) has been filed.

(5) In this rule "testamentary script" means a will or draft thereof, written instructions for a will made by or at the request or under the instructions of the testator and any document purporting to be evidence of the
contents, or to be a copy, of a will which is alleged to have been lost or destroyed.

AMENDMENT

This rule was amended by R.S.C. (Amendment No. 2) 1982 (S.I. 1982 No. 1111).

Failure to acknowledge service (O. 76, r. 6)

6.—(1) Order 13 shall not apply in relation to a probate action.

(2) Where any of several defendants to a probate action fails to acknowledge service of the writ, the plaintiff may, after the time for acknowledging service has expired and upon filing an affidavit proving due service of
the writ, or notice of the writ, on that defendant proceed with the action as
if that defendant had acknowledged service.

(3) Where the defendant, or all the defendants, to a probate action, fails
or fail to acknowledge service of the writ, then, unless on the application of
the plaintiff the Court orders the action to be discontinued, the plaintiff
may after the time limited for acknowledging service by the defendant
apply to the Court for an order for trial of the action.

(4) Before applying for an order under paragraph (3) the plaintiff must
file an affidavit providing due service of the writ, or notice of the writ, on
the defendant and, if no statement of claim is indorsed on the writ, he must
lodge a statement of claim in the judge's chambers.

(5) Where the Court grants an order under paragraph (3), it may direct
the action to be tried on affidavit evidence.

Service of statement of claim (O. 76, r. 7)

7. The plaintiff in a probate action must, unless the court gives leave to
the contrary or unless a statement of claim is indorsed on the writ, serve a
statement of claim on every defendant who acknowledges service of the
writ in the action and must do so before the expiration of six weeks after
acknowledgment of service by that defendant or of eight days after the filing by that defendant of an affidavit under rule 5, whichever is the later.

Counterclaim (O. 76, r. 8)

8.—(1) Notwithstanding anything in Order 15, rule 2(1), a defendant to
a probate action who alleges that he has any claim or is entitled to any
relief or remedy in respect of any matter relating to the grant of probate of
the will, or letters of administration of the estate, of the deceased person
which is the subject of the action must add to his defence a counterclaim in
respect of that matter.

(2) If the plaintiff fails to serve a statement of claim, any such defendant may, with the leave of the Court, serve a counterclaim and the action shall then proceed as if the counterclaim were the statement of claim.

Contents of pleadings (O. 76, r. 9)

9.—(1) Where the plaintiff in a probate action disputes the interest of a defendant he must allege in his statement of claim that he denies the interest of that defendant.

(2) In a probate action in which the interest by virtue of which a party claims to be entitled to a grant of letters of administration is disputed, the party disputing that interest must show in his pleading that if the allegations made therein are proved he would be entitled to an interest in the estate.

(3) Without prejudice to Order 18, rule 7, any party who pleads that at the time when a will, the subject of the action, was alleged to have been executed the testator did not know and approve of its contents must specify the nature of the case on which he intends to rely, and no allegation in support of that plea which would be relevant in support of any of the following other pleas, that is to say:

- (*a*) that the will was not duly executed,
- (*b*) that at the time of the execution of the will the testator was not of sound mind, memory and understanding, and
- (*c*) that the execution of the will was obtained by undue influence or fraud,

shall be made by that party unless that other plea is also pleaded.

Default of pleadings (O. 76, r. 10)

10.—(1) Order 19 shall not apply in relation to a probate action.

(2) Where any party to a probate action fails to serve on any other party a pleading which he is required by these rules to serve on that other party, then, unless the Court orders the action to be discontinued or dismissed, that other party may, after the expiration of the period fixed by or under these rules for service of the pleading in question, apply to the Court for an order for trial of the action; and if an order is made the Court may direct the action to be tried on affidavit evidence.

Discontinuance and dismissal (O. 76, r. 11)

11.—(1) Order 21 shall not apply in relation to a probate action.

(2) At any stage of the proceedings in a probate action the Court may, on the application of the plaintiff or of any party to the action who has entered acknowledged service of the writ therein, order the action to be discontinued or dismissed on such terms as to costs or otherwise as it thinks just, and may further order that a grant of probate of the will, or letters of

administration of the estate, of the deceased person, as the case may be, which is the subject of the action, be made to the person entitled thereto.

(3) An application for an order under this rule may be made by motion or summons or by notice under Order 25, rule 7.

Compromise of action: trial on affidavit evidence (O. 76, r. 12)

12. Where, whether before or after the service of the defence in a probate action, the parties to the action agree to a compromise, the Court may order the trial of the action on affidavit evidence.

Application for order to bring will, etc. (O. 76, r. 13)

13.—(1) Any application in a probate action for an order under section 122 of the Act shall be for an order requiring a person to bring a will or other testamentary paper into Chancery Chambers or to attend in court for examination.

(2) An application under paragraph (1) shall be made by summons in the action, which must be served on the person against whom the order is sought.

(3) Any application in a probate action of the issue of a subpoena under section 123 of the Act shall be for the issue of a subpoena requiring a person to bring into Chancery Chambers a will or other testamentary paper.

(4) An application under paragraph (3) may be made ex parte and must be supported by an affidavit setting out the grounds of the application.

(5) An application under paragraph (3) shall be made to a master who may, if the application is granted, authorise the issue of a subpoena accordingly.

(6) Any person against whom a subpoena is issued under section 123 of the Act and who denies that the will or other testamentary paper referred to in the subpoena is in his possession or under his control may file an affidavit to that effect.

AMENDMENT

The former rule 13 was revoked and rules 14–16 renumbered 13–15 by R.S.C. (Amendment No. 2) 1982 (S.I. 1982 No. 1111).

Administration pendente lite (O. 76, r. 14)

14.—(1) An application under section 117 of the Act for an order for the grant of administration may be made by summons issued in the Chancery Division.

(2) Where an order for a grant of administration is made under the said section 117, Order 30, rules 2, 4 and 6 and (subject to subsection (3) of the said section) rule 3, shall apply as if the administrator were a receiver appointed by the court; and every application relating to the conduct of the administration shall be made in the Chancery Division.

AMENDMENT

This rule was amended by R.S.C. (Amendment No. 2) 1982 (S.I. 1982 No. 1111).

Probate counterclaim in other proceedings (O. 76, r. 15)

15.—(1) In this rule "probate counterclaim" means a counterclaim in any action other than a probate action by which the defendant claims any such relief as is mentioned in rule 1(2).

(2) Subject to the following paragraphs, this Order shall apply with the necessary modifications to a probate counterclaim as it applies to a probate action.

(3) A probate counterclaim must contain a statement of the nature of the interest of the defendant and of the plaintiff in the estate of the deceased to which the counterclaim relates.

(4) Unless an application under Order 15, rule 5(2), is made within seven days after the service of a probate counterclaim for the counterclaim to be struck out and the application is granted, the Court shall, if necessary of its own motion, order the transfer of the action to the Chancery Division (if it is not already assigned to that Division) and to the Royal Courts of Justice (if it is not already proceeding there).

AMENDMENT

Added by R.S.C. (Amendment 1976 (S.I. 1976 No. 337) and re-numbered by R.S.C. (Amendment No. 2) 1982 (S.I. 1982 No. 1111). Amended by R.S.C. (Amendment) 1984 (S.I. 1984 No. 1051).

Rectification of wills (O. 76, r. 16)

16.—(1) Where an application is made for rectification of a will, and the grant has not been lodged in court, rule 4 shall apply, with the necessary modifications, as if the proceedings were a probate action.

(2) A copy of every order made for the rectification of a will shall be sent to the principal registry of the Family Division for filing, and a memorandum of the order shall be endorsed on, or permanently annexed to, the grant under which the estate is administered.

AMENDMENT
Added by R.S.C. (Amendment No. 3) 1982 (S.I. 1982 No. 1786).

ORDER 85

ADMINISTRATION AND SIMILAR ACTIONS

Interpretation (O. 85, r. 1)

1. In this Order "administration action" means an action for the administration under the direction of the Court of the estate of a deceased person or for the execution under the direction of the Court of a trust.

Determination of questions, etc., without administration (O. 85, r. 2)

2.—(1) An action may be brought for the determination of any question or for any relief which could be determined or granted, as the case may be, in an administration action and a claim need not be made in the action for the administration or execution under the direction of the Court of the estate or trust in connection with which the question arises or the relief is sought.

(2) Without prejudice to the generality of paragraph (1), an action may be brought for the determination of any of the following questions:

(a) any question arising in the administration of the estate of a deceased person or in the execution of a trust;

(b) any question as to the composition of any class of persons having a claim against the estate of a deceased person or a beneficial interest in the estate of such a person in any property subject to a trust;

(c) any question as to the rights or interests of a person claiming to be a creditor of the estate of a deceased person or to be entitled under a will or on the intestacy of a deceased person or to be beneficially entitled under a trust.

(3) Without prejudice to the generality of paragraph (1), an action may be brought for any of the following reliefs:

(a) an order requiring an executor, administrator or trustee to furnish and, if necessary, verify accounts;

(b) an order requiring the payment into court of money held by a person in his capacity as executor, administrator or trustee;

(c) an order directing a person to do or abstain from doing a particular act in his capacity as executor, administrator or trustee;

(d) an order approving any sale, purchase, compromise or other transaction by a person in his capacity as executor, administrator or trustee;

(e) an order directing any act to be done in the administration of the estate of a deceased person or in the execution of a trust which the Court could order to be done if the estate or trust were being administered or executed, as the case may be, under the direction of the Court.

Parties (O. 85, r. 3)

3.—(1) All the executors or administrators of the estate or trustees of the trust, as the case may be, to which an administration action or such an action as is referred to in rule 2 relates must be parties to the action, and where the action is brought by executors, administrators or trustees, any of them who does not consent to being joined as a plaintiff must be made a defendant.

(2) Notwithstanding anything in Order 15, rule 4(2), and without prejudice to the powers of the Court under that Order, all the persons having a beneficial interest in or claim against the estate or having a beneficial interest under the trust, as the case may be, to which such an action as is mentioned in paragraph (1) relates need not be parties to the action; but the plaintiff may make such of those persons, whether all or any one or more of them, parties as, having regard to the nature of the relief or remedy claimed in the action, he thinks fit.

(3) Where, in proceedings under a judgment or order given or made in an action for the administration under the direction of the Court of the estate of a deceased person, a claim in respect of a debt or other liability is made against the estate by a person not a party to the action, no party other than the executors or administrators of the estate shall be entitled to appear in any proceedings relating to that claim without the leave of the Court, and the Court may direct or allow any other party to appear either in addition to, or in substitution for, the executors or administrators on such terms as to costs or otherwise as it thinks fit.

Grant of relief in action begun by originating summons (O. 85, r. 4)

4. In an administration action or such an action as is referred to in rule 2, the Court may make any certificate or order and grant any relief to which the plaintiff may be entitled by reason of any breach of trust, wilful default or other misconduct of the defendant notwithstanding that the action was begun by originating summons, but the foregoing provision is without prejudice to the power of the Court to make an order under Order 28, rule 8, in relation to the action.

Judgments and orders in administration actions (O. 85, r. 5)

5.—(1) A judgment or order for the administration or execution under the direction of the Court of an estate or trust need not be given or made unless in the opinion of the Court the questions at issue between the parties cannot properly be determined otherwise than under such a judgment or order.

(2) Where an administration action is brought by a creditor of the estate

of a deceased person or by a person claiming to be entitled under a will or on the intestacy of a deceased person or to be beneficially entitled under a trust, and the plaintiff alleges that no or insufficient accounts have been furnished by the executors, administrators or trustees, as the case may be, then, without prejudice to its other powers, the Court may—

(a) order that proceedings in the action be stayed for a period specified in the order and that the executors, administrators or trustees, as the case may be, shall within that period furnish the plaintiff with proper accounts;

(b) if necessary to prevent proceedings by other creditors or by other persons claiming to be entitled as aforesaid, give judgment or make an order for the administration of the estate to which the action relates and include therein an order that no proceedings are to be taken under the judgment or order, or under any particular account or inquiry directed, without the leave of the judge in person.

Conduct of sale of trust property (O. 85, r. 6)

6. Where in an administration action an order is made for the sale of any property vested in executors, administrators or trustees, those executors, administrators or trustees, as the case may be, shall have the conduct of the sale unless the Court otherwise directs.

ORDER 99

INHERITANCE (PROVISION FOR FAMILY AND DEPENDANTS) ACT 1975

Interpretation (O. 99, r. 1)

1. In this Order "the Act" means the Inheritance (Provision for Family and Dependants) Act 1975 and a section referred to by number means the section so numbered in that Act.

Assignment to Chancery or Family Division (O. 99, r. 2)

2. Proceedings in the High Court under the Act may be assigned to the Chancery Division or to the Family Division.

Application for financial provision (O. 99, r. 3)

3.—(1) Any originating summons by which an application under section 1 is made may be issued out of Chancery Chambers, the principal registry of the Family Division or any district registry.

(2) The summons shall be in Form No. 10 in Appendix A.

(3) There shall be lodged with the Court an affidavit by the applicant in support of the summons, exhibiting an official copy of the grant of representation to the deceased's estate and of every testamentary document admitted to proof, and a copy of the affidavit shall be served on every defendant with the summons.

AMENDMENT

Paragraph (1) was amended by R.S.C. (Amendment No. 2) 1982 (S.I. 1982 No. 1111); paragraph (2) was substituted by R.S.C. (Writ and Appearance) 1979 (S.I. 1979 No. 1716).

Powers of Court as to parties (O. 99, r. 4)

4.—(1) Without prejudice to its powers under Order 15, the Court may at any stage of proceedings under the Act direct that any person be added as a party to the proceedings or that notice of the proceedings be served on any person.

(2) Order 15, rule 13, shall apply to proceedings under the Act as it applies to the proceedings mentioned in paragraph (1) of that rule.

Affidavit in answer (O. 99, r. 5)

5.—(1) A defendant to an application under section 1 who is a personal representative of the deceased shall and any other defendant may, within 21 days after service of the summons on him, inclusive of the day of service, lodge with the Court an affidavit in answer to the application.

(2) The affidavit lodged by a personal representative pursuant to paragraph (1) shall state to the best of the deponent's ability—

(*a*) full particulars of the value of the deceased's net estate, as defined by section 25(1);

(*b*) the person or classes of persons beneficially interested in the estate, giving the names and (in the case of those who are not already parties) the addresses of all living beneficiaries, and the value of their interests so far as ascertained;

(*c*) if such be the case, that any living beneficiary (naming him) is a minor or a patient within the meaning of Order 80, rule 1; and

(*d*) any facts known to the deponent which might affect the exercise of the Court's powers under the Act.

(3) Every defendant who lodges an affidavit shall at the same time serve a copy on the plaintiff and on every other defendant who is not represented by the same solicitor.

Separate representation (O. 99, r. 6)

6. Where an application under section 1 is made jointly by two or more applicants and the originating summons is accordingly issued by one solicitor on behalf of all of them, they may, if they have conflicting interests, appear on any hearing of the summons by separate solicitors or counsel or in person, and where at any stage of the proceedings it appears to the Court that one of the applicants is not but ought to be separately represented, the Court may adjourn the proceedings until he is.

Endorsement of memorandum on grant (O. 99, r. 7)

7. (On the hearing of an application under section 1 the personal representative shall produce to the Court the grant of representation to the deceased's estate and, if an order is made under the Act, the grant shall remain in the custody of the Court until a memorandum of the order has been endorsed on or permanently annexed to the grant in accordance with section 19(3).

Disposal of proceedings in chambers (O. 99, r. 8)

8. Any proceedings under the Act may, if the Court so directs, be disposed of in chambers and Order 32, rule 14(1) shall apply in relation to proceedings in the Family Division as if for the words "The masters of the Chancery Division shall" there were substituted the words "A registrar of the Family Division shall."

AMENDMENT

Rule 8 was amended by R.S.C. (Amendment No. 2) 1982 (S.I. 1982 No. 1111).

Subsequent applications in proceedings under section 1 (O. 99, r. 9)

9. Where an order has been made on an application under section 1, any subsequent application under the Act, whether made by a party to the proceedings or by any other person, shall be made by summons in those proceedings.

Drawing up and service of orders (O. 99, r. 10)

10. The provisions of the Matrimonial Causes Rules relating to the drawing up and service of orders shall apply to proceedings in the Family Division under this Order as if they were proceedings under those Rules.

Transfer to county court (O. 99, r. 11)

11.—(1) Where an application to which section 22(1) relates is within the jurisdiction of a county court, the Court may, if the parties consent or it appears to the Court to be desirable, order the transfer of the application to such county court as appears to the Court to be most convenient to the parties.

(2) An order under paragraph (1) may be made by the Court of its own motion or on the application of any party, but before making an order of its own motion otherwise than by consent the Court shall give the parties an opportunity of being heard on the question of transfer and for that purpose the master or registrar may give the parties notice of a date, time and place at which the question will be considered.

AMENDMENT

Rule 11 was substituted by R.S.C. (Amendment) 1976 (S.I. 1976 No. 337).

COUNTY COURT RULES

ORDER 48

FAMILY PROVISION

Interpretation (O. 48, r. 1)

1. In this Order—

"the Act of 1973" means the Matrimonial Causes Act 1973;
"the Act of 1975" means the Inheritance (Provision for Family and Dependants) Act 1975;
"the deceased" means, in the case of an application under section 36 of the Act of 1973, the deceased party to the agreement to which the application relates and, in the case of an application under section 1 of the Act of 1975, the person to whose estate the application relates.

Mode of application (O. 48, r. 2)

2.—(1) An application to a county court under section 1 of the Act of 1975 for provision to be made out of the estate of a deceased person shall be made by originating application stating—

(*a*) the name of the deceased, the date of his death and his country of domicile at that date;

(*b*) the relationship of the applicant to the deceased or other qualification of the applicant for making the application;

(*c*) the date on which representation with respect to the deceased's estate was first taken out and the names and addresses of the personal representatives;

(*d*) that to the best of the applicant's knowledge and belief the value of the deceased's net estate does not exceed the sum for the time being fixed under section 22(1) of the Act of 1975;

(*e*) whether the disposition of the deceased's estate effected by his will or the law relating to intestacy was such as to make any provision for the applicant and, if it was, the nature of the provision;

(*f*) to the best of the applicant's knowledge and belief, the persons or classes of persons interested in the deceased's estate and the nature of their interests;

(*g*) particulars of the applicant's present and foreseeable financial resources and financial needs and any other information which he desires to place before the court on the matters to which the court is required to have regard under section 3 of the Act of 1975;

(*h*) where appropriate, a request for the court's permission to make the application notwithstanding that the period of six months has expired from the date on which representation in regard to the estate of the deceased was first taken out, and the grounds of the request; and

(*i*) the nature of the provision applied for.

(2) An application to a county court under section 36 of the Act of 1973 for the alteration of a maintenance agreement after the death of one of the parties shall be made by originating application giving the information which would be required to be stated in a supporting affidavit if the application were made to the High Court and also, in the case of an application by the surviving party to the agreement, stating that to the best of the applicant's knowledge and belief the value of the deceased's net estate does not exceed the sum for the time being fixed under section 22(1) of the Act of 1975.

Filing of application (O. 48, r. 3)

3.—(1) An application to which rule 2(1) or (2) relates shall be filed—

(*a*) in the court for the district in which the deceased resided at the date of his death, or

(*b*) if the deceased did not then reside in England or Wales, in the court for the district in which the respondent or one of the respondents resides or carries on business or the estate or part of the estate is situate, or

(*c*) if neither of the foregoing sub-paragraphs is applicable, in the court for the district in which the applicant resides or carries on business.

(2) the applicant shall file with his originating application—

(*a*) an official copy of the grant of representation to the deceased's estate and of every testamentary document admitted to proof, and

(*b*) in the case of an application under section 36 of the Act of 1973, a copy of the agreement to which the application relates.

(3) Unless the court otherwise directs, the return day of the originating application shall be a day fixed for the pre-trial review of the proceedings.

Parties (O. 48, r. 4)

4.—(1) Without prejudice to its powers under Orders 5 and 15, the court may, at any stage of the proceedings, direct that any person be added as a party to the proceedings or that notice of the proceedings be served on any person.

(2) Order 5, rule 6, shall apply to an application under section 1 of the Act of 1975 or section 36 of the Act of 1973 as it applies to the proceedings mentioned in that rule.

Answer (O. 48, r. 5)

5. Every respondent shall, within 21 days after service of the originating application on him, file an answer, which, if the respondent is a personal representative, shall state to the best of his ability—

(a) full particulars of the value of the deceased's net estate, as defined by section 25(1) of the Act of 1975;

(b) the persons or classes of persons beneficially interested in the estate, giving the names and (in the case of those who are not already parties) the addresses of all living beneficiaries, and the value of their interests so far as ascertained;

(c) if such be the case, that any living beneficiary (naming him) is a minor or a mental patient; and

(d) in the case of an application under section 1 of the Act of 1975, any facts known to the personal representative which might affect exercise of the court's powers under that Act.

Subsequent application (O. 48, r. 6)

6. Where an order has been made on an application under section 1 of the Act of 1975, any subsequent application, whether made by a party to the proceedings or by any other person, shall be made in those proceedings in accordance with Order 13, rule 1.

Hearing (O. 48, r. 7)

7. Any application under section 1 of the Act of 1975 or section 36 of the Act of 1973 may be heard and determined by the registrar and may, if the court thinks fit, be dealt with in chambers.

Endorsement of memorandum on grant (O. 48, r. 8)

8. On the hearing of an application under section 1 of the Act of 1975, the personal representative shall produce to the court the grant of representation to the deceased's estate and, if an order is made under the Act, the proper officer shall send a sealed copy thereof, together with the grant of representation, to the principal registry of the Family Division for a memorandum of the order to be endorsed on, or permanently annexed to, the grant in accordance with section 19(3) of the Act of 1975.

Transfer to High Court (O. 48, r. 9)

9.—(1) The court in which an application under section 36 of the Act of 1973 or section 1 of the Act of 1975 is pending may order the transfer of the application to the High Court where the transfer appears to the court to be desirable.

(2) In considering whether an application should be transferred under paragraph (1) from a county court to the High Court, the court shall have

regard to all relevant considerations, including the nature and value of the property involved, the relative expense of proceeding in the High Court and the county court and the limit for the time being of the jurisdiction of county courts under section 22 of the Act of 1975.

(3) Any order of transfer shall state whether it is desired that the proceedings be assigned to the Chancery Division or to the Family Division of the High Court.

THE INTESTATE SUCCESSION (INTEREST AND CAPITALISATION) ORDER 1977

(S.I. 1977 No. 1491)

Dated September 4, 1977, made by the Lord Chancellor in exercise of the powers conferred on him by section 46(1)(i) of the Administration of Estates Act 1925, and by section 47A(3A) of that Act.

Citation and Interpretation

1.—(1) This Order may be cited as the Intestate Succession (Interest and Capitalisation) Order 1977 and shall come into operation on September 15, 1977.

(2) The Interpretation Act 1889 shall apply to the interpretation of this Order as it applies to the interpretation of an Act of Parliament.

Interest on Statutory Legacy

2. For the purposes of section 46(1)(i) of the Administration of Estates Act 1925, as it applies both in respect of persons dying before 1953 and in respect of persons dying after 1952, the specified rate of interest shall be 7 per cent. per annum.

Capitalisation of Life Interests

3.—(1) Where after the coming into operation of this Order an election is exercised in accordance with subsection (6) or (7) of section 47A of the Administration of Estates Act 1925, the capital value of the life interest of the surviving spouse shall be reckoned in accordance with the following provisions of this article.

(2) There shall be ascertained, by reference to the index compiled by the Financial Times, The Institute of Actuaries and the Faculty of Actuaries, the average gross redemption yield on medium coupon 15-year Government Stocks at the date on which the election was exercised or, if the index was not compiled on that date, by reference to the index on the last date before that date on which it was compiled; and the column which corresponds to that yield in whichever of the Tables set out in the Schedule hereto is applicable to the sex of the surviving spouse shall be the appropriate column for the purposes of paragraph (3) of this article.

(3) The capital value for the purposes of paragraph (1) of this article is the product of the part of the residuary estate (whether or not yielding income) in respect of which the election was exercised and the multiplier shown in the appropriate column opposite the age which the surviving spouse had attained at the date on which the election was exercised.

SCHEDULE

TABLE 1: **Multiplier to be applied to the part of the residuary estate in respect of which the election is exercised to obtain the capital value of the life interest of a surviving husband, when the average gross redemption yield on medium coupon fifteen-year Government Stocks is at the rate shown.**

AGE LAST BIRTHDAY OF HUSBAND	LESS THAN 8.50%	8.50% OR BETWEEN 8.50% AND 9.50%	9.50% OR BETWEEN 9.50% AND 10.50%	10.50% OR BETWEEN 10.50% AND 11.50%	11.50% OR BETWEEN 11.50% AND 12.50%	12.50% OR BETWEEN 12.50% AND 13.50%	13.50% OR BETWEEN 13.50% AND 14.50%	14.50% OR BETWEEN 14.50% AND 15.50%	15.50% OR MORE
16	0.882	0.897	0.908	0.917	0.923	0.927	0.931	0.934	0.936
17	0.879	0.895	0.906	0.915	0.921	0.926	0.930	0.933	0.935
18	0.876	0.892	0.904	0.913	0.920	0.925	0.929	0.932	0.934
19	0.873	0.890	0.902	0.911	0.918	0.923	0.928	0.931	0.933
20	0.870	0.887	0.900	0.909	0.917	0.922	0.926	0.930	0.933
21	0.866	0.884	0.897	0.907	0.915	0.921	0.925	0.929	0.932
22	0.863	0.881	0.895	0.905	0.913	0.919	0.924	0.928	0.931
23	0.859	0.878	0.892	0.903	0.911	0.918	0.923	0.927	0.930
24	0.855	0.875	0.890	0.901	0.909	0.916	0.921	0.925	0.929
25	0.852	0.872	0.887	0.898	0.907	0.914	0.920	0.924	0.928
26	0.847	0.868	0.884	0.896	0.905	0.912	0.918	0.923	0.926
27	0.843	0.864	0.880	0.893	0.903	0.910	0.916	0.921	0.925
28	0.838	0.860	0.877	0.890	0.900	0.908	0.914	0.919	0.923
29	0.834	0.856	0.873	0.887	0.897	0.905	0.912	0.917	0.922
30	0.828	0.851	0.869	0.883	0.894	0.903	0.910	0.915	0.920
31	0.823	0.847	0.865	0.879	0.891	0.900	0.907	0.913	0.918
32	0.818	0.842	0.861	0.876	0.887	0.897	0.904	0.911	0.916
33	0.812	0.837	0.856	0.871	0.884	0.893	0.901	0.908	0.913
34	0.806	0.831	0.851	0.867	0.880	0.890	0.898	0.905	0.911

Table 1—*continued*

AGE LAST BIRTHDAY OF HUSBAND	LESS THAN 8.50%	8.50% OR BETWEEN 8.50% AND 9.50%	9.50% OR BETWEEN 9.50% AND 10.50%	10.50% OR BETWEEN 10.50% AND 11.50%	11.50% OR BETWEEN 11.50% AND 12.50%	12.50% OR BETWEEN 12.50% AND 13.50%	13.50% OR BETWEEN 13.50% AND 14.50%	14.50% OR BETWEEN 14.50% AND 15.50%	15.50% OR MORE
35	0.799	0.825	0.846	0.862	0.875	0.886	0.895	0.902	0.908
36	0.792	0.819	0.840	0.857	0.871	0.882	0.891	0.899	0.905
37	0.785	0.813	0.834	0.852	0.866	0.878	0.887	0.895	0.902
38	0.778	0.806	0.828	0.846	0.861	0.873	0.883	0.891	0.898
39	0.771	0.799	0.822	0.840	0.856	0.868	0.879	0.887	0.894
40	0.763	0.792	0.815	0.834	0.850	0.863	0.874	0.883	0.890
41	0.755	0.784	0.808	0.828	0.844	0.857	0.869	0.878	0.886
42	0.746	0.776	0.801	0.821	0.838	0.852	0.863	0.873	0.881
43	0.737	0.768	0.793	0.814	0.831	0.845	0.857	0.868	0.876
44	0.728	0.759	0.785	0.806	0.824	0.839	0.851	0.862	0.871
45	0.719	0.750	0.776	0.798	0.816	0.832	0.845	0.856	0.866
46	0.709	0.741	0.768	0.790	0.809	0.825	0.838	0.850	0.860
47	0.699	0.731	0.758	0.781	0.801	0.817	0.831	0.843	0.853
48	0.688	0.721	0.749	0.772	0.792	0.809	0.823	0.836	0.847
49	0.678	0.711	0.739	0.763	0.783	0.800	0.815	0.828	0.839
50	0.666	0.700	0.729	0.753	0.774	0.791	0.807	0.820	0.832
51	0.655	0.689	0.718	0.743	0.764	0.782	0.798	0.812	0.824
52	0.643	0.678	0.707	0.732	0.754	0.772	0.789	0.803	0.815
53	0.631	0.666	0.695	0.721	0.743	0.762	0.779	0.794	0.807
54	0.619	0.654	0.684	0.710	0.732	0.752	0.769	0.784	0.797
55	0.606	0.641	0.671	0.698	0.721	0.741	0.758	0.774	0.787
56	0.594	0.628	0.659	0.685	0.709	0.729	0.747	0.763	0.777
57	0.580	0.615	0.646	0.673	0.696	0.717	0.735	0.752	0.766
58	0.567	0.602	0.633	0.660	0.683	0.705	0.723	0.740	0.755
59	0.553	0.588	0.619	0.646	0.670	0.692	0.711	0.728	0.743

Table 1—continued

Age Last Birthday of Husband	Less than 8.50%	8.50% or between 8.50% and 9.50%	9.50% or between 9.50% and 10.50%	10.50% or between 10.50% and 11.50%	11.50% or between 11.50% and 12.50%	12.50% or between 12.50% and 13.50%	13.50% or between 13.50% and 14.50%	14.50% or between 14.50% and 15.50%	15.50% or more
60	0.539	0.574	0.605	0.632	0.657	0.678	0.698	0.715	0.731
61	0.525	0.560	0.590	0.618	0.642	0.664	0.684	0.702	0.718
62	0.510	0.545	0.576	0.603	0.628	0.650	0.670	0.688	0.704
63	0.496	0.530	0.561	0.588	0.613	0.636	0.656	0.674	0.691
64	0.481	0.515	0.546	0.573	0.598	0.621	0.641	0.659	0.676
65	0.466	0.500	0.530	0.558	0.583	0.605	0.626	0.644	0.661
66	0.451	0.485	0.515	0.542	0.567	0.590	0.610	0.629	0.646
67	0.436	0.469	0.499	0.526	0.551	0.574	0.594	0.613	0.631
68	0.421	0.454	0.483	0.510	0.535	0.557	0.578	0.597	0.615
69	0.407	0.438	0.467	0.494	0.518	0.541	0.562	0.581	0.598
70	0.392	0.423	0.452	0.478	0.502	0.524	0.545	0.564	0.582
71	0.377	0.407	0.436	0.462	0.485	0.508	0.528	0.547	0.565
72	0.362	0.392	0.420	0.445	0.469	0.491	0.511	0.530	0.548
73	0.348	0.377	0.404	0.429	0.452	0.474	0.494	0.513	0.531
74	0.333	0.362	0.388	0.413	0.436	0.457	0.477	0.496	0.513
75	0.319	0.347	0.373	0.397	0.419	0.441	0.460	0.479	0.496
76	0.305	0.332	0.357	0.381	0.403	0.424	0.443	0.461	0.479
77	0.292	0.318	0.342	0.365	0.387	0.407	0.426	0.444	0.461
78	0.278	0.304	0.328	0.350	0.371	0.391	0.410	0.427	0.444
79	0.265	0.290	0.313	0.335	0.355	0.375	0.393	0.410	0.427
80	0.253	0.277	0.299	0.320	0.340	0.359	0.377	0.394	0.410
81	0.241	0.264	0.285	0.306	0.325	0.343	0.361	0.377	0.393
82	0.229	0.251	0.272	0.292	0.310	0.328	0.345	0.361	0.377
83	0.218	0.239	0.259	0.278	0.296	0.313	0.330	0.346	0.361
84	0.207	0.227	0.246	0.265	0.282	0.299	0.315	0.331	0.345

Table 1—*continued*

AGE LAST BIRTHDAY OF HUSBAND	LESS THAN 8.50%	8.50% OR BETWEEN 8.50% AND 9.50%	9.50% OR BETWEEN 9.50% AND 10.50%	10.50% OR BETWEEN 10.50% AND 11.50%	11.50% OR BETWEEN 11.50% AND 12.50%	12.50% OR BETWEEN 12.50% AND 13.50%	13.50% OR BETWEEN 13.50% AND 14.50%	14.50% OR BETWEEN 14.50% AND 15.50%	15.50% OR MORE
85	0.196	0.216	0.234	0.252	0.269	0.285	0.301	0.316	0.330
86	0.186	0.205	0.223	0.240	0.256	0.272	0.287	0.302	0.315
87	0.177	0.195	0.212	0.228	0.244	0.259	0.274	0.288	0.301
88	0.168	0.185	0.201	0.217	0.232	0.247	0.261	0.275	0.288
89	0.159	0.176	0.191	0.207	0.221	0.235	0.249	0.262	0.275
90	0.151	0.167	0.182	0.197	0.211	0.224	0.237	0.250	0.262
91	0.144	0.159	0.173	0.187	0.201	0.214	0.227	0.239	0.251
92	0.137	0.151	0.165	0.179	0.192	0.205	0.217	0.229	0.240
93	0.130	0.144	0.158	0.171	0.183	0.196	0.208	0.219	0.230
94	0.124	0.138	0.151	0.163	0.175	0.187	0.199	0.210	0.221
95	0.119	0.132	0.144	0.156	0.168	0.179	0.190	0.201	0.212
96	0.113	0.126	0.138	0.149	0.161	0.172	0.182	0.193	0.203
97	0.108	0.120	0.132	0.143	0.154	0.164	0.175	0.185	0.195
98	0.103	0.115	0.126	0.137	0.147	0.157	0.167	0.177	0.187
99	0.098	0.109	0.119	0.130	0.140	0.150	0.159	0.169	0.178
100 and over	0.093	0.103	0.112	0.123	0.133	0.143	0.151	0.161	0.169

TABLE 2: **Multiplier to be applied to the part of the residuary estate in respect of which the election is exercised to obtain the capital value of the life interest of a surviving husband, when the average gross redemption yield on medium coupon fifteen-year Government Stocks is at the rate shown.**

AGE LAST BIRTHDAY OF WIFE	LESS THAN 8.50%	8.50% OR BETWEEN 8.50% AND 9.50%	9.50% OR BETWEEN 9.50% AND 10.50%	10.50% OR BETWEEN 10.50% AND 11.50%	11.50% OR BETWEEN 11.50% AND 12.50%	12.50% OR BETWEEN 12.50% AND 13.50%	13.50% OR BETWEEN 13.50% AND 14.50%	14.50% OR BETWEEN 14.50% AND 15.50%	15.50% OR MORE
16	0.892	0.905	0.915	0.922	0.927	0.930	0.933	0.936	0.937
17	0.889	0.903	0.913	0.920	0.925	0.929	0.933	0.935	0.937
18	0.887	0.901	0.911	0.919	0.924	0.929	0.932	0.934	0.936
19	0.884	0.899	0.910	0.917	0.923	0.928	0.931	0.934	0.936
20	0.882	0.897	0.908	0.916	0.922	0.927	0.930	0.933	0.935
21	0.879	0.895	0.906	0.915	0.921	0.926	0.929	0.932	0.934
22	0.877	0.893	0.904	0.913	0.920	0.925	0.928	0.931	0.934
23	0.874	0.890	0.902	0.911	0.918	0.923	0.927	0.931	0.933
24	0.871	0.888	0.900	0.910	0.917	0.922	0.926	0.930	0.932
25	0.868	0.885	0.898	0.908	0.915	0.921	0.925	0.929	0.932
26	0.864	0.882	0.896	0.906	0.914	0.920	0.924	0.928	0.931
27	0.861	0.879	0.893	0.904	0.912	0.918	0.923	0.927	0.930
28	0.857	0.876	0.891	0.901	0.910	0.916	0.921	0.925	0.929
29	0.853	0.873	0.888	0.899	0.908	0.915	0.920	0.924	0.928
30	0.849	0.869	0.885	0.896	0.906	0.913	0.918	0.923	0.926
31	0.845	0.866	0.882	0.894	0.903	0.911	0.916	0.921	0.925
32	0.840	0.862	0.878	0.891	0.901	0.908	0.914	0.919	0.923
33	0.836	0.858	0.875	0.888	0.898	0.906	0.912	0.918	0.922
34	0.831	0.853	0.871	0.884	0.895	0.903	0.910	0.916	0.920
35	0.826	0.849	0.867	0.881	0.892	0.901	0.908	0.913	0.918
36	0.820	0.844	0.863	0.877	0.889	0.898	0.905	0.911	0.916
37	0.815	0.839	0.858	0.873	0.885	0.895	0.902	0.909	0.914

Table 2—continued

AGE LAST BIRTHDAY OF WIFE	LESS THAN 8.50%	8.50% OR BETWEEN 8.50% AND 9.50%	9.50% OR BETWEEN 9.50% AND 10.50%	10.50% OR BETWEEN 10.50% AND 11.50%	11.50% OR BETWEEN 11.50% AND 12.50%	12.50% OR BETWEEN 12.50% AND 13.50%	13.50% OR BETWEEN 13.50% AND 14.50%	14.50% OR BETWEEN 14.50% AND 15.50%	15.50% OR MORE
38	0.809	0.834	0.853	0.869	0.881	0.891	0.899	0.906	0.911
39	0.896	0.828	0.848	0.864	0.877	0.888	0.896	0.903	0.909
40	0.796	0.822	0.843	0.860	0.873	0.884	0.893	0.900	0.906
41	0.790	0.816	0.838	0.855	0.869	0.880	0.889	0.897	0.903
42	0.783	0.810	0.832	0.850	0.864	0.876	0.885	0.893	0.900
43	0.775	0.803	0.826	0.844	0.859	0.871	0.881	0.889	0.896
44	0.768	0.796	0.820	0.838	0.854	0.866	0.877	0.885	0.893
45	0.760	0.789	0.813	0.832	0.848	0.861	0.872	0.881	0.889
46	0.752	0.782	0.806	0.826	0.842	0.856	0.867	0.876	0.885
47	0.744	0.774	0.799	0.819	0.836	0.850	0.862	0.872	0.880
48	0.735	0.766	0.791	0.812	0.829	0.844	0.856	0.866	0.875
49	0.726	0.757	0.783	0.804	0.822	0.837	0.850	0.861	0.870
50	0.716	0.748	0.775	0.797	0.815	0.831	0.844	0.855	0.865
51	0.707	0.739	0.766	0.788	0.807	0.823	0.837	0.849	0.803
52	0.697	0.729	0.757	0.780	0.799	0.816	0.830	0.842	0.853
53	0.686	0.719	0.747	0.771	0.791	0.808	0.822	0.835	0.846
54	0.676	0.709	0.737	0.761	0.782	0.799	0.814	0.827	0.839
55	0.664	0.698	0.727	0.751	0.772	0.790	0.806	0.820	0.831
56	0.653	0.687	0.716	0.741	0.763	0.781	0.797	0.811	0.823
57	0.641	0.676	0.705	0.730	0.752	0.771	0.788	0.802	0.815
58	0.629	0.664	0.693	0.719	0.741	0.761	0.778	0.793	0.806
59	0.616	0.651	0.681	0.707	0.730	0.750	0.767	0.783	0.796
60	0.603	0.638	0.669	0.695	0.718	0.739	0.757	0.772	0.786
61	0.590	0.625	0.656	0.683	0.706	0.727	0.745	0.761	0.776
62	0.577	0.612	0.643	0.670	0.693	0.715	0.733	0.750	0.764

Table 2—*continued*

Age Last Birthday of Wife	Less than 8.50%	8.50% or between 8.50% and 9.50%	9.50% or between 9.50% and 10.50%	10.50% or between 10.50% and 11.50%	11.50% or between 11.50% and 12.50%	12.50% or between 12.50% and 13.50%	13.50% or between 13.50% and 14.50%	14.50% or between 14.50% and 15.50%	15.50% or more
63	0.563	0.598	0.629	0.656	0.680	0.702	0.721	0.738	0.753
64	0.549	0.584	0.615	0.642	0.667	0.688	0.859	0.725	0.740
65	0.534	0.569	0.600	0.628	0.653	0.674	0.694	0.712	0.728
66	0.520	0.555	0.586	0.613	0.638	0.660	0.680	0.698	0.714
67	0.505	0.540	0.570	0.598	0.623	0.645	0.666	0.684	0.700
68	0.490	0.524	0.555	0.583	0.608	0.630	0.651	0.669	0.686
69	0.475	0.509	0.539	0.567	0.592	0.615	0.635	0.654	0.671
70	0.459	0.493	0.523	0.551	0.576	0.599	0.619	0.638	0.655
71	0.444	0.477	0.507	0.535	0.560	0.582	0.603	0.622	0.640
72	0.428	0.461	0.491	0.518	0.543	0.566	0.586	0.606	0.623
73	0.413	0.445	0.475	0.501	0.526	0.549	0.570	0.589	0.606
74	0.398	0.429	0.458	0.485	0.509	0.532	0.552	0.572	0.589
75	0.382	0.413	0.442	0.468	0.492	0.514	0.535	0.554	0.572
76	0.367	0.397	0.425	0.451	0.475	0.497	0.517	0.536	0.554
77	0.352	0.381	0.408	0.434	0.457	0.479	0.499	0.518	0.536
78	0.337	0.365	0.392	0.417	0.440	0.461	0.482	0.500	0.518
79	0.322	0.350	0.376	0.400	0.423	0.444	0.464	0.482	0.500
80	0.307	0.334	0.360	0.383	0.406	0.426	0.446	0.464	0.482
81	0.293	0.319	0.344	0.367	0.389	0.409	0.428	0.446	0.463
82	0.279	0.304	0.328	0.351	0.372	0.392	0.410	0.428	0.445
83	0.265	0.290	0.313	0.335	0.355	0.375	0.393	0.410	0.427
84	0.252	0.276	0.298	0.319	0.339	0.358	0.376	0.393	0.409
85	0.239	0.262	0.284	0.304	0.323	0.342	0.359	0.376	0.392
86	0.227	0.249	0.269	0.289	0.308	0.326	0.343	0.359	0.374
87	0.215	0.236	0.256	0.275	0.293	0.310	0.327	0.342	0.357

Table 2—*continued*

AGE LAST BIRTHDAY OF WIFE	LESS THAN 8.50%	8.50% OR BETWEEN 8.50% AND 9.50%	9.50% OR BETWEEN 9.50% AND 10.50%	10.50% OR BETWEEN 10.50% AND 11.50%	11.50% OR BETWEEN 11.50% AND 12.50%	12.50% OR BETWEEN 12.50% AND 13.50%	13.50% OR BETWEEN 13.50% AND 14.50%	14.50% OR BETWEEN 14.50% AND 15.50%	15.50% OR MORE
88	0.204	0.224	0.243	0.261	0.279	0.295	0.311	0.327	0.341
89	0.193	0.212	0.230	0.248	0.265	0.281	0.296	0.311	0.325
90	0.182	0.201	0.218	0.235	0.251	0.267	0.282	0.296	0.310
91	0.173	0.190	0.207	0.223	0.239	0.254	0.268	0.282	0.296
92	0.164	0.180	0.197	0.212	0.227	0.242	0.256	0.269	0.282
93	0.155	0.171	0.187	0.202	0.216	0.230	0.243	0.256	0.269
94	0.147	0.162	0.177	0.192	0.205	0.219	0.232	0.244	0.256
95	0.139	0.154	0.168	0.182	0.195	0.208	0.221	0.233	0.244
96	0.132	0.146	0.159	0.173	0.185	0.198	0.210	0.222	0.233
97	0.125	0.138	0.151	0.164	0.176	0.188	0.199	0.211	0.222
98	0.118	0.130	0.143	0.155	0.167	0.178	0.189	0.200	0.210
99	0.110	0.122	0.134	0.146	0.157	0.168	0.178	0.189	0.199
100 and over	0.102	0.114	0.125	0.137	0.147	0.158	0.167	0.178	0.188

THE NON-CONTENTIOUS PROBATE FEES ORDER 1981

(S.I. 1981 No. 861)

Dated June 12, 1981, made by the Lord Chancellor, the Judges of the Supreme Court, and the Treasury, in exercise of the powers and authorities vested in them respectively by section 213 of the Supreme Court of Judicature (Consolidation) Act 1925 and sections 2 and 3 of the Public Offices Fees Act 1879.

Citation and commencement

1. This Order may be cited as the Non-Contentious Probate Fees Order 1981 and shall come into operation on August 3, 1981.

Interpretation

2.—(1) In this Order, unless the context otherwise requires—

"assessed value" means the value of the net real and personal estate (excluding settled land if any) passing under the grant as shown—

  (i) in the Inland Revenue affidavit (for a death occurring before March 13, 1971), or
 (ii) in the Inland Revenue account (for a death occurring on or after March 13, 1975), or
(iii) in a case in which, in accordance with arrangements made between the President of the Family Division and the Commissioners of Inland Revenue or regulations made under section 94(1)(a) of the Finance Act 1980 and from time to time in force, no such affidavit or account is required to be delivered, in the oath which is sworn to lead to the grant;

and in the case of an application to reseal a grant means the said value, as so shown, passing under the grant upon its being resealed;

"authorised place of deposit" means any place in which, by virtue of a direction given under section 170 of the Supreme Court of Judicature (Consolidation) Act 1925 original wills and other documents under the control of the High Court (either in the principal registry or in any district registry) are deposited and preserved;

"grant" means a grant of probate or letters of administration;

"district registry" includes the probate registry of Wales, any district probate registry and any sub-registry attached thereto;

"the principal registry" means the Principal Registry of the Family Division and any sub-registry attached thereto.

(2) A fee referred to by number means the fee so numbered in the Schedule to this Order.

Taking of fees

3.—(1) The fees set out in column 2 of the Schedule to this Order shall be taken in the principal registry and in each district registry in respect of the items set out opposite thereto in column 1.

(2) The fees prescribed by this Order shall be taken in cash.

Exclusion of certain death gratuities

4. In determining the value of any personal estate for the purpose of this Order there shall be excluded the value of a death gratuity payable under section 17(2) of the Judicial Pensions Act 1981 or payable to the personal representatives of a deceased civil servant by virtue of a scheme made under section 1 of the Superannuation Act 1972.

Reduction, remission and exemption

5.—(1) Where it appears to the Lord Chancellor that the payment of any fee specified in the Schedule would, owing to the exceptional circumstances of the particular case, involve undue hardship, the Lord Chancellor may reduce or remit the fee in that case.

(2) Where by any convention entered into by Her Majesty with any foreign power it is provided that no fee shall be required to be paid in respect of any proceedings, the fees specified in this Order shall not be taken in respect of those proceedings.

(3) Where any application for a grant is withdrawn before the issue of the grant, a registrar may reduce or remit a fee.

(4) Where, on application for a grant by a personal applicant, the papers leading to the grant are prepared by the applicant himself, a registrar may remit up to one-half of the fee prescribed by fee No. 2.

(5) Fee No. 7 shall not be taken where a search is made for research or similar purposes by permission of the President of the Family Division for a document over 100 years old filed in the principal registry or a district registry or another authorised place of deposit.

Revocation of orders

6. The Supreme Court (Non-Contentious Probate) Fees Order 1975, The Supreme Court (Non-Contentious Probate) Fees (Amendment) Order 1976, The Supreme Court (Non-Contentious Probate) Fees (Amendment) Order 1978, and The Supreme Court (Non-Contentious Probate) Fees (Amendment) Order 1980 are hereby revoked.

rule 3(1)   **SCHEDULE**

Column 1	Column 2
Item	Fee £

Application for grant: general

1. On an application for a grant (or for resealing a grant) other than an application to which fee No. 3 applies:—

    (*a*) if the assessed value

does not exceed £10,000	No fee
exceeds £10,000 but does not exceed £25,000	40.00
exceeds £25,000 but does not exceed £100,000	2.50 per £1,000 or part thereof

    (*b*) if the assessed value exceeds £100,000 ....   250.00

      and, for every additional £100,000 or part thereof, a further fee of 50.00

Personal application fee

2. On application for a grant by a personal applicant (or for resealing such a grant if the application is prepared in the registry) save where fee No. 3(*a*) is payable, in addition to any other fee:—

    (*a*) if the assessed value

does not exceed £500	1.00
exceeds £500 but does not exceed £1,000	2.00
exceeds £1,000 but does not exceed £5,000	5.00

    (*b*) if the assessed value exceeds £5,000, for each £1,000 or part thereof 1.00

Special applications

3. On an application for:—

    (*a*) a grant in respect of an estate exempt from estate duty by virtue of section 71 of the Finance Act 1952 (*a*) or from capital transfer tax by virtue of paragraph 1 of Schedule 7 to the Finance Act 1975 (*b*) (exemption for members of the armed forces, etc.);

    (*b*) a grant limited to settled land;

    (*c*) a grant limited to trust property;

    (*d*) A duplicate grant;

    (*e*) Any second or subsequent grant (including one following a revoked grant) in respect of the same deceased person, other than a grant preceded only by a grant limited to settled land, to trust property or to a part of the estate 2.00

Caveats

4. For the entry or the extension of a caveat 4.00

Column 1	Column 2
Item	Fee £

Search

5. On an application for a standing search to be carried out in an estate, for each period for six months 2.00

Deposit of will

6. On depositing a will for safe custody in the principal registry or a district registry 1.00

Inspection

7. On inspection of an original will or any other document including a copy of a will 0.25

Copies of documents

8.—(a) For a copy of all or part of any document, whether or not issued as an office copy, for each page 0.25
   (b) For a sealed and certified copy of any document 1.00
       and for each page after the first, a further fee of 1.00
   (c) For an exemplification of a copy signed by a registrar and countersigned by the President of the Family Division, including the fees for preparing the necessary documents 5.00

Postal application

9. For handling a postal application in the principal registry for a copy of a will or grant, in respect of each estate 1.00

Oaths and guarantees

10. Save on a personal application for a grant—
   (a) for administering an oath, for each deponent to each affidavit 2.00
   (b) for making each exhibit 0.50
   (c) for superintending and attesting execution of a guarantee, for each surety 1.00

Taxation of costs

11. For taxing a bill of costs in the principal registry inclusive of the registrar's certificate .... The same fees as are payable in an action.

Settling documents

12. For perusing and settling citations, advertisements, oaths, affidavits or other documents, for each document settled 5.00

EXPLANATORY NOTE
(*This Note is not part of the Order*)

This Order replaces the Supreme Court (Non-Contentious Probate) Fees Order 1975 as amended. By fee No. 1 in the Schedule the exemption from fees for small estates is raised from £2,000 in value to £10,000 in value, and a fixed fee of £40 is substituted for the *ad valorem* charge in respect of estates valued between £10,000 and £25,000. There is no change in fee No. 1 in respect of estates above £25,000 or in any of the other fees except that, instead of the former fee of £2, fee No. 1 will now be taken in respect of property in England and Wales on an application to reseal a grant under the Colonial Probates Act 1892. The Order applies to fees becoming due or payable on or after August 3, 1981.

DISTRIBUTION ON INTESTACY: TABLE OF VARIATIONS IN THE FIXED NET SUM

Where death occurred on or after:	Amount	Authority
January 1, 1926 up to and including December 31, 1952	£1,000	Administration of Estates Act 1925, s.46(1)
January 1, 1953 up to and including December 31, 1966	*issue alive* £5,000 *no living issue* £20,000	Administration of Estates Act 1925, s.46(1), as amended by Intestates' Estates Act 1952, s.1
January 1, 1967 up to and including June 30, 1972	*issue alive* £8,750 *no living issue* £30,000	Family Provision Act 1966, s.1
July 1, 1972 up to and including March 14, 1977	*issue alive* £15,000 *no living issue* £40,000	Family Provision Act 1966, s.1; Family Provision (Intestate Succession) Order 1972 (S.I. 1972 No. 916)
March 15, 1977 up to and including February 28, 1981	*issue alive* £25,000 *no living issue* £55,000	Family Provision Act 1966, s.1; Family Provision (Intestate Succession) Order 1977 (S.I. 1977 No. 415)
March 1, 1981 up to and including May 30, 1987	*issue alive* £40,000 *no living issue* £85,000	Family Provision Act 1966, s.1; Family Provision (Intestate Succession) Order 1981 (S.I. 1981 No. 255)
June 1, 1987 onwards	*issue alive* £75,000 *no living issue* £125,000	Family Provision Act 1966, s.1; Family Provision (Intestate Succession) Order 1987 (S.I. 1987 No. 799)

Appendix Three

TABLE OF DISTRIBUTION ON INTESTACY

APPENDIX 3

TABLE OF DISTRIBUTION OF INTESTACY WHERE DEATH OCCURRED AFTER DECEMBER 31, 1952[1]

Surviving relatives in order of precedence	Distribution of estate when spouse survives deceased	Distribution of estate when spouse does not survive deceased	Notes

1. Spouse	(a) Personal chattels,[2] *and*
	 (b) Fixed net sum[3] absolutely. *and*
	 (c) The residue on the following terms:
	   (i) one-half for life if issue alive, *or*
	   (ii) one-half absolutely if no living issue (even if other relatives are alive), *or*
	   (iii) all residue if no issue or other relatives alive
			The surviving spouse may call on the personal representatives to purchase the life interest for a lump sum within a year of grant of representation and may acquire by appropriation any matrimonial home owned by the deceased[4]

2. Issue on the statutory trusts[5]	(a) One-half the residue on statutory trusts,[6] *and* (b) The other half of the residue, on statutory trust,[6] on the death of the surviving spouse	All to issue on statutory trusts[6]	Children and issue must "account"[7] If the issue dies while an infant and unmarried during the lieftime of the surviving spouse, the residuary estate is dealt with as if the child had never existed

Where the deceased died after 1969, illegitimate children or their issue share equally with legitimate.[8] Prior to 1970 an illegitimate child was entitled only to his mother's estate

3. Parent(s)	One-half of the residue in equal shares absolutely[6]	All to parent or parents in equal shares absolutely	Parents do not "account"[7] The parents do not take on statutory trusts[6] Where the deceased died after 1969, the parents of an illegitimate child share the estate.[9] Before 1970 only the mother of an illegitimate child was entitled.
4. Brother(s) and/or sister(s) of the whole blood	One-half of the residue on statutory trusts[6]	All to brother(s) and/or sister(s) on statutory trusts[6]	Collaterals do not "account"[7] Deceased brothers and sisters are represented by their issue (i.e., nephews and nieces of the intestate)
5. Brother(s) and/or sister(s) of the half blood	Nothing	All to brother(s) and/or sister(s) of the half blood on statutory trusts[6]	See notes to No. 4
6. Grandparent(s)	Nothing	All to grandparent(s) in equal shares absolutely	The grandparents do not "account"[7] The grandparents do not take on statutory trusts[8]

7. Uncle(s) and/or aunt(s) of the whole blood	Nothing	All to uncle(s) and/or aunt(s) on statutory trusts[8]	These do not "account"[7] Deceased uncles and aunts are represented by their issue (i.e., cousins of the intestate)
8. Uncle(s) and/or aunt(s) of the half blood	Nothing	All to uncle(s) and/or aunt(s) on statutory trusts[8]	See note to No. 7
9. The Crown/Duchy of Lancaster/Duchy of Cornwall	Nothing	All to the Crown or appropriate Duchy	No relation more remote than a grandparent or the descendant of a grandparent can claim on intestacy. The Crown will usually modify its strict rights by providing for dependants of the intestate.. related or not, and certain others. This is a discretionary power[10]

[1] For details see Chaps. 20 and 82. For discussion of distribution on intestacy under the old rules, see Chap 83.
[2] As to the meaning of this phrase, see *ante*.
[3] This is currently £40,000 if there are issue alive, or £85,000 if there are no living issue.
[4] See *ante*.
[5] From this class downwards, the existence of relatives in one class means that there is no need to consider any further class.
[6] For the statutory trusts see *ante*.
[7] As to accounting by children and issue but not other relatives see *ante*.
[8] Family Law Reform Act 1969, s.14.
[9] *Ibid*.
[10] See *ante*.

INDEX

1291